W9-AOZ-355

Occupational Outlook Handbook

1996-97 Edition

U.S. Department of Labor
Robert B. Reich, Secretary

Bureau of Labor Statistics
Katharine G. Abraham, Commissioner

January 1996

Bulletin 2470

A sampling of JIST's career-related materials can be found in the back of this *Handbook*. Contact your bookstores, distributors, or wholesalers for complete information on our exceptional product line.

Guide to the *Handbook*

- Highlights of the job outlook for the year 2005 are presented in **Tomorrow's Jobs**, page 1.

- Additional career-oriented materials available from private and public organizations, and sources of state and local job market information are described in **Sources of Career Information**, page 8.

- Job search methods and tips on applying for a job and evaluation a job offer are discussed in **Finding a Job and Evaluating a Job Offer**, page 14.

- Highlights of the kind of information presented in detailed occupational descriptions, and pointers on interpreting this information appear in *Occupational Information Included in the Handbook*, **page 19.**

- For occupations not covered in detail in the *Handbook*, brief descriptions of the nature of the work, the number of jobs in 1994, the projected 1995-2005 change in employment, and the most significant source of training are presented in a section beginning on page 469.

- The assumptions and methods used in preparing Bureau of Labor Statistics employment projections are described briefly on page 477.

- A list of *Dictionary of Occupational Title* numbers that are related to *Handbook* occupations can be found on page 478.

- All occupational statements in the *Handbook* are available in reprint form. For a list of reprints, consult page 494.

- An alphabetical index of occupations found in the *Handbook* is on page 497.

Bureau of Labor Statistics Regional Offices

Atlanta—Suite 500, 1371 Peachtree St. NE,
Atlanta, GA 30367
Phone (404)347-4416

Boston—10th Floor, 1 Congress St.,
Boston, MA 02114
Phone (617)-565-2327

Chicago—9th Floor, Kluczynski Bldg.,
230 South Dearborn St.,
Chicago, IL 60604
Phone (312) 353-1880

Dallas—Room 221, A. Maceo Smith Federal Bldg.,
525 Griffin St.,
Dallas, TX 75202
Phone (214) 767-6970

Kansas City—Suite 600, 1100 Main St.,
Kansas City, MO 64106
Phone (816) 426-2481

New York—Room 808, 201 Varick St.,
New York, NY 10014
Phone (212) 337-2400

Philadelphia—Room 8000, 3535 Market St.,
P.O. Box 13309,
Philadelphia, PA 19101-3309
Phone (215) 596-1154

San Francisco—71 Stevenson St.,
P.O. Box 193766,
San Francisco, CA 94119
Phone (415) 975-4350

Occupational Outlook Handbook, 1996-97 Edition
© 1996 JIST Works, Inc.
720 N. Park Avenue
Indianapolis, IN 46202-3431
Phone: 317-264-3720 Fax: 317-264-3709 E-mail: JISTWorks@AOL.com

Printed in the United States of America

99 98 97 96   5 4 3 2 1

ISSN 0082-9072
ISBN 1-56370-278-9 Hardcover   ISBN 1-56370-277-0 Softcover

A reprint of the U.S. Department of Labor's *Occupational Outlook Handbook,* 1996-97 Edition.
To order additional copies of this book or other products found in the back of the *Handbook,*
contact JIST Works at 1-800-648-5478 or call our 24-hour fax line: 1-800-547-8329.

Message from the Secretary

The rules for competing in a technologically-advanced global economy are changing everyday. The jobs of the future and the challenges posed by global competitiveness will require a skilled American workforce that can quickly adapt to a changing workplace.

The *Occupational Outlook Handbook*, the Government's premier publication on career guidance, provides essential information about prospective changes in the world of work and the qualifications that will be needed by tomorrow's workers.

ROBERT B. REICH

Foreword

Global competition, changing technology and business practices, and shifts in the demand for goods and services continue to reshape America's job market—creating a widespread need for comprehensive, up-to-date, and reliable career information.

The Bureau's *Occupational Outlook Handbook*—a nationally recognized source of career information—describes what workers do on the job, working conditions, the training and education needed, earnings, and expected job prospects in a wide range of occupations. Employment in the approximately 250 occupations covered in the 1996-97 *Handbook* accounts for about 7 out of every 8 jobs in the economy. The occupational information presented this new edition should provide valuable assistance to individuals making career decisions about their future work lives.

KATHARINE G. ABRAHAM
Commissioner
Bureau of Labor Statistics

v

Acknowledgments

The *Handbook* was produced in the Bureau of Labor Statistics under the general guidance and direction of Ronald E. Kutscher, Associate Commissioner for Employment Projections and Neal H. Rosenthal, Chief, Division of Occupational Outlook. Mike Pilot, Manager, Occupational Outlook Program, was responsible for planning and day-to-day direction.

Project leaders supervising the research and preparation of material were Douglas Braddock, Alan Eck, Chester C. Levine, and Jon Q. Sargent. Occupational analysts who contributed material were Thomas A. Amirault, Megan Barkume, Verada P. Bluford, Theresa Cosca, Geof Gradler, Jeffrey C. Gruenert, Hall Dillon, Mark Mittelhauser, Rachel Moskowitz, Kurt Schrammel, Kristina Shelley, Gary Steinberg, Allison Thomson, Carolyn M. Veneri, and Drew A. Warwick.

Word processing support was handled by Beverly A. Williams.

Note

A great many trade associations, professional societies, unions, industrial organizations, and government agencies provide career information that is valuable to counselors and jobseekers. For the convenience of *Handbook* users, some of these organizations are listed at the end of each occupational statement. Although these references were carefully compiled, the Bureau of Labor Statistics has neither authority nor facilities for investigating the organizations or the information or publications that may be sent in response to a request and cannot guarantee the accuracy of such information. The listing of an organization, therefore, does not constitute in any way an endorsement or recommendation by the Bureau either of the organization and its activities or of the information it may supply. Each organization has sole responsibility for whatever information it may issue.

The occupational information contained in the *Handbook* presents a general, composite description of jobs and cannot be expected to reflect work situations in specific establishments or localities. The *Handbook*, therefore, is not intended and should not be used as a guide for determining wages, hours, the right of a particular union to represent workers, appropriate bargaining units, or formal job evaluation systems. Nor should earnings data in the *Handbook* be used to compute future loss of earnings in adjudication proceedings involving work injuries or accidental deaths.

Material in this publication is in the public domain and, with appropriate credit, may be reproduced without permission. Comments about the contents of this publication and suggestions for improving it are welcome. Please address them to Chief, Division of Occupational Outlook, Bureau of Labor Statistics, U.S. Department of Labor, Washington, DC 20212.

Photograph Credits

The Bureau of Labor Statistics wishes to express its appreciation for the cooperation and assistance of the many government and private sources—listed below—that either contributed photographs or made their facilities available to photographers working under contract to the U.S. Department of Labor. Photographs may not be free of every possible safety or health hazard. Depiction of company or trade name in no way constitutes endorsement by the Department of Labor.

American University; Baltimore Specialty Steels; Bell Atlantic; Black Magic Film Company; Brenda Schulz, A.I.A.; Brookland Branch of Riggs Bank of Washington; Brooks Upholstery; Chapel Opticians, Inc.; Continental Airlines, Inc.; Crist Air Maintenance Services, Inc.; D.L. Boyd, Inc.; Don Zuckerman; Dr. Joan Murrell Owens, Howard University; Dr. Pierre Palian, D.D.S.; Dravo Corporation; Ed Yoe, Artist Services, Inc.; Fontana Affiliated Lithograph; Frank's Well Drilling; George Hyman Construction Company; George Meany Labor Studies Center; George Washington University; George Washington University Hospital; Giant Supermarkets; Gladhill Tractor Mart; Glaziers Local #963/BCI; Globe Auto Body, Inc.; Goddard Space Flight Center (NASA); Grace Chemical Company; Herb Gordon Dodge; H. & H. Bindery; Hyatt Regency Washington on Capitol Hill; Judge Lee Sisler, Sixth District Court of Maryland; Local 10 of Ironworkers; Maryland National Capitol Park and Planning Commission; Memorial Hospital and Medical Center of Cumberland, Maryland; Midstate Coal Company; Midwest Photo and Video; M.P.I. Pharmacy Services, Inc.; National Institute of Standards and Technology, U.S. Government; NBC—Channel 4, Washington, DC; Northwestern Illinois Research and Development Center and the University of Illinois at Urbana—Champaign; Potomac Electric Power Company; Rabbi Warren Stone, Temple Emanuel; Representative Constance A. Morello (Maryland); Rock Terrace High School—Montgomery County, Maryland; Sandy Springs Friends School; Saspirilla Band; Strauss Technical Photo; Suburban Dental Laboratory, Inc.; Susan Sanders Fine Art Jewelry; The Treatment and Learning Centers; Toman Optician; Washington Hospital Center; Washington Fireworks Company; The Washington Times; Welch and Rushe, Inc.; WDCU—FM, Washington, DC; WGBQ—FM Radio, Galesburg, Illinois; The Woodner; Wyatt Company; University of Maryland, Electrical Engineering Department; Working Images Photographs—Martha Tabor.

Contents

Tomorrow's Jobs

Making informed career decisions requires reliable information about opportunities that should be available in the future. This chapter presents highlights of Bureau of Labor Statistics projections of industry and occupational employment and the labor force, that can help guide your career plans.

A slowdown in employment growth is expected.

- Over the 1994-2005 period, employment is projected to increase by 17.7 million or 14 percent. This is slower than the 24-percent increase attained during the 11-year period, 1983-94, when the economy added 24.6 million jobs.

- Wage and salary worker employment will account for 95 percent of this increase. In addition, the number of self-employed workers is expected to increase by 950,000, to 11.6 million in 2005, while the number of unpaid family workers will decline.

Service-producing industries will account for most new jobs. (See chart 1.)

- Employment growth is projected to be highly concentrated by industry. The services and retail trade industries will account for 16.2 million out of a total projected growth of 16.8 million wage and salary jobs.

- Business, health, and education services will account for 70 percent of the growth—9.2 million out of 13.6 million jobs—within services.

- Health care services will account for almost one-fifth of all job growth from 1994-2005. Factors contributing to continued growth in this industry include the aging population, which will continue to require more services, and the increased use of innovative medical technology for intensive diagnosis and treatment. Patients will increasingly be shifted out of hospitals and into outpatient facilities, nursing homes, and home health care in an attempt to contain costs.

- The personnel supply services industry, which provides temporary help to employers in other industries, is projected to add 1.3 million jobs from 1994 to 2005. Temporary workers tend to have low wages, low job stability, and poor job benefits.

The goods-producing sector will decline. (See chart 2.)

- The goods-producing sector faces declining employment in two of its four industries—manufacturing and mining. Employment in the other two industries—construction, and agriculture, forestry, and fishing—is expected to increase.

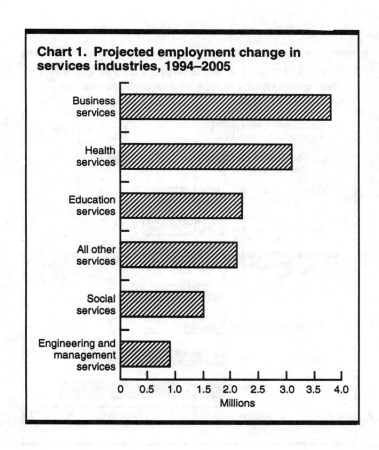

Chart 1. Projected employment change in services industries, 1994–2005

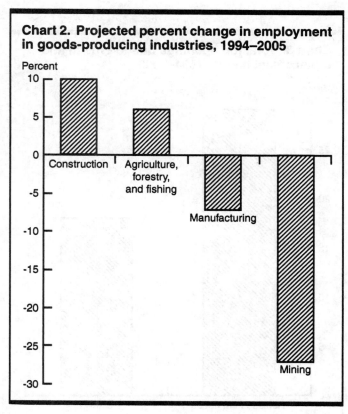

Chart 2. Projected percent change in employment in goods-producing industries, 1994–2005

- Employment in manufacturing is expected to continue to decline, losing 1.3 million jobs over the 1994-2005 period. Operators, fabricators, and laborers, and precision production, craft, and repair occupations are expected to account for more than 1 million of these lost jobs. Systems analysts and other computer-related occupations in manufacturing are expected to increase.

Job opportunities can arise in two ways—job growth and replacement needs. (See chart 3.)

- Job growth can be measured by percent change and numerical change. The fastest growing occupations do not necessarily provide the largest number of jobs. Even though an occupation is expected to grow rapidly, it may provide fewer openings than a slower growing, larger occupation.

- Opportunities in large occupations are enhanced by the additional job openings resulting from the need to replace workers who leave the occupation. Some workers leave the occupation as they are promoted or change careers; others stop working to return to school, assume household responsibilities, or retire.

- Replacement needs are greater in occupations with low pay and status, low training requirements, and a high proportion of young and part-time workers.

- Replacement needs will account for 29.4 million job openings from 1994 to 2005, far more than the 17.7 million openings projected to arise from employment growth.

Employment change will vary widely by broad occupational group. (See chart 4.)

- Employment in professional specialty occupations is projected to increase at a faster rate than any other major occupational group.

- Among the major occupational groups, employment in professional specialty occupations is also projected to account for the most job growth from 1994-2005.

- Professional specialty occupations—which require high educational attainment and offer high earnings—and service occupations—which require lower educational attainment and offer lower earnings—are expected to account for more than half of all job growth between 1994 and 2005.

- Agriculture, forestry, fishing, and related occupations is the only major occupational group projected to decline. All job openings in this group will stem from replacement needs.

- Office automation is expected to have a significant effect on many individual administrative and clerical support occupations.

- Precision production, craft, and repair occupations and operators, fabricators, and laborers are projected to grow much more slowly than average due to continuing advances in technology, changes in production methods, and the overall decline in manufacturing employment.

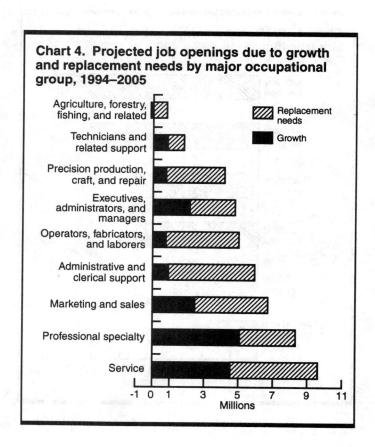

Chart 3. Total job openings due to growth and replacement needs, 1994–2005

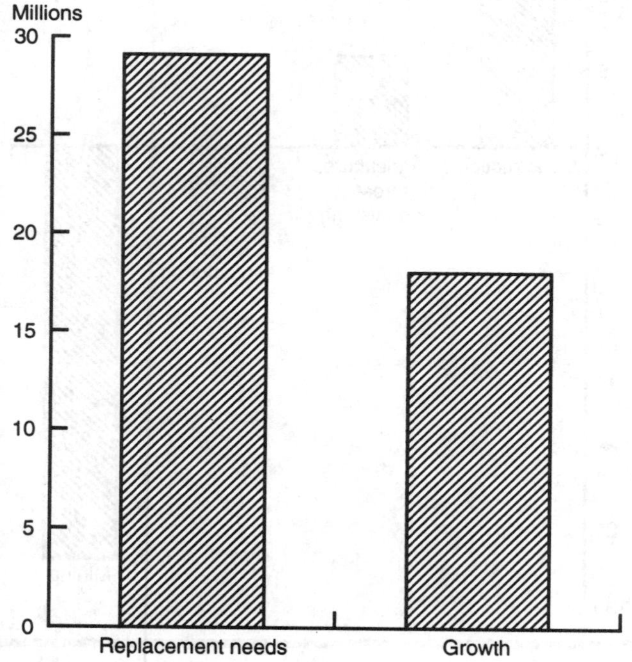

Chart 4. Projected job openings due to growth and replacement needs by major occupational group, 1994–2005

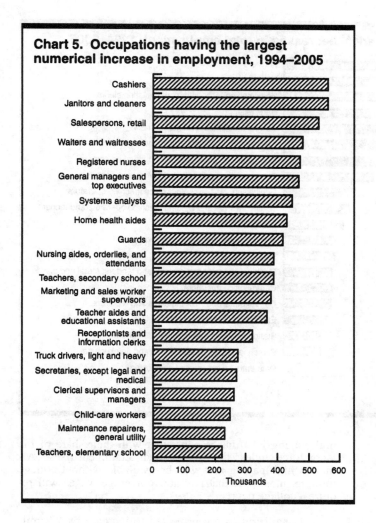

Chart 5. Occupations having the largest numerical increase in employment, 1994–2005

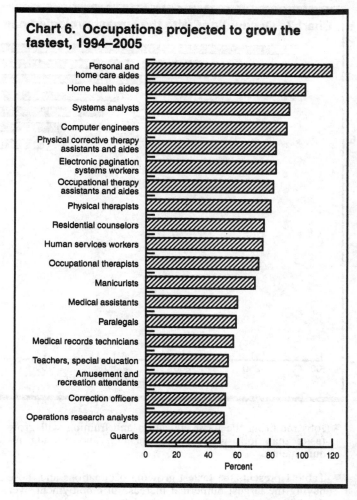

Chart 6. Occupations projected to grow the fastest, 1994–2005

Twenty occupations will account for half of all job growth over the 1994-2005 period. (See chart 5.)

- The 20 occupations accounting for half of all job growth over the 1994-2005 period tend to be large in size rather than fast growing. Three health care occupations are in the top 10, and 3 education-related occupations are in the second 10.

The fastest growing occupations reflect growth in computer technology and health services. (See chart 6.)

- Many of the fastest growing occupations are concentrated in health services, which is expected to increase more than twice as fast as the economy as a whole. Personal and home care aides, and home health aides, are expected to be in great demand to provide personal and physical care for an increasing number of elderly people and for persons who are recovering from surgery and other serious health conditions. This is occurring as hospitals and insurance companies mandate shorter stays for recovery to contain costs.

- Employment of computer engineers and systems analysts is expected to grow rapidly to satisfy expanding needs for scientific research and applications of computer technology in business and industry.

Declining occupational employment stems from declining industry employment and technological change. (See chart 7.)

- Farmers, garment sewing machine operators, and private household cleaners and servants are examples of occupations that will lose employment because of declining industry employment.

- Many declining occupations are affected by structural changes, resulting from technological advances, organizational changes, and other factors that affect the employment of workers. For example, the use of typists and word processors is expected to decline substantially because of productivity improvements resulting from office automation, and the increased use of word processing equipment by professional and managerial employees.

Education and training affect job opportunities. (See chart 8 and table 1.)

- Workers in jobs with low education and training requirements tend to have greater occupational mobility. Consequently, these jobs will provide a larger than proportional share of all job openings stemming from replacement needs.

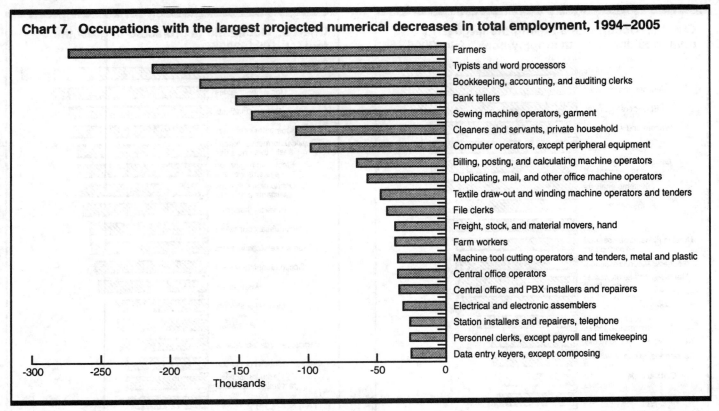

Chart 7. Occupations with the largest projected numerical decreases in total employment, 1994–2005

Farmers
Typists and word processors
Bookkeeping, accounting, and auditing clerks
Bank tellers
Sewing machine operators, garment
Cleaners and servants, private household
Computer operators, except peripheral equipment
Billing, posting, and calculating machine operators
Duplicating, mail, and other office machine operators
Textile draw-out and winding machine operators and tenders
File clerks
Freight, stock, and material movers, hand
Farm workers
Machine tool cutting operators and tenders, metal and plastic
Central office operators
Central office and PBX installers and repairers
Electrical and electronic assemblers
Station installers and repairers, telephone
Personnel clerks, except payroll and timekeeping
Data entry keyers, except composing

-300   -250   -200   -150   -100   -50   0
Thousands

- Jobs requiring the most education and training will grow faster than jobs with lower education and training requirements.

- Table 1 presents the fastest growing occupations and those having the largest numerical increase in employment over the 1994-2005 period, categorized by level of education and training.

Jobs requiring the most education and training will be the fastest growing and highest paying.

- Occupations which require a bachelor's degree or above will average 23 percent growth, almost double the 12-percent growth projected for occupations that require less education and training.

- Occupations that pay above average wages are projected to grow faster than occupations with below average wages. Jobs with above average wages are expected to account for 60 percent of employment growth over the 1994-2005 period. Jobs with higher earnings often require higher levels of education and training.

- Education is important in getting a high paying job. However, many occupations—for example, registered nurses, blue-collar worker supervisors, electrical and electronic technicians/technologists, carpenters, and police and detectives—do not require a college degree, yet offer higher than average earnings.

Groups in the labor force with lower than average educational attainment in 1994, including Hispanics and blacks, will continue to have difficulty obtaining a share of the high paying jobs that is consistent with their share of the labor force, unless their educational attainment rises. Although high paying jobs will be available without college training, most jobs that pay above average wages will require a college degree.

- Educational services are projected to increase by 2.2 million jobs and account for 1 out of every 8 jobs that will be added to the economy between 1994 and 2005. Most jobs will be for teachers, who are projected to account for about 20 percent of all jobs available for college graduates.

- Projected employment growth of the occupations whose earnings rank in the top quartile in the Nation was highly concentrated. Eight of the 146 occupations will account for about half of the new jobs: Registered nurses, systems analysts, blue-collar worker supervisors, general managers and top executives, and four teaching occupations—elementary school teachers, secondary school teachers, college faculty, and special education teachers.

Jobs requiring the least education and training will provide the most openings, but offer the lowest pay.
(See chart 9.)

- The distribution of jobs by education and training, and earnings, will change little over the 1994-2005 period, with jobs requiring the least amount of education and training, and generally offering low pay, continuing to account for about 4 of every 10 jobs.

- Jobs which require moderate-length and short-term training and experience (the two categories requiring the least amount of education and training) will provide over half of total job openings over the 1994-2005 period.

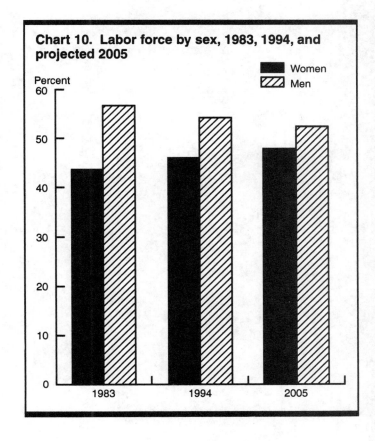

The labor force will continue to grow faster than the population.

- Spurred by the growing proportion of women who work, the labor force will grow slightly faster than the population over the 1994-2005 period.

Women will continue to comprise an increasing share of the labor force. (See chart 10.)

- Women, as a result of a faster rate of growth than men, are projected to represent a slightly greater portion of the labor force in 2005 than in 1994—increasing from 46 to 48 percent.

- The number of men in the labor force is projected to grow, but at a slower rate than in the past, in part reflecting declining employment in good-paying production jobs in manufacturing, and a continued shift in demand for workers from the goods-producing sector to the service-producing sector. Men with less education and training may find it increasingly difficult to obtain jobs consistent with their experience.

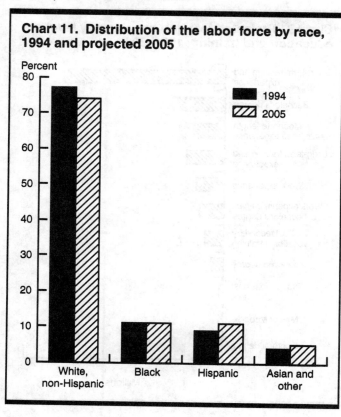

Chart 11. Distribution of the labor force by race, 1994 and projected 2005

The labor force will become increasingly diverse. (See chart 11.)

- The number of Hispanics, and Asians and other races, will increase much faster than blacks and white non-Hispanics. Blacks will increase faster than white non-Hispanics.

- Despite relatively slow growth, resulting in a declining share of the labor force, white non-Hispanics will still make up the vast majority of workers in 2005.

Interested in more detail?

- Readers interested in more information about projections and detail on the labor force, economic growth, industry and occupational employment, or methods and assumptions should consult the November 1995 *Monthly Labor Review*; *The Employment Outlook: 1994-2005*, BLS Bulletin 2472; or the Fall 1995 *Occupational Outlook Quarterly*. Information on the limitations inherent in economic projections also can be found in these publications.

- For more information about employment change, job openings, earnings, unemployment rates, and training requirements by occupation, consult *Occupational Projections and Training Data, 1996 Edition*, BLS Bulletin 2471.

Table 1. Jobs growing the fastest and having the largest numerical increase in employment from 1994-2005, by level of education and training

Fastest growing occupations	Occupations having the largest numerical increase in employment
First-professional degree	
Chiropractors	Lawyers
Lawyers	Physicians
Physicians	Clergy
Clergy	Chiropractors
Podiatrists	Dentists
Doctoral degree	
Medical scientists	College and university faculty
Biological scientists	Biological scientists
College and university faculty	Medical scientists
Mathematicians and all other mathematical scientists	Mathematicians and all other mathematical scientists
Master's degree	
Operations research analysts	Management analysts
Speech-language pathologists and audiologists	Counselors
Management analysts	Speech-language pathologists and audiologists
Counselors	Psychologists
Urban and regional planners	Operations research analysts
Work experience plus bachelor's degree	
Engineering, mathematics, and natural science managers	General managers and top executives
Marketing, advertising, and public relations managers	Financial managers
Artists and commercial artists	Marketing, advertising, and public relations managers
Financial managers	Engineering, mathematics, and natural science managers
Education administrators	Education administrators
Bachelor's degree	
Systems analysts	Systems analysts
Computer engineers	Teachers, secondary school
Occupational therapists	Teachers, elementary school
Physical therapists	Teachers, special education
Special education teachers	Social workers
Associate degree	
Paralegals	Registered nurses
Medical records technicians	Paralegals
Dental hygienists	Radiologic technologists and technicians
Respiratory therapists	Dental hygienists
Radiologic technologists and technicians	Medical records technicians
Postsecondary vocational training	
Manicurists	Secretaries, except legal and medical
Surgical technologists	Licensed practical nurses
Data processing equipment repairers	Hairdressers, hairstylists, and cosmetologists
Dancers and choreographers	Legal secretaries
Emergency medical technicians	Medical secretaries
Work experience	
Nursery and greenhouse managers	Marketing and sales worker supervisors
Lawn service managers	Clerical supervisors and managers
Food service and lodging managers	Food service and lodging managers
Clerical supervisors and managers	Instructors, adult education
Teachers and instructors, vocational and nonvocational training	Teachers and instructors, vocational education and training
Long-term training and experience (more than 12 months of on-the-job training)	
Electronic pagination systems workers	Maintenance repairers, general utility
Correction officers	Correction officers
Securities and financial services sales workers	Automotive mechanics
Patternmakers and layout workers, fabric and apparel	Cooks, restaurant
Producers, directors, actors, and entertainers	Police patrol officers
Moderate-length training and experience (1 to 12 months of combined on-the-job experience and informal training)	
Physical and corrective therapy assistants and aides	Human services workers
Occupational therapy assistants and aides	Medical assistants
Human services workers	Instructors and coaches, sports and physical training
Medical assistants	Dental assistants
Detectives, except public	Painters and paper hangers, construction and maintenance
Short-term training and experience (up to 1 month of on-the-job experience)	
Personal and home care aides	Cashiers
Home health aides	Janitors and cleaners, including maids and housekeepers
Amusement and recreation attendants	Salespersons, retail
Guards	Waiters and waitresses
Adjustment clerks	Home health aides

Sources of Career Information

This chapter identifies selected sources of information about occupations and career planning, counseling, training and education, and financial aid. Also, read the occupational statements in the *Handbook*, including the section on sources of additional information, which lists organizations you can contact for more information about particular occupations, training, and education.

Career information

Listed below are several good places to start collecting information you need on careers and job opportunities.

Personal contacts. The people closest to you—your family and friends—are often overlooked, but can be extremely helpful. They may be able to answer your questions directly or, more importantly, put you in touch with someone else who can. This "networking" can lead to an "informational interview," where you can meet with someone who is willing to answer your questions about a career or a company, and who can provide inside information on related fields and other helpful hints. This is a highly effective way to learn the recommended type of training for certain positions, how someone in that position entered and advanced, and what he or she likes and dislikes about the work.

Public libraries, career centers, and guidance offices. These places maintain a great deal of career material. To begin your library search, look at the computer listings under "vocations" or "careers" and then under specific fields. Check the periodicals section, where you will find trade and professional magazines and journals about specific occupations and industries. Familiarize yourself with the concerns and activities of potential employers by skimming their annual reports and other information they distribute to the public. You can also find occupational information on video cassettes, in kits, and through computerized information systems. Most public libraries maintain a relatively up-to-date collection of occupational or career materials. Don't forget the librarians; they can be a great source of information and can save you time by directing you to the information you need.

Check career centers for programs such as individual counseling, group discussions, guest speakers, field trips, and career days. Also, leaf through any files of pamphlets that describe employment in different organizations.

Always assess career guidance materials carefully. Information should be current. Beware of materials that seem to glamorize the occupation, overstate the earnings, or exaggerate the demand for workers; some schools may produce such materials to attract students.

Counselors. You may wish to seek help from a counselor. These professionals are trained to help you discover your strengths and weaknesses, guide you through an evaluation of your goals and values, and help you determine what you want in a career. The counselor will not tell you what to do, but will administer interest inventories and aptitude tests, interpret the results, and help you explore your options. Counselors also may be able to discuss local job markets, and the entry requirements and costs of the schools, colleges, or training programs offering preparation for the kind of work that interests you. You can find counselors in:

- high school guidance offices
- college career planning and placement offices
- placement offices in private vocational/technical schools and institutions
- vocational rehabilitation agencies
- counseling services offered by community organizations
- private counseling agencies and private practices
- State employment service offices affiliated with the U.S. Employment Service

Before employing the services of a private counselor or agency, seek recommendations and check their credentials. The International Association of Counseling Services (IACS) accredits counseling services throughout the country. To receive the listing of accredited services for your region, send a self-addressed, stamped, business-size envelope to:

☛IACS, 101 South Whiting St., Suite 211, Alexandria, VA 22304.

The *Directory of Counseling Services*, an IACS publication providing employment counseling and other assistance, may be available in your library or school career counseling center. A list of certified career counselors by State can be obtained from:

☛ The National Board of Certified Counselors, 3 Terrace Way, Suite D, Greensboro, NC 27403-3660. Phone: (910) 547-0607.

Internet networks and resources. The growth of on-line listings has made available a wide variety of resources at your fingertips—24 hours a day, 7 days a week—if you have access to the Internet. Companies, professional societies, academic institutions, and government agencies maintain on-line resources or "homepages" which are updated regularly with the latest information on their organization and it's activities.

Listings include information such as government documents, schedules of events, job openings, and even networking contacts. Listings for academic institutions provide links to career counseling and placement services through career resource centers, as well as information on financing your education. Colleges and universities also offer on-line guides to campus facilities and admission requirements and procedures.

The variety of career information databases available through the Internet provide much of the same information available through libraries, career centers, and guidance offices. However, no single network or resource will contain all desired information, so be prepared to search a lot of different places for what you need. As in a library search, look through various lists by field or discipline, or by using particular "keywords." It may even be helpful to consult a reference book such as *The Internet Yellow Pages*, which should be available in most libraries.

Professional societies, trade associations, labor unions, business firms, and educational institutions. These organizations provide a variety of free or inexpensive career material. Many of these are identified in the sources of additional information section of each *Handbook* statement. For information on occupations not covered in the *Handbook*, consult directories in your library's reference section for the names of potential sources. You may need to start with *The Guide to American Directories* or *The Directory of Directories*. Another useful resource is *The Encyclopedia of Associations*, an annual multivolume publication listing trade associations, professional societies, labor unions, and fraternal and patriotic organizations.

The National Technical Information Service Center, a central source for all audiovisual material produced by the U.S. Government, rents and sells material on jobs and careers. For a catalog, contact:

☛ NTIS, Springfield, VA 22161. Phone: 1-800-788-6282.

For first-hand experience in an occupation, you may wish to intern, or take a summer or part-time job. Some internships offer academic credit or pay a stipend. Check with guidance offices, college career resource centers, or directly with employers.

Organizations for specific groups. The organizations listed below provide information on career planning, training, job opportunities, or public policy support for specific groups. Consult directories in your library's reference center or a career guidance office for information on additional organizations and associations geared towards special groups.

Disabled:

☛ President's Committee on Employment of People with Disabilities, 1331 F St. NW., 3rd Floor, Washington, DC 20004. Phone: (202) 376-6200.

The blind: Information on the free national reference and referral service provided by the Federation of the Blind can be obtained by contacting:

☛ Job Opportunities for the Blind (JOB), National Federation of the Blind, 1800 Johnson St., Baltimore, MD 21230. Phone: toll-free, 1-800-638-7518, or locally (410) 659-9314.

Minorities: The National Urban League is a nonprofit community-based social service and civil rights organization that assists African-Americans in the achievement of social and economic equality. There are 113 local affiliates throughout the country that provide services related to employment and job training, and education and career development. Contact the affiliate nearest you for information.

☛ National Association for the Advancement of Colored People (NAACP), 4805 Mount Hope Dr., Baltimore, MD 21215. Phone: (410) 358-8900.

Older workers:

☛ National Association of Older Workers Employment Services, c/o National Council on the Aging, 409 3rd St. SW., Suite 200, Washington, DC 20024. Phone: (202) 479-1200.

☛ American Association of Retired Persons, Workforce Program Department, 601 E St. NW., Floor A5, Washington, DC 20049. Phone: (202) 434-2040.
☛ Asociación Nacional Por Personas Mayores (National Association for Hispanic Elderly), 2727 W. 6th St., Suite 20, Los Angeles, CA 90057. Phone: (231) 486-1922. (This organization specifically serves low-income, minority persons who are 55 years of age and older.)
☛ National Caucus/Center on Black Aged,Inc., 1424 K St. NW., Suite 500, Washington, DC 20005. Phone: (202) 637-8400.

Veterans: Contact the nearest regional office of the Department of Veterans Affairs or contact:

☛ Veterans' Employment and Training Service (VETS), 200 Constitution Ave. NW., Room S-1315, Washington, DC 20210. Phone: (202) 219-9116.

Women:

☛ Department of Labor, Women's Bureau, 200 Constitution Ave. NW., Washington, DC 20210. Phone: (202) 219-6652.
☛ Catalyst, 250 Park Ave. South, 5th floor, New York, NY 10003. Phone: (212) 777-8900.
☛ Wider Opportunities for Women, 815 15th St. NW., Suite 916, Washington, DC 20005. Phone: (202) 638-3143.

Federal laws, executive orders, and selected Federal grant programs bar discrimination in employment based on race, color, religion, sex, national origin, age, and handicap. Information on how to file a charge of discrimination is avail able from U.S. Equal Employment Opportunity Commission offices around the country. Their addresses and telephone numbers are listed in telephone directories under U.S. Government, EEOC, or are available from:

☛ Equal Employment Opportunity Commission, 1801 L St. NW., Washington, DC 20507. Phone: (202) 663-4900

Information on Federal laws concerning fair labor standards such as the minimum wage and equal employment opportunity can be obtained from:

☛ Office of Public Affairs, Employment Standards Administration, U.S. Department of Labor, Room C-4325, 200 Constitution Ave. NW., Washington, DC 20210. Phone: (202) 219-8743.

Education and training information

Colleges, schools, and training institutes readily reply to requests for information. When contacting these institutions, you may want to keep in mind the following items:

- admission requirements
- courses offered
- certificates or degrees awarded
- cost
- available financial aid
- location and size of school

Check with professional and trade associations for lists of schools that offer career preparation in a field you're interested in. Guidance offices and libraries usually have copies of the kinds of directories listed below, as well as college catalogs that can provide more information on specific institutions. Helpful resources include the *Directory of Private Career Schools and Colleges of Technology*, put out by the Accrediting Commission of Career Schools and Colleges of Technology. Be sure to use the latest edition because these directories and catalogs are often revised annually.

Information about home or correspondence study programs appears in the *Directory of Accredited Institutions*. Send requests for the *Directory* and a list of other publications to:

☛ Distance Education and Training Council, 1601 18th St. NW., Washington, DC 20009. Phone: (202) 234-5100.

Local labor unions, school guidance counselors, and State employment offices provide information about apprenticeships. Send requests for copies of *The National Apprenticeship Program* and *Apprenticeship Information* to:

☛ Bureau of Apprenticeship and Training, U.S. Department of Labor, 200 Constitution Ave. NW., Room N-4649, Washington, DC 20210. Phone: (202) 219-5921.

Financial aid information

Information about financial aid is available from a variety of sources. Contact your high school guidance counselor and college financial aid officer for information concerning scholarships, fellowships, grants, loans, and work-study programs. In addition, every State administers financial aid programs; contact State Departments of Education for information. Banks and credit unions can provide information about student loans. You also may want to consult the directories and guides to sources of student financial aid available in guidance offices and public libraries.

The Federal Government provides grants, loans, work-study programs, and other benefits to students. Information about programs administered by the U.S. Department of Education is presented in *The Student Guide to Federal Financial Aid Programs*, updated annually. To receive a copy, write to:

☛ Federal Student Aid Information Center, c/o Federal Student Aid Programs, P.O. Box 84, Washington, DC 20044-0084, or phone, toll-free, 1-800-433-3243.

The National and Community Service Trust Act of 1993 allows individuals aged 17 and over to serve in approved local programs before, during, or after postsecondary education, to earn money for education. A participant must complete at least 1 year of full-time or 2 years of part-time service to qualify. Awards may be used for past, present, or future expenses, including 2- and 4-year colleges, training programs, and graduate or professional programs. Information about service appointments may be found in high schools, colleges, and other placement offices, or can be obtained by contacting the commission on national service in your State, or by calling 1-800-94-ACORPS.

Meeting College Costs, an annual publication of the College Board, explains how student financial aid works and how to apply for it. The current edition is available to high school students through guidance counselors.

Need a Lift?, an annual publication of the American Legion, contains career and scholarship information. Copies cost $3 each, prepaid (including postage), and can be obtained from:

☛ American Legion, Attn: Emblem Sales, P.O. Box 1050, Indianapolis, IN 46206. Phone: (317) 630-1200.

Some student aid programs are designed to assist specific groups—Hispanics, blacks, native Americans, or women, for example. *Higher Education Opportunities for Minorities and Women*, published in 1991 by the U.S. Department of Education, is a guide to organizations offering assistance. This publication can be found in libraries and guidance offices, or copies may be obtained from:

☛ Department of Education, 400 Maryland Ave. SW., Washington, DC 20202. Phone: (202) 401-3550.

The Armed Forces have several educational assistance programs. These include the Reserve Officers' Training Corps (ROTC), the New G.I. bill, and tuition assistance. Information can be obtained from military recruiting centers, located in most cities.

State and local information

The *Handbook* provides information for the Nation as a whole. For help in locating State or local area information, you may contact the following:

State Occupational Information Coordinating Committee (SOICC). These committees may provide the information directly, or refer you to other sources. The addresses and telephone numbers of the directors of SOICC's are listed below.

State employment security agencies. These agencies develop detailed information about local labor markets, such as current and projected employment by occupation and industry, characteristics of the work force, and changes in State and local area economic activity. Addresses and telephone numbers of the directors of research and analysis in these agencies are listed below.

Most States have career information delivery systems (CIDS). Look for these systems in secondary schools, postsecondary institutions, libraries, job training sites, vocational rehabilitation centers, and employment service offices. Jobseekers can use the systems' computers, printed material, microfiche, and toll-free hotlines to obtain information on occupations, educational opportunities, student financial aid, apprenticeships, and military careers. Ask counselors and SOICC's for specific locations.

A computerized State Training Inventory (STI) developed by the National Occupational Information Coordinating Committee (NOICC) is also maintained by the SOICC's and available in every State. Education and training data are organized by occupation or training program title, type of institution, and geographic area. The database is compiled at the State level and includes more than 215,000 education and training programs offered by over 17,000 schools, colleges, and hospitals. If you are interested in STI, contact individual SOICC's for State-specific data.

Alabama
Director, Labor Market Information, Alabama Department of Industrial Relations, 649 Monroe St., Room 422, Montgomery, AL 36130. Phone: (205) 242-8855.

Director, Alabama Occupational Information Coordinating Committee, Room 424, 401 Adams Ave., P.O. Box 5690, Montgomery, AL 36103-5690. Phone: (334) 242-2990.

Alaska
Chief, Research and Analysis, Alaska Department of Labor, P.O. Box 25501, Juneau, AK 99802-5501. Phone: (907) 465-6022.

Executive Director, Alaska Department of Labor, Research and Analysis, P.O. Box 25501, Juneau, AK 99802-5501. Phone: (907) 465-4518.

American Samoa
Statistical Analyst, Research and Statistics, Office of Manpower Resources, American Samoa Government, Pago Pago, AS 96799. Phone: (684) 633-5172.

Director, Occupational Information Coordinating Council, Department of Human Resources, American Samoa Government, Pago Pago, AS 96799. Phone: (684) 633-4485.

Arizona
Research Administrator, Department of Economic Security, P.O. Box 6123, Site Code 733A, Phoenix, AZ 85005. Phone: (602) 542-3871.

Executive Director, Occupational Information Coordinating Council, P.O. Box 6123, Site Code 733A, 1789 West Jefferson St., First Floor, Phoenix, AZ 85005-6123. Phone: (602) 542-3871.

Arkansas
Chief, Arkansas Employment Security Department, P.O. Box 2981, Little Rock, AR 72203. Phone: (501) 682-3159.

Executive Director, Occupational Information Coordinating Council, Arkansas Employment Security Division, Employment and Training Services, P.O. Box 2981, Little Rock, AR 72203-2981. Phone: (501) 682-3159.

California
Chief, Labor Market Information Division, Employment Development Department, 700 Franklin Blvd., Suite 1100, Sacramento, CA 94280-0001. Phone: (916) 262-2160.

Executive Director, Occupational Information Coordinating Council, 1116 9th St. Lower Level, P.O. Box 944222, Sacramento, CA 94244-2220. Phone: (916) 323-6544.

Colorado
Director, Colorado Department of Labor, Tower 2, Suite 400, 1515 Arapahoe St., Denver, CO 80202-2117. Phone: (303) 620-4977.

Director, Occupational Information Coordinating Council, State Board Community College, 1391 Speer Blvd., Suite 600, Denver, CO 80204-2554. Phone: (303) 866-4488.

Connecticut
Director of Research, State Labor Department, 200 Folly Brook Blvd., Wethersfield, CT 06109. Phone: (203) 566-2120.

Executive Director, Occupational Information Coordinating Council, Connecticut Department of Education, 25 Industrial Park Rd., Middletown, CT 06457-1543. Phone: (203) 638-4042.

Delaware
Chief, Delaware Department of Labor, University Plaza, Building D, P.O. Box 9029, Newark, DE 19714. Phone: (302) 368-6962.

Executive Director, Office of Occupational and Labor Market Information, University Office Plaza, P.O. Box 9029, Newark, DE 19714-9029. Phone: (302) 368-6963.

District of Columbia
Chief, Labor Market Information, District of Columbia Department of Employment Services, 500 C St. NW., Room 201, Washington, DC 20001. Phone: (202) 724-7214.

Executive Director, Occupational Information Coordinating Council, Department of Employment Services, 500 C St. NW., Room 215, Washington, DC 20001-2187. Phone: (202) 724-7237.

Florida
Chief, Florida Department of Labor and Employment Security, 2012 Capitol Circle SE., Room 200 Hartman Bldg., Tallahassee, FL 32399-0674. Phone: (904) 488-1048.

Manager, Bureau of Labor Market Information/Department of Labor and Employment Security, 2012 Capitol Circle SE., Hartman Bldg., Suite 200, Tallahassee, FL 32399-0673. Phone: (904) 488-1048.

Georgia
Director, Labor Information Systems, Georgia Department of Labor, 223 Courtlnad St. NE., Atlanta, GA 30303-1751. Phone: (404) 656-3177.

Executive Director, Occupational Information Coordinating Council, Department of Labor, 148 International Blvd., Sussex Place, Atlanta, GA 30303-1751. Phone: (404) 656-9639.

Guam
Administrator, Department of Labor, Bureau of Labor Statistics, Government of Guam, P.O. Box 9970, Tamuning, GU 96911-9970.

Executive Director, Human Resource Development Agency, Jay Ease Bldg., Third Floor, P.O. Box 2817, Agana, GU 96910-2817. Phone: (671) 646-9341.

Hawaii
Chief, Department of Labor and Industrial Relations, 830 Punchbowl St., Rm 304, Honolulu, HI 96813. Phone: (808) 586-8999.

Executive Director, Occupational Information Coordinating Council, 830 Punchbowl St., Room 315, Honolulu, HI 96813-5080. Phone: (808) 586-8750.

Idaho
Chief, Research and Analysis, Idaho Department of Employment, 317 Main St., Boise, ID 83735. Phone: (208) 334-6169.

Director, Occupational Information Coordinating Council, Len B. Jordan Bldg., Room 301, 650 West State St., P.O. Box 83720, Boise, ID 83720-0095. Phone: (208) 334-3705.

Illinois
Director, Illinois Department of Employment Security, 401 South State St., Suite 215, Chicago, IL 60605. Phone: (312) 793-2316.

Executive Director, Occupational Information Coordinating Council, 217 East Monroe, Suite 203, Springfield, IL 62706-1147. Phone: (217) 785-0789.

Indiana
Director, Labor Market Information, Department of Employment and Training Services, 10 North Senate Ave., Indianapolis, IN 46204. Phone: (317) 232-7460.

Executive Director, Department of Workforce Development State Occupational Information Coordinating Committee, Indiana Government Center South, 10 North Senate Ave., Room SE 205, Indianapolis, IN 46204-2277. Phone: (317) 232-8528.

Iowa
Chief, Iowa Department of Employment Services, 1000 East Grand Ave., Des Moines, IA 50319. Phone: (515) 281-8181.

Acting Executive Director, Occupational Information Coordinating Council, Iowa Department of Economic Development, 200 East Grand Ave., Des Moines, IA 50309-1747. Phone: (515) 242-4889.

Kansas
Chief, Labor Market Information, Kansas Department of Human Resources, 401Topeka Blvd., Topeka, KS 66603-3182. Phone: (913) 296-5058.

Director, State Occupational Information Coordinating Committee, 401 Topeka Ave., Topeka, KS 66603-3182. Phone: (913) 296-2387.

Kentucky
Director, Labor Market Research and Analysis, Department of Employment Services, 275 East Main St., Frankfort, KY 40621. Phone: (502) 564-7976.

Information Liaison/Manager, Occupational Information Coordinating Council, 2031 Capital Plaza Tower, Frankfort, KY 40601. Phone: (502) 564-4258.

Louisiana
Director, Research and Statistics Division, Department of Employment and Training, P.O. Box 94094, Baton Rouge, LA 70804-9094. Phone: (504) 342-3141.

Acting Director, Louisiana Occupational Information Coordinating Committee, 1001 North 23rd, Baton Rouge, LA 70802. Phone: (504) 342-5149.

Maine
Director, Economic Analysis and Research, Maine Department of Labor, P.O. Box 309, Augusta, ME 04330-0309. Phone: (207) 287-2271.

Acting Executive Director, Maine Occupational Information Coordinating Committee, State House Station 71, Augusta, ME 04333. Phone: (207) 624-6200.

Maryland
Director, Office of Labor Market Analysis and Information, Department of Labor, Licensing, and Regulations, 1100 North Eutaw St., Room 601, Baltimore, MD 21201. Phone: (410) 767-2250.

Director, Occupational Information Coordinating Council, State Department of Employment and Training, 1100 North Eutaw St., Room 103, Baltimore, MD 21201-2298. Phone: (410) 767-2951.

Massachusetts
Director of Research, Division of Employment Security, 19 Staniford St., 2nd Floor, Boston, MA 02114. Phone: (617) 626-6556.

Director, Occupational Information Coordinating Council, Massachusetts Division of Employment Security, Charles F. Hurley Bldg., 2nd Floor, Government Center, Boston, MA 02114. Phone: (617) 727-5718.

Michigan
Director, Bureau of Research and Statistics, Michigan Employment Security Commission, 7310 Woodward Ave., Room 510, Detroit, MI 48202. Phone: (313) 876-5904.

Executive Coordinator, Michigan Occupational Information Coordinating Committee, Victor Office Center, Third Floor, 201 North Washington Square, Box 30015, Lansing, MI 48909-7515. Phone: (517) 373-0363.

Minnesota
Director, Research and Statistical Services, Minnesota Department of Economic Security, 390 North Robert St., 5th Floor, St. Paul, MN 55101. Phone: (612) 296-6546.

Director, Occupational Information Coordinating Council, Department of Jobs and Training, 390 North Robert Street., St. Paul, MN 55101. Phone: (612) 296-2072.

Mississippi
Chief, Labor Market Information Department, Mississippi Employment Security Commission, P.O. Box 1699, Jackson, MS 39215-1699. Phone: (601) 961-7424.

Director, Department of Economic and Community Development, Labor Assistance Division/ State Occupational Information Coordinating Committee Office, 301 West Pearl St., Jackson, MS 39203-3089. Phone: (601) 949-2240.

Missouri
Chief, Research and Analysis,Division of Employment Security, 421 East Dunkin St., P.O. Box 59, Jefferson City, MO 65104-0059. Phone: (314) 751-3591.

Director, Missouri Occupational Information Coordinating Committee, 400 Dix Rd., Jefferson City, MO 65109. Phone: (314) 751-3800.

Montana
Chief, Research and Analysis, Department of Labor and Industry, P.O. Box 1728, Helena, MT 59624. Phone: (406) 444-2430.

Program Manager, Montana Occupational Information Coordinating Committee, P.O. Box 1728, 1327 Lockey St., Second Floor, Helena, MT 59624-1728. Phone: (406) 444-2741.

Nebraska
Research Administrator, Labor Market Information, Nebraska Department of Labor, 550 South 16th St., P.O. Box 94600, Lincoln, NE 68509. Phone: (402) 471-2600.

Administrator, Nebraska Occupational Information Coordinating Committee, P.O. Box 94600, 550 South 16th St., Lincoln, NE 68509-4600. Phone: (402) 471-9953.

Nevada
Chief, Research and Analysis/LMI, Nevada Employment Security Division, 500 East 3rd St., Carson City, NV 89713-0001. Phone: (702) 687-4550.

Director, Nevada Occupational Information Coordinating Committee, 500 East 3rd St., Carson City, NV 89713. Phone: (702) 687-4550.

New Hampshire
Director, Labor Market Information, New Hampshire Department of Employment Security, 32 South Main St., Concord, NH 03301. Phone: (603) 228-4123.

Director, New Hampshire State Occupational Information Coordinating Committee, 64B Old Suncook Rd., Concord, NH 03301. Phone: (603) 228-3349.

New Jersey
Director, Labor Market and Demographic Research, New Jersey Department of Labor, CN383, Trenton, NJ 08625. Phone: (609) 292-0089.

Staff Director, New Jersey Occupational Information Coordinating Committee, Room 609, Labor and Industry Bldg., CN056, Trenton, NJ 08625-0056. Phone: (609) 292-2682.

New Mexico
Chief, Economic Research and Analysis Bureau, New Mexico Department of Labor, P.O. Box 1928, Albuquerque, NM 87103. Phone: (505) 841-8645.

Director, New Mexico Occupational Information Coordinating Committee, 401 Broadway NE., Tiwa Bldg., P.O. Box 1928, Albuquerque, NM 87103-1928. Phone: (505) 841-8455.

New York
Director, Division of Research and Statistics, New York State Department of Labor, State Office Building Campus, Bldg. 12, Room 402, Albany, NY 12240. Phone: (518) 457-6369.

Executive Director, New York Occupational Information Coordinating Committee, Research and Statistics Division, State Campus, Bldg. 12, Room 400, Albany, NY 12240. Phone: (518) 457-6182.

North Carolina
Director, Labor Market Information, Employment Security Commission of North Carolina, P.O. Box 25903, Raleigh, NC 27611. Phone: (919) 733-2936.

Executive Director, North Carolina Occupational Information Coordinating Committee, 700 Wade Avenue, P.O. Box 25903, Raleigh, NC 27611. Phone: (919) 733-6700.

North Dakota
Director, Research and Statistics, Job Service of North Dakota, P.O. Box 5507, Bismarck, ND 58502-5507. Phone: (701) 328-2860.

Coordinator, North Dakota State Occupational Information Coordinating Committee, 1720 Burnt Boat Dr., P.O. Box 1537, Bismarck, ND 58502-1537. Phone: (701) 328-2733.

Northern Mariana Islands
Executive Director, Northern Mariana Islands Occupational Information Coordinating Committee, P.O. Box 149, Saipan, CM 96950-0149. Phone: (670) 234-7394.

Ohio
Administrator, Labor Market Information Division, Ohio Bureau of Employment Services, 78-80 Chestnut, Columbus, OH 43215. Phone: (614) 752-9494.

Director, Ohio Occupational Information Coordinating Committee, Ohio Bureau of Employment Services, P.O. Box 1618, Columbus, OH 43266-0018. Phone: (614) 466-1109.

Oklahoma
Director, Research Division, Oklahoma Employment Security Commission, 305 Will Rogers Memorial Office Bldg., Oklahoma City, OK 73105. Phone: (405) 557-7265.

Executive Director, Occupational Information Coordinating Council, Department of Voc/Tech Education, 1500 W. 7th Ave., Stillwater, OK 74074-4364. Phone: (405) 743-5198.

Oregon
Adminstrator for Research, Tax and Analysis, Employment Department, 875 Union St. NE., Salem, OR 97311. Phone: (503) 378-5490.

Acting Director, Oregon Occupational Information Coordinating Committee, 875 Union St. NE., Salem, OR 97311-0101. Phone: (503) 378-5490.

Pennsylvania
Director, Bureau of Research and Statistics, Department of Labor and Industry, 300 Captiol Associates Building, 3rd Floor, Harrisburg, PA 17120-9969. Phone: (717) 787-3266.

Director, Pennsylvania Department of Labor and Industry, 1224 Labor and Industry Bldg., 7th and Foster, Harrisburg, PA 17120-0019. Phone: (717) 787-8646.

Puerto Rico
Director, Research and Statistics Division, Department of Labor and Human Resources, 505 Munoz Rivera Ave., 20th Floor, Hato Rey, PR 00918. Phone: (809) 754-5385.

Director, Puerto Rico Occupational Information Coordinating Committee, P.O. Box 366212, San Juan, PR 00936-6212. Phone: (809) 723-7110.

Rhode Island
Administrator, Labor Market Information, Rhode Island Department of Employment and Training, 101 Friendship St., Providence, RI 02903. Phone: (401) 277-2731.

Director, Rhode Island Occupational Information Coordinating Committee, 22 Hayes St., Room 133, Providence, RI 02908-5092. Phone: (401) 272-0830.

South Carolina
Director, Labor Market Information, South Carolina Employment Security Commission, P.O. Box 995, Columbia, SC 29202. Phone: (803) 737-2660.

Director, South Carolina Occupational Information Coordinating Committee, 1550 Gadsden St., P.O. Box 995, Columbia, SC 29202-0995. Phone: (803) 737-2733.

South Dakota
Director, Labor Information Center, South Dakota Department of Labor, 400 S. Roosevelt, P.O. Box 4730, Aberdeen, SD 57402-4730. Phone: (605) 626-2314.
Director, Occupational Information Coordinating Council, South Dakota Department of Labor, 420 South Roosevelt St., P.O. Box 4730, Aberdeen, SD 57402-4730. Phone: (605) 626-2314.

Tennessee
Director, Research and Statistics Division, Tennessee Department of Employment Security, 500 James Robertson Pkwy., 11th Floor-Volunteer Plaza, Nashville, TN 37245-1000. Phone: (615) 741-2284.

Executive Director, Tennessee Occupational Information Coordinating Committee, 500 James Robertson Pkwy., 11th Floor-Volunteer Plaza, Nashville, TN 37219-1215. Phone: (615) 741-6451.

Texas
Director, Economic Research and Analysis, Texas Employment Commission, 15th & Congress Ave., Room 208T, Austin, TX 78778. Phone: (512) 463-2616.

Director, Texas Occupational Information Coordinating Committee, Texas Employment Commission Building, 3520 Executive Center Dr., Suite 205, Austin, TX 78731-0000. Phone: (512) 502-3750.

Utah
Director, LMI & Research, Utah Department of Employment Security, P.O. Box 45249, Salt Lake City, UT 84145-0249. Phone: (801) 536-7425.

Executive Director, Utah Occupational Information Coordinating Committee, P.O. Box 45249, 140 East 300 South, Salt Lake City, UT 84145-0249. Phone: (801) 536-7806.

Vermont
Director, Policy and Information, Vermont Department of Employment and Training, P.O. Box 488, Montpelier, VT 05602. Phone: (802) 828-4135.

Director, Vermont Occupational Information Coordinating Committee, 5 Green Mountain Dr., P.O. Box 488, Montpelier, VT 05601-0488. Phone: (802) 229-0311.

Virginia
Director, Economic Information and Services Division, Virginia Employment Commission, P.O. Box 1358, Richmond, VA 23211. Phone: (804) 786-7496.

Executive Director, Virginia Occupational Information Coordinating Committee, Virginia Employment Commission, 703 East Main St., P.O. Box 1358, Richmond, VA 23211-1358. Phone: (804) 786-7496.

Virgin Islands
Chief, Bureau of Labor Statistics, Virgin Islands Department of Labor, 53A and 54B Kronprindsens Gade,Charlotte Amalie, St. Thomas, U.S. Virgin Islands 00820. Phone: (809) 776-3700.

Coordinator, Virgin Islands Occupational Information Coordinating Committee, P.O. Box 3359, St. Thomas, U.S. Virgin Islands 00801. Phone: (809) 776-3700.

Washington
Chief, Labor and Economic Analysis, Washington Employment Security Department, P.O. Box 9046, Olympia, WA 98507-9046. Phone: (360) 438-4804.

Acting Executive Director, Washington Occupational Information Coordinating Committee, c/o Employment Security Department, P.O. Box 9046, Olympia, WA 98507-9046. Phone: (206) 438-4803.

West Virginia
Assistant Director, Labor and Economic Research, Bureau of Employment Programs, 112 California Ave., Charleston, WV 25305-0112. Phone: (304) 558-2660.

Executive Director, West Virginia Occupational Information Coordinating Committee, 5088 Washington St. West, Cross Lanes, WV 25313. Phone: (304) 759-0724.

Wisconsin
Director, Bureau of Labor Market Information, Department of Industry, Labor, and Human Relations, P.O. Box 7944, Madison, WI 53707. Phone: (608) 266-5843.

Administrative Director, Wisconsin Occupational Information Coordinating Council, Division of Jobs, Employment and Training Services, 201 East Washington Ave., P.O. Box 7972, Madison, WI 53707-7972. Phone: (608) 266-8012.

Wyoming
Manager, Research and Planning, Division of Administration, Department of Employment, P.O. Box 2760, Casper, WY 82602-2760. Phone: (307) 473-3801.

Executive Director, Wyoming Occupational Information Coordinating Council, Post Office Box 2760, 100 West Midwest, Casper, WY 82602-2760. Phone: (307) 265-6715.

Finding a Job
and Evaluating a Job Offer

Information on Finding a Job

It takes some people a great deal of time and effort to find a job they enjoy. Others may walk right into an ideal employment situation. Don't be discouraged if you have to pursue many leads. Friends, neighbors, teachers, and counselors may know of available jobs in your field of interest. Read the want ads. Consult State employment service offices and private or nonprofit employment agencies, or contact employers directly.

Where To Learn About Job Openings

Parents, friends, and Neighbors
School or college placement services
Classified ads
—Local and out-of-town newspapers
—Professional journals
—Trade magazines
Employment agencies and career consultants
State employment service offices
Internet networks and resources
Civil service announements (Federal, State, local)
Labor unions
Professional associations (State and local chapters)
Libraries and community centers
Women's counseling and employment programs
Youth programs
Employers

Job search methods

Want ads. The "Help Wanted" ads in newspapers list hundreds of jobs. Realize, however, that many job openings are not listed. Also, be aware that the classified ads sometimes do not give some important information. Many offer little or no description of the job, working conditions, or pay. Some ads do not identify the employer. They may simply give a post office box for sending your resume. This makes follow-up inquiries very difficult. Furthermore, some ads offer out-of-town jobs; others advertise employment agencies rather than employment.

Keep the following in mind if you are using want ads:

- Do not rely solely on the classifieds to find a job; follow other leads as well.
- Answer ads promptly, since openings may be filled quickly, even before the ad stops appearing in the paper.
- Follow the ads diligently. Check them every day, as early as possible, to give yourself an advantage.

- Beware of "no experience necessary" ads. These ads often signal low wages, poor working conditions, or straight commission work.
- Keep a record of all ads to which you have responded, including the specific skills, educational background, and personal qualifications required for the position.

Internet networks and resources. A variety of information on jobs and job search resources and techniques is currently available on-line through the Internet. Once you have access, on-line resources are available 7 days a week, 24 hours a day. Internet resources include Usenet newsgroups, Telnet sites, and World Wide Web resources, just to name a few.

In addition to the listings of companies, professional societies, academic institutions, and government agencies, it is possible to search employment ad and career information databases directly. Available information includes government reports, salary surveys, job listings, and even "networking" contacts within organizations. You can find out about companies or academic institutions directly, as well as the cities in which they are located.

When searching employment ad databases, it is sometimes possible to post your resume on-line or send it to an employer via electronic mail. Some sources provide this service free of charge once you have access to the Internet. However, be careful that you are not going to incur any additional charges for postings or updates.

No single network or resource will contain all information on employment or career opportunities, so be prepared to search for what you need. Job listings may be posted by field or discipline so it is best to begin your search using topics or "keywords." It may be helpful to consult a reference book such as *The Internet Yellow Pages*, which should be available in most libraries.

Public employment service. The State employment service, sometimes called the Job Service, operates in coordination with the U.S. Employment Service of the U.S. Department of Labor. About 1,700 local offices, also known as employment service centers, help jobseekers find jobs and help employers find qualified workers at no cost to themselves. To find the office nearest you, look in the State government telephone listings under "Job Service" or "Employment."

A computerized job network system—*America's Job Bank*—run by the U.S. Department of Labor, lists approximately 100,000 job openings each week. A wide range of jobs are listed all over the country, and most are full-time jobs in the private sector. Jobseekers can access these listings through the use of a personal computer in any local public employment service office, as well as in several hundred military installations. In addition, some State employment agencies have set up *America's Job Bank* in other settings, including libraries, schools, shopping malls, and correctional facilities. *America's Job Bank* is also available on-line

through the Internet and can be accessed at the following World Wide Web address: *http://www.ajb.dni.us*

Tips for Finding the Right Job, a U.S. Department of Labor pamphlet, offers advice on determining your job skills, organizing your job search, writing a resume, and making the most of an interview. *Job Search Guide: Strategies For Professionals*, another U.S. Department of Labor publication, also discusses specific steps that jobseekers can follow to identify employment opportunities. This publication includes sections on handling your job loss, managing your personal resources, assessing your skills and interests, researching the job market, conducting the job search and networking, writing resumes and cover letters, employment interviewing and testing, and sources of additional information. Check with your State employment service office, or order a copy of these publications from the U.S. Government Printing Office. Phone: (202) 512-1800 for price and ordering information.

Job matching and referral. At a State employment service office, an interviewer will determine if you are "job ready" or if counseling and testing services would be helpful before you begin your job search. After you are "job ready," you may examine available job listings and select openings that interest you. A staff member can then describe the job openings in detail and arrange for interviews with prospective employers. Career counseling and testing centers can test for occupational aptitudes and interests and then help you choose and prepare for a career.

Services for special groups. By law, veterans are entitled to priority at State employment service centers. Veterans' employment representatives can inform you of available assistance and help you deal with any problems.

Summer Youth Programs provide summer jobs in city, county, and State government agencies for low-income youth. Students, school dropouts, or graduates entering the labor market who are between 16 and 21 years of age are eligible. In addition, the Job Corps, with more than 100 centers throughout the United States, helps young people learn skills or obtain education.

Service centers also refer applicants to opportunities available under the Job Training Partnership Act (JTPA) of 1982. JTPA prepares economically disadvantaged persons and those facing barriers to employment for jobs.

Federal job information. For information about employment with the U.S. Government, call the Federal Job Information Center's *Career America Connection*, operated by the Office of Personnel Management. The phone number is (202) 606-2700, or write to:

☛ Federal Job Information Center, 1900 E St. NW., Room 1416, Washington, DC 20415.

It is also possible to obtain this information directly on-line by accessing the *Fedworld* information network on the Internet. This is a central access point for locating and acquiring information about U.S. Government employment. Access *Fedworld* at the following World Wide Web address: *http://www.fedworld.gov*

Private employment agencies. These agencies can be very helpful, but don't forget that they are in business to make money. Most agencies operate on a commission basis, with the fee dependent upon a successful match. You or the hiring company will have to pay a fee for the matching service. Find out the exact cost and who is responsible for paying it before using the service.

While employment agencies can help you save time and contact employers who otherwise may be difficult to locate, in some cases, your costs may outweigh the benefits. Consider any guarantee they offer when figuring the cost.

College career planning and placement offices. College placement offices facilitate matching job openings with suitable jobseekers. You can set up schedules and use available facilities for interviews with recruiters or scan lists of part-time, temporary, and summer jobs maintained in many of these offices. You also can get counseling, testing, and job search advice and take advantage of their career resource library. Here you also will be able to identify and evaluate your interests, work values, and skills; attend workshops on such topics as job search strategy, resume writing, letter writing, and effective interviewing; critique drafts of resumes and videotapes of mock interviews; explore files of resumes and references; and attend job fairs conducted by the office.

Community agencies. Many nonprofit organizations offer counseling, career development, and job placement services, generally targeted to a particular group, such as women, youth, minorities, ex-offenders, or older workers.

Many communities have career counseling, training, placement, and support services for employment. These programs are sponsored by a variety of organizations, including churches and synagogues, nonprofit organizations, social service agencies, the State employment service, and vocational rehabilitation agencies. Many cities have commissions that provide services for these special groups.

Employers. It is possible to apply directly to employers without a referral. You may locate a potential employer in the *Yellow Pages*, in directories of local chambers of commerce, and in other directories that provide information about employers. When you find an employer you are interested in, you can send a cover letter and resume or file a job application even if you don't know for certain that an opening exists.

Applying for a Job

Resumes and application forms. Resumes and application forms are two ways to provide employers with written evidence of your skills and knowledge. Most information is common to both the resume and application form, but the way the information is presented differs. Some employers prefer a resume while others require an application form.

There are many ways of organizing a resume. Depending upon the job you are applying for, you should choose the format that best highlights your skills, training, and experience. It may be helpful to look at different examples. Examples can be found in a variety of books and publications

---

What Goes Into a Resume

A resume summarizes your qualifications and employment history. It usually is required when applying for managerial, administrative, professional, or technical positions. Although there is no set format, a resume should contain the following information:

- Name, address, and telephone number.
- Employment objective. State the type of work or specific job you are seeking.
- Education, including school name and address, dates of attendance, curriculum, and highest grade completed or degree awarded.
- Experience, paid or volunteer. Include the following for each job: Job title, name and address of employer, and dates of employment. Describe your job duties.
- Special skills, knowledge of machinery, proficiency in foreign languages, honors received, awards, or membership in organizations.
- Note on your resume that "references are available upon request."

---

available through public libraries or career guidance centers. Also, ask someone to read your resume and suggest ways to improve it.

In completing an application form, make sure you fill it out properly and follow all instructions. In general, the same type of information is included on an application form as in a resume. Don't omit any information asked for and be sure to check that all information provided is correct.

Cover letters. A cover letter should be sent with a resume or application form, as a way to introduce yourself to employers. It should capture the employer's attention, follow a business letter format, and should generally include the following information:

- The name and address of the specific person to whom the letter is addressed
- The reason for your interest in the company or position
- Your main qualifications for the position (in brief)
- A request for an interview
- Your phone number

Interviewing. An interview gives you the best opportunity to show an employer your qualifications, so it pays to be well prepared. Each interview is different, however. The box below provides some helpful information.

Evaluating a Job Offer

Once you receive a job offer, you are faced with a difficult decision and must evaluate each offer carefully. Fortunately, most organizations will not expect you to accept or reject an offer on the spot. You probably will be given at least a week to make up your mind.

There are many issues to consider when assessing a job offer. Will the organization be a good place to work? Will the job be interesting? How are opportunities for advance-

---

Job Interview Tips

Preparation:
  Learn about the organization.
  Have a specific job or jobs in mind.
  Review your qualifications for the job.
  Prepare answers to broad questions about yourself.
  Review your resume.
  Practice an interview with a friend or relative.
  Arrive before the scheduled time of your interview.

Personal Appearance:
  Be well groomed.
  Dress appropriately.
  Do not chew gum or smoke.

The Interview:
  Answer each question concisely.
  Respond promptly.
  Use good manners. Learn the name of your interviewer and shake hands as you meet.
  Use proper English and avoid slang.
  Be cooperative and enthusiastic.
  Ask questions about the position and the organization.
  Thank the interviewer, and follow up with a letter.

Test (if employer gives one):
  Listen closely to instructions.
  Read each question carefully.
  Write legibly and clearly.
  Budget your time wisely and don't dwell on one question.

Information To Bring to an Interview:
  Social Security number.
  Driver's license number.
  Resume. Although not all employers require applicants to bring a resume, you should be able to furnish the interviewer with information about your education, training, and previous employment.
  References. An employer usually requires three references. Get permission from people before using their names, and make sure they will give you a good reference. Try to avoid using relatives. For each reference, provide the following information: Name, address, telephone number, and job title.

---

ment? Is the salary fair? Does the employer offer good benefits? If you have not already figured out exactly what you want, the following discussion may help you develop a set of criteria for judging job offers, whether you are starting a career, reentering the labor force after a long absence, or planning a career change.

The organization. Background information on an organization can help you decide whether it is a good place for you to work. Factors to consider include the organization's business or activity, financial condition, age, size, and location. Information on growth prospects for the industry or industries that the company represents also is important. Here are some questions to ask.

Is the organization's business or activity in keeping with your own interests and beliefs?
It will be easier to apply yourself to the work if you are enthusiastic about what the organization does.

How will the size of the organization affect you?
Large firms generally offer a greater variety of training programs and career paths, more managerial levels for advancement, and better employee benefits than small firms. Large employers may also have more advanced technologies in their laboratories, offices, and factories. However, jobs in large firms may tend to be highly specialized.

Jobs in small firms may offer broader authority and responsibility, a closer working relationship with top management, and a chance to clearly see your contribution to the success of the organization.

Should you work for a fledgling organization or one that is well established?
New businesses have a high failure rate, but for many people, the excitement of helping create a company and the potential for sharing in its success more than offset the risk of job loss. It may also be as exciting and rewarding, however, to work for a young firm which already has a foothold on success.

Does it make any difference to you whether the company is private or public?
A privately owned company may be controlled by an individual or a family, which can mean that key jobs are reserved for relatives and friends. A publicly owned company is controlled by a board of directors responsible to the stockholders. Key jobs are open to anyone with talent.

Is the organization in an industry with favorable long-term prospects?
The most successful firms tend to be in industries that are growing rapidly.

Where is the job located?
If it is in another city, you need to consider the cost of living, the availability of housing and transportation, and the quality of educational and recreational facilities in the new location. Even if the place of work is in your area, consider the time and expense of commuting in your decision.

It is easy to get background information on an organization simply by telephoning its public relations office. A public company's annual report to the stockholders tells about its corporate philosophy, history, products or services, goals, and financial status. Most government agencies can furnish reports that describe their programs and missions. Press releases, company newsletters or magazines, and recruitment brochures also can be useful. Ask the organization for any other items that might interest a prospective employee.

Background information on the organization also may be available at your public or school library. If you cannot get an annual report, check the library for reference directories that provide basic facts about the company, such as earnings, products and services, and number of employees. Some directories widely available in libraries include the following:

- *Dun & Bradstreet's Million Dollar Directory*
- *Standard and Poor's Register of Corporations*
- *Directors and Executives*

- *Moody's Industrial Manual*
- *Thomas' Register of American Manufacturers*
- *Ward's Business Directory*

Stories about an organization in magazines and newspapers can tell a great deal about its successes, failures, and plans for the future. You can identify articles on a company by looking under its name in periodical or computerized indexes such as the following—however, it probably will not be useful to look back more than 2 or 3 years.

- *Business Periodicals Index*
- *Reader's Guide to Periodical Literature*
- *Newspaper Index*
- *Wall Street Journal Index*
- *New York Times Index*

The library also may have government publications that present projections of growth for the industry in which the organization is classified. Long-term projections of employment and output for more than 200 industries, covering the entire economy, are developed by the Bureau of Labor Statistics and revised every other year—see the November 1995 *Monthly Labor Review* for the most recent projections. The *U.S. Global Trade Outlook*, published annually by the U.S. Department of Commerce, is the successor to the *U.S. Industrial Outlook* and presents detailed analyses of the globalization of U.S. industry and growth prospects for six industrial sectors. Trade magazines also have frequent articles on the trends for specific industries.

Career centers at colleges and universities often have information on employers that is not available in libraries. Ask the career center librarian how to find out about a particular organization. The career center may have an entire file of information on the company.

The nature of the work. Even if everything else about the job is good, you will be unhappy if you dislike the day-to-day work. Determining in advance whether you will like the work may be difficult. However, the more you find out about it before accepting or rejecting the job offer, the more likely you are to make the right choice. You may want to ask yourself the following questions:

Does the work match your interests and make good use of your skills?
The duties and responsibilities of the job should be explained in enough detail to answer this question.

How important is the job in this company?
An explanation of where you fit in the organization and how you are supposed to contribute to its overall objectives should give you an idea of the job's importance.

Are you comfortable with the supervisor?
Do the other employees seem friendly and cooperative?
Does the work require travel?
Does the job call for irregular hours?
Some jobs involve regular hours—for example, 40 hours a week, during the day, Monday through Friday. Other jobs involve variable hours, including night, weekend, or holiday work. In addition, some jobs routinely require overtime to

meet deadlines or sales or production goals, or to better serve customers. Consider the effect of work hours on your personal life.

How long do most people who enter this job stay with the company?
High turnover can mean dissatisfaction with the nature of the work or something else about the job.

The opportunities. A good job offers you opportunities to learn new skills, increase your earnings, and rise to positions of greater authority, responsibility, and prestige. A lack of opportunities can dampen interest in the work and result in frustration and boredom.

The company should have a training plan for you. What valuable new skills does the company plan to teach you?

The employer should give you some idea of promotion possibilities within the organization. What is the next step on the career ladder? If you have to wait for a job to become vacant before you can be promoted, how long does this usually take? Employers differ on their policies regarding promotion from within the organization. When opportunities for advancement do arise, will you compete with applicants from outside the company? Can you apply for jobs for which you qualify elsewhere within the organization or is mobility within the firm limited?

The salary and benefits. Wait for the employer to introduce these subjects. Most companies will not talk about pay until they have decided to hire you. In order to know if their offer is reasonable, you need a rough estimate of what the job should pay. You may have to go to several sources for this information. Talk to friends who recently were hired in similar jobs. Ask your teachers and the staff in the college placement office about starting pay for graduates with your qualifications. Scan the help-wanted ads in newspapers.

If you are considering the salary and benefits for a job in another geographic area, make allowances for differences in the cost of living, which may be significantly higher in a large metropolitan area than in a smaller city, town, or rural area.

You also should learn the organization's policy regarding overtime. Depending on the job, you may or may not be exempt from laws requiring the employer to compensate you for overtime. Find out how many hours you will be expected to work each week and whether you receive overtime pay or compensatory time off for working more than the specified number of hours in a week.

Also take into account that the starting salary is just that, the start. Your salary should be reviewed on a regular basis—many organizations do it every 12 months. How much can you expect to earn after 1, 2, or 3 or more years? An employer cannot be specific about the amount of pay if it includes commissions and bonuses.

Benefits can also add a lot to your base pay, but they vary widely. Find out exactly what the benefit package includes and how much of the costs you must bear.

Check the library or your school's career center for salary surveys such as the College Placement Council Salary Survey or salary information compiled by professional associations.

Detailed data on wages and benefits are also available from:

☛ Bureau of Labor Statistics, Office of Compensation and Working Conditions, Division of Occupational Pay and Employee Benefit Levels, 2 Massachusetts Ave. NE., Room 4160, Washington, DC 20212-0001. Phone: (202) 606-6225.

Data on weekly earnings, based on the Current Population Survey, are available from:

☛ Bureau of Labor Statistics, Office of Employment and Unemployment Statistics, 2 Massachusetts Ave. NE., Room 4945, Washington, DC 20212-0001. Phone: (202) 606-6400.

Occupational Information Included in the *Handbook*

The *Occupational Outlook Handbook* is best used as a reference; it is not meant to be read from cover to cover. Instead, start by exploring the table of contents, where related occupations are grouped in clusters, or look in the alphabetical index at the end of the *Handbook* for specific occupations that interest you. This section is intended as an overview of how the occupational descriptions, or statements, are organized. Two earlier chapters—Tomorrow's Jobs, and Sources of Career Information—highlight the forces that are likely to determine employment opportunities in industries and occupations through the year 2005, and tell you where to obtain additional information.

Unless otherwise noted, the source of employment and earnings data presented in the *Handbook* is the Bureau of Labor Statistics. Many *Handbook* statements cite earnings data from the Current Population Survey (CPS), while other statements include earnings data from outside sources. Since the characteristics of these data vary, it is difficult to compare earnings precisely among occupations.

For any occupation that sounds interesting to you, use the *Handbook* to find out what the work entails; what education and training you need; what the advancement possibilities, earnings, and job outlook are; and what related occupations you might consider. Each occupational statement in the *Handbook* follows a standard format, making it easier for you to compare occupations. The following highlights information presented in each section of a *Handbook* statement, and gives some hints on how to interpret the information provided.

About Those Numbers at the Beginning of Each Statement

The numbers in parentheses that appear just below the title of most occupational statements are from the *Dictionary of Occupational Titles* (D.O.T.), Fourth Edition, Revised 1991, a U.S. Department of Labor publication. Each number classifies the occupation by the type of work, required training, physical demands, and working conditions. D.O.T. numbers are used primarily by State employment service offices to classify applicants and job openings. They are included in the *Handbook* because some career information centers and libraries use them for filing occupational information.

An index at the back of this book beginning on page 478 cross-references the Revised Fourth Edition D.O.T. numbers to occupations covered in the *Handbook*.

Nature of the Work

- What workers do on the job, the equipment they use, and how closely they are supervised.

- How the duties of workers vary by industry, establishment and size of firm.
- How the responsibilities of entry-level workers differ from those of experienced, supervisory, or self-employed workers.
- How technological innovations are changing what workers do and how they do it.
- Emerging specialties.

Working Conditions

- Typical hours worked.
- The workplace environment.
- Susceptibility to injury, illness, and job-related stress.
- Necessary protective clothing and safety equipment.
- Physical activities required.
- Extent of travel required.

Employment

- The number of jobs the occupation provided in 1994.
- Key industries employing workers in the occupation.
- Geographic distribution of jobs.
- The proportion of part-time (fewer than 35 hours a week) and self-employed workers in the occupation.

Training, Other Qualifications, and Advancement

- Most significant sources of training, typical length of training, and training preferred by employers.
- Whether workers acquire skills through previous work experience, informal on-the-job training, formal training (including apprenticeships) offered by employers or unions, the Armed Forces, home study, or hobbies and other activities.
- Formal educational requirements—high school, postsecondary vocational or technical training, college, or graduate or professional education.
- Desirable skills, aptitudes, and personal characteristics.
- Certification, examination, or licensing required for entry into the field, advancement, or for independent practice.
- Continuing education or skill improvement requirements.
- Paths of advancement.

Job Outlook

- Forces that will result in growth or decline in the number of jobs.

• Relative number of job openings an occupation provides. Occupations which are large and have high turnover rates generally provide the most job openings—reflecting the need to replace workers who transfer to other occupations or stop working.
• Degree of competition for jobs. Is there a surplus or shortage of jobseekers compared to the number of job openings available? Do opportunities vary by industry, size of firm,

---

Key Phrases in the *Handbook*

This box explains how to interpret the key phrases used to describe projected changes in employment. It also explains the terms used to describe the relationship between the number of job openings and the number of jobseekers. The descriptions of the relationship between the supply of and demand for workers in a particular occupation reflects the knowledge and judgment of economists in the Bureau's Office of Employment Projections.

Changing employment between 1994 and 2005

If the statement reads:	Employment is projected to:
Grow much faster than average	increase 36 percent or more
Grow faster than average	increase 21 to 35 percent
Grow about as fast as average	increase 10 to 20 percent
Grow more slowly than average, or little or no change	increase 0 to 9 percent
Decline	decrease 1 percent or more

Opportunities and Competition for Jobs

If the statement reads:	Job openings compared to jobseekers may be:
Excellent opportunities	Much more numerous
Very good opportunities	More numerous
Good or favorable opportunities	About the same
May face competition	Fewer
May face keen competition	Much fewer

---

or geographic location? Even in overcrowded fields, job openings do exist, and good students or well-qualified individuals should not be deterred from undertaking training or seeking entry.
• Susceptibility to layoffs due to imports, slowdowns in economic activity, technological advancements, or budget cuts.

Earnings

• Typical earnings of workers in the occupation.
• If earnings tend to vary with experience, location, and tenure.
• Whether workers are compensated through annual salaries, hourly wages, commissions, piece rates, tips, or bonuses.
• Earnings of wage and salary workers compared to self-employed persons, who held about 8 percent of all jobs in 1994.
• Benefits, including health insurance, pensions, paid vacation and sick leave, family leave, child care or elder care, employee assistance programs, summers off, sabbaticals, tuition for dependents, discounted airfare or merchandise, stock options, profit sharing plans, savings plans, or expense accounts.

Related Occupations

• Occupations involving similar aptitudes, interests, education, and training.

Sources of Additional Information

• Associations, government agencies, unions, and other organizations which provide useful occupational information.
• Free or relatively inexpensive publications offering more information, some of which may be available in libraries, school career centers, or guidance offices.

(For additional sources of information, read the earlier chapter, Sources of Career Information.)

Executive, Administrative, and Managerial Occupations

Accountants and Auditors

(D.O.T. 160 through .167-042, -054, .267-014)

Nature of the Work

Accountants and auditors prepare, analyze, and verify financial reports and taxes, and monitor information systems that furnish this information to managers in business, industrial, and government organizations.

Four major fields of accounting are public, management, and government accounting, and internal auditing. Public accountants have their own businesses or work for public accounting firms. They perform a broad range of accounting, auditing, tax, and consulting activities for their clients, who may be corporations, governments, nonprofit organizations, or individuals. Management accountants, also called industrial, corporate, or private accountants, record and analyze the financial information of the companies for which they work. They also are responsible for budgeting, performance evaluation, cost management, and asset management. They are usually part of executive teams that are involved in strategic planning or new product development. Internal auditors verify the accuracy of their organization's records and check for mismanagement, waste, or fraud. Government accountants and auditors maintain and examine the records of government agencies and audit private businesses and individuals whose activities are subject to government regulations or taxation.

Within each field, accountants often concentrate on one aspect of accounting. For example, many public accountants concentrate on tax matters, such as preparing individual income tax returns and advising companies of the tax advantages and disadvantages of certain business decisions. Others concentrate on consulting and offer advice on matters such as employee health care benefits, and compensation; the design of companies' accounting and data processing systems; and controls to safeguard assets. Some specialize in forensic accounting—investigating and interpreting bankruptcies and other complex financial transactions. Still others work primarily in auditing—examining a client's financial statements and reporting to investors and authorities that they have been prepared and reported correctly; however, fewer accounting firms are performing this type of work because of potential liability.

Increasing numbers of accounting graduates are working in private corporations. Management accountants are to analyze and interpret the financial information corporate executives need to make sound business decisions. They also prepare financial reports for nonmanagement groups, including stockholders, creditors, regulatory agencies, and tax authorities. Within accounting departments, they may work in financial analysis, planning and budgeting, cost accounting, and other areas.

Internal auditing is rapidly growing in importance. As computer systems make information more timely, top management can base its decisions on actual data rather than personal observation. Internal auditors examine and evaluate their firms' financial and information systems, management procedures, and internal controls to ensure that records are accurate and controls are adequate to protect against fraud and waste. They also review company operations—evaluating their efficiency, effectiveness, and compliance with corporate policies and procedures, laws, and government regulations. There are many types of highly specialized auditors, such as electronic data processing auditors, environmental auditors, engineering auditors, legal auditors, insurance premium auditors, bank auditors, and health care auditors.

Accountants employed by Federal, State, and local governments see that revenues are received and expenditures are made in accordance with laws and regulations. Many persons with an accounting background work for the Federal Government as Internal Revenue Service agents or in financial management, financial institution examination, and budget analysis and administration.

Computers are widely used in accounting and auditing. With the aid of special software packages, accountants summarize transactions in standard formats for financial records or organize data in special formats for financial analysis. These accounting packages greatly reduce the amount of tedious manual work associated with figures and records; some packages require few specialized computer skills,

Many accountants work long hours during the tax season.

21

while others require formal training. Personal and laptop computers enable accountants and auditors in all fields—even those who work independently—to use their clients' computer system and to extract information from large mainframe computers. Internal auditors may recommend controls for their organization's computer system to ensure the reliability of the system and the integrity of the data. A growing number of accountants and auditors have extensive computer skills and specialize in correcting problems with software or developing software to meet unique data needs.

Working Conditions

Accountants and auditors work in offices, but public accountants may frequently visit the offices of clients while conducting audits. Self-employed accountants may be able to do part of their work at home. Accountants and auditors employed by large firms and government agencies may travel frequently to perform audits at clients' places of business, branches of their firm, or government facilities.

Many accountants and auditors generally work a standard 40-hour week, but many work longer, particularly if they are self-employed and free to take on the work of as many clients as they choose. For example, about 4 out of 10 self-employed accountants and auditors work more than 50 hours per week, compared to 1 out of 4 wage and salary accountants and auditors. Tax specialists often work long hours during the tax season.

Employment

Accountants and auditors held about 962,000 jobs in 1994. They worked throughout private industry and government, but nearly one-third worked for accounting, auditing, and bookkeeping firms, or were self-employed.

Many accountants and auditors were unlicensed management accountants, internal auditors, or government accountants and auditors. However, in 1994 there were 501,000 State-licensed Certified Public Accountants (CPA's), Public Accountants (PA's), Registered Public Accountants (RPA's), and Accounting Practitioners (AP's).

Most accountants and auditors work in urban areas where public accounting firms and central or regional offices of businesses are concentrated. Roughly 10 percent of all accountants were self-employed, and less than 10 percent worked part time.

Some accountants and auditors teach full time in junior colleges and colleges and universities; others teach part time while working for private industry or government or as self-employed accountants.

Training, Other Qualifications, and Advancement

Most public accounting and business firms require applicants for accountant and internal auditor positions to have at least a bachelor's degree in accounting or a related field. Those wishing to pursue a bachelor's degree in accounting should carefully research accounting curricula before enrolling. Many States will soon require CPA candidates to complete 150 semester hours of coursework prior to taking the CPA exam—on January 1, 2001 at least 32 states will have this requirement—and many schools have altered their curricula accordingly. Some employers prefer those with a master's degree in accounting or a master's degree in business administration with a concentration in accounting. Most employers also prefer applicants who are familiar with computers and their applications in accounting and internal auditing.

For beginning accounting and auditing positions in the Federal Government, 4 years of college (including 24 semester hours in accounting or auditing) or an equivalent combination of education and experience is required.

Previous experience in accounting or auditing can help an applicant get a job. Many colleges offer students an opportunity to gain experience through summer or part-time internship programs conducted by public accounting or business firms. Such training is advantageous in gaining permanent employment in the field.

Professional recognition through certification or licensure also is helpful. In most States, CPA's are the only accountants who are licensed and regulated. Anyone working as a CPA must have a certificate and a license issued by a State board of accountancy. The vast majority of States require CPA candidates to be college graduates, but a few States substitute a certain number of years of public accounting experience for the educational requirement. Based on recommendations made by the American Institute of Certified Public Accountants, a small number of States currently require that CPA candidates complete 150 semester hours of college coursework, but most States are working toward adopting this recommendation. The 150-hour rule requires an additional 30 hours of coursework beyond the usual 4-year bachelor's degree in accounting. The composition of the additional 30 hours of coursework is unspecified by most States.

All States use the four-part Uniform CPA Examination prepared by the American Institute of Certified Public Accountants. The 2-day CPA examination is rigorous, and only about one-quarter of those who take it each year pass each part they attempt. Candidates are not required to pass all four parts at once, although most States require candidates to pass at least two parts for partial credit. Many States require all sections of the test to be passed within a certain period of time. Most States also require applicants for a CPA certificate to have some accounting experience.

The designations PA or RPA are also recognized by most States, and several States continue to issue these licenses. With the growth in the number of CPA's, however, the majority of States are phasing out the PA, RPA, and other non-CPA designations by not issuing any more new licenses. Accountants who hold PA or RPA designations have similar legal rights, duties, and obligations as CPA's, but their qualifications for licensure are less stringent. The designation Accounting Practitioner is also awarded by several States. It requires less formal training than a CPA license and covers a more limited scope of practice.

Nearly all States require both CPA's and PA's to complete a certain number of hours of continuing professional education before their licenses can be renewed. The professional associations representing accountants sponsor numerous courses, seminars, group study programs, and other forms of continuing education.

Professional societies bestow other forms of credentials on a voluntary basis. Voluntary certification can attest to professional competence in a specialized field of accounting and auditing. It also can certify that a recognized level of professional competence has been achieved by accountants and auditors who acquired some skills on the job, without the amount of formal education or public accounting work experience needed to meet the rigorous standards required to take the CPA examination. Employers increasingly seek applicants with these credentials.

The Institute of Management Accountants (IMA) confers the Certified Management Accountant (CMA) designation upon college graduates who pass a four-part examination, agree to meet continuing education requirements, comply with standards of professional conduct, and have at least 2 years' work in management accounting. The CMA program is administered through the Institute of Certified Management Accountants, an affiliate of the IMA.

The Institute of Internal Auditors confers the designation Certified Internal Auditor (CIA) to graduates from accredited colleges and universities who have completed 2 years' work in internal auditing and who have passed a four-part examination. The Information Systems Audit and Control Association confers the designation Certified Information Systems Auditor (CISA) upon candidates who pass an examination and who have 5 years of experience in auditing electronic data processing systems. However, auditing or data processing experience and college education may be substituted for up to 3 years. The Accreditation Council for Accountancy and Taxation, a satellite organization of the National Society of Public Accountants, awards a Certificate of Accreditation in Accountancy to those who pass a comprehensive examination, and a Certificate of Accreditation in Taxation to those with appropriate experience and education.

Other organizations, such as the National Association of Certified Fraud Examiners and the Bank Administration Institute, confer specialized auditing designations. It is not uncommon for a practitioner to hold multiple licenses and designations. For instance, an internal auditor might be a CPA, Certified Internal Auditor, and Certified Information Systems Auditor.

Persons planning a career in accounting should have an aptitude for mathematics, be able to analyze, compare, and interpret facts and figures quickly, and make sound judgments based on this knowledge. They must be able to clearly communicate the results of their work, orally and in writing, to clients and management.

Accountants and auditors must be good at working with people as well as with business systems and computers. Accuracy and the ability to handle responsibility with limited supervision are important. Perhaps most important, because millions of financial statement users rely on their services, accountants and auditors should have high standards of integrity.

Capable accountants and auditors should advance rapidly; those having inadequate academic preparation may be assigned routine jobs and find promotion difficult. Many graduates of junior colleges and business and correspondence schools, as well as bookkeepers and accounting clerks who meet the education and experience requirements set by their employers, can obtain junior accounting positions and advance to more responsible positions by demonstrating their accounting skills on the job.

Beginning public accountants usually start by assisting with work for several clients. They may advance to positions with more responsibility in 1 or 2 years and to senior positions within another few years. Those who excel may become supervisors, managers, partners, open their own public accounting firms, or transfer to executive positions in management accounting or internal auditing in private firms.

Beginning management accountants often start as cost accountants, junior internal auditors, or as trainees for other accounting positions. As they rise through the organization, they may advance to accounting manager, chief cost accountant, budget director, or manager of internal auditing. Some become controllers, treasurers, financial vice presidents, chief financial officers, or corporation presidents. Many senior corporation executives have a background in accounting, internal auditing, or finance.

There is a large degree of mobility among public accountants, management accountants, and internal auditors. Practitioners often shift into management accounting or internal auditing from public accounting, or between internal auditing and management accounting. However, it is less common for accountants and auditors to move from either management accounting or internal auditing into public accounting.

Job Outlook

Qualified accountants and auditors are expected to have fairly good job prospects. CPA's should continue to enjoy the widest range of job opportunities, especially as more States enact the 150-hour requirement, making it more difficult to become a CPA. Competition for the most prestigious jobs—such as those with major accounting and business firms—will remain keen. Applicants with a master's degree in accounting or a master's degree in business administration with a concentration in accounting are increasingly valued, particularly among large firms. As computers now perform many increasingly complex accounting functions and allow accountants and auditors to analyze more information, a broad base of computer experience is also advantageous. Expertise in specialized areas such as international business, specific industries, or current legislation may also be helpful in landing certain accounting and auditing jobs.

Employment of accountants and auditors is expected to grow about as fast as the average for all occupations through the year 2005. Although the profession is characterized by a relatively low rate of turnover, because the occupation is so large the need to replace accountants and auditors who retire or move into other occupations will produce thousands of additional job openings annually.

As the economy grows, the number of business establishments increases, requiring more accountants and auditors to set up their books, prepare their taxes, and provide management advice. As these businesses grow, the volume and complexity of information developed by accountants and auditors on costs, expenditures, and taxes will increase as well. More complex requirements for accountants and auditors also arise from changes in legislation related to taxes, financial reporting standards, business investments, mergers, and other financial matters. In addition, businesses will increasingly need quick, accurate, and individually tailored financial information due to the demands of growing international competition.

The changing role of public accountants, management accountants, and internal auditors also will spur job growth. Public accountants will perform less auditing work due to potential liability, and less tax work due to growing competition from tax preparation firms, but they will assume an even greater management advisory role and expand their consulting services. These rapidly growing services will lead to increased demand for public accountants in the coming years. Management accountants also will take on a greater advisory role as they develop more sophisticated and flexible accounting systems, and focus more on analyzing operations rather than just providing financial data. Similarly, management will increasingly need internal auditors to develop new ways to discover and eliminate waste and fraud.

Earnings

According to a salary survey conducted by the National Association of Colleges and Employers, bachelor's degree candidates in accounting received starting offers averaging $27,900 a year in 1995; master's degree candidates in accounting, $31,500.

According to a survey of workplaces in 160 metropolitan areas, accountants with limited experience had median earnings of $25,400 in 1993, with the middle half earning between $23,000 and $28,200. The most experienced accountants had median earnings of $77,200, with the middle half earning between $70,300 and $85,400. Public accountants—employed by public accounting firms—with limited experience had median earnings of $28,100 in 1993, with the middle half earning between $26,900 and $29,400. The most experienced public accountants had median earnings of $48,800, with the middle half earning between $41,300 and $54,400. Many owners and partners of firms earned considerably more.

Based on a survey by the Institute of Management Accountants, the average salary of IMA members was about $62,300 a year in 1994. IMA members who were certified public accountants averaged $68,500, while members who were certified management accountants averaged $67,000.

According to a salary survey conducted by Robert Half International, a staffing services firm specializing in accounting and finance, accountants and auditors with up to 1 year of experience earned between $23,000 and $35,500 in 1995. Those with 1 to 3 years of experience earned between $26,000 and $39,000. Senior accountants and auditors earned between $31,000 and $47,600; managers earned between $39,900 and $68,800; and directors of accounting and auditing earned between $50,300 and $84,500 a year. The variation in salaries reflects differences in location, level of education, and credentials.

In the Federal Government, the starting annual salary for junior accountants and auditors was about $18,700 in 1995. Candidates who had a superior academic record could start at $23,200, while applicants with a master's degree or 2 years of professional experience began at $28,300. Beginning salaries were slightly higher in selected areas where the prevailing local pay level was higher. Accountants employed by the Federal Government in nonsupervisory, supervisory, and managerial positions averaged $50,500 a year in 1995; auditors, $53,600.

Related Occupations

Accountants and auditors design internal control systems and analyze financial data. Others for whom training in accounting is invaluable include appraisers, budget officers, loan officers, financial analysts and managers, bank officers, actuaries, underwriters, tax collectors and revenue agents, FBI special agents, securities sales representatives, and purchasing agents.

Sources of Additional Information

Information about careers in certified public accounting and about CPA standards and examinations may be obtained from:

☞American Institute of Certified Public Accountants, Harborside Financial Center, 201 Plaza III, Jersey City, NJ 07311-3881.

Information on management accounting and other specialized fields of accounting and auditing is available from:

☞Institute of Management Accountants, 10 Paragon Dr., Montvale, NJ 07645-1760.

☞National Society of Public Accountants and the Accreditation Council for Accountancy and Taxation, 1010 North Fairfax St., Alexandria, VA 22314.

☞The Institute of Internal Auditors, 249 Maitland Ave., Altamonte Springs, FL 32701-4201.

☞The Information Systems Audit and Control Association, 3701 Algonquin Rd., Suite 1010, Rolling Meadows, IL 60008.

For information on accredited accounting programs and educational institutions offering a specialization in accounting or business management, contact:

☞American Assembly of Collegiate Schools of Business, 605 Old Ballas Rd., Suite 220, St. Louis, MO 63141.

Administrative Services Managers

(D.O.T. 162.117-014; 163.167-026; 169.167-034; 188.117-122, .167-106)

Nature of the Work

Administrative services managers are employed throughout private industry and government, and their range of duties is broad. They coordinate and direct support services, which may include: Secretarial and reception; administration; payroll; conference planning and travel; information and data processing; mail; facilities management; materials scheduling and distribution; printing and reproduction; records management; telecommunications management; personal property procurement, supply, and disposal; security; and parking.

In small organizations, a single administrative services manager may oversee all support services. In larger ones, however, first-line managers report to their mid-level superiors who, in turn, report to proprietors or top-level managers. These upper-level managers, such as vice president of administrative services, are included in the *Handbook* statement on general managers and top executives.

First-line administrative services managers directly oversee staffs involved in various support services. Mid-level managers develop departmental plans, set goals and deadlines, develop procedures to improve productivity and customer service, and define the responsibilities of supervisory-level managers. They often are involved in the hiring and dismissal of employees but generally have no role in the formulation of personnel policy.

As the size of the firm increases, administrative services managers are more likely to specialize in one or more support activities. For example, some administrative services managers work primarily as facilities managers, office managers, contract administrators, property managers, or unclaimed property officers. In many cases, the duties of these administrative services managers are quite similar to those of other managers and supervisors, some of whom are discussed in other *Handbook* statements.

Administrative services managers who specialize in facilities management may engage in facilities planning, including the buying,

Like other managers, administrative services managers should be able to communicate effectively.

selling, or leasing of facilities; redesign work areas to be more efficient and ergonomic (user-friendly); ensure that facilities comply with government regulations; and supervise maintenance, grounds, and custodial staffs. In some firms, they are called facilities managers.

Some mid-level administrative services managers work as office managers and oversee first-line supervisors from various departments, including the clerical staff. In small firms, however, clerical supervisors, who are discussed in the *Handbook* statement on clerical supervisors and managers, perform this function. Administrative services managers who work as contract administrators direct the preparation, analysis, negotiation, and review of contracts related to the purchase or sale of equipment, materials, supplies, products, or services. However, procurement functions are generally directed by purchasers and buyers, also discussed in a separate *Handbook* statement.

Property management is divided into the management and use of personal property such as office supplies, an administrative services management function, and real property management, which is a function of property and real estate managers, who are discussed elsewhere in the *Handbook*. Personal property managers acquire, distribute, and store supplies, and may sell or dispose of surplus property. Other property managers are engaged solely in surplus property disposal, which involves the resale of scraps, rejects, and surplus or unneeded supplies and machinery. This is an increasingly important source of revenue for many commercial organizations. In government, surplus property officers may receive surplus from various departments and agencies, and then sell or dispose of it to the public or other agencies.

Some administrative services managers oversee unclaimed property disposal. In government, this activity may entail auctioning off unclaimed liquid assets, such as stocks, bonds, savings accounts, and the contents of safe deposit boxes, or personal property, such as motor vehicles, after attempts to locate owners have failed.

Working Conditions

Administrative services managers generally work in comfortable offices. In smaller firms, where they may work alongside the people they supervise, the office may be crowded and noisy.

Their work can be stressful, as they attempt to schedule work to meet deadlines. Although the 40-hour week is standard, uncompensated overtime is often required to resolve problems. Managers involved in contract administration and personal property procurement, use, and disposal may travel extensively between home offices, branch offices, vendors' offices, and property sales sites. Facilities managers who are responsible for the design of work spaces often must spend time at construction sites. Facilities managers also may monitor the work of maintenance, grounds, and custodial staffs, and travel between different facilities.

Employment
Administrative services managers held about 279,000 jobs in 1994. Over two-fifths worked in services industries, including management, business, social, and health services organizations. Others were found in virtually every other industry. A few run their own management services, management consulting, or facilities support services firms.

Training, Other Qualifications, and Advancement
Many administrative services managers advance through the ranks in an organization, acquiring several years' work experience in various administrative positions before assuming first-line supervisory duties. All managers who oversee departmental supervisors should be familiar with office procedures and equipment. Those who supervise clerical supervisors must have a working knowledge of word processing, communications, data processing, and recordkeeping. Facilities managers may have a background in architecture, engineering, construction, interior design, or real estate, in addition to managerial or other administrative experience. Managers of personal property acquisition and disposal need experience in purchasing and sales and knowledge of a wide variety of supplies, machinery, and equipment. Managers concerned with supply, inventory, and distribution must be experienced in receiving, warehousing, packaging, shipping, transportation, and related operations. Contract administrators may have worked as contract specialists, cost analysts, or procurement specialists. Managers of unclaimed property often have experience in insurance claims analysis and records management.

Educational requirements vary widely. For first-line administrative services managers of secretarial, mail room, and related administrative support activities, many employers prefer an associate of arts degree in business or management, although a high school diploma may suffice. For managers of audiovisual, graphics, and other more technical activities, postsecondary technical school training is preferred. For managers of highly complex services such as contract administration, a bachelor's degree, preferably in business administration or finance, is usually required. The curriculum should include courses in office technology, accounting, business mathematics, computer applications, and business law. Similarly, facilities managers often need a bachelor's degree in engineering, architecture, or business administration. Some administrative services managers have advanced degrees. Whatever the manager's educational background, it must be accompanied by related work experience reflecting demonstrated ability.

Persons interested in becoming administrative services managers should be able to communicate and establish effective working relationships with many different people, ranging from managers, supervisors, and professionals, to clerks and blue-collar workers. They should be analytical, detail oriented, flexible, and decisive. The ability to coordinate several activities at once and to quickly analyze and resolve specific problems is important. Ability to work under stress and cope with deadlines is also important.

Advancement is easier in large firms that employ several levels of administrative services managers. Attainment of the Certified Administrative Manager (CAM) designation, through work experience and successful completion of examinations offered by the Institute of Certified Professional Managers, can increase one's advancement potential. A bachelor's degree enhances a first-level manager's opportunities to advance to a mid-level management position, such as director of administrative services, and eventually to a top-level management position, such as executive vice president for administrative services. Those with the required capital and experience can establish their own management consulting, management services, or facilities support services firm.

Job Outlook
Employment of administrative services managers is expected to grow about as fast as the average for all occupations through the year 2005. Like other managerial occupations, this occupation is characterized by low turnover. These factors, coupled with the ample supply of competent, experienced workers seeking managerial jobs, should result in keen competition for administrative services management positions in the coming years.

Many firms are increasingly contracting out administrative services positions and otherwise streamlining these functions in an effort to cut costs. Corporate restructuring has tempered growth in the number of administrative services managers in recent years, and this trend is expected to continue.

As it becomes more common for firms to contract out administrative services, however, demand for administrative services managers will increase in the management services, management consulting, and facilities support services firms that will provide the services. In addition, some categories of administrative services managers may grow more quickly than others. Facilities managers may not be subject to the same cost-cutting pressures as other administrative services managers. Also, the extent to which governments at all levels contract out for goods and services could affect demand for contract administrators and personal property managers.

Earnings
According to a salary survey by the Administrative Management Society Foundation, building services/facilities managers averaged about $50,300 a year in 1994; office/administrative services managers, about $40,700; and records managers, about $38,900. Average salaries ranged from $29,600 for the lowest paid records managers to $61,300 for the highest paid building services/facilities managers.

According to a survey by the International Facility Management Association, unit or first-line supervisors earned a median base salary of $41,600 in 1994; section heads or second-line supervisors $55,000; and managers with two levels of supervisors reporting to them, $65,000.

In the Federal Government, contract specialists in nonsupervisory, supervisory, and managerial positions averaged $47,890 a year in 1995; facilities managers, $45,660; administrative officers, $45,220; industrial property managers, $44,020; property disposal specialists, $40,940; and support services administrators, $35,990.

Related Occupations
Administrative services managers direct and coordinate support services and oversee the purchase, use, and disposal of personal property. Occupations with similar functions include administrative assistants, appraisers, buyers, clerical supervisors, contract specialists, cost estimators, procurement services managers, property and real estate managers, purchasing managers, and personnel managers.

Sources of Additional Information
For information about careers in facilities management, contact:
☛International Facility Management Association, 1 East Greenway Plaza, Suite 1100, Houston, TX 77046-0194.

Budget Analysts

(D.O.T. 161.117-010, .267-030)

Nature of the Work
Budget analysts play a primary role in the development, analysis, and execution of budgets. Budgets are financial plans used to estimate future requirements and organize and allocate operating and capital resources effectively. The analysis of spending behavior and the planning of future operations are an integral part of the decision-

making process in most corporations and government agencies.

Budget analysts work in private industry, nonprofit organizations, and the public sector. In private industry, a budget analyst examines, analyzes, and seeks new ways to improve efficiency and increase profits. Although analysts working in government generally are not concerned with profits, they too are interested in finding the most efficient distribution of funds and other resources among various departments and programs.

A major responsibility of budget analysts is to provide advice and technical assistance in the preparation of annual budgets. At the beginning of the budget cycle, managers and department heads submit proposed operating and financial plans to budget analysts for review. These plans outline expected programs—including proposed program increases or new initiatives, estimated costs and expenses, and capital expenditures needed to finance these programs.

Analysts begin by examining the budget estimates or proposals for completeness, accuracy, and conformance with established procedures, regulations, and organizational objectives. Sometimes they review financial requests by employing cost-benefit analysis, assessing program trade-offs, and exploring alternative funding methods. They also examine past and current budgets, and research economic and financial developments that affect the organization's spending. This process allows analysts to evaluate proposals in terms of the organization's priorities and financial resources.

After this review process, budget analysts consolidate the individual department budgets into operating and capital budget summaries. The analysts submit preliminary budgets to senior management, or sometimes, as is often the case in local and State governments, to appointed or elected officials, with comments and supporting statements that justify or deny funding requests. By reviewing different departments' operating plans, analysts gain insight into an organization's overall operations. This generally proves useful when they interpret and offer technical assistance to officials approving the budget. At this point in the budget process, budget analysts help the chief operating officer, agency head, or other top managers analyze the proposed plan and devise possible alternatives if the projected results are unsatisfactory. The final decision to approve the budget, however, is usually made by the organization head or elected officials, such as the state legislative body.

Throughout the rest of the year, analysts periodically monitor the budget by reviewing reports and accounting records to determine if allocated funds have been spent as specified. If deviations appear between the approved budget and actual performance, budget analysts may write a report explaining the causes of the variations along with recommendations for new or revised budget procedures. They suggest reallocation of excess funds or recommend program cuts to avoid or alleviate deficits. They also inform program managers and others within their organization of the status and availability of funds in different budget accounts. Before any changes are made to an existing program or a new one is started, a budget analyst assesses its efficiency and effectiveness. Analysts also may project budget needs for long-range planning.

Analysts assist in developing procedural guidelines and policies governing the development, formulation, and maintenance of the budget. If necessary, they conduct training sessions for agency or company personnel on new budget procedures.

Working Conditions

Budget analysts work in a normal office setting, generally 40 hours per week. However, during the initial development and mid-year and final reviews of budgets, they often experience the pressure of deadlines and tight work schedules. The work during these periods can be extremely stressful, and analysts are usually required to work more than the routine 40 hours a week.

Budget analysts spend the majority of their time working independently, compiling and analyzing data and preparing budget proposals. Nevertheless, their routine schedule can be interrupted by

Federal, State and local governments are major employers of budget analysts.

special budget requests, meetings, and training sessions. Others may travel to obtain budget details and explanations of variances from coworkers, and to personally observe what funding is being used for in the field.

Employment

Budget analysts held about 66,000 jobs throughout private industry and government in 1994. Federal, State, and local governments are major employers, accounting for 1 of every 3 budget analyst jobs. The Department of Defense employed 7 of every 10 budget analysts working for the Federal Government. Other major employers of budget analysts are schools, hospitals, banks, and manufacturers of transportation equipment, chemicals and allied products, electrical and electronic machinery, and industrial machines..

Training, Other Qualifications, and Advancement

Most private firms and government agencies require candidates for budget analyst positions to have at least a bachelor's degree. Within the Federal Government, a bachelor's degree in any field is sufficient background for an entry-level budget analyst position. State and local governments have varying requirements, but a bachelor's degree in one of many areas—accounting, finance, business or public administration, economics, political science, planning, statistics, or a social science such as sociology—may qualify one for entry into the occupation. Sometimes, a field closely related to the employing industry or organization within an industry, such as engineering, may be preferred. An increasing number of states and other employers require a candidate to possess a master's degree to ensure adequate analytical and communication skills. Some firms prefer candidates with business backgrounds because business courses emphasize quantitative analytical skills. Financial experience can occasionally be substituted for formal education when applying for a budget analyst position. An increasingly small number of companies prefer to promote from within; therefore, competent accounting or payroll clerks and other clerical staff who have worked closely with the budget process are sometimes given the opportunity to advance to entry-level budget analyst positions even if they do not meet the educational requirements.

Because developing a budget involves manipulating numbers and requires strong analytical skills, courses in statistics, or accounting are helpful, regardless of the prospective budget analyst's major field of study. Because most financial analysis performed by organizations is automated, a familiarity with the financial software packages used by most organizations in budget analysis, as well as word processing, is generally required by employers. Software packages commonly used by budget analysts include electronic spreadsheets and database and graphics software. Job candidates who already possess these computer skills may be preferred over those who need to be trained.

In addition to analytical and computer skills, those seeking a career as a budget analyst must also be able to work under strict time constraints. Strong oral and written communication skills are essential for analysts to prepare, present, and defend budget proposals to decision makers.

Entry-level budget analysts may receive some formal training when they begin their jobs. However, most employers feel that the best training is obtained by working through one complete budget cycle. During the cycle, analysts become familiar with all the steps involved in the budgeting process.

The Federal Government, on the other hand, offers extensive on-the-job and classroom training for entry-level analysts, who are initially called trainees. Analysts are encouraged to participate in the various classes offered throughout their careers.

Beginning analysts usually work under close supervision. Capable entry-level analysts can be promoted into intermediate level positions within 1 to 2 years, and then into senior positions within a few more years. Progressing to a higher level means added budgetary responsibility and can lead to a supervisory role.

In the Federal Government, for example, beginning budget analysts compare projected costs with prior expenditures; consolidate and enter data prepared by others; and assist higher grade analysts by doing research. As analysts progress, they begin to develop and formulate budget estimates and justification statements; perform in-depth analyses of budget requests; write statements supporting funding requests; advise program managers and others on the status and availability of funds in different budget activities; and present and defend budget proposals to senior managers.

Because financial and analytical skills are vital in any organization, budget analysts often are able to transfer to a related field in other organizations. Senior budget analysts in central staff functions are often candidates for senior management posistions in other parts of the organization.

Job Outlook

Despite the increase in demand for budget analysts, competition for jobs should remain keen because of the substantial number of qualified applicants. Job opportunities are usually best for candidates with a college degree, particularly a master's. In some cases, experience is more beneficial than a degree and can be used to offset a lack of education. A working knowledge of computer financial software packages can also enhance one's employment prospects in this field.

Employment of budget analysts is expected to grow about as fast as the average for all occupations through the year 2005. In addition to employment growth, many job openings will result from the need to replace experienced budget analysts who transfer to other occupations or leave the labor force.

The expanding use of automation may make analysts more productive, allowing them to process more data in less time. Also, computers are increasingly used to organize, summarize, and disseminate data to the top levels in organizations, thereby centralizing decision-making and reducing the need for middle managers. Any computer-induced effects on employment may be offset, however, by a greater demand for information and analysis. Easier manipulation of and accessibility to data provide management more considerations on which to base decisions.

Because of the growing complexity of business and the increasing specialization of functions within organizations, more attention is being given to planning and financial control. Many companies will continue to rely heavily on budget analysts to examine, analyze, and develop budgets to determine capital requirements and to allocate labor and other resources efficiently among all parts of the organization. Managers will continue to use budgets as a vehicle to plan, coordinate, control, and evaluate activities within their organizations more effectively.

The financial work performed by budget analysts is an important function in every organization. Financial and budget reports must be completed during periods of economic growth and slowdowns. Therefore, employment of budget analysts generally is not as adversely affected by changes in the economy.

Earnings

Salaries of budget analysts vary widely by experience, education, and employer. According to a survey conducted by Robert Half International, a staffing services firm specializing in accounting and finance, starting salaries of budget and other financial analysts in small firms ranged from $23,500 to $27,000 in 1995; in large organizations, from $26,000 to $30,800. Analysts in small firms with 1 to 3 years of experience earned from $27,000 to $33,000; in large companies, from $30,000 to $38,800. Senior analysts in small firms earned from $33,000 to $38,800; in large firms, from $38,000 to $46,500. Earnings of managers in this field ranged from $38,500 to $50,000 a year in small firms, while managers in large organizations earned between $46,000 and $65,000.

A survey of workplaces in 160 metropolitan areas reported that inexperienced budget analysts had median annual earnings of about $27,000 in 1993, with the middle half earning between $24,100 and $32,000 a year.

In the Federal Government, budget analysts generally started as trainees earning $18,700 or $23,200 a year in 1995. Candidates with a master's degree might begin at $28,300. Beginning salaries were slightly higher in selected areas where the prevailing local pay level was higher. The average annual salary for budget analysts employed by the Federal Government in nonsupervisory, supervisory, and managerial positions was $45,700 in 1995.

Related Occupations

Budget analysts review, analyze, and interpret financial data; make recommendations for the future; and assist in the implementation of new ideas. Workers who use these skills in other occupations include accountants and auditors, economists, financial analysts, financial managers, and loan officers.

Sources of Additional Information

Information about career opportunities as a budget analyst may be available from your State or local employment service.

Persons interested in working as a budget analyst in the Federal Government can obtain information from:

☛Office of Personnel Management, 1900 E St. NW., Washington, DC 20415.

Construction and Building Inspectors

(D.O.T. 168.167-030, -034, -038, -046, and -050; .267-010, -102; 182.267; 850.387, .467)

Nature of the Work

Construction and building inspectors examine the construction, alteration, or repair of buildings, highways and streets, sewer and water systems, dams, bridges, and other structures to ensure compliance with building codes and ordinances, zoning regulations, and contract specifications. Inspectors generally specialize in one particular type of construction work or construction trade, such as electrical work or plumbing. They make an initial inspection during the first phase of construction, and follow-up inspections throughout the construction project to monitor compliance with regulations. In areas where severe natural disasters—such as earthquakes or hurricanes—are more common, inspectors monitor compliance with additional safety regulations.

Building inspectors inspect the structural quality and general safety of buildings. Some specialize—for example, in structural steel or reinforced concrete structures. Before construction begins, *plan examiners* determine whether the plans for the building or other structure comply with building code regulations and are suited to the engineering and environmental demands of the building site. Inspectors visit the work site before the foundation is poured to inspect the soil condition and positioning and depth of the footings. Later they return to the site to inspect the foundation after it has been completed. The size and type of structure and the rate of completion determine the number of other site visits they must make. Upon completion of the entire project, they make a final comprehensive inspection.

A primary concern of building inspectors is fire safety. They inspect structure's fire sprinklers, alarms, and smoke control systems, as well as fire doors and exits. In addition, inspectors may calculate fire insurance rates by assessing the type of construction, building contents, adequacy of fire protection equipment, and risks posed by adjoining buildings.

Electrical inspectors inspect the installation of electrical systems and equipment to ensure that they function properly and comply with electrical codes and standards. They visit work sites to inspect new and existing wiring, lighting, sound and security systems, motors, and generating equipment. They also inspect the installation of the electrical wiring for heating and air-conditioning systems, appliances, and other components.

Elevator inspectors examine lifting and conveying devices such as elevators, escalators, moving sidewalks, lifts and hoists, inclined railways, ski lifts, and amusement rides.

Mechanical inspectors inspect the installation of the mechanical components of commercial kitchen appliances, heating and air-conditioning equipment, gasoline and butane tanks, gas and oil piping, and gas-fired and oil-fired appliances. Some specialize in inspecting boilers or ventilating equipment as well.

Plumbing inspectors examine plumbing systems, including private disposal systems, water supply and distribution systems, plumbing fixtures and traps, and drain, waste, and vent lines.

Public works inspectors ensure that Federal, State, and local government construction of water and sewer systems, highways, streets, bridges, and dams conforms to detailed contract specifications. They inspect excavation and fill operations, the placement of forms for concrete, concrete mixing and pouring, asphalt paving, and grading operations. They record the work and materials used so that contract payments can be calculated. Public works inspectors may specialize in highways, structural steel, reinforced concrete, or ditches. Others specialize in dredging operations required for bridges and dams or for harbors.

Home inspectors conduct inspections of newly built homes to check that they meet all regulatory requirements. Home inspectors are also increasingly hired by prospective home buyers to inspect and report on the condition of a home's major systems, components, and structure. Typically, home inspectors are hired either immediately prior to a purchase offer on a home or as a contingency to a sales contract.

Construction and building inspectors increasingly use computers to help them monitor the status of construction inspection activities and keep track of permits issued. Details about construction projects, building and occupancy permits, and other documentation are now generally stored on computers so that they can easily be retrieved and kept accurate and up to date.

Although inspections are primarily visual, inspectors often use tape measures, survey instruments, metering devices, and test equipment such as concrete strength measurers. They keep a daily log of their work, take photographs, file reports, and, if necessary, act on their findings. For example, construction inspectors notify the construction contractor, superintendent, or supervisor when they discover a code or ordinance violation or something that does not comply with the contract specifications or approved plans. If the problem is not corrected within a reasonable or specified period of time, government inspectors have authority to issue a "stop-work" order.

Many inspectors also investigate construction or alterations being done without proper permits. Violators of permit laws are directed to obtain permits and submit to inspection.

Working Conditions

Construction and building inspectors usually work alone. However, several may be assigned to large, complex projects, particularly because inspectors specialize in different areas of construction. Though they spend considerable time inspecting construction work sites, inspectors may spend much of their time in a field office reviewing blueprints, answering letters or telephone calls, writing reports, and scheduling inspections.

Inspection sites are dirty and may be cluttered with tools, materials, or debris. Inspectors may have to climb ladders or many flights of stairs, or may have to crawl around in tight spaces. Although their work is not considered hazardous, inspectors usually wear "hard hats" for safety.

Inspectors normally work regular hours. However, if an accident occurs at a construction site, inspectors must respond immediately and may work additional hours to complete their report.

Nearly 60 percent of all construction and building inspectors work for local governments.

Employment

Construction and building inspectors held about 64,000 jobs in 1994. Over 50 percent worked for local governments, primarily municipal or county building departments. Employment of local government inspectors is concentrated in cities and in suburban areas undergoing rapid growth. Local governments employ large inspection staffs, including many plan examiners or inspectors who specialize in structural steel, reinforced concrete, boiler, electrical, and elevator inspection.

About 18 percent of all construction and building inspectors worked for engineering and architectural services firms, conducting inspections for a fee or on a contract basis. Most of the remaining inspectors were employed by the Federal and State governments. Many construction inspectors employed by the Federal Government work for the U.S. Army Corps of Engineers or the General Services Administration. Other Federal employers include the Tennessee Valley Authority and the Departments of Agriculture, Housing and Urban Development, and Interior.

Training, Other Qualifications, and Advancement

Individuals who want to become construction and building inspectors should have a thorough knowledge of construction materials and practices in either a general area, like structural or heavy construction, or in a specialized area, such as electrical or plumbing systems, reinforced concrete, or structural steel. Construction or building inspectors need several years of experience as a manager, supervisor, or craft worker before becoming inspectors. Many inspectors have previously worked as carpenters, electricians, plumbers, or pipefitters.

Employers prefer to hire inspectors who have formal training as well as experience. Employers look for persons who have studied engineering or architecture, or who have a degree from a community or junior college, with courses in construction technology, blueprint reading, mathematics, and building inspection. Courses in drafting, algebra, geometry, and English are also useful. Most employers require inspectors to have a high school diploma or equivalent even when they qualify on the basis of experience.

Certification can enhance an inspector's opportunities for employment and advancement to more responsible positions. Most States and cities actually require some type of certification for employment. To become certified, inspectors with substantial experience and education must pass stringent examinations on code requirements, construction techniques, and materials. Many categories of certification are awarded for inspectors and plan examiners in a variety of disciplines, including the designation "CBO," Certified Building Official. (Organizations that administer certification programs are listed below in the section on Sources of Additional Information.)

Construction and building inspectors must be in good physical condition in order to walk and climb about construction sites. They also must have a driver's license. In addition, Federal, State, and many local governments may require that inspectors pass a civil service examination.

Construction and building inspectors usually receive most of their training on the job. At first, working with an experienced inspector, they learn about inspection techniques; codes, ordinances, and regulations; contract specifications; and record keeping and reporting duties. They usually begin by inspecting less complex types of construction, such as residential buildings, and then progress to more difficult assignments. An engineering or architectural degree is often required for advancement to supervisory positions.

Because they advise builders and the general public on building codes, construction practices, and technical developments, construction and building inspectors must keep abreast of changes in these areas. Many employers provide formal training programs to broaden inspectors' knowledge of construction materials, practices, and techniques. Inspectors who work for small agencies or firms that do not conduct training programs can expand their knowledge and upgrade their skills by attending State-sponsored training programs, by taking college or correspondence courses, or by attending seminars sponsored by the organizations that certify inspectors.

Job Outlook

Employment of construction and building inspectors is expected to grow faster than the average for all occupations through the year 2005. Growing concern for public safety and improvements in the quality of construction should continue to stimulate demand for construction and building inspectors. Despite the expected employment growth, most job openings will arise from the need to replace inspectors who transfer to other occupations or who leave the labor force. Replacement needs are relatively high because construction and building inspectors tend to be older, more experienced workers who have spent years working in other occupations.

Opportunities to become a construction and building inspector should be best for highly experienced supervisors and craft workers who have some college education, some engineering or architectural training, or who are certified as inspectors or plan examiners. Thorough knowledge of construction practices and skills in areas such as reading and evaluating blueprints and plans are essential. Governments—particularly Federal and State—should continue to contract out inspection work to engineering, architectural and management services firms as their budgets remain tight. However, the volume of real estate transactions will increase as the population grows, and greater emphasis on home inspections should result in rapid growth in employment of home inspectors. Inspectors are involved in all phases of construction, including maintenance and repair work, and are therefore less likely to lose jobs during recessionary periods when new construction slows.

Earnings

The median annual salary of construction and building inspectors was $32,300 in 1994. The middle 50 percent earned between $25,200 and $43,800. The lowest 10 percent earned less than $19,400 and the highest 10 percent earned more than $57,500 a year. Generally, building inspectors, including plan examiners, earn the highest salaries. Salaries in large metropolitan areas are substantially higher than those in small local jurisdictions.

Related Occupations

Construction and building inspectors combine a knowledge of construction principles and law with an ability to coordinate data, diagnose problems, and communicate with people. Workers in other occupations using a similar combination of skills include drafters, estimators, industrial engineering technicians, surveyors, architects, and construction contractors and managers.

Sources of Additional Information

Information about a career and certification as a construction or building inspector is available from the following model code organizations:

☛International Conference of Building Officials, 5360 Workman Mill Rd., Whittier, CA 90601-2298.

☛Building Officials and Code Administrators International, Inc., 4051 West Flossmoor Rd., Country Club Hills, IL 60478.

☛Southern Building Code Congress International, Inc., 900 Montclair Rd., Birmingham, AL 35213.

Information about a career as a home inspector is available from:

☛American Society of Home Inspectors, Inc., 85 West Algonquin Rd., Arlington Heights, IL 60005.

For information about a career as a State or local government construction or building inspector, contact your State or local employment service.

Construction Managers

(D.O.T. 182.167-010, -018, -026, -030, and -034)

Nature of the Work

Construction managers assume a wide variety of responsibilities and positions within construction firms. They are known by a range of job titles that are often used interchangeably—for example, *construction superintendent*, *general superintendent*, *project manager*, *general construction manager*, or *executive construction manager*. Construction managers may be owners or salaried employees of a construction management or contracting firm, or individuals working under contract or as salaried employees for the owner, developer, contractor, or management firm overseeing the construction project. The *Handbook* uses the term "construction manager" to encompass all supervisory-level salaried and self-employed construction managers who oversee construction supervisors and workers.

In the construction industry, managers and other professionals active in the industry—general managers, project engineers, cost estimators, and others—are increasingly referred to as *constructors*. The term constructor refers to a broad group of professionals in construction who, through education and experience, are capable of managing, coordinating, and supervising the construction process from conceptual development through final construction on a timely and economical basis. Given designs for buildings, roads, bridges, or other projects, constructors oversee the organization, scheduling, and implementation of the project to execute those designs. They are responsible for coordinating and managing people, materials, and equipment; budgets, schedules, and contracts; and the safety of employees and the general public.

In contrast with the *Handbook*, the term "construction manager" is used more narrowly within the construction industry to denote a firm, or an individual employed by the firm, involved in management oversight of a construction project. Under this narrower definition, construction managers generally act as agents or representatives of the owner or developer throughout the life of the project. Although they generally play no direct role in the actual construction of the building or other facility, they typically schedule and coordinate all design and construction processes. They develop and implement a management plan to complete the project according to the owner's goals that allows the design and construction processes to be carried out efficiently and effectively within budgetary and schedule constraints. In the *Handbook*, "construction manager" includes these workers as well as managers working directly for the contractors who actually perform the construction.

Generally, a *contractor* is the firm under contract to provide specialized construction services. On small projects such as remodeling a home, the construction contractor is usually a self-employed construction manager or skilled trades worker who directs and oversees employees. On larger projects, construction managers working for a *general contractor* have overall responsibility for completing the construction in accordance with the engineer or architect's drawings and specifications and prevailing building codes. They arrange for *subcontractors* to perform specialized craft work or other specified construction work.

Large construction projects, like an office building or industrial complex for example, are too complicated for one person to supervise. These projects are divided into many segments: Site preparation, including land clearing and earth moving; sewage systems; landscaping and road construction; building construction, including excavation and laying foundations, erection of structural framework, floors, walls, and roofs; and building systems, including fire protection, electrical, plumbing, air-conditioning, and heating. Construction managers may work as part of a team or may be in charge of one or more of these activities. They may have several subordinates, such as assistant project managers, superintendents, field engineers, or crew supervisors, reporting to them.

Construction managers plan, budget, and direct the construction project. They evaluate various construction methods and determine the most cost-effective plan and schedule. They determine the appropriate construction methods and schedule all required construction site activities into logical, specific steps, budgeting the time required to meet established deadlines. This may require sophisticated estimating and scheduling techniques, using computers with specialized software. Construction managers determine the labor requirements and, in some cases, supervise or monitor the hiring and dismissal of workers.

Managers direct and monitor the progress of field or site construction activities, at times through other construction supervisors. This includes the delivery and use of materials, tools, and equipment; the quality of construction, worker productivity, and safety. They are responsible for obtaining all necessary permits and licenses and, depending upon the contractual arrangements, direct or monitor compliance with building and safety codes and other regulations.

They regularly review engineering and architectural drawings and specifications to monitor progress and ensure compliance with plans and specifications. They track and control construction costs to avoid cost overruns. Based upon direct observation and reports by subordinate supervisors, managers may prepare daily reports of progress and requirements for labor, material, and machinery and equipment at the construction site. Construction managers meet regularly with owners, subcontractors, architects, and other design professionals to monitor and coordinate all phases of the construction project.

Working Conditions

Construction managers work out of a main office from which the overall construction project is monitored or out of a field office at the construction site. Management decisions regarding daily construction activities are usually made at the job site. Managers usually travel when the construction site is in another State or when they are responsible for activities at two or more sites. Management of construction projects overseas usually entails temporary residence in another country.

Construction managers must be "on call" to deal with delays, bad weather, or emergencies at the site. Most work more than a standard 40-hour week since construction may proceed around-the-clock. This type of work schedule can go on for days, even weeks, to meet special project deadlines, especially if there have been unforeseen delays.

Construction managers schedule construction site activities and are responsible for all necessary permits and licenses.

Although the work generally is not considered dangerous, construction managers must be careful while touring construction sites, especially when large machinery, heavy equipment, and vehicles are being operated. Managers must be able to establish priorities and assign duties. They need to observe job conditions and to be alert to changes and potential problems, particularly involving safety on the job site and adherence to regulations.

Employment

Construction managers held about 197,000 jobs in 1994. Over 85 percent were employed in the construction industry, primarily by specialty trade contractors—for example, plumbing, heating and air-conditioning, and electrical contractors—and general building contractors. Many also worked as self-employed independent contractors in the specialty trades. Others were employed by engineering, architectural, surveying, and construction management services firms, as well as local governments, educational institutions, and real estate developers.

Training, Other Qualifications, and Advancement

Persons interested in becoming a construction manager need a solid background in building science and management, as well as related work experience within the construction industry. They need to be able to understand contracts, plans, and specifications, and be knowledgeable about construction methods, materials, and regulations. Familiarity with computers and software programs for job costing, scheduling, and estimating is increasingly important.

Traditionally, persons advanced to construction management positions after having substantial experience as construction craft workers—for example, as carpenters, masons, plumbers, or electricians—or after having worked as construction supervisors or as independent specialty contractors overseeing workers in one or more construction trades. However, more and more employers—particularly, large construction firms—seek to hire managers with industry work experience and formal postsecondary education in building science or construction management.

In 1994, over 100 colleges and universities offered 4-year degree programs in construction management or construction science. These programs include courses in project control and development, site planning, design, construction methods, construction materials, value analysis, cost estimating, scheduling, contract administration, accounting, business and financial management, building codes and standards, inspection procedures, engineering and architectural sciences, mathematics, statistics, and computer science. Graduates from 4-year degree programs usually are hired as assistants to project managers, field engineers, schedulers, or cost estimators. An increasing number of graduates in related fields—engineering or architecture, for example—also enter construction management, often after having had substantial experience on construction projects.

Around 30 colleges and universities also offer a master's degree program in construction management or construction science, and at least two offer a Ph.D. in the field. Master's degree recipients, especially those with work experience in construction, typically become construction managers in very large construction or construction management companies. Often, individuals who hold a bachelor's degree in an unrelated field seek a master's degree in order to work in the construction industry. Doctoral degree recipients generally become college professors or work in an area of research.

Many individuals also attend training and educational programs sponsored by industry associations, often in collaboration with postsecondary institutions. A number of 2-year colleges throughout the country offer construction management or construction technology programs.

Construction managers should be adaptable and be able to work effectively in a fast-paced environment. They should be decisive and able to work well under pressure, particularly when faced with unexpected occurrences or delays. The ability to coordinate several major activities at once, while being able to analyze and resolve specific problems is essential, as is the ability to understand engineering, architectural, and other construction drawings. Managers must be able to establish a good working relationship with many different people including owners, other managers, design professionals, supervisors, and craft workers.

Advancement opportunities for construction managers vary depending upon the size and type of company for which one works. Within large firms, managers may eventually become top-level managers or executives. Highly experienced individuals may become independent consultants; some serve as expert witnesses in court or as arbitrators in disputes. Those with the required capital may establish their own firms offering construction management services or their own general contracting firms overseeing construction projects from start to finish.

Job Outlook

Employment of construction managers is expected to increase faster than the average for all occupations through the year 2005 as the level of construction activity and complexity of construction projects continues to grow. In addition, many job openings should result annually from the need to replace workers who transfer to other occupations or leave the labor force. Employers prefer applicants with previous construction work experience who can combine a strong background in building technology with proven supervisory or managerial skills. Prospects in construction management, engineering and architectural services, and construction contracting firms should be particularly favorable for persons with a bachelor's degree or higher in construction science, construction management, or construction engineering who have worked in construction.

Increased spending on the Nation's infrastructure—highways, bridges, dams, water and sewage systems, and electric power generation and transmission facilities—will result in a greater demand for construction managers, as will the need to build more residential housing, commercial and office buildings, and factories. In addition, continuing maintenance and repair of all kinds of existing structures will also contribute to demand for these professionals.

The increasing complexity of construction projects also should lead to the creation of more manager jobs. Advances in building materials and construction methods and the growing number of multipurpose buildings, electronically operated "smart" buildings, and energy-efficient structures will require the expertise of more construction managers. In addition, the proliferation of laws setting standards for buildings and construction materials, worker safety, energy efficiency, and environmental pollution have further complicated the construction process and should increase demand for managers. As project owners and construction companies strive to keep costs in line and reduce the causes of disputes and litigation, they will continue to depend on the services and expertise of highly effective managers.

Employment of construction managers is sensitive to the short-term nature of many construction projects and cyclical fluctuations in construction activity. During periods of diminished construction activity—when many construction workers are laid off—many construction managers remain employed to plan, schedule, or estimate costs of future construction projects, as well as to manage maintenance, repair and renovation work which remains ongoing.

Earnings

Earnings of salaried construction managers and incomes of self-employed independent construction contractors vary depending upon the size and nature of the construction project, its geographic location, and economic conditions. Based on limited information available, the average starting salary for construction managers in 1994 was around $30,000 annually. The average salary for experienced construction managers in 1994 ranged from around $40,000 to $100,000 annually. Many salaried construction managers receive benefits such as bonuses, use of company motor vehicles, paid vacations, and life and health insurance.

Related Occupations

Construction managers participate in the conceptual development of a construction project and oversee its organization, scheduling, and implementation. Occupations that perform similar functions include architects, civil engineers, construction supervisors, cost engineers, cost estimators, developers, electrical engineers, industrial engineers, landscape architects, and mechanical engineers.

Sources of Information

For information about a career as a construction manager contact:

☛American Institute of Constructors, 466 94th Ave. North, St. Petersburg, FL 33702.

☛Associated Builders and Contractors, 1300 North 17th St., Rosslyn, VA 22209.

☛Associated General Contractors of America, 1957 E St. NW., Washington, DC 20006-5199.

☛Construction Management Association of America, 7918 Jones Branch Dr., Suite 540, McLean, VA 22102.

Information on the accreditation requirements for construction science and management programs is available from:

☛American Council for Construction Education, 1300 Hudson Lane, Suite 3, Monroe, LA 71201-6054.

Cost Estimators

(D.O.T. 169.267-038; 221.362-018, and .367-014)

Nature of the Work

Accurately predicting the cost of future projects is vital to the survival of any business. Cost estimators develop cost information for owners or managers to use in making bids for contracts, in determining if a new product will be profitable, or in determining which of a firms' products are making a profit.

Regardless of the industry they work in, estimators compile and analyze data on all the factors that can influence costs—such as materials, labor, location, and special machinery requirements, including computer hardware and software. Job duties vary widely depending upon the type and size of the project. Estimators working in the construction industry and manufacturing businesses have different methods of and motivations for estimating costs.

On a large construction project, for example, the estimating process begins with the decision to submit a bid. After reviewing the architect's drawings and specifications, the estimator visits the site of the proposed project. The estimator needs to gather information on access to the site and availability of electricity, water, and other services, as well as surface topography and drainage. If the project is a remodeling or renovation job, the estimator might consider the need to control noise and dust and schedule work in order to accommodate occupants of the building. The information developed during the site visit generally is recorded in a signed report that is made part of the final project estimate.

After the site visit is completed, the estimator determines the quantity of materials and labor that the firm will have to furnish. This process, called the quantity survey or "takeoff," is completed by filling out standard estimating forms that provide spaces for the entry of dimensions, number of units, and other information. A cost estimator working for a general contractor, for example, will estimate the costs of all items the contractor must provide. Although subcontractors will estimate their costs as part of their own bidding process, the general contractor's cost estimator often analyzes bids made by subcontractors as well. Also during the takeoff process, the estimator must make decisions concerning equipment needs, sequence of operations, and crew size. Allowances for the waste of materials, inclement weather, shipping delays, and other factors that may increase costs are incorporated in the takeoff.

On completion of the quantity surveys, a total project cost summary is prepared by the chief estimator that includes the cost of labor, equipment, materials, subcontracts, overhead, taxes, insurance, markup, and any other costs that may affect the project. The chief estimator then prepares the bid proposal for submission to the developer.

Construction cost estimators also may be employed by the project's architect or owner to estimate costs or track actual costs relative to bid specifications as the project develops. In large construction companies that employ more than one estimator, it is common practice for them to specialize. For instance, one person may estimate only electrical work, whereas another may concentrate on excavation, concrete, and forms.

In manufacturing and other firms, cost estimators generally are assigned to the engineering or cost department. The estimators' goal in manufacturing is to accurately allocate the costs associated with making products. The job may begin when management requests an estimate of the costs associated with a major redesign of an existing product or the development of a new product or production process. When estimating the cost of developing a new product, for example, the estimator works with engineers, first reviewing blueprints or conceptual drawings to determine the machining operations, tools, gauges, and materials that would be required for the job. The estimator then prepares a parts list and determines whether it is more efficient to produce or to purchase the parts. To do this, the estimator must initiate inquiries for price information from potential suppliers. The next step is to determine the cost of manufacturing each component of the product. Some high technology products require a tremendous amount of computer programming during the design phase. The cost of software development is one of the fastest growing and most difficult activities to estimate. Some cost estimators now specialize in only estimating computer software development and related costs.

The cost estimator then prepares time-phase charts and learning curves. Time-phase charts indicate the time required for tool design and fabrication, tool "debugging"—finding and correcting all problems—manufacturing of parts, assembly, and testing. Learning curves graphically represent the rate at which performance improves with practice. These curves are commonly called "problem-elimination" curves because many problems—such as engineering changes, rework, parts shortages, and lack of operator skills—diminish as the number of parts produced increases, resulting in lower unit costs.

Using all of this information, the estimator then calculates the standard labor hours necessary to produce a predetermined number of units. Standard labor hours are then converted to dollar values, to

Cost estimators use computers to perform complex mathematical calculations.

which are added factors for waste, overhead, and profit to yield the unit cost in dollars. The estimator then compares the cost of purchasing parts with the firm's cost of manufacturing them to determine which is cheaper.

Computers are widely used because cost estimating may involve complex mathematical calculations and require advanced mathematical techniques. For example, to undertake a parametric analysis, a process used to estimate project costs on a per unit basis subject to the specific requirements of a project, cost estimators use a computer database containing information on costs and conditions of many other similar projects. Although computers cannot be used for the entire estimating process, they can relieve estimators of much of the drudgery associated with routine, repetitive, and time-consuming calculations. Computers also are used to produce all of the necessary documentation with the help of basic word-processing and spreadsheet software. This leaves estimators with more time to study and analyze projects and can lead to more accurate estimates. (More detailed information on various cost estimating techniques is available from the organizations listed under Sources of Additional Information below.)

Working Conditions
Although estimators spend most of their time in an office, construction estimators must make frequent visits to work sites that are dirty and cluttered with debris. Likewise, estimators in manufacturing must spend time on the factory floor where it can be hot, noisy, and dirty. Cost estimators usually operate under pressure, especially when facing deadlines. Inaccurate estimating can cause a firm to lose out on a bid or lose money on a job that proves to be unprofitable. Although estimators normally work a 40-hour week, much overtime is often required. In some industries, frequent travel between a firm's headquarters and its subsidiaries or subcontractors also may be required.

Employment
Cost estimators held about 179,000 jobs in 1994, primarily in construction industries. Others can be found primarily in manufacturing industries. Some cost estimators also worked for engineering and architectural services firms, business services firms, and throughout a wide range of other industries. Construction, operations research, production control, cost, and price analysts who work for government agencies also may do significant amounts of cost estimating in the course of their regular duties. (For more information, see the section on operations research analysts elsewhere in the *Handbook*.)

Cost estimators work throughout the country, usually in or near major industrial, commercial, and government centers, and in cities and suburban areas undergoing rapid change or development.

Training, Other Qualifications, and Advancement
Entry requirements for cost estimators vary significantly by industry. In the construction industry, employers prefer applicants with a thorough knowledge of construction materials, costs, and procedures in areas ranging from heavy construction to electrical work, plumbing systems, or masonry work. Most construction estimators have considerable previous experience as a construction craft worker or manager. Individuals who combine this experience with some postsecondary training in construction estimating, or with a bachelor's or associate degree in civil engineering, architectural drafting, or building construction, have a competitive edge in landing jobs.

In manufacturing industries, employers prefer to hire individuals with a degree in engineering, science, operations research, mathematics, or statistics, or in accounting, finance, business, or a related subject. In high-technology industries, great emphasis is placed on experience involving quantitative techniques.

Cost estimators should have an aptitude for mathematics, be able to quickly analyze, compare, and interpret detailed and sometimes poorly defined information, and be able to make sound and accurate judgments based on this knowledge. Assertiveness and self-con-

fidence in presenting and supporting their conclusions are important. Cost estimators should also be familiar with computers and their application to the estimating process, including word-processing and spreadsheet packages used to produce necessary documentation. In some instances, familiarity with special estimation software or programming skills may be useful.

Regardless of their background, estimators receive much training on the job. Working with an experienced estimator, they become familiar with each step in the process. Those with no experience reading construction specifications or blueprints first learn that aspect of the work. They then may accompany an experienced estimator to the construction site or shop floor where they observe the work being done, take measurements, or perform other routine tasks. As they become more knowledgeable, estimators learn how to tabulate quantities and dimensions from drawings and how to select the appropriate material prices.

Many colleges and universities include cost estimating as part of curriculums in civil engineering, industrial engineering, and construction management or construction engineering technology. Courses and programs in cost estimating techniques and procedures are offered by many technical schools, junior colleges, and universities. In addition, cost estimating is a significant part of master's degree programs in construction management offered by many colleges and universities. Organizations that represent cost estimators, such as American Association of Cost Engineers (AACE) International and the Society of Cost Estimating and Analysis, also sponsor educational programs. These programs help students, estimators-in-training, and experienced estimators stay abreast of changes affecting the profession.

Voluntary certification can be valuable to cost estimators because it provides professional recognition of the estimator's competence and experience. Both AACE International and the Society of Cost Estimating and Analysis administer certification programs. To become certified, estimators generally must have between 3 and 7 years of estimating experience and must pass both a written and an oral examination. In addition, certification requirements may include publication of at least one article or paper in the field.

For most estimators, advancement takes the form of higher pay and prestige. Some move into management positions, such as project manager for a construction firm or manager of the industrial engineering department for a manufacturer. Others may go into business for themselves as consultants, providing estimating services for a fee to government or construction and manufacturing firms.

Job Outlook
Overall employment of cost estimators is expected to grow about as fast as average for all occupations through the year 2005 as the levels of construction and manufacturing activity increase as the economy grows. However, even when construction and manufacturing activity decline, there should always remain a demand for cost estimators to accurately predict costs in all areas of business. Some job openings will also arise from the need to replace workers who transfer to other occupations or who leave the labor force altogether.

Growth of the construction industry, where over 60 percent of all cost estimators are employed, will be the driving force behind the rising demand for these workers. The fastest growing sectors of the construction industry are expected to be special trade contractors and those associated with heavy construction and spending on the Nation's infrastructure. Construction and repair of highways and streets, bridges, and construction of more subway systems, airports, water and sewage systems, and electric power plants and transmission lines will stimulate demand for many more cost estimators. Job prospects in construction should be best for those workers with a degree in construction management, engineering, or architectural drafting, or who have substantial experience in various phases of construction or a specialty craft area.

Employment of cost estimators in manufacturing should remain relatively stable as firms continue to use their services to identify and control their operating costs. Experienced estimators with degrees in engineering, science, mathematics, business administration, or economics and who have computer expertise should have the best job prospects in manufacturing.

Earnings

Salaries of cost estimators vary widely by experience, education, size of firm, and industry. According to limited data available, most starting salaries in the construction industry for cost estimators with limited training were between about $17,000 and $21,000 a year in 1994. College graduates with degrees in fields such as engineering or construction management that provide a strong background in cost estimating could start at about $30,000 annually or more. Highly experienced cost estimators earned $75,000 a year or more. Starting salaries and annual earnings in the manufacturing sector usually were somewhat higher.

Related Occupations

Other workers who quantitatively analyze information in a similar capacity include appraisers, cost accountants, cost engineers, economists, evaluators, financial analysts, loan officers, operations research analysts, underwriters, and value engineers.

Sources of Additional Information

Information about career opportunities, certification, and educational programs in cost estimating in the construction industry may be obtained from:

☛ AACE International, 209 Prairie Ave., Suite 100, Morgantown, WV 26505.
☛ Professional Construction Estimators Association of America, P.O. Box 11626, Charlotte, NC 28220-1626.

Similar information about cost estimating in government, manufacturing, and other industries is available from:

☛ Society of Cost Estimating and Analysis, 101 S. Whiting St., Suite 201, Alexandria, VA 22304.

Education Administrators

(D.O.T. 075.117-010, -018, -030; 090.117 except -034, .167; 091.107; 092.167, .117-010, .167-014; 096.167; 097.167; 099.117 except -022, .167-034; 100.117-010; 169.267-022; 239.137-010)

Nature of the Work

Smooth operation of an educational institution requires competent administrators. Education administrators provide direction, leadership, and day-to-day management of educational activities in schools, colleges and universities, businesses, correctional institutions, museums, and job training and community service organizations. (College presidents and school superintendents are covered in the Handbook statement on general managers and top executives.) Education administrators set educational standards and goals and aid in establishing the policies and procedures to carry them out. They develop academic programs; monitor students' educational progress; train and motivate teachers and other staff; manage guidance and other student services; administer recordkeeping; prepare budgets; handle relations with parents, prospective students, employers, and the community; and perform many other activities.

They also supervise managers, management support staff, teachers, counselors, librarians, coaches, and others. In an organization such as a small daycare center, there may be one administrator who handles all these functions. In universities or large school systems, responsibilities are divided among many administrators, each with a specific function.

Principals manage elementary and secondary schools. They set the academic tone and they hire teachers and other staff, help them improve their skills, and evaluate them. Principals confer with staff—advising, explaining, or answering procedural questions. They visit classrooms, observe teaching methods, review instructional objectives, and examine learning materials. They actively work with teachers to develop and maintain high curriculum standards, develop mission statements, and set performance goals and objectives. As pay-for-performance becomes an accepted standard for teachers, principals must ensure that they are using clear, objective guidelines for teacher appraisals.

Principals also meet and interact with other administrators, students, parents, and representatives of community organizations. As decision-making authority shifts from school district central offices to individual schools, parents, teachers, and other members of the community are playing an increasingly important role in setting school policies and goals. Principals must pay attention to the concerns of these groups when making administrative decisions.

Principals prepare budgets and reports on various subjects, including finances and attendance, and oversee the requisitioning and allocation of supplies. As school budgets become tighter, many principals are becoming more involved in public relations and fund raising in an effort to secure financial support for their schools from local businesses. Many principals take an active role in developing school/business partnerships and school-to-work transition programs for students.

In recent years, schools have become more involved with students' emotional welfare as well as their academic achievement. As a result, principals face new responsibilities. For example, in response to the growing number of dual-income and single-parent families and teenage parents, more schools have before- and after-school child- care programs or family resource centers, which also may offer parenting classes and social service referrals. With the help of community organizations, some principals have established programs to combat the increase in crime, drug and alcohol abuse, and sexually transmitted disease among students.

Assistant principals aid the principal in the overall administration of the school. Some assistant principals hold this position for several years to prepare for advancement to principal; others are career assistant principals. Depending on the number of students, the number of assistant principals a school employs may vary. They are responsible for programming student classes, ordering textbooks and supplies, and coordinating transportation, custodial, cafeteria, and other support services. They usually handle discipline, attendance, social and recreational programs, and health and safety. They also may counsel students on personal, educational, or vocational matters. As site-based management becomes more prevalent, assistant principals are playing a greater role in curriculum development, evaluating teachers, and school-community relations, responsibilities previously assumed solely by the principal.

Administrators in school district central offices manage public schools under their jurisdiction. This group includes those who direct subject area programs such as English, music, vocational education, special education, and mathematics. They plan, evaluate, standardize, and improve curriculums and teaching techniques, and help teachers improve their skills and learn about new methods and materials. They oversee career counseling programs, and testing which measures students' abilities and helps place them in appropriate classes. Central office administrators also include directors of programs such as guidance, school psychology, athletics, curriculum and instruction, and professional development. With the trend toward site-based management, principals and assistant principals, along with teachers and other staff, have primary responsibility for many of these programs in their individual schools.

In colleges and universities, academic deans, deans of faculty, provosts, and/or university deans assist presidents and develop budgets and academic policies and programs. They direct and coordinate activities of deans of individual colleges and chairpersons of academic departments.

College or university department heads or chairpersons are in charge of departments such as English, biological science, or mathematics. In addition to teaching, they coordinate schedules of classes and teaching assignments; propose budgets; recruit, interview, and hire applicants for teaching positions; evaluate faculty members; encourage faculty development; and perform other administrative duties. In overseeing their departments, chairpersons must consider and balance the concerns of faculty, administrators, and students.

Higher education administrators also provide student services. Vice presidents of student affairs or student life, deans of students, and directors of student services may direct and coordinate admissions, foreign student services, health and counseling services, career services, financial aid, and housing and residential life, as well as social, recreational, and related programs. In small colleges, they may counsel students. Registrars are custodians of students' education records. They register students, prepare student transcripts, evaluate academic records, oversee the preparation of college catalogs and schedules of classes, and analyze registration statistics. Directors of admissions manage the process of recruiting and admitting students, and work closely with financial aid directors, who oversee scholarship, fellowship, and loan programs. Registrars and admissions officers must adapt to technological innovations in student information systems such as touch-tone voice response, desk-top publishing, and presentation of information—college catalogs and schedules, for example—on computer systems, including the Internet. Directors of student activities plan and arrange social, cultural and recreational activities, assist student-run organizations, and may orient new students. Athletic directors plan and direct intramural and intercollegiate athletic activities, including publicity for athletic events, preparation of budgets, and supervision of coaches.

Working Conditions

Education administrators hold management positions with significant responsibility. Coordinating and interacting with faculty, parents, and students can be fast-paced and stimulating, but also stressful and demanding. Some jobs include travel. Principals and assistant principals whose main duty is often discipline may find working with difficult students frustrating, but challenging. The number of school-age children is rising, and some school systems have hired assistant principals when a school's population increased significantly. In other school systems, principals may manage larger student bodies, which can also be stressful.

Most education administrators work more than 40 hours a week, including many nights and weekends when they oversee school activities. Unlike teachers, they usually work year round.

Employment

Education administrators held about 393,000 jobs in 1994. About 9 out of 10 were in educational services—in elementary, secondary, and technical schools and colleges and universities. The rest worked in child daycare centers, religious organizations, job training centers, State departments of education, and businesses and other organizations that provide training activities for their employees.

Training, Other Qualifications, and Advancement

Education administrator is not usually an entry-level job. Most education administrators begin their careers in related occupations, and prepare for a job in education administration by completing a master's or doctoral degree. Because of the diversity of duties and levels of responsibility, their educational backgrounds and experience vary considerably. Principals, assistant principals, central office administrators, and academic deans usually have taught or held another related job before moving into administration. Some teachers move directly into principalships; others first become assistant principals, or gain experience in other central office administrative jobs at either the school or district level in positions such as department head, curriculum specialist, or subject matter advisor. In some cases, administrators move up from related staff jobs such as recruiter, guidance counselor, librarian, residence hall director, or financial aid or admissions counselor. Earning a graduate degree generally improves one's advancement opportunities in education administration.

To be considered for education administrator positions, workers must first prove themselves in their current jobs. In evaluating candidates, supervisors look for determination, confidence, innovativeness, motivation, leadership, and managerial attributes, such as ability to make sound decisions and organize and coordinate work efficiently. Since much of an administrator's job involves interacting with others, from students to parents to teachers, they must have strong interpersonal skills and be effective communicators and motivators. Knowledge of management principles and practices, gained through work experience and formal education, is important.

In public schools, principals, assistant principals, and school administrators in central offices need a master's degree in education administration or educational supervision, and a State teaching certificate. Some principals and central office administrators have a doctorate or specialized degree in education administration. In private schools, which are not subject to State certification requirements, some principals and assistant principals hold only a bachelor's degree. However, the majority have a master's or doctoral degree.

Education administrators meet with other administrators, students, parents, and representatives of community organizations.

Licensing standards for principals are currently being developed and are expected to be in place by 1997. The Interstate Principals Licensure Consortium will be the licensing body.

Academic deans and chairpersons usually have a doctorate in their specialty. Most have held a professorship in their department before advancing. Admissions, student affairs, and financial aid directors and registrars sometimes start in related staff jobs with bachelor's degrees—any field usually is acceptable—and obtain advanced degrees in college student affairs or higher education administration. A Ph.D. or Ed.D. usually is necessary for top student affairs positions. Computer literacy and a background in mathematics or statistics may be assets in admissions, records, and financial work.

Advanced degrees in higher education administration, educational supervision, and college student affairs are offered in many colleges and universities. The National Council for Accreditation of Teacher Education accredits programs. Education administration degree programs include courses in school management, school law, school finance and budgeting, curriculum development and evaluation, research design and data analysis, community relations, politics in education, counseling, and leadership. Educational supervision degree programs include courses in supervision of instruction and curriculum, human relations, curriculum development, research, and advanced pedagogy courses.

Education administrators advance by moving up an administrative ladder or transferring to larger schools or systems. They also may become superintendent of a school system or president of an educational institution.

Job Outlook

Substantial competition is expected for prestigious jobs as education administrators. Many teachers and other staff meet the education and experience requirements for these jobs, and seek promotion. However, the number of openings is relatively small; only the most highly qualified are selected. Candidates who have the most formal education and who are willing to relocate should have the best job prospects.

Employment of education administrators is expected to grow about as fast as the average for all occupations through the year 2005. Most job openings, particularly for principals and assistant principals, are likely to result from the need to replace administrators who retire. Additional openings will be created by workers who transfer to other occupations.

Employment of education administrators will grow as more services are provided to students; as efforts to improve the quality of education continue; and as institutions comply with government regulations. As school enrollments increase, job opportunities for assistant principals will grow. Rather than opening new schools, many existing school populations will grow, spurring demand for assistant principals to help with the increased workload.

The number of education administrators employed depends largely on State and local expenditures for education. Budgetary constraints could result in fewer administrators than anticipated; pressures to increase spending to improve the quality of education could result in more.

Earnings

Salaries of education administrators vary according to position, level of responsibility and experience, and the size and location of the institution. Generally, principals employed in public schools earn higher salaries than those in private schools.

Based on a salary survey conducted by the National Association of Colleges and Employers, master's degree candidates in education administration received starting salary offers averaging $31,600 a year in 1995; doctoral degree candidates in education administration, $58,600.

According to a survey of public schools, conducted by the Educational Research Service, average salaries for principals and assistant principals in the 1994-95 school year were as follows:

Principals:

Elementary school	$58,600
Junior high/middle school	62,300
Senior high school	66,600

Assistant principals:

Elementary school	$48,500
Junior high/middle school	52,900
Senior high school	55,600

In 1994-95, according to the College and University Personnel Association, median annual salaries for selected administrators in higher education were as follows:

Academic deans:

Medicine	$199,500
Law	139,000
Engineering	100,900
Arts and sciences	79,200
Business	78,600
Education	77,700
Social sciences	58,600
Mathematics	56,900

Student services directors:

Admissions and registrar	$50,600
Student financial aid	43,400
Student activities	33,400

Related Occupations

Education administrators apply organizational and leadership skills to provide services to individuals. Workers in related occupations include health services administrators, social service agency administrators, recreation and park managers, museum directors, library directors, and professional and membership organization executives. Since principals and assistant principals generally have extensive teaching experience, their backgrounds are similar to those of teachers and many school counselors.

Sources of Additional Information

For information on elementary and secondary school principals, assistant principals, and central office administrators, contact:
☛American Federation of School Administrators, 1729 21st St. NW., Washington, DC 20009.
☛American Association of School Administrators, 1801 North Moore St., Arlington, VA 22209

For information on elementary school principals and assistant principals, contact:
☛The National Association of Elementary School Principals, 1615 Duke St., Alexandria, VA 22314-3483.

For information on secondary school principals and assitant principals, contact:
☛The National Association of Secondary School Principals, 1904 Association Dr., Reston, VA 22091.

For information on college student affairs administrators, contact:
☛National Association of Student Personnel Administrators, 1875 Connecticut Ave. NW., Suite 418, Washington, DC 20009-5728.

For information on collegiate registrars and admissions officers, contact:
☛American Association of Collegiate Registrars and Admissions Officers, One Dupont Circle NW., Suite 330, Washington, DC 20036-1171.

Employment Interviewers

(D.O.T. 166.267-010)

Nature of the Work

Whether you are looking for a job or trying to fill one, you could find yourself turning to an employment interviewer for help. Sometimes called personnel consultants, human resources coordinators, personnel development specialists, or employment brokers, employment interviewers help jobseekers find employment and help employers find qualified staff.

Working largely in private personnel supply firms or State employment security offices (also known as job or employment service centers), employment interviewers act as brokers, putting together the best combination of applicant and job. To accomplish this, they obtain information from employers as well as jobseekers.

Being a private industry employment interviewer is being a salesperson. Counselors pool together a group of qualified applicants and try to sell them to many different companies. Often a consultant will call a company that has never been a client (cold-calling) with the aim of filling their employment needs.

Employers generally pay private (but not public) agencies to recruit workers. The employer places a "job order" with the agency describing the opening and listing requirements such as education, licenses or credentials, and experience. Employment interviewers often contact the employer to determine their exact personnel needs. Jobseekers are asked to fill out forms or present resumes that detail their education, experience, and other qualifications. They may be interviewed or tested and have their background, references, and credentials checked. The employment interviewer then reviews the job requirements and the jobseeker qualifications to determine the best possible match of position and employee. Although computers are increasingly used to keep records and match employers with jobseekers, personal contact with an employment interviewer remains an essential part of an applicant's job search.

Maintaining good relations with employers is an important part of the employment interviewer's job because this helps assure a steady flow of job orders. Being prepared to fill an opening quickly with a qualified applicant impresses employers most and keeps them as clients.

Besides helping firms fill job openings, employment interviewers help individuals find jobs. The services they provide depend upon the company or type of agency they work for and the clientele it serves.

Employment interviewers in personnel supply firms who place permanent employees are generally called counselors. They usually place job applicants who have the right qualifications but lack knowledge of the job market for their desired position. Counselors in these firms offer tips on personal appearance, suggestions on presenting a positive image of oneself, background on the company with which an interview is scheduled, and recommendations about interviewing techniques. Many firms specialize in placing applicants in particular kinds of jobs, for example secretarial, word processing, computer programming and computer systems analysis, engineering, accounting, law, or health. Counselors in such firms usually have 3 to 5 years of experience in the field into which they are placing applicants.

Some employment interviewers work in temporary help services companies. These companies send out their own employees to firms that need temporary help. Employment interviewers take job orders from client firms and match their requests against a list of available workers. Employment interviewers select the best qualified workers available and assign them to the firms requiring assistance. Sometimes employees placed with companies as temporaries are later hired as permanent employees.

Traditionally, firms that placed permanent employees usually dealt with highly skilled applicants, such as lawyers or accountants, and those placing temporary employees dealt with less skilled workers, such as secretaries or data entry operators. However, temporary help services increasingly place workers with a wide range of educational backgrounds and work experience; businesses are turning to temporary employees to fill all types of positions to reduce costs of pay and benefits associated with hiring permanent employees.

Regular evaluation of employee job skills is an important part of the job for those interviewers working in temporary help services companies. Initially, interviewers evaluate or test new employees' skills to determine their abilities and weaknesses. The results, which are kept on file, are referred to when filling job orders. In some cases, the temporary help company will train employees to improve their skills. Periodically, the interviewer may reevaluate or retest employees to identify any new skills they may have developed.

The duties of employment interviewers in job service centers differ somewhat because applicants may lack marketable skills. In these centers, jobseekers present resumes and fill out forms that ask about educational attainment, job history, skills, awards, certificates, and licenses. An employment interviewer reviews these forms and asks the applicant about the type of job sought and salary range desired. Applicants sometimes have exaggerated expectations. Employment interviewers must be tactful, but persuasive, if an applicant's job or salary requests are unreasonable.

Applicants may need help identifying the kind of work for which they are best suited. The employment interviewer evaluates the applicant's qualifications and either chooses an appropriate occupation or class of occupations, or refers the applicant for vocational testing.

After identifying an appropriate job type, the employment interviewer searches the file of job orders seeking a possible job match, and refers the applicant to the employer if a match is found. If no match is found, the interviewer shows the applicant how to use listings of available jobs.

Some applicants are hindered by problems such as poor English language skills, no high school diploma, a history of drug or alcohol dependency, or a prison record. The amount and nature of special help for such applicants vary from State to State. In some States, it is the employment interviewer's responsibility to counsel hard-to-place applicants and refer them elsewhere for literacy or language instruction, vocational training, transportation assistance, child care, and other services. In other States, specially trained counselors perform this task.

Rapid expansion of temporary help firms will spur growth in the number of employment interviewers.

Working Conditions

Employment interviewers usually work in comfortable, well-lighted offices, often using a computer to match information about employers and jobseekers. Some interviewers, however, may spend much of their time out of the office interviewing. The work can prove hectic, especially in temporary help service companies which supply clients with immediate help for short periods of time. Some overtime may be required, and temporary workers may need their own transportation to make employer visits. The private placement industry is competitive, so counselors feel pressed to give their client companies the best service.

Employment

Employment interviewers held about 77,000 jobs in 1994. About 65 percent worked in the private sector for personnel supply services, generally for employment placement firms or temporary help services companies. Another 21 percent worked for State or local government. Others were employed by organizations that provide various services, such as job training and vocational rehabilitation.

Employees of career consulting or outplacement firms are not included in these estimates. Workers in these firms help clients market themselves; they do not act as job brokers, nor do they match individuals with particular vacancies.

Training, Other Qualifications, and Advancement

Although most public and private agencies prefer to hire college graduates for interviewer jobs, a degree is not always necessary. Hiring requirements in the private sector reflect a firm's management approach as well as the placements in which its interviewers specialize. Those that place highly trained individuals such as accountants, lawyers, engineers, physicians, or managers generally have some training or experience in the field in which they are placing workers. Thus, a bachelor's, master's, or even a doctoral degree may be a prerequisite for some interviewers. Even with the right education, however, sales ability is still required to succeed in the private sector.

Educational requirements play a lesser role for interviewers placing secretaries, word processing operators, and other clerical personnel. In these positions, qualities such as energy level, telephone voice, and sales ability take precedence over educational attainment.

Entry-level employment interviewer positions in the public sector are generally filled by college graduates, even though the positions do not always require a bachelor's degree. Some States allow substitution of suitable work experience for college education. Suitable work experience is generally defined as public contact work or time spent at other jobs (including clerical jobs) in a job service office. In States that permit employment interviewers to engage in counseling, course work in counseling may be required.

Most States and many large city and county governments use some form of merit system for hiring interviewers. Applicants may take a written exam, undergo a preliminary interview, or submit records of their education and experience for evaluation. Those who meet the standards are placed on a list from which the top-ranked candidates are selected for later interviews and possible hiring.

Other desirable qualifications for employment interviewers include good communications skills, a desire to help people, office skills, and adaptability. A friendly, confidence-winning manner is an asset because personal interaction plays a large role in this occupation. Increasingly, employment interviewers use computers as a tool; thus, basic knowledge of computers is helpful.

Advancement as an employment interviewer in the public sector is often based on a system providing regular promotions and salary increases for those meeting established standards. Advancement to supervisory positions is highly competitive. In personnel supply firms, advancement often depends on one's success in placing workers and generally takes the form of greater responsibility and higher income. Successful individuals may form their own businesses.

Job Outlook

Employment in this occupation is expected to grow much faster than the average for all occupations through the year 2005. The overwhelming majority of new jobs will be with temporary help or personnel supply firms. Job growth is not anticipated in State job service offices because of budgetary problems and the increasing use of computerized job matching and information systems. Some additional job openings will result from the need to replace interviewers whose performance does not meet their employer's requirements for placing job applicants. Other openings will stem from the need to replace experienced interviewers who transfer to other occupations, retire, or leave the labor force for other reasons.

Rapid expansion of firms supplying temporary help will be responsible for much of the growth in this occupation. Businesses of all types are turning to temporary help services companies for additional workers during busy periods, for handling short-term assignments or one-time projects, for launching new programs, and to reduce costs of pay and benefits associated with hiring permanent employees.

Expansion of the personnel supply industry, in general, will also spur job growth. Job orders will increase as the economy expands and new businesses are formed; this is expected to heighten demand for employment interviewers. Firms that lack the time or resources to develop their own screening procedures will likely turn to personnel firms.

Employment opportunities should be better in private placement firms than in State job service centers. Entry to this occupation is relatively easy for college graduates, or people who have had some college courses, except in those positions specializing in placement of workers with highly specialized training, such as lawyers, doctors, and engineers.

Employment interviewers who place permanent workers may lose their jobs during recessions because employers reduce or eliminate hiring for permanent positions during downturns in the economy. Also, during periods of high unemployment, employers have fewer problems finding the workers they need, so they turn less often to employment agencies for help. However, during these times the need for the services of employment interviewers who place temporary employees may increase. Employers are increasingly turning to temporary services because temporary employees, who generally do not receive typical benefits such as health or life insurance, are less expensive than permanent employees and are more flexible in terms of hours and working conditions. Those who place permanent or temporary personnel are more susceptible to layoffs than State job service employment interviewers.

Earnings

Earnings in private firms vary, in part, because the basis for compensation varies. Workers in personnel supply firms tend to be paid on a commission basis; those in temporary help service companies receive a salary.

When workers are paid on a commission basis (or salary plus commission), total earnings depend on how much business they bring in. This is usually based on the type as well as the number of placements. Those who place more highly skilled or hard-to-find employees earn more. An interviewer or counselor working strictly on a commission basis often makes around 30 percent of what he or she bills the client, although this varies widely from firm to firm. Some work on a salary-plus-commission basis because they fill difficult or highly specialized positions requiring long periods of search. The salary, usually small by normal standards, guarantees these individuals security through slow times. The commission provides the incentive and opportunity for higher earnings.

Some personnel supply firms employ new workers for a 2- to 3-month probationary period during which they draw a regular salary. This gives new workers time to develop their skills and acquire some clients. At the end of the probationary period, the new employees are evaluated, and they are either let go or switched to a commission basis.

Related Occupations

Employment interviewers serve as intermediaries for jobseekers and employers. Workers in several other occupations do similar jobs.

Personnel officers screen and help hire new employees, but they concern themselves mainly with the hiring needs of the firm; they never represent individual jobseekers. Personnel officers may also have additional duties in areas such as payroll or benefits management.

Career counselors help students and alumni find jobs, but they primarily emphasize career counseling and decision making, not placement.

Counselors in community organizations and vocational rehabilitation facilities help clients find jobs, but they also assist with drug or alcohol dependencies, housing, transportation, child care, and other problems that stand in the way of finding and keeping a job.

Sources of Additional Information

For information on a career as an employment interviewer/counselor, contact:

☛National Association of Personnel Services, 3133 Mt. Vernon Ave., Alexandria, VA 22305.

☛National Association of Temporary Services, 119 S. Saint Asaph St., Alexandria, VA 22314.

For information on a career as an employment interviewer in State employment security offices, contact offices of the State government for which you are interested in working.

Engineering, Science, and Data Processing Managers

(D.O.T. 003.167-034 and -070; 005.167-010 and -022; 007.167-014; 008.167-010; 010.161-010, -014, and .167-018; 011.161-010; 012.167-058 and -062; 018.167-022; 019.167-014; 022.161-010; 024.167-010; 029.167-014; 162.117-030; 169.167-030 and -082; and 189.117-014)

Nature of the Work

Engineering, science, and data processing managers plan, coordinate, and direct research, development, design, production, and computer related activities. They supervise a staff which may include engineers, scientists, technicians, computer specialists, and data processing workers, along with support personnel.

Engineering, science, and data processing managers determine scientific and technical goals within broad outlines provided by top management. These goals may include the redesign of an industrial machine, improvements in manufacturing processes, the development of a large computer program, or advances in basic scientific research. Managers make detailed plans for the accomplishment of these goals—for example, they may develop the overall concepts of new products or identify problems standing in the way of project completion. They forecast costs and equipment and personnel needs for projects and programs. They hire and assign scientists, engineers, technicians, computer specialists, data processing workers, and support personnel to carry out specific parts of the projects, supervise their work, and review their designs, programs, and reports.

Managers coordinate the activities of their unit with other units or organizations. They confer with higher levels of management; with financial, industrial production, marketing, and other managers; and with contractors and equipment suppliers. They also establish working and administrative procedures and policies.

Engineering managers direct and coordinate production, operations, quality assurance, testing, or maintenance in industrial plants; or plan and coordinate the design and development of machinery, products, systems, and processes. Many are plant engineers, who direct and coordinate the maintenance, operation, design, and installation of equipment and machinery in industrial plants. Others manage research and development activities that produce new products and processes or improve existing ones.

Natural science managers oversee activities in agricultural science, chemistry, biology, geology, meteorology, or physics. They manage research and development projects and direct and coordinate testing, quality control, and production activities in research institutes and industrial plants.

Electronic data processing managers direct, plan, and coordinate data processing activities. Top level managers direct all computer-related activities in an organization. Others manage computer operations, software development, or data bases. They analyze the data processing requirements of their organization and assign, schedule, and review the work of systems analysts, computer programmers, and computer operators. They determine computer hardware requirements, evaluate equipment options, and make purchasing decisions.

Some engineering, science, and data processing managers head a section of perhaps 3 to 10 or more scientists, engineers, or computer professionals. Above them are heads of divisions composed of a number of sections, with as many as 15 to 50 scientists or engineers. A few are directors of large laboratories or directors of research.

Working Conditions

Engineering, science, and data processing managers spend most of their time in an office. Some managers, however, may also work in laboratories or industrial plants, where they normally are exposed to the same conditions as research scientists and may occasionally be exposed to the same conditions as production workers. Most work at least 40 hours a week and may work much longer on occasion to meet project deadlines. Some may experience considerable pressure to meet technical or scientific goals within a short time or within a tight budget.

Employment

Engineering, science, and data processing managers held about 337,000 jobs in 1994. Although these managers are found in almost all industries, nearly two-fifths are employed in manufacturing, especially in the industrial machinery and equipment, electrical and electronic equipment, instruments, transportation equipment, and chemicals industries. However, the largest single industry employing these managers was engineering and architectural services, where

Managers of research and development activities are often scientists directly involved in research.

almost 1 in 10 worked in 1994. Others work for management and computer and data processing services companies, government, colleges and universities, and nonprofit research organizations. The majority are most likely engineering managers, often managing industrial research, development, and design projects.

Training, Other Qualifications, and Advancement

Experience as an engineer, mathematician, natural scientist, or computer professional is the usual requirement for becoming an engineering, science, or data processing manager. Consequently, educational requirements are similar to those for scientists, engineers, and data processing professionals.

Engineering managers start as engineers. A bachelor's degree in engineering from an accredited engineering program is acceptable for beginning engineering jobs, but many engineers increase their chances for promotion to manager by obtaining a master's degree in engineering or business administration. A degree in business administration or engineering management is especially useful for becoming a general manager.

Natural science managers usually start as a chemist, physicist, biologist, or other natural scientist. Most natural scientists engaged in basic research have a Ph.D. degree. Some in applied research and other activities may have lesser degrees. First-level science managers are usually specialists in the work they supervise. For example, the manager of a group of physicists doing optical research is almost always a physicist who is an expert in optics.

Most data processing managers have been systems analysts, although some may have experience as programmers, operators, or in other computer specialties. There is no universally accepted way of preparing for a job as a systems analyst. Many have degrees in computer or information science, computer information systems, or data processing and have experience as computer programmers. A bachelor's degree is usually required and a graduate degree often is preferred. However, many data processing managers have associate degrees. A typical career advancement progression in a large organization would be from programmer to programmer/analyst, to systems analyst, and then to project leader or senior analyst. The first real managerial position might be as project manager, programming supervisor, systems supervisor, or software manager.

In addition to educational requirements, scientists, engineers, or computer specialists generally must have demonstrated above-average technical skills to be considered for promotion to manager. Superiors also look for leadership and communication skills, as well as managerial attributes such as the ability to make rational decisions, to manage time well, to organize and coordinate work effectively, to establish good working and personal relationships, and to motivate others. Also, a successful manager must have the desire to manage. Many scientists, engineers, and computer specialists want to be promoted but actually prefer doing technical work.

Some scientists and engineers become managers in marketing, personnel, purchasing, or other areas or become general managers.

Job Outlook

Opportunities for those who wish to become engineering, science, and data processing managers should be closely related to the growth of the occupations they supervise and the industries in which they are found. (See the accompanying chart and the statements on natural scientists, engineers, computer programmers, and computer scientists and systems analysts elsewhere in the *Handbook*.) Because many engineers, natural scientists, and computer specialists are eligible for management and seek promotion, there can be substantial competition for these openings.

Overall employment of engineering and science managers is expected to increase faster than the average for all occupations through the year 2005. Underlying much of the growth of managers in science and engineering are competitive pressures and advancing technologies which force companies to update and improve products more frequently. Research and investment in plants and equipment

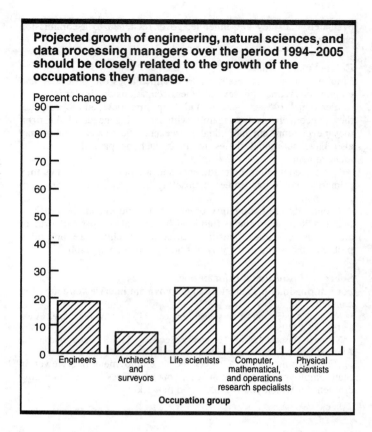

Projected growth of engineering, natural sciences, and data processing managers over the period 1994–2005 should be closely related to the growth of the occupations they manage.

to expand output of goods and services and to raise productivity also will add to employment requirements for science and engineering managers involved in research and development, design, and the operation and maintenance of production facilities.

Many of the industries which employ engineers and scientists derive a large portion of their business from defense contracts. Because defense expenditures are being reduced, employment has declined and job outlook for managers is not as favorable in these industries compared with less defense-oriented industries.

Employment of data processing managers will increase rapidly due to the fast paced expansion of the computer and data processing services industry and the increased employment of computer systems analysts. Large computer centers are consolidating or closing as small computers become more powerful, resulting in fewer opportunities for data processing managers at these centers. However, as the economy expands and as advances in technology lead to broader applications for computers, opportunities should increase and employment growth should be brisk.

Earnings

Earnings for engineering, science, and data processing managers vary by specialty and level of management. Science and engineering managers had average salaries that ranged from $44,000 to well over $100,000 for the most senior managers in large organizations, according to the limited data available. Data processing managers had salaries that ranged from $35,000 to $80,000. Managers often earn about 15 to 25 percent more than those they directly supervise, although there are cases where some employees are paid more than the manager who supervises them, especially in research.

According to a survey of workplaces in 160 metropolitan areas, lower-level engineering managers had median annual earnings of $78,100 in 1993, with the middle half earning between $71,700 and $84,800. The highest-level engineering managers had median annual earnings of $105,700 with the middle half earning between $96,300 and $118,200. Beginning systems analysts managers had median annual earnings of $52,300, with the middle half earning between

$51,400 and $61,800. The most senior systems analysts managers had median annual earnings of $96,500, with the middle half earning between $88,300 and $105,300.

In addition, engineering, science, and data processing managers, especially those at higher levels, often are provided more benefits (e.g., expense accounts, stock option plans, and bonuses) than non-managerial workers in their organizations.

Related Occupations

The work of engineering, science, and data processing managers is closely related to that of engineers, natural scientists, computer personnel, and mathematicians. It is also related to the work of other managers, especially general managers and top executives.

Sources of Additional Information

For information about a career as an engineering, science, or data processing manager, contact the sources of additional information on engineers, natural scientists, and systems analysts that are listed in statements on these occupations elsewhere in the *Handbook*.

Financial Managers

(D.O.T. 160.167-058; 161.117-018; 169.167-086; 186.117-066, -070, -078, -086; .167-054, -086; 189.117-038)

Nature of the Work

Practically every firm—whether in manufacturing, communications, finance, education, or health care—has one or more financial managers. Some of them are treasurers, controllers, credit managers, or cash managers; they prepare the financial reports required by the firm to conduct its operations and to ensure that the firm satisfies tax and regulatory requirements. Financial managers also oversee the flow of cash and financial instruments, monitor the extension of credit, assess the risk of transactions, raise capital, analyze investments, develop information to assess the present and future financial status of the firm, and communicate with stock holders and other investors.

In small firms, chief financial officers usually handle all financial management functions. However, in large firms, these officers oversee financial management departments and help top managers develop financial and economic policy and establish procedures, delegate authority, and oversee the implementation of these policies.

Highly trained and experienced financial managers head each financial department. Controllers direct the preparation of all financial reports—income statements, balance sheets, and special reports, such as depreciation schedules. They oversee the accounting, audit, or budget departments. Cash and credit managers monitor and control the flow of cash receipts and disbursements to meet the business and investment needs of the firm. For example, cash flow projections are needed to determine whether loans must be obtained to meet cash requirements, or whether surplus cash may be invested in interest-bearing instruments. Risk and insurance managers oversee programs to minimize risks and losses that may arise from financial transactions and business operations undertaken by the institution. Credit operations managers establish credit rating criteria, determine credit ceilings, and monitor their institution's extension of credit. Reserve officers review their institution's financial statements and direct the purchase and sale of bonds and other securities to maintain the asset-liability ratio required by law. User representatives in international accounting develop integrated international financial and accounting systems for the banking transactions of multinational organizations. A working knowledge of the financial systems of foreign countries is essential.

Financial institutions—such as banks, savings and loan associations, credit unions, personal credit institutions, and finance companies — may serve as depositories for cash and financial instruments

The need for skilled financial management is increasing.

and offer loans, investment counseling, consumer credit, trust management, and other financial services. Some specialize in specific financial services. Financial managers in financial institutions include vice presidents—who may head one or more departments—bank branch managers, savings and loan association managers, consumer credit managers, and credit union managers. These managers make decisions in accordance with policy set by the institution's board of directors and Federal and State laws and regulations.

Due to changing regulations and increased government scrutiny, financial managers in financial institutions must place greater emphasis on accurate reporting of financial data. They must have detailed knowledge of industries allied to banking—such as insurance, real estate, and securities—and a broad knowledge of business and industrial activities. With growing domestic and foreign competition, knowledge of an expanding and increasingly complex variety of financial services is becoming a necessity for financial managers in financial institutions and other corporations. Besides supervising financial services, financial managers in financial institutions may advise individuals and businesses on financial planning.

Working Conditions

Financial managers are provided with comfortable offices, often close to top managers and to departments which develop the financial data these managers need. Financial managers typically work 40 hours a week, but many work longer hours. Attendance at meetings of financial and economic associations and similar activities is often required. In very large corporations, some traveling to subsidiary firms and to customer accounts may be necessary.

Employment

Financial managers held about 768,000 jobs in 1994. Although these managers are found in virtually every industry, nearly one-third were employed by financial institutions—banks, savings institutions, finance companies, credit unions, insurance companies, securities dealers, and real estate firms, for example. Another third were employed by services industries, including business, health, social, and management services.

Training, Other Qualifications, and Advancement

A bachelor's degree in accounting or finance, or in business administration with an emphasis on accounting or finance, is the minimum academic preparation for financial managers. However, a Master of Business Administration (MBA) degree increasingly is valued by employers. Many financial management positions are filled by promoting experienced, technically skilled professional personnel—for example, accountants, budget analysts, credit analysts, insurance analysts, loan officers, and securities analysts—or accounting or related department supervisors in large institutions.

Due to the growing complexity of global trade, shifting Federal and State laws and regulations, and a proliferation of new, complex financial instruments, continuing education is becoming vital for financial mangers. Firms often provide opportunities for workers to broaden their knowledge and skills and encourage employees to take graduate courses at colleges and universities or attend conferences sponsored by the company. In addition, financial management, banking, and credit union associations, often in cooperation with colleges and universities, sponsor numerous national or local training programs. Persons enrolled prepare extensively at home, then attend sessions on subjects such as accounting management, budget management, corporate cash management, financial analysis, international banking, and data processing and management information systems. Many firms pay all or part of the costs for those who successfully complete courses. Although experience, ability, and leadership are emphasized for promotion, advancement may be accelerated by this type of special study.

In some cases, financial managers may also broaden their skills and exhibit their competency in specialized fields by attaining professional certification. For example, the Association for Investment Management and Research confers the Chartered Financial Analyst designation to investment professionals who have a bachelor's degree, pass three test levels, and have 3 or more years of experience in the field. The National Association of Credit Management administers a three-part certification program for business credit professionals. Through a combination of experience and examinations, these financial managers pass through the level of Credit Business Associate, to Credit Business Fellow, to Certified Credit Executive. The Treasury Management Association confers the Certified Cash Manager designation to those who pass an examination and have 2 years of relevant experience.

Persons interested in becoming financial managers should enjoy working independently, dealing with people, and analyzing detailed account information. The ability to communicate effectively, both orally and in writing, is also important. They also need tact, good judgment, and the ability to establish effective personal relationships to oversee staff.

Financial analysis and management have been revolutionized by technological improvements in personal computers and data processing equipment. Knowledge of their applications is vital to upgrade managerial skills and to enhance advancement opportunities.

Because financial management is critical for efficient business operations, well-trained, experienced financial managers who display a strong grasp of the operations of various departments within their organization are prime candidates for promotion to top management positions. Some financial managers transfer to closely related positions in other industries. Those with extensive experience and access to sufficient capital may head their own consulting firms.

Job Outlook

Like other managerial occupations, the number of applicants for financial management positions is expected to exceed the number of job openings, resulting in competition for jobs. Many opportunities will exist for the most skilled, adaptable, and knowledgeable financial managers. Those who keep abreast of the latest financial instruments and changing regulations, and those familiar with a range of financial services—for example, banking, business credit, credit unions, insurance, real estate, and securities—and with data processing and management information systems will enjoy the best employment opportunities. Developing expertise in a rapidly growing industry, such as health care, also may prove helpful.

Employment of financial managers is expected to increase faster than the average for all occupations through the year 2005. The need for skilled financial management will increase due to the demands of global trade, the proliferation of complex financial instruments, and

changing Federal and State laws and regulations. Many firms have reduced the ranks of middle managers in an effort to be more efficient and competitive, but much of the restructuring and consolidation is complete. The banking industry, on the other hand, is still undergoing mergers and consolidation, and may eliminate some financial management positions as a result.

Earnings

The median annual salary of financial managers was $39,700 in 1994. The lowest 10 percent earned $20,200 or less, while the top 10 percent earned over $77,800.

According to a 1995 survey by Robert Half International, a staffing services firm specializing in accounting and finance, salaries of assistant controllers ranged from $40,000 in the smallest firms to $77,800 in the largest firms; controllers, $46,000 to $134,000; and chief financial officers/treasurers, $60,000 to $295,000.

The salary level depends upon the manager's experience and the size and location of the organization, and is likely to be higher in larger organizations and cities. Many financial managers in private industry receive additional compensation in the form of bonuses, which also vary substantially by the size of the firm.

Related Occupations

Financial managers combine formal education with experience in one or more areas of finance—such as asset management, lending, credit operations, securities investment, or insurance risk and loss control. Workers in other occupations which require similar training and ability include accountants and auditors, budget officers, credit analysts, loan officers, insurance consultants, portfolio managers, pension consultants, real estate advisors, securities analysts, and underwriters.

Sources of Additional Information

For information about financial management careers in banking and related financial institutions, contact:

☞American Bankers Association, Center for Banking Information, 1120 Connecticut Ave. NW., Washington, DC 20036.

For information about financial careers in business credit management, the Certified Credit Executive program, and institutions offering graduate courses in credit and financial management, contact:

☞National Association of Credit Management (NACM), Credit Research Foundation, 8815 Centre Park Dr., Columbia, MD 21045-2117.

For information about careers in corporate cash management and the Certified Cash Manager program, contact:

☞Treasury Management Association, 7315 Wisconsin Ave., Bethesda, MD 20814.

For information about the Chartered Financial Analyst program, contact:

☞Association for Investment Management and Research, 5 Boar's Head Lane, P.O. Box 3668, Charlottesville, VA 22903.

For information about financial management careers in the health care industry, contact:

☞Healthcare Financial Management Association, Two Westbrook Corporate Center, Suite 700, Westchester, IL 60154.

State bankers' associations can furnish specific information about job opportunities in their respective States, or write directly to a particular bank to inquire about job openings. For the names and addresses of banks and savings and related institutions, as well as the names of their principal officers, consult the following directories.

☞The American Financial Directory (Norcross, Ga., McFadden Business Publications).

☞The U.S. Savings and Loan Directory (Chicago, Rand McNally & Co.).

☞Rand McNally Credit Union Directory (Chicago, Rand McNally & Co.).

☞Polk's World Bank Directory (Nashville, R.L. Polk & Co.).

Funeral Directors

(D.O.T. 187.167-030)

Nature of the Work

Since the earliest of times, most peoples have held funeral ceremonies. The dead have ritually been interred in pyramids, cremated on burning pyres, and sunk beneath the oceans' waves. Even today, funeral practices and rites vary greatly among various cultures and religions. Among the many diverse groups in the United States, funeral practices generally share some common elements: Removal of the remains of the deceased to a mortuary, preparation of the remains, performance of a ceremony that honors the deceased and addresses the spiritual needs of the living as well as the dead, and the burial or destruction of the remains. To unburden themselves of arranging and directing these tasks, grieving families turn to funeral directors.

Funeral directors are also called morticians or undertakers. Although this career does not appeal to everyone, the men and women who work as funeral directors take great pride in the fact that they provide efficient and appropriate services that give comfort to their customers.

Funeral directors interview the family to learn what they desire with regard to the nature of the funeral, the clergy members or other persons who will officiate, and the final disposition of the remains; sometimes the deceased leave detailed instructions for their own funerals. Together with the family, directors establish the location, dates, and times of wakes, memorial services, and burials. They also send a hearse to carry the body to the funeral home or mortuary.

Burial in a casket is the most common method of disposing of remains in this country, although entombments also occur. Cremation, which is the burning of a body in a special furnace, is increasingly selected. Even when remains are cremated, the ashes are often placed in an urn and buried. Funeral directors usually stock a selection of caskets and urns for families to purchase.

Directors arrange the details and handle the logistics of funerals. They prepare obituary notices and have them placed in newspapers, arrange for pallbearers and clergy, schedule with the cemetery the opening and closing of a grave, decorate and prepare the sites of all services, and provide for the transportation of the remains, mourners, and flowers between sites. They also direct preparation and shipment of remains for out-of-State burial.

Funeral services may take place in the home, a house of worship, or the funeral home and at the grave site or crematory. Services may be nonreligious, but often they reflect the religion of the family, so funeral directors must be familiar with the funeral and burial customs of many faiths, ethnic groups, and fraternal organizations. For example, members of some religions seldom have the bodies of the deceased embalmed or cremated.

Most funeral directors are also trained, licensed, and practicing embalmers. Embalming is a sanitary, cosmetic, and preservative process through which the body is prepared for interment. If more than 24 hours or so elapses between death and interment, State laws usually require that remains be refrigerated or embalmed. The *embalmer* washes the body with germicidal soap and replaces the blood with embalming fluid to preserve the body. Embalmers may reshape and reconstruct disfigured or maimed bodies using materials, such as clay, cotton, plaster of Paris, and wax. They also may apply cosmetics to provide a natural appearance, and then dress the body and place it in a casket. Embalmers maintain records such as embalming reports, and itemized lists of clothing or valuables delivered with the body. In large funeral homes, an embalming staff of two or more embalmers, plus several apprentices, may be employed.

Funeral directors also handle the paper work involved with the person's death. They may help family members apply for veterans' burial benefits, notify the Social Security Administration of the

Funeral directors interview the family to learn what type of funeral they desire.

death, apply on behalf of survivors for the transfer of any pensions, insurance policies, or annuities, and submit papers to State authorities so that a formal certificate of death may be issued and copies distributed to heirs.

Funeral directors are also responsible for the success and the profitability of their businesses. Directors keep records on expenses, purchases, and services rendered; prepare and send invoices for services; prepare and submit reports for unemployment insurance; prepare Federal, State, and local tax forms; and prepare itemized bills for customers. Directors also strive to foster a cooperative spirit and friendly attitude among employees and a compassionate demeanor toward the families. A growing number of funeral directors are also involved in helping individuals adapt to changes in their lives following a death through post-death counseling and support group activities.

Most funeral homes have a chapel, one or more viewing rooms, a casket-selection room, and a preparation room. Some also have a crematory on the premises. Equipment may include a hearse, a flower car, limousines, and sometimes an ambulance.

Working Conditions

Funeral directors often work long, irregular hours. Shift work is sometimes necessary because funeral home hours include evenings and weekends. In smaller funeral homes, working hours vary, but in larger homes employees generally work 8 hours a day, 5 or 6 days a week.

Funeral directors occasionally come into contact with the remains of persons who had contagious diseases, but the possibility of infection is remote if strict health regulations are followed.

To show proper respect and consideration for the families and the dead, funeral directors must dress appropriately. The profession usually requires short, neat hair cuts and trim beards if any, for men. Suits, ties, and dresses are customary for a conservative look.

Employment

Funeral directors held about 26,000 jobs in 1994. About 1 in 8 were self-employed. Nearly all worked in the funeral service and crematory industry, but a few worked for the Federal Government.

Training, Other Qualifications, and Advancement

Funeral directors must be licensed in all but one State, Colorado. Licensing laws vary from State to State, but most require applicants to be 21 years old, have a high school diploma, complete some college training in mortuary science, and serve an apprenticeship. After passing a State board licensing examination, new funeral directors may join the staff of a funeral home. Embalmers are required to be licensed in all States, and some States issue a single license for both funeral directors and embalmers. In States that have separate licensing and apprenticeship requirements for the two positions, most people in the field obtain both licenses. Persons interested in a career as a funeral director should contact their state board for specific state requirements.

College programs in mortuary science usually last from 1 to 4 years, depending on the school. There were 42 mortuary science programs accredited by the American Board of Funeral Service Education in 1994. One-year mortuary science programs offered by some vocational schools emphasize basic subjects such as anatomy, physiology, embalming techniques, and restorative art. Two-year programs are offered by a small number of community and junior colleges, and a few colleges and universities offer both 2- and 4-year programs. Mortuary science programs include courses in business management, accounting, and use of computers in funeral home management and client services. They also include courses in the social sciences and legal, ethical, and regulatory subjects, such as psychology, grief counseling, oral and written communication, funeral service law, business law, and ethics.

The National Foundation of Funeral Service offers a continuing education program designed for active practitioners in the field. It is a 3-week program in communications, counseling, and management. Over 25 States have continuing education requirements that funeral directors must meet before a license can be renewed.

Apprenticeships must be completed under an experienced and licensed funeral director or embalmer. Depending on State regulations, apprenticeships last from 1 to 2 years and may be served before, during, or after mortuary school. They provide practical experience in all facets of the funeral service from embalming to transporting remains.

State board licensing examinations vary, but they usually consist of written and oral parts and include a demonstration of practical skills. Persons who want to work in another State may have to pass the examination for that State, although many States will grant licenses to funeral directors from another State without further examination.

High school students can start preparing for a career as a funeral director by taking courses in biology and chemistry and participating public speaking or debating clubs. Part-time or summer jobs in funeral homes consist mostly of maintenance and clean-up tasks, such as washing and polishing limousines and hearses, but these tasks can help students become familiar with the operation of funeral homes.

Important personal traits for funeral directors are composure, tact, and the ability to communicate easily with the public. They also should have the desire and ability to comfort people in their time of sorrow.

Advancement opportunities are best in large funeral homes at which directors may earn promotions to higher paying positions such as branch manager or general manager. Some directors eventually acquire enough money and experience to establish their own funeral businesses.

Job Outlook

Employment opportunities for funeral directors are expected to be excellent, because the number of graduates in mortuary science is likely to continue to be less than the number of job openings in the field.

Employment of funeral directors is expected to increase about as fast as the average for all occupations through the year 2005. Demand for funeral services will rise as the population grows, and with it the number of deaths. The population is projected to become older because the number of persons age 55 and over is expected to increase significantly faster than the population as a whole.

Cremations have been increasing over the years. This trend may lessen the demand for embalming somewhat, because embalming is not required before cremation.

Earnings

Salaries of funeral directors depend on the size of the establishment and the number of services performed. A survey conducted by the National Funeral Directors Association found that the average salary, including bonus, for funeral directors who were owner-managers was $62,506 in 1994; mid-level managers averaged $44,062.

Related Occupations

The job of a funeral director requires tact, discretion, and compassion when dealing with grieving people. Others who need these qualities include members of the clergy, social workers, psychologists, psychiatrists, and other health care professionals.

Sources of Additional Information

For information on the funeral service profession and funeral service statistics, write to:

☛The National Funeral Directors Association, 11121 West Oklahoma Ave., Milwaukee, WI 53227.

For information about college programs in mortuary science, scholarships, and funeral service as a career, contact:

☛The American Board of Funeral Service Education, P.O. Box 1305, Brunswick, ME 04011.

For information on continuing education programs in funeral service, contact:

☛The National Foundation of Funeral Service, 2250 East Devon Ave., Suite 250, Des Plaines, IL 60018.

For information on programs, publications, and statistics on cremations write to:

☛The Cremation Association of North America, 401 N. Michigan, Chicago, IL 60611.

General Managers and Top Executives

(List of D.O.T. codes available upon request. See p. 478.)

Nature of the Work

Chief executive officer, president, executive vice president,, partner, financial institution president, brokerage office manager, college president, school superintendent, and police chief—all are examples of general managers and top executives who formulate the policies and direct the operations of corporations, nonprofit institutions, and government agencies. (The chief executives who formulate policy in government are discussed in detail in the *Handbook* statement on government chief executives and legislators.)

The fundamental objective of private for-profit companies is to make a profit for their shareholders or owners, or to increase shareholder value. Nonprofit organizations and government agencies must effectively implement programs that further their causes or policies within budgetary constraints and shifting public priorities. General managers and top executives work to ensure that their organizations meet these objectives.

A corporation's general goals and policies are established by the chief executive officer in collaboration with other top executives, who are overseen by a board of directors. In a large corporation, chief executive officers must frequently meet with other executives of the corporation to ensure that operations are being carried out in accordance with the organization's policies. Although the chief executive officer of a corporation retains overall accountability, a chief operating officer may be delegated the authority to oversee the executives who direct the activities of various departments and are responsible for implementing the organization's policies in these departments on a day-to-day basis. In publicly-held corporations it is the board of directors that is ultimately accountable for the success or failure of the enterprise, and the chief executive officer reports to the

General managers and top executives held over 3 million jobs in 1994.

board. In nonprofit corporations, the board of trustees fulfills the same role.

The scope of other high level executive's responsibilities depends greatly upon the size of the organization. In large organizations, their duties may be highly specialized. For example, they may oversee managers of marketing, sales promotion, purchasing, finance, personnel, training, industrial relations, administrative services, electronic data processing, property management, transportation, or legal services departments. (Some of these and other managerial occupations are discussed elsewhere in this section of the *Handbook*.) In smaller firms, the chief executive or general manager might be responsible for all or a number of these functions.

Middle managers, in turn, direct their individual departments' activities within the framework of the organization's overall plan. With the help of supervisory managers and their staffs, these managers oversee and motivate their workers to achieve their departments' goals as rapidly and economically as possible. In smaller organizations, such as independent retail stores or small manufacturers, a partner, owner, or general manager may be responsible for all purchasing, hiring, training, quality control, and other day-to-day supervisory duties. (See the *Handbook* statement on retail managers.)

Working Conditions

General managers in large firms or government agencies are usually provided with offices close to the top executives to whom they report. Top executives are generally provided with spacious offices and secretarial and support staff. Long hours, including evenings and weekends, are the rule for most top executives and general managers, though their schedules may be flexible.

Substantial travel is often required of managers and executives, who may travel between national, regional, and local offices or overseas to monitor operations and meet with customers and staff and other executives. Many attend meetings and conferences that are sponsored by associations which provide an opportunity to meet with prospective customers and keep abreast of technological and other developments.

In large corporations, frequent job transfers between local offices or subsidiaries are common. With increasing domestic and international competition, general managers and top executives are under intense pressure to attain ever higher profit, production, and marketing goals. Executives in charge of poorly performing companies or departments generally find their jobs in jeopardy.

Employment

General managers and top executives held over 3 million jobs in 1994. They are found in every industry, but wholesale and retail trade and services industries employ over 6 out of 10.

Training, Other Qualifications, and Advancement

The educational background of managers and top executives varies as widely as the nature of their responsibilities. Many general managers and top executives have a bachelor's degree or higher in liberal arts or business administration. Their major often is related to the departments they direct—for example, accounting for a manager of finance or computer science for a manager of information systems. Graduate and professional degrees are common. Many managers in administrative, marketing, financial, and manufacturing activities have a master's degree in business administration. Managers in highly technical manufacturing and research activities often have a master's degree in engineering or a doctoral degree in a scientific discipline. A law degree is mandatory for managers of legal departments; hospital administrators generally have a master's degree in health services administration or business administration. (For additional information, see the *Handbook* statement on health services managers.) College presidents and school superintendents generally have a doctorate, often in education administration. (See the *Handbook* statement on education administrators.) On the other hand, in some industries, such as retail trade or transportation, it is fairly common for individuals without a college degree to become managers.

In the public sector, many managers have liberal arts degrees in public administration or one of the social sciences. Park superintendents, for example, often have liberal arts degrees, while police chiefs are generally graduates of police academies, and hold degrees in police science or a related field.

Since most general manager and top executive positions are filled by promoting experienced, lower level managers, many are promoted from within the organization. Some companies prefer that their top executives have specialized backgrounds and hire individuals who are managers in other organizations. Qualities critical for success include leadership, self-confidence, motivation, decisiveness, flexibility, the ability to communicate effectively, sound business judgment, and stamina.

Advancement may be accelerated by participation in company training programs to gain a broader knowledge of company policy and operations. Through attendance at national or local training programs sponsored by various industry and trade associations and by continuing education, normally at company expense, managers can become familiar with the latest developments in management techniques and improve their chances of promotion. Every year, thousands of senior managers, who often have experience in a particular field, such as accounting, engineering, or science, attend executive development programs to facilitate their promotion from functional specialists to general managers. Participation in interdisciplinary conferences and seminars can expand knowledge of national and international issues influencing the firm and can help develop a network of useful business contacts.

General managers and top executives must have highly developed personal skills. An analytical mind able to quickly assess large amounts of information and data is very important, as is the ability to consider and evaluate the interrelationships of numerous factors. General managers and top executives also must be able to communicate clearly and persuasively with customers, subordinate managers, and others.

General managers may advance to top executive positions, such as executive vice president, in their own firm or they may land a corresponding position in another firm. They may even advance to peak corporate positions such as chief operating officer or chief executive officer. Chief executive officers and other top executives often become members of the board of directors of one or more firms. Typically the chief executive is also a director of his or her own firm and often chairs the board of directors. Some general managers and top executives go on to establish their own firms or become independent consultants.

Job Outlook

Employment of general managers and top executives is expected to grow about as fast as average for all occupations through the year 2005 as new companies start up and established companies seek managers who can help them maintain a competitive edge in domestic and world markets. In addition, because this is a large occupation, many openings will occur each year as executives transfer to other positions, start their own businesses, or retire. Nonetheless, competition for top managerial jobs will be keen. Many executives who leave their jobs transfer to other executive or managerial positions, limiting openings for new entrants. Continued management efforts to downsize and restructure—resulting in layoffs of, mostly, middle managers—will add to an ample supply of competent managers seeking positions.

Projected employment growth of general managers and top executives varies widely among industries. For example, employment growth is expected to be faster than average in all services industries combined, but only about as fast as average in all finance, insurance, and real estate industries combined. Employment of general managers and top executives is projected to decline in manufacturing industries overall. Because of the growing importance of the global market, overseas experience may give a prospective general manager an edge in seeking additional responsibility.

Experienced managers whose accomplishments reflect strong leadership qualities and the ability to improve the efficiency or competitive position of an organization will have the best opportunities. In an increasingly global economy, certain types of experience, such as international economics, marketing, information systems, or knowledge of several disciplines, will also help.

Earnings

General managers and top executives are among the highest paid workers in the Nation. However, salary levels vary substantially depending upon the level of managerial responsibility, length of service, and type, size, and location of the firm.

At the highest level, chief executive officers (CEOs) of medium and large corporations are extremely well paid. Salaries often are related to the size of the corporation—a top manager in a very large corporation can earn significantly more than a counterpart in a small firm. Total compensation often includes, in addition to salaries, stock options and dividends, and other performance bonuses.

Salaries also vary substantially by type and level of responsibilities and by industry. According to a salary survey by Robert Half International, senior vice presidents/heads of lending in banks with $1 billion or more in assets earned about $200,000 in 1995. Based on a survey sponsored by the Administrative Management Society, the average salary for managers of large plants with more than 500 employees ranged from $70,000 to $108,000 in 1994. In the nonprofit sector, three quarters of the CEOs make under $81,700, according to a survey by Abbott, Langer, & Associates.

Company-paid insurance premiums and physical examinations, the use of executive dining rooms and company cars, and expense allowances are among benefits commonly enjoyed by general managers and top executives in private industry. CEOs often enjoy company-paid club memberships, a limousine with driver, and other amenities. CEOs of very large corporations may have the use of private aircraft.

Related Occupations

General managers and top executives plan, organize, direct, control, and coordinate the operations of an organization and its major departments or programs. The members of the board of directors and supervisory managers are also involved in these activities. Occupations in State and local government with similar functions are governor, mayor, commissioner, and director.

Sources of Additional Information

For a wide variety of information on general managers and top executives, including educational programs and job listings, contact:
☛American Management Association, 135 West 50th St., New York, NY 10020
☛National Management Association, 2210 Arbor Blvd., Dayton, OH 45439.

Government Chief Executives and Legislators

Nature of the Work

Chief executives and legislators at the Federal, State, and local level direct governmental activities and make laws that affect all of us. They are elected or appointed officials who strive to meet the needs of their constituents through effective and efficient government.

Chief executives are officials who run governmental bodies that formulate and enforce laws. These officials include the President and Vice President of the United States, State governors and lieutenant governors, county executives, town and township officials, mayors, and city, county, town, and township managers. All except local government managers are elected by their constituents. Managers are appointed by the local government council or commission.

Government chief executives, like their counterparts in the private sector, have overall responsibility for how their organizations perform. Working in coordination with legislators, they establish goals and then organize programs and form policies to attain them. They appoint heads of departments, such as highway, health, law enforcement, park and recreation, economic development, education, and finance departments. Through these departmental heads, chief executives oversee the work of the civil servants who carry out programs and enforce laws enacted by the legislative bodies. They prepare budgets, specifying how government resources will be used, and insure that these resources are used properly and programs are carried out as planned.

Chief executives meet with legislators and constituents to discuss proposed programs and encourage their support. They also may confer with leaders of other governments to solve mutual problems. Chief executives nominate citizens for boards and commissions that oversee government activities addressing problems such as drug abuse, crime, deteriorating roads, and inadequate public education. They also solicit bids from and select contractors to do work for the government, encourage business investment and economic development in their jurisdictions, and seek Federal or State funds. Chief executives of large jurisdictions rely on a staff of aides and assistants, but those in small ones often do much of the work themselves. City, county, town, and other managers, although appointed officials, may act as chief executives.

Legislators are the elected officials who pass laws or amend existing ones in order to remedy problems or to promote certain activities. They include U.S. Senators and Representatives, State senators and representatives (called assemblypersons or delegates in some States), county legislators (called supervisors, commissioners, councilmembers, or freeholders in some States), and city and town council members (called trustees, clerks, supervisors, magistrates, and commissioners, among other titles).

Legislators introduce bills in the legislative body and examine and vote on bills introduced by other legislators. In preparing legislation, they read staff reports and work with constituents, representatives of interest groups, members of boards and commissions, the chief executive and department heads, and others with an interest in the legislation. They generally approve budgets and the appointments of department heads and commission members submitted by the chief executive. In some jurisdictions, the legislative body appoints

Many government chief executives have a staff to help do research, prepare legislation, and resolve problems.

a city, town, or county manager. Many legislators, especially at the State and Federal levels, have a staff to perform research, prepare legislation, and resolve constituents' problems.

Both chief executives and legislators perform many ceremonial duties such as opening new buildings, making proclamations, welcoming visitors, and leading celebrations.

Working Conditions

The working conditions of chief executives and legislators vary with the size and budget of the governmental unit. Time spent at work ranges from meeting once a month for a local council member to 60 or more hours per week for a U. S. Senator. U.S. Senators and Representatives, governors and lieutenant governors, and chief executives and legislators in large local jurisdictions usually work full time year round, as do county and city managers. Many State legislators work full time while legislatures are in session (usually for 2 to 6 months a year) and part time the rest of the year. Local elected officials in most jurisdictions work a schedule that is officially designated part time, but many incumbents actually work a full-time schedule when unpaid duties are taken into account. In addition to their regular schedules, chief executives are on call at all hours to handle emergencies.

Some jobs require only occasional out-of-town travel, but others involve long periods away from home to attend sessions of the legislature. Officials in rural districts covering a large area may drive long distances to perform their regular duties.

Employment

Chief executives and legislators held about 91,000 jobs in 1994. About 5 of 6 worked in local government, while the rest worked primarily in State governments. The Federal Government had 535 Senators and Representatives and the President and Vice President. There were about 7,500 State legislators and, according to the International City/County Management Association (ICMA), about 10,100 city managers. Executives and council members for local governments made up the remainder.

Chief executives and legislators who do not hold full-time, year-round positions often work in a second occupation as well. This is commonly the one they held before being elected. Business owner or manager, teacher, and lawyer are common primary occupations, and there are many others as well.

Training, Other Qualifications, and Advancement

Because voters seek to elect the individual believed to be most qualified from among a slate of candidates who meet the minimum

age, residency, and citizenship requirements, the question becomes not "How does one become qualified?" but "How does one get elected?"

Successful candidates usually have a strong record of accomplishment in paid and unpaid work. Some have business, teaching, or legal experience, but others come from a wide variety of occupations. In addition, many have served as volunteers on school boards or zoning commissions; with charities, political action groups, and political campaigns; or with religious, fraternal, and social organizations.

Management-level work experience and public service help develop the planning, organizing, negotiating, motivating, fundraising, budgeting, public speaking, and problem-solving skills needed to run a political campaign. Candidates must make decisions quickly, sometimes with little or contradictory information. They must inspire and motivate their constituents and their staff. They should appear sincere and candid, presenting their views thoughtfully and convincingly. Additionally, they must know how to hammer out compromises and satisfy the demands of constituents. National and Statewide campaigns also require massive amounts of energy and stamina, as well as superior fund raising skills.

Town, city, and county managers are appointed by a council or commission. Managers come from a variety of educational backgrounds. A master's degree in public administration—including courses such as public financial management and legal issues in public administration—is widely recommended but not required. Virtually all town, city, and county managers have at least a bachelor's degree and the majority hold a master's degree. Working as a student intern in government is recommended—the experience and personal contacts acquired can prove invaluable in eventually securing a position.

Generally, a town, city, or county manager in a smaller jurisdiction is required to have expertise in a wide variety of areas. Those who work for larger jurisdictions specialize in financial, administrative, and personnel matters. For all managers, communication skills and the ability to get along with others are essential.

Advancement opportunities for elected public officials are not clearly defined. Because elected positions normally require a period of residency and because local public support is critical, officials can usually advance to other offices only in the jurisdictions where they live. For example, council members may run for mayor or for a position in the State government, and State legislators may run for governor or for Congress. Many officials are not politically ambitious, however, and do not seek advancement. Others lose their bids for reelection or voluntarily leave the occupation. A lifetime career as a government chief executive or legislator is rare.

Town, city, and county managers have a clearer career path. They generally obtain a master's degree in public administration, then gain experience as management analysts or assistants in government departments working for councils or chief executives and learning about planning, budgeting, civil engineering, and other aspects of running a city. With sufficient experience, they may be hired to manage a town or a small city and may become manager of progressively larger cities over time.

Job Outlook

Little, if any, growth is expected in the number of government chief executives and legislators through the year 2005. Few, if any, new governments are likely to form, and the number of chief executives and legislators in existing governments rarely changes. Some small increase may occur as growing communities—in the rapidly growing South and West, for example—become independent cities and towns and elect a chief executive and legislators and, perhaps, appoint a town manager. A few new positions may also develop as cities and counties without managers hire them and as unpaid offices—which are not counted as employment—are converted to paid positions.

Elections give newcomers the chance to unseat incumbents or to fill vacated positions. In many elections, there is substantial competition, although the level of competition varies from jurisdiction to jurisdiction and from year to year. Generally, there is less competition in small jurisdictions, which have part-time positions offering relatively low salaries and little or no staff to help with routine work, than in large jurisdictions, which have full-time positions offering higher salaries, more staff, and greater status. In some cases, an incumbent runs unopposed, or an incumbent resigns, leaving only one candidate for a job. The high cost of running for such positions in large jurisdictions may serve as a deterrent, or may leave the challenger dependent on contributions from special interest groups.

Earnings

Earnings of public administrators vary widely, depending on the size of the government unit and on whether the job is part time, full time and year round, or full time for only a few months a year. Salaries range from little or nothing for a small town council member to $200,000 a year for the President of the United States.

According to the International City/County Management Association, the average annual salary of mayors was about $9,900 in 1994. ICMA data indicate that the average salary for city managers was about $65,700 in 1994. Salaries ranged from $30,800 in towns with fewer than 2,500 residents to $130,400 in cities with a population over 1 million.

According to the National Conference of State Legislatures, the salary for legislators in the 40 States that paid an annual salary ranged from about $10,000 to $47,000 per year. In 6 States, legislators received a daily salary plus an allowance for expenses while legislatures were in session. Two States paid no expenses and only nominal daily salaries, while 2 States paid no salary at all but did pay a daily expense allowance. Salaries and the expense allowance were generally higher in the larger States.

Data from *Book of the States, 1994-95* indicate that gubernatorial annual salaries ranged from $60,000 in Arkansas to $130,000 in New York. In addition to a salary, most governors received perquisites such as transportation and an official residence.

In 1995, U.S. Senators and Representatives earned $133,600, the Senate and House Majority and Minority leaders $148,400, and the Vice President $171,500.

Related Occupations

Related occupations include managerial positions that require a broad range of skills in addition to administrative expertise, such as corporate chief executives and board members, and high ranking officers in the military.

Sources of Additional Information

Information on appointed officials in local government can be obtained from:
☛International City/County Management Association, 777 North Capitol St. NE., Suite 500, Washington, DC 20002.

Health Services Managers

(D.O.T. 072.117-010; 074.167-010, 075.117-014, -022, -026, -030 and -034; 076.117-010; 077.117-010; 078.131-010, .161-010 and -014, .162-010; 079.117-010, .131-010, .151-010, and .167-014; 187.117-010, -058, 062, and .167-034, and -090; 188.117-082

Nature of the Work

Health care is a business, albeit a special one. Like every other business, it needs good management to keep it running smoothly, especially during times of change. The term "health services man-

ager" encompasses individuals in many different positions who plan, organize, coordinate, and supervise the delivery of health care. Health services managers include both generalists—administrators who manage or help to manage an entire facility—and health specialists—managers in charge of specific clinical departments or services found only in the health industry.

The structure and financing of health care is changing rapidly. Future health services managers must be prepared to deal with evolving integrated health care delivery systems, restructuring of work, and an increased focus on preventive care.

The top administrator or chief executive officer (CEO) and the assistant administrators without specific titles are health care generalists, who set the overall direction of the organization. They concentrate on such areas as community outreach, planning, marketing, human resources, finance, and complying with government regulations. Their range of knowledge is broad, including developments in the clinical departments as well as in the business arena. They often speak before civic groups, promote public participation in health programs, and coordinate the activities of the organization with those of government or community agencies. CEO's make long-term institutional plans by assessing the need for services, personnel, facilities, and equipment and recommending changes such as opening a home health service. CEO's need leadership ability as well as technical skills to provide quality health care while, at the same time, satisfying demand for financial viability, cost containment, and public and professional accountability.

Larger facilities typically have several assistant administrators to aid the top administrator and to handle day-to-day decisions. They may direct activities in clinical areas such as nursing, surgery, therapy, food service, and medical records; or the activities in nonhealth areas such as finance, housekeeping, human resources, and information management. (Because the nonhealth departments are not directly related to health care, these managers are not included in this statement. For information about them, see the statements on managerial occupations elsewhere in the *Handbook*). In smaller facilities, top administrators may handle more of the details of day-to-day operations. For example, many nursing home administrators directly manage personnel, finance, operations, and admissions.

Clinical managers have more narrowly defined responsibilities than generalists and have training and/or experience in a specific clinical area. For example, directors of physical therapy are experienced physical therapists, and most medical records administrators have a bachelor's degree in medical records administration. These managers establish and implement policies, objectives, and procedures for their departments; evaluate personnel and work; develop reports and budgets; and coordinate activities with other managers.

Health services managers coordinate the delivery of health care services.

In group practices, managers work closely with the physician owners. While an office manager may handle business affairs in small medical groups, leaving policy decisions to the physicians themselves, larger groups generally employ a full-time administrator to advise on business strategies and coordinate day-to-day business.

A small group of 10 or 15 physicians might employ a single administrator to oversee personnel matters, billing and collection, budgeting, planning, equipment outlays, and patient flow. A large practice of 40 or 50 physicians may have a chief administrator and several assistants, each responsible for different areas.

Health services managers in health maintenance organizations (HMO's) and other managed care settings perform functions similar to those in large group practices, except their staffs may be larger. Also, they may do more work in the areas of community outreach and preventive care than managers of a group practice. The size of the administrative staff in HMO's varies according to the size and type of HMO.

Some health services managers oversee the activities of a number of facilities in multifacility health organizations.

Working Conditions

Many health services managers work long hours. Facilities such as nursing homes and hospitals operate around the clock, and administrators and managers may be called at all hours to deal with problems. They may also travel to attend meetings or to inspect satellite facilities.

Employment

Health services managers held about 315,000 jobs in 1994. Over one-half of all jobs were in hospitals. About 1 in 4 were in nursing and personal care facilities or offices and clinics of physicians. The remainder worked in home health agencies, medical and dental laboratories, offices of dentists and other practitioners, and other health and allied services.

Training, Other Qualifications, and Advancement

Health services managers must be familiar with management principles and practices. Some learn from work experience. However, formal education is usually necessary for advancement. Most CEO positions require a graduate degree in health services administration, nursing administration, or business administration. For some generalist positions, employers seek applicants with clinical experience (as nurses or therapists, for example) as well as academic preparation in business or health services administration.

Bachelor's, master's, and doctoral degree programs in health administration are offered by colleges, universities, and schools of public health, medicine, allied health, public administration, and business administration. There are also some certificate or diploma programs, generally lasting less than 1 year, in health services administration and in medical office management. A master's degree—in health services administration, long term care administration, health sciences, public health, public administration, or business administration—is the standard credential for most generalist positions in this field. However, a bachelor's degree is adequate for some entry-level positions in smaller operations. A bachelor's degree is required to work in smaller nursing homes, and a master's degree in larger long-term care facilities. Physicians' offices and some other facilities may substitute on-the-job experience for formal education. For clinical department heads, a degree in the appropriate field and work experience are usually sufficient, but a master's degree in health services administration usually is required to advance.

In 1995, 69 schools had accredited programs leading to the master's degree in health services administration, according to the Accrediting Commission on Education for Health Services Administration.

Some graduate programs seek students with undergraduate degrees in business or health administration; however, many programs prefer students with a liberal arts or health professions background.

Competition for entry to these programs is keen, and applicants need above-average grades to gain admission. The programs generally last between 2 and 3 years. They may include up to 1 year of supervised administrative experience, and course work in areas such as hospital organization and management, marketing, accounting and budgeting, human resources administration, strategic planning, health economics, and health information systems. Some programs allow students to specialize in one type of facility—hospitals; nursing homes; mental health facilities; HMO's; or outpatient care facilities, including medical groups. Other programs encourage a generalist approach to health administration education.

New graduates with master's degrees in health services or hospital administration may start as department managers or in staff positions. The level of the starting position varies with the experience of the applicant and the size of the facility. Postgraduate residencies and fellowships are offered by hospitals and other health facilities; these usually are staff positions. Graduates from master's degree programs also take jobs in HMO's, large group medical practices, clinics, mental health facilities, and multifacility nursing home corporations.

Graduates with bachelor's degrees in health administration usually begin as administrative assistants or assistant department heads in larger hospitals, or as department heads or assistant administrators in small hospitals or in nursing homes.

A Ph.D. degree may be required to teach, consult, or do research. Nursing service administrators are usually chosen from among supervisory registered nurses with administrative abilities and a graduate degree in nursing administration.

All States and the District of Columbia require nursing home administrators to have a bachelor's degree, pass a licensing examination, complete a State-approved training program, and pursue continuing education. A license is not required in other areas of health services management.

Health services managers are often responsible for millions of dollars of facilities and equipment and hundreds of employees. To make effective decisions, they need to be open to different opinions and good at analyzing contradictory information. They must understand finance and information systems, and be able to interpret data. To motivate others to implement their decisions, they need strong leadership qualities. Tact, diplomacy, flexibility, and communication skills are essential.

Health services managers advance by moving into more responsible and higher paying positions such as assistant or associate administrator, or by moving to larger facilities.

Job Outlook

Employment of health services managers is expected to grow faster than the average for all occupations through the year 2005 as health services continue to expand and diversify. Opportunities will be good in home health care, long-term care and nontraditional health organizations such as managed care operations, particularly for health services managers with strong business and management skills.

Hospitals will continue to employ the most managers, although the number of jobs will not grow nearly as fast as in other areas, such as long-term and home health care. As hospitals continue to consolidate, centralize, and diversify functions, competition will increase at all job levels.

Employment in home health agencies, offices of other health practitioners, and nursing and personal care facilities will grow the fastest, due to an increased number of elderly who will need care. In addition, many services previously provided in hospitals will be shifted to these sectors. Demand in medical group practices will also grow as medical group practices and HMO's become larger and more complex. Health services managers will need to deal with the pressures of cost containment and financial accountability, as well as the increased focus on preventive and primary care.

Health services managers will also be employed by hospital management companies who provide expertise in areas such as emergency department assistance, information management systems, managed care contract negotiations, and physician recruiting. They may also provide consulting services to medical group practices.

Earnings

Earnings vary by type and size of the facility, as well as by level of responsibility. For example, the Medical Group Management Association reported that the median salary for administrators in group practices was $65,000 in 1994. The median salary for those in small group practices—with net revenues of $2 million or less—was $48,000; for those in very large group practices—with net revenues over $10 million—$116,000.

According to a survey by *Modern Healthcare* magazine, half of all hospital CEO's earned $165,500 or more in 1995. Salaries varied according to size of facility and geographic region. Clinical department heads' salaries varied too. Median total compensation in 1995 for heads of the following clinical departments were: Home health, $55,000; radiology, $58,000; physical therapy, $58,200; ambulatory/outpatient services, $62,400, rehabilitation services, $66,700; and nursing services, $88,000.

According to the Buck Survey conducted by the American Health Care Association, nursing home administrators had median annual compensation of about $47,400 in 1994. The middle 50 percent earned between $40,900 and $55,400. Assistant administrators earned about $32,000.

Executives often receive bonuses based on performance outcomes such as cost-containment, quality assurance, and patient satisfaction.

Related Occupations

Health services managers have training or experience in both health and management. Other occupations that require knowledge of both fields are public health directors, social welfare administrators, directors of voluntary health agencies and health professional associations, and underwriters in health insurance companies.

Sources of Additional Information

General information about health administration is available from:
☛American College of Healthcare Executives, One North Franklin St., Suite 1700, Chicago, IL 60606.

Information about undergraduate and graduate academic programs in this field is available from:
☛Association of University Programs in Health Administration, 1911 North Fort Myer Dr., Suite 503, Arlington, VA 22209.

For a list of accredited graduate programs in health services administration, contact:
☛Accrediting Commission on Education for Health Services Administration, 1911 North Fort Myer Dr., Suite 503, Arlington, VA 22209.

For information about career opportunities in long term care administration, contact:
☛American College of Health Care Administrators, 325 S. Patrick St., Alexandria, VA 22314.

For information about career opportunities in medical group practices and ambulatory care management, contact:
☛Medical Group Management Association, 104 Inverness Terrace East, Englewood, CO 80112.

Hotel Managers and Assistants

(D.O.T. 187.117-038, .137-018; .167-046, -078, -106, -122; and 320)

Nature of the Work

A comfortable room, good food, and a helpful hotel staff can make being away from home an enjoyable experience for both vacationing families and business travelers. Hotel managers and assistant managers strive to ensure their guests will have a pleasant stay.

Hotel managers are responsible for the efficient and profitable operation of their establishments. In a small hotel, motel, or inn with a limited staff, a single manager may direct all aspects of operations. However, large hotels may employ hundreds of workers, and the general manager may be aided by a number of assistant managers assigned to the various departments of the operation. Assistant managers must ensure that the day-to-day operations of their departments meet the standards set by the general manager.

The *general manager* has overall responsibility for the operation of the hotel. Within guidelines established by the owners of the hotel or executives of the hotel chain, the general manager sets room rates, allocates funds to departments, approves expenditures, and establishes standards for service to guests, decor, housekeeping, food quality, and banquet operations. Managers who work for chains also may be assigned to organize and staff a newly built hotel, refurbish an older hotel, or reorganize a hotel or motel that is not operating successfully. (For more information, see the statement on general managers and top executives elsewhere in the *Handbook*.)

Resident managers live in hotels and are on call 24 hours a day to resolve problems or emergencies. However, they typically work an 8-hour day, while overseeing the day-to-day operations of the hotel. In many hotels, the general manager also serves as the resident manager.

Executive housekeepers are responsible for ensuring guest rooms, meeting and banquet rooms, and public areas are clean, orderly, and well maintained. They train, schedule, and supervise the work of housekeepers, inspect rooms, and order cleaning supplies.

Front office managers coordinate reservations and room assignments as well as train and direct the hotel's front desk staff. They ensure guests are treated courteously, complaints and problems that may arise are resolved, and requests for special services are carried out.

Food and beverage managers direct the food service operations of hotels. They oversee the hotels' restaurants, cocktail lounges, and banquet facilities. They supervise and schedule food and beverage preparation and service workers, plan menus, estimate costs, and deal with food suppliers. (For more information, see the statement on restaurant and food service managers elsewhere in the *Handbook*.)

Convention services managers coordinate the activities of large hotels' various departments for meetings, conventions, and special events. They meet with representatives of groups or organizations to plan the number of rooms to reserve, the desired configuration of hotel meeting space, and any banquet services needed. During the meeting or event, they resolve unexpected problems and monitor activities to check that hotel operations conform to the expectations of the group.

Hotel managers are responsible for the efficient and profitable operation of their establishments.

Other assistant managers are responsible for personnel, accounting and office administration, marketing and sales, purchasing, security, maintenance, and recreational facilities. (For more information, see the related statements on personnel, training, and labor relations specialists and managers; financial managers; and marketing, advertising, and public relations managers elsewhere in the *Handbook*.)

Working Conditions

Because hotels are open around the clock, night and weekend work is common. Many hotel managers work considerably more than 40 hours per week. Managers who live in the hotel usually have regular work schedules, but they may be called to work at any time. Some employees of resort hotels are managers during the busy season and have other duties during the rest of the year.

Hotel managers sometimes experience the pressures of coordinating a wide range of functions. Conventions and large groups of tourists may present unusual problems. Dealing with irate patrons can be stressful. The job can be particularly hectic for front office managers around check-in and check-out time.

Employment

Hotel managers and assistant managers held about 105,000 wage and salary jobs in 1994. An additional number—primarily owners of small hotels and motels—were self-employed. Some were employed by companies that manage hotels and motels under contract.

Training, Other Qualifications, and Advancement

Postsecondary training in hotel or restaurant management is preferred for most hotel management positions, although a college liberal arts degree may be sufficient when coupled with related hotel experience. In the past, most managers were promoted from the ranks of front desk clerks, housekeepers, waiters and chefs, and hotel sales workers. Although some employees still advance to hotel management positions without the benefit of education or training beyond high school, postsecondary education is preferred. Nevertheless, experience working in a hotel—even part time while in school—is an asset to anyone seeking a career in hotel management. Restaurant management training or experience is also a good background for entering hotel management because the success of a hotel's food service and beverage operations is often of great importance to the profitability of the entire establishment.

A bachelor's degree in hotel and restaurant administration provides particularly strong preparation for a career in hotel management. In 1994, over 160 colleges and universities offered bachelor's and graduate programs in this field. Over 800 community and junior colleges, technical institutes, vocational and trade schools, and other academic institutions also have programs leading to an associate degree or other formal recognition in hotel or restaurant management. Graduates of hotel or restaurant management programs usually start as trainee assistant managers, or at least advance to such positions more quickly.

Hotel management programs include instruction in hotel administration, accounting, economics, marketing, housekeeping, food service management and catering, and hotel maintenance engineering. The widespread use of computers in hotel operations such as reservations, accounting, and housekeeping management is making some familiarity with computers essential. Programs encourage part-time or summer work in hotels and restaurants because the experience gained and the contacts made with employers may benefit students when they seek full-time employment after graduation.

Hotel managers must be able to get along with all kinds of people, even in stressful situations. They need initiative, self-discipline, and the ability to organize and direct the work of others. They must be able to solve problems and concentrate on details.

Sometimes large hotels sponsor specialized on-the-job management training programs which allow trainees to rotate among various departments and gain a thorough knowledge of the hotel's operation.

Other hotels may help finance the necessary training in hotel management for outstanding employees.

Most hotels promote employees who have proven their ability. Newly built hotels, particularly those without well-established on-the-job training programs, often prefer experienced personnel for managerial positions. Large hotel and motel chains may offer better opportunities for advancement than small, independently owned establishments, but relocation every several years often is necessary for advancement. The large chains have more extensive career ladder programs and offer managers the opportunity to transfer to another hotel or motel in the chain or to the central office if an opening occurs. Career advancement can be accelerated by completion of certification programs offered by the associations listed below. These programs generally require a combination of course work, examinations, and experience.

Job Outlook

Opportunities to enter hotel management are expected to be good for persons who have college degrees in hotel or restaurant management.

Employment of salaried hotel managers is expected to grow faster than the average for all occupations through the year 2005. Business travel will continue to grow, and increased domestic and foreign tourism will also create demand for additional hotels and motels. However, manager jobs are not expected to grow as rapidly as in the past because an increasing share of the hotel industry will be comprised of economy properties, which generally have fewer managers than full-service hotels. In the face of financial constraints, guests are becoming more bargain-conscious, and hotel chains are increasing the number of rooms in economy class hotels. Economy hotels offer clean, comfortable rooms and front desk services without costly extras like restaurants and room service. Because there are not as many departments in each hotel, fewer managers are needed on the hotel premises. Economy hotels have a general manager, and regional offices of the hotel management company employ department managers, such as executive housekeepers, to oversee several hotels.

Although new employment growth is expected to be concentrated in economy hotels, large full-service hotels will continue to offer many trainee and managerial opportunities. Most openings are expected to occur as experienced managers transfer to other occupations, retire, or stop working for other reasons.

Earnings

Salaries of hotel managers vary greatly according to their responsibilities and the segment of the hotel industry in which they are employed. In early 1995, annual salaries of assistant hotel managers averaged nearly $40,000, based on a hospitality industry survey conducted by Roth Young. Salaries of assistant managers also varied because of differences in duties and responsibilities. For example, food and beverage directors averaged $44,000, according to the same survey, whereas front office managers averaged $30,000. The manager's level of experience is also an important factor.

In 1995, salaries of general managers averaged nearly $57,000, according to the Roth Young survey. Their salaries ranged from $40,000 to $81,000 depending on the size and type of establishment. Managers may earn bonuses up to 25 percent of their basic salary in some hotels. In addition, they and their families may be furnished with lodging, meals, parking, laundry, and other services.

Most managers and assistants receive 3 to 11 paid holidays a year, paid vacation, sick leave, life insurance, medical benefits, and pension plans. Some hotels offer profit-sharing plans, educational assistance, and other benefits to their employees.

Related Occupations

Hotel managers and assistants are not the only workers concerned with organizing and directing a business where customer service is the cornerstone of their success. Other occupations sharing similar responsibilities include restaurant managers, apartment building managers, retail store managers, and office managers.

Sources of Additional Information

For information on careers and scholarships in hotel management, contact:

☛The American Hotel and Motel Association (AH&MA), Information Center, 1201 New York Ave. NW., Washington, DC 20005-3931.

For information on educational programs, including correspondence courses, in hotel and restaurant management, write to:

☛The Educational Institute of AH&MA, P.O. Box 1240, East Lansing, MI 48826.

Information on careers in housekeeping management may be obtained from:

☛National Executive Housekeepers Association, Inc., 1001 Eastwind Dr., Suite 301, Westerville, OH 43081, or 1-800-200-6342.

For information on hospitality careers, as well as how to purchase a directory of colleges and other schools offering programs and courses in hotel and restaurant administration, write to:

☛Council on Hotel, Restaurant, and Institutional Education, 1200 17th St. NW., Washington, DC 20036-3097.

General career information and a directory of accredited private trade and technical schools offering programs in hotel-motel management may be obtained from:

☛Accrediting Commission of Career Schools and Colleges of Technology, 2101 Wilson Blvd., Suite 302, Arlington, VA 22201.

Industrial Production Managers

(D.O.T. 180.167-054; 181.117-010; 182.167-022; 183.117-010, -014, .161-014, .167-010, -014, -018, -022, -026, -034, -038; 188.167-094; 189.117-042, .167-042, -046)

Nature of the Work

Industrial production managers coordinate the resources and activities required to produce millions of goods every year in the United States. Due to the wide variety of these goods and differences among factories, managers' duties vary from plant to plant. In general, industrial production managers share many of the same major functions, regardless of the industry. These functions include responsibility for production scheduling, staffing, equipment, quality control, inventory control, and the coordination of production activities with those of other departments.

The primary mission of industrial production managers is planning the production schedule within budgetary limitations and time constraints. This entails analyzing the plant's personnel and capital resources and selecting the best way to meet the production quota. Industrial production managers determine which machines will be used, whether overtime or extra shifts are necessary, and the sequence of production. They also monitor the production run to make sure that it stays on schedule and correct any problems that may arise.

Industrial production managers also monitor product standards. When quality drops below the established standard, they must determine why standards aren't being maintained and how to improve the product. If the problem is poor work, the manager may implement better training programs, reorganize the manufacturing process, or institute employee suggestion or involvement programs. If the cause is substandard materials, the manager works with the purchasing department to improve the quality of the product's components.

Working with the purchasing department, the production manager ensures that plant inventories are maintained at their optimal level. This is vital to a firm's operation because maintaining the inventory of materials necessary for production ties up the firm's financial resources, yet insufficient quantities of materials cause delays in production. A breakdown in communications between these departments can cause slowdowns and a failure to meet production schedules.

Industrial production managers must keep up to date with the latest production technologies.

Because the work of many departments is dependent upon others, managers work closely with heads of other departments such as sales, purchasing, and traffic to plan and implement companies' goals, policies, and procedures. Production managers also work closely with, and act as a liaison between, executives and first-line supervisors.

Production managers usually report to the plant manager or the vice president for manufacturing. (Information about these workers can be found in the statement on general managers and top executives elsewhere in the *Handbook*). In many plants, one production manager is responsible for all production. In large plants with several operations—aircraft assembly, for example—there are managers in charge of each operation, such as machining, assembly, or finishing.

Computers play an integral role in the coordination of the production process by providing up-to-date data on inventory, work-in-progress, and product standards. Industrial production managers analyze these data and, working with upper management and other departments, determine if adjustments need to be made.

As the trend toward a flatter management structure and worker empowerment continues, production managers will increasingly perform the role of facilitators. Instead of independently making decisions and giving and taking orders, production managers will review and discuss recommendations with subordinates and superiors in the hopes of improving productivity. Because of the additional duties resulting from corporate downsizing, production managers are delegating more authority and responsibility to first-line supervisors.

Working Conditions

Most industrial production managers divide their time between the shop floor and their office. While on the floor, they must follow established health and safety practices and wear the required protective clothing and equipment. The time in the office—often located on or near the production floor—is usually spent meeting with subordinates or other department managers, analyzing production data, and writing and reviewing reports.

Most industrial production managers work more than 40 hours a week, especially when production deadlines must be met. In facilities that operate around the clock, managers may have to work shifts or may be called at any hour to deal with emergencies. This could mean going to the plant to resolve the problem, regardless of the hour, and staying until the situation is under control. Dealing with production workers as well as superiors when working under the pressure of production deadlines or emergency situations can be stressful. In addition, restructuring has eliminated levels of management and support staff. As a result, production managers now have to accomplish more with less, and this has greatly increased job-related stress.

Employment

Industrial production managers held about 206,000 jobs in 1994. Although employed throughout manufacturing industries, about one-half are employed in industrial machinery and equipment, transportation equipment, electronic and electrical equipment, fabricated metal products, and food products manufacturing. Production managers work in all parts of the country, but jobs are most plentiful in areas where manufacturing is concentrated.

Training, Other Qualifications, and Advancement

Because of the diversity of manufacturing operations and job requirements, there is no standard preparation for this occupation. Many industrial production managers have a college degree in business administration or industrial engineering. Some have a master's degree in business administration (MBA). Others are former production line supervisors who have been promoted. Although many employers prefer candidates to have a degree in business or engineering, some companies hire liberal arts graduates.

As production operations become more sophisticated, an increasing number of employers are looking for candidates with MBA's. This, combined with an undergraduate degree in engineering, is considered particularly good preparation. Companies also are placing greater importance on a candidate's personality. Because the job demands technical knowledge and the ability to compromise, persuade, and negotiate, successful production managers must be well rounded and have excellent communication skills.

Those who enter the field directly from college or graduate school often are unfamiliar with the firm's production process. As a result, they may spend their first few months on the job in the company's training program. These programs familiarize trainees with the production line, company policies and procedures, and the requirements of the job. In larger companies, they may also include assignments to other departments, such as purchasing and accounting.

Blue-collar worker supervisors who advance to production manager positions already have an intimate knowledge of the production process and the firm's organization. To be selected for promotion, these workers must have demonstrated leadership qualities, and often take company-sponsored courses in management skills and communications techniques. Some companies hire college graduates as blue-collar worker supervisors and then promote them.

Once in their job, industrial production managers must stay abreast of new production technologies and management practices. To do this, they belong to professional organizations and attend trade shows where new equipment is displayed; they also attend industry conferences and conventions where changes in production methods and technological advances are discussed.

Although certification in production management and inventory control is not required for most positions, it demonstrates an individual's knowledge of the production process and related areas. Various certifications are available through the American Production and Inventory Control Society. To be certified in production and inventory management, candidates must pass a series of examinations that test their knowledge of inventory management, just-in-time systems, production control, capacity management, and materials planning.

Industrial production managers with a proven record of superior performance may advance to plant manager or vice president for manufacturing. Others transfer to jobs at larger firms with more responsibilities. Opportunities also exist as consultants. (For more information, see the statement on management analysts and consultants elsewhere in the *Handbook*.)

Job Outlook

Employment of industrial production managers is expected to decline slightly through the year 2005. Although manufacturing output is expected to rise significantly, the trend towards smaller management staffs and the lack of growth in production worker employment will limit demand for production managers. The widening use of computers for scheduling and planning is also making production managers more productive, allowing fewer of them to accomplish the same amount of work. Nevertheless, some openings will result from the need to replace workers who transfer to other occupations or leave the labor force. Many of these openings, however, may be filled through internal promotions.

Opportunities should be best for those with college degrees in industrial engineering or business administration, and those with MBA's and undergraduate engineering degrees. Employers also are likely to seek candidates who have excellent communication skills, and who are personable, flexible, and eager to participate in ongoing training.

Earnings

Salaries of industrial production managers vary significantly by industry and plant size. According to Abbott, Langer, and Associates, the average salary for all production managers was $63,000 in 1994. In addition to salary, industrial production managers usually receive bonuses based on job performance.

Benefits for industrial production managers tend to be similar to those offered many workers—vacation and sick leave, health and life insurance, and retirement plans.

Related Occupations

Industrial production managers oversee production staff and equipment, insure that production goals and quality standards are being met, and implement company policies. Individuals with similar functions include materials, operations, purchasing, and traffic managers.

Other occupations requiring similar training and skills are sales engineer, manufacturers' sales representative, and industrial engineer.

Sources of Additional Information

Information on industrial production management can be obtained from:

☛ National Management Association, 2210 Arbor Blvd., Dayton, OH 45439.
☛ American Management Association, 135 W. 50th St., New York, NY 10020.

Inspectors and Compliance Officers, Except Construction

(List of D.O.T. codes available upon request. See p. 478.)

Nature of the Work

Inspectors and compliance officers enforce a wide range of laws, regulations, policies, or procedures, and advise on standards that protect the public. They inspect and enforce rules on matters such as health, safety, food, immigration, licensing, interstate commerce, or international trade. Inspectors' duties vary widely, depending upon their employer.

Agricultural chemicals inspectors protect American agriculture by inspecting establishments where agricultural service products, such as livestock feed and remedies, fertilizers, and pesticides are manufactured, sold, or used. They may visit processing plants, distribution warehouses, sales outlets, agricultural service organizations, and farmers to collect product samples for analysis. They call on dealers to determine that licensing requirements have been met. They then prepare reports for supervisors and for use as evidence in legal actions.

Agricultural commodity graders apply quality standards to aid the buying and selling of commodities and to insure that retailers and consumers know the quality of the products they purchase. Although this grading is not required by law, buyers generally will not purchase ungraded commodities. Graders usually specialize in an area such as eggs and egg products, meat, poultry, processed or fresh fruits and vegetables, grain, tobacco, cotton, or dairy products. They examine product samples to determine quality and grade, and issue official grading certificates. Graders also may inspect the plant and equipment to maintain sanitation standards.

Attendance officers investigate continued absences of pupils from public schools.

Aviation safety inspectors ensure that Federal Aviation Administration (FAA) regulations which govern the quality and safety of aircraft equipment, aircraft operations, and personnel are maintained. Aviation safety inspectors may inspect aircraft and equipment manufacturing, maintenance and repair, or flight procedures. They may work in the areas of flight operations, maintenance, or avionics, and usually specialize in either commercial or general aviation aircraft. They also examine and certify aircraft pilots, pilot examiners, flight instructors, repair stations, schools, and instructional materials.

Bank examiners investigate financial institutions to enforce Federal and State laws and regulations governing the institution's operations and solvency. Examiners schedule audits, determine actions to protect the institution's solvency and the interests of shareholders and depositors, and recommend acceptance or rejection of applications for mergers, acquisitions, establishment of a new institution, or acceptance in the Federal Reserve System.

Consumer safety inspectors inspect food, feeds and pesticides, weights and measures, biological products, cosmetics, drugs and medical equipment, as well as radiation emitting products. Some are proficient in several areas. Working individually or in teams under a senior inspector, they check on firms that produce, handle, store, or market the products they regulate. They ensure that standards are maintained and respond to consumer complaints by questioning employees, vendors, and others to obtain evidence. Inspectors look for inaccurate product labeling, and for decomposition or chemical or bacteriological contamination that could result in a product becoming harmful to health. They may use portable scales, cameras, ultraviolet lights, thermometers, chemical testing kits, radiation monitors, or other equipment to find violations. They may send product samples collected as part of their examinations to laboratories for analysis.

After completing their inspection, inspectors discuss their observations with plant managers or officials and point out areas where corrective measures are needed. They write reports of their findings and, when necessary, compile evidence that may be used in court if legal action must be taken.

Customs inspectors enforce laws governing imports and exports. Stationed in the United States and overseas at airports, seaports, and border crossing points, they examine, count, weigh, gauge, measure, and sample commercial and noncommercial cargoes entering and leaving the United States to determine admissibility and the amount of duties that must be paid. They insure that all cargo is properly described on accompanying importers' declarations to determine the proper duty and interdict contraband. They inspect baggage and articles carried by passengers and crew members to insure that all merchandise is declared, proper duties are paid, and contraband is not present. They also ensure that people, ships, planes, and anything used to import or export cargo comply with all appropriate entrance and clearance requirements.

Dealer compliance representatives inspect franchised establishments to ascertain compliance with the franchiser's policies and procedures. They may suggest changes in financial and other operations.

Environmental health inspectors, or sanitarians, who work primarily for State and local governments, ensure that food, water, and air meet government standards. They check the cleanliness and safety of food and beverages produced in dairies and processing plants, or served in restaurants, hospitals, and other institutions. They often examine the handling, processing, and serving of food for compliance with sanitation rules and regulations and oversee the treatment and disposal of sewage, refuse, and garbage. In addition, inspectors may visit pollution sources and test for pollutants by collecting air, water, or waste samples for analysis. They try to determine the nature and cause of pollution and initiate action to stop it.

In large local and State health or agriculture departments, environmental health inspectors may specialize in milk and dairy products, food sanitation, waste control, air pollution, water pollution, institutional sanitation, or occupational health. In rural areas and small cities, they may be responsible for a wide range of environmental health activities.

Equal opportunity representatives ascertain and correct unfair employment practices through consultation with and mediation between employers and minority groups.

Federal and State laws require *food inspectors* to inspect meat, poultry, and their byproducts to ensure that they are safe for public consumption. Working onsite, frequently as part of a team, they inspect meat and poultry slaughtering, processing, and packaging operations. They also check for correct product labeling and proper sanitation.

Immigration inspectors interview and examine people seeking to enter the United States and its territories. They inspect passports to determine whether people are legally eligible to enter and to verify their citizenship status and identity. Immigration inspectors also prepare reports, maintain records, and process applications and petitions for immigration or temporary residence in the United States.

Logging operations inspectors review contract logging operations. They prepare reports and issue remedial instructions for violations of contractual agreements and of fire and safety regulations.

Mine safety and health inspectors work to ensure the health and safety of miners. They visit mines and related facilities to obtain information on health and safety conditions and to enforce safety laws and regulations. They discuss their findings with the management of the mine and issue citations describing violations and hazards that must be corrected. Mine inspectors also investigate and report on mine accidents and may direct rescue and firefighting operations when fires or explosions occur.

Motor vehicle inspectors verify the compliance of automobiles and trucks with State requirements for safe operation and emissions. They inspect truck cargoes to assure compliance with legal limitations on gross weight and hazardous cargoes.

Occupational safety and health inspectors visit places of employment to detect unsafe machinery and equipment or unhealthy working conditions. They discuss their findings with the employer or plant manager and order that violations be promptly corrected in accordance with Federal, State, or local government safety standards and regulations. They interview supervisors and employees in response to complaints or accidents, and may order suspension of activity posing threats to workers.

Park rangers enforce laws and regulations in State and national parks. Their duties range from registering vehicles and visitors, collecting fees, and providing information regarding park use and points of interest, to patrolling areas to prevent fire, participating in first aid and rescue activities, and training and supervising other park workers. Some rangers specialize in snow safety and avalanche control. With increasing numbers of visitors to our national parks, some rangers specialize as law enforcement officers.

Postal inspectors observe the functioning of the postal system and enforce laws and regulations. As law enforcement agents, postal inspectors have statutory powers of arrest and the authority to carry firearms. They investigate criminal activities such as theft and misuse of the mail. In instances of suspected mismanagement or fraud, inspectors conduct management or financial audits. They also collaborate with other government agencies, such as the Internal Revenue Service, as members of special task forces.

Quality control inspectors and coordinators inspect products manufactured or processed by private companies for government use to ensure compliance with contract specifications. They may specialize in specific products such as lumber, machinery, petroleum products, paper products, electronic equipment, or furniture. Others coordinate the activities of workers engaged in testing and evaluating pharmaceuticals in order to control quality of manufacture and ensure compliance with legal standards.

Railroad inspectors verify the compliance of railroad systems and equipment with Federal safety regulations. They investigate accidents and review railroads' operating practices.

Revenue officers investigate and collect delinquent tax returns from individuals or businesses. They investigate leads from various sources. They attempt to resolve tax problems with taxpayers and recommend penalties, collection actions, and recommend criminal prosecutions when necessary.

Securities compliance examiners implement regulations concerning securities and real estate transactions. They investigate applications for registration of securities sales and complaints of irregular securities transactions, and recommend necessary legal action.

Travel accommodations raters inspect hotels, motels, restaurants, campgrounds, and vacation resorts. They evaluate travel and tourist accommodations for travel guide publishers and organizations such as tourism promoters and automobile clubs.

Other inspectors and compliance officers include coroners, customs import specialists, code inspectors, mortician investigators, and dealer-compliance representatives. Closely related work is done by construction and building inspectors. (Construction and building inspectors are discussed elsewhere in the *Handbook*.)

Working Conditions

Inspectors and compliance officers meet all kinds of people and work in a variety of environments. Their jobs often involve considerable field work, and some inspectors travel frequently. They are generally furnished with an automobile or are reimbursed for travel expenses.

Inspectors may experience unpleasant, stressful, and dangerous working conditions. For example, mine safety and health inspectors often are exposed to the same hazards as miners. Some food inspectors examine and inspect the livestock slaughtering process in slaughterhouses and frequently come in contact with unpleasant conditions. Customs inspectors have to put up with an irritated public when they search individuals, luggage, and cargo, in addition to the danger inherent to making an occasional arrest. Park rangers often work outdoors—in many cases, on rugged terrain—in very hot or bitterly cold weather for extended periods.

Many inspectors work long and often irregular hours. Even those inspectors not engaged in some form of law enforcement may find themselves in adversarial roles when the organization or individual being inspected objects.

Employment

Inspectors and compliance officers held about 157,000 jobs in 1994. State governments employed 34 percent, the Federal Government— chiefly the Departments of Defense, Labor, Treasury, Agriculture, and Justice—employed 29 percent, and local governments employed 18 percent. The remaining 19 percent were employed in the U.S. Postal Service and throughout the private sector—primarily in education, hospitals, insurance companies, labor unions, and manufacturing firms.

Most consumer safety inspectors on the Federal level work for the U.S. Food and Drug Administration, but the majority of these inspectors work for State governments. Most food inspectors and agricultural commodity graders are employed by the U.S. Department of Agriculture. Many health inspectors work for State and local governments. Compliance inspectors are employed primarily by the Treasury, Justice, and Labor departments on the Federal level, as well as by State and local governments. The Department of Defense employs the most quality assurance inspectors. The Treasury Department employs internal revenue officers and customs inspectors. Aviation safety inspectors work for the Federal Aviation Administration. The Environmental Protection Agency employs inspectors to verify compliance with pollution control and other laws. The U.S. Department of Labor and many State governments employ occupational safety and health inspectors, equal-opportunity officers, and mine safety and health inspectors. Immigration inspectors are employed by the U.S. Department of Justice, while the U.S. Department of Interior employs park rangers. Immigration and customs inspectors work in the United States and overseas at airports, seaports, and border crossing points.

Training, Other Qualifications, and Advancement

Because of the diversity of the functions they perform, qualifications for inspector and compliance officer jobs differ greatly. Requirements include a combination of education, experience, and often a passing grade on a written examination. Employers may require

Many inspectors work long and irregular hours.

college training, including courses related to the job. The following examples illustrate the range of qualifications for various inspector jobs.

Postal inspectors must have a bachelor's degree and 1 year's work experience. It is desirable that they have one of several professional certifications, such as that of certified public accountant. They also must pass a background suitability investigation, and meet certain health requirements, undergo a drug screening test, possess a valid State driver's license, and be a U.S. citizen between 21 and 36 years of age when hired.

Aviation safety inspectors working in operations must be pilots with varying certificates, ratings, and numbers of flight hours to their credit. Maintenance and avionics inspectors must have considerable experience in aviation maintenance and knowledge of industry standards and relevant Federal laws. In addition, FAA medical certificates are required. Some also are required to have an FAA flight instructor rating. Many aviation safety inspectors have had flight and maintenance training in the Armed Forces. No written examination is required.

Applicants for positions as mine safety and health inspectors generally must have experience in mine safety, management, or supervision. Some may possess a skill such as that of an electrician (for mine electrical inspectors). Applicants must meet strict medical requirements and be physically able to perform arduous duties efficiently. Many mine safety inspectors are former miners.

Applicants for internal revenue officer jobs must be a U.S. citizen and have a bachelor's degree or 3 years of experience in business, legal, or financial, or investigative practices.

Park rangers need at least 2 years of college with at least 12 credits in science and criminal justice, although some start as part-time, seasonal workers with the U.S. Forest Service. Most positions require a bachelor's degree.

Environmental health inspectors, called sanitarians in many States, sometimes must have a bachelor's degree in environmental health or in the physical or biological sciences. In most States, they are licensed by examining boards.

All inspectors and compliance officers are trained in the applicable laws or inspection procedures through some combination of classroom and on-the-job training. In general, people who want to enter this occupation should be able to accept responsibility and like detailed work. Inspectors and compliance officers should be neat and personable and able to express themselves well orally and in writing.

Federal Government inspectors and compliance officers whose job performance is satisfactory advance through their career ladder to a specified full performance level. For positions above this level (usually supervisory positions), advancement is competitive, based on agency needs and individual merit. Advancement opportunities in State and local governments and the private sector are often similar to those in the Federal Government.

Some civil service specifications, including those for mine inspectors, aviation safety inspectors, and agricultural commodity graders, rate applicants solely on their experience and education. Others require a written examination.

Job Outlook

Employment of inspectors and compliance officers is expected to grow about as fast as the average for all occupations through the year 2005, reflecting a balance of growing public demand for a safe environment and quality products against the desire for smaller government and fewer regulations. Modest employment growth, particularly in local government, should stem from the expansion of regulatory and compliance programs in solid and hazardous waste disposal and water pollution. In private industry, employment growth will reflect industry growth, due to continuing self-enforcement of government and company regulations and policies, particularly among franchise operations in various industries. Job openings will also arise from the need to replace those who transfer

to other occupations, retire, or leave the labor force for other reasons.

Employment of inspectors and compliance officers is seldom affected by general economic fluctuations. Federal, State, and local governments—which employ most inspectors—provide workers with considerable job security. As a result, inspectors are less likely to lose their jobs than many other workers.

Earnings

The median weekly salary of inspectors and compliance officers, except construction, was about $667 in 1994. The lowest 10 percent earned less than $388; the highest 10 percent earned over $1,130. In the Federal Government, the annual starting salaries for inspectors varied substantially in 1995—from $18,700 to $41,100—depending upon the nature of the inspection or compliance activity. Beginning salaries were slightly higher in selected areas where the prevailing local pay level was higher. The following tabulation presents 1995 average salaries for selected inspectors and compliance officers in the Federal Government in nonsupervisory, supervisory, and managerial positions.

Aviation safety inspectors	$62,970
Highway safety inspectors	59,750
Railroad safety inspectors	52,790
Equal opportunity compliance officials	52,420
Mine safety and health inspectors	51,850
Internal revenue agent	50,720
Environmental protection specialists	49,170
Import specialists	47,550
Alcohol, tobacco, and firearms inspectors	47,050
Safety and occupational health managers	46,730
Quality assurance inspectors	43,970
Customs inspectors	39,050
Agricultural commodity graders	36,040
Immigration inspectors	35,540
Securities compliance examiners	35,400
Consumer safety inspectors	31,700
Food inspectors	31,280
Environmental protection assistants	26,630

Most inspectors and compliance officers work for Federal, State, and local governments and in large private firms, all of which generally offer more generous benefits than do smaller firms.

Related Occupations

Inspectors and compliance officers are responsible for seeing that laws and regulations are obeyed. Construction and building inspectors, fire marshals, Federal, State, and local law enforcement professionals, corrections officers, and fish and game wardens also enforce laws and regulations.

Sources of Additional Information

Information on Federal Government jobs is available from offices of the State employment service, area offices of the U.S. Office of Personnel Management, and Federal Job Information Centers in large cities throughout the country. For information on a career as a specific type of Federal inspector or compliance officer, a Federal department or agency that employs them may also be contacted directly.

Information about State and local government jobs is available from State civil service commissions, usually located in each State capital, or from local government offices.

Information about jobs in private industry is available from the State Employment Service, which is listed under "Job Service" or "Employment" in the State government section of local telephone directories.

Loan Officers and Counselors

(D.O.T. 186.167-078, .267-018, -022, -026)

Nature of the Work

Banks and other financial institutions need up-to-date information on companies and individuals applying for loans and credit. Customers and clients provide this information to the financial institution's loan officers and counselors, generally the first employees to be seen by them. Loan officers prepare, analyze, and verify loan applications, make decisions regarding the extension of credit, and help borrowers fill out loan applications. Loan counselors help consumers with low income or a poor credit history qualify for credit, usually a home mortgage.

Loan officers usually specialize in commercial, consumer, or mortgage loans. Commercial or business loans help companies pay for new equipment or to expand operations. Consumer loans include home equity, automobile, and personal loans. Mortgage loans are made to purchase real estate or to refinance an existing mortgage.

Loan officers represent lending institutions that provide funds for a variety of purposes. Personal loans can be made to consolidate bills, purchase expensive items such as an automobile or furniture, or finance a college education. Loan officers attempt to lower their firm's risk by receiving collateral—security pledged for the payment of a loan. For example, when lending money for a college education, the bank may insist that the borrower offer his or her home as collateral. If the borrower were ever unable to repay the loan, the borrower would have to sell the home to raise the necessary money. Loans backed by collateral also are beneficial to the customer because they generally carry a lower interest rate.

Loan officers and counselors must keep abreast of new financial products and services so they can meet their customers' needs; for example, banks and other lenders now offer a variety of mortgage products, including reverse equity mortgages, shared equity mortgages, and adjustable rate mortgages.

Loan officers meet with customers and gather basic information about the loan request. Often customers will not fully understand the information requested, and will call the loan officer for assistance. Once the customer completes the financial forms, the loan officer begins to process them. The loan officer reviews the completed financial forms for accuracy and thoroughness, and requests additional information if necessary. For example, the loan officer verifies that the customer has correctly identified the type and purpose of the loan. The loan officer then requests a credit report from one or more of the major credit reporting agencies. This information, along with comments from the loan officer, is included in a loan file, and is compared to the lending institution's requirements. Banks and other lenders have established requirements for the maximum percentage of income that can safely go to repay loans. At this point, the loan officer, in consultation with his or her manager, decides whether or not to grant the loan. A loan that would otherwise be denied may be approved if the customer can provide the lender appropriate collateral. Whether or not the loan request is approved, the loan officer informs the borrower of the decision.

Loan counselors meet with consumers who are attempting to purchase a home or refinance debt, but who do not qualify for loans with banks. Often clients rely on income from self-employment or government assistance to prove that they can repay the loan. Counselors also help to psychologically prepare consumers to be homeowners and to pay their debts. Counselors frequently work with clients who have little or no experience with financial matters.

Loan counselors provide positive reinforcement along with the financial tools needed to qualify for a loan—this assistance may take several forms. Occasionally, counselors simply need to explain what information loan officers need to complete a loan transaction. Most of the time loan counselors help clients qualify for a bank-financed

Mortgage loan officers typically are paid on a commission basis.

mortgage loan. The loan counselor helps the client complete an application, and researches Federal, State, and local government programs that could provide the money needed for the client to purchase the home. Often several government programs are combined to provide the necessary money.

Working Conditions

Loan officers and counselors usually work in offices, but mortgage loan officers frequently move from office to office and often visit homes of clients while completing a loan request. Commercial loan officers employed by large firms may travel frequently to prepare complex loan agreements.

Most loan officers and counselors work a standard 40-hour week, but may work longer, particularly mortgage loan officers who are free to take on as many customers as they choose. Loan officers and counselors usually carry a heavy caseload and sometimes cannot accept new clients until they complete current cases. They are especially busy when interest rates are low, resulting in a surge in loan applications.

Employment

Loan officers and counselors held about 214,000 jobs in 1994. About 6 out of 10 are employed by commercial banks, savings institutions, and credit unions. Others are employed by nonbank financial institutions, such as mortgage brokerage firms and personal credit firms. Most loan counselors work for State and local governments, or for nonprofit organizations. Loan officers and counselors generally work in urban areas where large banks are concentrated.

Training, Other Qualifications, and Advancement

Most loan officer positions require a bachelor's degree in finance, economics, or a related field. Most employers also prefer applicants who are familiar with computers and their applications in banking. A mortgage loan officer is the exception, with training or experience in sales more crucial to potential employers. Some loan officers advance through the ranks in an organization, acquiring several years of work experience in various other occupations, such as teller or customer service representative.

Persons planning a career as a loan officer or counselor should be skilled in mathematics and in oral and written communication. Developing effective working relationships with different people—managers, clients, and the public—is essential to success as a loan officer or counselor. Loan officers must enjoy public contact and be willing to attend community events as a representative of their employer.

Persons interested in counseling should have a strong interest in helping others and the ability to inspire trust, respect, and confidence.

Because loan counselors frequently explain the complicated world of banking to clients who have never been exposed to it, patience and an understanding of mortgage banking is necessary to be an effective loan counselor. Loan counselors should be sensitive to their clients' needs and must consider the importance and pride their clients attach to home ownership. Counselors should be able to work independently or as part of a team.

The American Institute of Banking, which is affiliated with the American Bankers Association, offers courses through correspondence and in some colleges and universities for students and others interested in lending, as well as for experienced loan officers. The certification program for lenders leads to the title, "Certified Lender in Business Banking." Completion of these courses and programs enhances one's employment and advancement opportunities.

Capable loan officers may advance to larger branches of the firm or to a managerial position, while less capable loan officers and those having inadequate academic preparation may be assigned to smaller branches and find promotion difficult. Advancement from a loan officer position usually includes becoming a supervisor over other loan officers and clerical staff.

Most loan counselors receive substantial on-the-job training, gaining a thorough understanding of the requirements and procedures for approval of loans. Some acquire this knowledge through work experience in a related field. In addition, accounting skills can be very helpful. Educational requirements vary—some counselors are high school graduates while others have a college degree in economics, finance, or a related field.

Like other workers, outstanding loan counselors can advance to supervisory positions. However, promotion potential is limited, and many loan counselors leave for better paying positions elsewhere.

Job Outlook

Employment of loan officers and counselors is expected to grow faster than the average for all occupations through the year 2005. As the population and economy grow, applications for commercial, consumer, and mortgage loans will increase, spurring demand for loan officers and counselors. Growth in the variety and complexity of loans, and the importance of loan officers to the success of banks and other lending institutions, also should assure rapid employment growth. Although increased demand will generate many new jobs, most openings will result from the need to replace workers who leave the occupation or retire. College graduates and those with banking or lending experience should have the best job prospects.

Loan officers are less likely to lose their jobs than other workers in banks and other lending institutions during difficult economic times. Because loans are the major source of income for banks, loan officers are fundamental to the success of their organizations. Also, many loan officers are compensated in part on a commission basis. Loan counselors typically have so many clients that a reduction in their numbers would lead to a decline in the services provided to the community. However, job security is influenced by the spending patterns of local governments. Budget reductions could result in less hiring or even layoffs of loan counselors.

Earnings

The form of compensation for loan officers varies, depending on the lending institution. Some banks offer salary plus commission as an incentive to increase the number of loans processed, while others pay only salaries.

According to a salary survey conducted by Robert Half International, a staffing services firm specializing in accounting and finance, residential real estate mortgage loan officers earned between $28,500 and $44,000 in 1995; commercial real estate mortgage loan officers earned between $43,300 and $70,500; consumer loan officers, between $27,200 and $45,700; and commercial lenders, between $36,100 and $82,500. Smaller banks generally paid 15 percent less than larger banks. Loan officers who are paid on a commission basis generally earn more than those on salary only.

The earnings for loan counselors varies widely, with local government employees in large cities earning the highest salaries.

Banks and other lenders sometimes offer their loan officers free checking privileges and somewhat lower interest rates on personal loans. Loan counselors sometimes get awards for their service to the community.

Related Occupations

Loan officers and counselors help the public manage financial assets and secure loans. Occupations that involve similar functions include securities and financial services sales representatives, financial aid officers, real estate agents and brokers, and insurance agents and brokers.

Sources of Additional Information

Information about a career as a loan officer may be obtained from:
☛American Bankers Association, 1120 Connecticut Ave. NW., Washington, DC 20036.

State bankers' associations can furnish specific information about job opportunities in their State. Or, contact individual banks to inquire about job openings, and for more details about the activities, responsibilities, and preferred qualifications of their loan officers. For the names and addresses of banks and savings and related institutions, as well as the names of their principal officers, consult one of the following directories.
☛The American Financial Directory (Norcross, Ga., McFadden Business Publications).
☛Polk's World Bank Directory (Nashville, R.L. Polk & Co.).
☛Rand McNally Bankers Directory (Chicago, Rand McNally & Co.).
☛The U.S. Savings and Loan Directory (Chicago, Rand McNally & Co.).
☛Rand McNally Credit Union Directory (Chicago, Rand McNally & Co.).

Your local State employment service office or municipal government also may have information on job opportunities, particularly for loan counselors.

Management Analysts and Consultants

(D.O.T. 100.117-014; 161.117-014, .167-010, -014, -018, and -022, .267 except -014 and -030; 169.167-074; 184.267; and 310.267-010)

Nature of the Work

Management analysts and consultants suggest solutions to management problems. For example, a rapidly growing small company may need help in designing a better system of control over inventories and expenses, or an established manufacturing company decides to relocate to another State and needs assistance planning the move, or a large company realizes that its corporate structure must be reorganized after acquiring a new division. These are just a few of the many organizational problems that management analysts, as they are called in government agencies, and management consultants, as business firms refer to them, help solve.

The work of management analysts and consultants varies by client or employer and from project to project. For example, some projects require a team of consultants, each specializing in one area; at other times, they will work independently with the client's managers. In general, analysts and consultants first collect, review, and analyze information. They then make recommendations to management and often assist in the implementation of their proposal.

Both public and private organizations use consultants for a variety of reasons. Some don't have the internal resources needed to handle a project; others need a consultant's expertise to determine what resources will be required, and what problems may be encountered, if they pursue a particular course of action. Still others want to get outside help on how to resolve organizational problems that have already been identified or to avoid troublesome problems that could arise.

Firms providing consulting services range in size from solo practitioners to large international organizations employing thousands of consultants. Some firms specialize by industry while others specialize by type of business function, such as human resources or information systems. In government, management analysts tend to specialize by type of agency. Consulting services usually are provided on a contract basis whereby a company solicits proposals from a number of consulting firms specializing in the area in which it needs assistance. These proposals include the estimated cost and scope of the project, staffing requirements, references from a number of previous clients, and the deadline. The company then selects the proposal which best meets its needs.

Upon getting an assignment or contract, consultants and analysts try to define the nature and extent of the problem. During this phase of the job, they may analyze data such as annual revenues, employment, or expenditures. Next they interview managers and employees and observe the operations of the organizational unit.

Next, they use their knowledge of management systems and their expertise in a particular area to develop solutions to the problem. In the course of preparing their recommendations, they must take into account the general nature of the business, the relationship the firm has with others in that industry, and the firm's internal organization and culture, as well as information gained through data collection and analysis.

Once they have decided on a course of action, consultants usually report their findings and recommendations to the client, often in writing. In addition, they generally make oral presentations regarding their findings. For some projects, this is all that is required; for others, consultants may assist in the implementation of their suggestions.

Management analysts in government agencies use the same skills as their private-sector colleagues to advise managers in government on many types of issues, most of which are similar to the problems faced by private firms. For example, if an agency is planning to purchase personal computers, it first must determine which type to buy, given its budget and data processing needs. Management analysts would assess the various types of machines available by price range and determine which best meets their department's needs.

Working Conditions

Management analysts and consultants usually divide their time between their offices and their client's site. Although much of their time is spent indoors in clean, well-lighted offices, they may have to visit a client's production facility where conditions may not be so favorable.

Typically, analysts and consultants work at least 40 hours a week. Overtime is common, especially when project deadlines are near. Since they must spend a significant portion of their time with clients, they may travel frequently.

Self-employed consultants can set their workload and hours and work at home. On the other hand, their livelihood depends on their ability to maintain and expand their client base. Wage and salary consultants also must favorably impress potential clients to get and keep clients for their company.

Employment

Management analysts and consultants held about 231,000 jobs in 1994. About half of these workers were self-employed. Most of the rest worked in management consulting firms and for Federal, State, and local governments. The majority of those working for the Federal Government were found in the Department of Defense.

Management analysts and consultants are found throughout the country, but employment is concentrated in large metropolitan areas.

Training, Other Qualifications, and Advancement

Educational requirements for entry level jobs in this field vary widely, but there is an increasing emphasis on scientific and technological applications at the undergraduate level. Employers in private industry generally seek individuals with a master's degree in business administration or a related discipline. Individuals hired straight out of school with only a bachelor's degree generally work as research associates, but find it difficult to advance up the career ladder unless they get an advanced degree. Most government agencies hire people with a bachelor's degree and no work experience as entry level management analysts, and often pay for graduate classes in management analysis.

Many fields of study provide a suitable educational background for this occupation because of the diversity of problem areas addressed by management analysts and consultants. These include most areas of business and management, as well as computer and information sciences and engineering.

Management analysts and consultants who are hired directly from school may participate in formal company or government training programs. Such programs often include instruction on policies and procedures, computer systems and software, research processes, and management practices and principles. Analysts and consultants routinely attend conferences to keep abreast of current developments in their field.

Many entrants to this occupation have, in addition to the appropriate formal education, several years of experience in management or in another specialization. The value of this experience enables many to land mid-level positions.

Management analysts and consultants often work with little or no supervision, so they should be self-motivated and disciplined. Analytical skills, the ability to get along with a wide range of people, strong oral and written communication skills, good judgment, the ability to manage time well, and creativity in developing solutions to problems are other desirable qualities for prospective management analysts and consultants.

In large consulting firms, beginners usually start as a researcher for a consulting team. The team is responsible for the entire project and each consultant is assigned to a particular area. As consultants gain experience, they may be assigned to work on one specific project full-time, taking on more responsibility and managing their own hours. At the senior level, consultants may supervise entry level workers and become increasingly involved in seeking out new business. Those with exceptional skills may eventually become a partner or principal in the firm. Others with entrepreneurial ambition may open their own firm.

A high percentage of management consultants are self-employed, partly because business start-up costs are low. Self-employed con-

Many innovative business ideas are contributed by management consultants.

sultants also can share office space, administrative help, and other resources with other self-employed consultants or small consulting firms—thus reducing overhead costs. Many such firms fail, however, because of an inability to acquire and maintain a profitable client base.

The Institute of Management Consultants (a division of the Council of Consulting Organizations, Inc.) offers the Certified Management Consultant (CMC) designation to those who pass an examination and meet minimum levels of education and experience. Certification is not mandatory for management consultants to practice, but it may give a jobseeker a competitive advantage.

Job Outlook

Employment of management analysts and consultants is expected to grow faster than the average for all occupations through the year 2005 as industry and government increasingly rely on outside expertise to improve the performance of their organizations. Growth is expected in large consulting firms, but also in small consulting firms whose consultants will specialize in specific areas of expertise.

Increased competition has forced American industry to take a closer look at its operations. As international and domestic markets become more competitive, firms must use what resources they have more efficiently. Management consultants are being increasingly relied upon to help reduce costs, streamline operations, and develop marketing strategies. As businesses downsize and eliminate needed functions as well as permanent staff, consultants will be used to perform those functions that were previously handled internally. Businesses attempting to expand, particularly into world markets, frequently need the skills of management consultants to help with organizational, administrative, and other issues. Continuing changes in the business environment also are expected to lead to demand for management consultants. Firms will use consultants to incorporate new technologies, to cope with more numerous and complex government regulations, and to adapt to a changing labor force. As businesses rely more on technology, there are increasing roles for consultants with a technical background, such as engineering or biotechnology, particularly when combined with an MBA.

Federal, State, and local agencies also are expected to expand their use of management analysts. In the era of budget deficits, analysts' skills at identifying problems and implementing cost reduction measures are expected to become increasingly important. However, because almost one-half of the management analysts employed by the Federal Government work for the Department of Defense, Federal employment growth will increase slowly because of cutbacks in the Nation's defense budget.

Despite projected rapid employment growth, competition for jobs as management consultants is expected to be keen in the private sector. Because management consultants can come from such diverse educational backgrounds, the pool of applicants from which employers hire is quite large. Additionally, the independent and challenging nature of the work combined with high earnings potential make this occupation attractive to many. Job opportunities are expected to be best for those with a graduate degree and some industry expertise.

Because many small consulting firms fail each year for lack of managerial expertise and clients, those interested in opening their own firm must have good organizational and marketing skills, plus several years of consulting experience.

Earnings

Salaries for management analysts and consultants vary widely by experience, education, and employer. In 1994, those who were wage and salary workers had median annual earnings of about $41,300. The middle 50 percent earned between $30,000 and $53,900.

In 1994, according to the Association of Management Consulting Firms (ACME), earnings—including bonuses and/or profit sharing—for research associates in ACME member firms averaged $30,400;

for entry level consultants, $41,800; for management consultants, $58,300; for senior consultants, $89,200; for junior partners, $120,100; and for senior partners, $194,000.

Typical benefits for salaried analysts and consultants include health and life insurance, a retirement plan, vacation and sick leave, profit sharing, and bonuses for outstanding work. In addition, all travel expenses usually are reimbursed by the employer. Self-employed consultants usually have to maintain their own office and provide their own benefits.

Related Occupations

Management analysts and consultants collect, review, and analyze data; make recommendations; and assist in the implementation of their ideas. Others who use similar skills are managers, computer systems analysts, operations research analysts, economists, and financial analysts.

Sources of Additional Information

Information about career opportunities in management consulting is available from:
☛ACME, The Association of Management Consulting Firms, 521 Fifth Ave., 35th Floor, New York, NY 10175-3598.

For information about a career as a State or local government management analyst, contact your State or local employment service.

Persons interested in a management analyst position in the Federal Government can obtain information from:
☛Office of Personnel Management, 1900 E St. NW., Washington, DC 20415.

Marketing, Advertising, and Public Relations Managers

(D.O.T. 096.161-010, 141.137-010; 159.167-022; 163.117-014, -018, -022, -026, .167-010, -014, -018, -022, .267-010; 164.117-010, -014, -018, .167-010; 165.117-010, -014; 185.157-014, .167-042; 187.167-162, -170; 189.117-018)

Nature of the Work

The fundamental objective of any firm is to market its products or services profitably. In small firms, all marketing responsibilities may be assumed by the owner or chief executive officer. In large firms, which may offer numerous products and services nationally or even worldwide, experienced marketing, advertising, and public relations managers coordinate these and related activities.

The executive vice president for marketing in large firms directs the overall marketing policy—including market research, marketing strategy, sales, advertising, promotion, pricing, product development, and public relations activities. (This occupation is included in the *Handbook* statement on general managers and top executives.) These activities are supervised by middle and supervisory managers who oversee staffs of professionals and technicians.

Marketing managers develop the firm's detailed marketing strategy. With the help of subordinates, including product development managers and market research managers, they determine the demand for products and services offered by the firm and its competitors and identify potential consumers—for example, business firms, wholesalers, retailers, government, or the general public. Mass markets are further categorized according to various factors such as region, age, income, and lifestyle. Marketing managers develop pricing strategy with an eye towards maximizing the firm's share of the market and its profits while ensuring that the firm's customers are satisfied. In collaboration with sales, product development, and other managers, they monitor trends that indicate the need for new products and services and oversee product development. Marketing managers work with advertising and promotion managers to best promote the firm's products and services and to attract potential users.

A wide range of educational backgrounds are suitable for entry into marketing, advertising, and public relations jobs, but many employers prefer a broad liberal arts background.

Sales managers direct the firm's sales program. They assign sales territories and goals and establish training programs for their sales representatives. Managers advise their sales representatives on ways to improve their sales performance. In large, multiproduct firms, they oversee regional and local sales managers and their staffs. Sales managers maintain contact with dealers and distributors. They analyze sales statistics gathered by their staffs to determine sales potential and inventory requirements and monitor the preferences of customers. Such information is vital to develop products and maximize profits.

Except in the largest firms, advertising and promotion staffs generally are small and serve as a liaison between the firm and the advertising or promotion agency to which many advertising or promotional functions are contracted out. Advertising managers oversee the account services, creative services, and media services departments. The account services department is managed by account executives, who assess the need for advertising and, in advertising agencies, maintain the accounts of clients. The creative services department develops the subject matter and presentation of advertising. This department is supervised by a creative director, who oversees the copy chief and art director and their staffs. The media services department is supervised by the media director, who oversees planning groups that select the communication media—for example, radio, television, newspapers, magazines, or outdoor signs—to disseminate the advertising.

Promotion managers supervise staffs of promotion specialists. They direct promotion programs combining advertising with purchase incentives to increase sales of products or services. In an effort to establish closer contact with purchasers—dealers, distributors, or consumers—promotion programs may involve direct mail, telemarketing, television or radio advertising, catalogs, exhibits, inserts in newspapers, in-store displays and product endorsements, and special events. Purchase incentives may include discounts, samples, gifts, rebates, coupons, sweepstakes, and contests.

Public relations managers supervise public relations specialists (see the *Handbook* statement on public relations specialists). These managers direct publicity programs to a targeted public. They use any necessary communication media in their effort to maintain the support of the specific group upon whom their organization's success depends, such as consumers, stockholders, or the general public. For example, public relations managers may clarify or justify the firm's point of view on health or environmental issues to community or special interest groups. They evaluate advertising and promotion programs for compatibility with public relations efforts. Public relations managers, in effect, serve as the eyes and ears of top man-

agement. They observe social, economic, and political trends that might ultimately have an effect upon the firm, and make recommendations to enhance the firm's public image in view of those trends. Public relations managers may confer with labor relations managers to produce internal company communications—such as news about employee-management relations—and with financial managers to produce company reports. They assist company executives in drafting speeches, arranging interviews, and other forms of public contact; oversee company archives; and respond to information requests. In addition, some public relations managers handle special events such as sponsorship of races, parties introducing new products, or other activities the firm supports in order to gain public attention through the press without advertising directly.

Working Conditions

Marketing, advertising, and public relations managers are provided with offices close to top managers. Long hours, including evenings and weekends, are common. Working under pressure is unavoidable as schedules change, problems arise, and deadlines and goals must be met. Marketing, advertising, and public relations managers meet frequently with other managers; some meet with the public and government officials.

Substantial travel may be involved. For example, attendance at meetings sponsored by associations or industries is often mandatory. Sales managers travel to national, regional, and local offices and to various dealers and distributors. Advertising and promotion managers may travel to meet with clients or representatives of communications media. At times, public relations managers travel to meet with special interest groups or government officials. Job transfers between headquarters and regional offices are common—particularly among sales managers—and can disrupt family life.

Employment

Marketing, advertising, and public relations managers held about 461,000 jobs in 1994. These managers are found in virtually every industry. Industries employing them in significant numbers include motor vehicle dealers; printing and publishing firms; advertising agencies; department stores; computer and data processing services firms; and management and public relations firms.

Training, Advancement, and Other Qualifications

A wide range of educational backgrounds are suitable for entry into marketing, advertising, and public relations managerial jobs, but many employers prefer a broad liberal arts background. A bachelor's degree in sociology, psychology, literature, or philosophy, among other subjects, is acceptable. However, requirements vary depending upon the particular job.

For marketing, sales, and promotion management positions, some employers prefer a bachelor's or master's degree in business administration with an emphasis on marketing. Courses in business law, economics, accounting, finance, mathematics, and statistics are also highly recommended. In highly technical industries, such as computer and electronics manufacturing, a bachelor's degree in engineering or science combined with a master's degree in business administration is preferred. For advertising management positions, some employers prefer a bachelor's degree in advertising or journalism. A course of study should include courses in marketing, consumer behavior, market research, sales, communications methods and technology, and visual arts—for example, art history and photography. For public relations management positions, some employers prefer a bachelor's or master's degree in public relations or journalism. The individual's curriculum should include courses in advertising, business administration, public affairs, political science, and creative and technical writing. For all these specialties, courses in management and completion of an internship while in school are highly recommended. Familiarity with computerized word processing and data base applications also are important for many marketing, advertising, and public relations management positions.

Most marketing, advertising, and public relations management positions are filled by promoting experienced staff or related professional or technical personnel—for example, sales representatives, purchasing agents, buyers, product or brand specialists, advertising specialists, promotion specialists, and public relations specialists. In small firms, where the number of positions is limited, advancement to a management position generally comes slowly. In large firms, promotion may occur more quickly.

Although experience, ability, and leadership are emphasized for promotion, advancement can be accelerated by participation in management training programs conducted by many large firms. Many firms also provide their employees with continuing education opportunities, either in-house or at local colleges and universities, and encourage employee participation in seminars and conferences, often provided by professional societies. Often in collaboration with colleges and universities, numerous marketing and related associations sponsor national or local management training programs. Courses include brand and product management, international marketing, sales management evaluation, telemarketing and direct sales, promotion, marketing communication, market research, organizational communication, and data processing systems procedures and management. Many firms pay all or part of the cost for those who successfully complete courses.

Some associations (listed under sources of additional information) offer certification programs for marketing, advertising, and public relations managers. Certification is a sign of competence and achievement in this field that is particularly important in a competitive job market. While relatively few marketing, advertising, and public relations managers currently are certified, the number of managers who seek certification is expected to grow. For example, Sales and Marketing Executives International offers a management certification program based on education and job performance. The Public Relations Society of America offers an accreditation program for public relations practitioners based on years of experience and an examination. The International Association of Business Communicators offers an accreditation program for the manager or the person ready to move into communication management. The American Marketing Association is developing a certification program for marketing managers.

Persons interested in becoming marketing, advertising, and public relations managers should be mature, creative, highly motivated, resistant to stress, and flexible, yet decisive. The ability to communicate persuasively, both orally and in writing, with other managers, staff, and the public is vital. Marketing, advertising, and public relations managers also need tact, good judgment, and exceptional ability to establish and maintain effective personal relationships with supervisory and professional staff members and client firms.

Because of the importance and high visibility of their jobs, marketing, advertising, and public relations managers often are prime candidates for advancement. Well-trained, experienced, successful managers may be promoted to higher positions in their own or other firms. Some become top executives. Managers with extensive experience and sufficient capital may open their own businesses.

Job Outlook

Marketing, advertising, and public relations manager jobs are highly coveted and will be sought by other managers or highly experienced professional and technical personnel, resulting in substantial job competition. College graduates with extensive experience, a high level of creativity, and strong communication skills should have the best job opportunities.

Employment of marketing, advertising, and public relations managers is expected to increase faster than the average for all occupations through the year 2005. Increasingly intense domestic and global competition in products and services offered to consumers should require greater marketing, promotional, and public relations efforts. Management and public relations firms may experience particularly rapid growth as businesses increasingly hire contractors for these services rather than support additional full-time staff.

Projected employment growth varies by industry. For example, employment of marketing, advertising, and public relations managers is expected to grow much faster than average in most business services industries, such as computer and data processing, and management and public relations firms, while average growth is projected in manufacturing industries overall. Many companies that eliminated in-house marketing and advertising departments during downsizing in recent years are now relying on firms which specialize in promotion, marketing, and advertising activities to provide these services.

Earnings

According to a National Association of Colleges and Employers survey, starting salary offers to marketing majors graduating in 1995 averaged about $25,000; advertising majors, about $22,000.

The median annual salary of marketing, advertising, and public relations managers was $44,000 in 1994. The lowest 10 percent earned $21,000 or less, while the top 10 percent earned $98,000 or more. Many earn bonuses equal to 10 percent or more of their salaries. Surveys show that salary levels vary substantially depending upon the level of managerial responsibility, length of service, education, and the employer's size, location, and industry. For example, manufacturing firms generally pay marketing, advertising, and public relations managers higher salaries than nonmanufacturing firms. For sales managers, the size of their sales territory is another important factor.

According to a 1994 survey by Abbot, Langer and Associates, of Crete, Illinois, annual incomes for sales/marketing managers varied greatly—from under $28,000 to over $250,000—depending on the manager's level of education, experience, industry, and the number of employees he or she supervised. The median annual income for top advertising managers was $44,000; top sales promotion managers was $45,000; product/brand managers, $57,000; top market research managers, $59,000; regional sales managers, $69,000; and chief marketing executives, $69,000.

According to a 1994 survey by Advertising Age Magazine, annual salaries of marketing, advertising, and public relations managers ranged from a low of $44,000 to a high of $145,000.

Related Occupations

Marketing, advertising, and public relations managers direct the sale of products and services offered by their firms and the communication of information about their firms' activities. Other personnel involved with marketing, advertising, and public relations include art directors, commercial and graphic artists, copy chiefs, copywriters, editors, lobbyists, marketing research analysts, public relations specialists, promotion specialists, sales representatives, and technical writers. (Some of these occupations are discussed elsewhere in the *Handbook*.)

Sources of Additional Information

For information about careers in sales and marketing management, contact:

☛American Marketing Association, 250 S. Wacker Dr., Chicago, IL 60606.

☛Sales and Marketing Executives International, 458 Statler Office Tower, Cleveland, OH 44115.

For information about careers in advertising management, contact:

☛American Advertising Federation, Education Services Department, 1101 Vermont Ave. NW., Suite 500, Washington, DC 20005.

Information about careers in promotion management is available from:

☛Council of Sales Promotion Agencies, 750 Summer St., Stamford, CT 06901.

☛Promotion Marketing Association of America, Inc., 322 Eighth Ave., Suite 1201, New York, NY 10001.

Information about careers in public relations management is available from:

☛Public Relations Society of America, 33 Irving Place, New York, NY 10003-2376.

Information on accreditation for business communicators is available from:

☛International Business Communicators, One Hallidie Plaza, Suite 600, San Francisco, CA 94102.

Personnel, Training, and Labor Relations Specialists and Managers

(D.O.T. 079.127; 099.167-010; 166.067, .117, .167 except -046, .257, .267-014 through -046; 169.107, .167-062, .207; 188.117-010, -086, .217)

Nature of the Work

Attracting the most qualified employees available and matching them to the jobs for which they are best suited is important for the success of any organization. However, many enterprises are too large to permit close contact between top management and employees. Instead, personnel, training, and labor relations specialists and managers, commonly known as human resources specialists and managers, provide this link. These individuals recruit and interview employees and advise on hiring decisions in accordance with policies and requirements that have been established in conjunction with top management. In an effort to improve morale and productivity and limit job turnover, they also help their firms effectively use employees' skills, provide training opportunities to enhance those skills, and boost employees' satisfaction with their jobs and working conditions. Although some jobs in the human resources field require only limited contact with people outside the office, most involve frequent contact. Dealing with people is an essential part of the job.

In a small organization, one person may handle all aspects of personnel, training, and labor relations work. In contrast, in a large corporation, the top human resources executive usually develops and coordinates personnel programs and policies. (Executives are included in the *Handbook* statement on general managers and top executives.) These policies usually are implemented by a director or manager of human resources and, in some cases, a director of industrial relations.

The director of human resources may oversee several departments, each headed by an experienced manager, who most likely specializes in one personnel activity such as employment, compensation, benefits, training and development, or employee relations.

Employment and placement managers oversee the hiring and separation of employees and supervise various workers, including equal employment opportunity specialists and recruitment specialists.

Recruiters maintain contacts within the community and may travel extensively—often to college campuses—to search for promising job applicants. Recruiters screen, interview, and, in some cases, test applicants. They may also check references and extend offers of employment to qualified candidates. These workers need to be thoroughly familiar with the organization and its personnel policies to discuss wages, working conditions, and promotional opportunities with prospective employees. They also need to keep informed about equal employment opportunity (EEO) and affirmative action guidelines and laws, such as the Americans With Disabilities Act.

EEO representatives or affirmative action coordinators handle this area in large organizations. They investigate and resolve EEO grievances, examine corporate practices for possible violations, and compile and submit EEO statistical reports.

Employer relations representatives—who usually work in government agencies—maintain working relationships with local employers and promote the use of public employment programs and services. Similarly, employment interviewers—sometimes called personnel consultants—help match jobseekers with employers. (For more information, see the statement on employment interviewers elsewhere in the *Handbook*.)

Job analysts, sometimes called position classifiers, perform very exacting work. They collect and examine detailed information about job duties to prepare job descriptions. These descriptions explain the duties, training, and skills each job requires. Whenever a large organization introduces a new job or reviews existing jobs, it calls upon the expert knowledge of the job analyst.

Occupational analysts conduct research, generally in large firms. They are concerned with occupational classification systems and study the effects of industry and occupational trends upon worker relationships. They may serve as technical liaison between the firm and industry, government, and labor unions.

Establishing and maintaining a firm's pay system is the principal job of the compensation manager. Assisted by staff specialists, compensation managers devise ways to ensure fair and equitable pay rates. They may conduct surveys to see how their rates compare with others and to see that the firm's pay scale complies with changing laws and regulations. In addition, compensation managers often oversee their firm's performance evaluation system, and they may design reward systems such as pay-for-performance plans.

Employee benefits managers handle the company's employee benefits program, notably its health insurance and pension plans. Expertise in designing and administering benefits programs continues to gain importance as employer-provided benefits account for a growing proportion of overall compensation costs, and as benefit plans increase in number and complexity. For example, pension benefits might include savings and thrift, profit-sharing, and stock ownership plans; health benefits may include long-term catastrophic illness insurance and dental insurance. Familiarity with health benefits is a top priority at present, as more firms struggle to cope with the rising cost of health care for employees and retirees. In addition to health insurance and pension coverage, some firms offer their employees life and accidental death and dismemberment insurance, disability insurance, and relatively new benefits designed to meet the needs of a changing work force, such as parental leave, child care and elder care, long-term nursing home care insurance, employee assistance and wellness programs, and flexible benefits plans. Benefits managers must keep abreast of changing Federal and State regulations and legislation that may affect employee benefits.

Employee assistance plan managers—also called employee welfare managers—are responsible for a wide array of programs covering occupational safety and health standards and practices; health promotion and physical fitness, medical examinations, and minor health treatment, such as first aid; plant security; publications; food service and recreation activities; car pooling; employee suggestion systems; child care and elder care; and counseling services. Child and elder care are increasingly important due to growth in the number of dual-income households and the elderly population. Counseling may help employees deal with emotional disorders, alcoholism, or marital, family, consumer, legal, and financial problems. Career counseling and second career counseling for employees approaching retirement age also may be provided. In large firms, some of these programs—such as security and safety—are in separate departments headed by other managers.

Training is supervised by training and development managers. Increasingly, management recognizes that training offers a way of developing skills, enhancing productivity and quality of work, and building loyalty to the firm. Training is widely accepted as a method of improving employee morale, but this is only one of the reasons for its growing importance. Other factors include the complexity of the work environment, the rapid pace of organizational and technological change, and the growing number of jobs in fields that constantly generate new knowledge. In addition, advances in learning theory have provided insights into how adults learn, and how training can be organized most effectively for them.

Training specialists plan, organize, and direct a wide range of training activities. Trainers conduct orientation sessions and arrange on-the-job training for new employees. They help rank-and-file workers maintain and improve their job skills and possibly prepare for jobs requiring greater skill. They help supervisors improve their interpersonal skills in order to deal effectively with employees. They may set up individualized training plans to strengthen an employee's existing skills or to teach new ones. Training specialists in some companies set up programs to develop executive potential among employees in lower-level positions. In government-supported training programs, training specialists function as case managers. They first assess the training needs of clients, then guide them through the most appropriate training method. After training, clients may either be referred to employer relations representatives or receive job placement assistance.

Planning and program development is an important part of the training specialist's job. In order to identify and assess training needs within the firm, trainers may confer with managers and supervisors or conduct surveys. They also periodically evaluate training effectiveness.

Depending on the size, goals, and nature of the organization, trainers may differ considerably in their responsibilities and in the methods they use. Training methods include on-the-job training; schools in which shop conditions are duplicated for trainees prior to putting them on the shop floor; apprenticeship training; classroom training; programmed instruction, which may involve interactive videos, videodiscs, and other computer-aided instructional technologies; simulators; conferences; and workshops.

The director of industrial relations forms labor policy, oversees industrial labor relations, negotiates collective bargaining agreements, and coordinates grievance procedures to handle complaints resulting from disputes under the contract for firms with unionized employees. The director of industrial relations also advises and collaborates with the director of human resources and other managers and members of their staff, because all aspects of personnel policy—such as wages, benefits, pensions, and work practices—may be involved in drawing up a new or revised contract.

Industrial labor relations programs are implemented by labor relations managers and their staff. When a collective bargaining agreement is up for negotiation, labor relations specialists prepare information for management to use during negotiation, which requires familiarity with economic and wage data as well as extensive knowledge of labor law and collective bargaining trends. The labor relations staff interprets and administers the contract with respect to grievances, wages and salaries, employee welfare, health care, pensions, union and management practices, and other contractual stipulations. As union membership is continuing to decline in most industries, industrial relations personnel are working more with employees who are not members of a labor union.

Dispute resolution—that is, attaining tacit or contractual agreements—has become increasingly important as parties to a dispute attempt to avoid costly litigation, strikes, or other disruptions. Dispute resolution also has become more complex, involving employees, management, unions, other firms, and government agencies. Specialists involved in dispute resolution must be highly knowledgeable and experienced, and often report to the director of industrial relations. Conciliators, or mediators, advise and counsel labor and management to prevent and, when necessary, resolve disputes over labor agreements or other labor relations issues. Arbitrators, sometimes called umpires or referees, decide disputes that bind both labor and management to specific terms and conditions of labor contracts. Labor relations specialists who work for unions perform many of the same functions on behalf of the union and its members.

Other emerging specialists include international human resources managers, who handle human resources issues related to a company's foreign operations, and human resources information system specialists, who develop and apply computer programs to process personnel information, match jobseekers with job openings, and handle other personnel matters.

Orientation for new employees is often the responsibility of personnel specialists.

Working Conditions

Personnel work generally takes place in clean, pleasant, and comfortable office settings. Many personnel, training, and labor relations specialists and managers work a standard 35- to 40-hour week. However, longer hours might be necessary for some workers—for example, labor relations specialists and managers—when contract agreements are being prepared and negotiated.

Although most personnel, training, and labor relations specialists and managers work in the office, some travel extensively. For example, recruiters regularly attend professional meetings and visit college campuses to interview prospective employees.

Employment

Personnel, training, and labor relations specialists and managers held about 513,000 jobs in 1994. They were employed in virtually every industry. Specialists accounted for 3 out of 5 positions; managers, 2 out of 5. About 9,000—mostly specialists—were self-employed, working as consultants to public and private employers.

The private sector accounted for about 85 percent of salaried jobs. Among these salaried jobs, services industries—including business, health, social, management, and educational services—accounted for 4 out of 10 jobs; labor organizations—the largest employer among specific industries—accounted for 1 out of 10. Manufacturing industries accounted for 2 out of 10 jobs, while finance, insurance, and real estate firms accounted for about 1 out of 10.

Federal, State, and local governments employed about 15 percent of salaried personnel, training, and labor relations specialists and managers. They handled the recruitment, interviewing, job classification, training, salary administration, benefits, employee relations, and related matters of the Nation's public employees.

Training, Other Qualifications, and Advancement

Because of the diversity of duties and level of responsibility, the educational backgrounds of personnel, training, and labor relations specialists and managers vary considerably. In filling entry-level jobs, firms generally seek college graduates. Some employers prefer applicants who have majored in human resources, personnel administration, or industrial and labor relations, while others look for college graduates with a technical or business background. Still others feel that a well-rounded liberal arts education is best.

Many colleges and universities have programs leading to a degree in personnel, human resources, or labor relations. Some offer degree programs in personnel administration or human resources management, training and development, or compensation and benefits. Depending on the school, courses leading to a career in human resources management may be found in departments of business administration, education, instructional technology, organizational development, human services, communication, or public administration, or within a separate human resources institution or department.

Because an interdisciplinary background is appropriate for work in this area, a combination of courses in the social sciences, business, and behavioral sciences is useful. Some jobs may require a background in engineering, science, finance, or law. Most prospective personnel specialists should take courses in compensation, recruitment, training and development, and performance appraisal, as well as courses in principles of management, organizational structure, and industrial psychology. Other relevant courses include business administration, public administration, psychology, sociology, political science, economics, and statistics. Courses in labor law, collective bargaining, labor economics, labor history, and industrial psychology also provide a valuable background for the prospective labor relations specialist. Knowledge of computers and information systems is important for some jobs.

An advanced degree is increasingly important for some jobs. Many labor relations jobs require graduate study in industrial or labor relations. A law degree seldom is required for entry-level jobs, but many people responsible for contract negotiations are lawyers, and a combination of industrial relations courses and law is highly desirable. A background in law is also desirable for employee benefits managers and others who must interpret the growing number of laws and regulations. A degree in dispute resolution provides an excellent background for mediators, arbitrators, and related personnel. A master's degree in personnel, training, or labor relations, or in business administration with a concentration in human resources management is desirable for those seeking general and top management positions.

For many specialized jobs in this field, previous experience is an asset; for managerial positions, it is essential. Many employers prefer entry-level workers who have gained some experience through an internship or work-study program while in school. Personnel administration and human resources development require the ability to work with individuals as well as a commitment to organizational goals. This field also demands other skills that people may develop elsewhere—computer usage, selling, teaching, supervising, and volunteering, among others. This field offers clerical workers opportunities for advancement to professional positions. Responsible positions sometimes are filled by experienced individuals from other fields, including business, government, education, social services administration, and the military.

Personnel, training, and labor relations specialists and managers should speak and write effectively. The growing diversity of the workforce demands the ability to work with or supervise people with various cultural backgrounds, levels of education, and experience. Personnel, training, and labor relations specialists and managers must be patient to cope with conflicting points of view and be able to handle the unexpected and the unusual. The ability to function under pressure is essential. Integrity, fair-mindedness, and a persuasive, congenial personality are also important qualities.

Entry-level workers often enter formal or on-the-job training programs, in which they learn how to classify jobs, interview applicants, or administer employee benefits. Next, they are assigned to specific areas in the personnel department to gain experience. Later, they may advance to a managerial position, overseeing a major element of the personnel program—compensation or training, for example.

Exceptional personnel, training, and labor relations workers may be promoted to director of personnel or industrial relations, which can eventually lead to a top managerial or executive position. Others may join a consulting firm or open their own business. A Ph.D. is an asset for teaching, writing, or consulting work.

Though not widespread, some organizations offer certification examinations to members who meet certain education and experience requirements. Certification is a sign of competence and can enhance one's advancement opportunities. (Several of these organizations are listed under sources of additional information.)

Job Outlook

The number of personnel, training, and labor relations specialists and managers is expected to grow faster than the average for all occupations through the year 2005. As in other occupations, job growth among specialists is projected to outpace job growth among managers. In addition, many job openings will result from the need to replace workers who leave this occupation to transfer to other jobs, retire, or for other reasons. However, the job market is likely to remain competitive in view of the abundant supply of qualified college graduates and experienced workers.

Most new jobs for personnel, training, and labor relations specialists and managers will be in the private sector as employers, increasingly concerned about productivity and quality of work, devote greater resources to job-specific training programs in response to the growing complexity of many jobs, the aging of the work force, and technological advances that can leave employees with obsolete skills. In addition, legislation and court rulings setting standards in occupational safety and health, equal employment opportunity, wages, and health, pension, family leave, and other benefits will increase demand for experts in these areas. Rising health care costs, in particular, should spur demand for specialists to develop creative compensation and benefits packages that firms can offer prospective employees. Employment of labor relations staff, including arbitrators and mediators, should grow as firms become more involved in labor relations, and attempt to resolve potentially costly labor-management disputes out of court. Increasing demand for international human resources managers and human resources information systems specialists may spur additional job growth.

Employment demand should be strong in management and consulting firms as well as personnel supply firms as businesses increasingly contract out personnel functions or hire personnel specialists on a contractual basis to meet the increasing cost and complexity of training and development programs. Demand should also increase in firms that develop and administer the increasingly complex employee benefits and compensation packages for other organizations.

Demand for personnel, training, and labor relations specialists and managers also is governed by the staffing needs of the firms where they work. A rapidly expanding business is likely to hire additional personnel workers—either as permanent employees or consultants—while a business that has experienced a merger or a reduction in its work force will require fewer personnel workers. Also, as human resources management becomes increasingly important to the success of an organization, some small and medium-size businesses that do not have a human resources department may employ workers to perform human resources duties on a part-time basis while maintaining other unrelated responsibilities within the company. In any particular firm, the size and the job duties of the human resources staff are determined by a variety of factors, including the firm's organizational philosophy and goals, the labor intensity and skill profile of the industry, the pace of technological change, government regulations, collective bargaining agreements, standards of professional practice, and labor market conditions.

Factors that could limit job growth include the widespread use of computerized human resources information systems that make workers more productive. Similar to other workers, employment of personnel, training, and labor relations specialists and managers, particularly in larger firms, may be adversely affected by corporate downsizing and restructuring.

Earnings

According to a salary survey conducted by the National Association of Colleges and Employers, bachelor's degree candidates majoring in human resources, including labor relations, received starting offers averaging $25,800 a year in 1995; master's degree candidates, $38,700.

According to a 1994 survey of compensation in the human resources field, conducted by Abbott, Langer, and Associates of Crete,

Illinois, the median total cash compensation for selected personnel and labor relations occupations were:

Regional human resources directors	$98,900
Industrial/labor relations directors	79,500
Compensation and benefits directors	75,300
Benefits directors	74,300
Employee/community relations directors	68,000
Training directors	64,400
Plant/location personnel managers	57,200
Recruitment and interviewing managers	55,000
Training generalists	54,600
Compensation and benefits supervisors	47,000
Benefits supervisors	45,900
Classroom instructors	45,900
Training material development specialists	42,000
E.E.O./affirmative action specialists	42,000
Employment interviewing supervisors	40,600
Employee/plant nurses	40,300
Safety specialists	39,400
Employee assistance/employee counseling specialists	39,100
Job evaluation specialists	37,900
Human resources information systems specialists	35,900
Employee services/employee recreation specialists	35,200
Benefits specialists	32,000
Personnel records specialists	26,600

According to a survey of workplaces in 160 metropolitan areas, personnel specialists with limited experience had median earnings of $25,000 a year in 1993. The middle half earned between $22,700 and $28,600 a year. Personnel supervisors/managers with limited experience had median earnings of $52,800 a year. The middle half earned between $46,300 and $58,600 a year.

In the Federal Government in 1995, persons with a bachelor's degree or 3 years' general experience in the personnel field generally started at $18,700 a year. Those with a superior academic record or an additional year of specialized experience started at $23,200 a year. Those with a master's degree may start at $28,300, and those with a doctorate in a personnel field started at $34,300. Beginning salaries were slightly higher in areas where the prevailing local pay level was higher. There are no formal entry-level requirements for managerial positions. Applicants must possess a suitable combination of educational attainment, experience, and record of accomplishment.

Labor relations specialists in the Federal Government averaged $54,000 a year in 1995; personnel managers, $52,100; equal employment opportunity specialists, $50,800; position classification specialists, $48,300; and personnel staffing specialists, $46,000.

Related Occupations

All personnel, training, and labor relations occupations are closely related. Other workers with skills and expertise in interpersonal relations include employment, rehabilitation, and college career planning and placement counselors; lawyers; psychologists; sociologists; social workers; public relations specialists; and teachers. These occupations are described elsewhere in the *Handbook*.

Sources of Additional Information

For information about careers in employee training and development, contact:

☛American Society for Training and Development, 1640 King St., Box 1443, Alexandria, VA 22313.

For information about careers and certification in employee compensation and benefits, contact:

☛American Compensation Association, 14040 Northsight Blvd., Scottsdale, AZ 85260.

Information about careers and certification in employee benefits is available from:

☛International Foundation of Employee Benefit Plans, 18700 W. Bluemound Rd., Brookfield, WI 53045.

For information about careers in arbitration and other aspects of dispute resolution, contact:

☛American Arbitration Association, 140 West 51st St., New York, NY 10020.

For information about academic programs in industrial relations, write to:

☛Industrial Relations Research Association, University of Wisconsin, 7226 Social Science Bldg., 1180 Observatory Dr., Madison, WI 53706.

Information about personnel careers in the health care industry is available from:

☛American Society for Healthcare Human Resources Administration, One North Franklin, 31st Floor, Chicago, IL 60606.

For information about personnel and labor relations careers in government, contact:

☛International Association of Personnel in Employment Security, 1801 Louisville Rd., Frankfort, KY 40601.

Property and Real Estate Managers

(D.O.T. 186.117-042, -046, -058, and -062, .167-018, -030, -038, -042, -046, -062, -066, and -090; 187.167-190; 191.117-046 and -050)

Nature of the Work

Many people own real estate in the form of a home, but, to businesses and investors, commercial real estate is a source of income and profits rather than simply a place for shelter. For them, real estate—including land and structures such as office buildings, shopping centers, and apartment complexes—is a valuable asset that can produce income and appreciate in value over time if well managed. Real estate can be a source of income when it is leased to others, and a substantial business expense when it is leased from others. For this reason, property and real estate managers perform an important function in increasing and maintaining the value of real estate investments for investors. Property managers oversee the performance of income-producing commercial and residential properties and manage the communal property and services of condominium and community associations. Real estate managers, also called real estate asset managers, plan and direct the purchase, development, and disposition of real estate for businesses and are usually employed by a sole owner, large corporation, bank, pension fund, or investment group. These managers are becoming increasingly involved in long-term strategic financial planning rather than the day-to-day operations of the property.

Most property and real estate managers work in the field of property management. When owners of apartments, office buildings, or retail and industrial properties lack the time or expertise to assume the day-to-day management of their real estate investments, they often hire a property manager, or contract for services with a real estate management company. Most property managers handle several properties simultaneously. Property managers act as the owners' agent and adviser for the property. They market vacant space to prospective tenants, through the use of a leasing agent, advertising, or by other means, and establish rental rates in accordance with prevailing local conditions. They negotiate and prepare lease or rental agreements with tenants and collect their rent payments and other fees. Property managers also handle the financial operations of the property. They see to it that rents are received and make sure that mortgages, taxes, insurance premiums, payroll, and maintenance bills are paid on time. They also supervise the preparation of financial statements and periodically report to the owners on the status of the property, occupancy rates, dates of lease expirations, and other matters.

Property managers negotiate contracts for janitorial, security, groundskeeping, trash removal, and other services. When contracts are awarded competitively, managers must solicit bids from several contractors and recommend to the owners which bid to accept. They monitor the performance of the contractors, and investigate and resolve complaints from residents and tenants. Managers also purchase all supplies and equipment needed for the property, and make arrangements with specialists for any repairs that cannot be handled by the regular property maintenance staff.

Property managers hire and direct the maintenance and on-site management personnel. At smaller properties, the property manager might employ only a building engineer who maintains the building's heating, ventilation, and air-conditioning systems and performs other routine maintenance and repair. Larger properties require a sizable maintenance staff supervised by a full-time on-site manager, who works under the direction of the property manager. Building managers have similar duties and responsibilities to property managers, except they are responsible for one site only.

Although some on-site managers oversee large office buildings or shopping centers, most manage apartments. They train, supervise, and assign duties to the maintenance staff as well as routinely inspect the grounds, facilities, and equipment to determine what repairs are needed. Occasionally, outside contractors are required, and the on-site manager may obtain bids for the work and submit them to the property manager. On-site managers schedule routine servicing of the heating, ventilation, and air-conditioning systems and ensure that the work of the maintenance staff and contract workers is up to standards or contract specifications. They keep records of expenditures incurred for operating the property and submit regular expense reports to the property manager or owners. They may recruit maintenance staff, interview job applicants, and make hiring recommendations to the property manager.

Property and on-site managers employed by condominium and homeowner associations—known as community association managers—must be particularly adept at dealing with people. Instead of tenants, they must deal on a daily basis with homeowners—members of the community association that employs the manager. Hired by the volunteer board of directors of the association, the community association manager administers its daily affairs and oversees the maintenance of property and facilities that the homeowners own and use jointly through the association. Smaller community associations usually cannot afford professional management, but managers of larger condominiums have many of the same responsibilities as the managers of large apartment complexes. Some homeowner associations encompass thousands of homes, and, in addition to administering the associations' financial records and budget, their managers may be responsible for the operation of community pools, golf courses, community centers, and the maintenance of landscaping, parking areas, and streets.

Tenant relations (in commercial properties) and resident relations (in residential properties) are an important part of the work of on-site managers, particularly apartment, condominium, and community association managers. On-site managers are responsible for enforcing rules and lease restrictions, such as pet restrictions or use of parking areas. Apartment and building managers handle requests for service or repairs and try to resolve complaints. They show vacant apartments or office space to prospective residents and explain the occupancy terms. Property managers must understand the provisions of legislation, such as the Americans With Disabilities Act and the Federal Fair Housing Amendment Act, and local fair housing laws to be sure they are not being discriminatory in the renting or advertising of apartments.

Some real estate managers are employed by businesses to locate, acquire, and develop real estate needed for their operations and to dispose of property no longer suited to their uses. These managers, sometimes referred to as corporate real estate managers, locate desirable sites for factories, retail stores, hotels and motels, and other business ventures and arrange to purchase or lease the property. They select a site based on their assessment of considerations such as property values, zoning, population growth, and traffic volume and patterns. They negotiate contracts for the purchase or lease of the property, securing the most beneficial terms for their company. Corporate real estate managers periodically review their company's real estate holdings, identifying properties that are no longer commercially attractive. They negotiate the sale or termination of the lease of properties selected for disposal.

Real estate managers who work for land development companies acquire land and plan the construction of shopping centers, houses and apartments, office buildings, or industrial parks. They negotiate with representatives of local government, other businesses, community and public interest groups, and public utilities to eliminate obstacles to the development of the land and to gain support for the planned project. It sometimes takes years to win approval for a project, and in the process managers may have to modify the plans for the project many times. Once they are free to proceed with a project, managers negotiate short-term loans to finance the construction of the project, and later negotiate long-term permanent mortgage loans. They then contract with architectural firms to draw up detailed plans, and with construction companies to build the project.

Working Conditions

Most property and real estate managers work in clean, modern, well-lighted offices, but many spend a major portion of their time away from their desks. Property managers frequently visit the properties they oversee, sometimes on a daily basis when contractors are doing major repair or renovation work. On-site managers may spend a large portion of their workday away from their office visiting the building engineer in the boiler room, checking up on the janitorial and maintenance staff, or investigating a problem reported by a tenant. Many real estate managers spend the majority of their time away from home, traveling to company real estate holdings or searching for properties that might be acquired.

Property managers often must attend meetings in the evening with property owners, community association boards of directors, or civic groups. Not surprisingly, many property and real estate managers put in long work weeks. Some apartment managers are required to live in the apartment complexes where they work so that they are available to handle any emergency that occurs while they are off duty. They usually receive compensatory time off, however, for working at night or on weekends. Many apartment managers receive time off during the week so that they are available on weekends to show apartments to prospective residents.

Employment

Property and real estate managers held about 261,000 jobs in 1994. Most worked for real estate operators and lessors or for property

Delegating responsibilities and communicating effectively are important to the success of property and real estate managers.

management firms. Others worked for real estate development companies, banks, government agencies that manage public buildings, and corporations with extensive holdings of commercial properties. Many were self-employed developers, apartment owner-managers, or owners of property management or full-service real estate firms that manage as well as sell real estate for clients.

Training, Other Qualifications, and Advancement

Most employers prefer to hire college graduates for property and real estate management positions. Degrees in business administration, finance, real estate, public administration, or related fields are preferred, but persons with degrees in the liberal arts are often accepted. Good speaking, writing, and financial skills, as well as an ability to deal tactfully with people, are essential. Most persons enter property and real estate management as on-site apartment or community association managers, or as assistants to property managers. Previous employment as a real estate agent may be an asset to apartment managers because it provides experience useful in showing apartments and dealing with people, as well as an understanding that an attractive, well-maintained property can command higher rental rates and result in lower turnover among residents. In the past, many persons with backgrounds in building maintenance have advanced to apartment manager positions on the strength of their knowledge of building mechanical systems, but this is becoming uncommon as employers are placing greater emphasis on administrative, financial, and communication abilities for managerial jobs.

On-site managers usually begin at smaller apartment complexes, condominiums, or community associations, or as an assistant manager at a large property or management company. As they acquire experience working under the direction of a property manager, they may advance to positions with greater responsibility at larger properties. Persons who excel as on-site managers often transfer to assistant property manager positions where they can acquire experience handling a broader range of property management responsibilities.

Although most persons who enter jobs as assistant property managers do so on the strength of on-site management experience, employers are increasingly hiring inexperienced college graduates with bachelor's or master's degrees in business administration, finance, or real estate for these jobs. Assistants work closely with a property manager and acquire experience performing a variety of management tasks, such as preparing the budget, analyzing insurance coverage and risk options, marketing the property to prospective tenants, and collecting overdue rent payments. In time, many assistants advance to property manager positions.

The responsibilities and compensation of property managers increase as they manage larger properties. Most property managers are responsible for several properties at a time, and as their careers advance they are gradually entrusted with properties that are larger or whose management is more complex. Many specialize in the management of one type of property, such as apartments, office buildings, condominiums, cooperatives, homeowner associations, or retail properties. Managers who excel at marketing properties to tenants may specialize in managing new properties, while those who are particularly knowledgeable about buildings and their mechanical systems might specialize in the management of older properties that require renovation or more frequent repairs. Some experienced property and real estate managers open their own property or real estate management firms.

Persons most commonly enter real estate manager jobs by transferring from positions as property managers or real estate brokers. Real estate managers must be good negotiators, adept at persuading and handling people, and good at analyzing data to assess the fair market value of property or its development potential. Resourcefulness and creativity in arranging financing are essential for managers who specialize in land development. Real estate managers may be required to hold a real estate broker's license.

Many property and real estate managers attend short-term formal training programs conducted by various professional and trade associations active in the real estate field. Employers send managers to these programs to improve their management skills and expand their knowledge of specialized subjects, such as the operation and maintenance of building mechanical systems, enhancing property values, insurance and risk management, personnel management, business and real estate law, resident/tenant relations, communications, and accounting and financial concepts. Managers also participate in these programs to prepare themselves for positions of greater responsibility in property and real estate management. Completion of these programs, together with meeting job experience standards and achieving a satisfactory score on a written examination, leads to certification, or the formal award of a professional designation, by the sponsoring association. In addition to these qualifications, some associations require their members to adhere to a specific code of ethics.

Managers of public housing subsidized by the Federal Government are required to be certified, but many property and real estate managers who work with all kinds of property choose to earn a professional designation voluntarily because it represents formal industry recognition of their achievements and status in the occupation. A number of organizations offer such programs. The Institute of Real Estate Management awards the designations Accredited Residential Manager and Certified Property Manager, while the National Association of Home Builders awards the designation Registered Apartment Manager. The National Apartment Association confers the designations Certified Apartment Manager and Certified Apartment Property Supervisor. The Community Associations Institute bestows the designation Professional Community Association Manager and Association Management Specialist, while the Building Owners and Managers Institute International awards the designations Real Property Administrator and Facilities Management Administrator.

Job Outlook

Employment of property and real estate managers is projected to increase as fast as the average for all occupations through the year 2005. In addition to rising demand for these workers, many job openings are expected to occur as property managers transfer to other occupations or leave the labor force. Opportunities should be best for persons with college degrees in business administration and related fields, as well as those who attain professional designations.

Growth in the demand for office buildings and retail establishments will spur employment of property and real estate managers. The projected expansion in wholesale and retail trade; finance, insurance, and real estate; and services industries is expected to require growth in the Nation's supply of office and retail space. Some additional growth will come from adding on to existing buildings. However, growth will be tempered by downsizing and consolidation, as well as by the leftover office space created during the building boom of the 1980s. Although some of these additions will be handled by the property manager already on the site, other additions will require the hiring of additional property managers. More complex responsibilities combined with larger facilities may lead to the hiring of more property managers per building.

In addition, the expected faster than average employment growth in some retail trade industries should require greater numbers of real estate managers to acquire and develop properties for expanding restaurant, food, apparel, and specialized merchandise chains.

Growth in the Nation's stock of apartments and houses also should require more property and real estate managers. Although the rate of new household formation is expected to slow somewhat over the 1994-2005 period, the high cost of purchasing a home is expected to force an increasing proportion of individuals to delay leaving rental housing. In addition, developments of new homes are increasingly being organized with community or homeowner associations that provide community services and oversee jointly owned common areas, requiring professional management. To help properties become more profitable, more commercial and multi-unit residential property owners are expected to place their investments in the hands of professional managers.

Growth in demand should also arise as a result of the changing demographic composition of the population. The number of older people will increase during the projection period, creating a need for various types of suitable housing, such as assisted living arrangements and retirement communities. Accordingly, there will be a need for property managers to operate these facilities, especially those who have a background in the operation and administrative aspects of running a health unit.

Earnings
Median earnings of all property and real estate managers were $22,600 a year in 1994. The middle 50 percent earned between $15,300 and $35,100. Ten percent earned less than $10,200 and 10 percent earned more than $52,500 annually.

Community association managers received compensation comparable to on-site and property managers employed by other types of properties. Many resident apartment managers receive the use of an apartment as part of their compensation package. Property and real estate managers often are given the use of a company automobile, and managers employed in land development often receive a small percentage of ownership in projects that they develop.

Related Occupations
Property and real estate managers plan, organize, staff, and manage the real estate operations of businesses. Workers who perform similar functions in other fields include restaurant and food service managers, hotel and resort managers and assistants, health services managers, education administrators, and city managers.

Sources of Additional Information
General information about careers in property and real estate management and programs leading to the award of a professional designation in the field is available from:

☛Building Owners and Managers Association International, 1201 New York Ave. NW., Suite 300, Washington, DC 20005.

☛Building Owners and Managers Institute International, 1521 Ritchie Hwy., Arnold, MD 21012.

☛Community Associations Institute, 1630 Duke St., Alexandria, VA 22314.

☛Institute of Real Estate Management, 430 N. Michigan Ave., Chicago, IL 60611.

☛National Apartment Association, 1111 14th St. NW., Suite 900, Washington, DC 20005.

☛National Association of Home Builders, 1201 15th St. NW., Washington, DC 20005.

☛International Association of Corporate Real Estate Executives, 440 Columbia Dr., Suite 100, West Palm Beach, FL 33409.

Purchasers and Buyers

(D.O.T. 162.117-018, .157-018, -022, -030, -034, and -038, .167-022, and -030; 163.117-010; 169.167-054; 184.117-078; and 185.167-034)

Nature of the Work
Purchasers and buyers seek to obtain the highest quality merchandise at the lowest possible price for their employers. In general, purchasers buy goods and services for the use of their company or organization and buyers buy items for resale. They determine which commodities or services are best, choose the suppliers of the product or service, negotiate the lowest price, and award contracts that ensure that the correct amount of the product or service is received at the appropriate time. In order to accomplish these tasks successfully, purchasers and buyers study sales records and inventory levels of current stock, identify foreign and domestic suppliers, and keep abreast of changes affecting both the supply of and demand for products and materials for which they are responsible.

Purchasers and buyers evaluate and select suppliers based upon price, quality, availability, reliability, and selection. They review listings in catalogs, industry periodicals, directories, and trade journals, research the reputation and history of the suppliers, and advertise anticipated purchase actions in order to solicit bids from suppliers. Meetings, trade shows, conferences, and visits to suppliers' plants and distribution centers also provide opportunities for purchasers and buyers to examine products, assess a supplier's production and distribution capabilities, as well as discuss other technical and business considerations that bear on the purchase. Specific job duties and responsibilities vary with the type of commodities or services to be purchased and the employer.

Purchasing professionals who are employed by government agencies or manufacturing firms are usually called purchasing directors, managers, or agents; industrial buyers; or contract specialists. These workers acquire product materials, intermediate goods, machines, supplies, and other materials used in the production of a final product. Some purchasing managers who work in the industrial sector and specialize in negotiating and supervising supply contracts are called contract specialists or supply managers. Purchasing agents and managers obtain items ranging from raw materials, fabricated parts, machinery, and office supplies to construction services and airline tickets. The flow of work—or even the entire production process—can be slowed or halted if the right materials, supplies, or equipment are not on hand when needed. In order to be effective, purchasers and buyers must have a working technical knowledge of the goods or services to be purchased.

In large industrial organizations, a distinction is often drawn between the work of a buyer or purchasing agent and that of a purchasing manager. Purchasing agents and buyers typically focus on routine purchasing tasks, often specializing in a commodity or group of related commodities—for example, steel, lumber, cotton, fabricated metal products, or petroleum products. This usually requires the purchaser to track such things as market conditions, price trends, or futures markets. Purchasing managers usually handle the more complex or critical purchases and may supervise a group of purchasing agents handling other goods and services. Whether a person is titled purchasing agent, buyer, or manager depends more on specific industry and employer practices than on specific job duties.

Changing business practices have altered the traditional roles of purchasing professionals. Manufacturing companies have begun to recognize the importance of purchasing professionals and increasingly involve them at most stages of product development. Their ability to forecast a part's or material's cost, availability, and suitability for its intended purpose can affect the entire product design. For example, potential problems with the supply of materials may be avoided by consulting the purchasing department in the early stages of product design.

In addition, there is a trend toward limited-source, long-term contracting. These contracts increase the importance of supplier selection because agreements are larger in scope and longer in duration. A major responsibility of most purchasers is to work out problems that may occur with a supplier because the success of the relationship directly affects the buying firm's performance.

Increasingly, purchasing professionals work closely with other employees in their own organization when deciding on purchases, an arrangement sometimes called team buying. For example, they may discuss the design of custom-made products with company design engineers, quality problems in purchased goods with quality assurance engineers and production supervisors, or shipment problems with managers in the receiving department before submitting an order.

Contract specialists in the Federal Government typically use sealed bids, but sometimes use negotiated agreements for complex items. Government purchasing agents and managers must follow strict laws and regulations in their work. These legal requirements are occasionally changed, so agents and contract specialists must stay informed about the latest regulations and their applications.

Other professionals, who buy finished goods for resale, are employed by wholesale and retail establishments where they are commonly referred to as "buyers" or "merchandise managers." Wholesale and retail buyers are an integral part of a complex system of distribution and merchandising that caters to the vast array of consumer needs and desires. Wholesale buyers purchase goods directly from manufacturers or from other wholesale firms for resale to retail firms, commercial establishments, institutions, and other organizations. In retail firms, buyers purchase goods from wholesale firms or directly from manufacturers for resale to the public. Buyers largely determine which products their establishment will sell. Therefore, it is essential that they have the ability to accurately predict what will appeal to consumers. They must constantly stay informed of the latest fashions and trends because failure to do so could jeopardize profits and the reputation of their company. Buyers also follow ads in newspapers and other media to check competitors' sales activities and watch general economic conditions to anticipate consumer buying patterns. Buyers working for large and medium-sized firms usually specialize in acquiring one or two lines of merchandise, whereas buyers working for small stores may purchase their complete inventory.

The use of private-label merchandise and the consolidation of buying departments have increased the responsibilities of retail buyers. Private-label merchandise, produced for a particular retailer, requires buyers to work closely with vendors to develop and obtain the desired product. The downsizing and consolidation of buying departments is also increasing the demands placed on buyers because, although the amount of work remains unchanged, there are fewer people needed to accomplish it. The result is an increase in the workloads and levels of responsibility.

Many merchandise managers assist in the planning and implementation of sales promotion programs. Working with merchandising executives, they determine the nature of the sale and purchase accordingly. They also work with advertising personnel to create the ad campaign. For example, they may determine the media in which the advertisement will be placed—newspapers, direct mail, television, or some combination of these. In addition, merchandising managers often visit the selling floor to ensure that the goods are properly displayed. Often, assistant buyers are responsible for placing orders and checking shipments.

Computers are having a major effect on the jobs of purchasers and buyers. In manufacturing and service industries, computers handle most of the more routine tasks—enabling purchasing professionals

Computers allow purchasers and buyers easy access to current product, sales, and inventory information.

to concentrate mainly on the analytical aspects of the job. Computers are used to obtain up-to-date product and price listings, to track inventory levels, process routine orders, and help determine when to make purchases. Computers also maintain bidders' lists, record the history of supplier performance, and issue purchase orders.

Computerized systems have dramatically simplified many of the routine buying functions and improved efficiency in determining which products are selling. For example, cash registers connected to computers, known as point-of-sale terminals, allow organizations to maintain centralized, up-to-date sales and inventory records. This information can then be used to produce weekly sales reports that reflect the types of products in demand. As well as monitoring their company's sales, buyers use computers to gain instant access to the specifications for thousands of commodities, inventory records, and their customers' purchase records. Some firms are linked with manufacturers or wholesalers by electronic purchasing systems. These systems speed selection and ordering and provide information on availability and shipment, allowing buyers to better concentrate on the selection of goods and suppliers.

Working Conditions

Most purchasers and buyers work in comfortable, well-lighted offices at stores, corporate headquarters, or production facilities. They frequently work more than a 40-hour week because of special sales, conferences, or production deadlines. Evening and weekend work is common. For those working in retail trade, this is especially true prior to holiday seasons. Consequently, many retail firms discourage the use of vacation time from late November until early January.

Buyers and merchandise managers often work under great pressure since wholesale and retail stores are so competitive; buyers need physical stamina to keep up with the fast-paced nature of their work.

Traveling is usually required and many purchasers and buyers spend at least several days a month on the road. High-fashion buyers and purchasers for worldwide manufacturing companies often travel outside the United States.

Employment

Purchasers and buyers held about 621,000 jobs in 1994. Purchasing agents and purchasing managers each accounted for slightly more than one-third of the total while buyers accounted for the remainder. Almost all worked full time.

About one-half of all buyers and purchasers worked in wholesale and retail trade establishments such as grocery or department stores. One-fourth worked in manufacturing.

Training, Other Qualifications, and Advancement.

Qualified persons usually begin as trainees, purchasing clerks, expediters, junior buyers, or assistant buyers. Retail and wholesale firms prefer to hire applicants who are familiar with the merchandise they sell as well as with wholesaling and retailing practices. Some retail firms promote qualified employees to assistant buyer positions; others recruit and train college graduates as assistant buyers. Most employers use a combination of methods.

Educational requirements tend to vary with the size of the organization. Large stores and distributors, especially those in wholesale and retail trade, prefer applicants who have completed a bachelor's degree program that focused on business related curriculum. Many manufacturing firms desire applicants with a bachelor's or master's degree in business, economics, or technical training such as engineering or one of the applied sciences and tend to put a greater emphasis on formal training. Regardless of academic preparation, new employees must learn the specifics of their employers' business.

Although training periods vary in length, most last several years. In wholesale and retail establishments, most trainees begin by selling merchandise, supervising sales workers, checking invoices on material received, and keeping track of stock on hand, although widespread use of computers has simplified some of these tasks. As they progress, retail trainees are given more buying-related responsibilities. In manufacturing, new purchasing employees are often enrolled in company training programs and spend a considerable amount of time learning about company operations and purchasing practices. They work with experienced purchasers to learn about commodities, prices, suppliers, and markets. In addition, they may be assigned to production planning to learn about the material requirements system and the inventory system.

Persons who wish to become wholesale or retail buyers should be good at planning and decision making and have an interest in merchandising. Anticipating consumer preferences and ensuring that goods are in stock when they are needed require resourcefulness, good judgment, and self-confidence. Buyers must be able to make decisions quickly and take risks. Marketing skills and the ability to identify products that will sell are also very important. Employers often look for leadership ability and communication skills because buyers spend a large portion of their time supervising assistant buyers and dealing with manufacturers' representatives and store executives.

Purchasing professionals must be able to analyze the technical data in suppliers' proposals, make buying decisions, and spend large amounts of money responsibly. The job requires the ability to work independently as well as a part of a team. In addition, these workers must be able to get along well with people to balance the needs of departments within the organization with budgetary constraints. They may consult with lawyers, engineers, and scientists when involved in complex procurements.

Experienced buyers may advance by moving to a department that manages a larger volume or by becoming a merchandise manager. Others may go to work in sales for a manufacturer.

An experienced purchasing agent or buyer may become an assistant purchasing manager in charge of a group of purchasing professionals before advancing to purchasing manager, supply manager, or director of materials management. At the top levels, duties may overlap into other management functions such as production, planning, and marketing.

In high technology manufacturing firms, continuing education is essential for advancement. Many purchasers participate in seminars offered by professional societies and take college courses in purchasing. Although no national standard exists, professional certification is becoming increasingly important.

In private industry, the recognized marks of experience and professional competence are the designations Certified Purchasing Manager (CPM), conferred by the National Association of Purchasing Management and Certified Purchasing Professional (CPP) and Certified Purchasing Executive (CPE), conferred by the American Purchasing Society upon candidates who pass examinations and meet specified educational, experience, and related requirements. In Federal, State, and local government, the indications of professional competence are the designations Certified Professional Public Buyer (CPPB) and Certified Public Purchasing Officer (CPPO), conferred by the National Institute of Governmental Purchasing, Inc. The CPPB is earned by passing a two-part written examination and meeting certain experience requirements. To earn the CPPO, a candidate must have additional purchasing and supervisory or management experience, pass a three-part written exam, and undergo an oral interview assessment.

As more materials purchasing is conducted on a long-term basis, both private and public purchasing professionals are specializing in the contractual aspects of purchasing. The National Contract Management Association confers the designations Certified Associate Contract Manager (CACM) or Certified Professional Contract Manager (CPCM). Candidates for these certifications must have related work experience, complete academic course-work, and pass written exams. These designations primarily apply to contract managers in the Federal Government and its suppliers.

Job Outlook

Employment of purchasers and buyers is expected to increase more slowly than the average for all occupations through the year 2005. Demand for these workers will not keep pace with the rising level of economic activity because the increasing use of computers has allowed much of the paperwork typically involved in ordering and procuring supplies to be done away with, reducing the demand for lower-level buyers who traditionally performed these duties. Also, limited sourcing and long-term contracting have allowed companies to negotiate with fewer suppliers less frequently. Another industry-wide trend is the increased use of credit cards by some employees to purchase supplies without using the services of the procurement or purchasing office.

In retail trade, mergers and acquisitions have forced the consolidation of buying departments, eliminating jobs. In addition, larger retail stores are removing their buying departments from geographic markets and centralizing them at their headquarters, eliminating more jobs.

The Federal Acquisition Streamlining Act of 1994 will restrict demand of purchasing agents within the Federal Government because it requires certain purchases under a mandated dollar value to be made electronically.

Consequently, most job openings will result from the need to replace workers who transfer to other occupations or leave the labor force.

Persons who have a bachelor's degree in business should have the best chance of obtaining a buyer job in wholesale or retail trade or within government. A master's degree or bachelor's degree in a technical field will be an advantage for those interested in working for a manufacturing or industrial company

Earnings

Median annual earnings of purchasers and buyers were $31,700 in 1994. The middle 50 percent earned between $24,100 and $43,000. The lowest 10 percent averaged less than $18,500 while the top 10 percent earned more than $57,400. Merchandise managers and purchasing managers generally earned higher salaries than buyers or agents. As a general rule, those with the most education in their field have the highest incomes.

The average annual salaries for purchasing agents and contract specialists in the Federal Government in 1995 were about $26,579 and $47,885, respectively.

Purchasers and buyers receive the same benefits package as their coworkers, frequently including vacations, sick leave, life and health insurance, and pension plans. In addition to standard benefits, retail buyers often earn cash bonuses based on their performance and may receive discounts on merchandise bought from the employer.

Related Occupations

Workers in other occupations who need a knowledge of marketing and the ability to assess demand are retail sales workers, sales managers, comparison shoppers, manufacturers' and wholesale sales representatives, insurance sales agents, services sales representatives, procurement services managers, and traffic managers.

Sources of Additional Information

Further information about careers in purchasing and certification is available from:

☛American Purchasing Society, 11910 Oak Trail Way, Port Richey, FL 34668.

☛National Association of Purchasing Management, Customer Service, 2055 East Centennial Circle, P.O. Box 22160, Tempe, AZ 85285.

☛National Institute of Governmental Purchasing, 11800 Sunrise Valley Dr., Suite 1050, Reston, VA 22091.

☛National Contract Management Association, 1912 Woodford Rd., Vienna, VA 22182.

Restaurant and Food Service Managers

(D.O.T. 185.137; 187.161-010 and .167-026, -106, -126, -206, and -210; 319.137-014, -018, and -030)

Nature of the Work

Food is consumed outside the home in a variety of settings. Eating places range from institutional cafeterias and fast food to elegant dining establishments. The cuisine, price, and setting where the meals are consumed vary, but managers of these dining facilities share many of the same responsibilities. Efficient and profitable operation of restaurants and institutional food service facilities requires managers and assistant managers to select and appropriately price menu items, use food and other supplies efficiently, and achieve consistent quality in food preparation and service. They also must attend to the various administrative aspects of the business, which includes recruiting, training, and supervising an adequate number of workers.

In most restaurants and institutional food service facilities, the manager is assisted by one or more assistant managers, depending on the size and operating hours of the establishment. In large establishments, as well as in many smaller ones, the management team consists of a *general manager*, one or more *assistant managers*, and an *executive chef*. The executive chef is responsible for the operation of the kitchen, while the assistant managers oversee service in the dining room and other areas of the operation. In smaller restaurants, the executive chef may be the general manager, and sometimes an owner. In fast-food restaurants and other food service facilities open for long hours or 7 days a week, the manager is aided by several assistant managers, each of whom supervises a shift of workers. (For additional information, see the *Handbook* statements on general managers and top executives and chefs, cooks, and other kitchen workers.)

Many restaurants rarely change their menu, while others make frequent alterations. Institutional food service facilities and some restaurants offer a new menu every day. Managers or executive chefs select menu items, taking into account the likely number of customers, and the past popularity of dishes. Other issues taken into consideration when planning a menu include food left over from prior meals that should not be wasted, the need for variety, and the availability of foods due to seasonality and other factors. Managers or executive chefs analyze the recipes of the dishes to determine food, labor, overhead costs and to assign prices to the various dishes. Menus must be developed far enough in advance that supplies can be ordered and received in time.

Ordering supplies and dealing with suppliers are important aspects of the work of restaurant and food service managers. On a daily basis, managers estimate food consumption, place orders with suppliers, and schedule the delivery of fresh food and beverages. They receive and check the content of deliveries, evaluating the quality of meats, poultry, fish, fruits, vegetables, and baked goods. Managers meet with the sales representatives from restaurant suppliers to place orders replenishing stocks of tableware, linens, paper, cleaning supplies, cooking utensils, and furniture and fixtures. They also arrange for equipment maintenance and repairs, and for a variety of services such as waste removal and pest control.

Managers interview, hire, and, when necessary, fire employees. They explain the establishment's policies and practices to newly hired workers and oversee their training. Managers schedule the work hours of employees, making sure there are enough workers present to cover peak dining periods.

Restaurant and food service managers supervise the kitchen and the dining room. They oversee food preparation and cooking, examining the quality and portion sizes to ensure that dishes are prepared and garnished correctly and in a timely manner. They also investigate and resolve customers' complaints about food quality or service. During busy periods, managers "roll up their sleeves" and help with the cooking, clearing of tables, or other tasks. They direct the cleaning of the kitchen and dining areas and the washing of tableware, kitchen utensils, and equipment to maintain company and government sanitation standards. They monitor the actions of their employees and patrons on a continual basis to ensure the health and safety standards and local liquor regulations are obeyed.

Managers have a variety of administrative responsibilities. In larger establishments, much of this work is delegated to a bookkeeper, but in others, managers must keep accurate records of the hours and wages of employees, prepare the payroll, and do paperwork to comply with licensing laws and reporting requirements of tax, wage and hour, unemployment compensation, and Social Security laws. They also maintain the records of supplies and equipment purchased, and ensure that accounts with suppliers are paid on a regular basis. In addition, managers record the number, type, and cost of items sold to exclude dishes that are unpopular or less profitable.

Many managers are able to ease the burden of record keeping and paperwork through the use of computers. Point-of-service-systems (POS) are used in many restaurants to increase employee productivity and allow managers to track the sales of specific menu items. Using a POS system, a server keys in the customer's order and the computer immediately sends the order to the kitchen so preparation can begin. The same system totals checks, acts as a cash register and credit card authorizer, and tracks daily sales. To minimize food costs and spoilage, many managers use inventory tracking software to compare the record of daily sales from the POS with a record of present inventory. In some establishments, when supplies needed for the preparation of popular menu items run low, additional inventory can be ordered directly from the supplier using the computer.

Managers are among the first to arrive and the last to leave. At the conclusion of each day, or sometimes each shift, managers tally the cash and charge receipts received and balance them against the record of sales. They are responsible for depositing the day's receipts at the bank, or securing it in a safe place. Managers are also responsible for locking up, checking that ovens, grills, and lights are off, and switching on alarm systems.

Working Conditions

Evenings and weekends are popular dining periods, making night and weekend work common. However, many managers of institutional

Managers select and appropriately price menu items so food and other supplies are used efficiently.

food service facilities work more conventional hours because factory and office cafeterias are generally open only on weekdays for breakfast and lunch. It is common for restaurant and food service managers to work 50 hours or more per week.

Managers often experience the pressure of simultaneously coordinating a wide range of activities. When problems occur, it is the responsibility of the manager to resolve them with minimal disruption to customers. The job can be hectic during peak dining hours, and dealing with irate customers or uncooperative employees can be stressful.

Employment

Restaurant and food service managers held about 526,500 jobs in 1994. Most worked in restaurants or for contract institutional food service companies, but a small number were also employed by educational institutions, hospitals, nursing and personal care facilities, and civic, social, and fraternal organizations. About two-fifths were self-employed. Jobs are located throughout the country, but are most plentiful in large cities and tourist areas.

Training, Other Qualifications, and Advancement

Many restaurant and food service manager positions are filled by promoting experienced food and beverage preparation and service workers. Waiters, waitresses, chefs, and fast-food workers who have demonstrated their potential for handling increased responsibility sometimes advance to assistant manager or management trainee jobs when openings occur. Executive chefs need extensive experience working as a chef, and general managers need experience working as assistant manager. However, most food service management companies and national or regional restaurant chains also recruit management trainees from 2- and 4-year college hospitality management programs. Food service and restaurant chains prefer to hire people with degrees in restaurant and institutional food service management, but they often hire graduates with degrees in other fields who have demonstrated interest and aptitude.

A bachelor's degree in restaurant and food service management provides a particularly strong preparation for a career in this occupation. In 1992, more than 160 colleges and universities offered 4-year programs in restaurant and hotel management or institutional food service management. For people not interested in pursing a 4-year degree, a good alternative is the more than 800 community and junior colleges, technical institutes, and other institutions that offer programs in these fields leading to an associate degree or other formal certification. Both 2 and 4-year programs provide instruction in subjects such as accounting, business law and management, food planning and preparation, and nutrition. Some programs combine classroom and laboratory study with internships that provide on-the-job experience. In addition, many educational institutions offer culinary programs that provide food preparation training which can lead to a career as a cook or chef and provide a foundation for advancement to an executive chef position.

Most employers emphasize personal qualities. Restaurant and food service management can be demanding, so good health and stamina are important. Self-discipline, initiative, and leadership ability are essential. Managers must be able to solve problems and concentrate on details. They need good communication skills to deal with customers and suppliers, as well as to motivate and direct their subordinates. A neat and clean appearance is a must because they are often in close personal contact with the public.

Most restaurant chains and food service management companies have rigorous training programs for their management positions. Through a combination of classroom and on-the-job training, trainees receive instruction and gain work experience in all aspects of the operations of a restaurant or institutional food service facility—food preparation, nutrition, sanitation, security, company policies and procedures, personnel management, record keeping, and preparation of reports. Usually after 6 months or a year, trainees receive their first permanent assignment as an assistant manager.

A measure of professional achievement for restaurant and food service managers is to earn the designation of certified Foodservice Management Professional (FMP). Although not a requirement for employment or advancement in the occupation, voluntary certification provides recognition of professional competence, particularly for managers who acquired their skills largely on the job. The Educational Foundation of the National Restaurant Association awards the FMP designation to managers who achieve a qualifying score on a written examination, complete a series of courses that cover a range of food service management topics, and who meet standards of work experience in the field.

Willingness to relocate often is essential for advancement to positions with greater responsibility. Managers advance to larger establishments, or regional management positions within restaurant chains. Some eventually open their own eating and drinking establishments. Others transfer to hotel management positions, because their restaurant management experience provides a good background for food and beverage manager jobs at hotels and resorts.

Job Outlook

Employment of restaurant and food service managers is expected to increase faster than the average for all occupations through the year 2005. In addition to growth in demand, the need to replace managers who transfer to other occupations or stop working will create many job openings. Job opportunities are expected to be best for people with bachelor's or associate degrees in restaurant and institutional food service management.

Employment growth is expected to vary by industry. Eating and drinking places will provide the most new jobs as the number of eating and drinking establishments increases and other industries continue to contract out their food services. Population growth, rising personal incomes, and increased leisure time will continue to produce growth in the number of meals consumed outside the home. To meet the demand for prepared food, more restaurants will be built, and more managers will be employed to supervise them. In addition, the number of manager jobs will increase in eating and drinking places as schools, hospitals, and other businesses contract out more of their food services to institutional food service companies located in the eating and drinking industry.

Employment of wage and salary managers in eating and drinking places is expected to increase more rapidly than self-employed managers. New restaurants are increasingly affiliated with national chains rather than being independently owned and operated. As this trend continues, fewer owners will manage restaurants themselves, and more restaurant managers will be employed to run the establishments.

Employment in eating and drinking establishments is not very sensitive to changes in economic conditions, so restaurant and food service managers are rarely laid off during hard times. However, competition among restaurants is always intense, and many restaurants do not survive.

Food service manager jobs are expected to increase in other industries, but growth will be slowed as contracting out becomes more common. Growth in the population of elderly people is expected to result in growth of food service manager jobs in nursing homes, residential care facilities, and other health care institutions.

Earnings

Median earnings for restaurant and food service managers were $421 a week in 1994. The middle 50 percent earned between about $295 and $599 a week. The lowest paid 10 percent earned $220 a week or less, while the highest paid 10 percent earned over $884 a week.

Earnings of restaurant and food service managers vary greatly according to their responsibilities and the type and size of establishment. Based on a survey conducted for the National Restaurant Association, the median base salary of managers in restaurants was estimated to be about $28,600 a year in 1994, but managers of the largest restaurants and institutional food service facilities often had annual salaries in excess of $45,000. Managers of fast-food restaurants had an estimated median base salary of $25,000 a year; managers of full-menu restaurants with table service, almost $30,000; and managers of commercial and institutional cafeterias, nearly $31,400 a year in 1994. Besides a salary, most managers received an annual bonus or incentive payment based on their performance. In 1994, most of these payments ranged between $2,000 and $8,000 a year.

Executive chefs had an estimated median base salary of about $37,000 a year in 1994, but those employed in the largest restaurants and institutional food service facilities often had base salaries over $43,000. Annual bonus or incentive payments of most executive chefs ranged between $1,500 and $6,000 a year.

The estimated median base salary of assistant managers was over $22,000 a year in 1994, but ranged from less than $19,000 in fast-food restaurants to over $25,000 in some of the largest restaurants and food service facilities. Annual bonus or incentive payments of most assistant managers ranged between $1,000 and $4,000 a year.

Manager trainees had an estimated median base salary of about $20,000 a year in 1994, but had salaries of nearly $30,000 in some of the largest restaurants and food service facilities. Annual bonus or incentive payments of most trainees ranged between $500 and $2,500 a year.

Most salaried restaurant and food service managers received free meals, sick leave, health and life insurance, 1 to 3 weeks of paid vacation a year, and the opportunity for additional training depending on their length of service.

Related Occupations
Restaurant and food service managers direct the activities of businesses which provide a service to customers. Other managers in service-oriented businesses include hotel managers and assistants, health services administrators, retail store managers, and bank managers.

Sources of Additional Information
Information about job opportunities may be obtained from local employers and local offices of the State employment service.

Information about a career as a restaurant and food service manager, 2- and 4-year college programs in restaurant and food service management, and certification as a Foodservice Management Professional is available from:
☛The Educational Foundation of the National Restaurant Association, Suite 1400, 250 South Wacker Dr., Chicago, IL 60606.

General information on hospitality careers may be obtained from:
☛Council on Hotel, Restaurant, and Institutional Education, 1200 17th St. NW., Washington, DC 20036-3097.

For general career information and a directory of accredited private trade and technical schools offering programs in restaurant and food service management, write to:
☛Accrediting Commission of Career Schools and Colleges of Technology, 2101 Wilson Blvd., Suite 302, Arlington, VA 22201.

Underwriters

(D.O.T. 169.267-046)

Nature of the Work
Insurance companies assume billions of dollars in risks each year by writing policies that transfer the risk of loss from their policyholders to themselves. Underwriters appraise and select the risks their company will insure. An insurance company may lose business to competitors if the underwriter appraises risks too conservatively, or it may have to pay more claims if the underwriting actions are too liberal.

Underwriters decide whether an applicant for insurance is an acceptable risk. They analyze information in insurance applications,

Underwriters should enjoy working with detail and analyzing information.

reports from loss control consultants, medical reports, and actuarial studies—reports that describe the probability of insured loss. They then decide whether to issue a policy and may outline the terms of the contract, including the amount of the premium. Underwriters sometimes correspond with policyholders, agents, and managers about policy cancellations or other matters. On rare occasions, they accompany sales representatives on appointments with prospective customers. (Life insurance agents and brokers are increasingly called "life underwriters;" they are included in the section on insurance agents and brokers elsewhere in the *Handbook*.)

Most underwriters specialize in one of three major categories of insurance: Life, property and casualty, or health. They further specialize in group or individual policies. Property and casualty underwriters specialize by type of risk insured, such as fire, homeowner, automobile, marine, property, or workers' compensation. In cases where casualty companies insure in a single "package" policy, covering various types of risks, the underwriter must be familiar with different lines of insurance. Some underwriters, called commercial account underwriters, handle business insurance exclusively. They often evaluate a firm's entire operation in appraising its application for insurance.

An increasing proportion of insurance sales, particularly in life and health insurance, are being made through group contracts. A standard group policy insures everyone in a specified group through a single contract at uniform premium rates. The group underwriter analyzes the overall composition of the group to ensure the total risk is not excessive. Another type of group policy provides members of a group—a labor union, for example—with individual policies reflecting their needs. These generally are casualty policies, such as those covering automobiles. The casualty underwriter analyzes the application of each group member and makes individual appraisals. Some group underwriters meet with union or employer representatives to discuss the types of policies available to their group.

Working Conditions
Underwriters have desk jobs that require no unusual physical activity. Their offices generally are comfortable and pleasant. Although some overtime may be required, underwriters generally work from 35 to 40 hours a week. They occasionally attend meetings away from home for several days. Construction and marine underwriters often travel to inspect work sites and assess risks.

Employment
Insurance underwriters held about 96,000 jobs in 1994. The following tabulation shows the percent distribution of wage and salary jobs by industry.

Total	100
Fire, marine, and casualty insurance carriers	38
Insurance agents, brokers, and service	31
Life insurance carriers	16
Pension funds and miscellaneous insurance carriers	4
Medical service and health insurance carriers	3
Other industries	8

The majority of underwriters worked for insurance companies, often called "carriers." Most of the remaining underwriters worked throughout the country in independent insurance agencies—firms which represent one or more insurance companies—and brokers—firms which may deal with any insurance company and represent the interests of the buyers of insurance, known as "insureds". A small number of underwriters worked for banks, mortgage companies, and real estate firms.

Office underwriters in the life insurance industry are most likely to work in an insurance company's home office. In some large general agencies, underwriters help life insurance agents, or "producers", determine if the risk will be accepted or rejected by the home office. However, most regional life insurance offices deal predominantly with sales, not underwriting. Property and casualty underwriters also work in home offices, but more work for agencies or regional branch offices, where they have the authority to underwrite risks and determine an appropriate rating without consulting the home office.

Training, Other Qualifications, and Advancement

For beginning underwriting jobs, most large insurance companies prefer college graduates who have a degree in business administration or finance, with courses or experience in accounting. However, a bachelor's degree in almost any field—plus courses in business law and accounting—provides a good general background and may be sufficient to qualify. Basic familiarity with computers is essential.

Beginners typically start as underwriter trainees or assistant underwriters. They may help collect information on applicants and evaluate routine applications under the supervision of an experienced risk analyst. Property and casualty trainees study claim files to become familiar with factors associated with certain types of losses. Many larger insurers offer a training program, lasting from a few months to a year, that combines study with work. As trainees develop the necessary judgment, they are assigned policy applications that are more complex and cover greater risks. These often require the use of computers for more efficient processing.

Continuing education is necessary for advancement. Insurance companies generally pay tuition for underwriting courses that their trainees successfully complete; some also offer salary incentives. Independent study programs for experienced property and casualty underwriters are also available. The American Institute for Chartered Property Casualty Underwriters awards the designations "Associate in Underwriting" (AU), and "Chartered Property Casualty Underwriter" (CPCU). To earn the AU designation, underwriters complete a series of courses and examinations; it usually takes about two years to earn the AU designation. Earning the more advanced CPCU designation generally takes about 5 years, and requires passing 10 examinations covering personal and commercial insurance, risk management insurance, business law, accounting, finance, management, economics, and ethics. Although CPCU's may be underwriters, the CPCU is intended for everyone working in any and all aspects of insurance. An AU designation is the first, formal step in developing a career in underwriting.

Underwriting can be a satisfying career for people who enjoy working with detail and analyzing information. In addition, underwriters must possess good judgment in order to make sound decisions. They must also be imaginative and aggressive, especially when they have to obtain information from outside sources.

Experienced underwriters who complete courses of study may advance to senior underwriter or underwriting manager. Some underwriting managers are promoted to senior managerial jobs. Others are attracted to the earnings potential of sales and obtain state licensing to sell insurance and insurance products as agents or brokers.

Job Outlook

Employment of underwriters is expected to increase more slowly than the average for all occupations through the year 2005. Most job openings are expected to result from the need to replace underwriters who transfer to other occupations or stop working altogether.

A number of factors underlie the continuing need for underwriters. Shifts in the age distribution of the population will result in an increase in the number of people who assume career and family responsibilities. People in this group have the greatest need for life and property and casualty insurance. In addition, expanding long-term healthcare and pension benefits for retirees—an increasing proportion of the population—will increase underwriting requirements. Growing concerns for financial security and liability should also contribute to demand for more insurance protection for homes, automobiles, pleasure craft, and other valuables. New or expanding businesses will need protection for new plants and equipment, product liability, and insurance for workers' compensation and employee benefits.

Employment of underwriters, however, is expected to increase more slowly than growth in demand for insurance. The trend toward self-insurance is expected to lower the demand for some property and casualty underwriters. Businesses that self-insure set a rate for their own company and pay premiums into a reserve fund. Additionally, many property and casualty companies are foregoing personal lines of insurance—especially automobile—and concentrating on commercial lines of business. The increased use of "intelligent" or "smart" underwriting software systems is also slowing the demand for new underwriters. These systems automatically analyze and rate insurance applications, then accept or deny the risk without human intervention.

Underwriters specializing in one particular area of insurance may find it difficult to transfer to another type of insurance if their jobs are threatened. Because insurance is usually regarded as a necessity, regardless of economic conditions, underwriters are unlikely to be laid off because of a recession.

Earnings

Median annual earnings of full-time wage and salaried underwriters in 1994 were about $30,800. The middle 50 percent earned between $22,000 and $40,500 a year. The lowest 10 percent earned less than $18,600; the top 10 percent, more than $54,800 a year.

Most insurance companies have liberal vacation policies and other employee benefits. Almost all insurance companies provide employer-financed group life and retirement plans.

Related Occupations

Underwriters make decisions on the basis of financial data. Other workers with the same type of responsibility include auditors, budget analysts, financial advisors, loan officers, credit managers, real estate appraisers, and risk managers.

Sources of Additional Information

General information about a career as an insurance underwriter is available from the home offices of many life insurance and property and liability insurance companies. Information about the insurance business in general and the underwriting function in particular also may be obtained from:

☛The American Institute for Chartered Property and Casualty Underwriters, 720 Providence Rd., P.O. Box 3016, Malvern, PA 19355-0716.

Professional Specialty Occupations

Engineers

Nature of the Work

Engineers apply the theories and principles of science and mathematics to the economical solution of practical technical problems. Usually their work is the link between a scientific discovery and its commercial application. Engineers design machinery, products, systems, and processes for efficient and economical performance. They design industrial machinery and equipment for manufacturing defense-related goods and weapons systems for the Armed Forces. They design, plan, and supervise the construction of buildings, highways, and rapid transit systems. They also design and develop systems for control and automation of manufacturing, business, and management processes.

Engineers consider many factors in developing a new product. For example, in developing an industrial robot, they determine precisely what function it needs to perform; design and test components; fit them together in an integrated plan; and evaluate the design's overall effectiveness, cost, reliability, and safety. This process applies to products as different as chemicals, computers, gas turbines, helicopters, and toys.

In addition to design and development, many engineers work in testing, production, or maintenance. They supervise production in factories, determine the causes of breakdowns, and test manufactured products to maintain quality. They also estimate the time and cost to complete projects. Some work in engineering management or in sales, where an engineering background enables them to discuss the technical aspects of a product and assist in planning its installation or use. (See the statements on engineering, science, and data processing managers and manufacturers' and wholesale sales representatives elsewhere in the *Handbook*.)

Most engineers specialize; more than 25 major specialties are recognized by professional societies, and within the major branches are numerous subdivisions. Structural, environmental, and transportation engineering, for example, are subdivisions of civil engineering. Engineers also may specialize in one industry, such as motor vehicles, or in one field of technology, such as propulsion or guidance systems.

This section, which contains an overall discussion of engineering, is followed by separate sections on 10 engineering branches: Aerospace; chemical; civil; electrical and electronics; industrial; mechanical; metallurgical, ceramic, and materials; mining; nuclear; and petroleum engineering. Branches of engineering not covered in detail here, but in which there are established college programs include: Architectural engineering—the design of a building's internal support structure; biomedical engineering—the application of engineering to medical and physiological problems; environmental engineering—a growing discipline involved with identifying, solving, and alleviating environmental problems; and marine engineering—the design and installation of ship machinery and propulsion systems.

Engineers in each branch have knowledge and training that can be applied to many fields. Electrical and electronics engineers, for example, work in the medical, computer, missile guidance, and power distribution fields. Because there are many separate problems to solve in a large engineering project, engineers in one field often work closely with specialists in other scientific, engineering, and business occupations.

Engineers often use computers to simulate and test how a machine, structure, or system operates. Many engineers also use computer-aided design systems to produce and analyze designs. They spend a great deal of time writing reports and consulting with other engineers, as complex projects often require an interdisciplinary team of engineers. Supervisory engineers are responsible for major components or entire projects.

Working Conditions

Many engineers work in laboratories, industrial plants, or at construction sites, where they inspect, supervise, or solve onsite problems. Others work in offices almost all of the time. Engineers in branches such as civil engineering may work outdoors part of the time. A few engineers travel extensively to plants or construction sites.

Many engineers work a standard 40-hour week. At times, deadlines or design standards may bring extra pressure to a job. When this happens, engineers may work long hours and experience considerable stress.

Employment

In 1994, engineers held 1,327,000 jobs. Chart 1 shows the employment of the engineering disciplines covered in this statement. Forty-seven percent of all engineering jobs were located in manufacturing

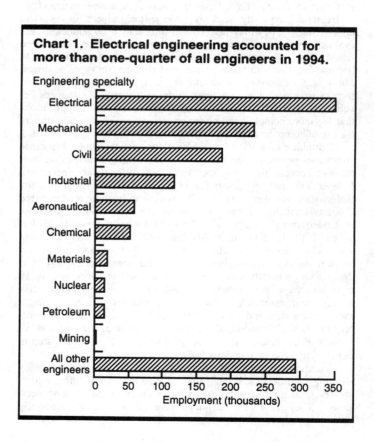

Chart 1. Electrical engineering accounted for more than one-quarter of all engineers in 1994.

industries—mostly in electrical and electronic equipment, industrial machinery, scientific instruments, aircraft and parts, motor vehicles, chemicals, guided missiles and space vehicles, fabricated metal products, and primary metals industries. In 1994, 684,000 jobs were in nonmanufacturing ndustries, primarily in engineering and architectural services, research and testing services, and business services, where firms designed construction projects or did other engineering work on a contract basis for organizations in other parts of the economy. Engineers also worked in the communications, utilities, and construction industries.

Federal, State, and local governments employed about 181,000 engineers. Over half of these were in the Federal Government, mainly in the Departments of Defense, Transportation, Agriculture, Interior, and Energy, and in the National Aeronautics and Space Administration. Most engineers in State and local government agencies worked in highway and public works departments. Some engineers are self-employed consultants.

Engineers are employed in every State, in small and large cities, and in rural areas. Some branches of engineering are concentrated in particular industries and geographic areas, as discussed in statements later in this chapter.

Training, Other Qualifications, and Advancement

A bachelor's degree in engineering from an accredited engineering program is usually required for beginning engineering jobs. College graduates with a degree in a physical science or mathematics may occasionally qualify for some engineering jobs, especially in engineering specialties in high demand. Most engineering degrees are granted in branches such as electrical, mechanical, or civil engineering. However, engineers trained in one branch may work in another. This flexibility allows employers to meet staffing needs in new technologies and specialties where engineers are in short supply. It also allows engineers to shift to fields with better employment prospects, or to ones that match their interests more closely.

In addition to the standard engineering degree, many colleges offer degrees in engineering technology, which are offered as either 2- or 4-year programs. These programs prepare students for practical design and production work rather than for jobs that require more theoretical, scientific and mathematical knowledge. Graduates of 4-year technology programs may get jobs similar to those obtained by graduates with a bachelor's degree in engineering. Some employers regard them as having skills between those of a technician and an engineer.

Graduate training is essential for engineering faculty positions but is not required for the majority of entry-level engineering jobs. Many engineers obtain graduate degrees in engineering or business administration to learn new technology, broaden their education, and enhance promotion opportunities; others obtain law degrees and become attorneys. Many high-level executives in government and industry began their careers as engineers.

About 340 colleges and universities offer a bachelor's degree in engineering, and nearly 300 colleges offer a bachelor's degree in engineering technology, although not all are accredited programs. Although most institutions offer programs in the larger branches of engineering, only a few offer some of the smaller specialties. Also, programs of the same title may vary in content. For example, some emphasize industrial practices, preparing students for a job in industry, while others are more theoretical and are better for students preparing to take graduate work. Therefore, students should investigate curricula and check accreditations carefully before selecting a college. Admissions requirements for undergraduate engineering schools include courses in advanced high school mathematics and the physical sciences.

Bachelor's degree programs in engineering are typically designed to last 4 years, but many students find that it takes between 4 and 5 years to complete their studies. In a typical 4-year college curriculum, the first 2 years are spent studying basic sciences (mathematics, physics, and chemistry), introductory engineering, and the humanities, social sciences, and English. In the last 2 years, most courses are in engineering, usually with a concentration in one branch. For example, the last 2 years of an aerospace program might include courses such as fluid mechanics, heat transfer, applied aerodynamics, analytical mechanics, flight vehicle design, trajectory dynamics, and aerospace propulsion systems. Some programs offer a general engineering curriculum; students then specialize in graduate school or on the job.

A few engineering schools and 2-year colleges have agreements whereby the 2-year college provides the initial engineering education and the engineering school automatically admits students for their last 2 years. In addition, a few engineering schools have arrangements whereby a student spends 3 years in a liberal arts college studying preengineering subjects and 2 years in the engineering school and receives a bachelor's degree from each. Some colleges and universities offer 5-year master's degree programs.

Some 5- or even 6-year cooperative plans combine classroom study and practical work, permitting students to gain valuable experience and finance part of their education.

All 50 States and the District of Columbia require registration for engineers whose work may affect life, health, or property, or who offer their services to the public. In 1994, between 250,000 and 300,000 engineers were registered. Registration generally requires a degree from an engineering program accredited by the Accreditation Board for Engineering and Technology, 4 years of relevant work experience, and passing a State examination. Some States will not register people with degrees in engineering technology. Engineers may be registered in several states.

Beginning engineering graduates usually do routine work under the supervision of experienced engineers and, in larger companies, may also receive formal classroom or seminar-type training. As they gain knowledge and experience, they are assigned more difficult tasks with greater independence to develop designs, solve problems, and make decisions. Engineers may become technical specialists or may supervise a staff or team of engineers and technicians. Some eventually become engineering managers or enter other managerial, management support, or sales jobs. (See the statements under executive, administrative, and managerial occupations; under sales occupations; and on computer scientists and systems analysts elsewhere in the *Handbook*.)

Engineers should be able to work as part of a team and should be creative, analytical, and detail-oriented. In addition, engineers should be able to communicate well—both orally and in writing.

Job Outlook

Employment opportunities in engineering are expected to be good through the year 2005 because employment is expected to increase about as fast as the average for all occupations while the number of degrees granted in engineering is expected to remain near present levels through the year 2005.

Many of the jobs in engineering are related to national defense. Because defense expenditures have declined, employment growth and job outlook for engineers may not be as strong as in times when defense expenditures were increasing. However, graduating engineers will continue to be in demand for jobs in engineering and other areas, possibly even at the same time other engineers, especially defense industry engineers, are being laid off.

Employers will rely on engineers to further increase productivity as they increase investment in plant and equipment to expand output of goods and services. In addition, competitive pressures and advancing technology will force companies to improve and update product designs more frequently. Finally, more engineers will be needed to improve deteriorating roads, bridges, water and pollution control systems, and other public facilities.

Freshman engineering enrollments began declining in 1983, and the number of bachelor's degrees in engineering began declining in 1987, as shown in chart 2. Although it is difficult to project engineering enrollments, this decline may continue through the late 1990s

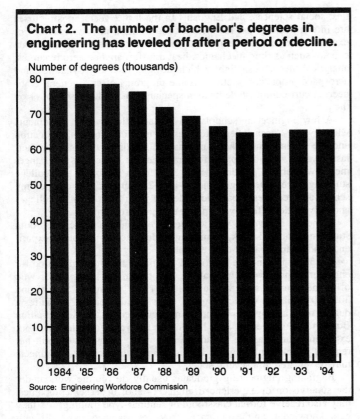

Chart 2. The number of bachelor's degrees in engineering has leveled off after a period of decline.

Number of degrees (thousands)

1984 '85 '86 '87 '88 '89 '90 '91 '92 '93 '94

Source: Engineering Workforce Commission

because the total college-age population is projected to decline. Furthermore, the proportion of students interested in engineering careers has declined as prospects for college graduates in other fields have improved and interest in other programs has increased. Also, engineering schools have restricted enrollments, especially in defense-related fields such as aerospace engineering, to accommodate the reduced opportunities in defense-related industries.

Only a relatively small proportion of engineers leave the profession each year. Despite this, over 70 percent of all job openings will arise from replacement needs. A greater proportion of replacement openings is created by engineers who transfer to management, sales, or other professional specialty occupations than by those who leave the labor force.

Most industries are less likely to lay off engineers than other workers. Many engineers work on long-term research and development projects or in other activities which may continue even during recessions. In industries such as electronics and aerospace, however, large government cutbacks in defense or research and development have resulted in significant layoffs for engineers.

New computer-aided design systems have improved the design process, enabling engineers to produce or modify designs much more rapidly. Engineers now produce and analyze many more design variations before selecting a final one. However, this technology is not expected to limit employment opportunities.

It is important for engineers to continue their education throughout their careers because much of their value to their employer depends on their knowledge of the latest technology. The pace of technological change varies by engineering specialty and industry. Engineers in high-technology areas such as advanced electronics may find that technical knowledge can become obsolete rapidly. Even those who continue their education are vulnerable if the particular technology or product they have specialized in becomes obsolete. Engineers who have not kept current in their field may find themselves passed over for promotions and are vulnerable should layoffs occur. On the other hand, it is often these high-technology areas that

offer the greatest challenges, the most interesting work, and the highest salaries. Therefore, the choice of engineering specialty and employer involves an assessment not only of the potential rewards but also of the risk of technological obsolescence.

Earnings

Starting salaries for engineers with the bachelor's degree are significantly higher than starting salaries of bachelor's degree graduates in other fields. According to the National Association of Colleges and Employers, engineering graduates with a bachelor's degree averaged about $34,100 a year in private industry in 1994; those with a master's degree and no experience, $40,200 a year; and those with a Ph.D., $55,300. Starting salaries for those with the bachelor's degree vary by branch, as shown in the following tabulation.

Aerospace	$30,860
Chemical	39,204
Civil	29,809
Electrical	34,840
Industrial	33,267
Mechanical	35,051
Metallurgical	33,429
Mining	32,638
Nuclear	33,603
Petroleum	38,286

A survey of workplaces in 160 metropolitan areas reported that beginning engineers had median annual earnings of about $33,900 in 1993, with the middle half earning between about $30,900 and $36,900 a year. Experienced midlevel engineers with no supervisory responsibilities had median annual earnings of about $54,400, with the middle half earning between about $49,800 and $59,600 a year. Median annual earnings for engineers at senior managerial levels were about $90,000. Median annual earnings for these and other levels of engineers are shown in the following tabulation.

Engineer I	$33,900
Engineer II	38,500
Engineer III	44,800
Engineer IV	54,400
Engineer V	65,400
Engineer VI	78,100
Engineer VII	90,000
Engineer VIII	105,700

Median annual salaries for all engineers was about $46,600 in 1994. Those with a bachelor's degree had median earnings of $47,100; master's degree holders, $53,200; and PhDs, $62,300. Median salaries for some engineering specialties were:

Aerospace	$50,200
Chemical	53,100
Civil	44,700
Electrical	48,000
Industrial	40,900
Mechanical	46,400
Engineers, nec	45,400

The average annual salary for engineers in the Federal Government in nonsupervisory, supervisory, and managerial positions was $58,080 in 1995.

Related Occupations

Engineers apply the principles of physical science and mathematics in their work. Other workers who use scientific and mathematical principles include physical scientists, life scientists, computer scientists, mathematicians, engineering and science technicians, and architects.

Sources of Additional Information

High school students interested in obtaining general information on a variety of engineering disciplines should contact the Junior Engineering Technical Society by sending a self-addressed business-size envelope with 6 first-class stamps affixed to:

☞JETS-Guidance, at 1420 King St., Suite 405, Alexandria, VA 22314.

Non-high school students and those wanting more detailed information should contact societies representing the individual branches of engineering. Each can provide information about careers in the particular branch.

Aeronautical and Aerospace Engineering, send $3 to:

☞American Institute of Aeronautics and Astronautics, Inc., AIAA Student Programs, The Aerospace Center, 370 L'Enfant Promenade SW., Washington, DC 20024-2518.

Chemical Engineering

☞American Institute of Chemical Engineers, 345 East 47th St., New York, NY 10017-2395.

☞American Chemical Society, Career Services, 1155 16th St. NW., Washington, DC 20036.

Civil Engineering

☞American Society of Civil Engineers, 345 E. 47th St., New York, NY 10017.

Electrical and Electronics Engineering

☞Institute of Electrical and Electronics Engineers, 1828 L St. NW., Suite 1202, Washington, DC 20036.

Industrial Engineering

☞Institute of Industrial Engineers, Inc., 25 Technology Park/Atlanta, Norcross, GA 30092.

Mechanical Engineering

☞The American Society of Mechanical Engineers, 345 E. 47th St., New York, NY 10017.

☞American Society of Heating, Refrigerating, and Air-Conditioning Engineers, Inc., 1791 Tullie Circle NE., Atlanta, GA 30329.

Metallurgical, Ceramic, and Materials Engineering

☞The Minerals, Metals, & Materials Society, 420 Commonwealth Dr., Warrendale, PA 15086-7514.

☞ASM International, Student Outreach Program, Materials Park, OH 44073-0002.

Mining Engineering

☞The Society for Mining, Metallurgy, and Exploration, Inc., P.O. Box 625002, Littleton, CO 80162-5002.

Nuclear Engineering

☞American Nuclear Society, 555 North Kensington Ave., LaGrange Park, IL 60525.

Petroleum Engineering

☞Society of Petroleum Engineers, 222 Palisades Creek Dr., Richardson, TX 75080.

Aerospace Engineers

D.O.T. 002.061 and .167)

Nature of the Work

Aerospace engineers design, develop, test, and help manufacture commercial and military aircraft, missiles, and spacecraft. They develop new technologies for use in commercial aviation, defense systems, and space exploration, often specializing in areas like structural design, guidance, navigation and control, instrumentation and communication, or production methods. They also may specialize in a particular type of aerospace product, such as commercial transports, helicopters, spacecraft, or rockets. Aerospace engineers may be experts in aerodynamics, propulsion, thermodynamics, structures, celestial mechanics, acoustics, or guidance and control systems.

Employment

Aerospace engineers held about 56,000 jobs in 1994. About half were in the aircraft and parts and guided missile and space vehicle

An aerospace engineer models the orbital position of a satellite.

manufacturing industries. Federal Government agencies, primarily the Department of Defense and the National Aeronautics and Space Administration, provided more than 1 out of 7 jobs. Business services, engineering and architectural services, research and testing services, and electrical and electronics manufacturing firms accounted for most of the remainder.

California, Washington, Texas, and Florida—States with large aerospace manufacturers—have the most aerospace engineers.

Job Outlook

Those seeking employment as aerospace engineers are likely to face keen competition because the number of job opportunities is expected to be significantly fewer than the relatively large pool of graduates. Defense Department expenditures for military aircraft, missiles, and other aerospace systems are declining, although funding for research and development of new systems has remained stable. Growth in the civilian sector, which needs to replace the present fleet of airliners with quieter and more fuel-efficient aircraft, is projected to be slow due to smaller orders from airlines and increasing foreign competition. This has caused a restructuring of firms and layoffs of personnel within both defense and civilian aircraft manufacturing that is expected to continue through the mid-1990s. Consequently, employment of aerospace engineers is expected to grow more slowly than the average through the year 2005. Future growth of employment in this field could also be limited because a higher proportion of engineers in aerospace manufacturing may come from the materials, mechanical, or electrical engineering fields. Most job openings will result from the need to replace aerospace engineers who transfer to other occupations or leave the labor force.

(See introductory section of this chapter for information on training requirements, earnings, and sources of additional information.)

Chemical Engineers

(D.O.T. 008.061)

Nature of the Work

Chemical engineers apply the principles of chemistry and engineering to solve problems involving the production or use of chemicals. Most work in the production of chemicals and chemical products. They design equipment and develop processes for manufacturing chemicals, plan and test methods of manufacturing the products, and supervise production. Chemical engineers also work in industries other than chemical manufacturing such as electronics or aircraft manufacturing. Because the knowledge and duties of chemical engineers cut across many fields, they apply principles of chemistry, physics, mathematics, and mechanical and electrical engineering in their work. They frequently specialize in a particular operation such as oxidation or polymerization. Others specialize in a particular area such as pollution control or the production of a specific product like automotive plastics or chlorine bleach.

Employment

Chemical engineers held over 50,000 jobs in 1994. Manufacturing industries employed sixty-nine percent, primarily in the chemical, petroleum refining, and related industries. Most of the rest worked for engineering services, research and testing services, or consulting firms that design chemical plants or do other work on a contract basis, or worked for government agencies or as independent consultants.

Job Outlook

Although employment in the chemical manufacturing industry is projected to grow very little through 2005, employment of chemical engineers should increase about as fast as the average for all occupations as chemical companies research and develop new chemicals and more efficient processes to increase output. Areas relating to the production of specialty chemicals, pharmaceuticals, and plastics materials may provide better opportunities than other portions of the chemical industry. Much of the projected growth in employment,

however, will be in nonmanufacturing industries, especially service industries.

(See introductory part of this section for information on training requirements, earnings, and sources of additional information.)

Civil Engineers

(D.O.T. 005.061 except-042, .167-014 and -018; and 019.167-018)

Nature of the Work

Civil engineers work in the oldest branch of engineering. They design and supervise the construction of roads, airports, tunnels, bridges, water supply and sewage systems, and buildings. Major specialties within civil engineering are structural, water resources, environmental, construction, transportation, and geotechnical engineering.

Many civil engineers hold supervisory or administrative positions, ranging from supervisor of a construction site to city engineer. Others may work in design, construction, research, and teaching.

Employment

Civil engineers held about 184,000 jobs in 1994. Over 40 percent of the jobs were in Federal, State, and local government agencies. Another 40 percent were in firms that provide engineering consulting services, primarily developing designs for new construction projects. The construction industry, public utilities, transportation, and manufacturing industries accounted for most of the rest.

Civil engineers usually are found working near major industrial and commercial centers, often at construction sites. Some projects are situated in remote areas or in foreign countries. In some jobs, civil engineers move from place to place to work on different projects.

Job Outlook

Those wishing to become civil engineers should find favorable opportunities through 2005. Spurred by general population growth and an expanding economy, more civil engineers will be needed to design and construct higher capacity transportation, water supply, and pollution control systems; large buildings and building complexes; and repair or replace existing roads, bridges, and other public structures. Employment of civil engineers is expected to increase about as fast as the average for all occupations through the year 2005. Most job openings, however, will result from the need to

A chemical engineer adjusts the mix of chemicals during production using automated controls.

A civil engineer construction manager reviews the progress of different components of the project.

replace civil engineers who transfer to other occupations or leave the labor force.

Because construction and related industries—including those providing design services—employ many civil engineers, employment opportunities will vary by geographic area and may decrease during economic slowdowns, when construction often is curtailed.

(See introductory part of this section for information on training requirements, earnings, and sources of additional information.)

Electrical and Electronics Engineers

(D.O.T. 003.061, .167 except -034 and -070, and .187)

Nature of the Work
Electrical and electronics engineers design, develop, test, and supervise the manufacture of electrical and electronic equipment. Electrical equipment includes power generating and transmission equipment used by electric utilities, and electric motors, machinery controls, and lighting and wiring in buildings, automobiles, and aircraft. Electronic equipment includes radar, computer hardware, and communications and video equipment.

The specialties of electrical and electronics engineers include several major areas—such as power generation, transmission, and distribution; communications; computer electronics; and electrical equipment manufacturing—or a subdivision of these areas—industrial robot control systems or aviation electronics, for example. Electrical and electronics engineers design new products, write performance requirements, and develop maintenance schedules. They also test equipment, solve operating problems, and estimate the time and cost of engineering projects.

Employment
Electrical and electronics engineers held about 349,000 jobs in 1994, making it the largest branch of engineering. Most jobs were in engineering and business consulting firms, manufacturers of electrical and electronic equipment, professional and scientific instruments, and government agencies. Communications and utilities firms, industrial machinery manufacturers, and computer and data processing services firms accounted for most of the remaining jobs.

Job Outlook
Employment opportunities for electrical and electronics engineers are expected to be good through the year 2005. Most job openings will result from job growth and the need to replace electrical engineers who transfer to other occupations or leave the labor force. These

openings should be sufficient to absorb the number of new graduates and other entrants.

Employment in this engineering specialty is expected to increase about as fast as the average for all occupations. Job growth is expected to be fastest in industrial sectors other than manufacturing. The need for electronics manufacturers to invest heavily in research and development to remain competitive will provide openings for graduates who have learned the latest technologies. Increased demand by businesses and government for computers and communications equipment is expected to account for much of the projected employment growth. Consumer demand for electrical and electronic goods should create additional jobs.

Because many electrical engineering jobs are defense related, expected cutbacks in defense spending could result in layoffs of electrical engineers, especially if a defense-related project or contract is unexpectedly canceled. Furthermore, engineers who fail to keep up with the rapid changes in technology in some specialties risk technological obsolescence, which makes them more susceptible to layoffs or, at a minimum, more likely to be passed over for advancement.

(See introductory part of this section for information on training requirements, earnings, and sources of additional information.)

Industrial Engineers

(D.O.T. 005.167-026; 012.061 -018, .067, .167 except -022, -026, -034, -058, and -062, and .187)

Nature of the Work
Industrial engineers determine the most effective ways for an organization to use the basic factors of production—people, machines, materials, information, and energy—to make or process a product. They are the bridge between management and operations. They are more concerned with increasing productivity through the management of people, methods of business organization, and technology than are engineers in other specialties, who generally work more with products or processes.

To solve organizational, production, and related problems most efficiently, industrial engineers carefully study the product and its requirements, design manufacturing and information systems, and use mathematical analysis methods such as operations research to meet those requirements. They develop management control systems to aid in financial planning and cost analysis, design production

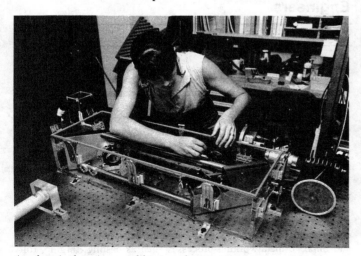

An electrical engineer calibrates a laser.

Industrial engineers work to make operations more efficient.

planning and control systems to coordinate activities and control product quality, and design or improve systems for the physical distribution of goods and services. Industrial engineers conduct surveys to find plant locations with the best combination of raw materials, transportation, and costs. They also develop wage and salary administration systems and job evaluation programs. Many industrial engineers move into management positions because the work is closely related.

Employment
Industrial engineers held about 115,000 jobs in 1994; about 75 percent of jobs were in manufacturing industries. Because their skills can be used in almost any type of organization, industrial engineers are more widely distributed among manufacturing industries than other engineers.

Their skills can be readily applied outside manufacturing as well. Some work for insurance companies, banks, hospitals, and retail organizations; others work for government agencies or as independent consultants.

Job Outlook
Employment of industrial engineers is expected to grow about as fast as the average for all occupations through the year 2005, making for favorable opportunities. Industrial growth, more complex business operations, and the greater use of automation in factories and in offices underlie the projected employment growth. Because the main function of an industrial engineer is to make a higher quality product as efficiently as possible, their services should be in demand in the manufacturing sector as firms seek to reduce costs and increase productivity through scientific management and safety engineering. Most job openings, however, will result from the need to replace industrial engineers who transfer to other occupations or leave the labor force.

(See introductory part of this section for information on training requirements, earnings, and sources of additional information.)

Mechanical Engineers

(D.O.T. 007.061, .161-022, -034, and -038, and .267-010)

Nature of the Work
Mechanical engineers plan and design tools, engines, machines, and other mechanical equipment. They design and develop power-producing machines such as internal combustion engines, steam and gas turbines, and jet and rocket engines. They also design and develop power-using machines such as refrigeration and air-conditioning equipment, robots, machine tools, materials handling systems, and industrial production equipment.

The work of mechanical engineers varies by industry and function. Specialties include, among others, applied mechanics, design engineering, heat transfer, power plant engineering, pressure vessels and piping, and underwater technology. Mechanical engineers design tools needed by other engineers for their work.

Mechanical engineering is the broadest engineering discipline, extending across many interdependent specialties. Mechanical engineers may work in production operations, maintenance, or technical sales. Many are administrators or managers.

Employment
Mechanical engineers held about 231,000 jobs in 1994. More than 6 out of 10 jobs were in manufacturing—of these, most were in the machinery, transportation equipment, electrical equipment, instruments, and fabricated metal products industries. Business and engineering consulting services and government agencies provided most of the remaining jobs.

A mechanical engineer reviews her titanium ring design and the final product.

Job Outlook
Employment of mechanical engineers is expected to grow about as fast as the average for all occupations through the year 2005. Although overall employment in manufacturing is expected to decline, employment of mechanical engineers in manufacturing should increase as the demand for machinery and machine tools grows and industrial machinery and processes become increasingly complex. Employment of mechanical engineers in other sectors of the economy, such as construction and services, is expected to grow faster than average as firms in these industries learn to apply these engineers' skills.

Job prospects in this field should be favorable through the year 2005. Most of the expected job openings resulting from employment growth and the need to replace those who will leave the occupation should be sufficient to absorb the supply of new graduates and other entrants.

Many mechanical engineering jobs are in defense-related industries. Reductions in defense spending has and may continue to result in layoffs in these industries.

(See introductory part of this section for information on training requirements, earnings, and sources of additional information.)

Metallurgical, Ceramic, and Materials Engineers

(D.O.T. 006.061; 011.061; and 019.061-014)

Nature of the Work
Metallurgical, ceramic, and materials engineers develop new types of metal alloys, ceramics, composites, and other materials which meet special requirements. Examples are graphite golf club shafts that are light but stiff, ceramic tiles on the space shuttle that protect it from burning up during reentry, and the alloy turbine blades in a jet engine.

Most metallurgical engineers work in one of the three main branches of metallurgy—extractive or chemical, physical, and mechanical or process. Extractive metallurgists are concerned with removing metals from ores and refining and alloying them to obtain useful metal. Physical metallurgists study the nature, structure, and physical properties of metals and their alloys, and methods of processing them into final products. Mechanical metallurgists develop and improve metalworking processes such as casting, forging, rolling, and drawing.

A materials engineer uses x-ray photoelectron spectroscopy to examine the structure of a new ceramic.

Ceramic engineers develop new ceramic materials and methods for making ceramic materials into useful products. Ceramics include all nonmetallic, inorganic materials which require high temperatures in their processing. Ceramic engineers work on products as diverse as glassware, semiconductors, automobile and aircraft engine components, fiber-optic phone lines, tile, and electric power line insulators.

Materials engineers evaluate technical requirements and material specifications to develop materials that can be used, for example, to reduce the weight, but not the strength of an object. Materials engineers also test and evaluate materials and develop new materials, such as the composite materials now being used in "stealth" aircraft.

Employment
Metallurgical, ceramic, and materials engineers held nearly 19,000 jobs in 1994. Over one-fourth worked in metal-producing and processing industries. They also worked in research and testing services, government agencies, industries that manufacture machinery, electrical equipment, and aircraft and aircraft parts, and in engineering consulting firms.

Job Outlook
Individuals seeking to become employed as metallurgical, ceramic, and materials engineers should find good opportunities, as the number of anticipated job openings should be sufficient to absorb the relatively low number of new graduates in this engineering discipline.

Employment of metallurgical, ceramic, and materials engineers is expected to increase more slowly than the average for all occupations through the year 2005. Many of the industries in which they are concentrated, such as stone, clay, and glass products, primary metals, fabricated metal products, and transportation equipment industries, are expected to experience little if any employment growth through the year 2005. Anticipated employment growth in service industries, such as research and testing services and engineering and architectural services, however, should provide significant job openings as these firms are employed to develop improved materials for their industrial customers.

(See introductory part of this section for information on training requirements, earnings, and sources of additional information.)

Mining Engineers

(D.O.T. 010.061 except -018)

Nature of the Work
Mining engineers find, extract, and prepare metals and minerals for use by manufacturing industries. They design open pit and underground mines, supervise the construction of mine shafts and tunnels in underground operations, and devise methods for transporting minerals to processing plants. Mining engineers are responsible for the safe, economical, and environmentally sound operation of mines. Some mining engineers work with geologists and metallurgical engineers to locate and appraise new ore deposits. Others develop new mining equipment or direct mineral processing operations to separate minerals from the dirt, rock, and other materials with which they are mixed. Mining engineers frequently specialize in the mining of one mineral or metal, such as coal or gold.

With increased emphasis on protecting the environment, many mining engineers work solving problems related to land reclamation and water and air pollution.

Employment
Mining engineers held about 3,200 jobs in 1994. Just under two-thirds worked in the mining industry. Other jobs were located in government agencies, manufacturing industries, or engineering consulting firms.

Mining engineers are usually employed at the location of mineral deposits, often near small communities. Those in research and

A mining engineer examines the plans of the current mine and the next phase to determine the best location for a conveyor system.

development, management, consulting, or sales, however, often are located in metropolitan areas.

Job Outlook

The mining industry traditionally has few openings. In fact, employment of mining engineers is expected to decline through the year 2005. Therefore, graduates in mining engineering will face competition despite the low number of mining engineering graduates.

Opportunities in the mining industry are closely related to the price of the metals and minerals they produce. If the price of these products is high, it makes it worthwhile for a mining company to invest the many millions of dollars in material moving equipment and ore processing technology necessary to operate a mine.

Although prices for mined products have been unstable, the increasing activity of auto manufacturing and expanded development and repair of the Nation's roadways will help provide demand for metals and minerals. The long-term business environment for mining generally is perceived to be favorable, but because a mine takes years of research, planning, and development to become fully operational, it may, even then, not contribute to expansion in employment opportunities for mining engineers.

(See introductory part of this section for information on training requirements, earnings, and sources of additional information.)

Nuclear Engineers

(D.O.T. 005.061-042; 015.061, .067, .137, and .167)

Nature of the Work

Nuclear engineers conduct research on nuclear energy and radiation. They design, develop, monitor, and operate nuclear power plants used to generate electricity and power Navy ships. They may work on the nuclear fuel cycle—the production, handling, and use of nuclear fuel and the safe disposal of waste produced by nuclear energy—or on fusion energy. Some specialize in the development of nuclear weapons; others develop industrial and medical uses for radioactive materials, such as equipment to diagnose and treat medical problems.

Employment

Nuclear engineers held about 15,000 jobs in 1994; about one-fifth each were in utilities, the Federal Government, and engineering consulting firms. Another 10 percent were in research and testing services. Nearly half of all federally employed nuclear engineers were civilian employees of the Navy, about one-third worked for the Nuclear Regulatory Commission, and most of the rest worked for the Department of Energy or the Tennessee Valley Authority. Most nonfederally employed nuclear engineers worked for public utilities or engineering consulting companies. Some worked for defense manufacturers or manufacturers of nuclear power equipment.

Job Outlook

Little change in employment of nuclear engineers is expected through the year 2005. Because of public concerns over the cost and safety of nuclear power, there are only a small number of nuclear power plants under construction in the United States, two of which are scheduled to begin operating before 2005. Nevertheless, nuclear engineers will be needed to operate existing plants. In addition, nuclear engineers will be needed to work in defense-related areas and to improve and enforce safety standards.

Despite the expected absence of employment growth, good opportunities for nuclear engineers should exist because the small number of nuclear engineering graduates is likely to be roughly in balance with the number of job openings. Most openings will arise as nuclear engineers transfer to other occupations or leave the labor force.

A team of nuclear engineers at the controls of a nuclear power plant.

(See introductory part of this section for information on training requirements, earnings, and sources of additional information.)

Petroleum Engineers

(D.O.T. 010.061 except -014 and -026, .161-010, and .167-010 and -014)

Nature of the Work

Petroleum engineers explore for workable reservoirs containing oil or natural gas. When one is discovered, petroleum engineers work to achieve the maximum profitable recovery from the reservoir by determining and developing the most efficient production methods.

Because only a small proportion of the oil and gas in a reservoir will flow out under natural forces, petroleum engineers develop and use various enhanced recovery methods. These include injecting water, chemicals, or steam into an oil reservoir to force more of the oil out, and horizontal drilling or fracturing to connect more of a gas reservoir to a well. Since even the best methods in use today recover only a portion of the oil and gas in a reservoir, petroleum engineers work to find ways to increase this proportion.

Employment

Petroleum engineers held about 14,000 jobs in 1994, mostly in the petroleum industry and closely allied fields. Employers include major oil companies and hundreds of smaller, independent oil exploration, production, and service companies. Engineering consulting

Petroleum engineers discuss a drilling problem on site.

firms, government agencies, oil field services, and equipment suppliers also employ petroleum engineers. Others work as independent consultants.

Because petroleum engineers specialize in the discovery and production of oil and gas, relatively few are employed in the refining, transportation, and retail sectors of the oil and gas industry.

Most petroleum engineers work where oil and gas are found. Large numbers are employed in Texas, Oklahoma, Louisiana, and California, including offshore sites. Many American petroleum engineers also work overseas in oil-producing countries.

Job Outlook

The price of oil has a major effect on the level of employment opportunities for petroleum engineers in the United States. A high price of oil and gas makes it profitable for oil exploration firms to seek oil and gas reservoirs, and they will hire petroleum engineers to do so. With low oil prices, however, it is cheaper to purchase needed oil from other countries, such as Saudi Arabia, which have vast oil reserves. Also, the best exploration opportunities are in other countries because many of the most likely petroleum-producing areas in the United States have already been explored.

Employment of petroleum engineers is expected to decline through the year 2005 unless oil and gas prices unexpectedly increase enough to encourage increased exploration for oil in this country. In spite of this projected decline, employment opportunities for petroleum engineers should be favorable because the number of degrees granted in petroleum engineering has traditionally been low. Therefore, new graduates are not likely to significantly exceed the number of job openings that will arise as petroleum engineers transfer to other occupations or leave the labor force.

(See introductory part of this section for information on training requirements, earnings, and sources of additional information.)

Architects and Surveyors

Architects

(D.O.T. 001.061-010 and .167-010)

Nature of the Work

Architects design buildings and other structures. The design of a building involves far more than its appearance. Buildings must also be functional, safe, and economical and must suit the needs of the people who use them. Architects take all these things into consideration when they design buildings and other structures.

Architects provide a wide variety of professional services to individuals and organizations planning a construction project. They may be involved in all phases of development, from the initial discussion of general ideas with the client through construction. Their duties require a number of skills—design, engineering, managerial, communication, and supervisory.

The architect and client first discuss the purposes, requirements, and budget of a project. Based on the discussions, architects may prepare a program—a report specifying the requirements the design must meet. In some cases, the architect assists in conducting feasibility and environmental impact analyses and selecting a site. The architect then prepares drawings and written information presenting ideas for the client to review.

After the initial proposals are discussed and accepted, architects develop final construction plans. These plans show the building's appearance and details for its construction. Accompanying these are drawings of the structural system; air-conditioning, heating, and ventilating systems; electrical systems; plumbing; and possibly site and landscape plans. They also specify the building materials and, in some cases, the interior furnishings. In developing designs, architects follow building codes, zoning laws, fire regulations, and other ordinances, such as those that require easy access by disabled persons. Throughout the planning stage, they make necessary changes. Although they have traditionally used pencil and paper to produce design and construction drawings, architects are increasingly turning to computer-aided design and drafting (CADD) technology for these important tasks.

Architects may also assist the client in obtaining construction bids, selecting a contractor, and negotiating the construction contract. As construction proceeds, they may be employed by the client to visit the building site to ensure that the contractor is following the design, meeting the schedule, using the specified materials, and meeting the specified standards for the quality of work. The job is not complete until all construction is finished, required tests are made, and construction costs are paid.

Architects design a wide variety of buildings, such as office and apartment buildings, schools, churches, factories, hospitals, houses, and airport terminals. They also design multibuilding complexes such as urban centers, college campuses, industrial parks, and entire communities. In addition to designing buildings, they may advise on the selection of building sites, prepare cost analysis and land-use studies, and do long-range planning for land development.

Architects sometimes specialize in one phase of work. Some specialize in the design of one type of building—for example, hospitals, schools, or housing. Others specialize in construction management or the management of their firm and do little design work.

Nearly one-third of all architects are self-employed.

They often work with engineers, urban planners, interior designers, landscape architects, and others.

During a training period leading up to licensure as architects, entry-level workers are called intern-architects. This training period gives them practical work experience while they prepare for the Architect Registration Examination. Typical duties may include preparing construction drawings on CADD, assisting in the design of one part of a project, or managing the production of a small project.

Working Conditions

Architects generally work in a comfortable environment. Most of their time is spent in offices advising clients, developing reports and drawings, and working with other architects and engineers. However, they also often work at construction sites reviewing the progress of projects.

Architects may occasionally be under great stress, working nights and weekends to meet deadlines; a 40-hour workweek, however, is usual.

Employment

Architects held about 91,000 jobs in 1994. Most jobs were in architecture firms—the majority of which employ fewer than five workers. Nearly one-third were self-employed architects, practicing as partners in architecture firms or on their own. A few worked for builders, real estate developers, and for government agencies responsible for housing, planning, or community development, such as the U.S. Departments of Defense, Interior, and Housing and Urban Development, and the General Services Administration.

Training, Other Qualifications, and Advancement

All States and the District of Columbia require individuals to be licensed (registered) before they may call themselves architects or contract to provide architectural services. Many architecture school graduates work in the field even though they are not licensed. However, a licensed architect is required to take legal responsibility for all work. Three requirements generally must be met for licensure: A professional degree in architecture, a period of practical training or internship (usually for 3 years), and passage of all sections of the Architect Registration Examination.

In many States, the professional degree in architecture must be from one of the approximately 100 schools of architecture with programs accredited by the National Architectural Accrediting Board (NAAB). However, State architectural registration boards set their own standards, so graduation from a non NAAB-accredited program may meet the education requirement for licensure in some States. There are several types of professional degrees in architecture. The

majority of all architecture degrees are from 5-year Bachelor of Architecture programs intended for students entering from high school or with no previous architecture training. Some schools offer a 2-year Master of Architecture program for students with a preprofessional undergraduate degree in architecture or a related area, or a 3- or 4-year Master of Architecture program for students with a degree in another discipline. In addition, there are many combinations and variations of these degree programs.

The choice of degree type depends upon each individual's preference and educational background. Prospective architecture students should carefully consider the available options before committing to a program. For example, although the 5-year Bachelor of Architecture program offers the fastest route to the professional degree, courses are specialized and, if the student does not complete the program, moving to a nonarchitecture program may be difficult. A typical program includes courses in architectural history and theory, building design, including its technical and legal aspects, professional practice, math, physical sciences, and liberal arts. Many architecture schools also offer graduate education for those who already have a bachelor's or master's degree in architecture or other areas. Although graduate education beyond the professional degree is not essential for practicing architects, it is normally required for research, teaching, and certain specialties.

Architects must be able to visually communicate their ideas to clients. Artistic and drawing ability is very helpful in doing this, but not essential. More important is a visual orientation and the ability to conceptualize and understand spatial relationships. Good communication skills (both written and oral), the ability to work independently or as part of a team, and creativity are important qualities for anyone interested in becoming an architect. Computer literacy is also required as most firms use computers for word processing, specifications writing, two- and three- dimensional drafting, and financial management. A knowledge of computer-aided design and drafting (CADD) is helpful and will become more important as architecture firms continue to adopt this technology.

New graduates usually begin in architecture firms, where they assist in preparing architectural documents or drawings. They also may do research on building codes and materials; or write specifications for building materials, installation criteria, the quality of finishes, and other related details. Graduates with degrees in architecture also enter related fields such as graphic, interior, or industrial design; urban planning; real estate development; civil engineering; or construction management.

In large firms, architects may advance to supervisory or managerial positions. Some architects become partners in established firms; others set up their own practice.

Job Outlook

Architects' employment has traditionally been affected by the level of local construction, particularly of noninstitutional structures such as office buildings, shopping centers, schools, and healthcare facilities. The boom in construction of commercial office space and some other types of non-residential structures during the 1980s means there will be less construction of this type between 1994 and 2005. Nevertheless, employment growth of architects is expected to increase as fast as the average for all occupations during this period.

The needed renovation and rehabilitation of old buildings, particularly in urban areas where space for new buildings is becoming limited, is expected to provide jobs for architects and to compensate somewhat for any slowdowns in jobs related to new construction. Also, the expected expansion of the population under age 15 and over age 65 should spur the demand for public and private buildings, such as schools and healthcare facilities. The need to replace architects who retire or leave the labor force for other reasons will provide many additional job openings.

Despite expected employment growth and the increased number of openings due to replacement needs, prospective architects may face competition, especially if the number of architecture degrees awarded remain at, or above, current levels. Traditionally, many individuals are attracted to this occupation, and there are often numerous applicants for available openings, especially in the most prestigious firms. Because noninstitutional construction is sensitive to cyclical changes in the economy, architects will face particularly strong competition for jobs or clients during recessions, and layoffs may occur. Those involved in the design of institutional buildings such as schools, hospitals, nursing homes, and correctional facilities, will be less affected by fluctuations in the economy.

Even in times of overall good opportunities, there may be areas of the country with poor opportunities. Architects who are licensed to practice in one State must meet the licensing requirements of other States before practicing elsewhere. These requirements are becoming more standardized, however, facilitating movement to other States.

Because the use of computer-aided design and drafting is becoming more prevalent in architecture firms, prospective architects who know CADD technology may experience better opportunities in the future, particularly in a competitive job market.

Earnings

According to The American Institute of Architects, the median salary for intern-architects in architecture firms was $24,700 in 1993. Licensed architects with 8 to 10 years' experience but who were not managers or principals of a firm earned a median salary of $38,900 in 1993; and principals or partners of firms earned a median salary of $50,000 in 1993. Partners in some large practices earned over $110,000. Most employers of wage and salary architects offer paid vacation and sick leave, and a majority also provide medical and life insurance plans to their employees. Employees of very small architecture firms (fewer than 5 employees) are less likely to receive these benefits.

Architects who are partners in well-established architecture firms generally earn much more than their salaried employees, but their income may fluctuate due to changing business conditions. Some architects may have difficulty getting established in their own practices and may go through a period when their expenses are greater than their income, requiring substantial financial resources.

Related Occupations

Architects design and construct buildings and related structures. Others who engage in similar work are landscape architects, building contractors, civil engineers, urban planners, interior designers, industrial designers, and graphic designers.

Sources of Additional Information

Information about education and careers in architecture can be obtained from:

☞Architecture Fact Book, The American Institute of Architects, 1735 New York Ave. NW., Washington, DC 20006.

☞Society of American Registered Architects, 1245 S. Highland Ave., Lombard, IL 60148.

Landscape Architects

(D.O.T. 001.061-018)

Nature of the Work

Everyone enjoys attractively designed residential areas, public parks, college campuses, shopping centers, golf courses, parkways, and industrial parks. Landscape architects design these areas so that they are not only functional but beautiful and compatible with the natural environment as well. They may plan the location of buildings, roads, and walkways and the arrangement of flowers, shrubs, and trees. Historic preservation and natural resource conservation and reclama-

tion are other important objectives to which landscape architects may apply their knowledge of the environment as well as their design and artistic talents.

Landscape architects are hired by many types of organizations—from real estate development firms starting new projects to municipalities constructing airports or parks. They are often involved with the development of a site from its conception. Working with architects, engineers, scientists, and other professionals, they help determine the best arrangement of roads and buildings, and the best way to conserve or restore natural resources. Once these decisions are made, landscape architects create detailed plans indicating new topography, vegetation, walkways, and landscape amenities.

In planning a site, landscape architects first consider the nature and purpose of the project and the funds available. They analyze the natural elements of the site, such as the climate, soil, slope of the land, drainage, and vegetation. They observe where sunlight falls on the site at different times of the day and examine the site from various angles. They assess the effect of existing buildings, roads, walkways, and utilities on the project.

After studying and analyzing the site, they prepare a preliminary design. To account for the needs of the client as well as the conditions at the site, they may have to make many changes before a final design is approved. They must also take into account any local, State, or Federal regulations such as those protecting wetlands or historic resources. An increasing number of landscape architects are using computer-aided design (CAD) systems to assist them in preparing their designs. Many landscape architects also use video simulation as a tool to help clients envision the proposed ideas and plans. For larger scale site planning, landscape architects also use geographic information systems technology, a computer mapping system.

Throughout all phases of the planning and design, landscape architects consult with other professionals involved in the project. Once the design is complete, they prepare a proposal for the client. They produce detailed plans of the site, including written reports, sketches, models, photographs, land-use studies, and cost estimates, and submit them for approval by the client and by regulatory agencies. If the plans are approved, landscape architects prepare working drawings showing all existing and proposed features. They also outline in detail the methods of construction and draw up a list of necessary materials.

Although many landscape architects supervise the installation of their design, some are involved in the construction of the site. However, this usually is done by the developer or landscape contractor.

Some landscape architects work on a wide variety of projects. Others specialize in a particular area, such as residential development, historic landscape restoration, waterfront improvement projects, parks and playgrounds, or shopping centers. Still others work in regional planning and resource management; feasibility, environmental impact, and cost studies; or site construction. Some landscape architects teach in colleges or universities.

Although most landscape architects do at least some residential work, relatively few limit their practice to landscape design for individual homeowners because most residential landscape design projects are too small to provide suitable income compared with larger commercial or multiunit residential projects. Some nurseries offer residential landscape design services, but these services often are performed by lesser qualified landscape designers or others with training and experience in related areas.

Landscape architects who work for government agencies do similar work at national parks, government buildings, and other government-owned facilities. In addition, they may prepare environmental impact statements and studies on environmental issues such as public land-use planning.

Working Conditions

Landscape architects spend most of their time in offices creating plans and designs, preparing models and cost estimates, doing research, or attending meetings. The remainder of their time is spent at

Landscape architects combine their knowledge of design, construction, plants, soils, and ecology to create their final designs.

the site. During the design and planning stage, landscape architects visit and analyze the site to verify that the design can be incorporated into the landscape. After the plans and specifications are completed, they may spend additional time at the site observing or supervising the construction. Those who work in large firms may spend considerably more time out of the office because of travel to sites outside the local area.

Salaried employees in both government and landscape architectural firms usually work regular hours, although they may work overtime to meet a project deadline. Hours of self-employed landscape architects may vary.

Employment

Landscape architects held about 14,000 jobs in 1994. Three-fifths worked for firms that provide landscape architecture services. Most of the rest were employed by architectural firms. The Federal Government also employs these workers; most were found in the U.S. Departments of Agriculture, Defense, and Interior. About 1 of every 5 landscape architects was self-employed.

Most employment for landscape architects is concentrated in urban and suburban areas in all parts of the country. Some landscape architects work in rural areas, particularly those in the Federal Government who plan and design parks and recreation areas.

Training, Other Qualifications, and Advancement

A bachelor's or master's degree in landscape architecture is usually necessary for entry into the profession. The bachelor's degree in landscape architecture takes 4 or 5 years to complete. There are two types of accredited master's degree programs. The master's degree as a first professional degree is a 3-year program designed for students with an undergraduate degree in another discipline; this is the most common type. The master's degree as the second professional degree is a 2-year program for students who have a bachelor's degree in landscape architecture and wish to demonstrate mastery or specialize in some aspect of landscape architecture.

In 1995, approximately 55 colleges and universities offered 72 undergraduate and graduate programs in landscape architecture that were accredited by the Landscape Architecture Accreditation Board of the American Society of Landscape Architects.

College courses required in this field usually include technical subjects such as surveying, landscape design and construction, landscape ecology, structural design, and city and regional planning. Other courses include history of landscape architecture, plant and soil science, geology, design and color theory, and general management. In addition, most students at the undergraduate level take a year of prerequisite courses such as English, mathematics, and social and physical science. The design studio is an important aspect of many landscape architecture curriculums. Whenever possible, students are assigned real projects to work on, providing them with valuable hands-on experience. While working on real projects, students may become more proficient in the use of technologies such as computer-aided design, geographic information systems, and video simulation.

Forty-five States require landscape architects to be licensed or registered. Licensing is based on the Landscape Architect Registration Examination (L.A.R.E.), sponsored by the Council of Landscape Architectural Registration Boards. Admission to the exam usually requires a degree from an accredited school plus 1 to 4 years of work experience, although standards vary from State to State. Many States require additional examinations focusing on laws and/or plant materials indigenous to their State.

Because States' requirements for licensure are not uniform, landscape architects may not find it easy to transfer their registration to another State to practice. However, those who meet the national standard of graduating from an accredited program, serving 3 years of internship under the supervision of a registered landscape architect, and passing the L.A.R.E. can satisfy requirements in most States.

In the Federal Government, candidates for entry positions should have a bachelor's or master's degree in landscape architecture. The Federal Government does not require its landscape architects to be licensed.

Persons planning a career in landscape architecture should appreciate nature and enjoy working with their hands. Although creativity and artistic talent are also desirable qualities, they are not absolutely essential to success as a landscape architect. High school courses in mechanical or geometric drawing, art, botany, and mathematics are helpful. Good oral communication skills are important, because these workers must be able to convey their ideas to other professionals and clients and to make presentations before large groups. Landscape architects do research and prepare reports and land impact studies, so strong writing skills are valuable. A knowledge of computer applications of all kinds, including computer-aided design and drafting (CADD), is becoming increasingly necessary. Those interested in starting their own firm should be skilled in small business management.

In States where licensure is required, new hires are technically called intern landscape architects until they become licensed. Their duties vary depending on the type and size of employing firm. They may do project research or prepare base maps of the area to be landscaped, while some are allowed to participate in the actual design of a project. However, interns must perform all work under the supervision of a licensed landscape architect. Additionally, all drawings and specifications must be signed and/or sealed by the licensed landscape architect, who takes legal responsibility for the work. After gaining experience and becoming licensed, landscape architects usually can carry a design through all stages of development. After several years, they may become associates, and eventually they may become partners in a firm or open their own offices.

Job Outlook

Despite expected stronger employment growth and higher replacement needs due to retirements than in the past decade, new graduates can expect to face competition for jobs as landscape architects. The number of professional degrees awarded in landscape architecture has remained steady over the years, even during times of fluctuating demand due to economic conditions. If this trend continues, the number of openings in this small occupation will be too few to absorb all jobseekers.

Traditionally, however, those with landscape architecture training qualify for jobs closely related to landscape architecture, and may become construction or landscape supervisors, landscape designers, drafters, land or environmental planners, or landscape consultants.

Opportunities will be best for landscape architects who develop strong technical skills and a knowledge of environmental issues, codes, and regulation.

Employment of landscape architects is expected to increase about as fast as the average for all occupations through the year 2005. The level of new construction plays an important role in determining demand for landscape architects. Anticipated growth in construction is expected to increase demand for landscape architectural services over the long run. An increasing proportion of office and other commercial and industrial development will occur outside cities. These projects are typically located on larger sites with more surrounding land which needs to be designed, in contrast to urban development, which often includes little or no surrounding land. Also, as the cost of land increases, the importance of good site planning and landscape design increases. Because employment is linked to new construction, however, landscape architects may face layoffs and competition for jobs when real estate sales and construction slow down, such as during a recession.

Increased development of open space into recreation areas, wildlife refuges, and parks will also require the skills of landscape architects. Continued concern for the environment should stimulate employment growth because of the need to design development projects which best fit in with the surrounding environment.

In addition to the work related to new development and construction, landscape architects are expected to be involved in historic preservation, local, city, and regional planning, land reclamation, and refurbishment of existing sites.

The need to replace landscape architects who retire or leave the labor force for other reasons is expected to result in nearly as many openings as new openings due to job growth.

Earnings

According to a 1994 American Society of Landscape Architects survey, the median salary for landscape architects in private practice was about $40,000; the median bonus, $4,000; and additional landscape architecture-related income, $5,000. Those who work in the public sector earned higher salaries—a median of $42,400—but median bonus amount and outside landscape architecture-related income were lower than for private practitioners. In 1995, the average annual salary for all landscape architects in the Federal Government in nonsupervisory, supervisory, and managerial positions was $49,570.

Because many landscape architects work for small firms or are self-employed, benefits tend to be less generous than those of other workers with similar skills who work for large organizations. With the exception of those who are self-employed, however, most landscape architects receive health insurance, paid vacations, and sick leave.

Related Occupations

Landscape architects use their knowledge of design, construction, and land-use planning to develop a landscape project. Others whose work requires similar skills are architects, interior designers, civil engineers, and urban and regional planners. Landscape architects also know how to grow and use plants in the landscape. Botanists, who study plants in general, and horticulturists, who study ornamental plants as well as fruit, vegetable, greenhouse, and nursery crops, do similar work.

Sources of Additional Information

Additional information, including a list of colleges and universities offering accredited programs in landscape architecture, is available from:

☛American Society of Landscape Architects, Career Information, 4401 Connecticut Ave. NW., Suite 500, Washington, DC 20008.

General information on registration or licensing requirements is available from:

☛Council of Landscape Architectural Registration Boards, 12700 Fair Lakes Circle, Suite 110, Fairfax, VA 22033.

Surveyors

(D.O.T. 018 except .167-022, and 024.061-014)

Nature of the Work

Three groups of workers measure and map the earth's surface. *Land surveyors* establish official land, air space, and water boundaries. They write descriptions of land for deeds, leases, and other legal documents; define air space for airports; and measure construction and mineral sites. *Survey technicians*, assist land surveyors by operating survey instruments and collecting information. *Mapping scientists* and other surveyors collect geographic information and prepare maps of large areas.

Land surveyors manage survey parties that measure distances, directions, and angles between points and elevations of points, lines, and contours on the earth's surface. They plan the fieldwork, select known survey reference points, and determine the precise location of important features in the survey area. Surveyors research legal records and look for evidence of previous boundaries. They record the results of the survey, verify the accuracy of data, and prepare plats, maps, and reports. Surveyors who establish boundaries must be licensed by the State in which they work.

The information needed by the land surveyor is gathered by a survey party. A typical survey party is made up of a party chief and several survey technicians and helpers. The party chief, who may be either a land surveyor or a senior survey technician, leads the day-to-day work activities. The party chief is assisted by survey technicians, who adjust and operate surveying instruments such as the theodolite (used to measure horizontal and vertical angles) and electronic distance-measuring equipment. Survey technicians or assistants position and hold the vertical rods or targets that the theodolite operator sights on to measure angles, distances, or elevations. They may also hold measuring tapes and chains if electronic distance-measuring equipment is not used. Survey technicians compile notes, make sketches, and enter the data obtained from these instruments into computers. Some survey parties include laborers or helpers to clear brush from sight lines, drive stakes, carry equipment, and perform other less skilled duties.

New technology is changing the nature of the work of surveyors and survey technicians. For larger surveying projects, surveyors are increasingly using the Global Positioning System (GPS), a satellite system which precisely locates points on the earth using radio signals transmitted by satellites. To use it, a surveyor places a satellite receiver—about the size of a backpack—on a desired point. The receiver collects information from several differently positioned satellites simultaneously to locate its precise position. Two receivers are generally operated in synchronization, one at a known point and the other at the unknown point. The receiver can also be placed in a vehicle to trace out road systems, or for other uses. The cost of the receivers has fallen and much more surveying work is being done by GPS.

Mapping scientists, like land surveyors, measure, map, and chart the earth's surface but generally cover much larger areas. Unlike land surveyors, however, mapping scientists work mainly in offices and seldom visit the sites they are mapping. Mapping scientists include workers in several occupations. *Cartographers* prepare maps using information provided by geodetic surveys, aerial photographs, and satellite data. *Photogrammetrists* prepare maps and drawings by measuring and interpreting aerial photographs, using analytical processes and mathematical formulas. Photogrammetrists make detailed maps of areas that are inaccessible or difficult to survey by other methods. *Map editors* develop and verify map contents from aerial photographs and other reference sources.

Some surveyors perform specialized functions which are closer to mapping science than traditional surveying. *Geodetic surveyors* use high-accuracy techniques, including satellite observations, to meas-

Land surveyors and technicians spend a lot of their time outdoors, and may be exposed to all types of weather.

sure large areas of the earth's surface. *Geophysical prospecting surveyors* mark sites for subsurface exploration, usually petroleum related. *Marine surveyors* survey harbors, rivers, and other bodies of water to determine shorelines, topography of the bottom, water depth, and other features.

The work of mapping scientists is changing due to advancements in technology. These advancements include the GPS, Geographic Information Systems (GIS)—which are computerized data banks of spatial data—new earth resources data satellites, and improved aerial photography. From the older specialties of photogrammetrist or cartographer, a new type of mapping scientist is emerging. The *geographic information specialist* combines the functions of mapping science and surveying into a broader field concerned with the collection and analysis of geographic spatial information.

Working Conditions

Surveyors usually work an 8-hour day, 5 days a week, and spend a lot of their time outdoors. Sometimes they work longer hours during the summer, when weather and light conditions are most suitable for fieldwork.

Land surveyors and technicians do active and sometimes strenuous work. They often stand for long periods, walk long distances, and climb hills with heavy packs of instruments and equipment. They are also exposed to all types of weather. Occasionally, they may commute long distances, stay overnight, or even temporarily relocate near a survey site.

Surveyors also spend considerable time in offices, planning surveys, analyzing data, and preparing reports and maps. Most computations and map drafting are performed on a computer. Mapping scientists spend virtually all their time in offices.

Employment

Surveyors held about 96,000 jobs in 1994. Engineering, architectural, and surveying firms employed over three-fifths of all surveyors. Federal, State, and local government agencies employed an additional quarter. Major Federal Government employers are the U.S. Geological Survey, the Bureau of Land Management, the Army Corps of Engineers, the Forest Service, the National Oceanic and Atmospheric Administration, and the Defense Mapping Agency. Most surveyors in State and local government work for highway departments and urban planning and redevelopment agencies. Construction firms, mining and oil and gas extraction companies, and public utilities also employ surveyors. About 7,000 surveyors were self-employed in 1994.

Training, Other Qualifications, and Advancement

Most people prepare for a career as a licensed surveyor by combining postsecondary school courses in surveying with extensive on-the-job training. About 25 universities offer 4-year programs leading to a B.S. degree in surveying. Junior and community colleges, technical institutes, and vocational schools offer 1-, 2-, and 3-year programs in both surveying and surveying technology.

All 50 States license land surveyors. For licensure, most State licensing boards require that individuals pass two written examinations, one prepared by the State and one given by the National Council of Examiners for Engineering and Surveying. In addition, they must meet varying standards of formal education and work experience in the field. In the past, many surveyors started as members of survey crews and worked their way up to licensed surveyor with little formal training in surveying. However, due to advancing technology and an increase in licensing standards, formal education requirements are increasing. Most States at the present time require some formal post-high school education coursework and 10 to 12 years of surveying experience to gain licensure. However, requirements vary among the States. Generally, the quickest route to licensure is a combination of 4 years of college, 2 to 4 years of experience (a few States do not require any), and passing the licensing examinations. An increasing number of States require a bachelor's degree in surveying or in a closely related field, such as civil engineering or forestry, with courses in surveying.

High school students interested in surveying should take courses in algebra, geometry, trigonometry, drafting, mechanical drawing, and computer science.

High school graduates with no formal training in surveying usually start as an apprentice. Beginners with postsecondary school training in surveying can generally start as technicians or assistants. With on-the-job experience and formal training in surveying—either in an institutional program or from a correspondence school—workers may advance to senior survey technician, then to party chief, and in some cases, to licensed surveyor (depending on State licensing requirements).

The American Congress on Surveying and Mapping has a voluntary certification program for survey technicians. Technicians are certified at four levels that require progressive amounts of experience and passing written examinations. Although not required for State licensure, many employers require certification for promotion to positions with greater responsibilities.

Cartographers and photogrammetrists usually have a bachelor's degree in engineering or a physical science. It also is possible to enter these positions through previous experience as a photogrammetric or cartographic technician. Most cartographic and photogrammetric technicians have had some specialized postsecondary school training. With the development of Geographic Information Systems, cartographers, photogrammetrists, and other mapping scientists need additional education and more experience with computers than in the past.

The American Society for Photogrammetry and Remote Sensing has voluntary certification programs for photogrammetrists and mapping scientists. To qualify for these professional distinctions, individuals must meet work experience standards and pass an oral or written examination.

Surveyors should have the ability to visualize objects, distances, sizes, and other abstract forms. They have to work with precision and accuracy because mistakes can be costly. Surveying is a cooperative process, so good interpersonal skills and the ability to work as part of a team are important. Leadership qualities are important for party chief and other supervisory positions.

Members of a survey party must be in good physical condition to work outdoors and carry equipment over difficult terrain. They need good eyesight, coordination, and hearing to communicate via hand and voice signals.

Job Outlook

Employment of surveyors is expected to decline slightly through the year 2005. The widespread use of GPS and remote sensing technologies is increasing both the accuracy and productivity of surveyors. Job openings will result from the need to replace workers who transfer to other occupations or leave the labor force.

Growth in construction through the year 2005 should require surveyors to lay out streets, shopping centers, housing developments, factories, office buildings, and recreation areas. Continuing road and highway construction and improvements should also require surveyors. However, employment may fluctuate from year to year along with construction activity.

The employment of mapping scientists and other surveyors by private firms, and the Federal Government is expected to decline due to budget cutbacks and technological efficiency.

Opportunities will be best for surveyors and mapping scientists who have at least a bachelor's degree as a result of trends towards more complex technology, upgraded licensing requirements, and the increased demand for geographic spatial data (as opposed to traditional surveying services). New technology such as GPS and GIS may increase productivity for larger projects and may enhance employment opportunities for surveyors and survey technicians who have the educational background to use it, but limit opportunities for those with less education.

Earnings

The median weekly earnings for surveyors and mapping scientists were about $590 a week in 1994. The middle 50 percent earned between $420 and $840 a week; 10 percent earned less than $340 a week; 10 percent earned more than $950 a week.

The median annual earnings for survey technicians were about $520 a week in 1994. The middle 50 percent earned between $390 and $750 a week; 10 percent earned less than $300 a week; 10 percent earned more than $960 a week.

In 1995, the Federal Government hired high school graduates with little or no training or experience at salaries or about $15,800 annually for entry level jobs on survey crews. Those with 1 year of related postsecondary training earned about $18,500 a year. Those with an associate degree that included coursework in surveying generally started as instrument assistants with an annual salary of about $21,300. In 1995, entry level land surveyors or cartographers with the Federal Government earned about $24,500 or $29,900 a year, depending on their qualifications. The average annual salary for Federal land surveyors in 1995 was about $44,200, for cartographers, about $47,700, and for geodesists, about $50,200. The average annual salary for Federal surveying technicians was about $24,400, for cartographic technicians, about $32,100, and for geodetic technicians, about $40,900.

Related Occupations

Surveying is related to the work of civil engineers and architects, since an accurate survey is the first step in land development and construction projects. Mapping science and geodetic surveying are related to the work of geologists and geophysicists, who study the earth's internal composition, surface, and atmosphere. Mapping science is also related to the work of geographers and urban planners, who study how the earth's surface is used.

Sources of Additional Information

Information about career opportunities, licensure requirements, and the survey technician certification program is available from:

☛American Congress on Surveying and Mapping, 5410 Grosvenor Lane, Bethesda, MD 20814-2122.

General information on careers in photogrammetry is available from:

☛American Society for Photogrammetry and Remote Sensing, 5410 Grosvenor Lane, Suite 200, Bethesda, MD 20814.

Computer, Mathematical, and Operations Research Occupations

Actuaries

(D.O.T. 020.167-010)

Nature of the Work

Actuaries answer questions about future risk, make pricing decisions, and formulate investment strategies. Some design insurance, financial, and pension plans and ensure that they are maintained on a sound financial basis. Most actuaries specialize in either life, health, or property and casualty insurance; others specialize in pension plans or in financial planning and investment.

Actuaries assemble and analyze statistics to calculate probabilities of death, sickness, injury, disability, retirement income level, property loss, or return on investment. They use this information to determine the expected insured loss, or to make other business decisions. For example, they may calculate the probability of claims due to automobile accidents, which can vary depending on the insured's age, sex, driving history, type of car, and other factors. They must

make sure that the price charged for such insurance will enable the company to pay all claims and expenses as they occur. Finally, this price must be profitable and yet be competitive with other insurance companies. The actuary calculates premium rates and determines policy contract provisions for each type of insurance offered.

To perform their duties effectively, actuaries must keep informed about general economic and social trends and legislative, health, business, finance, and other developments that may affect insurance or investment practices. Because of their broad knowledge of mathematics, actuaries may work in investment, risk classification, or pension planning. Actuaries in executive positions help determine company policy. In that role, they may be called upon to explain complex technical matters to other company executives, government officials, policyholders, and the public. They may testify before public agencies on proposed legislation affecting their businesses, for example, or explain changes in contract provisions to customers. They also may help companies develop plans to enter new lines of business.

Some actuaries work in the financial services industry, where they manage credit, prepayment, and other risks, and help price corporate offerings.

Actuaries need a strong background in mathematics.

Consulting actuaries provide advice for a fee to various clients including insurance companies, corporations, hospitals and other health care providers, labor unions, government agencies, and attorneys. Some consulting actuaries set up pension and welfare plans, calculate future benefits, and determine the amount of employer contributions. Others provide advice to health care and financial services firms. Consultants may be called upon to testify in court regarding the value of potential lifetime earnings lost by a person who has been disabled or killed in an accident, the current value of future pension benefits in divorce cases, or the calculation of automobile insurance rates. Pension actuaries enrolled under the provisions of the Employee Retirement Income Security Act of 1974 (ERISA) evaluate the pension plans covered by that act and report on their financial soundness to employers and regulators.

Working Conditions

Actuaries have desk jobs that require little physical activity; their offices generally are comfortable and pleasant. They usually work at least 40 hours a week. Some actuaries, particularly consulting actuaries, often travel to meet with clients. Consulting actuaries may also be expected to work more than 40 hours per week.

Employment

Actuaries held about 17,000 jobs in 1994. More than 1 in 10 were self-employed.

Over one-half of the actuaries who were wage and salary workers were in the insurance industry. Most worked for life insurance companies; others worked for property, casualty, and health insurance companies, pension funds, and insurance agents and brokers. Most of the remaining actuaries worked for firms providing services, especially management and public relations, and actuarial consulting services. A small number of actuaries worked for security and commodity brokers or government agencies. Some are employed developing computer software for actuarial calculations.

Training, Other Qualifications, and Advancement

A good educational background for a beginning job in a large life or casualty company is a bachelor's degree in mathematics or statistics, or a business-related discipline, such as actuarial science, economics, finance, or accounting. Some companies hire applicants with any major, provided the applicant has a working knowledge of mathematics, including calculus, probability, and statistics, and has demonstrated this ability by passing at least the beginning actuarial exams required for professional designation. Courses in accounting, computer science, and insurance also are useful. Companies increasingly prefer well-rounded individuals who, in addition to a strong technical background, have some training in liberal arts and business. Good communication and interpersonal skills are important, particularly for prospective consulting actuaries. Although only about 55 colleges and universities offer an actuarial science program, most colleges and universities offer a degree in mathematics or statistics.

A strong background in mathematics is essential for persons interested in a career as an actuary. It is an advantage to pass, while still in school, two or more of the examinations offered by professional actuarial societies. Two professional societies sponsor programs leading to full professional status in their specialty. The Society of Actuaries (SOA) gives a series of actuarial examinations for the life and health insurance, pension, and finance and investment fields. The Casualty Actuarial Society (CAS) gives a series of examinations for the property and casualty field, which covers risks such as fire, accidents, medical malpractice, and personal injury liability. Because the first parts of the examination series of each society are jointly sponsored and cover the same material, students need not commit themselves to a specialty until they have taken the initial examinations. These examinations test an individual's competence in subjects such as linear algebra, probability, calculus, statistics, risk theory, and actuarial mathematics. The first few examinations help students evaluate their potential as actuaries. Those who pass usually have better opportunities for employment and higher starting salaries.

Actuaries are encouraged to complete the entire series of examinations as soon as possible, advancing first to the associate level, and then to the fellowship level. Completion of the promotion process generally takes from 5 to 10 years. Examinations are given twice each year. Extensive home study is required to pass the examinations; many actuaries study for months to prepare for an examination. Most reach Associateship within 4 to 6 years. They generally specialize in the SOA courses leading to a career in either life insurance, health insurance, investment, or pension services, or else the CAS examinations in property and the casualty insurance careers. Fellowship candidates usually have several years of experience. Most actuaries complete the Fellowship exams a few years after reaching Associateship. Both levels of examinations are extremely difficult.

Pension actuaries who verify the financial status of defined benefit pension plans to the Federal Government must be enrolled by the Joint Board for the Enrollment of Actuaries. Applicants for enrollment must meet certain experience and examination requirements as stipulated by the Joint Board.

Beginning actuaries often rotate between jobs to learn various actuarial operations and phases of insurance work, such as marketing, underwriting, or product development. At first, they prepare data for actuarial projects or perform other simple tasks. As they gain experience, they may supervise clerks, prepare correspondence and reports, and do research. They may move from one company to another in their early careers, as they move up to progressively more responsible positions.

Advancement to more responsible work depends largely on job performance and the number of actuarial examinations passed. Actuaries with a broad knowledge of the insurance, pension, investment, or employee benefits fields can advance to administrative and executive positions in their companies. Actuaries with supervisory ability may advance to management positions in other areas, such as underwriting, accounting, data processing, marketing, advertising, or planning.

Job Outlook

Prospective actuaries will face competition for jobs. Employment of actuaries is expected to grow more slowly than the average for all occupations through the year 2005 due to expected slower growth in the insurance industry. Anticipated downsizing and merger activity in the insurance industry is likely to have the greatest negative effect on actuaries with the least experience. Since experience is of paramount importance in the actuarial field, experienced actuaries should enjoy a competitive edge when vying for available openings.

Employment growth of consulting actuaries is expected to be faster than employment growth in insurance carriers, traditionally the leading employer of actuaries. As many companies seek to boost profitability by streamlining operations, actuarial employment may be cut back in insurance carriers. At the same time, insurance companies will require fewer actuaries as a result of merger and acquisition activity within the insurance field. Investment firms and large corporations may increasingly turn to consultants to provide actuarial services formerly performed in-house.

The liability of companies for damage resulting from their products has received much attention in recent years. Casualty actuaries will continue to be involved in the development of product liability insurance, medical malpractice and workers' compensation coverage, and self-insurance, which may involve internal reserve funds established by some large corporations. The growing need to evaluate catastrophic risks such as earthquakes and calculate prices for insuring facilities against such risks, which may involve huge losses, will be an increasing source of demand for property and casualty actuaries. So is planning for the systematic financing of environmental risks, such as toxic waste clean-up.

Earnings

In 1995, starting salaries for actuaries averaged about $36,000 for those with a bachelor's degree, according to the National Association of Colleges and Employers. New college graduates entering the actuarial field without having passed any actuarial exams averaged slightly lower salaries.

Insurance companies and consulting firms give merit increases to actuaries as they gain experience and pass examinations. Some companies also offer cash bonuses for each professional designation achieved. A 1994 salary survey of insurance and financial services companies, conducted by the Life Office Management Association, Inc., indicated that the average base salary for a newly designated Associate, Society of Actuaries, was about $46,600. Newly designated Fellows, Society of Actuaries, received an average salary of nearly $72,700. Fellows with additional years of experience can earn substantially more. For example, the average base salary for a Fellow of the Society of Actuaries (FSA) who received the designation ten years previously (in 1984) was $96,000.

Actuaries typically receive other benefits including vacation and sick leave, health and life insurance, and pension plans.

Related Occupations

Actuaries determine the probability of income or loss from various risk factors. Other workers whose jobs involve related skills include accountants, economists, financial analysts, mathematicians, rate analysts, rate engineers, risk managers, statisticians, and value engineers.

Sources of Additional Information

For facts about actuarial careers, contact:
☛American Academy of Actuaries, 1100 17th St. NW., 7th Floor, Washington, DC 20036.

For information about actuarial careers in life and health insurance, contact:
☛Society of Actuaries, 475 N. Martingale Rd., Suite 800, Schaumburg, IL 60173-2226.

For information about actuarial careers in property and casualty insurance, contact:
☛Casualty Actuarial Society, 1100 N. Glebe Rd., Suite 600, Arlington, VA 22201.

Career information on actuaries specializing in pensions is available from:
☛American Society of Pension Actuaries, 4350 N. Fairfax Dr., Suite 820, Arlington, VA 22203.

Computer Scientists and Systems Analysts

(D.O.T. 030.062-010, .162-014, .167-014; 031; 032; 033; 039; and 109.067-010)

Nature of the Work

The rapid spread of computers and computer-based technologies over the past two decades has generated a need for skilled, highly trained workers to design and develop hardware and software systems and to incorporate these advances into new or existing systems. Although many narrow specializations have developed and no uniform job titles exist, this professional specialty group is widely referred to as computer scientists and systems analysts.

Computer scientists generally design computers and conduct research to improve their design or use, and develop and adapt principles for applying computers to new uses. Computer scientists perform many of the same duties as other computer professionals throughout a normal workday, but their jobs are distinguished by the higher level of theoretical expertise and innovation they apply to complex problems and the creation or application of new technology. Computer scientists include computer engineers, database administrators, computer support analysts, and a variety of other specialized workers.

Computer scientists employed by academic institutions work in areas ranging from theory, to hardware, to language design. Some work on multi-discipline projects, for example, developing and advancing uses for virtual reality. Their counterparts in private industry work in areas such as applying theory, developing specialized languages, or designing programming tools, knowledge-based systems, or computer games.

Computer engineers work with the hardware and software aspects of systems design and development. Computer engineers may often work as part of a team that designs new computing devices or computer-related equipment. Software engineers design and develop both packaged and systems software.

Database administrators work with database management systems software. They reorganize and restructure data to better suit the needs of users. They also may be responsible for maintaining the efficiency of the database, system security, and may aid in design implementation.

Computer support analysts provide assistance and advice to users, interpreting problems and providing technical support for hardware, software, and systems. They may work within an organization or directly for the computer or software vendor.

Far more numerous, *systems analysts* use their knowledge and skills in a problem solving capacity, implementing the means for computer technology to meet the individual needs of an organization. They study business, scientific, or engineering data processing problems and design new solutions using computers. This process may include planning and developing new computer systems or devising ways to apply existing systems to operations still completed manually or by some less efficient method. Systems analysts may design entirely new systems, including both hardware and software, or add a single new software application to harness more of the computer's power. They work to help an organization realize the maximum benefit from its investment in equipment, personnel, and business processes.

Analysts begin an assignment by discussing the data processing problem with managers and users to determine its exact nature. Much time is devoted to clearly defining the goals of the system and understanding the individual steps used to achieve them so that the problem can be broken down into separate programmable procedures. Analysts then use techniques such as structured analysis, data modeling, information engineering, mathematical model building, sampling, and cost accounting to plan the system. Analysts must specify the files and records to be accessed by the system and design the processing steps, as well as the format for the output that will meet the users' needs. Once the design has been developed, systems analysts prepare charts and diagrams that describe it in terms that managers and other users can understand. They may prepare a cost-benefit and return-on-investment analysis to help management decide whether the proposed system will be satisfactory and financially feasible.

When a system is accepted, systems analysts may determine what computer hardware and software will be needed to set up the system or implement changes to it. They coordinate tests and observe initial use of the system to ensure it performs as planned. They prepare specifications, work diagrams, and structure charts for computer programmers to follow and then work with them to "debug," or eliminate errors from the system.

Some organizations do not employ programmers; instead, a single worker called a programmer-analyst is responsible for both systems analysis and programming. As this becomes more commonplace, analysts will increasingly work with Computer Aided Software Engineering (CASE) tools and object-oriented programming languages, as well as client/server applications development and multimedia and Internet technology. (The work of programmers is described elsewhere in the *Handbook*.)

One obstacle associated with expanding computer use is the inability of different computers to communicate with each other. Many systems analysts are involved with connecting all the computers in an individual office, department, or establishment. This "networking" has many variations, and may be referred to as local area networks, wide area networks, or multi-user systems, for example. A primary goal of networking is to allow users of microcomputers— also known as personal computers or PCs—to retrieve data from a mainframe computer and use it on their machine. This connection also allows data to be entered into the mainframe from the PC.

Because up-to-date information—accounting records, sales figures, or budget projections, for example—is so important in modern organizations, systems analysts may be instructed to make the computer systems in each department compatible so that facts and figures can be shared. Similarly, electronic mail requires open pathways to send messages, documents, and data from one computer "mailbox" to another across different equipment and program lines. Analysts must design the gates in the hardware and software to allow free exchange of data, custom applications, and the computer power to process it all. They study the seemingly incompatible pieces and

Systems analysts design new solutions to business, scientific, and engineering data processing problems.

create ways to link them so that users can access information from any part of the system.

Working Conditions

Computer scientists and systems analysts normally work in offices or laboratories in comfortable surroundings. They usually work about 40 hours a week—the same as many other professional or office workers. However, evening or weekend work may be necessary to meet deadlines or solve problems. Given the technology available today, more work, including technical support, can be done from remote locations using modems, laptops, electronic mail, and even through the Internet.

Because computer scientists and systems analysts spend long periods of time in front of a computer terminal typing on a keyboard, they are susceptible to eye strain, back discomfort, and hand and wrist problems.

Employment

Computer scientists and systems analysts held about 828,000 jobs in 1994. Although they are found in most industries, the greatest concentration is in the computer and data processing services industry. This includes firms that design and install computer systems; integrate or network systems; perform data processing and database management; develop packaged software; and even operate entire computer facilities under contract. Many others work for government agencies, manufacturers of computer and related electronic equipment, insurance companies, and universities.

A growing number of computer scientists and systems analysts are employed on a temporary or contract basis, or as consultants. For example, a company installing a new computer system may need the services of several systems analysts just to get the system running. Because not all of them would be needed once the system is functioning, the company might contract directly with the systems analysts themselves or with a temporary help agency or consulting firm. Such jobs may last from several months up to 2 years or more.

Training, Other Qualifications, and Advancement

There is no universally accepted way to prepare for a job as a computer professional because employers' preferences depend on the work to be done. Prior work experience is very important. Many people develop advanced computer skills in other occupations in which they work extensively with computers and then transfer into computer occupations. For example, an accountant may become a systems analyst specializing in accounting systems development, or an individual may move into a systems analyst job after working as computer programmer.

Employers almost always seek college graduates for computer professional positions; for some of the more complex jobs, persons with graduate degrees are preferred. Generally, a Ph.D., or at least a master's degree in computer science or engineering, is required for computer scientist jobs in research laboratories or academic institutions. Some computer scientists are able to gain sufficient experience for this type of position with only a bachelor's degree, but this is difficult. Computer engineers generally require a bachelor's degree in computer engineering, electrical engineering, or math. Computer support analysts may also need a bachelor's degree in a computer-related field, as well as significant experience working with computers, including programming skills.

For systems analyst or even database administrator positions, many employers seek applicants who have a bachelor's degree in computer science, information science, computer information systems, or data processing. Regardless of college major, employers generally look for people who are familiar with programming languages and have broad knowledge of and experience with computer systems and technologies. Courses in computer programming or systems design offer good preparation for a job in this field. For jobs in a business environment, employers usually want systems analysts to have a background in business management or a closely related field, while a background in the physical sciences, applied mathematics, or engineering is preferred for work in scientifically oriented organizations.

Systems analysts must be able to think logically, have good communication skills, and like working with ideas and people. They often deal with a number of tasks simultaneously. The ability to concentrate and pay close attention to detail is important. Although both computer scientists and systems analysts often work independently, they also may work in teams on large projects. They must be able to communicate effectively with computer personnel, such as programmers and managers, as well as with other staff who have no technical computer background.

Technological advances come so rapidly in the computer field that continuous study is necessary to keep skills up to date. Continuing education is usually offered by employers, hardware and software vendors, colleges and universities, or private training institutions. Additional training may come from professional development seminars offered by professional computing societies.

The Institute for Certification of Computing Professionals offers the designation Certified Computing Professional (CCP) to those who have at least 4 years of work experience as a computer professional, or at least 2 years experience and a college degree. Candidates must pass a core examination testing general knowledge, plus exams in two specialty areas, or in one specialty area and two computer programming languages. The Quality Assurance Institute awards the designation Certified Quality Analyst (CQA) to those who meet education and experience requirements, pass an exam, and endorse a code of ethics. Neither designation is mandatory, but professional certification may provide a job seeker a competitive advantage.

Systems analysts may be promoted to senior or lead systems analysts after several years of experience. Those who show leadership ability also can advance to management positions, such as manager of information systems or chief information officer.

Computer engineers and scientists employed in industry may eventually advance into managerial or project leadership positions. Those employed in academic institutions can become heads of research departments or published authorities in their field. Computer professionals with several years of experience and considerable expertise in a particular area may choose to start their own computer consulting firms.

Job Outlook

Computer scientists and systems analysts will be among the fastest growing occupations through the year 2005. In addition, tens of thousands of job openings will result annually from the need to replace workers who move into managerial positions or other occupations or who leave the labor force.

The demand for computer scientists and engineers is expected to rise as organizations attempt to maximize the efficiency of their computer systems. There will continue to be a need for increasingly sophisticated technological innovation. Competition will place organizations under growing pressure to use technological advances in areas such as office and factory automation, telecommunications technology, and scientific research. As the complexity of these applications grows, more computer scientists and systems analysts will be needed to design, develop, and implement the new technology.

As more computing power is made available to the individual user, more computer scientists and systems analysts will be required to provide support. As users develop more sophisticated knowledge of computers, they become more aware of the machine's potential and better able to suggest how computers could be used to increase their own productivity and that of the organization. Increasingly, users are able to design and implement more of their own applications and programs. As technology continues to advance, computer scientists and systems analysts will continue to need to upgrade their levels of skill and technical expertise and their ability to interact with users will increase in importance.

The demand for "networking" to facilitate the sharing of information will be a major factor in the rising demand for systems analysts. Falling prices of computer hardware and software should continue to induce more small businesses to computerize their operations, further stimulating demand for these workers. In order to maintain a competitive edge and operate more cost effectively, firms will continue to demand computer professionals who are knowledgeable about the latest technologies and able to apply them to meet the needs of businesses. A greater emphasis on problem solving, analysis, and client/server environments will also contribute to the growing demand for systems analysts.

Individuals with an advanced degree in computer science should enjoy very favorable employment prospects because employers are demanding a higher level of technical expertise. College graduates with a bachelor's degree in computer science, computer engineering, information science, or information systems should also experience good prospects for employment. College graduates with non-computer science majors who have had courses in computer programming, systems analysis, and other data processing areas, as well as training or experience in an applied field, should be able to find jobs as computer professionals. Those who are familiar with CASE tools, object-oriented and client/server programming, and multimedia technology will have an even greater advantage, as will individuals with significant networking, database, and systems experience. Employers should increasing seek computer professionals who can combine strong programming and traditional systems analysis skills with good interpersonal and business skills.

Earnings

Median annual earnings of computer systems analysts and scientists who worked full time in 1994 were about $44,000. The middle 50 percent earned between $34,100 and $55,000. The lowest 10 percent earned less than $25,100 and the highest tenth, more than $69,400. Computer scientists with advanced degrees generally earn more than systems analysts.

According to Robert Half International Inc., starting salaries in 1994 for systems analysts employed by large establishments employing more than 50 staff members ranged from $43,500 to $54,000. Salaries for those employed in small establishments ranged from $35,000 to $45,000. Starting salaries ranged from $51,000 to $62,000 for data base administrators, and from $45,000 to $62,000 for software engineers.

In the Federal Government, the entrance salary for systems analysts who are recent college graduates with a bachelor's degree was about $18,700 a year in 1995; for those with a superior academic record, $23,200.

Related Occupations

Other workers who use research, logic, and creativity to solve business problems are computer programmers, financial analysts, urban planners, engineers, operations research analysts, management analysts, and actuaries.

Sources of Additional Information

Further information about computer careers is available from:
☛Association for Computing Machinery, 1515 Broadway, New York, NY 10036.

Information about the designation Certified Computing Professional is available from:
☛Institute for the Certification of Computing Professionals, 2200 East Devon Ave., Suite 268, Des Plaines, IL 60018.

Information about the designation Certified Quality Analyst is available from:
☛Quality Assurance Institute, 7575 Dr. Phillips Blvd., Suite 350, Orlando, FL 32819.

Mathematicians

(D.O.T. 020.067-014, .167-030; 199.267-014)

Nature of the Work

Mathematics is one of the oldest and most basic sciences. Mathematicians create new mathematical theories and techniques involving the latest technology and solve economic, scientific, engineering, and business problems using mathematical knowledge and computational tools.

Mathematical work falls into two broad classes: theoretical (pure) mathematics and applied mathematics. However, these classes are not sharply defined and often overlap.

Theoretical mathematicians advance mathematical science by developing new principles and new relationships between existing principles of mathematics. Although they seek to increase basic knowledge without necessarily considering its practical use, this pure and abstract knowledge has been instrumental in producing or furthering many scientific and engineering achievements.

Applied mathematicians use theories and techniques, such as mathematical modeling and computational methods, to formulate and solve practical problems in business, government, engineering, and the physical, life, and social sciences. For example, they may analyze the mathematical aspects of computer and communications networks, the effects of new drugs on disease, the aerodynamic characteristics of aircraft, or the distribution costs or manufacturing processes of businesses. Applied mathematicians working in industrial research and development may develop or enhance mathematical methods when confronted with difficult problems. Some mathematicians, called cryptanalysts, analyze and decipher encryption systems designed to transmit national security-related information.

Mathematicians use computers extensively to analyze relationships among variables, solve complex problems, develop models, and process large amounts of data.

Much work in applied mathematics, however, is carried on by persons other than mathematicians. In fact, because mathematics is the foundation upon which many other academic disciplines are built, the number of workers using mathematical techniques is many times greater than the number actually designated as mathematicians. Engineers, computer scientists, physicists, and economists are among those who use mathematics extensively but have job titles other than mathematician. Some workers, such as statisticians, actuaries, and operations research analysts, actually are specialists in a particular branch of mathematics. (See statements on actuaries, operations research analysts, and statisticians elsewhere in the *Handbook*.)

Working Conditions

Mathematicians working for government agencies or private firms usually have structured work schedules. They may work alone, in a small group of mathematicians, or as an integral part of a team that includes engineers, computer scientists, physicists, technicians, and others. Deadlines, overtime work, special requests for information or analysis, and travel to attend seminars or conferences may be part of their jobs.

Employment

Mathematicians held about 14,000 jobs in 1994. In addition, about 20,000 persons held mathematics faculty positions in colleges and universities, according to the American Mathematical Society. (See the statement on college and university faculty elsewhere in the *Handbook*.)

Many nonfaculty mathematicians work for either Federal or State governments. The Department of Defense is the primary Federal employer of mathematicians; more than three-fourths of the mathematicians employed by the Federal Government work for the Navy, Army, or Air Force. In the private sector, major employers include research and testing services, educational services, security and commodity exchanges, and management and public relations services. Within manufacturing, the drug industry is the key employer. Some mathematicians also work for banks, insurance companies, and public utilities.

Training, Other Qualifications, and Advancement

A bachelor's degree in mathematics is the minimum education needed for prospective mathematicians. In the Federal Government, entry-level job candidates usually must have a 4-year degree with a major in mathematics or a 4-year degree with the equivalent of a mathematics major—24 semester hours of mathematics courses.

In private industry, job candidates generally need a master's or a Ph.D. degree to obtain jobs as mathematicians. Most of the positions designated for mathematicians are in research and development labs as part of technical teams. These research scientists engage in either pure mathematical, or basic, research; or in applied research focusing on developing or improving specific products or processes. The majority of bachelor's and master's degree holders in private industry work, not as mathematicians, but in related fields such as computer science, where they are called computer programmers, systems analysts, or systems engineers.

A bachelor's degree in mathematics is offered by most colleges and universities. Mathematics courses usually required for this degree are calculus, differential equations, and linear and abstract algebra. Additional coursework might include probability theory and statistics, mathematical analysis, numerical analysis, topology, modern algebra, discrete mathematics, and mathematical logic. Many colleges and universities urge or even require students majoring in mathematics to take several courses in a field that uses or is closely related to mathematics, such as computer science, engineering, operations research, a physical science, statistics, or economics. A double major in mathematics and another discipline such as computer science, economics, or one of the sciences is particularly desirable. A prospective college mathematics major should take as many mathematics courses as possible while in high school.

In 1994, about 240 colleges and universities offered a master's degree as the highest degree in either pure or applied mathematics; 195 offered a Ph.D. in pure or applied mathematics. In graduate school, students conduct research and take advanced courses, usually specializing in a subfield of mathematics. Some areas of concentration are algebra, number theory, real or complex analysis, geometry, topology, logic, and applied mathematics.

For work in applied mathematics, training in the field in which the mathematics will be used is very important. Fields in which

A large majority of mathematicians have at least a master's degree.

applied mathematics is used extensively include physics, actuarial science, engineering, and operations research; of increasing importance are computer and information science, business and industrial management, economics, statistics, chemistry, geology, life sciences, and the behavioral sciences.

Mathematicians should have substantial knowledge of computer programming because most complex mathematical computation and much mathematical modeling is done by computer.

Mathematicians need good reasoning ability and persistence in order to identify, analyze, and apply basic principles to technical problems. Communication skills are also important, as mathematicians must be able to interact with others, including nonmathematicians, and discuss proposed solutions to problems.

Job Outlook

Employment of mathematicians is expected to increase more slowly than the average for all occupations through the year 2005. The number of jobs available for workers whose educational background is solely mathematics is not expected to increase significantly. Many firms engaged in civilian research and development that use mathematicians are not planning to expand their research departments much, and, in some cases, may reduce them. Expected reductions in defense-related research and development will also affect mathematicians' employment, especially in the Federal Government. Those whose educational background includes the study of a related discipline will have better job opportunities. However, as advancements in technology lead to expanding applications of mathematics, more workers with a knowledge of mathematics will be required. Many of these workers have job titles which reflect the end product of their work rather than the discipline of mathematics used in that work.

Bachelor's degree holders in mathematics are usually not qualified for most jobs as mathematicians. However, those with a strong background in computer science, electrical or mechanical engineering, or operations research should have good opportunities in industry. Bachelor's degree holders who meet State certification requirements may become high school mathematics teachers. (For additional information, see the statement on kindergarten, elementary, and secondary school teachers elsewhere in the *Handbook.*)

Holders of a master's degree in mathematics will face very strong competition for jobs in theoretical research. However, job opportunities in applied mathematics and related areas such as computer programming, operations research, and engineering design in industry and government will be more numerous.

Earnings

According to a 1995 survey by the National Association of Colleges and Employers, starting salary offers for mathematics graduates with a bachelor's degree averaged about $30,300 a year and for those with a master's degree, $35,600. Starting salaries were generally higher in industry and government than in educational institutions. For example, the American Mathematical Society reported that, based on a 1994 survey, median annual earnings for new recipients of doctorates in research were $35,000; for those in government, $45,500; and for those in business and industry, $52,500.

In the Federal Government in 1995, the average annual salary for mathematicians in supervisory, nonsupervisory, and managerial positions was $58,150; for mathematical statisticians, $60,510; and for cryptanalysts, $52,840.

Benefits for mathematicians tend to be similar to those offered to most professionals who work in office settings: Vacation and sick leave, health and life insurance, and a retirement plan, among others.

Related Occupations

Other occupations that require a degree in or extensive knowledge of mathematics include actuary, statistician, computer programmer, systems analyst, systems engineer, and operations research analyst. In addition, a strong background in mathematics facilitates employment in fields such as engineering, economics, finance, and physics.

Sources of Additional Information

For more information about the field of mathematics, including career opportunities and professional training, contact:

☛American Mathematical Society, Department of Professional Programs and Services, P.O. Box 6248, Providence, RI 02940-6248.

☛Mathematical Association of America, 1529 18th St. NW., Washington, DC 20036.

For a 1995 resource guide on careers in mathematical sciences, send a self-addressed envelope with two first-class stamps to:

☛Conference Board of the Mathematical Sciences, 1529 18th St. NW., Washington, DC 20036.

For specific information on careers in applied mathematics, contact:

☛Society for Industrial and Applied Mathematics, 3600 University City Science Center, Philadelphia, PA 19104-2688.

Information on Federal job opportunities is available from area offices of the State employment service and the U.S. Office of Personnel Management's Federal Job Information Centers located in various large cities throughout the country.

Operations Research Analysts

(D.O.T. 020.067-018)

Nature of the Work

Efficiently running a complex organization or operation such as a large manufacturing plant, an airline, or a military deployment requires the precise coordination of materials, machines, and people. Operations research analysts help organizations coordinate and operate in the most efficient manner by applying scientific methods and mathematical principles to organizational problems. Managers can then evaluate alternatives and choose the course of action that best meets the organizational goals.

Operations research analysts, sometimes also called management science analysts, are problem solvers. The problems they tackle are for the most part those encountered in large business and government organizations, including strategy, forecasting, resource allocation, facilities layout, inventory control, personnel schedules, and distribution systems. Their methods generally use a mathematical model consisting of a set of equations that explains how things happen within the organization. Use of models enables the analyst to break down real-world problems into their component parts, assign numerical values to different components, and determine the mathematical relationships between them. These values can be altered to examine what will happen to the system under different circumstances. The situation under consideration determines the mathematical method used. Some of the methods available include simulation, linear optimization, networks, waiting lines, and game theory.

Operations research analysts use computers extensively in their work. They are typically highly proficient in database collection and management, programming, and in the development and use of sophisticated software programs. Most of the models employed by operations research analysts are so large and complicated that only a computer can solve them efficiently.

The type of problem they usually handle varies by industry. For example, an analyst for an airline coordinates flight and maintenance schedules, passenger level estimates, and fuel consumption to produce an optimal schedule that ensures safety and produces the greatest profit. An analyst employed by a hospital concentrates on a different set of problems, such as scheduling admissions, managing patient flow, assigning shifts, monitoring use of pharmacy and laboratory services, and forecasting demand for adding hospital services.

The duties of the operations research analyst vary according to the structure and management philosophy of the employer or client. Some firms centralize operations research in one department, while others disperse operations research personnel throughout all divisions. Some operations research analysts specialize in one type of application, whereas others are generalists, especially at the beginning of their careers.

The degree of supervision varies by organizational structure and experience. In some organizations, analysts have a great deal of professional autonomy, while in others, analysts are more closely supervised. Operations research analysts work closely with senior managers, who have a wide variety of support needs. Analysts must adapt their work to reflect these requirements.

Regardless of the industry or structure of the organization, operations research entails a similar set of procedures. Managers begin the process by describing the symptoms of a problem to the analyst, who then formally defines the problem. For example, an operations research analyst for an auto manufacturer may be asked to determine the best inventory level for each of the materials for a new production line or, more specifically, to determine how many windshields should be kept in inventory.

Analysts study the problem, then break it into its component parts. Then they gather information about each of these parts. Usually this involves consulting a wide variety of people and other sources of information, such as professional journals. To determine the most efficient amount of inventory to be kept on hand, for example, operations research analysts might talk with engineers about production levels, discuss purchasing arrangements with industrial buyers, and examine data on storage costs provided by the accounting department.

With this information in hand, the operations research analyst is ready to select the most appropriate analytical technique. There may be several techniques that could be used, but in some cases, the analyst must construct an original model to examine and explain the system. In almost all cases, the computer program used to run the selected model must be modified repeatedly to reflect the different circumstances of various solutions.

A model for airline flight scheduling, for example, might include variables for the cities to be connected, amount of fuel required to fly the routes, projected levels of passenger demand, varying ticket and fuel prices, pilot scheduling, and maintenance costs. The analyst then chooses the values for these variables, enters them into a computer which he or she has already programmed to make the calculations required, and runs the program to produce the best flight schedule consistent with various sets of assumptions.

At this point, the operations research analyst presents the final work to management along with recommendations based on the results of the analysis. Additional computer runs based on different assumptions may be needed to help in making the final decision between various options. Once a decision has been reached, the analyst works with others in the organization to ensure the plan's successful implementation.

Working Conditions

Operations research analysts generally work regular hours in an office environment. Because they work on projects that are of immediate interest to management, analysts often are under pressure to meet deadlines and often work more than a 40-hour week.

Employment

Operations research analysts held about 44,000 jobs in 1994. They are employed in most industries. Major employers include computer and data processing services, commercial banks and savings institutions, insurance carriers, telecommunication companies, engineering and management services firms, manufacturers of transportation equipment, air carriers, and the Federal Government. About 2 out of 10 analysts work for management, research, public relations, and testing agencies that do operations research consulting for firms that do not have an in-house operations research staff.

Most analysts in the Federal Government work for the Armed Forces. In addition, many operations research analysts who work in

Operations research analysts rely on mathematics and computer skills to solve problems.

private industry do work directly or indirectly related to national defense.

Training, Other Qualifications, and Advancement

Employers strongly prefer applicants with at least a master's degree in operations research or management science, or other quantitative disciplines. A high level of computer skills is also required.

Employers often sponsor skill-improvement training for experienced workers, helping them keep up with new developments in operations research techniques as well as advances in computer science. Some analysts attend advanced university classes on these subjects at their employer's expense.

Operations research analysts must be able to think logically and work well with people, so employers prefer workers with good oral and written communication skills. The computer is the most important tool for quantitative analysis, and both training and experience in programming is a must.

Beginning analysts usually do routine work under the supervision of more experienced analysts. As they gain knowledge and experience, they are assigned more complex tasks, with greater autonomy to design models and solve problems. Operations research analysts advance by assuming positions as technical specialists or supervisors. The skills acquired by operations research analysts are useful for higher-level management jobs, and experienced analysts may leave the field altogether to assume nontechnical managerial or administrative positions.

Job Outlook

Organizations are increasingly using operations research and management science techniques to improve productivity and quality and to reduce costs. This reflects growing acceptance of a systematic approach to decisionmaking by top managers. This trend is expected to continue and should greatly stimulate demand for these workers in the years ahead.

Those seeking employment as operations research or management science analysts who hold a master's or Ph.D. degree should find good opportunities through the year 2005. The number of openings generated each year as a result of employment growth and the need to replace those leaving the occupation, is expected to exceed the number of persons graduating with master's and Ph.D. degrees from management science or operations research programs.

Graduates with only a bachelors degrees in operations research or management science should find opportunities as research assistants or analyst assistants in a variety of related fields, which allow them to use their quantitative abilities. Only the most highly qualified are likely to find employment as operations research or management science analysts.

Employment of operations research analysts is expected to grow much faster than the average for all occupations through the year 2005 due to the increasing importance of quantitative analysis in decisionmaking. Much of the job growth is expected to occur in the transportation, manufacturing, finance, and services sectors, areas where the use of quantitative analysis can achieve dramatic improvements in operating efficiency and profitability. More airlines, for example, are using operations research to determine the best flight and maintenance schedules, select the best routes to service, analyze customer characteristics, and control fuel consumption, among other things. Motel chains are beginning to use operations research to improve their efficiency by analyzing automobile traffic patterns and customer attitudes to determine location, size, and style of proposed new motels. Like other management support functions, operations research grows by its own success. When one firm in an industry increases productivity by adopting a new procedure, its competitors usually follow. This competitive pressure will contribute to demand for operations research analysts.

Demand also should be strong in the manufacturing sector as firms expand existing operations research staffs in the face of growing domestic and foreign competition. More manufacturers are using mathematical models to study the operations of the organization. For example, analysts will be needed to determine the best way to control product inventory, distribute finished products, and to decide where sales offices should be based. In addition, increasing factory automation will require more operations research analysts to alter existing models or develop new ones for production layout, robotics installation, work schedules, and inventory control.

Earnings

According to recruiters and national operations research associations, operations research analysts with a master's degree generally earned starting salaries of about $36,000 to $45,000 a year in 1995. Experienced operations research analysts earned about $50,000 to $60,000 a year in 1995. Top salaries exceed $90,000.

The average annual salary for operations research analysts in the Federal Government in nonsupervisory, supervisory, and managerial positions was $62,450 in 1995.

Related Occupations

Operations research analysts apply mathematical principles to large, complicated problems. Workers in other occupations that stress quantitative analysis include computer scientists, engineers, mathematicians, statisticians, and economists. Operations research is closely allied to managerial occupations in that its goal is improved organizational efficiency.

Sources of Additional Information

Information on career opportunities for operations research analysts is available from:

☛The Institute for Operations Research and the Management Sciences, 290 Westminster St., Providence, RI 02903.

For information on careers in the Armed Forces and Department of Defense, contact:

☛Military Operations Research Society, 101 South Whiting St., Suite 202, Alexandria, VA 22304.

Statisticians

(D.O.T. 020.067-022, .167-026)

Nature of the Work

Statistics is the collection, analysis, and presentation of numerical data. Statisticians design surveys and experiments, then collect and interpret the resulting information or data. In doing so, they often apply their knowledge of statistical methods to a particular subject area, such as biology, economics, engineering, medicine, or psychology. They use statistical techniques to predict population growth or economic conditions, develop quality control tests for manufactured products, assess the nature of environmental problems, analyze legal and social problems, or help business managers and government officials make decisions and evaluate the results of new programs. Some statisticians develop new statistical methods.

Often statisticians are able to obtain information about a group of people or things by surveying a small portion, called a sample, of the group. For example, to determine the size of the total audience for particular programs, television rating services ask only a few thousand families, rather than all viewers, which programs they watch. Statisticians decide where and how to gather the data, determine the type and size of the sample group, and develop the survey questionnaire or reporting form. They also prepare instructions for workers who will collect and tabulate the data. Finally, statisticians analyze, interpret, and summarize the data, usually using sophisticated statistical computer software packages.

In manufacturing industries, statisticians play an important role in the area of quality improvement. For example, a statistician in an automobile manufacturing company might design experiments using statistical models to estimate the failure time of an engine exposed to extreme weather conditions and to identify factors that lead to improved performance. In chemical companies, statisticians might

Computers are essential tools for statisticians who handle large amounts of data.

design experiments to determine what combination of several chemicals would lead to the best product. Statisticians working in all industries use computers extensively to process large amounts of data for statistical modeling and graphic analysis.

Because statistics are used in so many areas, it sometimes is difficult to distinguish statisticians from specialists in other fields who use statistics. For example, a statistician working with data on economic conditions may have the title of economist.

Working Conditions

Statisticians usually work regular hours in offices. Some statisticians travel to provide advice on research projects, supervise or set up surveys, or to gather statistical data. Some may have fairly repetitive tasks, while others may have a variety of tasks, such as designing experiments.

Employment

Statisticians held about 14,000 jobs in 1994. Over one-fourth of these jobs were in the Federal Government, where statisticians were concentrated in the Departments of Commerce (especially the Bureau of the Census); Agriculture; and Health and Human Services. Most of the remaining jobs were in private industry, especially in the transportation equipment, research and testing services, management and public relations, and insurance industries. In addition, many statisticians work as teachers in post-secondary institutions, but they are counted as college and university faculty in the *Handbook.*

Training, Other Qualifications, and Advancement

A bachelor's degree with a major in statistics or mathematics is the minimum educational requirement for many beginning jobs in statistics. The training required for employment as an entry level statistician in the Federal Government is a college degree including at least 15 semester hours of statistics—or a combination of 15 hours of mathematics and statistics if at least 6 semester hours are in statistics. An additional 9 semester hours in another academic discipline, such as economics, physical or biological science, medicine, education, engineering, or social science, are also required. To qualify as a mathematical statistician in the Federal Government requires 24 semester hours of mathematics and statistics with a minimum of 6 semester hours in statistics and 12 semester hours in advanced mathematics, such as calculus, differential equations, or vector analysis. Research positions in institutions of higher education and many positions in private industry require a graduate degree, often a doctorate, in statistics.

About 80 colleges and universities offered bachelor's degrees in statistics in 1994. Many other schools also offered degrees in mathematics, operations research, and other fields which included a sufficient number of courses in statistics to qualify graduates for some beginning positions, particularly in the Federal Government. Required subjects for statistics majors include differential and integral calculus, statistical methods, mathematical modeling, and probability theory. Additional courses that undergraduates should take include linear algebra, design and analysis of experiments, applied multivariate analysis, and mathematical statistics. Because computers are used extensively for statistical applications, a strong background in computer science is highly recommended. For positions involving quality and productivity improvement, training in engineering or physical science is useful. A background in biological, chemical, or health science is important for positions involving the preparation and testing of pharmaceutical or agricultural products. For many jobs in market research, business analysis, and forecasting, courses in economics and business administration are helpful.

In 1994, approximately 110 universities offered a master's degree program in statistics, and about 58 had statistics departments which offered a doctoral degree program. Many other schools also offered graduate-level courses in applied statistics for students majoring in biology, business, economics, education, engineering, psychology, and other fields. Acceptance into graduate statistics programs does not require an undergraduate degree in statistics although a good mathematics background is essential.

Good communications skills are important for prospective statisticians, not only for those who plan to teach, but also to qualify for many positions in industry, where the need to explain statistical processes to those who are not statisticians is common. A solid understanding of business and management is also important for those who plan to work in private industry.

Beginning statisticians who have only the bachelor's degree often spend much of their time doing routine work supervised by an experienced statistician. With experience, they may advance to positions of greater technical and supervisory responsibility. However, opportunities for promotion are best for those with advanced degrees. Master's and Ph.D. degree holders enjoy greater independence in their work and are qualified to engage in research, to develop statistical methods, or, after several years of experience in a particular area of technological application, to become statistical consultants.

Job Outlook

Although employment of statisticians is expected to grow more slowly than the average for all occupations through the year 2005, job opportunities should remain favorable for individuals with statistics training. Many statistics majors, particularly at the bachelor's degree level, but also at the master's degree level, may find positions in which they do not have the title of statistician. This is especially true for those involved in analyzing and interpreting data from other disciplines such as economics, biological science, psychology, or engineering.

Among graduates with a bachelor's degree in statistics, those with a strong background in mathematics, engineering, or health or computer science should have the best prospects of finding jobs related to their field of study in private industry or government. Federal Government agencies will need statisticians in fields such as demography, agriculture, consumer and producer surveys, Social Security, health, education, energy conservation, and environmental quality control. However, competition for entry level positions in the Federal Government is expected to be strong for those just meeting the minimum qualification standards for statisticians. Those who meet State certification requirements may become high school statistics teachers, a newly emerging field. (For additional information, see the statement on kindergarten, elementary, and secondary school teachers elsewhere in the *Handbook.*)

Private industry, in the face of increasing competition and strong government regulation, will continue to require statisticians, especially at the master's and Ph.D. degree levels, to not only monitor but improve productivity and quality in the manufacture of various products including pharmaceuticals, motor vehicles, chemicals, and food products. For example, pharmaceutical firms will need more statisticians to assess the safety and effectiveness of the rapidly expanding number of drugs. To meet continuing competition, motor vehicle manufacturers will need statisticians to improve and monitor the quality of automobiles, trucks, and their components by developing tests for new and existing designs. Statisticians with a knowledge of engineering and the physical sciences will find jobs in research and development, working with scientists and engineers to help improve design and production processes in order to ensure consistent quality of newly developed products. Business firms will rely more heavily than in the past on workers with a background in statistics to forecast sales, analyze business conditions, and help solve management problems. In addition, sophisticated statistical services will increasingly be contracted out to consulting firms.

Earnings

The average annual salary for statisticians in the Federal Government in nonsupervisory, supervisory, and managerial positions was $56,890 in 1995; mathematical statisticians averaged $60,510.

Statisticians who hold advanced degrees generally earn higher starting salaries.

Benefits for statisticians tend to resemble those offered most professionals who work in an office setting: Vacation and sick leave, health and life insurance, and a retirement plan, among others.

Related Occupations

People in numerous occupations work with statistics. Among them are actuaries, mathematicians, operations research analysts, computer programmers, computer systems analysts, engineers, economists, financial analysts, information scientists, life scientists, physical scientists, and social scientists.

Sources of Additional Information

For information about career opportunities in statistics, contact:

☛American Statistical Association, 1429 Duke St., Alexandria, VA 22314.

For information on a career as a mathematical statistician, contact:

☛Institute of Mathematical Statistics, 3401 Investment Blvd., No. 7, Hayward, CA 94545.

Information on Federal job opportunities is available from area offices of the State employment service and the U.S. Office of Personnel Management or from Federal Job Information Centers located in various large cities throughout the country.

Life Scientists

Agricultural Scientists

(D.O.T. 040.061-010, -014, -018, -038, -042, and -058; 041.061-014, -018, -046, and -082; and 041.081)

Nature of the Work

The work agricultural scientists do plays an important part in maintaining and increasing the Nation's agricultural productivity. Agricultural scientists study farm crops and animals and develop ways of improving their quantity and quality. They look for ways to improve crop yield and quality with less labor, control pests and weeds more safely and effectively, and conserve soil and water. They research methods of converting raw agricultural commodities into attractive and healthy food products for consumers.

Agricultural science is closely related to biological science, and agricultural scientists use the principles of biology, chemistry, and other sciences to solve problems in agriculture. They often work with biological scientists on basic biological research and in applying to agriculture the advances in knowledge brought about by biotechnology.

Many agricultural scientists work in basic or applied research and development. Others manage or administer research and development programs or manage marketing or production operations in companies that produce food products or agricultural chemicals, supplies, and machinery. Some agricultural scientists are consultants to business firms, private clients, or to government.

Depending on the agricultural scientist's area of specialization, the nature of the work performed varies.

Food science. Food scientists or technologists are usually employed in the food processing industry, universities, or the Federal Government, and help meet consumer demand for food products that are healthful, safe, palatable, and convenient. To do this, they use their knowledge of chemistry, microbiology, and other sciences to develop new or better ways of preserving, processing, packaging, storing, and delivering foods. Some engage in basic research, discovering new food sources; analyzing food content to determine levels of vitamins, fat, sugar, or protein; or searching for substitutes for harmful or undesirable additives, such as nitrites. Many food technologists work in product development. Others enforce government regulations, inspecting food processing areas and ensuring that sanitation, safety, quality, and waste management standards are met.

Plant science. Plant science includes the disciplines of agronomy, crop science, entomology, and plant breeding, among others. These scientists study plants and their growth in soils, helping producers of food, feed, and fiber crops to continue to feed a growing population while conserving natural resources and maintaining the environment. Agronomists and crop scientists not only help increase productivity, but also study ways to improve the nutritional value of crops and the quality of seed. Some crop scientists study the breeding, physiology, and management of crops and use genetic engineering to develop crops resistant to pests and drought.

Soil science. Soil scientists study the chemical, physical, biological, and mineralogical composition of soils as they relate to plant or crop growth. They study the responses of various soil types to fertilizers, tillage practices, and crop rotation. Many soil scientists who work for the Federal Government conduct soil surveys, classifying and mapping soils. They provide information and recommendations to farmers and other landowners regarding the best use of land and how to avoid or correct problems such as erosion. They may also consult with engineers and other technical personnel working on construction projects about the effects of, and solutions to, soil problems. Since soil science is closely related to environmental science, persons trained in soil science also apply their knowledge to ensure environmental quality and effective land use.

Animal science. Animal scientists develop better, more efficient ways of producing and processing meat, poultry, eggs, and milk.

An entomologist talks to local farmers about insect problems in growing corn.

Dairy scientists, poultry scientists, animal breeders, and other related scientists study the genetics, nutrition, reproduction, growth, and development of domestic farm animals. Some animal scientists inspect and grade livestock food products, purchase livestock, or work in technical sales or marketing. As extension agents or consultants, animal scientists advise agricultural producers on how to upgrade animal housing facilities properly, lower mortality rates, or increase production of animal products, such as milk or eggs.

Working Conditions

Agricultural scientists involved in management or basic research tend to work regular hours in offices and laboratories. The working environment for those engaged in applied research or product development varies, depending on the discipline of agricultural science and the type of employer. For example, food scientists in private industry may work in test kitchens while investigating new processing techniques. Animal scientists working for Federal or State research stations may spend part of their time at dairies, farrowing houses, feedlots, farm animal facilities, or outdoors conducting research associated with livestock. Soil and crop scientists also spend time outdoors conducting research on farms or agricultural research stations.

Employment

Agricultural scientists held about 26,000 jobs in 1994. In addition, several thousand persons held agricultural science faculty positions in colleges and universities. (See the statement on college and university faculty elsewhere in the *Handbook*.)

About one-third of all nonfaculty agricultural scientists work for Federal, State, or local governments. Nearly 1 out of 4 worked for the Federal Government in 1994, mostly in the Department of Agriculture. In addition, large numbers worked for State governments at State agricultural colleges or agricultural research stations. Some worked for agricultural service companies; others worked for commercial research and development laboratories, seed companies, pharmaceutical companies, wholesale distributors, and food products companies. About 4,000 agricultural scientists were self-employed in 1994, mainly as consultants.

Training, Other Qualifications, and Advancement

Training requirements for agricultural scientists depend on specialty and the type of work they perform. A bachelor's degree in agricultural science is sufficient for some jobs in applied research or in assisting in basic research, but a master's or doctoral degree is required for basic research. A Ph.D. degree in agricultural science is usually needed for college teaching and for advancement to administrative research positions. Degrees in related sciences such as biology, chemistry, or physics or in related engineering specialties also may qualify persons for some agricultural science jobs.

All States have a land-grant college which offers agricultural science degrees. Many other colleges and universities also offer agricultural science degrees or some agricultural science courses. However, not every school offers all specialties. A typical undergraduate agricultural science curriculum includes communications, economics, business, and physical and life sciences courses, in addition to a wide variety of technical agricultural science courses. For prospective animal scientists, these technical agricultural science courses might include animal breeding, reproductive physiology, nutrition, and meats and muscle biology; students preparing as food scientists take courses such as food chemistry, food analysis, food microbiology, and food processing operations; and those preparing as crop or soil scientists take courses in plant pathology, soil chemistry, entomology, plant physiology, and biochemistry, among others. Advanced degree programs include classroom and fieldwork, laboratory research, and a thesis based on independent research.

Agricultural scientists should be able to work independently or as part of a team and be able to communicate clearly and concisely, both orally and in writing. Most agricultural scientists also need an understanding of basic business principles.

Agricultural scientists who have advanced degrees usually begin in research or teaching. With experience, they may advance to jobs such as supervisors of research programs or managers of other agriculture-related activities.

Job Outlook

Employment of agricultural scientists is expected to grow about as fast as the average for all occupations through the year 2005. Additionally, the need to replace agricultural scientists who retire or otherwise leave the occupation permanently will account for many more job openings than projected growth. Although the number of degrees awarded in agricultural science programs has been steady or even declined since the 1980s, new entrants, even those with advanced degrees, may still face competition for jobs as agricultural scientists. Animal and plant scientists with a background in molecular biology, microbiology, genetics, or biotechnology, soil scientists with an interest in the environment, and food technologists may find the best opportunities.

Generally speaking, those with advanced degrees will be in the best position to enter jobs as agricultural scientists. However, competition for teaching positions in colleges or universities and for some basic research jobs may be keen, even for doctoral holders. Federal and State budget cuts may limit funding for these positions through the year 2005.

Bachelor's degree holders can work in some applied research and product development positions, but usually only in certain subfields, such as food science and technology. Also, the Federal Government hires bachelor's degree holders to work as soil scientists. Despite the more limited opportunities for those with only a bachelor's degree to obtain jobs as agricultural scientists, a bachelor's degree in agricultural science is useful for managerial jobs in businesses that deal with ranchers and farmers such as feed, fertilizer, seed, and farm equipment manufacturers; retailers or wholesalers; and farm credit institutions. Four-year degrees may also help persons enter occupations such as farmer or farm or ranch manager, cooperative extension service agent, agricultural products inspector, technician, landscape architect, or purchasing or sales agent for agricultural commodities or farm supplies.

Earnings

According to the National Association of Colleges and Employers, beginning salary offers in 1995 for graduates with a bachelor's degree in animal science averaged about $24,200 a year, and for graduates in plant science, $22,500.

Average Federal salaries for employees in nonsupervisory, supervisory, and managerial positions in certain agricultural science specialties in 1995 were as follows: Animal science, $61,480; agronomy, $49,270; soil science, $46,140; horticulture, $48,210; entomology, $58,200.

Related Occupations

The work of agricultural scientists is closely related to that of biologists and other natural scientists such as chemists, foresters, and conservation scientists. It is also related to agricultural production occupations such as farmer and farm manager and cooperative extension service agent. Certain specialties of agricultural science are also related to other occupations. For example, the work of animal scientists is related to that of veterinarians; horticulturists, to landscape architects; and soil scientists, to soil conservationists.

Sources of Additional Information

Information on careers in agricultural science is available from:

☛American Society of Agronomy, Crop Science Society of America, Soil Science Society of America, 677 S. Segoe Rd., Madison, WI 53711.

☛Food and Agricultural Careers for Tomorrow, Attn.: Dr. Allan Goecker, Purdue University, 1140 Agricultural Administration Bldg., West Lafayette, IN 47907-1140.

For information on careers in food technology, write to:

☛Institute of Food Technologists, Attn.: Dean Duxbury, Suite 300, 221 N. LaSalle St., Chicago IL 60601.

For information on careers in animal science, write to:

☛The American Society of Animal Science, 309 West Clark St., Champaign, IL 61820.

Information on Federal job opportunities is available from local offices of State employment security agencies or offices of the U.S. Office of Personnel Management, located in major metropolitan areas.

Biological and Medical Scientists

(D.O.T. 022.081-010; 041.061, except -014, -018, -046, and -082; 041.067-010; 041.261-010)

Nature of the Work

Biological and medical scientists study living organisms and their relationship to their environment. Most specialize in some area of biology such as zoology (the study of animals) or microbiology (the study of microscopic organisms).

Many biological scientists and virtually all medical scientists work in research and development. Some conduct basic research to increase knowledge of living organisms. Others, in applied research, use knowledge provided by basic research to develop new medicines, increase crop yields, and improve the environment. Biological and medical scientists who conduct research usually work in laboratories and use electron microscopes, computers, thermal cyclers, or a wide variety of other equipment. Some may conduct experiments on laboratory animals or greenhouse plants. For some biological scientists, a good deal of research is performed outside of laboratories. For example, a botanist may do research in tropical rain forests to see what plants grow there, or an ecologist may study how a forest area recovers after a fire.

Some biological and medical scientists work in management or administration. They may plan and administer programs for testing foods and drugs, for example, or direct activities at zoos or botanical gardens. Some biological scientists work as consultants to business firms or to government, while others test and inspect foods, drugs, and other products or write for technical publications. Some work in sales and service jobs for companies manufacturing chemicals or other technical products. (See the statement on manufacturers' and wholesale sales representatives elsewhere in the Handbook.)

Advances in basic biological knowledge, especially at the genetic and molecular levels, continue to spur the field of biotechnology. Biological and medical scientists using this technology manipulate the genetic material of animals or plants, attempting to make organisms more productive or disease resistant. The first application of this technology has been in the medical and pharmaceutical areas. Many substances not previously available in large quantities are starting to be produced by biotechnological means; some may be useful in treating cancer and other diseases. Advances in biotechnology have opened up research opportunities in almost all areas of biology, including commercial applications in agriculture and the food and chemical industries.

Most biological scientists who come under the broad category of biologist are further classified by the type of organism they study or by the specific activity they perform, although recent advances in the understanding of basic life processes at the molecular and cellular levels have blurred some traditional classifications.

Aquatic biologists study plants and animals living in water. Marine biologists study salt water organisms and limnologists study fresh water organisms. Marine biologists are sometimes erroneously called oceanographers, but oceanography usually refers to the study of the physical characteristics of oceans and the ocean floor. (See the statement on geologists and geophysicists elsewhere in the Handbook.)

Biochemists study the chemical composition of living things. They try to understand the complex chemical combinations and reactions involved in metabolism, reproduction, growth, and heredity. Much of the work in biotechnology is done by biochemists and molecular biologists because this technology involves understanding the complex chemistry of life.

Botanists study plants and their environment. Some study all aspects of plant life; others specialize in areas such as identification and classification of plants, the structure and function of plant parts, the biochemistry of plant processes, the causes and cures of plant diseases, and the geological record of plants.

Microbiologists investigate the growth and characteristics of microscopic organisms such as bacteria, algae, or fungi. Medical microbiologists study the relationship between organisms and disease or the effect of antibiotics on microorganisms. Other microbiologists may specialize in environmental, food, agricultural, or industrial microbiology, virology (the study of viruses), or immunology (the study of mechanisms that fight infections). Many microbiologists are using biotechnology to advance knowledge of cell reproduction and human disease.

Physiologists study life functions of plants and animals, both in the whole organism and at the cellular or molecular level, under normal and abnormal conditions. Physiologists may specialize in functions such as growth, reproduction, photosynthesis, respiration, or movement, or in the physiology of a certain area or system of the organism.

Zoologists study animals—their origin, behavior, diseases, and life processes. Some experiment with live animals in controlled or natural surroundings while others dissect dead animals to study their structure. Zoologists are usually identified by the animal group studied—ornithologists (birds), mammalogists (mammals), herpetologists (reptiles), and ichthyologists (fish).

Ecologists study the relationship among organisms and between organisms and their environments and the effects of influences such as population size, pollutants, rainfall, temperature, and altitude.

Agricultural scientists, who may also be classified as biological scientists, are included in a separate statement elsewhere in the Handbook.

Biological scientists who do biomedical research are usually called medical scientists. Medical scientists working on basic research into normal biological systems often do so in order to understand the causes of and to discover treatment for disease and other health problems. Medical scientists may try to identify the kinds of changes in a cell, chromosome, or even gene that signal the development of medical problems, such as different types of cancer. After identifying structures of or changes in organisms that provide clues to health problems, medical scientists may then work on the treatment of problems. For example, a medical scientist involved in cancer research might try to formulate a combination of drugs which will lessen the effects of the disease. Medical scientists who have a medical degree might then administer the drugs to patients in clinical trials, monitor their reactions, and observe the results. (Medical scientists who do not have a medical degree normally collaborate with a medical doctor who deals directly with patients.) The medical scientist might then return to the laboratory to examine the results and, if necessary, adjust the dosage levels to reduce negative side effects or to try to induce even better results. In addition to using basic research to develop treatments for health problems, medical scientists attempt to discover ways to prevent health problems from developing, such as affirming the link between smoking and increased risk of lung cancer, or alcoholism and liver disease.

Working Conditions

Biological and medical scientists generally work regular hours in offices or laboratories and usually are not exposed to unsafe or

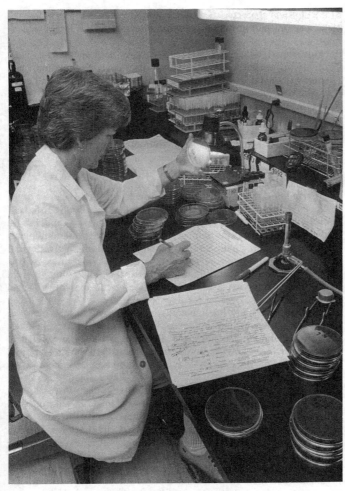

Demand will remain strong for biological and medical scientists to research health problems and discover new treatments.

unhealthy conditions. Some work with dangerous organisms or toxic substances in the laboratory, so strict safety procedures must be followed to avoid contamination. Medical scientists also spend time working in clinics and hospitals administering drugs and treatments to patients in clinical trials. Many biological scientists such as botanists, ecologists, and zoologists take field trips which involve strenuous physical activity and primitive living conditions.

Employment
Biological and medical scientists held about 118,000 jobs in 1994. In addition, many biological and medical scientists held biology faculty positions in colleges and universities. (See the statement on college and university faculty elsewhere in the *Handbook*.)

Almost 1 in 3 nonfaculty biological scientists were employed by Federal, State, and local governments. Federal biological scientists worked mainly in the U.S. Departments of Agriculture, the Interior, and Defense, and in the National Institutes of Health. Most of the rest worked in the drug industry, which includes pharmaceutical and biotechnology establishments; hospitals; or research and testing laboratories. About 6 percent of medical scientists worked in research and testing laboratories, with most of the remainder found in hospitals and the drug industry.

Training, Other Qualifications, and Advancement
For biological scientists, the Ph.D. degree generally is required for college teaching, independent research, and for advancement to administrative positions. A master's degree is sufficient for some jobs in applied research and for jobs in management, inspection, sales, and service. The bachelor's degree is adequate for some nonresearch jobs. Some graduates with a bachelor's degree start as biological scientists in testing and inspection, or get jobs related to biological science such as technical sales or service representatives. In some cases, graduates with a bachelor's degree are able to work in a laboratory environment on their own projects, but this is unusual. Some may work as research assistants. Others become biological technicians, medical laboratory technologists or, with courses in education, high school biology teachers. (See the statements on clinical laboratory technologists and technicians; science technicians; and kindergarten, elementary, and secondary school teachers elsewhere in the *Handbook*.) Many with a bachelor's degree in biology enter medical, dental, veterinary, or other health profession schools. Some enter a wide range of occupations with little or no connection to biology.

Most colleges and universities offer bachelor's degrees in biological science and many offer advanced degrees. Curriculums for advanced degrees often emphasize a subfield such as microbiology or botany but not all universities offer all curriculums. Advanced degree programs include classroom and field work, laboratory research, and a thesis or dissertation. Biological scientists who have advanced degrees often take temporary post-doctoral research positions which provide specialized research experience. In private industry, some may become managers or administrators within biology; others leave biology for nontechnical managerial, administrative, or sales jobs.

Biological scientists should be able to work independently or as part of a team and be able to communicate clearly and concisely, both orally and in writing. Those in private industry who aspire to management or administrative positions should possess good business skills and be familiar with regulatory issues and marketing and management techniques. Those doing field research in remote areas must have physical stamina.

The Ph.D. degree in a biological science is the minimum education required for prospective medical scientists because the work of medical scientists is almost entirely research oriented. A Ph.D. degree qualifies one to do research on basic life processes or on particular medical problems or diseases, and to analyze and interpret the results of experiments on patients. Medical scientists who administer drug or gene therapy to human patients, or who otherwise interact medically with patients (such as drawing blood, excising tissue, or performing other invasive procedures) must have a medical degree. It is particularly helpful for medical scientists to earn both Ph.D. and medical degrees.

In addition to the formal education, medical scientists are usually expected to spend several years in a post-doctoral position before they are offered permanent jobs. Post-doctoral work provides valuable laboratory experience, including experience in specific processes and techniques (such as gene splicing) which are transferable to other research projects later on. In some institutions, the post-doctoral position can lead to a permanent position.

Job Outlook
Employment of biological and medical scientists is expected to increase faster than the average for all occupations through the year 2005. Nevertheless, jobseekers can expect to face considerable competition for highly sought-after basic research positions. Biological and medical scientists will continue to conduct genetic and biotechnological research and help develop and produce products developed by new biological methods. In addition, efforts to clean up and preserve the environment will continue to add to growth. More biological scientists will be needed to determine the environmental impact of industry and government actions and to correct past environmental problems. Expected expansion in research related to health issues, such as AIDS, cancer, and the Human Genome project, should also result in growth. However, much research and develop-

ment, including many areas of medical research, is funded by the Federal Government. Anticipated budget tightening should lead to smaller increases in research and development expenditures, further limiting the dollar amount of each grant and slowing the growth of the number of grants awarded to researchers. If, at the same time, the number of newly trained scientists continues to increase at a rate similar to that of the 1980s, both new and established scientists will experience greater difficulty winning and renewing research grants.

Persons with a bachelor's degree in biological science are usually not called biological scientists, but find jobs as science or engineering technicians or health technologists and technicians. Some become high school biology teachers, where they are regarded as teachers rather than biologists. Those with a doctorate in biological science may become college and university faculty. (See statements on science and engineering technicians, health technologists and technicians, high school teachers, and college and university faculty elsewhere in the *Handbook.*)

Biological and medical scientists are less likely to lose their jobs during recessions than those in many other occupations because most are employed on long-term research projects or in agricultural research. However, a recession could influence the amount of money allocated to new research and development efforts, particularly in areas of risky or innovative research. A recession could also limit the possibility of extension or renewal of existing projects.

Earnings

Median annual earnings for biological and life scientists were about $37,500 in 1994; the middle 50 percent earned between $26,700 and $49,600. Ten percent earned less than $16,300, and 10 percent earned over $67,000. For medical scientists, median annual earnings were about $36,300; the middle 50 percent earned between $27,800 and $56,700. Ten percent earned less than $20,000, and 10 percent earned over $73,900. According to the National Association of Colleges and Employers, beginning salary offers in private industry in 1995 averaged $22,900 a year for bachelor's degree recipients in biological science; about $29,400 for master's degree recipients; and about $48,000 for doctoral degree recipients.

In the Federal Government in 1995, general biological scientists in nonsupervisory, supervisory, and managerial positions earned an average salary of $48,290; microbiologists averaged $54,280; ecologists, $47,840; physiologists, $61,150; and geneticists, $60,110.

Related Occupations

Many other occupations deal with living organisms and require a level of training similar to that of biological and medical scientists. These include the conservation occupations of forester, range manager, and soil conservationist; animal breeders, horticulturists, soil scientists, and most other agricultural scientists. Many health occupations are also related to those in the biological sciences, such as medical doctors, dentists, and veterinarians.

Sources of Additional Information

For information on careers in physiology, contact:
☛American Physiological Society, Membership Services Dept., 9650 Rockville Pike, Bethesda, MD 20814.

For information on careers in biotechnology, contact:
☛Biotechnology Industry Organization, 1625 K St., NW., Suite 1100, Washington, DC 20006.

For information on careers in biochemistry, contact:
☛American Society for Biochemistry and Molecular Biology, 9650 Rockville Pike, Bethesda, MD 20814.

For information on careers in botany, contact:
☛Business Office, Botanical Society of America, 1725 Neil Ave., Columbus, OH 43210-1293.

For information on careers in microbiology, contact:
☛American Society for Microbiology, Office of Education and Training—Career Information, 1325 Massachusetts Ave. NW., Washington, DC 20005.

Information on Federal job opportunities is available from local offices of State employment services or offices of the U.S. Office of Personnel Management, located in major metropolitan areas.

Foresters and Conservation Scientists

(D.O.T. 040.061-030, -046, -050, -054, and -062; .167-010; 049.127)

Nature of the Work

Forests and rangelands serve a variety of needs: They supply wood products, livestock forage, minerals, and water; serve as sites for recreational activities; and provide habitats for wildlife. Foresters and conservation scientists manage, develop, use, and help protect these and other natural resources.

Foresters manage forested lands for a variety of purposes. Those working in private industry may procure timber from private landowners. To do this, foresters contact local forest owners and gain permission to take inventory of the type, amount, and location of all standing timber on the property, a process known as timber cruising. Foresters then appraise the timber's worth, negotiate the purchase of timber, and draw up a contract for procurement. Next, they subcontract with loggers or pulpwood cutters for tree removal, aid in road layout, and maintain close contact with the subcontractor's workers and the landowner to ensure that the work meets the landowner's requirements, as well as Federal, State, and local environmental specifications. Forestry consultants often act as agents for the forest owner, performing the above duties and negotiating timber sales with industrial procurement foresters.

Throughout the process, foresters consider the economics of the purchase as well as the environmental impact on natural resources, a function which has taken on added importance in recent years. To do this, they determine how best to conserve wildlife habitats, creek beds, water quality, and soil stability and how best to comply with environmental regulations. Foresters must balance the desire to conserve forested ecosystems for future generations with the need to use forest resources for recreational or economic purposes.

Foresters also supervise the planting and growing of new trees, a process called regeneration. They choose and prepare the site, using controlled burning, bulldozers, or herbicides to clear weeds, brush, and logging debris. They advise on the type, number, and placement of trees to be planted. Foresters then monitor the trees to ensure healthy growth and to determine the best time for harvesting. If they detect signs of disease or harmful insects, they decide on the best course of treatment to prevent contamination or infestation of healthy trees.

Foresters who work for State and Federal governments manage public forests and parks and also work with private landowners to protect and manage forest land outside of the public domain. They may also design campgrounds and recreation areas.

Foresters use a number of tools to perform their jobs: Clinometers measure the heights, diameter tapes measure the diameter, and increment borers and bark gauges measure the growth of trees so that timber volumes can be computed and future growth estimated. Photogrammetry and remote sensing (aerial photographs taken from airplanes and satellites) are often used for mapping large forest areas and for detecting widespread trends of forest and land use. Computers are used extensively, both in the office and in the field, for the storage, retrieval, and analysis of information required to manage the forest land and its resources.

Range managers, also called range *conservationists*, range *ecologists*, or range *scientists*, manage, improve, and protect rangelands to maximize their use without damaging the environment. Rangelands cover about 1 billion acres of the United States, mostly in the western States and Alaska. They contain many natural resources, including grass and shrubs for animal grazing, wildlife habitats, water from vast watersheds, recreation facilities, and valuable mineral and energy resources. Range managers help ranchers attain optimum livestock production by determining the number and kind of animals to graze, the grazing system to use, and the best season for grazing. At the same time, however, they maintain soil stability and vegetation for other uses such as wildlife habitats and outdoor recreation. They also plan and implement revegetation of disturbed sites.

Soil conservationists provide technical assistance to farmers, ranchers, State and local governments, and others concerned with the conservation of soil, water, and related natural resources. They develop programs designed to get the most productive use of land without damaging it. Conservationists visit areas with erosion problems, find the source of the problem, and help landowners and managers develop management practices to combat it.

Foresters and conservation scientists often specialize in one area such as forest resource management, urban forestry, wood technology, or forest economics.

Foresters and conservation scientists spend much time working outdoors.

Working Conditions

Working conditions vary considerably. Although some of the work is solitary, foresters and conservation scientists also deal regularly with landowners, loggers, forestry technicians and aides, farmers, ranchers, government officials, special interest groups, and the public in general. Some work regular hours in offices or labs.

The work can be physically demanding. Many foresters and conservation scientists often work outdoors in all kinds of weather, sometimes in isolated areas. Some foresters may need to walk long distances through densely wooded land to carry out their work. Foresters also may work long hours fighting fires. Conservation scientists are often called in to prevent erosion after a forest fire, and they provide emergency help after floods, mudslides, and tropical storms.

Employment

Foresters and conservation scientists held about 41,000 jobs in 1994. About 12,000 of the salaried workers were in the Federal Government, primarily in the Department of Agriculture's Forest Service and Natural Resource Conservation Service and in the Department of the Interior's Bureau of Land Management. Another 24 percent worked for State governments, and 7 percent worked for local governments. The remainder worked in private industry, mainly in the forestry industry. Other significant employers included logging and lumber companies and sawmills. Some were self-employed as consultants for private landowners, State and Federal governments, and forestry-related businesses.

Most soil conservationists work for the Department of Agriculture's Natural Resource Conservation Service. Others are employed by State and local governments in their soil conservation districts.

Although foresters and conservation scientists work in every State, employment of foresters is concentrated in the western and southeastern States, where many national and private forests and parks are, and where most of the lumber and pulpwood-producing forests are. Range managers work almost entirely in the western States, where most of the rangeland is located. Soil conservationists, on the other hand, are employed in almost every county in the country.

Training, Other Qualifications, and Advancement

A bachelor's degree in forestry is the minimum educational requirement for professional careers in forestry. In the Federal Government, a combination of experience and appropriate education may occasionally substitute for a 4-year forestry degree, but job competition makes this difficult.

Fourteen States have either mandatory licensing or voluntary registration requirements which a forester must meet in order to acquire the title "professional forester." Becoming licensed or registered usually requires a 4-year degree in forestry, a minimum period of training time, and passing an exam.

Foresters who wish to perform specialized research or teach should have an advanced degree, preferably a Ph.D.

In 1995, about 60 colleges and universities offered bachelor's or higher degrees in forestry; 47 of these were accredited by the Society of American Foresters. Curriculums stress science, mathematics, communications skills, and computer science, as well as technical forestry subjects. Courses in forest economics and business administration supplement the student's scientific and technical knowledge. Prospective foresters should also have a strong grasp on policy issues and on the increasingly numerous and complex environmental regulations which affect many forestry-related activities. Many colleges require students to complete a field session either in a camp operated by the college or in a cooperative work-study program with a Federal or State agency or private industry. All schools encourage students to take summer jobs that provide experience in forestry or conservation work.

A bachelor's degree in range management or range science is the usual minimum educational requirement for range managers; graduate degrees generally are required for teaching and research positions. In 1994, 31 colleges and universities offered degrees in range management or range science or in a closely related discipline with a range management or range science option. A number of other schools offered some courses in range management or range science. Specialized range management courses combine plant, animal, and soil sciences with principles of ecology and resource management. Desirable electives include economics, forestry, hydrology, agronomy, wildlife, animal husbandry, computer science, and recreation.

Very few colleges and universities offer degrees in soil conservation. Most soil conservationists have degrees in environmental studies, agronomy, general agriculture, hydrology, or crop or soil science; a few have degrees in related fields such as wildlife biology, forestry, and range management. Programs of study generally include 30 semester hours in natural resources or agriculture, including at least 3 hours in soil science. The Soil and Water Conservation Society sponsors a certification program based on education, experience, and testing. Upon completion of the program, individuals are designated as Certified Professional Erosion and Sediment Control specialist.

In addition to meeting the demands of forestry and conservation research and analysis, foresters and conservation scientists generally must enjoy working outdoors, be physically hardy, and be willing to move to where the jobs are. They must also work well with people and have good communications skills.

Recent forestry and range management graduates usually work under the supervision of experienced foresters or range managers. After gaining experience, they may advance to more responsible positions. In the Federal Government, most entry level foresters work in forest resource management. An experienced Federal forester may supervise a ranger district, and may advance to forest supervisor, regional forester, or to a top administrative position in the national headquarters. In private industry, foresters start by learning the practical and administrative aspects of the business and acquiring comprehensive technical training. They are then introduced to contract writing, timber harvesting, and decision making. Some foresters work their way up to top managerial positions within their companies. Foresters in management usually leave the fieldwork behind, spending more of their time in an office, working with teams to develop management plans and supervising others. After gaining several years of experience, some foresters may become consulting foresters, working alone or with one or several partners. They contract with State or local governments, private landowners, private industry, or other forestry consulting groups.

Soil conservationists usually begin working within one county or conservation district and with experience may advance to the area, State, regional, or national level. Also, soil conservationists can transfer to related occupations such as farm or ranch management advisor or land appraiser.

Job Outlook
Employment of foresters and conservation scientists is expected to grow as fast as the average for all occupations through the year 2005. At the State and local government level, demand will be spurred by a continuing emphasis on environmental protection and responsible land management. For example, urban foresters are increasingly needed to do environmental impact studies in urban areas and to help regional planning commissions make land use decisions, particularly in the Northeast and in other major population centers of the country. At the State level, more numerous and complex environmental regulations have created demand for more foresters and conservation scientists to deal with these issues. Also, the nationwide Stewardship Incentive Program, funded by the Federal Government, provides money to the States to encourage landowners to practice multiple-use forest management. Foresters will be needed to assist landowners in making decisions about how to manage their forested property. Job opportunities for soil conservationists will also grow as government regulations, such as those regarding the management of stormwater and coastlines, has created demand for persons knowledgeable about erosion, not only on farms, but in cities and suburbs. In private industry, more foresters should be needed to improve forest and logging practices, increase output and profitability, and deal with environmental regulations.

Opportunities for foresters will be fewer in the Federal government, partly due to budgetary constraints. Also, Federal land management agencies, such as the Forest Service, are de-emphasizing their timber programs and focusing increasingly on wildlife, recreation, and sustaining ecosystems, increasing demand for other life and social scientists relative to foresters. However, a large number of foresters is expected to retire or leave the labor force for other reasons, which will provide additional opportunities for jobseekers.

Although job openings between 1994 and 2005 are expected to be fewer than during the 1980s, the number of degrees awarded in forestry each year is also expected to be lower, creating good opportunities. However, if the number of students graduating with forestry degrees increases quickly, jobseekers may face increased competition.

Certain areas of the country offer greater job opportunities for foresters and range conservationists than others. Employment for range conservationists is concentrated in the West and Midwest, and most forestry-related employment is in the South and West.

Earnings
Most graduates entering the Federal Government as foresters, range managers, or soil conservationists with a bachelor's degree started at $18,700 or $23,200 a year, in 1995, depending on academic achievement. Those with a master's degree could start at $23,200 or $28,300. Holders of doctorates could start at $34,300 or, in research positions, at $41,100. Beginning salaries were slightly higher in selected areas where the prevailing local pay level was higher. In 1995, the average Federal salary for foresters in nonsupervisory, supervisory, and managerial positions was $44,700; for soil conservationists, $42,220; and for forest products technologists, $58,680.

In private industry, starting salaries for students with a bachelor's degree were comparable to starting salaries in the Federal Government, but starting salaries in State and local governments were generally lower.

Foresters and conservation scientists who work for Federal, State, and local governments and large private firms generally receive more generous benefits—for example, pension and retirement plans, health and life insurance, and paid vacations—than those working for smaller firms.

Related Occupations
Foresters and conservation scientists are not the only workers who manage, develop, and protect natural resources. Other workers with similar responsibilities include agricultural scientists, agricultural engineers, biological scientists, environmental scientists, farm and ranch managers, soil scientists and soil conservation technicians, and wildlife managers.

Sources of Additional Information
For information about the forestry profession and lists of schools offering education in forestry, send a self-addressed, stamped business envelope to:
☛ Society of American Foresters, 5400 Grosvenor Ln., Bethesda, MD 20814.

Information about a career as a range manager as well as a list of schools offering training is available from:
☛ Society for Range Management, 1839 York St., Denver, CO 80206.

Information about a career as a soil conservationist is available from:
☛ Soil and Water Conservation Society, 7515 Northeast Ankeny Rd., RR #1, Ankeny, IA 50021-9764.

For information about career opportunities in forestry in the Federal Government, contact:
☛ Chief, U.S. Forest Service, U.S. Department of Agriculture, P.O. Box 96090, Washington, DC 20090-6090.

Physical Scientists

Chemists

(D.O.T. 022.061-010, -014, and .137-010)

Nature of the Work
Chemists search for and put to practical use new knowledge about chemicals. Although chemicals are often thought of as artificial or toxic substances, all physical things, whether naturally occurring or of human design, are composed of chemicals. Chemists have devel-

oped a tremendous variety of new and improved synthetic fibers, paints, adhesives, drugs, cosmetics, electronic components, lubricants, and thousands of other products. They also develop processes which save energy and reduce pollution, such as improved oil refining and petrochemical processing methods. Research on the chemistry of living things spurs advances in medicine, agriculture, food processing, and other areas.

Many chemists work in research and development. In basic research, chemists investigate the properties, composition, and structure of matter and the laws that govern the combination of elements and reactions of substances. In applied research and development, they create new products and processes or improve existing ones, often using knowledge gained from basic research. For example, synthetic rubber and plastics resulted from research on small molecules uniting to form large ones (polymerization).

Chemists also work in production and quality control in chemical manufacturing plants. They prepare instructions for plant workers which specify ingredients, mixing times, and temperatures for each stage in the process. They also monitor automated processes to ensure proper product yield, and they test samples to ensure they meet industry and government standards. Chemists also record and report on test results. Others are marketing or sales representatives who sell and provide technical information on chemical products.

Chemists often specialize in a subfield. *Analytical chemists* determine the structure, composition, and nature of substances and develop analytical techniques. They also identify the presence and concentration of chemical pollutants in air, water, and soil. *Organic chemists* study the chemistry of the vast number of carbon compounds. Many commercial products, such as drugs, plastics, and fertilizers, have been developed by organic chemists. *Inorganic chemists* study compounds consisting mainly of elements other than carbon, such as those in electronic components. *Physical chemists* study the physical characteristics of atoms and molecules and investigate how chemical reactions work. Their research may result in new and better energy sources.

Biochemists, whose work encompasses both biology and chemistry, are included under biological scientists elsewhere in the *Handbook*.

Working Conditions

Chemists usually work regular hours in offices and laboratories. Research chemists spend much time in laboratories, but also work in offices when they do theoretical research or plan, record, and report on their lab research. Although some laboratories are small, others are large and may incorporate prototype chemical manufacturing facilities as well as advanced equipment. Chemists may also do

Chemists who work in production and quality control test samples to ensure product specifications are met.

some of their research in a chemical plant or outdoors—while gathering samples of pollutants, for example. Some chemists are exposed to health or safety hazards when handling certain chemicals, but there is little risk if proper procedures are followed.

Employment

Chemists held about 97,000 jobs in 1994. The majority of chemists are employed in manufacturing firms—mostly in the chemical manufacturing industry, which includes firms that produce plastics and synthetic materials, drugs, soaps and cleaners, paints, industrial organic chemicals, and other miscellaneous chemical products. Chemists also work for State and local governments, primarily in health and agriculture, and for Federal agencies, chiefly in the Departments of Defense, Health and Human Services, and Agriculture. Others work for research and testing services. In addition, thousands of persons held chemistry faculty positions in colleges and universities. (See the statement on college and university faculty elsewhere in the *Handbook*.)

Chemists are employed in all parts of the country, but they are mainly concentrated in large industrial areas.

Training, Other Qualifications, and Advancement

A bachelor's degree in chemistry or a related discipline is usually the minimum education necessary to work as a chemist. However, many, if not most, research jobs require a Ph.D. degree.

Many colleges and universities offer a bachelor's degree program in chemistry, 606 of which are approved by the American Chemical Society. Several hundred colleges and universities also offer advanced degree programs in chemistry.

Students planning careers as chemists should enjoy studying science and mathematics, and should like working with their hands building scientific apparatus and performing experiments. Perseverance, curiosity, and the ability to concentrate on detail and to work independently are essential. In addition to required courses in analytical, inorganic, organic, and physical chemistry, undergraduate chemistry majors usually study biological sciences, mathematics, and physics. Computer courses are invaluable, as employers increasingly prefer job applicants to be not only computer literate, but able to apply computer skills to modeling and simulation tasks. Laboratory instruments are also computerized, and the ability to operate and understand equipment is essential.

Because research and development chemists are increasingly expected to work on interdisciplinary teams, some understanding of other disciplines, including business and marketing or economics, is desirable, along with leadership ability and good oral and written communication skills. Experience, either in academic laboratories or through internships or co-op programs in industry, also is useful. Some employers of research chemists, particularly in the pharmaceutical industry, prefer to hire individuals with several years of postdoctoral experience.

Although graduate students typically specialize in a subfield of chemistry, such as analytical chemistry or polymer chemistry, students usually need not specialize at the undergraduate level. In fact, undergraduates who are broadly trained have more flexibility when job hunting or changing jobs than if they narrowly define their interests. Most employers provide new bachelor's degree chemists with additional training or education.

In government or industry, beginning chemists with a bachelor's degree work in technical sales or services, quality control, or assist senior chemists in research and development laboratories. Some may work in research positions, analyzing and testing products, but these may be technicians' positions, with limited upward mobility. Many employers prefer chemists with a Ph.D. to work in basic and applied research. A Ph.D. is also generally preferred for advancement to many administrative positions. Chemists who work in sales, marketing, or professional research positions often move into management eventually.

Many people with a bachelor's degree in chemistry enter other occupations in which a chemistry background is helpful, such as technical writers or sales representatives in chemical marketing. Some enter medical, dental, veterinary, or other health profession schools. Others choose from a wide range of occupations with little or no connection to chemistry.

Chemistry graduates may become high school teachers, and those with a Ph.D. may teach at the college or university level. However, they usually are then regarded as science teachers, or college or university faculty, rather than chemists. Others may qualify as engineers, especially if they have taken some courses in engineering.

Job Outlook
Employment of chemists is expected to grow about as fast as the average for all occupations through the year 2005. The chemical industry, the major employer of chemists, should face continued demand for goods such as new and better pharmaceuticals and personal care products, as well as more specialty chemicals designed to address specific problems or applications. To meet these demands, research and development expenditures in the chemical industry will continue to increase, contributing to employment opportunities for chemists.

Within the chemical industry, job opportunities are expected to be most plentiful in pharmaceutical and biotechnology firms. Stronger competition among drug companies and an aging population are among the several factors contributing to the need for innovative and improved drugs discovered through scientific research. Although employment growth is expected to be slower in the remaining segments of the chemical industry, there will still be a need for chemists to develop and improve products, such as cosmetics and cleansers, as well as the technologies and processes used to produce chemicals for all purposes. Job growth will also be spurred by the need for chemists to monitor and measure air and water pollutants to ensure compliance with local, state, and federal environmental regulations.

Because much employment growth of chemists is expected to relate to drug research and development and environmental issues, analytical, environmental, and synthetic organic chemists should have the best job prospects.

During periods of economic recession, layoffs of chemists may occur—especially in the oil refining and industrial chemicals industries. Chemists are vulnerable to temporary slowdowns in automobile manufacturing and construction, end users of many of the products of the chemical industry.

Earnings
According to a 1995 survey by the National Association of Colleges and Employers, the average starting salary offer for recently graduated chemists with a bachelor's degree was about $29,300 a year; with a master's degree, $38,000; with a Ph.D., $52,900.

A survey by the American Chemical Society reports that the median salary of all their members with a bachelor's degree was $45,400 a year in 1994; with a master's degree, $53,500; and with a Ph.D., $66,000.

In 1995, chemists in nonsupervisory, supervisory, and managerial positions in the Federal Government earned an average salary of $56,070.

Related Occupations
The work of chemical engineers, agricultural scientists, biological scientists, and chemical technicians is closely related to the work done by chemists. The work of other physical and life science occupations, such as physicists and medical scientists, may also be similar to that of chemists.

Sources of Additional Information
General information on career opportunities and earnings for chemists is available from:

American Chemical Society, Department of Career Services, 1155 16th St. NW., Washington, DC 20036.

Information on Federal job opportunities is available from local offices of State employment services or offices of the U.S. Office of Personnel Management, located in major metropolitan areas.

Geologists and Geophysicists

(D.O.T. 024.061 except -014, and .161)

Nature of the Work
Geologists and geophysicists, also known as geological scientists or geoscientists, study the physical aspects and history of the earth. They identify and examine rocks, study information collected by remote sensing instruments in satellites, conduct geological surveys, construct maps, and use instruments to measure the earth's gravity and magnetic field. They also analyze information collected through seismic studies, which involves bouncing energy waves off buried rock layers. Many geologists and geophysicists search for oil, natural gas, minerals, and groundwater.

Other geological scientists play an important role in preserving and cleaning up the environment. Their activities include designing and monitoring waste disposal sites, preserving water supplies, and reclaiming contaminated land and water to comply with Federal environmental regulations. They also help locate safe sites for hazardous waste facilities and landfills.

Geologists and geophysicists examine chemical and physical properties of specimens in laboratories. They study fossil remains of animal and plant life or experiment with the flow of water and oil through rocks. Some geoscientists use two- or three-dimensional computer modeling to portray water layers and the flow of water or other fluids through rock cracks and porous materials. They use a variety of sophisticated laboratory instruments, including x-ray diffractometers, which determine the crystal structure of minerals, and petrographic microscopes, for the study of rock and sediment samples. Geoscientists also use seismographs, instruments which measure energy waves resulting from movements in the earth's crust, to determine the locations and intensities of earthquakes.

Geoscientists working in the oil and gas industry sometimes process and interpret the maps produced by remote sensing satellites to help identify potential new oil or gas deposits. Seismic technology is also an important exploration tool. Seismic waves are used to develop 3-dimensional computer models of underground or underwater rock formations.

Geologists and geophysicists also apply geological knowledge to engineering problems in constructing large buildings, dams, tunnels, and highways. Some administer and manage research and exploration programs; others become general managers in petroleum and mining companies.

Geology and geophysics are closely related fields, but there are major differences. Geologists study the composition, structure, and history of the earth's crust. They try to find out how rocks were formed and what has happened to them since their formation. Geophysicists use the principles of physics and mathematics to study not only the earth's surface but its internal composition, ground and surface waters, atmosphere, and oceans as well as its magnetic, electrical, and gravitational forces. Both, however, commonly apply their skills to the search for natural resources and to solve environmental problems.

There are numerous subdisciplines or specialties that fall under the two major disciplines of geology and geophysics which further differentiate the kind of work geoscientists do. For example, *petroleum geologists* explore for oil and gas deposits by studying and mapping the subsurface of the ocean or land. They use sophisticated geophysical instrumentation, well log data, and computers to collect information. *Mineralogists* analyze and classify minerals and precious stones according to composition and structure. *Paleontologists* study fossils found in geological formations to trace the evolution of plant and animal life and the geologic history of the earth. *Stratigraphers* help to locate minerals by studying the distribution and arrangement of sedimentary rock layers and by examining the fossil and mineral content of such layers. Those who study marine geology are usually called *oceanographers* or *marine geologists*. They study and map the ocean floor, and collect information using remote sensing devices aboard surface ships or underwater research craft.

Geophysicists may specialize in areas such as geodesy, seismology, or marine geophysics, also known as physical oceanography. *Geodesists* study the size and shape of the Earth, its gravitational field, tides, polar motion, and rotation. *Seismologists* interpret data from seismographs and other geophysical instruments to detect earthquakes and locate earthquake-related faults. *Physical oceanographers* study the physical aspects of oceans such as currents and the interaction of the surface of the sea with the atmosphere.

Hydrology is a discipline closely related to geology and geophysics. *Hydrologists* study the distribution, circulation, and physical properties of underground and surface waters. They study the form and intensity of precipitation, its rate of infiltration into the soil, movement through the earth, and its return to the ocean and atmosphere. The work they do is particularly important in environmental preservation and remediation.

Geologists are able to classify rock and mineral specimens by examining the composition and structure of each.

Working Conditions

Some geoscientists spend the majority of their time in an office, others divide their time between fieldwork and office or laboratory work. Geologists often travel to remote field sites by helicopter or four-wheel drive vehicles and cover large areas on foot. Exploration geologists and geophysicists often work overseas or in remote areas, and job relocation is not unusual. Marine geologists and oceanographers may spend considerable time at sea.

Employment

Geologists and geophysicists held about 46,000 jobs in 1994. Many more individuals held geology, geophysics, and oceanography faculty positions in colleges and universities, but they are counted as college and university faculty, not geologists, geophysicists, or oceanographers. (See the statement on college and university faculty elsewhere in the *Handbook*.)

About 1 in 5 were employed in oil and gas companies or oil and gas field service firms. Many other geologists worked for consulting firms and business services, especially engineering services. About 1 geologist in 7 was self-employed; most of whom were consultants to industry or government.

The Federal Government employed about 6,100 geologists, geophysicists, oceanographers, and hydrologists in 1994. Over one-half worked for the Department of the Interior, mostly within the U.S. Geological Survey. Others worked for the Departments of Defense, Agriculture, Commerce, Energy, and the Environmental Protection Agency. Some worked for State agencies such as State geological surveys and State departments of conservation. Geologists and geophysicists also worked for nonprofit research institutions.

Training, Other Qualifications, and Advancement

A bachelor's degree in geology or geophysics is adequate for entry into some lower level geology jobs, but better jobs with good advancement potential usually require at least a master's degree in geology or geophysics. Persons with strong backgrounds in physics, chemistry, mathematics, or computer science also may qualify for some geophysics or geology jobs. A Ph.D. degree is required for most research positions in colleges and universities, and is also important for work in Federal agencies and some State geological surveys that involve basic research.

Hundreds of colleges and universities offer a bachelor's degree in geology, geophysics, oceanography, or other geoscience. Other programs offering related training for beginning geological scientists include geophysical technology, geophysical engineering, geophysical prospecting, engineering geology, petroleum geology, hydrology, and geochemistry. In addition, several hundred more universities award advanced degrees in geology or geophysics.

Geologists and geophysicists need to be able to work as part of a team. Computer modeling, data processing, and effective oral and written communication skills are important, as well as the ability to think independently and creatively. Those involved in fieldwork must have physical stamina.

Traditional geoscience courses emphasizing classical geologic methods and topics (such as mineralogy, paleontology, stratigraphy, and structural geology) are important for all geoscientists. However, those students interested in working in the environmental or regulatory fields should take courses in hydrology, hazardous waste management, environmental legislation, chemistry, fluid mechanics, and geologic logging. Also, some employers seek applicants with field experience, so a summer internship or employment in an environmentally-related area may be beneficial to prospective geoscientists.

Geologists and geophysicists often begin their careers in field exploration or as research assistants in laboratories. They are given more difficult assignments as they gain experience. Eventually they may be promoted to project leader, program manager, or another management and research position.

Job Outlook

Many jobs for geologists and geophysicists are in or related to the petroleum industry, especially the exploration for oil and gas. This industry is subject to cyclical fluctuations. Low oil prices, higher production costs, improvements in energy efficiency, shrinking oil reserves, and restrictions on potential drilling sites have caused exploration activities to be curtailed in the United States. If these conditions continue, there will be limited openings in the petroleum industry for geoscientists working in the United States.

As a result of generally poor job prospects in the past few years, the number of students enrolling in geology and geophysics has dropped considerably. Although enrollments are rising again, the number of students trained in petroleum geology is likely to be so low that even a small increase in openings in the oil industry will be greater than the number of petroleum geologists and geophysicists available to fill them, creating good employment opportunities if exploration activities increase significantly. Employment prospects will be best for jobseekers who hold a master's degree and are familiar with the advanced technologies, such as computer modeling, which are increasingly used to locate new oil and gas fields or pinpoint hidden deposits in existing fields. Because of the cyclical nature of the oil and gas industry, hiring on a contractual basis is common.

Despite the generally poor job prospects encountered by geoscientists in recent years in the petroleum industry, employment of geologists and geophysicists is expected to grow as fast as the average for all occupations through the year 2005. Recent setbacks have been offset by increased demand for these professionals in environmental protection and reclamation. Geologists and geophysicists will continue to be needed to help clean up contaminated sites in the United States, and to help private companies and government comply with more numerous and complex environmental regulations. In particular, jobs requiring training in engineering geology, hydrology and geochemistry should be in demand. However, the number of geoscientists obtaining training in these areas has been increasing, so they may experience competition despite the increasing number of jobs available.

Earnings

Surveys by the National Association of Colleges and Employers indicate that graduates with bachelor's degrees in geology and the geological sciences received an average starting offer of about $27,900 a year in 1995. However, the starting salaries can vary widely depending on the employing industry. For example, according to a 1994 American Association of Petroleum Geologists survey, the average salary in the oil and gas industry for geoscientists with less than 2 years of experience was about $42,500.

Although the petroleum, mineral, and mining industries offer higher salaries, the competition in these areas is normally intense, and the job security less than in other areas.

In 1995, the Federal Government's average salary for geologists in managerial, supervisory, and nonsupervisory positions was $55,540; for geophysicists, $62,220; for hydrologists, $51,080; and for oceanographers, $58,980.

Related Occupations

Many geologists and geophysicists work in the petroleum and natural gas industry. This industry also employs many other workers in the scientific and technical aspects of petroleum and natural gas exploration and extraction, including engineering technicians, science technicians, petroleum engineers, and surveyors. Also, some life scientists, physicists, chemists, and meteorologists, as well as mathematicians, computer scientists, soil scientists, and mapping scientists, perform related work in both petroleum and natural gas exploration and extraction and in environment-related activities.

Sources of Additional Information

Information on training and career opportunities for geologists is available from:

☛American Geological Institute, 4220 King St., Alexandria, VA 22302-1507.

☛Geological Society of America, P.O. Box 9140, 3300 Penrose Pl., Boulder, CO 80301.

☛American Association of Petroleum Geologists, Communications Department, P.O. Box 979, Tulsa, OK 74101.

Information on training and career opportunities for geophysicists is available from:

☛American Geophysical Union, 2000 Florida Ave. NW., Washington, DC 20009.

A list of curricula in colleges and universities offering programs in oceanography and related fields is available from:

☛Marine Technology Society, 1828 L St. NW., Suite 906, Washington, DC 20036.

Information on Federal job opportunities is available from local offices of State employment services or branches of the U.S. Office of Personnel Management located in major metropolitan areas.

Meteorologists

(D.O.T. 025.062-010)

Nature of the Work

Meteorology is the study of the atmosphere, the air that covers the earth. Meteorologists study the atmosphere's physical characteristics, motions, and processes, and the way it affects the rest of our environment. The best-known application of this knowledge is in forecasting the weather. However, weather information and meteorological research also are applied in air-pollution control, agriculture, air and sea transportation, defense, and the study of trends in the earth's climate such as global warming or ozone depletion.

Meteorologists who forecast the weather, known professionally as *operational meteorologists*, are the largest group of specialists. They study information on air pressure, temperature, humidity, and wind velocity, and they apply physical and mathematical relationships to make short- and long-range weather forecasts. Their data come from weather satellites, weather radar, and remote sensors and observers in many parts of the world. Meteorologists use sophisticated computer models of the world's atmosphere to make long-term, short-term, and local-area forecasts. These forecasts inform not only the general public, but also those who need accurate weather information for both economic and safety reasons, as in the shipping, aviation, agriculture, fishing, and utilities industries.

The use of weather balloons, launched several times a day, to measure wind, temperature, and humidity in the upper atmosphere, is supplemented by far more sophisticated weather equipment which transmits data as frequently as every few minutes. Doppler radar, for example, can detect rotational patterns in violent storm systems, allowing forecasters to better predict thunderstorms, tornadoes, flash floods, as well as their direction and intensity.

Some meteorologists work in research. *Physical meteorologists*, for example, study the atmosphere's chemical and physical properties; the transmission of light, sound, and radio waves; and the transfer of energy in the atmosphere. They also study factors affecting formation of clouds, rain, snow, and other weather phenomena, such as severe storms. *Climatologists* collect, analyze, and interpret past records of wind, rainfall, sunshine, and temperature in specific areas or regions. Their studies are used to design buildings and to plan heating and cooling systems, to aid in effective land use, and in agricultural production. Other research meteorologists examine the most effective ways to control or diminish air pollution or improve weather forecasting using mathematical models.

The Federal Government's National Weather Service is the largest employer of civilian meteorologists.

Working Conditions

Jobs in weather stations, most of which operate around the clock 7 days a week, often involve night, weekend, and holiday work and rotating shifts. During times of weather emergencies, such as hurricanes, operational meteorologists may work overtime. Operational meteorologists are also often under pressure to meet forecast deadlines. Weather stations are found all over the country: At airports, in or near cities, and in isolated and remote areas. Some meteorologists also spend time observing weather conditions and collecting data from aircraft. Meteorologists in smaller weather offices often work alone; in larger ones, they work as part of a team. Meteorologists not doing forecasting work regular hours, usually in offices. Those who work for private consulting firms or for companies that analyze and monitor emissions to improve air quality often work with other science or engineering professionals.

Employment

Meteorologists held about 6,600 jobs in 1994. The largest employer of civilian meteorologists is the National Oceanic and Atmospheric Administration (NOAA), which employs about 2,700 meteorologists. Nearly 90 percent of NOAA's meteorologists work in the National Weather Service at stations in all parts of the United States. The remainder of NOAA's meteorologists work mainly in research or in program management. The Department of Defense employs about 280 civilian meteorologists. Others work for private weather consultants, research and testing services, and computer and data processing services.

Although hundreds of people teach meteorology and related courses in college and university departments of meteorology or atmospheric science, physics, earth science, and geophysics, these individuals are classified as college or university faculty, rather than meteorologists. (See the statement on college and university faculty elsewhere in the *Handbook*.)

In addition to civilian meteorologists, thousands of members of the Armed Forces do forecasting and other meteorological work.

Training, Other Qualifications, and Advancement

A bachelor's degree with a major in meteorology or a closely related field with coursework in meteorology is the usual minimum requirement for a beginning job as a meteorologist.

The preferred educational requirement for entry level meteorologists in the Federal Government is a bachelor's degree—not necessarily in meteorology—with at least 20 semester hours of meteorology courses, including 6 hours in weather analysis and forecasting and 6 hours in dynamic meteorology. In addition to meteorology coursework, differential and integral calculus and 6 hours of college physics are required. These requirements have recently been upgraded to include coursework in computer science and additional coursework appropriate for a physical science major, such as statistics, chemistry, physical oceanography, or physical climatology. Sometimes, a combination of experience and education may be substituted for a degree.

Although positions in operational meteorology are available for those with only a bachelor's degree, obtaining a graduate degree enhances advancement potential. A master's degree is usually necessary for conducting research and development, and a Ph.D. may be required for some research positions. Students who plan a career in research and development need not necessarily major in meteorology as an undergraduate. In fact, a bachelor's degree in mathematics, physics, or engineering is excellent preparation for graduate study in meteorology.

Because meteorology is a small field, relatively few colleges and universities offer degrees in meteorology or atmospheric science, although many departments of physics, earth science, geography, and geophysics offer atmospheric science and related courses. Prospective students should make certain that courses required by the National Weather Service and other employers are offered at the college they are considering. Computer science courses, additional meteorology courses, and a strong background in mathematics and physics are important to prospective employers. Many programs combine the study of meteorology with another field, such as agriculture, engineering, or physics. For example, hydrometeorology is the blending of hydrology (the science of the earth's water) and meteorology, and is the field concerned with the effect of precipitation on the hydrologic cycle and the environment.

Beginning meteorologists often do routine data collection, computation, or analysis and some basic forecasting. Entry level meteorologists in the Federal Government are usually placed in intern positions for training and experience. Experienced meteorologists may advance to various supervisory or administrative jobs, or may handle more complex forecasting jobs. Increasing numbers of meteorologists establish their own weather consulting services.

Job Outlook

Persons seeking employment as meteorologists are likely to face competition because the National Weather Service—the largest single employer of meteorologists—has curtailed hiring following an extensive modernization of its weather forecasting equipment. Employment of meteorologists is expected to grow more slowly than the average for all occupations through the year 2005. Employment of meteorologists in other parts of the Federal Government is not expected to increase either. Some employment growth is anticipated in private industry as the use of private weather forecasting and meteorological services by farmers, commodity investors, utilities, transportation and construction firms, and radio and television stations increases. For people in these and other areas, additional weather information, which is more closely targeted to their needs than the more general information provided by the National Weather Service, can yield significant benefits. However, because many customers for private weather services are in industries sensitive to fluctuations in the economy, the sales and growth of private weather services depend on the health of the economy.

There will continue to be demand for meteorologists to analyze and monitor the dispersion of pollutants into the air to ensure compliance with the Federal environmental regulations outlined in the Clean Air Act of 1990.

Earnings

According to an American Meteorological Society survey, the average salary for meteorologists in entry level positions with a bachelor's degree was about $22,000 in 1992; for those with a master's degree, $27,000; and for those with a Ph.D. degree, $37,000.

The average salary for meteorologists in nonsupervisory, supervisory, and managerial positions employed by the Federal Government was $50,540 in 1995. In 1995, meteorologists in the Federal Government with a bachelor's degree and no experience received a starting salary of about $18,700 or $23,200 a year, depending on their college grades. Those with a master's degree could start at $23,200 or $28,300; those with the Ph.D. degree, at $34,300 or $41,100. Beginning salaries for all degree levels were slightly higher in selected areas of the country where the prevailing local pay level was higher.

Related Occupations

Workers in other occupations concerned with the physical environment include oceanographers; geologists and geophysicists; hydrologists; civil, chemical, and environmental engineers; physicists; and mathematicians.

Sources of Additional Information

Information on career opportunities in meteorology is available from:

☛American Meteorological Society, 45 Beacon St., Boston, MA 02108.

☛National Oceanic and Atmospheric Administration, Human Resources Management Office, 1315 East West Hwy., Route Code OA/22, Silver Spring, MD 20910.

Physicists and Astronomers

(D.O.T. 015.021-010; 021.067-010; 023.061-010, -014, and .067; 079.021-014)

Nature of the Work

Physicists explore and identify basic principles governing the structure and behavior of matter, the generation and transfer of energy, and the interaction of matter and energy. Some physicists use these principles in theoretical areas, such as the nature of time and the origin of the universe; others apply their physics knowledge to practical areas such as the development of advanced materials, electronic and optical devices, and medical equipment.

Physicists design and perform experiments with lasers, cyclotrons, telescopes, mass spectrometers, and other equipment. Based on observations and analysis, they attempt to discover the laws that describe the forces of nature, such as gravity, electromagnetism, and nuclear interactions. They also find ways to apply physical laws and theories to problems in nuclear energy, electronics, optics, materials, communications, aerospace technology, navigation equipment, and medical instrumentation.

Astronomy is sometimes considered a subfield of physics. Astronomers use the principles of physics and mathematics to learn about the fundamental nature of the universe, including the sun, moon, planets, stars, and galaxies. They also apply their knowledge to problems in navigation and space flight.

Most physicists work in research and development. Some do basic research to increase scientific knowledge. Physicists who conduct applied research build upon the discoveries made through basic research and work to develop new devices, products, and processes. For instance, basic research in solid-state physics led to the development of transistors and then to the integrated circuits used in computers.

Physicists also design research equipment. This equipment often has additional unanticipated uses. For example, lasers are used in surgery; microwave devices are used for ovens; and measuring instruments can analyze blood or the chemical content of foods. A small number work in inspection, testing, quality control, and other production-related jobs in industry.

Astronomers occasionally use high powered telescopes to observe stars and planets.

Much physics research is done in small or medium-size laboratories. However, experiments in plasma, nuclear, high energy, and some other areas of physics require extremely large, expensive equipment such as particle accelerators. Physicists in these subfields often work in large teams. Although physics research may require extensive experimentation in laboratories, research physicists still spend time in offices planning, recording, analyzing, and reporting on research.

Almost all astronomers do research. They analyze large quantities of data gathered by observatories and satellites and write scientific papers or reports on their findings. Most astronomers spend only a few weeks each year making observations with optical telescopes, radio telescopes, and other instruments. Contrary to the popular image, astronomers almost never make observations by looking directly through a telescope because enhanced photographic and electronic detecting equipment can see more than the human eye.

Physicists generally specialize in one of many subfields— elementary particle physics; nuclear physics; atomic and molecular physics; physics of condensed matter (solid-state physics); optics; acoustics; plasma physics; or the physics of fluids. Some specialize in a subdivision of one of these subfields; for example, within condensed matter physics, specialties include superconductivity, crystallography, and semiconductors. However, all physics involves the same fundamental principles, so specialties may overlap, and physicists may switch from one subfield to another. Also, growing numbers of physicists work in combined fields such as biophysics, chemical physics, and geophysics.

Working Conditions

Physicists often work regular hours in laboratories and offices. At times, however, those who are deeply involved in research may work long or irregular hours. Most do not encounter unusual hazards in their work. Some physicists temporarily work away from home at national or international facilities with unique equipment such as particle accelerators. Astronomers who make observations may travel to observatories, which are usually in remote locations, and routinely work at night.

Employment

Physicists and astronomers held nearly 20,000 jobs in 1994. Also, a significant number held physics or astronomy faculty positions in colleges and universities. (See the statement on college and university faculty elsewhere in the *Handbook*.) About one-fourth of all nonfaculty physicists and astronomers worked for commercial or noncommercial research, development, and testing laboratories. The

Federal Government employed almost one-fifth, mostly in the Departments of Defense and Commerce and in the National Aeronautics and Space Administration. Others worked in colleges and universities in nonfaculty positions and for State governments, electrical and electronic equipment manufacturers, drug companies, and search and navigation equipment manufacturers.

Although physicists and astronomers are employed in all parts of the country, most work in areas that have universities and large research and development laboratories or observatories.

Training, Other Qualifications, and Advancement

A doctoral degree is the usual educational requirement for physicists and astronomers, because most jobs are in research and development. (Many physics and astronomy Ph.D. holders ultimately take jobs teaching at the college or university level. See the statement on college and university faculty elsewhere in the *Handbook*.) Additional experience and training in a post-doctoral research assignment, although not required, is helpful in preparing physicists and astronomers for permanent research positions.

Those having bachelor's or master's degrees in physics are rarely qualified to fill positions as physicists. They are, however, usually qualified to work in an engineering-related area or other scientific fields, to work as technicians, or to assist in setting up laboratories. Some may qualify for applied research jobs in private industry or nonresearch positions in the Federal Government, and a master's degree often suffices for teaching jobs in 2-year colleges. Astronomy bachelor's degree holders often enter a field unrelated to astronomy, but they are also qualified to work in planetariums running science shows or to assist astronomers doing research. (See statements on engineers, geologists and geophysicists, computer programmers, and computer scientists and systems analysts elsewhere in the *Handbook*.)

Hundreds of colleges and universities offer a bachelor's degree in physics. The undergraduate program provides a broad background in the natural sciences and mathematics. Typical physics courses include mechanics, electromagnetism, optics, thermodynamics, atomic physics, and quantum mechanics.

About 180 colleges and universities have physics departments which offer Ph.D. degrees in physics. Graduate students usually concentrate in a subfield of physics such as elementary particles or condensed matter. Many begin studying for their doctorate immediately after their bachelor's degree.

About 40 universities offer the Ph.D. degree in astronomy, either through an astronomy department, a physics department, or a combined physics/astronomy department. Applicants to astronomy doctoral programs face keen competition for available slots. Those planning a career in astronomy should have a very strong physics background. In fact, an undergraduate degree in physics is excellent preparation, followed by a Ph.D. in astronomy.

Mathematical ability, computer skills, an inquisitive mind, imagination, and the ability to work independently are important traits for anyone planning a career in physics or astronomy. Prospective physicists who hope to work in industrial laboratories applying physics knowledge to practical problems should broaden their educational background to include courses outside of physics, such as economics, computer technology, and current affairs. Good oral and written communication skills are also important because many physicists work as part of a team or have contact with persons with non-physics backgrounds, such as clients or customers.

The beginning job for most Ph.D. physics and astronomy graduates is conducting research in a postdoctoral position, where they may work with experienced physicists as they continue to learn about their specialty and develop ideas and results to be used in later work. The initial work may be routine and under the close supervision of senior scientists. After some experience, they perform more complex tasks and work more independently. Physicists who develop new products or processes sometimes form their own companies or join new firms to exploit their own ideas.

Job Outlook

A large proportion of physicists and astronomers are employed on research projects, many of which, in the past, were defense related. Expected reductions in defense-related research and an expected slowdown in the growth of civilian physics-related research will cause employment of physicists and astronomers to decline through the year 2005. Proposed employment cutbacks and overall budget tightening in the Federal government will also affect employment of physicists, especially those dependent on Federal research grants. The number of doctorates granted in physics has been much greater than the number of openings for physicists for several years. Although physics enrollments are starting to decline slightly, the number of new Ph.D. graduates is likely to continue to be high enough to result in keen competition for the kind of research and academic jobs that those with new doctorates in physics have traditionally sought. Also, more prospective researchers will likely compete for less grant money.

Although research and development budgets in private industry will continue to grow, many research laboratories in private industry are expected to reduce basic research, which is where much physics research takes place, in favor of applied or manufacturing research and product and software development. Furthermore, although the median age of physicists and astronomers is higher than the average for all occupations and many will be eligible for retirement in the next decade, it is possible that many of them will not be replaced when they retire.

Persons with only a bachelor's degree in physics or astronomy are not qualified to enter most physicist or astronomer jobs. However, many find jobs as high school physics teachers and in engineering, technician, mathematics, and computer- and environment-related occupations. (See the statements on these occupations elsewhere in the *Handbook*.) Despite the strong competition for, and expected employment declines in, traditional physics and astronomical research oriented jobs, individuals with a physics degree at any level will find their skills useful for entry to many other occupations.

Earnings

The American Institute of Physics reported a median salary of $64,000 in 1994 for its members with Ph.D.'s. Those working in 4-year colleges (9-10 months a year) earned the least—$45,000—while those employed in industry and hospitals earned the most—$75,000 and $77,000, respectively.

Average earnings for physicists in nonsupervisory, supervisory, and managerial positions in the Federal Government in 1995 were $67,240 a year, and for astronomy and space scientists, $71,660.

Related Occupations

The work of physicists and astronomers relates closely to that of other scientific and mathematics occupations such as chemist, geologist, geophysicist, and mathematician. Engineers and engineering and science technicians also use the principles of physics in their work.

Sources of Additional Information

General information on career opportunities in physics is available from:

☛American Institute of Physics, Career Planning and Placement, One Physics Ellipse, College Park, MD 20740-3843.

☛American Physical Society, Education Department, One Physics Ellipse, College Park, MD 20740-3844.

For a pamphlet containing information on careers in astronomy, send your request to:

☛American Astronomical Society, Education Office, University of Texas, Department of Astronomy, Austin, TX 78712-1083.

Lawyers and Judges

(D.O.T. 110; 111; 119.107, .117, .167-010, .267-014; 169.267-010)

Nature of the Work

Lawyers. Lawyers, also called *attorneys*, act as both advocates and advisors in our society. As advocates, they represent one of the opposing parties in criminal and civil trials by presenting evidence that supports their client in court. As advisors, lawyers counsel their clients as to their legal rights and obligations, and suggest particular courses of action in business and personal matters. Whether acting as advocates or advisors, all attorneys interpret the law and apply it to specific situations. This requires excellent research and communication skills.

Lawyers perform in-depth research into the purposes behind the applicable laws and into judicial decisions that have been applied to those laws under circumstances similar to those currently faced by the client. While all lawyers continue to make use of law libraries to prepare cases, some supplement their search of the conventional printed sources with computer software packages. Software can be used to automatically search legal literature and identify legal texts relevant to a specific case. In litigation involving many supporting documents, lawyers may use computers to organize and index the material. Tax lawyers are increasingly using computers for making tax computations and exploring alternative tax strategies for clients.

Lawyers then communicate to others the information obtained by research. They advise what actions clients may take and draw up legal documents, such as wills and contracts, for clients. Lawyers must deal with people in a courteous, efficient manner and not disclose matters discussed in confidence with clients. They hold positions of great responsibility and are obligated to adhere to a strict code of ethics.

The more detailed aspects of a lawyer's job depend upon his or her field of specialization and position. While all lawyers are licensed to represent parties in court, some appear in court more frequently than others. Some lawyers specialize in trial work. These lawyers need an exceptional ability to think quickly and speak with ease and authority, and must be thoroughly familiar with courtroom rules and strategy. Trial lawyers still spend most of their time outside the courtroom conducting research, interviewing clients and witnesses, and handling other details in preparation for trial.

Besides trials, lawyers may specialize in other areas, such as bankruptcy, probate, or international law. Environmental lawyers, for example, may represent public interest groups, waste disposal companies, or construction firms in their dealings with the Environmental Protection Agency (EPA) and other State and Federal agencies. They help clients prepare and file for licenses and applications for approval before certain activities can occur. They also represent clients' interests in administrative adjudications and during drafting of new regulations.

Some lawyers concentrate in the emerging field of intellectual property. These lawyers help protect clients' claims to copyrights, art work under contract, product designs, and computer programs. Still other lawyers advise insurance companies about the legality of insurance transactions. They write insurance policies to conform with the law and to protect companies from unwarranted claims. They review claims filed against insurance companies and represent the companies in court.

The majority of lawyers are in private practice where they may concentrate on criminal or civil law. In criminal law, lawyers represent individuals who have been charged with crimes and argue their cases in courts of law. In civil law, attorneys assist clients with litigation, wills, trusts, contracts, mortgages, titles, and leases. Some manage a person's property as a trustee or, as an executor, to ensure the provisions of a client's will are carried out. Others handle only public interest cases—civil or criminal—which have a potential impact extending well beyond the individual client.

Lawyers sometimes are employed full time by a single client. If the client is a corporation, the lawyer is known as "house counsel" and usually advises the company about legal issues related to its business activities. These issues might involve patents, government regulations, contracts with other companies, property interests, or collective bargaining agreements with unions.

Attorneys employed at the various levels of government make up still another category. Lawyers that work for State attorneys general, prosecutors, public defenders, and courts play a key role in the criminal justice system. At the Federal level, attorneys investigate cases for the Department of Justice or other agencies. Also, lawyers at every government level help develop programs, draft laws, interpret legislation, establish enforcement procedures, and argue civil and criminal cases on behalf of the government.

Other lawyers work for legal aid societies—private, nonprofit organizations established to serve disadvantaged people. These lawyers generally handle civil rather than criminal cases.

A relatively small number of trained attorneys work in law schools. Most are faculty members who specialize in one or more subjects, and others serve as administrators. Some work full time in nonacademic settings and teach part time. (For additional information, see the section on college and university faculty elsewhere in the *Handbook*.) Some lawyers become judges, although not all judges have practiced law.

Judges. Judges apply the law. They oversee the legal process in courts of law, resolving civil disputes and determining guilt in criminal cases according to local, State, and Federal statutes. They preside over cases touching on virtually every aspect of society, from traffic offenses to disputes over management of professional sports, from the rights of huge corporations to questions of disconnecting life support equipment for terminally ill persons. They must ensure trials and hearings are conducted fairly and that the court administers justice in a manner safeguarding the legal rights of all parties involved.

Judges preside over trials or hearings and listen as attorneys representing the parties present and argue their cases. They rule on the admissibility of evidence and methods of conducting testimony, and settle disputes between the opposing attorneys. They ensure the rules and procedures are followed, and if unusual circumstances arise for which standard procedures have not been established, judges direct how the trial will proceed based on their knowledge of the law.

Judges often hold pretrial hearings for cases. They listen to allegations and, based on the evidence presented, determine whether there is enough merit for a trial to be held. In criminal cases, judges may decide that persons charged with crimes should be held in jail pending their trial, or may set conditions for release through the trial. In civil cases, judges may impose restrictions upon the parties until a trial is held.

When trials are held, juries are often selected to decide cases. However, judges decide cases when the law does not require a jury trial, or when the parties waive their right to a jury. Judges instruct juries on applicable laws, direct them to deduce the facts from the evidence presented, and hear their verdict. Judges sentence those convicted in criminal cases in many States. They also award relief to litigants including, where appropriate, compensation for damages in civil cases.

Judges also work outside the courtroom "in chambers." In their private offices, judges read documents on pleadings and motions, research legal issues, hold hearings with lawyers, write opinions, and oversee the court's operations. Running a court is like running a small business, and judges manage their courts' administrative and clerical staff, too.

Judges' duties vary according to the extent of their jurisdictions and powers. *General trial court judges* of the Federal and State court systems have jurisdiction over any case in their system. They generally try civil cases that transcend the jurisdiction of lower courts, and all cases involving felony offenses. Federal and State *appellate court judges*, although few in number, have the power to overrule decisions made by trial court or administrative law judges if they determine that legal errors were made in a case, or if legal precedent does not support the judgment of the lower court. They rule on fewer cases and rarely have direct contacts with the people involved.

The majority of State court judges preside in courts in which jurisdiction is limited by law to certain types of cases. A variety of titles are assigned to these judges, but among the most common are *municipal court judge*, *county court judge*, *magistrate*, or *justice of the peace*. Traffic violations, misdemeanors, small claims cases, and pretrial hearings constitute the bulk of the work of these judges, but some States allow them to handle cases involving domestic relations, probate, contracts, and selected other areas of the law.

Administrative law judges, formerly called *hearing officers*, are employed by government agencies to rule on appeals of agency administrative decisions. They make decisions on a person's eligibility for various Social Security benefits or worker's compensation, protection of the environment, enforcement of health and safety regulations, employment discrimination, and compliance with economic regulatory requirements.

Working Conditions

Lawyers and judges do most of their work in offices, law libraries, and courtrooms. Lawyers sometimes meet in clients' homes or places of business and, when necessary, in hospitals or prisons. They frequently travel to attend meetings; to gather evidence; and to appear before courts, legislative bodies, and other authorities.

Salaried lawyers in government and private corporations generally have structured work schedules. Lawyers in private practice may work irregular hours while conducting research, conferring with clients, or preparing briefs during nonoffice hours. Lawyers often work long hours, and about half regularly work 50 hours or more per week. They are under particularly heavy pressure, for example, when a case is being tried. Preparation for court includes keeping abreast of the latest laws and judicial decisions.

Lawyers and judges often work long and irregular hours.

Although work generally is not seasonal, the work of tax lawyers and other specialists may be an exception. Because lawyers in private practice can often determine their own workload and when they will retire, many stay in practice well beyond the usual retirement age.

Many judges work a standard 40-hour week, but a third of all judges work over 50 hours per week. Some judges with limited jurisdiction are employed part time and divide their time between their judicial responsibilities and other careers.

Employment

Lawyers and judges held about 735,000 jobs in 1994. About three-fourths of the 656,000 lawyers practiced privately, either in law firms or in solo practices. Most of the remaining lawyers held positions in government, the greatest number at the local level. In the Federal Government, lawyers work for many different agencies but they are concentrated in the Departments of Justice, Treasury, and Defense. Other lawyers are employed as house counsel by public utilities, banks, insurance companies, real estate agencies, manufacturing firms, welfare and religious organizations, and other business firms and nonprofit organizations. Some salaried lawyers also have part-time independent practices; others work as lawyers part time while working full time in another occupation.

Judges held 79,000 jobs in 1994. All worked for Federal, State, or local governments, with about 40 percent holding positions in the Federal Government. The remainder were mostly employed at the State level.

Many people trained as lawyers are not employed as lawyers or judges; they work as law clerks, law school professors, managers and administrators, and in a variety of other occupations.

Training, Other Qualifications, and Advancement

Lawyers. To practice law in the courts of any State or other jurisdiction, a person must be licensed, or admitted to its bar, under rules established by the jurisdiction's highest court. Nearly all require that applicants for admission to the bar pass a written bar examination. Most jurisdictions also require applicants to pass a separate written ethics examination. Lawyers who have been admitted to the bar in one jurisdiction occasionally may be admitted to the bar in another without taking an examination if they meet that jurisdiction's standards of good moral character and have a specified period of legal experience. Federal courts and agencies set their own qualifications for those practicing before them.

To qualify for the bar examination in most States, an applicant must complete at least 3 years of college and graduate from a law school approved by the American Bar Association (ABA) or the proper State authorities. (ABA approval signifies that the law school—particularly its library and faculty—meets certain standards developed by the Association to promote quality legal education.) In 1994, the American Bar Association approved 178 law schools. Others were approved by State authorities only. With certain exceptions, graduates of schools not approved by the ABA are restricted to taking the bar examination and practicing in the State or other jurisdiction in which the school is located; most of these schools are in California. Seven States accept the study of law in a law office or in combination with study in a law school; only California accepts the study of law by correspondence as qualifying for taking the bar examination. Several States require registration and approval of students by the State Board of Law Examiners, either before they enter law school or during the early years of legal study.

Although there is no nationwide bar examination, 47 States, the District of Columbia, Guam, the Northern Mariana Islands, and the Virgin Islands require the 6-hour Multistate Bar Examination (MBE) as part of the bar examination; the MBE is not required in Indiana, Louisiana, Washington, and Puerto Rico. The MBE, covering issues of broad interest, is given in addition to a locally prepared 6-hour State bar examination. The 3-hour Multistate Essay Examination (MEE) is used as part of the State bar examination in a few States. States vary in their use of MBE and MEE scores.

The required college and law school education usually takes 7 years of full-time study after high school—4 years of undergraduate study followed by 3 years in law school. Although some law schools accept a very small number of students after 3 years of college, most require applicants to have a bachelor's degree. To meet the needs of students who can attend only part time, a number of law schools have night or part-time divisions which usually require 4 years of study. In 1994, about one 1 in 8 graduates from ABA-approved schools attended part time.

Preparation for a career as a lawyer really begins in college. Although there is no recommended "prelaw" major, the choice of an undergraduate program is important. Certain courses and activities are desirable because they give the student the skills needed to succeed both in law school and in the profession. Essential skills—proficiency in writing, reading and analyzing, thinking logically, and communicating verbally—are learned during high school and college. An undergraduate program that cultivates these skills while broadening the student's view of the world is desirable. Courses in English, a foreign language, public speaking, government, philosophy, history, economics, mathematics, and computer science, among others, are useful. Whatever the major, students should study a variety of disciplines.

Students interested in a particular aspect of law may find related courses helpful. For example, many law schools with patent law tracks require bachelor's degrees, or at least several courses, in engineering and science. Future tax lawyers should have a strong undergraduate background in accounting.

Acceptance by most law schools depends on the applicant's ability to demonstrate an aptitude for the study of law, usually through good undergraduate grades, the Law School Admission Test (LSAT), the quality of the applicant's undergraduate school, any prior work experience, and sometimes a personal interview. However, law schools vary in the weight that they place on each of these factors.

All law schools approved by the American Bar Association require that applicants take the LSAT. Nearly all law schools require applicants to have certified transcripts sent to the Law School Data Assembly Service, which then sends applicants' LSAT scores and their standardized records of college grades to the law schools of their choice. Both this service and the LSAT are administered by the Law School Admission Council.

Competition for admission to many law schools is intense. Enrollments rose very rapidly during the 1970s, with applicants far outnumbering available seats. Since then, law school enrollments have remained relatively unchanged, and the number of applicants has fluctuated. However, the number of applicants to most law schools still greatly exceeds the number that can be admitted. Enrollments are expected to remain at about their present level through the year 2005, and competition for admission to the more prestigious law schools will remain keen.

During the first year or year and a half of law school, students generally study fundamental courses such as constitutional law, contracts, property law, torts, civil procedure, and legal writing. In the remaining time, they may elect specialized courses in fields such as tax, labor, or corporation law. Law students often acquire practical experience by participation in school sponsored legal aid or legal clinic activities, in the school's moot court competitions in which students conduct appellate arguments, in practice trials under the supervision of experienced lawyers and judges, and through research and writing on legal issues for the school's law journal.

In 1994, law students in 38 States were required to pass the Multistate Professional Responsibility Examination (MPRE), which tests their knowledge of the ABA codes on professional responsibility and judicial conduct. In some States, the MPRE may be taken during law school, usually after completing a course on legal ethics.

A number of law schools have clinical programs where students gain legal experience through practice trials and law school projects under the supervision of practicing lawyers and law school faculty.

Law school clinical programs might include work in legal aid clinics, for example, or on the staff of legislative committees. Part-time or summer clerkships in law firms, government agencies, and corporate legal departments also provide experience that can be extremely valuable later on. Such training can provide references or lead directly to a job after graduation, and can help students decide what kind of practice best suits them. Clerkships also may be an important source of financial aid.

Graduates receive the degree of *juris doctor* (J.D.) or *bachelor of law* (LL.B.) as the first professional degree. Advanced law degrees may be desirable for those planning to specialize, do research, or teach. Some law students pursue joint degree programs, which generally require an additional year. Joint degree programs are offered in a number of areas, including law and business administration and law and public administration.

After graduation, lawyers must keep informed about legal and nonlegal developments that affect their practice. Thirty-seven States and jurisdictions mandate Continuing Legal Education (CLE). Furthermore, many law schools and State and local bar associations provide continuing education courses that help lawyers stay abreast of recent developments.

The practice of law involves a great deal of responsibility. Individuals planning careers in law should like to work with people and be able to win the respect and confidence of their clients, associates, and the public. Integrity and honesty are vital personal qualities. Perseverance and reasoning ability are essential to analyze complex cases and reach sound conclusions. Lawyers also need creativity when handling new and unique legal problems.

Most beginning lawyers start in salaried positions. Newly hired salaried attorneys usually act as research assistants to experienced lawyers or judges. After several years of progressively more responsible salaried employment, some lawyers are admitted to partnership in their firm, or go into practice for themselves. Some lawyers, after years of practice, become full-time law school faculty or administrators; a growing number have advanced degrees in other fields as well.

Some attorneys use their legal training in administrative or managerial positions in various departments of large corporations. A transfer from a corporation's legal department to another department often is viewed as a way to gain administrative experience and rise in the ranks of management.

Judges. Most judges, although not all, have been lawyers first. All Federal judges and State trial and appellate court judges are required to be lawyers or "learned in law." About 40 States presently allow nonlawyers to hold limited jurisdiction judgeships, but opportunities are better with law experience. Federal administrative law judges must be lawyers and pass a competitive examination administered by the U.S. Office of Personnel Management. Many State administrative law judges and other hearing officials are not required to be lawyers, but law degrees are preferred for most positions.

Federal judges are appointed for life by the President, with the consent of the Senate. Federal administrative law judges are appointed by the various Federal agencies with virtually lifetime tenure. About half of all State judges are appointed, while the remainder are elected in partisan or nonpartisan State elections. Most State and local judges serve fixed terms, which range from 4 or 6 years for most limited jurisdiction judgeships to as long as 14 years for some appellate court judges. Judicial nominating commissions, composed of members of the bar and the public, are used to screen candidates for judgeships in many States, as well as for Federal judgeships.

All States have some type of orientation for newly elected or appointed judges. The National Judicial College and the National Center for State Courts provide judicial education and training for judges and other judicial branch personnel. General and continuing education courses usually run from a couple of days to 3 weeks in length. Over half of the States, including Puerto Rico, require judges to enroll in continuing education courses while serving on the bench.

Job Outlook

Individuals interested in pursuing careers as lawyers or judges should encounter keen competition through the year 2005. Law schools still attract large numbers of applicants and are not expected to decrease their enrollments, so the supply of persons trained as lawyers should continue to exceed job openings. As for judges, the prestige associated with serving on the bench should insure continued intense competition for openings.

Lawyers. Employment of lawyers has grown very rapidly since the early 1970s, and is expected to continue to grow faster than the average for all occupations through the year 2005. New jobs created by growth in the profession should exceed job openings that arise from the need to replace lawyers who stop working or leave the profession. The strong growth in demand for lawyers will result from growth in the population and the general level of business activities. Demand will also be spurred by growth of legal action in such areas as employee benefits, health care, intellectual property, sexual harassment, the environment, and real estate. Legal services can be expensive, but the availability of legal clinics and prepaid legal service programs should increase the use of legal services by middle-income groups.

Even though jobs for lawyers are expected to increase rapidly, competition for job openings should continue to be keen because of the large numbers graduating from law school each year. During the 1970s, the annual number of law school graduates more than doubled, outpacing the rapid growth of jobs. Growth in the yearly number of law school graduates tapered off during the 1980s, but again increased in the early 1990s. The high number of graduates will strain the economy's capacity to absorb them. Although graduates with superior academic records from well-regarded law schools will continue to enjoy good opportunities, most graduates will encounter competition for jobs. As in the past, some graduates may have to accept positions in areas outside their field of interest or for which they feel they are overqualified. They may have to enter jobs for which legal training is an asset but not normally a requirement. For example, banks, insurance firms, real estate companies, government agencies, and other organizations seek law graduates to fill many administrative, managerial, and business positions.

Due to the competition for jobs, a law graduate's geographic mobility and work experience assume greater importance. The willingness to relocate may be an advantage in getting a job, but to be licensed in a new State, a lawyer may have to take an additional State bar examination. In addition, employers increasingly seek graduates who have advanced law degrees and experience in a particular field such as tax, patent, or admiralty law.

Employment growth of lawyers will continue to be concentrated in salaried jobs, as businesses and all levels of government employ a growing number of staff attorneys, and as employment in the legal services industry is increasingly concentrated in larger law firms. The number of self-employed lawyers is expected to continue to increase slowly, reflecting the difficulty of establishing a profitable new practice in the face of competition from larger, established law firms. Also, the growing complexity of law—which encourages specialization—and the cost of maintaining up-to-date legal research materials favor larger firms.

Nevertheless, for lawyers who wish to work independently, establishing a new practice probably will continue to be easiest in small towns and expanding suburban areas, as long as an active market for legal services exists. In such communities, competition from larger established law firms is likely to be less than in big cities, and new lawyers may find it easier to become known to potential clients. Additionally, rent and other business costs are somewhat lower in small towns than metropolitan areas. Yet, starting a new practice will remain an expensive and risky undertaking that should be weighed carefully. Most salaried positions will remain in urban areas where government agencies, law firms, and big corporations are concentrated.

Some lawyers are adversely affected by cyclical swings in the economy. During recessions, the demand declines for some discretionary legal services, such as planning estates, drafting wills, and handling real estate transactions. Also, corporations are less likely to litigate cases when declining sales and profits result in budgetary restrictions. Although few lawyers actually lose their jobs during these times, earnings may decline for many. Some corporations and law firms will not hire new attorneys until business improves. Several factors, however, mitigate the overall impact of recessions on lawyers. During recessions, individuals and corporations face other legal problems, such as bankruptcies, foreclosures, and divorces, that require legal action. Furthermore, new laws and legal interpretations will create new opportunities for lawyers.

Judges. Employment of judges is expected to grow more slowly than the average for all occupations. Contradictory social forces affect the demand for judges. Pushing up demand are public concerns about crime, safety, and efficient administration of justice; on the other hand, tight public funding should slow job growth.

Competition for judgeships should remain keen. Most job openings will arise as judges retire. Traditionally, many judges have held their positions until late in life. Now, early retirement is becoming more common, creating more job openings. However, becoming a judge will still be difficult. Besides competing with other qualified people, judicial candidates must gain political support in order to be elected or appointed.

Earnings

Annual salaries of beginning lawyers in private industry averaged about $37,000 in 1993, but top graduates obtaining positions at the Nation's largest law firms in some cases started at over $80,000 a year. In the Federal Government, annual starting salaries for attorneys in 1994 were about $29,200 or $36,400, depending upon academic and personal qualifications. Factors affecting the salaries offered to new graduates include: Academic record; type, size, and location of employer; and the specialized educational background desired. The field of law makes a difference, too. Patent lawyers, for example, generally are among the highest paid attorneys.

Salaries of experienced attorneys also vary widely according to the type, size, and location of their employer. The average salary of the most experienced lawyers in private industry in 1993 was nearly $115,000, but some senior lawyers who were partners in the Nation's top law firms earned over $1 million. General attorneys in the Federal Government averaged around $67,900 a year in 1995; the relatively small number of patent attorneys in the Federal Government averaged around $76,300.

Lawyers on salary receive increases as they assume greater responsibility. Lawyers starting their own practice may need to work part time in other occupations during the first years to supplement their income. Their incomes usually grow as their practices develop. Lawyers who are partners in law firms generally earn more than those who practice alone.

Federal district court judges had salaries of $133,600 in 1995, as did judges in the Court of Federal Claims. Circuit court judges earned $141,700 a year. Federal judges with limited jurisdiction, such as magistrates and bankruptcy court judges, had salaries of $122,900 in 1995. Full-time Federal administrative law judges had average salaries of $94,800 in 1995. The Chief Justice of the United States Supreme Court earned $171,500 in 1995, and the Associate Justices earned $164,100.

Annual salaries of associate justices of States' highest courts averaged $91,093 in 1995, according to a survey by the National Center for State Courts, and ranged from about $64,452 to $131,085. Salaries of State intermediate appellate court judges averaged $93,970, but ranged from $75,589 to $122,893. Salaries of State judges with limited jurisdiction varied widely; many salaries are set locally.

Most salaried lawyers and judges were provided health and life insurance, and contributions were made on their behalf to retirement plans. Lawyers who practiced independently were only covered if they arranged and paid for such benefits themselves.

Related Occupations

Legal training is useful in many other occupations. Some of these are paralegal, arbitrator, journalist, patent agent, title examiner, legislative assistant, lobbyist, FBI special agent, political office holder, and corporate executive.

Sources of Additional Information

The American Bar Association annually publishes *A Review of Legal Education in the United States*, which provides detailed information on each of the 178 law schools approved by the ABA, State require-

ments for admission to legal practice, a directory of State bar examination administrators, and other information on legal education. Single copies are free from the ABA, but there is a fee for multiple copies. Free information on the bar examination, financial aid for law students, and law as a career may also be obtained from:

☛American Bar Association, 750 North Lake Shore Dr., Chicago, IL 60611.

Information on the LSAT, the Law School Data Assembly Service, applying to law school, and financial aid for law students may be obtained from:

☛Law School Admission Council, P.O. Box 40, Newtown, PA 18940. Telephone: (215) 968-1001.

The specific requirements for admission to the bar in a particular State or other jurisdiction may also be obtained at the State capital from the clerk of the Supreme Court or the administrator of the State Board of Bar Examiners.

Social Scientists

(D.O.T. 029.067; 045.061, .067, .107-022, -026, -030, -034, -046; 050.067; 051; 052 except .067-014; 054; 055; 059)

Nature of the Work

Social scientists study all aspects of human society—from the distribution of goods and services to the beliefs of newly formed religious groups to modern mass transportation systems. Their research provides insights that help us understand the different ways in which individuals and groups make decisions, exercise power, or respond to change. Through their studies and analyses, social scientists and urban planners assist educators, government officials, business leaders, and others in solving social, economic, and environmental problems.

Research is a basic activity for many social scientists. They use established or newly discovered methods to assemble facts and theory that contribute to human knowledge. Applied research usually is designed to produce information that will enable people to make better decisions or manage their affairs more effectively. Interviews and surveys are widely used to collect facts, opinions, or other information. Data collection takes many forms, however, such as living and working among the population being studied, including speaking their native language; field investigations, including the analysis of historical records and documents; experiments with human or animal subjects in a laboratory; the administration of standardized tests and questionnaires; and the preparation and interpretation of maps and computer graphics.

Social sciences are interdisciplinary in nature. Specialists in one field often find that their research overlaps work that is being conducted in another discipline.

Anthropologists study the origin and the physical, social, and cultural development and behavior of humans. They may study the way of life, remains, language, or physical characteristics of people in various parts of the world. Some compare the customs, values, and social patterns of different cultures. Anthropologists generally concentrate in sociocultural anthropology, archaeology, linguistics, or biological-physical anthropology. Sociocultural anthropologists study the customs, cultures, and social lives of groups in settings from nonindustrialized societies to modern urban centers. Archaeologists engage in the systematic recovery and examination of material evidence, such as tools and pottery remaining from past human cultures, in order to determine the history, customs, and living habits of earlier civilizations. Linguistic anthropologists study the role of

language in various cultures. Biological-physical anthropologists study the evolution of the human body, look for the earliest evidences of human life, and analyze how culture and biology influence one another. Most anthropologists specialize in one particular region of the world.

Economists study the production, distribution, and consumption of goods and services. They may analyze data to determine public demand for a specific mix of goods and services. Most economists are concerned with the practical applications of economic policy in a particular area, such as finance, labor, agriculture, transportation, energy, or health. Others develop theories to explain economic phenomena such as unemployment or inflation. *Marketing research analysts* study market conditions in localities, regions, the Nation, or the world to determine potential sales of a product or service. They analyze data on past sales and trends to develop forecasts, and conduct extensive market surveys to test their conclusions.

Geographers analyze distributions of physical and cultural phenomena on local, regional, continental, and global scales. Geographers specialize, as a rule. Economic geographers study the distribution of resources and economic activities. Political geographers are concerned with the relationship of geography to political phenomena, while cultural geographers study the geography of cultural phenomena. Physical geographers study the variations in climates, vegetation, soil, and land forms, and their implications for human activity. Urban and transportation geographers study cities and metropolitan areas, while regional geographers study the physical, economic, political, and cultural characteristics of regions, ranging in size from a congressional district to entire continents. Medical geographers study health care delivery systems, epidemiology, and the effect of the environment on health. (Some occupational classification systems include geographers under physical scientists rather than social scientists.)

Historians research, analyze, and interpret the past. They use many sources of information in their research, including government and institutional records, newspapers and other periodicals, photographs, interviews, films, and unpublished manuscripts such as personal diaries and letters. Historians usually specialize in a specific country or region; in a particular time period; or in a particular field, such as social, intellectual, political, or diplomatic history. Biographers collect detailed information on individuals. Genealogists trace family histories. Other historians help study and preserve archival materials, artifacts, and historic buildings and sites.

Political scientists study the origin, development, and operation of political systems and public policy. They conduct research on a wide range of subjects such as relations between the United States and all other countries, the institutions and political life of all nations, the politics of small towns or a major metropolis, or the decisions of the U.S. Supreme Court. Studying topics such as public opinion, political decisionmaking, ideology, and public policy, they analyze the structure and operation of governments as well as various political entities. Depending on the topic under study, a political scientist might conduct a public opinion survey, analyze election results, analyze public documents, or interview public officials.

Psychologists, who constitute over half of all social scientists, study human behavior and counsel or advise individuals or groups. Their research also assists business advertisers, politicians, and others interested in influencing or motivating people. While clinical psychology is the largest specialty, psychologists specialize in many other fields such as counseling, experimental, social, and industrial psychology.

Sociologists study human society and social behavior by examining the groups and social institutions that people form, as well as various social, religious, political, and business organizations. They also study the behavior and interaction of groups, trace their origin and growth, and analyze the influence of group activities on individual members. They are concerned with the characteristics of social groups, organizations, and institutions; the ways individuals are affected by each other and by the groups to which they belong; and the effect of social traits such as sex, age, or race on a person's daily life. The results of sociological research aid educators, lawmakers, administrators, and others interested in resolving social problems and formulating public policy.

Expanding opportunities exist for practicing sociologists, who apply sociological knowledge, theory and methods to effect interventions at the individual, group or community levels. Practicing sociologists, including clinical sociologists, work in business, government, social service and education, performing evaluations, counseling, substance abuse prevention and treatment, and economic and community development.

Most sociologists work in one or more specialties, such as social organization, stratification, and mobility; racial and ethnic relations; education; family; social psychology; urban, rural, political, and comparative sociology; sex roles and relations; demography; gerontology; criminology; and sociological practice.

Urban and regional planners develop comprehensive plans and programs for the use of land. Planners prepare for situations that are likely to develop as a result of population growth or social and economic change.

Working Conditions

Most social scientists have regular hours. Generally working behind a desk, either alone or in collaboration with other social scientists, they read and write research reports. Many experience the pressures of writing and publishing articles, deadlines and tight schedules, and sometimes they must work overtime, for which they generally are not reimbursed. Social scientists often work as an integral part of a research team. Their routine may be interrupted frequently by telephone calls, letters to answer, special requests for information, meetings, or conferences. Travel may be necessary to collect information or attend meetings. Social scientists on foreign assignment must adjust to unfamiliar cultures, climates, and languages.

Some social scientists do fieldwork. For example, anthropologists, archaeologists, and geographers often travel to remote areas, live among the people they study, learn their languages, and stay for long periods at the site of their investigations. They may work under rugged conditions, and their work may involve strenuous physical exertion.

Social scientists employed by colleges and universities generally have flexible work schedules, often dividing their time among teaching, research and writing, consulting, or administrative responsibilities.

Employment

Social scientists held about 259,000 jobs in 1994. Over half of all social scientists are psychologists. Almost one-third of all social scientists—overwhelmingly psychologists—are self-employed, involved in counseling, consulting, or research.

Salaried social scientists worked as researchers, administrators, and counselors for a wide range of employers, including Federal, State, and local governments, educational institutions, hospitals, research and testing services, and management and public relations firms. Other employers include social service agencies, international organizations, associations, museums, historical societies, computer and data processing firms, and business firms.

In addition, many persons with training in a social science discipline teach in colleges and universities, and in secondary and elementary schools. (For more information, see the *Handbook* statements on college and university faculty, and kindergarten, elementary, and secondary school teachers.) The proportion of social scientists who teach varies by occupation—for example, the academic world generally is a more important source of jobs for graduates in sociology than for graduates in psychology.

Training, Other Qualifications, and Advancement

Educational attainment of social scientists is among the highest of all occupations. The Ph.D. or equivalent degree is a minimum requirement for most positions in colleges and universities and is important for advancement to many top level nonacademic research and administrative posts. Graduates with master's degrees in applied specialties generally have better professional opportunities outside of colleges and universities, although the situation varies by field. For example, job prospects for master's degree holders in urban or regional planning are brighter than for master's degree holders in history. Graduates with a master's degree in a social science qualify for teaching positions in junior colleges. Bachelor's degree holders have limited opportunities and in most social science occupations do not qualify for "professional" positions. The bachelor's degree does, however, provide a suitable background for many different kinds of entry level jobs, such as research assistant, administrative aide, or management or sales trainee. With the addition of sufficient education courses, social science graduates also can qualify for teaching positions in secondary and elementary schools.

Training in statistics and mathematics is essential for many social scientists. Mathematical and quantitative research methods are increasingly used in economics, geography, political science, experimental psychology, and other fields. The ability to use computers for research purposes is mandatory in most disciplines.

Depending on their jobs, social scientists and urban planners may need a wide range of personal characteristics. Because they constantly seek new information about people, things, and ideas, intellectual curiosity and creativity are fundamental personal traits. The ability to think logically and methodically is important to a political scientist comparing the merits of various forms of government. The ability to analyze data is important to an economist studying proposals to reduce Federal budget deficits. Objectivity, openmindedness, and systematic work habits are important in all kinds of social science research. Perseverance is essential for an anthropologist, who might spend years accumulating artifacts from an ancient civilization. Emotional stability and sensitivity are vital to a clinical psychologist working with mental patients. Written and oral communication skills are essential for all these professionals.

Job Outlook

Employment of social scientists is expected to grow faster than the average for all occupations through the year 2005, due to concern over the environment, crime, the increasingly competitive global economy, and a wide range of other issues. The largest social science occupation, psychologists, is expected to grow faster than average, as are economists and marketing research analysts, and urban and regional planners. All other social scientists combined, including anthropologists, geographers, historians, political scientists, and sociologists, should experience average growth. Most job openings, however, will result from the need to replace social scientists who transfer to other occupations or stop working altogether.

Prospects are best for those with advanced degrees, and generally are better in disciplines such as economics, psychology, and urban and regional planning, which offer many opportunities in nonacademic settings. However, graduates in all social science fields are expected to find enhanced job opportunities in applied fields due to the excellent research, communication, and quantitative skills they develop in graduate school. Government agencies, health and social service organizations, marketing, research and consulting firms, and a wide range of businesses seek social science graduates.

Social scientists currently face stiff competition for academic positions. However, the growing importance and popularity of social science subjects in secondary schools is strengthening the demand for social science teachers at this level.

Other considerations that affect employment opportunities in these occupations include specific skills and technical expertise, salary requirements, and geographic mobility. In addition, experience acquired through internships can prove invaluable later in obtaining a full-time position in a social science field.

Earnings

Median annual earnings of all social scientists were about $38,000 in 1994. The middle 50 percent earned between $23,200 and $52,600 annually. The lowest 10 percent earned under $17,300, while the highest 10 percent earned over $70,800.

According to a 1995 survey by the National Association of Colleges and Employers, people with a bachelor's degree in a social science field received starting offers averaging about $22,000 a year in 1995.

In the Federal Government, social scientists with a bachelor's degree and no experience could start at $18,700 or $23,200 a year in 1995, depending on their college records. Those with a master's degree could start at $28,300, and those having a Ph.D. degree could begin at $34,300, while some individuals with experience and an advanced degree could start at $41,100. Beginning salaries were slightly higher in selected areas of the country where the prevailing local pay level was higher. The average salary of social scientists working for the Federal Government in 1995 in nonsupervisory, supervisory, and managerial positions in geography was about $45,230; in history was $51,180; in sociology was $56,780; and in archeology was $38,770.

Related Occupations

A number of fields that require training and personal qualities similar to those of the various social science fields are covered elsewhere in the *Handbook*. These include lawyers, statisticians, mathematicians, computer programmers, computer scientists and systems analysts, reporters and correspondents, social workers, college and university faculty, and counselors.

Sources of Additional Information

More detailed information about economists and marketing research analysts, psychologists, and urban and regional planners is presented in the *Handbook* statements that follow this introductory statement.

Anthropology

For information about careers in anthropology, contact:
☛The American Anthropological Association, 4350 N. Fairfax Dr., Suite 640, Arlington, VA 22203.

Archaeology

For information about careers in archaeology, contact:
☛Society for American Archaeology, 900 2nd Street NE., Suite 12, Washington, DC 20002.
☛Archaeological Institute of America, 656 Beacon Street, Boston, MA 02215.

Geography

For information about careers in geography, contact:
☛Association of American Geographers, 1710 16th St. NW., Washington, DC 20009.

History

Information on careers for historians is available from:
☛American Historical Association, 400 A St. SE., Washington, DC 20003.
☛Organization of American Historians, 112 North Bryan St., Bloomington, IN 47408.
☛American Association for State and Local History, 530 Church St., 6th Floor, Nashville, TN 37219.

Political Science

For information about careers in political science, contact:
☛American Political Science Association, 1527 New Hampshire Ave. NW., Washington, DC 20036.
☛National Association of Schools of Public Affairs and Administration, 1120 G St. NW., Suite 730, Washington, DC 20005.

Sociology

Information about careers in sociology is available from:
☛American Sociological Association, 1722 N St. NW., Washington, DC 20036-2981.

For information about careers in demography, contact:
☛Population Association of America, 1722 N St. NW., Washington, DC 20036.

For information about careers and certification in clinical and applied sociology, contact:
☛Sociological Practice Association, Department of Pediatrics/Human Development, B240 Life Sciences, Michigan State University, East Lansing, MI 48824-1317.

Economists and Marketing Research Analysts

(D.O.T. 050.067)

Nature of the Work

Economists. Economists study the ways a society distributes scarce resources such as land, labor, raw materials, and machinery to produce goods and services. They conduct research, collect and analyze data, monitor economic trends, and develop forecasts. They might research topics such as energy costs, inflation, interest rates, farm prices, rents, imports, or employment levels.

Most economists are concerned with practical applications of economic policy in a particular area. They use their understanding of economic relationships to advise businesses and other organizations, including insurance companies, banks, securities firms, industry and trade associations, labor unions, and government agencies. Economists use mathematical models to develop programs predicting the nature and length of business cycles, the effects of inflation on the economy, or the effects of tax legislation on unemployment levels.

Economists devise methods and procedures for obtaining the data they need. For example, sampling techniques may be used to conduct a survey, and various mathematical modeling techniques may be used to develop forecasts. Preparing reports on the results of their research is an important part of the economist's job. Relevant data must be reviewed and analyzed, applicable tables and charts prepared, and the results presented in clear, concise language that can be understood by non-economists. Being able to present economic and statistical concepts in a meaningful way is particularly important for economists whose research is directed toward making policy for their organization.

Economists who work for government agencies may assess economic conditions in the United States or abroad in order to estimate the economic effects of specific changes in legislation or public policy. They may study areas such as how the dollar's fluctuation against foreign currencies affects import and export levels. The majority of government economists work in the area of agriculture, labor, or quantitative analysis, and some economists work in almost every area of government. For example, economists in the U.S. Department of Commerce study domestic production, distribution, and consumption of commodities or services, while economists employed with the Bureau of Labor Statistics analyze data on prices, wages, employment, productivity, and safety and health. An economist working in State or local government might analyze data on trade and commerce, industrial growth, and employment and unemployment rates in order to project employment trends.

Marketing Research Analysts. Marketing research analysts are concerned with the potential sales of a product or service. They analyze statistical data on past sales to predict future sales. They gather data on competitors and analyze prices, sales, and methods of marketing and distribution. Like economists, marketing research analysts devise methods and procedures for obtaining the data they need. They often design telephone, personal, or mail interview surveys to assess consumer preferences. The surveys usually are conducted by trained interviewers under the marketing research analyst's direction. Once the data are compiled, marketing research analysts evaluate it. They then make recommendations based upon their findings. They provide a company's management with information needed to make decisions on the promotion, distribution, design, and pricing of company products or services, or to determine the advisability of adding new lines of merchandise, opening new branches, or otherwise diversifying the company's operations. Analysts may conduct opinion research to determine public attitudes on various issues. This can help political or business leaders and others assess public support for their policies or products.

Working Conditions

Economists and marketing research analysts who work for government agencies and private firms have structured work schedules. They often work alone writing reports, preparing statistical charts, and using computers, but they may also be an integral part of a research team. Most work under pressure of deadlines and tight schedules, and sometimes must work overtime. Their routine may be interrupted by special requests for data, letters, meetings, or conferences. Regular travel may be necessary to collect data or attend conferences or meetings.

Employment

Economists and marketing research analysts held about 48,000 jobs in 1994. Private industry, particularly economic and marketing research firms, management consulting firms, banks, securities and commodities brokers, and computer and data processing companies, employed about 8 out of 10 salaried workers. The remainder, primarily economists, were employed by a wide range of government agencies, primarily in the State Government. The Departments of Labor, Agriculture, and Commerce are the largest Federal employers of economists. A number of economists and marketing research analysts combine a full-time job in government or business with part-time or consulting work in academia or another setting.

Employment of economists and marketing research analysts is concentrated in large cities. Some economists work abroad for companies with major international operations, for U.S. Government agencies, and for international organizations like the World Bank and the United Nations.

Besides the jobs described above, many economists and marketing research analysts held economics and marketing faculty positions in colleges and universities. Economics and marketing faculty have flexible work schedules, and may divide their time among teaching, research, consulting, and administration. (See the statement on college and university faculty elsewhere in the *Handbook*.)

Economists and marketing research analysts are concerned with practical applications of their work.

Training, Other Qualifications, and Advancement

Graduate training is required for most private sector economist and marketing research analyst jobs, and for advancement to more responsible positions. Economics includes many specialties at the graduate level, such as advanced economic theory, econometrics, international economics, and labor economics. Students should select graduate schools strong in specialties in which they are interested. Marketing research analysts may earn advanced degrees in economics, business administration, marketing, statistics, or some closely related discipline. Some schools help graduate students find internships or part-time employment in government agencies, economic consulting firms, financial institutions, or marketing research firms prior to graduation.

In the Federal Government, candidates for entry level economist positions must have a bachelor's degree with a minimum of 21 semester hours of economics and 3 hours of statistics, accounting, or calculus. Competition is keen for those positions which require only a bachelor's degree, however, and additional education or superior academic performance is likely to be required.

For a job as an instructor in many junior and some community colleges, a master's degree is the minimum requirement. In most colleges and universities, however, a Ph.D. is necessary for appointment as an instructor. A Ph.D. and extensive publications in academic journals are required for a professorship, tenure, and promotion.

Whether working in government, industry, research organizations, marketing, or consulting firms, economists and marketing research analysts who have a graduate degree usually qualify for more responsible research and administrative positions. A Ph.D. is necessary for top economist or marketing positions in many organizations. Many corporation and government executives have a strong background in economics or marketing.

A bachelor's degree with a major in economics or marketing is generally not sufficient to obtain positions as economist or marketing analyst, but is excellent preparation for many entry level positions as a research assistant, administrative or management trainee, marketing interviewer, or any of a number of professional sales jobs.

Economics majors can choose from a variety of courses, ranging from those which are intensely mathematical such as microeconomics, macroeconomics, and econometrics, to more philosophical courses such as the history of economic thought.

In addition to courses in business, marketing, and consumer behavior, marketing majors should take courses in related disciplines, including economics, psychology, organizational behavior, sociology, finance, business law, and international relations. Because of the importance of quantitative skills to economists and marketing researchers, courses in mathematics, statistics, econometrics, sampling theory and survey design, and computer science are extremely helpful.

Aspiring economists and marketing research analysts should gain experience gathering and analyzing data, conducting interviews or surveys, and writing reports on their findings while in college. This experience can prove invaluable later in obtaining a full-time position in the field, since much of their work in the beginning may center around these duties. With experience, economists and marketing research analysts eventually are assigned their own research projects.

Persons considering careers as economists or marketing research analysts should be able to work accurately because much time is spent on data analysis. Patience and persistence are necessary qualities since economists and marketing research analysts must spend long hours on independent study and problem solving. At the same time, they must be able to work well with others, especially marketing research analysts, who often interview or oversee interviews for a wide variety of individuals. Economists and marketing research analysts must be able to present their findings, both orally and in writing, in a clear, meaningful way.

Job Outlook

Employment of economists and marketing research analysts is expected to grow faster than average for all occupations through the year 2005. Most job openings, however, are likely to result from the need to replace experienced workers who transfer to other occupations, or retire or leave the labor force for other reasons.

Opportunities for economists should be best in private industry, especially in research, testing, and consulting firms, as more companies contract out for economic research services. Competition, the growing complexity of the global economy, and increased reliance on quantitative methods for analyzing business trends, forecasting sales, and planning purchasing and production should spur demand for economists. The continued need for economic analyses in virtually every industry should result in additional jobs for economists. Employment of economists in the Federal Government should decline in line with the rate of growth projected for the Federal workforce as a whole. Slower than average employment growth is expected among economists in State and local government.

A strong background in economic theory, mathematics, statistics, and econometrics provides the basis for acquiring any specialty within the field. Those skilled in quantitative techniques and their application to economic modeling and forecasting, including the use of computers, coupled with good communications skills, should have the best job opportunities.

Persons who graduate with a bachelor's degree in economics through the year 2005 will face keen competition for the limited number of economist positions for which they qualify. They will

qualify for a number of other positions, however, where they can take advantage of their economic knowledge in conducting research, developing surveys, or analyzing data. Many graduates with bachelor's degrees will find good jobs in industry and business as management or sales trainees, or administrative assistants. Economists with good quantitative skills are qualified for research assistant positions in a broad range of fields. Those who meet State certification requirements may become high school economics teachers. The demand for secondary school economics teachers is expected to grow as economics becomes an increasingly important and popular course. (See the statement on kindergarten, elementary, and secondary school teachers elsewhere in the *Handbook*.)

Candidates who hold a master's degree in economics have much better employment prospects than bachelor's degree holders. Many businesses, research and consulting firms, and government agencies seek master's degree holders who have strong computer and quantitative skills and can perform complex research, but do not command the higher salary of a Ph.D. Ph.D. degree holders are likely to face competition for teaching positions in colleges and universities.

Demand for marketing research analysts should be strong due to an increasingly competitive global economy. Marketing research provides organizations valuable feedback from purchasers, allowing companies to evaluate consumer satisfaction and more effectively plan for the future. As companies seek to expand their market and consumers become better informed, the need for marketing professionals is increasing. Opportunities for marketing research analysts should be good in a wide range of employment settings, particularly in marketing research firms, as companies find it more profitable to contract out for marketing research services rather than supporting their own marketing department. Other organizations, including financial services organizations, health care institutions, advertising firms, manufacturing firms that produce consumer goods, and insurance companies may offer job opportunities for marketing research analysts.

A strong background in economic theory, mathematics, statistics, and econometrics provides the basis for acquiring any specialty within the field. Those skilled in quantitative techniques and their application to marketing research, including the use of computers, should have the best job opportunities. Like economists, marketing research graduates with related work experience and an advanced degree in marketing or a closely related business field should have the best job opportunities.

Those with only a bachelor's degree but who have a strong background in mathematics, statistics, survey design, and computer science may be hired by private firms as assistants to marketing research professionals.

Earnings

According to a 1995 salary survey by the National Association of Colleges and Employers, persons with a bachelor's degree in economics received offers averaging $27,600 a year; for those with a bachelor's degrees in marketing, $25,400.

The median base salary of business economists in 1994 was $70,000, according to a survey by the National Association of Business Economists. Ninety two percent of the respondents held advanced degrees. The highest salaries were reported by those who had a Ph.D., with a median salary of $80,000. Master's degree holders earned a median salary of $62,000, while bachelor's degree holders earned $60,500. The highest paid business economists were in the securities and investment industry, which reported a median income of $95,000, followed by the nondurable manufacturing at $94,000 and the banking industry at $85,000. The lowest paid were in academia, wholesale and retail trade, and publishing.

The Federal Government recognizes education and experience in certifying applicants for entry level positions. In general, the entrance salary for economists having a bachelor's degree averaged about $18,700 a year in 1995; however, those with superior academic records could begin at $23,200. Those having a master's degree could qualify for positions at an annual salary of $28,300. Those with a Ph.D. could begin at $34,300, while some individuals with experience and an advanced degree could start at $41,100. Starting salaries were slightly more in selected areas where the prevailing local pay was higher. Economists in the Federal Government in nonsupervisory, supervisory, and managerial positions averaged around $59,030 a year in 1995.

Related Occupations

Economists are concerned with understanding and interpreting financial matters, among other subjects. Other jobs in this area include financial managers, financial analysts, underwriters, actuaries, securities and financial services sales workers, credit analysts, loan officers, and budget officers.

Marketing research analysts do research to find out how well products or services sell. This may include the planning, implementation, and analysis of surveys to determine people's needs and preferences. Other jobs using these skills include psychologists, sociologists, and urban and regional planners.

Sources of Additional Information

For information on careers in economics and business, contact:
☛National Association of Business Economists, 1233 20th St. NW., Suite 505, Washington, DC 20036.

For information about careers and salaries in marketing research, contact:
☛Marketing Research Association, 2189 Silas Deane Hwy., Suite 5, Rocky Hill, CT 06067.
☛Council of American Survey Research Organizations, 3 Upper Devon, Port Jefferson, NY 11777.

Psychologists

(D.O.T. 045.061, .067, .107-022, -026, -030, -034, and -046)

Nature of the Work

Psychologists study human behavior and the mental processes related to that behavior. Research psychologists investigate the physical, cognitive, emotional, or social aspects of human behavior. Psychologists in applied fields provide mental health services in hospitals, clinics, schools, or private settings.

Like other social scientists, psychologists formulate hypotheses and collect data to test their validity. Research methods depend on the topic under study. Psychologists may gather information through controlled laboratory experiments, as well as through personality, performance, aptitude, and intelligence tests. Other methods include observation, interviews, questionnaires, clinical studies, and surveys. Computers are widely used to record and analyze this information.

Psychologists apply their knowledge and techniques to a wide range of endeavors including human services, management, education, law, and sports. In addition to a variety of work settings, psychologists specialize in many different areas. *Clinical psychologists* —who constitute the largest specialty—generally work in independent or group practice or in hospitals or clinics. They assist mentally or emotionally disturbed clients adjust to life and increasingly help medical and surgical patients deal with their illnesses or injuries. Some work in physical rehabilitation settings, treating patients with spinal cord injuries, chronic pain or illness, stroke, arthritis, and neurologic conditions such as multiple sclerosis. Others help people deal with life stresses such as divorce or the death of a loved one. Clinical psychologists interview patients and give diagnostic tests. They provide individual, family, and group psychotherapy, and design and implement behavior modification programs. They may collaborate with physicians and other specialists in developing and implementing treatment and intervention programs that patients can understand and comply with. Some clinical psychologists work in universities, where they train graduate students in the delivery of mental health and behavioral medicine services. Others administer community mental health programs.

Relatively new specialties within clinical psychology include cognitive psychology, health psychology, neuropsychology, and geropsychology. *Cognitive psychologists* deal with memory, thinking, and perceptions. Some conduct research related to computer programming and artificial intelligence. *Health psychologists* promote good health through health maintenance counseling programs that are designed to help people achieve goals such as to stop smoking or lose weight. *Neuropsychologists* study the relation between the brain and behavior. They often work in stroke and head injury programs. *Geropsychologists* deal with the special problems faced by the elderly. The emergence and growth of these specialties reflects the increasing participation of psychologists in providing direct services to special patient populations.

Counseling psychologists use various techniques, including interviewing and testing, to advise people on how to deal with problems of everyday living, including career choices. (Also see the statements on counselors and social workers elsewhere in the *Handbook*.)

Developmental psychologists study the patterns and causes of behavioral change as people progress from infancy to adulthood. Some specialize in behavior during infancy, childhood, and adolescence, while others study changes that take place during maturity or old age. The study of developmental disabilities and how they affect people is a relatively new area within developmental psychology.

Experimental psychologists study behavior processes as they work with human beings and animals, such as rats, monkeys, and pigeons. Prominent areas of study in experimental research include motivation, thinking, attention, learning and retention, sensory and perceptual processes, effects of substance use and abuse, and genetic and neurological factors affecting behavior.

Industrial-organizational psychologists (I/O) apply psychological techniques to personnel administration, management, and marketing problems. They are involved in applicant screening, training and development, counseling, and organizational development and analysis. An industrial psychologist might work with management to develop better training programs and to reorganize the work setting to improve worker productivity or quality of worklife. They may also act as consultants to management.

School psychologists work with students, teachers, parents, and administrators to resolve students' learning and behavior problems. They collaborate with teachers, parents, and school personnel about classroom management strategies, parenting skills, substance abuse,

Many psychologists are self-employed.

working with students with disabilities or gifted and talented students, and teaching and learning strategies. They may evaluate the effectiveness of academic programs, behavior management procedures, and other services provided in the school setting.

Social psychologists examine people's interactions with others and with the social environment. Prominent areas of study include group behavior, leadership, attitudes, and interpersonal perception.

Working Conditions

A psychologist's specialty and place of employment determine working conditions. Clinical, school, and counseling psychologists in private practice have pleasant, comfortable offices and set their own hours. However, they often must offer evening hours to accommodate their clients. Those employed in hospitals, nursing homes, and other health facilities may work evenings and weekends, while those who work in schools and clinics generally work regular hours. Psychologists employed as faculty by colleges and universities divide their time between teaching and research, and a few have administrative responsibilities as well. Many have part-time consulting practices as well. Most psychologists in government and industry have structured schedules. Psychologists often work alone, reading and writing reports. Many experience pressures due to deadlines, tight schedules, and overtime work. Their routine may be interrupted frequently. Travel may be required to attend conferences or conduct research.

Employment

Psychologists held about 144,000 jobs in 1994. Educational institutions employed nearly 4 out of 10 salaried psychologists in positions other than teaching, involving counseling, testing, research, and administration. Three out of 10 were employed in health services, primarily in hospitals, mental health clinics, rehabilitation centers, nursing homes, and other health facilities. Government agencies at the Federal, State, and local levels employed one-sixth. Governments employ psychologists in hospitals, clinics, correctional facilities, and other settings. The Department of Veterans Affairs and the Department of Defense employ about 80 percent of the psychologists working for Federal agencies. Some psychologists work in social service organizations, research organizations, management consulting firms, marketing research firms, and other businesses.

After several years of experience, some psychologists—usually those with doctoral degrees—enter private practice or set up their own research or consulting firms. Over 40 percent of all psychologists are self-employed.

In addition to the jobs described above, many persons held positions as psychology faculty at colleges and universities, and as high school psychology teachers. (See the statements on college and university faculty and kindergarten, elementary, and secondary school teachers elsewhere in the *Handbook*.)

Training, Other Qualifications, and Advancement

A doctoral degree generally is required for employment as a clinical or counseling psychologist. Psychologists with a Ph.D. qualify for a wide range of teaching, research, clinical, and counseling positions in universities, elementary and secondary schools, private industry, and government. Psychologists with a Psy.D.—Doctor of Psychology—generally work in clinical positions. Persons with a master's degree in psychology can work as organizational or industrial psychologists. Others work as psychological assistants, under the supervision of doctoral-level psychologists, and may conduct research or psychological evaluations or counsel patients. Many work as school psychologists or counselors, and some teach in high schools or 2-year colleges.

A bachelor's degree in psychology qualifies a person to assist psychologists and other professionals in community mental health centers, vocational rehabilitation offices, and correctional programs. They may work as research or administrative assistants or become sales or management trainees in business. However, without additional academic training, their opportunities in psychology are severely limited.

In the Federal Government, candidates having at least 24 semester hours in psychology and one course in statistics qualify for entry-level positions. Because this is one of the few areas where one can work as a psychologist without an advanced degree, competition for these jobs is keen. Clinical psychologists generally must have completed the Ph.D. or Psy.D. requirements and have served an internship. Vocational and guidance counselors usually need 2 years of graduate study in counseling and 1 year of counseling experience. School psychology requires a master's degree followed by a 1-year internship.

Most students need at least 2 years of full-time graduate study to earn a master's degree in psychology. Requirements usually include practical experience in an applied setting or a master's thesis based on an original research project.

A doctoral degree usually requires 5 to 7 years of graduate study. The Ph.D. degree culminates in a dissertation based on original research. Courses in quantitative research methods, which include the use of computer-based analysis, are an integral part of graduate study and are necessary to complete the dissertation. The Psy.D. usually is based on practical work and examinations rather than a dissertation. In clinical or counseling psychology, the requirements for the doctoral degree generally include a year or more of internship.

Competition for admission into graduate programs is keen. Some universities require an undergraduate major in psychology. Others prefer only basic psychology with courses in the biological, physical, and social sciences, statistics, and mathematics.

Most colleges and universities offer a bachelor's degree in psychology. Over 600 departments offer either a master's or a full Ph.D. program. A smaller number of professional schools of psychology offer the Psy.D.

The American Psychological Association (APA) presently accredits doctoral training programs in clinical, counseling, and school psychology. The National Council for Accreditation of Teacher Education, with the assistance of the National Association of School Psychologists, also is involved in the accreditation of advanced degree programs in school psychology. The APA also accredits institutions that provide internships for doctoral students in school, clinical, and counseling psychology.

Psychologists in independent practice or those who offer any type of patient care, including clinical, counseling, and school psychologists, must meet certification or licensing requirements. All States and the District of Columbia have such requirements. Licensing laws vary by State and by type of position. Clinical and counseling psychologists generally require a doctorate in psychology, completion of an approved internship, and 1 to 2 years of professional experience. In addition, most States require that applicants pass an examination. Most State boards administer a standardized test and many supplement that with additional oral or essay questions. Most States certify those with a master's degree as school psychologists after completion of an internship. Some States require continuing education for license renewal.

Most States require that licensed or certified psychologists limit their practice to those areas in which they have developed professional competence through training and experience.

The American Board of Professional Psychology recognizes professional achievement by awarding certification, primarily in clinical psychology, clinical neuropsychology, counseling, forensic, industrial and organizational, and school psychology. Candidates need a doctorate in psychology, 5 years of experience, professional endorsements, and a passing grade on an examination.

Aspiring psychologists who are interested in direct patient care must be emotionally stable, mature, and able to deal effectively with people. Sensitivity, compassion, and the ability to lead and inspire others are particularly important for clinical work and counseling. Research psychologists should be able to do detailed work independently and as part of a team. Verbal and writing skills are necessary to communicate research findings. Patience and perseverance are vital qualities because results from psychological treatment of patients or from research usually take a long time.

Job Outlook

Employment of psychologists is expected to grow faster than the average for all occupations through the year 2005. The need to combat alcohol and drug abuse, marital strife, family violence, crime, and other problems plaguing society should stimulate employment growth. Other factors spurring demand for psychologists include increased emphasis on mental health maintenance in conjunction with the treatment of physical illness and public concern for the development of human resources, including the growing elderly population and children in school.

Job opportunities in health care should remain strong in health care provider networks, such as health maintenance and preferred provider organizations, and in nursing homes and alcohol and drug abuse programs. Job opportunities will arise in businesses, nonprofit organizations, and research and computer firms for psychologists working as consultants. Companies will use psychologists' expertise in survey design, analysis, and research to provide marketing evaluation and statistical analysis. The increase in employee assistance programs, which offer employees help with personal problems, also should spur job growth.

Opportunities are best for candidates with a doctoral degree. Persons holding doctorates from leading universities in applied areas, such as clinical, counseling, health, industrial, and educational psychology should have particularly good prospects. Psychologists with extensive training in quantitative research methods and computer science may have a competitive edge over applicants without this background.

Graduates with a master's degree in psychology will encounter competition for the limited number of jobs for which they qualify. Graduates of master's degree programs in school psychology should have the best job prospects, as schools are expected to increase student counseling and mental health services. Other master's degree holders may find jobs as psychological assistants in the community mental health field, which often requires direct supervision by a licensed psychologist. Still others may find jobs involving research and data collection and analysis in universities, government, or private companies.

Bachelor's degree holders can expect very few opportunities directly related to psychology. Some may find jobs as assistants in rehabilitation centers or in other jobs involving data collection and analysis. Those who meet State certification requirements may become high school psychology teachers.

Earnings

According to a 1993 survey by the American Psychological Association, the median starting salary of psychologists with a doctoral degree was $39,100 in counseling psychology; $39,000 in research positions; $40,000 in clinical psychology; and $45,000 in school psychology. The median annual salary of master's degree holders was $26,000 in counseling psychology; $24,000 in clinical psychology; $28,000 in research positions; $34,500 in school psychology, and $58,000 in industrial-organizational psychology. Some psychologists have much higher earnings, particularly those in private practice.

The Federal Government recognizes education and experience in certifying applicants for entry level positions. In general, the starting salary for psychologists having a bachelor's degree was about $18,700 a year in 1995; those with superior academic records could begin at $23,200. Counseling and school psychologists with a master's degree and 1 year of counseling experience could start at $28,300. Clinical psychologists having a Ph.D. or Psy.D. degree and 1 year of internship could start at $34,300 and some individuals with experience could start at $41,100. Beginning salaries were slightly higher in selected areas of the country where the prevailing local pay level was higher. The average salary for psychologists in the Federal Government in nonsupervisory, supervisory, and managerial positions was about $58,300 a year in 1995.

Related Occupations

Psychologists are trained to conduct research and teach, evaluate, counsel, and advise individuals and groups with special needs. Others who do this kind of work include psychiatrists, clinical social workers, sociologists, clergy, special education teachers, and counselors.

Sources of Additional Information

For information on careers, educational requirements, financial assistance, and licensing in all fields of psychology, contact:

☛American Psychological Association, Research Office and Education in Psychology and Accreditation Offices, 750 1st St. NE., Washington, DC 20002.

For information on careers, educational requirements, and licensing of school psychologists, contact:

☛National Association of School Psychologists, 4030 East West Highway, Suite 402, Bethesda, MD 20814.

Information about State licensing requirements is available from:

☛Association of State and Provincial Psychology Boards, P.O. Box 4389, Montgomery, AL 36103-4389.

Information on traineeships and fellowships also is available from colleges and universities that have graduate departments of psychology.

Urban and Regional Planners

(D.O.T. 188.167-110 and 199.167-014)

Nature of the Work

Urban and regional planners are often referred to as community or city planners because many are employed by local governments. They develop long and short-term land use plans to provide for growth and revitalization of urban, suburban, and rural communities, while helping local officials make decisions on social, economic, and environmental problems.

Planners devise plans promoting the best use of a community's land and resources for residential, commercial, and recreational activities. Planners also are involved in various other planning activities, including social services, transportation, resource development, and the protection of ecologically sensitive regions. They address issues such as traffic congestion, air pollution, and the effect of growth and change on an area. They may formulate capital improvement plans for the construction of new school buildings, public housing, or sewage systems. Planners are involved in environmental issues ranging from pollution control to wetland preservation, forest conservation, and the location of new landfills. Planners also may be involved with drafting legislation on social issues such as the needs of the elderly, sheltering the homeless, or meeting the demand for new correctional facilities.

Planners examine proposed community facilities such as schools to be sure these facilities will meet the demands placed upon them over time by population growth. They keep abreast of the economic and legal issues involved in zoning codes, building codes, and environmental regulations. They ensure that builders and developers follow these codes and regulations. Planners also deal with land use and environmental issues created by population movements. For example, as suburban growth increases the need for traveling, some planners design new transportation systems and parking facilities.

Before preparing plans for community development, planners report on the current use of land for residential, business, and community purposes. These reports include information on the location of streets, highways, water and sewer lines, schools, libraries, and cultural and recreational sites, and provide data on the types of industries in the community, characteristics of the population, and employment and economic trends. With this information, along with input from citizens' advisory committees, planners design the layout of recommended buildings and other facilities such as subway lines and stations, and prepare reports that show how their programs can be carried out and what they will cost.

Planners increasingly use computers to record and analyze information and to prepare their reports and recommendations for government leaders and others. Computer databases, spreadsheets, and analytical techniques are widely used to determine program costs and forecast future trends in employment, housing, transportation, or population. Computerized geographic information systems enable planners to map land areas and overlay maps with geographic variables, such as population density, as well as to combine and manipulate geographic information to produce alternative plans for land use or development.

Urban and regional planners often confer with land developers, civic leaders, and public officials. They may function as mediators in community disputes by presenting alternatives that are acceptable to opposing parties. Planners may prepare material for community relations programs, speak at civic meetings, and appear before legislative committees and elected officials to explain and defend their proposals.

In large organizations, planners usually specialize in a single area such as transportation, housing, historic preservation, urban design, environmental and regulatory issues, or economic development. In small organizations, planners must be generalists, able to do various kinds of planning.

Working Conditions

Urban and regional planners spend much of their time in offices. To be familiar with areas that they are developing, however, they periodically spend time outdoors inspecting the features of land under consideration for development, including its current use and the types of structures on it. Some local government planners involved in site development inspections spend most of their time in the field. Although most planners have a scheduled 40-hour workweek, they frequently attend evening or weekend meetings or public hearings with citizens' groups. Planners may experience the pressure of deadlines and tight work schedules, as well as political pressure generated by interest groups affected by their land use proposals.

Most entry level jobs for urban and regional planners require a master's degree.

Employment

Urban and regional planners held about 29,000 jobs in 1994, 2 out of 3 of whom were employed by local governments. An increasing proportion of planners work in the private sector for companies involved with real estate and transportation. Others are employed in State agencies that deal with housing, transportation, or environmental protection, and a small number work for the Federal Government.

Many planners do consulting work, either part time as a supplement to their regular jobs, or full time. They provide services to private developers or government agencies. Private sector employers include architectural and surveying firms, management and public relations firms, educational institutions, large land developers, and law firms specializing in land use.

Training, Other Qualifications, and Advancement

Employers prefer workers who have advanced training. Most entry level jobs in Federal, State, and local government agencies require a master's degree in urban or regional planning or urban design, or the equivalent in work experience. A bachelor's degree from an accredited planning program, coupled with a master's degree in architecture, landscape architecture, or civil engineering, is good preparation for entry-level planning jobs in areas such as urban design, traffic, or the environment. A master's degree from an accredited planning program provides the best training for a number of planning fields. Although graduates from one of the limited number of accredited bachelor's degree programs qualify for many beginning positions, their advancement opportunities often are limited unless they acquire an advanced degree. Courses in related disciplines such as architecture, law, earth sciences, demography, economics, finance, health administration, geographic information systems, and management are highly recommended. In addition, familiarity with computer models and statistical techniques is necessary because of the increasing use of computerized modeling and geographic information systems in planning analyses.

In 1994, about 80 colleges and universities offered an accredited master's degree program and about 10 offered an accredited bachelor's degree program in urban or regional planning. These programs are accredited by the Planning Accreditation Board, which consists of representatives of the American Institute of Certified Planners and the Association of Collegiate Schools of Planning. Most graduate programs in planning require a minimum of 2 years.

Specializations most commonly offered by planning schools are environmental planning, land use and comprehensive planning, economic development, and housing. Other popular offerings include community development, transportation, and urban design. Graduate students spend considerable time in studios, workshops, and laboratory courses learning to analyze and solve planning problems. They often are required to work in a planning office part time or during the summer. Local government planning offices frequently offer students internships that provide experience that proves invaluable in obtaining a full-time planning position after graduation.

The American Institute of Certified Planners (AICP), a professional institute within the American Planning Association (APA), grants certification to individuals who have the appropriate combination of education and professional experience and who pass an examination. Certification may be helpful for promotion.

Planners must be able to think in terms of spatial relationships and visualize the effects of their plans and designs. Planners should be flexible and able to reconcile different viewpoints and to make constructive policy recommendations. The ability to communicate effectively, both orally and in writing, is necessary for anyone interested in this field.

After a few years' experience, planners may advance to assignments requiring a high degree of independent judgment, such as designing the physical layout of a large development or recommending policy and budget options. Some public sector planners are promoted to jobs as planning directors and spend a great deal of time meeting with officials, speaking to civic groups, and supervising a staff. Further advancement occurs through a transfer to a larger jurisdiction with more complex problems and greater responsibilities, or into related occupations, such as director of community or economic development. In the private sector, experience leads to increases in independence and compensation.

Job Outlook

A master's degree from an accredited planning program, or a master's degree in civil engineering or landscape architecture coupled with training in transportation, environmental planning, geographic information systems, or urban design, provide the most marketable background. Graduates with a bachelor's degree in planning but no graduate degree will have more difficulty finding a job in this field, although prospects are much brighter for entry-level jobs for those from one of the ten undergraduate programs in the country with an accredited bachelor's degree.

Employment of urban and regional planners is expected to grow faster than the average for all occupations through the year 2005. Most job openings, however, are expected to arise from the need to replace experienced planners who transfer to other occupations, or retire or leave the labor force for other reasons.

The continuing importance of transportation, environmental, and housing planning will increase demand for urban and regional planners. Specific factors contributing to job growth include the need to regulate commercial development of suburban areas with rapidly growing populations and legislation related to the environment, transportation, housing, and land use and development. Movements such as historic preservation and central city redevelopment will provide additional openings. However, local communities have limited resources and many demands for services. When communities need to cut expenditures, planning services may be cut before more basic services such as police or education.

Most new jobs for urban and regional planners will arise in rapidly expanding communities. Local governments need planners to address an array of problems associated with population growth. For example, new housing developments require roads, sewer systems, fire stations, schools, libraries, and recreation facilities that must be planned while considering budgetary constraints. Small town chambers of commerce, economic development authorities and tourism bureaus are eager to hire planners, provided that the candidate has some background in marketing and public relations.

Earnings

Salaries of planners vary by educational attainment, type of employer, experience, size of community in which they work, and geographic location. According to a 1994 report by the APA, urban and regional planners with less than 5 years of experience earned median annual salaries of about $30,000 to $37,000. Planners with between 5 and 10 years' experience earned median salaries of about $39,000 to $42,000. Those with more than 10 years' experience earned median annual salaries of about $52,000 to $63,000.

According to limited data, median annual earnings of full-time wage and salary urban and regional planners were about $45,000 in 1994.

Planners with a master's degree were hired by the Federal Government at a starting average salary of $28,300 a year in 1994. In some cases, persons having less than 2 years of graduate work could enter Federal service as interns at yearly salaries of about $18,700 or $23,200. Salaries of community planners employed by the Federal Government in nonsupervisory, supervisory, and managerial positions averaged about $55,500 a year in 1995.

Related Occupations

Urban and regional planners develop plans for the orderly growth of urban and rural communities. Others whose work is similar to the work of planners include architects, landscape architects, city managers, civil engineers, environmental engineers, and geographers.

Sources of Additional Information

Information on careers, salaries, and certification in urban and regional planning is available from:

☛American Planning Association, Education Division, 122 South Michigan Avenue, Suite 1600, Chicago, IL 60630-6107.

Social and Recreation Workers

Human Services Workers

(D.O.T. 195.367 except -026 and -030)

Nature of the Work

"Human services worker" is a generic term for people with various job titles, such as social service assistant, case management aide, social work assistant, residential counselor, community support worker, alcohol or drug abuse counselor, mental health technician, child-care worker, community outreach worker, life skill counselor, and gerontology aide. They generally work under the direction of professionals from a wide variety of fields, such as nursing, psychiatry, psychology, rehabilitation, or social work. The amount of responsibility and supervision they are given varies a great deal. Some are on their own most of the time and have little direct supervision; others work under close direction.

Human services workers provide direct and indirect client services. They assess clients' needs, establish their eligibility for benefits and services, and help clients obtain them. They examine financial documents such as rent receipts and tax returns to determine whether the client is eligible for food stamps, Medicaid, welfare, and other human service programs. They also arrange for transportation and escorts, if necessary, and provide emotional support. Human services workers monitor and keep case records on clients and report progress to supervisors.

Human services workers may transport or accompany clients to group meal sites, adult daycare programs, or doctors' offices; telephone or visit clients' homes to make sure services are being received; or help resolve disagreements, such as those between tenants and landlords.

Human services workers play a variety of roles in community settings. They may organize and lead group activities, assist clients in need of counseling or crisis intervention, or administer a food bank or emergency fuel program. In halfway houses, group homes, and government-supported housing programs, they assist adult residents who need supervision in personal hygiene and daily living skills. They review clients' records, ensure they take correct doses of medication, talk with their families, and confer with medical personnel to gain better insight into clients' backgrounds and needs. They also provide emotional support and help clients become involved in community recreation programs and other activities.

Human services workers may accompany clients to adult daycare programs.

In psychiatric hospitals, rehabilitation programs, and outpatient clinics, they may help clients master everyday living skills and teach them how to communicate more effectively and get along better with others. They support the client's participation in the treatment plan, such as individual or group counseling and occupational therapy.

Working Conditions

Working conditions of human services workers vary. They work in offices, group homes, shelters, day programs, sheltered workshops, hospitals, clinics, and in the field visiting clients. Most work a regular 40-hour week, although some work may be in the evening and on weekends. Human services workers in residential settings generally work in shifts because residents need supervision around the clock.

The work, while satisfying, can be emotionally draining. Understaffing and an inadequate work environment may add to the pressure. Turnover is reported to be high, especially among workers without academic preparation for this field.

Employment

Human services workers held about 168,000 jobs in 1994. About one-fourth were employed by State and local governments, primarily in public welfare agencies and facilities for mentally disabled and developmentally delayed individuals. Another fourth worked in private social or human services agencies offering a variety of services, including adult daycare, group meals, crisis intervention, and counseling. Many human services workers supervised residents of group homes and halfway houses. Human services workers also held jobs in clinics, detoxification units, community mental health centers, psychiatric hospitals, day treatment programs, and sheltered workshops.

Training, Other Qualifications, and Advancement

While some employers hire high school graduates, most prefer applicants with some college preparation in human services, social work, or one of the social or behavioral sciences. Some prefer to hire persons with a 4-year college degree. The level of formal education of human service workers often influences the kind of work they are assigned and the amount of responsibility entrusted to them. Workers with no more than a high school education are likely to receive on-the-job training to work in direct care services, while those with a college degree might be assigned to do supportive counseling, coordinate program activities, or manage a group home. Employers may also look for experience in other occupations, leadership experience in an organization, or human service volunteer exposure. Some enter the field on the basis of courses in human services, psychology, rehabilitation, social work, sociology, or special education. Most employers provide in-service training such as seminars and workshops.

Because so many human services jobs involve direct contact with people who are vulnerable to exploitation or mistreatment, employers try to select applicants with appropriate personal qualifications. Relevant academic preparation is generally required, and volunteer or work experience is preferred. A strong desire to help others, patience, and understanding are highly valued characteristics. Other important personal traits include communication skills, a strong sense of responsibility, and the ability to manage time effectively. Hiring requirements in group homes tend to be more stringent than in other settings. In some settings, applicants may need a valid driver's license and must meet the Criminal Offense Record Investigation (CORI) requirement. Special licensure or State certifications may also apply.

In 1994, 375 certificate and associate degree programs in human services or mental health were offered at community and junior colleges, vocational-technical institutes, and other postsecondary institutions. In addition, 390 programs offered a bachelor's degree in human services. Master's degree programs in human services administration are offered as well.

Generally, academic programs in this field educate students for specialized roles. Human services programs have a core curriculum that trains students in observation and recording, interviewing, communication techniques, behavior management, group dynamics, counseling, crisis intervention, case management, and referral. General education courses in liberal arts, sciences, and the humanities are also part of the curriculum. Many degree programs require completion of an internship.

Formal education is almost always necessary for advancement. In general, advancement requires a bachelor's or master's degree in counseling, rehabilitation, social work, or a related field.

Job Outlook

Opportunities for human services workers are expected to be excellent for qualified applicants. The number of human services workers is projected to grow much faster than the average for all occupations between 1994 and the year 2005—ranking among the most rapidly growing occupations. Also, the need to replace workers who retire or stop working for other reasons will create additional job opportunities. These jobs are not attractive to everyone due to the emotionally draining work and relatively low pay, so qualified applicants should have little difficulty finding employment.

Opportunities are expected to be best in job training programs, residential settings, and private social service agencies, which include such services as adult daycare and meal delivery programs. Demand for these services will expand with the growing number of older people, who are more likely to need services. In addition, human services workers will continue to be needed to provide services to the mentally disabled and developmentally delayed, those with substance abuse problems, the homeless, and pregnant teenagers. Faced with rapid growth in the demand for services, but slower growth in resources to provide the services, employers are expected to rely increasingly on human services workers rather than other occupations that command higher pay.

Job training programs are expected to require additional human services workers as the economy grows and businesses change their mode of production, requiring workers to be retrained. Human services workers help determine workers' eligibility for public assistance programs and help them obtain services while unemployed.

Residential settings should expand also as pressures to respond to the needs of the chronically mentally ill persist. For many years, chronic mental patients have been deinstitutionalized and left to their own devices. Now, more community-based programs, supported independent living sites, and group residences are expected to be established to house and assist the homeless and chronically mentally ill, and demand for human services workers will increase accordingly.

Jobs for human services workers will grow more rapidly than overall employment in State and local governments. State and local governments employ most of their human services workers in corrections and public assistance departments. Corrections departments are growing faster than other areas of government, so human services workers should find that their job opportunities increase along with other corrections jobs. Public assistance programs have been employing more human services workers in an attempt to employ fewer social workers, who are more educated and higher paid.

Earnings

Based on limited information, starting salaries for human services workers ranged from about $13,000 to $20,000 a year in 1994. Experienced workers generally earned between $18,000 and $27,000 annually, depending on their education, experience, and employer.

Related Occupations

Workers in other occupations that require skills similar to those of human services workers include social workers, religious workers, occupational therapy assistants, physical therapy assistants, psychiatric aides, and activity leaders.

Sources of Additional Information

Information on academic programs in human services may be found in most directories of 2- and 4-year colleges, available at libraries or career counseling centers.

For information on programs and careers in human services, contact:

☛National Organization for Human Service Education, Brookdale Community College, Lyncroft, NJ 07738.

☛Council for Standards in Human Service Education, Northern Essex Community College, Haverhill, MA 01830.

Information on job openings may be available from State employment service offices or directly from city, county, or State departments of health, mental health and mental retardation, and human resources.

Recreation Workers

(D.O.T. 153.137-010; 159.124-010; 187.167-238; 195.227-010, -014; 352.167-010)

Nature of the Work

Many people spend some of their leisure time participating in organized recreation ranging from aerobics or crafts to hiking or softball. Recreation programs, as diverse as the people they serve, are offered at local playgrounds and recreation areas, parks, community centers, health clubs, churches and synagogues, camps, and theme parks and tourist attractions. Recreation workers plan, organize, and direct these activities.

Recreation workers organize and lead programs and watch over recreational facilities and equipment. They help people to pursue their interest in crafts, art, or sports. They enable people to share common interests in physical or mental activities for their mutual entertainment, physical fitness, and self-improvement. Recreation workers organize teams and leagues and also teach the correct use of equipment and facilities.

In the workplace, recreation workers oganize and direct leisure activities and athletic programs for all ages, such as bowling and softball leagues, social functions, travel programs, discount services, and, to an increasing extent, exercise and fitness programs. These activities are generally for adults.

Camp counselors lead and instruct children and teenagers in outdoor-oriented forms of recreation, such as swimming, hiking, and horseback riding as well as camping. Activities often are intended to enhance campers' appreciation of nature and responsible use of the environment. In addition, counselors provide campers with specialized instruction in activities such as archery, boating, music, drama, gymnastics, tennis, or computers. In resident camps, counselors also provide guidance and supervise daily living and general socialization.

Recreation workers occupy a variety of positions at different levels of responsibility. *Recreation leaders* are responsible for a recreation program's daily operation and organize and direct participants. They may lead and give instruction in dance, drama, crafts, games, and sports; schedule use of facilities and keep records of equipment use; and monitor the use of recreation facilities and equipment to make sure they are used properly. Workers who provide instruction in specialties such as art, music, drama, swimming, or tennis may be called *activity specialists*. They often conduct classes and coach teams in the activity in which they specialize.

Recreation supervisors plan programs to meet the needs of the population they serve and supervise recreation leaders and activity specialists, sometimes over a large region. They may also direct specialized activities and special events. A growing number of supervisors use computers in their work.

In a related occupation, *recreational therapists* help individuals recover or adjust to illness, disability, or specific social problems; this occupation is described elsewhere in the *Handbook*.

Working Conditions

Recreation workers must work while others engage in leisure time activities. While most recreation workers put in about 40 hours a week, people entering this field—especially camp counselors—should expect some night and weekend work and irregular hours. About 3 out of 10 worked part time and many jobs are seasonal. The work setting for recreation workers may be anywhere from a cruise ship to a woodland recreational park. Recreation workers often spend much of their time outdoors and may work under a variety of weather conditions. Recreation supervisors may spend most of their time in an office. Since full-time recreation workers spend more time acting as managers than hands-on activities leaders, they engage in less physical activity. However, as is the case for anyone engaged in physical activity, recreation workers risk injuries, and the work can be physically tiring.

Employment

Recreation workers held about 222,000 jobs in 1994, and many additional workers held summer jobs in this occupation. Of those who held full-time jobs as recreation workers, about half worked in park and recreation departments of municipal and county governments. About 17 percent worked in membership organizations with a

Recreation workers often work outdoors with children.

civic, social, fraternal, or religious orientation—the Boy Scouts, the YWCA, and Red Cross, for example. Another 11 percent were in programs run by social service organizations—senior centers and adult daycare programs, or residential care facilities such as halfway houses, group homes, and institutions for delinquent youth. An additional 10 percent worked for nursing and other personal care facilities.

Other employers included commercial recreation establishments, amusement parks, sports and entertainment centers, wilderness and survival enterprises, tourist attractions, vacation excursion companies, hotels and resorts, summer camps, health and athletic clubs, and apartment complexes.

The recreation field has an unusually large number of part-time, seasonal, and volunteer jobs. These jobs include summer camp counselors, lifeguards, craft specialists, and after-school and weekend recreation program leaders. Teachers and college students take many jobs as recreation workers when school is not in session.

Many unpaid volunteers assist paid recreation workers. The vast majority of volunteers serve as activity leaders at local day-camp programs, or in youth organizations, camps, nursing homes, hospitals, senior centers, YMCA's, and other settings. Some volunteers serve on local park and recreation boards and commissions. Volunteer experience, part-time work during school, or a summer job can lead to a full-time job.

Training, Other Qualifications, and Advancement

Education needed for recreation worker jobs ranges from a high school diploma, or sometimes less, for many summer jobs to graduate education for some administrative positions in large public systems. Full-time career professional positions usually require a college degree with a major in parks and recreation or leisure studies, but a bachelor's degree in any liberal arts field may be sufficient for some jobs in the private sector. In industrial recreation, or "employee services" as it is more commonly called, companies prefer to hire those with a bachelor's degree in recreation or leisure studies and a background in business administration.

Specialized training or experience in a particular field, such as art, music, drama, or athletics, is an asset for many jobs. Some jobs also require a certification. For example, when teaching or coaching water-related activities, a lifesaving certificate is a prerequisite. Graduates of associate degree programs in parks and recreation, social work, and other human services disciplines also enter some career recreation positions. Occasionally high school graduates are able to enter career positions, but this is not common. Some college students work part time as recreation workers while earning degrees.

A bachelor's degree and experience are preferred for most recreation supervisor jobs and required for most higher level administrator jobs. However, increasing numbers of recreation workers who aspire to administrator positions are obtaining master's degrees in parks and recreation or related disciplines. Also, many persons in other disciplines, including social work, forestry, and resource management, pursue graduate degrees in recreation.

Programs leading to an associate or bachelor's degree in parks and recreation, leisure studies, or related fields are offered at several hundred colleges and universities. Many also offer master's or doctoral degrees in this field.

In 1995, approximately 90 bachelor's degree programs in parks and recreation were accredited by the National Recreation and Park Association (NRPA). Accredited programs provide broad exposure to the history, theory, and philosophy of park and recreation management. Courses offered include community organization, supervision and administration, recreational needs of special populations, such as older adults or the disabled, and supervised fieldwork. Students may specialize in areas such as therapeutic recreation, park management, outdoor recreation, industrial or commercial recreation, and camp management.

The American Camping Association has developed a curriculum for camp director education. Many national youth associations offer training courses for camp directors at the local and regional levels.

Persons planning recreation careers should be outgoing, good at motivating people, and sensitive to the needs of others. Good health and physical fitness are required. Activity planning calls for creativity and resourcefulness. Willingness to accept responsibility and the ability to exercise good judgment are important qualities since recreation personnel often work without close supervision. Part-time or summer recreation work experience while in high school or college may help students decide whether their interests really point to a human services career. Such experience also may increase their leadership skills and understanding of people.

Individuals contemplating careers in recreation at the supervisory or administrative level should develop managerial skills. College courses in management, business administration, accounting, and personnel management are likely to be useful.

Certification for this field is offered by the NRPA National Certification Board and the American Camping Association. The National Recreation and Parks Association, along with its State chapters, offers certification as a Certified Leisure Professional (CLP) for those with a college degree in recreation, and as a Certified Leisure Associate (CLA) for those with less than 4 years of college, for example. The American Camping Association offers a certification program for camp directors. Continuing education is necessary to remain certified in either field.

Certification is not usually required for employment or advancement in this field, but it is an asset. Employers choosing among qualified job applicants may opt to hire the person with a demonstrated record of professional achievement represented by certification.

Job Outlook

Applicants for full-time career positions in recreation will face keen competition. All college graduates can enter recreation jobs, regardless of major, as well as some high school and junior college graduates, so the number of full-time career jobseekers often greatly exceed the number of job openings. Opportunities for staff positions should be best for persons with job experience gained in part-time or seasonal recreation jobs, together with formal recreation training. Those with graduate degrees should have the best opportunities for supervisory or administrative positions.

Prospects are better for the large number of temporary seasonal jobs. These positions, typically filled by high school or college students, do not generally have formal education requirements and are open to anyone with the desired personal qualities. Employers compete for a share of the vacationing student labor force, and, while salaries in recreation are often lower than those in other fields, the nature of the work and the opportunity to work outdoors is attractive to many. Seasonal employment prospects should be good for applicants with specialized training and certification in an activity like swimming. These workers may obtain jobs as program directors.

Employment of recreation workers is expected to grow about as fast as the average for all occupations through the year 2005 as growing numbers of people possess both the time and the money to purchase leisure services. Growth in these jobs will also stem from increased interest in fitness and health and the rising demand for recreational opportunities for older adults in senior centers and retirement communities. However, overall job growth in local government—where half of all recreation workers are employed—is expected to be slow due to budget constraints, and local park and recreation departments are expected to do less hiring for permanent, full-time positions than in the past. As a result, this sector's share of recreation worker employment will continue to shrink. Nonetheless, opportunities will vary widely by region, since resources as well as priorities for public services differ from one community to another. Thus, hiring prospects for recreation workers will be much better in some park and recreation departments than overall projections would suggest, but worse in others.

Recreation worker jobs should also increase in social services—

more recreation workers will be needed to develop and lead activity programs in senior centers, halfway houses, children's homes, and daycare programs for the mentally retarded or developmentally disabled. Similarly, the increasing elderly population will spur job growth in nursing homes and other personal care facilities.

Recreation worker jobs in employee services and recreation will continue to increase as more businesses recognize the benefits to their employees of recreation programs and other services such as wellness programs and elder care. Job growth will also occur in the commercial recreation industry, composed of amusement parks, athletic clubs, camps, sports clinics, and swimming pools.

Earnings

Median annual earnings of recreation workers who worked full time in 1994 were about $15,500. The middle 50 percent earned between about $10,600 and $24,800, while the top 10 percent earned $38,900 or more. However, earnings of recreation directors and others in supervisory or managerial positions can be substantially higher.

Most public and private recreation agencies provide full-time recreation workers with vacation and other benefits, such as paid vacation, sick leave, and health insurance. Part-time workers receive few, if any, benefits.

Related Occupations

Recreation workers must exhibit leadership and sensitivity in dealing with people. Other occupations that require similar personal qualities include recreational therapists, social workers, parole officers, human relations counselors, school counselors, clinical and counseling psychologists, and teachers.

Sources of Additional Information

For information on jobs in recreation, contact employers such as local government departments of parks and recreation, nursing and personal care facilities, and YMCA's.

Ordering information for materials describing careers and academic programs in recreation is available from:

☛National Recreation and Park Association, Division of Professional Services, 2775 South Quincy St., Suite 300, Arlington, VA 22206.

For information on careers in employee services and recreation, contact:

☛National Employee Services and Recreation Association, 2211 York Rd., Suite 207, Oakbrook, IL 60521.

For information on careers in camping and summer counselor opportunities, contact:

☛American Camping Association, 5000 State Rd. 67 North, Martinsville, IN 46151.

Social Workers

(D.O.T. 045.107-058; 189.267-010; 195.107, .137, .164, .167-010, -014, .267-018, -022, and .367-026)

Nature of the Work

Social workers help people deal with a wide range of problems. They help individuals and families cope with mental illness and problems such as inadequate housing, unemployment, lack of job skills, financial mismanagement, serious illness, disability, substance abuse, unwanted pregnancy, or antisocial behavior. They also work with families who have serious conflicts, including those involving child or spousal abuse.

Through direct counseling, social workers help clients identify their concerns, consider solutions, and find resources. Often, social workers provide concrete information such as where to go for debt counseling, how to find child care or elder care, how to apply for public assistance or other benefits, or how to get an alcoholic or drug addict admitted to a rehabilitation program. Social workers may also arrange for services in consultation with clients and then follow through to assure the services are actually helpful. They may review eligibility requirements, fill out forms and applications, arrange for services, visit clients on a regular basis, and provide support during crises.

Most social workers specialize in a clinical field such as child welfare and family services, mental health, or school social work. Clinical social workers offer psychotherapy or counseling and a range of services in public agencies, clinics, as well as in private practice. Other social workers are employed in community organization, administration, or research.

Social workers in child welfare or family services may counsel children and youths who have difficulty adjusting socially, advise parents on how to care for disabled children, or arrange for homemaker services during a parent's illness. If children have serious problems in school, child welfare workers may consult with parents, teachers, and counselors to identify underlying causes and develop plans for treatment. Some social workers assist single parents, arrange adoptions, and help find foster homes for neglected, abandoned, or abused children. Child welfare workers also work in residential institutions for children and adolescents.

Social workers in child or adult protective services investigate reports of abuse and neglect and intervene if necessary. They may institute legal action to remove children from homes and place them temporarily in an emergency shelter or with a foster family.

Mental health social workers provide services for persons with mental or emotional problems, such as individual and group therapy, outreach, crisis intervention, social rehabilitation, and training in skills of everyday living. They may also help plan for supportive services to ease patients' return to the community. (Also see the statements on counselors and psychologists elsewhere in the *Handbook*.)

Health care social workers help patients and their families cope with chronic, acute, or terminal illnesses and handle problems that may stand in the way of recovery or rehabilitation. They may organize support groups for families of patients suffering from cancer, AIDS, Alzheimer's disease, or other illnesses. They also advise family caregivers, counsel patients, and help plan for their needs after discharge by arranging for at-home services—from meals-on-wheels to oxygen equipment. Some work on interdisciplinary teams that evaluate certain kinds of patients—geriatric or transplant patients, for example.

School social workers diagnose students' problems and arrange needed services, counsel children in trouble, and help integrate disabled students into the general school population. School social workers deal with problems such as student pregnancy, misbehavior in class, and excessive absences. They also advise teachers on how to deal with problem students.

Social workers in criminal justice make recommendations to courts, do pre-sentencing assessments, and provide services for prison inmates and their families. Probation and parole officers provide similar services to individuals sentenced by a court to parole or probation.

Occupational social workers generally work in a corporation's personnel department or health unit. Through employee assistance programs, they help workers cope with job-related pressures or personal problems that affect the quality of their work. They offer direct counseling to employees, often those whose performance is hindered by emotional or family problems or substance abuse. They also develop education programs and refer workers to specialized community programs.

Some social workers specialize in gerontological services. They run support groups for family caregivers or for the adult children of aging parents; advise elderly people or family members about the choices in such areas as housing, transportation, and long-term care; and coordinate and monitor services.

Social workers must establish and maintain good relationships with their clients.

Social workers also focus on policy and planning. They help develop programs to address such issues as child abuse, homelessness, substance abuse, poverty, and violence. These workers research and analyze policies, programs, and regulations. They identify social problems and suggest legislative and other solutions. They may help raise funds or write grants to support these programs.

Working Conditions

Most social workers have a standard 40-hour week. However, they may work some evenings and weekends to meet with clients, attend community meetings, and handle emergencies. Some, particularly in voluntary nonprofit agencies, work part time. They may spend most of their time in an office or residential facility, but may also travel locally to visit clients or meet with service providers.

The work, while satisfying, can be emotionally draining. Understaffing and large caseloads add to the pressure in some agencies.

Employment

Social workers held about 557,000 jobs in 1994. Nearly 40 percent of the jobs were in State, county, or municipal government agencies, primarily in departments of human resources, social services, child welfare, mental health, health, housing, education, and corrections. Most in the private sector were in voluntary social service agencies, community and religious organizations, hospitals, nursing homes, or home health agencies.

Although most social workers are employed in cities or suburbs, some work in rural areas.

Training, Other Qualifications, and Advancement

A bachelor's degree is the minimum requirement for most positions. Besides the bachelor's in social work (BSW), undergraduate majors in psychology, sociology, and related fields satisfy hiring requirements in some agencies, especially small community agencies. A master's degree in social work (MSW) is generally necessary for positions in health and mental health settings. Jobs in public agencies may also require an MSW. Supervisory, administrative, and staff training positions usually require at least an MSW. College and University teaching positions and most research appointments normally require a doctorate in social work.

In 1994, the Council on Social Work Education accredited 383 BSW programs and 117 MSW programs. There were 56 doctoral programs for Ph.D.'s in social work and DSW's (Doctor of Social Work). BSW programs prepare graduates for direct service positions such as case worker or group worker. They include courses in social work practice, social welfare policies, human behavior and the social

environment, and social research methods. Accredited BSW programs require at least 400 hours of supervised field experience.

An MSW degree prepares graduates to perform assessments, manage cases, and supervise other workers. Master's programs usually last 2 years and include 900 hours of supervised field instruction, or internship. Entry into an MSW program does not require a bachelor's in social work, but courses in psychology, biology, sociology, economics, political science, history, social anthropology, urban studies, and social work are recommended. Some schools offer an accelerated MSW program for those with a BSW.

Social workers may advance to supervisor, program manager, assistant director, or executive director of an agency or department. Advancement generally requires an MSW, as well as experience. Although some social workers with a BSW may be promoted to these positions after gaining experience, some employers choose to hire managers directly from MSW programs that focus specifically on management. These graduates often have little work experience but have an understanding of management through their education and training. Other career options for social workers include teaching, research, and consulting. Some help formulate government policies by analyzing and advocating policy positions in government agencies, in research institutions, and on legislators' staffs.

Some social workers go into private practice. Most private practitioners are clinical social workers who provide psychotherapy, usually paid through health insurance. Private practitioners must have a MSW and a period of supervised work experience. A network of contacts for referrals is also essential.

Since 1993, all States and the District of Columbia have had licensing, certification, or registration laws regarding social work practice and the use of professional titles. Standards for licensing vary by State. In addition, voluntary certification is offered by the National Association of Social Workers (NASW), which grants the title ACSW (Academy of Certified Social Worker) or ACBSW (Academy of Certified Baccalaureate Social Worker) to those who qualify. For clinical social workers, who are granted the title QCSW (Qualified Clinical Social Worker), professional credentials include listing in the *NASW Register of Clinical Social Workers*. Advanced credentials include the NASW Diplomate in Clinical Social Work, and School Social Work Specialist. An advanced credential is also offered by the *Directory of American Board of Examiners in Clinical Social Work*. Credentials are particularly important for those in private practice; some health insurance providers require them for reimbursement.

Social workers should be emotionally mature, objective, and sensitive to people and their problems. They must be able to handle responsibility, work independently, and maintain good working relationships with clients and coworkers. Volunteer or paid jobs as a social work aide offer ways of testing one's interest in this field.

Job Outlook

Employment of social workers is expected to increase faster than the average for all occupations through the year 2005. The number of older people, who are more likely to need social services, is growing rapidly. In addition, rising crime and juvenile delinquency as well as increasing concern about services for the mentally ill, the mentally retarded, AIDS patients, and individuals and families in crisis will spur demand for social workers. Many job openings will also arise due to the need to replace social workers who leave the occupation.

Projected employment growth among social workers in hospitals reflects greater emphasis on discharge planning, which facilitates early discharge of patients by assuring that the necessary medical services and social supports are in place when individuals leave the hospital.

Employment of social workers in private social service agencies will grow, but not as rapidly as demand for their services. Agencies will increasingly restructure services and hire more lower paid human services workers instead of social workers. Employment in government should also grow in response to increasing needs for public welfare and family services. However, employment levels will depend on government funding for various social service programs.

Social worker employment in home health care services is growing, not only because hospitals are releasing patients more quickly, but because a large and growing number of people have impairments or disabilities that make it difficult to live at home without some form of assistance.

Opportunities for social workers in private practice will expand because of the anticipated availability of funding from health insurance and public-sector contracts. Also, with increasing affluence, people will be better able to pay for professional help to deal with personal problems. The growing popularity of employee assistance programs is also expected to spur demand for private practitioners, some of whom provide social work services to corporations on a contractual basis.

Employment of school social workers is expected to grow, due to expanded efforts to respond to the adjustment problems of immigrants, children from single-parent families, and rising rates of teen pregnancy. Moreover, continued emphasis on integrating disabled children into the general school population—a requirement under the Education for All Handicapped Children Act—will lead to more jobs. Availability of State and local funding will dictate the actual increase in jobs in this setting, however.

Competition for social worker jobs is stronger in cities where training programs for social workers abound; rural areas often find it difficult to attract and retain qualified staff.

Earnings

According to a membership survey of the National Association of Social Workers, social workers with MSW degrees had median earnings of $30,000 in 1993. For those with BSW degrees, median earnings were between $17,500 and $20,000.

In hospitals, social workers who worked full-time averaged about $33,300 in 1994, according to a survey conducted by the University of Texas Medical Branch. Salaries ranged from a minimum of about $26,700 to a maximum of about $40,100.

The average annual salary for all social workers in the Federal Government in nonsupervisory, supervisory, and managerial positions was about $44,000 in 1995.

Related Occupations

Through direct counseling or referral to other services, social workers help people solve a range of personal problems. Workers in occupations with similar duties include the clergy, counselors, counseling psychologists, and vocational rehabilitation counselors.

Sources of Additional Information

For information about career opportunities in social work, contact:
☛National Association of Social Workers, IC-Career Information, 750 First St. NE., Suite 700, Washington, DC 20002-4241.
☛National Network For Social Work Managers, Inc., 1316 New Hampshire Ave. NW., Suite 602, Washington, DC 20036.

An annual *Directory of Accredited BSW and MSW Programs* is available for a nominal charge from:
☛Council on Social Work Education, 1600 Duke St., Alexandria, VA 22314-3421.

Clergy

(D.O.T. 120.107-010)

Nature of the Work

Religious beliefs, be they Buddist, Christian, Jewish, Moslem, or based on some other religion, are significant influences in the lives of millions of Americans and prompt many believers to participate in organizations that reinforce their faith. In the United States about 95 percent of all religious organization members are Christians. Protestants (52 percent) comprise the largest group but consist of many denominations such as Baptists, Lutherans, Methodists, and Presbyterians. The Christian Roman Catholic Church accounts for 37 percent of religious organization membership and is the single largest religious body in the United States. Other Christians belong to the Church of Jesus Christ of the Latter Day Saints (3 percent) and Eastern Orthodox sects (1 percent). Non-Christians account for the remaining 5 percent of religious organization members; 4 out of 5 are Jewish.

Clergy are religious and spiritual leaders, and teachers and interpreters of their traditions and faith. They organize and lead regular religious services on the Sabbath and on religious holidays, and conduct special wedding and funeral ceremonies upon request. They may lead worshipers in prayer, administer sacraments, deliver sermons, and read from sacred texts such as the Bible, Talmud, or Koran. When not conducting worship services, clergy organize, supervise, and lead religious education programs for their congregations. Clergy often visit the sick or bereaved to provide comfort, and counsel persons who are seeking religious or moral guidance, or who are troubled by family or personal problems. They also may work to expand the membership of their congregations and solicit donations to support its activities and facilities.

Clergy serving large congregations often share their duties with an associate or have more junior members of the clergy to assist them. They often spend considerable time on administrative duties. They oversee the management of buildings, order supplies, contract for services and repairs when necessary, and supervise the work of paid staff and volunteers. Clergy also work with committees and officials, elected by the congregation, who guide the management of the congregation's finances and real estate.

Working Conditions

Members of the clergy typically work long and irregular hours. Of those who served full time as clergy, about one-third spent at least 60 hours a week on their duties. Although many of their activities are sedentary and intellectual in nature, they are frequently called upon at short notice to visit the sick, comfort the dying and their families, and provide counseling to those in need. Involvement in community, administrative, and educational activities may require clergy to work evenings, early mornings, holidays, and weekends.

Training and Other Qualifications

Educational requirements for entry into the clergy vary greatly. About 3 out of 4 members of the clergy have completed at least a bachelor's degree. Many denominations require that clergy complete a bachelor's degree and a program of theological study; others will admit anyone who has been "called" to the vocation. Some sects do not allow women to become clergy. The following statements on Protestant ministers, Rabbis, and Roman Catholic priests provide more detailed information; those considering careers in the clergy should check with their religious leaders to verify specific entrance requirements.

Individuals considering a career in the clergy should realize they are choosing not only a career but a way of life. Religious leaders need to exude self-confidence and self motivation, while remaining tolerant and able to listen to the needs of others. They should be capable of making difficult decisions, working under pressure, and living up to the moral standards set by their community.

Protestant Ministers

(D.O.T. 120.107-010)

Nature of the Work

Protestant ministers lead their congregations in worship services and administer the various rites of the church, such as baptism, confirmation, and Holy Communion. There are many Protestant denominations. The services that ministers conduct differ among denominations and also among congregations within a denomination. In many denominations, ministers follow a traditional order of worship; in others, they adapt the services to the needs of youth and other groups within the congregation. Most services include Bible reading, hymn singing, prayers, and a sermon. In some denominations, Bible reading by a member of the congregation and individual testimonials may constitute a large part of the service.

Each Protestant denomination has its own hierarchical structure. Some ministers are responsible only to the congregation they serve, while others are assigned duties by elder ministers, or by the bishops of the diocese they serve. In some denominations, ministers are reassigned to a new pastorate by a central governing body or diocese every few years.

Ministers serving small congregations generally work personally with parishioners. Those serving large congregations may share specific aspects of the ministry with one or more associates or assistants, such as a minister of education who assists in educational programs for different age groups, or a minister of music.

Employment

In 1994, there were an estimated 300,000 Protestant ministers who served individual congregations. Thousands of others served without a regular congregation, or worked in closely related fields, such as chaplains in hospitals, the Armed Forces, universities, and correctional institutions. While there are numerous denominations, most ministers are employed by the five largest Protestant bodies—Baptist, Episcopalian, Lutheran, Methodist, and Presbyterian.

All cities and most towns in the United States have at least one Protestant church with a full-time minister. Although most ministers are located in urban areas, many serve two or more small congregations in less densely populated areas. Some small

Many Protestant denominations allow women to attend seminary and be ordained.

churches increasingly are employing part-time ministers who may be seminary students, retired ministers, or holders of secular jobs. Unpaid pastors serve other churches with meager funds. Some churches employ specially trained members of the laity to conduct nonliturgical functions.

Training and Other Qualifications

Educational requirements for entry into the Protestant ministry vary greatly. Many denominations require—or at least strongly prefer—a college bachelor's degree followed by study at a theological school. However, some denominations have no formal educational requirements, and others ordain persons having various types of training in Bible colleges, Bible institutes, or liberal arts colleges. Many denominations now allow women to be ordained, but others do not. Persons considering a career in the ministry should verify the entrance requirements with their particular denomination before deciding on a career as a minister.

In general, each large denomination has its own school or schools of theology that reflect its particular doctrine, interests, and needs. However, many of these schools are open to students from other denominations. Several interdenominational schools associated with universities give both undergraduate and graduate training covering a wide range of theological points of view.

In 1994, over 200 American Protestant theological schools were accredited by the Association of Theological Schools in the United States and Canada. These admit only students who have received a bachelor's degree or its equivalent in liberal arts from an accredited college. After college graduation, many denominations require a 3-year course of professional study in one of these accredited schools or seminaries for the degree of Master of Divinity.

The standard curriculum for accredited theological schools consists of four major categories: Biblical, historical, theological, and practical. Courses of a practical nature include pastoral care, preaching, religious education, and administration. Many accredited schools require that students work under the supervision of a faculty member or experienced minister. Some institutions offer Doctor of Ministry degrees to students who have completed additional study, usually 2 or more years, and served at least 2 years as a minister. Scholarships and loans are available for students of theological institutions.

Persons who have denominational qualifications for the ministry usually are ordained after graduation from a seminary or after serving a probationary pastoral period. Denominations that do not require seminary training ordain clergy at various appointed times. Some evangelical churches may ordain ministers with only a high school education.

Men and women entering the clergy often begin their careers as pastors of small congregations or as assistant pastors in large churches.

Job Outlook

Competition is expected to continue for paid Protestant ministers through the year 2005 due to slow growth of church membership and the large number of qualified candidates. Opportunities are expected to be best for graduates of theological schools. The amount of competition for paid positions will vary among denominations and geographic regions. Competition will still be strong for more responsible positions serving large, urban congregations. Relatively favorable prospects are expected for ministers in evangelical churches. Ministers willing to work part time or for smaller, rural congregations also should have relatively favorable opportunities. Most of the openings for ministers through the year 2005 will arise from the need to replace retirees and, to a lesser extent, those who die or leave the ministry.

Employment alternatives for newly ordained Protestant ministers who are unable to find positions in parishes include working in youth counseling, family relations, and welfare organizations; teaching in religious educational institutions; and serving as chaplains in the Armed Forces, hospitals, universities, and correctional institutions.

Earnings

Salaries of Protestant clergy vary substantially, depending on age, experience, denomination, size and wealth of congregation, and geographic location. Based on limited information, the estimated average annual income of Protestant ministers was about $20,000 in 1993. Including benefits such as housing, insurance, and transportation, average compensation was an estimated $40,000. In large, wealthier denominations, ministers often earned significantly higher salaries. Increasingly, ministers with modest salaries earn additional income from employment in secular occupations.

Sources of Additional Information

Persons who are interested in entering the Protestant ministry should seek the counsel of a minister or church guidance worker. Theological schools can supply information on admission requirements. Prospective ministers also should contact the ordination supervision body of their particular denomination for information on special requirements for ordination.

Rabbis

(D.O.T. 120.107-010)

Nature of the Work

Rabbis serve either Orthodox, Conservative, Reform, or Reconstructionist Jewish congregations. Regardless of their particular point of view, all preserve the substance of Jewish religious worship. Congregations differ in the extent to which they follow the traditional form of worship—for example, in the wearing of head coverings, the use of Hebrew as the language of prayer, or the use of instrumental music or a choir. The format of the worship service and, therefore, the ritual that the rabbi uses may vary even among congregations belonging to the same branch of Judaism.

Rabbis have a large amount of independence compared to other clergy since there is no formal hierarchy in their religion. They are only responsible to the Board of Trustees of the congregation they serve. Rabbis serving large congregations may spend considerable time in administrative duties, working with their staffs and committees. Large congregations frequently have an associate or assistant rabbi. Many assistant rabbis serve as educational directors.

Rabbis also may write for religious and lay publications and teach in theological seminaries, colleges, and universities.

Employment

In 1994, there were approximately 1,800 Reform, 1,250 Conservative, 1,000 Orthodox, and 175 Reconstructionist rabbis. Although the majority served congregations, many rabbis functioned in other settings. Some taught in Jewish studies programs at colleges and universities. Others served as chaplains in the military services, in hospitals, in college settings, and other institutions, or in one of the many Jewish community service agencies.

Although rabbis serve Jewish communities throughout the Nation, they are concentrated in major metropolitan areas with large Jewish populations.

Training and Other Qualifications

To become eligible for ordination as a rabbi, a student must complete a course of study in a seminary. Entrance requirements and the curriculum depend upon the branch of Judaism with which the seminary is associated.

In general, the curriculums of Jewish theological seminaries provide students with a comprehensive knowledge of the Bible,

Rabbis teach and interpret Jewish law and tradition.

Talmud, Rabbinic literature, Jewish history, theology, and courses in education, pastoral psychology, and public speaking. Students get extensive practical training in dealing with social problems in the community. Training for alternatives to the pulpit, such as leadership in community services and religious education, is increasingly stressed. Some seminaries grant advanced academic degrees in such fields as Biblical and Talmudic research. All Jewish theological seminaries make scholarships and loans available.

About 35 seminaries educate and ordain Orthodox rabbis. The Rabbi Isaac Elchanan Theological Seminary and the Beth Medrash Govoha Seminary are representative of the two basic kinds of Orthodox seminaries. The former requires a bachelor's degree for entry and has a formal 4-year ordination program. The latter has no formal admission requirements but may require more years of study for ordination. The training is rigorous. When students have become sufficiently learned in the Talmud, the Bible, and other religious studies, they may be ordained with the approval of an authorized rabbi, acting either independently or as a representative of a rabbinical seminary.

The Jewish Theological Seminary of America educates rabbis for the Conservative branch. The Hebrew Union College—Jewish Institute of Religion educates rabbis for the Reform branch. For admission to their rabbinical programs leading to ordination, both seminaries require the completion of a 4-year college course, as well as earlier preparation in Jewish studies. The Conservative seminary usually requires 5 years to complete the course of study. Normally, 5 years of study are also required to complete the rabbinical course at the Reform seminary, including 1 year of preparatory study in Jerusalem. Exceptionally well-prepared students can shorten this 5-year period to a minimum of 3 years.

The Reconstructionist Rabbinical College educates rabbis in the newest branch of Judaism. A bachelor's degree is required for admission. The rabbinical program is based on a 5-year course of study which emphasizes, in each year, a period in the history of Jewish civilization. A preliminary preparatory year is required for students without sufficient grounding in Hebrew and Jewish studies. Graduates are awarded the title Rabbi and the Master of Arts in Hebrew Letters and, with special study, can earn the Doctor of Hebrew Letters degree.

Newly ordained rabbis usually begin as spiritual leaders of small congregations, assistants to experienced rabbis, directors of Hillel Foundations on college campuses, teachers in educational institutions, or chaplains in the Armed Forces. As a rule, experienced rabbis fill the pulpits of large and well-established Jewish congregations.

Job Outlook

Job opportunities for rabbis are expected to be generally favorable in the four major branches of Judaism through the year 2005. Present unmet needs for rabbis, together with the need to replace the many rabbis approaching retirement age, should insure that the numbers of persons completing rabbinical training in the years ahead will encounter good job prospects. Since most rabbis prefer to serve in large, urban areas, employment opportunities generally are best in nonmetropolitan areas, particularly in smaller communities in the South, Midwest, and Northwest.

Graduates of Orthodox seminaries who seek pulpits should have good opportunities as growth in enrollments slows and as many graduates choose not to seek pulpits. Orthodox rabbis willing to work in small communities should have particularly good prospects.

Conservative and Reform rabbis are expected to have good employment opportunities throughout the country.

Reconstructionist rabbis are expected to have very good employment opportunities since membership is expanding rapidly.

Earnings

Based on limited information, annual average earnings of rabbis generally ranged from $38,000 to $62,000 in 1993, including benefits. Benefits may include housing, health insurance, and a retirement plan. Income varies widely, depending on the size and financial status of the congregation, as well as its denominational branch and geographic location. Rabbis may earn additional income from gifts or fees for officiating at ceremonies such as bar mitzvahs and weddings.

Sources of Additional Information

Persons who are interested in becoming rabbis should discuss their plans for a vocation with a practicing rabbi. Information on the work of rabbis and allied occupations can be obtained from:

☞Rabbinical Council of America, 305 7th Ave., New York, NY 10001. (Orthodox)

☞The Jewish Theological Seminary of America, 3080 Broadway, New York, NY 10027. (Conservative)

☞Hebrew Union College-Jewish Institute of Religion, 3101 Clifton Avenue, Cincinnati, OH 45220-2488. (Reform)

☞Reconstructionist Rabbinical College, Church Rd. and Greenwood Ave., Wyncote, PA 19095.

Roman Catholic Priests

(D.O.T. 120.107-010)

Nature of the Work

Roman Catholic priests attend to the spiritual, pastoral, moral, and educational needs of the members of their church. A priest's day usually begins with morning meditation and mass and may end with an individual counseling session or an evening visit to a hospital or home. Many priests direct and serve on church committees, work in civic and charitable organizations, and assist in community projects.

Priests in the Catholic church belong to one of two groups—diocesan or religious. Both types of priests have the same powers, acquired through ordination by a bishop. Their differences lie in their way of life, their type of work, and the church authority to whom they are responsible. *Diocesan priests* commit their lives to serving the people of a diocese, a church administrative region, and generally work in parishes assigned by the bishop of their diocese. *Religious priests* belong to a religious order, such as the Jesuits, Dominicans, or Franciscans. Religious priests are assigned duties by their superiors in their respective religious orders. Some religious priests specialize in teaching, while others serve as missionaries in foreign countries, where they may live under difficult and primitive conditions. Others live a communal life in monasteries, where they devote their lives to prayer, study, and assigned work.

Both religious and diocesan priests hold teaching and administrative posts in Catholic seminaries, colleges and universities, and high schools. Priests attached to religious orders staff a large proportion of the church's institutions of higher education and many high schools, whereas diocesan priests are usually concerned with the parochial schools attached to parish churches and with diocesan high schools. The members of religious orders do most of the missionary work conducted by the Catholic Church in this country and abroad.

Employment

There were approximately 51,000 priests in 1994, about two-thirds of them diocesan priests, according to the Official Catholic Directory. There are priests in nearly every city and town and in many rural communities. The majority are in metropolitan areas, where most Catholics reside. Large numbers of priests are located in communities near Catholic educational and other institutions.

Training and Other Qualifications

Preparation for the priesthood generally requires 8 years of study beyond high school in one of 349 seminaries. Priests commit themselves to celibacy, remaining unmarried. Only men are ordained as priests; women, may serve in only select church positions.

Preparatory study for the priesthood may begin either in the first year of high school, at the college level, or in theological seminaries after college graduation. Today, most candidates for the priesthood take a 4-year degree at a conventional college or university. After graduation from college, candidates generally receive 2 years of "Pre-theology" preparatory study (philosophy, religious studies, and prayer) before entering the seminary. Theology coursework in the seminary includes sacred scripture; dogmatic, moral, and pastoral theology; homiletics (art of preaching); church history; liturgy (sacraments); and canon (church) law. Fieldwork experience usually is required; in recent years, this aspect of a priest's training has been emphasized. Diocesan and religious priests attend different major seminaries, where slight variations in the training reflect the differences in their duties.

Alternatively, high school seminaries provide a college preparatory program that emphasizes English grammar, speech, literature, and social studies. Latin may be required, and modern languages are encouraged. In Hispanic communities, knowledge of Spanish is mandatory. Candidates may also choose to enter a seminary college that offers a liberal arts program stressing philosophy and religion, the study of humankind through the behavioral sciences and history, and the natural sciences and mathematics. In many college seminaries, a student may concentrate in any one of these fields.

Young men never are denied entry into seminaries because of lack of funds. In seminaries for secular priests, scholarships or loans are available. Those in religious seminaries are financed by contributions of benefactors.

Postgraduate work in theology is offered at a number of American Catholic universities or at ecclesiastical universities around the world, particularly in Rome. Also, many priests do graduate work in fields unrelated to theology. Priests are encouraged by the Catholic Church to continue their studies, at least informally, after ordination. In recent years, continuing education for ordained priests has stressed

Diocesan priests perform mass, administer sacraments, and hear confession, in addition to teaching and performing administrative work.

social sciences, such as sociology and psychology.

A newly ordained secular priest usually works as an assistant pastor or curate. Newly ordained priests of religious orders are assigned to the specialized duties for which they are trained. Depending on the talents, interests, and experience of the individual, many opportunities for greater responsibility exist within the church.

Job Outlook

The job outlook for Roman Catholic priests is expected to be very favorable through the year 2005. Many priests will be needed in the years ahead to provide for the spiritual, educational, and social needs of the increasing number of Catholics. In recent years, the number of ordained priests has been insufficient to fill the needs of newly established parishes and other Catholic institutions, and to replace priests who retire, die, or leave the priesthood. This situation is likely to continue—even if the recent modest increase in seminary enrollments continues—as an increasing proportion of priests approach retirement age.

In response to the shortage of priests, certain traditional functions increasingly are being performed by permanent deacons and by teams of clergy and laity. Presently about 10,400 permanent deacons have been ordained to preach and perform liturgical functions such as baptisms, distributing Holy Communion, and reading the gospel at the mass. The only services a deacon cannot perform are saying mass and hearing confessions. Teams of clergy and laity undertake nonliturgical functions such as hospital visits and religious teaching. Priests will continue to perform mass, administer sacraments, and hear confession, but may be less involved in teaching and administrative work.

Earnings

Diocesan priests' salaries vary from diocese to diocese. Based on limited information, salaries averaged about $9,000 in 1993. In addition to a salary, diocesan priests receive a package of benefits which may include a car allowance, free room and board in the parish rectory, health insurance, and a retirement plan. Including benefits, the total value of a priest's compensation package averaged about $29,000 a year in 1993.

Priests who do special work related to the church, such as teaching, usually receive a partial salary which is less than a lay person in the same position would receive. The difference between the usual salary for these jobs and the salary that the priest receives is called "contributed service." In some of these situations, housing and related expenses may be provided; in other cases, the priest must make his own arrangements. Some priests doing special work receive the same compensation that a lay person would receive.

Religious priests take a vow of poverty and are supported by their religious order. Any personal earnings are given to the order. Their vow of poverty is recognized by the Internal Revenue Service, which exempts them from paying Federal income tax.

Sources of Additional Information

Young men interested in entering the priesthood should seek the guidance and counsel of their parish priests. For information regarding the different religious orders and the secular priesthood, as well as a list of the seminaries which prepare students for the priesthood, contact the diocesan director of vocations through the office of the local pastor or bishop.

Individuals seeking additional information about careers in the Catholic Ministry should contact their local diocese.

Teachers, Librarians, and Counselors

Adult Education Teachers

(D.O.T. 075.127-010; 090.222, .227-018; 097.221, .227; 099.223, .224-014, .227-014, -018, -026, -030, -038; 149.021; 150.027-014; 151.027-014; 152.021; 153.227-014; 159.227; 166.221, .227; 235.222; 239.227; 375.227; 522.264; 621.221; 683.222; 689.324; 715.221; 740.221; 788.222; 789.222; 919.223; and 955.222)

Nature of the Work

Adult education teachers work in four main areas—adult vocational-technical education, adult remedial education, adult continuing education, and prebaccalaureate training. Some adult education teachers provide instruction for occupations that do not require a college degree, such as welder, dental hygienist, automated systems manager, x-ray technician, farmer, and cosmetologist. Other instruc-

tors help people update their job skills or adapt to technological advances. For example, an adult education teacher may train students how to use new computer software programs. Other teachers provide instruction in basic education courses for school dropouts or others who need to upgrade their skills to find a job. Some adult education teachers in junior or community colleges prepare students for a 4-year degree program, teaching classes for credit that can be applied towards that degree. Adult education teachers also teach courses which students take for personal enrichment, such as cooking, dancing, writing, exercise and physical fitness, photography, and finance.

Adult education teachers may lecture in classrooms and also give students hands-on experience. Increasingly, adult vocational-technical education teachers integrate academic and vocational curriculums so that students obtain a variety of skills. For example, an electronics student may be required to take courses in principles of mathematics and science in conjunction with hands-on electronics skills. Generally, teachers demonstrate techniques, have students apply them, and critique the students' work. For example, welding instructors show students various welding techniques, including the use of tools and equipment, watch them use the techniques, and have them repeat procedures until specific standards required by the trade are met.

Adult education teachers who instruct in adult basic education programs may work with students who do not speak English; teach adults reading, writing, and mathematics up to the 8th-grade level; or teach adults through the 12th-grade level in preparation for the General Educational Development Examination (GED). The GED offers the equivalent of a high school diploma. These teachers may refer students for counseling or job placement. Because many people who need adult basic education are reluctant to seek it, teachers also may recruit participants.

Adult education teachers also prepare lessons and assignments, grade papers and do related paperwork, attend faculty and professional meetings, and stay abreast of developments in their field. (For information on vocational education teachers in secondary schools, see the *Handbook* statement on kindergarten, elementary, and secondary school teachers.)

Working Conditions

Since adult education teachers work with adult students, they do not encounter some of the behavioral or social problems sometimes found when teaching younger students. The adults are there by

Many adult education teachers instruct part time while working other jobs related to their subjects.

choice, and usually are highly motivated—attributes that can make teaching these students rewarding and satisfying. However, teachers in adult basic education deal with students at different levels of development who may lack effective study skills and self-confidence, and who may require more attention and patience than other students.

Many adult education teachers work part time. To accommodate students who may have job or family responsibilities, many courses are offered at night or on weekends, and range from 2- to 4-hour workshops and 1-day minisessions to semester-long courses. Some adult education teachers have several part-time teaching assignments or work a full-time job in addition to their part-time teaching job, leading to long hours and a hectic schedule.

Although most adult education teachers work in a classroom setting, some may act as consultants to a business and teach classes at the job site.

Employment

Adult education teachers held about 590,000 jobs in 1994. About half taught part time, a larger proportion than for other teachers, and many taught only intermittently. However, many of them also held other jobs, in many cases doing work related to the subject they taught. Many adult education teachers are self-employed.

Adult education teachers are employed by public school systems; community and junior colleges; universities; businesses that provide formal education and training for their employees; automotive repair, bartending, business, computer, electronics, medical technology, and similar schools and institutes; dance studios; health clubs; job training centers; community organizations; labor unions; and religious organizations.

Training, Other Qualifications, and Advancement

Training requirements vary widely by State and by subject. In general, teachers need work or other experience in their field, and a license or certificate in fields where these usually are required for full professional status. In some cases, particularly at educational institutions, a master's or doctoral degree is required to teach nonvocational courses which can be applied towards a 4-year degree program. Many vocational teachers in junior or community colleges do not have a master's degree but draw on their work experience and knowledge, bringing valuable practical experience to the classroom. For general adult education classes that are taken for interest or enjoyment, an acceptable portfolio of work is required. For example, to secure a job teaching a flower arranging course, an applicant would need to show examples of previous work.

Most States and the District of Columbia require adult basic education teachers and adult literacy instructors to have a bachelor's degree from an approved teacher training program, and some require teacher certification.

Adult education teachers update their skills through continuing education to maintain certification—requirements vary among institutions. Teachers may take part in seminars, conferences, or graduate courses in adult education, training and development, or human resources development, or may return to work in business or industry for a limited time. Businesses are playing a growing role in adult education, forming consortiums with training institutions and junior colleges and providing input to curriculum development. In this way, adult education teachers maintain an ongoing dialogue with businesses to determine the most current skills required in the workplace.

Adult education teachers should communicate and relate well with students, enjoy working with them, and be able to motivate them. Adult basic education instructors, in particular, must be patient, understanding, and supportive to make students comfortable, develop trust, and help them better understand their needs and aims.

Some teachers advance to administrative positions in departments of education, colleges and universities, and corporate training departments. Such positions may require advanced degrees, such as a doctorate in adult and continuing education. (See the statement on education administrators elsewhere in the *Handbook*.)

Job Outlook

Employment of adult education teachers is expected to grow faster than the average for all occupations through the year 2005 as the demand for adult education programs continues to rise. The 35-44 year old population—the largest users of adult education—is expected to grow, contributing to increasing enrollment. Participation in continuing education grows as the educational attainment of the population increases. More people are realizing that life-long learning is important to success in their careers. To keep abreast of changes in their fields and advances in technology, an increasing number of adults are taking courses for career advancement, personal enrichment, and to upgrade their skills, spurring demand for adult education teachers. In addition, enrollment in adult basic education programs is increasing because of changes in immigration policy that require basic competency in English and civics, and an increased awareness of the difficulty in finding a good job without basic academic skills.

Employment growth of adult vocational-technical education teachers will result from the need to train young adults for entry-level jobs, and experienced workers who want to switch fields or whose jobs have been eliminated due to changing technology or business reorganization. Businesses are finding it essential to provide training to their workers to remain productive and globally competitive. Cooperation between businesses and educational institutions is increasing to insure that students are taught the skills employers desire. This should result in greater demand for adult education teachers, particularly at community and junior colleges. Since adult education programs receive State and Federal funding, employment growth may be affected by government budgets.

Many job openings for adult education teachers will stem from the need to replace persons who leave the occupation. Many teach part time and move into and out of the occupation for other jobs, family responsibilities, or to retire. Opportunities should be best in fields such as computer technology, automotive mechanics, and medical technology, which offer very attractive, and often higher paying, job opportunities outside of teaching.

Earnings

In 1994, salaried adult education teachers who usually worked full time had median earnings around $27,600 a year. The middle 50 percent earned between $18,700 and $39,700. The lowest 10 percent earned about $12,600, while the top 10 percent earned more than $50,000. Earnings varied widely by subject, academic credentials, experience, and region of the country. Part-time instructors generally are paid hourly wages and do not receive benefits or pay for preparation time outside of class.

Related Occupations

Adult education teaching requires a wide variety of skills and aptitudes, including the ability to influence, motivate, train, and teach; organizational, administrative, and communication skills; and creativity. Workers in other occupations that require these aptitudes include other teachers, counselors, school administrators, public relations specialists, employee development specialists and interviewers, and social workers.

Sources of Additional Information

Information on adult basic education programs and teacher certification requirements is available from State departments of education and local school districts.

For information about adult vocational-technical education teaching positions, contact State departments of vocational-technical education.

For information on adult continuing education teaching positions, contact departments of local government, State adult education departments, schools, colleges and universities, religious organizations, and a wide range of businesses that provide formal training for their employees.

General information on adult education is available from:
☛American Association for Adult and Continuing Education, 1200 19th St. NW., Suite 300, Washington, DC 20036.
☛American Vocational Association, 1410 King St., Alexandria, VA 22314.
☛ERIC Clearinghouse on Adult, Career, and Vocational Education, 1900 Kenny Rd., Columbus, OH 43210-1090.

Archivists and Curators

(D.O.T. 099.167-030; 101; 102 except .261-014 and .367-010; 109.067-014, .267-010, .281, .361, .364)

Nature of the Work

Archivists, curators, museum and archives technicians, and conservators search for, acquire, appraise, analyze, describe, arrange, catalogue, restore, preserve, exhibit, maintain, and store items of lasting value so that they can be used by researchers or for exhibitions, publications, broadcasting, and other educational programs. Depending on the occupation, these items may consist of historical documents, audiovisual materials, institutional records, works of art, coins, stamps, minerals, clothing, maps, living and preserved plants and animals, buildings, computer records, or historic sites.

Archivists and curators plan and oversee the arrangement, cataloguing, and exhibition of collections and, along with technicians and conservators, maintain collections. Archivists and curators may coordinate educational and public outreach programs, such as tours, workshops, lectures, and classes, and may work with the boards of institutions to administer plans and policies. They also may conduct research on topics or items relevant to their collections. Although some duties of archivists and curators are similar, the types of items they deal with differ. Curators usually handle objects found in cultural, biological, or historical collections, such as sculptures, textiles, and paintings, while archivists mainly handle valuable records, documents, or objects that are retained because they originally accompanied and relate specifically to the document.

Archivists determine what portion of the vast amount of records maintained by various organizations, such as government agencies, corporations, or educational institutions, or by families and individuals, should be made part of permanent historical holdings, and which of these records should be put on exhibit. They maintain records in their original arrangement according to the creator's organizational scheme, and describe records to facilitate retrieval. Records may be saved on any medium, including paper, film, videotape, audiotape, electronic disk, or computer. They also may be copied onto some other format to protect the original from repeated handling, and to make them more accessible to researchers who use the records. As computers and various storage media evolve, archivists must keep abreast of technological advances in electronic information storage.

Archives may be part of a library, museum, or historical society, or may exist as a distinct archival unit within an organization. Archivists consider any medium containing recorded information as documents, including letters, books, and other paper documents, photographs, blueprints, audiovisual materials, and computer records, among others. Any document which reflects organizational transactions, hierarchy, or procedures can be considered a record. Archivists often specialize in an area of history or technology so they can better determine what records in that area qualify for retention and should become part of the archives. Archivists also may work with specialized forms of records—for example, manuscripts, electronic records, photographs, cartographic records, motion pictures, and sound recordings.

Computers are increasingly used to generate and maintain archival records. However, professional standards for use of computers in handling archival records are still evolving.

Curators oversee collections in museums, zoos, aquariums, botanic gardens, nature centers, and historic sites. They acquire items through purchases, gifts, field exploration, intermuseum exchanges, or, in the case of some plants and animals, reproduction. Curators also plan and prepare exhibits. In natural history museums, curators collect and observe specimens in their natural habitat. Their work involves describing and classifying species, while specially trained collection managers and technicians provide hands-on care of natural history collections. Most curators use computers to catalogue and organize their collections, and to make information about the collection available to other curators and the public.

Most curators specialize in a specific field, such as botany, art, paleontology, or history. Those working in large institutions may be highly specialized. A large natural history museum, for example, would have specialists in birds, fishes, insects, and mollusks. Some curators maintain the collection while others perform administrative tasks. Registrars, for example, are responsible for keeping track of and moving objects in the collection. In small institutions, with only one or a few curators, one curator may be responsible for multiple tasks, from maintaining collections to directing the affairs of museums.

Conservators—also called preservation specialists or preparators—manage, care for, preserve, treat, and document works of art, artifacts, and specimens. This may require substantial historical, scientific, and archaeological research. They use x rays, chemical testing, microscopes, special lights, and other laboratory equipment and techniques to examine objects and determine their condition, the need for treatment or restoration, and the appropriate method for preservation. Conservators usually specialize in a particular material or group of objects, such as documents, paintings, decorative arts, textiles, metals, or architectural material. Emerging specialties in conservation include collections care, exhibit conservation, and environmental monitoring.

Museum directors formulate policies, plan budgets, and raise funds for their museums. They coordinate activities of their staff to establish and maintain collections. As their role has evolved, museum directors increasingly need business backgrounds in addition to an understanding and empathy for the subject matter of their collections.

Museum technicians assist curators and conservators by performing various preparatory and maintenance tasks on museum items. Some museum technicians may also assist curators with research. Archives technicians help archivists organize, maintain, and provide access to historical documentary materials.

Employment as an archivist or curator generally requires a master's degree and substantial practical or work experience.

Working Conditions

The working conditions of archivists and curators vary. Some spend most of their time working with the public, providing reference assistance and educational services. Others perform research or process records, which often means working alone or in offices with only one or two other persons. Those who restore and install exhibits or work with bulky, heavy record containers may climb, stretch, or lift, and those in zoos, botanical gardens, and other outdoor museums or historic sites frequently walk great distances.

Curators may travel extensively to evaluate potential additions to the collection, to organize exhibitions, and to conduct research in their area of expertise.

Employment

Archivists and curators held about 19,000 jobs in 1994. About a quarter were employed in museums, botanical gardens, and zoos, and approximately 2 in 10 worked in educational services, mainly in college and university libraries. About 4 in 10 worked in Federal, State, and local government. Most Federal archivists work for the National Archives and Records Administration; others manage military archives in the Department of Defense. Most Federal Government curators work at the Smithsonian Institution, in the military museums of the Department of Defense, and in archaeological and other museums managed by the Department of Interior. All State governments have archival or historical records sections employing archivists. State and local governments have numerous historical museums, parks, libraries, and zoos employing curators.

Some large corporations have archives or records centers, employing archivists to manage the growing volume of records created or maintained as required by law or necessary to the firms' operations. Religious and fraternal organizations, professional associations, conservation organizations, major private collectors, and research firms also employ archivists and curators.

Conservators may work under contract to treat particular items, rather than as a regular employee of a museum or other institution. These conservators may work on their own as private contractors, or as an employee of a conservation laboratory which contracts their services to museums.

Training, Other Qualifications, and Advancement

Employment as an archivist, conservator, or curator generally requires graduate education and substantial practical or work experience. Many archivists and curators work in archives or museums while completing their formal education, to gain the "hands-on" experience that many employers seek when hiring.

Employers generally look for archivists with undergraduate and graduate degrees in history or library science, with courses in archival science. Some positions may require knowledge of the discipline related to the collection, such as business or medicine. An increasing number of archivists have a double master's degree in history and library science. Approximately 65 colleges and universities offer courses or practical training in archival science as part of history, library science, or other discipline; some also offer a master's degree in archival studies. The Academy of Certified Archivists offers voluntary certification for archivists. Certification requires the applicant to have experience in the field and to pass an examination offered by the Academy.

Archivists need research and analytical ability to understand the content of documents and the context in which they were created, and to decipher deteriorated or poor quality printed matter, handwritten manuscripts, or photographs and films. A background in preservation management is often required of archivists since they are responsible for taking proper care of their records. Archivists also must be able to organize large amounts of information and write clear instructions for its retrieval and use. In addition, computer skills and the ability to work with electronic records and databases are increasingly important.

Many archives are very small, including one-person shops, with limited promotion opportunities. Archivists typically advance by transferring to a larger unit with supervisory positions. A doctorate in history, library science, or a related field may be needed for some advanced positions, such as director of a State archives.

In most museums, a master's degree in an appropriate discipline of the museum's specialty—for example, art, history, or archaeology—or museum studies is required for employment as a curator. Many employers prefer a doctoral degree, particularly for curators in natural history or science museums. Earning two graduate degrees—in museum studies (museology) and a specialized subject—gives a candidate a distinct advantage in this competitive job market. In small museums, curatorial positions may be available to individuals with a bachelor's degree. For some positions, an internship of full-time museum work supplemented by courses in museum practices is needed.

Museum technicians generally need a bachelor's degree in an appropriate discipline of the museum's specialty, museum studies training, or previous museum work experience, particularly in exhibit design. Similarly, archives technicians generally need a bachelor's degree in library science or history, or relevant work experience. Technician positions often serve as a stepping stone for individuals interested in archival and curatorial work. With the exception of small museums, a master's degree is needed for advancement.

When hiring conservators, employers look for a master's degree in conservation, or in a closely related field, and substantial experience. There are only a few graduate programs in museum conservation techniques in the United States. Competition for entry to these programs is keen; to qualify, a student must have a background in chemistry, studio art, and art history, as well as work experience. For some programs, knowledge of a foreign language is also helpful. Conservation apprenticeships or internships as an undergraduate can also enhance one's admission prospects. Graduate programs last 2 to 4 years; the latter years include internship training. A few individuals enter conservation through apprenticeships with museums, nonprofit organizations, and conservators in private practice. Apprenticeships should be supplemented with courses in chemistry, studio art, and history. Apprenticeship training, although accepted, generally is a more difficult route into the conservation profession.

Students interested in museum work may take courses or obtain a bachelor's or master's degree in museum studies. Colleges and universities throughout the country offer bachelor's and master's degrees in museum studies. However, many employers feel that, while museum studies are helpful, a thorough knowledge of the museum's specialty and museum work experience are more important.

Curatorial positions often require knowledge in a number of fields. For historic and artistic conservation, courses in chemistry, physics, and art are desirable. Since curators—particularly those in small museums—may have administrative and managerial responsibilities, courses in business administration and public relations also are recommended. Similar to archivists, curators need computer skills and the ability to work with electronic databases.

Curators must be flexible because of their wide variety of duties. They need an aesthetic sense to design and present exhibits, and, in small museums, manual dexterity is needed to erect exhibits or restore objects. Leadership ability and business skills are important for museum directors, while public relations skills are valuable in increasing museum attendance and fundraising.

In large museums, curators may advance through several levels of responsibility, eventually to museum director. Curators in smaller museums often advance to larger ones. Individual research and publications are important for advancement.

Continuing education, which enables archivists, curators, conservators, and museum technicians to keep up with developments in the field, is available through meetings, conferences, and workshops sponsored by archival, historical, and curatorial associations. Some larger organizations, such as the National Archives, offer such training in-house.

Job Outlook

Despite the anticipated increase in the employment of archivists and curators, competition for jobs is expected to be keen. Graduates with highly specialized training, such as master's degrees in both library science and history, with a concentration in archives or records management, may have the best opportunities for jobs as archivists. A job as a curator is attractive to many people, and many have the necessary subject knowledge; yet there are only a few openings. Consequently, candidates may have to work part time, or as an intern, or even as a volunteer assistant curator or research associate after completing their formal education, and substantial work experience in collection management, exhibit design, or restoration will be necessary for permanent status. Job opportunities for curators should be best in art and history museums, since these are the largest employers in the museum industry.

The job outlook for conservators may be more favorable, particularly for graduates of conservator programs. However, competition is stiff for the limited number of openings in these programs, and applicants need a technical background. Students who qualify and successfully complete the program, have knowledge of a foreign language, and are willing to relocate, will have an advantage over less qualified candidates in obtaining a position.

Employment of archivists and curators is expected to increase about as fast as the average for all occupations through the year 2005. Archival and curator jobs are expected to grow as public and private organizations put more emphasis on establishing archives and organizing records and information, and as public interest in science, art, history, and technology increases. Although the rate of turnover among archivists and curators is relatively low, the need to replace workers who leave the occupation or stop working will create some additional job openings.

Museums and other cultural institutions may be subject to cuts in funding during recessions, reducing demand for archivists and curators during these periods.

Earnings

Earnings of archivists and curators vary considerably by type and size of employer, and often by specialty. Average salaries in the Federal Government, for example, are generally higher than those in religious organizations. Salaries of curators in large, well-funded museums may be several times higher than those in small ones.

Salaries in the Federal Government depend on education and experience. In 1995, inexperienced archivists and curators with a bachelor's degree started at $18,700, while those with some experience started at $23,200. Those with a master's degree typically started at $28,300, and with a doctorate, $34,300 or $41,100. Beginning salaries were slightly higher in selected areas where the prevailing local pay level was higher. The average annual salary for all museum curators in the Federal Government in nonsupervisory, supervisory, and managerial positions was about $51,600 in 1995. Archivists averaged $50,000; museum specialists and technicians, $32,800; and archives technicians, $29,500.

According to a survey by the Association of Art Museum Directors, salaries generally are highest for museum workers in Western and Mid-Atlantic States and in metropolitan areas having populations over 2 million. The following tabulation shows median salaries for selected workers in art museums in 1995:

Director	$100,000
Senior conservator	48,900
Chief curator	48,600
Curator	47,000
Curatorial assistant	22,500

Related Occupations

Archivists' and curators' interests in preservation and display are shared by anthropologists, arborists, archaeologists, artifacts conservators, botanists, ethnologists, folklorists, genealogists, historians, horticulturists, information specialists, librarians, paintings restorers, records managers, and zoologists.

Sources of Additional Information
For information on archivists and on schools offering courses in archival studies, contact:

☛Society of American Archivists, 600 South Federal St., Suite 504, Chicago, IL 60605.

For information about certification for archivists, contact:

☛Academy of Certified Archivists, 600 South Federal St., Suite 504, Chicago, IL 60605.

For general information about careers as a curator and schools offering courses in museum studies, contact:

☛American Association of Museums, 1225 I St. NW., Suite 200, Washington, DC 20005.

For information about curatorial careers and internships in botanical gardens, contact:

☛American Association of Botanical Gardens and Arboreta, 786 Church Rd., Wayne, PA 19087.

For information about conservation and preservation careers and education programs, contact:

☛American Institute for Conservation of Historic and Artistic Works, 1717 K St. NW., Suite 301, Washington, DC 20006.

For information on curatorial and other positions in natural history museums, contact:

☛Association of Systematics Collections, 730 11th St. NW., Second Floor, Washington, DC 20001.

College and University Faculty

(D.O.T. 090.227-010)

Nature of the Work
College and university faculty teach and advise over 15 million full- and part-time college students and perform a significant part of our Nation's research. They also study and meet with colleagues to keep up with developments in their field and consult with government, business, nonprofit, and community organizations.

Faculty generally are organized into departments or divisions, based on subject or field. They usually teach several different courses in their department—algebra, calculus, and differential equations, for example. They may instruct undergraduate or graduate students, or both.

College and university faculty may give lectures to several hundred students in large halls, lead small seminars, or supervise students in laboratories. They prepare lectures, exercises, and laboratory experiments, grade exams and papers, and advise and work with students individually. In universities, they counsel, advise, teach, and supervise graduate student teaching and research. Technology is increasingly used in the classroom as well as in research. Faculty may use computers—including the Internet, electronic mail, and CD-ROMs—videotapes, and other teaching aids. Some professors may teach "satellite" courses that are broadcast to students through closed-circuit or cable television. New technology permits the collaboration and sharing of classes between institutions.

Faculty keep abreast of developments in their field by reading current literature, talking with colleagues, and participating in professional conferences. They also do their own research to expand knowledge in their field. They experiment, collect and analyze data, and examine original documents, literature, and other source material. From this, they develop hypotheses, arrive at conclusions, and publish their findings in scholarly journals, books, and electronic media.

Most faculty members serve on academic or administrative committees which deal with the policies of their institution, depart-

Many college and university faculty hold a doctoral degree.

mental matters, academic issues, curricula, budgets, equipment purchases, and hiring. Some work with student as well as community organizations. Department chairpersons are faculty members who usually teach some courses but generally have heavier administrative responsibilities.

The amount of time spent on each of these activities varies by individual circumstance and type of institution. Faculty members at universities generally spend a significant part of their time doing research; those in 4-year colleges, somewhat less; and those in 2-year colleges, relatively little. However, the teaching load usually is heavier in 2-year colleges and somewhat lower at 4-year institutions.

Working Conditions
College faculty generally have flexible schedules. They must be present for classes, usually 12 to 16 hours a week, and for faculty and committee meetings. Most establish regular office hours for student consultations, usually 3 to 6 hours per week. Otherwise, faculty have some flexibility to decide when and where they will work, and how much time to devote to course preparation, grading papers and exams, study, research, graduate student supervision, and other activities. Initial adjustment to these responsibilities can be challenging as new faculty adapt to switching roles from student to teacher. This adjustment may be even more difficult as class size grows in response to faculty and budget cutbacks, increasing an instructor's workload.

Some faculty members work staggered hours and teach classes at night and on weekends. This is particularly true for faculty who teach students with full-time jobs or family responsibilities on weekdays. Most faculty are employed on a 9-month contract. This provides them with great flexibility during the summer and school holidays, when they may teach or do research, travel, or pursue nonacademic interests. Most colleges and universities have funds to support faculty research or other professional development needs, including travel to conferences and research sites.

Faculty may experience a conflict between their responsibilities to teach students and the pressure to do research. This may be a particular problem for young faculty seeking advancement. Increasing emphasis on undergraduate teaching performance in tenure decisions may alleviate some of this pressure, however.

Part-time faculty generally spend little time on campus, because they usually don't have an office. In addition, they may teach at more than one college, requiring travel between their various places of employment. Colleges increasingly rely on part-time faculty to stretch shrinking budgets. Part-time faculty are usually not eligible for tenure. Dealing with this lack of job security and low pay can be stressful.

Employment

College and university faculty held about 823,000 jobs in 1994, mostly in public institutions.

About 4 out of 10 college and university faculty work part time. Some part-timers, known as "adjunct faculty," have primary jobs outside of academia—in government, private industry, or in non-profit research—and teach "on the side." Others seek full-time jobs but are unable to obtain them due to intense competition for available openings. Some work part time in more than one institution.

Training, Other Qualifications, and Advancement

Most college and university faculty are in four academic ranks: Professor, associate professor, assistant professor, and instructor. A small number are lecturers.

Most faculty members are hired as instructors or assistant professors. Four-year colleges and universities generally only consider doctoral degree holders for full-time, tenure-track positions, but may hire master's degree holders or doctoral candidates for certain disciplines, such as the arts, or for part-time and temporary jobs. In 2-year colleges, master's degree holders often qualify for full-time positions. However, with increasing competition for available jobs, institutions can be more selective in their hiring practices. Master's degree holders may find it increasingly difficult to obtain employment as they are passed over in favor of candidates holding a Ph.D.

Doctoral programs usually take 6 to 8 years of full-time study beyond the bachelor's degree (including time spent completing a master's degree and a dissertation). Some programs, such as the humanities, may take longer to complete; others, such as engineering, generally are shorter. Candidates usually specialize in a subfield of a discipline—for example, organic chemistry, counseling psychology, or European history—but also take courses covering the whole discipline. Programs include 20 or more increasingly specialized courses and seminars plus comprehensive examinations on all major areas of the field. Candidates also must complete a dissertation. This is a report on original research to answer some significant question in the field; it sets forth an original hypothesis or proposes a model and tests it. Students in the natural sciences and engineering usually do laboratory work; in the humanities, they study original documents and other published material. The dissertation, done under the guidance of one or more faculty advisors, usually takes 1 or 2 years of full-time work.

In some fields, particularly the natural sciences, some students spend an additional 2 years on postdoctoral research and study before taking a faculty position.

A major step in the traditional academic career is attaining tenure. Newly hired tenure-track faculty serve a certain period (usually 7 years) under term contracts. Then, their record of teaching, research, and overall contribution to the institution is reviewed; tenure is granted if the review is favorable. With tenure, a professor cannot be fired without just cause and due process. Those denied tenure usually must leave the institution. Tenure protects the faculty's academic freedom—the ability to teach and conduct research without fear of being fired for advocating unpopular ideas. It also gives both faculty and institutions the stability needed for effective research and teaching, and provides financial stability for faculty members. About 6 out of 10 full-time faculty are tenured, and many others are in the probationary period. Some institutions have adopted post-tenure review policies to encourage ongoing evaluation of tenured faculty members.

The number of tenure-track positions is expected to decline. Some institutions have placed "caps" on the percentage of faculty that can be tenured. Other institutions offer prospective faculty limited term contracts—typically 2-, 3-, or 5-year full-time contracts—in an effort to adapt to changes in the budget and the size of the student body. These contracts may be terminated or extended at the end of the period. Institutions are not obligated to grant tenure to these contract holders.

Some faculty—based on teaching experience, research, publication, and service on campus committees and task forces—move into administrative and managerial positions, such as departmental chairperson, dean, and president. At 4-year institutions, such advancement requires a doctoral degree. At 2-year colleges, a doctorate is helpful but not generally required, except for advancement to some top administrative positions. (Deans and departmental chairpersons are covered in the *Handbook* statement on education administrators, while college presidents are included in the *Handbook* statement on general managers and top executives.)

College faculty need intelligence, inquiring and analytical minds, and a strong desire to pursue and disseminate knowledge. They must be able to communicate clearly and logically, both orally and in writing. They should be able to establish rapport with students and, as models for them, be dedicated to the principles of academic integrity and intellectual honesty. Finally, they must be able to work in an environment where they receive little direct supervision.

Job Outlook

Employment of college and university faculty is expected to increase about as fast as the average for all occupations through the year 2005 as enrollments in higher education increase. Many additional openings will arise as faculty members retire. Faculty retirements should increase significantly from the late 1990s through 2005 as a large number of faculty who entered the profession during the 1950s and 1960s reach retirement age. Most faculty members likely to retire are full-time tenured professors. However, in an effort to cut costs, institutions are expected to either leave many of these positions vacant or hire part-time faculty members as replacements. Prospective job applicants should be prepared to face intense competition for available jobs as growing numbers of Ph.D. graduates vie for fewer full-time openings.

Enrollments in institutions of higher education increased in the 1980s and early 1990s despite a decline in the traditional college-age (18-24) population. This resulted from a higher proportion of 18- to 24-year-olds attending college, along with a growing number of part-time, female, and older students. Enrollments are expected to continue to grow through the year 2005, particularly as the traditional college-age population begins increasing after 1996, when the leading edge of the baby-boom "echo" generation (children of the baby boomers) reaches college age (see accompanying chart).

In the past two decades, keen competition for faculty jobs forced some applicants to accept part-time or short-term academic appointments that offered little hope of tenure, and others to seek nonacademic positions. This trend of hiring adjunct or part-time faculty is likely to continue due to financial difficulties faced by colleges and universities. Many States have reduced funding for higher education. As a result, colleges have increased the hiring of part-time faculty to save money on pay and benefits. With uncertainty over future funding, many colleges and universities are taking steps to cut costs. They are emphasizing certain academic programs while eliminating others, increasing class size, stepping up fundraising efforts, and closely monitoring expenses.

Once enrollments and retirements start increasing at a faster pace in the late 1990s, opportunities for college faculty positions may begin to improve somewhat. Job prospects will continue to be better in certain fields—business, engineering, health science, computer science, physical sciences, and mathematics, for example—largely because very attractive nonacademic jobs will be available for many potential faculty.

Employment of college faculty is related to the nonacademic job market through an "echo effect." Excellent job prospects in a field—for example, computer science from the late 1970s to the mid-1980s—cause more students to enroll, increasing faculty needs in that field. On the other hand, poor job prospects in a field, such as history in recent years, discourages students and reduces demand for faculty.

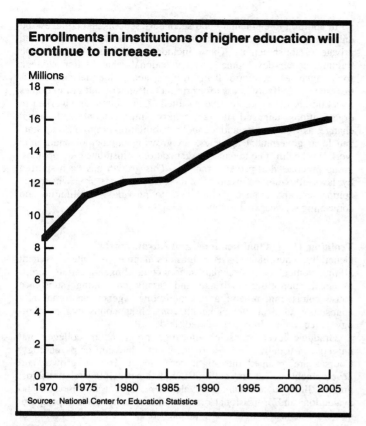

Enrollments in institutions of higher education will continue to increase.

Millions

Source: National Center for Education Statistics

Earnings

Earnings vary according to faculty rank and type of institution and, in some cases, by field. Faculty in 4-year institutions earn higher salaries, on the average, than those in 2-year schools. According to a 1994-95 survey by the American Association of University Professors, salaries for full-time faculty on 9-month contracts averaged $49,500. By rank, the average for professors was $63,500; associate professors, $47,000; assistant professors, $39,100; lecturers, $32,600; and instructors, $29,700. Those on 11- or 12-month contracts obviously earned more. In fields with high-paying nonacademic alternatives—notably medicine and law but also engineering and business, among others—earnings exceed these averages. In others—the fine arts, for example—they are lower.

Many faculty members have added earnings, both during the academic year and the summer, from consulting, teaching additional courses, research, writing for publication, or other employment.

Most college and university faculty enjoy some unique benefits, including access to campus facilities, tuition waivers for dependents, housing and travel allowances, and paid sabbatical leaves. Part-time faculty have fewer benefits than full-time faculty, and usually do not receive health insurance, retirement benefits, or sabbatical leave.

Related Occupations

College and university faculty function both as teachers and researchers. They communicate information and ideas. Related occupations include elementary and secondary school teachers, librarians, writers, consultants, lobbyists, trainers and employee development specialists, and policy analysts. Faculty research activities often are similar to those of scientists, as well as managers and administrators in industry, government, and nonprofit research organizations.

Sources of Additional Information

Professional societies generally provide information on academic and nonacademic employment opportunities in their fields. Names and addresses of these societies appear in statements elsewhere in the *Handbook*.

For information about faculty union activities on 2- and 4-year college campuses, contact:

☛American Federation of Teachers, 555 New Jersey Ave. NW., Washington, DC 20001.

Special publications on higher education, available in libraries, list specific employment opportunities for faculty.

Counselors

(D.O.T. 045.107-010, -014, -018, -038, -042 -050, -054, .117; 090.107; and 169.267-026)

Nature of the Work

Counselors assist people with personal, family, social, educational, mental health, and career decisions, problems, and concerns. Their duties depend on the individuals they serve and the settings in which they work.

School and college counselors—who work at the elementary, middle, secondary, and postsecondary school levels—help students understand their abilities, interests, talents, and personality characteristics so that the student can develop realistic academic and career options. Counselors use interviews, counseling sessions, tests, or other tools when evaluating and advising students. They may operate career information centers and career education programs. High school counselors advise on college majors, admission requirements, entrance exams, and financial aid, and on trade, technical school, and apprenticeship programs. They help students develop jobfinding skills such as resume writing and interviewing techniques. College career planning and placement counselors may assist alumni or students with career development and job hunting techniques.

Counselors also help students understand and deal with their social, behavioral, and personal problems. They emphasize preventive and developmental counseling to provide students with the life skills needed to deal with problems before they occur, and to enhance personal, social, and academic growth. Counselors provide special services, including alcohol and drug prevention programs, and classes that teach students to handle conflicts without resorting to violence. Counselors also try to identify cases involving domestic abuse and other family problems that can affect a student's development.

Counselors work with students individually, in small groups, or with entire classes. Counselors consult and work with parents, teachers, school administrators, school psychologists, school nurses, and social workers. Elementary school counselors do more social and personal counseling, and less vocational and academic counseling than secondary school counselors. They observe younger children during classroom and play activities and confer with their teachers and parents to evaluate their strengths, problems, or special needs. They also help students develop good study habits.

Rehabilitation counselors help persons deal with the personal, social, and vocational effects of their disabilities. They may counsel people with disabilities resulting from birth defects, illness or disease, accidents, or the stress of daily life. They evaluate the strengths and limitations of individuals, provide personal and vocational counseling, and may arrange for medical care, vocational training, and job placement. Rehabilitation counselors interview individuals with disabilities and their families, evaluate school and medical reports, and confer and plan with physicians, psychologists, occupational therapists, and employers to determine the capabilities and skills of the individual. Conferring with the client, they develop and implement a rehabilitation program, which may include training to help the person become more independent and employable. They also work toward increasing the client's capacity to adjust and live independently.

A master's degree, including a period of supervised clinical experience, is typically required for employment as a counselor.

Employment counselors help individuals make wise career decisions. They help clients explore and evaluate their education, training, work history, interests, skills, personal traits, and physical capacities, and may arrange for aptitude and achievement tests. They also work with individuals in developing jobseeking skills and assist clients in locating and applying for jobs.

Mental health counselors emphasize prevention and work with individuals and groups to promote optimum mental health. They help individuals deal with addictions and substance abuse, family, parenting, and marital problems, suicide, stress management, problems with self-esteem, issues associated with aging, job and career concerns, educational decisions, and issues of mental and emotional health. Mental health counselors work closely with other mental health specialists, including psychiatrists, psychologists, clinical social workers, psychiatric nurses, and school counselors. (See the statements on psychologists and social workers elsewhere in the *Handbook*.)

Counselors can specialize in a particular area, such as marriage and family, multicultural, and gerontological counseling. A gerontological counselor may provide services to elderly persons who face changing lifestyles due to health problems, as well as help families cope with these changes. A multicultural counselor might help employers adjust to an increasingly diverse workforce.

Working Conditions

Most school counselors work the traditional 9- to 10-month school year with a 2- to 3-month vacation, although an increasing number are employed on 10 1/2- or 11-month contracts. They generally have the same hours as teachers.

Rehabilitation and employment counselors generally work a standard 40-hour week. Self-employed counselors and those working in mental health and community agencies often work evenings to counsel clients who work during the day. College career planning and placement counselors may work long and irregular hours during recruiting periods.

Counselors must possess high physical and emotional energy to handle the array of problems they must address. Dealing with these day to day problems can cause stress and emotional burnout.

Since privacy is essential for confidential and frank discussions with clients, counselors usually have private offices.

Employment

Counselors held about 165,000 jobs in 1994. About 7 out of 10 were school counselors.

In addition to elementary and secondary schools and colleges and universities, counselors worked in a wide variety of public and private establishments. These include health care facilities; job training, career development, and vocational rehabilitation centers; social agencies; correctional institutions; and residential care facilities, such as halfway houses for criminal offenders and group homes for children, the aged, and the disabled. Counselors also worked in organizations engaged in community improvement and social change, as well as drug and alcohol rehabilitation programs and State and local government agencies. A growing number of counselors work in health maintenance organizations, insurance companies, group practice, and private practice. This growth has been spurred by laws allowing counselors to receive payments from insurance companies, and requiring employers to provide rehabilitation and counseling services to employees.

Training, Other Qualifications, and Advancement

Generally, counselors have a master's degree in college student affairs, elementary or secondary school counseling, education, gerontological counseling, marriage and family counseling, substance abuse counseling, rehabilitation counseling, agency or community counseling, clinical mental health counseling, counseling psychology, career counseling, or a related field.

Graduate level counselor education programs in colleges and universities usually are in departments of education or psychology. Courses are grouped into eight core areas: Human growth and development; social and cultural foundations; helping relationships; groups; lifestyle and career development; appraisal; research and evaluation; and professional orientation. In an accredited program, 48 to 60 semester hours of graduate study, including a period of supervised clinical experience in counseling, are required for a master's degree. In 1995, the Council for Accreditation of Counseling and Related Educational Programs (CACREP) accredited 105 graduate counseling programs in counselor education, and in career, community, gerontological, mental health, school, student affairs, and marriage and family counseling.

In 1995, 41 States and the District of Columbia had some form of counselor credentialing legislation, licensure, certification, or registry for practice outside schools. Requirements vary from State to State. In some States, credentialing is mandatory; in others, voluntary.

Many counselors elect to be nationally certified by the National Board for Certified Counselors (NBCC), which grants the general practice credential, "National Certified Counselor." To be certified, a counselor must hold a master's degree in counseling from a regionally accredited institution, have at least 2 years of supervised professional counseling experience, and pass NBCC's National Counselor Examination for Licensure and Certification. This national certification is voluntary and distinct from State certification. However, in some States those who pass the national exam are exempt from taking a State certification exam. NBCC also offers specialty certification in career, gerontological, school, clinical mental health, and addictions counseling. To maintain their certification, counselors must complete 100 hours of acceptable continuing education credit every 5 years.

All States require school counselors to hold State school counseling certification; however, certification varies from State to State. Some States require public school counselors to have both counseling and teaching certificates. Depending on the State, a master's degree in counseling and 2 to 5 years of teaching experience may be required for a counseling certificate.

Vocational and related rehabilitation agencies generally require a master's degree in rehabilitation counseling, counseling and guidance, or counseling psychology for rehabilitation counselor jobs. Some, however, may accept applicants with a bachelor's degree in rehabilitation services, counseling, psychology, sociology, or related fields. A bachelor's degree may qualify a person to work as a counseling aide, rehabilitation aide, or social service worker. Experience in employment counseling, job development, psychology, education, or social work may be helpful.

The Council on Rehabilitation Education (CORE) accredits graduate programs in rehabilitation counseling. A minimum of 2 years of study—including 600 hours of supervised clinical internship experience—are required for the master's degree.

In most State vocational rehabilitation agencies, applicants must pass a written examination and be evaluated by a board of examiners to obtain licensure. In addition, many employers require rehabilitation counselors to be nationally certified. To become certified by the Commission on Rehabilitation Counselor Certification, counselors must graduate from an accredited educational program, complete an internship, and pass a written examination. They are then designated as "Certified Rehabilitation Counselors." To maintain their certification, counselors must complete 100 hours of acceptable continuing education credit every 5 years.

Some States require counselors in public employment offices to have a master's degree; others accept a bachelor's degree with appropriate counseling courses.

Clinical mental health counselors generally have a master's degree in mental health counseling, another area of counseling, or in psychology or social work. They are voluntarily certified by the National Board for Certified Counselors. Generally, to receive certification as a clinical mental health counselor, a counselor must have a master's degree in counseling, 2 years of post-master's experience, a period of supervised clinical experience, a taped sample of clinical work, and a passing grade on a written examination.

Some employers provide training for newly hired counselors. Many have work-study programs so that employed counselors can earn graduate degrees. Counselors must participate in graduate studies, workshops, institutes, and personal studies to maintain their certificates and licenses.

Persons interested in counseling should have a strong interest in helping others and the ability to inspire respect, trust, and confidence. They should be able to work independently or as part of a team. Counselors follow the code of ethics associated with their respective certifications and licenses.

Prospects for advancement vary by counseling field. School counselors may move to a larger school; become directors or supervisors of counseling, guidance, or pupil personnel services; or, usually with further graduate education, become counselor educators, counseling psychologists, or school administrators. (See the statements on psychologists and education administrators elsewhere in the *Handbook*.) Some counselors also may advance to work at the State department of education.

Rehabilitation, mental health, and employment counselors may become supervisors or administrators in their agencies. Some counselors move into research, consulting, or college teaching, or go into private or group practice.

Job Outlook

Overall employment of counselors is expected to grow faster than the average for all occupations through the year 2005. In addition, replacement needs should increase significantly as a large number of counselors reach retirement age.

Employment of school counselors is expected to grow as a result of increasing enrollments, particularly in secondary schools, State legislation requiring counselors in elementary schools, and the expanded responsibilities of counselors. Counselors increasingly are becoming involved in crisis and preventive counseling, helping students deal with issues ranging from drug and alcohol abuse to death and suicide. Despite the increasing use of counselors, however, employment growth may be dampened by budgetary constraints—some counselors serve more than one school. Also, counselor positions are usually cut before teacher positions when funding is tight.

Rehabilitation and mental health counselors should be in strong demand. Under managed care systems, insurance companies increasingly provide for reimbursement of counselors, enabling many counselors to move from schools and government agencies to private practice. Counselors are also forming group practices to receive expanded insurance coverage. The number of people who need rehabilitation services will rise as advances in medical technology continue to save lives that only a few years ago would have been lost. In addition, legislation requiring equal employment rights for persons with disabilites will spur demand for counselors. Counselors not only will help individuals with disabilities with their transition into the work force, but also will help companies comply with the law. An increasing number of employers are also offering employee assistance programs which provide mental health and alcohol and drug abuse services. More rehabilitation and mental health counselors will be needed as the elderly population grows, and as society focuses on ways of developing mental well-being, such as controlling stress associated with job and family responsibilities.

Similar to other government jobs, the number of employment counselors, who work primarily for State and local government, could be limited by budgetary constraints. Opportunities for employment counselors working in private job training services, however, should grow as counselors provide skill training and other services to a growing number of laid-off workers, experienced workers seeking a new or second career, full-time homemakers seeking to enter or reenter the work force, and workers who want to upgrade their skills.

Earnings

Median earnings for full-time educational and vocational counselors were about $36,100 a year in 1994. The middle 50 percent earned between $26,500 and $46,200 a year. The bottom 10 percent earned less than $20,000 a year, while the top 10 percent earned over $50,000 a year.

According to the Educational Research Service, the average salary of public school counselors in the 1994-95 academic year was about $42,500. Many school counselors are compensated on the same pay scale as teachers. School counselors can earn additional income working summers in the school system or in other jobs.

Self-employed counselors who have well-established practices, as well as counselors employed in group practices, generally have the highest earnings, as do some counselors working for private firms, such as insurance companies and private rehabilitation companies.

Related Occupations

Counselors help people evaluate their interests, abilities, and disabilities, and deal with personal, social, academic, and career problems. Others who help people in similar ways include college and student personnel workers, teachers, personnel workers and managers, human services workers, social workers, psychologists, psychiatrists, members of the clergy, occupational therapists, training and employee development specialists, and equal employment opportunity/affirmative action specialists.

Sources of Additional Information

For general information about counseling, as well as information on specialties such as school, college, mental health, rehabilitation, multicultural, career, marriage and family, and gerontological counseling, contact:

☛American Counseling Association, 5999 Stevenson Ave., Alexandria, VA 22304.

For information on accredited counseling and related training programs, contact:

☛Council for Accreditation of Counseling and Related Educational Programs, American Counseling Association, 5999 Stevenson Ave., Alexandria, VA 22304.

For information on national certification requirements for counselors, contact:

☛National Board for Certified Counselors, 3 Terrace Way, Suite D, Greensboro, NC 27403.

For information about rehabilitation counseling, contact:

☛National Rehabilitation Counseling Association, 1910 Association Dr., Reston, VA 22091.

☛National Council on Rehabilitation Education, Department of Special Education, Utah State University, Logan, UT 84322-2870.

For information on certification requirements for rehabilitation counselors and a list of accredited rehabilitation education programs, contact:

☛Council on Rehabilitation Counselor Certification, 1835 Rohlwing Rd., Suite E, Rolling Meadows, IL 60008.

For general information about school counselors, contact:

☛American School Counselor Association, 5999 Stevenson Ave., Alexandria, VA 22304.

State departments of education can supply information on colleges and universities that offer approved guidance and counseling training for State certification and licensure requirements.

State employment service offices have information about job opportunities and entrance requirements for counselors.

Librarians

(D.O.T. 100 except .367-018; 109.267-014)

Nature of the Work

Librarians assist people in finding information and using it effectively in their personal and professional lives. They must have knowledge of a wide variety of scholarly and public information sources, and follow trends related to publishing, computers, and the media to effectively oversee the selection and organization of library materials. Librarians manage staff and develop and direct information programs and systems for the public, to ensure information is being organized to meet the needs of users.

There are generally three aspects of library work—user services, technical services, and administrative services. Increasingly, distinctions between these services is blurred, and many librarian positions incorporate all three aspects of the work. Even librarians who specialize in one of these areas may perform other responsibilities. Librarians in user services, such as reference and children's librarians, work with the public to help them find the information they need. This may involve analyzing users' needs to determine what information is appropriate, and searching for, acquiring, and providing the information. Librarians in technical services, such as acquisitions and cataloguing, acquire and prepare materials for use and may not deal directly with the public. Librarians in administrative services oversee the management and planning of libraries, negotiate contracts for services, materials, and equipment, supervise library employees, perform public relations and fundraising duties, prepare budgets, and direct activities to ensure that everything functions properly.

In small libraries or information centers, librarians generally handle all aspects of the work. They read book reviews, publishers' announcements, and catalogues to keep up with current literature and other available resources, and select and purchase materials from publishers, wholesalers, and distributors. Librarians prepare new materials for use by classifying them by subject matter, and describe books and other library materials in a way that users can easily find them. They supervise assistants who prepare cards, computer records, or other access tools that direct users to resources. In large libraries, librarians may specialize in a single area, such as acquisitions, cataloguing, bibliography, reference, special collections, or administration. Teamwork is increasingly important to ensure quality service to the public.

Librarians also compile lists of books, periodicals, articles, and audiovisual materials on particular subjects, analyze collections, and recommend materials to be acquired. They may collect and organize books, pamphlets, manuscripts, and other materials in a specific field, such as rare books, genealogy, or music. In addition, they coordinate programs such as storytelling for children, and literacy skills and book talks for adults; publicize services; provide reference help; supervise staff; prepare budgets; write grants; and oversee other administrative matters.

Librarians may be classified according to the type of library in which they work—public libraries, school library media centers, academic libraries, and special libraries. They may work with specific groups, such as children, young adults, adults, or the disadvantaged. In school library media centers, librarians help teachers develop curricula, acquire materials for classroom instruction, and sometimes team teach.

Librarians may also work in information centers or libraries maintained by government agencies, corporations, law firms, advertising agencies, museums, professional associations, medical centers, hospitals, religious organizations, and research laboratories. They build and arrange the organization's information resources, usually limited to subjects of special interest to the organization. These special librarians can provide vital information services by preparing abstracts and indexes of current periodicals, organizing bibliographies, or analyzing background information and preparing reports on areas of particular interest. For instance, a special librarian working for a corporation may provide the sales department with information on competitors or new developments affecting their field.

Many libraries have access to remote databases, as well as maintaining their own computerized databases. The widespread use of automation in libraries makes database searching skills important to librarians. Librarians develop and index databases and act as trainers to help users develop searching skills to obtain the information they need. Some libraries are forming consortiums with other libraries through electronic mail (e-mail). This allows patrons to submit information requests to several libraries at once. Use of Internet and other world-wide computer systems is also expanding the amount of available reference information. Librarians must be increasingly aware of how to use these resources to locate information.

Libraries may employ automated systems librarians who plan and operate computer systems, and information science librarians who design information storage and retrieval systems and develop procedures for collecting, organizing, interpreting, and classifying information. These librarians may analyze and plan for future information needs. (See statement on computer scientists and systems analysts elsewhere in the *Handbook.*) The increasing use of automated information systems enables librarians to focus on administrative and budgeting responsibilities, grant writing, and specialized research requests, while delegating more technical and user services responsibilities to technicians. (See statement on library technicians elsewhere in the *Handbook.*)

Some librarians apply their information management and research skills to other arenas outside libraries—for example, database development, reference tool development, information systems, publishing, Internet coordination, marketing, and training of database users. Entrepreneurial librarians may start their own consulting practices. They act as free-lance librarians or information brokers and provide services to other libraries, businesses, or government agencies.

Working Conditions

Working conditions in user services are different from those in technical services. Assisting users in obtaining the information for their jobs or for recreational and other needs can be challenging and satisfying. Working with users under deadlines may be demanding and stressful. In technical services, selecting and ordering new materials can be stimulating and rewarding. However, librarians may spend a significant portion of time at their desks or in front of computer terminals. Extended work at video display terminals may cause eyestrain and headaches.

Nearly 1 out of 4 librarians works part time. Public and college librarians often work weekends and evenings and may have to work

A master's degree in library science (M.L.S.) is necessary for most librarian jobs.

some holidays. School librarians generally have the same workday schedule as classroom teachers and similar vacation schedules. Special librarians may work normal business hours, but in fast-paced industries, such as advertising or legal services, may work longer hours during peak times.

Employment

Librarians held about 148,000 jobs in 1994. Most were in school and academic libraries; others were in public libraries and special libraries. A small number of librarians worked for hospitals and religious organizations. Others worked for governments at all levels.

Training, Other Qualifications, and Advancement

A master's degree in library science (M.L.S.) is necessary for librarian positions in most public, academic, and special libraries, and in some school libraries. In the Federal Government, an M.L.S. or the equivalent in education and experience is needed. Many colleges and universities offer M.L.S. programs, but many employers prefer graduates of the approximately 50 schools accredited by the American Library Association. Most M.L.S. programs require a bachelor's degree; any liberal arts major is appropriate.

Most programs take 1 year to complete; others take 2. A typical graduate program includes courses in the foundations of library and information science, including the history of books and printing, intellectual freedom and censorship, and the role of libraries and information in society. Other basic courses cover material selection and processing; the organization of information; reference tools and strategies; and user services. Courses are being adapted to educate librarians to use new resources brought about by advancing technology such as on-line reference systems and automated circulation systems. Course options can include resources for children or young adults; classification, cataloguing, indexing, and abstracting; library administration; and library automation.

The M.L.S. provides general, all-round preparation for library work, but some people specialize in a particular area such as reference, technical services, or children's services. A Ph.D. degree in library and information science is advantageous for a college teaching or top administrative position, particularly in a college or university library or in a large library system.

In special libraries, the M.L.S. is usually required. In addition, most special librarians supplement their education with knowledge of the subject specialization, or a master's, doctoral, or professional degree in the subject. Subject specializations include medicine, law, business, engineering, and the natural and social sciences. For example, a librarian working for a law firm may also be a licensed attorney, holding both library science and law degrees. In some jobs, knowledge of a foreign language is needed.

State certification requirements for public school librarians vary widely. Most States require that school librarians—often called library media specialists—be certified as teachers and have courses in library science. In some cases, the M.L.S., perhaps with a library media specialization, or a master's in education with a specialty in school library media or educational media is needed. Some States require certification of public librarians employed in municipal, county, or regional library systems.

Experienced librarians may advance to administrative positions, such as department head, library director, or chief information officer.

Job Outlook

Employment of librarians is expected to grow more slowly than the average for all occupations through the year 2005. However, the number of job openings resulting from the need to replace librarians who leave the occupation is expected to increase by 2005, as many workers reach retirement age. Willingness to relocate will greatly enhance job prospects.

Budgetary constraints will likely contribute to the slow growth in employment of librarians in school, public, and college and university libraries as libraries reduce staff to cut costs. Although fewer new positions have become available in recent years, the number of MLS graduates has been increasing. Thus, more applicants are competing for fewer jobs.

The increasing use of computerized information storage and retrieval systems may also dampen the demand for librarians. For example, computerized systems make cataloguing easier, and this task can now be handled by other library staff. In addition, many libraries are equipped for users to access library computers directly from their homes or offices. These systems allow users to bypass librarians and conduct research on their own. However, librarians will be needed to manage staff, help users develop database searching techniques, address complicated reference requests, and define users' needs.

Opportunities will be best for librarians outside traditional settings. Nontraditional library settings include information brokers, private corporations, and consulting firms. Many companies are turning to librarians because of their excellent research and organizational skills, and knowledge of library automation systems. Librarians can review the vast amount of information that is available and analyze, evaluate, and organize it according to a company's specific needs. Librarians are also moving into organizations to set up information on the Internet. Librarians working in these settings are often classified as systems analysts, database specialists and trainers, managers, and researchers.

Earnings

Salaries of librarians vary by the individual's qualifications and the type, size, and location of the library.

According to a survey by the American Library Association, the average salary of children's librarians in academic and public libraries was $35,000 in 1995; reference/information librarians averaged $35,600; cataloguers and classifiers earned $36,300; and department heads earned $42,000. Library directors had an average salary of $58,200. Beginning librarians with a master's degree but no professional experience averaged $28,300 in 1995.

According to the Educational Research Service, experienced librarians in public schools averaged about $40,400 during the 1994-95 school year.

According to the Special Libraries Association, 1994 salaries for special librarians with 2 years or less of library experience averaged $31,100, and those with 3 to 5 years of experience averaged $35,200. Salaries for special librarians with primarily administrative responsibilities averaged $54,600.

Salaries for medical librarians with 1 year or less experience averaged $25,300 in 1994, according to the Medical Library Association. The average salary for all medical librarians was $38,000.

The average annual salary for all librarians in the Federal Government in nonsupervisory, supervisory, and managerial positions was $48,200 in 1995.

Related Occupations

Librarians play an important role in the transfer of knowledge and ideas by providing people with access to the information they need and want. Jobs requiring similar analytical, organizational, and communicative skills include archivists, information scientists, museum curators, publishers' representatives, research analysts, information brokers, and records managers. The management aspect of a librarian's work is similar to the work of managers in a variety of business and government settings. School librarians have many duties similar to those of school teachers.

Sources of Additional Information

Information on librarianship, including a listing of accredited education programs and information on scholarships or loans, is available from:

☞American Library Association, Office for Library Personnel Resources, 50 East Huron St., Chicago, IL 60611.

For information on a career as a special librarian, write to:

☞Special Libraries Association, 1700 18th St. NW., Washington, DC 20009.

Material about a career in information science is available from:

☞American Society for Information Science, 8720 Georgia Ave., Suite 501, Silver Spring, MD 20910.

Information on graduate schools of library and information science can be obtained from:

☞Association for Library and Information Science Education, 4101 Lake Boone Trail, Suite 201, Raleigh, NC 27607.

Information on schools receiving Federal financial assistance for library training is available from:

☞Office of Educational Research and Improvement, Library Programs, Library Development Staff, U.S. Department of Education, 555 New Jersey Ave. NW., Room 402, Washington, DC 20208-5571.

For information on a career as a law librarian, as well as a list of ALA-accredited schools offering programs in law librarianship and scholarship information, contact:

☞American Association of Law Libraries, 53 West Jackson Blvd., Suite 940, Chicago, IL 60604.

For information on employment opportunities as a health sciences librarian, a list of ALA-accredited schools offering programs in health sciences librarianship and scholarship information, and credentialing information, contact:

☞Medical Library Association, 6 N. Michigan Ave., Suite 300, Chicago, IL 60602.

Those interested in a position as a librarian in the Federal service should write to:

☞Office of Personnel Management, 1900 E St. NW., Washington, DC 20415.

Information concerning requirements and application procedures for positions in the Library of Congress may be obtained directly from:

☞Personnel Office, Library of Congress, 101 Independence Ave. SE., Washington, DC 20540.

State library agencies can furnish information on scholarships available through their offices, requirements for certification, and general information about career prospects in the State. Several of these agencies maintain job hotlines which report openings for librarians.

State departments of education can furnish information on certification requirements and job opportunities for school librarians.

Many library science schools offer career placement services to their alumni and current students. Some will allow non-affiliated students and jobseekers to use their services.

School Teachers—Kindergarten, Elementary, and Secondary

D.O.T. 091.221, .227; 092.227-010, -014; 099.224-010, .227-022)

Nature of the Work

The role of a teacher is changing from that of a lecturer or presenter to one of a facilitator or coach. Interactive discussions and "hands-on" learning are replacing rote memorization. For example, rather than merely telling students about science, mathematics, or psychology, teachers ask students to help solve a mathematical problem or perform a laboratory experiment and discuss how these apply to the real world. Similarly, some teachers arrange to bring 3- and 4-year-olds into the classroom to demonstrate certain concepts of child psychology.

As teachers move away from the traditional repetitive drill approaches, they are using more "props" or "manipulatives" to help children understand abstract concepts, solve problems, and develop critical thought processes. For example, they teach the concepts of numbers or adding and subtracting by playing board games. As children get older, they may use more sophisticated materials such as tape recorders, science apparatus, or cameras.

Classes are becoming less structured, and students are working in groups to discuss and solve problems together. Preparing students for the future workforce is the major stimulus generating the changes in education. To be prepared, students must be able to interact with others, adapt to new technology, and logically think through problems. Teachers provide the tools and environment for their students to develop these skills.

Kindergarten and elementary school teachers—who generally teach 5- to 13-year olds—play a vital role in the development of children. What children learn and experience during their early years can shape their views of themselves and the world, and affect later success or failure in school, work, and their personal lives. Kindergarten and elementary school teachers introduce children to numbers, language, science, and social studies. They use games, music, artwork, films, slides, computers, and other teaching technology to teach basic skills.

Most elementary school teachers instruct one class of children in several subjects. In some schools, two or more teachers work as a team and are jointly responsible for a group of students in at least one subject. In other schools, a teacher may teach one special subject—usually music, art, reading, science, arithmetic, or physical education—to a number of classes. A small but growing number of teachers instruct multilevel classrooms—those with students at several different learning levels.

Secondary school teachers—who generally teach 14- to 17-year olds—help students delve more deeply into subjects introduced in elementary school and expose them to more information about the world and themselves. Secondary school teachers specialize in a specific subject, such as English, Spanish, mathematics, history, or biology. They teach a variety of related courses—for example, American history, contemporary American problems, and world geography.

Special education teachers—who instruct students with a variety of disabilities in lower grades and high schols—are discussed separately in this section of the *Handbook*.

Teachers may use films, slides, overhead projectors, and the latest technology in teaching, such as computers, telecommunication systems, and video discs. Telecommunication technology exposes students to a vast range of experiences and promotes interactive learning. Through telecommunications, American students can communicate with students in other countries to share personal experiences or research projects of interest to both groups. Computers are used in many classroom activities, from helping students solve math problems to learning English as a second language. Increasingly, students are using the Internet for research and information gathering. Many teachers also use computers to record grades and for other administrative and clerical duties. Teachers must continually update their skills to use the latest technology in the classroom.

Teachers work with students from increasingly diverse ethnic, racial, and religious backgrounds. With growing minority populations, it is important for teachers to learn about and establish rapport with a diverse student population. Teachers factor multicultural programming into their lesson plans so that no student, regardless of his or her cultural background, is at a disadvantage. Some schools offer training to help teachers enhance their awareness and understanding of different cultures.

Teachers design their classroom presentations to meet student needs and abilities. They also work with students individually. Teachers assign lessons, give tests, listen to oral presentations, and maintain classroom discipline. They observe and evaluate a student's performance and potential, and increasingly use new assessment methods, such as examining a portfolio of a student's artwork or writing, to measure student achievement. Teachers assess the portfolio at the end of a learning period to judge a student's overall progress. They then provide additional assistance in areas where a student needs help.

In addition to classroom activities, teachers plan and evaluate lessons, sometimes in collaboration with teachers of related subjects. They also prepare tests, grade papers, prepare report cards, oversee study halls and homerooms, supervise extracurricular activities, and meet with parents and school staff to discuss a student's academic progress or personal problems. They identify physical or mental problems and refer students to the proper agency for treatment. Secondary school teachers assist students in choosing courses, colleges, and careers. Teachers also participate in education conferences and workshops.

In recent years, site-based management, which allows teachers and parents to participate actively in management decisions, has gained popularity. In many schools, teachers help make decisions regarding the budget, personnel, textbook choices, curriculum design, and teaching methods.

Working Conditions

Seeing students develop new skills and gain an appreciation of the joy of learning can be very rewarding. However, teaching may be frustrating when dealing with unmotivated and disrespectful students. In urban areas, teachers may experience stress when dealing with large classes, a large number of students from disadvantaged backgrounds, and heavy workloads. Also, the relatively low pay causes some teachers to leave the profession.

Teachers must understand the emotional and educational needs of their students.

Teachers face isolation from their colleagues since they often work alone in a classroom of students. However, this autonomy provides teachers considerable freedom to choose their own teaching styles and methods.

Including school duties performed outside the classroom, many teachers work more than 40 hours a week. Most teachers work the traditional 10-month school year with a 2-month vacation during the summer. Those on the 10-month schedule may teach in summer sessions, take other jobs, travel, or pursue other personal interests. Many enroll in college courses or workshops to continue their education. Teachers in districts with a year-round schedule typically work 8 weeks, are on vacation for 1 week, and have a 5-week midwinter break.

Most States have tenure laws that prevent teachers from being fired without just cause and due process. Teachers may obtain tenure after they have satisfactorily completed a probationary period of teaching, normally 3 years. Tenure does not absolutely guarantee a job, but it does provide some security.

Employment

Teachers held over 2.9 million jobs in 1994. Of those, nearly 1.6 million were kindergarten and elementary school teachers, and over 1.3 million were secondary school teachers. Employment is distributed geographically, much the same as the population.

Training, Other Qualifications, and Advancement

All 50 States and the District of Columbia require public school teachers to be licensed. Licensure is generally offered for one or several related subjects. Usually licensure is granted by the State board of education or a licensure advisory committee. Teachers may be licensed to teach the early childhood grades (usually nursery school through grade 3); the elementary grades (grades 1 through 6 or 8); or a special subject, such as reading or music.

Requirements for regular licenses vary by State. However, all States require a bachelor's degree and completion of an approved teacher training program with a prescribed number of subject and education credits and supervised practice teaching. Many States require teachers to obtain a master's degree in education, which involves at least 1 year of additional coursework beyond the bachelor's degree with a specialization in a particular subject.

The National Council for Accreditation of Teacher Education currently accredits over 500 teacher education programs across the United States. Generally, 4-year colleges require students to wait until their sophomore year before applying for admission to teacher education programs. Traditional education programs for kinde garden.

ten and elementary school teachers include courses—designed specifically for those preparing to teach—in mathematics, physical science, social science, music, art, and literature, as well as prescribed professional education courses, such as philosophy of education, psychology of learning, and teaching methods. Aspiring secondary school teachers either major in the subject they plan to teach while also taking education courses, or major in education and take subject courses. Most programs require students to perform student teaching. Some States require specific grade point averages for teacher licensure.

Many States now offer professional development schools, which involve partnerships between universities and elementary or secondary schools. Students enter these 1-year programs after completion of their bachelor's degree. Professional development schools merge theory with practice and allow the student to experience a year of teaching first-hand, with professional guidance.

Many States offer alternative teacher licensure programs for people who have bachelor's degrees in the subject they will teach, but lack the necessary education courses required for a regular license. Alternative licensure programs were originally designed to ease teacher shortages in certain subjects, such as mathematics and science. The programs have expanded to attract other people into teaching, including recent college graduates and midcareer changers. In some programs, individuals begin teaching quickly under provisional licensure. After working under the close supervision of experienced educators for 1 or 2 years while taking education courses outside school hours, they receive regular licensure if they have progressed satisfactorily. Under other programs, college graduates who do not meet licensure requirements take only those courses that they lack, and then become licensed. This may take 1 or 2 semesters of full-time study. States may issue emergency licenses to individuals who do not meet requirements for a regular license when schools cannot attract enough qualified teachers to fill positions. Teachers who need licensure may enter programs that grant a master's degree in education, as well as licensure.

Almost all States require applicants for teacher licensure to be tested for competency in basic skills such as reading and writing, teaching skills, or subject matter proficiency. Most States require continuing education for renewal of the teacher's license—some require a master's degree. Many States have reciprocity agreements that make it easier for teachers licensed in one State to become licensed in another.

Recently, the National Board for Professional Teaching Standards began offering voluntary national certification for teachers. Teachers are required to obtain State licensure, but may choose whether they wish to obtain national certification. A teacher who is nationally certified may find it easier to obtain employment in another State. Certified teachers may also earn higher salaries, have more senior titles, and be eligible for more bonuses than non-certified teachers. Policies vary by State and since this is a fairly new credential, many States' policies regarding recognition of national certification have not been established.

In addition to being knowledgeable in their subject, the ability to communicate, inspire trust and confidence, and motivate students, as well as understand their educational and emotional needs, is essential for teachers. Teachers must be able to recognize and respond to individual differences in students, and employ different teaching methods that will result in high student achievement. They also should be organized, dependable, patient, and creative. Teachers must also be able to work cooperatively and communicate effectively with other teaching staff, support staff, and parents and other members of the community.

With additional preparation and certification or licensure, teachers may move into positions as school librarians, reading specialists, curriculum specialists, or guidance counselors. Teachers may become administrators or supervisors, although the number of these positions is limited. In some systems, highly qualified, experienced teachers can become senior or mentor teachers, with higher pay and additional responsibilities. They guide and assist less experienced teachers while keeping most of their teaching responsibilities.

Job Outlook

The job market for teachers varies widely among States and school districts. Some central cities and rural areas have difficulty attracting enough teachers, so job prospects should continue to be better in these areas than in suburban districts. Teachers in some subjects—mathematics, science (especially chemistry and physics), bilingual education, and computer science, for example—seem to be in short supply. Areas that seem to be experiencing an oversupply of teachers, on the other hand, include general elementary education, physical education, and social studies. Teachers who are geographically mobile and who obtain licensure in more than one subject should have a distinct advantage in finding a job. With enrollments of minorities increasing, and a shortage of minority teachers, efforts to recruit minority teachers should intensify.

Overall employment of kindergarten, elementary, and secondary school teachers is expected to increase faster than the average for all occupations through the year 2005. However, projected employment growth varies among individual teaching occupations. Job openings for all teachers are expected to increase substantially by the end of the decade as the large number of teachers now in their forties and fifties reach retirement age.

Employment of secondary school teachers is expected to grow faster than the average for all occupations through the year 2005, while average employment growth is projected for kindergarten and elementary school teachers. Assuming relatively little change in average class size, employment growth of teachers depends on population growth rates and corresponding student enrollments. Enrollment of 14- to 17-year-olds is expected to experience relatively strong growth through the year 2005, spurring demand for secondary school teachers (see chart 1). Enrollment of 5- to 13-year olds also is projected to increase, but at a slower rate, resulting in divergent growth rates for individual teaching occupations (see chart 2).

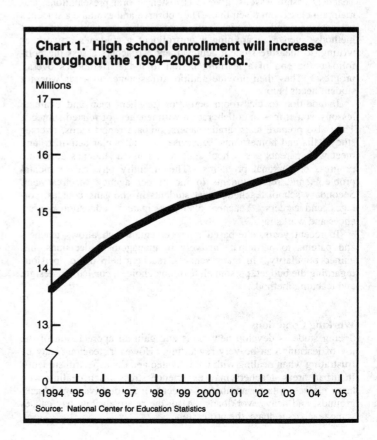

Chart 1. High school enrollment will increase throughout the 1994–2005 period.

Millions

Source: National Center for Education Statistics

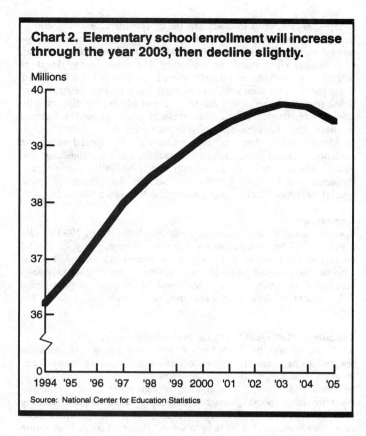

Chart 2. Elementary school enrollment will increase through the year 2003, then decline slightly.

Source: National Center for Education Statistics

The number of teachers employed is also dependent on State and local expenditures for education. Pressures from taxpayers to limit spending could result in fewer teachers than projected; pressures to spend more to improve the quality of education could increase the teacher workforce.

The supply of teachers also is expected to increase in response to reports of improved job prospects, more teacher involvement in school policy, and greater public interest in education. In fact, enrollments in teacher training programs already have increased in recent years. In addition, more teachers will be drawn from a reserve pool made up of career changers, teachers completing alternative certification programs, teachers relocating to different schools, substitute teachers, and teachers reentering the workforce.

Earnings
According to the National Education Association, the estimated average salary of all elementary and secondary school teachers in 1995 was $36,900. Public secondary school teachers averaged about $37,800 a year, while public elementary school teachers averaged $36,400. Starting salaries for teachers in 1995 ranged from about $20,000 to $25,000 a year. Private school teachers generally earn less than public school teachers.

In 1994, over half of all public school teachers belonged to unions—mainly the American Federation of Teachers and the National Education Association—that bargain with school systems over wages, hours, and the terms and conditions of employment.

In some schools, teachers receive extra pay for coaching sports and working with students in extracurricular activities. Some teachers earn extra income during the summer working in the school system or in other jobs.

Related Occupations
Kindergarten, elementary, and secondary school teaching requires a wide variety of skills and aptitudes, including a talent for working with children; organizational, administrative, and recordkeeping abilities; research and communication skills; the power to influence, motivate, and train others; patience; and creativity. Workers in other occupations requiring some of these aptitudes include college and university faculty, counselors, education administrators, employment interviewers, librarians, preschool teachers, public relations specialists, sales representatives, social workers, and trainers and employee development specialists.

Sources of Additional Information
Information on licensure or certification requirements and approved teacher training institutions is available from local school systems and State departments of education.

Information on teachers' unions and education-related issues may be obtained from:
☛American Federation of Teachers, 555 New Jersey Ave. NW., Washington, DC 20001.
☛National Education Association, 1201 16th St. NW., Washington, DC 20036.

A list of institutions with accredited teacher education programs can be obtained from:
☛National Council for Accreditation of Teacher Education, 2010 Massachusetts Ave. NW., 5th Floor, Washington, DC 20036.

For information on voluntary teacher certification requirements, contact:
☛National Board for Professional Teaching Standards, 300 River Pl., Detroit, MI 48207.

Special Education Teachers

D.O.T. 094.107, .224, .227, .267; 099.227-042; 195.227-018)

Nature of the Work
Special education teachers work with students—from toddlers to those in their early 20s—who have a variety of disabilities. Most special education teachers are found at the elementary, middle, and secondary school level. Special education teachers design and modify instruction to meet a student's special needs. Teachers also work with students who have other special instructional needs, including those who are gifted and talented.

The various types of disabilities delineated in federal special education programs include specific learning disabilities, mental retardation, speech or language impairment, serious emotional disturbance, visual and hearing impairment, orthopedic impairment, autism, traumatic brain injury, and other health impairments. Students are classified under one of the categories, and special education teachers are prepared to work with specific groups.

Special education teachers use various teaching techniques to promote learning. Depending on the disability, teaching methods can include individualized instruction, problem-solving assignments, and group or individual work. Since special education students often progress at slower rates than their peers in certain areas, teachers tailor a program to meet a student's specific needs.

Special education teachers are legally required to participate in the development of an Individualized Education Program (IEP) for each special education student. The IEP sets personalized goals for each student and is tailored to a student's individual learning style and ability. This program includes a transition plan which outlines specific steps and procedures to prepare special education students for a job or for postsecondary study. Teachers review the IEP with the student's parents, school administrators, and often the student's general education teacher. Teachers work closely with parents to inform them of their child's progress and suggest techniques to promote learning at home.

Teachers design curricula, assign work geared toward each student's ability, and grade papers and homework assignments. Special education teachers are involved in a student's behavioral as well as academic development. They help special education students develop emotionally, be comfortable in social situations, and be aware of socially acceptable behavior. Preparing special education students for daily life after graduation is an important aspect of the job. Teachers may help students with routine skills, such as balancing a check book, or provide them with career counseling.

As schools become more inclusive, special education teachers and general education teachers are working together in general education classrooms. Special education teachers help general educators adapt curriculum materials and teaching techniques to meet the needs of students with disabilities.

Special education teachers work in a variety of settings. Some have their own classrooms and teach classes comprised entirely of special education students; others work as special education resource teachers and offer individualized help to students in general education classrooms; others teach along with general education teachers in classes composed of both general and special education students. Some teachers work in a resource room, where special education students work several hours a day, separate from their general education classroom. A significantly smaller proportion of special education teachers work in residential facilities or tutor students in homebound or hospital environments.

A large part of a special education teacher's job involves interacting with others. They communicate frequently with social workers, school psychologists, occupational and physical therapists, parents, school administrators, and other teachers.

Early identification of children with special needs is another important part of a special education teacher's job. Early intervention is recognized as essential to educating children with special needs.

Technology is playing an increasingly important role in special education. Special education teachers may use specialized equipment such as computers with synthesized speech, interactive educational software programs, and audio tapes in the classroom.

Working Conditions

Helping students with disabilities achieve goals and making a difference in their lives can be highly rewarding. Special education teachers enjoy the challenge of working with these students and the opportunity to establish meaningful relationships. However, the work can also be intensely demanding, and attending to physical needs of students can be draining. These demands, coupled with relatively low wages and lack of prestige, result in a high "burnout" rate among special education teachers.

Many school districts throughout the Nation are experiencing shortages of special education teachers.

Special education teachers are under considerable stress due to heavy workloads and tedious administrative tasks. They must produce a substantial amount of paperwork and records documenting each student's progress. Exacerbating this stress is the threat of litigation by students' parents if correct procedure is not followed or if the parent feels their child is not receiving an adequate education. Some special educators feel that they are not adequately supported by school administrators, and feel isolated from general education teachers. Lack of support can lead to frustration.

Many schools offer year-round education for special education students, but most special education teachers work the traditional 10-month school year with a 2-month vacation during the summer. Including school duties performed outside the classroom, most special education teachers work more than 40 hours a week.

Employment

Special education teachers held about 388,000 jobs in 1994 in elementary, middle, and secondary schools. The majority of special education teachers were employed in public schools. The rest worked in separate educational facilities—public or private—residential facilities, or in homebound or hospital environments. Employment is distributed geographically, much the same as the population.

Training, Other Qualifications, and Advancement

All 50 States and the District of Columbia require special education teachers to be licensed. Special education licensure varies by State. In many States, special education teachers receive a general education credential to teach kindergarten through grade 12. These teachers train in a specialty, such as teaching children with learning disabilities or behavioral disorders. Some States offer general special education licensure, others license several different specialties within special education, while others require teachers to first obtain general education licensure and then additional licensure in special education. Usually licensure is granted by the State board of education or a licensure advisory committee.

All States require a bachelor's degree and completion of an approved teacher preparation program with a prescribed number of subject and education credits and supervised practice teaching. Many States require special education teachers to obtain a master's degree in special education, involving at least one year of additional coursework, including a specialization, beyond the bachelor's degree.

Some States have reciprocity agreements which allow special education teachers to transfer their licensure from one State to another, but many still require special education teachers to pass licensure requirements for that State. National certification standards for special education teachers are being developed by the National Board for Professional Teaching Standards. Voluntary national certification should be available in 1998.

About 700 colleges and universities across the United States offer programs in special education, including undergraduate, master's, and doctoral programs. Special education teachers usually undergo longer periods of training than general education teachers. Most bachelor's degree programs are 4-year programs that include general and specialized courses in special education. However, an increasing number of institutions require a fifth year or other postbaccalaureate preparation. Courses include educational psychology, legal issues of special education, child growth and development, and knowledge and skills needed for teaching students with disabilities. Some programs require a specialization, such as teaching students with specific learning disabilities. Others offer generalized special education degrees, or study in several specialized areas. The last year of the program is usually spent student teaching in a classroom supervised by a certified teacher.

Alternative and emergency licensure is available in many States due to the need to fill special education teaching positions. Alternative licensure is designed to bring college graduates and those changing careers into teaching more quickly. Requirements for alternative licensure may be less stringent than for regular licensure and vary by State. In some programs, individuals begin teaching quickly under provisional licensure. They can obtain regular licensure by teaching under the supervision of licensed teachers for a period of one to two years while taking education courses. Emergency licensure is enacted when States are having difficulty finding licensed special education teachers to fill positions.

Special education teachers must be able to motivate students, understand their students' special needs, and be accepting of differences in others. Teachers must be creative and apply different types of teaching methods to reach students who are having difficulty. Communication and cooperation are also essential traits since special education teachers spend a great deal of time interacting with others, including students, parents, and school faculty and administrators.

Special education teachers can advance to become supervisors or administrators. They may also earn advanced degrees and become instructors in colleges that prepare other special education teachers. In some school systems, highly experienced teachers can become mentor teachers to less experienced ones. They provide guidance to these teachers while maintaining a light teaching load.

Job Outlook

Special education teachers have excellent job prospects, as many school districts report shortages of qualified teachers. Job outlook varies by geographic area and subject specialty. Positions in rural areas and inner cities are more plentiful than job openings in suburban or wealthy urban areas. Also, job opportunities may be better in certain specialties—such as multiple disabilities, mental retardation, visual impairment, learning disabilities, and preschool special education—due to the considerable shortages of teachers in these fields. Special education teachers who are bilingual or have multicultural experience are also needed to work with an increasingly diverse student population.

Employment of special education teachers is expected to increase much faster than the average for all occupations through the year 2005, spurred by continued growth in the number of special education students needing services, legislation emphasizing training and employment for individuals with disabilities, growing public interest in individuals with special needs, and educational reform. Many job openings also arise when special education teachers switch to general education or change careers altogether. Job openings stemming from rapid employment growth and job turnover, coupled with a declining number of graduates from special education teaching programs, are expected to result in a favorable job market for special education teachers.

The number of students requiring special education services has been steadily increasing, as indicated by the accompanying chart. This trend is expected to continue due to Federal legislation which expanded the age range of special education students to include those ages 3 to 21; medical advances which result in more survivors of accidents and illness; the postponement of childbirth by more women, resulting in a greater number of premature births and children born with birth defects; and the increase in the general population.

The growing use of inclusive school settings, where special education students are integrated into general education settings, will also necessitate more reliance on special education teachers. The role of special education teachers is expanding to include acting as a consultant to general education teachers, in addition to teaching special education students in resource rooms, general education

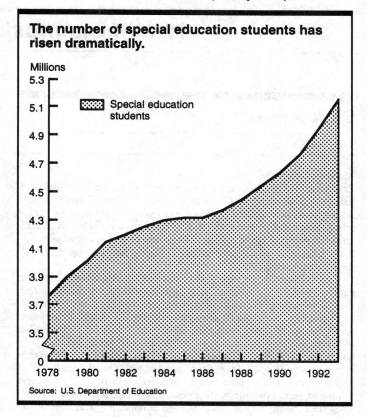

The number of special education students has risen dramatically.

Millions

Special education students

Source: U.S. Department of Education

classrooms, and separate classrooms made up entirely of special education students.

Earnings

Salaries of special education teachers generally follow the same scale as those for general education teachers. According to the National Education Association, the estimated average salary of all teachers was $36,900 in 1995. The estimated average salary for public secondary school teachers was $37,800; public elementary school teachers averaged $36,400. Starting salaries for teachers were in the $20,000 to $25,000 range. Earnings in private schools generally are lower than in public schools.

Related Occupations

Special education teachers work with students who have disabilities and special needs. Other occupations involved with the identification, evaluation, and development of students with disabilities include school psychologists, social workers, speech pathologists, rehabilitation counselors, adapted physical education teachers, and occupational, physical, creative arts, and recreational therapists.

Sources of Additional Information

For information on a career as a special education teacher, a list of accredited schools and financial aid information, and general information on special education-related personnel issues, contact:
☛National Clearinghouse for Professions in Special Education, Council for Exceptional Children, 1920 Association Dr., Reston, VA 22091.

To learn more about the special education teacher certification and licensing requirements in your State, contact your State's department of education.

Health Diagnosing Occupations

Chiropractors

(D.O.T. 079.101-010)

Nature of the Work

Chiropractors, also known as chiropractic doctors, diagnose and treat patients whose health problems are associated with the body's muscular, nervous, and skeletal systems, especially the spine. Chiropractors believe interference with these systems impairs normal functions and lowers resistance to disease. They also hold that spinal or vertebral dysfunction alters many important body functions by affecting the nervous system.

The chiropractic approach to health care is holistic, stressing the patient's overall well-being. It recognizes that many factors affect health, including exercise, diet, rest, environment, and heredity. Chiropractors use natural, drugless, nonsurgical health treatments, and rely on the body's inherent recuperative abilities. They also recommend lifestyle changes—in eating, exercise, and sleeping habits, for example—to their patients. When appropriate, chiropractors consult with and refer patients to other health practitioners.

Like other health practitioners, chiropractors follow a standard routine to secure the information needed for diagnosis and treatment: They take the patient's medical history, conduct physical, neurological, and orthopedic examinations, and may order laboratory tests. X rays and other diagnostic images are important tools because of the emphasis on the spine and its proper function. Chiropractors also employ a postural and spinal analysis unique to chiropractic diagnosis.

In cases where difficulties can be traced to involvement of musculoskeletal structures, chiropractors manually manipulate or adjust the spinal column. Many chiropractors also use water, light, massage, ultrasound, electric, and heat therapy and may apply supports such as straps, tapes, and braces. They may also counsel patients about nutrition, exercise, and stress management, but do not prescribe drugs or perform surgery.

Some chiropractors specialize in sports injuries, neurology, orthopedics, nutrition, internal disorders, or diagnostic imaging.

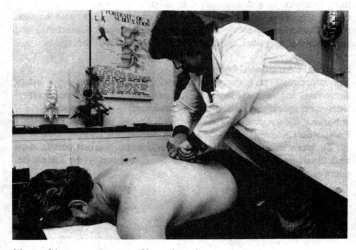

Many chiropractors are self-employed.

Almost all chiropractors are solo or group practitioners who also have the administrative responsibilities of running a practice. In larger offices, chiropractors delegate these tasks to office managers and chiropractic assistants. Chiropractors in private practice are responsible for developing a patient base, hiring employees, and keeping records.

Working Conditions

Chiropractors work in clean, comfortable offices. The average workweek is about 42 hours, although longer hours are not uncommon. Solo practitioners set their own hours, but may work evenings or weekends to accommodate patients.

Chiropractors who take x rays must take appropriate precautions against the dangers of repeated exposure to radiation.

Employment

Chiropractors held about 42,000 jobs in 1994. About 70 percent of active chiropractors are in solo practice. The remainder are in group practice or work for other chiropractors. A small number teach, conduct research at chiropractic colleges, or work in hospitals and HMO's.

Many chiropractors are located in small communities. There are geographic imbalances in the distribution of chiropractors, in part because many establish practices close to colleges of chiropractic.

Training, Other Qualifications, and Advancement

All States and the District of Columbia regulate the practice of chiropractic and grant licenses to chiropractors who meet educational requirements and pass a State board examination. Chiropractors can only practice in States where they are licensed. Some States have reciprocity agreements that permit chiropractors licensed in one State to obtain a license in another without further examination.

Most State licensing boards require completion of a 4-year chiropractic college course following at least 2 years of undergraduate education, although a few States require a bachelor's degree. All State boards recognize academic training in chiropractic colleges accredited by the Council on Chiropractic Education.

For licensure, most State boards recognize either all or part of the three-part test administered by the National Board of Chiropractic Examiners. State examinations may supplement the National Board tests, depending on State requirements.

To maintain licensure, almost all States require completion of a specified number of hours of continuing education each year. Continuing education programs are offered by accredited chiropractic colleges and chiropractic associations. Special councils within some chiropractic associations also offer programs leading to clinical specialty certification, called "diplomate" certification, in areas such as orthopedics, neurology, sports injuries, occupational and industrial health, nutrition, radiology, thermography, and internal disorders.

In 1994, 15 of the 17 chiropractic colleges in the United States were accredited by the Council on Chiropractic Education. All chiropractic colleges require applicants to have at least 2 years of undergraduate study, including courses in English, the social sciences or humanities, organic and inorganic chemistry, biology, physics, and psychology. Many applicants have a bachelors' degree, which may eventually become the minimum entry requirement. Several chiropractic colleges offer prechiropractic study, as well as a bachelors' degree program.

During the first 2 years, most chiropractic colleges emphasize classroom and laboratory work in basic science subjects such as anatomy, physiology, public health, microbiology, pathology, and biochemistry. The last 2 years stress courses in skeletal manipulation and spinal adjustments and provide clinical experience in physical and laboratory diagnosis, neurology, orthopedics, geriatrics, physiotherapy, and nutrition. Colleges grant the degree of Doctor of Chiropractic (D.C.).

Chiropractic requires keen observation to detect physical abnormalities. It also takes considerable hand dexterity to perform manipulations, but not unusual strength or endurance. Chiropractors should be able to work independently and handle responsibility. As in other health-related occupations, empathy, understanding, and the desire to help others are desirable qualities for dealing effectively with patients.

Newly licensed chiropractors can set up a new practice, purchase an established one, or enter into partnership with an established practitioner. They may also take a salaried position with an established chiropractor, a group practice, or a health care facility.

Job Outlook

Employment of chiropractors is expected to grow faster than the average for all occupations through the year 2005. Demand for chiropractic is related to the ability of patients to pay, either directly or through health insurance, and to public awareness of the profession, which is growing. The rapidly expanding older population, with their increased likelihood of mechanical and structural problems, will also increase demand.

In this occupation, replacement needs arise almost entirely from retirements. Chiropractors generally remain in the occupation until they retire; few transfer to other occupations.

Earnings

In 1994, median income for chiropractors was about $75,000, after expenses, according to the American Chiropractic Association. In chiropractic, as in other types of independent practice, earnings are relatively low in the beginning, and increase as the practice grows. In 1994, the lowest 10 percent of chiropractors had median net incomes of $28,000 or less, and the highest 10 percent earned $150,000 or more. Earnings are also influenced by the characteristics and qualifications of the practitioner, and geographic location. Self-employed chiropractors must provide for their own health insurance and retirement.

Related Occupations

Chiropractors diagnose, treat, and work to prevent bodily disorders and injuries. So do physicians, dentists, optometrists, podiatrists, veterinarians, occupational therapists, and physical therapists.

Sources of Additional Information

General information on chiropractic as a career is available from:

☛American Chiropractic Association, 1701 Clarendon Blvd., Arlington, VA 22209.

☛International Chiropractors Association, 1110 North Glebe Rd., Suite 1000, Arlington, VA 22201.

☛World Chiropractic Alliance, 2950 N. Dobson Rd., Suite 1, Chandler, AZ 85224-1802.

For a list of chiropractic colleges, as well as general information on chiropractic as a career, contact:

☛Council on Chiropractic Education, 7975 North Hayden Rd., Suite A-210, Scottsdale, AZ 85258.

For information on State education and licensure requirements, contact:

☛Federation of Chiropractic Licensing Boards, 901 54th Ave., Suite 101, Greeley, CO 80634.

For information on requirements for admission to a specific chiropractic college, as well as scholarship and loan information, contact the admissions office of the individual college.

Dentists

(D.O.T. 072, except .117)

Nature of the Work

Dentists diagnose, prevent, and treat problems of the teeth and tissues of the mouth. They remove decay and fill cavities, examine x rays, place protective plastic sealants on children's teeth, straighten teeth, and repair fractured teeth. They also perform corrective surgery of the gums and supporting bones to treat gum diseases. Dentists extract teeth and make molds and measurements for dentures to replace missing teeth. Dentists provide instruction in diet, brushing, flossing, the use of fluorides, and other aspects of dental care, as well. They also administer anesthetics and write prescriptions for antibiotics and other medications.

Dentists use a variety of equipment including x-ray machines, drills, and instruments such as mouth mirrors, probes, forceps, brushes, and scalpels.

Dentists in private practice oversee a variety of administrative tasks, including bookkeeping, and buying equipment and supplies. They may employ and supervise dental hygienists, dental assistants, dental laboratory technicians, and receptionists. (These occupations are described elsewhere in the *Handbook.*)

Most dentists are general practitioners who handle a wide variety of dental needs. Other dentists practice in one of eight specialty areas. Orthodontists, the largest group of specialists, straighten teeth. The next largest group, oral and maxillofacial surgeons, operate on the mouth and jaws. The remainder specialize in pediatric dentistry (dentistry for children); periodontics (treating the gums and the bone supporting the teeth); prosthodontics (making artificial teeth or dentures); endodontics (root canal therapy); dental public health; and oral pathology (studying diseases of the mouth).

Working Conditions

Most dentists work 4 or 5 days a week. Some dentists work evenings and weekends to meet their patients' needs. Most full-time dentists work about 40 hours a week; some worked more. Younger dentists may work fewer hours as they establish their practice, while older dentists often work fewer hours. A considerable number continue in part-time practice well beyond the usual retirement age.

Most dentists are "solo practitioners," that is they own their own businesses and work alone or with a small staff. Some dentists have partners, and a few work for other dentists as associate dentists.

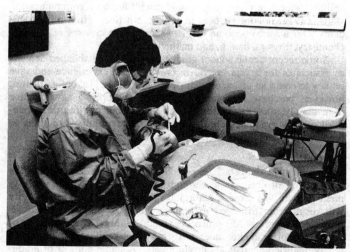

Most dentists own their own businesses and work alone or with a small staff.

Dentists wear masks, gloves, and safety glasses to protect themselves and their patients from infectious diseases like hepatitis.

Employment

Dentists held about 164,000 jobs in 1994. About 9 out of 10 dentists are in private practice. Others work in private and public hospitals and clinics, and in dental research.

Training, Other Qualifications, and Advancement

All 50 States and the District of Columbia require dentists to be licensed. To qualify for a license in most States, a candidate must graduate from a dental school accredited by the American Dental Association's Commission on Dental Accreditation and pass written and practical examinations. Candidates may fulfill the written part of the State licensing by passing the National Board Dental Examinations. Individual States or regional testing agencies give the written and/or practical examinations.

Currently, about 17 States require dentists to obtain a specialty license before practicing as a specialist. Requirements include 2 to 4 years of post graduate education and, in some cases, completion of a special State examination. Most State licenses permit dentists to engage in both general and specialized practice. Dentists who want to teach or do research usually spend an additional 2 to 5 years in advanced dental training in programs operated by dental schools or hospitals.

Dental schools require a minimum of 2 years of college-level predental education. However, most dental students have at least a bachelor's degree. Predental education emphasizes course work in the sciences.

All dental schools require applicants to take the Dental Admissions Test (DAT). They consider scores earned on the DAT, the applicants' overall grade point average (GPA), science course GPA, and information gathered through recommendations and interviews when selecting students.

Dental school generally lasts 4 academic years. Studies begin with classroom instruction and laboratory work in basic sciences including anatomy, microbiology, biochemistry, and physiology. Beginning courses in clinical sciences, including laboratory technique courses, also are provided at this time. During the last 2 years, students treat patients, usually in dental clinics under the supervision of licensed dentists.

Most dental schools award the degree of Doctor of Dental Surgery (D.D.S). The rest award an equivalent degree, Doctor of Dental Medicine (D.M.D.).

Dentistry requires diagnostic ability and manual skills. Dentists should have good visual memory, excellent judgment of space and shape, and a high degree of manual dexterity, as well as scientific ability. Good business sense, self-discipline, and communication skills, are helpful for success in private practice. High school students who want to become dentists should take courses in biology, chemistry, physics, health, and mathematics.

Some recent dental school graduates work for established dentists as associates for a year or two in order to gain experience and save money to equip an office of their own. Most dental school graduates, however, purchase an established practice or open a new practice immediately after graduation. Each year about one-fourth to one-third of new graduates enroll in postgraduate training programs to prepare for a dental specialty.

Job Outlook

Employment of dentists is expected to grow more slowly than the average for all occupations through the year 2005. While employment growth will provide some job opportunities, the vast majority will result from the need to replace the large number of dentists projected to retire. Job prospects should be good if the number of dental school graduates does not grow thus keeping the supply of newly qualified dentists at current levels. A stable number of graduates is consistent with data showing that first-year enrollees in dental school programs have changed little since the late-1980s.

Demand for dental care should grow substantially through 2005. As members of the baby boom generation advance into middle age, a large number will need maintenance on complicated dental work like bridges. Plus, elderly people are more likely to retain their teeth than their predecessors, so they will require much more care than in the past. The younger generation will continue to need preventive check-ups despite treatments like fluoridation of the water supply which decrease the incidence of dental caries.

However, the employment of dentists is not expected to grow as rapidly as the demand for dental services. As their practices expand, dentists are likely to hire more dental hygienists and dental assistants to handle routine services that they now perform themselves.

Earnings

The net median income of dentists in private practice was about $100,000 a year in 1994, according to the American Dental Association. Net median income of those in specialty practices was about $132,500 a year, and for those in general practice, $97,450 a year. Dentists in the beginning years of their practice often earn less, while those in mid-careers earn more.

A relatively large proportion of dentists are self-employed. Like other business owners, these dentists must provide their own health insurance, life insurance, and retirement benefits.

Related Occupations

Dentists examine, diagnose, prevent, and treat diseases and abnormalities. So do clinical psychologists, optometrists, physicians, chiropractors, veterinarians, and podiatrists.

Sources of Additional Information

For information on dentistry as a career and a list of accredited dental schools, contact:

☛American Dental Association, Department of Career Guidance, 211 E. Chicago Ave., Chicago, IL 60611.

☛American Association of Dental Schools, 1625 Massachusetts Ave. NW., Washington, DC 20036.

The American Dental Association also will furnish a list of State boards of dental examiners. Persons interested in practicing dentistry should obtain the requirements for licensure from the board of dental examiners of the State where they plan to work.

Prospective dental students should contact the office of student financial aid at the schools to which they apply for information on scholarships, grants, and loans, including Federal financial aid.

Optometrists

(D.O.T. 079.101-018)

Nature of the Work

Over half the people in the United States wear glasses or contact lenses. Optometrists (doctors of optometry, also known as O.D.'s) provide most of the primary vision care people need.

Optometrists examine people's eyes to diagnose vision problems and eye diseases. They treat vision problems, and in most States, they treat certain eye diseases such as conjunctivitis, glaucoma, or corneal infections. Optometrists use instruments and observation to examine eye health and to test patients' visual acuity, depth and color perception, and their ability to focus and coordinate the eyes. They analyze test results and develop a treatment plan. Optometrists prescribe eyeglasses, contact lenses, and vision therapy. They use drugs for diagnosis in all States and, as of 1995, may use topical and oral drugs to treat some eye diseases in 46 States. Optometrists often provide postoperative care to cataract and other eye surgery patients. When optometrists diagnose conditions that require care beyond the optometric scope of practice such as diabetes or high blood pressure, they refer patients to other health practitioners.

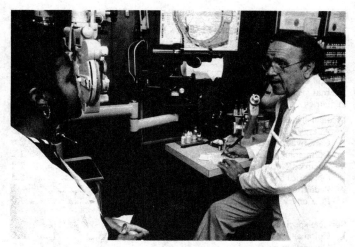

Optometrists examine people's eyes to diagnose vision problems and eye disease.

Optometrists should not be confused with ophthalmologists or dispensing opticians. Ophthalmologists are physicians who diagnose and treat eye diseases and injuries. They perform surgery and prescribe drugs. Like optometrists, they also examine eyes and prescribe eyeglasses and contact lenses. Dispensing opticians fit and adjust eyeglasses and in some States may fit contact lenses according to prescriptions written by ophthalmologists or optometrists. (See statements on physicians and dispensing opticians elsewhere in the *Handbook*.)

Most optometrists are in general practice. Some specialize in work with the elderly, children, or partially sighted persons who need specialized visual aids to improve their vision. Others develop and implement ways to protect workers' eyes from on-the-job strain or injury. Some specialize in contact lenses, sports vision, or vision therapy. A few teach optometry, do research, or consult.

Most optometrists are private practitioners who also handle the business aspects of running an office, such as developing a patient base, hiring employees, keeping records, and ordering equipment and supplies. Optometrists who operate franchise optical stores may also have some of these duties.

Working Conditions

Optometrists work in places—usually their own offices—that are clean, well lighted, and comfortable. The work requires attention to detail and manual dexterity. Most full-time optometrists work about 40 hours a week, but a substantial number work more than 50 hours a week. Many work Saturdays and evenings to suit the needs of patients, but emergency calls are few.

Employment

Optometrists held about 37,000 jobs in 1994. The number of jobs is greater than the number of practicing optometrists because some optometrists hold two or more jobs. For example, an optometrist may have a private practice, but also work in another practice, clinic, or vision care center. About one-half of all optometrists are self-employed.

Although many optometrists practice alone, a growing number are in a partnership or group practice. Some optometrists work as salaried employees of other optometrists or of ophthalmologists, hospitals, health maintenance organizations (HMO's), or retail optical stores. A small number of optometrists are consultants for industrial safety programs, insurance companies, manufacturers of ophthalmic products, HMO's, and others.

Training, Other Qualifications, and Advancement

All States and the District of Columbia require that optometrists be licensed. Applicants for a license must have a Doctor of Optometry degree from an accredited optometry school and pass both a written and a clinical State board examination. In many States, applicants can substitute the examinations of the National Board of Examiners in Optometry, usually taken during the student's academic career, for part or all of the written examination. Licenses are renewed every 1 to 2 years and in most States, continuing education credits are needed for renewal.

The Doctor of Optometry degree requires completion of a 4-year program at an accredited optometry school preceded by at least 3 years of preoptometric study at an accredited college or university (most optometry students hold a bachelor's degree). In 1995, 17 U.S. schools and colleges of optometry were accredited by the Council on Optometric Education of the American Optometric Association.

Requirements for admission to schools of optometry include courses in English, mathematics, physics, chemistry, and biology. A few schools require or recommend courses in psychology, history, sociology, speech, or business. Applicants must take the Optometry Admissions Test (OAT), which measures academic ability and scientific comprehension. Most applicants take the test after their sophomore or junior year. Competition for admission is keen.

Optometry programs include classroom and laboratory study of health and visual sciences, as well as clinical training in the diagnosis and treatment of eye disorders. Included are courses in pharmacology, optics, vision science, biochemistry, and systemic disease.

Business ability, self-discipline, and the ability to deal tactfully with patients are important for success.

Optometrists wishing to teach or do research may study for a master's or Ph.D. degree in visual science, physiological optics, neurophysiology, public health, health administration, health information and communication, or health education. One-year postgraduate clinical residency programs are available for optometrists who wish to specialize in family practice optometry, pediatric optometry, geriatric optometry, vision therapy, contact lenses, hospital based optometry, primary care optometry, or ocular disease.

Job Outlook

Employment of optometrists is expected to grow about as fast as the average for all occupations through the year 2005 in response to the vision care needs of a growing and aging population. The maturing of the baby-boom generation, together with rapid growth in the oldest age group will drive this growth. As baby boomers reach the age of 45 they will be more likely to visit optometrists and ophthalmologists because of the onset of vision problems in middle age. The demand for optometric services will also increase because of growth in the oldest age group, with their increased likelihood of cataracts, glaucoma, diabetes, and hypertension. Employment of optometrists will also grow due to greater recognition of the importance of vision care, rising personal incomes, and growth in employee vision care plans.

Employment of optometrists would grow more rapidly were it not for anticipated productivity gains which will allow each optometrist to see more patients. These gains will result from greater use of optometric assistants and other support personnel, and the introduction of new equipment and procedures.

Replacement needs are low. In this occupation, replacement needs arise almost entirely from retirements. Optometrists generally remain in practice until they retire; few transfer to other occupations.

Earnings

According to the American Optometric Association, new optometry graduates in their first year of practice earned median net incomes of about $55,500 in 1994. Overall, optometrists earned median net incomes of about $80,000.

Incomes vary depending upon location, specialization, and other factors. Salaried optometrists tend to earn more initially than optometrists who set up their own independent practice. In the long run, those in private practice generally earn more.

Related Occupations

Workers in other occupations who apply scientific knowledge to prevent, diagnose, and treat disorders and injuries are chiropractors, dentists, physicians, podiatrists, veterinarians, speech-language pathologists, and audiologists.

Sources of Additional Information

For information on optometry as a career and a listing of accredited optometric educational institutions, as well as required preoptometry courses write to:

☛American Optometric Association, Educational Services, 243 North Lindbergh Blvd., St. Louis, MO 63141-7881.

☛Association of Schools and Colleges of Optometry, 6110 Executive Blvd., Suite 690, Rockville, MD 20852.

The Board of Optometry in each State can supply information on licensing requirements.

For information on specific admission requirements and sources of financial aid, contact the admissions officer of individual optometry schools.

Physicians

(D.O.T. 070 and 071)

Nature of the Work

Physicians serve a fundamental role in our society and have an effect upon all our lives. They diagnose illnesses, and prescribe and administer treatment for people suffering from injury or disease. Physicians examine patients; obtain medical histories; and order, perform, and interpret diagnostic tests. They counsel patients on diet, hygiene, and preventive health care. They may be part of a team that coordinates care for a population of patients.

There are two types of physicians: The M.D.—Doctor of Medicine—and the D.O.—Doctor of Osteopathic Medicine. M.D.'s are also known as allopathic physicians. While M.D.'s and D.O.'s may use all accepted methods of treatment, including drugs and surgery, D.O.'s place special emphasis on the body's musculoskeletal system. They believe that good health requires proper alignment of bones, muscles, ligaments, and nerves. D.O's use osteopathic manipulative techniques to diagnose and treat patients.

About one third of M.D.'s are primary care physicians—pediatricians, general and family practitioners, or general internists—who are usually the first health professionals patients consult. They tend to see the same patients on a regular basis for preventive care and to treat a variety of ailments. When appropriate, they refer patients to other specialists (See table 1.) D.O.'s are more likely to be primary care providers than allopathic physicians, although they can be found in all specialties.

Working Conditions

Many physicians work long, irregular hours. About one-half of all full-timers in 1994 worked 60 hours a week or more. In general, as doctors approach retirement age, they may accept fewer new patients and tend to work shorter hours. Physicians who are on-call may make emergency visits to hospitals. Increasingly, physicians are practicing in groups or health care organizations that provide back-up coverage and allow for more time off. Many physicians must travel frequently between office and hospital to care for their patients.

Table 1. Percent distribution of M.D.'s by specialty, 1993

	Percent
Total	100.0
General and family practice	10.7
Internal medicine	16.5
Pediatrics	6.9
Medical specialties	
Allergy	.5
Cardiovascular diseases	2.6
Dermatology	1.2
Gastroenterology	1.2
Obstetrics and gynecology	5.3
Pediatric cardiology	.2
Pulmonary diseases	1.0
Surgical specialties	
Colon and rectal surgery	.1
General surgery	5.7
Neurological surgery	.7
Ophthalmology	2.5
Orthopedic surgery	3.1
Otalaryngology	1.3
Plastic surgery	.7
Thoracic surgery	.3
Urological surgery	1.4
Other specialties	
Aerospace medicine	.1
Anesthesiology	4.4
Child psychiatry	.7
Diagnostic radiology	2.8
Emergency medicine	2.4
Forensic pathology	.1
General preventive medicine	.2
Neurology	1.5
Nuclear medicine	.2
Occupational medicine	.4
Pathology	2.6
Physical medicine and rehabilitation	.7
Psychiatry	5.5
Public health	.3
Radiology	1.1
Radiation oncology	.5
Other specialty	1.1
Unspecified/unknown/inactive	13.4

SOURCE: American Medical Association

Employment

Physicians (M.D.'s and D.O.'s) held about 539,000 jobs in 1994. About 2 out of 3 were in office-based practice, including clinics and HMO's; about one-quarter were employed in hospitals. Others practiced in the Federal Government, most in Department of Veterans Affairs hospitals and clinics or in the Public Health Service of the Department of Health and Human Services.

A growing number of physicians are partners or salaried employees of group practices. Organized as clinics or as groups of physicians, medical groups can afford expensive medical equipment and realize other business advantages.

The Northeast and West have the highest ratio of physicians to population; the South, the lowest. D.O.'s are more likely than M.D.'s to practice in small cities and towns and in rural areas. M.D.'s tend to locate in urban areas, close to hospital and educational centers. Some rural and inner city areas remain underserved, although the situation has improved.

Osteopathic physicians locate chiefly in States that have osteopathic schools and hospitals. In 1995, 3 out of 4 D.O.'s practiced in 12 States. Michigan had the most D.O.'s, followed by Pennsylvania, Ohio, Florida, New Jersey, and Texas.

Job prospects are good for primary care physicians such as family practitioners and internists.

Training and Other Qualifications

It usually takes about 11 years to become a physician: 4 years of undergraduate school, 4 years of medical school, and 3 years in residency. However, a few medical schools offer a combined college and medical school program that lasts 6 years instead of the customary 8 years. For some specialties, residency may take longer, up to 8 years.

Premedical students must complete undergraduate work in physics, biology, mathematics, English, and inorganic and organic chemistry. Students should also take courses in humanities and the social sciences. Applicants may also want to volunteer at a local hospital or clinic to gain practical experience in the health professions.

The minimum educational requirement for entry to a medical or osteopathic school is 3 years of college; most applicants, however, have at least a bachelor's degree, and many have advanced degrees. There are 141 medical schools in the United States—125 teach allopathic medicine and award a Doctor of Medicine (M.D.); 16 teach osteopathic medicine and award the Doctor of Osteopathy (D.O.). Acceptance to medical school is very competitive. Applicants must submit transcripts, scores from the Medical College Admission Test (MCAT), and letters of recommendation. Most schools require an interview with an admissions officer. Schools also consider character, personality, leadership qualities, and participation in extracurricular activities.

Students spend most of the first 2 years of medical school in laboratories and classrooms taking courses such as anatomy, biochemistry, physiology, pharmacology, psychology, microbiology, pathology, medical ethics, and laws governing medicine. They also learn to take medical histories, examine patients, and recognize symptoms. During the last 2 years, students work with patients under the supervision of experienced physicians in hospitals and clinics to learn acute, chronic, preventive, and rehabilitative care. Through rotations in internal medicine, family practice, obstetrics and gynecology, pediatrics, psychiatry, and surgery, they gain experience in the diagnosis and treatment of illness.

Following medical school, almost all M.D.'s go directly on to graduate medical education, called a residency. All students, including foreign medical school graduates, applying for licensure—a requirement for the job of resident—take a standard examination. Most D.O.'s serve a 12-month rotating internship after graduation. The National Board of Osteopathic Medical Examiners gives an examination for internship application. Following their internship, many D.O.'s take a residency program in a specialty area.

All States, the District of Columbia, and U.S. territories license physicians. To be licensed, physicians must graduate from an accredited medical school, pass a licensing examination, and complete

1 to 7 years of graduate medical education—a residency for M.D.'s and an internship and residency for D.O.'s. Although physicians licensed in one State can usually get a license to practice in another without further examination, some States limit reciprocity. Graduates of foreign medical schools can qualify for licensure after passing an examination and completing a U.S. hospital residency training program.

M.D.'s and D.O.'s seeking board certification in a specialty may spend up to 7 years—depending on the specialty—in residency training. A final examination immediately after residency, or after 1 or 2 years of practice, is also necessary for board certification by the American Board of Medical Specialists (ABMS) or the American Osteopathic Association (AOA). There are 24 specialty boards: Allergy and immunology; anesthesiology; colon and rectal surgery; dermatology; emergency medicine; family practice; internal medicine; neurological surgery; nuclear medicine; obstetrics and gynecology; ophthalmology; orthopedic surgery; otolaryngology; pathology; pediatrics; physical medicine and rehabilitation; plastic surgery; preventive medicine; psychiatry and neurology; radiology; surgery; thoracic surgery; and urology. For those training in a subspecialty, another 1 to 2 years of residency is usual.

To teach or do research, physicians may need a master's or Ph.D. in such fields as biochemistry or microbiology. They may otherwise spend 1 year or more in research or in an advanced clinical training fellowship.

A physician's training is costly. While education costs have increased, student financial assistance has not. Over 80 percent of medical students borrow money to cover their expenses.

People who wish to become physicians must have a desire to serve patients, be self-motivated, and be able to survive the pressures and long hours of medical education and practice. Prospective physicians must also be willing to study throughout their career to keep up with medical advances. Physicians should have a good bedside manner, emotional stability, and the ability to make decisions in emergencies.

Job Outlook

Employment of physicians is expected to grow faster than the average for all occupations through the year 2005 due to continued expansion of the health industry. New technologies permit more intensive care: Physicians can do more tests, perform more procedures, and treat conditions previously regarded as untreatable. In addition, the population is growing and aging, and health care needs increase sharply with age. The need to replace physicians is lower than for most occupations because almost all physicians remain in the profession until they retire.

Job prospects are good for primary care physicians such as family practitioners and internists, and for geriatric and preventive care specialists. Because of efforts to control health care costs and increased reliance on utilization guidelines that often limit the use of specialty services, a lower percentage of specialists will be in demand. Some shortages have been reported in the specialty area of general surgery, and in some rural and low income areas. This is because physicians find these areas unattractive due to low earnings potential, isolation from medical colleagues, or other reasons, not because of any overall shortage.

Some health care analysts believe that there is, or that there soon could be a general oversupply of physicians; others disagree. In analyzing job prospects, it should be kept in mind that an oversupply may not necessarily limit the ability of physicians to find employment or to set up and maintain a practice. It could result in physicians delegating fewer tasks and working fewer hours. Physicians might be able to spend more time with each patient, give more attention to preventive care, and provide more services in rural and poor areas. It is also possible that physicians trained in specialties would provide services outside their specialty area.

Unlike their predecessors, newly trained physicians face radically different choices of where and how to practice. Many new physicians are less likely to enter solo practice and more likely to take salaried jobs in group medical practices, clinics, and HMO's in order to have regular work hours and the opportunity for peer consultation. Others will take salaried positions simply because they cannot afford the high costs of establishing a private practice while paying off student loans.

Earnings

Physicians have among the highest earnings of any occupation. According to the American Medical Association, average (mean) income, after expenses, for allopathic physicians was about $189,300 in 1993, and median income was $156,000. The middle 50 percent earned between $108,000 and $240,000. Self-employed physicians–those who own or are part owners of their medical practice–had higher median incomes than salaried physicians. Earnings vary according to number of years in practice; geographic region; hours worked; and skill, personality, and professional reputation. As shown in table 2, median income of allopathic physicians, after expenses, also varies by specialty.

Table 2. Median net income of M.D.'s after expenses, 1993

All physicians	$156,000
Radiology	240,000
Surgery	225,000
Anesthesiology	220,000
Obstetrics/gynecology	200,000
Pathology	170,000
Emergency medicine	164,000
Internal medicine	150,000
Psychiatry	120,000
Pediatrics	120,000
General/Family practice	110,000

SOURCE: American Medical Association

Average salaries of medical residents ranged from $30,753 in 1994-95 for those in their first year of residency to $41,895 for those in their eighth year, according to the Association of American Medical Colleges.

Related Occupations

Physicians work to prevent, diagnose, and treat diseases, disorders, and injuries. Professionals in other occupations that require similar kinds of skill and critical judgment include acupuncturists, audiologists, chiropractors, dentists, nurse practitioners, optometrists, podiatrists, speech pathologists, and veterinarians.

Sources of Additional Information

For a list of allopathic medical schools, as well as general information on premedical education, financial aid, and medicine as a career, contact:

☛American Medical Association, 515 N. State St., Chicago, IL 60610.

☛Association of American Medical Colleges, Section for Student Services, 2450 N St. NW., Washington, DC 20037-1131.

For general information on osteopathic medicine as a career, contact:

☛American Osteopathic Association, Department of Public Relations, 142 East Ontario St., Chicago, IL 60611.

☛American Association of Colleges of Osteopathic Medicine, 6110 Executive Blvd., Suite 405, Rockville, MD 20852.

Information on Federal scholarships and loans is available from the directors of student financial aid at schools of allopathic and osteopathic medicine.

Information on licensing is available from State boards of examiners.

Podiatrists

(D.O.T. 079.101-022)

Nature of the Work

The human foot is a complex structure. It contains 26 bones—plus muscles, nerves, ligaments, and blood vessels—and is designed for balance and mobility. Podiatrists, also known as doctors of podiatric medicine (DPM's), diagnose and treat disorders, diseases and injuries of the foot and lower leg to keep this part of the body working properly.

Podiatrists treat corns, calluses, ingrown toenails, bunions, heel spurs, and arch problems; ankle and foot injuries, deformities and infections; and foot complaints associated with diseases such as diabetes. To treat these problems, podiatrists prescribe drugs, order physical therapy, set fractures, and perform surgery. They also fit corrective inserts called orthotics, design plaster casts and strappings to correct deformities, and design custom-made shoes. Podiatrists may use a force plate to help design the orthotics and shoes. Patients walk across a plate connected to a computer that "reads" the patients' feet. From the computer readout, podiatrists order the correct design.

To diagnose a foot problem, podiatrists order x rays and laboratory tests. The foot may be the first area to show signs of serious conditions such as arthritis, diabetes, and heart disease. For example, diabetics are prone to foot ulcers and infections due to their poor circulation. Podiatrists consult with and refer patients to other health practitioners when they detect symptoms of these disorders.

Most podiatrists have a general practice. Some specialize in surgery, orthopedics, or public health. Besides these certified specialties, podiatrists may practice a subspecialty such as sports medicine, pediatrics, dermatology, radiology, geriatrics, or diabetic foot care. Podiatrists generally are in private practice, which means that they run a small business. They may hire employees, order supplies, and keep records.

Working Conditions

Podiatrists usually work independently in their own offices. They may also spend time visiting patients in nursing homes or performing surgery at a hospital. Those with private practices set their own hours, but to meet the needs of their patients, they may work evenings and weekends.

Employment

Podiatrists held about 13,000 jobs in 1994. Most podiatrists are solo practitioners, although more are entering partnerships and multi-

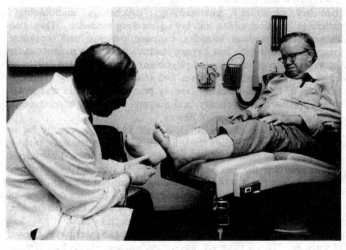

Most podiatrists are solo practitioners.

specialty group practices. Others are employed in hospitals, nursing homes, and offices and clinics of physicians, including health maintenance organizations (HMO's). Public health departments employ podiatrists, too.

Geographic imbalances are pronounced in podiatric medicine. Most podiatry graduates establish their practices in or near one of the seven States that have colleges of podiatric medicine—California, Florida, Illinois, Iowa, New York, Pennsylvania, and Ohio. Large areas of the country—particularly the South, the Southwest, and nonmetropolitan areas—have few podiatrists. In these areas, foot care is typically provided by primary care physicians and orthopedists.

Training, Other Qualifications, and Advancement

All States and the District of Columbia require a license for the practice of podiatric medicine. Each defines its own licensing requirements. Generally, the applicant must be a graduate of an accredited college of podiatric medicine and pass written and oral examinations. Some States permit applicants to substitute the examination of the National Board of Podiatric Examiners, given in the second and fourth years of podiatric medical college, for part or all of the written State examination. Thirty-two States also require completion of an accredited residency program. Certain States grant reciprocity to podiatrists who are licensed in another State. Thirty-eight States require continuing education for licensure renewal.

Prerequisites for admission to a college of podiatric medicine include the completion of at least 90 semester hours of undergraduate study, an acceptable grade point average, and suitable scores on the Medical College Admission Test (MCAT). All require 8 semester hours each of biology, inorganic chemistry, organic chemistry, and physics and 6 hours of English. Over 90 percent of podiatric students have a bachelor's degree.

Colleges of podiatric medicine offer a 4-year program whose core curriculum is similar to that in other schools of medicine. During the first 2 years, students receive classroom instruction in basic sciences, including anatomy, chemistry, pathology, and pharmacology. Third- and fourth-year students have clinical rotations in private practices, hospitals, and clinics. During these rotations, they learn how to take general and podiatric histories, perform routine physical examinations, interpret tests and findings, make diagnoses, and perform therapeutic procedures. Graduates receive the doctor of podiatric medicine (DPM) degree.

Most graduates complete a hospital residency program after receiving a DPM. Residency programs last from 1 to 3 years. Residents receive advanced training in podiatric medicine and surgery and serve clinical rotations in anesthesiology, internal medicine, pathology, radiology, emergency medicine, and orthopedic and general surgery. Residencies lasting more than 1 year provide more extensive training in specialty areas.

There are a number of certifying boards for podiatric specialties. Certification means that the DPM meets higher standards than those required for licensure. Each board requires advanced training, completion of written and oral examinations, and experience as a practicing podiatrist.

People planning a career in podiatry should have scientific aptitude, manual dexterity, interpersonal skills, and good business sense.

Podiatrists may advance to become professors at colleges of podiatric medicine, department chiefs of hospitals, or general health administrators. They may also enter a higher degree program.

Job Outlook

Employment of podiatrists is expected to grow about as fast as the average for all occupations through the year 2005. More people will turn to podiatrists for foot care as the elderly population grows. The elderly have more years of wear and tear on their feet and lower legs than most younger people, so they are more prone to foot ailments.

In addition to growth, the need to replace podiatrists who leave the occupation will create employment opportunities. Relatively few opportunities from this source are expected, however, since most podiatrists continue to practice until they retire; few transfer to other occupations. Even when combined, the number of job openings resulting from both growth and replacement needs is very low because the occupation is small.

Like dental services, podiatric care is more dependent on disposable income than other medical services. Medicare and most private health insurance programs cover acute medical and surgical foot services, as well as diagnostic x rays and leg braces. However, routine foot care—including the removal of corns and calluses—is ordinarily not covered. Because disposable income is expected to rise, more people are expected to pay for podiatric care out-of-pocket.

Establishing a new podiatric practice will be most difficult in the areas surrounding the seven colleges of podiatric medicine and in the Northeast since podiatrists are concentrated in these locations. Newly trained podiatrists will be more likely to work in group medical practices, clinics, and HMO's than in a traditional solo practice.

Earnings

According to a survey by *Podiatry Management*, median net income of podiatrists was about $95,600 in 1994. Earnings vary according to practice size and location, and years of experience.

Related Occupations

Workers in other occupations who apply scientific knowledge to prevent, diagnose, and treat disorders and injuries are chiropractors, dentists, optometrists, physicians, and veterinarians.

Sources of Additional Information

For information on podiatric medicine as a career, contact:

☛American Podiatric Medical Association, 9312 Old Georgetown Rd., Bethesda, MD 20814-1621.

Information on colleges of podiatric medicine, entrance requirements, curriculums, and student financial aid is available from:

☛American Association of Colleges of Podiatric Medicine, 1350 Piccard Dr., Suite 322, Rockville, MD 20850-4307.

Veterinarians

(D.O.T. 073.)

Nature of the Work

Veterinarians care for pets, livestock, sporting and laboratory animals, and protect humans against diseases carried by animals. Veterinarians diagnose medical problems, dress wounds, set broken bones, perform surgery, prescribe and administer medicines, and vaccinate animals against diseases. They also advise owners on care and breeding.

Most veterinarians are in private practice. Some have a general practice, treating all kinds of animals. The majority, however, just treat small companion animals such as dogs, cats, and birds. Others treat both small and larger animals, and some treat only large animals, such as cattle and horses.

Veterinarians in companion animal medicine provide services in over 20,000 animal hospitals or clinics.

Veterinarians for large animals treat and care for cattle, horses, sheep, and swine. They also advise ranchers and farmers on the care, breeding, and management of livestock. Others specialize in fish and poultry.

Veterinarians contribute to human as well as animal health. A number of veterinarians engage in research, food safety inspection, or education. Some work with physicians and scientists on research to prevent and treat diseases in humans. Veterinarians are also in regulatory medicine or public health. Those who are livestock inspectors

Most veterinarians are in private practice.

check animals for disease, advise owners on treatment, and may quarantine animals. Veterinarians who are meat inspectors examine slaughtering and processing plants, check live animals and carcasses for disease, and enforce government food purity as well as sanitation regulations. Some veterinarians care for zoo or aquarium animals or for laboratory animals.

Veterinarians help prevent the outbreak and spread of animal diseases, some of which—like rabies—can be transmitted to humans, and perform autopsies on diseased animals. Some specialize in epidemiology or animal pathology to control diseases transmitted through food animals and to deal with problems of residues from herbicides, pesticides, and antibiotics in animals used for food.

Working Conditions

Veterinarians usually treat pets in hospitals and clinics. Often these facilities are noisy. Those in large animal practice usually work out of well-equipped mobile clinics and may drive considerable distances to farms and ranches. They may work outdoors in all kinds of weather. Veterinarians can be exposed to disease and infection and may be kicked, bitten, or scratched.

Most veterinarians work 50 or more hours a week, however, about a fifth worked 40 hours. Those in private practice may work nights and weekends.

Employment

Veterinarians held about 56,000 jobs in 1994. About a third was self-employed, in solo or group practices. Most others were employees of a practice. The Federal Government employed about 2,800 civilian veterinarians, chiefly in the U.S. Departments of Agriculture, Defense, and Health and Human Services. Other employers of veterinarians are State and local governments, colleges of veterinary medicine, medical schools, research laboratories, animal food companies, and pharmaceutical companies. A few veterinarians work for zoos. Most veterinarians caring for zoo animals are private practitioners who contract with zoos to provide services, usually on a part-time basis.

Training, Other Qualifications, and Advancement

All States and the District of Columbia require that veterinarians be licensed. To obtain a license, applicants must have a Doctor of Veterinary Medicine (D.V.M. or V.M.D.) degree from an accredited college of veterinary medicine and pass a State board examination. The majority of States allow an individual to apply for licensure upon receiving the D.V.M. degree without a residency and without completing a prescribed number of hours of practice. Some States issue licenses without further examination to veterinarians already licensed by another State.

For research and teaching jobs, a master's or Ph.D. degree usually is required. Veterinarians who seek specialty certification in a field such as ophthalmology, pathology, surgery, radiology, or laboratory animal medicine must complete a 3-year residency program, and pass an examination.

The D.V.M. degree requires a minimum of 6 years of college consisting of at least 2 years of preveterinary study that emphasizes the physical and biological sciences and a 4-year veterinary program. Most successful applicants to veterinary programs have completed 4 years of college. In addition to academic instruction, training includes clinical experience in diagnosing and treating animal diseases, performing surgery, and performing laboratory work in anatomy, biochemistry, and other scientific and medical subjects.

In 1994, all 27 colleges of veterinary medicine were accredited by the Council on Education of the American Veterinary Medical Association (AVMA). Admission is highly competitive. There are approximately 3.5 applicants for every position. Applicants usually have grades of "B" or better, especially in sciences. Applicants must take the Veterinary Aptitude Test, Medical College Admission Test, or the Graduate Record Examination and submit evidence they have experience working with animals. Colleges usually give preference to in-State applicants, because most are State supported. There are regional educational agreements in which States without veterinary schools send students to designated regional schools. In other areas, schools give preference to applicants from nearby States that do not have veterinary schools.

To meet State licensure requirements, foreign-trained veterinarians must fulfill the English language and clinical evaluation requirements of the Educational Commission for Foreign Veterinary Graduates.

Most veterinarians begin as employees or partners in established practices. With experience, they may set up their own practice or purchase an established one.

Newly trained veterinarians may become U.S. Government meat and poultry inspectors, disease-control workers, epidemiologists, research assistants, or commissioned officers in the U.S. Public Health Service. A State license may be required.

Veterinarians need good manual dexterity. They should be able to calm animals that are upset, and get along with animal owners, and be able to make decisions in emergencies.

Job Outlook

The outlook for veterinarians is good, especially for those with specialty training in toxicology, laboratory animal medicine, animal behavior, or pathology. Prospects for veterinarians who specialize in farm animals are also better than average because most veterinarians prefer working in metropolitan areas.

Employment of veterinarians is expected to grow about as fast as the average for all occupations through the year 2005. The number of pets is expected to show a steady increase because of rising incomes and the movement of baby boomers into the 34-59 year age group, for which pet ownership is highest. Pet owners may also more willingly pay for more intensive care than in the past. In addition, emphasis on scientific methods of breeding and raising livestock and poultry, and continued support for public health and disease control programs will contribute to the demand for veterinarians. Jobs will also open as veterinarians retire.

Earnings

The average starting salary of 1994 veterinary medical college graduates was $30,694, according to the American Veterinary Medical Association. The average income of veterinarians in private practice was $59,188 in 1994.

The average annual salary for veterinarians in the Federal Government in nonsupervisory, supervisory, and managerial positions was $53,929 in 1995.

Related Occupations
Veterinarians prevent, diagnose, and treat diseases, disorders, and injuries in animals. Workers who do this for humans include audiologists, chiropractors, dentists, optometrists, physicians, podiatrists, and speech pathologists. Other occupations that involve working with animals include animal trainers, zoologists, marine biologists, naturalists, and veterinary technicians.

Sources of Additional Information
For more information on careers in veterinary medicine and veterinary technology write to:

☛American Veterinary Medical Association, 1931 N. Meacham Rd., Suite 100, Schaumburg, IL 60173-4360.

For information on scholarships, grants, and loans, contact the financial aid officer at the veterinary schools to which you wish to apply.

For information on veterinary education, write to:

☛Association of American Veterinary Medical Colleges, 1101 Vermont Ave. NW., Suite 710, Washington, DC 20005.

Health Assessment and Treating Occupations

Dietitians and Nutritionists

(D.O.T. 077 except .117-010 and .124-010)

Nature of the Work
Dietitians and nutritionists plan nutrition programs and supervise the preparation and serving of meals. They help prevent and treat illnesses by promoting healthy eating habits, scientifically evaluating clients' diets, and suggesting modifications such as less salt for those with high blood pressure or reduced fat and sugar intake for those who are overweight.

Dietitians run food service systems for institutions such as hospitals and schools, promote sound eating habits through education, and conduct research. Major areas of practice are clinical, community, management, and consultant dietetics.

Clinical dietitians provide nutritional services for patients in institutions such as hospitals and nursing homes. They assess patients' nutritional needs, develop and implement nutrition programs, and evaluate and report the results. They also confer with doctors and other health care professionals in order to coordinate medical and nutritional needs. Some clinical dietitians specialize in the management of overweight patients, care of the critically ill, or care of renal (kidney) and diabetic patients. In addition, clinical dietitians in nursing homes or small hospitals may also manage the food service department.

Community dietitians counsel individuals and groups on nutritional practices designed to prevent disease and to promote good health. Working in such places as public health clinics, home health agencies, and health maintenance organizations, they evaluate individual needs, develop nutritional care plans, and instruct individuals and their families. Dietitians working in home health agencies may provide instruction on grocery shopping and food preparation to the elderly, or patients with AIDS, cancer, or diabetes.

Popular interest in nutrition has led to opportunities in food manufacturing, advertising, and marketing, where dietitians analyze foods, prepare literature for distribution, or report on issues such as the nutritional content of recipes, dietary fiber, or vitamin supplements.

Management dietitians oversee large-scale meal planning and preparation in such places as health care facilities, company cafeterias, prisons, and schools. They hire, train, and direct other dietitians and food service workers; budget for and purchase food, equipment, and supplies; enforce sanitary and safety regulations; and prepare records and reports.

Consultant dietitians work under contract with health care facilities or in their own private practice. They perform nutrition screening for their clients, and offer advice on diet-related concerns such as weight loss or cholesterol reduction. Some work for wellness programs, sports teams, supermarkets, and other nutrition-related businesses. They may consult with food service managers, providing expertise in sanitation, safety procedures, budgeting, and planning.

Working Conditions
Most dietitians work a regular 40-hour week, although some work weekends. Many dietitians work part time.

Dietitians and nutritionists spend much of their time in clean, well-lighted, and well-ventilated areas. However, some dietitians spend time in hot, steamy kitchens. Dietitians and nutritionists may be on their feet for most of the workday.

Employment
Dietitians and nutritionists held about 53,000 jobs in 1994. Over half were in hospitals and nursing homes.

State and local governments provided about 1 job in 6—mostly in health departments and other public health related areas. Other jobs were in social service agencies, residential care facilities, diet workshops, physical fitness facilities, school systems, colleges and uni-

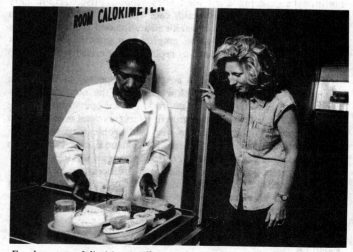

Employment of dietitians will grow due to increased emphasis on the prevention of disease by improved health habits.

versities, and the Federal Government—mostly in the Department of Veterans Affairs. Others were employed by firms that provide food services on contract to such facilities as colleges and universities, airlines, and company cafeterias.

Some dietitians were self-employed, working as consultants to facilities like hospitals and nursing homes and seeing individual clients.

Training, Other Qualifications, and Advancement

The basic educational requirement is a bachelor's degree with a major in dietetics, foods and nutrition, food service systems management, or a related area. Students take courses in foods, nutrition, institution management, chemistry, biology, microbiology, and physiology. Other suggested courses include business, mathematics, statistics, computer science, psychology, sociology, and economics.

Of the 37 States that have laws governing dietetics, 24 require licensure, 12 require certification, and 1 requires registration. The Commission on Dietetic Registration of the American Dietetic Association (ADA) awards the Registered Dietitian credential to those who pass a certification exam after completing their academic education and supervised experience.

As of 1995, there were 233 ADA-approved bachelor's degree programs. Supervised practice experience can be acquired in two ways. There are 51 ADA-accredited coordinated programs that combine academic and supervised practice experience in a 4-year program. The second option requires completion of 900 hours of supervised practice experience, either in one of the 157 ADA-accredited internships or in one of the 91 ADA-approved preprofessional practice programs. Internships and preprofessional practice programs may be full-time programs lasting 9 to 12 months or part time programs lasting 2 years. Students interested in research, advanced clinical positions, or public health should get a graduate degree.

Recommended high school courses include biology, chemistry, mathematics, health, and home economics.

Experienced dietitians may advance to assistant, associate, or director of a dietetic department or become self-employed. Some dietitians specialize in areas such as renal or pediatric dietetics. Others may leave the occupation to become sales representatives for equipment or food manufacturers.

Job Outlook

Employment of dietitians is expected to grow about as fast as the average for all occupations through the year 2005 due to increased emphasis on the prevention of disease by improved health habits. A growing and aging population will increase demand for meals and nutritional counseling in nursing homes, schools, prisons, community health programs, and home health care agencies. Public interest in nutrition and the emphasis on health education and prudent lifestyles will also spur demand. Besides employment growth, job openings will also result from the need to replace experienced workers who leave the occupation.

Employment of dietitians in hospitals is expected to show little change because of anticipated slow growth in the number of inpatients, and as hospitals contract out food service operations. On the other hand, faster than average growth in employment is expected in nursing homes as the number of very old people rises sharply, in contract providers of food services, in residential care facilities, in offices and clinics of physicians, and in other social services.

Employment growth for dietitians and nutritionists may be somewhat constrained by the substitutability of other workers such as nurses, health educators, food service managers, and dietetic technicians. Growth would also be faster except for limitations on insurance reimbursement for dietetic services.

Earnings

According to the American Dietetic Association, full-time registered dietitians with 5 years or less experience earned a median annual salary of $29,600 a year in 1993; those with 6-10 years of experience, $34,400; 11-15 years, $37,900; 16-20 years, $40,400; and 20 years or more, $41,600. Management and self-employed dietitians earned more than clinical and community dietitians. Salaries also vary by educational level, geographic region, and size of community.

According to a University of Texas Medical Branch survey of hospitals and medical centers, the median annual salary of dietitians was $31,372 in October 1994. The average minimum salary was $26,138 and the average maximum was $38,987.

Related Occupations

Dietitians and nutritionists apply the principles of nutrition in a variety of situations. Workers with duties similar to those of management dietitians include home economists and food service managers. Nurses and health educators often provide services related to those of community dietitians.

Sources of Additional Information

For a list of academic programs, scholarships, and other information about dietetics, contact:

☛The American Dietetic Association, 216 West Jackson Blvd., Chicago, IL 60606-6995.

Occupational Therapists

(D.O.T. 076.121-010 and .167-010)

Nature of the Work

Occupational therapists help individuals with mentally, physically, developmentally, or emotionally disabling conditions to develop, recover, or maintain daily living and work skills. They not only help patients improve basic motor functions and reasoning abilities, but also to compensate for permanent loss of function. Their goal is to help patients have independent, productive, and satisfying lifestyles.

Occupational therapists assist patients in performing activities of all kinds, ranging from using a computer to caring for daily needs, such as dressing, cooking, and eating. Physical exercises may be used to increase strength and dexterity, while paper and pencil games may be chosen to improve visual acuity and the ability to discern patterns. A patient suffering short-term memory loss, for instance, might be encouraged to make lists to aid recall. One with coordination problems might be given extra tasks to improve hand-eye coordination. Computer programs have been designed to help patients improve decisionmaking, abstract reasoning, problem solving, and perceptual skills, as well as memory, sequencing, and coordination—all of which are important for independent living.

For those with permanent functional disabilities, such as spinal cord injuries, cerebral palsy, or muscular dystrophy, therapists provide such adaptive equipment as wheelchairs, splints, and aids for eating and dressing. They also design or make special equipment needed at home or at work. Therapists develop and teach patients to operate computer-aided adaptive equipment, such as microprocessing devices that permit individuals with severe limitations to communicate, walk, operate telephones and television sets, and control other aspects of their environment.

Some occupational therapists, called industrial therapists, help patients find and hold a job. They arrange employment, plan work activities and evaluate the patient's progress.

Occupational therapists may work exclusively with individuals in a particular age group or with particular disabilities. In schools, for example, they evaluate children's abilities, recommend therapy, modify classroom equipment, and in general, help children participate as fully as possible in school programs and activities.

Occupational therapists in mental health settings treat mentally ill, mentally retarded, or emotionally disturbed individuals. To treat

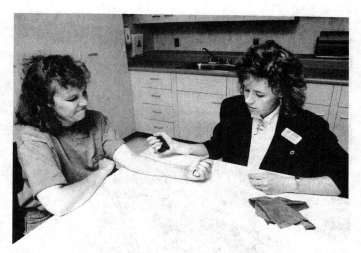

Occupational therapists may use physical exercises to increase patients' strength and dexterity.

these problems, therapists choose activities that help people learn to cope with daily life. Activities include time management skills, budgeting, shopping, homemaking, and use of public transportation. They may also work with patients suffering from alcoholism, drug abuse, depression, eating disorders, and stress related disorders.

Recording a patient's activities and progress is an important part of an occupational therapist's job. Accurate records are essential for evaluating patients, billing, and reporting to physicians.

Working Conditions

Occupational therapists in hospitals and other health care settings generally work a regular 40-hour week. Those in schools may also participate in meetings and other activities, during and after the school day. In large rehabilitation centers, therapists may work in spacious rooms equipped with machines, tools, and other devices that may generate noise. The job can be tiring because therapists are on their feet much of the time. Those providing home health care may spend several hours a day driving from appointment to appointment. Therapists also face hazards such as backstrain from lifting and moving patients and equipment.

Employment

Occupational therapists held about 54,000 jobs in 1994. The largest number of jobs were in hospitals, including many in rehabilitation and psychiatric hospitals. School systems are the second largest employer of occupational therapists. Other major employers include offices of occupational therapists and other health practitioners, nursing homes, community mental health centers, adult daycare programs, job training services, and residential care facilities.

A small but rapidly growing number of occupational therapists are in private practice. Some are solo practitioners, while others are in group practices. They see patients referred by physicians or other health professionals, or provide contract or consulting services to nursing homes, adult daycare programs, and home health agencies.

Training, Other Qualifications, and Advancement

A bachelor's degree in occupational therapy is the minimal requirement for entry into this field. In addition, 39 States, Puerto Rico, and the District of Columbia require a license to practice occupational therapy. To obtain a license, applicants must have a degree or a post-bachelor's certificate from an accredited educational program and pass a national certification examination given by the American Occupational Therapy Certification Board. Those who pass the test are awarded the title of registered occupational therapist.

In 1994, entry level education was offered in 69 bachelor's degree programs; 9 post-bachelor's certificate programs for students with a degree other than occupational therapy; and 19 entry level master's degree programs. Most schools have full-time programs, although a growing number also offer weekend or part-time programs.

Occupational therapy coursework includes physical, biological, and behavioral sciences and the application of occupational therapy theory and skills. Completion of 6 months of supervised clinical internship is also required.

Persons considering this profession should take high school courses in biology, chemistry, physics, health, art, and the social sciences. College admissions offices also look with favor on paid or volunteer experience in the health-care field.

Warmth and patience are needed to inspire both trust and respect. Ingenuity and imagination in adapting activities to individual needs are assets. Individuals working in home health care must be able to successfully adapt to a variety of settings.

Job Outlook

Job opportunities for occupational therapists are expected to continue to be excellent. Employment of occupational therapists is expected to increase much faster than the average for all occupations through the year 2005 due to anticipated growth in demand for rehabilitation and long-term care services. Several factors are increasing the need for rehabilitative services. Medical advances are now making it possible for more patients with critical problems to survive. These patients, however, may need extensive therapy. Also, there is the anticipated demand generated by the baby-boom generation's move into middle age, a period during which the incidence of heart attack and stroke increases. Additional services will also be demanded by the population 75 years of age and above, a rapidly growing age group that suffers from a very high incidence of disabling conditions. Finally, additional therapists will be needed to help children with disabilities prepare to enter special education programs, as required by recent Federal legislation.

Due to industry growth and more intensive care, hospitals will continue to employ the largest number of occupational therapists. Hospitals will also need occupational therapists to staff their growing home health-care and outpatient rehabilitation programs.

Moderate growth in schools will result from expansion of the school-age population and extended services for disabled students.

Movement into private practice has been made more attractive by a legislative change which permits occupational therapists to bill Medicare directly for services provided. Previously, billings were submitted through a hospital, home health agency, or other Medicare-approved facility.

Employment of occupational therapists in the home health field is expected to grow very fast. The rapidly growing number of people age 75 and older who are more likely to need home health care, and the greater use of at-home followup care will encourage this growth.

Earnings

According to a national survey of hospitals and medical centers conducted by the University of Texas Medical Branch, the median annual salary for occupational therapists, based on a 40-hour week and excluding shift or area differentials, was $39,634 in October 1994. The average minimum was $33,728 and the average maximum was $49,392. Some States classify occupational therapists employed in public schools as teachers and pay accordingly.

Therapists in private practice generally earned more than salaried workers.

Related Occupations

Occupational therapists use specialized knowledge to help individuals perform daily living skills and achieve maximum independence. Other workers performing similar duties include orthotists, prosthetists, physical therapists, chiropractors, speech pathologists and audiologists, rehabilitation counselors, recreational therapists, art therapists, music therapists, dance therapists, horticultural therapists, and manual arts therapists.

Sources of Additional Information

For more information on occupational therapy as a career, a list of education programs, and requirements for certification, write to:

☛The American Occupational Therapy Association, 4720 Montgomery Ln., P.O. Box 31220, Bethesda, MD 20824-1220.

Pharmacists

(D.O.T. 074.161-010 and -014)

Nature of the Work

Pharmacists dispense drugs prescribed by physicians and other health practitioners and provide information to patients about medications and their use. They advise physicians and other health practitioners on the selection, dosages, interactions, and side effects of medications. Pharmacists must understand the use, composition, and effects of drugs. Compounding–the actual mixing of ingredients to form powders, tablets, capsules, ointments, and solutions–is only a small part of a pharmacist's practice, because most medicines are produced by pharmaceutical companies in a standard dosage and form.

Pharmacists in community (retail) pharmacies answer customers' questions about prescription drugs, such as possible adverse reactions and interactions. They provide information about over-the-counter drugs and make recommendations after asking a series of health questions, such as whether the customer is on any other medication. They also give advice about durable medical equipment and home health care supplies. Those who own or manage community pharmacies may buy and sell nonhealth-related merchandise, hire and supervise personnel, and oversee the general operation of the pharmacy.

Pharmacists in hospitals and clinics dispense medications and advise the medical staff on the selection and effects of drugs. They may make sterile solutions and buy medical supplies. They also monitor drug regimens, advise patients on the use of drugs when they are discharged from the hospital, and evaluate drug use patterns in the hospital.

Pharmacists who work in home health care prepare medications for use in the home and monitor drug therapy.

Most pharmacists keep computerized records of patients' drug therapies to ensure that harmful drug interactions do not occur. They may also teach health professions students.

Some pharmacists specialize in specific aspects of drug therapy, such as drugs for psychiatric disorders, intravenous nutrition, or the diagnostic use of radiopharmaceuticals.

Working Conditions

Pharmacists usually work in clean, well-lighted, and well-ventilated areas. Many pharmacists spend most of their time on their feet. When working with potentially dangerous or sterile pharmaceutical products, pharmacists wear gloves and masks and work with special protective equipment. Many community and hospital pharmacies are open long hours or around the clock, so pharmacists may work evenings, nights, weekends, and holidays. Pharmacists who consult may travel to nursing homes or other facilities.

About 1 out of 6 pharmacists worked part time in 1994. Most full-time salaried pharmacists worked about 40 hours a week. Some, including most self-employed pharmacists, worked more than 50 hours a week.

Employment

Pharmacists held about 168,000 jobs in 1994. Three out of 5 worked in community pharmacies, either independently owned, part of a

Community pharmacies employed 3 out of 5 pharmacists.

drug store chain, or part of a grocery or department store. Most community pharmacists were salaried, but a substantial number were self employed. About one-quarter worked in hospitals, and some worked for health maintenance organizations (HMO's), clinics, home health care services, nursing homes, and the Federal Government.

Some pharmacists hold more than one job. They may work a standard week in their primary work setting and also work part time elsewhere.

Training, Other Qualifications, and Advancement

A license to practice pharmacy is required in all States, the District of Columbia, and U.S. territories. To obtain a license, one must graduate from an accredited college of pharmacy (a few States allow graduation from certain foreign pharmacy programs), pass a State examination, and serve an internship under a licensed pharmacist. In 1995, all States except California and Florida usually granted a license without extensive reexamination to qualified pharmacists already licensed by another State. Many pharmacists are licensed to practice in more than one State. Most States require continuing education for license renewal.

At least 5 years of study beyond high school are required to graduate from programs accredited by the American Council on Pharmaceutical Education. A Bachelor of Science (B.S.) in Pharmacy, the degree received by most graduates, takes 5 years. A Doctor of Pharmacy (Pharm.D.) normally requires at least 6 years, during which an intervening bachelor's degree usually is not awarded. Those who already hold the bachelor's degree may enter

Pharm.D. programs, but the combined period of study is usually longer than 6 years. In 1995, 75 colleges of pharmacy conferred degrees. The number of schools offering the Pharm.D. as the only professional degree increased to 27 and the number offering the B.S. in Pharmacy as the only professional degree continued to decline, reaching 25.

Requirements for admission to colleges of pharmacy vary. A few colleges admit students directly from high school. Most colleges of pharmacy, however, require 1 or 2 years of college-level prepharmacy education. Entry requirements usually include mathematics and basic sciences, such as chemistry, biology, and physics, as well as courses in the humanities and social sciences. Some colleges require the applicant to take the Pharmacy College Admissions Test (P-CAT).

All colleges of pharmacy offer courses in pharmacy practice, designed to teach students to dispense prescriptions, communicate with patients and other health professionals, and to strengthen their understanding of professional ethics and practice management responsibilities. Pharmacists' training increasingly emphasizes direct patient care as well as consultative services to other health professionals.

The bachelor's degree in pharmacy is generally acceptable for most positions in community pharmacies. However, a growing number of hospital employers prefer that a pharmacist have a Pharm.D. degree. A master's or Ph.D. degree in pharmacy or a related field usually is required to do research, and a Pharm.D. with additional residency or fellowship training, master's, or Ph.D. usually is necessary for faculty positions.

In 1994-95, 60 colleges of pharmacy awarded the Master of Science degree or the Ph.D. degree. Although a number of pharmacy graduates interested in further training pursue an advanced degree in pharmacy, there are other options. Some enter 1- or 2-year residency programs or fellowships. Pharmacy residencies are organized, directed, postgraduate training programs in a defined area of pharmacy practice, such as pediatrics, cardiology, oncology, or hospital pharmacy management. Pharmacy fellowships are directed, highly individualized programs designed to prepare participants to do independent research.

Areas of graduate study include pharmaceutics and pharmaceutical chemistry (physical and chemical properties of drugs and dosage forms), pharmacology (effects of drugs on the body), and pharmacy administration, including social-behavioral aspects of patient care.

Prospective pharmacists should have scientific aptitude, manual dexterity, and good interpersonal skills.

In community pharmacies, pharmacists usually begin at the staff level. After they gain experience and secure the necessary capital, many become owners or part owners of pharmacies. Pharmacists in chain drug stores may be promoted to supervisory pharmacist at the store level and then at the district level, and later to an executive position within the chain's headquarters.

Hospital pharmacists may advance to director of pharmacy services or to other administrative positions. Pharmacists in the pharmaceutical industry may advance in marketing, sales, research, quality control, production, packaging, and other areas.

Job Outlook

Employment of pharmacists is expected to grow as fast as the average for all occupations through the year 2005, due to the increased pharmaceutical needs of a larger and older population and greater use of medication. As in other occupations, most job openings will result from the need to replace pharmacists who leave the profession.

The increased number of middle-aged and elderly people will spur demand in all practice settings. Projected rapid growth in the elderly population is especially important because the number of prescriptions influences demand for pharmacists, and the elderly use more prescription drugs, on average, than younger people.

Other factors likely to increase demand for pharmacists through the year 2005 include the likelihood of scientific advances that will make more drug products available; new developments in administering medication; and increasingly sophisticated consumers seeking more information about drugs.

The number of pharmacists in health services is expected to grow as pharmacists consult more and become more actively involved in patient drug therapy decision-making. The increased severity of the typical hospital patient's illness, together with rapid strides in drug therapy, will sustain demand for pharmacists in hospitals, HMO's, and other health care settings.

Because of efforts to control prescription drug costs, retail pharmacies are taking steps to increase their prescription volume to make up for declining dispensing fees. Employment of community pharmacists would grow even more rapidly were it not for automation of drug dispensing that allows pharmacists to fill more prescriptions, and greater use of pharmacy technicians. If enrollments in colleges of pharmacy continue to rise, pharmacists may face competition for jobs.

Earnings

Median weekly earnings of full-time, salaried pharmacists were $954 in 1994. Half earned between $757 and $1,111. The lowest 10 percent earned less than $511 and the top 10 percent more than $1,319.

According to a survey by *Drug Topics* magazine, published by Medical Economics, Inc., average base salaries of full-time, salaried pharmacists were $53,600 per year in 1994. Pharmacists working in chain drug stores had an average base salary of $54,900 per year, while pharmacists working in independent drug stores averaged $49,000, and hospital pharmacists averaged $54,300. Overall, salaries for pharmacists were highest in the West and second highest in the East. Many pharmacists also receive compensation in the form of bonuses, overtime, and profit-sharing.

Related Occupations

Persons in other professions who work with pharmaceutical compounds are pharmaceutical chemists and pharmacologists.

Sources of Additional Information

For information on pharmacy as a career, preprofessional and professional requirements, programs offered by all the colleges of pharmacy, and student financial aid, contact:
☛American Association of Colleges of Pharmacy, 1426 Prince St., Alexandria, VA 22314.

Information on requirements for licensure in a particular State is available from the Board of Pharmacy of the State or from:
☛National Association of Boards of Pharmacy, 700 Busse Hwy., Park Ridge, IL 60068.

Information on specific college entrance requirements, curriculums, and financial aid is available from the dean of any college of pharmacy.

Physical Therapists

(D.O.T. 076.121-014)

Nature of the Work

Physical therapists improve mobility, relieve pain, and prevent or limit permanent physical disabilities of patients suffering from injuries or disease. Their patients include accident victims and disabled individuals with conditions such as multiple sclerosis, cerebral palsy, nerve injuries, burns, amputations, head injuries, fractures, low back pain, arthritis, and heart disease.

Therapists evaluate patients' medical histories, test and measure their strength, range of motion, and ability to function, and then develop treatment plans accordingly. These plans, which may be based on physician's orders, describe the treatment strategy, its purpose, and the anticipated outcome. After devising a treatment strategy, physical therapists often delegate specific procedures to physical therapy assistants and aides. (Physical therapy assistants and aides are discussed elsewhere in the *Handbook*.)

Treatment often includes exercise for patients who have been immobilized and lack flexibility. Using a technique known as passive exercise, therapists increase the patient's flexibility by stretching and manipulating stiff joints and unused muscles. Later in the treatment, they encourage patients to use their own muscles to further increase flexibility and range of motion before finally advancing to weights and other exercises that improve strength, balance, coordination, and endurance.

Physical therapists also use electrical stimulation, hot or cold compresses, and ultrasound to relieve pain, improve the condition of muscles or related tissues, and to reduce swelling. They may use traction or deep-tissue massage to relieve pain and restore function. Therapists also teach patients to use crutches, prostheses, and wheelchairs to perform day-to-day activities, and show them exercises to do at home to expedite their recovery.

As treatment continues, physical therapists document progress, conduct periodic evaluations, and modify treatments when necessary. Such documentation is used to track the patient's progress, identify areas requiring more or less attention, justify billings, and for legal purposes.

Some physical therapists treat a wide range of ailments; others specialize in areas such as pediatrics, geriatrics, orthopedics, sports medicine, neurology, and cardiopulmonary physical therapy.

Working Conditions

Physical therapists work in hospitals, clinics, and private offices that have specially equipped facilities, or they treat patients in hospital rooms, homes, or schools.

Most physical therapists work a 40-hour week, which may include some evenings and weekends. The job can be physically demanding because therapists often have to stoop, kneel, crouch, lift, and stand for long periods of time. In addition, therapists move heavy equipment and lift patients or help them turn, stand, or walk.

Employment

Physical therapists held about 102,000 jobs in 1994; about 1 in 4 worked part time.

Hospitals employed one-third and offices of physical therapists employed about one-quarter of all salaried physical therapists in 1994. Other jobs were in offices of physicians, home health agencies, nursing homes, and schools. Some physical therapists are self

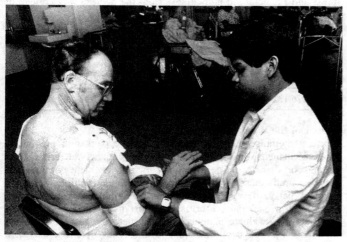

Competition for entry into physical therapy programs is intense.

employed in private practices. They may provide services to individual patients or contract to provide services in hospitals, rehabilitation centers, nursing homes, home health agencies, adult daycare programs, and schools. They may be in solo practice or be part of a consulting group. Some physical therapists teach in academic institutions and conduct research.

Training, Other Qualifications, and Advancement

All States require physical therapists to pass a licensure exam after graduating from an accredited physical therapy program, before they can practice.

According to the American Physical Therapy Association (APTA), there were 145 accredited and 39 developing professional physical therapist programs as of June 1995. Of the accredited programs, 65 offered bachelor's degrees and 80 were master's degree programs. The bachelor's degree curriculum usually starts with basic science courses such as biology, chemistry, and physics, and then introduces specialized courses such as biomechanics, neuroanatomy, human growth and development, manifestations of disease and trauma, evaluation and assessment techniques, research, and therapeutic procedures. Besides classroom and laboratory instruction, students receive supervised clinical experience in hospitals.

Individuals who have a 4-year degree in a related field, such as genetics or biology, and want to be a physical therapist, should enroll in a master's level physical therapy program. A master's degree is also recommended for those with a bachelor's degree in physical therapy who are interested in promotion to an administrative position, or attaining a research or teaching job.

Competition for entry to physical therapy programs is very intense, so interested students should attain superior grades in high school and college, especially in science courses. Courses useful when applying to physical therapy programs include anatomy, biology, chemistry, social science, mathematics, and physics. Before granting admission, many education programs require experience as a volunteer in the physical therapy department of a hospital or clinic.

Physical therapists should have strong interpersonal skills so they can make patients understand the treatments. They should also be compassionate and posses a desire to help the patient adjust to their disabilities. Similar traits are also needed to deal with the patient's family. Physical therapists should also have manual dexterity and physical stamina.

Physical therapists are expected to continue to develop professionally by participating in continuing education courses and workshops from time to time. A number of States require continuing education for maintaining licensure.

Job Outlook

Anecdotal reports about shortages of physical therapists that existed in recent years are no longer common. The number of physical therapy education programs has increased and more graduates have moved into the labor force. Nonetheless, most graduates receive multiple job offers and job prospects are expected to continue to be excellent. Physical therapists who are willing to work in rural areas will experience even better job opportunities.

Physical therapists is expected to be one of the fastest growing occupations through the year 2005. The rapidly growing elderly population is particularly vulnerable to chronic and debilitating conditions that require therapeutic services. Also, the baby-boom generation is entering the prime age for heart attacks and strokes, increasing the demand for cardiac and physical rehabilitation. More young people will also need physical therapy as medical advances save the lives of a larger proportion of newborns with severe birth defects. Future medical developments will also permit a higher percentage of trauma victims to survive, creating additional demand for rehabilitative care.

Growth will also result from advances in medical technology which permit treatment of more disabling conditions. In the past, for example, the development of hip and knee replacements for those with arthritis gave rise to employment for physical therapists to improve flexibility and strengthen weak muscles.

The widespread interest in health promotion should also increase demand for physical therapy services. A growing number of employers are using physical therapists to evaluate worksites, develop exercise programs, and teach safe work habits to employees in the hope of reducing injuries.

Earnings

In 1994, median annual earnings of salaried physical therapists who usually work full time were $37,596. The middle 50 percent earned between $26,34 and $46,956. The top 10 percent earned at least $61,776 and the bottom 10 percent earned less than $19,968.

According to a University of Texas Medical Branch survey of hospitals and medical centers, the median salary of physical therapists, based on a 40-hour week and excluding shift or area differentials, was $41,288 a year in October 1994. The average minimum salary was $35,074 and the average maximum salary was $51,950.

Physical therapists in private practice tend to earn more than salaried workers. Also, many sources report that salaries are higher in rural areas as employers try to attract therapists to where there are severe shortages.

Related Occupations

Physical therapists treat and rehabilitate persons with physical disabilities. Others who work in the rehabilitation field include occupational therapists, corrective therapists, recreational therapists, manual arts therapists, speech pathologists and audiologists, orthotists, prosthetists, respiratory therapists, chiropractors, acupuncturists, and athletic trainers.

Sources of Additional Information

Additional information on a career as a physical therapist and a list of accredited educational programs in physical therapy are available from:
☛American Physical Therapy Association, 1111 North Fairfax St., Alexandria, VA 22314-1488.

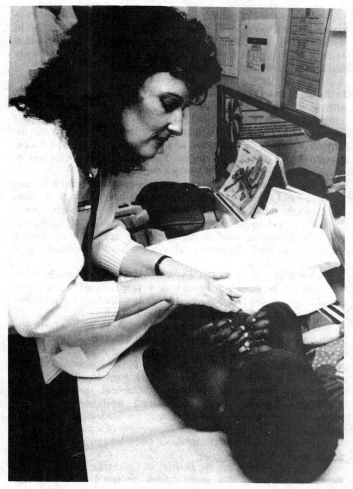

Employment opportunities are expected to be excellent for physician assistants.

Physician Assistants

(D.O.T. 079.364-018)

Nature of the Work

As their title suggests, physician assistants (PA's) support physicians. However, they should not be confused with medical assistants (see separate statement elsewhere in the *Handbook*). PA's are formally trained to provide routine diagnostic, therapeutic, and preventive health care services under the direction and supervision of a physician. They take medical histories, examine patients, order and interpret laboratory tests and X-rays, and make preliminary diagnoses. They also treat minor injuries by suturing, splinting, and casting. PA's record progress notes, instruct and counsel patients, and order or carry out therapy. In 39 States and the District of Columbia, physician assistants may prescribe medications. PA's may have managerial duties too. Some order medical and laboratory supplies and equipment; others supervise technicians and assistants.

Physician assistants always work under the supervision of a physician. The extent of supervision, however, depends upon the location. For example, PA's working in rural or inner city clinics, where a physician may be available just 1 or 2 days each week, may provide most of the health care for patients and consult with the supervising physician by telephone. Other PA's may make house calls or go to hospitals and nursing homes to check on patients and report back to the physician.

In some States, the duties of a physician assistant are determined by the supervising physician; in others, they are determined by the State's regulatory agency. Aspiring PA's should investigate the laws and regulations in the States where they wish to practice.

Many PA's work in primary care areas such as general internal medicine, pediatrics, and family practice. Others work in specialty areas, such as general and thoracic surgery, emergency medicine, orthopedics, and geriatrics. PA's specializing in surgery, also called surgeon assistants, provide pre- and post-operative care and may work as first or second assistants during major surgery.

Working Conditions

Although PA's generally work in a comfortable, well-lighted environment, those in surgery often stand for long periods, and others do considerable walking. Schedules vary according to practice setting and often depend on the hours of the supervising physician. The workweek of PA's in physicians' offices may include weekends, night hours, or early morning hospital rounds to visit patients. They may be on-call. PA's in clinics usually work a 5-day, 40-hour week.

Employment

Physician assistants held about 56,000 jobs in 1994. Most PA's work in physicians' offices and clinics. Others work in hospitals. The rest work for public health clinics, nursing homes, prisons, and rehabilitation centers.

About one-third of all PA's provide health care to communities having fewer than 50,000 residents where physicians may be in limited supply, according to the American Academy of Physician Assistants. Many PA's work in primary care areas such as family medicine, general internal medicine, and pediatrics.

Training, Other Qualifications, and Advancement

Almost all States require that new PA's complete an accredited, formal education program. In 1995, there were 61 such educational programs for physician assistants, including three programs for surgeon assistants. Thirty-seven of these programs offered a baccalaureate degree or a degree option. The rest offered either a certificate, an associate degree, or a master's degree.

Admission requirements vary, but many programs require 2 years of college and some work experience in the health care field. Students should take courses in biology, English, chemistry, math, psychology, and social sciences. More than half of all applicants hold a bachelor's or master's degree. Many applicants are former emergency medical technicians, other allied health professionals, or nurses.

PA programs generally last 2 years. Most programs are in medical schools, schools of allied health, or 4-year colleges; a few are in community colleges and in hospitals. Many accredited PA programs have clinical teaching affiliations with medical schools.

PA education includes classroom instruction in biochemistry, nutrition, human anatomy, physiology, microbiology, clinical pharmacology, clinical medicine, geriatric and home health care, disease prevention, and medical ethics. Students obtain supervised clinical training in several areas, including family medicine, inpatient and ambulatory medicine, general surgery, obstetrics and gynecology, geriatrics, emergency medicine, internal medicine, ambulatory psychiatry, and pediatrics. Sometimes, PA students serve one or more of these "rotations" under the supervision of a physician who is seeking to hire a PA. These rotations often lead to permanent employment.

As of 1995, 49 States, the District of Columbia, and Guam had legislation governing the qualifications or practice of physician assistants. Mississippi did not. Forty-nine States required physician assistants to pass a certifying exam that is only open to graduates of an accredited educational program. Only those successfully completing the examination may use the credential "Physician Assistant-Certified (PA-C)." In order to remain certified, PA's must have 100 hours of continuing medical education every 2 years and pass a recertification examination every 6 years.

PA postgraduate residency training programs, as yet unaccredited, are available in gynecology, geriatrics, surgery, pediatrics, neonatology, and occupational medicine. Candidates must be graduates of an accredited program and be certified by the National Commission on Certification of Physician Assistants.

Physician assistants need leadership skills, self-confidence, and emotional stability. They must be willing to continue studying throughout their career to keep up with medical advances.

Some PA's pursue additional education in order to practice in a specialty area such as surgery, neonatology, or emergency medicine. Others—as they attain greater clinical knowledge and experience—advance to added responsibilities and higher earnings. However, by the very nature of the profession, individual PA's are always supervised by physicians.

Job Outlook

Employment opportunities are expected to be excellent for physician assistants, particularly in areas or settings that have difficulty attracting enough physicians, such as rural and inner city clinics.

Employment of PA's is expected to grow faster than the average for all occupations through the year 2005 due to anticipated expansion of the health services industry and an emphasis on cost containment. Physicians and institutions are expected to employ more PA's to provide primary care and assist with medical and surgical procedures, thus freeing physicians to perform more complicated and revenue generating tasks. The public and third party payers also seem to approve of PA's use. For example, Medicare now allows physicians to bill the government for services provided by PA's in hospitals and nursing homes. Opportunities will be best in States that allow PA's a wider scope of practice, such as the ability to prescribe medication.

Besides the traditional office-based setting, PA's should find a growing number of jobs in institutional settings such as hospitals, academic medical centers, public clinics, and prisons. The growth of managed care and group medical practices should also lead to more jobs since they use PA's to provide a wide variety of services because their salaries are lower than those of physicians.

Earnings

According to a University of Texas Medical Branch survey of hospitals and medical centers, the median annual salary of physician assistants, based on a 40 hour week and excluding shift or area differentials, was $48,264 in October 1994. The average minimum salary was $37,639 and the average maximum was $57,005.

According to the American Academy of Physician Assistants, median income for all physician assistants in 1994 was $53,284; median income for first year graduates was $44,176. Income varies by specialty, practice setting, geographical location, and years of experience.

Related Occupations

Other health workers who provide direct patient care that requires a similar level of skill and training include nurse practitioners, physical therapists, occupational therapists, clinical psychologists, speech-language pathologists, and audiologists.

Sources of Additional Information

For information on a career as a physician assistant, contact:

☞American Academy of Physician Assistants, 950 North Washington St., Alexandria, VA 22314.

For a list of accredited programs and a catalog of individual PA training programs, contact:

☞Association of Physician Assistant Programs, 950 North Washington St., Alexandria, VA 22314.

For eligibility requirements and a description of the Physician Assistant National Certifying Examination, write to:

☞National Commission on Certification of Physician Assistants, Inc., 2845 Henderson Mill Rd. NE., Atlanta, GA 30341.

Recreational Therapists

(D.O.T. 076.124-014)

Nature of the Work

Recreational therapists employ activities to treat or maintain the physical, mental, and emotional well-being of patients. Activities include sports, games, dance, drama, arts and crafts, and music, as well as field trips for sightseeing, ball games, or picnics. They help individuals build confidence, socialize effectively, and remediate the effects of illness or disability. Recreational therapists should not be confused with recreation workers, who organize recreational activities primarily for enjoyment. (Recreation workers are discussed elsewhere in the *Handbook*.)

In clinical settings, such as hospitals and rehabilitation centers, recreational therapists treat and rehabilitate individuals with specific medical problems, usually in cooperation with physicians, nurses, psychologists, social workers, and physical and occupational therapists. In nursing homes, residential facilities, and community recreation departments, they use leisure activities—mostly group oriented—to improve general health and well-being, but may also treat medical problems. In these settings they may be called activity directors or therapeutic recreation specialists.

Recreational therapists assess patients based on information from medical records, medical staff, family, and patients themselves. They then develop and carry out therapeutic activity programs consistent with patient needs and interests. For instance, patients having trouble socializing may be helped to play games with others, a right-handed person with a right-side paralysis may be helped to use their left arm to throw a ball or swing a racket. They may instruct patients in relaxation techniques to reduce stress and tension, in stretching and limbering exercises, and in individual and group sports.

Community based recreational therapists work in park and recreation departments, special education programs, or programs for the elderly or disabled. In these programs therapists help patients develop leisure activities and provide them with opportunities for exercise, mental stimulation, creativity, and fun.

Recreational therapists observe and record patients' participation, reactions, and progress. These records are used by the medical staff and others, to monitor progress, to justify changes or end treatment, and for billing.

Working Conditions

Recreational therapists often plan events and keep records in offices and provide services in special activity rooms. In community settings they might also work with clients in a recreation room, on a playing field, or in a swimming pool.

Therapists often lift and carry equipment as well as participate in activities. Recreational therapists generally work a 40-hour week, which may include some evenings, weekends, and holidays.

Employment

Recreational therapists held about 31,000 jobs in 1994. About one-half were in hospitals and one-third were in nursing homes. Others were in residential facilities, community mental health centers, adult day care programs, correctional facilities, community programs for people with disabilities, and substance abuse centers. Some therapists were self-employed, generally contracting with nursing homes or community agencies to develop and oversee programs.

Training, Other Qualifications, and Advancement

A bachelor's degree in therapeutic recreation (or in recreation with an option in therapeutic recreation) is the usual requirement for hospital and other clinical positions. An associate degree in recreational therapy; training in art, drama, or music therapy; or qualifying work experience may be sufficient for activity director positions in nursing homes.

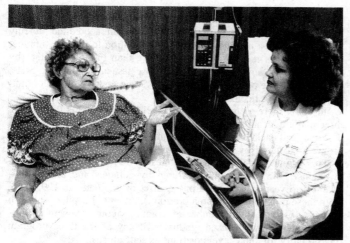

Recreational therapists should not be confused with recreation workers, who organize activities for enjoyment.

The National Council for Therapeutic Recreation Certification certifies therapeutic recreation specialists. Specialists must have a bachelor's degree and pass a certification exam. Some employers require individuals to be certified.

There are about 150 programs that prepare recreational therapists. As of 1994, 73 programs were accredited by the National Council on Accreditation. Most offer bachelor's degrees, although some offer associate, master's, or doctoral degrees.

In addition to therapeutic recreation courses in clinical practice and helping skills, program design, management, and professional issues, students study human anatomy, physiology, abnormal psychology, medical and psychiatric terminology, characteristics of illnesses and disabilities, and the concepts of mainstreaming and normalization. Courses cover professional ethics, assessment and referral procedures, and the use of adaptive and medical equipment. In addition, 360 hours of internship under the supervision of a certified therapeutic recreation specialist are required.

Recreational therapists should be comfortable working with disabled people and be patient, tactful, and persuasive. Ingenuity and imagination are needed in adapting activities to individual needs and good physical coordination is necessary when demonstrating or participating in recreational events.

Job Outlook

Employment of recreational therapists is expected to grow faster than the average for all occupations through the year 2005, because of anticipated expansion in long-term care, physical and psychiatric rehabilitation, and services for the disabled. Job prospects are expected to be favorable for those with a strong clinical background.

Hospitals will provide a large number of recreational therapy jobs through the year 2005. A growing number of these will be in hospital-based adult day care and out-patient programs, or in units offering short-term mental health and alcohol or drug abuse services. Long-term rehabilitation and psychiatric hospitals will provide additional jobs.

The rapidly growing number of older people is expected to spur job growth for activity directors in nursing homes, retirement communities, adult day care programs, and social service agencies. Continued growth is expected in community residential facilities as well as day care programs for people with disabilities.

Earnings

According to a survey by the National Therapeutic Recreation Society, the average salary for recreational therapists was $31,472 in 1994. The average annual salary for all recreational therapists in the Federal Government in nonsupervisory, supervisory, and managerial positions was about $35,954 in 1995.

Related Occupations

Recreational therapists design activities to help people with disabilities lead more fulfilling and independent lives. Other workers who have similar jobs are orientation therapists for the blind, art therapists, drama therapists, dance therapists, music therapists, occupational therapists, and rehabilitation counselors.

Sources of Additional Information

For information on how to order materials describing careers and academic programs in recreational therapy, write to:

☛American Therapeutic Recreation Association, C.O. Associated Management Systems, P.O. Box 15215, Hattiesburg, MS 39402-5215.

☛National Therapeutic Recreation Society, 2775 S. Quincy St., Suite 300, Arlington, VA 22206-2204.

Certification information may be obtained from:

☛National Council for Therapeutic Recreation Certification, P.O. Box 479, Thiells, NY 10984-0479.

Registered Nurses

(D.O.T. 075.124-010 and -014, .127-014, -026, -030 and -034, .137-010 and -014, .167-010 and -014, .264-010 and -014, .364-010, .371-010, .374-014, -018, and -022)

Nature of the Work

Registered nurses (R.N.'s) care for the sick and injured and help people stay well. They are typically concerned with the "whole person," providing for the physical, mental, and emotional needs of their patients. They observe, assess, and record symptoms, reactions, and progress; assist physicians during treatments and examinations; administer medications; and assist in convalescence and rehabilitation. R.N.'s also develop and manage nursing care plans; instruct patients and their families in proper care; and help individuals and groups take steps to improve or maintain their health. While State laws govern the tasks R.N.'s may perform, it is usually the work setting which determines their day-to-day job duties.

Hospital nurses form the largest group of nurses. Most are staff nurses, who provide bedside nursing care and carry out the medical regimen prescribed by physicians. They may also supervise licensed practical nurses and aides. Hospital nurses usually are assigned to one area such as surgery, maternity, pediatrics, emergency room, intensive care, or treatment of cancer patients or may rotate among departments.

Office nurses assist physicians in private practice, clinics, surgicenters, emergency medical centers, and health maintenance organizations (HMO's). They prepare patients for and assist with examinations, administer injections and medications, dress wounds and incisions, assist with minor surgery, and maintain records. Some also perform routine laboratory and office work.

Home health nurses provide periodic services, prescribed by a physician, to patients at home. They care for and instruct patients and their families. Home health nurses care for a broad range of patients, such as those recovering from illnesses and accidents, cancer, and child birth. They must be able to work independently.

Nursing home nurses manage nursing care for residents with conditions ranging from a fracture to Alzheimer's disease. Although they generally spend most of their time on administrative and supervisory tasks, R.N.'s also assess residents' medical condition, develop treatment plans, supervise licensed practical nurses and nursing aides, and perform difficult procedures such as starting intravenous fluids. They also work in specialty-care departments, such as long-term rehabilitation units for strokes and head-injuries.

Public health nurses work in government and private agencies and clinics, schools, retirement communities and other community settings. They instruct individuals, families, and other groups in health education, disease prevention, nutrition, and child care. They arrange for immunizations, blood pressure testing, and other health screening. These nurses also work with community leaders, teachers, parents, and physicians in community health education.

Occupational health or *industrial nurses* provide nursing care at worksites to employees, customers, and others with minor injuries and illnesses. They provide emergency care, prepare accident reports, and arrange for further care if necessary. They also offer health counseling, assist with health examinations and inoculations, and work on accident prevention programs.

Head nurses or *nurse supervisors* direct nursing activities. They plan work schedules and assign duties to nurses and aides, provide or arrange for training, and visit patients to observe nurses and to insure that care is proper. They may also insure that records are maintained and that equipment and supplies are ordered.

At the advanced level, *nurse practitioners* provide basic health care. They diagnose and treat common acute illnesses and injuries. Nurse practitioners can prescribe medications in some States. Other advanced practice nurses include *clinical nurse specialists, nurse anesthetists,* and *certified nurse-midwives.*

Registered nurses held over 1.9 million jobs in 1994.

Working Conditions

Most nurses work in well-lighted, comfortable medical facilities. Home health and public health nurses travel to patients' homes and to schools, community centers, and other sites. Nurses may spend considerable time walking and standing. They need emotional stability to cope with human suffering, emergencies, and other stresses. Because patients in hospitals and nursing homes require 24-hour care, nurses in these institutions may work nights, weekends, and holidays. They may also be on-call. Office, occupational health, and public health nurses are more likely to work regular business hours.

Nursing has its hazards, especially in hospitals, nursing homes, and clinics where nurses may care for individuals with infectious diseases such as hepatitis and AIDS. Nurses must observe rigid guidelines to guard against these and other dangers such as radiation, chemicals used for sterilization of instruments, and anesthetics. In addition, they face back injury when moving patients, shocks from electrical equipment, and hazards posed by compressed gases.

Employment

Registered nurses held about 1,906,000 jobs in 1994. About 2 out of 3 jobs were in hospitals. Others were in offices and clinics of physicians, home health care agencies, nursing homes, temporary help agencies, schools, and government agencies. More than one-fourth of all R.N.'s worked part time.

Training, Other Qualifications, and Advancement

In all States, students must graduate from an accredited nursing school and pass a national licensing examination to obtain a nursing license. Nurses may be licensed in more than one State, either by examination or endorsement of a license issued by another State. Licenses must be periodically renewed. Some States require continuing education for licensure renewal.

In 1993, there were 1,493 entry level R.N. programs. There are three major educational paths to nursing: Associate degree (A.D.N.), diploma, and bachelor of science degree in nursing (B.S.N.). A.D.N. programs, offered by community and junior colleges, take about 2 years. About two-thirds of graduates in 1993 were from A.D.N. programs. B.S.N. programs, offered by colleges and universities, take 4 or 5 years. More than one-quarter of graduates in 1993 were from these programs. Diploma programs, given in hospitals, last 2 to 3 years. Only a small number of graduates come from these programs. Generally, licensed graduates of any of the three program types qualify for entry level positions as staff nurses.

There have been attempts to raise the educational requirements for an R.N. license to a bachelor's degree and, possibly, create new job titles. However, such proposals have been around for years. These changes, should they occur, will be made State by State, through legislation or regulation. Changes in licensure requirements would not affect currently licensed R.N.'s, who would be "grandfathered" in, no matter what their educational preparation. However, individuals considering nursing should carefully weigh the pros and cons of enrolling in a B.S.N. program, since their advancement opportunities are broader. In fact, some career paths are open only to nurses with bachelor's or advanced degrees.

While A.D.N. or diploma preparation may be sufficient for a nursing home nurse to advance to director of nursing, a bachelor's degree is generally necessary for administrative positions in hospitals and for positions in community nursing. Moreover, the B.S.N. is a prerequisite for admission to graduate nursing programs in research, consulting, teaching, or a clinical specialization.

A growing number of A.D.N. and diploma-trained nurses are entering bachelor's programs to prepare for a broader scope of nursing practice. They can often find a hospital position and then take advantage of tuition reimbursement programs to get a B.S.N.

Nursing education includes classroom instruction and supervised training in hospitals and other health facilities. Students take courses in anatomy, physiology, microbiology, chemistry, nutrition, psychology and other behavioral sciences, and nursing.

Supervised clinical experience is provided in hospital departments such as pediatrics, psychiatry, maternity, and surgery. A growing number of programs include courses in gerontological nursing and clinical practice in nursing homes. Some provide clinical training in public health departments and home health agencies.

Nurses should be caring and sympathetic. They must be able to accept responsibility, direct or supervise others, follow orders precisely, and determine when consultation is required.

Experience and good performance can lead to promotion to increasingly more responsible positions. Nurses can advance, in management, to assistant head nurse or head nurse. From there, they can advance to assistant director, director, and vice president. Increasingly, management level nursing positions require a graduate degree in nursing or health services administration. They also require leadership, negotiation skills, and good judgment. Graduate programs preparing executive level nurses usually last 1 to 2 years.

Within patient care, nurses can advance to clinical nurse specialist, nurse practitioner, certified nurse-midwife, or nurse anesthetist. These positions require 1 or 2 years of graduate education, leading to a certificate or master's degree.

Some nurses move into the business side of health care. Their nursing expertise and experience on a health care team equip them to manage ambulatory, acute, home health, and chronic care services. Some are employed by health care corporations in health planning and development, marketing, and quality assurance.

Job Outlook

Job prospects in nursing are good. Employment of registered nurses is expected to grow faster than the average for all occupations through the year 2005 and, because the occupation is large, many new jobs will result. Job prospects will be even better if nursing school enrollments level off or decline, as they have on a cyclical basis in the past, thus reducing the number of qualified applicants. There will always be a need for traditional hospital nurses, but a large number of new nurses will be employed in home health, long-term, and ambulatory care.

Faster than average growth will be driven by technological advances in patient care, which permit a greater number of medical problems to be treated, and increasing emphasis on primary care. In addition, the number of older people, who are much more likely than younger people to need medical care, is projected to grow very rapidly. Many job openings also will result from the need to replace experienced nurses who leave the occupation, especially as the average age of the registered nurse population continues to rise.

Employment in hospitals, the largest sector, is expected to grow more slowly than in other health-care sectors. While the intensity of nursing care is likely to increase, requiring more nurses per patient, the number of inpatients (those who remain overnight) is not likely to increase much. Also, patients are being released earlier and more procedures are being done on an outpatient basis, both in and outside hospitals. Most rapid growth is expected in hospitals' outpatient facilities, such as same-day surgery, rehabilitation, and chemotherapy.

Employment in home health care is expected to grow the fastest. This is in response to a growing number of older persons with functional disabilities, consumer preference for care in the home, and technological advances which make it possible to bring increasingly complex treatments into the home. The type of care demanded will require nurses who are able to perform complex procedures.

Employment in nursing homes is expected to grow much faster than average due to increases in the number of people in their eighties and nineties, many of whom will require long-term care. In addition, the financial pressure on hospitals to release patients as soon as possible should produce more nursing home admissions. Growth in units to provide specialized long-term rehabilitation for stroke and head injury patients or to treat Alzheimer's victims will also increase employment.

An increasing proportion of sophisticated procedures, which once were performed only in hospitals, are being performed in physicians' offices and clinics, including HMO's, ambulatory surgicenters, and emergency medical centers. Accordingly, employment is expected to grow faster than average in these places as health care in general expands.

In evolving integrated health care networks, nurses may rotate among employment settings. Since jobs in traditional hospital nursing positions are no longer the only option, R.N.'s will need to be flexible. Opportunities will be best for nurses with advanced training.

Earnings

Median weekly earnings of full-time salaried registered nurses were $682 in 1994. The middle 50 percent earned between $542 and $838. The lowest 10 percent earned less than $395; the top 10 percent, more than $1,005.

According to a University of Texas Medical Branch survey of hospitals and medical centers, the median annual salary of staff nurses, based on a 40-hour week and excluding shift or area differentials, was $35,256 in October 1994. The average minimum salary was $28,531 and the average maximum was $43,711. For head nurses, the median was $50,700; clinical nurse specialists, $47,674; professional nurse practitioners, $47,432; and nurse anesthetists, $73,444.

According to the Buck Survey conducted by the American Health Care Association, staff R.N.'s in chain nursing homes had median annual earnings of about $32,200 in 1994. The middle 50 percent earned between $29,200 and $35,400.

Many employers offer flexible work schedules, child care, educational benefits, bonuses, and other incentives.

Related Occupations

Workers in other occupations with responsibilities and duties related to those of registered nurses are occupational therapists, paramedics, physical therapists, physician assistants, and respiratory therapists.

Sources of Additional Information

The National League for Nursing (NLN) publishes a variety of nursing and nursing education materials, including a list of nursing schools and information on student financial aid. For a complete list of NLN publications, write for a career information brochure. Send your request to:

☛Communications Department, National League for Nursing, 350 Hudson St., New York, NY 10014.

For a list of B.S.N. and graduate programs, write to:

☛American Association of Colleges of Nursing, 1 Dupont Circle, Suite 530, Washington, DC 20036.

Information on career opportunities as a registered nurse is available from:

☛American Nurses' Association, 600 Maryland Ave. SW., Washington, DC 20024-2571.

For information on nursing careers in long-term care, write to:

☛American Health Care Association, 1201 L St. NW., Washington, DC 20005-4014.

Respiratory Therapists

(D.O.T. 076.361-014)

Nature of the Work

You may live without water for a few days and without food for a few weeks. But without air, you will suffer brain damage within a few minutes and die after 9 minutes or more. Respiratory therapists, also known as respiratory care practitioners, evaluate, treat, and care for patients with breathing disorders.

In evaluating patients, therapists test the capacity of the lungs and analyze the oxygen and carbon dioxide concentration and potential of hydrogen (pH), a measure of the acidity or alkalinity level of the blood. To measure lung capacity, therapists have patients breathe into an instrument that measures the volume and flow of air during inhalation and exhalation. By comparing the reading with the norm for the patient's age, height, weight, and sex, respiratory therapists can determine whether lung deficiencies exist. To analyze oxygen, carbon dioxide, and pH levels, therapists draw an arterial blood sample, place it in a blood gas analyzer, and relay the results to a physician.

Respiratory therapists treat all sorts of patients, be they premature infants whose lungs are not fully developed or elderly people whose lungs are diseased. They provide temporary relief to patients with chronic asthma or emphysema and emergency care for heart failure, stroke, drowning, or shock victims. Respiratory therapists most commonly use oxygen or oxygen mixtures, chest physiotherapy, and aerosol medications. Therapists may place an oxygen mask or nasal cannula on a patient and set the oxygen flow at the level prescribed by a physician to increase a patient's concentration of oxygen. Therapists also connect patients who cannot breathe on their own to ventilators which deliver pressurized air into the lungs. They insert a tube into a patient's trachea, or windpipe; connect the tube to the ventilator; and set the rate, volume, and oxygen concentration of the air entering the patient's lungs. Therapists regularly check on patients and equipment. If the patient appears to be having difficulty or if the oxygen, carbon dioxide, or pH level of the blood is abnormal, they change the ventilator setting according the doctor's order or check equipment for mechanical problems. In homecare, therapists teach patients and their families to use ventilators and other life support systems. They visit several times a month to inspect and clean equipment and ensure its proper use and make emergency visits if equipment problems arise.

Respiratory therapists perform chest physiotherapy on patients to remove mucus from their lungs to make it easier for them to breathe. For example, during surgery, anesthesia depresses respiration, so this treatment may be prescribed to help get the patient's lungs back to normal and prevent congestion. Chest physiotherapy also is used on patients suffering from lung diseases, such as cystic fibrosis, that cause mucus to collect in the lungs. Therapists place patients in positions to help drain mucus, thump and vibrate patients' rib cages, and instruct them to cough.

Respiratory therapists also administer aerosols—generally liquid medications suspended in a gas that forms a mist which is inhaled

About 9 out of 10 jobs in respiratory therapy are in hospitals.

and teach patients how to inhale the aerosol properly to assure its effectiveness.

Therapists are increasingly working under the supervision of nurses and are being asked to perform tasks that fall outside of their traditional role. They are expanding into cardiopulminary procedures like electrocardiograms and stress testing, but also perform other tasks like drawing blood samples from patients. They also keep records of the materials used and charges to patients. Some therapists teach or supervise other respiratory therapy personnel.

Working Conditions

Respiratory therapists generally work between 35 and 40 hours a week. Because hospitals operate around the clock, therapists may work evenings, nights, or weekends; they spend long periods standing and walking between patients' rooms. In an emergency, they work under a great deal of stress. Gases used by respiratory therapists are potentially hazardous because they are used and stored under pressure. However, adherence to safety precautions and regular maintenance and testing of equipment minimize the risk of injury. As with many health occupations, respiratory therapists run a risk of catching infectious diseases. Careful adherence to proper procedures minimizes this risk as well.

Employment

Respiratory therapists held about 73,000 jobs in 1994. About 9 out of 10 jobs were located in hospitals in departments of respiratory care, anesthesiology, or pulmonary medicine. Durable medical equipment rental companies, home health agencies, and nursing homes accounted for most of the remaining jobs.

Training, Other Qualifications, and Advancement

Formal training is necessary for entry to this field. Training is offered at the postsecondary level by hospitals, medical schools, colleges and universities, trade schools, vocational-technical institutes, and the Armed Forces. Some programs prepare graduates for jobs as respiratory therapists; other, shorter programs lead to jobs as respiratory therapy technicians. In 1994, 275 programs for respiratory therapists were accredited by the Commission on Accreditation of Allied Health Education Programs (CAAHEP) of the American Medical Association (AMA). Another 174 programs offered CAAHEP-accredited preparation for respiratory therapy technicians.

Formal training programs vary in length and in the credential or degree awarded. Most of the CAAHEP-accredited therapist programs last 2 years and lead to an associate degree. Some, however, are 4-year bachelor's degree programs. Technician programs last about 1 year, and award certificates. Areas of study for respiratory therapist programs include human anatomy and physiology, chemistry, physics, microbiology, and mathematics. Technical courses deal with procedures, equipment, and clinical tests.

More and more therapists receive on-the-job training, allowing them to administer electrocardiograms and stress tests, as well as draw blood samples from patients.

Therapists should be sensitive to patients' physical and psychological needs. Respiratory care workers must pay attention to detail, follow instructions, and work as part of a team. Operating complicated respiratory therapy equipment requires mechanical ability and manual dexterity.

High school students interested in a career in respiratory care are encouraged to take courses in health, biology, mathematics, chemistry, and physics. Respiratory care involves basic mathematical problem-solving. An understanding of basic chemical and physical principles is also important. Computing medication dosages and calculating gas concentrations are just two examples of the need for knowledge of science and mathematics.

Thirty-eight States license respiratory care personnel. The National Board for Respiratory Care offers voluntary certification and registration to graduates of CAAHEP-accredited programs. Two credentials are awarded to respiratory care practitioners who satisfy the requirements: Certified Respiratory Therapy Technician (CRTT) and Registered Respiratory Therapist (RRT). All graduates—those from 2- and 4-year programs in respiratory therapy, as well as those from 1-year technician programs—may take the CRTT examination first. CRTT's who meet education and experience requirements can take a separate examination, leading to the award of the RRT.

Individuals who have completed a 4-year program in a nonrespiratory field, but have college level courses in anatomy, physiology, chemistry, biology, microbiology, physics, and mathematics, can become a CRTT after graduating from an AMA accredited 1- or 2-year program. After they receive 2 years of clinical experience, they are eligible to take the registry exam to become an RRT.

Most employers require that applicants for entry level or generalist positions hold the CRTT or are eligible to take the certification examination. Supervisory positions and those in intensive care specialties, usually require the RRT (or RRT eligibility).

Respiratory therapists advance in clinical practice by moving from care of "general" to "critical" patients, whom have significant problems in other organ systems such as the heart or kidneys. Respiratory therapists, especially those with 4-year degrees, may also advance to supervisory or managerial positions in a respiratory therapy department. Respiratory therapists in home care and equipment rental firms may become branch manager. Others leave the occupation to work as sales representatives or as equipment designers for equipment manufacturers.

Job Outlook

Job opportunities are expected to remain good. Employment of respiratory therapists is expected to increase much faster than the average for all occupations through the year 2005 because of substantial growth of the middle-aged and elderly population, a development that will heighten the incidence of cardiopulmonary disease.

The elderly are the most common sufferers from respiratory ailments and cardiopulmonary diseases such as pneumonia, chronic bronchitis, emphysema, and heart disease. As their numbers increase, the need for respiratory therapists will increase as well. In addition, advances in treating victims of heart attacks, accident victims, and premature infants (many of whom may be dependent on a ventilator during part of their treatment) will require the services of respiratory care practitioners. Rapid growth in the number of patients with AIDS also will boost demand because lung disease often accompanies AIDS.

Opportunities are expected to be highly favorable for respiratory therapists having cardiopulmonary care skills and experience working with infants.

Very rapid growth is expected in home health agencies, equipment rental companies, and firms that provide respiratory care on a contract basis.

Earnings

Median annual earnings for respiratory therapists who worked year round full time in 1994 were $30,212. The middle 50 percent earned between $24,544 and $34,996. The lowest 10 percent earned less than $18,200; the top 10 percent, more than $43,420.

According to the the University of Texas Medical Branch, median annual salary, based on a 40-hour week and excluding shift and area differentials, for respiratory therapists in hospitals and medical centers was about $30,888 in October 1994. The average minimum annual salary was $25,978 and the average maximum was $38,233.

Related Occupations

Respiratory therapists, under the supervision of a physician, administer respiratory care and life support to patients with heart and lung difficulties. Other workers who care for, treat, or train people to improve their physical condition include dialysis technicians, registered nurses, occupational therapists, physical therapists, and radiation therapy technologists.

Sources of Additional Information

Information concerning a career in respiratory care is available from:
☛American Association for Respiratory Care, 11030 Ables Ln., Dallas, TX 75229.

Information on gaining credentials as a respiratory therapy practitioner can be obtained from:
☛The National Board for Respiratory Care, Inc., 8310 Nieman Rd., Lenexa, KS 66214.

For the current list of CAAHEP-accredited educational programs for respiratory therapy occupations, write to:
☛Joint Review Committee for Respiratory Therapy Education, 1701 W. Euless Blvd., Suite 300, Euless, TX 76040.

Speech-Language Pathologists and Audiologists

(D.O.T. 076.101-010, .104-010, and .107-010)

Nature of the Work

Speech-language pathologists assess and treat persons with speech, language, voice, and fluency disorders; audiologists assess and treat those with hearing and related disorders.

Speech-language pathologists work with people who cannot make speech sounds, or cannot make them clearly; those with speech rhythm and fluency problems, such as stuttering; people with speech quality problems, such as inappropriate pitch or harsh voice; and those with problems understanding and producing language. They may also work with people who have oral motor problems that cause eating and swallowing difficulties.

Speech and language problems may result from causes such as hearing loss, brain injury or deterioration, cerebral palsy, stroke, cleft palate, voice pathology, mental retardation, or emotional problems. Speech-language pathologists use special instruments, as well as written and oral tests, to determine the nature and extent of impairment, and to record and analyze speech irregularities. For individuals with little or no speech, speech-language pathologists select alternative communication systems, including automated devices and sign language, and teach their use. They teach other patients how to make sounds, improve their voices, or increase their language skills.

Audiologists work with people who have hearing and related problems. They use audiometers and other testing devices to measure the loudness at which a person begins to hear sounds, the ability to distinguish between sounds, and other tests of the nature and extent of their hearing loss. Audiologists may coordinate these results with medical, educational, and psychological information, make a diagnosis, and determine a course of treatment.

Hearing disorders may result from causes such as viral infections, genetic disorders, or exposure to loud noise. Treatment may include examining and cleaning the ear canal, fitting a hearing aid, auditory training, and instruction in speech or lip reading. They may recommend use of amplifiers and alerting devices. Audiologists also test noise levels in workplaces and conduct hearing protection programs.

Most speech-language pathologists and audiologists provide direct clinical services to individuals with communication disorders. In speech, language, and hearing clinics, they may independently develop and carry out a treatment program. In medical facilities, they may work with physicians, social workers, psychologists, and other therapists to develop and execute a treatment plan. Speech-language pathology and audiology personnel in schools also develop individual or group programs, counsel parents, and assist teachers with classroom activities.

Speech-language pathologists and audiologists keep records on the initial evaluation, progress, and discharge of clients. This helps pinpoint problems, tracks client progress, and justifies the cost of treatment when applying for reimbursement. They counsel individuals and their families about communication disorders and how to cope with the stress and misunderstanding that often accompany them. They also work with family members to recognize and change behavior patterns that impede communication and treatment, and show them communication-enhancing techniques to use at home.

Some speech-language pathologists and audiologists conduct research on how people speak and hear. Others design and develop equipment or techniques for diagnosing and treating problems.

Working Conditions

Speech-language pathologists and audiologists usually work at a desk or table in clean comfortable surroundings. The job is not physically demanding, but does require attention to detail and intense concentration. The emotional needs of clients and their families may be demanding and there may be frustration when clients do not improve. Most full-time speech-language pathologists and audiologists work about 40 hours per week. Some work part-time. Those who work on a contract basis may spend a substantial amount of time traveling between facilities.

Most speech-language pathologists and audiologists provide direct clinical services to individuals with communication disorders.

Employment

Speech-language pathologists and audiologists held about 85,000 jobs in 1994. About one-half provided services in preschools, elementary and secondary schools, or colleges and universities. More than 10 percent were in hospitals. Others were in offices of physicians; offices of speech-language pathologists and audiologists; speech, language, and hearing centers; home health care agencies; and other facilities. Some were in private practice, working either as solo practitioners or in a group practice.

Some experienced speech-language pathologists or audiologists contract to provide services in schools, hospitals, or nursing homes or work as consultants to industry.

Training, Other Qualifications, and Advancement

A master's degree in speech-language pathology or audiology is the standard credential in this field. By the year 2005, a doctoral degree may be required for entry into audiology practice. Of the 45 States that regulate speech-language pathologists and/or audiologists, all currently require a master's degree or equivalent, 300-375 hours of supervised clinical experience, a passing score on a national examination, and 9 months of post-graduate professional experience. For licensure renewal, 27 States have continuing education requirements. Medicaid, Medicare, and private insurers generally require a license to qualify for reimbursement.

In some States, people with bachelor's degrees in speech-language pathology may work in schools with students who have communication problems. They may have to be certified by the State educational agency, and may be classified as special education teachers rather than speech-language pathologists or audiologists. Federal law requires speech-language pathologists in school systems in almost every State to have a minimum of a master's degree or equivalent. All States require audiologists to hold a master's degree or equivalent.

About 230 colleges and universities offered master's programs in speech-language pathology and/or audiology in 1995. Courses cover anatomy and physiology of the areas involved in speech, language, and hearing; the development of normal speech, language, and hearing and the nature of disorders; acoustics; and psychological aspects of communication. Graduate students also learn to evaluate and treat speech, language, and hearing disorders and receive supervised clinical training in communication disorders.

Those with a master's degree can acquire the Certificate of Clinical Competence (CCC) offered by the American Speech-Language-Hearing Association or the Fellowship-AAA (F-AAA) offered by the American Academy of Audiology. To earn the CCC or F-AAA, a person must have a master's degree, have 300-375 hours of supervised clinical experience, complete a 9-month post-graduate internship, and pass a written examination.

Speech-language pathologists and audiologists should be able to effectively communicate test results, diagnoses, and proposed treatment in a manner easily understood by their clients. They also need to be able to approach problems objectively and provide support to clients and their families. Patience and compassion are important because a client's progress may be slow.

With experience, some salaried speech-language pathologists and audiologists enter private practice; others become directors or administrators of services in schools, hospitals, health departments, and clinics. Some become researchers.

Job Outlook

Employment of speech-language pathologists and audiologists is expected to increase much faster than the average for all occupations through the year 2005. Some job openings also will arise from the need to replace speech-language pathologists and audiologists who leave the occupation.

Employment in the health services industry will increase as a result of several factors. Because hearing loss is strongly associated with older age, rapid growth in the population age 75 and over will cause the number of hearing-impaired persons to increase markedly. In addition, baby boomers are now entering middle age, when the possibility of neurological disorders and their associated speech, language, and hearing impairments increases. Medical advances are also improving the survival rate of premature infants and trauma victims, who then need treatment.

Employment in schools will increase as elementary and secondary school enrollments grow. Federal law guarantees special education and related services to all eligible children with disabilities. Greater awareness of the importance of early identification and diagnosis of speech, language, and hearing disorders will also increase employment.

The number of speech-language pathologists and audiologists in private practice, though small, is likely to rise sharply by the year 2005. Encouraging this growth is the increasing use of contract services by hospitals, schools, and nursing homes.

Earnings

Median weekly earnings of full-time salaried speech-language pathologists and audiologists were $693 in 1994. The middle 50 percent earned between $548 and $782. The lowest 10 percent earned less than $424 and the top 10 percent more than $1,015.

According to a 1994 survey by the American Speech-Language-Hearing Association, the median annual salary for full-time certified speech-language pathologists with 1 to 3 years experience was about $31,000; for certified audiologists, it was about $29,000. Speech-language pathologists with 16 years or more experience earned a median annual salary of about $42,430, while experienced audiologists earned about $50,000. Salaries also vary according to geographic location.

Speech-language pathologists and audiologists in hospitals earned a median annual salary of about $35,372, according to a 1994 survey conducted by the University of Texas Medical Branch.

Related Occupations

Speech-language pathologists and audiologists specialize in the prevention, diagnosis, and treatment of speech, language, and hearing problems. Workers in related occupations include occupational therapists, optometrists, physical therapists, psychologists, recreational therapists, and rehabilitation counselors.

Sources of Additional Information

State licensing boards in each State can provide information on licensure requirements. State departments of education can supply information on certification requirements for those who wish to work in public schools.

General information on speech-language pathology and audiology is available from:

☛American Speech-Language-Hearing Association, 10801 Rockville Pike, Rockville, MD 20852.

Information on a career in audiology is also available from:

☛American Academy of Audiology, 1735 N. Lynn St., #900, Arlington, VA 22209.

Communications Occupations

Public Relations Specialists

(D.O.T. 165.017, .167)

Nature of the Work

An organization's reputation, profitability, and even its continued existence can depend on the degree to which its goals and policies are supported by its targeted "publics." Public relations specialists serve as advocates for businesses, governments, universities, hospitals, schools, and other organizations, and strive to build and maintain positive relationships with the public. As managers recognize the growing importance of good public relations to the success of their organizations, they increasingly rely on public relations specialists for advice on strategy and policy.

Public relations specialists handle such functions as media, community, consumer, and governmental relations; political campaigns; interest-group representation; conflict mediation; or employee and investor relations. Public relations is not only "telling the organization's story," however. Understanding the attitudes and concerns of consumers, employees, and various other groups also is a vital part of the job. To improve communications, public relations specialists establish and maintain cooperative relationships with representatives of community, consumer, employee, and public interest groups and those in print and broadcast journalism.

Public relations specialists put together information that keeps the general public, interest groups, and stockholders aware of an organization's policies, activities, and accomplishments. Their work keeps management aware of public attitudes and concerns of the many groups and organizations with which it must deal.

Public relations specialists prepare press releases and contact people in the media who might print or broadcast their material. Many radio or television special reports, newspaper stories, and magazine articles start at the desks of public relations specialists. Sometimes the subject is an organization and its policies towards its employees or its role in the community. Often the subject is a public issue, such as health, nutrition, energy, or the environment.

Public relations specialists also arrange and conduct programs for contact between organization representatives and the public. For example, they set up speaking engagements and often prepare the speeches for company officials. These specialists represent employers at community projects; make film, slide, or other visual presentations at meetings and school assemblies; and plan conventions. In addition, they are responsible for preparing annual reports and writing proposals for various projects.

In government, public relations specialists—who may be called press secretaries, information officers, public affairs specialists, or communications specialists—keep the public informed about the activities of government agencies and officials. For example, public affairs specialists in the Department of Energy keep the public informed about the proposed lease of offshore land for oil exploration. A press secretary for a member of Congress keeps constituents aware of their elected representative's accomplishments.

In large organizations, the key public relations executive, who is often a vice president, may develop overall plans and policies with other executives. In addition, public relations departments employ public relations specialists to write, do research, prepare materials, maintain contacts, and respond to inquiries.

People who handle publicity for an individual or who direct public relations for a small organization may deal with all aspects of the job. They contact people, plan and do research, and prepare

Creativity, initiative, good judgement, and the ability to express thoughts clearly and simply are essential for public relations specialists.

material for distribution. They may also handle advertising or sales promotion work to support marketing.

Working Conditions

Some public relations specialists work a standard 35- to 40-hour week, but unpaid overtime is common. In addition, schedules often have to be rearranged to meet deadlines, deliver speeches, attend meetings and community activities, and travel out of town. Occasionally they have to be at the job or on call around the clock, especially if there is an emergency or crisis.

Employment

Public relations specialists held about 107,000 jobs in 1994. About two-thirds worked in services industries—management and public relations firms, educational institutions, membership organizations, health care organizations, social service agencies, and advertising agencies, for example. Others worked for a wide range of employers, including manufacturing firms, financial institutions, and government agencies. Some were self-employed.

Public relations specialists are concentrated in large cities where press services and other communications facilities are readily available, and where many businesses and trade associations have their headquarters. Many public relations consulting firms, for example, are in New York, Los Angeles, Chicago, and Washington, DC. There is a trend, however, for public relations jobs to be dispersed throughout the Nation.

Training, Other Qualifications, and Advancement

Although there are no defined standards for entry into a public relations career, a college degree combined with public relations experience, usually gained through an internship, is considered excellent preparation for public relations work. The ability to write and speak well is essential. Many beginners have a college major in public relations, journalism, advertising, or communications. Some firms seek college graduates who have worked in electronic or print journalism. Other employers seek applicants with demonstrated communications skills and training or experience in a field related to the firm's business—science, engineering, sales, or finance, for example.

In 1994, well over 200 colleges and about 100 graduate schools offered degree programs or special curricula in public relations, usually in a journalism or communications department. In addition, many other colleges offered at least one course in this field. A commonly used public relations sequence includes the following courses: Public relations principles and techniques; public relations management and administration, including organizational development; writing, emphasizing news releases, proposals, annual reports, scripts, speeches, and related items; visual communications, including desktop publishing and computer graphics; and research, emphasizing social science research and survey design and implementation. Courses in advertising, journalism, business administration, political science, psychology, sociology, and creative writing also are helpful, as is familiarity with word processing and other computer applications. Specialties are offered in public relations for business, government, or nonprofit organizations.

Many colleges help students gain part-time internships in public relations that provide valuable experience and training. The Armed Forces also can be an excellent place to gain training and experience. Membership in local chapters of the Public Relations Student Society of America or the International Association of Business Communicators provides an opportunity for students to exchange views with public relations specialists and to make professional contacts that may help them find a full-time job in the field. A portfolio of published articles, television or radio programs, slide presentations, and other work is an asset in finding a job. Writing for a school publication or television or radio station provides valuable experience and material for one's portfolio.

Creativity, initiative, good judgment, and the ability to express thoughts clearly and simply are essential. Decision making, problem solving, and research skills are also important.

People who choose public relations as a career need an outgoing personality, self-confidence, an understanding of human psychology, and an enthusiasm for motivating people. They should be competitive, yet flexible and able to function as part of a team.

Some organizations—particularly those with large public relations staffs—have formal training programs for new employees. In smaller organizations, new employees work under the guidance of experienced staff members. Beginners often maintain files of material about company activities, scan newspapers and magazines for appropriate articles to clip, and assemble information for speeches and pamphlets. After gaining experience, they write news releases, speeches, and articles for publication, or design and carry out public relations programs. Public relations specialists in smaller firms generally get all-around experience, whereas those in larger firms tend to be more specialized.

The Public Relations Society of America accredits public relations specialists who have at least 5 years of experience in the field and have passed a comprehensive 6-hour examination (5 hours written, 1 hour oral). The International Association of Business Communicators also has an accreditation program for professionals in the communications field, including public relations specialists. Those who meet all the requirements of the program earn the designation, Accredited Business Communicator. Candidates must have at least 5 years of experience in a communication field and pass a written and oral examination. They also must submit a portfolio of work samples demonstrating involvement in a range of communication projects and a thorough understanding of communication planning. Employers consider professional recognition through accreditation a sign of competence in this field, and it may be especially helpful in a competitive job market.

Promotion to supervisory jobs may come as public relations specialists show they can handle more demanding managerial assignments. In public relations firms, a beginner may be hired as a research assistant or account assistant and be promoted to account executive, account supervisor, vice president, and eventually senior vice president. A similar career path is followed in corporate public relations, although the titles may differ. Some experienced public relations specialists start their own consulting firms. (For more information on public relations managers, see the *Handbook* statement on marketing, advertising, and public relations managers.)

Job Outlook

Keen competition for public relations jobs will likely continue among recent college graduates with a degree in communications—journalism, public relations, advertising, or a related field—as the number of applicants is expected to exceed the number of job openings. People without the appropriate educational background or work experience will face the toughest obstacles in finding a public relations job.

Employment of public relations specialists is expected to increase about as fast as the average for all occupations through the year 2005. Recognition of the need for good public relations in an increasingly competitive business environment should spur demand for public relations specialists in organizations of all sizes. However, corporate restructuring and downsizing, in an effort to cut costs, could limit employment growth. Employment in public relations firms should grow as firms hire contractors to provide public relations services rather than support full-time staff. The vast majority of job opportunities should result from the need to replace public relations specialists who leave the occupation to take another job, retire, or for other reasons.

Earnings

Median annual earnings for salaried public relations specialists who usually worked full time were about $23,000 in 1994. The middle 50 percent earned between $16,000 and $33,000 annually; the lowest 10 percent earned less than $13,000; and the top 10 percent earned more than $47,000.

A National Association of Colleges and Employers survey indicated new college graduates entering the public relations field were offered average starting salaries of $21,000 in 1995.

According to a 1993 salary survey by the *Public Relations Journal*, the median entry level salary of public relations account executives was almost $21,500 a year. Median annual salaries of all public relations account executives ranged from $29,000 in public relations firms to about $36,000 in corporations. Manufacturers, utilities, and scientific and technical firms were among the highest paying employers; museums and miscellaneous nonprofit organizations, religious and charitable organizations, and advertising agencies were among the lowest paying employers. The survey indicated an annual median salary for all respondents, including managers, of about $46,000. Some highly successful public relations workers earn considerably more.

Public affairs specialists in the Federal Government in nonsupervisory, supervisory, and managerial positions averaged about $49,180 a year in 1995.

Related Occupations

Public relations specialists create favorable attitudes among various organizations, special interest groups, and the public through effective communication. Other workers with similar jobs include fundraisers, lobbyists, promotion managers, advertising managers, and police officers involved in community relations.

Sources of Additional Information

A comprehensive directory of schools offering degree programs or a sequence of study in public relations, a brochure on careers in public relations, and a $5 brochure entitled *Where Shall I go to Study Advertising and Public Relations* are available from:

☛Public Relations Society of America, Inc., 33 Irving Place, New York, NY 10003-2376.

Current information on the public relations field, salaries, and other items is available from:

☛*PR Reporter*, P.O. Box 600, Exeter, NH 03833.

Career information on public relations in hospitals/health care is available from:

☛The American Society for Health Care Marketing and Public Relations, American Hospital Association, One North Franklin St., Chicago, IL 60606.

Radio and Television Announcers and Newscasters

(D.O.T. 131.067-010, .262-010; 159.147-010, -014, and ˉ018)

Nature of the Work

Announcers and newscasters are well-known to radio and television audiences. Radio announcers, often called disk jockeys, select and introduce recorded music; present news, sports, weather, and commercials; interview guests; and report on community activities and other matters of interest to their audience. If a written script is required, they may do the research and writing. They often "ad-lib" much of the commentary. They also may operate the control board, sell commercial time to advertisers, and write commercial and news copy.

Some announcers at large stations usually specialize in sports or weather, or in general news, and may be called newscasters or anchors. Others are news analysts. In small stations, one announcer may do everything.

News anchors, or a pair of co-anchors, present news stories and introduce in-depth videotaped news or live transmissions from on-the-scene reporters. (See statement on reporters and correspondents elsewhere in the *Handbook*.) Weathercasters, also called weather reporters or meteorologists, report and forecast weather conditions. They gather information from national satellite weather services, wire services, and other local and regional weather bureaus. Sportscasters select, write, and deliver the sports news. This may include interviews with sports personalities and coverage of games played.

Broadcast news analysts, called commentators, present news stories and also interpret them and discuss how they may affect the Nation or listeners.

Show hosts interview guests about their lives, work, or topics of current interest.

Announcers frequently participate in community activities. Sports announcers, for example, are masters of ceremonies at touchdown club banquets or are on hand to greet customers at openings of sporting goods stores.

Working Conditions

Announcers and newscasters usually work in well-lighted, air-conditioned, soundproof studios.

The broadcast day is long for radio and TV stations—some are on the air 24 hours a day—so announcers can expect to work unusual

Radio and television announcers use computers to create and edit stories.

hours. Many announcers present early morning shows, when many people are getting ready for work or commuting, or do late night newscasts.

They work within tight schedule constraints, which can be physically and mentally stressful. For many announcers, the intangible rewards—creative work, many personal contacts, and the satisfaction of becoming widely known—far outweigh the disadvantages of irregular and often unpredictable hours, work pressures, and disrupted personal lives.

Employment

Radio and television announcers and newscasters held about 50,000 jobs in 1994. Nearly all were staff announcers, but some were freelance announcers who sold their services for individual assignments to networks and stations, or to advertising agencies and other independent producers.

Training, Other Qualifications, and Advancement

Entry to this occupation is highly competitive. While formal training in broadcast journalism from a college or technical school (private broadcasting school) is valuable, station officials pay particular attention to taped auditions that show an applicant's delivery and—in television—appearance and style on commercials, news, and interviews. Those hired by television stations usually start out as production secretaries, production assistants, researchers, or reporters and are given a chance to move into announcing if they show an aptitude for "on-air" work. Newcomers to TV broadcasting also may begin as news camera operators. (See the statement on photographers and camera operators elsewhere in the *Handbook*.) A beginner's chance of landing an on-air newscasting job is remote, except possibly for a small radio station. In radio, newcomers generally start out taping interviews and operating equipment.

Announcers usually begin at a station in a small community and, if qualified, may move to a better paying job in a large city. Announcers also may advance by hosting a regular program as a disc jockey, sportscaster, or other specialist. In the national networks, competition for jobs is particularly intense, and employers look for college graduates with at least several years of successful announcing experience.

Announcers must have a pleasant and well-controlled voice, good timing, excellent pronunciation, and correct English usage. Television announcers need a neat, pleasing appearance as well. Knowledge of theater, sports, music, business, politics, and other subjects likely to be covered in broadcasts improves chances for success. Announcers also must be computer literate because stories are created and edited on the computer. In addition, they should be able to "ad-lib" all or part of a show and to work under tight deadlines. The most successful announcers attract a large audience by combining a pleasing personality and voice with an appealing style.

High school courses in English, public speaking, drama, foreign languages, and electronics are valuable, and hobbies such as sports and music are additional assets. Students may gain valuable experience at campus radio or TV facilities and at commercial stations. Some stations and cable systems offer financial assistance and on-the-job training in the form of internships, apprentice programs, co-op work programs, scholarships, or fellowships.

Persons considering enrolling in a broadcasting school should contact personnel managers of radio and television stations as well as broadcasting trade organizations to determine the school's reputation for producing suitably trained candidates.

Announcers who operate transmitters must obtain a Federal Communications Commission (FCC) restricted radiotelephone operator permit. (For additional information on FCC requirements, see the statement on broadcast technicians elsewhere in the *Handbook*.)

Job Outlook

Competition for jobs as announcers will be very keen because the broadcasting field typically attracts many more jobseekers than there are jobs. Small radio stations are more inclined to hire beginners, but the pay is low. Because competition for ratings is so intense in major metropolitan areas, large stations will continue to seek announcers and newscasters who have proven that they can attract and retain a large audience.

Newscasters who are knowledgeable in such areas as business, consumer, and health news may have an advantage over others. While specialization is more common at larger stations and the networks, many smaller stations also encourage it.

Little change in the employment of announcers is expected through the year 2005 due to the slowing in the growth of new radio and television stations and cable systems. Most openings in this relatively small field will arise from the need to replace those who transfer to other kinds of work or leave the labor force. Many announcers leave the field because they can not advance to better paying jobs.

Employment in this occupation is not significantly affected by downturns in the economy. If recessions cause advertising revenues to fall, stations tend to cut "behind-the-scenes" workers rather than announcers and broadcasters.

Earnings

Salaries in broadcasting vary widely. They are higher in television than in radio, higher in larger markets than in small ones, and higher in commercial than in public broadcasting.

According to a survey conducted by the National Association of Broadcasters and the Broadcast Cable Financial Management Association, the average salary for radio news announcers was $27,901 a year in 1994. Salaries ranged from $23,000 in the smallest markets to $39,291 in the largest markets. Sports announcers' average was $38,950, ranging from $26,663 in the smallest to $75,029 in the largest markets.

Among television announcers, news anchors' average salary was $65,520, ranging from $24,935 in the smallest to $199,741 in the largest markets. Weathercasters' average was $52,562, ranging from $25,638 to $130,919. Sportscasters' average was $48,704, ranging from $22,400 to $128,877.

Related Occupations

The success of announcers and news broadcasters depends upon how well they speak to their audiences. Others for whom oral communication skills are vital are interpreters, sales workers, public relations specialists, teachers, and actors.

Sources of Additional Information

For a list of schools that offer programs and courses in broadcasting, contact:

☛Broadcast Education Association, 1771 N St. NW., Washington, DC 20036.

For information on FCC licenses, write to:

☛Federal Communications Commission, Consumer Assistance Office, 1270 Fairfield Rd., Gettysburg, PA 17325-7245 or call toll free 1-800-322-1117.

General information on the broadcasting industry is available from:

☛National Association of Broadcasters, 1771 N St. NW., Washington, DC 20036.

For information on careers in broadcast news, contact:

☛Radio-Television News Directors Association, 1717 K St. NW., Suite 615, Washington, DC 20006.

Reporters and Correspondents

(D.O.T. 131.262-018)

Nature of the Work

Reporters and correspondents play a key role in our society. They gather information and prepare stories that inform us about local, State, national, and international events; present points of view on current issues; and report on the actions of public officials, corporate executives, special interest groups, and others who exercise power.

In covering a story, they investigate leads and news tips, look at documents, observe on the scene, and interview people. Reporters take notes and may also take photographs or shoot videos. At their office, they organize the material, determine their focus or emphasis, write their stories, and may also edit videos. Many enter information or write stories on portable computers, then submit them t to their offices using a telephone modem. In some cases, newswriters write the story from information collected and submitted by the reporter.

Radio and television reporters often compose stories and report "live" from the scene. Later, they may tape a commentary in the studio.

General assignment reporters write up news as assigned, such as an accident, a political rally, the visit of a celebrity, or a company going out of business. Large newspapers and radio and television stations assign reporters to gather news at specific locations or "beats," such as police stations or courts. Some reporters specialize in fields such as health, politics, foreign affairs, sports, theater, consumer affairs, social events, science, business, and religion. Investigative reporters cover stories that take many days or weeks of information gathering.

News correspondents are stationed in large U.S. and foreign cities to report on news occurring there. Reporters on small publications cover all aspects of the news: They take photographs, write headlines, lay out pages, edit wire service copy, and write editorials. They also may solicit advertisements, sell subscriptions, and perform general office work.

Radio and television reporters often compose stories and report "live" from the scene.

Working Conditions

The work of reporters and correspondents is usually hectic. They are under great pressure to meet deadlines. Some reporters work in comfortable, private offices; others work in large rooms filled with the sound of keyboards and computer printers as well as the voices of other reporters. Those reporting from the scene for radio and television may be distracted by curious onlookers or police or other emergency workers. Covering wars, political uprisings, fires, floods, and similar events often is dangerous.

Working hours vary. Reporters on morning papers often work from late afternoon until midnight. Those on afternoon or evening papers generally work from early morning until early or midafternoon. Radio and television reporters usually are assigned to a day or evening shift. Magazine reporters generally work during the day. Reporters may have to change their work hours to meet a deadline or to follow late-breaking developments. Their work demands long hours, irregular schedules, and some travel.

Employment

Reporters and correspondents held about 59,000 jobs in 1994. About 7 of every 10 worked for newspapers, either large city dailies or suburban and small town dailies or weeklies. Almost 2 in 10 worked in radio and television broadcasting, and others worked for magazines and wire services.

Training, Other Qualifications, and Advancement

Most employers prefer people with a bachelor's degree in journalism, but some hire graduates with other majors. They look for experience on school newspapers or broadcasting stations and internships with news organizations. Large city newspapers and stations may also prefer candidates with a degree in a subject-matter specialty such as economics, political science, or business. Large newspapers and broadcasters also require a minimum of 3 to 5 years experience as a reporter.

Bachelor's degree programs in journalism are available in over 400 colleges. About three-fourths of the courses in a typical curriculum are in liberal arts; the remainder are in journalism. Journalism courses include introductory mass media, basic reporting and copy editing, history of journalism, and press law and ethics. Students planning a career in broadcasting take courses in radio and television newscasting and production. Those planning newspaper or magazine careers usually specialize in news-editorial journalism.

Many community and junior colleges offer journalism courses or programs; credits may be transferable to 4-year journalism programs.

A master's degree in journalism was offered by over 100 schools in 1994; about 20 schools offered a Ph.D. degree. Some graduate programs are intended primarily as preparation for news careers, while others prepare journalism teachers, researchers and theorists, and advertising and public relations workers.

High school courses in English, journalism, and social studies, provide a good foundation. Useful college liberal arts courses include English with an emphasis on writing, sociology, political science, economics, history, and psychology. Courses in computer science, business, and speech are useful as well. Fluency in a foreign language is necessary in some jobs.

Reporters need good word processing skills, and computer graphics and desktop publishing skills are useful. A knowledge of news photography is valuable for entry level positions which are for combination reporter/camera operator or reporter/photographer.

Experience in a part-time or summer job or an internship with a news organization is important. The Dow Jones Newspaper Fund and newspapers, magazines, and broadcast news organizations offer summer reporting and editing internships. Work on high school and college newspapers and broadcasting stations, community papers, and Armed Forces publications also helps. In addition, more than 3,000 journalism scholarships, fellowships, and assistantships were awarded to college journalism students by universities, newspapers, foundations, and professional organizations in 1994.

Experience as a "stringer"—a part-time reporter who is paid only for stories printed—is also helpful.

Reporters should be dedicated to providing accurate and impartial news. Accuracy is important both to serve the public and because untrue or libelous statements can lead to costly lawsuits. A "nose for news," persistence, initiative, poise, resourcefulness, a good memory, and the physical stamina and emotional stability to deal with pressing deadlines, irregular hours, and sometimes dangerous assignments are important. Broadcast reporters need to be at ease on camera. All reporters must be at ease in unfamiliar places with all kinds of people.

Most reporters start with small publications or broadcast stations as general assignment reporters or copy editors. Large publications and stations hire very few recent graduates; they generally require their new reporters to have several years of experience.

Beginning reporters cover court proceedings and civic and club meetings, summarize speeches, and write obituaries. With experience, they report more difficult assignments, cover an assigned "beat," or specialize in a particular field.

Some reporters may advance by moving to larger papers or stations. A few experienced reporters become columnists, correspondents, writers, announcers, or public relations specialists. Others become editors in print journalism or program managers in broadcast journalism, who supervise reporters. Some eventually become broadcasting or publications industry managers.

Job Outlook
Competition for reporting jobs on large metropolitan newspapers and broadcast stations and on national magazines will continue to be keen. Small town and suburban newspapers will continue to offer better opportunities for beginners. Many openings arise on small publications as reporters become editors or reporters on larger publications or leave the field. Talented writers who can handle highly specialized scientific or technical subjects have an advantage. Also, "stringers" and freelancers are being hired by more newspapers.

Employment of reporters and correspondents is expected to decline through the year 2005—the result of mergers, consolidations and closures of newspapers, decreased circulations, increased expenses, and a decline in advertising profits. Some growth is expected in radio and television stations.

Most job openings will arise from the need to replace reporters and correspondents who leave the occupation. Turnover is relatively high in this occupation—some find the work too stressful and hectic, or don't like the lifestyle and transfer to other occupations where their skills are valuable, especially public relations and advertising work. Others leave because they are unable to move up to better paid jobs in bigger cities.

Journalism graduates have the background for work in such closely related fields as advertising and public relations and many take jobs in these fields. Other graduates accept sales, managerial, and other nonmedia positions, in many cases because it is difficult to find media jobs.

The newspaper and broadcasting industries are sensitive to economic ups and downs. During recessions, few new reporters are hired and some reporters lose their jobs.

Earnings
The Newspaper Guild negotiates with individual newspapers on minimum salaries for both starting reporters and those still on the job after 3 to 6 years. The median minimum salary for reporters was about $443 a week as of August 1, 1994. Ten percent of the contracts called for minimums of $326 or less; 10 percent, $618 or more. The median minimum weekly salary for reporters after 3 to 6 years on the job was about $713 a week. Ten percent of the contracts called for top minimums of $522 or less; 10 percent, $933 or more.

Annual average salaries of radio reporters ranged from $18,600 in the smallest stations to $28,989, in the largest stations in 1994, according to a survey conducted by the National Association of Broadcasters. For all stations, the median salary was $23,612. Salaries of television reporters ranged from $17,435 in the smallest stations to $79,637 in the largest ones. For all stations, the median salary was $31,239.

Related Occupations
Reporters and correspondents must write clearly and effectively to succeed in their profession. Others for whom writing ability is essential include technical writers, advertising copy writers, public relations workers, educational writers, fiction writers, biographers, screen writers, and editors.

Sources of Additional Information
Career information, including pamphlets entitled *Facts about Newspapers*, and *Newspaper: What's In It For Me?* is available from:
☛Newspaper Association of America Foundation, 11600 Sunrise Valley Dr., Reston, VA 22091-1412.

Information on careers in journalism, colleges and universities that offer degree programs in journalism or communications, and journalism scholarships and internships may be obtained from:
☛The Dow Jones Newspaper Fund, Inc., P.O. Box 300, Princeton, NJ 08543-0300.

Information on union wage rates for newspaper and magazine reporters is available from:
☛The Newspaper Guild, Research and Information Department, 8611 Second Ave., Silver Spring, MD 20910.

For a list of schools with accredited programs in their journalism departments, send a stamped, self-addressed envelope to:
☛Accrediting Council on Education in Journalism and Mass Communications, University of Kansas School of Journalism, Stauffer-Flint Hall, Lawrence, KS 66045.

For general information about careers in journalism, contact:
☛Association For Education in Journalism and Mass Communication, University of South Carolina, 1621 College St., Columbia, SC 29208-0251.

A pamphlet titled *A Career in Newspapers*, can be obtained from:
☛National Newspaper Association, 1627 K St. NW., Suite 400, Washington, DC 20006.

Names and locations of newspapers and a list of schools and departments of journalism are published in the *Editor and Publisher International Year Book*, available in most public libraries and newspaper offices.

Writers and Editors

(D.O.T. 052.067-010; 131 except .262-010 and -018; 132; and 203.362-026)

Nature of the Work
Writers and editors communicate through the written word. Writers develop original fiction and nonfiction for books, magazines and trade journals, newspapers, technical reports, company newsletters, radio and television broadcasts, movies, and advertisements. Editors select and prepare material for publication or broadcasting and supervise writers.

Writers first select a topic or are assigned one by an editor. They then gather information through personal observation, library research, and interviews. Writers select and organize the material and put it into words that effectively convey it to the reader, and often revise or rewrite sections, searching for the best organization of the material or just the right phrasing.

Newswriters prepare news items for newspapers or news broadcasts, based on information supplied by reporters or wire services. Columnists analyze news and write commentaries, based on personal knowledge and experience. Editorial writers write comments to stimulate or mold public opinion, in accordance with their publication's viewpoint. Reporters and correspondents, who may also write articles or copy for broadcast, are described elsewhere in this section of the *Handbook*.

Technical writers make scientific and technical information easily understandable to a nontechnical audience. They prepare operating and maintenance manuals, catalogs, parts lists, assembly instructions, sales promotion materials, and project proposals. They also plan and edit technical reports and oversee preparation of illustrations, photographs, diagrams, and charts.

Copy writers write advertising copy for use by publication or broadcast media to promote the sale of goods and services.

Established writers may work on a freelance basis; they sell their work to publishers or publication units, manufacturing firms, and public relations and advertising departments or agencies. They sometimes contract to complete specific assignments such as writing about a new product or technique.

Editors frequently write and almost always review, rewrite, and edit the work of writers. However, their primary duties are to plan the contents of books, magazines, or newspapers and to supervise their preparation. They decide what will appeal to readers, assign topics to reporters and writers, and oversee the production of the publications. In small organizations, a single editor may do everything. In larger ones, an executive editor oversees associate or assistant editors who have responsibility for particular subjects, such as fiction, local news, international news, or sports, or who edit one or a few publications. Editors hire writers, reporters, or other employees, plan budgets, and negotiate contracts with freelance writers. In broadcasting companies, program directors have similar responsibilities.

Editors and program directors often have assistants, with the title of assistant editor, editorial assistant, copy editor, or production assistant. Many assistants hold entry level jobs. They review copy for errors in grammar, punctuation, and spelling. They check manuscripts for readability, style, and agreement with editorial policy. They add and rearrange sentences to improve clarity or delete incorrect and unnecessary material. Editorial assistants do research for writers and verify facts, dates, and statistics. Assistants also may arrange page layouts of articles, photographs, and advertising. They also may compose headlines, prepare copy for printing, and proofread printer's galleys. Some editorial assistants read and evaluate manuscripts submitted by freelance writers or answer letters about published or broadcast material. Production assistants on small papers or in radio stations clip stories that come over the wire services' printers, answer phones, and make photocopies. Most writers and editors use personal computers or word processors; many use desktop or electronic publishing systems.

Working Conditions

Some writers and editors work in comfortable, private offices; others work in noisy rooms filled with the sound of keyboards and computer printers as well as the voices of other writers tracking down information over the telephone. The search for information sometimes requires travel and visits to diverse workplaces, such as factories, offices, laboratories, the ballpark, or the theater, but many have to be content with telephone interviews and the library.

The workweek usually runs 35 to 40 hours. Those who prepare morning or weekend publications and broadcasts work nights or weekends. Writers may work overtime to meet deadlines or to cover late-developing stories. They often face deadlines and the pressure to meet them. On some jobs, deadlines are daily.

Employment

Writers and editors held about 272,000 jobs in 1994. Nearly a third of salaried writers and editors work for newspapers, magazines, and book publishers. Substantial numbers also work in advertising agencies, in radio and television broadcasting, in public relations firms, and on journals and newsletters published by business and nonprofit organizations, such as professional associations, labor unions, and religious organizations. Others develop publications for government agencies or write for motion picture companies.

Nearly a third of salaried writers and editors work for newspapers, magazines, and book publishers.

Many technical writers work for computer software firms or manufacturers of aircraft, chemicals, pharmaceuticals, and computers and other electronic equipment.

Jobs with major book publishers, magazines, broadcasting companies, advertising agencies and public relations firms, and the Federal Government are concentrated in New York, Chicago, Los Angeles, Boston, Philadelphia, San Francisco, and Washington, D.C. More widely dispersed throughout the country are jobs with newspapers; and professional, religious, business, technical, and trade union magazines or journals. Technical writers are employed throughout the country but the largest concentrations are in the Northeast, Texas, and California.

Thousands of other persons work as freelancers—earning some income from their articles, books, and, less commonly, television and movie scripts. Most support themselves primarily with income from other sources.

Training, Other Qualifications, and Advancement

A college degree generally is required. Although some employers look for a broad liberal arts background, most prefer to hire people with degrees in communications, journalism, or English.

Technical writing requires a degree in or some knowledge about a specialized field—engineering, business, or one of the sciences, for example. In many cases, people with good writing skills can pick up specialized knowledge on the job. Some transfer from jobs as technicians, scientists, or engineers. Some begin as research assistants, editorial assistants, or trainees in a technical information department, develop technical communication skills, and then assume writing duties.

Writers and editors must be able to express ideas clearly and logically and should love to write. Creativity, curiosity, a broad range of knowledge, self-motivation, and perseverance are also valuable. For some jobs, the ability to concentrate amid confusion and to produce under pressure is essential. Familiarity with electronic publishing, graphics, and video production equipment is increasingly needed. Editors must have good judgment in deciding what material to accept and what to reject. They need tact and the ability to guide and encourage others in their work.

High school and college newspapers, literary magazines, and community newspapers and radio and television stations all provide valuable—but sometimes unpaid—practical writing experience. Many magazines, newspapers, and broadcast stations have internships for students. Interns write short pieces, conduct research and interviews, and learn about the publishing or broadcasting business.

In small firms, beginning writers and editors may not only work as editorial or production assistants but also write or edit material right away. They often advance by moving to other firms. In larger firms, jobs usually are structured more formally. Beginners generally do research, fact checking, or copy editing. They take on full-scale writing or editing duties less rapidly than do the employees of small companies. Advancement comes as they are assigned more important articles.

Job Outlook

Through the year 2005, the outlook for most writing and editing jobs is expected to continue to be keenly competitive primarily because so many people are attracted to the field. However, opportunities will be good for technical writers because of the more limited number of writers who can handle technical material. Opportunities should be better on small dailies and weekly newspapers and in small radio and television stations, where the pay is low. Persons preparing to be writers and editors should also have academic preparation in another field as well, either to qualify them as writers specializing in that field or to enter that field if they are unable to get a writing job.

Employment of writers and editors is expected to increase faster than the average for all occupations through the year 2005. Employment of salaried writers and editors by newspapers, periodicals, book publishers, and nonprofit organizations is expected to increase with growing demand for their publications. Growth of advertising and public relations agencies should also be a source of new jobs. Demand for technical writers is expected to increase because of the continuing expansion of scientific and technical information and the continued need to communicate it. Many job openings will also occur as experienced workers transfer to other occupations or leave the labor force. Turnover is relatively high in this occupation—many freelancers leave because they can not earn enough.

Earnings

In 1994, beginning salaries for writers and editorial assistants averaged $18,000 annually, according to the Dow Jones Newspaper Fund. Those who had at least 5 years experience averaged more than $30,000 and senior editors at the largest newspapers earned over $60,000 a year.

According to the 1994 Technical Communicator's Salary Survey, the median annual salary for technical writers was $42,469 annually.

The average annual salary for technical writers and editors in the Federal Government in nonsupervisory, supervisory, and managerial positions was about $44,041 in 1995; other writers and editors averaged about $43,161.

Related Occupations

Writers and editors communicate ideas and information. Other communications occupations include newspaper reporters and correspondents, radio and television announcers, advertising and public relations workers, and teachers.

Sources of Additional Information

For a guide to journalism careers and scholarships, contact:
☛The Dow Jones Newspaper Fund, P.O. Box 300, Princeton, NJ 08540.

For information on college internships in magazine editing, contact:
☛American Society of Magazine Editors, 919 3rd. St., New York, NY 10022.

For information on careers in technical writing, contact:
☛Society for Technical Communication, Inc., 901 N. Stuart St., Suite 904, Arlington, VA 22203.

Visual Arts Occupations

Designers

(D.O.T. 141.051, .061, .067; 142 except .051-010, .061-030, -054)

Nature of the Work

Designers organize and design articles, products, and materials so they serve the purpose for which they were intended and are visually pleasing. Pleasant surroundings, beautiful clothes, and floral arrangements can boost our spirits, and products and packaging that are eye catching are more likely to attract buyers than those that are not.

Many designers specialize in one particular area of design—for example, automobiles, clothing, furniture, home appliances, industrial equipment, interiors of homes and office buildings, exhibits, movie and theater sets, packaging, or floral arrangements. Others work in more than one design field. The first step in developing a new design or altering an existing one is to determine the needs of the client. Then the designer considers various factors, including the size, shape, weight, color, materials used, and the way the product functions. The ease of use, safety, and cost of the design are additional factors. Designers may compare similar or competitive products. They take into account, and often set, style and fashion trends. Designers develop, by hand or with the aid of a computer, sketches of several design concepts that they present for final selection to a client, an art or design director, a product development team, or producer of a play, film, or television production. The designer then makes a model, a prototype, or detailed plans drawn to scale. Designers in some specialties increasingly use computer-aided design (CAD) tools to create and better visualize a final product. Computers greatly reduce the cost and time necessary to create a model or prototype, which gives a real idea of what the product will look like. Industrial designers use computer-aided industrial design (CAID) to create designs and to communicate them to automated production tools.

Designers may supervise craft workers who carry out their designs. Those who run their own businesses also may devote a considerable amount of time to developing new business contacts and to administrative tasks such as reviewing catalogs and ordering samples.

Design encompasses a number of different fields. *Industrial designers* develop and design countless manufactured products like cars, home appliances, children's toys, computer equipment, and medical, office, or recreational equipment. They combine artistic talent with research on product use, marketing, materials, and production methods to create the most functional and appealing design and to make the product competitive with others in the marketplace.

Furniture designers design furniture for manufacture, according to knowledge of design trends, competitors' products, production costs, capability of production facilities, and characteristics of a company's market. They may also prepare detailed drawings of fixtures, forms, or tools required to be used in production of furniture, along with designing custom pieces or styles according to a specific period or country. They must be strongly involved with the fashion industry and must be aware of current trends and styles.

Interior designers plan the space and furnish the interiors of private homes, public buildings, and commercial establishments, such as offices, restaurants, hospitals, hotels, and theaters. They also may plan additions and renovations. With a client's tastes, needs, and budget in mind, they develop designs and prepare working drawings and specifications for interior construction, furnishings, lighting, and finishes. Increasingly, designers use computers to plan layouts that can be changed easily to include ideas received from the client. They also design lighting and architectural details such as crown molding, coordinate colors, and select furniture, floor coverings, and curtains. Interior designers must design space in accordance with Federal, State, and local laws, including building codes. Increasingly, they plan spaces that meet accessibility standards for the disabled and elderly.

Set designers design movie, television, and theater sets. They study scripts, confer with directors, and conduct research to determine appropriate architectural styles.

Fashion designers design clothing and accessories. Some high-fashion designers are self-employed and design for individual clients. They make fashion news by establishing the "line," colors, and kinds of materials that will be worn each season. Other high-fashion designers cater to specialty stores or high-fashion department stores. They design original garments as well as follow the established fashion trends. Most fashion designers, however, work for apparel manufacturers, adapting men's, women's, and children's fashions for the mass market.

Creativity is crucial in all design occupations.

Textile designers design fabric for garments, upholstery, rugs, and other products, using their knowledge of textile materials and fashion trends. Computers are widely used in pattern design and grading. In the future, intelligent pattern engineering (IPE) systems will enable even greater automation in generating patterns.

Floral designers cut and arrange live, dried, or artificial flowers and foliage into designs to express the sentiments of the customer. They trim flowers and arrange bouquets, sprays, wreaths, dish gardens, and terrariums. They usually work from a written order indicating the occasion, customer preference for color and type of flower, price, and the date, time, and place the floral arrangement or plant is to be delivered. The variety of duties performed by a floral designer depends on the size of the shop and the number of designers employed. In a small operation, the floral designer may own the shop and do almost everything from growing flowers to keeping books.

Working Conditions

Working conditions and places of employment vary. Designers employed by manufacturing establishments or design firms generally work regular hours in well-lighted and comfortable settings. Self-employed designers tend to work longer hours—especially at first, when they are trying to establish themselves and cannot afford to hire assistants or clerical help.

Designers frequently adjust their workday to suit their clients, meeting with them evenings or on weekends when necessary. They may transact business in their own offices, clients' homes or offices, or may travel to other locations such as showrooms or manufacturing facilities.

Industrial designers usually work regular hours but occasionally work overtime to meet deadlines. In contrast, set designers, especially those in television broadcasting, often work long and irregular hours. The pace of television production is very fast, and set designers are often under pressure to make rapid changes in the sets. Fashion designers who work in the apparel industry usually have regular hours. During production deadlines or before fashion shows, however, they may be required to put in overtime. In addition, fashion designers may be required to travel to production sites overseas and across the United States. Interior designers generally work under deadlines and often work overtime to finish a job. Floral designers usually work regular hours in a pleasant work environment, except during holidays when overtime usually is required.

All designers face frustration at times when their designs are rejected or when they cannot be as creative as they would like. Independent consultants, who are paid by the assignment, are under pressure to please clients and to find new ones to maintain their incomes.

Employment

Designers held about 301,000 jobs in 1994. About one-third were self-employed, a much higher proportion than in most occupations.

Salaried designers work in a number of different industries, depending on their design specialty. Most industrial designers, for example, work for consulting firms or for large corporations. Interior designers usually work for design or architectural firms, department stores and home furnishing stores, or hotel and restaurant chains. Many do freelance work—full time, part time, or in addition to a salaried job in another occupation.

Set designers work for theater companies and film and television production companies. Fashion designers generally work for textile, apparel, and pattern manufacturers, or for fashion salons, high-fashion department stores, and specialty shops. Some work in the entertainment industry, designing costumes for theater, dance, television, and movies. Most floral designers work for retail flower shops but growing numbers work in floral departments of grocery stores.

Training, Other Qualifications, and Advancement

Creativity is crucial in all design occupations. People in this field must have a strong sense of color, an eye for detail, a sense of balance and proportion, and sensitivity to beauty. Sketching ability is especially important for fashion designers. A good portfolio—a collection of examples of a person's best work—is often the deciding factor in landing a job. However, formal preparation in design is important in all fields with the exception of floral design.

Educational requirements for entry-level positions vary. Some design occupations, notably industrial design, require a bachelor's degree. Interior designers also generally need a college education, preferably a bachelor of arts or a bachelor of applied arts degree. Few clients—especially commercial clients—are willing to entrust responsibility for designing living and working space to a designer with no formal credentials. Interior designers must also be knowledgeable about Federal, State, and local codes, and toxicity and flammability standards for furniture and furnishings.

In fashion design, some formal career preparation such as a 2-year or 4-year degree, is usually needed to enter the field. Employers seek individuals who are knowledgeable about textiles, fabrics, and ornamentation as well as trends in the fashion world.

In contrast to the other design occupations, a high school diploma ordinarily suffices for floral design jobs. Most floral designers learn their skills on the job. When they hire trainees, employers generally look for high school graduates who have a flair for color and a desire to learn. However, completion of formal training is an asset for floral designers, particularly for advancement to the lead floral designer level. Vocational and technical schools offer programs in floral design that usually last less than a year, while 2- and 4-year programs in floriculture, horticulture, floral design, or ornamental horticulture are offered by community and junior colleges, and colleges and universities.

Formal training for some design professions is also available in 2- and 3-year professional schools which award certificates or associate degrees in design. Graduates of 2-year programs generally qualify as assistants to designers. Four-year colleges and universities grant the Bachelor of Fine Arts degree. The curriculum in these schools includes art and art history, principles of design, designing and sketching, and specialized studies for each of the individual design disciplines such as garment construction, textiles, mechanical and architectural drawing, computerized design, sculpture, architecture, and basic engineering. A liberal arts education, with courses in merchandising, business administration, marketing, and psychology, along with training in art is also a good background for most design fields, excluding industrial design. Persons with training or experience in architecture also qualify for some design occupations, particularly interior design.

Computer-aided design (CAD) courses are very useful. CAD is used in various areas of design, and many employers expect new designers to be familiar with the use of the computer as a design tool. For example, industrial designers extensively use computers in the aerospace, automotive, and electronics industries. Interior designers are using computers to create numerous versions of space designs. Images can be inserted, edited, or replaced—making it possible for a client to see and choose among several designs. In furniture design, a chair's basic shape and structure may be duplicated and updated by applying new upholstery styles and fabrics with the use of computers.

In 1994, the National Association of Schools of Art and Design accredited 179 postsecondary institutions with programs in art and design. Most of these schools award a degree in art. Some award degrees in industrial design, interior design, textile design, graphic design, or fashion design. Many schools do not allow formal entry into a bachelor's degree program until a student has successfully finished a year of basic art and design courses. Applicants may be required to submit sketches and other examples of their artistic ability.

The Foundation for Interior Design Education Research accredits interior design programs and schools. Currently, there are over 100 accredited programs in the United States and Canada located in schools of art, architecture, and home economics.

People in the design field must be creative, imaginative, persis-

tent, and able to communicate their ideas both visually and verbally. Because tastes in style and fashion can change quickly, designers need to be open to new ideas and influences. Problem-solving skills and the ability to work independently are important traits. People in this field need self-discipline to start projects on their own, budget their time, and meet deadlines and production schedules. Business sense and sales ability are important for those who are freelancers or run their own businesses.

Beginning designers usually receive on-the-job training and normally need 1 to 3 years of training before they advance to higher level positions. Experienced designers in large firms may advance to chief designer, design department head, or other supervisory positions. Some experienced designers open their own firms.

Interior design is the only design field subject to government regulation: The District of Columbia licenses interior designers, and 16 States regulate use of the title. Since licensing is not mandatory in all States, membership in a professional association is universally recognized as a mark of achievement for designers. Professional membership usually requires the completion of 3 or 4 years of postsecondary education in design, at least 2 years of practical experience in the field, and completion of the National Council for Interior Design qualification examination.

Job Outlook

Many talented individuals are attracted to careers as designers. Consequently, designers in most fields—with the exception of floral and furniture design—can expect to face competition throughout their careers. Due to this competition, individuals with little or no formal education in design, and without the necessary personal traits—particularly creativity and perseverance—may find it very difficult to establish and maintain a career in design.

While most areas of design are highly competitive, this is not the case in floral design. Relatively low pay and limited opportunities for advancement restrict the supply of suitable applicants. As a result, finding a job as a floral designer should be relatively easy. Opportunities should also be good for qualified persons in specialized fields, such as furniture design.

Employment in design occupations is expected to grow faster than the average for all occupations through the year 2005. Demand for industrial designers will stem from continued emphasis on product quality and safety; design of new products that are easy and comfortable to use; high-technology products in medicine, transportation, and other fields; and increasing global competition among businesses. Increasing demand for professional design of private homes, office space, restaurants and other retail establishments, and institutions that care for the elderly should spur employment growth among interior designers. Floral design should experience healthy growth with the addition of floral departments in many grocery stores. Growth in population and in personal incomes is expected to encourage increased demand for fashion, textile, and set designers. In addition to employment growth, many job openings will result from the need to replace designers who leave the field.

Earnings

Median weekly earnings of experienced full-time designers in all fields of design were about $590 in 1994. The middle 50 percent earned between $380 and $840 a week. The bottom 10 percent earned less than $330, while the top 10 percent earned over $1,100.

Earnings of floral designers were lower than most types of designers. According to a survey conducted by Floral Finance Inc., beginning floral designers had average earnings of $5.52 an hour in 1994. Designers with 1 to 3 years of experience earned $6.44, while designers with over 3 years of experience averaged $7.68. Managers had average earnings of $9.63 an hour in 1994.

According to the Industrial Designers Society of America, the average base salary for an entry-level industrial designer with 1 to 2 years of experience was about $25,800 in 1994. Staff designers with 5 years of experience earned $33,500, while senior designers with 8 years of experience earned $42,800. Industrial designers in managerial or executive positions earned substantially more—up to $140,000 annually.

Related Occupations
Workers in other occupations who design or arrange objects, materials, or interiors to improve their appearance and function include visual artists, architects, landscape architects, engineers, photographers, and merchandise displayers.

Sources of Additional Information
For a list of accredited schools of art and design, contact:
☛National Association of Schools of Art and Design, 11250 Roger Bacon Dr., Suite 21, Reston, VA 22090.

For price and ordering information regarding a brochure that describes careers in industrial design and lists academic programs in the field, write to:
☛Industrial Designers Society of America, 1142-E Walker Rd., Great Falls, VA 22066.

For information about careers in interior design, contact:
☛American Society for Interior Designers, 608 Massachusetts Ave. NE., Washington, DC 20002-6006.

For a list of accredited programs in interior design, contact:
☛Foundation for Interior Design Education Research, 60 Monroe Center NW., Grand Rapids, MI 49503.

For information about careers in floral design, contact:
☛Society of American Florists, 1601 Duke St., Alexandria, VA 22314.

For a list of schools with accredited programs in furniture design, contact:
☛American Society of Furniture Designers, P.O. Box 1613, Lexington, NC 27293.

Photographers and Camera Operators

(D.O.T. 143)

Nature of the Work
Photographers and camera operators use cameras to capture the special feeling or mood that sells products, provides entertainment, highlights news stories, or brings back memories.

Photographers use a wide variety of cameras that can accept lenses designed for close-up, medium-range, or distance photography. Some cameras also offer adjustment settings that allow the photographer greater creative and technical control over the picture-taking process. In addition to cameras and film, photographers and camera operators use an array of equipment, from filters, tripods, and flash attachments to specially constructed motorized vehicles and lighting equipment.

Photography increasingly involves the use of computers. A photographer may take a picture, scan it to digital form, and, using a computer, manipulate it to create a desired effect. The images may be stored on a compact disk (CD) in the same way that music is stored on a CD. Currently, some photographers use this technology to create an electronic portfolio. However, due to inferior image quality and high cost, this technology has not been widely adopted.

Camera operators generally use 35- or 16-millimeter cameras or video cameras to film commercial motion pictures and documentary or industrial films. Some film events for television news, or film private ceremonies and special events.

Making commercial quality photographs and movies requires technical expertise and creativity. Composing a picture includes choosing and presenting a subject to achieve a particular effect and selecting equipment to accomplish the desired goal. By creatively using lighting, lenses, film, filters, and camera settings, photographers and camera operators produce pictures that capture a mood or tell a story. For example, photographers and camera operators may enhance the subject's appearance with lighting or by drawing attention to a particular aspect by blurring the background.

Some photographers develop and print their own photographs, especially those requiring special effects, but this requires a fully equipped darkroom and the technical skill to operate it. As a result, many professional photographers send their film to laboratories for processing. This is especially true for color film, which requires very expensive equipment and exacting conditions for processing and printing. (See the statement on photographic process workers elsewhere in the *Handbook*.)

Most photographers specialize in commercial, portrait, or media photography. Some specialize in weddings or school photographs. Portrait photographers take pictures of individuals or groups of people and often work in their own studios. Portrait photographers who are business owners arrange for advertising, schedule appointments, set and adjust equipment, develop and retouch negatives, and mount and frame pictures. They also hire and train employees, purchase supplies, keep records, and bill customers.

Self-employed photographers may license the use of their photographs through stock photo agencies. These agencies grant magazines and other customers the right to purchase the use of a photograph, and, in turn, pay the photographer on a commission basis. Stock photo agencies require an application from the photographer and a sizable portfolio. Once accepted, a large number of new submissions are generally required each year. Photographers frequently have their photos placed on CD's for this purpose.

Commercial and industrial photographers take pictures of such subjects as manufactured articles, buildings, livestock, landscapes, and groups of people. Their work is used in a wide variety of mediums, such as reports, advertisements, and catalogs. Industrial photographers use photographs or videotapes for analyzing engineering projects, publicity, or as records of equipment development or deployment, such as the placement of an off-shore oil rig. Automobile manufacturers hire photographers every year to publicize their new models. Companies use photographs in publications to report to stockholders or to advertise company products or services. This photography frequently is done on location.

Scientific photographers provide illustrations and documentation for scientific publications, research reports, and textbooks. They usually specialize in a field such as engineering, medicine, biology, or chemistry. Some use photographic or video equipment as research tools. For example, biomedical photographers use photomicrography, photographs of small objects magnified many times to obtain information not visible under normal conditions, and time-lapse photography, where time is stretched or condensed. Biomedical photographers record medical procedures such as surgery.

Photojournalists photograph newsworthy events, places, people, and things for newspapers, journals, magazines, or television. Some are salaried staff, while others are independent and known as freelance photographers.

Photography also is an art medium. Some photographers sell their photographs as artwork, placing even greater emphasis on self-expression and creativity, in addition to technical proficiency. Unlike other specializations, however, very few artistic photographers are successful enough to support themselves in this manner.

Many camera operators are employed by independent television stations, local affiliates, or networks. They often cover news events as part of a reporting team.

Camera operators employed in the entertainment field use motion picture cameras to film movies, television programs, and commercials. Some camera operators specialize in filming cartoons or other special effects for television and movies.

Camera operators and photographers need good eyesight, artistic ability, and manual dexterity.

Working Conditions

Working conditions for photographers and camera operators vary considerably. Photographers employed in government, commercial studios, and advertising agencies usually work a 5-day, 40-hour week. News photographers and camera operators often work long and irregular hours and must be available on short notice.

Self-employment allows for greater autonomy, freedom of expression, and flexible scheduling. However, income is uncertain and necessitates a continuous, time consuming, and sometimes stressful search for new clients. Some photographers hire an assistant solely for this responsibility.

Portrait photographers often work in their own studios but may travel to take photographs at schools and other places and weddings and other events. Press and commercial photographers and camera operators frequently travel locally or overnight; some travel to distant places for long periods of time. Their work may put them in uncomfortable or even dangerous surroundings. This is especially true for photojournalists covering natural disasters, civil strife, or military conflicts.

Some photographers and camera operators wait long hours in all kinds of weather for an event to take place and stand or walk for long periods while carrying heavy equipment. Photographers often work under severe time restrictions to meet deadlines and satisfy customers.

Employment

Photographers and camera operators held about 139,000 jobs in 1994. About 4 out of 10 were self-employed, a much higher proportion than the average for all occupations. Some self-employed photographers contracted with advertising agencies, magazines, or others to do individual projects at a predetermined fee, while others operated portrait studios or provided photographs to stock photo agencies.

Most salaried photographers worked in portrait or commercial photography studios. Others were employed by newspapers, magazines, advertising agencies, and government agencies. Most camera operators were employed in television broadcasting or in motion picture studios; relatively few were self-employed. Most photographers and camera operators worked in metropolitan areas.

Training, Other Qualifications, and Advancement

Employers usually seek applicants with a good technical understanding of photography who are imaginative and creative. Entry level positions in photojournalism, and in industrial, scientific, or technical photography are likely to require a college degree in photography

with courses in the specific field being photographed, such as industrial products or botany. Camera operators generally acquire their skills through formal post-secondary training at colleges, photographic institutes, universities, or through on-the-job training. Those in entry level jobs, including photography and cinematography assistants, learn to set up lights and cameras. They may receive routine assignments requiring few camera adjustments or decisions on what subject matter to capture. With increasing experience, they may advance to more demanding assignments. Photography assistants often learn to mix chemicals, develop film, print photographs, and the various skills vital to running their own business.

Individuals interested in this occupation should subscribe to photographic newsletters and magazines, join camera clubs, and seek work in camera stores or photo studios. Individuals also should decide on an area of interest and specialize in it. Completing a course of study at a private photographic institute, university, or community college provides many of the necessary skills to be successful. Summer or part-time work for a photographer, network, newspaper, or magazine is an excellent way to gain experience and eventual entry to this field.

Many sources, including universities, community and junior colleges, vocational-technical institutes, and private trade and technical schools, offer courses in photography. Courses in cinematography are most often offered by photography institutes and universities. Many photographers enhance their technical expertise by attending seminars.

Basic courses in photography cover equipment, processes, and techniques. Bachelor's degree programs provide a well-rounded education, including business courses. Art schools offer useful training in design and composition, but may be weak in the technical and commercial aspects of photography.

Photographers who wish to operate their own business need business skills as well as talent. They must know how to submit bids; write contracts; hire models, if needed; get permission to take on-site photographs at locations normally not open to the public; get clearances to use photographs of people; price photographs; and keep financial records. They should develop an individual style of photography to differentiate themselves from the competition. Some self-employed photographers enter the field by submitting unsolicited photographs to magazines or art directors at advertising agencies.

Photographers and camera operators need good eyesight, artistic ability, and manual dexterity. They should be patient, accurate, and enjoy working with detail. They should be able to work alone or with others, as photographers frequently deal with clients, graphic designers, and advertising and publishing specialists. Knowledge of mathematics, physics, and chemistry is helpful for understanding the workings of lenses, films, light sources, and developing processes.

Commercial photographers must be imaginative and original. Portrait photographers need the ability to help people relax in front of the camera. Photojournalists must not only be good with a camera but also understand the story behind an event so that their pictures match the story. They must be decisive in recognizing a potentially good photograph and act quickly to capture it. This requires journalistic skills and explains why such employers increasingly look for individuals with a 4-year degree in photojournalism or journalism with an emphasis on photography.

Camera operators can become directors of photography for movie studios, advertising agencies, or television programs. Magazine and news photographers may become photography editors. A few photographers and camera operators become teachers and provide instruction in their own area of expertise.

Job Outlook

Photography, particularly commercial photography and photojournalism, is a highly competitive field because there are more people who want to be photographers than there is employment to support them. Only the most skilled and those with the best business ability, and who have developed the best reputations in the industry, are able to find salaried positions or attract enough work to support themselves as self-employed photographers. Many have full-time jobs in other fields and take photographs or videos of weddings and other events on weekends.

Employment of photographers is expected to grow faster than the average for all occupations through the year 2005. The growing demand for visual images in education, communication, entertainment, marketing, research and development, and other areas should spur demand for photographers. Demand for portrait photographers should increase as the population grows.

Digital cameras use electronic memory rather than a film negative to record the image, which, in turn, can be transmitted instantly via a computer modem and telephone lines. For this reason, they are used widely by news photographers. However, these cameras are much more expensive than conventional cameras, and are not capable of producing an equally clear image, or one where the subject is in motion. As the technology improves and the prices drop, however, they may be more widely used, increasing demand for commercial photographers with a high degree of computer skills.

Employment of camera operators also is expected to grow more slowly than the average for all occupations through the year 2005, even though businesses are making greater use of videos for training films, business meetings, sales campaigns, and public relations work. Expansion of the entertainment industry will create additional openings, but competition will be keen for what generally is regarded as an exciting field.

Earnings
The median annual earnings for salaried photographers and camera operators who worked full time were about $25,100 in 1994. The middle 50 percent earned between $16,300 and $39,200. The top 10 percent earned more than $46,300, while the lowest 10 percent earned less than $12,400.

Most salaried photographers work full time and earn more than the majority of self-employed photographers, who work part time, but some self-employed photographers have very high earnings. Earnings are affected by the number of hours worked, skills, marketing ability, and general business conditions.

Unlike photojournalists and commercial photographers, very few artistic photographers are successful enough to support themselves solely through this specialty.

Related Occupations
Other jobs requiring visual arts talents include illustrators, designers, painters, sculptors, and photo editors.

Sources of Additional Information
Career information on photography is available from:
☛Professional Photographers of America, Inc., 57 Forsythe Street, Suite 1600, Atlanta, GA 30303

For reprints of a publication describing the work of various types of photographers and lists of colleges and universities offering courses or a degree in photography, write to:
☛American Society of Media Photographers, Washington Rd., Suite 502, Princeton Junction, NJ 08550-1033.

Visual Artists

(D.O.T. 102.261-014; 141.031-010, .061-010, -014, -018, -022, -026, -030, -034, .081-010; 142.061-030, -054; 144; 149.041, .051, .261; 970.131-014, .281-014, .361-018)

Nature of the Work
Visual artists use a variety of methods and materials to communicate ideas, thoughts, and feelings, including computers, oils, watercolors, acrylics, pastels, magic markers, pencils, pen and ink, silkscreen, plaster, clay, or any of a number of other media, such as photographs and sound. They create realistic and abstract works or images of objects, people, nature, topography, or events. (Designers, a closely related occupation, are discussed in a separate *Handbook* statement.)

Visual artists generally fall into one of two categories—"graphic artists" and "fine artists"—depending not so much on the medium, but on the artist's purpose in creating a work of art. Graphic artists, many of whom own their own studios, put their artistic skills and vision at the service of commercial clients, such as major corporations, retail stores, and advertising, design, or publishing firms. Fine artists, on the other hand, often create art to satisfy their own need for self-expression, and may display their work in museums, corporate collections, art galleries, and private homes. Some of their work may be done on request from clients, but not as exclusively as that of graphic artists.

Graphic artists, whether freelancers or employed by a firm, use a variety of print, electronic, and film media to create art that meets a client's needs. Most graphic artists use computer software to design new images. As the computer software becomes increasingly sophisticated, more artists are likely to become involved with this medium. Some graphic artists create packaging, promotional displays, and marketing brochures for new products, visual designs of annual reports and other corporate literature, or distinctive logos for products or businesses. They are responsible for the overall layout and design of magazines, newspapers, journals, and other publications, and they create graphics for television and computer-generated media.

Fine artists may sell their works to stores, commercial art galleries, and museums, or directly to collectors. Commercial galleries may sell artists' works on consignment. The gallery and artist predetermine how much each earns from a sale. Only the most successful fine artists are able to support themselves solely through sale of their works, however. Most fine artists hold other jobs as well. Those with teaching certification may teach art in elementary or secondary schools, while those with a master's or Ph.D. degree may teach in colleges or universities. Some fine artists work in arts administration in city, State, or Federal arts programs. Others may work as art critics, art consultants, or as directors or representatives in fine art galleries; give private art lessons; or work as curators setting up art exhibits in museums. Sometimes fine artists work in a totally unrelated field in order to support their careers as artists.

Fine artists usually work independently, choosing whatever subject matter and medium suits them. Usually, they specialize in one or two forms of art. *Painters* generally work with two-dimensional art forms. Using techniques of shading, perspective, and color mixing, painters produce works that depict realistic scences or may evoke different moods and emotions, depending on the artist's goals. Sometimes artists combine mediums and include sound and motion in their works.

Sculptors design three-dimensional art works—either molding and joining materials such as clay, glass, wire, plastic, or metal, or cutting and carving forms from a block of plaster, wood, or stone. Some sculptors combine various materials such as concrete, metal, wood, plastic, and paper.

Printmakers create printed images from designs cut into wood, stone, or metal, or from computer driven data. The designs may be engraved, as in the case of woodblocking; etched, as in the production of etchings; or derived from computers in the form of inkjet or laser prints.

Painting restorers preserve and restore damaged and faded paintings. They apply solvents and cleaning agents to clean the surfaces, reconstruct or retouch damaged areas, and apply preservatives to protect the paintings. This is very detailed work and is usually reserved for experts in the field.

Illustrators paint or draw pictures for books, magazines, and other publications, films, and paper products, including greeting cards, calenders, wrapping paper, and stationery. Many do a variety of illustrations, while others specialize in a particular style. Some illustrators draw "story boards" for television commercials, movies, and animated features. Story boards present television commercials in a series of scenes similar to a comic strip, so an advertising agency and client (the company doing the advertising) can evaluate proposed commercials. Story boards may also serve as guides to placement of actors and cameras and to other details during the production of commercials.

Medical and *scientific illustrators* combine artistic skills with knowledge of the biological sciences. Medical illustrators draw illustrations of human anatomy and surgical procedures. Scientific illustrators draw illustrations of animals and plants. These illustrations are used in medical and scientific publications, and in audiovisual presentations for teaching purposes. Medical illustrators also work for lawyers, producing exhibits for court cases, and for doctors. *Fashion artists* draw illustrations of women's, men's, and children's clothing and accessories for newspapers, magazines, and other media.

Cartoonists draw political, advertising, social, and sports cartoons. Some cartoonists work with others who create the idea or story and write the captions. Most cartoonists, however, have humorous, critical, or dramatic talents in addition to drawing skills.

Animators work in the motion picture and television industries. They draw by hand and use computers to create the large series of pictures which, when transferred to film or tape, form the animated cartoons seen in movies and on television.

Art directors, also called visual journalists, read the material to be printed in periodicals, newspapers, and other printed media, and decide how to best visually present the information in an eye-catching, yet organized manner. They make decisions about which photographs or artwork to use, and in general oversee production of the printed material.

Working Conditions

Graphic and fine artists generally work in art and design studios located in office buildings or their own studios. While their surroundings are usually well lighted and ventilated, odors from glues, paint, ink, or other materials may be present. They may use computers for extended periods of time.

Graphic artists employed by publishing companies and art and design studios generally work a standard 40-hour week. During busy periods, they may work overtime to meet deadlines. Self-employed graphic artists can set their own hours, but may spend much time and effort selling their services to potential customers or clients and establishing a reputation.

Visual artists communicate ideas, thoughts, and feelings through original artwork.

Employment

Visual artists held about 273,000 jobs in 1994. About 3 out of 5 were self-employed. Self-employed artists are either graphic artists who freelance, offering their services to advertising agencies, publishing firms, and other businesses, or fine artists who earn income when they sell a painting or other art work.

Of the artists who were not self-employed, many were graphic artists who worked for advertising agencies, design firms, commercial art and reproduction firms, or publishing and publishing firms. Other artists were employed by the motion picture and television industries, wholesale and retail trade establishments, and public relations firms.

Training, Other Qualifications, and Advancement

In the fine arts field, formal training requirements do not exist, but it is very difficult to become skilled enough to make a living without some basic training. Bachelor's and graduate degree programs in fine arts are offered in many colleges and universities. In the graphic arts field, demonstrated ability and appropriate training or other qualifications are needed for success. Evidence of appropriate talent and skill, displayed in an artist's "portfolio," is an important factor used by art and design directors and others in deciding whether to hire or contract out work to an artist. The portfolio is a collection of handmade, computer-generated, or printed examples of the artist's best work. Assembling a successful portfolio requires skills generally developed in a postsecondary art or design school program, such as a bachelor's degree program in fine art, graphic design, or visual communications. Internships also provide excellent opportunities for artists to develop and enhance their portfolios. Most programs in art and design also provide training in computer design techniques. This training is increasingly important as a qualification for many jobs in commercial art.

The appropriate training and education for prospective medical illustrators is more specific. Medical illustrators must not only demonstrate artistic ability but also have a detailed knowledge of living organisms, surgical and medical procedures, and human and sometimes animal anatomy. A 4-year bachelor's degree combining art and pre-medical courses is usually required, followed by a master's degree in medical illustration, a degree offered in only a few accredited schools in the United States.

Persons hired in advertising agencies or graphic design studios often start with relatively routine work. While doing this work, however, they may observe and practice their skills on the side. Many graphic artists work part time as freelancers while continuing to hold a full-time job until they get established. Others have enough talent, perseverance, and confidence in their ability to start out freelancing full-time immediately after they graduate from art school. Many freelance part time while still in school in order to develop experience and a portfolio of published work.

The freelance artist develops a set of clients who regularly contract for work. Some successful freelancers are widely recognized for their skill in specialties such as children's book illustration, design, or magazine illustration. These artists can earn high incomes and can pick and choose the type of work they do.

Fine artists and illustrators advance as their work circulates and as they establish a reputation for a particular style. The best artists and illustrators continue to grow in ideas, and their work constantly evolves over time. Graphic artists may advance to assistant art director, art director, design director, and in some companies, creative director of an art or design department. Some may gain enough skill to succeed as a freelancer or may prefer to specialize in a particular area. Others decide to open their own businesses.

Job Outlook

The graphic and fine arts fields have a glamorous and exciting image. Many people with a love for drawing and creative ability qualify for entry to these fields. As a result, the supply of aspiring artists will continue to exceed the number of job openings, resulting in keen competition for both salaried jobs and freelance work. Freelance work may be hard to come by, especially at first, and many freelancers earn very little until they acquire experience and establish a good reputation. Fine artists, in particular, may find it difficult to earn a living solely by selling their artwork. Nonetheless, graphic arts studios, clients, and galleries alike are always on the lookout for artists who display outstanding talent, creativity, and style. Talented artists who have developed a mastery of artistic techniques and skills, including computer skills, will be in high demand.

Employment of visual artists is expected to grow faster than the average for all occupations through the year 2005. Demand for graphic artists will be strong as producers of information, goods, and services put even more emphasis on visual appeal in product design, advertising, marketing, and television. Employment growth for graphic artists, however, may be limited by increases in productivity due to computers, and because some firms are turning to employees without formal artistic or design training to operate computer-aided design systems. Employment of fine artists is expected to grow because of population growth, rising incomes, and growth in the number of people who appreciate fine arts.

Demand for artists may also depend on the level of government funding for certain programs. For example, the National Endowment for the Arts offers a variety of grants to artists; however, competition is intense for most awards.

Earnings

Median earnings for salaried visual artists who usually work full time were about $25,500 a year in 1994. The middle 50 percent earned between $18,800 and $34,500 a year. The top 10 percent earned more than $46,600, and the bottom 10 percent earned less than $14,100.

According to the Society of Publication Designers, entry-level graphic designers earned between $21,000 and $24,000 annually.

Earnings for self-employed visual artists vary widely. Those struggling to gain experience and a reputation may be forced to charge what amounts to less than the minimum wage for their work. Well-established freelancers and fine artists may earn much more than salaried artists. Self-employed artists do not receive benefits such as paid holidays, sick leave, health insurance, or pensions.

Related Occupations

Many occupations in the advertising industry, such as account executive or creative director, are related to commercial and graphic art and design. Workers in other occupations which apply visual art skills are architects, display workers, floral designers, industrial designers, interior designers, landscape architects, and photographers. The various printing occupations are also related to graphic art, as is the work of art and design teachers.

Sources of Additional Information

Students in high school or college who are interested in careers as illustrators should contact:
☛The Society of Illustrators, 128 East 63rd St., New York, NY 10021-7392.
☛The National Association of Schools of Art and Design, 11250 Roger Bacon Dr., Suite 21, Reston, VA 22090-5202.

For information on careers in medical illustration, contact:
☛The Association of Medical Illustrators, 1819 Peachtree St. NE., Suite 602, Atlanta, GA 30309-1848.

For information on careers in scientific illustration, contact:
☛Guild of Natural Science Illustrators, P.O. Box 652, Ben Franklin Station, Washington, DC 20044-0652.

For a list of schools offering degree programs in graphic design, contact:
☛The American Institute of Graphic Arts, 164 Fifth Ave., New York, NY 10010.

For information on art careers in the publishing industry, contact:
☛The Society of Publication Designers, 60 East 42nd St., Suite 721, New York, NY 10165-1416.

Performing Arts Occupations

Actors, Directors, and Producers

(D.O.T. 139.167; 150 except .027-014; 159.041, .044, .047, .067, .117, .167-010 through -022, .267, .341, .344-010 -014, .347 except -010, .367, .647 except -018; 184.117-010, .162, .167-014, -022, -034; 187.167-174, -178, -182; 961.364, .667-014; 962.162-010, .167-014)

Nature of the Work

Actors, directors, and producers include stage and screen actors; narrators; magicians; clowns; comedians; impersonators; acrobats; jugglers; equestrians; amusement park entertainers; stunt, rodeo, and aquatic performers; casting, stage, news, sports, and public service directors; production, stage, and artist and repertoire managers; and producers and their assistants. This *Handbook* statement focuses on actors, directors, and producers.

Actors, directors, and producers express ideas and create images, based on a script, in theaters, film, television, and radio. They "make the words come alive" for their audiences.

Actors entertain and communicate with people through their interpretation of dramatic roles. But, only a few actors achieve recognition as stars on the stage, in motion pictures, or on television. A somewhat larger number are well-known, experienced performers, who frequently are cast in supporting roles. Most actors struggle for a toehold in the profession and pick up parts wherever they can.

Many successful actors continue to accept small roles, including commercials and product endorsements. Some actors employed by theater companies teach acting courses to the public.

In addition to the actors with speaking parts, "extras," who have small parts with no lines to deliver, are used throughout the industry.

Directors interpret plays or scripts. In addition, they audition and select cast members, conduct rehearsals, and direct the work of the cast and crew. Directors use their knowledge of acting, voice, and movement to achieve the best possible performance and usually approve the scenery, costumes, choreography, and music.

Producers are entrepreneurs. They select plays or scripts, arrange financing, and decide on the size and content of the production and its budget. They hire directors, principal members of the cast, and key production staff members, and they negotiate contracts with artistic personnel, often in accordance with collective bargaining agreements. Producers also coordinate the activities of writers, directors, managers, and other personnel.

Working Conditions

Acting demands patience and total commitment, because there are often long periods of unemployment between jobs. While under contract, actors are frequently required to work long hours and travel. Evening work is a regular part of a stage actor's life. Flawless performances require tedious memorizing of lines and repetitive rehearsals. On television, actors must deliver a good performance with

Directors conduct rehearsals, guiding the work of the cast and crew.

very little preparation. Actors need stamina to withstand the heat of stage or studio lights, heavy costumes, the long, irregular hours, and the adverse weather conditions that may exist "on location." When plays are "on the road," traveling is necessary. Actors often face the anxiety of intermittent employment and rejections when auditioning for work.

Directors and producers often work under stress as they try to meet schedules, stay within budgets, and resolve personnel problems while putting together a production.

Employment

In 1994, actors, directors, and producers held an average of about 93,000 jobs in motion pictures, stage plays, television, and radio. Many others were between jobs, so that the total number of people actually employed as actors, directors, and producers over the course of the year was higher. In the winter, most employment opportunities on the stage are in New York and other large cities, many of which have established professional regional theaters. In the summer, stock companies in suburban and resort areas also provide employment. Cruise Lines and amusement parks also provide opportunities. In addition, many cities have small nonprofit professional companies such as "little theaters," repertory companies, and dinner theaters, which provide opportunities for local amateur talent as well as for professional entertainers. Normally, casts are selected in New York City for shows that go on the road.

Employment in motion pictures and films for television is centered in Hollywood and New York City. However, studios are also located in Florida, Seattle, and other parts of the country. In addition, many films are shot on location and employ local professionals and nonprofessionals as day players and extras. In television, opportunities are at the network entertainment centers in New York and Los Angeles and at local television stations around the country.

Training, Other Qualifications, and Advancement

Aspiring actors and directors should take part in high school and college plays, or work with little theaters and other acting groups for experience.

Formal dramatic training or acting experience is generally necessary, although some people enter the field without it. Most people take college courses in theater, arts, drama, and dramatic literature. Many experienced actors get additional formal training to learn new skills and improve old ones. Training can be obtained at dramatic arts schools in New York and Los Angeles, and at colleges and universities throughout the country offering bachelor's or higher degrees in dramatic and theater arts. College drama curriculums usually include courses in liberal arts, stage speech and movement,

directing, playwriting, play production, design, and history of the drama, as well as practical courses in acting.

The best way to start is to use local opportunities and to build on them. Local and regional theater experience may help in obtaining work in New York or Los Angeles. Modeling experience may also be helpful. Actors need talent, creative ability, and training that will enable them to portray different characters. Training in singing and dancing is especially useful. Actors must have poise, stage presence, the ability to affect an audience, plus the ability to follow directions. Physical appearance is often a deciding factor in being selected for particular roles.

Many professional actors rely on agents or managers to find work, negotiate contracts, and plan their careers. Agents generally earn a percentage of an actor's contract.

To become a movie extra, one must usually be listed by a casting agency, such as Central Casting, a no-fee agency that supplies all extras to the major movie studios in Hollywood. Applicants are accepted only when the number of persons of a particular type on the list—for example, athletic young women, old men, or small children—is below the foreseeable need. In recent years, only a very small proportion of the applicants have succeeded in being listed.

There are no specific training requirements for directors and producers. However, talent, experience, and business acumen are very important. Directors and producers come from different backgrounds. Actors, writers, film editors, and business managers often enter these fields. Producers often start in the industry working behind the scenes with successful directors. Formal training in directing and producing is available at some colleges and universities.

As actors', directors', and producers' reputations grow, they work on larger productions or in more prestigious theaters. Actors also advance to lead or specialized roles. A few actors move into acting-related jobs as drama coaches or directors of stage, television, radio, or motion picture productions. Some teach drama in colleges and universities.

The length of a performer's working life depends largely on training, skill, versatility, and perseverance. Some actors, directors, and producers continue working throughout their lives; however, many leave the occupation after a short time because they cannot find enough work to make a living.

Job Outlook

The large number of people desiring acting careers and the lack of formal entry requirements should continue to cause keen competition for actor, director, and producer jobs. Only the most talented will find regular employment.

Employment of actors, directors, and producers is expected to grow faster than the average for all occupations through the year 2005. Rising foreign demand for American productions, combined with a growing domestic market—fueled by the growth of cable television, home movie rentals, and television syndications—should stimulate demand for actors and other production personnel. Growth of opportunities in recorded media should be accompanied by increasing jobs in live productions. Growing numbers of people who enjoy live theatrical entertainment will continue to go to theaters for excitement and aesthetics. Touring productions of Broadway plays and other large shows are providing new opportunities for actors and directors. However, employment may be somewhat affected by government funding for the arts—a decline in funding could dampen future employment growth in this segment of the entertainment industry. Workers leaving the field will continue to create more job openings than will growth.

Earnings

Minimum salaries, hours of work, and other conditions of employment are covered in collective bargaining agreements between producers of shows and unions representing workers in this field. The Actors' Equity Association represents stage actors; the Screen Actors

Guild and the Screen Extras Guild cover actors in motion pictures, including television, commercials, and films; and the American Federation of Television and Radio Artists (AFTRA) represents television and radio performers. Most stage directors belong to the Society of Stage Directors and Choreographers, and film and television directors belong to the Directors Guild of America. Of course, any actor or director may negotiate for a salary higher than the minimum.

According to limited information, the minimum weekly salary for actors in Broadway stage productions was $1,000 in 1995. Those in small "off-Broadway" theaters received minimums ranging from $380 to $650 a week, depending on the seating capacity of the theater. For shows on the road, actors receive about $100 per day more for living expenses.

Actors usually work long hours during rehearsals. Once the show opens, they have more regular hours, working about 30 hours a week.

According to the Screen Actors Guild, motion picture and television actors with speaking parts earned a minimum daily rate of about $500, or $1,750 for a 5-day week, in 1995. Those without speaking parts, "extras," earned a minimum daily rate of about $100. Actors also receive contributions to their health and pension plans and additional compensation for reruns.

Earnings from acting are low because employment is so irregular. The Screen Actors Guild also reports that the average income its members earned from acting was $1,400 a year, and 80 percent of its members earned less than $5,000 a year from acting. Therefore, many actors must supplement their incomes by holding jobs in other fields.

Some well-known actors have salary rates well above the minimums, and the salaries of the few top stars are many times the figures cited, creating a false impression that all actors are highly paid.

Many actors who work more than a set number of weeks per year are covered by a union health, welfare, and pension fund, including hospitalization insurance, to which employers contribute. Under some employment conditions, Actors' Equity and AFTRA members have paid vacations and sick leave.

Earnings of stage directors vary greatly. According to the Society of Stage Directors and Choreographers, summer theatres offer compensation, including "royalties" (based on the number of performances), usually ranging from $2,000 to $8,000 for a 3- to 4-week run of a production. Directing a production at a dinner theater will usually pay less than a summer theatre but has more potential for royalties. Regional theaters may hire directors for longer periods of time, increasing compensation accordingly. The highest paid directors work on Broadway productions, typically earning $80,000 plus royalties.

Producers seldom get a set fee; instead, they get a percentage of a show's earnings or ticket sales.

Related Occupations

People who work in occupations requiring acting skills include dancers, choreographers, disc jockeys, drama teachers or coaches, and radio and television announcers. Others working in occupations related to acting are playwrights, scriptwriters, stage managers, costume designers, makeup artists, hair stylists, lighting designers, and set designers. Workers in occupations involved with the business aspects of theater productions include managing directors, company managers, booking managers, publicists, and actors', directors', and playwrights' agents.

Sources of Additional Information

Information about opportunities in regional theaters may be obtained from:

☛Theatre Communications Group, Inc., 355 Lexington Ave., New York, NY 10017.

A directory of theatrical programs may be purchased from:

☛National Association of Schools of Theatre, 11250 Roger Bacon Dr., Suite 21, Reston, VA 22090.

Dancers and Choreographers

(D.O.T. 151.027-010 and .047-010)

Nature of the Work

From ancient times to the present, dancers have expressed ideas, stories, rhythm, and sound with their bodies. Many perform in classical ballet. Others perform modern dance, which allows more free movement and self-expression. Still others perform in dance adaptations for musical shows, in folk, ethnic, tap, and jazz dances, and in other popular kinds of dancing. In addition to being an art form for its own sake, dance also complements opera, musical comedy, television, movies, music videos, and commercials. Therefore, many dancers sing and act, as well as dance.

Dancers most often perform as a group, although a few top artists dance solo. Many dancers combine stage work with teaching or choreographing.

Choreographers create original dances. They may also create new interpretations to traditional dances like the ballet, "Nutcracker", since few dances are written down. Choreographers instruct performers at rehearsals to achieve the desired effect. They also audition performers.

Working Conditions

Dancing is strenuous. Rehearsals require very long hours and usually take place daily, including weekends and holidays. For shows on the

Dance routines require many hours of rehearsals.

road, weekend travel often is required. Most performances take place in the evening, while rehearsals and practice generally are scheduled during the day. Dancers must also work late hours.

Due to the physical demands, most dancers stop performing by their late thirties, but they sometimes continue to work in the dance field as choreographers, dance teachers and coaches, or as artistic directors. Some celebrated dancers, however, continue performing beyond the age of 50.

Employment

Professional dancers held an average of about 24,000 jobs at any one time in 1994. Many others were between engagements so that the total number of people employed as dancers over the course of the year was greater. Dancers work in a variety of settings, including eating and drinking establishments, theatrical and television productions, dance studios and schools, dance companies and bands, and amusement parks.

In addition, there were many dance instructors in secondary schools, colleges and universities, and private studios. Many teachers also perform from time to time.

New York City is the home of many of the major dance companies. Other cities with full-time professional dance companies include Atlanta, Boston, Chicago, Cincinnati, Cleveland, Columbus, Dallas, Houston, Miami, Milwaukee, Philadelphia, Pittsburgh, Salt Lake City, San Francisco, Seattle, and Washington, D.C.

Training, Other Qualifications, and Advancement

Training depends upon the type of dance. Early ballet training for women usually begins at 5 to 8 years of age and is often given by private teachers and independent ballet schools. Serious training traditionally begins between the ages of 10 and 12. Men often begin their training between the ages of 10 and 15. Students who demonstrate potential in the early teens receive more intensive and advanced professional training at regional ballet schools or schools conducted under the auspices of the major ballet companies. Leading dance school companies often have summer training programs from which they select candidates for admission to their regular full-time training program. Most dancers have their professional auditions by age 17 or 18; however, training and practice never end. Professional ballet dancers have 1 to 1 1/2 hours of lessons every day and spend many additional hours practicing and rehearsing.

Early and intensive training also is important for the modern dancer, but modern dance generally does not require as many years of training as ballet.

Because of the strenuous and time-consuming training required, a dancer's formal academic instruction may be minimal. However, a broad, general education including music, literature, history, and the visual arts is helpful in the interpretation of dramatic episodes, ideas, and feelings.

Many colleges and universities confer bachelor's or higher degrees in dance, generally through the departments of physical education, music, theater, or fine arts. Most programs concentrate on modern dance, but also offer courses in ballet/classical techniques, dance composition, dance history, dance criticism, and movement analysis.

A college education is not essential to obtaining employment as a professional dancer. In fact, ballet dancers who postpone their first audition until graduation may compete at a disadvantage with younger dancers. On the other hand, a college degree can help the dancer who retires at an early age, as often happens, and wishes to enter another field of work.

Completion of a college program in dance and education is essential to qualify for employment as a college or elementary/high school dance teacher. Colleges, as well as conservatories, generally require graduate degrees, but performance experience often may be substituted. However, a college background is not necessary for teaching dance or choreographing professionally. Studio schools usually require teachers to have experience as performers.

The dancer's life is one of rigorous practice and self-discipline; therefore, patience, perseverance, and a devotion to dance are essential. Good health and physical stamina are necessary in order to practice and perform and to follow the rugged schedule often required. Above all, one must have flexibility, agility, coordination, grace, a sense of rhythm, and a feeling for music, as well as a creative ability to express oneself through movement.

Dancers seldom perform unaccompanied, so they must be able to function as part of a team, highly motivated, and should be prepared to face the anxiety of intermittent employment and rejections when auditioning for work. For dancers, advancement takes the form of a growing reputation, more frequent work, bigger and better roles, and higher pay.

Job Outlook

Dancers and choreographers face very keen competition for jobs. The number of applicants will continue to exceed the number of job openings, and only the most talented will find regular employment.

Employment of dancers and choreographers is expected to grow faster than the average for all occupations through the year 2005 due to the public's continued interest in this form of artistic expression. However, cuts in funding for the National Endowment for the Arts and related organizations could adversely affect employment in this field. Although jobs will arise each year due to increased demand, most job openings will occur as dancers and choreographers retire and leave the occupation for other reasons, and as dance companies search for and find outstanding talent.

The best job opportunities are expected to be with national dance companies because of the demand for performances outside of New York City. Opera companies will also provide some employment opportunities. Dance groups affiliated with colleges and universities and television and motion pictures will also offer some opportunities. Moreover, the growing popularity of dance in recent years has resulted in increased employment opportunities in teaching dance.

With innovations such as electronic sounds and music videos, choreography is becoming a more challenging field of endeavor, and will offer some employment opportunities for highly talented and creative individuals.

Earnings

Earnings of many professional dancers are governed by union contracts. Dancers in the major opera ballet, classical ballet, and modern dance corps belong to the American Guild of Musical Artists, Inc., AFL-CIO; those on live or videotaped television belong to the American Federation of Television and Radio Artists; those who perform in films and on TV belong to the Screen Actors Guild or the Screen Extras Guild; and those in musical comedies are members of the Actors' Equity Association. The unions and producers sign basic agreements specifying minimum salary rates, hours of work, benefits, and other conditions of employment. However, the contract each dancer signs with the producer of the show may be more favorable than the basic agreement.

For 1994-95, the minimum weekly salary for dancers in ballet and modern productions was $610. According to the American Guild of Musical Artists, new first year dancers being paid for single performances under a union agreement earned about $475 per week and $70 per rehearsal hour. Dancers on tour received an additional allowance for room and board. The minimum performance rate for dancers in theatrical motion pictures was around $100 per day of filming. The normal workweek is 30 hours including rehearsals and matinee and evening performances, but may be longer. Extra compensation is paid for additional hours worked.

Earnings of choreographers vary greatly. Earnings from fees and performance royalties range from about $970 a week in small professional theaters, to over $30,000 for an 8- to 10-week rehearsal period for a Broadway production. In high budget films, choreographers make $3,000 for a 5-day week; in television, $7,500 to $10,000 for up to 14 work days.

Earnings from dancing are generally low because dancers' employment is irregular. They often must supplement their income by taking temporary jobs unrelated to dancing.

Dancers covered by union contracts are entitled to some paid sick leave, paid vacations, and various health and pension benefits, including extended sick pay and child birth provisions, provided by their unions. Employers contribute toward these benefits. Most other dancers do not receive any benefits.

Related Occupations

Other occupations require the dancer's knowledge of conveying ideas through physical motion. These include ice skaters, dance critics, dance instructors, dance notators, and dance therapists. Athletes in most sports also need the same strength, flexibility, agility, and body control as dancers.

Sources of Additional Information

For information on purchasing directories about colleges and universities that teach dance, including details on the types of courses offered, and scholarships, write to:

☛National Dance Association, 1900 Association Dr., Reston, VA 22091; or call 1-800-321-0789.

A directory of dance, art and design, music, and theater programs may be purchased from:

☛National Association of Schools of Dance, 11250 Roger Bacon Dr., Suite 21, Reston, VA 22090.

For information on all aspects of dance, including job listings, send a self-addressed stamped envelope to:

☛American Dance Guild, 31 West 21st St., Third Floor, New York, NY 10010.

A directory of dance companies and related organizations, plus other information on professional dance, is available from:

☛Dance/USA, 777 14th St. NW., Suite 540, Washington, DC 20005.

Musicians

(D.O.T. 152 except .021)

Nature of the Work

Musicians may play musical instruments, sing, compose,arrange, or conduct groups in instrumental or vocal performances. Musicians may perform alone or as part of a group, before live audiences or on radio, or in recording studios, television, or movie productions.

Musicians may specialize in a particular kind of music or performance. Instrumental musicians play a musical instrument in an orchestra, band, rock group, or jazz group. Musicians may play any of a wide variety of string, brass, woodwind, or percussion instruments or electronic synthesizers. Musicians may learn several related instruments, such as the flute and clarinet, often improving their employment opportunities.

Singers interpret music using their knowledge of voice production, melody, and harmony. They sing character parts or perform in their own individual style. Singers are often classified according to their voice range—soprano, contralto, tenor, baritone, or bass—or by the type of music they sing, such as opera, rock, reggae, folk, rap, or country and western.

Composers create original music such as symphonies, operas, sonatas, or popular songs. They transcribe ideas into musical notation using harmony, rhythm, melody, and tonal structure. Many songwriters now compose and edit music using computers. Some even have a musical keyboard linked to a computer which compiles the digital information into musical notation while they play. Also, they may program the composition in musical notation into the computer, which can play back the piece. Arrangers transcribe and adapt musical composition to a particular style for orchestras, bands, choral groups, or individuals.

Many professional musicians began studying at an early age.

Orchestra conductors lead instrumental music groups, such as orchestras, dance bands, and various popular ensembles. Conductors audition and select musicians, choose the music to accommodate the talents and abilities of the musicians, and direct rehearsals and performances, applying conducting techniques to achieve desired musical effects.

Choral directors lead choirs and glee clubs, sometimes working with a band or orchestra conductor. Directors audition and select singers and direct them at rehearsals and performances to achieve harmony, rhythm, tempo, shading, and other desired musical effects.

All musicians spend a considerable amount of time practicing, individually and with their band, orchestra, or other musical group.

Working Conditions

Musicians often perform at night and on weekends and spend considerable time in practice and rehearsal. Performances frequently require travel. Because many musicians find only part-time work or experience unemployment between engagements, they often supplement their income with other types of jobs. In fact, many decide they cannot support themselves as musicians and take permanent, full-time jobs in other occupations, while working only part time as musicians.

Most instrumental musicians come into contact with a variety of other people, including their colleagues, agents, employers, sponsors, and audiences. They usually work indoors, although some may perform outdoors for parades, concerts, and dances. Certain performances create noise and vibration. In some taverns and restaurants, smoke and odors may be present, and lighting and ventilation may be inadequate.

Employment

An average of about 256,000 musicians held jobs in 1994. Many were between engagements, so that the total number of people employed as musicians during the course of the year might have been greater. Nearly 3 out of 5 musicians employed in 1994 worked part time; over 1 out of 4 were self-employed.

Many work in cities in which entertainment and recording activities are concentrated, such as New York, Los Angeles, and Nashville. Classical musicians may perform with professional orchestras or in small chamber music groups like quartets or trios. Musicians may work in opera, musical comedy, and ballet productions. Many are organists who play in churches and synagogues—2 out of 3 musicians who are paid a wage or salary work in religious organizations. Musicians also perform in clubs and restaurants, and for weddings and other events. Well-known musicians and groups give their own concerts, appear "live" on radio and television, make recordings and music videos, or go on concert tours. The Armed Forces, too, offer careers in their bands and smaller musical groups.

Training, Other Qualifications, and Advancement

Many people who become professional musicians begin studying an instrument at an early age. They may gain valuable experience playing in a school or community band or orchestra, or with a group of friends. Singers usually start training when their voices mature. Participation in school musicals or in a choir often provides good early training and experience. Musicians need extensive and prolonged training to acquire the necessary skill, knowledge, and ability to interpret music. This training may be obtained through private study with an accomplished musician, in a college or university music program, in a music conservatory, or through practice with a group. For study in an institution, an audition frequently is necessary. Formal courses include musical theory, music interpretation, composition, conducting, and instrumental and voice instruction. Composers, conductors, and arrangers need advanced training in these subjects as well.

Many colleges, universities, and music conservatories grant bachelor's or higher degrees in music. Many also grant degrees in music education to qualify graduates for a State certificate to teach music in an elementary or secondary school.

Those who perform popular music must have an understanding of and feeling for the style of music that interests them, but classical training can expand their employment opportunities, as well as their musical abilities. Although voice training is an asset for singers of popular music, many with untrained voices have successful careers. As a rule, musicians take lessons with private teachers when young, and seize every opportunity to make amateur or professional appearances.

Young persons who are considering careers in music should have musical talent, versatility, creative ability, and poise and stage presence to face large audiences. Since quality performance requires constant study and practice, self-discipline is vital. Moreover, musicians who play concert and nightclub engagements must have physical stamina because frequent travel and night performances are required. They must also be prepared to face the anxiety of intermittent employment and rejections when auditioning for work.

Advancement for musicians generally means becoming better known and performing for greater earnings with better known bands and orchestras. Successful musicians often rely on agents or managers to find them performing engagements, negotiate contracts, and plan their careers.

Job Outlook

Competition for musician jobs is keen, and talent alone is no guarantee of success. The glamour and potentially high earnings in this occupation attract many talented individuals. However, being able to play several instruments and types of music enhances a musician's employment prospects.

Overall employment of musicians is expected to grow faster than the average for all occupations through the year 2005. Almost all new wage and salary jobs for musicians will arise in religious organizations and bands, orchestras, and other entertainment groups. A decline in employment is projected for salaried musicians in restaurants and bars, although they comprise a very small proportion of all wage and salary musicians. Bars, which regularly employ musicians, are expected to grow more slowly than eating establishments because consumption of alcoholic beverages outside the home is expected to continue to decline. The fastest growing segment of restaurants is the moderately priced, family dining restaurants, which seldom

provide live entertainment to their customers. Overall, most job openings for musicians will arise from the need to replace those who leave the field each year because they are unable to make a living solely as musicians.

Earnings

Earnings often depend on a performer's professional reputation, place of employment, and on the number of hours worked. The most successful musicians can earn far more than the minimum salaries indicated below.

According to the American Federation of Musicians, minimum salaries in major orchestras ranged from about $1,000 to $1,200 per week during the 1994-95 performing season. Each orchestra works out a separate contract with its members. The season of these top orchestras ranged from 48 to 52 weeks, with most being 52 weeks. In regional orchestras, the minimum salaries were between $400 and $700 per week, and the seasons lasted 25 to 38 weeks, with an average of 30 weeks; some now work a 52-week season. Community orchestras, however, had more limited levels of funding and offered salaries that were much lower for seasons of shorter duration.

Musicians employed in motion picture or television recording and those employed by recording companies were paid a minimum ranging from about $200 to $260 a week in 1995, depending on the size of the ensemble.

Musicians employed by some symphony orchestras work under master wage agreements, which guarantee a season's work up to 52 weeks. Many other musicians may face relatively long periods of unemployment between jobs. Even when employed, however, many work part time. Thus, their earnings generally are lower than those in many other occupations. Moreover, since they may not work steadily for one employer, some performers cannot qualify for unemployment compensation, and few have either sick leave or vacations with pay. For these reasons, many musicians give private lessons or take jobs unrelated to music to supplement their earnings as performers.

Many musicians belong to a local of the American Federation of Musicians. Professional singers usually belong to a branch of the Associated Actors and Artists of America.

Related Occupations

There are many music-related occupations. These include librettists, songwriters, and music therapists. A large number of music teachers work in elementary and secondary schools, music conservatories, and colleges and universities, or are self-employed. Many who teach music also perform.

Technical knowledge of musical instruments is required by instrument repairers, tuners, and copyists. In addition, there are a number of occupations in the business side of music such as booking agents, concert managers, music publishers, and music store owners and managers, as well as salespersons of records, sheet music, and musical instruments. Others whose work involves music include disc jockeys, music critics, sound and audio technicians, music librarians, and radio and television announcers.

Sources of Additional Information

For a directory of accredited programs in music teacher education, contact:

☛National Association of Schools of Music, 11250 Roger Bacon Dr., Suite 21, Reston, VA 22091.

Information on careers and employment opportunities for organists is available from:

☛American Guild of Organists, 475 Riverside Dr., Suite 1260, New York, NY 10115.

Technicians and Related Support Occupations

Health Technologists and Technicians

Cardiovascular Technologists and Technicians

D.O.T. 078.264-010, .362-018, -030, -050, -062, .364-014, and .367-010)

Nature of the Work

Cardiovascular technologists and technicians assist physicians in diagnosing and treating cardiac (heart) and peripheral vascular (blood vessel) ailments.

Cardiovascular technicians who obtain electro (electrical)- cardio (heart)- grams (record), abbreviated EKG's or ECG's, which trace electrical impulses transmitted by the heart, are known as *electrocardiograph (ECG or EKG) technicians*. To take a "basic" EKG, technicians attach electrodes to the patient's chest, arms, and legs, then manipulate switches on a electrocardiograph machine to obtain the reading. The test is done before most kinds of surgery and as part of a routine physical examination, especially for persons who have reached middle age or have a history of cardiovascular problems.

More skilled EKG technicians perform Holter monitor and stress testing. For a Holter monitoring, technicians place electrodes on the patient's chest and attach a portable EKG monitor to the patient's belt. Following 24-48 hours of normal routine for the patient, the technician removes a cassette tape from the monitor and places it in a scanner. After checking the quality of the recorded impulses on an electronic screen, the technician prints the information from the tape so that it can be interpreted later. The printed output from the scanner is eventually used by a physician to diagnose heart ailments.

For a treadmill stress test, EKG technicians document the patient's medical history, explain the procedure, connect the patient to an EKG monitor, and obtain a baseline reading and resting blood pressure. Next, they monitor the heart's performance while the patient is walking on a treadmill, gradually increasing the treadmill's speed to observe the effect of increased exertion. Those cardiovascular technicians who perform EKG and stress tests are known as noninvasive technicians because the techniques they use do not require the insertion of probes or other instruments into the patient's body.

Cardiovascular technologists who specialize in cardiac catheterization procedures are called *cardiology technologists*. They assist physicians with invasive procedures in which a small tube, or catheter, is wound through a patient's blood vessel from a spot on the patient's leg into the heart to determine if a blockage exists or for other diagnostic purposes. In balloon angioplasty, a procedure used to treat blockages of blood vessels, technologists assist physicians who insert a catheter with a balloon on the end to the point of the obstruction. Technologists may prepare patients for these procedures by positioning them on an examining table, then shaving, cleaning, and administering anesthesia to the top of the patient's leg near the groin. During the procedures, they monitor patients' blood pressure and heart rate using EKG equipment and notify the physician if something appears wrong. Technologists may also prepare and monitor patients during open heart surgery and the implantation of pacemakers.

Cardiovascular technologists and technicians may also specialize in noninvasive peripheral vascular tests. They use ultrasound equipment that transmits sound waves, then collects the echoes to form an image on a screen. Individuals who focus on blood flows and circulation problems are known as *vascular technologists*, while those who use ultrasound on the heart are referred to as *echocardiographers*.

Some cardiovascular technologists and technicians schedule appointments, type doctor's interpretations, maintain patient's files, and care for equipment.

Working Conditions

Technologists and technicians generally work a 5-day, 40- hour week, which may include Saturdays and Sundays. Those in catheterization labs tend to work longer hours and also may work evenings. They may also be on call during the night and on weekends.

Cardiovascular technologists and technicians spend a lot of time walking and standing. Those who work in catheterzation labs may face stressful working conditions, because they are in close contact with patients who have serious heart ailments. Some patients, for example, may encounter complications from time to time that have life or death implications.

Employment

Cardiovascular technologists and technicians held about 30,000 jobs in 1994. Most worked in hospital cardiology departments, while some worked in cardiologists' offices, cardiac rehabilitation centers, or health maintenance organizations. About one-half were EKG technicians.

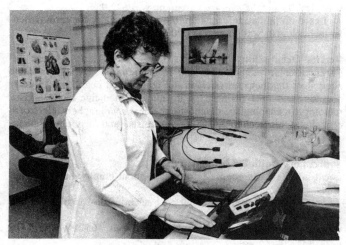

Cardiovascular technologists and technicians spend a lot of time walking or standing.

Training, Other Qualifications, and Advancement

For basic EKGs, Holter monitoring, and stress testing, 1-year certificate programs exist, although most EKG technicians are still trained on the job by an EKG supervisor or a cardiologist. On-the-job training usually lasts about 8 to 16 weeks. Applicants must be high school graduates. Most employers prefer to train people already in the health care field, nursing aides, for example. Some EKG technicians are students who are enrolled in 2-year programs to become technologists, but work part-time to get experience and make contact with employers. Most vascular technologists are trained on the job although some have backgrounds in nursing and sonography.

Cardiology technologists need to complete a 2-year junior or community college program. One year is dedicated to core courses followed by a year of specialized instruction in either invasive, noninvasive, or noninvasive peripheral cardiology. Those who are qualified in a related allied health profession only need to complete the year of specialized instruction.

Cardiovascular technologists must be reliable, have mechanical aptitude, and be able to follow detailed instructions. A pleasant, relaxed manner for putting patients at ease is an asset.

Job Outlook

Employment of cardiovascular technologists and technicians is expected to grow more slowly than the average for all occupations through the year 2005, with technologists and technicians experiencing different patterns of employment change. Employment of cardiology technologists is expected to grow faster than average for all occupations. Growth will occur as the population ages, because older people have a higher incidence of heart problems. In contrast, employment of EKG technicians is expected to decline as hospitals train registered nurses and others to perform basic EKG procedures. Individuals trained in Holter monitoring and stress testing are expected to have more favorable job prospects than those who can only perform a basic EKG.

Most job openings for cardiovascular technologists and technicians should arise from replacement needs as individuals transfer to other jobs or leave the labor force. Relatively few job opportunities due to both growth and replacement needs are expected, however, because these occupations are small.

Earnings

According to a University of Texas Medical Branch survey of hospitals and medical centers, the median annual salary of EKG technicians, based on a 40 hour week and excluding shift and area differentials, was $18,396 in October 1994. The average minimum salary was $15,793 and the average maximum was $22,985.

Based on limited information, the average salary for cardiovascular technologists was about $32,000 in 1994.

Related Occupations

Cardiovascular technologists and technicians operate sophisticated equipment that helps physicians and other allied health practitioners diagnose and treat patients, so do nuclear medicine technologists, radiologic technologists, diagnostic medical sonographers, electroencephalographic technologists, perfusionists, and respiratory therapists.

Sources of Additional Information

Local hospitals can supply information about employment opportunities.

For general information about a career in cardiovascular technology contact:

☛American Society for Cardiovascular Professionals, 10500 Wakeman Dr., Fredericksburg, VA 22407.

For a list of accredited programs in cardiovascular technology, contact:

☛Division of Allied Health Education and Accreditation, American Medical Association, 515 N. State St., Chicago, IL 60610.

For information on vascular technology, contact:

☛The Society of Vascular Technology, 4601 Presidents Dr., Suite 260, Lanham, MD 20706-4365.

Clinical Laboratory Technologists and Technicians

(D.O.T. 078.221-010, .261-010, -014, -026, -030, and -038, .281-010, .381-014, .687-010, and 559.361-010)

Nature of the Work

Clinical laboratory testing plays a crucial role in the detection, diagnosis, and treatment of disease. Clinical laboratory technologists and technicians, also known as medical technologists and technicians, perform most of these tests.

Clinical laboratory personnel examine and analyze body fluids, tissues, and cells. They look for bacteria, parasites, or other micro-organisms; analyze the chemical content of fluids; match blood for transfusions, and test for drug levels in the blood to show how a patient is responding to treatment. They also prepare specimens for examination, count cells, and look for abnormal cells. They use automated equipment and instruments that perform a number of tests simultaneously, as well as microscopes, cell counters, and other kinds of sophisticated laboratory equipment to perform tests. Then they analyze the results and relay them to physicians.

The complexity of tests performed, the level of judgment needed, and the amount of responsibility workers assume depend largely on the amount of education and experience they have.

Medical technologists generally have a bachelor's degree in medical technology or in one of the life sciences, or have a combination of formal training and work experience. They perform complex chemical, biological, hematological, immunologic, microscopic, and bacteriological tests. Technologists microscopically examine blood, tissue, and other body substances; make cultures of body fluid or tissue samples to determine the presence of bacteria, fungi, parasites, or other micro-organisms; analyze samples for chemical content or reaction; and determine blood glucose or cholesterol levels. They also type and cross-match blood samples for transfusions.

They may evaluate test results, develop and modify procedures, and establish and monitor programs to insure the accuracy of tests. Some medical technologists supervise medical laboratory technicians.

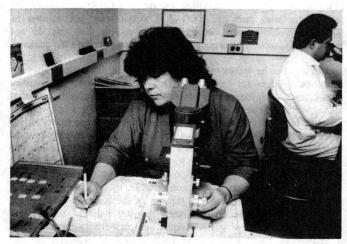

Clinical laboratory personnel analyze body bluids, tissues, and cells to detect disease.

Technologists in small laboratories perform many types of tests, while those in large laboratories generally specialize. Technologists who prepare specimens and analyze the chemical and hormonal contents of body fluids are *clinical chemistry technologists*. Those who examine and identify bacteria and other micro-organisms are *microbiology technologists*. *Blood bank technologists* collect, type, and prepare blood and its components for transfusions; *immunology technologists* examine elements and responses of the human immune system to foreign bodies. *Cytotechnologists*, prepare slides of body cells and microscopically examine these cells for abnormalities which may signal the beginning of a cancerous growth.

Medical laboratory technicians perform less complex tests and laboratory procedures than technologists. Technicians may prepare specimens and operate automatic analyzers, for example, or they may perform manual tests following detailed instructions. Like technologists, they may work in several areas of the clinical laboratory or specialize in just one. *Histology technicians* cut and stain tissue specimens for microscopic examination by pathologists, and *phlebotomists* draw and test blood. They usually work under the supervision of medical technologists or laboratory managers.

Working Conditions

Hours and other working conditions vary according to the size and type of employment setting. In large hospitals or in independent laboratories that operate continuously, personnel usually work the day, evening, or night shift, and may work weekends and holidays. Laboratory personnel in small facilities may work on rotating shifts rather than on a regular shift. In some facilities, laboratory personnel are on call, available in case of an emergency, several nights a week or on weekends.

Clinical laboratory personnel are trained to work with infectious specimens. When proper methods of infection control and sterilization are followed, few hazards exist.

Laboratories generally are well lighted and clean; however, specimens, solutions, and reagents used in the laboratory sometimes produce odors. Laboratory workers may spend a great deal of time on their feet.

Employment

Clinical laboratory technologists and technicians held about 274,000 jobs in 1994. More than half worked in hospitals. Most others worked in medical laboratories and offices and clinics of physicians. Some worked in blood banks, research and testing laboratories, and in the Federal Government—at Department of Veterans Affairs hospitals and U.S. Public Health Service facilities.

About 1 laboratory worker in 6 worked part-time.

Training, Other Qualifications, and Advancement

The usual requirement for an entry level position as a medical technologist is a bachelor's degree with a major in medical technology or in one of the life sciences. Universities and hospitals offer medical technology programs. It is also possible to qualify through a combination of on-the-job and specialized training.

Bachelor's degree programs in medical technology include courses in chemistry, biological sciences, microbiology, and mathematics, and specialized courses devoted to knowledge and skills used in the clinical laboratory. Many programs also offer or require courses in management, business, and computer applications.

Masters degrees in medical technology and related clinical laboratory sciences provide training for specialized areas of laboratory work or teaching, administration, or research.

After September 1, 1997, the Clinical Laboratory Improvement Act (CLIA) will require technologists who perform certain highly complex tests to have at least an associate's degree. A grandfather clause will allow experienced workers to continue performing these tests.

Medical laboratory technicians generally have an associate's degree from a community or junior college, or a certificate from a hospital, vocational or technical school, or from one of the Armed Forces. A few technicians learn on the job.

Nationally recognized accrediting agencies in the clinical laboratory science include the National Accrediting Agency for Clinical Laboratory Sciences, and the Accrediting Bureau of Health Education Schools (ABHES). National Accrediting Agency for Clinical Laboratory Sciences accredits over 391 programs that provide education for medical technologists, cytotechnologists, histologic technicians, specialists in blood bank technology, and medical laboratory technicians. ABHES accredits training programs for medical laboratory technicians.

Licensure and certification are methods of assuring the skill and competence of workers. Licensure refers to the process by which a government agency authorizes individuals to engage in a given occupation and use a particular job title. Some States require laboratory personnel to be licensed or registered. (Information on licensure is available from State departments of health, boards of occupational licensing, or occupational information coordinating committees.)

Certification is a voluntary process by which a nongovernmental organization such as a professional society or certifying agency grants recognition to an individual whose professional competence meets prescribed standards. Widely accepted by employers in the health industry, certification is a prerequisite for most jobs and often is necessary for advancement. Agencies that certify medical laboratory technologists and technicians include the Board of Registry of the American Society of Clinical Pathologists, the American Medical Technologists, the National Certification Agency for Medical Laboratory Personnel, and the Credentialing Commission of the International Society for Clinical Laboratory Technology. These agencies have different requirements for certification and different organizational sponsors.

Clinical laboratory personnel need analytical judgment and the ability to work under pressure. Close attention to detail is essential because small differences or changes in test substances or numerical readouts can be crucial for patient care. Manual dexterity and normal color vision are highly desirable. With the widespread use of automated laboratory equipment, computer skills are important. In addition, technologists in particular are expected to be good at problem solving.

Technologists may advance to supervisory positions in laboratory work or become chief medical technologists or laboratory managers in hospitals. Manufacturers of home diagnostic testing kits and laboratory equipment and supplies seek experienced technologists to work in product development, marketing, and sales. Graduate education in medical technology, one of the biological sciences, chemistry, management, or education usually speeds advancement. A doctorate is needed to become a laboratory director. Technicians can become technologists through additional education and experience.

Job Outlook

Overall, employment of clinical laboratory workers is expected to grow about as fast as the average for all occupations through the year 2005. The rapidly growing older population will spur demand, since older people generally have more medical problems. Technological changes will have two opposite effects on employment. New, more powerful diagnostic tests will encourage more testing and spur employment. However, advances in laboratory automation and simpler tests, which make it possible for each worker to perform more tests, should slow growth. Research and development efforts are targeted at simplifying routine testing procedures so that nonlaboratory personnel—physicians and patients in particular—can perform tests now done in laboratories. Also, robots may prepare specimens, a job now done by technologists and technicians. Because the Clinical Laboratory Improvement Act regulations that are to take effect will impose academic standards for persons conducting some evaluations, job opportunities will be best for technologists who have at least an associate's degree.

Fastest growth is expected in independent medical laboratories, as hospitals continue to send them a greater share of their testing. Rapid growth is also expected in offices and clinics of physicians. Slower growth is expected in hospitals. Although significant, growth will not be primary source of opportunities. As in most occupations, most will result from the need to replace workers who transfer to other occupations, retire, or stop working for some other reason.

Earnings

Median annual earnings of full time, salaried clinical laboratory technologists and technicians were $26,988 in 1994. Half earned between $19,240 and $35,204. The lowest 10 percent earned less than $14,820 and the top 10 percent more than $44,304.

Table 1 presents salary data for selected medical technology occupations from a University of Texas Medical Branch survey of hospitals and medical centers. The data are based on a 40 hour week and exclude shift and area differentials.

Table 1: Median annual salary, medical technology occupations, 1994

Occupation	Minimum	Median	Maximum
Cytotechnologist	$29,772	$37,107	$43,477
Histology technician	21,975	26,624	32,337
Medical laboratory technician	20,443	24,461	30,414
Medical technologist	26,033	32,282	38,844
Phlebotomist	15,344	17,166	22,339

Source: National Survey of Hospitals and Medical Centers, University of Texas Medical Branch

Related Occupations

Clinical laboratory technologists and technicians analyze body fluids, tissue, and other substances using a variety of tests. Similar or related procedures are performed by analytical, water purification, and other chemists; science technicians; crime laboratory analysts; food testers; and veterinary laboratory technicians.

Sources of Additional Information

Career and certification information is available from:

☛American Society of Clinical Pathologists, Board of Registry, P.O. Box 12277, Chicago, IL 60612.

☛American Medical Technologists, 710 Higgins Rd., Park Ridge, IL 60068.

☛American Society of Cytopathology 400 West 9th St., Suite 201, Wilmington, DE 19801.

☛National Certification Agency for Medical Laboratory Personnel, 7910 Woodmont Ave., Suite 1301, Bethesda, MD 20814.

☛International Society for Clinical Laboratory Technology, 818 Olive St., Suite 918, St. Louis, MO 63101.

For more career information, write to:

☛American Association of Blood Banks, 8101 Glenbrook Rd., Bethesda, MD 20814-2749.

☛Clinical Ligand Assay Society, 3139 S. Wayne Rd., Wayne, MI 48184.

For a list of educational programs accredited for clinical laboratory personnel, write to:

☛National Accrediting Agency for Clinical Laboratory Sciences, 8410 W. Bryn Mawr Ave., Suite 670, Chicago, IL 60631.

For a list of training programs for medical laboratory technicians accredited by the Accrediting Bureau of Health Education Schools, write to:

☛Secretary-ABHES, 29089 U.S. 20 West, Elkhart, IN 46514.

Information about employment opportunities in Department of Veterans Affairs medical centers is available from local medical centers and also from:

☛Title 38 Employment Division (054D), Department of Veterans Affairs, 810 Vermont Ave. NW., Washington, DC 20420.

Dental Hygienists

(D.O.T. 078.361-010)

Nature of the Work

Dental hygienists clean teeth and provide other preventive dental care as well as teach patients how to practice good oral hygiene. Hygienists examine patients' teeth and gums, recording the presence of diseases or abnormalities. They remove calculus, stains, and plaque from teeth; apply cavity preventive agents such as fluorides and pit and fissure sealants; take and develop dental x rays; place temporary fillings and periodontal dressings; remove sutures; and smooth and polish metal restorations. In some States, hygienists administer local anesthetics and anesthetic gas, and place and carve filling materials.

Dental hygienists also help patients develop and maintain good oral health. For example, they may explain the relationship between diet and oral health, inform patients how to select toothbrushes, and show patients how to brush and floss their teeth.

Dental hygienists use hand and rotary instruments to clean teeth, x-ray machines to take dental pictures, syringes with needles to administer local anesthetics, and models of teeth to explain oral hygiene.

Working Conditions

Flexible scheduling is a distinctive feature of this job. Full-time, part-time, evening, and weekend work is widely available. Dentists frequently hire hygienists to work only 2 or 3 days a week, so hygienists may hold jobs in more than one dental office.

Dental hygienists work in clean, well-lighted offices. Important health safeguards include strict adherence to proper radiological procedures and use of appropriate protective devices when administering anesthetic gas. Dental hygienists also wear safety glasses, surgical masks and gloves to protect themselves from infectious diseases such as hepatitis. The occupation is one of several covered by the Consumer-Patient Radiation Health and Safety Act of 1981,

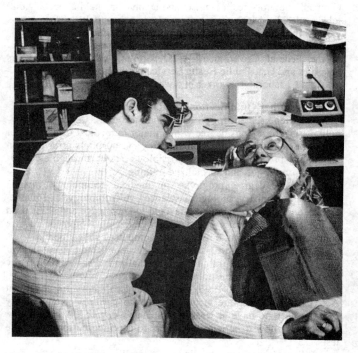

Dental hygienists must be licensed by the State in which they practice.

which encourages the States to adopt uniform standards for the training and certification of individuals who perform medical and dental radiological procedures.

Employment

Dental hygienists held about 127,000 jobs in 1994. Because multiple jobholding is common in this field, the number of jobs greatly exceeds the number of hygienists. About half of all dental hygienists usually worked part time—less than 35 hours a week.

Almost all dental hygienists work in private dental offices. Some work in public health agencies, school systems, hospitals, and clinics.

Training, Other Qualifications, and Advancement

Dental hygienists must be licensed by the State in which they practice. To qualify for licensure, a candidate must graduate from an accredited dental hygiene school and pass both a written and a clinical examination. The American Dental Association Joint Commission on National Dental Examinations administers the written examination that is accepted by all States and the District of Columbia. State or regional testing agencies administer the clinical examination. In addition, examinations on legal aspects of dental hygiene practice are required by most States. Alabama also allows candidates to take its examination if they have been trained through a State-regulated on-the-job program in a dentist's office.

In 1995, 212 programs in dental hygiene were accredited by the Commission on Dental Accreditation. Although some programs lead to a bachelor's degree, most grant an associate degree. Ten universities offer master's degree programs in dental hygiene.

An associate degree is sufficient for practice in a private dental office. A bachelor's or master's degree is usually required for research, teaching, or clinical practice in public or school health programs.

About half of the dental hygiene programs prefer applicants who have completed at least 1 year of college. Some of the bachelor's degree programs require applicants to have completed 2 years. However, requirements vary from school to school. These schools offer laboratory, clinical, and classroom instruction in subjects such as anatomy, physiology, chemistry, microbiology, pharmacology, nutrition, radiography, histology (the study of tissue structure), periodontology (the study of gum diseases), pathology, dental materials, clinical dental hygiene, and social and behavioral sciences.

Dental hygienists should work well with others and must have manual dexterity because they use dental instruments with little room for error within a patient's mouth. Recommended high school courses for aspiring dental hygienists include biology, chemistry, and mathematics.

Job Outlook

Employment of dental hygienists is expected to grow much faster than the average for all occupations through the year 2005 in response to increasing demand for dental care and the greater substitution of hygienists for services previously performed by dentists. Job prospects are expected to remain very good unless the number of dental hygienist program graduates grows much faster than during the last decade and results in a much larger pool of qualified applicants.

Demand will be stimulated by population growth, and greater retention of natural teeth by the larger number of middle-aged and elderly people. Also, dentists are likely to employ more hygienists, for several reasons. Older dentists, who are less likely to employ dental hygienists, will leave and be replaced by recent graduates, who are more likely to do so. In addition, as dentists' workloads increase, they are expected to hire more hygienists to perform preventive dental care such as cleaning, so they may use their own time more profitably.

Earnings

Earnings of dental hygienists are affected by geographic location, employment setting, and education and experience. Dental hygienists who work in private dental offices may be paid on an hourly, daily, salary, or commission basis.

According to the American Dental Association, dental hygienists who worked 32 hours a week or more averaged $675.50 a week in 1993; the average hourly earnings for all dental hygienists was $21.10.

Benefits vary substantially by practice setting, and may be contingent upon full-time employment. Dental hygienists who work for school systems, public health agencies, the Federal Government, or State agencies usually have substantial benefits.

Related Occupations

Workers in other occupations supporting health practitioners in an office setting include dental assistants, ophthalmic medical assistants, podiatric assistants, office nurses, medical assistants, physician assistants, physical therapy assistants, and occupational therapy assistants.

Sources of Additional Information

For information on a career in dental hygiene and the educational requirements to enter this occupation, contact:

☛Division of Professional Development, American Dental Hygienists' Association, 444 N. Michigan Ave., Suite 3400, Chicago, IL 60611.

☛American Dental Association, Department of Career Guidance, 211 E. Chicago Ave., Suite 1804, Chicago, IL 60611.

For information about accredited programs and educational requirements, contact:

☛Commission on Dental Accreditation, American Dental Association, 211 E. Chicago Ave., Suite 1814, Chicago, IL 60611.

The State Board of Dental Examiners in each State can supply information on licensing requirements.

Dispensing Opticians

(D.O.T. 299.361-010 and -014)

Nature of Work

Dispensing opticians fit eyeglasses and contact lenses, following prescriptions written by ophthalmologists or optometrists. (The work of optometrists is described in a statement elsewhere in the *Handbook*. See the statement on physicians for information about ophthalmologists.)

Dispensing opticians help customers select appropriate frames, order the necessary ophthalmic laboratory work, and adjust the finished eyeglasses. In some States, they fit contact lenses under the supervision of an optometrist or ophthalmologist.

Dispensing opticians examine written prescriptions to determine lens specifications. They recommend eyeglass frames, lenses, and lens coatings after considering the prescription and the customer's occupation, habits, and facial features. Dispensing opticians measure clients' eyes, including the distance between the centers of the pupils and the distance between the eye surface and the lens. For customers without prescriptions, dispensing opticians may use a lensometer to record the present eyeglass prescription. They also may obtain a customer's previous record, or verify a prescription with the examining optometrist or ophthalmologist.

Dispensing opticians prepare work orders that give ophthalmic laboratory technicians information needed to grind and insert lenses into a frame. The work order includes lens prescriptions and information on lens size, material, color, and style. Some dispensing opticians grind and insert lenses themselves. After the glasses are made, dispensing opticians verify that the lenses have been ground to specifications. Then they may reshape or bend the frame, by hand or using pliers, so that the eyeglasses fit the customer properly and comfortably. Dispensing opticians also fix, adjust, and refit broken frames. They instruct clients about adapting to, wearing, or caring for eyeglasses.

Some dispensing opticians specialize in fitting contacts, artificial eyes, or cosmetic shells to cover blemished eyes. To fit contact lenses, dispensing opticians measure eye shape and size, select the type of contact lens material, and prepare work orders specifying the prescription and lens size. Fitting contact lenses requires considerable skill, care, and patience. Dispensing opticians observe customers' eyes, corneas, lids, and contact lenses with special instruments and microscopes. During several visits, opticians show customers how to insert, remove, and care for their contacts, and ensure the fit is correct.

Dispensing opticians keep records on customer prescriptions, work orders, and payments; track inventory and sales; and perform other administrative duties.

Working Conditions

Dispensing opticians work indoors in attractive, well lighted, and well ventilated surroundings. They may work in medical offices or small stores where customers are served one at a time, or in large stores where several dispensing opticians serve a number of customers at once. Opticians spend a lot of time with customers, most of it on their feet. If they also prepare lenses, they need to take precautions against the hazards associated with glass cutting, chemicals, and machinery.

Most dispensing opticians work a 40-hour week, although some work longer hours. Those in retail stores may work evenings and weekends. Some work part time.

Employment

Dispensing opticians held about 63,000 jobs in 1994. About half work for ophthalmologists or optometrists who sell glasses directly to patients. Many also work in optical stores that offer one-stop shopping. Customers may have their eyes examined, choose frames, and have glasses made on the spot. Some work in optical departments of drug and department stores.

Training, Other Qualifications, and Advancement

Employers generally hire individuals with no background in opticianry or those who have worked as ophthalmic laboratory technicians and then provide the required training. (See the statement on ophthalmic laboratory technicians elsewhere in the *Handbook*.) Training may be informal, on-the-job or formal apprenticeship. Some employers, however, seek people with postsecondary training in opticianry.

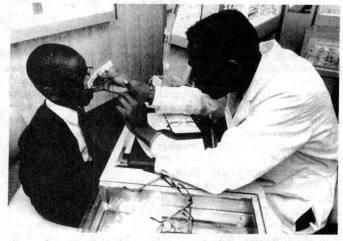

About one-half of dispensing opticians work for opthalmologists or optometrists who sell glasses directly to patients.

Knowledge of physics, basic anatomy, algebra, geometry, and mechanical drawing is particularly valuable because training usually includes instruction in optical mathematics, optical physics, and the use of precision measuring instruments and other machinery and tools. Because dispensing opticians deal directly with the public, they should be tactful and pleasant and communicate well.

Large employers generally offer structured apprenticeship programs, and small employers provide more informal on-the-job training. In the 21 States that license dispensing opticians, individuals without postsecondary training work from 2 to 4 years as apprentices. Apprenticeship or formal traineeship is offered in most of the other States as well.

Apprentices receive technical training and learn office management and sales. Under the supervision of an experienced optician, optometrist, or ophthalmologist, apprentices work directly with patients, fitting eyeglasses and contact lenses. In States requiring licensure, information about apprenticeships and licensing procedures is available from the State board of occupational licensing.

Formal opticianry training is offered in community colleges and a few colleges and universities. In 1995, there were about 40 programs. Of these, 24 were accredited by the Commission on Opticianry Accreditation and awarded 2-year associate degrees in ophthalmic dispensing or optometric technology. There are also shorter programs, including some under 1 year. Some States that license dispensing opticians allow graduates to take the licensure exam immediately upon graduation; others require a few months to a year of experience.

Dispensing opticians may apply to the American Board of Opticianry and the National Contact Lens Examiners for certification of their skills. Certification must be renewed every 3 years through continuing education.

Many experienced dispensing opticians open their own optical stores. Others become managers of optical stores or sales representatives for wholesalers or manufacturers of eyeglasses or lenses.

Job Outlook

Employment in this occupation is expected to increase faster than the average for all occupations through the year 2005 in response to rising demand for corrective lenses. The number of middle-aged and elderly persons is projected to increase rapidly. Middle age is a time when many people use corrective lenses for the first time, and elderly persons require more vision care, on the whole, than others.

Fashion, too, influences demand. Frames come in a growing variety of styles and colors—encouraging people to buy more than one pair. Finally, demand is expected to grow in response to products such as special lens treatments; photochromic lenses (glasses with lenses that become darker in sunlight), now available in plastic as well as glass; tinted lenses; and bifocal, extended wear, and disposable contact lenses.

Like other occupations in retail trade, a disproportionate number of openings will occur as young workers transfer to jobs in other occupations. Nevertheless, the need to replace those who leave the occupation and employment growth will result in relatively few job openings—because the occupation is small. This occupation is vulnerable to changes in the business cycle, with employment falling somewhat during downturns.

Earnings

According to the Opticians Association of America, salaries for nonmanagerial dispensing opticians averaged about $26,700 in 1994, while managers averaged about $30,400. Apprentice opticians averaged about $19,400 a year. Those who run their own stores earned more than salaried workers. In addition to base salaries, many employers provide commissions, bonuses, and profitsharing.

Related Occupations

Other workers who deal with customers and perform delicate work include jewelers, locksmiths, ophthalmic laboratory technicians, orthodontic technicians, dental laboratory technicians, prosthetics technicians, camera repairers, and watch repairers.

Sources of Additional Information

For general information about this occupation, contact:

☛Opticians Association of America, 10341 Democracy Lane, Fairfax, VA 22030-2521.

For a list of accredited training programs, contact:

☛Commission on Opticianry Accreditation, 10111 Martin Luther King, Jr. Hwy., Suite 100, Bowie, MD 20720-4299.

For general information on opticianry and a list of home-study programs, seminars, and review materials, contact:

☛National Academy of Opticianry, 10111 Martin Luther King, Jr. Hwy., Suite 112, Bowie, MD 20720-4299.

Electroneurodiagnostic Technologists

(D.O.T. 078.362-022, -042)

Nature of the Work

Electroneurodiagnostic technologists use an electroencephalograph (EEG) machine to record electrical impulses transmitted by the brain and the nervous system. They help physicians diagnose brain tumors, strokes, toxic/metabolic disorders, epilepsy and sleep disorders. They also measure the effects of infectious diseases on the brain, as well as determine whether individuals with mental or behavioral problems have an organic impairment such as Alzheimer's disease. Furthermore, they determine "cerebral" death, the absence of brain activity, and assess the probability of a recovery from a coma.

Electroneurodiagnostic technologists who specialize in basic or, "resting" EEG's are called EEG technologists. The range of tests performed by electroneurodiagnostic technologists is broader than, but includes, those conducted by EEG technologists. Because it provides a more accurate description of work typically performed in the field, the title electroneurodiagnostic technologists generally has replaced that of EEG technologist.

Electroneurodiagnostic technologists take patients' medical histories and help them relax, then apply electrodes to designated spots on the patient's head. They must choose the most appropriate combination of instrument controls and electrodes to correct for mechanical or electrical interference that come from somewhere other than the brain, such as eye movement or radiation from electrical sources.

Increasingly, technologists perform EEG's in the operating room, which requires that they understand anesthesia's effect on brain waves. For special procedure EEG's, technologists may secure electrodes to the chest, arm, leg, or spinal column to record activity from both the central and peripheral nervous systems.

In ambulatory monitoring, technologists monitor the brain, and sometimes the heart, while patients carry out normal activities over a 24-hour period. Then they remove the small recorder carried by the patients and obtain a readout. Technologists review the readouts, selecting sections for the physician to examine.

Using "evoked potential" testing, technologists measure sensory and physical responses to specific stimuli. After the electrodes have been attached, they set the instrument for the type and intensity of the stimulus, increase the intensity until the patient reacts, and note the sensation level. The tests may take from 1 to 4 hours.

For nerve conduction tests, used to diagnose muscle and nerve problems, technologists place electrodes on the patient's skin over a nerve and over the muscle. Then they stimulate the nerve with an electrical current and record how long it takes the nerve impulse to reach the muscle.

Electroneurodiagnostic technicians record electrical activity of the brain and other nervous system functions.

Technologists who specialize in and administer sleep disorder studies are called polysomnographic technologists. The sleep studies are conducted in a clinic called a "sleep center." During the procedure technologists monitor the patient's respiration and heart activity in addition to brain wave activity and must know the dynamics of the cardiopulmonary systems during each stage of sleep. They coordinate readings from several organ systems, separating them according to the stages of sleep, and relay them to the physician. For quantitative EEG's, technologists decide which sections of the EEG should be transformed into color-coded pictures of brain wave frequency and intensity, for interpretation by a physician. They may also write technical reports summarizing test results.

Technologists also look for changes in the patient's neurologic, cardiac, and respiratory status, which may indicate an emergency, such as a heart attack, and provide emergency care until help arrives.

Electorneurodiagnostic technologists may have supervisory or administrative responsibilities. They may manage an eletroneurodiagnostic laboratory, arrange work schedules, keep records, schedule appointments, order supplies, provide instruction to less experienced technologists, and may also be responsible for the equipment's upkeep.

Working Conditions

Electroneurodiagnostic technologists usually work in clean, well-lighted surroundings, and spend about half of their time on their feet. Bending and lifting are necessary because they may work with patients who are very ill and require assistance. Technologists who are employed in hospitals may do all their work in a single room, or may push equipment to a patient's bedside and obtain recordings there.

Most technologists work a standard workweek, although those in hospitals may be "on call" evenings, weekends, and holidays. Those performing sleep studies usually work evenings and nights.

Employment

Electroneurodiagnostic technologists held more than 6,000 jobs in 1994. Most worked in neurology laboratories of hospitals. Others worked in offices and clinics of neurologists and neurosurgeons, health maintenance organizations, and psychiatric facilities.

Training, Other Qualifications, and Advancement

Although most electroneurodiagnostic technologists currently employed learned their skills on the job, employers are beginning to favor those who have completed formal training. Some hospitals require applicants for trainee positions to have postsecondary training while others only expect a high school diploma. Often, on-the-job trainees are transfers from another hospital job, such as a licensed practical nurse.

Formal postsecondary training is offered in hospitals and communities colleges. In 1994, the Joint Review Committee on Education in Electroneurodiagnostic Technology had approved 14 formal programs. Programs usually last from 1 to 2 years and include laboratory experience as well as classroom instruction in human anatomy and physiology, neurology, neuroanatomy, neurophysiology, medical terminology, computer technology, electronics and instrumentation. Graduates receive associate degrees or certificates.

The American Board of Registration of Electroencephalographic and Evoked Potential Technologists awards the credential "Registered EEG Technologist" and "Registered Evoked Potential Technologist" to qualified applicants. The Association of Polysomnographic Technologists registers polysomnographic technologists. Applicants interested in taking the registration exam must have worked in a sleep center for at least 1 year. Although not generally required for staff level jobs, registration indicates professional competence, and usually is necessary for supervisory or teaching jobs.

Technologists should have manual dexterity, good vision, writing skills, an aptitude for working with electronic equipment, and the ability to work with patients as well as with other health personnel. High school courses in health, biology, and mathematics are useful.

Electorneurodiagnostic technologists who have significant experience can advance to chief or manager of a electroneurodiagnostic laboratory in a large hospital. Chief technologists generally are supervised by a physician—an electroencephalographer, neurologist, or neurosurgeon. Technologists may also teach or go into research.

Job Outlook

Job prospects for qualified applicants are expected to be good. Employment of electroneurodiagnostic technologists is expected to grow faster than the average for all occupations through the year 2005, reflecting the increased numbers of neurodiagnostic tests performed. There will be more testing as new procedures are developed and as the size of the population grows. A very low number of openings each year are expected, however, because the occupation is very small. Most jobs will be found in hospitals but growth will be fastest in offices and clinics of neurologists.

Earnings

According to a University of Texas Medical Branch survey of hospitals and medical centers, the median annual salary of EEG technologists, based on a 40 hour week and excluding shift or area differentials, was $24,710 in October 1994. The average minimum salary was $20,356 and the average maximum was $29,691.

Related Occupations

Other health personnel who operate medical equipment include radiologic technologists, nuclear medicine technologists, sonographers, perfusionists, and cardiovascular technologists.

Sources of Additional Information

Local hospitals can supply information about employment opportunities.

For general information about a career in electroneurodiagnostics as well as a list of accredited training programs, contact:

☞Executive Office, American Society of Electroneurodiagnostic Technologists, Inc., 204 W. 7th, Carroll, IA 51401.

For information on work in sleep studies, contact:

☞Association of Polysomnographic Technology, P.O. Box 14861, Lenexa, KS 66285-4861.

Information about specific accredited training programs is also available from:

☞Joint Review Committee on Electroneurodiagnostic Technology, Route 1, Box 63A, Genoa, WI 54632.

Information on becoming a registered Electroneurodiagnostic technologist is available from:

☞American Board of Registration of Electroencephalgraphic and Evoked Potential Technologists, P.O. Box 916633, Longwood, FL 32791-6633.

Emergency Medical Technicians

(D.O.T. 079.364-026 and .374-010)

Nature of the Work

Automobile accident injuries, heart attacks, near drownings, unscheduled childbirths, poisonings, and gunshot wounds all demand urgent medical attention. Emergency medical technicians (EMT's) give immediate care and then transport the sick or injured to medical facilities.

Following instructions from a dispatcher, EMT's—who usually work in teams of two—drive specially equipped vehicles to the scene of emergencies. If necessary, they request additional help from police or fire department personnel. They determine the nature and extent of the patient's injuries or illness while also trying to determine whether the patient has epilepsy, diabetes, or other preexisting medical conditions. EMT's then give appropriate emergency care following strict guidelines for which procedures they may perform. All EMT's, including those with basic skills, the EMT-Basic, may open airways, restore breathing, control bleeding, treat for shock, administer oxygen, immobilize fractures, bandage wounds, assist in childbirth, manage emotionally disturbed patients, treat and assist heart attack victims, give initial care to poison and burn victims, and treat patients with anti-shock trousers (which prevent a person's blood pressure from falling too low).

EMT-Intermediates, or EMT-I's, have more advanced training that allows them to administer intravenous fluids; use defibrillators to give lifesaving shocks to a stopped heart, as well as other intensive care procedures.

EMT-Paramedics, EMT-P's, provide the most extensive prehospital care. In addition to the procedures already described, paramedics may administer drugs orally and intravenously, interpret eletrocardiograms (EKG's), perform endotracheal intubations, and use monitors and other complex equipment.

When victims are trapped, as in the case of an automobile accident, cave-in, or building collapse, EMT's free them or provide emergency care while others free them. Some conditions are simple enough to be handled following general rules and guidelines. More complicated problems can only be carried out under the step-by-step direction of medical personnel by radio contact.

When transporting patients to a medical facility, EMT's may use special equipment such as backboards to immobilize them before placing them on stretchers and securing them in the ambulance. While one EMT drives, the other monitors the patient's vital signs and gives additional care as needed. Some EMT's work for hospital trauma centers or jurisdictions which use helicopters to transport critically ill or injured patients.

At a medical facility, EMT's transfer patients to the emergency department, report to the staff their observations and the care they provided, and help provide emergency treatment.

In rural areas, some EMT-P's are trained to treat patients with minor injuries on the scene of an accident or at their home without transporting them to a medical facility.

After each run, EMT's replace used supplies and check equipment. If patients have had a contagious disease, EMT's decontaminate the interior of the ambulance and report cases to the proper authorities.

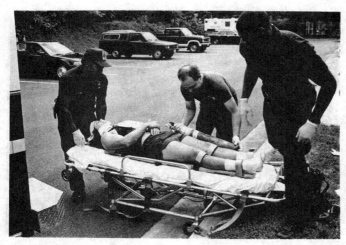

Many emergency medical technicians find their work exciting despite its stressful working conditions.

Working Conditions

EMT's work both indoors and outdoors, in all kinds of weather. Much of their time is spent standing, kneeling, bending, and lifting. They may risk noise-induced hearing loss from ambulance sirens and back injuries from lifting patients. EMT's may be exposed to diseases such as Hepatitis-B and AIDS, as well as violence from drug overdose victims. The work is not only physically strenuous, but stressful—not surprising in a job that involves life-or-death situations. Nonetheless, many people find the work exciting and challenging.

EMT's employed by fire departments often have about a 50-hour workweek. Those employed by hospitals frequently work between 45 and 58 hours a week and those in private ambulance services between 48 and 51 hours. Some EMT's, especially those in police and fire departments, are on call for extended periods. Because most emergency services function 24 hours a day, EMT's have irregular working hours that add to job stress.

Employment

EMT's held about 138,000 jobs in 1994. Two-fifths were in private ambulance services, about a third were in municipal fire, police, or rescue squad departments, and a quarter were in hospitals. In addition, there are many volunteer EMT's. Most paid EMT's work in metropolitan areas. In many smaller cities, towns, and rural areas, there are no paid EMT jobs.

Training, Other Qualifications, and Advancement

Formal training is needed to become an EMT. EMT-Basic training is 100 to 120 hours of classroom work plus 10 hours of internship in a hospital emergency room. Training is available in all 50 States and the District of Columbia, and is offered by police, fire, and health departments; in hospitals; and as a nondegree course in colleges and universities.

The EMT-Basic program provides instruction and practice in dealing with bleeding, fractures, airway obstruction, cardiac arrest, and emergency childbirth. Students learn to use and care for common emergency equipment, such as backboards, suction devices, splints, oxygen delivery systems, and stretchers.

EMT-Intermediate training varies from State to State, but includes 35-55 hours of additional instruction in patient assessment as well as the use of esophageal airways, intravenous fluids, and antishock garments. Training programs for EMT-Paramedics, of which there were about 85 in 1993, generally last between 750 and 2,000 hours. Refresher courses and continuing education are available for EMT's at all levels.

Applicants to an EMT training course generally must be at least 18 years old and have a high school diploma or the equivalent and a driver's license. Recommended high school subjects for prospective EMT's are driver education, health, and science. Training in the Armed Forces as a "medic" is also good preparation.

In addition to EMT training, EMT's in fire and police departments must be qualified as firefighters or police officers.

Graduates of approved EMT-Basic training programs who pass a written and practical examination administered by the State certifying agency or the National Registry of Emergency Medical Technicians earn the title of Registered EMT-Basic. Prerequisites for taking the EMT-Intermediate examination include registration as an EMT-Basic, required classroom work, and a specified amount of clinical experience and field internship. Registration for EMT-Paramedics by the National Registry of Emergency Medical Technicians or a State emergency medical services agency requires current registration or State certification as an EMT-Basic, completion of an EMT-Paramedic training program and required clinical and field internships as well as passing of a written and practical examination. Although not a general requirement for employment, registration acknowledges an EMT's qualifications and makes higher paying jobs easier to obtain.

All 50 States have some kind of certification procedure. In 31 States and the District of Columbia, registration with the National Registry is required at some or all levels of certification. Other States require their own certification examination or provide the option of taking the National Registry examination.

To maintain their certification, all EMT's must reregister, usually every 2 years. In order to reregister, an individual must be working as an EMT and meet a continuing education requirement.

EMT's should be emotionally stable, have good dexterity, agility, an physical coordination, and be able to lift and carry heavy loads. EMT's need good eyesight (corrective lenses may be used) with accurate color vision.

Advancement beyond the EMT-Paramedic level usually means leaving fieldwork. An EMT-Paramedic can become a supervisor, operations manager, administrative director, or executive director of emergency services. Some EMT's become EMT instructors, firefighters, dispatchers, or police officers, or others move into sales or marketing of emergency medical equipment. Finally, some become EMT's to assess their interest in health care and then decide to return to school and become registered nurses, physicians, or other health workers.

Job Outlook

Competition for jobs will be keen in fire, police, and rescue squad departments because of attractive pay and benefits and good job security. Opportunities for EMT's are expected to be excellent in hospitals and private ambulance services, where pay and benefits usually are low.

Employment of EMT's is expected to grow much faster than average for all occupations through the year 2005. Driving the growth will be an expanding population. Also, the number of older people, who are more likely to need emergency services, is increasing rapidly. Additional job openings will occur as more States begin to allow EMT-Paramedics to perform primary care on the scene without transporting the patient to a medical facility.

Most job openings will occur because of this occupation's substantial replacement needs. Turnover is quite high, reflecting this occupation's stressful working conditions, limited advancement potential, and the modest pay and benefits in the private sector.

Earnings

Earnings of EMT's depend on the employment setting and geographic location as well as the individual's training and experience. According to a survey conducted by the *Journal of Emergency Medical Services*, average starting salaries in 1995 were $19,919 for EMT-Ambulance or Basic, $21,818 for EMT-Intermediate, and

$23,861 for EMT-Paramedic. EMT's working in fire departments command the highest salaries, as the accompanying table shows.

Table 1: Average annual salaries of emergency medical technicians, by type of employer, 1995

Employer	Paramedic	EMT-I	EMT-Basic
All employers	$31,137	$26,102	$26,333
Private ambulance services	28,619	23,330	22,238
Hospitals	29,264	28,000	22,500
Fire departments	37,690	28,667	33,962

Source: *Journal of Emergency Medical Services*

Those in emergency medical services which are part of fire or police departments receive the same benefits as firefighters or police officers.

Related Occupations

Other workers in occupations that require quick and level-headed reactions to life-or-death situations are police officers, firefighters, air traffic controllers, workers in other health occupations, and members of the Armed Forces.

Sources of Additional Information

Information concerning training courses, registration, and job opportunities for EMT's can be obtained by writing to the State Emergency Medical Service Director.

General information about EMT's is available from:

☛National Association of Emergency Medical Technicians, 102 W. Leake St., Clinton, MS 39056.

☛National Registry of Emergency Medical Technicians, P.O. Box 29233, Columbus, OH 43229.

Licensed Practical Nurses

(D.O.T. 079.374-014)

Nature of the Work

Licensed practical nurses (L.P.N.'s), or licensed vocational nurses (L.V.N.'s) as they are called in Texas and California, care for the sick, injured, convalescing, and handicapped, under the direction of physicians and registered nurses. (The work of registered nurses is described elsewhere in the *Handbook*.)

Most L.P.N.'s provide basic bedside care. They take vital signs such as temperature, blood pressure, pulse, and respiration. They also treat bedsores, prepare and give injections and enemas, apply dressings, give alcohol rubs and massages, apply ice packs and hot water bottles, and insert catheters. L.P.N's observe patients and report adverse reactions to medications or treatments. They may collect samples from patients for testing and perform routine laboratory tests. They help patients with bathing, dressing, and personal hygiene, feed them and record food and liquid intake and output, keep them comfortable, and care for their emotional needs. In States where the law allows, they may administer prescribed medicines or start intravenous fluids. Some L.P.N.'s help deliver, care for, and feed infants. Some experienced L.P.N.'s supervise nursing assistants and aides.

L.P.N.'s in nursing homes, in addition to providing routine bedside care, may also help evaluate residents' needs, develop care plans, and supervise nursing aides. In doctors' offices and clinics, including health maintenance organizations, they may also make appointments, keep records, and perform other clerical duties. L.P.N.'s who work

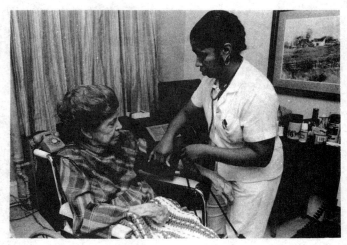

Most practical nursing programs last about 1 year and include both classroom study and supervised clinical practice.

in private homes may also prepare meals and teach family members simple nursing tasks.

Working Conditions

Most licensed practical nurses in hospitals and nursing homes work a 40-hour week, but because patients need round-the-clock care, some work nights, weekends, and holidays. They often stand for long periods and help patients move in bed, stand, or walk. They also face the stress of working with sick patients and their families.

L.P.N.'s may face hazards from caustic chemicals, radiation, and infectious diseases such as AIDS and hepatitis. L.P.N.'s also are subject to back injuries when moving patients and shock from electrical equipment. They often face heavy workloads. In addition, the people they take care of may be confused, irrational, agitated, or uncooperative.

Employment

Licensed practical nurses held about 702,000 jobs in 1994. About a quarter worked part time. Two out of 5 L.P.N.'s worked in hospitals, about one-quarter worked in nursing homes, and over a tenth in doctors' offices and clinics. Others worked for temporary help agencies, home health care services, or government agencies.

Training, Other Qualifications, and Advancement

All States require L.P.N.'s to pass a licensing examination after completing a State-approved practical nursing program. A high school diploma is usually required for entry, but some programs accept people without a diploma.

In 1993, approximately 1,098 State-approved programs provided practical nursing training. Almost 6 out of 10 students were enrolled in technical or vocational schools, while 3 out of 10 were in community and junior colleges. Others were in high schools, hospitals, and colleges and universities.

Most practical nursing programs last about 1 year and include both classroom study and supervised clinical practice (patient care). Classroom study covers basic nursing concepts and patient-care related subjects, including anatomy, physiology, medical-surgical nursing, pediatrics, obstetrics, psychiatric nursing, administration of drugs, nutrition, and first aid. Clinical practice is usually in a hospital, but sometimes includes other settings.

L.P.N.'s should have a caring, sympathetic nature. They should be emotionally stable because work with the sick and injured can be stressful. As part of a health care team, they must be able to follow orders and work under close supervision.

Job Outlook

Job prospects for L.P.N.'s are expected to be good if the current balance between jobs and job seekers continues. Over the past few years, the number of graduates from L.P.N. training programs has increased in pace with the need for additional workers. However, if enrollments in L.P.N. training programs level off or decline as they have on a cyclical basis in the past, job prospects will be even better.

Employment of L.P.N.'s is expected to increase faster than the average for all occupations through the year 2005 in response to the long-term care needs of a rapidly growing population of very old people and to the general growth of health care. As in most other occupations, replacement needs will be the main source of job openings.

Employment in nursing homes is expected to grow much faster than the average. Nursing homes will offer the most new jobs for L.P.N.'s as the number of aged and disabled persons in need of long-term care rises rapidly. In addition to caring for the aged, nursing homes will be called on to care for the increasing number of patients who have been released from the hospital and have not yet recovered enough to return home.

Much faster than average growth is also expected in home health care services. This is in response to a growing number of older persons with functional disabilities, consumer preference for care in the home, and technological advances which make it possible to bring increasingly complex treatments into the home.

An increasing proportion of sophisticated procedures, which once were performed only in hospitals, are being performed in physicians' offices and clinics, including health maintenance organizations, ambulatory surgicenters, and emergency medical centers—thanks largely to advances in technology. As a result, employment is projected to grow much faster than average in these places as health care in general expands.

Employment of L.P.N.'s in hospitals is expected to show only a small increase, largely because the number of inpatients, with whom most work, is not expected to increase much.

Earnings

Median weekly earnings of full-time salaried L.P.N's were $450 in 1994. The middle 50 percent earned between $383 and $537. The lowest 10 percent earned less than $316; the top 10 percent, more than $636.

According to a University of Texas Medical Branch survey of hospitals and medical centers, the median annual salary of L.P.N's, based on a 40-hour week and excluding shift or area differentials, was $23,394 in October 1994. The average minimum salary was $19,122 and the average maximum was $28,234.

According to the Buck Survey conducted by the American Health Care Association, staff L.P.N.'s in chain nursing homes had median annual earnings of about $23,900 in 1994. The middle 50 percent earned between $21,500 and $27,100.

Related Occupations

L.P.N.'s work closely with people while helping them. So do emergency medical technicians, social service aides, human service workers, and teacher aides.

Sources of Additional Information

A list of State-approved training programs and information about practical nursing are available from:

☛Communications Department, National League for Nursing, 350 Hudson St., New York, NY 10014.

☛National Association for Practical Nurse Education and Service, Inc., 1400 Spring St., Suite 310, Silver Spring, MD 20910.

For information on nursing careers in long-term care, write to:

☛American Health Care Association, 1201 L St. NW., Washington, DC 20005.

Medical Record Technicians

(D.O.T. 079.362-014, -018)

Nature of the Work

When you enter a hospital, you see a whirl of white coats of physicians, nurses, radiologic technologists, and others. Every time these health care personnel treat a patient, they record what they observed and did to the patient. This record includes information the patient provides about their symptoms and medical history, and also the results of examinations, reports of x rays and laboratory tests, and diagnoses and treatment plans. Medical record technicians organize and evaluate these records for completeness and accuracy.

When assembling a patient's medical record, technicians, who may also be called health information technicians, first make sure that the medical chart is complete. They ensure that all forms are present and properly identified and signed, and that all necessary information is on a computer file. Sometimes, they talk to physicians or others to clarify diagnoses or get additional information.

Technicians assign a code to each diagnosis and procedure. They consult a classification manual and rely, too, on their knowledge of disease processes. Technicians then use a software program to assign the patient to one of several hundred "diagnosis-related groups" or DRG's. The DRG determines the amount the hospital will be reimbursed if the patient is covered by Medicare or other insurance programs that use the DRG system. Technicians who specialize in coding are called medical record coders, coder/abstractors, or coding specialists.

Technicians also use computer programs to tabulate and analyze data to help improve patient care, to control costs, to be used in legal actions, or to respond to surveys. *Tumor registrars* compile and maintain records of patients who have cancer to provide information to physicians and for research studies.

Medical record technicians' duties vary with the size of the facility. In large to medium facilities, technicians may specialize in one aspect of medical records or supervise medical record clerks and transcribers while a *medical record administrator* manages the department (see the statement on health services managers elsewhere in the *Handbook*). In small facilities an accredited record technician

Working Conditions

Medical record technicians generally work a 40-hour week. Some overtime may be required. In hospitals where medical record

Medical record technicians are one of the only health occupations that have little or no contact with patients.

departments are open 18-24 hours a day, 7 days a week, they may work on day, evening, and night shifts.

They work in pleasant and comfortable offices. Medical record technician is one of the few health occupations in which there is little or no contact with patients. Accuracy is essential, and this demands concentration and close attention to detail. Medical record technicians who work at video display terminals for prolonged periods may experience eyestrain and muscle pain.

Employment
Medical record technicians held about 81,000 jobs in 1994. About one half of the jobs were in hospitals. Most of the remainder were in nursing homes, medical group practices, health maintenance organizations, and clinics.

In addition, insurance, accounting, and law firms that deal in health matters employ medical record technicians to tabulate and analyze data from medical records. Public health departments hire technicians to supervise data collection from health care institutions and to assist in research.

Some self-employed medical record technicians are consultants to nursing homes and physicians' offices.

Training, Other Qualifications, and Advancement
Medical record technicians entering the field usually have formal training in a 2-year associate degree program offered at community and junior colleges. Courses include medical terminology and diseases, anatomy and physiology, legal aspects of medical records, coding and abstraction of data, statistics, databases, quality assurance methods, and computers as well as general education. Applicants can improve their chances of admission into a program by taking biology, chemistry, health and computer courses in high school.

Technicians may also gain training through an Independent Study Program in Medical Record Technology offered by the American Health Information Management Association (AHIMA). Hospitals sometimes advance promising medical record clerks to jobs as medical record technicians, although this practice may be less common in the future. Advancement generally requires 2-4 years of job experience and completion of the hospital's in-house training program.

Most employers prefer to hire Accredited Record Technicians (ART). Accreditation is obtained by passing a written examination offered by the AHIMA. To take the examination, a person must be a graduate of a 2-year associate degree program accredited by the Commission on Accreditation of Allied Health Education Programs (CAAHEP) of the American Medical Association, or a graduate of the Independent Study Program in Medical Record Technology who has also obtained 30 semester hours of academic credit in prescribed areas. Technicians who have received training in non-CAAHEP accredited programs or on the job are not eligible to take the examination. In 1995, CAAHEP accredited 134 programs for medical record technicians.

Experienced medical record technicians generally advance in one of two ways—by specializing or managing. Many senior medical record technicians specialize in coding, particularly Medicare coding, or in tumor registry.

In large medical record departments, experienced technicians may become section supervisors, overseeing the work of the coding, correspondence, or discharge sections, for example. Senior technicians with ART credentials may become director or assistant director of a medical record department in a small facility. However, in larger institutions the director is a medical records administrator, with a bachelor's degree in medical record administration. (See the statement on health services managers elsewhere in the *Handbook*.)

Job Outlook
Job prospects for formally trained technicians should be very good. Employment of medical record technicians is expected to grow much faster than the average for all occupations through the year 2005 due

to rapid growth in the number of medical tests, treatments, and procedures and because medical records will be increasingly scrutinized by third-party payers, courts, and consumers.

Hospitals will continue to employ the most medical record technicians, but growth will not be as fast as in other areas. The need for detailed records in offices and clinics of doctors of medicine should result in faster employment growth in large group practices and offices of specialists. Rapid growth is also expected in health maintenance organizations, nursing homes, and home health agencies.

Earnings
According to a 1994 survey by American Health Consultant's, the median annual salary for accredited record technicians was $36,700 a year. The average annual salary for medical record technicians in the Federal Government in nonsupervisory, supervisory, and managerial positions was $23,779 in 1995.

Related Occupations
Medical record technicians need a strong clinical background to analyze the contents of medical records. Other occupations that require a knowledge of medical terminology, anatomy, and physiology without directly touching the patient are medical secretaries, medical transcribers, medical writers, and medical illustrators.

Sources of Additional Information
Information on careers in medical record technology, including the Independent Study Program, and a list of CAAHEP-accredited programs is available from:
☛American Health Information Management Association, 919 N. Michigan Ave., Suite 1400, Chicago, IL 60611.

Nuclear Medicine Technologists

(D.O.T. 078.361-018)

Nature of the Work
In nuclear medicine, radionuclides—unstable atoms that emit radiation spontaneously—are used to diagnose and treat disease. Radionuclides are purified and compounded like other drugs to form radiopharmaceuticals. Nuclear medicine technologists administer these radiopharmaceuticals to patients, then monitor the characteristics and functions of tissues or organs in which they localize. Abnormal areas show higher or lower concentrations of radioactivity than normal.

Nuclear medicine technologists operate cameras that detect and map the radioactive drug in the patient's body to create an image on photographic film. Radiologic technologists also operate diagnostic imaging equipment, but their equipment creates an image by projecting an x ray through the patient. (See the statement on radiologic technologists elsewhere in the *Handbook*.)

Nuclear medicine technologists explain test procedures to patients. They prepare a dosage of the radiopharmaceutical and administer it by mouth, injection, or other means. When preparing radiopharmaceuticals, technologists adhere to safety standards that keep the radiation dose to workers and patients as low as possible.

Technologists position patients and start a gamma scintillation camera, or scanner, which creates images of the distribution of a radiopharmaceutical as it passes through or localizes in the patient's body. Technologists produce the images on a computer screen or on film for a physician to interpret. Some nuclear medicine studies, such as cardiac function studies, are processed with the aid of a computer.

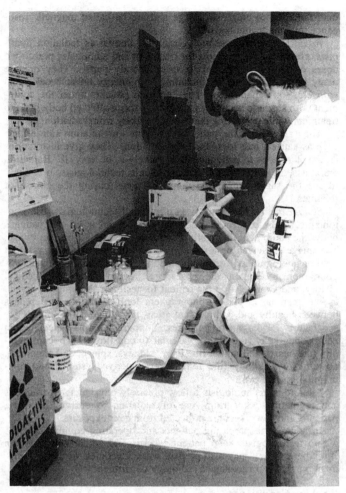

Nuclear medicine technologists may work evenings and on weekends.

Nuclear medicine technologists also perform radioimmunoassay studies which assess the behavior of a radioactive substance inside the body. For example, technologists may add radioactive substances to blood or serum to determine levels of hormones or therapeutic drug content.

Technologists keep patient records and record the amount and type of radionuclides received, used, and disposed of.

Working Conditions

Nuclear medicine technologists generally work a 40-hour week. This may include evening or weekend hours in departments which operate on an extended schedule. Opportunities for part-time and shift work are also available. In addition, technologists in hospitals may be on call duty on a rotational basis.

Because technologists are on their feet much of the day, and may lift or turn disabled patients, physical stamina is important.

Although there is potential for radiation exposure in this field, it is kept to a minimum by the use of shielded syringes, gloves, and other protective devices. Technologists also wear badges that measure radiation levels. Because of safety programs, however, badge measurements rarely exceed established safety levels.

Employment

Nuclear medicine technologists held about 13,000 jobs in 1994. About 9 out of 10 jobs were in hospitals. The rest were in physicians' offices and clinics, including imaging centers.

Training, Other Qualifications, and Advancement

Nuclear medicine technology programs range in length from 1 to 4 years and lead to a certificate, associate's degree, or bachelor's degree. Generally, certificate programs are offered in hospitals; associate programs in community colleges; and bachelor's programs in 4-year colleges and in universities. Courses cover physical sciences, the biological effects of radiation exposure, radiation protection and procedures, the use of radiopharmaceuticals, imaging techniques, and computer applications. Associate's and bachelor's programs also cover liberal arts.

One-year certificate programs are for health professionals, especially radiologic technologists and ultrasound technologists wishing to specialize in nuclear medicine. They also attract medical technologists, registered nurses, and others who wish to change fields or specialize. Others interested in the nuclear medicine technology field have three options: A 2-year certificate program, a 2-year associate program, or a 4-year bachelor's program.

The Joint Review Committee on Education Programs in Nuclear Medicine Technology accredits most formal training programs in nuclear medicine technology. In 1994, there were 120 accredited programs.

All nuclear medicine technologists must meet the minimum Federal standards on the administration of radioactive drugs and the operation of radiation detection equipment. In addition, about half of all States require technologists to be licensed. Technologists also may obtain voluntary professional certification or registration. Registration or certification is available from the American Registry of Radiologic Technologists and from the Nuclear Medicine Technology Certification Board. Most employers prefer to hire certified or registered technologists.

Technologists may advance to supervisor, then to chief technologist, and to department administrator or director. Some technologists specialize in a clinical area such as nuclear cardiology or computer analysis or leave patient care to take positions in research laboratories. Some become instructors or directors in nuclear medicine technology programs, a step that usually requires a bachelor's degree or a master's in nuclear medicine technology. Others leave the occupation to work as sales or training representatives for health equipment and radiopharmaceutical manufacturing firms, or as radiation safety officers in regulatory agencies or hospitals.

Job Outlook

Job prospects for nuclear medicine technologists are expected to be good. The number of openings each year, however, will be very low because the occupation is small.

Employment of nuclear medicine technologists is expected to grow faster than the average for all occupations through the year 2005. Substantial growth in the number of middle-aged and older persons will spur demand for diagnostic procedures, including nuclear medicine tests. Furthermore, technological innovations seem likely to increase the diagnostic uses of nuclear medicine. One example is the use of radiopharmaceuticals in combination with monoclonal antibodies to detect cancer at far earlier stages than is customary today, and without resorting to surgery. Another is the use of radionuclides to examine the heart's ability to pump blood. Wider use of nuclear medical imaging to observe metabolic and biochemical changes for neurology, cardiology, and oncology procedures, will also spur demand for nuclear medicine technologists.

Cost considerations will affect the speed with which new applications of nuclear medicine grow. Some promising nuclear medicine procedures, such as positron emission tomography, are extremely costly, and hospitals contemplating them will have to consider equipment costs, reimbursement policies, and the number of potential users.

Earnings

According to a University of Texas Medical Branch survey of hospitals and medical centers, the median annual salary of nuclear medicine technologists, based on a 40-hour week and excluding shift or area differentials, was $35,027 in October 1994. The average minimum salary was $28,044 and the average maximum was $41,598.

Related Occupations

Nuclear medical technologists operate sophisticated equipment to help physicians and other health practitioners diagnose and treat patients. Radiologic technologists, diagnostic medical sonographers, cardiovascular technologists, electroneurodiagnostic technologists, clinical laboratory technologists, perfusionists, and respiratory therapists also perform similar functions.

Sources of Additional Information

Additional information on a career as a nuclear medicine technologist is available from:

☛The Society of Nuclear Medicine-Technologist Section, 1850 Samuel Morse Dr., Reston, VA 22090.

For information on a career as a nuclear medicine technologist, enclose a stamped, self-addressed business size envelope with your request to:

☛American Society of Radiologic Technologists, 15000 Central Ave., SE,. Albuquerque, NM 87123-3917.

For a list of accredited programs in nuclear medicine technology, write to:

☛Joint Review Committee on Educational Programs in Nuclear Medicine Technology, 1144 West 3300 South, Salt Lake City, UT 84119-3330.

Information on certification is available from:

☛Nuclear Medicine Technology Certification Board, 2970 Clairmont Rd., Suite 610, Atlanta, GA 30329.

Radiologic Technologists

(D.O.T. 078.361-034, .362-026, -046, -054, -058, .364-010)

Nature of the Work

Perhaps the most familiar use of the x ray is the diagnosis of broken bones. However, medical uses of radiation go far beyond that. Radiation is used not only to produce images of the interior of the body, but to treat cancer as well. At the same time, the use of imaging techniques that do not involve x rays, such as ultrasound and magnetic resonance scans, is growing rapidly. The term "diagnostic imaging" embraces these procedures as well as the familiar x ray.

Radiographers produce x-ray films (radiographs) of parts of the human body for use in diagnosing medical problems. They prepare patients for radiologic examinations by explaining the procedure, removing articles such as jewelry, through which x rays cannot pass, and positioning patients so that the correct parts of the body can be radiographed. To prevent unnecessary radiation exposure, technologists surround the exposed area with radiation protection devices, such as lead shields, or limit the size of the x-ray beam. Radiographers position radiographic equipment at the correct angle and height over the appropriate area of a patient's body. Using instruments similar to a measuring tape, technologists may measure the thickness of the section to be radiographed and set controls on the machine to produce radiographs of the appropriate density, detail, and contrast. They place the x-ray film under the part of the patient's body to be examined and make the exposure. They then remove the film and develop it.

Experienced radiographers may perform more complex imaging tests. For fluoroscopies, radiographers prepare a solution of contrast medium for the patient to drink, allowing the radiologist, a physician who interprets x rays, to see soft tissues in the body. Some radiographers who operate computerized tomography scanners to produce cross sectional views of patients, are be called CT technologists. Others operate machines using giant magnets and radiowaves rather than radiation to create an image and are be called magnetic resonance imaging technologists.

Radiation therapy technologists, also known as radiation therapists, prepare cancer patients for treatment and administer prescribed doses of ionizing radiation to specific body parts. They operate many kinds of equipment, including high-energy linear accelerators with electron capabilities. They position patients under the equipment with absolute accuracy in order to expose affected body parts to treatment while protecting the rest of the body from radiation.

They also check the patient's reactions for radiation side effects such as nausea, hair loss, and skin irritation. They give instructions and explanations to patients who are likely to be very ill. Radiation therapists, in contrast to other radiologic technologists, are likely to see the same patient a number of times during the course of treatment.

Sonographers, also known as ultrasound technologists, use nonionizing, high frequency sound waves into areas of the patient's body; the equipment then collects reflected echoes to form an image. The image is viewed on a screen and may be recorded on a printout strip or photographed for interpretation and diagnosis by physicians. Sonographers explain the procedure, record additional medical history, and then position the patient for testing. Viewing the screen as the scan takes place, sonographers look for subtle differences between healthy and pathological areas, and judge if the images are satisfactory for diagnostic purposes. Sonographers may specialize in neurosonography (the brain), vascular (blood flows), echocardiography (the heart), abdominal (the liver, kidneys, spleen, and pancreas), obstetrics/gynecology (the female reproductive system), and ophthalmology (the eye).

Radiologic technologists follow precisely physicians' instructions and regulations concerning use of radiation to ensure that they, patients, and coworkers are protected from over exposure.

In addition to preparing patients and operating equipment, radiologic technologists keep patient records and adjust and maintain equipment. They may also prepare work schedules, evaluate equipment purchases, or manage a radiology department.

Working Conditions

Most full-time radiologic technologists work about 40 hours a week; they may have evening, weekend, or on-call hours.

Technologists are on their feet for long periods and may lift or turn disabled patients. They work at radiologic machines but may also do some procedures at patients' bedsides. Some radiologic technologists travel to patients in large vans equipped with sophisticated diagnostic equipment.

Hospitals will continue to employ the most radiologic technologists through 2005.

Radiation therapists are prone to emotional "burn out" because they regularly treat extremely ill and dying patients on a daily basis. Although potential radiation hazards exist in this occupation, they have been minimized by the use of lead aprons, gloves, and other shielding devices, as well as by instruments that monitor radiation exposure. Technologists wear badges that measure radiation levels in the radiation area, and detailed records are kept on their cumulative lifetime dose.

Employment

Radiologic technologists held about 167,000 jobs in 1994. Most technologists were radiographers. Some were sonographers and radiation therapists. About 1 radiologic technologist in 5 worked part time. About 3 out of 5 jobs are in hospitals. The rest are in physicians' offices and clinics, including diagnostic imaging centers.

Training, Other Qualifications, and Advancement

Preparation for this profession is offered in hospitals, colleges and universities, vocational-technical institutes, and the Armed Forces. Hospitals, which employ most radiologic technologists, prefer to hire those with formal training.

Formal training is offered in radiography, radiation therapy, and diagnostic medical sonography (ultrasound). Programs range in length from 1 to 4 years and lead to a certificate, associate's degree, or bachelor's degree. Two-year programs are most prevalent.

Some 1-year certificate programs are for individuals from other health occupations such as medical technologists and registered nurses who want to change fields or experienced radiographers who want to specialize in radiation therapy technology or sonography. A bachelor's or master's degree in one of the radiologic technologies is desirable for supervisory, administrative, or teaching positions.

The Joint Review Committee on Education in Radiologic Technology accredits most formal training programs for this field. They accredited 692 radiography programs, 125 radiation therapy programs. The Joint Review Committee on Education in Diagnostic Medical Sonography accredited 65 programs in sonography in 1995.

Radiography programs require, at a minimum, a high school diploma or the equivalent. High school courses in mathematics, physics, chemistry, and biology are helpful. The programs provide both classroom and clinical instruction in anatomy and physiology, patient care procedures, radiation physics, radiation protection, principles of imaging, medical terminology, positioning of patients, medical ethics, radiobiology, and pathology.

For training programs in radiation therapy and diagnostic medical sonography, applicants with a background in science, or experience in one of the health professions, generally are preferred. Some programs consider applicants with liberal arts backgrounds, however, as well as high school graduates with courses in math and science.

Radiographers and radiation therapists are covered by provisions of the Consumer-Patient Radiation Health and Safety Act of 1981, which aims to protect the public from the hazards of unnecessary exposure to medical and dental radiation by ensuring operators of radiologic equipment are properly trained. The act requires the Federal Government to set standards that the States, in turn, may use for accrediting training programs and certifying individuals who engage in medical or dental radiography.

By January 1995, 31 States required radiographers to be licensed, and 26 required radiation therapists to be licensed. (Puerto Rico requires a license for the practice of either specialty.)

Voluntary registration is offered by the American Registry of Radiologic Technologists (ARRT) in both radiography and radiation therapy. The American Registry of Diagnostic Medical Sonographers (ARDMS) certifies the competence of sonographers. To become registered, technologists must be graduates of an accredited program or meet other prerequisites and have passed an examination. Many employers prefer to hire registered technologists.

With experience and additional training, staff technologists may become specialists, performing CT scanning, ultrasound, angiogra-

phy, and magnetic resonance imaging. Experienced technologists may also be promoted to supervisor, chief radiologic technologist, and—ultimately—department administrator or director. Depending on the institution, courses or a master's degree in business or health administration may be necessary for the director's position. Some technologists progress by becoming instructors or directors in radiologic technology programs; others take jobs as sales representatives or instructors with equipment manufacturers.

With additional education, available at major cancer centers, radiation therapy technologists can specialize as medical radiation dosimetrists. Dosimetrists work with health physicists and oncologists (physicians who specialize in the study and treatment of tumors) to develop treatment plans.

Radiographers and radiation therapists are required to fulfill 24 hours of continuing education every other year and provide documentation to prove that they are complying with these requirements.

Job Outlook

While a significant increase in radiologic technologist employment is anticipated, jobseekers are likely to face competition from many other qualified applicants for most openings. Reports of shortages of radiographers and radiation therapists that were common during the last decade no longer exist. As more people entered the field, the number of qualified applicants increased faster than the number of job openings. The imbalance that resulted caused competition for jobs to become intense. While reduced, the imbalance is expected to persist through the year 2005. Sonographers should experience somewhat better job opportunities than other radiologic technologist occupations as technology spawns many new ultrasound procedures.

Employment of radiologic technologists is expected to grow faster than the average for all occupations through 2005, as the health care industries grow, and because of the vast clinical potential of diagnostic imaging and therapeutic technology. Current as well as new uses of imaging equipment should increase the demand for radiologic technologists.

Radiation therapy will continue to be used—alone or in combination with surgery or chemotherapy—to treat cancer. More treatment of cancer is anticipated due to the aging of the population, educational efforts aimed at early detection, and improved ability to detect malignancies through radiologic procedures such as mammography.

Although physicians are enthusiastic about the clinical benefits of new technologies, the extent to which they are adopted depends largely on cost and reimbursement considerations. Some promising new technologies may not come into widespread use because they are too expensive and third-party payers may not be willing to pay for their use. But on the whole, it appears that radiologic procedures will be used more widely.

Hospitals will remain the principal employer of radiologic technologists. However, employment is expected to grow most rapidly in offices and clinics of physicians, including diagnostic imaging centers. Health facilities such as these are expected to grow very rapidly through 2005 due to the strong shift toward outpatient care, encouraged by third-party payers and made possible by technological advances that permit more procedures to be performed outside the hospital. Some jobs will also come from the need to replace technologists who leave the occupation.

Earnings

In 1994, the median annual earnings for radiologic technologists who worked year round full time were $29,432. The middle 50 percent earned between $24,596 and $36,244 a week; 10 percent earned less than $20,696 a week; and 10 percent earned more than $49,036.

According to a University of Texas Medical Branch survey of hospitals and medical centers, the median salary for radiologic technologists, based on a 40 hour week and excluding shift or area differentials, was $27,008 in October 1994. The average minimum salary was $23,265 and the average maximum was $34,687. For radiation therapy technologists the median was $35,877 and for ultrasound technologists, $33,522.

Related Occupations

Radiologic technologists operate sophisticated equipment to help physicians, dentists, and other health practitioners diagnose and treat patients. Workers in related occupations include radiation dosimetrists, nuclear medicine technologists, cardiovascular technologists and technicians, perfusionists, respiratory therapists, clinical laboratory technologists, and electroneurodiagnostic technologists.

Sources of Additional Information

For career information, enclose a stamped, self-addressed business size envelope with your request to:

☛American Society of Radiologic Technologists, 15000 Central Ave. SE., Albuquerque, NM 87123-3917.

☛Society of Diagnostic Medical Sonographers, 12770 Coit Rd., Suite 508, Dallas, TX 75251.

☛American Healthcare Radiology Administrators, 111 Boston Post Rd., Suite 215, P.O. Box 334, Sudbury, MA 01776.

For the current list of accredited education programs in radiography, radiation therapy technology, write to:

☛Joint Review Committee on Education in Radiologic Technology, 20 N. Wacker St., Chicago, IL 60606-2901.

For a current list of accredited education programs in diagnostic medical sonography, write to:

☛The Joint Review Committee on Education in Diagnostic Medical Sonography, 7108 S. Alton Way, Building C., Englewood, CO 80112.

For information on certification in sonography, contact:

☛American Registry of Diagnostic Medical Sonographers, 600 Jefferson Plaza, Rockville, MD 20852-1150.

Surgical Technologists

(D.O.T. 079.374-022)

Nature of the Work

Surgical technologists, also called surgical or operating room technicians, assist in operations under the supervision of surgeons, registered nurses, or other surgical personnel. Before an operation, surgical technologists help set up the operating room with surgical instruments and equipment, sterile linens, and sterile solutions. They assemble, adjust, and check nonsterile equipment to ensure that it is working properly. Technologists also prepare patients for surgery by washing, shaving, and disinfecting incision sites. They transport patients to the operating room, help position them on the operating table, and cover them with sterile surgical "drapes." Technologists also observe patients' vital signs, check charts, and help the surgical team scrub and put on gloves, gowns, and masks.

During surgery, technologists pass instruments and other sterile supplies to surgeons and surgeon assistants. They may hold retractors, cut sutures, and help count sponges, needles, supplies, and instruments. Surgical technologists help prepare, care for, and dispose of specimens taken for laboratory analysis and may help apply dressings. They may operate sterilizers, lights, or suction machines, and help operate diagnostic equipment. Technologists may also maintain supplies of fluids, such as plasma and blood.

After an operation, surgical technologists may help transfer patients to the recovery room and clean and restock the operating room.

Working Conditions

Surgical technologists work in clean, well-lighted, cool environments. They must stand for long periods of time and remain alert

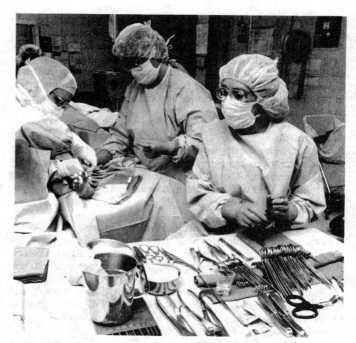

Surgical technologists must stand for long periods of time and remain alert during operations.

during operations. At times they may be exposed to communicable diseases and unpleasant sights, odors, and materials.

Most surgical technologists work a regular 40-hour week, although they may be on call or work nights, weekends and holidays on a rotating basis.

Employment

Surgical technologists held about 46,000 jobs in 1994. Most surgical technologists are employed by hospitals, mainly in operating and delivery rooms. Others are employed in clinics and surgical centers, and in the offices of physicians and dentists who perform outpatient surgery. A few, known as private scrubs, are employed directly by surgeons who have special surgical teams like those for liver transplants.

Training, Other Qualifications, and Advancement

Surgical technologists receive their training in formal programs offered by community and junior colleges, vocational schools, universities, hospitals, and the military. In 1995, the Commission on Accreditation of Allied Health Education Programs (CAAHEP) recognized 147 accredited programs. High school graduation normally is required for admission. Programs last 9 to 24 months and lead to a certificate, diploma, or associate degree. Shorter programs are designed for students who are already licensed practical nurses or military personnel.

Programs provide classroom education and supervised clinical experience. Students take courses in anatomy, physiology, microbiology, pharmacology, professional ethics, and medical terminology. Other studies cover the care and safety of patients during surgery, aseptic techniques, and surgical procedures. Students also learn to sterilize instruments; prevent and control infection; and handle special drugs, solutions, supplies, and equipment.

Technologists may obtain voluntary professional certification from the Liaison Council on Certification for the Surgical Technologist by graduating from a formal program and passing a national certification examination. They may then use the designation Certified Surgical Technologist, or CST. Continuing education or reexamination is required to maintain certification, which must be renewed every 6 years. Some employers prefer to hire certified technologists.

Surgical technologists need manual dexterity to handle instruments quickly. They also must be conscientious, orderly, and emotionally stable to handle the demands of the operating room environment. Technologists must respond quickly and know procedures well so that they may have instruments ready for surgeons without having to be told. They are expected to keep abreast of new developments in the field. Recommended high school courses include health, biology, chemistry, and mathematics.

Technologists advance by specializing in a particular area of surgery, such as neurosurgery or open heart surgery. They may also work as circulating technologists. A circulating technologist is the "unsterile" member of the surgical team who prepares patients; helps with anesthesia; gets, opens, and holds packages for the "sterile" persons during the procedure; interviews the patient before surgery; keeps a written account of the surgical procedure; and answers the surgeon's questions about the patient during the surgery. With additional training, some technologists advance to first assistants, who help with retracting, sponging, suturing, cauterizing bleeders, and closing and treating wounds. Some surgical technologists manage central supply departments in hospitals, or take positions with insurance companies, sterile supply services, and operating equipment firms.

Job Outlook

Employment of surgical technologists is expected to grow much faster than the average for all occupations through the year 2005, as the volume of surgery increases and operating room staffing patterns change.

The number of surgical procedures is expected to rise as the population grows and ages. Older people require more surgical procedures. Technological advances, such as fiber optics and laser technology, will also permit new surgical procedures. Some employers may seek to substitute surgical technologists for operating room nurses to reduce costs.

Hospitals will continue to be the primary employer of surgical technologists. Nonetheless, the shift to outpatient or ambulatory surgery will create much faster than average growth for technologists in offices and clinics of physicians, including surgical centers.

Earnings

According to a University of Texas Medical Branch survey of hospitals and medical centers, the median annual salary of surgical technologists, based on a 40 hour week and excluding shift or area differentials, was $22,285 in October 1994. The average minimum salary was $18,881 and the average maximum was $27,690.

Related Occupations

Other health occupations requiring approximately 1 year of training after high school include licensed practical nurses, respiratory therapy technicians, medical laboratory assistants, medical assistants, dental assistants, optometric assistants, and physical therapy aides.

Sources of Additional Information

For additional information on a career as a surgical technologist and a list of CAAHEP-accredited programs, contact:

☛Association of Surgical Technologists, 7108-C S. Alton Way, Englewood, CO 80112.

For information on certification, contact:

☛Liaison Council on Certification for the Surgical Technologist, 7108-C S. Alton Way, Englewood, CO 80112.

Technicians, Except Health

Aircraft Pilots

(D.O.T. 196, except .163 and .167-014, and 621.261-018)

Nature of the Work

Pilots are highly trained professionals who fly airplanes and helicopters to carry out a wide variety of tasks. Although most pilots transport passengers and cargo, others are involved in more unusual tasks, such as dusting crops, spreading seed for reforestation, testing aircraft, directing firefighting efforts, tracking criminals, monitoring traffic, and rescuing and evacuating injured persons.

Except on small aircraft, two pilots usually make up the cockpit crew. Generally, the most experienced pilot, the *captain*, is in command and supervises all other crew members. The *First officer* assists in communicating with air traffic controllers, monitoring the instruments, and flying the aircraft. Some large aircraft still have a third pilot in the cockpit—the *flight engineer*—who assists the other pilots by monitoring and operating many of the instruments and systems, making minor inflight repairs, and watching for other aircraft. New technology can perform many flight tasks, however, and virtually all new aircraft now fly with only two pilots, who rely more heavily on computerized controls. Flight engineer jobs could be completely eliminated in the future.

Before departure, pilots plan their flights carefully. They thoroughly check their aircraft to make sure that the engines, controls, instruments, and other systems are functioning properly. They also make sure that baggage or cargo has been loaded correctly. They confer with flight dispatchers and aviation weather forecasters to find out about weather conditions enroute and at their destination. Based on this information, they choose a route, altitude, and speed that should provide the fastest, safest, and smoothest flight. When flying under instrument flight rules—procedures governing the operation of the aircraft when there is poor visibility—the pilot in command, or the company dispatcher, normally files an instrument flight plan with air traffic control so that the flight can be coordinated with other air traffic.

Takeoff and landing are the most difficult parts of the flight and require close coordination between the pilot and first officer. For example, as the plane accelerates for takeoff, the pilot concentrates on the runway while the first officer scans the instrument panel. To calculate the speed they must attain to become airborne, pilots consider the altitude of the airport, outside temperature, weight of the plane, and the speed and direction of the wind. The moment the plane reaches takeoff speed, the first officer informs the pilot, who then pulls back on the controls to raise the nose of the plane.

Unless the weather is bad, the actual flight is relatively easy. Airplane pilots with the assistance of autopilot and the flight management computer, steer the plane along their planned route and are monitored by the air traffic control stations they pass along the way. They regularly scan the instrument panel to check their fuel supply, the condition of their engines, and the air-conditioning, hydraulic, and other systems. Pilots may request a change in altitude or route if circumstances dictate. For example, if the ride is rougher than expected, they may ask air traffic control if pilots flying at other altitudes have reported better conditions. If so, they may request a change. This procedure also may be used to find a stronger tailwind or a weaker headwind to save fuel and increase speed.

In contrast, helicopters are used for short trips at relatively low altitude, so pilots must be constantly on the lookout for trees, bridges, power lines, transmission towers, and other dangerous obstacles. Regardless of the type of aircraft, all pilots must monitor warning devices designed to help detect sudden shifts in wind conditions that can cause crashes.

If visibility is poor, pilots must rely completely on their instruments. Using the altimeter readings, they know how high above ground they are and whether or not they can fly safely over mountains and other obstacles. Special navigation radios give pilots precise information which, with the help of special maps, tell them their exact position. Other very sophisticated equipment provides directions to a point just above the end of a runway and enables pilots to land completely "blind."

Once on the ground, pilots must complete records on their flight for their organization and the Federal Aviation Administration (FAA).

The number of nonflying duties that pilots have depends on the employment setting. Airline pilots have the services of large support staffs, and consequently, perform few nonflying duties. Pilots employed by other organizations such as charter operators or businesses have many other duties. They may load the aircraft, handle all passenger luggage to ensure a balanced load, and supervise refueling;

Before takeoff, pilots check equipment and controls.

other nonflying responsibilities include keeping records, scheduling flights, arranging for major maintenance, and performing minor aircraft maintenance and repair work.

Some pilots are instructors. They teach their students the principles of flight in ground-school classes and demonstrate how to operate aircraft in dual-controlled planes and helicopters. A few specially trained pilots are "examiners" or "check pilots." They periodically fly with other pilots or pilot's license applicants to make sure that they are proficient.

Working Conditions
By law, airline pilots cannot fly more than 100 hours a month or more than 1,000 hours a year. Most airline pilots fly an average of 75 hours a month and work an additional 75 hours a month performing nonflying duties. Fifty percent of all pilots work more than 40 hours a week. The majority of flights involve overnight layovers. When pilots are away from home, the airlines provide hotel accommodations, transportation between the hotel and airport, and an allowance for expenses. Airlines operate flights at all hours of the day and night, so work schedules often are irregular. Flight assignments are based on seniority.

Those pilots not employed by the airlines often have irregular schedules as well; they may fly 30 hours one month and 90 hours the next. Because these pilots frequently have many nonflying responsibilities, they have much less free time than airline pilots. Except for business pilots, most do not remain away from home overnight. They may work odd hours . In addition, pilots working as instructors often give lessons at night or on weekends.

Airline pilots, especially those on international routes, often suffer jet lag—fatigue caused by many hours of flying through different time zones. The work of test pilots, who check the flight performance of new and experimental planes, may be dangerous. Pilots who are crop dusters may be exposed to toxic chemicals and seldom have the benefit of a regular landing strip. Helicopter pilots involved in police work may be subject to personal injury.

Although flying does not involve much physical effort, the mental stress of being responsible for a safe flight, no matter what the weather, can be tiring. Particularly during takeoff and landing, pilots must be alert and quick to react if something goes wrong.

Employment
Civilian pilots held about 90,000 jobs in 1994. Three-fifths worked for airlines. Many others worked as flight instructors at local airports or for large businesses that fly company cargo and executives in their own airplanes or helicopters. Some pilots flew small planes for air taxi companies, usually to or from lightly traveled airports not served by the airlines. Others worked for a variety of businesses performing tasks such as crop dusting, inspecting pipelines, or conducting sightseeing trips. Federal, State, and local governments also employed pilots. Several thousand pilots were self-employed.

The employment of airplane pilots is not distributed like the population. Pilots are more concentrated in the States of California, Texas, Georgia, Washington, Nevada, Hawaii, and Alaska which have a higher amount of flying activity relative to their population.

Training, Other Qualifications, and Advancement
All pilots who are paid to transport passengers or cargo must have a commercial pilot's license with an instrument rating issued by the FAA. Helicopter pilots must hold a commercial pilot's certificate with a helicopter rating. To qualify for these licenses, applicants must be at least 18 years old and have at least 250 hours of flight experience. The time can be reduced through participation in certain flight school curricula approved by the FAA. They also must pass a strict physical examination to make sure that they are in good health and have 20/20 vision with or without glasses, good hearing, and no physical handicaps that could impair their performance. Applicants must pass a written test that includes questions on the principles of

safe flight, navigation techniques, and FAA regulations. They also must demonstrate their flying ability to FAA or designated examiners.

To fly in periods of low visibility, pilots must be rated by the FAA to fly by instruments. Pilots may qualify for this rating by having a total of 105 hours of flight experience, including 40 hours of experience in flying by instruments; they also must pass a written examination on procedures and FAA regulations covering instrument flying and demonstrate to an examiner their ability to fly by instruments.

Airline pilots must fulfill additional requirements. They must pass FAA written and flight examinations to earn a flight engineer's license. Captains and first officers also must have an airline transport pilot's license. Applicants for this license must be at least 23 years old and have a minimum of 1,500 hours of flying experience, including night and instrument flying. Because pilots must be able to make quick decisions and accurate judgments under pressure, many airline companies reject applicants who do not pass required psychological and aptitude tests.

All licenses are valid as long as a pilot can pass the periodic physical examinations and tests of flying skills required by Government and company regulations.

The Armed Forces have always been an important source of trained pilots for civilian jobs. Military pilots gain valuable experience on jet aircraft and helicopters, and persons with this experience are generally preferred for civilian pilot jobs. This primarily reflects the extensive flying time military pilots receive. Persons without armed forces training also become pilots by attending flight schools. The FAA has certified about 600 civilian flying schools, including some colleges and universities that offer degree credit for pilot training. Over the projected period, Federal budget reductions are expected to reduce military pilot training. As a result, FAA certified schools will train a larger share of pilots than in the past.

Although some small airlines will hire high school graduates, most airlines require at least 2 years of college and prefer to hire college graduates; almost ninety percent of all pilots have completed some college.. In fact, most entrants to this occupation have a college degree. If the number of college educated applicants continues to increases, employers may make a college degree an educational requirement.

Depending on the type of aircraft in use, new airline pilots start as first officers or flight engineers. Although some airlines favor applicants who already have a flight engineer's license, they may provide flight engineer training for those who have only the commercial license. All new pilots receive several weeks of intensive training in simulators and classrooms before being assigned to a flight.

Organizations other than airlines generally require less flying experience. However, a commercial pilot's license is a minimum requirement, and employers prefer applicants who have experience in the type of craft they will be flying. New employees usually start as first officers, or fly less sophisticated equipment. Test pilots often are required to have an engineering degree.

Advancement for all pilots generally is limited to other flying jobs. Many pilots start as flight instructors, building up their flying hours while they earn money teaching. As they become more experienced, these pilots occasionally fly charter planes or perhaps get jobs with small air transportation firms, such as air taxi companies. Some advance to business flying jobs. A small number get flight engineer jobs with the airlines.

In the airlines, advancement usually depends on seniority provisions of union contracts. After 1 to 5 years, flight engineers advance according to seniority to first officer and, after 5 to 15 years, to captain. Seniority also determines which pilots get the more desirable routes. In a nonairline job, a first officer may advance to pilot and, in large companies, to chief pilot or director of aviation in charge of aircraft scheduling, maintenance, and flight procedures.

Job Outlook

Pilots are expected to face considerable competition for jobs through the year 2005 because the number of applicants for new positions is expected to exceed the number of job openings. Competition will be especially keen early in the projection period due to a temporary increase in the pool of qualified pilots seeking jobs. Mergers and bankruptcies during the recent restructuring of the industry caused a large number of airline pilots to lose their jobs. Also, Federal budget reductions resulted in many pilots leaving the Armed Forces. These and other qualified pilots seek jobs in this occupation because it offers very high earnings, glamour, prestige, and free or low cost travel benefits. As time passes, some pilots will fail to maintain their qualifications and the number of applicants competing for each opening should decline. Factors affecting demand, however, are not expected to ease that competition.

Relatively few jobs will be created from rising demand for pilots as employment is expected to increase more slowly than the average for all occupations through the year 2005. The expected growth in airline passenger and cargo traffic will create a need for more airliners, pilots, and flight instructors. However, computerized flight management systems on new aircraft will eliminate the need for flight engineers on those planes thus restricting pilot employment growth. In addition, the trend toward using larger planes in the airline industry will increase pilot productivity. Employment of business pilots is expected to grow more slowly than in the past as more businesses opt to fly with regional and smaller airlines serving their area rather than buy and operate their own aircraft. On the other hand, helicopter pilots are expected to grow more rapidly as the demand for the type of services they can offer expands.

Opportunities resulting from the need to replace pilots who leave the occupation also are expected to be limited. Aircraft pilots understandably have an extremely strong attachment to their occupation because it requires a substantial investment in specialized training that is not transferable to other fields and it generally offers very high earnings. Nevertheless, pilots who reach the mandatory retirement age will generate several thousand job openings each year.

Pilots who have logged the greatest number of flying hours in the more sophisticated equipment generally have the best prospects. This is the reason military pilots usually have an advantage over other applicants. Job seekers with the most FAA licenses will also have a competitive advantage. Opportunities for pilots in the regional commuter airlines and international service are expected to be more favorable as these segments are expected to grow faster than other segments of the industry.

Employment of pilots is sensitive to cyclical swings in the economy. During recessions, when a decline in the demand for air travel forces airlines to curtail the number of flights, airlines may temporarily furlough some pilots. Commercial and corporate flying, flight instruction, and testing of new aircraft also decline during recessions, adversely affecting pilots employed in those areas.

Earnings

Earnings of airline pilots are among the highest in the Nation. According to the Future Aviation Professionals of America (FAPA), the 1995 average starting salary for airline pilots ranged from about $13,000 at the smaller turboprop airlines to $27,900 at the larger major airlines. Average earnings for experienced pilots with six years of experience ranged from $37,500 at the turboprop airlines to almost $81,000 at the largest airlines. Some senior captains on the largest aircraft earned as much as $200,000 a year. Earnings depend on factors such as the type, size, and maximum speed of the plane, and the number of hours and miles flown. Extra pay may be given for night and international flights.

Generally, pilots working outside the airlines earn lower salaries. It was estimated that the median salary for chief pilots was $63,000 a year in 1994, for captains/pilots, $58,900 and for first officers, $42,800. Usually, pilots who fly jet aircraft earn higher salaries than nonjet pilots.

Data from the Future Aviation Professionals of America show that helicopter pilots averaged $29,200 a year. Average pay for helicopter pilots with five years of experience was about $45,600. Some helicopter pilots earn $65,000 to $75,00 a year.

Airline pilots generally are eligible for life and health insurance plans financed by the airlines. They also receive retirement benefits and if they fail the FAA physical examination at some point in their careers, they get disability payments. Some airlines provide allowances to pilots for purchasing and cleaning their uniforms. As an additional benefit, pilots and their immediate families usually are entitled to free or reduced fare transportation on their own and other airlines.

Most airline pilots are members of unions. Most airline pilots are members of the Airline Pilots Association, International, but those employed by one major airline are members of the Allied Pilots Association. Some flight engineers are members of the Flight Engineers' International Association.

Related Occupations

Although they are not in the cockpit, air traffic controllers and dispatchers also play an important role in making sure flights are safe and on schedule, and participate in many of the decisions pilots must make.

Sources of Additional Information

Information about job opportunities in a particular airline and the qualifications required may be obtained by writing to the personnel manager of the airline. For addresses of airline companies and information about job opportunities and salaries, contact:

☞FAPA, 4959 Massachusetts Blvd., Atlanta, GA 30032. (This organization may be called toll free at 1-800-JET-JOBS, extension 190.)

For information on airline pilots, contact:

☞Airline Pilots Association, 1625 Massachusetts Ave. NW., Washington, DC 20036.

☞Air Transport Association of America, 1301 Pennsylvania Ave. NW., Suite 1110, Washington, DC 20006.

For information on helicopter pilots, contact:

☞Helicopter Association International, 1619 Duke St., Alexandria, VA 22314.

For a copy of *List of Certificated Pilot Schools*, write to:

☞Superintendent of Documents, U.S. Government Printing Office, Washington, DC 20402.

For information about job opportunities in companies other than airlines, consult the classified section of aviation trade magazines and apply to companies that operate aircraft at local airports.

Air Traffic Controllers

(D.O.T. 193.162 except -022, .167-010)

Nature of the Work

The air traffic control system is a vast network of people and equipment that ensures the safe operation of commercial and private aircraft. Air traffic controllers coordinate the movement of air traffic to make certain that planes stay a safe distance apart. Their immediate concern is safety, but controllers also must direct planes efficiently to minimize delays. Some regulate airport traffic; others regulate flights between airports.

Although *airport tower or terminal controllers* watch over all planes traveling through the airport's airspace, their main responsibility is to organize the flow of aircraft in and out of the airport. Relying on radar and visual observation, they closely monitor each plane to ensure a safe distance between all aircraft and to guide pilots between the hangar or ramp and the end of the airport's airspace. In addition, controllers keep pilots informed about changes in weather conditions such as wind shear—a sudden change in the velocity or direction of the wind that can cause the pilot to lose control of the aircraft.

During arrival or departure, several controllers handle each plane. As a plane approaches an airport, the pilot radios ahead to inform the terminal of its presence. The controller in the radar room just beneath the control tower has a copy of the plane's flight plan and already has observed the plane on radar. If the way is clear, the controller directs the pilot to a runway; if the airport is busy, the plane is fitted into a traffic pattern with other aircraft waiting to land. As the plane nears the runway, the pilot is asked to contact the tower. There, another controller, who also is watching the plane on radar, monitors the aircraft the last mile or so to the runway, delaying any departures that would interfere with the plane's landing. Once the plane has landed, a ground controller in the tower directs it along the taxiways to its assigned gate. The ground controller usually works entirely by sight, but may use radar if visibility is very poor.

The procedure is reversed for departures. The ground controller directs the plane to the proper runway. The local controller then informs the pilot about conditions at the airport, such as the weather, speed and direction of wind, and visibility. The local controller also issues runway clearance for the pilot to take off. Once in the air, the plane is guided out of the airport's airspace by the departure controller.

After each plane departs, airport tower controllers notify *enroute controllers* who will next take charge. There are 22 enroute control centers located around the country, each employing 300 to 700 controllers, with more than 150 on duty during peak hours at the busier facilities. Airplanes generally fly along designated routes; each center is assigned a certain airspace containing many different routes. Enroute controllers work in teams of up to three members, depending on how heavy traffic is; each team is responsible for a section of the center's airspace. A team, for example, might be responsible for all planes that are between 30 to 100 miles north of an airport and flying at an altitude between 6,000 and 18,000 feet.

To prepare for planes about to enter the team's airspace, the radar associate controller organizes flight plans coming off a printer. If two planes are scheduled to enter the team's airspace at nearly the same time, location, and altitude, this controller may arrange with the preceding control unit for one plane to change its flight path. The previous unit may have been another team at the same or an adjacent center, or a departure controller at a neighboring terminal. As a plane approaches a team's airspace, the radar controller accepts responsibility for the plane from the previous controlling unit. The controller also delegates responsibility for the plane to the next controlling unit when the plane leaves the team's airspace.

The radar controller, who is the senior team member, observes the planes in the team's airspace on radar and communicates with the pilots when necessary. Radar controllers warn pilots about nearby planes, bad weather conditions, and other potential hazards. Two planes on a collision course will be directed around each other. If a pilot wants to change altitude in search of better flying conditions, the controller will check to determine that no other planes will be along the proposed path. As the flight progresses, the team responsible for the aircraft notifies the next team in charge. Through team coordination, the plane arrives safely at its destination.

Both airport tower and enroute controllers usually control several planes at a time and often have to make quick decisions about completely different activities. For example, a controller might direct a plane on its landing approach and at the same time provide pilots entering the airport's airspace with information about conditions at the airport. While instructing these pilots, the controller also would observe other planes in the vicinity, such as those in a holding pattern waiting for permission to land, to ensure that they remain well separated. Currently, the Federal Aviation Administration (FAA) is in the midst of developing and implementing a new automated air traffic control system. As a result, more powerful computers will help controllers deal with the demands of increased air traffic. Some

Air traffic controllers carefully monitor each plane.

traditional air traffic controller tasks—like determining how far apart planes should be kept—will be done by computer. Improved communication between computers on airplanes and those on the ground also is making the controller's job a little easier.

At present controllers sit at consoles with green-glowing screens that display radar images generated by a computer. In the future, controllers will work at a modern workstation computer that depicts air routes in full-color on a 20 by 20 inch screen. The controllers will select radio channels simply by touching on-screen buttons instead of turning dials or switching switches.

In addition to airport towers and enroute centers, air traffic controllers also work in flight service stations operated at over 100 locations. These *flight service specialists* provide pilots with information on the station's particular area, including terrain, preflight and inflight weather information, suggested routes, and other information important to the safety of a flight. Flight service station specialists help pilots in emergency situations and participate in searches for missing or overdue aircraft. However, they are not involved in actively managing air traffic.

Working Conditions

Controllers work a basic 40-hour week; however, they may work additional hours for which they receive overtime pay or equal time off. Because most control towers and centers operate 24 hours a day, 7 days a week, controllers rotate night and weekend shifts.

During busy times, controllers must work rapidly and efficiently. This requires total concentration to keep track of several planes at the same time and make certain all pilots receive correct instructions. The mental stress of being responsible for the safety of several aircraft and their passengers can be exhausting for some persons.

Employment

Air traffic controllers held about 23,000 jobs in 1994. They were employed by the Federal Government at airports—in towers and flight service stations—and in enroute traffic control centers. The overwhelming majority worked for the FAA. About 17,500 controllers were actively working controlling air traffic; 3,600 worked at flight service stations and another 750 worked in administrative staff positions. Some professional controllers conduct research at the FAA's national experimental center in Atlantic City, New Jersey. Others serve as instructors at the FAA Academy in Oklahoma City, Oklahoma. A small number of civilian controllers worked for the Department of Defense. In addition to controllers employed by the Federal Government, some worked for private air traffic control companies providing service to non-FAA towers.

Training, Other Qualifications, and Advancement

Air traffic controller trainees are selected through the competitive Federal Civil Service system. Applicants must pass a written test that measures their ability to learn the controller's duties. Applicants with experience as a pilot, navigator, or military controller can improve their rating by scoring well on the occupational knowledge portion of the examination. Abstract reasoning and three-dimensional spatial visualization are among the aptitudes the exam measures. In addition, applicants generally must have 3 years of general work experience or 4 years of college, or a combination of both. Applicants also must survive a 1 week screening at the FAA Academy in Oklahoma City which includes aptitude tests using computer simulator and physical and psychological examinations. Successful applicants receive drug screening tests. For airport tower and enroute center positions, applicants must be less than 31 years old. Those 31 years old and over are eligible for positions at flight service stations.

Controllers must be articulate, because directions to pilots must be given quickly and clearly. Intelligence and a good memory also are important because controllers constantly receive information that they must immediately grasp, interpret, and remember. Decisiveness is also required because controllers often have to make quick decisions. The ability to concentrate is crucial because controllers must make these decisions in the midst of noise and other distractions.

Trainees learn their craft through a combination of formal and on-the-job training. They receive 7 months of intensive training at the FAA academy, where they learn the fundamentals of the airway system, FAA regulations, controller equipment, aircraft performance characteristics, as well as more specialized tasks. To receive a job offer, trainees must successfully complete the training and pass a series of examinations, including a controller skills test that measures speed and accuracy in recognizing and correctly solving air traffic control problems. Based on aptitude and test scores, trainees are selected to work at either an enroute center or a tower.

After graduation, it takes several years of progressively more responsible work experience, interspersed with considerable classroom instruction and independent study, to become a fully qualified controller. This training includes instruction in the operation of the new, more automated air traffic control system—including the automated Microwave Landing System that enables pilots to receive instructions over automated data links—that is being installed in control sites across the country.

Controllers who fail to complete either the academy or the on-the-job portion of the training are usually dismissed. Controllers must pass a physical examination each year and a job performance examination twice each year. Failure to become certified in any position at a facility within a specified time may also result in dismissal. Controllers also are subject to drug screening as a condition of continuing employment.

At airports, new controllers begin by supplying pilots with basic flight data and airport information. They then advance to ground controller, then local controller, departure controller, and finally, arrival controller. At an enroute traffic control center, new controllers first deliver printed flight plans to teams, gradually advancing to radar associate controller and then radar controller.

Controllers can transfer to jobs at different locations or advance to supervisory positions, including management or staff jobs in air traffic control and top administrative jobs in the FAA. However, there are only limited opportunities for a controller to switch from a position in an enroute center to a tower.

Job Outlook

Competition for air traffic controller jobs is expected to remain extremely keen because the occupation attracts many more qualified applicants than the small number of job openings stemming from growth of the occupation and replacement needs. Turnover is very low; because of the relatively high pay and liberal retirement benefits, controllers have a very strong attachment to the occupation. Most of the current work force was hired as a result of the controller's strike during the 1980's, so the average age of current controllers is fairly young. Most controllers will not be eligible to retire until 2005 or later.

Employment of air traffic controllers is expected to show little or no change through the year 2005. Employment growth is not expected to keep pace with growth in the number of aircraft flying because of the implementation of a new air traffic control system over the next 10 years. This computerized system will assist the controller by automatically making many of the routine decisions. Automation will allow controllers to handle more traffic, thus increasing their productivity.

Air traffic controllers who continue to meet the proficiency and medical requirements enjoy more job security than most workers. The demand for air travel and the workloads of air traffic controllers decline during recessions, but controllers seldom are laid off.

Earnings

Air traffic controllers who started with the FAA in 1995 earned about $22,700 a year. Controllers at higher Federal pay grade levels earned 5 percent more than other Federal workers in an equivalent grade. A controller's pay is determined by both the worker's job responsibilities and the complexity of the particular facility. Earnings are higher at facilities where traffic patterns are more complex. In 1995, controllers averaged about $59,800 a year.

Depending on length of service, they receive 13 to 26 days of paid vacation and 13 days of paid sick leave each year, life insurance, and health benefits. In addition, controllers can retire at an earlier age and with fewer years of service than other Federal employees. Air traffic controllers are eligible to retire at age 50 with 20 years of service as an active air traffic controller or after 25 years of active service at any age. There is a mandatory retirement age of 56 for controllers who manage air traffic.

Related Occupations

Other occupations that involve the direction and control of traffic in air transportation are airline-radio operator and airplane dispatcher.

Sources of Additional Information

A pamphlet providing general information about controllers and instructions for submitting an application is available from any U.S. Office of Personnel Management Job Information Center. Look under U.S. Government, Office of Personnel Management, in your telephone book to obtain a local Job Information Center telephone number, and call for a copy of the Air Traffic Controller Announcement. If there is no listing in your telephone book, dial the toll-free number 1-800-555-1212 and request the number of the Office of Personnel Management Job Information Center for your location.

Broadcast Technicians

(D.O.T. 193.167-014, .262-018, and -038; 194.062, .122, .262-010, -014, -018, -022, .282, .362, and .382-014, -018, 962.167-010, and .382-010)

Nature of the Work

Broadcast technicians install, test, repair, set up, and operate the electronic equipment used to record and transmit radio and television programs. They work with television cameras, microphones, tape recorders, light and sound effects, transmitters, antennas, and other equipment. Some broadcast technicians develop movie sound tracks in motion picture production studios.

In the control room of a radio or television broadcasting studio, these technicians operate equipment that regulates the signal strength, clarity, and range of sounds and colors of recording or broadcasts. They also operate control panels to select the source of

the material. Technicians may switch from one camera or studio to another, from film to live programming, or from network to local programs. By means of hand signals and, in television, telephone headsets, they give technical directions to studio personnel.

Broadcast technicians in small stations perform a variety of duties. In large stations and at the networks, technicians are more specialized, although job assignments may change from day to day. The terms "operator," "engineer," and "technician" often are used interchangeably to describe these jobs. *Transmitter operators* monitor and log outgoing signals and operate transmitters. *Maintenance technicians* set up, adjust, service, and repair electronic broadcasting equipment. *Audio control engineers* regulate sound pickup, transmission, and switching of television pictures while *video control engineers* regulate their quality, brightness, and contrast. *Recording engineers* operate and maintain video and sound recording equipment. They may operate equipment designed to produce special effects, such as the illusions of a bolt of lightning or a police siren. *Field technicians* set up and operate broadcasting portable field transmission equipment outside the studio.

Television news coverage requires so much electronic equipment, and the technology is changing so fast, that many stations assign technicians exclusively to news. *Chief engineers*, *transmission engineers*, and *broadcast field supervisors* supervise the technicians who operate and maintain broadcasting equipment.

Technicians in the motion picture industry are called *sound mixers* or *rerecording mixers*. Mixers produce the sound track of a movie using a process called dubbing. They sit at sound consoles facing the screen and fade in and fade out each sound and regulate its volume. Each technician is responsible for certain sounds. Technicians follow a script that tells at precisely what moment, as the film runs through the projector, each of the sounds must be faded in and out. All the sounds for each shot are thus blended on a master sound track.

Working Conditions

Broadcast technicians generally work indoors in pleasant surroundings. However, those who broadcast from disaster areas or crime scenes may work under less favorable conditions. Technicians doing maintenance may climb poles or antenna towers, while those setting up equipment do heavy lifting.

Technicians in large stations and the networks usually work a 40-hour week, but may occasionally work overtime under great pressure to meet broadcast deadlines. Technicians in small stations routinely work more than 40 hours a week. Evening, weekend, and holiday work is usual because most stations are on the air 18 to 24 hours a day, 7 days a week.

Broadcast technicians generally work indoors in pleasant surroundings.

Those who work on motion pictures may be on a tight schedule to finish according to contract agreements.

Employment

Broadcast technicians held about 42,000 jobs in 1994. About 7 out of 10 broadcast technicians were in radio and television broadcasting. Almost 2 in 10 worked in the motion picture industry. About 8 percent worked for cable and other pay television services. Some were self employed. Television stations employ, on average, many more technicians than radio stations. Some are employed in other industries, producing employee communications, sales, and training programs. Technician jobs in television are located in virtually all cities, while jobs in radio are also found in most smaller towns. The highest paying and most specialized jobs are concentrated in New York City, Los Angeles, Chicago, and Washington, D.C.—the originating centers for most of network programs. Motion picture production jobs are concentrated in Los Angeles and New York City.

Training, Other Qualifications, and Advancement

The best way to prepare for a broadcast technician job in radio and television—particularly for those who hope to advance to supervisory positions or to jobs in large stations and at the networks—is to obtain technical school, community college, or college training in broadcast technology or in engineering or electronics. On the other hand, there is no formal training for jobs in the motion picture industry. People are hired as apprentice editorial assistants and work their way up to more skilled jobs. Reputation, determination, and luck are important in getting jobs.

Federal law requires a restricted radiotelephone operator permit for persons who operate and maintain broadcast transmitters in radio and television stations. No examination is required to obtain one. The Federal Communications Commission no longer requires persons working with microwave to have a general radiotelephone operator license; however, some States may require a license.

Beginners learn skills on the job from experienced technicians and supervisors. They generally begin their careers in small stations and, if qualified, move on to larger ones. Large stations generally only hire technicians with experience. Many employers pay tuition and expenses for courses or seminars to help technicians keep abreast of developments in the field.

Certification by the Society of Broadcast Engineers is a mark of competence and experience. The certificate is issued to experienced technicians who pass an examination.

Prospective technicians should take high school courses in math, physics, and electronics. Building electronic equipment from hobby kits and operating a "ham" or amateur radio are good experience, as is work in college radio and television stations.

Broadcast technicians must have an aptitude for working with electrical and mechanical systems and equipment and manual dexterity.

Experienced technicians may become supervisory technicians or chief engineers. A college degree in engineering is generally needed to become chief engineer at a large TV station.

Job Outlook

People seeking beginning jobs as radio and television broadcast technicians are expected to face strong competition in major metropolitan areas, where the number of qualified jobseekers greatly exceeds the number of openings. There, stations seek highly experienced personnel. Prospects for entry level positions generally are better in small cities and towns for people with appropriate training.

Employment of broadcast technicians is expected to decline through the year 2005. Employment in radio and television broad

casting is expected to decline because of laborsaving technical advances such as computer-controlled programming and remote control of transmitters. This has shifted the emphasis from operations to maintenance work, which frequently is performed by commercial and industrial electronic equipment repairers employed by broadcasting equipment manufacturers. (See the statement on this occupation elsewhere in the *Handbook.*)

Employment in the motion picture industry will grow about as fast as the average for all occupations. Job prospects are expected to remain competitive, however, because of the large number of people attracted to this relatively small field.

Virtually all job openings will result from the need to replace experienced technicians who leave the occupation. Turnover is relatively high for broadcast technicians. Many leave the occupation for electronic jobs in other areas such as computer technology or commercial and industrial repair because the number of jobs is limited in large cities where pay is high.

Earnings

Television stations usually pay higher salaries than radio stations; commercial broadcasting usually pays more than educational broadcasting; and stations in large markets pay more than those in small ones.

According to a survey conducted by the National Association of Broadcasters and the Broadcast Cable Financial Management Association, the average earnings for technicians at radio stations were $23,569 a year in 1994. For chief engineer, average earnings were $43,500 and the range was $34,256 to $57,937. In television, the average earnings for operator technician were $24,260 a year, and salaries ranged from $16,422 in the smallest markets to $45,158 in the largest markets; for technical director, the average earnings were $25,962 and the range was $18,444 to $44,531; for maintenance technician, the average was $32,533 and the range was $24,210 to $50,235; and for chief engineer, the average was $53,655 and the salaries ranged from $38,178 in the smallest markets to $91,051 in the largest markets.

Earnings in the motion picture industry depend on skill and reputation, and, based on limited information, range from $20,000 to $100,000 a year.

Related Occupations

Broadcast technicians need the electronics training and hand coordination necessary to operate technical equipment, and they generally complete specialized postsecondary programs. Others with similar jobs and training include drafters, engineering and science technicians, surveyors, air traffic controllers, radiologic technologists, respiratory therapy workers, cardiovascular technologists and technicians, electroneurodiagnostic technicians, and clinical laboratory technologists and technicians.

Sources of Additional Information

For information about licensing, write to:

☛Federal Communications Commission, Consumer Assistance Office, 1270 Fairfield Rd., Gettysburg, PA 17325-7245 or call 1 800 322-1117.

For information on careers for broadcast technicians, write to:

☛National Association of Broadcasters Employment Clearinghouse, 1771 N St. NW., Washington, DC 20036.

For a list of schools that offer programs or courses in broadcasting, contact:

☛Broadcast Education Association, National Association of Broadcasters, 1771 N St. NW., Washington, DC 20036.

For information on certification, contact:

☛Society of Broadcast Engineers, 8445 Keystone Crossing, Suite 140, Indianapolis, IN 46240.

Computer Programmers

(D.O.T. 030.162-010, -018, -022, and .167-010)

Nature of the Work

Computer programmers write, and maintain the detailed instructions—called "programs" or "software"—that list in a logical order the steps that computers must execute to perform their functions. In many large organizations, programmers follow descriptions prepared by systems analysts who have carefully studied the task that the computer system is going to perform. These descriptions list the input required, the steps the computer must follow to process data, and the desired arrangement of the output. (A more detailed description of the work of systems analysts is presented in the statement on computer scientists and systems analysts elsewhere in the *Handbook*.) Some organizations, particularly smaller ones, do not employ systems analysts. Instead, workers called *programmer-analysts* are responsible for both systems analysis and programming.

Regardless of setting, programmers write specific programs by breaking down each step into a logical series of instructions the computer can follow. They then code these instructions in a conventional programming language, such as C and FORTRAN, or one of the more advanced artificial intelligence or object oriented languages, such as LISP, Prolog, C++, or Ada.

The transition from a mainframe environment to primarily a PC-based environment has blurred the once rigid distinction between the programmer and the user. Increasingly adept users are taking over many of the tasks previously performed by programmers. For example, the growing use of packaged software, like spreadsheet and data base management software packages, allows users to write simple programs to access data and perform calculations.

Programmers in software development companies may work directly with experts from various fields to create software—either programs designed for specific clients or packaged software for general use—ranging from games and educational software to programs for desktop publishing, financial planning, and spreadsheets. Much of the programming being done today is the preparation of packaged software, one of the most rapidly growing segments of the computer industry.

Despite the prevalence of packaged software, many programmers are involved in updating, repairing, and modifying code for existing programs. When making changes to a section of code, called a "routine," programmers need to make other users aware of the task that the routine is to perform. They do this by inserting comments in the coded instructions so others can understand the program. Programmers using Computer-Aided Software Engineering (CASE) tools can concentrate on writing the unique parts of the program because the tools automate various pieces of the program being built. This also yields more reliable and consistent programs and increases programmers' productivity by eliminating some of the routine steps.

When a program is ready to be tested, programmers run it to ensure that the instructions are correct and will produce the desired information. They prepare sample data that test every part of the program and, after trial runs, review the results to see if any errors were made. If errors do occur, the programmer must make the appropriate change and recheck the program until it produces the correct results. This is called "debugging" the program.

Finally, programmers working in a mainframe environment prepare instructions for the computer operator who will run the program. (The work of computer operators is described in the statement on computer and peripheral equipment operators elsewhere in the *Handbook*.) They may also contribute to a user's manual for the program.

Programs vary depending upon the type of information to be accessed or generated. For example, the instructions involved in updating financial records are different from those required to

Applications programmers may write software for a specific job or modify existing packaged software to meet an organization's needs.

duplicate conditions onboard an aircraft for pilots training in a flight simulator. Although simple programs can be written in a few hours, programs that use complex mathematical formulas or many data files may require more than a year of work. In most cases, several programmers may work together as a team under a senior programmer's supervision.

Programmers often are grouped into two broad types: Applications programmers and systems programmers. *Applications programmers* usually are oriented toward business, engineering, or science. They write software to handle specific jobs, such as a program used in an inventory control system or one to guide a missile after it has been fired. They also may work alone to revise existing packaged software. *Systems programmers*, on the other hand, maintain the software that controls the operation of an entire computer system. These workers make changes in the sets of instructions that determine how the central processing unit of the system handles the various jobs it has been given and communicates with peripheral equipment, such as terminals, printers, and disk drives. Because of their knowledge of the entire computer system, systems programmers often help applications programmers determine the source of problems that may occur with their programs.

Working Conditions

Programmers generally work in offices in comfortable surroundings. Although they usually work about 40 hours a week, their hours are not always from 9 to 5. Programmers may work longer hours or weekends in order to meet deadlines or fix critical problems that occur during off hours.

Because programmers spend long periods of time in front of a computer monitor typing at a keyboard, they are susceptible to eyestrain, back discomfort, and hand and wrist problems.

Employment

Computer programmers held about 537,000 jobs in 1994. Programmers are employed in most industries, but the largest concentrations are in data processing service organizations, including firms that write and sell software; firms that provide engineering and management services; manufacturers of computer and office equipment; financial institutions; insurance carriers; educational institutions; and government agencies. Applications programmers work for all types of firms, whereas systems programmers usually work for organizations with large computer centers or for firms that manufacture computers or develop software.

A growing number of programmers are employed on a temporary or contract basis. Rather than hiring programmers as permanent employees and then laying them off after a job is completed, employers increasingly are contracting with temporary help agencies, consulting firms, or directly with programmers themselves. A marketing firm, for example, may only require the services of several programmers to write and "debug" the software necessary to get a new database management system running. Such jobs may last from several months to a year or longer.

Training, Other Qualifications, and Advancement

There are no universal training requirements for programmers because employers' needs are so varied. Computer applications have become so widespread that computer programming is taught at most public and private vocational schools, community and junior colleges, and universities. However, the level of education and quality of training that employers seek have been rising due to the growth in the number of qualified applicants and the increasing complexity of some programming tasks. Although some programmers obtain 2 year degrees or certificates, bachelor's degrees are now commonly required. In the absence of a degree, substantial specialized experience or expertise may be needed.

The majority of programmers hold a 4-year degree. Of these, some hold a B.A. or B.S. in computer science or information systems while others have taken special courses in computer programming to supplement their study in fields such as accounting, inventory control, or other business areas. College graduates who are interested in changing careers or developing an area of expertise may return to a junior college or technical school for more training.

Employers using computers for scientific or engineering applications prefer college graduates who have degrees in computer or information science, mathematics, engineering, or the physical sciences. Graduate degrees are required for some jobs. Employers who use computers for business applications prefer to hire people who have had college courses in management information systems (MIS) and business, and who possess strong programming skills. Knowledge of FORTRAN, COBOL, C, Fourth Generation Languages (4GL), CASE tools, systems programming, C++, Smalltalk, and other object oriented programming languages is highly desirable. General business skills and experience related to the operations of the firm are preferred by employers as well.

Most systems programmers hold a 4-year degree in computer science. Extensive knowledge of a variety of operating systems is essential. This includes being able to configure the operating system to work with different types of hardware, and adapting the operating system to best meet the needs of the particular organization. They also must be able to work with database systems such as DB2, Oracle, or Sybase, for example.

The Institute for Certification of Computing Professionals confers the designation Certified Computing Professional (CCP) to those who have at least 4 years of experience or 2 years of experience and a college degree. To qualify, individuals must pass a core examination plus exams in two specialty areas, or an exam in one specialty area and two computing languages. Those with little or no experience may be tested for certification as an Associate Computer Professional (ACP). Certification is not mandatory, but it may give a job seeker a competitive advantage.

When hiring programmers, employers look for people with the necessary programming skills who can think logically and pay close attention to detail. The job calls for patience, persistence, and the ability to work on exacting analytical work, especially under pressure. Ingenuity and imagination are also particularly important when programmers design solutions and test their work for potential failures. Increasingly, interpersonal skills are important as programmers are expected to work in teams and interact directly with users. The ability to work with abstract concepts and do technical analysis is especially important for systems programmers because they work with the software that controls the computer's operation.

Beginning programmers may spend their first weeks on the job attending training classes since each business has its own development methodology, processes, and tools. After this initial instruc-

tion, they may work alone on simple assignments, or on a team with more experienced programmers. Either way, they generally must spend at least several months working under close supervision. Because of rapidly changing technology, programmers must continuously update their training by taking courses sponsored by their employer or software vendors.

For skilled workers, the prospects for advancement are good. In large organizations, they may be promoted to lead programmer and be given supervisory responsibilities. Some applications programmers may move into systems programming after they gain experience and take courses in systems software. With general business experience, both applications programmers and systems programmers may become systems analysts or be promoted to a managerial position. Other programmers, with specialized knowledge and experience with a language or operating system, may work in research and development areas such as multimedia or Internet technology. As employers increasingly contract out programming jobs, more opportunities should arise for experienced programmers with expertise in a specific area to work as consultants.

Job Outlook

Employment of programmers is expected to grow about as fast as the average for all occupations through the year 2005. Employment is not expected to grow as rapidly as in the past as improved software and programming techniques continue to simplify programming tasks. In addition, greater use of packaged software—such as word processing and spreadsheet packages—should continue to moderate the growth in demand for applications programmers. As the level of technological innovation and sophistication increases, users will be able to design, write, and implement more of their own programs to meet their changing needs.

Although the proportion of programmers leaving the occupation each year is smaller than that of most occupations, most of the job openings for programmers will result from replacement needs. The majority of programmers who leave transfer to other occupations, such as manager or systems analyst. Jobs for both systems and applications programmers, however, should remain particularly plentiful in data processing service firms, software houses, and computer consulting businesses. These types of establishments remain part of one of the fastest growing industries—computer and data processing services. As companies look to control costs, those in need of programming services should look to this industry to meet these needs.

As computer usage expands, however, the demand for skilled programmers will increase as organizations seek new applications for computers and improvements to the software already in use. Employers are increasingly interested in programmers who can combine areas of technical expertise or who are adaptable and able to learn and incorporate new skills. One area of progress will be data communications. Networking computers so they can communicate with each other is necessary to achieve the greater efficiency that organizations require to remain competitive. Object-oriented languages will increasingly be used in the years ahead, further enhancing the productivity of programmers. Programmers will be creating and maintaining expert systems and embedding these technologies in more and more products.

The number and quality of applicants for programmer jobs have increased, so employers have become more selective. Graduates of 2-year programs in data processing, and people with less than a 2-year degree or its equivalent in work experience, are facing especially strong competition for programming jobs. Competition for entry-level positions even affects applicants with a bachelor's degree. Many observers expect opportunities for people without college degrees to diminish in coming years as programming tasks become more complex and more sophisticated skills and experience are demanded by employers. Prospects should be good for college graduates with knowledge of a variety of programming languages, particularly C++ and other object oriented languages, as well as newer languages that apply to computer networking, data base management, and artificial intelligence. In order to remain competitive, college graduates should keep up to date with the latest skills and technologies.

Many employers prefer to hire applicants with previous experience in the field. Firms also desire programmers who develop a technical specialization in areas such as client/server programming, multimedia technology, graphic user interface, or 4th and 5th generation programming tools. Therefore, people who want to become programmers can enhance their chances by combining work experience with the appropriate formal training. Students should try to gain experience by participating in a college work-study program, or undertaking an internship. Students also can greatly improve their employment prospects by taking courses such as accounting, management, engineering, or science—allied fields in which applications programmers are in demand. With the expansion of client/server environments, employers will continue to look for programmers with strong technical skills, as well as good interpersonal and business skills.

Earnings

Median earnings of programmers who worked full time in 1994 were about $38,400 a year. The middle 50 percent earned between about $30,000 and $49,200 a year. The lowest 10 percent earned less than $22,000, and the highest 10 percent, more than $60,600.

According to Robert Half International Inc., starting salaries in large establishments for 1994 ranged from $29,500 to $36,500 for programmers; $36,000 to $47,000 for programmer analysts; and $44,000 to $54,000 for systems programmers. Starting salaries in small establishments ranged from $25,000 to $34,000 for programmers and from $30,000 to $40,000 for programmer analysts.

Programmers working in the West and Northeast earned somewhat more than those working in the South and Midwest. On average, systems programmers earn more than applications programmers.

In the Federal Government, the entrance salary for programmers with a college degree or qualifying experience was about $18,700 a year in 1995; for those with a superior academic record, $23,200.

Related Occupations

Programmers must pay great attention to detail as they write and "debug" programs. Other professional workers who must be detail-oriented include statisticians, engineers, financial analysts, accountants, auditors, actuaries, and operations research analysts.

Sources of Additional Information

State employment service offices can provide information about job openings for computer programmers. Also check with your city's chamber of commerce for information on the area's largest employers.

For information about certification as a computing professional, contact:

☞Institute for the Certification of Computing Professionals, 2200 East Devon Ave., Suite 268, Des Plaines, IL 60018.

Further information about computer careers is available from:

☞The Association for Computing Machinery, 1515 Broadway, New York, NY 10036.

Drafters

(D.O.T. 001.261; 002.261; 003.131, .261 except -010, .281; 005.281; 007.161-010, -014, and -018, .261, and .281; 010.281 except -022; 014.281; 017 except .261-010 and .684; 019.161-010, .261-014; and 726.364-014)

Nature of the Work

Drafters prepare technical drawings followed by production and construction workers to build everything from spacecraft or industrial machinery and other manufactured products to structures such as office buildings or oil and gas pipelines. Their drawings show the technical details of the products and structures from all sides, including exact dimensions, specific materials to be used, and procedures to be followed. Drafters fill in technical details, using drawings, rough sketches, specifications, codes, and calculations previously made by engineers, surveyors, architects, or scientists. For example, they use their knowledge of standardized building techniques to draw in the details of a structure. Some drafters employ a knowledge of engineering and manufacturing theory and standards to draw the parts of a machine in order to determine the number and kind of fasteners needed to assemble it. They may use technical handbooks, tables, calculators, and computers.

Traditionally, drafters sat at drawing boards and used compasses, dividers, protractors, triangles, and other drafting devices to prepare a drawing manually. Many drafters now use computer-aided drafting (CAD) systems to prepare drawings. These systems employ computer work stations to create a drawing on a video screen. They store it electronically so that revisions and/or duplications can be made easily. These systems also permit drafters to easily and quickly prepare variations of a design. A person who produces a technical drawing using CAD is still functioning as a drafter, and needs most of the knowledge of traditional drafters as well as CAD skills.

Because the cost of CAD systems is dropping rapidly, by the year 2005 it is likely that almost all drafters will use CAD systems regularly. However, manual drafting probably will still be used in certain applications, especially in specialty firms that produce many one-of-a-kind drawings with little repetition.

Many drafters specialize. *Architectural drafters* draw architectural and structural features of buildings and other structures. They may specialize by the type of structure, such as schools or office buildings, or by material used, such as reinforced concrete, masonry, steel, or timber.

Aeronautical drafters prepare engineering drawings used for the manufacture of aircraft and missiles.

Electrical drafters draw wiring and layout diagrams used by workers who erect, install, and repair electrical equipment and wiring in powerplants, electrical distribution systems, and buildings.

Electronic drafters draw wiring diagrams, circuit board assembly diagrams, schematics, and layout drawings used in the manufacture, installation, and repair of electronic equipment.

Civil drafters prepare drawings and topographical and relief maps used in civil engineering projects such as highways, bridges, pipelines, flood control projects, and water and sewage systems.

Employment of drafters is expected to change little through the year 2005.

Mechanical drafters draw detailed diagrams of machinery and mechanical devices, such as process piping systems, including dimensions, fastening methods, and other engineering information.

Working Conditions
Drafters usually work in offices with lighting appropriate to their tasks. They often sit at drawing boards or computer terminals for long periods of time doing detailed work, which may cause eyestrain and back discomfort.

Employment
Drafters held about 304,000 jobs in 1994. Over one-third of all drafters worked in engineering and architectural services, firms that design construction projects or do other engineering work on a contract basis for organizations in other parts of the economy; about one-third worked in durable goods manufacturing industries, such as machinery, electrical equipment, and fabricated metals; and the remainder were mostly employed in the construction, communications, utilities, and personnel supply services industries.

About 10,000 drafters worked in government in 1994, primarily at the State and local level.

Training, Other Qualifications, and Advancement
Employers prefer applicants for drafting positions who have completed post-high school training in drafting, which is offered by technical institutes, junior and community colleges, and the extension divisions of colleges and universities. Employers are most interested in applicants who have well-developed drafting and mechanical drawing skills, a knowledge of standards and a solid background in computer-aided design techniques, and courses in mathematics, science, and engineering technology. In addition, communication and problem-solving skills are required.

Many types of publicly and privately operated schools provide some form of drafting training. The kind and quality of programs can vary considerably. Therefore, prospective students should be careful in selecting a program. They should contact prospective employers regarding their preferences and ask schools to provide information about the kinds of jobs obtained by graduates, type and condition of instructional facilities and equipment, and faculty qualifications.

Technical institutes offer intensive technical training but less theory and general education than junior and community colleges. Many offer 2-year associate degree programs, which are similar to or part of the programs offered by community colleges or State university systems. Other technical institutes are run by private, often for-profit, organizations, sometimes called proprietary schools; their programs vary considerably in both length and type of courses offered.

Junior and community colleges offer curriculums similar to those in technical institutes but include more courses on theory and liberal arts. Often there is little or no difference between technical institute and community college programs. However, courses taken at junior or community colleges are more likely to be accepted for credit at 4-year colleges than those at technical institutes. After completing a 2-year program, many graduates obtain jobs as drafters while others continue their education in a related field at 4-year colleges.

Four-year colleges usually do not offer drafting training, but college courses in engineering, architecture, and mathematics are useful for obtaining a job as a drafter.

Area vocational-technical schools are postsecondary public institutions that serve local students and emphasize training needed by local employers. Most require a high school diploma or its equivalent for admission. Many offer introductory drafting instruction.

Other training may be obtained in the Armed Forces in technical areas which can be applied in civilian drafting jobs. Some additional training may be needed, depending on the military specialty, but often this can be gained on the job.

Those planning careers in drafting should be able to draw free-hand three-dimensional objects and do detailed work accurately and neatly. Artistic ability is helpful in some specialized fields, as is knowledge of manufacturing and construction methods. In addition, prospective drafters should have good communication skills because they work closely with engineers, surveyors, architects, and other professionals.

Both the American Design Drafting Association (ADDA) and the American Institute of Building Design (AIBD) have established certification programs for drafters. Although drafters are not generally required to be certified by employers, certification demonstrates that nationally recognized standards have been met. Individuals who wish to become certified must pass the Drafter Certification Test, which is administered periodically at ADDA-authorized test sites. Applicants are tested on their knowledge and understanding of basic drafting concepts such as geometric construction, working drawings, and architectural terms and standards.

Entry level or junior drafters usually do routine work under close supervision. After gaining experience, they do more difficult work with less supervision and may advance to senior drafter, designer, or supervisor. Many employers pay for ongoing education, and with appropriate college degrees, drafters may become engineers or architects.

Job Outlook
Employment of drafters is expected to change little through the year 2005. Industrial growth and increasingly complex design problems associated with new products and manufacturing increase the demand for drafting services. However, greater use of CAD equipment by architects and engineers, as well as drafters, may offset this growth in demand. Although productivity gains from CAD have been relatively modest since its use became widespread, the technology continues to advance. CAD is expected to become an increasingly powerful tool, simplifying many traditional drafting tasks and enabling some engineers and architects to do some drafting tasks themselves. Individuals who have at least 2 years of training in a technically strong drafting program and who have experience with CAD systems will have the best opportunities. Although few, if any, jobs will be generated by employment growth, many job openings are expected to arise as drafters move to other occupations, retire, or leave the labor force for other reasons.

Employment of drafters is highly concentrated in industries that are sensitive to cyclical swings in the economy, such as engineering and architectural services and durable goods manufacturing. During recessions, drafters may be laid off.

Earnings
Median annual earnings of drafters who worked year round, full time were about $28,500 in 1994; the middle 50 percent earned between $21,500 and $38,600 annually. The top 10 percent earned more than $50,200, while the bottom 10 percent earned less than $16,400.

According to a survey of workplaces in 160 metropolitan areas, the most experienced drafters had median earnings of about $38,600 a year in 1993, with the middle half earning between about $35,500 and $42,600 a year.

Related Occupations
Other workers who prepare or analyze detailed drawings and make precise calculations and measurements include architects, landscape architects, engineers, engineering technicians, science technicians, cartographers, and surveyors.

Sources of Additional Information
Information on schools offering programs in drafting and other areas is available from:

☛ Accrediting Commission of Career Schools and Colleges of Technology, 2101 Wilson Blvd., Suite 302, Arlington, VA 22201.

Engineering Technicians

(D.O.T. 002.261-014, .262-010; 003.161, .261-010, .362; 005.261; 006.261; 007.161-026 and -030, .167-010, .181 and .267-014; 008.261; 010.261-010 and -026; 011.261-010, -014, -018, and -022, .281, .361; 012.261-014, .267; 013.161; 017.261-010; 017.684; 019.161-014, .261-018, -022, -026, -030, and -034, .267, .281; 194.381, .382-010; 199.261-014; 726.261-010 and -014; 806.281-014; 761.281-014; 828.261-018; and 869.261-026)

Nature of the Work

Engineering technicians use the principles and theories of science, engineering, and mathematics to solve technical problems in research and development, manufacturing, sales, construction, and customer service. Their jobs are more limited in scope and more practically oriented than those of scientists and engineers. Many engineering technicians assist engineers and scientists, especially in research and development. Others work in production or inspection jobs.

Engineering technicians who work in research and development build or set up equipment, prepare and conduct experiments, calculate or record the results, and help engineers in other ways. Some make prototype versions of newly designed equipment. They also assist in routine design work, often using computer-aided design equipment.

Engineering technicians who work in manufacturing follow the general directions of engineers. They may prepare specifications for materials, devise and run tests to ensure product quality, or study ways to improve manufacturing efficiency. They may also supervise production workers to make sure they follow prescribed procedures.

Civil engineering technicians help civil engineers plan and build highways, buildings, bridges, dams, wastewater treatment systems, and other structures and perform related surveys and studies. Some inspect water and wastewater treatment systems to ensure that pollution control requirements are met. Others estimate construction costs and specify materials to be used. (See statement on cost estimators elsewhere in the *Handbook*.)

Electronics engineering technicians use their knowledge of electronic circuits to help design, develop, and manufacture electronic equipment such as radios, radar, sonar, television, industrial and medical measuring or control devices, navigational equipment, and computers. They use measuring and diagnostic devices to test, adjust, and repair equipment. Workers who only repair electrical and electronic equipment are discussed in several other statements elsewhere in the *Handbook*. Many of these repairers are often called electronics technicians.

Job duties for some engineering technicians include testing, calibrating, and repairing electronic equipment.

Industrial engineering technicians study the efficient use of personnel, materials, and machines in factories, stores, repair shops, and offices. They prepare layouts of machinery and equipment, plan the flow of work, make statistical studies, and analyze production costs.

Mechanical engineering technicians help engineers design, develop, test, and manufacture machinery, industrial robotics, and other equipment. They may assist in the testing of a guided missile, or in the planning and design of an electric power generation plant. They make sketches and rough layouts, record data, make computations, analyze results, and write reports. When planning production, mechanical engineering technicians prepare layouts and drawings of the assembly process and of parts to be manufactured. They estimate labor costs, equipment life, and plant space. Some test and inspect machines and equipment in manufacturing departments or work with engineers to eliminate production problems.

Chemical engineering technicians are usually employed in industries producing pharmaceuticals, chemicals, and petroleum products, among others. They help design, install, and test or maintain process equipment or computer control instrumentation, monitor quality control in processing plants, and make needed adjustments.

Working Conditions

Most engineering technicians work regular hours in laboratories, offices, electronics and industrial plants, or construction sites. Some may be exposed to hazards from equipment, chemicals, or toxic materials.

Employment

Engineering technicians held about 685,000 jobs in 1994. About two-fifths worked in manufacturing, mainly in the electrical and electronic machinery and equipment, industrial machinery and equipment, instruments and related products, and transportation equipment industries. Nearly one-fourth worked in service industries, mostly in engineering or business services companies who do engineering work on contract for government, manufacturing, or other organizations.

In 1994, the Federal Government employed about 55,000 engineering technicians. The major employer was the Department of Defense, followed by the Departments of Transportation, Agriculture, and the Interior, the Tennessee Valley Authority, and the National Aeronautics and Space Administration. State governments employed about 36,000 and local governments about 27,000.

Training, Other Qualifications, and Advancement

Although it is possible to qualify for some engineering technician jobs with no formal training, most employers prefer to hire someone who will require less on-the-job training and supervision. Training is available at technical institutes, junior and community colleges, extension divisions of colleges and universities, public and private vocational-technical schools, and through some technical training programs in the Armed Forces. Persons with college courses in science, engineering, and mathematics may also qualify for some positions but may need additional specialized training and experience.

Many types of publicly and privately operated schools provide technical training. The kind and quality of programs vary considerably. Therefore, prospective students should be careful in selecting a program. They should contact prospective employers regarding their preferences and ask schools to provide information about the kinds of jobs obtained by graduates, instructional facilities and equipment, and faculty qualifications. Graduates of programs accredited by the Accreditation Board for Engineering and Technology (ABET) are generally recognized to have achieved a minimum level of competence in the mathematics, science, and technical courses required for this occupation.

Technical institutes offer intensive technical training but less theory and general education than junior and community colleges.

Many offer 2-year associate degree programs, and are similar to or are part of a community college or State university system. Other technical institutes are run by private, often for-profit, organizations, sometimes called proprietary schools; their programs vary considerably in length and types of courses offered. Some are 2-year associate degree programs.

Junior and community colleges offer curriculums similar to those in technical institutes but may include more theory and liberal arts. Often there may be little or no difference between technical institute and community college programs, as both offer associate degrees. After completing the 2-year program, some graduates get jobs as engineering technicians, while others continue their education at 4-year colleges. However, there is a difference between an associate degree in pre-engineering and one in engineering technology. Students who enroll in a 2-year pre-engineering program may find it very difficult to find work as an engineering technician should they decide not to enter a 4-year engineering program because pre-engineering programs usually focus less on hands-on applications and more on academic preparatory work. Conversely, graduates of 2-year engineering technology programs may not receive credit for many of the courses they have taken if they choose to transfer to a 4-year engineering program.

Four-year colleges usually do not offer engineering technician training, but college courses in science, engineering, and mathematics are useful for obtaining a job as an engineering technician. Many 4-year colleges offer bachelor's degrees in engineering technology, but graduates of these programs are often hired to work as applied engineers, not technicians.

Area vocational-technical schools include postsecondary public institutions that serve local students and emphasize training needed by local employers. Most require a high school diploma or its equivalent for admission.

Other training in technical areas may be obtained in the Armed Forces. Many military technical training programs are highly regarded by employers. However, skills acquired in military programs often are narrowly focused, so they are not necessarily transferable to civilian industry, which often requires broader training. Therefore, some additional training may be needed, depending on the skills acquired and the kind of job.

Prospective engineering technicians should take as many high school science and math courses as possible to prepare for postsecondary programs in engineering technology. Most ABET-accredited 2-year associate programs require, at a minimum, college algebra and trigonometry, and one or two basic science courses. More math or science may be required depending on the area of specialty. The type of technical courses required varies depending on the area of specialty, as well. For example, prospective mechanical engineering technicians may take courses in fluid mechanics, thermodynamics, and mechanical design; electrical engineering technicians may take classes in electric circuits, microprocessors, and digital electronics; and those preparing to work in environmental engineering technology need courses in environmental regulations and safe handling of hazardous materials. Because many engineering technicians may become involved in design work, creativity is desirable. Good communication skills and the ability to work well with others is also important since they are often part of a team of engineers and other technicians.

Engineering technicians usually begin by performing routine duties under the close supervision of an experienced technician, engineer, or scientist. As they gain experience, they are given more difficult assignments with only general supervision. Some engineering technicians eventually become supervisors.

Job Outlook
Employment of engineering technicians is expected to increase more slowly than the average for all occupations through the year 2005. The output of technical products will continue to grow, and competitive pressures will force companies to improve and update manufacturing facilities and product designs more rapidly than in the past. However, the growing availability and use of advanced technologies, such as computer-aided design and drafting and computer simulation, is expected to curtail employment growth of engineering technicians.

Like engineers, employment of engineering technicians is influenced by local and national economic conditions. The employment outlook also varies with the area of specialization and industry. Some types of engineering technicians, such as civil engineering and aeronautical engineering technicians, experience greater cyclical fluctuations than others. Technicians whose jobs are defense related may experience fewer opportunities because of defense cutbacks.

In addition to growth, nearly as many job openings will be to replace technicians who retire or leave the labor force for other reasons.

Earnings
According to a survey of workplaces in 160 metropolitan areas, engineering technicians at the most junior level had median earnings of about $16,590 in 1993, with the middle half earning between $14,560 and $19,500 a year. Engineering technicians with more experience and the ability to work with little supervision had median earnings of about $34,530, and those in supervisory or senior level positions earned about $51,060.

In the Federal Government, engineering technicians could start at about $14,900, $16,700, or $18,700 in 1995, depending on their education and experience. Beginning salaries were slightly higher in selected areas of the country where the prevailing local pay level was higher. In 1995, the average annual salary for engineering technicians in supervisory, nonsupervisory, and management positions in the Federal Government was $38,850; for electronics technicians, $43,540; and for industrial engineering technicians, $41,080.

Related Occupations
Engineering technicians apply scientific and engineering principles usually acquired in postsecondary programs below the baccalaureate level. Similar occupations include science technicians, drafters, surveyors, broadcast technicians, and health technologists and technicians.

Sources of Additional Information
A number of engineering technology-related organizations provide information on engineering technician and technology careers. The Junior Engineering Technical Society (JETS), at 1420 King St., Suite 405, Alexandria, VA 22314-2715, serves as a central distribution point for information from most of these organizations. Enclose a self-addressed, business-size envelope with four first class stamps to obtain a sampling of materials available.

Library Technicians

(D.O.T. 100.367-018)

Nature of the Work
Library technicians help librarians acquire, prepare, and organize material, and assist users in finding materials and information. Technicians in small libraries handle a wide range of duties; those in large libraries usually specialize.

Depending on the employer, library technicians may have other titles, such as library technical assistants. Library technicians assist in the use of public catalogues, direct library users to standard references, organize and maintain periodicals, prepare volumes for binding, handle interlibrary loan requests, prepare invoices, perform routine cataloguing and coding of library materials, retrieve information from computer databases, and supervise other support staff.

Library technicians use computerized information systems to help users locate reference materials.

The widespread use of computerized information storage and retrieval systems has resulted in technicians handling more technical and user services, such as entering catalogue information into the library's computer, that were once performed by librarians. (See the statement on librarians elsewhere in the *Handbook*.) Technicians may assist with customizing databases. In addition, technicians may instruct patrons how to use computer systems to access data. The increased use of automation has cut down on the amount of clerical work performed by library technicians. Many libraries now offer self-service registration and circulation with computers, decreasing the time that library technicians spend manually recording and inputting records.

Some library technicians operate and maintain audiovisual equipment, such as projectors, tape recorders, and videocassette recorders, and assist library users with microfilm or microfiche readers. They may also design posters, bulletin boards, or displays.

Those in school libraries teach students to use the library and media center and encourage them to do so. They also help teachers obtain instructional materials and assist students with special assignments. Some work in special libraries maintained by government agencies, corporations, law firms, advertising agencies, museums, professional societies, medical centers, and research laboratories, where they conduct literature searches, compile bibliographies, and prepare abstracts, usually on subjects of particular interest to the organization.

Working Conditions

Technicians who work with users answer questions and provide assistance. Those who prepare library materials sit at desks or computer terminals for long periods and may develop headaches or eyestrain from working with video display terminals. Some duties like calculating circulation statistics can be repetitive and boring. Others, such as performing computer searches using local and regional library networks and cooperatives, can be interesting and challenging.

Library technicians in school libraries work regular school hours. Those in public libraries and college and university (academic) libraries may work weekends, evenings and some holidays. Library technicians in special libraries usually work normal business hours, although they are often called upon to work overtime.

Library technicians usually work under the supervision of a professional librarian, although they may work independently in certain situations.

Employment

Library technicians held about 75,000 jobs in 1994. Most worked in school, academic, or public libraries. Some worked in hospitals and religious organizations. The Federal Government, primarily the Department of Defense and the Library of Congress, and State and local governments also employed library technicians.

Training, Other Qualifications, and Advancement

Training requirements for library technicians vary widely, ranging from a high school diploma to specialized postsecondary training. Some libraries require that technicians have a bachelor's degree. Some employers hire individuals with work experience or other training; others train inexperienced workers on the job. Given the widespread use of automation in libraries, computer skills are needed for many jobs. Knowledge of databases, library automation systems, on-line library systems, on-line public access systems, and circulation systems is valuable.

Some 2-year colleges offer an associate of arts degree in library technology. Programs include both liberal arts and library-related study. Students learn about library and media organization and operation and how to order, process, catalogue, locate, and circulate library materials, and work with library automation. Libraries and associations offer continuing education courses to keep technicians abreast of new developments in the field.

Library technicians usually advance by assuming added responsibilities. For example, technicians may start at the circulation desk, checking books in and out. After gaining experience, they may be responsible for storing and verifying information. As they advance, they may become involved in budget and personnel matters in their department. Some library technicians advance to supervisory positions and are in charge of the day-to-day operation of their department.

Job Outlook

Employment of library technicians is expected to grow about as fast as the average for all occupations through the year 2005. Additional job openings will result from the need to replace library technicians who transfer to other fields or leave the labor force. Willingness to relocate enhances an aspiring library technician's job prospects.

The increasing use of library automation may spur job growth among library technicians. Computerized information systems have simplified certain tasks, such as descriptive cataloguing, which can now be handled by technicians instead of librarians. For instance, technicians can now easily retrieve information from a central database and store it in the library's own computer. Although budgetary constraints may dampen employment growth of library technicians in school, public, and college and university libraries, libraries may use technicians to perform some librarian duties in order to stretch shrinking budgets. Growth in the number of professional and other workers who use special libraries should result in relatively fast employment growth among library technicians in special libraries.

Earnings

Salaries for library technicians vary widely, depending on the type of library and geographic location. Salaries of library technicians in the Federal Government averaged $25,100 in 1995.

Related Occupations

Library technicians perform organizational and administrative duties. Workers in other occupations with similar duties include library clerks, information clerks, record clerks, medical record technicians, and title searchers. Library technicians also assist librarians. Other workers who assist professional workers include museum technicians, teacher aides, legal assistants, and engineering and science technicians.

Sources of Additional Information

Information about a career as a library technician and a directory of schools offering training programs in this field can be obtained from:
☞Council on Library/Media Technology, P.O. Box 951, Oxon Hill, MD 20750.

For information on training programs for library/media technical assistants, write to:
☞American Library Association, Office for Library Personnel Resources, 50 East Huron St., Chicago, IL 60611.

Information on schools receiving Federal financial assistance for library training is available from:
☞Office of Educational Research and Improvement, Library Programs, Library Development Staff, U.S. Department of Education, 555 New Jersey Ave. NW., Washington, DC 20208-5571.

Those interested in a position as a library technician in the Federal service should write to:
☞Office of Personnel Management, 1900 E St. NW., Washington, DC 20415.

Information concerning requirements and application procedures for positions in the Library of Congress may be obtained directly from:
☞Personnel Office, Library of Congress, Washington, DC 20540.

State library agencies can furnish information on requirements for technicians, and general information about career prospects in the State. Several of these agencies maintain job hotlines which report openings for library technicians.

State departments of education can furnish information on requirements and job opportunities for school library technicians.

Paralegals

(D.O.T. 119.267-022 and -026)

Nature of the Work

Not all legal work requires a law degree. Lawyers are often assisted in their work by paralegals or legal assistants. Paralegals perform many of the same tasks as lawyers, except for those tasks considered to be the practice of law.

Paralegals work under the direct supervision of lawyers. Although the lawyers assume responsibility for the legal work, they often delegate many of the tasks they perform to paralegals. Paralegals are prohibited from setting legal fees, giving legal advice, and presenting cases in court.

Paralegals generally do the background work for lawyers. To help prepare cases for trial, paralegals investigate the facts of cases ensuring all relevant information is uncovered. Paralegals may conduct legal research to identify the appropriate laws, judicial decisions, legal articles, and other materials that may be relevant to assigned cases. After organizing and analyzing all the information, paralegals may prepare written reports that attorneys use in determining how cases should be handled. Should attorneys decide to file lawsuits on behalf of clients, paralegals may help prepare the legal arguments, draft pleadings and motions to be filed with the court, obtain affidavits, and assist the attorneys during trials. Paralegals also keep files of all documents and correspondence important to cases.

Besides litigation, paralegals may also work in areas such as bankruptcy, corporate law, criminal law, employee benefits, patent and copyright law, and real estate. They help draft documents such as contracts, mortgages, separation agreements, and trust instruments. They may help prepare tax returns and plan estates. Some paralegals coordinate the activities of the other law office employees and keep the financial records for the office.

Paralegals who work for corporations help attorneys with such matters as employee contracts, shareholder agreements, stock option plans, and employee benefit plans. They may help prepare and file annual financial reports, maintain corporate minute books and reso-

lutions, and help secure loans for the corporation. Paralegals may also review government regulations to ensure the corporation operates within the law.

The duties of paralegals who work in government vary depending on the agency with whom they are employed. Generally, paralegals in government analyze legal material for internal use, maintain reference files, conduct research for attorneys, collect and analyze evidence for agency hearings, and prepare informative or explanatory material on the law, agency regulations, and agency policy for general use by the agency and the public.

Paralegals employed in community legal service projects help the poor, the aged, and others in need of legal assistance. They file forms, conduct research, and prepare documents. When authorized by law, they may represent clients at administrative hearings.

Some paralegals, usually those in small and medium-sized law firms, perform a variety of duties. They may research judicial decisions on improper police arrests or help prepare a mortgage contract. Paralegals must have a general knowledge of the law to perform these duties.

Some paralegals employed by large law firms, government agencies, and corporations, specialize in one aspect of the law, including real estate, estate planning, family law, labor law, litigation, and corporate law. Even within specialties, functions often are broken down further so paralegals may deal with a specific area of the specialty. For example, paralegals specializing in labor law may deal exclusively with employee benefits.

A growing number of paralegals use computers in their work. Computer software packages and on-line legal research are increasingly used to search legal literature stored in computer databases and on CD-ROM. In litigation that involves many supporting documents, paralegals may use computers to organize and index the material. They may also use computer software packages to perform tax computations and explore the consequences of possible tax strategies for clients.

Working Conditions

Paralegals do most of their work at desks in offices and law libraries. Occasionally, they travel to gather information and perform other duties.

Paralegals investigate the facts of cases to make sure all relevant information is uncovered.

Paralegals employed by corporations and government work a standard 40-hour week. Although most paralegals work year round, some are temporarily employed during busy times of the year, then released when the workload diminishes. Paralegals who work for law firms sometimes work very long hours and when they are under pressure to meet deadlines. Some law firms reward such loyalty with bonuses and additional time off.

Paralegals handle many routine assignments, particularly when they are inexperienced. Some find that these assignments offer little challenge and become frustrated with their duties. However, paralegals usually assume more responsible and varied tasks as they gain experience. Furthermore, as new laws and judicial interpretations emerge, paralegals are exposed to many new legal problems that make their work more interesting and challenging.

Employment

Paralegals held about 111,000 jobs in 1994. Private law firms employed the vast majority; most of the remainder worked for the various levels of government. Paralegals are found in nearly every Federal Government agency; the Departments of Justice, Treasury, Interior, and Health and Human Services, and the General Services Administration are the largest employers. State and local governments and publicly funded legal service projects employ paralegals as well. Banks, real estate development companies, and insurance companies also employ small numbers of paralegals. Some paralegals own their own businesses; as freelance legal assistants they contract their services to attorneys or corporate legal departments.

Training, Other Qualifications, and Advancement

There are several ways to enter the paralegal profession. Employers generally require formal paralegal training; several types of training programs are acceptable. Increasingly employers prefer to hire either graduates of 4-year paralegal programs, or persons with bachelor's degrees who have earned paralegal certificates through short-term programs after graduation. However, some employers prefer to train their paralegals on the job, promoting experienced legal secretaries or hiring college graduates with no legal experience. Other entrants have experience in a technical field that is useful to law firms, such as a background in tax preparation for tax and estate practice or nursing or health administration for personal injury practice.

Over 800 formal paralegal training programs are offered by 4-year colleges and universities, law schools, community and junior colleges, business schools, and proprietary schools. In 1995, about 200 programs had been approved by the American Bar Association (ABA). Although this approval is neither required nor sought by many programs, graduation from an ABA-approved program can enhance one's employment opportunities. The requirements for admission to formal training programs vary widely. Some require some college courses or a bachelor's degree. Others accept high school graduates or those with legal experience. A few schools require standardized tests and personal interviews.

Some paralegal programs are completed in 2 years, while others take as long as 4 years and award a bachelor's degree upon completion. Certificate programs take only a few months to complete, but require a bachelor's degree for admission. Programs typically include general courses on the law and legal research techniques, in addition to courses covering specialized areas of the law, such as real estate, estate planning and probate, litigation, family law, contracts, and criminal law. Many employers prefer applicants with training in a specialized area of the law. Programs increasingly include courses introducing students to the legal applications of computers. Many paralegal training programs include an internship in which students gain practical experience by working for several months in a law office, corporate legal department, or government agency. Experience gained in internships is an asset when seeking a job after graduation. Depending on the program, graduates may receive a certificate, an associate degree, or a bachelor's degree.

The quality of paralegal training programs varies; the better programs generally emphasize job placement. Prospective students should examine the experiences of recent graduates of programs in which they are considering enrolling.

Paralegals need not be certified, but the National Association of Legal Assistants has established standards for voluntary certification which require various combinations of education and experience. Paralegals who meet these standards are eligible to take a 2-day examination given each year at several regional testing centers by the Certifying Board of Legal Assistants of the National Association of Legal Assistants. Those who pass this examination may use the designation Certified Legal Assistant (CLA). This designation is a sign of competence in the field and may enhance employment and advancement opportunities. The Paralegal Advanced Competency Exam, administered through the National Federation of Paralegal Associations to qualified paralegals, offers a similar level of professional recognition.

Paralegals must be able to handle legal problems logically and communicate, both orally and in writing, their findings and opinions to their supervising attorney. They must understand legal terminology and have good research and investigative skills. Familiarity with the operation and applications of computers in legal research and litigation support is increasingly important. Paralegals must always stay abreast of new developments in the law that affect their area of practice.

Because paralegals often deal with the public, they must be courteous and uphold the high ethical standards of the legal profession. A few States and the National Federation of Paralegal Associations have established ethical guidelines which paralegals must follow.

Experienced paralegals usually are given progressively more responsibilities and less supervision. In large law firms, corporate legal departments, and government agencies, experienced paralegals may supervise other paralegals and clerical staff and delegate work assigned by the attorneys. Advancement opportunities include promotion to managerial and other law-related positions within the firm or corporate legal department. However, some paralegals find it easier to move to another law firm when seeking increased responsibility or advancement.

Job Outlook

Employment of paralegals is expected to grow much faster than the average for all occupations through the year 2005. Job opportunities are expected to expand as more employers become aware that paralegals are able to do many legal tasks for lower salaries than lawyers. Both law firms and other employers with legal staffs should continue to emphasize hiring paralegals so that the cost, availability, and efficiency of legal services can be improved.

New jobs created by rapid employment growth will create most of the job openings for paralegals in the future. Other job openings will arise as people leave the occupation. Although the number of job openings for paralegals is expected to increase significantly through the year 2005, so will the number of people pursuing this career. Thus, keen competition for jobs should continue as the growing number of graduates from paralegal education programs keeps pace with employment growth. Still, job prospects are expected to be favorable for persons with bachelor's degrees who graduate from well regarded paralegal training programs.

Private law firms will continue to be the largest employers of paralegals as a growing population demands additional legal services. The growth of prepaid legal plans should also contribute to the demand for the services of law firms. A growing array of other organizations, such as corporate legal departments, insurance companies, real estate and title insurance firms, and banks will also hire paralegals.

Job opportunities for paralegals will expand even in the public sector. Community legal service programs—which provide assistance to the poor, aged, minorities, and middle-income families—

operate on limited budgets. They will seek to employ additional paralegals in order to minimize expenses and serve the most people. Federal, State, and local government agencies, consumer organizations, and the courts should continue to hire paralegals in increasing numbers.

To a limited extent, paralegal jobs are affected by the business cycle. During recessions, demand declines for some discretionary legal services, such as planning estates, drafting wills, and handling real estate transactions. Corporations are less inclined to initiate litigation when falling sales and profits lead to fiscal belt tightening. As a result, full-time paralegals employed in offices adversely affected by a recession may be laid off or have their work hours reduced. On the other hand, during recessions, corporations and individuals are more likely to face other legal problems, such as bankruptcies, foreclosures, and divorces, that require legal assistance. Furthermore, the continuous emergence of new laws and judicial interpretations of existing ones creates new business for lawyers and paralegals without regard to the business cycle.

Earnings

Earnings of paralegals vary greatly. Salaries depend on the education, training, and experience the paralegal brings to the job, the type and size of employer, and the geographic location of the job. Generally, paralegals who work for large law firms or in large metropolitan areas earn more than those who work for smaller firms or in less populated regions.

Paralegals had an average annual salary of about $31,700 in 1993, according to a compensation survey by Kenneth Leventhal & Company for the National Federation of Paralegal Associations. Starting salaries of entry-level paralegals ranged from a low of $14,000 to a high of $32,000 an year, according to the same survey. In addition to a salary, many paralegals received an annual bonus, which averaged more than $1,600 in 1993. Employers of the majority of paralegals provided life and health insurance benefits and contributed to a retirement plan on their behalf.

Paralegal Specialists hired by the Federal Government in 1994 started at about $20,000 or $25,200 a year, depending on their training and experience. The average annual salary of paralegals who worked for the Federal Government in 1995 was about $39,800.

Related Occupations

Several other occupations also call for a specialized understanding of the law and the legal system but do not require the extensive training of a lawyer. Some of these are abstractors, claim examiners, compliance and enforcement inspectors, occupational safety and health workers, patent agents, police officers, and title examiners.

Sources of Additional Information

General information on a career as a paralegal and the *Guide for Legal Assistant Education Programs* by the American Bar Association may be purchased for $7.50 from:
☛Standing Committee on Legal Assistants, American Bar Association, 750 North Lake Shore Dr., Chicago, IL 60611.

For information on certification of paralegals, schools that offer training programs in a specific State, and standards and guidelines for paralegals, contact:
☛National Association of Legal Assistants, Inc., 1516 South Boston St., Suite 200, Tulsa, OK 74119.

Information on a career as a paralegal, schools that offer training programs, the Paralegal Advanced Competency Exam, and local paralegal associations can be obtained from:
☛National Federation of Paralegal Associations, P.O. Box 33108, Kansas City, MO 64114; or on the internet http://www.paralegals.org.

Information on paralegal training programs, including the pamphlet "How to Choose a Paralegal Education Program" may be obtained from:
☛American Association for Paralegal Education, P.O. Box 40244, Overland Park, KS 66204; (913) 381-4458.

Science Technicians

(List of D.O.T. codes available on request. See p. 478.)

Nature of the Work

Science technicians use the principles and theories of science and mathematics to solve problems in research and development and to help invent and improve products. Their jobs are more practically oriented than those of scientists. Technicians set up, operate, and maintain laboratory instruments, monitor experiments, make observations, calculate and record results, and often develop conclusions. Those who work in production test products for proper proportions of ingredients or for strength and durability.

In recent years, as laboratory instrumentation and procedures have become more complex, the role of science technicians in research and development has expanded. In addition to performing routine tasks under the direction of scientists, many technicians also develop and adapt laboratory procedures to achieve the best results, interpret data, and devise solutions to problems. The increasing use of robotics to perform many routine tasks formerly done by technicians has freed technicians to operate other, more sophisticated laboratory equipment. Science technicians make extensive use of computers, computer-interfaced equipment, robotics, and high-technology industrial applications such as biological engineering.

Agricultural technicians work with agricultural scientists in food and fiber research, production, and processing. Some conduct tests and experiments to improve the yield and quality of crops or to increase the resistance of plants and animals to disease, insects, or other hazards. Other agricultural technicians do animal breeding and nutrition work.

Biological technicians work with biologists, studying living organisms. They may assist scientists who conduct medical research, helping to find a cure for cancer or AIDS, for example. Those who work in pharmaceutical companies help develop and manufacture medicinal and pharmaceutical preparations. Biological technicians also analyze organic substances such as blood, food, and drugs, and some examine evidence in criminal investigations. Biological technicians working in biotechnology labs use the knowledge and techniques gained from basic research by scientists, including gene splicing and recombinant DNA, and apply these techniques in product development.

Chemical technicians work with chemists and chemical engineers, developing and using chemicals and related products and equipment. Most do research and development, testing, or other laboratory work. For example, they might test packaging for design, materials, and environmental acceptability; assemble and operate new equipment to develop new products; monitor product quality; or develop new production techniques. Some chemical technicians collect and analyze samples of air and water to monitor pollution levels. Those who focus on basic research might produce compounds through complex organic synthesis.

Nuclear technicians operate nuclear test and research equipment, monitor radiation, and assist nuclear engineers and physicists in research. Some also operate remote control equipment to manipulate radioactive materials or materials to be exposed to radioactivity.

Petroleum technicians measure and record physical and geologic conditions in oil or gas wells using instruments lowered into wells or by analysis of the mud from wells. In oil and gas exploration, they collect and examine geological data or test geological samples to determine petroleum and mineral content. Some petroleum technicians, called scouts, collect information about oil and gas well drilling operations, geological and geophysical prospecting, and land or lease contracts.

Other science technicians collect weather information or assist oceanographers.

Working Conditions

Science technicians work under a wide variety of conditions. Most work indoors, usually in laboratories, and have regular hours. Some occasionally work irregular hours to monitor experiments that can't be completed during regular working hours. Some, such as agricultural and petroleum technicians, perform much of their work outdoors, sometimes in remote locations, and some may be exposed to hazardous conditions. Chemical technicians sometimes work with toxic chemicals or radioactive isotopes; nuclear technicians may be exposed to radiation; and biological technicians sometimes work with disease-causing organisms or radioactive agents. However, there is little risk if proper safety procedures are followed.

Employment

Science technicians held about 231,000 jobs in 1994. Over one-third worked in manufacturing, mostly in the chemical industry, but also in the food processing industry. About 15 percent worked in education services and another 15 percent worked in research and testing services.

In 1994, the Federal Government employed about 17,500 science technicians, mostly in the Departments of Defense, Agriculture, and Interior.

A science technician prepares slides of diseased tissue for study.

Training, Other Qualifications, and Advancement

There are several ways to qualify for a job as a science technician. Most employers prefer applicants who have at least 2 years of specialized training. Many junior and community colleges offer associate degrees in a specific technology or a more general education in science and mathematics. A number of 2-year associate degree programs are designed to provide easy transfer to a 4-year college or university if desired. Technical institutes generally offer technician training but provide less theory and general education than junior or community colleges. The length of programs at technical institutes varies, although 2-year associate degree programs are common. Some of these schools offer cooperative-education programs, allowing students the opportunity to work at a local company while attending classes in alternate terms. Many science technicians have a bachelor's degree in chemistry or biology, or have at least had several science and math courses in 4-year colleges.

Two-year formal training programs that combine the teaching of scientific principles and theory with practical hands-on application in a laboratory setting with up-to-date equipment provide very good preparation for prospective science technicians. Graduates of 4-year bachelor's degree programs in science who have completed internships or held summer jobs in laboratories are also well-qualified for science technician positions.

Persons interested in careers as science technicians should take as many high school science and math courses as possible. Science courses taken beyond high school, in an associate's or bachelor's program, should be laboratory oriented, with an emphasis on "bench" skills. Because computers and computer-interfaced equipment are often used in research and development laboratories, technicians should have strong computer skills. Communication skills are important, since technicians are often asked to report their finding both verbally and in writing. Technicians should also be able to work well with others since they often are part of a team.

Technicians usually begin work as trainees in routine positions under the direct supervision of a scientist or experienced technician. Job candidates whose training or educational background encompasses extensive hands-on experience with a variety of laboratory equipment, including computers and related equipment, usually require a much shorter period of on-the-job training. As they gain experience, they take on more responsibility and carry out assignments under only general supervision. Some eventually become supervisors.

Job Outlook

Employment of science technicians is expected to increase about as fast as the average for all occupations through the year 2005. Continued growth of scientific and medical research and development and the production of technical products should spur demand for all science technicians. The growing number of agricultural and medicinal products developed using biotechnology techniques will increase the need for biological technicians in particular. Employment growth will also be fueled by the demand for science technicians to work in environmental research and testing. Technicians will be needed to help regulate waste products, collect air and water samples to measure levels of pollutants, and clean up contaminated sites. However, growth of job openings will be moderated somewhat by an expected slowdown in overall employment growth in the chemical industry, where many chemical technicians are employed.

Job opportunities are expected to be very good for graduates of science technician training programs who are well-trained on the equipment currently in use in industrial and government laboratories. As the instrumentation and techniques used in industrial research and development laboratories becomes more complex, employers are seeking well trained individuals with highly developed technical and communication skills.

In addition to the projected growth, nearly as many job openings will arise from the need to replace technicians who retire or leave the labor force for other reasons.

Earnings

Median annual earnings of science technicians were about $26,900 in 1994; the middle 50 percent earned between $19,600 and $37,300. Ten percent earned less than $14,700, and 10 percent earned over $46,800. At all income levels, chemical technicians earned significantly more than biological technicians.

In the Federal Government in 1995, science technicians could start at $14,900, $16,700, or $18,700, depending on their education and experience. Beginning salaries were slightly higher in selected areas of the country where the prevailing local pay level was higher. The average annual salary for biological science technicians in nonsupervisory, supervisory, and managerial positions employed by the Federal Government in 1995 was $23,790; for mathematical technicians, $26,640; for physical science technicians, $32,490; for geodetic technicians, $40,860; for hydrologic technicians, $28,850; and for meteorologic technicians, $36,750.

Related Occupations

Other technicians who apply scientific principles at a level usually taught in 2-year associate degree programs include engineering technicians, broadcast technicians, drafters, and health technologists and technicians. Some of the work of agricultural and biological technicians is related to that in agriculture and forestry occupations.

Sources of Additional Information

For information about a career as a chemical technician, contact:
☞American Chemical Society, Education Division, Career Publications, 1155 16th St. NW., Washington, DC 20036.

Marketing and Sales Occupations

Cashiers

(D.O.T. 209.567-014; 211.362-010, .367, .462, .467, .482-010; 249.467; and 294.567)

Nature of the Work

Supermarkets, department stores, gasoline service stations, movie theaters, restaurants, and many other businesses employ cashiers to register the sale of their merchandise. Most cashiers total bills, receive money, make change, fill out charge forms, and give receipts. Bank tellers, who perform similar duties but work in financial institutions, are discussed elsewhere in the *Handbook*.

Although specific job duties vary by employer, cashiers are usually assigned to a register and given a drawer containing a "bank" of money at the beginning of their shifts. They must count their bank to ensure that it contains the correct amount of money and that there is an adequate supply of change. At the end of their shift, they once again count the drawers' contents and compare the totals with sales data. An occasional shortage of small amounts may be overlooked, but repeated shortages are grounds for dismissal in many establishments.

In addition to counting the contents of their drawer at the end of their shift, cashiers usually separate charge forms, return slips, coupons, and any other noncash items.

Cashiers also handle returns and exchanges. They must ensure that the merchandise is in good condition and determine where and when it was purchased and the type of payment used.

Cashiers traditionally have rung up customers' purchases using a cash register—manually entering the price of each product the consumer was buying. However, most establishments are now using more sophisticated equipment, such as scanners and computers. In stores with scanners, the cashier passes the product's Universal Product Code over the scanning device, which transmits the code number to a computer. The computer identifies the item and its price. In other establishments, cashiers manually enter a code into a computer, and a description of the item and its price appear on the screen.

After entering all items and subtracting the value of any coupons or special discounts, cashiers total the bill and take payment. Depending on the type of establishment, payment may be by cash, check, charge, or increasingly, debit cards. Cashiers must know the store's policies and procedures for accepting each type of payment. For checks and charges, they may have to request additional identification from the customer or call in for an authorization. When the sale is complete, cashiers issue a receipt to the customer and return the appropriate change. They may also wrap or bag the purchase.

Depending on the type of establishment, cashiers may have other duties as well. In many supermarkets, for example, they weigh produce and bulk food as well as return unwanted items to the shelves. In convenience stores, cashiers may be required to know how to use a variety of machines other than cash registers, and how to furnish money orders. Operating ticket-dispensing machines and answering questions are common duties for cashiers who work at movie theaters and ticket agencies. Counter and rental clerks, who perform many similar duties, are discussed elsewhere in the *Handbook*.

Working Conditions

More than one-half of all cashiers are on part-time schedules. Hours of work often vary depending on the needs of the employer. Generally, cashiers are expected to work weekends, evenings, and holidays to accommodate customers' needs. However, because of this, many employers offer flexible schedules. For example, full-time workers who work on weekends may receive time off during the week. Because the holiday season is the busiest time for most retailers, many employers restrict the use of vacation time from Thanksgiving through the beginning of January.

Most cashiers work indoors, usually standing in booths or behind counters. In addition, they are often unable to leave their workstations without supervisory approval since they are responsible for large sums of money. The work of cashiers can be very repetitious but improvements in machine design are being made to combat problems caused by repetitive motion.

Employment

Cashiers held about 3,005,000 jobs in 1994. Although employed in nearly every industry, more than one-third of all jobs were in supermarkets and other food stores. Department stores, gasoline service stations, drug stores, and other retail establishments also employed large numbers of these workers. Because cashiers are needed in businesses and organizations of all types and sizes, job opportunities are found throughout the country.

Training, Other Qualifications, and Advancement

Cashier jobs tend to be entry level positions requiring little or no previous work experience. Although there are no specific educational requirements, employers filling full-time jobs often prefer applicants with a high school diploma.

Nearly all cashiers are trained on the job. In small firms, beginners are often trained by an experienced worker. The first day is usually spent observing the operation and becoming familiar with the store's equipment, policies, and procedures. After this, trainees are assigned to a register—frequently under the supervision of a more experienced worker. In larger firms, before being placed at a cash register, trainees first spend several days in classes. Topics typically covered include a description of the industry and the company, instruction on the store's policies, procedures, and equipment operation, and security.

Nearly 9 out of 10 cashiers work in retail trade.

Training for experienced workers is not common except when new equipment is introduced or when procedures change. In these cases, training is given on the job by the employer or a representative of the equipment manufacturer.

Persons who want to become cashiers should be able to do repetitious work accurately. They also need basic arithmetic skills, good manual dexterity and, because they deal constantly with the public, cashiers should be neat in appearance and be able to deal tactfully and pleasantly with customers. In addition, some firms seek persons who have operated specialized equipment or who have business experience, such as typing, selling, or handling money.

Advancement opportunities for cashiers vary. For those working part time, promotion may be to a full-time position. Others advance to head cashier or cash office clerk. In addition, the job offers a good opportunity to learn an employer's business and serves as a stepping-stone to a more responsible position.

Job Outlook

Employment of cashiers is expected to increase about as fast as the average for all occupations through the year 2005 due to expanding demand for goods and services by a growing population. Although growth will account for numerous openings, most jobs will result from the need to replace experienced workers who transfer to other occupations or leave the labor force. Workers under the age of 25 traditionally have filled many of the openings in this occupation. Recently, however, more openings are being filled by nontraditional workers, such as elderly and disabled persons. As in the past, replacement needs will create a significant number of job openings, for the occupation is large and turnover is much higher than average. Opportunities for part-time work are expected to continue to be excellent.

Earnings

Cashiers have earnings ranging from the minimum wage to several times that amount. Wages tend to be higher in areas where there is intense competition for workers. In establishments covered by Federal law, those beginning at the minimum wage earned $4.25 an hour in 1994. In some States, the minimum wage in many establishments is governed by State law, and where State minimums are higher, the establishment must pay at least that amount.

In 1994, median weekly earnings for full-time cashiers were $228. The middle 50 percent earned between $188 and $303; 10 percent earned below $153; and 10 percent earned above $421.

Benefits for full-time cashiers tend to be better than for those working part time. Cashiers often receive health and life insurance and paid vacations. In addition, those working in retail establishments often receive discounts on purchases and those in restaurants may receive free or low-cost meals.

Related Occupations

Cashiers receive payment for the purchase of goods and services. Other workers with similar duties include food counter clerks, bank tellers, counter and rental clerks, postal service clerks, and sales clerks.

Sources of Additional Information

For information about employment opportunities as a cashier, contact:

☛National Association of Convenience Stores, 1605 King St., Alexandria, VA 22314-2792.

☛Service Station Dealers of America, 9420 Annapolis Rd., Suite 307, Lanham, MD 20706.

☛United Food and Commercial Workers Union, 1775 K St. NW., Washington, DC 20006-1502.

Counter and Rental Clerks

(D.O.T. 216.482-030; 249.362-010; .366-010; 295.357-010, -014 and -018; .367-010, -014, and -026; .467; 299.367-018; 369.367-010 and -014; . 467-010; .477; and .677-010)

Nature of the Work

Whether renting video tapes, dropping off clothes to be dry-cleaned, or getting appliances serviced, we rely on counter and rental clerks to handle these transactions efficiently. Although specific duties vary by establishment, counter and rental clerks are responsible for answering questions involving product availability, cost, and rental provisions. They may give other types of advice as well. Counter and rental clerks also take orders, calculate fees, receive payments, and accept returns. (Cashiers and retail sales workers, occupations with similar duties, are discussed elsewhere in the *Handbook*.)

Regardless of where they work, counter and rental clerks must be knowledgeable about the company's services, policies, and procedures. Depending on the type of establishment, counter and rental clerks use their special knowledge to give advice on a wide variety of products and services, which may range from hydraulic tools to shoe repair. For example, in the car rental industry, they inform customers about the features of the different types of automobiles available and their daily and weekly rental costs, ensure that customers meet age or other requirements, and indicate when and in what condition the car must be returned. In dry-cleaning establishments, counter clerks inform customers when items will be ready.

When taking orders counter and rental clerks use various types of equipment. In some establishments, they write out tickets and order forms. However, computers and bar code scanners are quickly becoming the norm. Most computer systems are user friendly and usually require very little data entry. Scanners "read" the product code and display a description of the item on a computer screen. Clerks must insure, however, that the data on the screen matches the actual product.

Working Conditions

Because firms employing counter and rental clerks generally operate at the convenience of their customers, these workers often work night and weekend hours. However, because of this many employers offer flexible schedules. Some counter and rental clerks work a 40-hour week but over one-half are on part-time schedules—usually during rush periods such as weekends, evenings, and holidays.

Counter and rental clerks must be aware of the goods and services their company offers.

Working conditions are usually pleasant; most stores and service establishments are clean, well-lighted, and temperature controlled. However, clerks are on their feet much of the time and may be confined behind a small counter area. This job requires constant interaction with the public and can be taxing—especially during busy periods.

Employment

Counter and rental clerks held over 341,000 jobs in 1994. About 1 of every 4 clerks worked for a video tape rental establishment. Other large employers included laundries or dry cleaners, automobile or truck rental firms, equipment rental firms, and miscellaneous entertainment and recreation establishments.

Counter and rental clerks are employed throughout the country but are concentrated in metropolitan areas where personal services and renting and leasing services are in greater demand.

Training, Other Qualifications, and Advancement

Counter and rental clerk jobs are primarily entry level and require little or no experience and little formal education. However, many employers prefer those with at least a high school diploma for these positions.

In most companies, counter and rental clerks are trained on the job, sometimes through the use of video tapes, brochures, and pamphlets. Clerks usually learn how to operate the equipment and become familiar with the establishment's policies and procedures under the observation of a more experienced worker. However, some employers have formal classroom training programs lasting from a few hours to a few weeks. Topics covered in this training usually include a description of the industry, the company and its policies and procedures, equipment operation, sales techniques, and customer service. Counter and rental clerks must also become familiar with the different products and services rented or provided by their company in order to give customers the best possible service.

Persons who want to become counter and rental clerks should enjoy working with people and have the ability to deal tactfully with difficult customers. In addition, good oral and written communication skills are essential.

Advancement opportunities depend on the size and type of company. However, jobs as counter and rental clerks offer good opportunities for workers to learn about their company's products and business practices. These jobs can be steppingstones to more responsible positions, because it is common in many establishments to promote counter and rental clerks into assistant manager positions.

In certain industries, such as equipment repair, counter and rental jobs may be an additional or alternate source of income for workers who are unemployed or entering semi-retirement. For example, a retired mechanic could prove invaluable at a tool rental center because of his or her relevant knowledge.

Job Outlook

Employment in this occupation is expected to increase faster than the average for all occupations through the year 2005 due to anticipated employment growth in the industries where they are concentrated—video tape rental, laundries and dry cleaners, automotive rentals, amusement and recreation services, and equipment rental and leasing. Despite this growth, however, most job openings will arise from the need to replace experienced workers who transfer to other occupations or leave the labor force. Part-time employment opportunities are expected to be plentiful.

Earnings

Counter and rental clerks typically start at the minimum wage, which, in establishments covered by Federal law, was $4.25 an hour in 1994. In areas where there is intense competition for workers, however, wages are often higher. In addition to their wages, some counter and rental clerks receive commissions based on the number of contracts they complete or services they sell.

Retail counter clerks earned a median weekly income of $266 in 1994. The middle 50 percent earned between $195 and $391 a week. The bottom 10 percent earned less than $157; the top 10 percent earned more than $586.

Full-time workers typically receive health and life insurance and paid vacation and sick leave. Benefits for counter and rental clerks who work part time tend to be significantly less than for those who work full time. Many companies offer discounts to both full- and part-time employees on the services they provide.

Related Occupations

Counter and rental clerks take orders and receive payment for services rendered. Other workers with similar duties include cashiers, retail sales workers, food counter clerks, postal service clerks, and bank tellers.

Sources of Additional Information

For more information about employment opportunities in the equipment rental industry contact:

☛American Rental Association, 1900 19th St., Moline, IL 61625.

Insurance Agents and Brokers

(D.O.T. 169.167-050, 239.267-010, and 250.257-010)

Nature of the Work

Most people have their first contact with an insurance company through an insurance agent or broker. These professionals sell insurance policies to individuals and businesses to provide protection against loss. Insurance agents and brokers help individuals, families, and businesses select the policy that provides the best insurance protection for their lives and health, as well as for their automobiles, jewelry, personal valuables, furniture, household items, businesses, and other properties. Agents and brokers prepare reports, maintain records, and, in the event of a loss, help policyholders settle insurance claims. Specialists in group policies may help an employer provide employees the opportunity to buy insurance through payroll deductions. *Insurance agents* may work for one insurance company or as "independent agents" selling for several companies. *Insurance brokers* do not sell for a particular company, but place insurance policies for their clients with the company that offers the best rate and coverage.

Insurance agents sell one or more of several types of insurance: Life, property and casualty, health, disability, and long-term care. Life insurance agents specialize in selling policies that pay beneficiaries when a policyholder dies. Depending on the policyholder's circumstances, a whole-life policy can be designed to provide retirement income, funds for the education of children, or other benefits. Life insurance agents and brokers are sometimes referred to as *life underwriters*. (See the section on underwriters elsewhere in the *Handbook*.)

Property and casualty insurance agents and brokers sell policies that protect individuals and businesses from financial loss as a result of automobile accidents, fire or theft, tornados and storms, and other events that can damage property. For businesses, property and casualty insurance can also cover injured workers' compensation, product liability claims, or medical malpractice payments. Many life and property and casualty insurance agents also sell health insurance policies covering the costs of hospital and medical care, or loss of income due to illness or injury.

An increasing number of insurance agents and brokers offer comprehensive financial planning services to their clients, such as retirement planning counseling. As a result, many insurance agents and brokers are also licensed to sell mutual funds, annuities, and

An increasing number of agents and brokers offer comprehensive financial planning services to their clients.

other securities. (See the section on securities and financial services sales representatives elsewhere in the *Handbook*.)

Since insurance sales agents obtain many new accounts through referrals, it is important that agents maintain regular contact with their clients to ensure their financial needs are being met as personal and business needs change. Developing a satisfied clientele who will recommend an agent's services to other potential customers is a key to success in this field.

Working Conditions

Most insurance agents and brokers work in small offices, contacting clients and providing insurance policy information. However, most of their time is spent outside their offices, traveling locally to meet with clients and close sales. They generally arrange their own hours of work, and often schedule evening and weekend appointments for the convenience of clients. Although the majority of agents and brokers work no more than 40 hours a week, some work as much as 60 hours a week or even longer.

Employment

Insurance agents and brokers held about 418,000 jobs in 1994. About 30 percent of all agents and brokers were self-employed. While most insurance agents specialize in life insurance, a growing number of "multiline agents" offer life, property/casualty, and health and disability policies. The following tabulation shows the percent distribution of wage and salary jobs by industry.

Total	100
Insurance agents, brokers, and service	42
Life insurance carriers	38
Fire, marine, and casualty insurance carriers	12
Medical service and health insurance carriers	4
Pension funds and miscellaneous insurance carriers	1
Other industries	3

Agents and brokers are employed in cities and towns throughout the country, but most work in or near large population centers. Some insurance agents and brokers are employed in the headquarters of insurance companies, but the majority work out of local company offices or independent agencies.

Training, Other Qualifications, and Advancement

For jobs selling insurance, most companies and independent agencies prefer to hire college graduates—particularly those who have majored in business or economics. Some hire high school graduates with potential or proven sales ability or who have been successful in

other types of work. In fact, most entrants to agent and broker jobs transfer from other occupations. As a result, agents and brokers tend to be older than the entrants of many other occupations.

College training may help agents or brokers grasp the technical aspects of insurance policies and the fundamentals and procedures of selling insurance. Many colleges and universities offer courses in insurance, and some schools offer a bachelor's degree in insurance. College courses in finance, mathematics, accounting, economics, business law, government, and business administration enable insurance agents or brokers to understand how social, marketing, and economic conditions relate to the insurance industry. It is important for insurance agents and brokers to keep up to date with issues concerning clients. Changes in tax laws, government benefit programs, and other State and Federal regulations can affect the insurance needs of clients and how agents conduct business. Courses in psychology, sociology, and public speaking can prove useful in improving sales techniques. In addition, some basic familiarity with computers and popular software packages is very important. The use of computers to provide instantaneous information on a wide variety of financial products has greatly improved agents' and brokers' efficiency and enabled them to devote more time to clients.

Insurance agents and brokers must obtain a license in the States where they plan to sell insurance. By law in most States, licenses are issued only to applicants who complete specified courses and then pass written examinations covering insurance fundamentals and the State insurance laws. Agents and brokers who plan to sell mutual funds and other securities must also obtain a separate securities license. New agents usually receive training in a classroom setting at pre-licensing schools conducted by state insurance agents associations or at the home offices of the insurance company. Often they attend company-sponsored classes to prepare for examinations. Others study on their own and accompany experienced agents when they call on prospective clients.

As the diversity of financial products sold by insurance agents and brokers increases, employers are placing greater emphasis on continuing professional education. Agents and brokers can hone their practical selling skills and broaden their knowledge of insurance and other financial services and planning by taking courses at colleges and universities and attending institutes, conferences, and seminars sponsored by insurance organizations. In 1995, 43 States had mandatory continuing education requirements focusing on insurance laws, consumer protection, and the technical details of various insurance policies.

A number of organizations offer professional designation programs which certify expertise in specialties such as life, health, or property and casualty insurance or financial consulting. Although voluntary, professional designation assures clients and employers that an agent has a thorough understanding of the relevant specialty. Many professional societies now require agents to commit to continuing education in order to retain the designation.

Insurance agents and brokers should be enthusiastic, outgoing, self-confident, disciplined, hard working, and able to communicate effectively. They should be able to inspire customer confidence. Some companies give personality tests to prospective employees because personality attributes are important in sales work. Because they usually work without supervision, agents and brokers must be able to plan their time well and have the initiative to locate new clients.

An insurance agent who shows sales ability and leadership may become a sales manager in a local office. A few advance to agency superintendent or executive positions. However, many who have built up a good clientele prefer to remain in sales work. Some, particularly in the property/casualty field, establish their own independent agencies or brokerage firms.

Job Outlook

Employment of insurance agents and brokers is expected to grow more slowly than the average for all occupations through the year

2005. Most job openings are expected to result from the need to replace agents and brokers who leave the occupation. Many beginners find it difficult to establish a sufficiently large clientele in this highly competitive business; consequently, many eventually leave for other jobs. Opportunities should be best for ambitious people who enjoy sales work and who develop expertise in a wide range of insurance and financial services.

Future demand for agents and brokers depends on the volume of sales of insurance and other financial products. The growing number of working women should increase insurance sales. Rising incomes as well as a concern for financial security should stimulate sales of mutual funds, variable annuities, and other financial products and services. Growing demand for long-term health care and pension benefits for retirees—an increasing proportion of the population—should spur insurance sales. Sales of property and casualty insurance should rise as more people seek coverage not only for their homes, cars, and valuables, but also for expensive, advanced technology products such as home computers. As new businesses emerge and existing firms expand coverage, sales of commercial insurance should increase. In addition, complex types of commercial coverage such as product liability, workers' compensation, employee benefits, and pollution liability insurance are increasingly in demand.

Employment of agents and brokers will not keep pace with the rising level of insurance sales. Using computers, agents can access an abundance of information on potential clients, allowing them to save time and money by carefully crafting individually tailored plans. Consequently, agents will be able to handle a greater volume of sales. Many companies and agencies are diversifying their marketing techniques to include some direct mail or telephone sales, as well as other methods. These methods reduce the time agents must spend developing sales leads, allowing them to concentrate on following up on leads. In some cases, clients can purchase policies without a visit from an agent. Also, customer service representatives are increasingly assuming some sales functions, such as expanding accounts, and, occasionally, generating new accounts. Trends toward multiline agents, self-insurance, and group policies will also contribute to employment rising slower than the volume of insurance sales. In addition, large firms may increasingly hire risk managers to analyze their insurance needs and select the best policies.

Most individuals and businesses consider insurance a necessity, regardless of economic conditions. Therefore, agents are not likely to face unemployment because of a recession.

Earnings

The median annual earnings of salaried insurance sales workers was $31,620 in 1994. The middle 50 percent earned between $22,050 and $46,380 a year. The lowest 10 percent earned $15,500 or less, while the top 10 percent earned over $69,990.

Most independent agents are paid on a commission only basis, whereas sales workers who are employees of an agency may be paid in one of three ways: Salary only, salary plus commission, or salary plus bonus. Commissions, however, are the most common form of compensation, especially for experienced agents. The amount of the commission depends on the type and amount of insurance sold, and whether the transaction is a new policy or a renewal. Bonuses are usually awarded when agents meet their sales goals or when an agency's profit goals are met. Some agents involved with financial planning receive an hourly fee for their services rather than a commission.

Company-paid benefits to sales agents generally include continuing education, paid licensing training, group insurance plans, and office space and support services. Some may pay for automobile and transportation expenses, attendence at conventions and meetings, promotion and marketing expenses, and retirement plans. Independent agents working for insurance agencies receive fewer benefits, but their commissions may be higher to help them pay for promotion and marketing expenses. They are typically responsible for their own travel and automobile expenses, life insurance, and retirement plans.

In addition, all agents are legally responsible for any mistakes that they make, and independent agents must purchase their own insurance to cover damages from their errors and omissions.

Related Occupations

Other workers who sell financial products or services include real estate agents and brokers, securities and financial services sales representatives, financial advisors, estate planning specialists, and manufacturers' sales workers.

Sources of Additional Information

General occupational information about insurance agents and brokers is available from the home office of many life and casualty insurance companies. Information on State licensing requirements may be obtained from the department of insurance at any State capital.

Information about a career as a life insurance agent also is available from:

☛National Association of Life Underwriters, 1922 F St. NW., Washington, DC 20006.

For information about insurance sales careers in independent agencies and brokerages, contact:

☛Independent Insurance Agents of America, 127 S. Peyton St., Alexandria, VA 22314.

☛National Association of Professional Insurance Agents, 400 N. Washington St., Alexandria, VA 22314.

For information about professional designation programs, contact:

☛American Society of CLU and ChFC, 270 Bryn Mawr Ave., Bryn Mawr, PA 19010-2195.

☛Society of Certified Insurance Counselors, 3630 North Hills Dr., Austin, TX 78731, or call 1-800-633-2165.

☛Society of Chartered Property and Casualty Underwriters, 720 Providence Rd., Malvern, PA 19355.

Manufacturers' and Wholesale Sales Representatives

(List of D.O.T. codes available on request. See p. 478.)

Nature of the Work

Computers, compact discs, and clothing are among the thousands of products bought and sold each day. Manufacturers' and wholesale sales representatives are an important part of the sales process. They market their company's products to manufacturers, wholesale and retail establishments, government agencies, and other institutions. Regardless of the type of product they sell, their primary duties are to interest wholesale and retail buyers and purchasing agents in their merchandise and ensure that any questions or concerns of current clients are addressed. Sales representatives also provide advice to clients on how to increase sales. (Retail sales workers, who sell directly to consumers, are discussed elsewhere in the *Handbook*.)

Depending on where they work, sales representatives have different job titles. Many of those working directly for manufacturers are referred to as *manufacturers' representatives* and those employed by wholesalers generally are called *sales representatives*. Those selling technical products, for both manufacturers and wholesalers, are usually called *industrial sales workers* or *sales engineers*. In addition to those employed directly by firms, *manufacturers' agents* are self-employed sales workers who contract their services to all types of companies. Many of these titles, however, are used interchangeably.

Manufacturers' and wholesale sales representatives spend much of their time traveling to and visiting with prospective buyers and current clients. During a sales call, they discuss the customers' needs and suggest how their merchandise or services can meet those needs.

They may show samples or catalogs that describe items their company stocks and inform customers about prices, availability, and how their products can save money and improve productivity. Because of the vast number of manufacturers and wholesalers selling similar products, they also try to emphasize the unique qualities of the products and services offered by their company. They also take orders and resolve any problems or complaints with the merchandise.

Depending on the products they sell, sales representatives may have additional duties. For example, sales engineers, who are among the most highly trained sales workers, typically sell products whose installation and optimal use require a great deal of technical expertise and support—products such as material handling equipment, numerical-control machinery, and computer systems. In addition to providing information on their firm's products, these workers help prospective and current buyers with technical problems by recommending improved materials and machinery for a firm's manufacturing process, drawing up plans of proposed machinery layouts, and estimating cost savings from the use of their equipment. They present this information and negotiate the sale, a process that may take several months. During their presentation, they may use a portable computer so they can have instant access to technical, sales, and other information.

Increasingly, sales representatives who lack technical expertise work as a team with a technical expert. In this arrangement, the duties of a sales representative are to make the preliminary contact with customers, introduce the company's product, and close the sale. The technical expert will attend the sales presentation to explain and answer questions and concerns. In this way, the sales representative is able to spend more time maintaining and soliciting accounts and less time acquiring technical knowledge. After the sale, sales representatives may make frequent follow-up visits to ensure that the equipment is functioning properly and may even help train customers' employees to operate and maintain new equipment.

Those selling consumer goods often suggest how and where their merchandise should be displayed. Working with retailers, they may help arrange promotional programs, store displays, and advertising.

Obtaining new accounts is an important part of the job. Sales representatives follow leads suggested by other clients, from advertisements in trade journals, and from participation in trade shows and conferences. At times, they make unannounced visits to potential clients. In addition, they may spend a lot of time meeting with and entertaining prospective clients during evenings and weekends.

Sales representatives also analyze sales statistics, prepare reports, and handle administrative duties, such as filing their expense account reports, scheduling appointments, and making travel plans. They

Some manufacturers' and wholesale sales representatives travel frequently.

study literature about new and existing products and monitor the sales, prices, and products of their competitors.

In addition to all these duties, manufacturers' agents who operate a sales agency must also manage their business. This requires organizational skills as well as knowledge of accounting, marketing, and administration.

Working Conditions

Some manufacturers' and wholesale sales representatives have large territories and do considerable traveling. Because a sales region may cover several States, they may be away from home for several days or weeks at a time. Others work near their "home base" and do most of their traveling by automobile. Due to the nature of the work and the amount of travel, sales representatives typically work more than 40 hours per week.

Although the hours are long and often irregular, most sales representatives have the freedom to determine their own schedule. As a result, they may be able to arrange their appointments so that they can have time off when they want it.

Dealing with different types of people can be demanding but stimulating. In addition, sales representatives often face competition from representatives of other companies as well as from fellow workers. Companies may set goals or quotas that the representatives are expected to meet. Because their earnings depend upon commissions, manufacturers' agents are also under the added pressure to maintain and expand their clientele.

Employment

Manufacturers' and wholesale sales representatives held about 1,503,000 jobs in 1994. Three of every 4 worked in wholesale trade—mostly for distributors of machinery and equipment, groceries and related products, and motor vehicles and parts. Others were employed in manufacturing and mining. Due to the diversity of products and services sold, employment opportunities are available in every part of the country.

In addition to those working directly for a firm, many sales representatives are self-employed manufacturers' agents who work for a straight commission based on the value of their sales. However, these workers generally gain experience and recognition with a manufacturer or wholesaler prior to going into business for themselves.

Training, Other Qualifications, and Advancement

The background needed for sales jobs varies by product line and market. As the number of college graduates has increased and the job requirements have become more technical and analytical, most firms have placed a greater emphasis on a strong educational background. Nevertheless, many employers still hire individuals with previous sales experience who do not have a college degree. In fact, for some consumer products, sales ability, personality, and familiarity with brands are as important as a degree. On the other hand, firms selling industrial products often require a degree in science or engineering in addition to some sales experience. In general, companies are looking for the best and brightest individuals who display the personality and desire necessary to sell.

Many companies have formal training programs for beginning sales representatives that last up to 2 years. However, most businesses are accelerating these programs to reduce costs and expedite the return from training. In some programs, trainees rotate among jobs in plants and offices to learn all phases of production, installation, and distribution of the product. In others, trainees take formal classroom instruction at the plant, followed by on-the-job training under the supervision of a field sales manager.

In some firms, new workers are trained by accompanying more experienced workers on their sales calls. As these workers gain familiarity with the firm's products and clients, they are given increasing responsibility until they are eventually assigned their own territory. As businesses experience greater competition, increased pressure is placed upon sales representatives to produce faster.

These workers must stay abreast of new merchandise and the changing needs of their customers. They may attend trade shows where new products are displayed or conferences and conventions where they meet with other sales representatives and clients to discuss new product developments. In addition, many companies sponsor meetings of their entire sales force where presentations are made on sales performance, product development, and profitability.

Manufacturers' and wholesale sales representatives should be goal oriented, persuasive, and able to work both as part of a team and independently. A pleasant personality and appearance, the ability to communicate well with people, and problem-solving skills are important as well. In addition, patience and perseverance are needed because completing a sale can take several months. Because these workers may be on their feet for long periods and may have to carry heavy sample cases, some physical stamina is necessary. Sales representatives should also enjoy traveling because much of their time is spent visiting current and prospective clients.

Frequently, promotion takes the form of an assignment to a larger account or territory where commissions are likely to be greater. Experienced sales representatives may move into jobs as sales trainers—workers who train new employees on selling techniques and company policies and procedures. Those who have good sales records and leadership ability may advance to sales supervisor or district manager.

In addition to advancement opportunities within a firm, some go into business for themselves as manufacturers' agents. Others find opportunities in buying, purchasing, advertising, or marketing research.

Job Outlook

Overall, employment of manufacturers' and wholesale sales representatives is expected to grow about as fast as the average for all occupations through the year 2005 due to continued growth in the amount of goods provided which need to be sold. Many job openings will also result from the need to replace workers who transfer to other occupations or leave the labor force.

Job opportunities as manufacturers agents should be a little better than those for sales representatives as companies are expected to continue outsourcing their sales duties to these workers rather than using in-house or direct selling personnel because agents are more likely to work in a sales area or territory longer than representatives, creating a better working relationship and understanding how customers operate their businesses. Also, by using agents who usually lend their services to more than one company, companies can share costs with the other companies involved with that agent.

Unlike other occupations, technology is not expected to have a dramatic effect on the demand for these workers because sales workers will still needed to go to the prospective customer in order to demonstrate or illustrate the particulars about the good or service. It is expected, however, to make them more effective and productive since they are allowed to provide accurate and current information to customers during sales presentations.

Those interested in this occupation should keep in mind that direct selling opportunities in manufacturing are likely to be best for products with strong demand. Furthermore, jobs will be most plentiful in small wholesale and manufacturing firms because a growing number of these companies will rely on wholesalers and manufacturers' agents to market their products as a way to control their costs and expand their customer base.

Employment opportunities and earnings may fluctuate from year to year because sales are affected by changing economic conditions, legislative issues, and consumer preferences. Prospects will be best for those with the appropriate knowledge or technical expertise as well as the personal traits necessary for successful selling.

Earnings

Compensation methods vary significantly by the type of firm and product sold. However, most employers use a combination of salary and commission or salary plus bonus. Commissions are usually based on the amount of sales, whereas bonuses may depend on individual performance, on the performance of all sales workers in the group or district, or on the company's performance.

Median annual earnings of full-time manufacturers' and wholesale sales representatives were about $32,600 in 1994. The middle 50 percent earned between $22,600 and $48,100 per year. The bottom 10 percent earned less than $15,500; the top 10 percent earned more than $69,200 per year. Earnings vary by experience and the type of goods or services sold.

In addition to their earnings, sales representatives are usually reimbursed for expenses such as transportation costs, meals, hotels, and entertaining customers. They often receive benefits such as health and life insurance, a pension plan, vacation and sick leave, personal use of a company car, and "frequent flyer" mileage. Some companies offer incentives such as free vacation trips or gifts for outstanding sales workers.

Unlike those working directly for a manufacturer or wholesaler, manufacturers' agents work strictly on commission. Depending on the type of product they are selling, their experience in the field, and the number of clients, their earnings can be significantly higher or lower than those working in direct sales. In addition, because manufacturers' agents are self-employed, they must pay their own travel and entertainment expenses as well as provide for their own benefits, which can be a significant cost.

Related Occupations

Manufacturers' and wholesale sales representatives must have sales ability and knowledge of the products they sell. Other occupations that require similar skills are retail, services, real estate, insurance, and securities sales workers, as well as wholesale and retail buyers.

Sources of Additional Information

Information on manufacturers' agents is available from:
☛ Manufacturers' Agents National Association, P.O. Box 3467, Laguna Hills, CA 92654-3467.

Career and certification information is available from:
☛ Sales and Marketing Executives International, Suite 977, Statler Office Tower, 1127 Euclid Ave., Cleveland OH, 44115.
☛ Manufacturers Representatives Educational Research Foundation, P.O. Box 247, Geneva, IL 60134.

Real Estate Agents, Brokers, and Appraisers

(D.O.T. 191.267-010 and 250.157-010, .357-010, -014, and -018)

Nature of the Work

The purchase or sale of a home, or an investment property, is not only one of the most important financial events in peoples' lives, but one of the most complex transactions as well. As a result, people generally seek the help of real estate agents, brokers, and appraisers when buying, selling, or establishing a price for real estate.

Real estate agents and brokers have a thorough knowledge of the housing market in their community. They know which neighborhoods will best fit their clients' needs and budgets. They are familiar with local zoning and tax laws, and know where to obtain financing. Agents and brokers also act as an intermediary in price negotiations between buyer and seller.

Brokers are independent business people who, for a fee, sell real estate owned by others and rent and manage properties. In closing sales, brokers often provide buyers with information on loans to finance their purchase. They also arrange for title searches and for meetings between buyers and sellers when details of the transactions are agreed upon and the new owners take possession. A broker's knowledge, resourcefulness, and creativity in arranging financing that is most favorable to the prospective buyer often mean the difference between success and failure in closing a sale. In some cases, agents assume the responsibilities in closing sales, but, in many areas, this is done by lawyers or lenders. Brokers also manage their own offices, advertise properties, and handle other business matters. Some combine other types of work, such as the sale of insurance or the practice of law, with their real estate business.

Real estate agents generally are independent sales workers who provide their services to a licensed broker on a contract basis. In return, the broker pays the agent a portion of the commission earned from property sold through the firm by the agent. Today, relatively few agents receive salaries as employees of a brokerage or realty firm. Instead, most derive their income solely from commissions.

Before showing properties to potential buyers, the broker or agent has an initial meeting with them to get a feeling for the type of home they would like and can afford. Often, an agent or broker uses a computer to generate lists of properties for sale, their location and description, and to identify available sources of financing. Then, they take the clients to see a number of homes that are likely to meet their needs and income. Because buying real estate is such an important part of the average person's life, agents may have to meet several times with a prospective buyer to discuss available properties. In answering questions, agents emphasize those selling points that are likely to be most important to the buyer. To a young family looking at a house, for example, they may point out the convenient floor plan and the fact that quality schools and shopping centers are close by. To a potential investor seeking the tax advantages of owning a rental property, they may point out the proximity to the city and the ease of finding a renter. If bargaining over price becomes necessary, agents must carefully follow their client's instructions and may have to present counteroffers in order to get the best possible price.

Once the contract has been signed by both parties, the real estate broker or agent must see to it that all special terms of the contract are met before the closing date. For example, if the seller has agreed to a home inspection or a termite and radon inspection, the agent must make sure that this is done. Also, if the seller has agreed to any repairs, the broker or agent must see to it that they have been made. Increasingly, brokers and agents must handle environmental problems or make sure the property they are selling meets environmental regulations. For example, they may be responsible for dealing with problems such as lead paint on the walls. While many details are handled by loan officers, attorneys, or other persons, the agent must check to make sure that they also are completed.

There is more to an agent's and broker's job, however, than just making a sale. Because they must have properties to sell, they may spend a significant amount of time obtaining "listings" (owner agreements to place properties for sale with the firm). When listing property for sale, agents and brokers compare the listed property with similar properties that have been sold recently to determine its competitive market price.

Most real estate agents and brokers sell residential property. A few, usually in large firms or small specialized firms, sell commercial, industrial, agricultural, or other types of real estate. Each specialty requires knowledge of that particular type of property and clientele. Selling or leasing business property, for example, requires an understanding of leasing practices, business trends, and location needs. Agents who sell or lease industrial properties must know about transportation, utilities, and labor supply. To sell residential properties, the agent or broker must know the location of schools, religious institutions, shopping facilities, and public transportation, and be familiar with tax rates and insurance coverage.

Because real estate transactions involve substantial financial commitments, parties to the transactions may seek the advice of real estate appraisers, who are objective experts who do not have a vested interest in the property. An appraisal is an unbiased estimate of the quality, value, and best use of a specific property. Appraisals may be used by prospective sellers to set a competitive price, by a lending institution to estimate the market value of a property as a condition for a mortgage loan, or by local governments to determine the assessed value of a property for tax purposes. Many real estate appraisers are independent fee appraisers or work for real estate appraisal firms while others are employees of banks, savings and loan associations, mortgage companies, government agencies, or multiservice real estate companies.

During a property inspection, real estate appraisers investigate the quality of the construction, the overall condition of the property, and its functional design. They gather information on properties by taking measurements, interviewing persons familiar with the properties' history, and searching public records of sales, leases, assessments, and other transactions. Appraisers compare the subject property with similar properties for which recent sale prices or rental data are available to arrive at an estimate of value. They may also estimate the current cost of reproducing any structures on the properties and how much the value of existing structures may have depreciated over time. Appraisers must consider the influence of the location of the properties, potential income, current market conditions, and real estate trends or impending changes that could influence the present and future value of the property. Depending on the purpose of the appraisal, they may estimate the market value of the property, the insurable value, the investment value, or other kinds of value. Appraisers must prepare formal written reports of their findings that meet the standards of The Appraisal Foundation.

Real estate appraisers often specialize in certain types of properties. Most appraise only homes, but others specialize in appraising apartment or office buildings, shopping centers, or a variety of other types of commercial, industrial, or agricultural properties.

Working Conditions

Although real estate agents, brokers, and appraisers generally work in offices, much of their time is spent outside the office—showing properties to customers, analyzing properties for sale, meeting with prospective clients, researching the state of the market, inspecting properties for appraisal, and performing a wide range of other duties. Brokers provide office space, but agents generally furnish their own automobiles.

Agents, brokers, and appraisers often work more than a standard 40-hour week; nearly 1 of every 4 worked 50 hours or more a week in 1994. They often work evenings and weekends to suit the convenience of their clients.

Real estate appraisers determine the value of industrial plants.

Employment

Real estate agents, brokers, and appraisers held about 374,000 jobs in 1994. Many worked part time, combining their real estate activities with other careers. Most were self-employed, working on a commission basis.

Most real estate and appraisal firms are relatively small; indeed, some are a one-person business. Some large real estate firms have several hundred real estate agents operating out of many branch offices. Many brokers have franchise agreements with national or regional real estate organizations. Under this type of arrangement, the broker pays a fee in exchange for the privilege of using the more widely known name of the parent organization. Although franchised brokers often receive help in training salespeople and in running their offices, they bear the ultimate responsibility for the success or failure of the firm.

Real estate is sold and appraised in all areas, but employment is concentrated in large urban areas and in smaller but rapidly growing communities.

Training, Other Qualifications, and Advancement

Real estate agents and brokers must be licensed in every State and in the District of Columbia. All States require prospective agents to be a high school graduate, be at least 18 years old, and pass a written test. The examination—more comprehensive for brokers than for agents—includes questions on basic real estate transactions and on laws affecting the sale of property. Most States require candidates for the general sales license to complete between 30 and 90 hours of classroom instruction, whereas those seeking the broker's license are required to complete between 60 and 90 hours of formal training in addition to a specified amount of experience in selling real estate (generally 1 to 3 years). Some States waive the experience requirements for the broker's license for applicants who have a bachelor's degree in real estate. State licenses generally must be renewed every year or two, usually without reexamination. Many States, however, require continuing education for license renewal.

Federal law requires appraisers of most types of real estate (all property being financed by a Federally regulated lender) to be State licensed or certified. In most States, appraisers who are not involved with Federally regulated institutions do not have to be certified. State certification requirements for appraisers must meet Federal standards, but States are free to set more stringent requirements. Formal courses, appraisal experience, and a satisfactory score on an examination are needed to be certified, but college education may be substituted for a portion of the experience requirement in some States. Requirements for licensure vary by State but are somewhat less stringent than for certification.

Individuals enter real estate appraisal from a variety of backgrounds. Traditionally, persons enter from real estate sales, management, and finance positions. However, a growing number of people are entering appraiser jobs directly from college. College courses in real estate, finance and business administration, statistics, computer science, economics, and English are helpful. Many junior and community colleges offer 2-year degrees in real estate or appraisal. Trainee appraisers usually assist experienced appraisers until they become licensed.

Persons who are real estate agents, brokers, and appraisers are older, on average, than those in most other occupations. Many homemakers and retired persons are attracted to real estate sales by the flexible and part-time work schedules characteristic of this field and may enter, leave, and later reenter the occupation, depending on the strength of the real estate market, family responsibilities, or other personal circumstances. In addition to those who are entering or reentering the labor force, some transfer into real estate jobs from a wide range of occupations, including clerical and other sales jobs.

As real estate transactions have become more complex, involving complicated legal requirements, many firms have turned to college graduates to fill positions. A large number of agents, brokers, and appraisers have some college training, and the number of college graduates selling real estate has risen substantially in recent years. However, personality traits are fully as important as academic background. Brokers look for applicants who possess a pleasant personality, honesty, and a neat appearance. Maturity, tact, and enthusiasm for the job are required in order to motivate prospective customers in this keenly competitive field. Agents also should be well organized and detail oriented as well as have a good memory for names and faces and business details, such as taxes, zoning codes, and local land-use regulations. Appraisers should have good judgment, writing, and math skills.

Persons interested in beginning jobs as real estate agents often apply in their own communities, where their knowledge of local neighborhoods is an advantage. The beginner usually learns the practical aspects of the job, including the use of computers to locate or list available properties or identify sources of financing, under the direction of an experienced agent.

Many firms offer formal training programs for both beginners and experienced agents. Larger firms generally offer more extensive programs than smaller firms. Over 1,000 universities, colleges, and junior colleges offer courses in real estate. At some, a student can earn an associate or bachelor's degree with a major in real estate; several offer advanced degrees. Many local real estate associations that are members of the National Association of Realtors sponsor courses covering the fundamentals and legal aspects of the field. Advanced courses in appraisal, mortgage financing, property development and management, and other subjects also are available through various affiliates of the National Association of Realtors.

Many real estate appraisers voluntarily earn professional designations that represent formal recognition of their professional competence and achievements. A number of appraisal organizations have programs that, through a combination of experience, professional education, and examinations, lead to the award of such designations. These professional designations are desirable because requirements for them are more stringent than State standards.

Advancement opportunities for agents often take the form of higher commission rates and more and bigger sales, both of which increase compensation. This occurs as agents gain knowledge and expertise and become more efficient in closing a greater number of transactions. Experienced agents can advance in many large firms to sales or general manager. Persons who have received their broker's license may open their own offices. Others with experience and training in estimating property value may become real estate appraisers, and people familiar with operating and maintaining rental properties may become property or real estate managers. (See the statement on property and real estate managers elsewhere in the *Handbook*). Agents, brokers, and appraisers who gain general experience in real estate and a thorough knowledge of business conditions and property values in their localities may enter mortgage financing or real estate investment counseling.

Job Outlook

Employment of real estate agents, brokers, and appraisers is expected to grow more slowly than the average for all occupations through the year 2005. However, a large number of job openings will arise due to replacement needs. Each year, tens of thousands of jobs will become available as workers transfer to other occupations or leave the labor force. Because turnover is high, real estate sales positions should continue to be relatively easy to obtain. Not everyone is successful in this highly competitive field; many beginners become discouraged by their inability to get listings and to close a sufficient number of sales. Lacking financial sustenance and motivation, they subsequently leave the occupation. Well-trained, ambitious people who enjoy selling should have the best chance for success.

Employment growth in this field will stem primarily from increased demand for home purchases and rental units. Shifts in the age distribution of the population over the next decade or so will result in a large number of persons in the prime working ages (25-54 years old) with careers and family responsibilities. This is the most geographically mobile group in our society and the one that traditionally makes most of the home purchases. As their incomes rise, they also may be expected to invest in additional real estate.

Increasing use of technology and electronic information may increase the productivity of agents, brokers, and appraisers as the use of computers, faxes, modems, and databases becomes more commonplace. Some real estate companies are using computer generated images to show houses to customers without even leaving the office. These devices enable one agent to serve a greater number of customers. Use of this technology may eliminate some of the more marginal agents such as those practicing real estate part time or between jobs. These workers will not be able to compete as easily with full-time agents who have invested in this technology.

Employment of real estate agents, brokers, and appraisers is sensitive to swings in the economy. During periods of declining economic activity and tight credit, the volume of sales and the resulting demand for sales workers may decline. During these periods, the earnings of agents, brokers, and appraisers decline, and many work fewer hours or leave the occupation.

Earnings

Commissions on sales are the main source of earnings of real estate agents and brokers—few receive a salary. The rate of commission varies according to the type of property and its value; the percentage paid on the sale of farm and commercial properties or unimproved land usually is higher than that paid for selling a home.

Commissions may be divided among several agents and brokers. The broker and the agent in the firm who obtained the listing generally share their part of the commission when the property is sold; the broker and the agent in the firm who made the sale also generally share their part of the commission. Although an agent's share varies greatly from one firm to another, often it is about half of the total amount received by the firm. The agent who both lists and sells the property maximizes his or her commission.

Real estate agents, brokers, and appraisers who usually worked full time had median weekly earnings of $593 in 1994. The middle 50 percent earned between $375 and $943. The top 10 percent earned more than $1,447 and the lowest 10 percent earned less than $198.

Income usually increases as an agent gains experience, but individual ability, economic conditions, and the type and location of the property also affect earnings. Sales workers who are active in community organizations and local real estate associations can broaden their contacts and increase their earnings. A beginner's earnings often are irregular because a few weeks or even months may go by without a sale. Although some brokers allow an agent a drawing account against future earnings, this practice is not usual with new employees. The beginner, therefore, should have enough money to live on for about 6 months or until commissions increase.

Related Occupations

Selling expensive items such as homes requires maturity, tact, and a sense of responsibility. Other sales workers who find these character traits important in their work include motor vehicle sales workers, securities and financial services sales workers, insurance agents and brokers, travel agents, and manufacturers' representatives. Other appraisers specialize in performing many types of appraisals besides real estate, including aircraft, antiques and fine arts, and business valuations.

Sources of Additional Information

Details on licensing requirements for real estate agents, brokers, and appraisers are available from most local real estate and appraiser organizations or from the State real estate commission or board.

For more information about opportunities in real estate work, contact:

☛National Association of Realtors, 430 North Michigan Ave., Chicago, IL 60611.

Information on careers and licensing and certification requirements in real estate appraising is available from:

☛Appraisal Institute, 875 North Michigan Ave., Suite 2400, Chicago, IL 60611-1980.

☛National Association of Real Estate Appraisers, 8383 East Evans Rd., Scottsdale, AZ 85260.

☛American Society of Appraisers, P.O. Box 17265, Washington, DC 20041. (This organization may be called toll free at 1-800-ASA-VALU.)

Retail Sales Worker Supervisors and Managers

(D.O.T. 185.167-010, -014, -022, -030, -038, and -046; 291.157; 299.137-010 and -026)

Nature of the Work

In every one of the thousands of retail stores across the country, there is at least one retail sales worker supervisor or manager. Because the retail trade industry provides goods and services directly to customers, the retail supervisor or manager is responsible for ensuring that customers receive prompt service and quality goods. They also answer customers' complaints and inquiries.

Retail supervisors and managers oversee the work of sales associates, cashiers, customer service workers, stock and inventory clerks, and grocery clerks. (Some of these occupations are discussed elsewhere in the *Handbook*.) Retail supervisors and managers also are responsible for interviewing, hiring, and training employees, as well as preparing work schedules and assigning workers to their specific duties. (Managers in eating and drinking places are discussed in the *Handbook* statement on restaurant and food service managers.)

The responsibilities of retail sales worker supervisors and managers vary depending on the size and type of establishment as well as the level of management. As the size of the retail store and the types of goods and services increase, these workers increasingly specialize in one department or one aspect of merchandising. Larger organizations tend to have many layers of management. Similar to other industries, supervisory-level retail managers usually report to their mid-level counterparts who, in turn, report to top-level managers. Small stores and stores that carry specialized merchandise typically have fewer levels of management.

Supervisory-level retail managers, often known as department managers, provide the day-to-day oversight of individual departments such as shoes, cosmetics, or housewares in large department stores, produce and meat in grocery stores, and service and sales in automotive dealerships. Department managers commonly are found in large retail stores. They establish and implement policies, goals, objectives, and procedures for their specific departments; coordinate activities with other department heads; and strive for smooth operations within their departments. They supervise employees who price and ticket goods and place them on display; clean and organize shelves, displays, and inventory in stockrooms; and inspect merchandise to ensure that none is outdated. Department managers also may greet and assist customers and promote sales and good public relations. Department managers also review inventory and sales records, develop merchandising techniques, and coordinate sales promotions.

In smaller or independent retail stores, retail sales worker supervisors and managers not only directly supervise sales associates, but are also responsible for the operation of the entire store. In these instances, they may also be called a store manager. Some are also store owners.

Retail sales worker supervisors and managers often work nights and weekends.

Working Conditions

Most retail sales worker supervisors and managers have offices within the store itself. Although some of their time is spent in the office completing merchandise orders or arranging work schedules, a large portion of a their time is spent on the sales floor.

Work hours vary greatly among retail establishments. The work schedule of retail supervisors and managers usually depends on consumers' needs. Most work around 40 hours a week, but longer hours are common, especially during holidays, busy shopping hours and seasons, sales, and store inventory. They are expected to work evenings and weekends, but usually are compensated by getting a weekday off. Hours can change weekly, and managers sometimes may have to report to work on short notice, especially when many employees are absent. Independent owners can set their own schedules, but hours must be convenient to their customers.

Employment

Retail sales worker supervisors and managers who work in retail trade held about 888,000 wage and salary jobs in 1994. In addition, there were thousands of self-employed retail sales managers, mainly store owners. Managers are found in every retail trade industry—grocery stores, department stores, clothing and shoe stores, automotive dealers, and furniture stores are among the largest industries.

Training, Other Qualifications, and Advancement

Knowledge of management principles and practices is the essential requirement for a management position in retail trade, and such knowledge usually is acquired through work experience. Many supervisors and managers begin their careers on the sales floor as sales clerks, cashiers, or customer service workers. In these positions they learn merchandising, customer service, and the basic policies and procedures of the store.

The educational background of retail sales worker supervisors and managers varies widely. Regardless of the education received, business courses including accounting, administration, marketing, management, and sales, as well as courses in psychology, sociology, and communication, are helpful. Supervisors and managers also must be computer literate as cash registers and inventory control systems become more computerized.

Most supervisors and managers who have postsecondary education hold an associate or a bachelor's degree in liberal arts, social science, business, or management. To gain experience, many postsecondary students participate in internship programs which usually are planned between individual schools and retail firms.

Once on the job, the type and amount of training available for supervisors and managers varies from store to store. Many national chains have formal training programs for management trainees, which include both classroom and in-store training. Training may last from 1 week to 1 year or more, as many retail organizations require their trainees to gain experience during all shopping seasons. Other retail organizations may not have formal training programs.

Classroom training may include such topics as interviewing and customer service skills, and employee and inventory management and scheduling. Management trainees may be placed in one specific department while training on the job, or they may be rotated among several departments to gather a well-rounded knowledge of the store's operation. Training programs in franchises generally are extensive, covering all functions of the operation, including promotion, marketing, management, finance, purchasing, product preparation, human resource management, and compensation. College graduates usually enter management training programs directly.

Retail sales worker supervisors and managers must get along with all kinds of people. They need initiative, self-discipline, good judgment, and decisiveness. Patience and a mild temperament are necessary when dealing with demanding customers. They also must be able to motivate and organize and direct the work of subordinates and communicate clearly and persuasively with customers and other managers.

Individuals who display leadership skills, self-confidence, motivation, and decisiveness become candidates for promotion to assistant store manager or store manager. Increasingly, a postsecondary degree is needed for advancement because it is viewed by employers as a sign of motivation and maturity—qualities deemed important for promotion to more responsible positions. In many retail establishments, managers are promoted from within the company. In small retail establishments, where the number of positions is limited, advancement to a higher management position may come slowly. Larger establishments have more extensive career ladder programs and offer managers the opportunity to transfer to another store in the chain or to the central office if an opening occurs. Promotion may occur more quickly in larger establishments, but relocation every several years may be necessary for advancement. Positions within the central office to which sales supervisors and managers can move include marketing, advertising, and public relations managers, who coordinate marketing plans, monitor sales, and propose advertisements and promotions, and purchasers and buyers, who purchase goods and supplies for their organization or for resale. (Both occupations are covered in other *Handbook* statements.)

Some supervisors and managers who have worked in the retail industry for a long time decide to open their own store. However, retail trade is highly competitive, and although many independent retail owners succeed, some fail to cover expenses and eventually go out of business. Retail owners need good business sense and strong customer service and public relations skills.

Job Outlook

Jobs in retail management vary greatly in earnings, weekly hours, number of employees supervised, and type of goods and services provided. Since most jobs for retail sales worker supervisors and managers do not require postsecondary education, competition is expected for jobs with the most attractive earnings and working conditions. Candidates who have retail experience will have the best opportunities.

Overall employment of wage and salary retail sales worker supervisors and managers is expected to grow about as fast as the average for all occupations through the year 2005 as grocery stores, department stores, automotive dealerships, and other retail establishments grow in number and size. Establishment size has been increasing as retailers seek to accommodate consumers' desires for a greater selection of merchandise and one-stop shopping. The specialization arising from creation of new departments within existing stores and the offering of additional product lines should spur the demand for store-level retail sales worker supervisors and managers.

Projected employment growth of retail managers will mirror, in part, the patterns of employment growth in industries in which they are concentrated. For example, faster than average growth is expected in miscellaneous shopping goods stores and in appliance, radio, television, and music stores. Average growth is expected in drug stores and proprietary stores, shoe stores, gasoline service stations, and motor vehicle dealers. On the other hand, slower than average growth is expected in department stores.

Unlike middle- and upper-level management positions, store-level retail supervisors and managers generally will not be affected by the restructuring and consolidating that is taking place at the corporate and headquarters level of many retail chain companies.

Because retail supervisors and managers comprise a large occupation, most job openings are expected to occur as experienced supervisors and managers move into higher levels of management, transfer to other occupations, or leave the labor force.

Earnings

Salaries of retail managers vary substantially, depending upon the level of responsibility, length of service, and type, size, and location of the firm.

Supervisors or managers of sales workers in the retail trade industry who usually worked full time had median weekly earnings of $445 in 1994. The middle 50 percent earned between $310 and $623. The top 10 percent earned more than $907 and the lowest 10 percent earned less than $240.

According to a survey sponsored by the Association of Convenience Stores, the average total compensation for assistant store managers in the U.S. and Canada ranged between $13,700 and $16,300 a year in 1994, depending on the size of the organization. Store managers received between $21,900 and $26,300 on average.

Compensation systems vary by type of establishment and merchandise sold. Many managers receive a commission or a combination of salary and commission. Under a commission system, retail managers receive a percentage of department or store sales. These systems offer managers the opportunity to significantly increase their earnings, but they may find that their earnings depend on their ability to sell their product and the condition of the economy. Those managers who sell large amounts of merchandise often are rewarded with bonuses and awards, and receive recognition throughout the store or chain.

Retail managers receive typical benefits and, in some cases, stock options. In addition, retail managers generally are able to buy their store's merchandise at a discount.

Related Occupations

Retail supervisors and managers serve customers, supervise workers, and direct and coordinate the operations of an establishment. Others with similar responsibilities include managers in wholesale trade, hotels, banks, hospitals, law firms, and a wide range of other industries.

Sources of Additional Information

Information on employment opportunities for retail managers may be obtained from the employment offices of various retail establishments, or State employment service offices.

General information on management careers in retail establishments is available from:

☛National Retail Federation, 325 Seventh St. NW., Suite 1000, Washington, DC 20004-2802.

Information on management careers in grocery stores, and schools offering related programs, is available from:

☛Food Marketing Institute, 800 Connecticut Ave. NW., Washington, DC 20006-2701.

Information about management careers and training programs in the motor vehicle dealers industry is available from:

☛National Automobile Dealers Association, 8400 Westpark Dr., McLean, VA 22102-3591.

Information about management careers in convenience stores is available from:

☛National Association of Convenience Stores, 1605 King St., Alexandria, VA 22314.

Information about management careers in service stations is available from:

☛Service Station Dealers of America, 9420 Annapolis Rd., Suite 307, Lanham, MD 20706.

Retail Sales Workers

(List of D.O.T. codes available on request. See page 478.)

Nature of the Work

Millions of dollars are spent each day on all types of merchandise—everything from sweaters and cosmetics to lumber and plumbing supplies. Sales workers are employed by many types of retailers to assist customers in the selection and purchase of these items.

Whether selling shoes, computer equipment, or automobiles, a sales worker's primary job is to assist customers in finding what they are looking for and to interest them in the merchandise. This may be done by describing the product's features, demonstrating its use, or showing various models and colors. For some jobs, particularly those selling expensive and complex items, special knowledge or skills are needed. For example, workers who sell personal computers must be able to explain to customers the features of various brands and models, the meaning of manufacturers' specifications, and the types of software that are available.

In addition to selling, most retail sales workers, especially those who work in department and apparel stores, make out sales checks; receive cash, check, and charge payments; bag or package purchases; and give change and receipts. Depending on the hours they work, they may have to open or close the cash register. This may include counting the money in the cash register; separating charge slips, coupons, and exchange vouchers; and making deposits at the cash office. Sales workers are often held responsible for the contents of their register, and repeated shortages are cause for dismissal in many organizations. (Cashiers, who have similar job duties, are discussed elsewhere in the *Handbook*.)

Sales workers also handle returns and exchanges of merchandise, perform gift wrapping services, and keep their work areas neat. In addition, they may help stock shelves or racks, arrange for mailing or delivery of a purchase, mark price tags, take inventory, and prepare displays.

Sales workers must be aware of not only the promotions their store is sponsoring, but also those that are being sponsored by competitors. Also, they often must recognize possible security risks and know how to handle such situations.

Consumers often form their impressions of a store by its sales force. The retail industry is very competitive and, increasingly, employers are stressing the importance of providing courteous and efficient service. When a customer wants an item that is not on the sales floor, for example, the sales worker may check the stockroom and, if there are none there, place a special order or call another store to locate the item.

To provide better customer service, some firms employ personal shoppers. Some personal shoppers assist consumers in purchasing a particular item. For example, personal shoppers employed in department stores can assist customers in updating their wardrobes. Others actually choose the item for the client based on information provided. Those personal shoppers who work in food stores may buy groceries and arrange for their delivery for people confined to their homes.

Retail sales workers help customers select merchandise.

Although most sales workers have many duties and responsibilities, in jobs selling standardized articles such as food, hardware, linens, and housewares, they often do little more than take payments and wrap purchases.

Working Conditions
Most sales workers in retail trade work in clean, comfortable, well-lighted stores. They often stand for long periods and may need supervisory approval when they want to leave the sales floor.

The Monday through Friday, 9 to 5 work week is the exception rather than the rule in retail trade. Most salespersons can expect to work some evening and weekend hours and longer than normal hours may be scheduled during Christmas and other peak periods. In addition, most retailers restrict the use of vacation time from Thanksgiving until early January.

This job can be rewarding for those who enjoy working with people. Patience is required, however, when the work is repetitious and the customers demanding.

Employment
Retail sales workers held about 4,261,000 jobs in 1994. They worked in stores ranging from small specialty shops employing several workers to the giant department store with hundreds of salespersons. In addition, some were self-employed representatives of direct sales companies and mail-order houses. The largest employers of retail sales workers, however, are department stores, clothing and accessories stores, motor vehicle dealers, and grocery stores.

This occupation offers many opportunities for part-time work and is especially appealing to students, retirees, and others looking to supplement their income. However, most of those selling "big ticket" items, such as cars, furniture, and electronic equipment, work full time and have substantial experience.

Because retail stores are found in every city and town, employment is distributed geographically in much the same way as the population.

Training, Other Qualifications, and Advancement
There usually are no formal education requirements for this type of work, although a high school diploma or equivalent is increasingly preferred. Employers look for persons who enjoy working with people and have the tact and patience to deal with difficult customers. Among other desirable characteristics are an interest in sales work, a neat appearance, and the ability to communicate clearly and effectively. Before hiring, some employers may conduct a background check, especially for jobs in selling high-priced items.

In most small stores, an experienced employee or the proprietor instructs newly hired sales personnel in making out sales checks and operating the cash register. In larger stores, training programs are more formal and usually are conducted over several days. Topics usually discussed are customer service, security, the store's policies and procedures, and how to work the cash register. Depending on the type of product they are selling, they may be given additional specialized training by manufacturers' representatives. For example, those working in cosmetics receive instruction on the types of products available and for whom they would be most beneficial. Likewise, sales workers employed by motor vehicle dealers may be required to participate in training programs designed to provide information on the technical details of standard and optional equipment available on new models.

As salespersons gain experience and seniority, they usually move to positions of greater responsibility and are given their choice of departments. This often means moving to areas with potentially higher earnings and commissions. The highest earnings potential is usually found in selling big-ticket items. This work often requires the most knowledge of the product and the greatest talent for persuasion.

Traditionally, capable sales workers without a college degree could advance to management positions, but today, large retail businesses generally prefer to hire college graduates as management trainees, making a college education increasingly important. Despite this trend, capable employees without a college degree should still be able to advance to administrative or supervisory work in large stores.

Opportunities for advancement vary in small stores. In some establishments, advancement opportunities are limited because one person, often the owner, does most of the managerial work. In others, however, some sales workers are promoted to assistant managers.

Retail selling experience may be an asset when applying for sales positions with larger retailers or in other industries, such as financial services, wholesale trade, or manufacturing.

Job Outlook
Employment of retail sales workers is expected to increase about as fast as the average for all workers through the year 2005 due to anticipated growth in retail sales. In addition, numerous job openings will be created as sales workers transfer to other occupations or leave the labor force. As in the past, replacement needs will generate an exceptionally large number of sales jobs because the occupation is large and turnover is much higher than average. There will continue to be many opportunities for part-time workers, and demand will be strong for temporary workers during peak selling periods such as the Christmas season.

During economic downturns, sales volume and the resulting demand for sales workers generally decline. Purchases of costly items such as cars, appliances, and furniture tend to be postponed during difficult economic times. In areas of high unemployment, sales of all types of goods may decline. However, since turnover of sales workers is usually very high, employers often can control employment simply by not replacing all those who leave.

In some geographic areas, employers face a shortage of qualified applicants. As a result, employers can be expected to improve efforts to attract and retain workers by offering higher wages, more generous benefits, and more flexible schedules.

Earnings
The starting wage for many part-time retail sales positions is the Federal minimum wage, $4.25 an hour. In some areas where employers are having difficulty attracting and retaining workers, wages are much higher than the established minimum. The following tabulation shows 1994 median weekly earnings by class of sales worker.

Motor vehicle and boats $534
Furniture and home furnishings 427
Radio, television, hi-fi, and appliances 401
Parts 378
Hardware and building supplies.. 333
Street and door-to-door sales workers...................................... 323
Shoes.. 280
Apparel 265

Compensation systems vary by type of establishment and merchandise sold. Most sales workers receive an hourly wage. Others receive a commission or a combination of wages and commissions. Under a commission system, salespersons receive a percentage of the sales that they make. These systems offer sales workers the opportunity to significantly increase their earnings, but they may find their earnings depend on their ability to sell their product and the ups and downs of the economy. Employers also use incentive programs such as awards, banquets, and profit sharing plans to promote teamwork among the sales staff.

Benefits may be limited in smaller stores, but in large establishments they are usually comparable to those offered by other employers. In addition, nearly all sales workers are able to buy their store's merchandise at a discount, with the savings depending upon on the type of merchandise.

Related Occupations
Sales workers use sales techniques coupled with their knowledge of merchandise to assist customers and encourage purchases. These skills are used by people in a number of other occupations, including manufacturers' and wholesale trade sales representatives, service sales representatives, securities and financial services sales representatives, counter and rental clerks, real estate sales agents, purchasers and buyers, insurance agents and brokers, and cashiers.

Sources of Additional Information
Information on careers in retail sales may be obtained from the personnel offices of local stores; from State merchants' associations; or from local unions of the United Food and Commercial Workers International Union.

General information about retailing is available from:
☛National Retail Federation, 325 Seventh St. NW., Suite 1000, Washington, DC 20004-2802.

Information about training for a career in automobile sales is available from:
☛National Automobile Dealership Association, 8400 Westpark Dr., McLean, VA 22102-3591.

Securities and Financial Services Sales Representatives

(D.O.T. 162.167-034 and -038; 250.257-014, -018, and -022.)

Nature of the Work
Most investors, whether they are individuals with a few hundred dollars to invest or large institutions with millions, use *securities sales representatives* when buying or selling stocks, bonds, shares in mutual funds, insurance annuities, or other financial products. Securities sales representatives often are called stock brokers, registered representatives, or account executives.

When an investor wishes to buy or sell securities, sales representatives may relay the order through their firms' offices to the floor of a securities exchange, such as the New York Stock Exchange. There, securities sales representatives known as brokers' floor representa-

tives buy and sell securities. If a security is not traded on an exchange, the sales representative sends the order to the firm's trading department, where a security trader trades it directly with a dealer in an over-the-counter market, such as the NASDAQ computerized trading system. After the transaction has been completed, the sales representative notifies the customer of the final price.

Securities sales representatives also provide many related services for their customers. Depending on a customer's knowledge of the market, they may explain the meaning of stock market terms and trading practices; offer financial counseling; devise an individual financial portfolio for the client including securities, life insurance, corporate and municipal bonds, mutual funds, certificates of deposit, annuities, and other investments; and offer advice on the purchase or sale of particular securities.

Not all customers have the same investment goals. Some individuals may prefer long-term investments designed either for capital growth or to provide income over the years; others might want to invest in speculative securities that they hope will rise in price quickly. Securities sales representatives furnish information about the advantages and disadvantages of an investment based on each person's objectives. They also supply the latest price quotations on any security in which the investor is interested, as well as information on the activities and financial positions of the corporations issuing these securities.

The growing need for investment advice is expected to create a favorable outlook for securities and financial services sales representatives.

Most securities sales representatives serve individual investors, but others specialize in institutional investors. In institutional investing, most sales representatives concentrate on a specific financial product such as stocks, bonds, options, annuities, or commodity futures. Some handle the sale of new issues, such as corporate securities issued to finance plant expansion.

The most important part of a sales representative's job is finding clients and building a customer base. Thus, beginning securities sales representatives spend much of their time searching for customers—relying heavily on telephone solicitation. They may meet some clients through business and social contacts. Many sales representatives find it useful to get additional exposure by teaching adult education investment courses or by giving lectures at libraries or social clubs. Brokerage firms may give sales representatives lists of people with whom the firm has done business with in the past. Sometimes sales representatives may inherit the clients of representatives who have retired.

Financial services sales representatives sell banking and related services. They contact potential customers to explain their services and to ascertain the customer's banking and other financial needs. They may discuss services such as deposit accounts, lines of credit, sales or inventory financing, certificates of deposit, cash management, or investment services. They may solicit businesses to participate in consumer credit card programs. At most small and medium-size banks, branch managers and commercial loan officers are responsible for marketing the bank's financial services. As banks offer more and increasingly complex financial services—for example, securities brokerage and financial planning—the job of the financial services sales representative is assuming greater importance.

Financial planners develop and implement financial plans for individuals and businesses using their knowledge of tax and investment strategies, securities, insurance, pension plans, and real estate. They interview clients to determine their assets, liabilities, cash flow, insurance coverage, tax status, and financial objectives. Then they analyze all this information and develop a financial plan tailored to the clients' needs.

Working Conditions

Securities sales representatives usually work in offices where there is much activity. They have access to "quote boards" or computer terminals that continually provide information on the prices of securities. When sales activity increases, due perhaps to unanticipated changes in the economy, the pace may become very hectic.

Established securities sales representatives usually work the same hours as others in the business community. Beginners who are seeking customers may work much longer hours, however. Most securities sales representatives accommodate customers by meeting with them in the evenings or on weekends.

Financial services sales representatives normally work in a comfortable, less stressful office environment. They generally work 40 hours a week. They may spend considerable time outside the office meeting with present and prospective clients, attending civic functions, and participating in trade association meetings. Some financial services sales representatives work exclusively inside banks, providing service to "walk-in" customers.

Employment

Securities and financial services sales representatives held almost 246,000 jobs in 1994. In addition, a substantial number of people in other occupations sold securities. These include partners and branch office managers in securities firms as well as insurance agents and brokers offering securities to their customers.

Securities sales representatives are employed by brokerage and investment firms in all parts of the country. Many of these firms are very small. Most sales representatives, however, work for a small number of large firms with main offices in large cities, especially New York.

Financial services sales representatives are employed by banks, savings and loan associations, and other credit institutions.

Training, Other Qualifications, and Advancement

Because securities sales representatives must be well informed about economic conditions and trends, a college education is increasingly important, especially in the larger securities firms. In fact, the overwhelming majority of workers in this occupation are college graduates. Although employers seldom require specialized academic training, courses in business administration, economics, and finance are helpful.

Many employers consider personal qualities and skills more important than academic training. Employers seek applicants who have sales ability and good communication skills, are well groomed, and have a strong desire to succeed. Self-confidence and an ability to handle frequent rejections also are important ingredients for success.

Because maturity and the ability to work independently also are important, many employers prefer to hire those who have achieved success in other jobs. Some firms prefer candidates with sales experience, particularly those who have worked on commission in areas such as real estate or insurance. Therefore, most entrants to this occupation transfer from other jobs. Some begin working as securities sales representatives following retirement from other fields.

Securities sales representatives must meet State licensing requirements, which generally include passing an examination and, in some cases, furnishing a personal bond. In addition, sales representatives must register as representatives of their firm according to regulations of the securities exchanges where they do business or the National Association of Securities Dealers, Inc. (NASD). Before beginners can qualify as registered representatives, they must pass the General Securities Registered Representative Examination, administered by the NASD, and be an employee of a registered firm for at least 4 months. Most States require a second examination—the Uniform Securities Agents State Law Examination. These tests measure the prospective representative's knowledge of the securities business, customer protection requirements, and recordkeeping procedures. Many take correspondence courses in preparation for the securities examinations.

Most employers provide on-the-job training to help securities sales representatives meet the requirements for registration. In most firms, the training period generally takes about 4 months. Trainees in large firms may receive classroom instruction in securities analysis, effective speaking, and the finer points of selling; take courses offered by business schools and associations; and undergo a period of on-the-job training lasting up to 2 years. Many firms like to rotate their trainees among various departments in the firm to give them a broader perspective of the securities business. In small firms, sales representatives generally receive training in outside institutions and on the job.

Securities sales representatives must understand the basic characteristics of a wide variety of financial products offered by brokerage firms. Representatives periodically take training, through their firms or outside institutions, to keep abreast of new financial products as they are introduced on the market and to improve their sales techniques. Training in the use of computers is important, as the securities sales business is highly automated.

The principal form of advancement for securities sales representatives is an increase in the number and size of the accounts they handle. Although beginners usually service the accounts of individual investors, eventually they may handle very large institutional accounts such as those of banks and pension funds. Some experienced sales representatives become branch office managers and supervise other sales representatives while continuing to provide services for their own customers. A few representatives advance to top management positions or become partners in their firms.

Banks and other credit institutions prefer to hire college graduates for financial services sales jobs. A business administration degree with a specialization in finance or a liberal arts degree including courses in accounting, economics, and marketing serves as excellent preparation for this job.

Financial services sales representatives learn through on-the-job training under the supervision of bank officers. Outstanding performance can lead to promotion to managerial positions.

Job Outlook

Employment of securities and financial sales representatives is expected to grow much faster than the average for all occupations through the year 2005 as economic growth, rising personal incomes, and greater inherited wealth increase the funds available for investment. However, employment of financial services sales representatives is expected to grow somewhat slower than securities sales representatives as more and more people are expected to do their banking from home via their personal computer.

More individual investors are expected to purchase common stocks, mutual funds, and other financial products after seeking advice from securities sales representatives regarding the increasing array of investment alternatives. Deregulation has enabled brokerage firms to sell certificates of deposit, offer checking and deposit services through cash management accounts, and sell insurance products such as annuities and life insurance. Growth in the number and size of institutional investors will be strong as more people enroll in pension plans, set up individual retirement accounts, establish trust funds, and contribute to the endowment funds of colleges and other nonprofit institutions. More representatives also will be needed to sell securities issued by new and expanding corporations, by State and local governments financing public improvements, and by foreign governments, whose securities have become attractive to U.S. investors as international trade expands.

Investors increasingly rely on the growing number of financial planners to assist them in selecting the proper options among a wide variety of financial alternatives. In addition, demand should increase as banks and credit institutions expand the range of financial services they offer and issue more loans for personal and commercial use.

Due to the highly competitive nature of securities sales work, many beginners leave the field because they are unable to establish a sufficient clientele. Once established, however, securities and financial services sales representatives have a very strong attachment to their occupation because of high earnings and the considerable investment in training.

The demand for securities sales representatives fluctuates as the economy expands and contracts. Thus, in an economic downturn, the number of persons seeking jobs usually exceeds the number of openings—sometimes by a great deal. Even during periods of rapid economic expansion, however, competition for securities sales training positions—particularly in larger firms—is keen because of potentially high earnings.

Job opportunities should be best for mature individuals with successful work experience. Opportunities for inexperienced sales representatives should be best in smaller firms.

Earnings

In 1994, median annual earnings of securities and financial services sales representatives were $37,300; the middle 50 percent earned between $24,800 and $70,800. Ten percent earned less than $17,600 and 10 percent earned more than $120,700. On average, financial services sales representatives earn considerably less than securities sales representatives.

Trainees usually are paid a salary until they meet licensing and registration requirements. After candidates are licensed and registered, their earnings depend on commissions from the sale or purchase of stocks and bonds, life insurance, or other securities for customers. Commission earnings are likely to be high when there is much buying and selling and lower when there is a slump in market activity. Most firms provide sales representatives with a steady

income by paying a "draw against commission"—that is, a minimum salary based on the commissions which they can be expected to earn. Securities sales representatives who can provide their clients with the most complete financial services should enjoy the greatest income stability.

Financial services sales representatives usually are paid a salary; some receive a bonus if they meet certain established goals.

Related Occupations

Similar sales jobs requiring specialized knowledge include insurance agents and real estate agents.

Sources of Additional Information

Information about job opportunities as a securities sales representative may be obtained from the personnel departments of individual securities firms.

For information about job opportunities for financial services sales representatives in various States, contact State bankers' associations or write directly to a particular bank to inquire about job openings.

Services Sales Representatives

(D.O.T. 165.157; 236.252; 250.357-022; 251.157, .257, .357; 252.257, .357; 253; 254; 259 except .257-014; 269.357-018; 273.357-014; 279.357-042; and 293 except .137-010 and .357-018)

Nature of the Work

Services sales representatives sell a wide variety of services. For example, sales representatives for data processing services firms sell complex services such as inventory control, payroll processing, sales analysis, and financial reporting systems. Hotel sales representatives contact government, business, and social groups to solicit convention and conference business. Sales representatives for temporary help services firms locate and acquire clients who will hire the firm's employees. Telephone services sales representatives visit commercial customers to review their telephone systems, analyze their communications needs, and recommend services, such as installation of additional equipment. Other representatives sell automotive leasing, public utility, burial, shipping, protective, and management consulting services. (Information on other sales workers, including insurance agents and brokers, real estate agents and brokers, securities and financial services sales representatives, retail sales workers, manufacturers' and wholesale sales representatives, and travel agents, appears in other *Handbook* statements.)

Services sales representatives act as industry experts, consultants, and problem solvers when selling their firm's services. The sales representative, in some cases, creates demand for his or her firm's services. A prospective client who is asked to consider buying a particular service may never have used, or even been aware of a need for, that service. For example, wholesalers might be persuaded to order a list of credit ratings for checking their customers' credit prior to making sales, and discover that the list could be used to solicit new business.

There are several different categories of services sales jobs. *Outside sales representatives* call on clients and prospects at their homes or offices. They may have an appointment, or they may practice "cold calls," arriving without an appointment. *Inside sales representatives* work on their employer's premises, assisting individuals interested in the company's services. *Telemarketing sales representatives* sell over the telephone. They make large numbers of calls to prospects, attempting to sell the company's service themselves, or to arrange an appointment between the prospect and an outside sales representative. Some sales representatives deal exclusively with one, or a few, major clients.

Despite the diversity of services being sold, the jobs of all services sales representatives have much in common. All sales representatives must fully understand and be able to discuss the services their company offers. Also, the procedures they follow are similar. Many sales representatives develop lists of prospective clients through telephone and business directories, asking business associates and customers for leads, and calling on new businesses as they cover their assigned territory. Some services sales representatives acquire clients through inquiries about their company's services.

Regardless of how they first meet the client, all services sales representatives must explain how the services being offered can meet the client's needs. This often involves demonstrations of their company's services. They answer questions about the nature and cost of the services and try to overcome objections in order to persuade potential customers to purchase the services. If they fail to make a sale on the first visit, they may follow up with more visits, letters, or phone calls. After closing a sale, services sales representatives generally follow up to see that the purchase meets the customer's needs, and to determine if additional services can be sold.

Because services sales representatives obtain many of their new accounts through referrals, their success hinges on developing a satisfied clientele who will continue to use the services and will recommend them to other potential customers. Like other types of sales jobs, a services sales representative's reputation is crucial to his or her success.

Services sales work varies with the kind of service sold. Selling highly technical services, such as communications systems or computer consulting services, involves complex and lengthy sales negotiations. In addition, sales of such complex services may require extensive after-sale support. In these situations, sales representatives may operate as part of a team of sales representatives and experts from other departments. Sales representatives receive valuable technical assistance from these experts. For example, those who sell data processing services might work with a systems engineer or computer scientist, and those who sell telephone services might receive technical assistance from a communications consultant. Teams enhance customer service and build strong long-term relationships with customers, resulting in increased sales.

Because of the length of time between the initial contact with a customer and the actual sale, representatives who sell complex technical services generally work with several customers simultaneously. Sales representatives must be well organized and efficient in scheduling their time. Selling less complex services, such as linen supply or exterminating services, generally involves simpler and shorter sales negotiations.

A sales representative's job may also vary with the size of the employer. Those working for large companies generally are more

Services sales representatives frequently seek new accounts.

specialized and are assigned a specific territory, a specific line of services, and their own accounts. In smaller companies, sales representatives may have broader responsibilities—administrative, marketing, or public relations, for example—in addition to their sales duties.

A sales representative often services a specific territory. A representative for a company offering services widely used by the general public, such as pest control, generally has numerous clients in a relatively small territory. On the other hand, a sales representative for a more specialized organization, such as a standardized testing service, may need to service several States to acquire an adequate customer base.

Working Conditions

Working conditions for sales representatives vary. Outside sales representatives responsible for a large territory may spend a great deal of time traveling, sometimes for weeks at a time. Representatives who cover a small territory may spend time in the office each day keeping records, preparing various documents, and setting up appointments with customers. Inside sales representatives and telemarketers spend all their time in their offices, which can range from bright and cheerful customer showrooms to cramped and noisy rooms. Many outside sales representatives have the flexibility to set their own schedules as long as they meet their company's goals.

Selling is stressful work. Sales representatives face competition not only from other companies but also from their fellow sales workers. Companies generally set sales quotas and have contests with prizes for those who make the most sales. There often is considerable pressure on the sales representative to meet monthly sales quotas.

Employment

Services sales representatives held over 612,000 wage and salary jobs in 1994. Over half were in firms providing business services, including computer and data processing, advertising, personnel supply, equipment rental and leasing, and mailing, reproduction, and stenographic services. Other sales representatives worked for firms that offer a wide range of other services, as the following tabulation shows.

Total (percent)	100
Business services	57
Computer and data processing	9
Advertising	7
Personnel supply	9
Mailing, reproduction, and stenographic	3
Miscellaneous equipment rental and leasing	3
Other business services	26
Engineering and management services	11
Personal services	6
Amusement and recreation services	5
Automotive repair services	4
Membership organizations	3
Hotels and other lodging places	2
Health services	2
Education, public and private	2
Other services	7

Training, Other Qualifications, and Advancement

Many employers require that services sales representatives have a college degree, but requirements may vary depending on the industry a particular company represents. Employers who market advertising services seek individuals with a college degree in advertising or marketing or a master's degree in business administration; companies that market educational services prefer individuals with an advanced degree in marketing or a related field. Many hotels seek graduates from college hotel administration programs, and companies that sell computer services and telephone systems prefer sales representatives with a background in computer science or engineering. College courses in business, economics, communications, and marketing are helpful in obtaining other jobs as services sales representatives.

Employers may hire sales representatives with a high school diploma if they have a proven sales record. This is particularly true for those who sell nontechnical services, such as linen supply, exterminating, laundry, or funeral services.

Many firms conduct intensive training programs for their sales representatives. A sound training program covers the history of the business, origin, development, and uses of the service, effective prospecting methods, presentation of the service, answering customer objections, creating customer demand, closing a sale, writing an order, company policies, and the use of technical support personnel. Sales representatives also may attend seminars on a wide range of subjects given by outside or in-house training institutions. These sessions acquaint them with new services and products and help them maintain and update their sales techniques, and may include motivational or sensitivity training to make sales representatives more effective in dealing with people. They generally receive training in the use of computers and communications technology in order to increase their productivity.

Very large companies often prefer to hire sales representatives directly out of college, while smaller companies often prefer to hire individuals with a proven sales record. Smaller companies generally prefer not to incur the expense of providing formal training programs for their sales representatives.

In order to be successful, sales representatives should have a pleasant, outgoing personality and good rapport with people. They must be highly motivated, well organized, and efficient. Good grooming and a neat appearance are essential, as are self-confidence, reliability, and the ability to communicate effectively. Sales representatives should be self-starters who have the ability to work under pressure to meet sales goals.

Sales representatives who have good sales records and leadership ability may advance to supervisory and managerial positions. Frequent contact with business people in other firms provides sales workers with leads about job openings, enhancing advancement opportunities.

Job Outlook

Employment of services sales representatives, as a group, is expected to grow much faster than the average for all occupations through the year 2005 in response to growth of the services industries that employ them. However, the projected growth of particular services industries varies. For example, the continued growth in factory and office automation should lead to much faster than average employment growth for computer and data processing services sales representatives. Growth will be tempered in some industries due to downsizing of the sales force, as well as the growing use of various technologies, such as voice mail, cellular telephones, and laptop computers, that increase sales workers' productivity.

In addition to the jobs generated by this growth, openings will occur each year because of the need to replace sales workers who transfer to other occupations or leave the labor force. Each year, many sales representatives discover that they are unable to earn enough money and leave the occupation. Turnover generally is higher among representatives who sell nontechnical services, since they have invested less time and effort in specialized training. Because of this turnover, job opportunities should be good, especially for those with a college degree and a proven sales record.

Earnings

In 1994, the median annual income for full-time advertising sales representatives was $28,800, while representatives selling other business services earned $32,900. Earnings of representatives who sold technical services generally were higher than earnings of those who sold nontechnical services.

Earnings of experienced sales representatives depend on performance. Successful sales representatives who establish a strong customer base can earn more than managers in their firm. According to Dartnell Corporation's 1994-95 Sales Compensation Survey, the average total cash compensation for entry level sales representatives was $27,800 in business services, $31,600 in educational services, and $24,600 in health services.

Sales representatives are paid in a variety of ways. Some get a straight salary; others are paid solely on a commission basis—a percentage of the dollar value of their sales. Most firms use a combination of salary and commissions. Some services sales representatives receive a base salary plus incentive pay that can add 25 to 75 percent to the sales representative's base salary. In addition to the same benefits package received by other employees of the firm, outside sales representatives have expense accounts to cover meals and travel, and some drive a company car. Many employers offer bonuses, including vacation trips and prizes, for sales that exceed company quotas.

Because sales are affected by changing economic conditions and consumer and business expectations, earnings may fluctuate widely from year to year.

Related Occupations

Services sales representatives must have sales ability and knowledge of the service they sell. Workers in other occupations that require these skills include real estate agents, insurance agents, securities and financial services sales representatives, retail sales workers, manufacturers' and wholesale sales representatives, and travel agents.

Sources of Additional Information

For details about employment opportunities for services sales representatives, contact employers who sell services in your area.

Travel Agents

(D.O.T. 252.152-010)

Nature of the Work

Constantly changing air fares and schedules, a proliferation of vacation packages, and business/pleasure trip combinations can make travel planning frustrating and time consuming. Many people who travel, therefore, turn to travel agents, who assess their needs and make the best possible travel arrangements for them.

Depending on the needs of the client, travel agents give advice on destinations, make arrangements for transportation, hotel accommodations, car rentals, tours, and recreation, or plan the right vacation package or business/pleasure trip combination. They may also advise on weather conditions, restaurants, and tourist attractions and recreation. For international travel, agents also provide information on customs regulations, required papers (passports, visas, and certificates of vaccination), and currency exchange rates.

Travel agents consult a variety of published and computer-based sources for information on departure and arrival times, fares, and hotel ratings and accommodations. They may visit hotels, resorts, and restaurants to judge, firsthand, their comfort, cleanliness, and quality of food and service so they can base recommendations on their own travel experiences or those of colleagues or clients.

Travel agents also promote their services. They make presentations to social and special interest groups, arrange advertising displays, and suggest company-sponsored trips to business managers.

Depending on the size of the travel agency, an agent may specialize by type of travel, such as leisure or business, or destination, such as Europe or Africa.

It is increasingly important for travel agents to have formal or specialized training.

Working Conditions

Travel agents spend most of their time behind a desk conferring with clients, completing paperwork, contacting airlines and hotels for travel arrangements, and promoting group tours. They may be under a great deal of pressure at times, such as during vacation seasons. Many agents, especially those who are self-employed, frequently work long hours.

Employment

Travel agents held about 122,000 jobs in 1994 and are found in every part of the country. More than 9 out of 10 salaried agents worked for travel agencies; some worked for membership organizations. About 1 out of 10 agents are self-employed.

Training, Other Qualifications, and Advancement

The minimum requirement for those interested in becoming a travel agent is a high school diploma or equivalent. With technology and computerization having a profound effect on the work of travel agents, however, formal or specialized training is becoming increasingly important. Many vocational schools offer 6- to 12-week full-time travel agent programs, as well as evening and Saturday programs. Travel courses are also offered in public adult education programs and in community and 4-year colleges. A few colleges offer bachelor's or master's degrees in travel and tourism. Although few college courses relate directly to the travel industry, a college education is sometimes desired by employers to establish a background in areas such as computer science, geography, communication, foreign languages, and world history. Courses in accounting and business management also are important, especially for those who expect to manage or start their own travel agencies. Other desirable qualifications include good typing and letter writing skills, and an ability to work with computers.

The American Society of Travel Agents (ASTA) offers a correspondence course that provides a basic understanding of the travel industry. Travel agencies also provide on-the-job training for their employees, a significant part of which consists of computer instruction. Computer skills are required by employers to operate airline and centralized reservation systems.

Experienced travel agents can take advanced self or group study courses from the Institute of Certified Travel Agents (ICTA) that lead to the designation of Certified Travel Counselor (CTC). The ICTA also offers sales skills development programs and destination specialist programs, which provide a detailed knowledge of the geographic areas of North America, Western Europe, the Caribbean, and the Pacific Rim.

Travel experience is an asset since personal knowledge about a city or foreign country often helps to influence clients' travel plans, as is experience as an airline reservation agent. Selling skills, patience, and the ability to gain the confidence of clients also are useful qualities.

Some employees start as reservation clerks or receptionists in travel agencies. With experience and some formal training, they can take on greater responsibilities and eventually assume travel agent duties. In agencies with many offices, travel agents may advance to office manager or to other managerial positions.

Those who start their own agencies generally have experience in an established agency. They must generally gain formal supplier or corporation approval before they can receive commissions. Suppliers or corporations are organizations of airlines, ship lines, or rail lines. The Airlines Reporting Corporation and the International Airlines Travel Agency Network, for example, are the approving bodies for airlines. To gain approval, an agency must be in operation, be financially sound, and employ at least one experienced manager/travel agent.

There are no Federal licensing requirements for travel agents. However, nine States require some form of registration or certification of retail sellers of travel services: California, Florida, Hawaii, Illinois, Iowa, Ohio, Oregon, Rhode Island, and Washington. More information may be obtained by contacting the Office of the Attorney General or Department of Commerce for each State.

Job Outlook

Employment of travel agents is expected to grow faster than the average for all occupations through the year 2005. Many job openings will arise as new agencies open and existing agencies expand, but most openings will occur as experienced agents transfer to other occupations or leave the labor force.

Spending on travel is expected to increase significantly through the year 2005. As business activity expands, so will business-related travel. Employment of managerial, professional specialty, and sales representative occupations—those who do most business travel—is projected to grow at least as fast as the average. Also, with rising household incomes, smaller families, and an increasing number of older people who are more likely to travel, more people are expected to travel on vacation—and to do so more frequently—than in the past. In fact, many people take more than one vacation a year.

Charter flights and larger, more efficient planes have brought air transportation within the budgets of more people. Also, the easing of Government regulation of air fares and routes has fostered greater competition among airlines, resulting in more affordable service. In addition, American travel agents organize tours for the growing number of foreign visitors. Although most travel agencies now have automated reservation systems, this has not weakened demand for travel agents.

Some developments, however, may reduce opportunities for travel agents in the future. The development of on-line computer systems has allowed people with access to such systems to make their own travel arrangements. Suppliers of travel services are increasingly able to make their services available through less conventional means, such as electronic ticketing machines and remote ticket printers. Also, airline companies have put a cap on the amount of commissions they will pay to travel agencies. The full impact of these practices on travel agents, though, has yet to be determined.

The travel industry generally is sensitive to economic downturns and political crises, when travel plans are likely to be deferred. Therefore, the number of job opportunities fluctuates.

Earnings

Median annual earnings of travel agents were $21,300 in 1994. The middle 50 percent earned between $16,000 and $28,900 annually. Ten percent earned less than $13,000 and 10 percent earned more than $38,400 annually. Experience, sales ability, and the size and location of the agency determine the salary of a travel agent. According to a Louis Harris survey, conducted for *Travel Weekly Magazine*, the 1994 median annual earnings of travel agents on straight salary with less than 1 year experience were $12,990; from 1 to 3 years, $16,481; from 3 to 5 years, $19,491; from 5 to 10 years, $22,122; and more than 10 years, $24,645. Salaried agents usually have standard benefits, such as medical insurance coverage and paid vacations, that self-employed agents must provide for themselves. Among agencies, those focusing on corporate sales pay higher salaries and provide more extensive benefits, on average, than those who focus on leisure sales.

Earnings of travel agents who own their agencies depend mainly on commissions from airlines and other carriers, cruise lines, tour operators, and lodging places. Commissions for domestic travel arrangements, cruises, hotels, sightseeing tours, and car rentals are about 7-10 percent of the total sale; and for international travel, about 11 percent. They may also charge clients a service fee for the time and expense involved in planning a trip.

During the first year of business or while awaiting corporation approval, self-employed travel agents generally have low earnings. Their income usually is limited to commissions from hotels, cruises, and tour operators and to nominal fees for making complicated arrangements. Even established agents have lower profits during economic downturns.

When they travel, agents usually get reduced rates for transportation and accommodations.

Related Occupations

Travel agents organize and schedule business, educational, or recreational travel or activities. Other workers with similar responsibilities include tour guides, meeting planners, airline reservation agents, rental car agents, and travel counselors.

Sources of Additional Information

For further information on training opportunities, contact:

☛American Society of Travel Agents, Education Department, 1101 King St., Alexandria, VA 22314.

For information on certification qualifications, contact:

☛The Institute of Certified Travel Agents, 148 Linden St., P.O. Box 812059, Wellesley, MA 02181-0012, or phone toll free 1-800-542-4282.

Administrative Support Occupations, Including Clerical

Adjusters, Investigators, and Collectors

(D.O.T. 168.267-014 and -038; 191.167-022; 195.267-010; 203.382-014; 205.367-018, -034 and -046; 209.382-014 and .687-018; 219.362-042, and -050, .367-014, and .482-014; 241.217, .267-014, -018, -030, and -034, .357, 362, .367-010, -014, -022, and -034, and .387; and 249.367-030)

Nature of the Work
Organizations must deal smoothly and efficiently with a variety of problems to maintain good relations with their customers. Handling complaints, interpreting and explaining policies or regulations, resolving billing disputes, collecting delinquent accounts, and determining eligibility for governmental assistance are just a few examples. Organizations like insurance companies, department stores, banks, and government social services agencies employ adjusters, investigators, and collectors to act as intermediaries with the public in these situations. The following is a discussion of occupations that make up this group of workers.

Claim Representatives. Claim representatives at insurance companies investigate claims, negotiate settlements, and authorize payments to claimants. When a policyholder files a claim for damage or a loss, the *claim adjuster, claim examiner,* or *claim investigator* must initially determine whether the customer's insurance policy covers it and the amount of the loss.

Minor claims filed by automobile or homeowner policyholders are usually handled by "inside adjusters" or "telephone adjusters." These workers contact claimants by telephone or by mail to get information on repair costs, medical expenses, or other details the company needs. Many companies centralize this operation in a drive-in claims center, where the cost of repair is determined and a check is issued immediately.

More complex cases are referred to an "independent adjuster" or "outside adjuster." Claim adjusters plan and schedule the work required to process a claim. They investigate claims by interviewing the claimant and witnesses, consulting police and hospital records, and inspecting property damage to determine the extent of the company's liability. They keep photographs, written or taped statements, or computer files of information obtained from witnesses and prepare reports of their findings. When the policy holder's claim is legitimate, the claim adjuster negotiates with the claimant and settles the claim. When claims are contested, adjusters may testify in court.

Some adjusters work with multiple lines of insurance. Others specialize in claims associated with fire damage, marine loss, automotive damage, product liability, or workers' compensation. Material damage adjusters inspect automobile damage and use the latest computerized estimating equipment to prepare estimates of the damage.

In life and health insurance companies, the counterpart of the claim adjuster is the claim examiner. In property and casualty insurance companies, the claim examiner may supervise claim adjusters. In both cases, they investigate questionable claims or authorize payment for those exceeding a designated amount. Larger claims are referred to senior examiners. Examiners may check claim applications for completeness and accuracy, interview medical specialists, consult policy files to verify information on a claim, or calculate

benefit payments. They also maintain records of settled claims and prepare reports to be submitted to their company's data processing department.

Claim representatives are making greater use of computers to keep records of clients and actions taken in various claims. Most have computer terminals on their desks, and a growing number use portable lap-top computers to enter or access information when they are on assignment outside the office.

Insurance Processing Clerks. *Policy processing clerks* process new insurance policies, modifications to existing policies, and claims. They begin the new policy process by reviewing the insurance application to ensure that all the questions have been answered. After an application has been reviewed by underwriters and the company determines that it will issue a policy, a policy processing clerk prepares the necessary forms and informs the insurance sales agent of an application's processing status. Policy processing clerks also update existing policies—such as a change in beneficiary, amount of coverage, or type of insurance—and recalculate premiums. They mail correspondence notices regarding changes to the sales agent and to the policyholder. Policy processing clerks maintain files for each policyholder, including policies that are to be reinstated or canceled.

Claim clerks, also called *claim interviewers,* obtain information from policyholders regarding claims. Claims may concern a number of things, such as fire damage, personal injury, or an automobile accident. They prepare reports and review insurance claim forms and related documents for completeness. They call or write the insured or other party involved for missing information and update claim files. They may transmit routine claims for payment or advise the claim supervisor if further investigation is needed.

Like claim representatives, insurance processing clerks use computers extensively in their work. Most spend a large part of their time creating and updating records at a personal computer or terminal.

Adjustment Clerks. Adjustment clerks investigate and resolve customers' complaints about merchandise, service, billing, or credit rating. They may work for banks, department stores, utility companies, and other large organizations selling products and services to the public. Sometimes they are called *customer service representatives, customer complaint clerks,* or *adjustment correspondents.*

Adjustment clerks examine all pertinent information to determine the validity of a customer's complaint. In a department store, this may mean checking sales slips or warranties, as well as the merchandise in question. In a bank, it could mean reviewing records and videotapes of automated teller machine transactions. In a utility company, they review meter books, microfilm, computer printouts, and machine accounting records. Regardless of the setting, these clerks get information—in person, by telephone, or through written correspondence—from all parties involved.

After an investigation and evaluation of the facts, adjustment clerks report their findings, adjustments, and recommendations. These may include exchanging merchandise, refunding money, crediting customers' accounts, or adjusting customers' bills. Adjustment clerks also ensure that the appropriate changes are set in motion and follow up on the recommendations to ensure customer satisfaction. To prevent similar complaints in the future, they may recommend to management improvements in product, packaging, shipping methods, service, or billing methods and procedures. Adjustment clerks keep records of all relevant matters, using them to prepare reports for their supervisors.

Adjustment clerks also respond to inquiries from customers. Clerks frequently can answer these inquiries with a form letter, but other times they must compose a letter themselves. Upon request, adjustment clerks issue duplicate or additional credit cards for banks and department stores.

Bill and Account Collectors. Bill and account collectors, sometimes called *collection correspondents*, are responsible for ensuring customers pay their overdue accounts. Some are employed by third party collection agencies, while others, known as "inside collectors," work directly for the original creditors, like department stores, hospitals, or banks.

Many companies automatically notify customers by mail if their account is overdue. When customers do not respond, collectors are called on to locate and notify them of the delinquent account, usually over the telephone, sometimes by letter. When customers move without leaving a forwarding address, collectors may check with the post office, telephone companies, credit bureaus, or former neighbors to obtain their new address. This is called "skip-tracing."

Once collectors find the debtor, they inform them of the overdue account and solicit payment. If necessary, they review the terms of the sale, service, or credit contract with the customer. Collectors may attempt to learn the cause of the delay in payment. Where feasible, they offer the customer advice and counsel on how to pay off the debts, such as by taking out a bill consolidation loan. However, the collector's objective is always to ensure that the customer first pays the debt in question.

If customers agree to pay, collectors note that for the record and check later to verify that the payment was indeed made. Collectors may have authority to grant an extension of time if customers ask for one. If customers fail to respond at all, collectors prepare a statement to that effect for the credit department of the establishment. In more extreme cases, collectors may initiate repossession proceedings or service disconnections, or hand the account over to an attorney for legal action.

Most collectors handle other administrative functions for the accounts assigned to them. This may include recording changes of addresses, and purging the records of the deceased. Bill and account collectors keep records of the amounts collected and the status of the accounts. Some fill out daily reports to keep their supervisors apprised of their progress. In some organizations, inside collectors receive payments and post the amounts to the customers' account. In most operations, however, the posting and receiving are done by other clerical workers. Collectors employed by collection agencies do not receive payments; rather, their primary responsibility is to get customers to pay their obligation.

Increasingly, collectors use computers and a variety of automated systems to keep track of overdue accounts. Typically, collectors work at video display terminals that are linked to computers. In sophisticated predicted dialer systems, the computer dials the telephone automatically and the collector speaks only when a connection has been made. Such systems eliminate time spent calling busy or nonanswering numbers. Many collectors use regular telephones; some wear headsets like those used by telephone operators. Occasionally, supervisors may listen in on collectors' conversations with customers to evaluate their job performance.

Welfare Eligibility Workers and Interviewers. Welfare eligibility workers and interviewers—sometimes referred to as *intake workers, eligibility determination workers, eligibility specialists,* or *income maintenance specialists*—determine who can receive welfare and other types of social assistance. They do so by interviewing and investigating applicants and recipients to see who is eligible. Based on the personal and financial information they obtain and the rules and regulations of each program, they initiate procedures to grant, modify, deny, or terminate individuals' eligibility for various aid programs. This information is recorded and evaluated to determine the amounts of the grants.

Welfare eligibility workers and interviewers work with various public assistance programs. The best-known are Aid to Families with Dependent Children, Medicaid, Food Stamps, and the Work Incentive Program. Depending on local circumstances, there may be other programs, such as those for public housing, refugee assistance, and fuel assistance.

Most welfare eligibility workers and interviewers specialize in a specific area, such as housing, but some are responsible for several areas. They may assist social workers by informing them of pertinent information they have gathered during their interviews with applicants. In some areas, particularly rural ones, eligibility workers may also perform other welfare duties.

These workers often provide information to applicants and current recipients. For example, they may explain and interpret eligibility rules and regulations or identify other resources available in the community for financial or social welfare assistance. More experienced workers may help train new workers. In addition, they may be assigned to special units whose responsibility is to detect fraud.

An increasing number of jurisdictions are using computers to increase worker productivity and to reduce the incidence of welfare fraud. In these settings, welfare eligibility workers and interviewers sit in front of computer terminals when they interview applicants and recipients. Welfare eligibility workers then enter the information provided. In the most advanced systems, the computer terminal prompts them with questions.

Although these workers usually interview applicants and recipients who visit their offices, they may make occasional home visits, especially if the applicant or recipient is elderly or disabled. They may also check with employers or other references to verify answers and get further information.

The authority of welfare eligibility workers and interviewers varies from one jurisdiction to another. In some places, these workers are authorized to decide on an applicant's eligibility, subject to review by their supervisor. In other places, however, they can only make recommendations to their supervisors, who in turn make the ultimate decision.

Working Conditions

Most claim examiners have desk jobs that require no unusual physical activity. They typically work a standard 5-day, 40-hour week. Claim examiners may work longer hours during peak periods or when quarterly and annual statements are prepared. Sometimes they

Welfare eligibility workers interview clients before they receive benefits.

travel from time to time to obtain information by personal interview.

Many claim adjusters work outside the office, visiting and inspecting damaged buildings, for example. Occasionally, experienced adjusters are away from home for days when they travel to the scene of a disaster—such as a tornado, hurricane, or flood—to work with local adjusters and government officials. Some adjusters are on "emergency call" in the case of such incidents. Material damage adjusters work at local claim centers where policy holders take their cars for estimates of damage.

Adjusters generally have the flexibility to arrange their work schedule to accommodate evening and weekend appointments with clients. Some report to the office every morning to get their assignments while others simply call from home and spend their days traveling to claim sites. This enables some adjusters to work independently.

Most insurance processing clerks work 40 hours a week in an office. Much of the work is routine and requires remaining at work stations for extended periods of time. Because most insurance information is stored on computers, many of these workers sit at video display terminals and enter or access information while the customer is on the phone. Because most companies provide 24-hour claim service to their policyholders, some claim clerks work evenings and weekends. Many claim clerks work part time.

Adjustment clerks, bill and account collectors, and welfare eligibility workers and interviewers work in offices, usually during regular business hours. Some work part time. A few bill and account collectors work as temporaries. From their offices, they deal with customers, clients, or applicants, either by telephone or in person. Dealing with upset or angry clients is often part of the daily routine in these jobs, making the work stressful at times.

Some welfare eligibility workers and interviewers may be hired on a seasonal basis to help administer a specific program. For example, some States hire these workers for the winter to help run emergency fuel assistance programs.

Adjusters, investigators, and collectors who spend a lot of time working at video display terminals may experience musculoskeletal strain and eyestrain.

Employment

Adjusters, investigators, and collectors held about 1,286,000 jobs in 1994. The following tabulation shows the percent distribution of employment by detailed occupation:

Total	100
Adjustment clerks	29
Bill and account collectors	20
Insurance policy processing clerks	14
Insurance adjusters, examiners, and investigators	13
Insurance claims clerks	9
Welfare eligibility workers and interviewers	8
Claims examiners, property and casualty insurance	4
All other adjusters and investigators	3

Insurance companies employ the vast majority of claim adjusters, examiners, investigators, property and casualty insurance claim examiners, policy processing clerks, and claim clerks. The remainder are employed by real estate firms and government agencies.

About one-fifth of all adjustment clerks are employed by department stores, grocery stores, or catalog and mail order houses. Manufacturing firms, banks and other financial institutions, and telephone companies are other major employers of these workers.

One in 6 bill and account collectors works for a credit reporting and collection agency. Many others work in banks, department stores, and other institutions that extend credit.

Nine of every 10 welfare eligibility workers and interviewers work for State or local government agencies. In 37 States, these workers are employed exclusively by the State government. In the remainder, they are employed by the county or municipal government. Most of those not employed by government work for private social service agencies.

Training, Other Qualifications, and Advancement

Training and entry requirements vary widely for adjuster, investigator, and collector jobs. A high school education is sufficient to qualify for most insurance processing clerk, adjustment clerk, and bill and account collector positions, while a bachelor's degree is preferred for most claim representative positions. While some college education is preferred for positions as adjuster or welfare eligibility worker or interviewer, many people qualify for these positions on the strength of related prior work experience. Because a significant and growing proportion of adjusters, investigators, and collectors use computers, courses in typing or word processing are recommended. Employers increasingly view experience with computers as an asset.

Claim Representatives. Most companies prefer to hire college graduates for claim representative positions. Entry-level workers may be hired without college coursework if they have specialized experience. For example, people with knowledge of automobile mechanics or body repair may qualify as material damage adjusters and those with extensive clerical experience might be hired as inside adjusters. Both adjusters and examiners should be observant and enjoy working with details.

No specific college major is recommended as the best preparation for these occupations. Although courses in insurance, economics, or other business subjects are helpful, a degree in almost any field is adequate. An adjuster who has a business or an accounting background might specialize in claims of financial loss due to strikes, breakdowns in equipment, or damage to merchandise. College training in engineering is helpful in adjusting industrial claims, such as damage from fires and other accidents. A legal background is most helpful to those handling workers' compensation and product liability cases. Knowledge of computer applications is increasingly important, and in most instances essential.

Most States require adjusters to be licensed. Applicants usually must comply with one or more of the following: Pass a written examination covering the fundamentals of adjusting; complete an approved course in insurance or loss adjusting; furnish character references; be at least 20 or 21 years of age and a resident of the State; and file a surety bond.

Because they often work closely with claimants, witnesses, and other insurance professionals, claim representatives must be able to communicate effectively with others. Some companies require applicants to pass a battery of written aptitude tests designed to measure communication, analytical, and general mathematical skills. Examiners must understand Federal and State insurance laws and regulations.

Some large insurance companies provide on-the-job training and home-study courses for entry-level claim adjusters and examiners. For example, material damage adjusters would learn about automobile body construction, analysis of collision data, and repair cost estimation, including computerized estimating equipment. They also learn how to deal with customers.

Workers may receive their training through courses offered by the Insurance Institute of America, a nonprofit organization offering educational programs and professional certification to persons in the property-liability insurance industry. The Insurance Institute of America offers an Associate in Claims designation upon successful completion of four essay examinations. Adjusters can prepare for the examination by independent home study or through company or public classes.

The International Claim Association offers a program on life and health insurance claim administration. Completion of the six-examination program leads to the professional designation, Associate, Life and Health Claims.

The Life Office Management Association offers a comprehensive 10-course life and health insurance educational program that leads to the professional designation, Fellow, Life Management Institute (FLMI). LOMA also offers the Master Fellow Program that is designed specifically to meet the continuing education needs of life and health insurance professionals. Students can prepare for FLMI exams through independent home study or through insurance company or FLMI Society classes.

Beginning adjusters and examiners work on small claims under the supervision of an experienced worker. As they learn more about claim investigation and settlement, they are assigned larger, more complex claims. Trainees are promoted as they demonstrate competence in handling assignments and as they progress in their course work. Because of the complexity of insurance regulations and claim procedures, workers who lack formal academic training tend to advance slower than those with additional education. Employees who demonstrate competence in claim work or administrative skills may be promoted to department supervisor in a field office or to a managerial position in the home office.

Insurance Processing Clerks. High school graduation is considered adequate preparation for most insurance processing clerk positions. Courses in typing and word processing, and business arithmetic are desirable. Employers view favorably previous office experience and familiarity with computers. Most new workers begin as file clerks and move into insurance processing positions as they demonstrate their ability. However, people with considerable clerical experience may begin processing insurance policies immediately.

Some experienced insurance processing clerks may be promoted to a clerical supervisor position. Advancement to a claim representative or an underwriting technician position is possible for clerks who demonstrate potential, have college coursework, or have taken specialized courses in insurance. Many companies offer home-study courses for their employees so they can acquire the knowledge necessary to advance.

Adjustment Clerks. Many employers do not require any formal education for adjustment clerk positions. Instead, they look for people who can read and write and who possess good communications and interpersonal skills. Typing ability is also viewed favorably.

Adjustment clerk is an entry level position in some, but not all, organizations. Depending on their assignment, new adjustment clerks may receive training on the job from a supervisor or an experienced coworker, or they may enter a formal training course offered by the organization. Training covers such topics as how to use computers, what standard forms to use, whom to contact in other departments of the organization, and how to deal with customers. Some employers provide more advanced training for experienced adjustment clerks. This training may be offered in-house or from trade associations or local colleges.

Bill and Account Collectors. While high school graduation sometimes is required by employers when they hire bill and account collectors, formal education beyond high school is not stressed. Previous work experience as a collector is particularly valuable. Experience in the field of telemarketing or as a telephone operator also is helpful, as is knowledge of the billing process. Employers seek individuals who speak well and who are persistent and detail-oriented.

Employers normally provide training to new bill and account collectors. This training, which may last up to a couple of months, is usually conducted in a classroom or on the job. It may use lectures, videotapes, computer programs, role-playing, and hands-on experience. In addition to learning about skip-tracing and the firm's billing procedure, new collectors learn communications and negotiating skills. Learning to use the firm's computer and telephone systems is an integral part of their training.

Successful bill and account collectors may become supervisors. Some even start their own collection agencies.

Welfare Eligibility Workers and Interviewers. Hiring requirements for welfare eligibility workers and interviewers vary widely.

Depending on the jurisdiction, applicants may need a high school diploma, some post-secondary training, or a bachelor's degree. Previous work experience may be substituted for education in some places, particularly if it is in a closely related field like employment interviewing, social work, or insurance claims. Fluency in a foreign language may be an advantage in parts of the country with a high concentration of non-English speaking people.

Because they deal with people who are in difficult economic circumstances, welfare eligibility workers and interviewers should be compassionate and empathetic. Attention to detail is important because there are many procedures, and regulations that must be observed.

After they are hired, eligibility workers are given training, sometimes in a formal classroom setting, other times in a more informal manner. They are taught the policies, procedures, and program regulations that they are expected to use to determine eligibility. If a formal training program is selected, it generally is followed by on-the-job training provided by the supervisor.

Advancement to the job of social worker is possible, although additional formal education such as a bachelor's or master's degree usually is needed.

Job Outlook
Overall employment of adjusters, investigators, and collectors is expected to grow faster than the average for all occupations through the year 2005. Most job openings will result from the need to replace workers who transfer to other occupations or leave the labor force.

Growth rates will vary considerably by occupation. Employment of insurance claim examiners is expected to grow about as fast as the average as the increasing volume of insurance results in more insurance claims. Shifts in the age distribution of the population will result in a large increase in the number of people who assume career and family responsibilities. People in this group have the greatest need for life and health insurance, as well as protection for homes, automobiles, and other possessions. A growing demand for insurance coverage for working women is also expected. New or expanding businesses will need protection for new plants and equipment and for insurance covering their employees' health and safety. Opportunities should be particularly good for claim representatives who specialize in complex business insurance such as marine cargo, workers' compensation, and product and pollution liability.

Employment of insurance processing clerks is expected to grow more slowly than the average as computerization automates some functions performed by these workers, although the increasing number of policyholders will require more workers to provide customer service. Within this group, employment of adjusters and claim clerks will increase about as fast as the average because their work requires much interpersonal contact, which cannot be automated. However, employment of policy processing clerks will decline because their jobs can be automated. The number of job openings for workers in the insurance industry should not fluctuate greatly from year to year. This industry, particularly the health insurance component, is less sensitive to cyclical swings in the economy than most industries.

Employment of adjustment clerks is expected to grow much faster than the average as business establishments place an increased emphasis on maintaining good customer relations. An important aspect of good customer service is resolving customers' complaints in a friendly and timely fashion. Because much of their work involves direct communication with customers, demand for adjustment clerks is expected to keep pace with the growth in the number of customers.

Bill and account collector jobs also are expected to grow much faster than average as the level of consumer debt rises. As the economy expands, firms will strive to increase the efficiency of their debt collection to keep losses at a minimum. Contrary to the pattern in most occupations, employment of bill and account collectors tends to rise during recessions. This is due primarily to the difficulty that many individuals have in meeting their financial obligations.

Employment of welfare eligibility workers and interviewers is expected to grow more slowly than average as State and local governments attempt to curb the growth in their expenditures for public assistance.

Earnings

Earnings of adjusters, investigators, and collectors vary significantly. For adjusters and investigators, the median weekly earnings in 1994 were $418. The middle 50 percent earned between about $327 and $564 a week. Adjusters are also furnished a company car or are reimbursed for use of their own vehicle for business purposes.

Specific information on earnings of insurance processing clerks and is not available. However, median weekly earnings for records clerks, a category that includes policy processing clerks, were $398 in 1994. Interviewers, whose work is similar to that of claim clerks, also had median weekly earnings of $361.

Median weekly earnings of full-time bill and account collectors were $378 in 1994; the middle 50 percent earned between $304 and $466 a week. Ten percent earned less than $231 and 10 percent more than $605. Some bill and account collectors receive a base salary and work on commission beyond that.

Median weekly earnings of full-time welfare eligibility workers and interviewers were about $452 in 1994; the middle 50 percent earned between $342 and $548 a week. The lowest 10 percent earned less than $268 and the top 10 percent earned more than $651.

Welfare eligibility workers and interviewers are twice as likely to belong to unions than workers in all occupations. In 1994, about one-third of all welfare eligibility workers and interviewers were union members compared to less than one-sixth for all occupations. The two principal unions representing these workers are the American Federation of State, County, and Municipal Employees and the Service Employees International Union.

Related Occupations

Insurance adjusters and examiners investigate, analyze, and determine the validity of their firm's liability concerning personal, casualty, or property loss or damages and effect settlement with claimants. Workers in other occupations that require similar skills include cost estimators, budget analysts, and private investigators.

The work of insurance processing clerks and adjustment clerks is similar to that of other workers who compile, review, or maintain records, including coding, contract, auditing, and reservation clerks and title searchers.

The work of bill and account collectors is related to that of customer service representatives, telemarketers, telephone interviewers, and other workers who deal with the public over the telephone.

The work of welfare eligibility workers is similar to that of human services workers, financial aid counselors, loan counselors, credit counselors, probation officers, and other workers who interview customers or clients.

Sources of Additional Information

General information about a career as a claim representative or an insurance processing clerk is available from the home offices of many life and property and liability insurance companies.

Information about career opportunities in these occupations may be obtained from:

☛Insurance Information Institute, 110 William St., New York, NY 10038.

Information about licensing requirements for claim adjusters may be obtained from the department of insurance in each State.

For more information on claim representatives, contact:

☛Alliance of American Insurers, 1501 Woodfield Rd., Suite 400 West, Schaumburg, IL 60173-4980.

For information about the voluntary designation Associate in Claims, contact:

☛Insurance Institute of America, 720 Providence Rd., P.O. Box 3016, Malvern, PA 19355-0716.

☛National Association of Independent Insurance Adjusters, 300 West Washington St., Suite 805, Chicago, IL 60606.

Information on the Associate, Life and Health Claims and the Fellow, Life Management Institute designations can be obtained from:

☛Life Office Management Association, 5770 Powers Ferry Rd., Atlanta, GA 30327-4308.

Career information on bill and account collectors is available from:

☛American Collectors Association, Inc., P.O. Box 39106, Minneapolis, MN 55439-0106.

Employment information on welfare eligibility workers and interviewers is available at social service offices of municipal, county, and State governments.

Bank Tellers

(D.O.T. 211.362 except -010; 211.382-010; 219.462-010)

Nature of the Work

Bank tellers interact with the majority of bank customers. Tellers generally handle a wide range of banking transactions, such as cashing checks, accepting deposits and loan payments, and processing withdrawals. They sell savings bonds; accept payment for customers' utility bills; receive deposits for special accounts; keep records and perform the necessary paperwork for customer loans; process the proliferating variety of certificates of deposit and money market accounts; and sell travelers' checks. Some tellers specialize in handling foreign currencies or commercial or business accounts.

Before cashing a check, the teller must verify the date, bank name, and identity of the person to receive payment, and see that the document is legal tender, that written and numerical amounts agree, and that the account has sufficient funds to cover the check. The teller must carefully count out the cash to avoid errors. Sometimes a customer withdraws money in the form of a cashier's check, which the teller prepares and verifies. When accepting a deposit, the teller checks the accuracy of the deposit slip and processes the transaction. Tellers may use machines to calculate and record transactions and to prepare documents, such as receipts and drafts. In some banks, they type or write deposit receipts and passbook entries by hand, but this is uncommon. In most banks, tellers use computer terminals to record deposits and withdrawals. Some banks use very sophisticated computer systems that give tellers quick access to detailed information on customer accounts. Tellers may use this information to tailor their services to fit the customer's needs, or recommend an appropriate bank product or service.

The duties of tellers begin before the bank opens and end after the bank closes. They begin the day by receiving and counting an amount of working cash for their drawer; this amount is verified by a supervisor, usually the head teller. Tellers use this cash for payments during the day and are responsible for its safe and accurate handling. After banking hours, tellers count cash on hand, list the currency-received tickets on a balance sheet, and balance the day's accounts. They sort checks and deposit slips. Tellers also spend time learning about the bank's products and services and changes in the bank's procedures. They also spend time training to refresh and upgrade their skills.

Tellers process numerous mail transactions. Some tellers replenish cash drawers and corroborate deposits and payments to automated teller machines (ATMs). Head tellers supervise the work of other tellers and ensure that ATMs function properly.

Because banks offer more and increasingly complex financial services, most bank tellers are now being trained to act as customer

Employment of bank tellers is projected to decline.

service representatives in addition to their other duties. These tellers can briefly explain to customers the various types of accounts and financial services offered by their bank, and refer customers to more experienced customer service representatives or bank managers. (New accounts clerks, who also may act as customer service representatives, are discussed in the *Handbook* statement on interviewing and new accounts clerks. Bank managers are covered in the *Handbook* statement on financial managers.)

Working Conditions

Tellers generally work during the day, Monday through Friday; some evening and weekend work may be required. The job offers ample opportunity to work part time with flexible hours; in some banks, 90 percent of tellers work part time. Banks often hire part-time, or "peak-time," tellers for busy banking periods such as lunch hours and weekend mornings. Increasing numbers of tellers work outside the traditional bank setting—in shopping malls, grocery stores, or other large retail establishments. Continual communication with customers, repetitive tasks, long periods within a fairly small area, and a high level of attention to security also characterize the job.

Employment

Bank tellers held about 559,000 jobs in 1994; over one-fourth worked part time. The overwhelming majority, about 97 percent, worked in commercial banks, savings institutions, or credit unions. The rest worked in personal, business, or Federal credit institutions; mortgage banks; security and commodity brokerages; and holding and other investment offices.

Training, Other Qualifications, and Advancement

When hiring tellers, banks seek applicants who enjoy public contact and have good numerical, clerical, and communication skills.. Tellers must feel comfortable handling large amounts of cash and working with computers and video terminals, since their work is highly automated. In some metropolitan areas, employers seek multilingual tellers.

Although tellers work independently, their recordkeeping is closely supervised. Accuracy and attention to detail are vital. Tellers should be courteous, attentive, and patient in dealing with the public, because customers often judge a bank by the way they are treated at the teller window. Maturity, tact, and the ability to quickly explain bank procedures and services are important in helping customers complete transactions or make financial decisions.

Many entrants transfer from other occupations; virtually all have at least a high school education. In general, banks prefer applicants who have had high school courses in mathematics, accounting, bookkeeping, economics, and public speaking. New tellers at larger

banks receive at least 1 week of formal classroom training. Formal training is followed by several weeks of on-the-job training where tellers observe experienced workers before doing the work themselves. Smaller banks rely primarily upon on-the-job training. In addition to instruction in basic duties, many banks now include extensive training in the bank's products and services—so that tellers can refer customers to appropriate products—communication and sales skills, and instruction on equipment such as ATMs and on-line video terminals.

In large banks, beginners usually start as limited-transaction tellers, cashing checks and processing simple transactions for a few days, before becoming full-service tellers. Often banks simultaneously train tellers for other clerical duties.

Advancement opportunities are good for well-trained, motivated employees. Experienced tellers may advance to head teller, customer service representative, or new accounts clerk. Outstanding tellers who have had some college or specialized training offered by the banking industry may be promoted to a managerial position. Banks encourage this upward mobility by providing access to education and other sources of additional training.

Tellers can prepare for better jobs by taking courses offered or accredited by the American Institute of Banking, an educational affiliate of the American Bankers Association, or the Institute of Financial Education. These organizations have several hundred chapters in cities across the country and numerous study groups in small communities, and they offer correspondence courses. They also work closely with local colleges and universities in preparing courses of study. Most banks use the facilities of these organizations, which assist local banks in conducting cooperative training programs or developing independent training programs. In addition, many banks refund college tuition fees to their employees upon successful completion of their courses. Although most courses are meant for employed tellers, some community colleges offer preemployment training programs. These programs can help prepare applicants for a job in banking, and can give them an advantage over other jobseekers.

Job Outlook

Opportunites for employment as a bank teller should be good for qualified applicants. While employment of bank tellers is expected to decline through the year 2005 and growth will not contribute to opportunities, many job openings should arise from the need to replace tellers who transfer to other occupations or stop working. Replacement needs will create many opportunities because the job turnover rate is high—characteristic of occupations that generally require little formal education and offer relatively low pay—and the occupation is large. Banks should continue to have difficulty finding prospective tellers with the desired skills, particularly as the duties of these workers become more complex.

The number of bank tellers is projected to decrease for a variety of reasons. One reflects changes in the banking industry. Banks are expected to decline in number and increase in size as interstate banking grows. As banks become larger, the operations, duties and responsibilities, and staffing of branch offices will change, and some branches will close. These changes are reducing the demand for tellers.

New banking technology is also decreasing the demand for tellers. The adoption of new technology in banking has been slow historically, but banks are increasingly using the available technology to gain a competitive edge. Some banks have introduced branches that consist entirely of ATMs and Kiosks. Kiosks use ATM technology and video screens and cameras to allow customers at several remote locations to conduct transactions with tellers at a central location. There are also banks which allow banking by computer and by telephone from one's home or office. Banks are also opening branches inside supermarkets and department stores; instead of tellers, they have ATMs and more highly trained customer service representatives, who can perform the standard duties of tellers, but who can also open new accounts and arrange for customers to receive other services or products sold by the bank.

Earnings

In 1994, median annual earnings of full-time tellers were $15,300. The lowest 10 percent earned about $9,900 while the top 10 percent earned around $24,200. Some banks offer incentives whereby tellers earn supplemental rewards for inducing customers to use other financial products and services offered by the bank. In general, a greater range of responsibilities results in a higher salary. Experience, length of service, and, especially, the location and size of the bank also are important.

Some part-time tellers may not be eligible for certain benefits such as life and health insurance, although they may have higher hourly earnings in lieu of benefits.

Related Occupations

Tellers combine customer service and a knowledge of bank procedures with quickness and accuracy to process money, checks, and other financial items for customers. Other workers with similar duties include new accounts clerks, cashiers, toll collectors, post office clerks, auction clerks, and ticket sellers.

Sources of Additional Information

General information about banking occupations, training opportunities, and the banking industry is available from:

☛American Bankers Association, Center for Banking Information, 1120 Connecticut Ave. NW., Washington, DC 20036.

For information on continuing education, preemployment training, and banking jobs, contact:

☛Institute of Financial Education, 111 E. Wacker Dr., Suite 900, Chicago, IL 60601-4389.

☛American Institute of Banking, 1120 Connecticut Ave. NW., Washington, DC 20036.

State bankers' associations can furnish specific information about job opportunities in their State. Or contact individual banks to inquire about job openings, and for more details about the activities, responsibilities, and preferred qualifications of tellers. For the names and addresses of banks and savings and related institutions, as well as the names of their principal officers, consult one of the following directories.

☛The American Financial Directory, (Norcross, Ga., McFadden Business Publications).

☛Polk's World Bank Directory, (Nashville, R.L. Polk & Co.).

☛Rand McNally Bankers Directory, (Chicago, Rand McNally & Co.).

☛The U.S. Savings and Loan Directory, (Chicago, Rand McNally & Co.).

☛Rand McNally Credit Union Directory, (Chicago, Rand McNally & Co.).

Clerical Supervisors and Managers

(List of D.O.T. codes available on request. See page 478.)

Nature of the Work

All organizations need timely and effective clerical and administrative support to operate efficiently. Coordinating this support is the responsibility of clerical supervisors and managers. They can be found in nearly every sector of the economy, working in positions as varied as office manager, customer services supervisor, or chief telephone operator.

Although some functions may vary considerably, many duties are common to all. Supervisors perform administrative tasks to ensure that their staffs can work efficiently. For example, equipment and machinery used in their departments must be in good working order. If the computer system goes down or a photocopier malfunctions, they must try to correct the problem or alert repair personnel. They

also request new equipment or supplies for their department when necessary.

Planning and supervising the work of their staff is another key function of this job. To do this effectively, the supervisor must know the strengths and weaknesses of each member of the staff as well as the required level of quality and time allotted to each job. They must make allowances for unexpected absences and other disruptions and adjust assignments or perform the work themselves if the situation requires it.

After allocating work assignments and issuing deadlines, clerical supervisors oversee the work to ensure that it is proceeding on schedule and meets established quality standards. This may involve reviewing each person's work on a computer, as in the case of accounting clerks, or, in the case of cashiers, listening to how they deal with customers. When supervising long-term projects, the supervisor may establish regular meetings with staff members to discuss their progress.

Clerical supervisors also evaluate each worker's performance. If a worker has done a good job, the supervisor records it in the employee's personnel file and may recommend a promotion or other award. Alternatively, if a worker is performing poorly, the supervisor discusses the problem with the employee to determine the cause and helps the worker improve his or her performance. This might entail sending the employee to a training course or arranging personal counseling. If the situation does not improve, the supervisor may recommend a transfer, demotion, or dismissal.

Clerical supervisors and managers generally interview and evaluate prospective clerical employees. When new workers arrive on the job, supervisors greet them and provide orientation to acquaint them with the organization and its operating routines. Some may be actively involved in recruiting new workers by performing functions like making presentations at high schools and business colleges. They may also serve as the primary liaisons between their offices and the general public through direct contact and helping to prepare promotional information.

Supervisors also help train new employees in organization and office procedures. They may teach them to use the telephone system and to operate office equipment. Because much clerical work is computerized, they must also teach new employees to use the organization's computer system. When new office equipment or updated computer software is introduced, supervisors retrain experienced employees to use it efficiently. If this is not possible, they may arrange for special outside training for their employees.

Clerical supervisors often act as liaisons between the clerical staff and the professional, technical, and managerial staff. This may

The ability to communicate effectively is vital for clerical supervisors.

involve implementing new company policies or restructuring the workflow in their departments. They must also keep their superiors informed of their progress and abreast of any potential problems. Often this communication takes the form of research projects and progress reports. Because they have access to information like their department's performance records, they may compile and present these data for use in planning or designing new policies.

Clerical supervisors may be called upon to resolve interpersonal conflicts among the staff. In organizations covered by union contracts, supervisors must know the provisions of labor-management agreements and run their departments accordingly. They may meet with union representatives to discuss work problems or grievances.

Working Conditions

Clerical supervisors and managers are employed in a wide variety of work settings, but most work in offices that are clean, well-lit, and generally comfortable.

Most work a standard 40-hour week. Because some organizations operate around the clock, however, clerical supervisors may have to work nights, weekends, and holidays. In some cases, supervisors rotate among the three shifts. In others, shifts are assigned on the basis of seniority.

Employment

Clerical supervisors and managers held over 1.3 million jobs in 1994. Although jobs for clerical supervisors are found in practically every industry, the largest number are found in organizations with a large clerical work force, such as government agencies, retail establishments, wholesalers, business service firms, banks, and insurance companies. Due to the need in most organizations for continuity of supervision, few clerical supervisors and managers work on a temporary or part-time basis.

Training, Other Qualifications, and Advancement

Most people entering this occupation transfer from other occupations within the organization, very often from the ranks of those they subsequently supervise. To be promoted to a supervisory position, clerical or administrative support workers must prove that they are capable of handling additional responsibilities. When evaluating candidates, superiors look for strong teamwork skills, determination, loyalty, poise, and confidence. They also look for more specific supervisory attributes, such as the ability to organize and coordinate work efficiently, set priorities, and motivate others. Increasingly, supervisors need a broad base of office skills coupled with personal flexibility to adapt to changes in organizational structure and move among departments when necessary.

In addition, supervisors must pay close attention to detail in order to identify and correct errors made by subordinates. Good working knowledge of the organization's computer system is also an advantage. Many employers require some postsecondary training. An associate degree is sufficient in many cases, but some organizations prefer candidates to hold bachelor's degrees.

A clerk with potential supervisory abilities may be given occasional supervisory assignments. To prepare for full-time supervisory duties, he or she may attend in-house training or take courses in time management or personal relations, for example, at a local community college or vocational school.

Some clerical supervisors are hired from outside the organization for positions with more managerial duties. These positions may serve as entry-level training for potential higher-level managers. New college graduates may rotate through departments of an organization at this level to learn the work of the entire organization.

Job Outlook

Employment of clerical supervisors and managers is expected to grow about as fast as the average for all occupations through the year 2005. Although growth in the demand for clerical supervisors will generate many job openings, most openings will result from the need to replace experienced supervisors who transfer to other occupations or leave the labor force. Because the occupation is large, replacement needs will create many job openings.

Employment of clerical supervisors is affected by the demand for clerical workers, which is determined by the volume of clerical work and the development of office automation. As the amount of clerical work continues to increase, more managers will be needed to coordinate it. With the help of office automation, however, this work may now be accomplished with fewer clerical workers. As office automation causes employment in some clerical occupations to slow or even decline, supervisors may have smaller staffs and perform more professional tasks. In other areas, fewer supervisors will be needed. In most cases, though, the relatively higher skills and longer tenure of clerical supervisors and managers will make them among the clerical workers most likely to be retained by an organization.

Earnings

Median annual earnings of full-time clerical supervisors were about $28,000 in 1994; the middle 50 percent earned between $21,000 and $37,600 a year. The lowest paid 10 percent earned less than $16,300, while the highest paid 10 percent earned more than $47,200. Employers in major metropolitan areas tend to pay higher salaries than those in rural areas.

Depending on their employer, clerical supervisors may receive a variety of benefits. These may include health and life insurance, paid vacations, tuition assistance, and a pension plan. Some clerical supervisors in the private sector may receive additional compensation in the form of bonuses and stock options.

Related Occupations

Clerical supervisors and managers must understand and sometimes perform the work of people whom they oversee, including accounting clerks, cashiers, bank tellers, and telephone operators. Their supervisory and administrative duties are similar to those of other managers.

Sources of Additional Information

State employment service offices can provide information about earnings, hours, and employment opportunities in this and other clerical jobs.

Computer and Peripheral Equipment Operators

(D.O.T. 213.362, .382, and .582)

Nature of the Work

Computer and peripheral equipment operators oversee the operation of computer hardware systems, ensuring that these machines are used as efficiently as possible. This means that operators must anticipate problems before they occur and take preventive action as well as solve problems that do occur.

The duties of computer and peripheral equipment operators vary with the size of the installation, the type of equipment used, and the policies of the employer. Working from operating instructions prepared by programmers, users, or operations managers, computer operators set controls on the computer and on peripheral devices required to run a particular job. Computer operators or, in some large installations peripheral equipment operators, load the equipment with tapes, disks, and paper as needed. While the computer is running—which may be 24 hours a day for large computers—computer operators monitor the computer console and respond to operating and computer messages. Messages indicate the individual specifications of each job being run. If an error message occurs, operators must locate and solve the problem or terminate the program.

Traditionally, peripheral equipment operators have to prepare printouts and other output for distribution to computer users. Operators also maintain log books listing each job that is run and events such as machine malfunctions that occurred during their shift. In addition, computer operators may supervise and train peripheral equipment operators and computer operator trainees. They also may help programmers and systems analysts test and debug new programs. (Detailed descriptions of these occupations are presented elsewhere in the *Handbook*.)

As the trend toward networking computers accelerates, a growing number of these workers are operating personal computers (PCs) and minicomputers. More and more establishments are realizing the need to connect all their computers in order to enhance productivity. In many offices, factories, and other work settings, PCs and minicomputers serve as the center of such networks, often referred to as local area networks or multi-user systems. While some of these computers are operated by users in the area, many require the services of full-time operators. The tasks performed are very similar to those performed on the larger computers.

As organizations continue to use computers in more areas of operation, they are also realizing opportunities to increase the productivity of computer operations. Automation, which traditionally has been the application of computer technology to other functional areas of an organization, is now reaching the computer room. Sophisticated software coupled with robotics now exist, enabling the computer to perform many routine tasks formerly done by computer and peripheral equipment operators. Scheduling, loading and downloading programs, mounting tapes, rerouting messages, and running periodic reports can be done without the intervention of an operator. These improvements will change what computer operators do in the future. However, in the computer centers that lack this level of automation, some computer operators still may be responsible for tasks traditionally done by peripheral equipment operators. As technology advances, many computer operators will essentially monitor an automated system. As the role of operators changes due to new technology, their responsibilities may shift to system security, troubleshooting, desk help, network problems, and maintaining large databases.

Working Conditions

Computer operating personnel generally work in well-lighted, well-ventilated, comfortable rooms. Because many organizations use their computers 24 hours a day, 7 days a week, computer and peripheral equipment operators may be required to work evening or night shifts and weekends. Shift assignments generally are made on the basis of seniority. Automated operations will lessen the need for shift work because many companies let the computer take over all operations during less desirable working hours. Because computer operators spend a lot of time in front of a computer monitor, as well as performing repetitive tasks such as loading and unloading printers, they may be susceptible to eyestrain, back discomfort, and hand and wrist problems.

Employment

In 1994, computer operators and peripheral equipment operators held about 259,000 and 30,000 jobs, respectively. Although jobs for computer and peripheral equipment operators are found in almost every industry, most are in wholesale trade establishments; manufacturing companies; data processing service firms; financial institutions; and government agencies. These organizations have data processing needs that require large computer installations. A growing number are employed by firms in the computer and data processing services industry, as more companies contract out the operation of their data processing centers.

More than 1 out of 10 computer and peripheral equipment operators works part time.

Computer operators set controls on the computer and load tapes, disks, and paper as needed.

Training, Other Qualifications, and Advancement

Previous work experience is the key to landing an operator job in many large establishments. Employers look for specific, hands-on experience in the type of equipment and related operating systems that they use. Additionally, computer-related formal training, perhaps through a junior college or technical school, is recommended. As computer technology changes and data processing centers become more automated, more employers will require candidates for the remaining operator jobs to have formal training as well as experience.

Workers usually receive on-the-job training in order to become acquainted with their employer's equipment and routines. The length of training varies with the job and the experience of the worker. Training is also offered by the Armed Forces and by some computer manufacturers.

Because computer technology changes so rapidly, operators must be adaptable and willing to learn. Greater analytical and technical expertise are also needed to deal with the unique or higher level problems that the computer is not programmed to handle, particularly by operators who work in automated data centers.

Computer and peripheral equipment operators must be able to communicate well in order to work effectively with programmers or users, as well as with other operators. Computer operators also must be able to work independently because they may have little or no supervision.

Peripheral equipment operators may advance to computer operator jobs. A few computer operators may advance to supervisory jobs. Through on-the-job experience and additional formal education, some computer and peripheral equipment operators may advance to jobs as programmers or analysts, although the move into these jobs is becoming more difficult as employers increasingly require candidates for more skilled computer professional jobs posses at least a bachelor's degree. Others may become specialists in areas such as network operations or support.

Job Outlook

Employment of computer and peripheral equipment operators is expected to decline sharply through the year 2005. Many experienced operators are expected to compete for the small number of openings that will arise each year to replace workers who transfer to other occupations or leave the labor force.

Advances in technology have reduced both the size and the cost of computer equipment while increasing the capacity for data storage and processing. These improvements in technology have fueled an expansion in the use of computers in such areas as factory and office automation, telecommunications, medicine, and education.

The expanding use of software that automates computer operations gives companies the option of making systems user-friendly, greatly reducing the need for operators. Even if firms continue to employ operators in some capacity—which, for many, is extremely likely in the near future—these new technologies will require operators to monitor a greater number of operations at the same time and be capable of solving a broader range of problems that may arise. The result is that fewer and fewer operators will be needed to perform more highly skilled work.

Computer operators or peripheral equipment operators who are displaced by automation may be reassigned to support staffs that maintain personal computer networks or assist other members of the organization. Operators who keep up with changing technology, by updating their skills and enhancing their training, should have the best prospects of moving into other areas such as network administration. Others may be retrained to perform different job duties, such as supervising an entire operations center, maintaining automation packages, or analyzing computer operations to recommend ways to increase productivity. In the future, operators who wish to continue in the computer field will need to know more about programming, automation software, graphics interface, and open systems in order to take advantage of changing opportunities.

Earnings

In 1994, full-time computer operators had median earnings of $21,300 a year. The middle 50 percent earned between $16,200 and $29,900. The lowest 10 percent earned less than $12,800 and the top 10 percent earned more than $39,500.

According to Robert Half International Inc., the average starting salaries for computer operator ranged from $20,000 to $31,500 in 1994. Salaries generally are higher in large organizations than in small ones.

In the Federal Government, computer operators with a high school diploma started at about $14,900 a year in 1995. Those with 1 year of college started at $16,700. Applicants with operations experience started at higher salaries. The average annual salary for all computer operators employed by the Federal Government in non supervisory, supervisory, and managerial positions was about $28,800 in 1994.

Related Occupations

Other occupations involving work with computers include computer scientists and systems analysts, programmers, and computer service technicians. Other occupations in which workers operate electronic office equipment include data entry keyers, secretaries, typists and word processors, and typesetters and compositors.

Sources of Additional Information

For information about work opportunities in computer operations, contact firms that use computers such as banks, manufacturing and insurance firms, colleges and universities, and data processing service organizations. The local office of the State employment service can supply information about employment and training opportunities.

Credit Clerks and Authorizers

(D.O.T. 205.367-022; 209.362-018; 219.362-038, .367-046; 237.367-014; 241.367-018, -026, -030; 249.362-014, -018, -022, .367-022)

Nature of the Work

Credit clerks or authorizers review credit history and obtain the information needed to determine the creditworthiness of loan and credit card applicants. Credit clerks contact applicants, credit bureaus, and other sources for information, and verify the completeness of loan documents. Credit authorizers refer to credit records and reports to decide whether to approve a customer's credit card purchase.

Clerks in credit bureaus secure, update, and verify information for credit reports. These workers are often called credit investigators or reporters. Clerks in banks and other financial institutions process loan and credit applications. Some clerks verify employment and financial information of credit card applicants. Loan processing clerks prepare loan applications for underwriters. They review loan applications, contact credit bureaus and reporting agencies for applicant records, and contact employers, banks, and references to verify personal and financial information. Clerks order appraisals from appraisal companies and secure tax forms, bank statements, and any required government forms from applicants. They calculate debt-to-income ratios to see that applicants meet the minimum guidelines for a loan. If any information in the loan package is inaccurate or incomplete, clerks contact the proper source for further information. Closing clerks obtain and prepare documents needed for real estate settlements. The closing clerks check to see that all documents are complete, accurate and correctly signed including deeds of trust, hazard insurance papers, and title commitments—and that all loan conditions required for settlement have been met.

Credit authorizers approve charges against customers' existing accounts. Most charges are approved automatically by computer. However, when accounts are past due, overextended, invalid, or show a change of address, sales persons refer transactions to credit

Credit clerks and authorizers use computers to enter and retrieve data.

authorizers located in a central office. Authorizers evaluate the customers' computerized credit records and payment histories and quickly decide whether or not to approve new charges. Authorizers may enter address changes and credit extensions into computer credit files.

Working Conditions
Credit clerks and authorizers usually work a 35- to 40-hour week. However, during particularly busy periods, they may work overtime. For credit clerks handling residential real estate, the busy periods are spring and summer and at the end of the month. For credit authorizers, busy periods are during the holiday shopping seasons and on store sale days. In fact, temporary workers are often hired as credit authorizers during peak workloads. In retail establishments, authorizers may work nights and weekends during store hours.

Credit authorizers and some credit clerks sit for long periods in front of video display terminals, which may cause eyestrain and headaches.

Employment
Credit clerks and authorizers held about 258,000 jobs in 1994. About 8 out of 10 were employed by commercial banks and other depository institutions, and mortgage banks and other nondepository institutions. Other credit clerks and authorizers were employed by insurance and real estate firms, credit reporting and collection agencies, and wholesale and retail trade establishments.

Training, Other Qualifications, and Advancement
No specific training is needed for entry-level positions in credit clerking and authorizing, with the exception of loan closing and loan interviewing. Closers and interviewers are often required to have previous work experience, preferably in financial institutions, and some knowledge of underwriting.

New employees are generally trained on the job, working under the close supervision of more experienced workers, although some firms offer formal training. Some credit workers also take courses in credit offered by banking and credit associations, public and private vocational schools, and colleges and universities. As workers demonstrate competence, they can advance to team leader of a small group of clerks, loan or credit department supervisor, underwriter, loan officer, or management. For management positions, employers prefer applicants with a bachelor's degree in business or a related field, or at least some college-level business or management courses.

Because positions in these fields involve much telephone contact, good communication skills are a necessity. Good organizational skills and the ability to pay attention to detail are also important. Many credit checkers use computers to enter and retrieve data, so some computer skills and good typing speed are required.

Job Outlook
Little change is expected in the employment of credit clerks and authorizers over the 1994-2005 period. The year 1994 was characterized by significant growth over previous years in the number of real estate, retail sales, and other transactions requiring credit. Projected employment reflects a slowdown in loan activity. The interpersonal nature of loan clerking and the judgment required of authorizers ensure that computers will not significantly affect employment. In addition to jobs created by growth, many jobs will become available as credit clerks and authorizers leave the occupation for various reasons.

Job outlook in this occupation is affected by changes in the economy. During periods when credit or loans are restricted, the number of job openings for credit clerks and authorizers may be limited.

Earnings
According to a 1994 survey of mortgage banking companies conducted by Carl D. Jacobs & Associates, the average salary for loan processors was $22,500, and the average salary for loan closers was $23,500.

Full-time workers generally receive health insurance, vacation and sick leave, and other standard benefits; part-timers may not. In addition, workers in retail establishments usually receive a discount on store purchases.

Related Occupations
Occupations with duties similar to those of credit clerks and authorizers include claim examiners and adjusters, customer-complaint clerks, procurement clerks, probate clerks, and collection clerks.

Sources of Additional Information
Information about local job opportunities for credit clerks and authorizers may be obtained from banking institutions, retail stores, and credit reporting agencies.

General Office Clerks

(D.O.T. 209.362-030, .562-010; 219.362-010, -022, -026; 243.362-014; 245.362-014, .367-010, -014, -018; 249.367-010, -014; 375.362-010)

Nature of the Work
The duties of general office clerks are too varied and diverse for them to be classified in any specific administrative support occupation. Rather than performing a single specialized task, the duties of a general office clerk change with the needs of their employer. They may spend some days filing or typing; others entering data at a computer terminal. They also may operate photocopiers, fax machines, or other office equipment; prepare mailings; proofread copy; and answer telephones and deliver messages.

Duties vary significantly depending upon the office in which a clerk works. A general office clerk in a doctor's office may not perform the same tasks as a clerk in a large financial institution or in the office of an auto parts wholesaler. Although they all may sort checks, keep payroll records, take inventory, or access information, they also may perform duties unique to their employer, such as organizing medications, making transparencies for a presentation, or filling orders received by fax machine.

Duties of general office clerks are diverse, ranging from entering data at a computer terminal to maintaining records.

Duties also vary by level of experience. Inexperienced employees may transcribe data, operate calculators, or record inquiries while more experienced workers may handle greater responsibilities. They might maintain financial or other records, verify statistical reports for accuracy and completeness, handle and adjust customer complaints, take inventory of equipment and supplies, answer questions on departmental services and functions, and help prepare budgetary requests. In addition to performing more complex duties, senior general office clerks may be expected to oversee and direct the work of lower level clerks.

Working Conditions

For the most part, working conditions for general office clerks are the same as those for other office employees within the same company. Those on a full-time schedule usually work a standard 40-hour week. Some may work shifts or overtime during busy periods and about 1 in 3 works part time. In addition, many general office clerks work as temporaries.

Employment

General office clerks held about 2,946,000 jobs in 1994. They work in every sector of the economy. Most general office clerks are employed in relatively small businesses, with over 50 percent working in the services or wholesale and retail trade industries.

Training, Other Qualifications, and Advancement

Most general office clerk jobs are entry level administrative support positions, although they may require previous office or business experience. Employers usually require a high school diploma, and some require typing, basic computer skills, and other general office skills. Familiarity with computer word processing software and applications is becoming increasingly important.

Training for this occupation is available through business education programs offered in high schools, community and junior colleges, and postsecondary vocational schools. Courses in word-processing, microcomputer applications, and office practices are particularly helpful.

Because general office clerks usually work with other office staff they should be cooperative and able to work as part of a team. They should be able to communicate with a wide range of people and have good organizational skills and attention to detail. They also must be willing to change to meet the unexpected requirements of the job or take on additional responsibilities.

General office clerks who exhibit strong communication, interpersonal, and analytical skills may be promoted to supervisory positions. Others move into different clerical jobs, such as receptionist, secretary, or administrative assistant. Advancement to professional occupations within an establishment usually requires more formal education including a college degree.

Job Outlook

Employment of general office clerks is expected to grow more slowly than the average for all occupations through the year 2005. Nonetheless, good job opportunities should continue to exist. The large size of this occupation and the high turnover associated with it will continue to produce a large number of job openings. After gaining some work experience or specialized skills, many workers transfer to jobs with higher pay or greater advancement potential.

Increasing use of computers and expanding office automation mean a wider variety of duties can be performed by fewer office workers. As more small businesses consolidate their clerical staffs and job responsibilities become more diverse, it may become more common to find a single general office clerk in charge of all clerical work. However, as duties expand, employers will seek workers with greater computer skills and a broader range of office skills or experience.

Job seekers who have computer word-processing and other secretarial skills, and knowledge of the operation of basic office machinery, such as fax machines and copiers, should have the best opportunities. Because they must be so versatile, general office clerks find work in virtually every kind of industry. In addition, they should find many opportunities for part-time or temporary work, especially during peak business periods in industries where these jobs are concentrated.

Earnings

Median annual earnings of full-time general office clerks were about $19,300 in 1994; the middle 50 percent earned between $14,900 and $25,000 annually. Ten percent earned less than $11,300, and 10 percent more than $32,200.

According to a survey of workplaces in 160 metropolitan areas, beginning general office clerks had median annual earnings of $13,000 in 1993, with the middle half earning about $11,600 to $15,000 a year. The most experienced general office clerks had median annual earnings of about $24,000, with the middle half earning between about $21,500 and $27,200 a year. General office clerks' salaries varied by industry. They tended to be higher in transportation and public utilities and lower in construction and finance, insurance, and real estate.

In 1995, the Federal Government paid general office clerks a starting salary of between $13,650 and $16,721 a year, depending on education and experience. In 1995, general office clerks in the Federal Government earned an average annual salary of about $23,730.

Related Occupations

General office clerk usually is an entry-level office job. The duties of general office clerks may include a combination of bookkeeping, typing, office machine operation, and filing; a variety of other administrative support workers perform similar duties. Entry-level jobs in other settings include cashier, medical assistant, teacher aide, and food and beverage service worker.

Sources of Additional Information

State employment service offices and agencies that specialize in placing administrative support personnel can provide information about job openings for general office clerks.

Information Clerks

Nature of the Work

Information clerks gather information from and provide information to the public. Since they are found in a variety of organizations, they have a variety of different job titles and duties. *Hotel and motel desk clerks* are a guest's first contact for check-in, check-out, and other services. *Interviewing* and *new account clerks*, often found in medical facilities and financial institutions, assist the public in completing forms, applications or questionnaires. *Receptionists* are often a visitor's or caller's first contact within an organization, providing information and routing calls. *Reservation and transportation ticket agents*, as well as *travel clerks*, assist the public in making travel plans, reservations, and purchasing tickets for a variety of transportation services.

Although their day-to-day duties vary widely, most information clerks greet customers, guests, or other visitors, and after determining their needs, either assist them or refer them to someone else who can be of help. Others answer telephones or elicit information from the public. Most information clerks use office equipment such as multi-line telephones, fax machines, and personal computers in their work. More information on four information clerk occupations follows this section.

Working Conditions

Information clerks who greet customers and visitors usually work in areas that are highly visible and designed and furnished to make a good impression. Most work stations are clean, well lighted, and relatively quiet, and overall working conditions usually are pleasant. Reservation agents and interviewing clerks, who do much of their work over the telephone, generally work away from the public; a number of agents or clerks may share the same work space, which may be crowded and noisy. Occasionally, interviewing clerks may conduct surveys on the street or in shopping malls, or go door to door.

Although most information clerks work a standard 40-hour week, about 3 out of 10 work part time. Some high school and college students work part time as information clerks after school or during vacations. Some jobs—such as those in the transportation industry, hospitals, and hotels, in particular—may require working evenings, late night shifts, weekends, and holidays. In many cases, employees with the least seniority may be assigned the least desirable shifts. Interviewing clerks conducting surveys or other research may mainly work evenings or weekends.

The work performed by information clerks may be tiring, repetitious, and stressful. Many receptionists spend all day answering continuously ringing telephones. Many reservation agents and travel clerks must work under stringent guidelines for the use of their time. Management may electronically monitor their use of the computer systems, monitor or tape record their telephone calls, limit the time that they can spend on each call, and have quotas on the number of reservations made. Such practices may make stress-related complaints more common. In addition, prolonged exposure to a video display terminal may lead to eye strain.

The work of hotel and motel desk clerks and transportation ticket agents also can be stressful when trying to serve the needs of difficult or angry customers. During holidays and other busy travel periods, these clerks may find the work extremely hectic. When flights are canceled, reservations mishandled, or guests are dissatisfied, these clerks must act as a buffer between the establishment and its customers. Both hotel desk clerks and ticket agents may be on their feet most of the time, and ticket agents may have to lift heavy baggage.

Employment

Information clerks held over 1.4 million jobs in 1994. The following tabulation shows 1994 employment for the individual occupations.

Receptionists	1,019,000
Interviewing and new account clerks	183,000
Reservation and transportation ticket agents and travel clerks	139,000
Hotel and motel desk clerks	136,000

Though information clerks are employed throughout the economy, they are concentrated in hotels and motels, the health services industry, banks and savings institutions, the transportation industry, and firms providing business or real estate services.

Training, Other Qualifications, and Advancement

Although hiring requirements for information clerk jobs vary from industry to industry, a high school diploma or its equivalent is the most common educational requirement. However, good interpersonal skills and familiarity or experience with computers often are more important to employers. For airline reservation and ticket agent jobs, some college education may be preferred.

With the exception of airline reservation and transportation ticket agents, orientation and training for information clerks generally takes place on the job. For example, orientation for hotel and motel desk clerks usually includes an explanation of the job duties and information about the establishment, such as room locations and available services. New employees learn job tasks through on-the-job training under the guidance of a supervisor or an experienced clerk. They often need additional training in how to use the computerized reservation, room assignment, and billing systems and equipment.

Receptionists generally receive on-the-job training. However, employers often look for applicants who already possess certain skills, such as prior computer and word processing experience. Some employers also may prefer some formal office education or training. On the job, they learn how to operate the telephone system, computers, and the proper procedures for greeting visitors, and distributing mail, fax, and parcel deliveries.

Most airline reservation agents learn their skills through formal company training programs. They spend some time in a classroom setting, learning company and industry policies, computer systems, and ticketing procedures. They learn to use a computer to obtain information on schedules, seat availability, and fares; to reserve space for passengers; and to plan passenger itineraries. They must learn airport and airline code designations, and may be tested on this knowledge. After completing classroom instruction, new agents work on the job with supervisors or experienced agents for a period of time. During this period, monitoring of telephone conversations may serve as a training device to improve the quality of customer service. Agents are expected to provide good service while limiting the time spent on each call without being discourteous to customers. In contrast, automobile clubs, bus lines, and railroads tend to train their ticket agents or travel clerks on the job, through short in-house classes that can last several days. Most information clerks continue to receive instruction on new procedures and company policies after their initial training ends.

Because many information clerks deal directly with the public, a good appearance and a pleasant personality are imperative, as are good problem-solving and interpersonal skills. A clear speaking voice and fluency in the English language are essential because these employees frequently use the telephone or public address system. Coursework useful to persons wanting to enter these occupations include basic math, English, geography, U.S. history, psychology, communications, and public speaking. Good spelling, typing ability, and computer literacy often are needed, particularly since most work involves considerable computer use. Some employers may require applicants to take a typing and spelling test to gauge their skills, often requiring a minimum typing speed of 35 to 50 words per minute. It also is increasingly helpful for those wishing to enter the hotel and motel industry to speak a foreign language fluently.

Advancement for information clerks generally comes about either by transfer to a different, more responsible occupation or by promotion to a supervisory position. The more skills, experience, and additional training an employee possesses, the better their advancement opportunities in most establishments. Receptionists, interviewers, and new accounts clerks with typing or other clerical skills may advance to a better paying job as a secretary or administrative assistant. In the airline industry, a ticket agent may advance to lead worker on the shift. Additional training is helpful in preparing information clerks for promotion. In the lodging industry, clerks can improve their chances for advancement by taking home or group study courses in lodging management, such as those sponsored by the Educational Institute of the American Hotel and Motel Association. In some industries—such as lodging, banking, or the airline industry—workers commonly are promoted through the ranks. Positions such as airline reservation agent or hotel and motel desk clerk offer good opportunities for qualified workers to get started in the business. In many industries, a college degree may be required for advancement to management ranks.

Job Outlook

Overall employment of information clerks is expected to increase faster than the average for all occupations through the year 2005. In addition to the many openings that will occur as businesses and organizations expand, numerous job openings for information clerks will result from the need to replace experienced workers who transfer to other occupations or leave the labor force. Replacement needs will reflect the relatively high turnover among these jobs. Many young people work as information clerks for a few years before switching to other, better paying jobs. This work is well suited to flexible work schedules, and many opportunities for part-time work will continue to be available, particularly as organizations look to cut labor costs by hiring more part-time or temporary workers.

Economic growth and general business expansion are expected to stimulate faster than average growth in the large number of receptionist jobs. Other information clerk jobs, however, are expected to increase more slowly or decline, reflecting the impact of new technology and trends in the industries where their employment is concentrated.

Earnings

In 1994, median weekly earnings of full-time information clerks were about $322. The middle 50 percent earned between $263 and $417. The bottom 10 percent earned less than $209, while the top 10 percent earned more than $562. Earnings vary widely by occupation and experience. Weekly earnings ranged from less than $193 for the lowest paid hotel clerks to over $732 for the highest paid reservation agents. Salaries of reservation and ticket agents tend to be significantly higher than for other information clerks, while hotel and motel desk clerks tend to earn quite a bit less, as the following tabulation of median weekly earnings shows.

Reservation and transportation ticket agents and travel clerks....................$407
Interviewing and new account clerks... 361
Receptionists.. 308
Hotel and motel desk clerks 286

In 1995, the Federal Government commonly paid beginning receptionists with a high school diploma or 6 months of experience salaries ranging from $12,100 to $14,900 a year. The average annual salary for all receptionists employed by the Federal Government was about $19,530 in 1995.

Earnings of hotel and motel desk clerks depend on the location, size, and type of establishment in which they work. Large luxury hotels and those located in metropolitan and resort areas generally pay clerks more than less exclusive or "budget" establishments and those located in less populated areas. In general, hotels pay higher salaries than motels or other types of lodging establishments.

In addition to their hourly wage, full-time information clerks who work evenings, nights, weekends, or holidays may receive shift differential pay. Some employers offer educational assistance to their employees. Reservation and transportation ticket agents and travel clerks receive free or reduced rate travel on their company's carriers for themselves and their immediate family and, in some companies, free uniforms. Relatively few information clerks belong to unions. However, unions representing these workers include the Transportation Communications International Union, the Amalgamated Transit Union, and the Hotel Employees and Restaurant Employees International Union.

Related Occupations

A number of other workers deal with the public, receive and provide information, or direct people to others who can assist them. Among these are dispatchers, security guards, bank tellers, guides, telephone operators, record clerks, counter and rental clerks, survey workers, and ushers and lobby attendants.

Hotel and Motel Desk Clerks

(D.O.T. 238.367-038)

Nature of the Work

Hotel and motel desk clerks perform a variety of services for guests of hotels, motels, and other lodging establishments. They register arriving guests and assign them rooms, and check guests out at the

Hotel desk clerks answer questions about services, the local community, and other matters of interest to guests.

end of their stay. In assigning rooms, clerks consider their guests' preferences while trying to maximize the establishment's revenues. They keep records of room assignments and other registration information on computers, and when guests check out, they prepare and explain the bill of charges, as well as process payments.

Desk clerks are always in the public eye and, through their attitude and behavior, greatly influence the public's impressions of the establishment. They answer questions about services, checkout times, the local community, and other matters of public interest. Should guests report problems with their rooms, clerks contact members of the housekeeping or maintenance staff to correct them.

In some smaller hotels and motels, clerks have a variety of additional responsibilities that in most larger establishments are usually performed by specialized employees. Clerks also may perform the work of a bookkeeper, advance reservation agent, cashier, laundry attendant, and telephone switchboard operator.

Employment

Hotel and motel desk clerks held about 136,000 jobs in 1994. This occupation is well suited to flexible work schedules, with over 1 in 4 desk clerks working part time. Since hotels and motels are found in all parts of the country, so are these jobs.

Job Outlook

Job opportunities for hotel and motel desk clerks should remain relatively good because turnover is very high. Each year thousands of workers transfer to other occupations offering better pay and advancement opportunities, or simply leave the workforce altogether. Opportunities for part-time work should continue to be plentiful since the front desk must be staffed 24 hours a day, 7 days a week.

Employment of hotel and motel desk clerks is expected to grow about as fast as the average for all occupations through the year 2005 as more hotels, motels, and other lodging establishments are built and as occupancy rates rise. Employment of hotel and motel desk clerks should be favorably affected by an increase in business and leisure travel. Shifts in travel preference away from long vacations and toward long weekends and other, more frequent, short trips also should increase demand.

However, changes within the hotel and motel industry are expected to somewhat slow the growth of desk clerk employment. Expansion of smaller budget hotels and less construction of larger, luxury establishments with big staffs should result in slower employment growth in the occupation than in the past. Also, new technology that automates guest check-in and check-out—an effort to cut labor costs while moving towards more efficient service—will require fewer desk clerks to be on duty at peak arrival and departure times.

Employment of desk clerks is sensitive to cyclical swings in the economy. During recessions, vacation and business travel declines and hotels and motels need fewer clerks.

Sources of Additional Information
Information on working conditions, training requirements, and earnings appears in the *Information clerks* introduction to this section.

Information on careers in the lodging industry, as well as information about professional development and training programs, may be obtained from:

☛The Educational Institute of the American Hotel and Motel Association, P.O. Box 1240, East Lansing, MI 48826-1240.

Interviewing and New Accounts Clerks

(D.O.T. 205.362-018, -026, -030, .367-014, -026, -042, -054, and -058)

Nature of the Work
Interviewing and new accounts clerks obtain information from people by mail, by telephone, or in person that organizations need to enable individuals to open bank accounts, gain admission to medical facilities, participate in consumer surveys, and complete various other forms. They solicit and verify information, create files, and perform various processing tasks. The specific duties and job titles of these workers depend upon the type of employer.

New accounts clerks also are known as *customer service representatives.* They work for financial institutions such as commercial banks, credit unions, and savings and loan associations. They interview people who want to open a checking or savings account and record the data directly into a computer. They must be familiar with the products and services of the bank for which they work since it is their job to explain the increasing array of financial services that are available. They help people fill out enrollment forms for special services, such as automated teller machine (ATM) cards. They also may answer telephone inquiries about bank services or procedures for opening or closing accounts. (Bank tellers, who also may perform customer service representative duties, are discussed elsewhere in the *Handbook.*)

Many *interviewing clerks* work in hospitals, doctors' offices, and other health care facilities, where they are also known as *admitting interviewers.* They interview patients to obtain all preliminary information required for admission, such as the patient's name,

Interviewing clerks often read from a prepared script on a computer screen when asking individuals questions about topics such as customer satisfaction.

address, age, medical history, present medications, previous hospitalizations, religion, persons to notify in case of emergency, attending physician, and the party responsible for payment. They may assign patients to rooms and summon escorts to conduct patients to the rooms; sometimes they may escort patients themselves. Using a computer, they prepare admitting and discharge records and route them to the appropriate departments. They also may bill patients, receive payments, and answer the telephone. In an outpatient setting, they schedule appointments, keep track of cancellations, and provide general information about care.

Interviewing clerks also conduct market research surveys and polls for research firms. They ask individuals questions on such topics as their occupation and earnings, political preferences, buying habits, or customer satisfaction. Market research is not limited to the consumer market, but also includes executive, medical, and industrial research. No selling is involved. Often reading from a prepared script, interviewers ask a carefully worded series of questions, record the responses, and forward the results to management.

Employment
Interviewing and new accounts clerks held about 183,000 jobs in 1994. More than 6 out of 10 were employed by commercial banks and other depository institutions. Most of the rest worked in hospitals and other health-care facilities, while a small number of clerks worked for market research firms in the business services industry. About 1 of every 4 interviewing clerks worked part time.

Job Outlook
Overall employment of interviewing and new accounts clerks is expected to increase about as fast as the average for all occupations through the year 2005, but growth rates will vary by industry. Opportunities will be best for applicants with a broad range of job skills.

Employment of interviewing clerks in the health services industry is expected to grow as fast as the average. As hospitals consolidate their staffs, however, the duties of admitting interviewers should expand. Additionally, much faster than average employment growth of interviewing clerks will occur in personnel supply services, as more organizations contract out for the services of these types of clerks rather than support a full-time staff. On the other hand, almost no employment growth is expected for new accounts clerks, reflecting the general lack of employment growth among commercial banks and savings and loan institutions as consolidation, electronic banking, and ATM technology decrease the role of branch offices.

Sources of Additional Information
Information on working conditions, training requirements, and earnings appears in the *Information clerks* introduction to this section.

State employment service offices can provide information about employment opportunities.

A brochure on careers in banking, including information on new accounts clerks, referred to as customer service representatives in the brochure, is available from:

☛American Bankers Association Education Foundation, 1120 Connecticut Ave. NW., Washington, DC 20036.

Receptionists

(D.O.T. 203.362-014; 205.367-038; 237.267, .367-010, -018, -022, -026, -038, -042, -046, and -050; 238.367-022 and -034; 249.262 and .367-082)

Nature of the Work
All organizations want to make a good first impression, and this is the job of the receptionist, who is often the first representative of the organization that a visitor encounters. In addition to traditional

Many receptionists are expected to perform secretarial duties when they are not busy with callers.

duties such as answering telephones, routing calls to the appropriate individuals, and greeting visitors, a receptionist may serve a security function—monitoring the access of visitors and determining who belongs and who does not.

Receptionists generally are expected to answer questions from the public and provide information about the organization. Their day-to-day duties, however, can vary depending upon where they work. Receptionists in hospitals and doctors' offices may obtain personal and financial information and direct patients to the proper waiting rooms. At beauty or hair salons, they arrange appointments, direct customers to the hairstylist, and also may serve as cashier—taking payments for services and products. In factories, large corporations, and government offices, they may provide identification cards and arrange for escorts to take visitors to the proper office. Those working for bus and train companies respond to inquiries about departures, arrivals, stops, and related matters.

Increasingly, receptionists use multiline telephone systems, personal computers, and facsimile (fax) machines. Many receptionists take messages and may inform other employees of a visitors' arrival or cancellation of an appointment. When they are not busy with callers, they may be expected to perform a variety of secretarial duties including opening and sorting mail, collecting and distributing parcels, making fax transmittals and deliveries, updating appointment calendars, preparing travel vouchers, and doing simple bookkeeping, typing, and filing.

Employment

Receptionists held about 1,019,000 jobs in 1994, accounting for over two-thirds of all information clerk jobs. More than two-thirds of all receptionists worked in services industries, and almost half of these were located in the health services industry—doctors' and dentists' offices, hospitals, nursing homes, urgent care centers, surgical centers, and clinics. Manufacturing, wholesale and retail trade, government, and real estate industries also employed large numbers of receptionists. About 3 of every 10 receptionists worked part time.

Job Outlook

Job opportunities for receptionists should be plentiful due to strong employment growth and high turnover. Employment of receptionists is expected to grow faster than the average for all occupations through the year 2005 because so many receptionists work for firms in services industries—industries that include physician's offices, law firms, temporary help agencies, and consulting firms and that are expected to continue to show strong growth. In addition to openings from growth, several hundred thousand openings are expected each year from the need to replace receptionists who transfer to other

occupations, seeking better pay or career advancement, or who leave the labor force altogether.

Opportunities should be best for persons with a wide range of clerical skills and experience. Many receptionists also perform secretarial duties and often employers look to hire receptionists with good word processing and computer skills, coupled with strong interpersonal and communications skills.

The demand for receptionists may be tempered somewhat by the increasing use of voice mail and other telephone automation. Where several receptionists may have been required to answer the company's telephones in the past, voice mail now makes it possible for one person to do the job of many.

Since establishments need someone to perform their duties even during economic downturns, receptionists are less subject to layoffs during recessions than other clerical workers.

Sources of Additional Information

Information on working conditions, training requirements, and earnings appears in the *Information clerks* introduction to this section.

State employment offices can provide information on job openings for receptionists.

Reservation and Transportation Ticket Agents and Travel Clerks

(D.O.T. 214.362-030; 238.167, .362, .367-010, -014, -018, -026, -030; and 248.382)

Nature of the Work

Each year, millions of Americans travel by plane, train, ship, bus, and automobile. When they make reservations for travel or accommodations, purchase tickets, or check their luggage, they deal with reservation and transportation ticket agents and travel clerks.

Most *reservation agents* work for large hotel chains or airlines helping people plan trips and make reservations. They usually work in large central offices answering telephone inquiries and offering suggestions on travel arrangements such as routes, time schedules, rates, and types of accommodation. They quote fares and room rates, make and confirm transportation and hotel reservations, and sell tickets. Agents use computer terminals to quickly obtain information needed to make, change, or cancel reservations for customers. After a ticket has been purchased, they arrange for it to be sent to or picked up by the traveler.

Transportation ticket agents sometimes are known as passenger service agents, passenger-booking clerks, reservation clerks, ticket clerks, or ticket sellers. They work in airports, train, and bus stations selling tickets, assigning seats to passengers, and checking baggage. In addition, they may answer inquiries and give directions, examine passports and visas, or check in animals. Other ticket agents, more commonly known as *gate* or *station agents*, work in airport terminals assisting passengers when boarding airplanes. They direct passengers to the correct boarding area, check tickets and seat assignments, make boarding announcements, and provide special assistance to young, elderly, or disabled passengers when they board or disembark.

Passenger rate clerks work for bus companies. They sell tickets for regular bus routes and arrange nonscheduled or chartered trips. They plan travel routes, compute rates, and keep customers informed of appropriate details. They also may arrange travel accommodations.

Most *travel clerks* are employed by automobile clubs. These workers, sometimes called member services counselors or travel counselors, plan trips, calculate mileage, and offer travel suggestions for club members. They highlight the best route from the point of

In addition to selling tickets, transportation ticket agents assign seats, check baggage, and answer inquiries.

origin to the destination, as well as the return. They also may prepare an itinerary which indicates points of interest, restaurants, overnight accommodations, and availability of emergency services during the trip. In some cases, they may make rental car, hotel, or restaurant reservations for club members.

Reservation and transportation ticket agents and travel clerks must be knowledgeable about their companies' policies and about industry procedures. They must be able to use computers to ascertain the availability of special promotions or services, reservation information, and find answers to any questions customers may have.

Employment

Reservation and transportation ticket agents and travel clerks held about 139,000 jobs in 1994. More than 2 of every 3 workers are employed by the airlines. Others work for membership organizations like automobile clubs, hotels and other lodging places, railroad companies, bus lines, and other companies that provide transportation services.

Although agents and clerks are found throughout the country, most work at large metropolitan airports, downtown ticket and reservation offices, large reservation centers, as well as train and bus stations. The remainder work in smaller communities served only by intercity bus or railroad lines.

Job Outlook

Applicants for reservation and transportation ticket agent jobs are likely to encounter considerable competition because the supply of qualified applicants exceeds the expected number of job openings. Entry requirements for these jobs are minimal and many people seeking to get into the airline industry or travel business often start out in these types of positions. Also, these jobs provide excellent travel benefits and many people view airline jobs as glamorous.

Employment of reservation and transportation ticket agents and travel clerks is expected to decline slightly through the year 2005. The work of these occupations is being affected significantly by technology. Automated reservations and ticketing, as well as "ticketless" travel, reduces the need for some of these positions. Nevertheless, job openings will become available as workers transfer to other occupations, retire, or leave the labor force altogether.

Employment of reservation and transportation ticket agents and travel clerks is sensitive to cyclical swings in the economy. During recessions, discretionary passenger travel declines and transportation service companies are less likely to hire new workers and even may resort to layoffs.

Sources of Additional Information

Information on working conditions, training requirements, and earnings appears in the *Information clerks* introduction to this section.

For information about job opportunities as reservation and transportation ticket agents and travel clerks, write the personnel manager of individual transportation companies. Addresses of airlines are available from:

☞Air Transport Association of America, 1301 Pennsylvania Ave. NW., Suite 1100, Washington, DC 20004-1707.

A brochure describing airline jobs is available from:

☞Air Line Employees Association, Job Opportunity Program, 6520 South Cicero Ave., Chicago, IL 60638.

Mail Clerks and Messengers

(D.O.T. 209.587-018 and .687-026; 215.563; 222.367-022, .387-038, .567-018, and .587-030 and -032; 230.647-010 and .663-010; 239.567, .677, and .687; 243.367-010; 248.367-030; and 249.687-010)

Nature of the Work

Mail clerks and messengers help businesses, institutions, and government agencies run efficiently by moving and distributing information, documents, and small packages.

Most large organizations employ *mail clerks* to handle their internal mail. Internal mail goes back and forth among people, offices, or departments within a firm or institution. It ranges from memos to key personnel to bulletins on job issues to all employees. Mail clerks sort internal mail and deliver it to their fellow employees, often using carts to carry the mail between offices.

Mail clerks also handle external mail, serving as the link between the U.S. Postal Service and individual offices and workers. They sort incoming mail and deliver mail within large office buildings. They also prepare outgoing mail—which may range from advertising flyers, to customers' orders, to legal documents—for delivery to the post office. To facilitate delivery of outgoing mail, mail clerks often determine if the mail is to be sent registered, certified, special delivery, or first, second, third, or fourth class, and may group mailings by ZIP code. When necessary, they contact delivery services to send important letters or parcels. In larger organizations, or organizations with a large volume of outgoing mail, mail clerks often operate machines which collate, fold, and insert material to be mailed into envelopes. They also operate machines which affix postage. In addition, mail clerks increasingly use computers to keep records of incoming and outgoing items.

Messengers pick up and deliver letters, important business documents, or packages which need to be sent or received in a hurry from within a local area. By sending an item by messenger, the sender ensures that it reaches its destination the same day or even within the hour. Messengers, also called couriers, also deliver items which the sender is unwilling to entrust to other means of delivery, such as important legal or financial documents. Some messengers pick up and deliver important packages, such as medical samples to be tested.

Messengers receive their instructions either by reporting to their office in person, by telephone, or by two-way radio. They then pick up the item and carry it to its destination. After a delivery, they check with their office and receive instructions about the next delivery. Consequently, most messengers spend most of their time outdoors or in their vehicle. Messengers usually maintain records of deliveries and often obtain signatures from the persons receiving the items.

Most messengers deliver items within a limited geographic area, such as a city or metropolitan area. Items which need to go longer distances usually are sent by mail or by an overnight delivery service. Some messengers carry items only for their employer,

Messengers often use bicycles in congested urban areas.

which typically might be a law firm, bank, or financial institution. Other messengers may act as part of an organization's internal mail system and mainly carry items between an organization's buildings or entirely within one building. Many messengers work for messenger or courier services; for a fee they pick up items from anyone and deliver them to specified destinations within a local area.

Messengers reach their destination by several methods. Many drive vans or cars or ride motorcycles. A few travel by foot, especially in urban areas or when making deliveries nearby. In congested urban areas, messengers often use bicycles, since this is the fastest way to travel in heavy traffic. Bicycle messengers usually are employed by messenger or courier services. Although fax machines and computerized electronic mail (e-mail) can deliver information faster than messengers, for many types of business transactions an electronic copy cannot substitute for the original document.

Working Conditions

Working conditions for mail clerks are much different from the working conditions for most messengers. Most mail clerks work regular hours, spending much of their time in mailrooms, which are usually located in office buildings. Most of the rest of their time is spent making mail deliveries throughout an office building. Although mailrooms are usually clean and well lighted, there may be noise from mail-handling machines. While sorting and delivering mail and operating machinery, mail clerks spend most of their time on their feet, which can be tiring and physically demanding. They are sometimes required to lift heavy objects or operate a motor vehicle to make deliveries and pick-ups.

Messengers work in a less structured environment than mail clerks because they spend most of their time alone making deliveries and usually are not closely supervised. Although many messengers work full time during regular business hours, some messengers work nights and weekends.

Messengers who deliver by bicycle must be physically fit and are exposed to all weather conditions as well as the many hazards connected with heavy traffic. The pressure to make as many deliveries as possible to increase earnings can be stressful and may lead to unsafe driving or bicycling practices.

Employment

Messengers and mail clerks together held about 260,000 jobs in 1994; about 127,000 were mail clerks and 133,000 were messengers. About 12 percent of the messengers were employed by trucking and warehousing companies, another 15 percent worked for law firms, and 16 percent worked for hospitals and medical and dental laboratories. Financial institutions, such as commercial banks, saving

institutions, and credit unions, employed 7 percent. The rest were employed in a wide variety of other industries.

In 1994, about 19 percent of all mail clerks worked in Federal, State, and local governments. Others were employed in a wide range of industries. Technically, many messengers are self-employed independent contractors because they provide their vehicles and set their own schedules to a certain extent, but in many respects they are like employees since they usually work for one company.

Training, Other Qualifications, and Advancement

There are no formal qualifications or training required to be a mail clerk or messenger, although some employers prefer high school graduates. This is a first job for many.

Mail clerks must be careful and dependable workers. They must be able to do routine work and work well with their hands. They are usually trained on the job. If they operate computers and mail-handling machinery to help prepare mailings, training may be provided by another employee or by a representative of the machinery manufacturer. Mail clerks are sometimes required to have a driver's license if they make deliveries to other buildings.

Messengers who work as independent contractors for a messenger or delivery service may be required to have a valid drivers license, a registered and inspected vehicle, a good driving record, and insurance coverage. Many messengers who are employees, not independent contractors, are also required to provide and maintain their own vehicle. A good knowledge of the geographic area in which they travel as well as a good sense of direction are also important.

Some mail clerks, depending on the size of the operation, advance to positions as clerical staff supervisors or office managers. Other mail clerks transfer to related jobs with the U.S. Postal Service, if they pass the competitive entrance examination. (Information on postal clerk and mail carrier careers appears elsewhere in the *Handbook*.) Messengers, especially those who work for messenger or courier services, have limited advancement opportunities.

Job Outlook

Employment of mail clerks and messengers is expected to decline through the year 2005 despite an increasing volume of internal mail, parcels, business documents, promotional materials, and other written information that must be handled and delivered as the economy expands. Nevertheless, job openings are expected to be plentiful for mail clerks and messengers through the year 2005 and will stem from the need to replace workers who leave the occupation. Mail clerk and messenger jobs are attractive to many persons seeking their first job or a short-term source of income because the limited formal education and training requirements allow easy entry. This is especially true for messengers, many of whom work in this occupation a relatively short time.

Businesses' growing reliance on directly mailing advertising and promotional materials to prospective customers will result in increasing amounts of mail to be handled. However, increasing automation of mail-handling will enable mail clerks to handle a growing volume of mail. In addition, employment of mail clerks will be limited by more widespread use of robot mail carts to distribute mail in large office buildings.

Employment of messengers will grow slowly as new electronic information-handling technology comes into more widespread use. Fax machines, for example, allow copies of documents to be immediately sent across town or across the country and have become standard office equipment. The transmission of information through telephone lines between computers (e-mail) will also reduce the demand for messengers as more computers are connected to networks. However, messengers will still be needed to transport materials which cannot be sent electronically, such as legal documents, blueprints and other over-sized materials, large multipage documents, and securities. Also, messengers will still be required by medical and dental laboratories to pick up and deliver medical samples, specimens, and other materials.

Earnings

Median weekly earnings of full-time mail clerks were about $322 in 1994; the middle 50 percent earned between $254 and $437 a week. Median weekly earnings of full-time messengers were about $338. The middle 50 percent of messengers earned between $269 and $515 a week. Messengers occasionally receive tips from clients, but this is not a significant part of their earnings.

Some messengers are paid by commission rather than earning a regular wage. The commission usually is based on the number of deliveries made, the distance traveled, and the fee charged to the customer. They must provide their own transportation and must pay fuel and maintenance costs. The more deliveries they make and the faster they travel, the more they earn. Unlike other messengers, they are independent contractors and therefore seldom receive paid vacations, sick leave, health insurance, or other benefits from the messenger or delivery company. Messengers working for employers other than messenger and courier services usually are paid by the hour and receive the benefits offered to all employees.

Mail clerks are usually paid by the hour and benefits often include health and life insurance, sick leave, vacation pay, and pension plan.

Related Occupations

Messengers and mail clerks sort and deliver letters, parcels, and other items. They also keep accurate records of their work. Others who do similar work are postal clerks and mail carriers, route drivers, traffic, shipping, and receiving clerks, and parcel post clerks.

Sources of Additional Information

Information about job opportunities may be obtained from local employers and local offices of the State employment service. Persons interested in mail clerk and messenger jobs may also contact messenger and courier services, mail order firms, banks, printing and publishing firms, utility companies, retail stores, or other large firms.

For information on training and certification programs in mail systems management, contact:

☛ Mail Systems Management Association, J.A.F. Building, P.O. Box 2155, New York, NY 10116-2155.

Material Recording, Scheduling, Dispatching, and Distributing Occupations

(A list of D.O.T. codes is available on request. See page 478.)

Nature of the Work

Workers in this group are responsible for a variety of communications and recordkeeping operations in business and government. In general, they coordinate, expedite, and keep track of orders for personnel, equipment, and materials.

Dispatchers receive requests for service and initiate action to provide that service. Duties vary, depending on the needs of the employer. Police, fire, and ambulance dispatchers, also called public safety dispatchers, handle calls from people reporting crimes, fires, and medical emergencies; truck, bus, and train dispatchers schedule and coordinate the movement of these vehicles to ensure that they arrive on schedule; taxicab dispatchers relay requests for cabs to individual drivers; tow truck dispatchers take calls for emergency road service; and utility company dispatchers handle calls related to utility and telephone service.

Stock clerks receive, unpack, store, issue, and maintain an inventory. The inventory may be merchandise in wholesale and retail establishments, and equipment, supplies, or materials in other kinds of organizations. In small firms, they may perform all of the above tasks, as well as those usually handled by shipping and receiving clerks. In large establishments, they may be responsible for only one task.

Traffic, shipping, and receiving clerks keep track of all incoming and outgoing shipments of goods transferred between businesses, suppliers, and customers. Traffic clerks keep a record of destination, weight, and charges of all incoming and outgoing shipments. Shipping clerks assemble, address, stamp, and ship merchandise or materials. Receiving clerks unpack, verify, and record incoming merchandise. In a small company, one clerk may perform all of these tasks. More detail on these occupations is available in the statements that follow.

Other administrative support occupations in this group include *production, planning, and expediting clerks*—who coordinate and expedite the flow of work and material according to production schedules; *procurement clerks*—who draw up purchase orders to obtain merchandise or material; *weighers, measurers, checkers, and samplers*—who weigh, measure, and check materials; and *utility meter readers*—who read electric, gas, water, or steam meters and record the quantity used by their customers.

Working Conditions

Working conditions vary considerably by occupation and employment setting. Meter readers spend a good portion of their workday traveling around communities and neighborhoods taking readings, either directly or with remote reading equipment. The work of dispatchers can be very hectic when a large number of calls come in at the same time. The job of public safety dispatcher is particularly stressful because slow or improper response to a call can result in further destruction of property, serious injury, or death. Also, callers who are anxious or afraid may become hysterical and be unable to provide the needed information; some may even become abusive. Despite provocations, the dispatcher must remain calm, objective, and in control of the situation.

Dispatchers work in surroundings that are typical of office jobs. They sit for long periods, often using telephones, computers, and two-way radios. If much time is spent at a video display terminal, as is increasingly common, they can experience eyestrain and back discomfort. Dispatchers generally work a standard 40-hour week. However, evening, weekend, and holiday work is common because many service providers operate around the clock. Some employers rotate dispatchers among three shifts to divide daytime, weekend, and holiday work equally.

Traffic, shipping, receiving, and stock clerks work in a wide variety of businesses, institutions, and industries. Some work in warehouses, stock rooms, or in shipping and receiving rooms that may not be temperature controlled. Others may spend time in cold storage rooms or outside on loading platforms, where they are exposed to the weather. Most jobs involve frequent standing, bending, walking, stretching, lifting, and carrying. Although many use mechanical material-handling equipment to move heavy items, the work still can be strenuous. The typical workweek is 40 hours, Monday through Friday, although evening and weekend hours are standard for some jobs and may be required in others when large shipments are involved or when inventory is taken.

Employment

In 1994, material recording, scheduling, dispatching, and distributing workers held about 3,556,000 million jobs. Employment was distributed among the occupations in this group as follows:

Total	3,556,000
Stock clerks	1,759,000
Traffic, shipping, and receiving clerks	798,000
Production, planning, and expediting clerks	239,000
Dispatchers	224,000
Order fillers, wholesale and retail sales	215,000
Procurement clerks	57,000
Meter readers, utilities	57,000
Weighers, measurers, checkers, and samplers	45,000
All other	161,000

Nearly 3 out of 4 material recording, scheduling, dispatching, and distributing jobs were in manufacturing and wholesale and retail trade. Although these workers are found throughout the country, most work near population centers where stores, warehouses, factories, and large communications centers are concentrated.

Training, Other Qualifications, and Advancement

Employers prefer to hire high school graduates, especially those who have taken business courses. Preference also may be given to candidates who have previous business, dispatching, or specific job-related experience. Good reading and writing skills, as well as a basic knowledge of business arithmetic are necessary. Typing, filing, record-keeping, and other clerical skills are also important. Some employers give applicants typing tests.

Traffic, shipping, and receiving clerks and stock clerks who handle jewelry, liquor, or drugs may have to be bonded. Police, fire, and ambulance dispatching jobs generally are governed by State or local government civil service regulations. Candidates for these jobs may have to pass written, oral, and performance tests. A familiarity with personal computers or computer systems is an asset, because computers are increasingly used for inventory control and for dispatching.

Trainees usually develop the necessary skills on the job. This informal training lasts from several days to a few months, depending on the complexity of the job. Dispatchers usually require the most extensive training. Working under an experienced dispatcher, they monitor calls and learn how to operate telephones, radio transmitters and receivers, radio consoles, teletypewriters, and data communications terminals. As trainees gain confidence, they begin to handle calls themselves. Many public safety dispatchers also participate in structured training programs provided by their employer. Some employers offer a course designed by the Associated Public Safety Communications Officers (APCO). This course covers topics such as interpersonal communications; overview of the police, fire, and rescue functions; modern public safety telecommunications systems; basic radio broadcasting; local, State, and national crime information computer systems; and telephone complaint/report processing procedures. Other employers develop in-house programs based on their own needs. Emergency medical dispatchers often get special training or have special skills. Some agencies bring in trained paramedics or nurses to work as dispatchers, but because this is so costly, many agencies expand the training of their dispatchers to include instruction on how to help callers begin appropriate lifesaving procedures while trained professionals are on their way.

Although there are no mandatory licensing or certification requirements, some States require that public safety dispatchers possess a certificate to work on a State network such as the Police Information Network. Voluntary certification programs are offered by both APCO and the International Municipal Signal Association. Many dispatchers participate in these programs in order to improve their prospects for career advancement.

Stock clerks and traffic, shipping, and receiving clerks usually learn the job by doing simple tasks under close supervision. They learn how to count and mark stock and then start keeping records and taking inventory. Stock clerks whose sole responsibility is to bring merchandise to the sales floor and stock shelves and racks need little or no training. Traffic, shipping, and receiving clerks start out by checking items to be shipped and then attaching labels and making sure the addresses are correct. Training in the use of automated equipment is usually done informally on the job.

Communications skills and the ability to work under pressure are important personal qualities for dispatchers. Residency in the city or county of employment is frequently required for public safety dispatchers. Dispatchers in transportation industries must be able to deal with sudden influxes of shipments and disruptions of shipping schedules caused by bad weather, road construction, or accidents. Strength, stamina, good eyesight, and an ability to work at repetitive tasks, sometimes under pressure, are important characteristics for stock clerks and traffic, shipping, and receiving clerks.

Advancement opportunities vary with the place of employment. Dispatchers who work for private firms, which are usually small, will find few opportunities for advancement. Public safety dispatchers, on the other hand, may become a shift or divisional supervisor or chief of communications, or move to higher paying administrative jobs. Some go on to become police officers or firefighters. In large firms, stock clerks can advance to invoice clerk, stock control clerk, or procurement clerk. Traffic, shipping, and receiving clerks are promoted to head clerk, and those with a broad understanding of shipping and receiving may enter a related field such as industrial traffic management. With additional training, some stock clerks and traffic, shipping, and receiving clerks advance to jobs as warehouse manager or purchasing agent.

Job Outlook

Overall employment of material recording, scheduling, dispatching, and distributing workers is expected to grow more slowly than the average for all occupations through the year 2005. Employment growth among the occupations in this group is expected to vary, however. Employment of stock clerks is expected to grow more slowly than the average. The volume of business transactions will increase as the economy grows, but automation will enable clerks to handle more stock, holding down employment growth somewhat. The effect of automation will be greatest in warehouses and stockrooms. Employment of traffic, shipping, and receiving clerks is also expected to grow more slowly than the average as automation and other productivity improvements will enable these clerks to handle materials more efficiently, reducing potential employment opportunities. Employment of dispatchers is expected to grow about as fast as the average as the population increases and with it the need to protect property and to coordinate the transportation and shipment of a larger amount of goods.

Because employment in material recording, scheduling, dispatching, and distributing occupations is substantial, workers who leave the labor force or transfer to other occupations are expected to create many job openings each year.

Earnings

Median weekly earnings of workers in all material recording, scheduling, dispatching, and distributing occupations were $402 in 1994. The middle 50 percent earned between $297 and $555. The lowest 10 percent earned $231 or less; the top 10 percent earned over $713.

Earnings vary somewhat by occupation and industry. Dispatchers earn slightly more than the average for these occupations, and stock clerks and traffic, shipping, and receiving clerks generally earn less. Median weekly earnings of dispatchers were $405 in 1994, whereas the median weekly earnings of traffic, shipping, and receiving clerks and stock clerks were $383 and $394, respectively, in 1994.

Workers in material recording, scheduling, dispatching, and distributing occupations usually receive the same benefits as most other workers. If uniforms are required, employers usually either provide the uniforms or an allowance to purchase them.

Dispatchers

(D.O.T. 184.167-010, -262; 215.167, .367-018; 221.362-014, .367-070, -082; 239.167-014; .367-014, -022, -030; 248.367-026; 249.167-014, .367-070; 372.167-010; 379.162; .362-010, and -018; 579.137-030; 910.167-014, .367-018; 911.167; 913.167-010; .367; 914.167-014; 919.162; 932.167; 939.362-010; 952.167-010; 953.167; 954.367; 955.167; and 959.167)

Nature of the Work

The work of dispatchers varies greatly depending on the industry in which they work.

Police, fire, and ambulance dispatchers, also called public safety dispatchers, are usually the first people the public talks to when they call for emergency assistance. Dispatchers receive these calls in a variety of settings; they may work in a police station, a fire station, a hospital, or a centralized city communications center. In many cities, the police department serves as the communications center. In these situations, all 911 emergency calls go to the police department where a dispatcher handles the police calls and screens the others before transferring them to the appropriate service.

When handling a call, dispatchers carefully question the caller to determine the type, seriousness, and location of the emergency. They then quickly decide on the kind and number of units needed, locate the closest and most suitable ones available, and send them to the scene of the emergency. They keep in touch with the units until the emergency has been handled, in case further instructions are needed. When appropriate, they stay in close contact with other service providers—for example, a police dispatcher would monitor the response of the fire department when there is a major fire. In a medical emergency, dispatchers not only keep in close touch with the dispatched units but also with the caller. They may give extensive pre-arrival first aid instructions while the caller is waiting for the ambulance. They continuously give updates on the patient's condition to the ambulance personnel and often serve as a link between the medical staff in a hospital and the emergency medical technicians in the ambulance. (The work of emergency medical technicians is described elsewhere in the *Handbook*.)

Truck dispatchers who work for local and long distance trucking companies coordinate the movement of trucks and freight between cities. They direct the pickup and delivery activities of drivers. They receive customers' requests for pickup and delivery of freight, consolidate freight into truckloads for specific destinations, assign drivers and trucks, make up routes and pickup and delivery schedules, and provide other information. *Bus dispatchers* make sure that local and long distance buses stay on schedule. They handle all problems that may disrupt service and dispatch other buses or arrange for repairs to restore service and schedules. *Train dispatchers* are responsible for the timely movement of trains according to train orders and schedules. They must be aware of track switch positions

Most police, fire, and ambulance dispatchers work for State or local governments.

and the location of other trains running on the track. *Taxicab dispatchers*, or starters, dispatch taxis in response to requests for service and keep logs on all road service calls. *Tow truck dispatchers* take calls for emergency road service. They relay the problem to a nearby service station or a tow truck service and see to it that the emergency road service is completed. *Gas and water service dispatchers* monitor gas lines and water mains and send out service trucks and crews to take care of emergencies. Other dispatchers coordinate deliveries, service calls, and related activities for a variety of firms.

Regardless of where they work, all dispatchers keep records, logs, and schedules of the calls they receive and the actions they take. They may type and file cards on each call and then prepare detailed reports on all activities occurring during their shift. Those who work with a computer-aided dispatch system make the appropriate entries and corrections into the computer as they occur, and then print a log or report at the end of their shift.

Many police, ambulance, taxicab, and tow truck dispatchers work as part of a two-person team. One person usually receives incoming calls while the other dispatches and follows up on them. This is commonplace in large communications centers or companies.

Employment

Dispatchers held over 224,000 jobs in 1994. About one-third were police, fire, and ambulance dispatchers, almost all of whom worked for State and local governments—primarily for local police and fire departments. Most of the remaining dispatchers worked for local and long distance trucking companies and bus lines; telephone, electric, and gas utility companies; wholesale and retail establishments; railroads; and companies providing business services.

Although dispatching jobs are found throughout the country, most dispatchers work in urban areas where large communications centers and businesses are located.

Job Outlook

Overall employment of dispatchers is expected to grow about as fast as the average for all occupations through the year 2005 due to the growing need for the various services that dispatchers provide. Most job openings will result from the need to replace those who transfer to other occupations or leave the labor force.

Employment of police, fire, and ambulance dispatchers is expected to grow more slowly than the average for all occupations. Increasingly intense competition among government functions for available resources should limit the ability of many growing communities to keep pace with rapidly growing emergency services needs.

Although population growth and economic expansion are expected to increase overall employment of other dispatchers not involved in public safety, not all specialties will be affected in the same way. Employment of taxicab, train, and truck dispatchers is sensitive to economic conditions. When economic activity falls, demand for transportation services declines. They may experience layoffs or a shortened workweek, and jobseekers may have some difficulty finding entry-level jobs. Employment of tow truck dispatchers, on the other hand, is seldom affected by general economic conditions because of the emergency nature of their business.

Computerization is making inroads into all areas of dispatching, increasing productivity and dampening employment growth somewhat. However, computer-aided dispatch systems are very expensive, making them affordable only to relatively large establishments.

Related Occupations

Other occupations that involve directing and controlling the movement of vehicles, freight, and personnel, as well as information and message distribution, are airline-radio operators, airline dispatchers, air traffic controllers, radio and television transmitter operators, telephone operators, customer service representatives, and transportation agents.

Sources of Additional Information

For further information on training for police, fire, and emergency dispatchers contact:

☛Associated Public Safety Communications Officers, 2040 S. Ridgewood, South Daytona, FL 32119-8437.

☛International Municipal Signal Association, 165 East Union St., P.O. Box 539, Newark, NY 14513-1526.

For general information on dispatchers contact:

☛Service Employees International Union, AFL-CIO; CLC, 1313 L St. NW., Washington, DC 20005-4100.

☛American Train Dispatchers Association, 1370 Ontario St., Cleveland, OH 44113.

Information on job opportunities for police, fire, and emergency dispatchers is available from the personnel offices of State and local governments or police departments. Information about work opportunities for other types of dispatchers is available from local employers and State employment service offices. (Information on training and earnings is in the introduction to material recording, scheduling, dispatching, and distributing occupations.)

Stock Clerks

(D.O.T. 219.367-018, .387-026 and -030; 221.587-018 and -022; 222.167, .367-014, -026, -038, -042, -050, and -062, .387-018, -026, -030, -034, -042, -058, and -062, .487, .587-022 and -054, .684, .687-038 and -046; 229.367, .587-014; 249.367-058; 299.367-014, .677-014; 339.687; 381.687-010; and 969.367)

Nature of the Work

Stock clerks receive, unpack, check, store, and keep track of merchandise or materials. They keep records of items entering or leaving the stock room and report damaged or spoiled goods. They organize and, when necessary, mark items with identifying codes or prices so that inventories can be located quickly and easily. In many firms, stock clerks use hand-held scanners, which they can connect to computers to keep inventories up to date. In stores, stock clerks bring merchandise to the sales floor and stock shelves and racks. In stockrooms and warehouses, they store materials in bins, on the floor, or on shelves. In large establishments where they may be responsible for only one specific task, they may be known as inventory clerk, stock control clerk, merchandise distributor, order filler, property custodian, or storekeeper. In small firms they may also be responsible for tasks usually handled by shipping and receiving clerks.

Employment

Stock clerks held about 1,759,000 jobs in 1994 with almost 80 percent working in wholesale or retail trade. The greatest numbers were employed by department and grocery stores. Jobs for stock clerks are found in all parts of the country, but most work in urban areas where stores, warehouses, and factories are concentrated.

Job Outlook

Job prospects for stock clerks should be favorable even though employment is expected to grow more slowly than the average for all occupations through the year 2005. This occupation is very large, and many job openings will occur each year to replace those who transfer to other jobs or leave the labor force. Many jobs are entry level, and therefore vacancies are also created by normal career progression.

Growing use of computers for inventory control and new automated equipment are expected to slow growth in demand for stock clerks. This is especially true in manufacturing and in wholesale trade, the industries whose operations are most easily automated. In addition to computerized inventory control systems, firms in these industries are expected to rely more and more on sophisticated conveyor belts, automatic high stackers to store and retrieve goods,

Computerized inventory control systems are expected to slow the growth of stock clerks.

and automatic guided vehicles, which are battery powered and driverless.

Employment of stock clerks who work in grocery, general merchandise, department, apparel, and accessories stores is expected to be somewhat less affected by automation since much of their work is done manually on the sales floor and is difficult to automate.

Related Occupations

Other workers who also handle, move, organize, and store materials include shipping and receiving clerks, distributing clerks, routing clerks, stock supervisors, and cargo checkers.

Sources of Additional Information

State employment service offices can provide information about job openings for stock clerks. Also, see clerical and sales occupations elsewhere in the *Handbook* for sources of additional information.

General information about stock clerks can be obtained by contacting:

☛National Retail Federation, 701 Pennsylvania Ave. NW., Washington, DC 20004-2608.

(Information on training and earnings is in the introduction to material recording, scheduling, dispatching, and distributing occupations.)

Traffic, Shipping, and Receiving Clerks

(D.O.T. 209.367-042; 214.587-014; 219.367-022 and -030; 221.367-022;
222.367-066, .387-014, -022, -050, and -054, .485, .567-010 and -014,
.587-018, -034, and -058, .687-022 and -030; 248.362-010, .367-014 and
-022; 919.687-010; and 976.687-018)

Nature of the Work

Traffic, shipping, and receiving clerks keep records of all goods
shipped and received. Their duties depend on the size of the establishment. In a small company, one clerk may be responsible for
accepting deliveries, preparing shipments, and maintaining records.
In a large company, the responsibilities are usually divided among
several clerks who have specialized duties.

Traffic clerks maintain records on the destination, weight, and
charges on all incoming and outgoing freight. They sometimes enter
this information into a computer to be used by the accounting and
other departments within the firm. They make sure that the rate
charges are accurate by comparing the classification of materials
with rate charts. They also keep a file of claims for overcharges and
for damage to goods in transit.

Shipping clerks are record keepers responsible for all outgoing
shipments. They prepare shipping documents and mailing labels, and
make sure orders have been filled correctly. They also record items
taken from inventory and note when orders were filled. Sometimes
they fill the order themselves; obtaining merchandise from the stockroom and wrapping it or packing it in shipping containers. They also
address and label packages, look up and compute freight or postal
rates, and record the weight and cost of each shipment. Sometimes
they prepare invoices and furnish information about shipments to
another part of the company, such as the accounting department.
Once a shipment is checked and ready to go, shipping clerks may
move the goods from the plant—sometimes by forklift truck—to the
shipping dock and direct its loading.

When shipments arrive, *receiving clerks* perform tasks similar to
those of shipping clerks. They determine whether their employer's

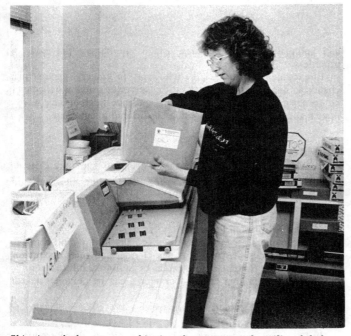

*Shipping clerks prepare shipping documents and mailing labels
and make sure orders have been filled correctly.*

orders have been correctly filled by verifying incoming shipments
against the original order and the accompanying bill of lading or
invoice. They record the shipment and the condition of its contents.
In many firms, receiving clerks record the information by using
hand-held scanners to read the bar codes on incoming products.
They then connect the scanner or reader to a personal computer and
transfer the data to the appropriate department. Depending on the
computer system used, this information is then compared with the
information transferred from a similar type of scanner used by the
truck driver. The shipment is checked for any discrepancies in
quantity, price, and discounts. Receiving clerks may route or move
shipments to the proper department, warehouse section, or stockroom. They also arrange for adjustments with shippers whenever
merchandise is lost or damaged. Shipping and receiving clerks in
small businesses may also perform some stock clerk duties.

Employment

Traffic, shipping, and receiving clerks held about 798,000 jobs in
1994. Nearly 3 out of every 4 were employed by wholesale or retail
establishments, or manufacturing firms. Although jobs for traffic,
shipping, and receiving clerks are found throughout the country, most
clerks work in urban areas, where factories and wholesale establishments generally are located. Many traffic, shipping, and receiving
clerks work for the U.S. Postal Service. For information on these
workers, see the statement on postal clerks and mail carriers, elsewhere in the *Handbook*.

Job Outlook

Employment of traffic, shipping, and receiving clerks is expected to
increase more slowly than the average for all occupations through the
year 2005. Employment growth will continue to be affected by
automation, as all but the smallest firms move to hold down labor
costs by using computers to store and retrieve shipping and receiving
records.

Methods of materials handling have changed significantly in
recent years. Large warehouses are increasingly automated, using
equipment such as computerized conveyor systems, robots, com-
puter-directed trucks, and automatic storage and retrieval systems.
Automation, coupled with the growing use of hand-held scanners and
personal computers in receiving departments has increased the
productivity of these workers.

Despite automation, job openings will arise due to increasing
economic activity and because certain functions cannot be automated. For example, someone needs to check shipments before they
go out and when they arrive to ensure that everything is in order.
However, most job openings will occur because of the need to replace traffic, shipping, and receiving clerks who leave the occupation. Because this is an entry level occupation, vacancies are also
created by normal career progression.

Related Occupations

Traffic, shipping, and receiving clerks record, check, and often store
the materials that a company receives. They also process and pack
goods for shipment. Other workers who perform similar duties are
stock clerks, material clerks, distributing clerks, routing clerks,
express clerks, expediters, and order fillers.

Sources of Additional Information

General information about traffic, shipping, and receiving clerks can
be obtained by contacting:
☛National Retail Federation, 701 Pennsylvania Ave. NW., Washington, DC
20004-2608.

(Information on training and earnings is in the introduction to
material recording, scheduling, dispatching, and distributing occupations.)

Postal Clerks and Mail Carriers

(D.O.T. 209.687-014; 230.363-010, .367-010; 239.367-018; and 243.367-014)

Nature of the Work

Each day, the U.S. Postal Service receives, sorts, and delivers millions of letters, bills, advertisements, and packages. To do this, it employs about 818,000 workers. Almost 6 out of 10 of these workers are either postal clerks, who sort mail and serve customers in post offices, or mail carriers, who deliver the mail.

Clerks and carriers are distinguished by the type of work they do. Clerks are usually classified by the mail processing function they perform, whereas carriers are classified by their type of route—city or rural.

About 350 mail processing centers throughout the country service post offices in surrounding areas and are staffed primarily by postal clerks. Some clerks, more commonly referred to as mail handlers, unload the sacks of incoming mail; separate letters, parcel post, magazines, and newspapers; and transport these to the proper sorting and processing area. In addition, they may load mail into automated letter sorting machines, perform postage canceling operations, and rewrap packages damaged in processing.

After letters have been put through stamp-canceling machines, they are taken to other workrooms to be sorted according to destination. Clerks operating older electronic letter-sorting machines push keys corresponding to the ZIP code of the local post office to which each letter will be delivered; the machine then drops the letters into the proper slots. This older, less automated method of letter sorting is being slowly phased out. Other clerks sort odd-sized letters, magazines, and newspapers by hand. Finally, the mail is sent to local post offices for sorting according to delivery route and delivered.

A growing proportion of clerks operate optical character readers (OCR's) and bar code sorters. Optical character readers "read" the zip code and spray a bar code onto the mail. Bar code sorters then scan the code and sort the mail. Because this is significantly faster than older sorting methods, it is becoming the standard sorting technology in mail processing centers.

Postal clerks at local post offices sort local mail for delivery to individual customers; sell stamps, money orders, postal stationary, and mailing envelopes and boxes; weigh packages to determine postage; and check that packages are in satisfactory condition for mailing. Increasingly, mail is being sorted in delivery route sequence by machines. Clerks also register, certify, and insure mail and answer questions about postage rates, post office boxes, mailing restrictions, and other postal matters. They also may help customers file claims for damaged packages.

Once the mail has been processed and sorted, it is ready to be delivered by mail carriers. Duties of city and rural carriers are very similar. Most travel established routes delivering and collecting mail. Mail carriers start work at the post office early in the morning, where they spend a few hours arranging their mail in delivery sequence and taking care of other details. Recently, automated equipment has begun to be used to sort most of the mail for city and rural carriers, allowing them to spend less time sorting and more time delivering mail. This sorting equipment should be used in most post offices by 1998.

Carriers cover their routes on foot, by vehicle, or a combination of both. On foot, they carry a heavy load of mail in a satchel or push it in a cart. In some urban and most rural areas, they use a car or small truck. Although the Postal Service provides vehicles to city carriers, most rural carriers use their own automobiles. Deliveries are made house-to-house, to roadside mailboxes, and to large buildings, such as offices or apartments, which generally have all the mailboxes on the first floor.

Besides delivering and collecting mail, carriers collect money for postage-due and c.o.d. (cash on delivery) fees and obtain signed receipts for registered, certified, and insured mail. If a customer is not home, the carrier leaves a notice that tells where special mail is being held.

After completing their routes, carriers return to the post office with mail gathered from street collection boxes, homes, and businesses. They turn in the mail receipts and money collected during the day and may separate letters and parcels for further processing by clerks.

The duties of some city carriers may be very specialized; some deliver only parcel post while others collect mail from street boxes and receiving boxes in office buildings. In contrast, rural carriers provide a wide range of postal services. In addition to delivering and picking up mail, they sell stamps and money orders and accept parcels, letters, and items to be registered, certified, or insured.

All carriers answer customers' questions about postal regulations and services and provide change-of-address cards and other postal forms when requested. In addition to their regularly scheduled duties, carriers often participate in neighborhood service programs in which they check on elderly or shut-in patrons or notify the police of any suspicious activities along their route.

Postal clerks and mail carriers are classified as casual, part-time flexible, part-time regular, or full time. Casual workers, hired for 90 days at a time, help process and deliver mail during peak mailing or vacation periods. Part-time flexible workers do not have a regular work schedule or weekly guarantee of hours; they replace absent

Automated mail sorting machines will reduce the amount of hand sorting to be done by mail carriers.

workers and help with extra work as the need arises. Part-time regulars have a set work schedule of fewer than 40 hours per week. Full-time postal employees work a 40-hour week over a 5-day period.

Working Conditions

Postal clerks usually work in clean, well-ventilated, and well-lit buildings. However, other conditions vary according to work assignments and the type of machinery in operation. In small post offices, mail handlers use handtrucks to move heavy mail sacks from one part of the building to another and clerks may sort mail by hand. In large post offices and mail processing centers, chutes and conveyors move the mail, and much of the sorting is done by machines. Despite the use of automated equipment, the work of mail handlers and postal clerks can be physically demanding. These workers are usually on their feet, reaching for sacks and trays of mail or placing packages and bundles into sacks and trays.

Mail handlers and distribution clerks may become bored with the routine of moving and sorting mail. Many work at night or on weekends because most large post offices process mail around the clock, and the largest volume of mail is sorted during the evening and night shifts. Workers may experience stress as they process and deliver ever larger quantities of mail under tight production deadlines and quotas.

Window clerks, on the other hand, have a greater variety of duties, frequent contact with the public, and rarely have to work at night. However, they may have to deal with upset customers, and they are held accountable for the assigned stock of stamps and for postal funds.

Most carriers begin work early in the morning, in some cases as early as 4 a.m. if they have routes in the business district. A carrier's schedule has its advantages, however. Carriers who begin work early in the morning are through by early afternoon, and they spend most of the day on their own, relatively free from direct supervision. Overtime hours may be required during peak delivery times, such as the holidays.

Carriers spend most of their time outdoors, and deliver mail in all kinds of weather. Even those who drive often must walk when making deliveries and must lift heavy sacks of parcel post items when loading their vehicles. In addition, carriers always must be cautious of potential hazards on their routes. Wet roads and sidewalks can be treacherous, and each year numerous carriers are bitten by dogs.

Employment

The U.S. Postal Service employed 154,000 postal clerks and 320,000 mail carriers in 1994. About 90 percent of them worked full time. Most postal clerks provided window service and sorted mail at local post offices, although some worked at mail processing centers. Although most mail carriers worked in cities and suburban communities, 46,000 were rural carriers.

In addition to the postal clerks mentioned above, there were about 91,000 traffic, shipping, and receiving clerks employed in the U.S. Postal Service in 1994. (Many of the duties of these clerks are described in the Nature of the Work section of this statement. For more information about these workers, see the statement on traffic, shipping, and receiving clerks elsewhere in the *Handbook*.)

Training, Other Qualifications, and Advancement

Postal clerks and mail carriers must be U.S. citizens or have been granted permanent resident-alien status in the United States. They must be at least 18 years old (or 16, if they have a high school diploma). Qualification is based on a written examination that measures speed and accuracy at checking names and numbers and ability to memorize mail distribution procedures. Applicants must pass a physical examination as well, and may be asked to show that they can lift and handle mail sacks weighing up to 70 pounds. Applicants

for jobs as postal clerks operating electronic sorting machines must pass a special examination that includes a machine aptitude test. Applicants for mail carrier positions must have a driver's license, a good driving record, and a passing grade on a road test.

Applicants should apply at the post office or mail processing center where they wish to work in order to determine when an exam will be given. Applicants' names are listed in order of their examination scores. Five points are added to the score of an honorably discharged veteran, and 10 points to the score of a veteran wounded in combat or disabled. When a vacancy occurs, the appointing officer chooses one of the top three applicants; the rest of the names remain on the list to be considered for future openings until their eligibility expires, usually 2 years from the examination date.

Relatively few people under the age of 25 are hired as career postal clerks or mail carriers, a result of keen competition for these jobs and the customary waiting period of 1-2 years or more after passing the examination. It is not surprising, therefore, that most entrants transfer from other occupations.

New postal clerks and mail carriers are trained on the job by experienced workers. Many post offices offer classroom instruction. Workers receive additional instruction when new equipment or procedures are introduced. They usually are trained by another postal employee or, sometimes, a training specialist hired under contract by the Postal Service.

A good memory, good coordination, and the ability to read rapidly and accurately are important. In addition, mail handlers should be in good physical condition. Mail handlers and distribution clerks work closely with other clerks, frequently under the tension and strain of meeting dispatch transportation deadlines. Window clerks and mail carriers must be courteous and tactful when dealing with the public, especially when answering questions or receiving complaints.

Postal clerks and mail carriers often begin on a part-time flexible basis and become regular or full time in order of seniority as vacancies occur. Full-time clerks may bid for preferred assignments such as the day shift, a window job, or a higher level nonsupervisory position as expediter or window service technician. Carriers can look forward to obtaining preferred routes as their seniority increases, or to higher level jobs such as carrier technician. Both clerks and carriers can advance to supervisory positions.

Job Outlook

Those seeking a job in the Postal Service can expect to encounter keen competition—the number of applicants for postal clerk and mail carrier positions is expected to continue to far exceed the number of openings. Job opportunities will vary by occupation and duties performed.

Overall employment of postal clerks is expected to increase more slowly than the average through the year 2005. Increasingly, mail will be moved using automated materials-handling equipment and sorted using optical character readers, bar code sorters, and other automated sorting equipment. In spite of increased use of this productivity-increasing machinery, the expected increase in the volume of mail will require additional clerks. However, demand for window clerks will be moderated by the increased sales of stamps and other postal products by grocery and department stores and other retail outlets.

Conflicting factors also are expected to influence demand for mail carriers. Despite competition from alternative delivery systems and new forms of electronic communication, the volume of mail handled by the Postal Service is expected to continue to grow. Population growth and the formation of new households will stimulate demand for mail delivery. However, increased use of the "ZIP + 4" system, which is used to sort mail to the carrier route, and other automated sorting equipment should decrease the amount of time carriers spend sorting their mail, allowing them more time to handle longer routes. In addition, the Postal Service is moving toward more centralized mail delivery, such as the use of more cluster boxes, to cut down on the number of door-to-door deliveries. These trends are expected to increase carrier productivity. Employment of mail carriers is expected to change little through the year 2005.

Jobs will become available because of the need to replace postal clerks and mail carriers who retire or stop working for other reasons. However, the factors that make entry to these occupations highly competitive—attractive salaries, a good pension plan, job security, and modest educational requirements—contribute to a high degree of job attachment. Accordingly, replacement needs produce relatively fewer job openings than in other occupations of this size. In contrast to the typical pattern, postal workers generally remain in their jobs until they retire; relatively few transfer to other occupations.

Although the volume of mail to be processed and delivered rises and falls with the level of business activity, as well as with the season of the year, full-time postal clerks and mail carriers have never been laid off. When mail volume is high, full-time clerks and carriers work overtime, part-time clerks and carriers work additional hours, and casual clerks and carriers may be hired. When mail volume is low, overtime is curtailed, part-timers work fewer hours, and casual workers are discharged.

Earnings

In 1995, base pay for beginning full-time carriers and postal clerks was $25,240 a year, rising to a maximum of $35,604 after 12 1/2 years of service. For those working between 6 p.m. and 6 a.m, a supplement is paid. Experienced, full-time, city delivery mail carriers earn an average salary of $34,566 a year. Postal clerks and carriers working part-time flexible schedules begin at $12.59 an hour and, based on the number of years of service, increase to a maximum of $17.76 an hour.

Rural delivery carriers had average base salaries of $33,980 in 1995. Their earnings are determined through an evaluation of the amount of work required to service their routes. Carriers with heavier workloads generally earn more than those with lighter workloads. Rural carriers also receive an equipment maintenance allowance when required to use their own vehicles. In 1995, this was approximately 35 cents per mile.

Postal workers enjoy a variety of employer-provided benefits. These include health and life insurance, vacation and sick leave, and a pension plan.

In addition to their hourly wage and benefits package, some postal workers receive a uniform allowance. This group includes those workers who are in the public view for 4 or more hours each day and various maintenance workers. The amount of the allowance depends on the job performed—some workers are only required to wear a partial uniform, and their allowance is lower. In 1995, for example, the allowance for a letter carrier was $252 per year, compared to $108 for a window clerk and $50 for a mailhandler.

Most of these workers belong to one of four unions: American Postal Workers Union, National Association of Letter Carriers, National Postal Mail Handlers Union, and National Rural Letter Carriers Association.

Related Occupations

Other workers whose duties are related to those of postal clerks include mail clerks, file clerks, routing clerks, sorters, material moving equipment operators, clerk typists, cashiers, data entry operators, and ticket sellers. Others with duties related to those of mail carriers include messengers, merchandise deliverers, and delivery-route truckdrivers.

Sources of Additional Information

Local post offices and State employment service offices can supply details about entrance examinations and specific employment opportunities for postal clerks and mail carriers.

Record Clerks

Nature of the Work

Organizations of all kinds—businesses, government agencies, unions, health care facilities, and colleges and universities—must keep accurate records. Maintaining and updating records, ranging from payrolls to information on the shipment of goods to bank statements, is the job of record clerks. (Additional information about specific record clerk occupations is provided in the separate statements in this section.)

Record clerks perform a wide variety of recordkeeping duties. Billing clerks and billing machine operators prepare bills and invoices. Bookkeeping, accounting, and auditing clerks maintain financial data in computer and paper files. Brokerage clerks prepare and maintain the records generated when stocks, bonds, and other types of investments are traded. Statement clerks prepare monthly statements for bank customers. File clerks store and retrieve various kinds of office information for use by staff members. Library assistants and bookmobile drivers assist library patrons. Order clerks process incoming orders for goods and services. Payroll and timekeeping clerks compute wages for payroll records. Personnel clerks maintain employee records.

Record clerks' duties may vary with the size of the firm. In a small business, one bookkeeping clerk may handle all financial records and transactions as well as payroll and personnel duties, while a large firm may employ specialized accounting clerks to work on each aspect of the balance sheet, as well as specialized payroll and personnel clerks.

Increased computerization has changed the duties of most record clerks. In the past, clerks made calculations with adding machines and entered figures into ledgers and paper files. Now, many workers use financial software to enter and manipulate data. In many cases, these computer programs can automatically perform calculations on data that previously had to be calculated manually. Computers enable clerks to access data within files more quickly than by leafing through stacks of paper. Despite increased automation, however, workers still keep backup paper records for research, auditing, and reference purposes.

Interaction with the public and with coworkers is a basic part of the job of many record clerks. Payroll clerks, for example, may answer employees' questions concerning benefits; bookmobile drivers help patients in nursing homes and hospitals select books; and order clerks call customers to verify special mailing instructions.

Other administrative support occupations in this group include *advertising clerks*—who receive orders for classified advertising from customers for newpapers or magazines; prepare copy according to customer specifications; and verify conformance of published ads to specifications for purposes of billing, and *correspondence clerks*—who reply to customers regarding damage claims, delinquent accounts, incorrect billing, complaints of unsatisfactory service, and requests for merchandise exchanges or returns.

Working Conditions

With the exception of library clerks and bookmobile drivers, record clerks typically work in an office environment. Most work alongside the organization's other clerical workers, but some work in centralized units away from the organization's front office. Clerks who review detailed data may have to sit for extended periods. Although they do not do heavy lifting, file clerks and library assistants frequently stoop, bend, reach, and spend a lot of time on their feet. Bookmobile drivers must maneuver large vehicles in all kinds of traffic and weather conditions. In addition, some are responsible for the maintenance of the bookmobile.

An increasing number of record clerks use computers as part of their daily routine. Workers who spend a lot of time at computers may experience eye and muscle strain, backaches, headaches, and repetitive motion injuries.

Most of these workers work regular business hours. Some, such as library assistants, may work evenings and weekends. Library assistants employed in school libraries generally work only during the school year. Accounting clerks may work longer hours to meet deadlines at the end of the fiscal year, during tax time, or when monthly and yearly accounting audits are performed. Billing, bookkeeping, and accounting clerks in hotels, restaurants, and stores may work overtime during peak holiday and vacation seasons. Brokerage clerks may have to work overtime if there is a high volume of activity in the stock or bond markets. Order clerks in retail establishments often work overtime when sales volume is high, especially around Christmas.

Employment

Record clerks held more than 3.7 million jobs in 1994. The following tabulation shows employment in individual occupations.

Bookkeeping, accounting, and auditing clerks	2,181,000
Billing clerks and billing machine operators	419,000
Order clerks	310,000
File clerks	278,000
Payroll and timekeeping clerks	157,000
Personnel clerks, except payroll and timekeeping	123,000
Library assistants and bookmobile drivers	121,000
Brokerage and statement clerks	98,000
Correspondence clerks	29,000
Advertising clerks	17,000

These workers are employed in virtually every industry. The largest number work for firms providing health, business, and other types of services. Large numbers also work in trade; finance, insurance, and real estate; manufacturing; and government.

Training, Other Qualifications, and Advancement

Most record clerk jobs are entry-level positions. Most employers require applicants to have at least a high school diploma or its equivalent. A higher level of education will usually be favored over a high school diploma, but it is not generally required. However, in some cases, more extensive education is mandatory. For example, order clerks in high-technology firms often need to understand scientific and mechanical processes, which may require some college education. Regardless of the type of work being done, most employers prefer those who are computer literate. Knowledge of word processing and spreadsheet software is especially valuable, as is experience working in an office and good interpersonal skills.

High schools, business schools, and community colleges teach office skills. Business education programs typically include courses in typing (keyboarding), word processing, shorthand, business communications, records management, and office systems and procedures. Technical training needed for some specialized order clerk positions can be obtained in technical institutes and in 2- and 4-year colleges.

Some entrants are college graduates with degrees in business, finance, or the liberal arts. Although a degree is rarely required, many graduates take entry-level clerical positions to get into a company or into the finance and accounting field, with the hope of being promoted to professional or managerial jobs. Some companies, such as brokerage and accounting firms, have a set plan of advancement that tracks college graduates from entry-level clerk jobs into management positions. These workers may start at higher salaries and advance more rapidly than those without a degree.

Once hired, record clerks generally receive on-the-job training. Under the guidance of a supervisor or senior worker, new employees learn company procedures. Some formal classroom training may be necessary, such as training in operating specific computer software.

Record clerks must be careful, orderly, and detail oriented in order to avoid making errors and to be able to recognize errors made by others. These workers must also be honest, discreet, and trustworthy because they frequently come in contact with confidential material. Payroll clerks, billing clerks, and bookkeeping, accounting, and auditing clerks should have a strong aptitude for numbers. Because statement clerks have access to individuals' financial information, they must be bonded. Many bookmobile drivers are now required to have a commercial driver's license.

Workers usually advance by taking on more duties in the same occupation with higher pay. Others advance to closely related occupations. For example, some order clerks use their experience to move into sales positions. Others move into other clerical jobs, such as secretary, or advance to a supervisory position. With appropriate experience and education, some clerks may become accountants, personnel specialists, brokers, or librarians.

Job Outlook

Turnover in this very large occupation places it among those occupations providing the most job openings. Opportunities will be plentiful for full-time, part-time, and seasonal employment as record clerks transfer to other occupations or leave the labor force.

Employment of record clerks is expected to decline through the year 2005. Despite continued growth in the volume of business transactions, fewer record clerks will be needed because of rising productivity. The main factor affecting productivity in these occupations is the spread of office automation. Many of these jobs are "back office" clerical positions, which have already been heavily automated in many organizations. Productivity has increased significantly as workers use word processors and personal computers instead of more time-consuming equipment such as typewriters, adding machines, and calculators. The growing use of equipment such as bar code readers, point-of-sale terminals, and optical scanners by other employees also reduces much of the data entry handled by record clerks. Managers and professionals now do much of their own clerical work, using computers to access, create, and store data directly in the computer system. The growing use of local area networks is also facilitating electronic data interchange—the sending of data from computer to computer, without the need for clerks to reenter the data. To further eliminate duplicate functions, more large companies may consolidate all their clerical operations in a central office where accounting, billing, personnel, and payroll functions are performed for all satellite offices in the organization.

Earnings

Salaries of record clerks vary considerably. Region of the country, size of city, and type and size of establishment all influence salary levels. The level of industry or technical expertise required and the complexity and uniqueness of a clerk's responsibilities may also affect earnings. Median earnings of full-time record clerks in 1994 are shown in the following tabulation.

Personnel clerks	$25,100
Order clerks	24,300
Payroll and timekeeping clerks	21,300
Bookkeeping, accounting, and auditing clerks	19,500
Billing clerks	19,500
Library clerks	18,800
Billing machine operators	17,800
File clerks	16,200

In the Federal Government in 1995, record clerks with a high school diploma or clerical experience typically started at $16,700 a year. Beginning salaries were slightly higher in selected areas where the prevailing local pay level was higher. In 1995, the average salary for all personnel clerks was $25,600.

In addition to salary, record clerks receive the same package of benefits as other employees in the organization. Sick and annual leave, life and health insurance, and retirement plans are common.

Related Occupations

Most record clerks today enter data into a computer system and perform basic analysis of the data. Other clerical workers who enter and manipulate data are bank tellers, statistical clerks, receiving clerks, medical record clerks, hotel and motel clerks, credit clerks, and reservation and transportation ticket agents.

Sources of Additional Information

State employment service offices can provide information about job openings for record clerks.

Public libraries and libraries in academic institutions can provide information about job openings for library assistants and bookmobile drivers.

Specific information on bookmobile drivers is available from:
☛The State Library of Ohio, Field Operations Department, 65 South Front St., Columbus, OH 43215.

Information on careers in records and information management can be obtained from:
☛Association of Record Managers and Administrators (ARMA), 4200 Somerset Dr., Suite 215, Prairie Village, KS 66208. Phone: 1-800-422-2762.

Billing Clerks and Billing Machine Operators

(D.O.T. 184.387-010; 210.382-022, -026, -066; 211.482-014, -018; 214.267-010, .362-010, -014, -022, -026, -038, -042, .382-014, -018, -030, .387-010, -014, -018, .462-010, .467-010, -014; 214.482-010, -014, -018, -022, .587-010; 216.382-022, -034, -050, -054; 217.382-010; 241.267-026; and 249.367-034)

Nature of the Work

Billing clerks keep the records, calculate the charges, and maintain the files of payments made for goods or services. Billing machine operators run the machines that generate the bills, statements, and invoices.

Billing clerks review purchase orders, bills of lading, sales tickets, hospital records, or charge slips to calculate the total amount due from a customer. In accounting, law, consulting, and similar firms, billing clerks calculate client fees based on the actual time required to perform the task. They keep track of the accumulated hours and dollar amounts to charge to each job, the type of job performed for a customer, and the percentage of work completed. In hospitals, calculating the charges for an individual's hospital stay may require a letter to an insurance company, whereas a clerk computing trucking rates for machine parts may consult a rate book. After billing clerks review all necessary information, they compute the charges using calculators or computers. They then prepare the itemized statements, bills, or invoices—depending on the organization's needs—used for billing and recordkeeping purposes. In one organization, the clerk might prepare a simple bill that only contains the amount due and the date and type of service; in another, the clerk would produce a detailed invoice that includes the codes for all goods and services provided. This latter form might list the items sold, credit terms, date of shipment or dates services were provided, a salesperson's or doctor's identification, if necessary, and the sales total.

Once all the information has been entered, billing machine operators then run off the bill that will be sent to the customer. In a growing number of firms, billing machines are being replaced by computers and specialized billing software that allow clerks to

Billing clerks check statements, bills, and invoices for accuracy.

calculate charges and prepare bills in one step. Computer packages prompt clerks to enter data from hand-written forms and manipulate the necessary entries of quantities, labor, and rates to be charged. Billing clerks verify the entry of information and check for errors before the bill is printed by the computer. After the bills are printed, billing clerks check them again for accuracy.

Employment

In 1994, billing clerks held about 323,000 jobs, and billing machine operators held about 96,000. About 4 of every 10 billing clerks and billing machine operators were employed by banks and other financial institutions, insurance companies, and other organizations providing business and health services. About 1 of every 5 employees was found in wholesale and retail establishments, and a significant number worked in manufacturing, transportation, communications, and utilities. Approximately 1 in 6 billing clerks and billing machine operators works part time.

Job Outlook

Job openings for persons seeking work as billing clerks or billing machine operators are expected to be numerous through the year 2005. Despite the lack of employment growth, many job openings will occur as these workers transfer to other occupations or leave the labor force. Turnover in this occupation is relatively high, characteristic of an entry-level occupation requiring only a high school diploma.

Little change is expected in the employment of billing clerks through the year 2005. A growing economy and a greater demand for billing services will result in more business transactions, but productivity increases will keep employment from rising. Billing clerks will be affected as computers are increasingly used to manage account information. Less routine, more complex billing applications will increasingly require workers with greater technical expertise.

Employment of billing machine operators is expected to decline through the year 2005 as billing machines are replaced by more advanced machines and computers which enable billing clerks to perform the jobs formerly done by billing machine operators. In smaller firms, accounting clerks are taking over the responsibilities of billing clerks and billing machine operators due to productivity gains from billing software.

(See introductory part of this section for information on working conditions, training requirements, and earnings, as well as sources of additional information.)

Bookkeeping, Accounting, and Auditing Clerks

(D.O.T. 209.687-010; 210.362-010, .367-010, -014, .382-010, -014, -030, -038, -042, -046, -050, -054, -062; 216.362-014, -022, -026, -034, -038, -042, .382-022, -026, -058, .482-010, -026, .587-010; 219.362-066, .367-042, .387-018, .487-010, and .587-010)

Nature of the Work

Bookkeeping, accounting, and auditing clerks are an organization's financial recordkeepers. They compute, classify, record, and verify numerical data in order to develop and maintain financial records.

In smaller establishments, bookkeeping clerks handle all aspects of financial transactions. They record debits and credits, compare current and past balance sheets, summarize details of separate ledgers, and prepare reports for supervisors and managers. They may also prepare bank deposits by compiling data from cashiers, verifying and balancing receipts, and sending the cash, checks, or other forms of payment to the bank.

In larger offices and accounting departments, accounting clerks are more specialized. Their title may reflect the type of accounting they do, such as accounts payable clerk or accounts receivable clerk. Entry-level accounting clerks post details of transactions, total accounts, and compute interest charges. They may also monitor loans and accounts payable and receivable to ensure that payments are up to date. More advanced clerks may total, balance, and reconcile billing vouchers; ensure completeness and accuracy of data on accounts; and code documents according to company procedures. They post transactions in journals and on computer files, and update these files when needed. They also review computer printouts against manually maintained journals, and make necessary corrections. Senior workers review invoices and statements to make sure all information is accurate and complete, and may reconcile computer reports with operating reports.

Auditing clerks verify records of transactions posted by other workers. They check figures, postings, and documents for correct entry, mathematical accuracy, and proper codes. They also correct or note errors for accountants or other workers to adjust.

As organizations computerize their financial records, more bookkeeping, accounting, and auditing clerks are using specialized accounting software on personal computers. They increasingly post charges to accounts on computer spreadsheets and data bases; manual posting to general ledgers is becoming a thing of the past. Information is entered into the computer from receipts or bills and then is stored either electronically or as computer printouts, or both.

Job openings for bookkeeping, accounting, and auditing clerks should be plentiful.

Employment

Bookkeeping, accounting, and auditing clerks held nearly 2.2 million jobs in 1994. About 1 of every 4 was in wholesale and retail trade. About one-third were in organizations providing business, health, educational, and social services. Approximately 1 in 4 bookkeeping, accounting, and auditing clerks works part time.

Job Outlook

Virtually all job openings for bookkeeping, accounting, and auditing clerks through the year 2005 will stem from replacement needs. Each year, several hundred thousand jobs will become available as these clerks transfer to other occupations or leave the labor force. Turnover is lower than among other record clerks, but the large size of the occupation ensures a large number of openings and plentiful job opportunities for jobseekers. Many opportunities for temporary and part-time work should be available.

Employment of bookkeeping, accounting, and auditing clerks is expected to decline through 2005. A growing economy should result in more financial transactions and other activities and, therefore, more demand for accounting services. However, automation of office functions is expected to continue, with resulting productivity increases. Virtually all new jobs will be created in small, rapidly growing organizations. Large organizations are likely to continue the consolidation of departments to eliminate duplicate functions and reduce the demand for these clerks.

(See introductory part of this section for information on working conditions, training requirements, and earnings, as well as sources of additional information.)

Brokerage Clerks and Statement Clerks

(D.O.T. 214.362-046; 216.362-046, .382-046, .482-034; 219.362-018, -054, .482-010)

Nature of the Work

Brokerage clerks and statement clerks work behind the scenes to produce records associated with financial transactions.

Brokerage clerks, who work in the operations areas of securities firms, perform many duties to facilitate the sale and purchase of stocks, bonds, commodities, and other kinds of investments. These clerks produce the necessary records of all transactions that occur in their area of the business.

Job titles depend upon the type of work performed. Purchase-and-sale clerks match orders to buy with orders to sell. They balance and verify stock trades by comparing the records of the selling firm to those of the buying firm. Dividend clerks ensure timely payments of stock or cash dividends to clients of a particular brokerage firm. Transfer clerks execute customer requests for changes to security registration and examine stock certificates for adherence to banking regulations. Receive-and-deliver clerks facilitate the receipt and delivery of securities among firms and institutions. Margin clerks post accounts and monitor activity in customers' accounts. Their job is to ensure that customers make their payments and stay within legal boundaries concerning stock purchases.

A significant and growing number of brokerage clerks use custom designed software programs to process transactions, allowing transactions to be processed quicker than if they were done manually. Currnetly, only a few customized accounts are handled manually.

Statement clerks assemble, verify, and send individual and commercial bank statements every month.

In most banks, statement clerks, sometimes called statement operators, run sophisticated, high-speed machines. These machines fold the computer-printed statement, collate it if it is more than one page, insert the statement and cancelled checks into an envelope, seal it, and weigh it for postage. Statement clerks load the machine with the statements, cancelled checks, and envelopes. They then monitor

With appropriate experience and education, brokerage clerks may become securities sales representatives.

the equipment and correct minor problems. For serious problems, they call repair personnel.

In banks that do not have such machines, statement clerks perform all operations manually. They may also be responsible for verifying signatures and checking for missing information on checks, placing cancelled checks into trays, and retrieving them to send with the statements.

In a growing number of banks, only the statement is printed and sent to the account holder. The cancelled checks are not returned; this is known as check truncation.

Statement clerks are employed primarily by large banks. In smaller banks, their function is usually handled by a teller or a bookkeeping clerk who performs other duties during the rest of the month. Some small banks send their statement information to larger banks for processing, printing, and mailing.

Employment

Brokerage clerks held about 73,000 jobs in 1994, and statement clerks held about 25,000 jobs. Brokerage clerks worked in firms involved in the sales of securities and commodities. Almost all statement clerks were employed by banking institutions.

Job Outlook

No change is expected in the employment of brokerage clerks through the year 2005. Employment of statement clerks is projected to decline. Nevertheless, some jobs will become available each year to replace brokerage and statement clerks who transfer to other occupations or leave the labor force.

Similar to other record clerks, employment will be adversely affected by automation and changes in business practices. For example, computers now calculate the dividends due on stocks, something done for decades by brokerage clerks with adding machines and calculators. However, brokerage clerks are still needed to enter data into the computer and to process information. In the past, the record of security ownership was a piece of paper—a stock certificate. Today, most securities are stored in computer form and traded using electronic data interchange. Although less paper changes hands, clerks continue to enter and verify all transactions. Automated statement processing will grow as the increased volume of transactions justifies the cost of the necessary equipment, and this will dampen demand for statement clerks. In addition, the further spread of check truncation is expected to hold down employment of statement clerks. The use of ATM card systems and other electronic money transfers should increase as well, resulting in significantly fewer checks being written and processed.

(See introductory part of this section for information on working conditions, training requirements, and earnings, as well as sources of additional information.)

File Clerks

(D.O.T. 206.362-010, .367-014, -018; .387-010, -014, -022, -034)

Nature of the Work

File clerks classify, store, retrieve, and update information generated by their employers. They are employed by all kinds of organizations, including businesses, nonprofit organizations, and government agencies.

File clerks, also called records and information clerks or record center clerks, examine incoming material and code it numerically, alphabetically, or by subject matter. They then store forms, letters, receipts, or reports in paper form or enter necessary information into other storage devices. Some clerks operate mechanized files that rotate to bring the needed records to them. Others film documents that are then stored on microforms (microfilm or microfiche). A small but growing number of file clerks use imaging systems that scan paper files or film and store the material on optical disks.

Records must be current to be useful. File clerks ensure that new information is added to the files in a timely manner and may destroy outdated file materials or transfer them to inactive storage. They also check files at regular intervals to make sure that all items are correctly sequenced and placed. Whenever records cannot be located, the file clerk searches for the missing material. As an organization's needs for information change, file clerks implement changes to the filing system established by supervisory personnel.

When records are requested, file clerks locate them and give them to the borrower. The document may be a sheet of paper stored in a drawer in a file cabinet or an image on microform. In the first example, the clerk manually retrieves the document and hands or forwards it to the borrower. In the latter example, the clerk retrieves the microform and displays it on a microform reader. If necessary, file clerks make copies of records and distribute them. They keep track of materials removed from the files and ensure that those given out are returned.

A growing number of file clerks are using computerized filing and retrieval systems. There are a variety of computerized storage systems—an organization may store data on a mainframe, magnetic

File clerks should find many opportunities for temporary and part-time work.

tape, CD-ROM, or even floppy disk, depending on their needs. To retrieve a document, the clerk enters the document's identification code, obtains the location, and pulls the document. Even when files are stored electronically, backup paper or electronic copies generally are also kept. Accessing files in a computer data base is much quicker than locating and physically retrieving paper files.

In small offices, file clerks often have expanded responsibilities. These may include data entry, word processing, sorting mail, and operating copying machines.

Employment

File clerks held about 278,000 jobs in 1994. Many other clerical workers also perform filing in connection with their work. While file clerk jobs are found in nearly every sector of the economy, more than 4 out of every 5 file clerks are employed in services, government, finance, insurance, and real estate. More than 1 out of every 10 is employed in temporary services, and about 1 out of 3 works part time.

Job Outlook

Employment of file clerks is expected to decline through the year 2005 because of productivity gains stemming from office automation and the restructuring of work as use of personal computers by professionals and managers increases. Despite the projected decline in employment, job opportunities for file clerks should be plentiful because a large number of workers will be needed to replace workers who leave the occupation each year. Turnover is the highest among all record clerk occupations. This reflects the lack of formal training requirements, limited advancement potential, and relatively low pay.

Jobseekers who have typing (keyboarding) and other secretarial skills and are familiar with a wide range of office machines, especially personal computers, should have better opportunities than less experienced applicants. File clerks should find many opportunities for temporary or part-time work, especially during peak business periods. Demand for file clerk services will be strongest in the rapidly growing health sector.

(See introductory part of this section for information on working conditions, training requirements, and earnings, as well as sources of additional information.)

Library Assistants and Bookmobile Drivers

(D.O.T. 209.387-026; 222.587-014; 249.363-010, .365-010, .367-046, .687-014)

Nature of the Work

Library assistants and bookmobile drivers keep library resources in order and make them readily available to a variety of users. They work under the direction of librarians.

Library assistants—sometimes referred to as library media assistants, library aides, or circulation assistants—register patrons so they can borrow materials from the library. They record the borrower's name and address from an application and then issue a library card. Many library assistants now enter and update patrons' records using computers.

At the circulation desk, assistants lend and collect books, periodicals, video tapes, and other materials. When an item is borrowed, assistants stamp the due date on the material and record the patron's identification from his or her library card. They inspect returned materials for damage, check the due dates, and compute any fines that may be owed. They review records to compile a list of overdue materials and send out notices. They also answer patrons' questions in person and on the telephone and refer those they cannot answer to a librarian.

Throughout the library, assistants sort returned books, periodicals, and other items and return them to their designated shelves, files, or storage areas. They locate materials to be loaned, either to a patron or to another library. Many card catalogues are computerized, so library assistants must be familiar with the computer system for their particular library. If any of the materials have been damaged, these workers repair them, if possible. For example, they use tape or paste to repair torn pages or book covers and other specialized processes to repair more valuable materials.

Some library assistants specialize in helping patrons with vision problems. Sometimes referred to as talking-books library clerks or braille-and-talking-books clerks, they review the borrower's list of desired reading material. They select those materials or closely related substitutes from the library collection of large type or braille volumes, tape cassettes, and open-reel talking books. They complete the necessary paperwork and give or mail them to the borrower.

To extend library services to as wide an audience as possible, many libraries operate bookmobiles. Bookmobile drivers drive trucks stocked with books or drive light trucks that pull book trailers to designated sites on a regular schedule. Bookmobiles serve community organizations such as shopping centers, apartment complexes, schools, and nursing homes. Depending on local conditions, they may drive alone or may be accompanied by a library technician.

When working alone, the drivers perform many of the same functions as a library assistant in a main or branch library. They answer patrons' questions, receive and check out books, collect fines, maintain the book collection, and shelve materials. Bookmobile drivers participate and may assist in planning programs sponsored by the library such as reader advisory programs, used book sales, or outreach programs. They must keep track of their mileage, the materials lent out, and the amount of fines collected. In some areas they are responsible for the maintenance of the vehicle and any photocopiers or other equipment in it. They record statistics on circulation and the number of people visiting the bookmobile. Drivers may also record requests for special items from the main library and arrange for the materials to be mailed or delivered to a patron during the next scheduled visit. Increasingly, bookmobiles are equipped with personal computers and CD-ROM systems linked to the main library system; this allows bookmobile drivers to reserve or locate books immediately.

Because bookmobile drivers may be the only link some people have to the library, much of their work is helping the public. They may assist handicapped or elderly patrons to the bookmobile or shovel snow to assure their safety. They may enter hospitals or nursing homes to deliver books directly to patrons who are bedridden. Bookmobile drivers also should be familiar with audiovisual equipment for showing slides or films.

Library assistants should enjoy interacting with people.

The schedules of bookmobile drivers depend on the size of the area being served. Some of these workers go out on their routes every working day, while others do so only certain days of the week. On the other days, they perform library assistant duties at the library. Some now work evenings and weekends to give patrons as much access to the library as possible.

Employment

Library assistants and bookmobile drivers held about 121,000 jobs in 1994. Over one-half of these workers were employed school libraries; most of the remainder worked in public libraries. Opportunities for flexible schedules are abundant; over one-half of these workers were on part-time schedules.

Job Outlook

Opportunities should be good for persons interested in jobs as library assistants or bookmobile drivers through the year 2005. Turnover of these workers is quite high, reflecting the relatively weak attachment to the occupation. This work is attractive to retirees and others who want a part-time schedule, and there is a lot of movement into and out of the occupation. Many openings will become available each year to replace workers who transfer to another occupation or leave the labor force. Some positions become available as library assistants move within the organization. Library assistants can be promoted to supervisory positions in public service or technical service areas. Advancement opportunities are greater in larger libraries and may be more limited in smaller ones.

Employment is expected to grow more slowly than the average for all occupations through the year 2005. The vast majority of library assistants and bookmobile drivers work in public or school libraries of some kind. Slow employment growth is expected due to budgetary constraints in local governments and academic institutions of all types. Because so many are employed by public institutions, library assistants and bookmobile drivers are not directly affected by the ups and downs of the business cycle. Some of these workers may lose their jobs, however, if there are cuts in government budgets.

(See introductory part of this section for information on working conditions, training requirements, and earnings, as well as sources of additional information.)

Order Clerks

(D.O.T. 209.387-018; 245.367-026; 249.367-042, -054; 295.367-018; and 659.462-010)

Nature of the Work

Order clerks receive and process incoming orders for such items as spare parts for machines, consumer appliances, gas and electric power connections, film rentals, and articles of clothing. They are sometimes called order-entry clerks, customer service representatives, order processors, or order takers.

Orders for materials, merchandise, or services can come from within an organization or from outside of it. In large companies with many work sites, such as automobile manufacturers, parts and equipment need to be ordered from the company's warehouses. Inside order clerks receive orders from other workers employed by the same company or from salespersons in the field. Many other order clerks, however, receive orders from other companies or from individuals. Order clerks in wholesale businesses, for instance, receive orders for merchandise from retail establishments that the retailer in turn sells to the public. An increasing number of order clerks work in catalog sales, receiving orders from individual customers either by phone, by fax, or by mail. Order clerks dealing primarily with the public sometimes are referred to as outside order clerks.

Today, most order clerks sit at computers and receive orders directly by telephone, entering the required information as the customer places the order. Some orders are received through the computer system; they are sent directly from the customer's terminal to the order clerk's terminal.

The computer provides the order clerk with ready access to information such as stock numbers, prices, and inventory. Orders frequently depend on which products are in stock and which products are most appropriate for the customer's needs. Some order clerks, especially those in industrial settings, must be able to give price estimates for entire jobs, not just single parts. Others must be able to take special orders or give expected arrival dates.

Although the large majority of orders are now placed by phone, some order clerks also receive orders by mail and increasingly by fax machine. These clerks review the hand-written or typed orders for completeness and clarity. They extract the checks or money orders, sort them, and send them for processing. The clerk may complete missing information or contact the customer for the information. Similarly, if customers need additional information, such as prices, shipping dates, or anticipated delays, the order clerk contacts them. These orders may be processed by order clerks in small establishments or, in large organizations, entered into the computer system by data-entry clerks.

After an order has been verified and entered, the customer's final cost is calculated. The clerk then routes the order to the proper department—such as the warehouse—that actually sends out or delivers the item in question.

In organizations with computer systems, inventory records are adjusted automatically as sales are made. In less automated organizations, order clerks adjust inventory records. For example, after processing an order for bolts, the clerk verifies that the bolts were sent and subtracts the order from the inventory control form. Clerks may also notify other departments when inventories are low or when orders would deplete supplies.

Some order clerks must establish priorities in filling orders. For example, an order clerk in a blood bank may receive a request from a hospital for a certain type of blood. The clerk must first find out if the request is routine or an emergency, and then take appropriate action.

Employment

Order clerks held about 310,000 jobs in 1994. Most worked for wholesale and retail establishments and manufacturing firms.

Order clerks in retail establishments often work overtime when sales volume is high.

Job Outlook

Job openings for order clerks should be plentiful through the year 2005 due to sizeable replacement needs. Numerous jobs will become available each year to replace order clerks who transfer to other occupations or who leave the labor force. Many of these openings will be for seasonal work, especially in catalogue companies that cater to holiday gift buyers.

Employment of order clerks is expected to grow more slowly than average through the year 2005 as office automation continues to increase the productivity of these workers. As the economy grows, more orders for goods and services will be placed. How this growing business activity relates to employment of order clerks depends in large measure on the setting. Demand for outside order clerks who deal mainly with the public should remain fairly strong. The greater use of toll-free numbers that makes "home shopping" easier and more convenient will stimulate demand for these workers. However, productivity gains from the increasing use of automation will absorb some of the growth in the volume of orders.

Demand for inside order clerks will be much weaker, however. The spread of electronic data interchange, a system that enables computers to communicate directly with each other, allows orders between establishments to be placed with little human intervention. Although currently limited to large organizations, it is expected that orders will increase between computers of different companies and from home computers.

Other types of automation should also depress the demand for order clerks. Sophisticated inventory control and automatic billing systems allow companies to track their inventory and accounts with much less help from order clerks. A large and increasing number of companies are using fax machines to receive orders. Increasingly, data-entry keyers enter the information from faxed or mailed orders. Some companies use automated menus that can be accessed with a touch tone phone to receive orders, and others use answering machines. Interactive voice recognition equipment is expected to be available by the year 2005, further reducing the demand for order clerks.

(See introductory part of this section for information on working conditions, training requirements, and earnings, as well as sources of additional information.)

Payroll and Timekeeping Clerks

(D.O.T. 215.362-018, .367-022, .382-014, .482-010)

Nature of the Work

Payroll and timekeeping clerks perform a vital function—ensuring that employees are paid on time and that their paychecks are correct. They adjust monetary errors or incorrect amounts of vacation time, research these records, and perform other clerical tasks.

Timekeeping clerks distribute and collect timecards each pay period. These workers review employee workcharts, timesheets, and timecards to ensure that information is properly recorded, and that the records have the signatures of authorizing officials. For example, they may recalculate total hours on a timesheet that has many complex entries. In companies that bill for the time spent by staff, such as law or accounting firms, timekeeping clerks make sure the hours recorded are charged to the correct job so the client can be properly billed. They review computer reports listing timecards that cannot be processed because of errors and contact the employee or the employee's supervisor to resolve the problem. Timekeeping clerks also keep informed of new payroll policies and inform managers and other employees of procedural changes.

In the payroll department, payroll clerks, also called payroll technicians, screen the timecards for calculating, coding, or other errors. Then they compute pay by subtracting allotments like retirement, Federal and State taxes, insurance, or savings from gross

Timekeeping clerks ensure that employees' timecards are accurate.

earnings. Increasingly, computers perform these calculations and alert payroll clerks to problems or errors in the data. For small organizations or for new employees whose records are not yet entered into a computer system, clerks may perform all the necessary calculations. In some small offices, payroll is processed by clerks or other employees in the accounting department.

Payroll clerks also maintain paper backup files for research and reference. They record changes in employee addresses; close out files when workers retire, resign, or transfer; and advise employees on income tax withholding and other mandatory deductions. They also issue and record adjustments to pay because of previous errors or retroactive increases. Payroll clerks must follow changes in tax and deduction laws, so they have to be aware of the most current revisions. They prepare and mail earnings and tax withholding statements in early January for employees' use in preparing their income tax returns.

In small offices, payroll and timekeeping duties are more likely to be included in the duties of a general office clerk or secretary. Larger organizations employ specialized payroll and timekeeping clerks to perform these functions.

Employment

Payroll and timekeeping clerks held about 157,000 jobs in 1994. About 1 of every 3 worked in business, health, education, and social services. One in 4 worked in manufacturing, and more than 2 of every 10 were in wholesale and retail trade or in government. About 1 in 10 payroll and timekeeping clerks works part time.

Job Outlook

Numerous job openings for persons seeking work as payroll and timekeeping clerks should be available through the year 2005. Many jobs will open up each year as these workers transfer to other occupations—many payroll clerks use this position as a steppingstone to higher level accounting jobs—or leave the labor force.

Employment of payroll and timekeeping clerks is expected to decline through the year 2005 as continuing automation of the payroll and timekeeping function makes these workers more productive. The technology having the greatest effect on employment is the expanding use of automated timeclocks to calculate employees' hours and balances. These automated timeclocks allow large organizations to centralize their timekeeping duties in one location. At individual sites, employee hours are increasingly tracked by computer and verified by managers. Then, this information is compiled and sent to a central office to be processed by payroll clerks. This eliminates the need to have payroll clerks at every site. Also, timekeeping duties are more commonly being distributed to secretaries and general office clerks or being contracted out to organizations that specialize in these services.

(See introductory part of this section for information on working conditions, training requirements, and earnings, as well as sources of additional information.)

Personnel Clerks

(D.O.T. 205.362-010, -014, -022, .367-062, .567-010; 209.362-026; 241.267-010; 249.367-090)

Nature of the Work

Personnel clerks maintain the personnel records of the organization's employees. These records include information such as name, address, job title, earnings, benefits such as health and life insurance, and tax withholding. On a daily basis, they record and answer questions about employees' absences and supervisory reports on job performance. When an employee receives a promotion or switches health insurance plans, the personnel clerk updates the appropriate form. Personnel clerks may also prepare reports for managers elsewhere in the organization. For example, they might compile a list of employees eligible for an award.

In smaller organizations, some personnel clerks perform a variety of other clerical duties. They answer telephone or letter inquiries from the public, send out announcements of job openings or job examinations, and issue application forms. When credit bureaus and finance companies request confirmation of a person's employment, the personnel clerk provides authorized information from the employee's personnel records. Payroll departments and insurance companies may also be contacted to verify changes to records.

Some personnel clerks are also involved in hiring. As part of their job, they screen job applicants to obtain information such as education and work experience; administer aptitude, personality, and interest tests; explain the organization's employment policies and refer qualified applicants to the employing official; and request references from present or past employers. Personnel clerks inform job applicants, by telephone or letter, of their acceptance or rejection for employment.

Other personnel clerks are known as assignment clerks. Their role is to notify a firm's existing employees of position vacancies and to identify and assign qualified applicants. They keep track of vacancies throughout the organization and complete and distribute vacancy advertisement forms. The clerks review applications in response to the advertisement and verify the information using personnel records. After the selection is made, they notify all the applicants of their acceptance or rejection.

In some job settings, personnel clerks have more specific job titles. Identification clerks are responsible for security matters at defense installations. They compile and record personal data about vendors, contractors, and civilian and military personnel and their dependents. Their job duties include interviewing applicants, corresponding with law enforcement authorities, and preparing badges, passes, and identification cards.

Employment

Personnel clerks held about 123,000 jobs in 1994. Although these workers are found in most industries, more than 1 in every 4 works for a government agency. Colleges and universities, hospitals, department stores, and banks also employ large numbers of personnel clerks.

Job Outlook

Replacement needs will account for most job openings for personnel clerks through the year 2005. Jobs will open up as clerks advance within the personnel department, take a job unrelated to personnel administration, or leave the labor force.

Personnel clerks are employed throughout private industry and government.

Employment of personnel clerks is expected to decline through the year 2005. Contributing to the declining number of personnel clerks is the increased use of computers. The growing use of computers and electronic data interchange in personnel or human resource departments means that a lot of data entry work done by personnel clerks can be eliminated as employees themselves enter the data and send it to the personnel office. This is most feasible in large organizations with multiple personnel offices. In addition, as professionals in personnel offices increasingly use computers and other automated office equipment, there could be less work for personnel clerks.

(See introductory part of this section for information on working conditions, training requirements, and earnings, as well as sources of additional information.)

Secretaries

(D.O.T. 201 and 219.362-074)

Nature of the Work

Secretarial work continues to evolve along with new office automation and organizational restructuring. In many cases, secretaries have assumed new responsibilities and learned to operate different office equipment. In the midst of these changes, though, their central responsibilities remain much as they were. Most organizations still employ secretaries to perform and coordinate office activities and to ensure that information gets disseminated to staff and clients. Managers, professionals, and other support staff still rely on them to keep administrative operations under control.

Secretaries are responsible for a variety of administrative and clerical duties that are necessary to run and maintain organizations efficiently. They schedule appointments, give information to callers, organize and maintain files, complete forms, and take dictation. They may also type letters, make travel arrangements, or contact clients. In addition, secretaries operate office equipment like facsimile machines, photocopiers, and telephones with voice mail capabilities.

Secretaries increasingly use personal computers to run spreadsheet, word processing, data base management, desktop publishing, and graphics programs—tasks previously handled by managers and professionals. Because they are often relieved from dictation and typing, they can support several members of the professional staff. Secretaries sometimes work in clusters of three or four so that they can work more flexibly and share their expertise.

Executive secretaries or administrative assistants perform fewer clerical tasks than lower level secretaries. In addition to receiving visitors, arranging conference calls, and answering letters, they may handle more complex responsibilities like conducting research, preparing statistical reports, training employees, and supervising other clerical staff.

Some secretaries do highly specialized work that requires a knowledge of technical terminology and procedures. Further specialization in various types of law is common among legal secretaries, for example. They prepare correspondence and legal papers such as summonses, complaints, motions, and subpoenas under the supervision of an attorney. They also may review legal journals and assist in other ways with legal research. Medical secretaries comprise another type of specialized secretary. These workers transcribe dictation, prepare correspondence, and assist physicians or medical scientists with reports, speeches, articles, and conference proceedings. They also record simple medical histories, arrange for patients to be hospitalized, and order supplies. Most medical secretaries need to be familiar with insurance rules, billing practices, and hospital or laboratory procedures. Other technical secretaries assist engineers or scientists. They may prepare correspondence, maintain the technical library, and gather and edit materials for scientific papers.

Secretaries must be able to juggle many tasks simultaneously.

Working Conditions

Secretaries usually work in offices with other professionals or in schools, hospitals, or doctors' offices. Their jobs often involve sitting for long periods. If they spend a lot of time typing, particularly at a video display terminal, they may encounter problems of eyestrain, stress, and repetitive motion problems such as carpal tunnel syndrome.

Office work lends itself to alternative or flexible working arrangements, like telecommuting, and 1 secretary in 6 works part time. In addition, a significant number of secretaries work as temporaries. A few participate in job sharing arrangements in which two people divide responsibility for a single job. The majority of secretaries, however, are full-time employees who work a standard 40-hour week.

Employment

Secretaries held over 3.3 million jobs in 1994, making this one of the largest occupations in the U.S. economy. The following tabulation shows the distribution of employment by secretarial specialty.

Secretaries, total	3,349,000
Legal secretaries	281,000
Medical secretaries	226,000
Secretaries, except legal and medical	2,842,000

Secretaries are employed in organizations of every description. About one-half of all secretaries are employed in firms providing services, ranging from education and health to legal and business services. Others work for firms that engage in manufacturing, construction, wholesale and retail trade, transportation, and communications. Banks, insurance companies, investment firms, and real estate firms are important employers, as are Federal, State, and local government agencies.

Training, Other Qualifications, and Advancement

High school graduates may qualify for secretarial positions provided they have basic office skills. Secretaries should be proficient in keyboarding and good at spelling, punctuation, grammar, and oral communication. Shorthand is necessary for some positions. Knowledge of word processing, spreadsheet, and database management programs is becoming increasingly important to most employers. Because secretaries must be tactful in their dealings with many different people, employers also look for good interpersonal skills. Discretion, judgment, organizational ability, and initiative are especially important for higher level secretarial positions.

As office automation continues to evolve, retraining and continuing education will remain an integral part of many jobs. Continuing changes in the office environment have increased the demand for secretaries who are adaptable and versatile. Secretaries may have to attend classes to learn to operate new office equipment such as word processing equipment, information storage systems, personal computers, or new updated software packages.

The skills needed for a secretarial job can be acquired in various ways. Secretarial training ranges from high school vocational education programs that teach office practices, shorthand, and keyboarding skills to 1- to 2-year programs in secretarial science offered by business schools, vocational-technical institutes, and community colleges. Many temporary help agencies provide formal training in computer and keyboarding skills. These skills are most often acquired, however, through instruction offered at the workplace by other employees or by equipment and software vendors. Specialized training programs are available for students planning to become medical or legal secretaries or office automation specialists.

Testing and certification for entry-level office skills is available through the Office Proficiency Assessment and Certification (OPAC) program offered by Professional Secretaries International (PSI). As secretaries gain experience, they can earn the designation Certified Professional Secretary (CPS) by passing a series of examinations given by the Institute for Certifying Secretaries, a department of PSI. This designation is recognized by many employers as the mark of excellence for senior level office professionals. Similarly, those without experience who want to be certified as a legal support professional may be certified as an Accredited Legal Secretary (ALS) by the Certifying Board of the National Association of Legal Secretaries. They also administer an examination to certify a legal secretary with 3 years of experience as a Professional Legal Secretary (PLS).

Advancement for secretaries generally comes about by promotion to a secretarial position with more responsibilities. Qualified secretaries who broaden their knowledge of the company's operations and enhance their skills may be promoted to other positions such as senior or executive secretary, clerical supervisor, or office manager.

Secretaries with word processing experience can advance to jobs as word processing trainers, supervisors, or managers within their own firms or in a secretarial or word processing service bureau. Their experience as a secretary can lead to jobs such as instructor or sales representative with manufacturers of word processing or computer equipment. With additional training, many legal secretaries become legal assistants and paralegals.

Job Outlook

Projected employment growth for secretaries varies by occupational specialty. Growth in the legal services and health services industries will drive faster than average employment growth for legal and medical secretaries through the year 2005. Employment of the 85 percent of secretaries who are not legal or medical secretaries, however, is expected to grow more slowly than the average for all occupations. Nevertheless, employment opportunities should be quite plentiful, especially for well qualified and experienced secretaries, who, according to many employers, are in short supply. The very large size of the occupation, coupled with a moderate turnover rate, will generate several hundred thousand secretarial positions each year as experienced workers transfer to other occupations or leave the labor force.

The major factor limiting employment growth for most secretaries is the widespread application of new office automation. Secretaries have become more productive with the help of word processing machines, personal computers, electronic mail, scanners, facsimile machines, and voice message systems. These technologies will continue to be purchased by firms, ensuring that employment growth for secretaries will lag behind the rapidly growing amount of office work.

The use of automated equipment is also changing the workflow in many offices. Administrative duties are being reassigned and the functions of entire departments are being restructured. In some cases, such traditional secretarial duties as typing or keyboarding, filing, copying, and accounting are being assigned to workers in other units or departments. In some law offices and physicians' offices, for example, paralegals and medical assistants are assuming some tasks formerly done by secretaries. Professionals and managers increasingly do their own word processing rather than submit the work to secretaries and other support staff. In addition, there is a trend in many offices for groups of professionals and managers to "share" secretaries. The traditional arrangement of one secretary per manager is becoming less prevalent; instead, secretaries increasingly support systems or units. This approach often means that secretaries assume added responsibilities and are seen as valuable members of a team, but it also contributes to slower rates of employment growth.

Developments in office technology are certain to continue, and they will bring about further changes in the secretary's work environment. However, many secretarial job duties are of a personal, interactive nature and, therefore, not easily automated. Duties such as planning conferences, receiving clients, and transmitting staff instructions require tact and communication skills. Because automated equipment cannot substitute for these personal skills, secretaries will continue to play a key role in the office activities of most organizations.

Earnings

Based on a survey of metropolitan areas, the average annual salary for all secretaries was $26,700 in 1993. Salaries vary a great deal, however, reflecting differences in skill, experience, and level of responsibility, ranging from $19,100 to $38,400.

Salaries in different parts of the country also vary; earnings generally are lowest in southern cities, and highest in northern and western cities. In addition, salaries vary by industry; salaries of secretaries tend to be highest in transportation, legal services, and public utilities, and lowest in retail trade and finance, insurance, and real estate.

The starting salary for inexperienced secretaries in the Federal Government was $16,700 a year in 1995. Beginning salaries were slightly higher in selected areas where the prevailing local pay level was higher. All secretaries employed by the Federal Government averaged about $25,800 in 1995.

Related Occupations

A number of other workers type, record information, and process paperwork. Among these are bookkeepers, receptionists, stenographers, personnel clerks, typists and word processors, legal assistants, medical assistants, and medical record technicians. A growing number of secretaries share in managerial and human resource responsibilities. Occupations requiring these skills include clerical supervisor, systems manager, office manager, and human resource officer.

Sources of Additional Information

For career information, contact:
☛Professional Secretaries International, P.O. Box 20404, Kansas City, MO 64195-0404. (Phone: 1-816-891-6600.)

Persons interested in careers as legal secretaries can request information from:
☛National Association of Legal Secretaries (International), 2250 East 73rd St., Suite 550, Tulsa, OK 74136.

State employment offices can provide information about job openings for secretaries.

Stenographers, Court Reporters, and Medical Transcriptionists

(D.O.T. 202.362, .382-010, and 203.582-058)

Nature of the Work

When written accounts of spoken words are necessary for correspondence, records, or legal proof, verbatim reports of speeches, conversations, legal proceedings, meetings, or other events are taken by stenographers, court reporters and medical transcriptionists.

Stenographers and *stenotype operators* take dictation and then transcribe their notes on a word processor or onto a computer diskette. They may take dictation using either shorthand or a stenotype machine, which prints shorthand symbols. General stenographers, including most beginners, take routine dictation and perform other office tasks such as typing, filing, answering telephones, and operating office machines. Experienced and highly skilled stenographers take more difficult dictation. For example, they sit in on staff meetings and provide word-for-word records or summary reports of the proceedings to the participants. They also supervise other stenographers, typists, and clerical workers. Some experienced stenographers take dictation in foreign languages; others work as public stenographers serving traveling business people and others. Technical stenographers must know the medical, legal, engineering, or scientific terminology used in a particular profession.

Court reporters record all statements made in an official proceeding, usually using a stenotype machine. They take down all

Many court reporters do freelance work, recording out-of-court depositions for attorneys.

statements and present their record as the official transcript. Because there is only one person creating an official transcript, accuracy is vitally important. Some reporters still dictate notes on magnetic tapes that a typist can transcribe later. Others transcribe their own notes, or give them to *note readers*, persons skilled in reading back shorthand notes.

Many reporters do freelance work recording out-of-court depositions for attorneys, proceedings of meetings and conventions, and other private activities. Still others record the proceedings in the U.S. Congress, in State and local governing bodies, and in government agencies at all levels.

Most court reporters use stenotype machines that print shorthand symbols on paper and record them on computer disks. The disks are then loaded into a computer that translates and displays the symbols in English. This is called computer-aided transcription. Stenotype machines that link directly to the computer are used for real-time captioning. That is, as the reporter types the symbols, they are instantly transcribed by the computer. This is used for closed captioning for the deaf or hearing-impaired on television, in courts, or in meetings. Court reporters who specialize in captioning television news stories are called *stenocaptioners*.

Medical transcriptionists listen to audio recordings from physicians and other health care professionals that note diagnoses of patients' ailments and courses of treatment. They transcribe the notes into the requested printed or computer-based format to become part of patients' medical records and edit the notes for format, proper

medical terminology, and grammar. Often medical professionals use abbreviations or technical jargon, which transcriptionists must be able to expand upon to ensure the accuracy of patient and health care facility records; transcriptionists must be medical language specialists and familiar with patient assessment, therapeutic procedures, diagnoses, and prognoses. In addition to transcribing letters, reports, and the like, they may have other clerical duties. (Medical secretaries and assistants may also transcribe as part of their jobs. These occupations are covered elsewhere in the *Handbook.*)

Working Conditions

Stenographers usually work in clean, well-lighted offices. Court reporters sometimes record depositions in the offices of attorneys, but they more often work in non-office settings, such as court rooms, legislatures, and conventions. Most medical transcriptionists work in hospitals, doctors' offices, or outpatient medical care facilities. An increasing number of freelance court reporters and transcriptionists are working from home-based offices as subcontractors for law firms, hospitals, and transcription services. Although the work of stenographers, court reporters, and medical transcriptionists is not physically demanding, sitting in the same position for long periods can be tiring. The pressure to be accurate and fast can be stressful, and like other administrative support positions workers risk repetitive motion injuries, such as carpel tunnel syndrome.

Many stenographers, court reporters, and medical transcriptionists work a standard 40-hour week, although about one-fourth work part time. Some court reporters and medical transcriptionists, however, are self-employed and freelance their services, which may result in irregular working hours.

Employment

Stenographers, court reporters, and medical transcriptionists held 105,000 jobs in 1994. Nearly one-fifth were self-employed freelance court reporters or medical transcriptionists. Of those who worked for a wage or salary, about one-third worked for State and local governments, a reflection of the large number of court reporters working in courts, legislatures, and various agencies. Over one-fourth worked for hospitals, and physicians' offices as medical transcriptionists. Other stenographers and court reporters worked for colleges and universities, secretarial and court reporting services, temporary help supply services, and law firms.

Training, Other Qualifications, and Advancement

Stenographic skills are taught in high schools, vocational schools, community colleges, and proprietary business schools. For stenographer jobs, employers prefer to hire high school graduates and seldom have a preference among the many different shorthand methods. Although requirements vary in private firms, applicants with the best speed and accuracy usually receive first consideration in hiring. To qualify for jobs in the Federal Government, stenographers must be able to take dictation at a minimum of 80 words per minute and type at least 40 words per minute. Workers must achieve higher rates to advance to more responsible positions.

For court reporter jobs, however, most employers require knowledge of stenotype, not only because reporters can write faster using stenotype, but also because they can feed stenotype notes to a computer for high-speed transcription. Speed and accuracy are the most important factors in hiring. Court reporters in the Federal Government generally must take at least 175 words a minute, and many court reporting jobs require at least 225 words of dictation per minute. There are 350 post secondary schools and colleges that offer 2- or 4-year training programs in court reporting. About 110 programs have been approved by the National Court Reporters Association, and all of them teach computer-aided transcription.

Some States require court reporters who stenotype depositions to be notary publics, and 18 States require each court reporter to be a Certified Court Reporter (CCR). A certification test is administered by a board of examiners in each State that has CCR laws. The

National Court Reporters Association confers the designation Registered Professional Reporter (RPR) upon those who pass a two-part examination and participate in continuing education programs. Although voluntary, the RPR designation is recognized as a mark of distinction in the profession.

For medical transcriptionist jobs, understanding medical terminology is essential. Good English grammar and punctuation skills are required, as well as familiarity with personal computers and word processing software. Many employers prefer to hire transcriptionists who have completed some college coursework. Many vocational schools and community colleges offer programs and associate degrees in medical transcription. Courses in the various programs often include computer applications, business communication, English composition, grammar, keyboarding, medical terminology, and medical transcription. The American Association for Medical Transcription awards the voluntary designation Certified Medical Transcriptionist to those who earn passing scores on written and practical examinations.

Stenographers can advance to more responsible secretarial positions, especially if they develop their interpersonal skills, such as the ability to communicate well. Stenographers who get the necessary education can become court reporters. Court reporters, on the other hand, have little advancement opportunities, although some reporters choose to specialize in captioning television programs.

Job Outlook

Overall employment of stenographers, court reporters, and medical transcriptionists is expected to decline slightly. Decreases in stenographer and court reporter jobs should more than offset growth in transcriptionist jobs.

The widespread use of dictation machines has greatly reduced the need for office stenographers. The traditional "steno pool" is practically a thing of the past. Audio recording equipment and the use of personal computers by managers and other professionals should continue to greatly decrease the demand for these workers.

The demand for skilled court reporters should decline as video recordings are increasingly recognized as legal records of proceedings. Also, budget constraints should limit the ability of Federal, State, and local courts to expand, even in the face of rising numbers of criminal court cases and civil lawsuits. Demand should grow for court reporters willing to take depositions for court reporting service bureaus or those willing to freelance. Competition for entry level jobs is increasing as more workers are attracted to the occupation. Opportunities should be best for those who earn certification by the National Court Reporters Association.

Demand for medical transcriptionists is expected to increase rapidly with growth in the need for health care and the industries that provide it. Growing numbers of medical transcriptionists will be needed to amend patients' records, edit for grammar, and watch out for medical discrepancies.

Contributing to the demand for court reporters and transcriptionists is the growing number of conventions, conferences, depositions, seminars, and similar meetings whose proceedings are recorded. Although many of these events are being videotaped, a written transcript must still be created for legal purposes or if the proceedings are to be published. Also, the trend to provide instantaneous written captions for the deaf and hearing impaired should strengthen demand for stenocaptioners.

Earnings

Stenographers, court reporters, and medical transcriptionists had median earnings of $399 a week in 1994. The middle 50 percent earned between $306 and $629 a week. The lowest paid 10 percent earned less than $232, while the highest paid 10 percent earned over $790 a week. Court reporters generally earn higher salaries than stenographers or medical transcriptionists. Regardless of specialty, earnings depend on speed, education, experience, and geographic location.

Related Occupations

A number of other workers type, record information, and process paperwork. Among these are bookkeepers, receptionists, secretaries, personnel clerks, administrative assistants, and medical assistants.

Sources of Additional Information

For information about job openings for stenographers, contact State employment service offices.

For information about shorthand court reporting, contact:

☞National Court Reporters Association, 8224 Old Courthouse Rd., Vienna, VA 22182. Telephone 1-800-272-6272.

Information on medical transcription is available from:

☞American Association for Medical Transcription, P.O. Box 576187, Modesto, CA 95357. Telephone 1-800-982-2182.

Teacher Aides

(D.O.T. 099.327; 219.467; 249.367-074, -086)

Nature of the Work

Teacher aides, also called paraprofessionals or paraeducators, provide instructional and clerical support for classroom teachers, allowing teachers more time for lesson planning and teaching. Aides assist and supervise students in the classroom, cafeteria, schoolyard, or on field trips. They record grades, set up equipment, or help prepare materials for instruction. They also tutor and assist children in learning class material using the teacher's lesson plans.

Aides' responsibilities vary greatly. Some teacher aides handle routine nonteaching and clerical tasks. They grade tests and papers, check homework, keep health and attendance records, type, file, and duplicate materials. They also may stock supplies, operate audiovisual equipment, and keep classroom equipment in order.

Other aides instruct children, under the direction and guidance of teachers. They work with students individually or in small groups—listening while students read, reviewing or reinforcing class work, or helping them find information for reports. Instructional teacher aides usually specialize in a certain subject, such as English or math. Teacher aides also assist students working with computers and educational software. Some teacher aides work in computer laboratories.

Teacher aides provide valuable assistance to students in the classroom.

Teacher aides also may provide personal attention to students whose families live in poverty, or to students who speak English as a second language, for example. In addition, schools are becoming more inclusive, integrating special education students into general education classrooms. As a result, teacher aides increasingly assist students with disabilities. Aides may attend to a student's physical needs, including feeding, teaching good grooming habits, or using physical restraint. Aides help assess a student's progress by observing a student's performance and recording relevant data.

Many aides have a combination of instructional and clerical duties, designed to most effectively assist classroom teachers. Sometimes aides take charge of special projects and prepare equipment or exhibits, such as for a science demonstration.

Working Conditions
Over half of all teacher aides worked part time during the school year in 1994. Most aides who provide educational instruction work the traditional 9- to 10-month school year, usually in a classroom setting. Aides also may work outdoors supervising recess when weather allows, and spend much of their time standing, walking, or kneeling.

Seeing students develop and gain appreciation of the joy of learning can be very rewarding. However, working closely with students can be both physically and emotionally tiring. Aides who perform clerical work may feel overwhelmed by tedious administrative duties, such as making copies or assembling handouts containing information for students. The relatively low pay may deter some from entering this occupation.

Employment
Teacher aides held about 932,000 jobs in 1994. About 9 out of 10 worked in elementary and secondary schools, mostly in the lower grades. A significant number assisted special education teachers in working with children who have disabilities. Most of the others worked in child daycare centers and religious organizations.

Training, Other Qualifications, and Advancement
Educational requirements for teacher aides range from a high school diploma to some college training. Aides with teaching responsibilities usually require more training than those who don't perform teaching tasks. Increasingly, employers prefer aides who have some college training. Some teacher aides are aspiring teachers who are working towards their degree while gaining experience. Many schools require previous experience in working with children. Schools may also require a valid driver's license and perform a background check on applicants.

A number of 2-year and community colleges offer associate degree programs that prepare graduates to work as teacher aides. However, most teacher aides receive on-the-job training. Aides who tutor and review lessons with students must have a thorough understanding of class materials and instructional methods, and must be familiar with the organization and operation of a school. Aides also must know how to operate audiovisual equipment, keep records, and prepare instructional materials, as well as have adequate computer skills.

Teacher aides should enjoy working with children from a wide range of cultural backgrounds, and be able to handle classroom situations with fairness and patience. Aides also must demonstrate initiative and a willingness to follow a teacher's directions. They must have good oral and writing skills and be able to communicate effectively with students and teachers. Teacher aides who speak a second language are in great demand to communicate with growing numbers of students and parents whose primary language is not English.

Some States have established certification and training requirements for general teacher aides. To qualify, an individual may need a high school diploma or general equivalency degree (G.E.D.), or even some college training.

Advancement for teacher aides, usually in the form of higher earnings or increased responsibility, comes primarily with experience or additional education. Some school districts provide time away from the job so that aides may take college courses. Aides who earn bachelor's degrees may become licensed teachers.

Job Outlook
Employment of teacher aides is expected to grow much faster than the average for all occupations through the year 2005. Including special education students in general education classrooms, restructuring of schools, emphasis on early education, and the rising number of students who speak English as a second language will spur rapid growth among teacher aides. Numerous job openings also will arise as workers transfer to other occupations, leave the labor force for family responsibilities, return to school, or leave for other reasons—characteristic of occupations that require limited formal education and offer relatively low pay.

Projected rapid employment growth in special education will also spur strong demand for teacher aides. The number of special education programs is rising in response to Federal legislation which mandates appropriate education for all children with disabilities, and emphasizes placing disabled children into regular school settings. Children with special needs require much personal attention, and special education teachers, as well as general education teachers with special education students, rely heavily on teacher aides.

In addition, school reforms which call for more individual instruction should further enhance employment opportunities for teacher aides. More paraprofessionals are being employed to provide students with the personal instruction and remedial education they need. Most students greatly benefit from additional attention, individual instruction, and positive feedback.

Teacher aide employment is sensitive to changes in State and local expenditures for education. Pressures on education budgets are greater in some States and localities than in others. A number of teacher aide positions, such as Head Start assistant teachers, are financed through Federal programs, which also may be affected by budget constraints.

Earnings
According to a survey of salaries in public schools, conducted by the Educational Research Service, aides involved in teaching activities averaged $8.77 an hour in 1994-95; those performing only nonteaching activities averaged $8.29 an hour. Earnings varied by region, work experience, and academic qualifications. Many aides are covered by collective bargaining agreements and have benefits similar to those of the teachers in their schools.

Related Occupations
Teacher aides who instruct children have duties similar to those of preschool, elementary, and secondary school teachers and librarians. However, teacher aides do not have the same level of responsibility or training. The support activities of teacher aides and their educational backgrounds are similar to those of child-care workers, family daycare providers, library technicians, and library assistants.

Sources of Additional Information
For information on teacher aides, including training and unionization, and on a wide range of education-related subjects, contact:
☛American Federation of Teachers, Organizing Department, 555 New Jersey Ave. NW., Washington, DC 20001.

For information on a career as a teacher aide, contact:
☛National Resource Center for Paraprofessionals in Education and Related Services, 25 West 43rd St., Room 620, New York, NY 10036.

School superintendents and State departments of education can provide details about employment requirements.

Telephone Operators

(D.O.T. 235.222-010, .462-010, .562-014, .662-014, -018, -022, and -026)

Nature of the Work

Although most telephone numbers are dialed directly, some still require the assistance of a telephone operator. Telephone company central office operators help customers with person-to-person or collect calls or with special billing requests, such as charging a call to a third number or giving customers credit or a refund for a wrong number or a bad connection. Operators also are called upon to handle emergency calls and assist children or people with physical limitations.

Technological innovations have changed the responsibilities of central office operators. Electronic switching systems have eliminated the need for manual switching, and new systems automatically record information about the length and cost of calls into a computer that processes the billing statements. It is also now possible in most places to call other countries, person-to-person, or collect without the help of an operator. The task of responding to "intercept" calls (vacant, changed, or disconnected numbers) also is automated, and a computerized recording explains the reason for the interception and gives the new number. The monitoring and computing of charges on calls from pay telephones also have an automated function formerly performed by operators.

Directory assistance operators answer inquiries by accessing computerized alphabetical and geographical directories. They generally no longer read numbers; this is done by a computerized recording.

Many organizations like hotels and medical centers employ operators to run private branch exchange (PBX) switchboards. These switchboard, or PBX operators, connect interoffice or house calls, answer and relay outside calls, connect outgoing calls, supply information to callers, and record charges. Many also act as receptionists or information clerks, relaying messages or announcing visitors. (Receptionists are described elsewhere in this section of the *Handbook*.)

Operators also work in other settings. Telephone-answering-service operators manage switchboards to provide answering service for clients. Communication-center operators handle airport authority communication systems. For example, they use the public address system to page passengers or visitors. They also monitor electronic equipment alarms.

Telephone company operators work at video display terminals in pleasant, well-lighted, air-conditioned surroundings.

Private-branch-exchange service advisors, sometimes called customer instructors or telephone usage counselors, train switchboard operators. Service advisors monitor conversations between operators and customers to observe the operator's behavior, technical accuracy, and adherence to company policies.

Working Conditions

The hours of PBX or switchboard operators generally are the same as those of other clerical workers in the firm. In some organizations, they work 40 hours a week during regular business hours. Operators in hotels, hospitals, and other places where telephone service is needed on a 24-hour basis, work shifts, even on holidays and weekends. Telephone company operators generally work 32 1/2 to 37 1/2 hours a week. They also may work day, evening, or night shifts, which include weekends and holidays.

Some operators work split shifts, that is, they are on duty during the peak calling periods in the late morning and early evening and have time off in between. Telephone companies normally assign shifts by seniority, allowing the most experienced workers to choose when they will work. These operators, like all telephone company employees, may be subject to 24-hour call. In general, though, they work overtime only during emergencies.

Telephone company operators work at video display terminals in pleasant, well-lighted, air-conditioned surroundings. But if the work site is not well designed, these operators may experience eyestrain and back discomfort.

The job of a telephone operator requires little physical exertion; during peak calling periods, however, the pace at the switchboard may be hectic. Telephone companies continually strive to increase operator efficiency, and this can create a tense work environment. An operator's work generally is quite repetitive and, in telephone companies, is closely supervised. Computerized pacing and monitoring by supervisors, combined with the rapid pace, may cause stress. Operators must sit for long periods and usually need supervisory approval to leave their work stations.

Employment

Telephone operators held about 310,000 jobs in 1994. About 3 out of 4 worked as PBX operators in hotels, hospitals, department stores, or other organizations. The remainder worked in telephone companies. Roughly one-fifth of all operators worked part time, although relatively few of those employed by telephone companies were part-timers.

Training, Other Qualifications, and Advancement

Telephone operators should be pleasant, courteous, and patient. A clear, pleasing voice and good hearing are important. In addition to being a good listener, prospective operators should have good reading, spelling, and arithmetic skills. Good eye-hand coordination and manual dexterity are useful, as is an ability to work well under pressure. Many employers require operators to pass a physical examination. Some employers require a high school diploma. High school courses in speech, office practices, and business math provide a helpful background. Fluency in a foreign language is also looked upon favorably.

New operators are taught how to use the equipment. In telephone companies, classroom instruction lasts up to 3 weeks and is followed by on-the-job training. Classroom instruction covers time zones and geography so that central office operators understand rates and know where major cities are located. Tapes are used to familiarize trainees with the dial tone, busy signal, and other telephone sounds and to improve diction and courtesy by giving them an opportunity to hear their own voices. Close supervision continues after training is completed.

PBX operators who handle routine calls usually have a somewhat shorter training period than telephone company operators. These workers usually are trained informally by experienced personnel, although, in some organizations, it may be done by a telephone company instructor.

After 1 or 2 years of experience, telephone company operators may be promoted to service assistant, aiding the supervisor by monitoring telephone conversations. Direct promotion to supervisor may also be possible in some companies. Some operators advance to other clerical jobs or to telephone craft jobs such as installer or repairer. Large firms may promote PBX operators to more responsible clerical positions; however, many small businesses have limited advancement opportunities.

Job Outlook

Job opportunities for telephone operators are expected to be extremely limited over the next decade. Overall employment is expected to decline but variations in growth will occur among different groups of operators. Employment of operators in telephone companies is expected to decline sharply through the year 2005 as automation continues to increase these workers' productivity and deregulations increase competition for phone services from other industries. Many telephone companies do not plan to replace operators who leave and many are laying off operators. In contrast, the number of switchboard or PBX operators is expected to grow, but more slowly than the average for all workers. As older switchboards that require operators to make connections are replaced by ones that route calls automatically, fewer operators will be needed. In addition, voice message systems have proliferated as computers became smaller, cheaper, and more powerful. These systems record, store, play, and forward telephone messages—work currently performed by PBX operators. When callers need to speak to an operator, they may be helped by receptionists who have been trained to make telephone connections. However, many firms may still keep switchboard operators for the "personal touch," which would somewhat limit the effects of new technology.

Voice recognition technology, which gives computers the capacity to understand speech and to talk back, is now here and has replaced many directory assistance operators and central office operators.

Earnings

Telephone operators who worked full time earned a median weekly salary of $398 in 1994. The middle 50 percent earned between $285 and $513. The bottom 10 percent earned less than $227; the top 10 percent earned more than $604 a week.

According to a survey of workplaces in 160 metropolitan areas, switchboard operators had median weekly earnings of $320 in 1993. The middle half earned between $273 and $372 a week.

Telephone company operators generally earn more than switchboard operators. Most telephone company operators are members of the Communications Workers of America or the International Brotherhood of Electrical Workers. The average hourly earnings for operators represented by these unions were $12.52 in 1994, with an average low of $9.09 and an average high of $18.56. For these operators, union contracts govern wage rates, wage increases, and the time required to advance from one step to the next (it normally takes 4 years to rise from the lowest paying, nonsupervisory operator position to the highest). Contracts also call for extra pay for work beyond the normal 6 1/2 to 7 1/2 hours a day or 5 days a week, for Sunday and holiday work, and for a pay differential for nightwork and split shifts. Many contracts provide for a 1-week vacation with 6 months of service; 2 weeks for 1 to 6 years; 3 weeks for 7 to 14 years; 4 weeks for 15 to 24 years; and 5 weeks for 25 years and over. Holidays range from 9 to 11 days a year.

Related Occupations

Other workers who provide information to the general public include customer service representatives, dispatchers, hotel clerks, information clerks, police aides, receptionists, reservation agents, and travel clerks.

Sources of Additional Information

For more details about employment opportunities, contact a telephone company. For general information on the telephone industry and career opportunities contact:

☛United States Telephone Association, 1401 H St. NW., Suite 600, Washington, DC 20005-2136.

☛Communications Workers of America, Research Department, 501 3rd St. NW., Washington, DC 20001.

☛International Brotherhood of Electrical Workers, Telecommunications Department, 1125 15th. St. NW., Room 807, Washington, DC 20005.

Typists, Word Processors, and Data Entry Keyers

(D.O.T. 203.362-010, -022, .382-018, -026, .582-014, -038, -042, -046, -054, -062, -066, -078; 208.382-010; and 209.382-010)

Nature of the Work

The information that many of today's organizations need to process is growing at a dizzying pace. Typists, word processors, and data entry keyers help to insure that this work is handled smoothly and efficiently.

Typists and word processors usually set up and enter reports, letters, mailing labels, and other text material. Typists make neat, typed copies of materials written by other clerical, professional, or managerial workers. They may begin as entry-level workers by typing headings on form letters, addressing envelopes, or preparing standard forms on electric or electronic typewriters. As they gain experience, they may begin to do work that requires a higher degree of accuracy and independent judgment. Senior typists may work with highly technical material, plan and type complicated statistical tables, combine and rearrange materials from different sources, or prepare master copies to be reproduced on photocopiers.

Although it is becoming less common, some centralized word processing teams handle the transcription and typing for several departments. Regardless of how work is organized, though, most keyboarding is now done on word processing equipment. Word processors use this equipment to record, edit, store, and revise letters, memos, reports, statistical tables, forms, and other printed materials. Word processing equipment—usually a personal computer or part of a larger computer system—normally includes a keyboard, a video display terminal, and a printer, and may have "add-on" capabilities such as optical character recognition readers.

Typists and word processors often perform other office tasks as well. They answer telephones, file, and operate copiers, calculators, and other office machines. Job titles of typists vary by duties performed and by work setting. For example, clerk typists combine typing with filing, sorting mail, answering telephones, and other general office work. Notereaders transcribe stenotyped notes of court proceedings into standard formats.

Data entry keyers usually fill forms that appear on a computer screen or enter lists of items or numbers. They also may manipulate existing data, edit current information, or proofread new entries to a database. Some examples of data sources include customers' personal information, medical records, and membership lists. Usually this information is used internally by a company and may be reformatted before use by other departments or by customers.

Keyers can enter data on a variety of typewriter-like equipment. Many keyers use a machine that converts the information they type to magnetic impulses on tapes or disks for entry into a computer system. Others prepare materials for printing or publication by using data entry composing machines. Some keyers operate on-line terminals or personal computers. Data entry keyers increasingly work with non-keyboard forms of data entry like scanners and electronically transmitted files. When working with these new optical character

Experienced typists may work with highly technical materials.

recognition systems, data entry keyers often enter only those data which cannot be recognized by machines. In some offices, keyers also operate computer peripheral equipment such as printers and tape readers, act as tape librarians, and perform other clerical duties.

Working Conditions

Typists, word processors, and data entry keyers usually work in clean offices. They sit for long periods and sometimes must contend with high noise levels caused by various office machines such as printers. These workers are susceptible to repetitive strain injuries like carpal tunnel syndrome and neck, back, and eye strain. To help prevent these from occurring, some offices have scheduled exercise breaks and installed ergonomically designed keyboards and workstations that allow workers to stand or sit as they wish. They generally work a standard 40-hour week.

Employment

Typists, word processors, and data entry keyers held nearly 1.1 million jobs in 1994, and were employed in every sector of the economy. Office work lends itself to alternative or flexible working arrangements, so many of these workers hold temporary jobs and 1 in 5 works part time. Some workers "telecommute" by working from their homes via personal computers linked by telephone lines to those in the main office. This enables them to type material at home and almost instantly produce printed copy in their offices.

Twenty-four percent of all typists, word processors, and data entry keyers held jobs in firms that provide business services, including temporary help agencies and word processing service bureaus. Eighteen percent worked in government agencies at various levels, while 9 percent were employed in educational institutions.

Training, Other Qualifications, and Advancement

Employers generally hire high school graduates who can meet their requirements for keyboarding speed. Keyboarding skills can be learned in different ways—in high schools, community colleges, business schools, or on one's own—using self-teaching aids such as books, records, and personal computers. Spelling, punctuation, and grammar skills are also important, as is familiarity with standard office equipment and procedures.

Increasingly, employers also expect applicants to have word processing or data entry training or experience. Many community colleges, business schools, and temporary help agencies teach students to use word processing, spreadsheet, and database management computer software packages.

For many people, a job as a typist, word processor, or data entry keyer is their first job after graduating from high school or after a period of full-time family responsibilities. This work frequently serves as a steppingstone to higher paying jobs with more responsibilities. Large companies and government agencies generally have training programs to help clerical employees upgrade their skills and advance to other positions. It is common for typists, word processors, and data entry keyers to transfer to other clerical jobs, such as secretary, statistical clerk, or court reporter, or to be promoted to a supervisory job in a word processing or data entry center.

Job Outlook

Employment of typists, word processors, and data entry keyers is expected to decline through the year 2005 despite rapid growth in the production of information and volume of business transactions. This decline is largely the result of productivity gains and organizational restructuring brought about by new technologies. Most important among these is the proliferation of personal computers, which has enabled other workers to perform work formerly done by typists, word processors, and data entry keyers. Most professionals and managers now use desktop personal computers or work stations to enter data and do their own word processing.

Further automation of tasks is expected and should continue to reduce the demand for typists, word processors, and data entry keyers. For example, bar code scanners, which are now used in many retail establishments, should continue to spread to smaller establishments. More sophisticated optical character recognition readers, which scan documents and enter their text and data into a computer, are being used in more workplaces. This technology is being improved and should be more widely used in coming years. Researchers are also developing voice recognition technologies that enable people to enter text and data by simply speaking to a computer.

In addition to these technologies designed to make traditional data entry more productive, others are being implemented which aim to make it unnecessary. Data are being captured at the point of origin and entered into the system without human intervention. An example of this in the banking industry is automatic teller machines. As telecommunications technology improves, many organizations will take advantage of computer networks that allow more data to be transmitted electronically, thereby avoiding the reentry of data.

Employment in this occupation will also be influenced by international and service sector outsourcing. Some large data entry and processing firms employ workers in nations with low wages to enter data. As international trade barriers continue to fall and telecommunications technology improves, this transfer will continue to have a negative impact on employment of data entry keyers in the United States. Employment is also shifting between industries within the U.S. As organizations have demanded more flexibility from workers, they have reduced in-house staff and have opted to use a staffing service firm. This trend has led to a redistribution of employment to temporary and staffing services firms.

In spite of declining employment, a couple of hundred thousand openings will still occur each year as workers transfer to other occupations or leave the labor force. Job prospects will be brightest for those typists, word processors, and data entry keyers with the best technical skills. Applicants for these positions, however, will need to be flexible and willing to continuously develop their skills. In particular, the more expertise these workers have in computer equipment and software packages, the better their job opportunities will be.

Earnings

Based on a survey of metropolitan areas, word processors averaged $22,900 a year in 1993; data entry keyers averaged $17,600.

highest in transportation and public utilities, and lowest in retail trade and finance, insurance, and real estate. Similarly, their salaries tend to vary by region, with salaries in the West being the highest. Regardless of industry or region, typists generally receive higher salaries if they have word processing experience.

In the Federal Government, clerk-typists and data entry keyers without work experience started at about $14,900 a year in 1995. Beginning salaries were slightly higher in selected areas where the prevailing local pay level was higher. The average annual salary for all clerk-typists in the Federal Government was about $19,400 in 1995.

Related Occupations
Typists, word processors, and data entry keyers must transcribe information quickly. Other workers who deliver information in a timely manner are stenographers, court reporters, dispatchers, and telephone operators. They must also be comfortable working with office automation, and in this regard they are similar to secretaries and computer and peripheral equipment operators.

Sources of Additional Information
For information about job opportunities in data entry, contact the nearest office of the State employment service.

Service Occupations

Protective Service Occupations

Correctional Officers

(D.O.T. 372.367-014, .567-014, .667-018, and .677; and 375.367-010)

Nature of the Work

Correctional officers are charged with overseeing individuals who have been arrested, are awaiting trial or other hearing, or who have been convicted of a crime and sentenced to serve time in a jail, reformatory, or penitentiary. They maintain security and observe inmate conduct and behavior to prevent disturbances and escapes. Many correctional officers work in small county and municipal jails or precinct station houses as deputy sheriffs or police officers with wide ranging responsibilities. (See the statement on Police, Detectives, and Special Agents elsewhere in the *Handbook*.) Others are assigned to large State and Federal prisons where job duties are more specialized. A relatively small number supervise aliens being held by the Immigration and Naturalization Service before being released or deported. Regardless of the setting, correctional officers maintain order within the institution, enforce rules and regulations, and may supplement whatever counseling inmates receive from psychologists, social workers, or other mental health professionals.

To make sure inmates are orderly and obey rules, correctional officers monitor inmates' activities, including working, exercising, eating, and bathing. They assign and supervise inmates' work assignments. Sometimes it is necessary to search inmates and their living quarters for weapons or drugs, to settle disputes between inmates, and to enforce discipline. Correctional officers cannot show favoritism and must report any inmate who violates the rules. A few officers hold staff security positions in towers, where they are equipped with high-powered rifles. Other, unarmed officers are responsible for direct supervision of inmates. They are locked in a cell-block alone, or with another officer, among the 50 to 100 inmates who reside there. The officers enforce regulations primarily through their communications skills and moral authority.

Other correctional officers periodically inspect the facilities. They may, for example, check cells and other areas of the institution for unsanitary conditions, weapons, drugs, fire hazards, and any evidence of infractions of rules. In addition, they routinely inspect locks, window bars, grille doors, and gates for signs of tampering.

Correctional officers report orally and in writing on inmate conduct and on the quality and quantity of work done by inmates. Officers also report disturbances, violations of rules, and any unusual occurrences. They usually keep a daily record of their activities. In the most modern facilities, correctional officers can monitor the activities of prisoners from a centralized control center with the aid of closed circuit television cameras and a computer tracking system. In such an environment, the inmates may not see anyone but officers for days or weeks at a time.

Depending on the offender's classification within the institution, correctional officers may escort inmates to and from cells and other areas and admit and accompany authorized visitors to see inmates. Officers may also escort prisoners between the institution and courtrooms, medical facilities, and other destinations. They inspect mail and visitors for contraband (prohibited items). Should the situation arise, they assist law enforcement authorities by investigating crimes

Correctional officers are responsible for the safety and well being of individuals in their keeping.

committed within their institution and by helping search for escaped inmates.

Correctional officers may arrange a change in a daily schedule so that an inmate can visit the library, help inmates get news of their families, or help inmates in other ways. In a few institutions, officers receive specialized training, have a more formal counseling role, and may lead or participate in group counseling sessions.

Correctional sergeants directly supervise correctional officers. They usually are responsible for maintaining security and directing the activities of a group of inmates during an assigned watch or in an assigned area.

Working Conditions

Correctional officers may work indoors or outdoors, depending on their specific duties. Some indoor areas of correctional institutions are well lighted, heated, and ventilated, but others are overcrowded, hot, and noisy. Outdoors, weather conditions may be disagreeable, for example when standing watch on a guard tower in cold weather. Working in a correctional institution can be stressful and hazardous; correctional officers occasionally have been injured or killed by inmates.

Correctional officers usually work an 8-hour day, 5 days a week, on rotating shifts. Prison security must be provided around the clock, which often means that junior officers work weekends, holidays, and nights. In addition, officers may be required to work overtime.

Employment

Correctional officers held about 310,000 jobs in 1994. Six of every 10 worked at State correctional institutions such as prisons, prison camps, and reformatories. Most of the remainder worked at city and county jails or other institutions run by local governments. About 9,000 correctional officers worked at Federal correctional institutions, and about 4,000 worked in privately owned and managed prisons.

Most correctional officers work in relatively large institutions located in rural areas, although a significant number work in jails and other smaller facilities located in law enforcement agencies throughout the country.

Training, Other Qualifications, and Advancement

Most institutions require that correctional officers be at least 18 or 21 years of age, have a high school education or its equivalent, have no felony convictions, and be a United States citizen. In addition, correctional institutions increasingly seek correctional officers with postsecondary education, particularly in psychology, criminal justice, police science, criminology, and related fields.

Correctional officers must be in good health. The Federal System and many States require candidates to meet formal standards of physical fitness, eyesight, and hearing. Strength, good judgment, and the ability to think and act quickly are indispensable. Other common requirements include a driver's license, and work experience that demonstrates reliability. The Federal System and some States screen applicants for drug abuse and require candidates to pass a written or oral examination, along with a background check.

Federal, State, and local departments of corrections provide training for correctional officers based on guidelines established by the American Correctional Association, the American Jail Association, and other professional organizations. Some States have special training academies. All States and local departments of correction provide informal on-the-job training at the conclusion of formal instruction. On-the-job trainees receive several weeks or months of training in an actual job setting under an experienced officer.

Academy trainees generally receive instruction on institutional policies, regulations, and operations; constitutional law and cultural awareness; crisis intervention, inmate behavior, and contraband control; custody and security procedures; fire and safety; inmate rules and legal rights; administrative responsibilities; written and oral communication, including preparation of reports; self-defense, including the use of firearms and physical force; first aid including cardiopulmonary resuscitation (CPR); and physical fitness training. New Federal correctional officers must undergo 200 hours of formal training within the first year of employment. They must complete 120 hours of specialized correctional instruction at the Federal Bureau of Prisons residential training center at Glynco, Georgia, within the first 60 days after appointment. Experienced officers receive inservice training to keep abreast of new ideas and procedures.

Entry requirements and on-the-job training vary widely from agency to agency. For instance, correctional officers in North Dakota need 2 years of college with emphasis on criminal justice or behavioral science, or 3 years as a correctional, military police, or licensed peace officer. The department then provides 80 hours of training at the start, and follows up with 40 hours of training annually. On the other hand, Connecticut requires only that candidates be 18 years of age, have a high school diploma or GED Certificate, and pass a medical/physical examination, including drug screening. It then provides 520 hours of initial training, and follows up with 40 hours annually.

Correctional officers have the opportunity to join prison tactical response teams, which are trained to respond to riots, hostage situations, forced cell moves, and other potentially dangerous confrontations. Team members often receive monthly training and practice with weapons, chemical agents, forced entry methods, and other tactics.

With education, experience, and training, qualified officers may advance to correctional sergeant or other supervisory or administrative positions. Many correctional institutions require experience as a correctional officer for other corrections positions. Ambitious correctional officers can be promoted up to assistant warden. Officers sometimes transfer to related areas, such as probation and parole officer.

Job Outlook

Job opportunities for correctional officers are expected to be plentiful through the year 2005. The need to replace correctional officers who transfer to other occupations or leave the labor force, coupled with rising employment demand, will generate many thousands of job openings each year. Some local and a few State correctional agencies have traditionally experienced difficulty in attracting qualified applicants, largely due to relatively low salaries and unattractive rural locations. This situation is expected to continue, ensuring highly favorable job prospects.

Employment of correctional officers is expected to increase much faster than the average for all occupations through the year 2005 as additional officers are hired to supervise and control a growing inmate population. Expansion and new construction of correctional facilities also are expected to create many new jobs for correctional officers, although State and local government budgetary constraints could affect the rate at which new facilities are built. Increasing public concern about the spread of crime and illegal drugs—resulting in more convictions—and the adoption of mandatory sentencing guidelines calling for longer sentences and reduced parole for inmates also will spur demand for correctional officers.

Layoffs of correctional officers are rare because security must be maintained in correctional institutions at all times.

Earnings

According to a 1994 survey in *Corrections Compendium,* a national journal for corrections professionals, starting salaries of State correctional officers averaged about $19,100 a year, ranging from $13,700 in Kentucky to $29,700 in New Jersey. Professional correctional officers' salaries, overall, averaged about $22,900 and ranged from $17,000 in Wyoming to $34,100 in New York.

At the Federal level, the starting salary was about $18,700 to $20,800 a year in 1995; supervisory correctional officers started at about $28,300 a year. Starting salaries were slightly higher in selected areas where prevailing local pay levels were higher. The 1995 average salary for all Federal nonsupervisory correctional officers was about $31,460; for supervisors, about $57,100.

Correctional officers usually are provided uniforms or a clothing allowance to purchase their own uniforms. Most are provided or can participate in hospitalization or major medical insurance plans; many officers can get disability and life insurance at group rates. They also receive vacation and sick leave and pension benefits. Officers employed by the Federal Government and most State governments are covered by civil service systems or merit boards. Their retirement coverage entitles them to retire at age 50 after 20 years of service or at any age with 25 years of service. In the Federal system and some States, correctional officers are represented by labor unions.

Related Occupations

A number of related careers are open to high school graduates who are interested in protective services and the field of security. Bailiffs supervise offenders and maintain order in local and State courtrooms during legal proceedings. Bodyguards escort people and protect them from injury or invasion of privacy. House or store detectives patrol business establishments to protect against theft and vandalism and to enforce standards of good behavior. Security guards protect government, commercial, and industrial property against theft, vandalism, illegal entry, and fire. Police officers and deputy sheriffs maintain law and order, prevent crime, and arrest offenders.

Other corrections careers are open to persons interested in working with offenders. Probation and parole officers monitor and counsel offenders, process their release from correctional institutions, and evaluate their progress in becoming productive members of society. Recreation leaders organize and instruct offenders in sports, games, arts, and crafts. Some of these related occupations are discussed elsewhere in the *Handbook.*

Sources of Additional Information

Information about entrance requirements, training, and career opportunities for correctional officers on the State level may be obtained from State civil service commissions, State departments of corrections, or nearby correctional institutions and facilities.

Additional information on careers in corrections on the local level is available from:

☛The American Jail Association, 2053 Day Road, Hagerstown, MD 21740-9795.

Information on entrance requirements, training, and career opportunities for correctional officers on the Federal level may be obtained from:

☛Federal Bureau of Prisons, National Recruitment Office, 320 First St. NW., Room 460, Washington, DC 20534.

☛International Association of Correctional Officers, 1333 S. Wabash-Box 53, Chicago, IL 60605.

Firefighting Occupations

(D.O.T. 373 except .117; 379.687-010; 452.134, .167, .364-014, .367-010, -014, .687-014)

Nature of the Work

Firefighters respond to a variety of emergency situations where life, property, or the environment are at risk. They frequently are the first emergency response team at the scene of an accident, fire, flood, earthquake, or act of terrorism. Every year, fires and other emergency conditions take thousands of lives and destroy property worth billions of dollars. Firefighters help protect the public against these dangers. This statement provides information only about career firefighters; it does not cover volunteer firefighters, who perform the same duties, and who may comprise the majority of firefighters in your area.

Most calls that firefighters respond to involve medical emergencies, and many fire departments provide ambulance service for victims. Firefighters receive training in emergency medical procedures, and many fire departments require them to be certified as emergency medical technicians. (For more information on this occupation, see the *Handbook* statement on emergency medical technicians.)

During duty hours, firefighters must be prepared to respond immediately to a fire or other emergency situation that arises. Each situation a firefighter encounters is unique. Because firefighting is dangerous and complex, it requires organization and teamwork. At every emergency scene, firefighters perform specific duties assigned by a superior officer. They may connect hose lines to hydrants, operate a pump, or position ladders. They may rescue victims and administer emergency medical aid, ventilate smoke-filled areas, operate equipment, and salvage the contents of buildings. Their duties may change several times while the company is in action. Sometimes they remain at the site of a disaster for several days or more, rescuing survivors and assisting with medical emergencies.

The job of firefighter has become more complicated in recent years due to the use of increasingly sophisticated equipment. In addition, many firefighters have assumed a wider range of responsibilities—for example, working with ambulance services that provide emergency medical treatment, assisting in the recovery from natural disasters such as earthquakes and tornadoes, and becoming involved with the control and cleanup of oil spills and other hazardous materials incidents.

Firefighters are primarily involved with protecting structures, but they also work at airports on crash and rescue crews, at chemical plants, by waterfronts, and in forests and wildland areas. In forests, air patrols locate fires and report their findings to headquarters by telephone or radio. Fire rangers patrol areas of the forest to locate and report fires and hazardous conditions and to ensure that travelers and campers are complying with fire regulations. When fires break out, firefighters use hand tools and water hoses to battle the blaze. Some specialized firefighters parachute from airplanes when necessary to reach inaccessible areas.

Most fire departments have a fire prevention division which is usually headed by a fire marshall. Fire inspectors are specially trained to conduct inspections of structures to prevent fires and to ensure fire code compliance. These firefighters may also check and approve plans for new buildings, working with developers and planners in that process. Fire prevention personnel often speak on these subjects before public assemblies and civic organizations. Some firefighters become fire investigators, who determine the origin and cause of fires. They collect evidence, interview witnesses, and prepare reports on fires where there may be arson or criminal negligence. Some investigators have police powers and may arrest suspects. They may also be called upon to testify in court.

Between alarms, firefighters have classroom training, clean and maintain equipment, conduct practice drills and fire inspections, and participate in physical fitness activities. They prepare written reports on fire incidents and review fire science literature to keep abreast of technological developments and administrative practices and policies.

Working Conditions

Firefighters spend much of their time at fire stations, which usually have facilities for dining and sleeping. When an alarm comes in, firefighters must respond rapidly, regardless of the weather or hour. They may spend long periods on their feet, sometimes in adverse weather, tending to fires, medical emergencies, hazardous materials incidents, and other emergencies.

Firefighting is a very hazardous occupation. It involves risk of death or injury from sudden cave-ins of floors or toppling walls and from exposure to flames and smoke. Strong winds and falling trees and branches can make fighting forest fires particularly dangerous. Firefighters also may come in contact with poisonous, flammable, and explosive gases and chemicals, and radiation or other hazardous materials, that may have immediate or long-term effects on their health. For these reasons, they must wear all kinds of protective gear, which can be very heavy.

Work hours of firefighters are longer and vary more widely than hours of most other workers. Many work more than 50 hours a week; during some weeks, they may work significantly longer hours. In some cities, they are on duty for 24 hours, then off for 48 hours, and receive an extra day off at intervals. In other cities, they work a day shift of 10 hours for 3 or 4 days, a night shift of 14 hours for 3 or 4 nights, have 3 or 4 days off, and then repeat the cycle. In addition,

Firefighting is one of the most hazardous occupations.

firefighters often work extra hours at fires and other emergencies and are regularly assigned to work on holidays. Fire lieutenants and fire captains often work the same hours as the firefighters they supervise. Duty hours include time when firefighters study, train, and perform fire prevention duties.

Employment

Firefighters held about 284,000 jobs in 1994. Nine of every 10 worked in municipal or county fire departments. Some very large cities have several thousand firefighters, while many small towns have only a few. Most of the remainder worked in fire departments on Federal and State installations, including airports. Private firefighting companies employ a small number.

Training, Other Qualifications, and Advancement

Applicants for municipal firefighting jobs may have to pass a written test; tests of strength, physical stamina, coordination, and agility; and a medical examination—including drug screening. Workers also may be monitored on a random basis for drug use after accepting employment. Examinations are open to persons who are at least 18 years of age and have a high school education or the equivalent. Those who receive the highest scores have the best chances for appointment. The completion of community college courses in fire science may improve an applicant's chances for appointment. In fact, in recent years, an increasing proportion of entrants to this occupation have some postsecondary education.

As a rule, beginners in large fire departments are trained for several weeks at the department's training center. Through classroom instruction and practical training, the recruits study firefighting techniques, fire prevention, hazardous materials, local building codes, and emergency medical procedures, including first aid and cardiopulmonary resuscitation. Also, they learn how to use axes, saws, chemical extinguishers, ladders, and other firefighting and rescue equipment. After successfully completing this training, they are assigned to a fire company, where they undergo a period of probation.

A number of fire departments have accredited apprenticeship programs lasting 3 to 4 years. These programs combine formal, technical instruction with on-the-job training under the supervision of experienced firefighters. Technical instruction covers subjects such as firefighting techniques and equipment, chemical hazards associated with various combustible building materials, emergency medical procedures, and fire prevention and safety.

Most experienced firefighters continue studying to improve their job performance and prepare for promotion examinations. Today, firefighters need more training to operate increasingly sophisticated equipment and to deal safely with the greater hazards associated with fighting fires in larger, more elaborate structures. To progress to higher level positions, they must acquire expertise in the most advanced firefighting equipment and techniques and in building construction, emergency medical procedures, writing, public speaking, management and budgeting procedures, and labor relations. Fire departments frequently conduct training programs, and some firefighters attend training sessions sponsored by the National Fire Academy. These training sessions cover various topics, including executive development, anti-arson techniques, and public fire safety and education. Some States also have extensive firefighter training programs.

Many colleges and universities offer courses leading to 2- or 4-year degrees in fire engineering or fire science. Many fire departments offer firefighters incentives such as tuition reimbursement or higher pay for completing advanced training.

Among the personal qualities firefighters need are mental alertness, courage, mechanical aptitude, endurance, strength, and a sense of public service. Initiative and good judgment are extremely important because firefighters often must make quick decisions in emergencies. Because members of a crew eat, sleep, and work closely together under conditions of stress and danger, they should be de-

pendable and able to get along well with others in a group. Leadership qualities are necessary for officers, who must establish and maintain discipline and efficiency as well as direct the activities of firefighters in their companies.

Opportunities for promotion are good in most fire departments. As firefighters gain experience, they may advance to a higher rank. The line of promotion usually is to engineer, lieutenant, captain, battalion chief, assistant chief, deputy chief, and finally to chief. Advancement generally depends upon scores on a written examination, job performance, and seniority. Increasingly, fire departments are using assessment centers—which simulate a variety of actual job performance tasks—to screen for the best candidates for promotion. Many fire departments now require a bachelor's degree, preferably in public administration or a related field, for promotion to positions higher than battalion chief. Some departments now require a master's degree for the chief and for executive fire officer certification from the National Fire Academy, or for a State chief officer certification.

Job Outlook

Firefighters are expected to face considerable competition for available job openings. Firefighting attracts many people because a high school education usually is sufficient, earnings are relatively high, and a pension is guaranteed upon retirement. In addition, the work is frequently exciting and challenging and affords an opportunity to perform a valuable public service. Consequently, the number of qualified applicants in most areas generally exceeds the number of job openings, even though the written examination and physical requirements eliminate many applicants. This situation is expected to persist through the year 2005.

Employment of firefighters is expected to increase about as fast as the average for all occupations through the year 2005 as a result of the increase in the Nation's population and fire protection needs. In addition, the number of paid firefighter positions is expected to increase as a percentage of all firefighter jobs. The increased level of specialized training required in this occupation makes it more difficult for volunteer firefighters to remain qualified for duty. Much of the expected job growth will occur in smaller communities with expanding populations that augment volunteers with career firefighters to better meet growing, increasingly complex fire protection needs. However, little growth is expected in large, urban fire departments. A small number of local governments are expected to contract for firefighting services with private companies.

In response to the expanding role of firefighters, some municipalities have combined fire prevention, public fire education, safety, and emergency medical services into a single organization commonly referred to as a public safety organization. Some local and regional fire departments are being consolidated into county-wide establishments in order to cut overhead, take advantage of economies of scale, reduce administrative staffs, and establish consistent training standards and work procedures.

Turnover of firefighter jobs is unusually low, particularly for an occupation that requires a relatively limited investment in formal education. Nevertheless, most job openings are expected to result from the need to replace those who retire or stop working for other reasons, or who transfer to other occupations.

Layoffs of firefighters are not common. Fire protection is an essential service, and citizens are likely to exert considerable pressure on city officials to expand or at least preserve the level of fire-protection coverage. Even when budget cuts do occur, local fire departments usually cut expenses by postponing equipment purchases or not hiring new firefighters, rather than by laying off staff.

Earnings

Median weekly earnings for firefighting occupations were around $630 in 1994. The middle 50 percent earned between $490 and $775 weekly. The lowest 10 percent earned less than $380, while the highest 10 percent earned more than $975. The average annual salary for all firefighters in the Federal Government in nonsupervisory, supervisory, and managerial positions was about $27,100 in 1995. Fire lieutenants and fire captains may earn considerably more.

The law requires that overtime be paid to those firefighters who average 53 or more hours a week during their work period—which ranges from 7 to 28 days. Firefighters often earn overtime for working extra shifts to maintain minimum staffing levels or for special emergencies.

Firefighters receive benefits that usually include medical and liability insurance, vacation and sick leave, and some paid holidays. Practically all fire departments provide protective clothing (helmets, boots, and coats) and breathing apparatus, and many also provide dress uniforms. Firefighters generally are covered by pension plans that often provide retirement at half pay at age 50 after 25 years of service or at any age if disabled in the line of duty.

Many career firefighters are unionized, and belong to the International Association of Firefighters. Many company officers and chief officers belong to the International Association of Fire Chiefs.

Related Occupations

A related fire protection occupation is the fire-protection engineer, who identifies fire hazards in homes and workplaces and designs prevention programs and automatic fire detection and extinguishing systems. Other occupations in which workers respond to emergencies include police officers and emergency medical technicians.

Sources of Additional Information

Information about a career as a firefighter may be obtained from local fire departments and:

☛International Association of Fire Chiefs, 4025 Fair Ridge Dr., Fairfax, VA 22033-2868.

☛International Association of Firefighters, 1750 New York Ave. NW., Washington, DC 20006.

☛Fire Administration, 16825 South Seaton Ave., Emittsburg, MD 21727.

Information about firefighter professional qualifications and a list of colleges and universities that offer 2- or 4-year degree programs in fire science or fire prevention may be obtained from:

☛National Fire Protection Association, Batterymarch Park, Quincy, MA 02269.

Guards

(D.O.T. 372.563, .567-010, .667-010, -014, -030 through -038; 376.667-010; 379.667-010)

Nature of the Work

Guards, also called security officers, patrol and inspect property to protect against fire, theft, vandalism, and illegal entry. Their duties vary with the size, type, and location of their employer. Correction officers—guards who work in prisons and other correctional institutions—and police, detectives, and special agents are discussed separately in this section of the *Handbook.*

In office buildings, banks, hospitals, and department stores, guards protect records, merchandise, money, and equipment. In department stores, they often work with undercover detectives to watch for theft by customers or store employees. Some guards patrol the outside of these buildings.

At ports, airports, and railroads, guards protect merchandise being shipped as well as property and equipment. They screen passengers and visitors for weapons, explosives, and other contraband. They ensure that nothing is stolen while being loaded or unloaded, and watch for fires, prowlers, and trouble among work crews. Sometimes they direct traffic.

Guards who work in public buildings, such as museums or art galleries, protect paintings and exhibits by inspecting people and

packages entering the building. They also answer routine questions from visitors and sometimes guide tours.

In factories, laboratories, government buildings, data processing centers, and military bases where valuable property or information—such as information on new products, computer codes, or defense secrets—must be protected, guards check the credentials of persons and vehicles entering and leaving the premises. University, park, or recreation guards perform similar duties and also may issue parking permits and direct traffic. Golf course patrollers prevent unauthorized persons from using the facility and help keep play running smoothly.

At social affairs, sports events, conventions, and other public gatherings, guards provide information, assist in crowd control, and watch for persons who may cause trouble. Some guards patrol places of entertainment such as nightclubs to preserve order among customers and to protect property.

Armored car guards protect money and valuables during transit. Bodyguards protect individuals from bodily injury, kidnapping, or invasion of privacy.

In a large organization, a security officer often is in charge of the guard force; in a small organization, a single worker may be responsible for all security measures. Patrolling usually is done on foot, but if the property is large, guards may make their rounds by car or motor scooter. As more businesses purchase advanced electronic security systems to protect their property, more guards are being assigned to stations where they monitor perimeter security, environmental functions, communications, and other systems. In many cases, these guards maintain radio contact with other guards patrolling on foot or in motor vehicles. Some guards use computers to store information on matters relevant to security—for example, visitors or suspicious occurrences—during their hours on duty.

As they make their rounds, guards check all doors and windows, see that no unauthorized persons remain after working hours, and ensure that fire extinguishers, alarms, sprinkler systems, furnaces, and various electrical and plumbing systems are working properly. They sometimes set thermostats or turn on lights for janitorial workers.

Although some guards carry weapons, the trend is toward less use of armed guards. Guards may carry a flashlight, whistle, two-way radio, and a watch clock—a device that indicates the time at which they reach various checkpoints.

Working Conditions

Most guards spend considerable time on their feet patrolling buildings, industrial plants, and grounds. Indoors, they may be stationed at a guard desk to monitor electronic security and surveillance de-

The need for security will spur rapid employment growth among guards.

vices or to check the credentials of persons entering or leaving the premises. They also may be stationed at gate shelters or may patrol grounds in all weather.

Because guards often work alone, there may be no one nearby to help if an accident or injury occurs. Some large firms use a reporting service that enables guards to be in constant contact with a central station outside the plant. If they fail to transmit an expected signal, the central station investigates. Guard work is usually routine, but guards must be constantly alert for threats to themselves and to the property that they are protecting. Guards who work during the day may have a great deal of contact with other employees and members of the public.

Many guards work alone at night; the usual shift lasts 8 hours. Some employers have three shifts, and guards rotate to divide daytime, weekend, and holiday work equally. Guards usually eat on the job instead of taking a regular break away from the site.

Employment

Guards held about 867,000 jobs in 1994. Industrial security firms and guard agencies employed 55 percent of all guards. These organizations provide security services on contract, assigning their guards to buildings and other sites as needed. The remainder were in-house guards, employed in many settings including banks, building management companies, hotels, hospitals, retail stores, restaurants and bars, schools, and government.

Although guard jobs are found throughout the country, most are located in metropolitan areas.

Training, Other Qualifications, and Advancement

Most States require that guards be licensed. To be licensed as a guard, individuals generally must be 18 years old, have no convictions for perjury or acts of violence, pass a background examination, and complete classroom training in such subjects as property rights, emergency procedures, and seizure of suspected criminals.

Most employers prefer guards who are high school graduates. Some jobs require a driver's license. Employers also seek people who have had experience in the military police or in State and local police departments. Most persons entering guard jobs have prior work experience, although it is usually unrelated. Because of limited formal training requirements and flexible hours, this occupation attracts some persons seeking a second job. For some entrants—for example, those retired from military careers or other protective services—guard employment is a second career.

Applicants are expected to have good character references, no police record, good health—especially in hearing and vision—and good personal habits such as neatness and dependability. They should be mentally alert, emotionally stable, and physically fit in order to cope with emergencies. Guards who have frequent contact with the public should be friendly and personable. Some employers require applicants to take a polygraph examination or a written test of honesty, attitudes, and other personal qualities. Many employers require applicants and experienced workers to submit to drug screening tests as a condition of employment.

Candidates for guard jobs in the Federal Government must have some experience as a guard and pass a written examination. Armed Forces experience also is an asset. For most Federal guard positions, applicants must qualify in the use of firearms.

The amount of training guards receive varies. Training requirements generally are increasing as modern, highly sophisticated security systems become more commonplace. Many employers give newly hired guards instruction before they start the job and also provide several weeks of on-the-job training. More and more States are making ongoing training a legal requirement. For example, New York State now requires guards to complete 40 hours of training after starting work. Illinois requires 20 hours for unarmed guards, plus an additional 20 hours for armed guards. Guards receive training in protection, public relations, report writing, crisis deterrence, first aid, drug control, and specialized training relevant to their particular assignment. Guards employed at establishments that place a heavy emphasis on security usually receive extensive formal training. For example, guards at nuclear power plants may undergo several months of training before being placed on duty under close supervision. Guards may be taught to use firearms, administer first aid, operate alarm systems and electronic security equipment, and spot and deal with security problems. Guards who are authorized to carry firearms may be periodically tested in their use according to State or local laws. Some guards are periodically tested for strength and endurance.

Although guards in small companies receive periodic salary increases, advancement is likely to be limited. However, most large organizations use a military type of ranking that offers advancement in position and salary. Higher level guard experience may enable persons to transfer to police jobs that offer higher pay and greater opportunities for advancement. Guards with some college education may advance to jobs that involve administrative and management duties. A few guards with management skills open their own contract security guard agencies.

Job Outlook

Job openings for persons seeking work as guards are expected to be plentiful through the year 2005. High turnover and this occupation's large size ranks it among those providing the greatest number of job openings in the entire economy. Many opportunities are expected for persons seeking full-time employment, as well as for those seeking part-time or second jobs at night or on weekends. However, some competition is expected for the higher paying in-house guard positions. Compared to contract security guards, in-house guards enjoy higher earnings and benefits, greater job security, and more advancement potential, and are usually given more training and responsibility.

Employment of guards is expected to grow much faster than the average for all occupations through the year 2005. Increased concern about crime, vandalism, and terrorism will heighten the need for security in and around plants, stores, offices, and recreation areas. The level of business investment in increasingly expensive plant and equipment, including sophisticated computer systems, is expected to rise, resulting in growth in the number of guard jobs. Demand for guards will also grow as private security firms increasingly perform duties—such as monitoring crowds at airports and providing security in courts—formerly handled by government police officers and marshals. Because engaging the services of a security guard firm is easier and less costly than assuming direct responsibility for hiring, training, and managing a security guard force, job growth is expected to be concentrated among contract security guard agencies.

Guards employed by industrial security and guard agencies occasionally are laid off when the firm at which they work does not renew its contract with their agency. Most are able to find employment with other agencies, however. Guards employed directly by the firm at which they work are seldom laid off because a plant or factory must still be protected even when economic conditions force it to close temporarily.

Earnings

According to a survey of workplaces in 160 metropolitan areas, guards with the least responsibilty and training had median hourly earnings of $6.00 in 1993. The middle half earned between $5.00 and $7.35 an hour. Guards with more specialized training and experience had median hourly earnings of $11.20.

Unionized in-house guards tend to earn more than the average. Many guards are represented by the United Plant Guard Workers Of America. Other guards belong to the International Guards Union of America or the International Union Of Security Officers.

Depending on their experience, newly hired guards in the Federal Government earned $14,900 or $16,700 a year in 1995. Beginning salaries were slightly higher in selected areas where the prevailing local pay level was higher. Guards employed by the Federal Government averaged about $23,300 a year in 1995. These workers usually receive overtime pay as well as a wage differential for the second and third shifts.

Related Occupations

Guards protect property, maintain security, and enforce regulations for entry and conduct in the establishments at which they work. Related security and protective service occupations include bailiffs, border guards, correction officers, deputy sheriffs, fish and game wardens, house or store detectives, police officers, and private investigators.

Sources of Additional Information

Further information about work opportunities for guards is available from local detective and guard firms and the nearest State employment service office.

Information about licensing requirements for guards may be obtained from the State licensing commission or the State police department. In States where local jurisdictions establish licensing requirements, contact a local government authority such as the sheriff, county executive, or city manager.

Police, Detectives, and Special Agents

(D.O.T. 168.167-010; 372.167-018, .267, .363 and .367-010; 375.133, .137 except -022 and -038, .163, .167 except -018, -026, and -054, .263, .264, .267, .363 through .384, and .587-010; 376.167 and .667-018; 377; and 379.167 and .263-014)

Nature of the Work

Police officers, detectives, and special agents are responsible for enforcing statutes, laws, and regulations designed to protect life and property. Many law enforcement officers spend much of their time interviewing witnesses and suspects, apprehending fugitives and criminals, collecting evidence, and providing testimony in court. After being incarcerated, many individuals are held under the care of correctional officers. (See the statement on correctional officers elsewhere in the *Handbook.*) Others spend most of their time patrolling a designated area to preserve the peace and to prevent crime. They resolve problems within the community and enforce laws governing motor vehicle operations. All law enforcement officers are required to file reports of their activities, often involving long hours of paperwork. In most jurisdictions, whether on or off duty, these officers are expected to exercise their authority whenever necessary.

In recent years, American voters have expressed their desire for government to place increasing emphasis on law enforcement efforts to reduce serious crime. As one response to serious crime, law enforcement officers are becoming more involved in community policing—building partnerships with the citizens of high-crime, urban neighborhoods, thus increasing public confidence in the police and mobilizing the public to help the police fight crime. Through the use of government, volunteer, and commercial resources, police encourage people in the community to help identify and solve recurring problems. This involves making the police officer a permanent, highly visible figure in the neighborhood rather than merely an officer reacting to a crime.

Police officers and detectives who work in small communities and rural areas have general law enforcement duties. In the course of a day's work, they may direct traffic at the scene of a fire, investigate a burglary, or give first aid to an accident victim. In large police departments and Federal agencies, officers and special agents usually are assigned to a specific detail for a fixed length of time. Some may become experts in chemical and microscopic analysis, firearms identification, handwriting and fingerprint identification, or serve on mounted and motorcycle patrol, harbor patrol, canine corps, special weapons and tactics or emergency response teams, or task forces formed to combat specific types of crime.

Sheriffs and *deputy sheriffs* generally enforce the law in rural areas or places where there is no local police department. They may serve legal processes of courts. Sheriffs' duties resemble those of local or county police departments, but generally on a smaller scale. Most sheriffs' departments employ fewer than 25 sworn officers, and many employ fewer than 10.

Detectives and special agents work as plainclothes investigators, gathering facts and collecting evidence for criminal cases. They conduct interviews, examine records, observe the activities of suspects, and participate in raids or arrests.

Special agents employed by the U.S. Department of Justice work for the Drug Enforcement Administration, the Federal Bureau of Investigation, the U.S. Border Patrol, and the U.S. Marshals Service. *Drug Enforcement Administration (DEA) special agents* specialize in enforcement of drug laws and regulations. Agents may conduct complex criminal investigations, carry out surveillance of criminals, and infiltrate illicit drug organizations using undercover techniques. They may work closely with confidential sources of information to collect evidence leading to the seizure of assets gained from the sale of illegal drugs. *Federal Bureau of Investigation (FBI) special agents* are the Government's principal investigators, responsible for investigating violations of more than 260 statutes. Agents may be required to do surveillance, monitor court-authorized wiretaps, examine business records to investigate white-collar crime, track the interstate movement of stolen property, collect evidence of espionage activities, or be assigned to sensitive undercover assignments designed to apprehend terrorists. Some special agents investigate violations of Federal laws in connection with bank robberies, theft of Government property, organized crime, espionage, sabotage, kidnapping, and terrorism. Agents with specialized training usually work on cases related to their background. For example, agents with an accounting background may investigate bank embezzlements or fraudulent bankruptcies. *U.S. marshals and deputy marshals* provide security for Federal courts, including judges, witnesses, and prisoners. They apprehend fugitives and operate the Special Operations Group (SOG)—a tactical unit which responds to high-threat and emergency situations. Some deputies provide security to the Department of Defense and the U.S. Air Force during movements of missiles between military facilities. *U.S. Border Patrol special agents* are responsible for protecting more than 8,000 miles of international land and water boundaries. Their primary mission is to detect and prevent the smuggling and unlawful entry of undocumented aliens into the United States and to apprehend those persons found in violation of the immigration laws. The Border Patrol is the primary interdicting agency along the land borders between the ports of entry for illicit drugs and various contraband. They accomplish their mission through activities such as: tracking, traffic checks on roads and highways leading away from the border, and participating in various task force operations with other law enforcement agencies.

Special agents employed by the U.S. Department of the Treasury work for The Bureau of Alcohol, Tobacco, and Firearms, the U.S. Customs Service, Internal Revenue Service, and U.S. Secret Service. *Bureau of Alcohol, Tobacco, and Firearms (BATF) special agents* investigate violations of Federal explosives laws, including bombings and arson-for-profit schemes affecting interstate commerce. They may investigate suspected illegal sales, possession, or use of firearms. Other BATF agents investigate violations related to the illegal sale of liquor and interstate smuggling of untaxed cigarettes. These investigations involve surveillance, participation in raids, interviewing suspects, and searching for physical evidence. *Customs agents* enforce laws to prevent smuggling of goods across U.S. borders. *Internal Revenue Service special agents* collect evidence against individuals and companies that are evading the payment of Federal taxes. *U.S. Secret Service special agents* are charged with two main missions—protection and investigation. During the course of their careers, they may be assigned to protect the President, Vice President, and their immediate families, Presidential candidates, ex-Presidents, and foreign dignitaries visiting the United States. Secret Service agents also investigate counterfeiting, the forgery of Government checks or bonds, and the fraudulent use of credit cards.

Special agents employed by the U.S. Department of State work for the Diplomatic Security Service. *Diplomatic Security Service special agents* advise ambassadors on security matters and manage a complex range of security programs overseas. In the United States, they investigate passport and visa fraud, conduct personnel security investigations, issue security clearances, and protect the Secretary of State and certain foreign dignitaries. They train foreign civilian police who then return to their own countries better able to fight terrorism.

Various other Federal agencies employ special agents with sworn police powers and the authority to carry firearms and make arrests. These agencies generally evolved from the need for security for the agency's property and personnel. The largest such agency is the Federal Protective Service, which has personnel nationwide. Other examples include the U.S. Mint police, the Government Printing Service police, and the Central Intelligence Agency's Special Protective Service.

State police officers (sometimes called State troopers or highway patrol officers) patrol highways and enforce motor vehicle laws and regulations. They issue traffic citations to motorists who violate the law. At the scene of an accident, they may direct traffic, give first aid, and call for emergency equipment. They also write reports that may be used to determine the cause of the accident. In addition, State police officers may provide services to motorists on the highways, such as calling for road service for drivers with mechanical trouble.

State police also enforce criminal laws. They are frequently called upon to render assistance to officers of other law enforcement agencies. In rural areas that do not have a police force or a local representative from the sheriff's department, the State police are the primary law enforcement agency, investigating any crimes that occur, such as burglary or assault.

Most new police recruits begin their careers in an urban setting. They generally start on patrol duty, riding in a police vehicle. In smaller agencies, they may work alone; in larger agencies, they ride with experienced officers. Patrols generally cover an area such as old and congested business districts or outlying residential neighborhoods. Officers attempt to become thoroughly familiar with conditions throughout their patrol area and, while on patrol, remain alert for anything unusual. They note suspicious circumstances, such as open windows or lights in vacant buildings, as well as hazards to public safety. Officers on patrol enforce traffic regulations and also watch for stolen vehicles and wanted individuals. At regular intervals, officers report to police headquarters by radio, or by telephone when they are imparting information that is confidential, since scanners which pick up police radio communications are in popular usage.

Regardless of where they work, police, detectives, and special agents spend considerable time writing reports and maintaining records. They are called to testify in court when their arrests result in legal action. Some senior officers, such as chief inspectors, commanders, division and bureau chiefs, and agents-in-charge, are responsible for operation of geographic divisions of an agency, certain kinds of criminal investigations, and various agency functions. Such managers have administrative and supervisory duties.

Working Conditions

Police, detectives, and special agents usually work a 40-hour week, but paid overtime work is common. Shift work is necessary because police protection must be provided around the clock. More junior officers frequently must work weekends, holidays, and nights. Police officers, detectives, and special agents are subject to call at any time

Educational requirements for law enforcement professionals have increased in recent years.

their services are needed and may work long hours during criminal investigations.

The jobs of some special agents such as U.S. Secret Service and DEA special agents require extensive travel, often on very short notice.

Some police, detectives, and special agents with agencies such as the U.S. Border Patrol have to work outdoors for long periods in all kinds of weather. While police work is inherently dangerous, good training, team work, and equipment such as bullet-resistant vests minimize the number of injuries and fatalities. The risks associated with pursuing speeding motorists, apprehending criminals, and dealing with public disorders can be very stressful for the officer as well as for his or her family.

Employment

Police, detectives, and special agents held about 682,000 jobs in 1994. About 81 percent were employed by local governments, primarily in cities with more than 25,000 inhabitants. Some cities have very large police forces, while hundreds of small communities employ fewer than 25 officers each. State police agencies employed about 13 percent of all police, detectives, and special agents; various Federal agencies employed an additional 6 percent. There are about 17,000 Federal, State, special (such as park police, transit police, and county police) and local police agencies in the Nation.

Training, Other Qualifications, and Advancement

Civil service regulations govern the appointment of police and detectives in practically all State and large city agencies and in many smaller ones. Candidates must be U.S. citizens, usually at least 20 years of age, and must meet rigorous physical and personal qualifications. Eligibility for appointment generally depends on performance in competitive written examinations as well as on education and experience. Physical examinations often include tests of vision, hearing, strength, and agility.

Because personal characteristics such as honesty, judgment, integrity, and a sense of responsibility are especially important in law enforcement work, candidates are interviewed by senior officers, and their character traits and background are investigated. In some agencies, candidates are interviewed by a psychiatrist or a psychologist, or given a personality test. Most applicants are subjected to lie detector examinations and drug testing. Some agencies subject sworn personnel to random drug testing as a condition of continuing employment. Although police, detectives, and special agents work independently, they must perform their duties in accordance with the law and departmental rules. They should enjoy working with people and meeting the public.

In larger police departments, where the majority of law enforcement jobs are found, applicants usually must have at least a high school education. A small but growing proportion of local, special, and State departments require some college training. Some agencies hire police science or criminal justice students as police interns or cadets; some police departments and virtually all Federal agencies require a college degree. A few police departments accept applicants as recruits who have less than a high school education, but the number is declining.

The Federal agency with the largest number of special agents is the FBI. To be considered for appointment as an FBI special agent, an applicant either must be a graduate of an accredited law school; be a college graduate with a major in accounting; or be a college graduate with either fluency in a foreign language or 3 years of full-time work experience. Applicants must be U.S. citizens, possess a valid driver's license, be between 23 and 37 years of age at the time of appointment, and be willing to accept an assignment anywhere in the United States. They also must be in excellent physical condition with at least 20/200 vision corrected to 20/40 in one eye and 20/20 in the other eye. All new agents undergo 16 weeks of training at the FBI academy on the U.S. Marine Corps base in Quantico, Virginia.

Applicants for special agent jobs with the U.S. Department of Treasury's Secret Service and BATF must have a bachelor's degree, or a minimum of 3 years' work experience which demonstrates the ability to deal effectively with individuals or groups, collect and assemble pertinent facts, and prepare clear and concise reports. Candidates must be in excellent physical condition and be less than 37 years of age at the time they enter the agency unless they have previous qualifying Federal law enforcement experience. Prospective special agents undergo 8 weeks of training at the Federal Law Enforcement Training Center in Glynco, Georgia, and another 8-11 weeks of specialized training with their particular agencies.

Applicants for special agent jobs with the U.S. Drug Enforcement Administration must be U.S. citizens, have a college degree in any field and either 1 year of experience conducting criminal investigations, 1 year of graduate school, or have achieved at least a 2.95 grade point average while in college. The minimum age for entry is 21 and the maximum age is 37 unless they have previous qualifying Federal law enforcement experience. DEA special agents undergo 14 weeks of specialized training at the FBI Academy in Quantico, Virginia.

More and more, police departments are encouraging applicants to take postsecondary school training in law enforcement. Many entry level applicants to police jobs have completed some formal postsecondary education and a significant number are college graduates. Many junior colleges, colleges, and universities offer programs in law enforcement or administration of justice. Other courses helpful in preparing for a career in law enforcement include accounting, finance, electrical engineering or computer science, and foreign languages. Physical education and sports are helpful in developing the competitiveness, stamina, and agility needed for law enforcement work. Knowledge of a foreign language is an asset in many agencies.

Some large cities hire high school graduates who are still in their teens as police cadets or trainees. They do clerical work and attend classes, and can be appointed to the regular force at the conclusion of their training, usually in 1 to 2 years, upon reaching the minimum age requirement.

Before their first assignments, officers usually go through a period of training. In small agencies, recruits often get on the job training with more experienced officers, rather than formal training. In State and large local departments, they get training at a police academy for 12 to 14 weeks, as mandated by the State. This training includes classroom instruction in constitutional law and civil rights, State laws and local ordinances, and accident investigation. Recruits also receive training and supervised experience in patrol, traffic control, use of firearms, self-defense, first aid, and handling emergencies.

Police officers usually become eligible for promotion after a probationary period ranging from 6 months to 3 years. In a large department, promotion may enable an officer to become a detective or specialize in one type of police work such as laboratory analysis of evidence, traffic control, communications, or working with juveniles. Promotions to sergeant, lieutenant, and captain usually are made according to a candidate's position on a promotion list, as determined by scores on a written examination and on-the-job performance, and are very competitive.

Continuing training helps police officers, detectives, and special agents improve their job performance. Through police department academies, regional centers for public safety employees established by the States, and Federal agency training centers, instructors provide annual training in defensive tactics, firearms, use-of-force policies, sensitivity and communications skills, crowd-control techniques, legal developments that affect their work, and advances in law enforcement equipment. Many agencies pay all or part of the tuition for officers to work toward degrees in law enforcement, police science, administration of justice, or public administration, and pay higher salaries to those who earn such a degree.

Job Outlook
The opportunity for public service through law enforcement work is attractive to many. The job is challenging and involves much personal responsibility. Furthermore, in many agencies, law enforcement officers may retire with a pension after 20 or 25 years of service, allowing them to pursue a second career while still in their 40s. Because of relatively attractive salaries and benefits, the number of qualified candidates exceeds the number of job openings in Federal law enforcement agencies and in most State, local, and special police departments—resulting in increased hiring standards and selectivity by employers. Competition is expected to remain keen for the higher paying jobs with State and Federal agencies and police departments in more affluent areas. Persons having college training in police science, military experience, or both should have the best opportunities. Opportunities will be best in those urban communities whose departments offer relatively low salaries and where the crime rate is relatively high. Such departments are having difficulty attracting an adequate supply of high quality police officer candidates. Competition is extremely keen for special agent positions with the Justice and Treasury Departments and other Federal law enforcement agencies. Positions with these prestigious agencies tend to attract a far greater number of applicants than the number of job openings. Consequently, only the most highly qualified candidates obtain jobs.

Employment of police officers, detectives, and special agents is expected to increase faster than average for all occupations through the year 2005. A more security-conscious society and growing concern about drug-related crimes should contribute to the increasing demand for police services. At the local and State levels, growth is likely to continue as long as crime remains a serious concern. However, employment growth at the Federal level will be tempered by continuing budgetary constraints faced by law enforcement agencies. Turnover in police, detective, and special agent positions is among the lowest of all occupations; nevertheless, the need to replace workers who retire, transfer to other occupations, or stop working for other reasons will be the source of most job openings.

The level of government spending determines the level of employment for police officers, detectives, and special agents. The number of job opportunities, therefore, can vary from year to year and from place to place. Layoffs, on the other hand, are rare because retirements enable most staffing cuts to be handled through attrition. Trained law enforcement officers who lose their jobs because of budget cuts usually have little difficulty finding jobs with other agencies.

Earnings

In 1994, the median salary of nonsupervisory police officers and detectives was about $34,000 a year. The middle 50 percent earned between about $25,500 and $43,900; the lowest 10 percent were paid less than $17,900, while the highest 10 percent earned over $56,100 a year. Generally, salaries tend to be higher in urban, more affluent jurisdictions, which usually have best funded police departments.

Police officers and detectives in supervisory positions had a median salary of about $42,800 a year, also in 1994. The middle 50 percent earned between about $30,100 and $52,500; the lowest 10 percent were paid less than $19,800, while the highest 10 percent earned over $62,100 annually.

Sheriffs and other law enforcement officers had a median annual salary of about $26,800 in 1994. The middle 50 percent earned between about $20,800 and $37,200; the lowest 10 percent were paid less than $16,500, while the highest 10 percent earned over $48,600.

Federal law provides special salary rates to Federal employees who serve in law enforcement. Additionally, many Federal special agents receive administratively uncontrolled overtime (AUO)—equal to 25 percent of the agent's grade and step—awarded because of the large amount of overtime that these agents are expected to work. For example, in 1995 FBI agents started at a base salary of $31,200 a year, therefore earning $39,000 a year with AUO. Other Justice and Treasury Department special agents started at about $23,200 or $28,300 a year, therefore earning $29,000 or 35,400 per year including AUO, depending on their qualifications. Salaries of Justice and Treasury Department special agents progress to $66,800 including AUO, while supervisory agents started at $61,100 including AUO. Salaries were slightly higher in selected areas where the prevailing local pay level was higher. Since Federal agents may be eligible for a special law enforcement benefits package, applicants should ask their recruiter for more information.

Total earnings for local, State, and special police detectives frequently exceed the stated salary due to payments for overtime, which can be significant. In addition to the common benefits—paid vacation, sick leave, and medical and life insurance—most police and sheriffs' departments provide officers with special allowances for uniforms and furnish weapons, handcuffs, and other required equipment. In addition, because police officers generally are covered by liberal pension plans, many retire at half-pay after 20 or 25 years of service.

Related Occupations

Police, detectives, and special agents maintain law and order. Workers in related occupations include correctional officers, guards, fire marshals, and inspectors.

Sources of Additional Information

Information about entrance requirements may be obtained from Federal, State, and local law enforcement agencies.

Further information about qualifications for employment as an FBI Special Agent is available from the nearest State FBI office; the address and phone number are listed in the local telephone directory.

Information about career opportunities, qualifications, and training to become a deputy marshal is available from:

☛United States Marshals Service, Employment and Compensation Division, Field Staffing Branch, 600 Army Navy Dr., Arlington, VA 22202.

Information on careers as a DEA Special Agent may be obtained from:

☛Drug Enforcement Administration, Special Agent Staffing Unit, Washington, DC 20537.

An overview of career opportunities, qualifications, and training for U.S. Secret Service Special Agents is available from:

☛Secret Service, Personnel, 1800 G St. NW., Washington, DC 20223.

Private Detectives and Investigators

(D.O.T. 189.167-054; 343.367-014; 376.137, .267; 367; and .667-014)

Nature of the Work

Private detectives and investigators assist attorneys, government agencies, businesses, and the public with a variety of problems, such as gathering facts, tracing debtors, or conducting background investigations. The main job of private investigators and some private detectives is to obtain information and locate assets or individuals. Some private detectives protect stores and hotels from theft, vandalism, and disorder.

Private detectives working as general investigators have duties ranging from locating missing persons to exposing fraudulent workers' compensation claims. Some investigators specialize in one field, such as finance, where they might use accounting skills to investigate the financial standing of a company or locate funds stolen by an embezzler.

About half of all private investigators are self-employed or work for detective agencies. They specialize in missing persons, infidelity, and background investigations, including financial profiles and asset searches; physical surveillance; on-line computer database searches; and insurance investigations. They may obtain information, interview witnesses, and assemble evidence for litigation or criminal trials. They get cases from clients or are assigned to cases by the owner or manager of the firm.

Many investigators spend considerable time conducting surveillance, seeking to observe inconsistencies in a subject's behavior. For example, a person who has recently filed a workers' compensation claim that an injury has made walking difficult should not be able to jog or mow the lawn. If such behavior is observed, the investigator takes video or still photographs to document the activity and reports back to the supervisor or client.

"Stakeouts" are a common form of surveillance. On a stakeout, an investigator regularly observes a site, such as the home of a subject, until the desired evidence is obtained. The investigator sits in a car or other inconspicuous location. They are equipped with cameras—including still and video cameras—binoculars, and a citizen's band radio or a car phone.

Some investigations involve verification of facts, such as an individual's place of employment or income. This might involve a phone call or a visit to the workplace. In other investigations, especially in missing persons cases, the investigator interviews people to learn as much as possible about someone's previous movements. These interviews can be formal or informal and sometimes turn into confrontations if the person is uncooperative.

Legal investigators specialize in cases involving the courts and lawyers. To assist in preparing criminal defenses, investigators locate witnesses, interview police, gather and review evidence, take photographs, and testify in court. To assist attorneys in the preparation of litigation for injured parties, they interview prospective witnesses, collect information on the parties to the litigation, and search out testimonial, documentary, or physical evidence.

Corporate investigators work for companies other than investigative firms—often large corporations. In contrast to most private investigators, they report to a corporate chain of command. They conduct internal or external investigations. External investigations consist of preventing criminal schemes, thefts of company assets, and fraudulent deliveries of products by suppliers. In internal investigations, they insure that expense accounts are not abused and catch employees who are stealing.

Investigators who specialize in finance may be hired to investigate the financial standing of companies or individuals. These investigators often work with investment bankers and lawyers. They generally develop confidential financial profiles of individuals or companies who may be parties to large financial transactions. An asset search is a common type of such an investigation.

Private detectives and investigators who work for large retail stores or malls are responsible for loss control and asset protection. *Store detectives* safeguard the assets of retail stores by apprehending persons attempting to steal merchandise or destroy store property. They detect theft by shoplifters, vendor representatives, delivery personnel, and even store employees. Store detectives also conduct periodic inspections of stock areas, dressing rooms, and rest rooms, and sometimes assist in the opening and closing of the store. They may prepare loss prevention and security reports for management and testify in court against persons they apprehend.

Computers have changed the nature of this profession and have become an integral part of investigative work. They allow investigators to obtain massive amounts of information in a short period of time from the dozens of on-line data bases containing probate records, motor-vehicle registrations, credit reports, association membership lists, and, other information.

Working Conditions

Private investigators often work irregular hours. Early morning, evening, weekend, and holiday work is common. The irregular hours result from the need to conduct surveillance and contact people who may not be available during normal working hours. Investigators who work solely for insurance companies and corporate investigators have more normal work hours.

Many investigators spend much time away from their offices conducting interviews or doing surveillance, but some work in their office most of the day conducting computer searches and making phone calls. Corporate investigators often split their time between the office and the field; work done in the office generally consists of computer research.

When away from the office, the environment might range from plush boardrooms to seedy bars. Store and hotel detectives work mostly in the businesses that they protect. Investigators generally work alone, but sometimes work with others during surveillance or stake-outs.

Much of the work that detectives and investigators do can be confrontational because the person being observed may not want to be observed. As a result, the job can be quite stressful and sometimes dangerous. Some investigators carry handguns, but most do not since it is difficult to obtain a permit to carry a concealed weapon in many jurisdictions. Owners of investigations firms have the added stress of having to deal with demanding and sometimes distraught clients.

Employment

Private detectives and investigators held about 55,000 jobs in 1994.

Most jurisdictions require that private detectives be licensed.

About 20 percent were self employed. About 34 percent of wage and salary workers worked for detective agencies and about 40 percent were employed as store detectives in department or clothing and accessories stores. Others worked for hotels and other lodging places, legal services firms, and many other industries.

Training, Other Qualifications, and Advancement

There are no formal education requirements for most private detective and investigator jobs, although most employers prefer high school graduates and many private detectives have college degrees. Some private detectives and investigators get their entry-level training on the job while working for insurance or collections companies or in the security industry. Many investigators enter from the military or law enforcement jobs and apply their experience as law enforcement officers, military police, or government agents. Other investigators enter from such diverse fields as finance, accounting, investigative reporting, insurance, and law. These individuals often can apply their prior work experience in a related investigation specialty.

The vast majority of States and the District of Colombia require that private investigators be licensed. Licensing requirements vary widely among the States, but, in most, the State police is the licensing authority. Some States have very liberal requirements, while others have stringent regulations. For example, the California Department of Consumer Affairs Bureau of Security and Investigative Services requires 6,000 hours of investigative experience, a background check, a qualifying score on a written examination, payment of a $50 application fee and a $32 fingerprint fee, and payment of an annual $175 license fee upon approval. In contrast, other States may have little or no licensing requirements. A growing number of States are enacting mandatory training programs for private investigators. In States that require licensing, a felony conviction generally disqualifies a candidate from being granted a license.

In most investigations firms, the screening process for potential employees includes a background check, consisting of confirmation of education, work experience, and criminal history, and interviews with references and others known to the applicant. Corporate and industrial security positions may require a criminal history check, a personal interview, an ethics interview, a practical test, verification of education claims, and license review as well as personal and employment references checks.

For private detective and investigator jobs, most employers look for individuals with ingenuity who are aggressive, persistent, and assertive. A candidate must not be afraid of being confrontational, should communicate well, and should be able to think on his or her feet. The courts are often the ultimate judge of a properly conducted investigation, so the investigator must be able to present the facts in a manner a jury will believe.

Training in subjects such as criminal justice are helpful to the aspiring private detective. Most corporate investigators must have a bachelor's degree, preferably in a business-related field. Some corporate investigators have Masters of Business Administration or law degrees, while others are Certified Public Accountants.

Corporate investigators hired by larger companies may receive formal training from their employers on business practices, management structure, and various finance related topics. Interview and interrogation training is frequently included.

Most investigations firms are small, with little room for advancement. Usually there are no defined ranks or steps, so advancement is in terms of salary and assignment status. Many investigators work for an investigations firm in the beginning of their investigative careers and after a few years try to start their own investigations firms. Corporate and legal investigators may rise to supervisor or manager of the security or investigations department.

Job Outlook

Employment of private detectives and investigators is expected to grow much faster than average for all occupations through the year

2005. In addition, job turnover should create many additional job openings, particularly among wage and salary workers. Nevertheless, competition is expected for the available openings because private detective and investigator careers are attractive to many.

Demand for private detectives and investigators is expected to be generated by increases in the size of the population, increased economic activity, and global and domestic competition. These forces are expected to produce increases in crime, litigation, and the need for confidential information of all kinds. As crime continues to increase, more firms will hire or contract for the service of private detectives. Drug abuse continues to be a problem in our society, contributing to the high crime rate, and some companies will hire private investigators to determine the extent of their internal drug problems. Additional private detectives and investigators will be needed to meet the needs for information associated with criminal defenses and litigation among companies and individuals. Greater financial activity also will increase the demand for investigators. In addition, as competition becomes more intense, growing numbers of companies will hire investigators to control internal and external financial losses, as well as to find out what their competitors are doing and to prevent industrial spying.

In spite of the rapid growth in employment of private detectives and investigators, competition should continue to be very intense for full-time, salaried job openings due to a large supply of workers qualified for these jobs. Many individuals leave law enforcement, military, and intelligence jobs in the public sector, often at a relatively young age, and decide to become private investigators. Opportunities should be best for entry-level jobs as store detectives or with detective agencies on a part-time basis. Persons seeking store detective jobs may find the best opportunities with private guard and security firms since some retail businesses are replacing their own workers with outside contract workers.

Earnings

Earnings of private detectives and investigators vary greatly depending on their employer, specialty, and geographic area in which they work. According to a study by Abbott, Langer & Associates, private investigators averaged about $36,700 a year in 1993, and store detectives about $16,100.

According to other limited information, legal investigators earned an estimated $15,000 to $18,000 a year to start, and experienced legal investigators earned $20,000 to $35,000. Entry level corporate investigators earned an estimated $40,000 to $45,000 annually, and experienced corporate investigators, $50,000 to $55,000.

Most private investigator bill their clients between $50 and $150 per hour to conduct investigations. Most private investigators, except for those working for large corporations, do not receive paid vacation or sick days, health or life insurance, retirement packages, or other benefits. Investigators are usually reimbursed for expenses and generally given a car allowance.

Most corporate investigators received health insurance, pension plans, profit-sharing plans, and paid vacation.

Related Occupations

Private detectives and investigators often collect information and protect property and assets of companies. Others with related concerns include security guards, insurance claims examiners, inspectors, collectors, and law enforcement officers. Corporate investigators and investigators who specialize in conducting financial profiles and asset searches do work closely related to that of accountants and financial analysts.

Sources of Additional Information

Most States have associations for private detectives and investigators that provide career information. For information on local licensing requirements, contact your local State police headquarters.

Food and Beverage Preparation and Service Occupations

Chefs, Cooks, and Other Kitchen Workers

(D.O.T. 311.674-014; 313 except .131; 315.361, .371, and .381; 316.661 and .684-014; 317; 318.687; and 319.484)

Nature of the Work

A reputation for serving good food is essential to any restaurant, whether it prides itself on hamburgers and french fries or exotic foreign cuisine. Chefs, cooks, and other kitchen workers are largely responsible for the reputation a restaurant acquires. Some restaurants offer a varied menu featuring meals that are time consuming and difficult to prepare, requiring a highly skilled cook or chef. Other restaurants emphasize fast service, offering hamburgers and sandwiches that can be prepared in advance or in a few minutes by a fast-food or short-order cook with only limited cooking skills.

Chefs and cooks are responsible for preparing meals that are pleasing to the palate and the eye. Chefs are the most highly skilled, trained, and experienced of all kitchen workers. Although the terms chef and cook are still used interchangeably, cooks are less skilled. Many chefs have earned fame for both themselves and the establishments where they work due to their skillful preparation of traditional dishes and refreshing twists in creating new ones. (For information

on *executive chefs*, see the *Handbook* statement on restaurant and food service managers.)

Institutional chefs and cooks work in the kitchens of schools, industrial cafeterias, hospitals, and other institutions. For each meal, they prepare a small selection, but large quantity of entrees, vegetables, and desserts. *Restaurant chefs and cooks* generally prepare a wider selection of dishes for each meal, cooking most orders individually. Whether in institutions or restaurants, chefs and cooks measure, mix, and cook ingredients according to recipes. In the course of their work they use a variety of pots, pans, cutlery, and equipment, including ovens, broilers, grills, slicers, grinders, and blenders. They are often responsible for directing the work of other kitchen workers, estimating food requirements, and ordering food supplies. Some chefs and cooks also assist in planning meals and developing menus.

Bread and pastry bakers, called pastry chefs in some kitchens, produce baked goods for restaurants, institutions, and retail bakery shops. Unlike bakers who work in large, automated industrial bakeries, bread and pastry bakers need only to supply the customers who visit their establishment. They bake smaller quantities of breads, rolls, pastries, pies, and cakes, doing most of the work by hand. They measure and mix ingredients, shape and bake the dough, and apply fillings and decorations.

Short-order cooks prepare foods to order in restaurants and coffee shops that emphasize fast service. They grill and garnish hamburgers, prepare sandwiches, fry eggs, and cook french fried potatoes, often working on several orders at the same time. Prior to busy periods, they may slice meats and cheeses or prepare coleslaw or potato salad. During slow periods, they may clean the grill, food preparation surfaces, counters, and floors.

Specialty fast-food cooks prepare a limited selection of menu items in fast-food restaurants. They cook and package batches of food such as hamburgers and fried chicken, which are prepared to order or kept warm until sold.

Other kitchen workers, under the direction of chefs and cooks, perform tasks requiring less skill. They weigh and measure ingredients, fetch pots and pans, and stir and strain soups and sauces. They clean, peel, and slice potatoes, other vegetables, and fruits and make salads. They may cut and grind meats, poultry, and seafood in preparation for cooking. Their responsibilities also include cleaning work areas, equipment and utensils, and dishes and silverware.

The number and types of workers employed in kitchens depends on the type of establishment. For example, fast-food outlets offer only a few items, which are prepared by fast-food cooks. Smaller, full-service restaurants offering a casual dining atmosphere often feature a limited number of easy-to-prepare items, supplemented by short-order specialties and ready-made desserts. Typically, one cook prepares all of the food with the help of a short-order cook and one or two kitchen workers.

Large eating places tend to have varied menus and prepare more of the food they serve from start to finish. Kitchen staffs often include several chefs and cooks, sometimes called assistant or apprentice chefs or cooks, a bread and pastry baker, and many less skilled kitchen workers. Each chef or cook usually has a special assignment and often a special job title—vegetable, fry, or sauce cook, for example. Executive chefs coordinate the work of the kitchen staff and often direct the preparation of certain foods. They decide the size of servings, sometimes plan menus, and buy food supplies.

Working Conditions
Many restaurant and institutional kitchens have modern equipment, convenient work areas, and air-conditioning; but in older and smaller eating places, the kitchens often are not as well equipped. Working conditions depend on the type and quantity of food being prepared and the local laws governing food service operations. Workers generally must withstand the pressure and strain of working in close quarters, standing for hours at a time, lifting heavy pots and kettles, and working near hot ovens and grills. Job hazards include slips and falls, cuts, and burns, but injuries are seldom serious.

Work hours in restaurants may include late evenings, holidays, and weekends, while hours in factory, and school cafeterias may be more regular. Half of all short-order and fast-food cooks and other kitchen workers worked part time; a third of all bakers and restaurant and institutional cooks worked part time. Kitchen workers employed by public and private schools may work during the school year only, usually for 9 or 10 months. Similarly, establishments at vacation resorts generally only offer seasonal employment.

Employment
Chefs, cooks, and other kitchen workers held more than 3.2 million jobs in 1994. Short-order and fast-food cooks held 760,000 of the jobs; restaurant cooks, 704,000; institutional cooks, 412,000; bread and pastry bakers, 170,000; and other kitchen workers, 1,190,000.

About three-fifths of all chefs, cooks, and other kitchen workers were employed in restaurants and other retail eating and drinking places. One-fifth worked in institutions such as schools, universities, hospitals, and nursing homes. The remainder were employed by grocery stores, hotels, and many other organizations.

Training, Other Qualifications, and Advancement
Most kitchen workers start as fast-food or short-order cooks, or in one of the other less skilled kitchen positions. These positions

Chefs are often responsible for planning meals, estimating food requirements, and ordering supplies.

require little education or training and most skills are learned on the job. After acquiring some basic food handling, preparation, and cooking skills, they may be able to advance to an assistant cook or short-order cook position. To achieve the level of skill required of an executive chef or cook in a fine restaurant, many years of training and experience are necessary. Even though a high school diploma is not required for beginning jobs, it is recommended for those planning a career as a cook or chef. High school or vocational school courses in business arithmetic and business administration are particularly helpful.

Many school districts, in cooperation with State departments of education, provide on-the-job training and sometimes summer workshops for cafeteria kitchen workers with aspirations of becoming cooks. Employees who have participated in these training programs are often selected for jobs as cooks.

An increasing number of chefs and cooks obtain their training through high school, post-high school vocational programs, and 2- or 4-year colleges. Chefs and cooks also may be trained in apprenticeship programs offered by professional culinary institutes, industry associations, and trade unions. An example is the 3-year apprenticeship program administered by local chapters of the American Culinary Federation in cooperation with local employers and junior colleges or vocational education institutions. In addition, some large hotels and restaurants operate their own training programs for cooks and chefs.

People who have had courses in commercial food preparation may be able to start in a cook or chef job without having to spend time in a lower skilled kitchen job. Their education may give them an advantage when looking for jobs in better restaurants and hotels, where hiring standards often are high. Some vocational programs in high schools offer this kind of training, but usually these courses are given by trade schools, vocational centers, colleges, professional associations, and trade unions. Post secondary courses range from a few months to 2 years or more and are open in some cases only to high school graduates. The Armed Forces are also a good source of training and experience.

Although curricula may vary, students usually spend most of their time learning to prepare food through actual practice. They learn to bake, broil, and otherwise prepare food, and to use and care for kitchen equipment. Training programs often include courses in menu planning, determination of portion size, food cost control, purchasing food supplies in quantity, selection and storage of food, and use of leftover food to minimize waste. Students also learn hotel and restaurant sanitation and public health rules for handling food. Training in supervisory and management skills sometimes is emphasized in courses offered by private vocational schools, professional associations, and university programs.

Culinary courses are given by 550 schools across the Nation. The American Culinary Federation accredited 70 of these programs in 1993. Accreditation is an indication that a culinary program meets recognized standards regarding course content, facilities, and quality of instruction. The American Culinary Federation has only been accrediting culinary programs for a relatively short time, and many programs have yet to seek accreditation.

Certification provides valuable formal recognition of the skills of a chef or cook. The American Culinary Federation certifies chefs and cooks at the levels of cook, working chef, executive chef, and master chef. It also certifies pastry professionals and culinary educators. Certification standards are based primarily on experience and formal training.

Important qualifications for chefs, cooks, and other kitchen workers include the ability to work as part of a team, possessing a keen sense of taste and smell, and personal cleanliness. Most States require health certificates indicating workers are free from communicable diseases.

Advancement opportunities for chefs and cooks are better than for most other food and beverage preparation and service occupations. Many acquire higher paying positions and new cooking skills by moving from one job to another. Besides culinary skills, advancement also depends on ability to supervise lesser skilled workers and limit food costs by minimizing waste and accurately anticipating the amount of perishable supplies needed. Some cooks and chefs gradually advance to executive chef positions or supervisory or management positions, particularly in hotels, clubs, or larger, more elegant restaurants. Some eventually go into business as caterers or restaurant owners, while others become instructors in vocational programs in high schools, community colleges, and other academic institutions.

Job Outlook
Job openings for chefs, cooks, and other kitchen workers are expected to be plentiful through the year 2005. Growth in demand for these workers will create many new positions, but most openings will arise from the need to replace the high proportion of workers who leave this occupation every year. There is substantial turnover in many of these jobs because of the minimal educational and training requirements. The occupation also offers many part-time positions, attractive to people seeking a short-term source of income rather than a career. Many of the workers who leave these jobs transfer to other occupations, while others stop working to assume household responsibilities or to attend school full time.

Workers under the age of 25 have traditionally filled a significant proportion of the lesser skilled jobs in this occupation. The pool of young workers is expected to continue to shrink through the 1990's, but begin to expand after the year 2000. Many employers will be forced to offer higher wages, better benefits, and more training to attract and retain workers.

Employment of chefs, cooks, and other kitchen workers is expected to increase about as fast as the average for all occupations through the year 2005. Since a significant proportion of food and beverage sales by eating and drinking establishments is associated with the overall level of economic activity, sales and employment will increase with the growth of the economy. Other factors contributing to employment growth will be population growth, rising household incomes, and an increase in leisure time that will allow people to dine out and take vacations more often. As two income households are becoming more common, families may increasingly find dining out a convenience.

Employment in restaurants is expected to grow. As the average age of the population increases, demand will grow for restaurants that offer table service and more varied menus—which will require higher skilled cooks and chefs. The popularity of fresh baked breads and pastries in fine dining establishments should ensure continued rapid growth in the employment of bakers. However, employment of short-order and specialty fast-food cooks is expected to increase more slowly than other occupations in this group because most work in fast-food restaurants, which are expected to grow at a slower rate than in the past.

Employment of institutional and cafeteria chefs and cooks will grow more slowly than the average. Their employment is concentrated in the educational and health services sectors. Although employment in both sectors is expected to increase rapidly, growth of institutional and cafeteria cooks will not keep pace. Many high schools and hospitals are trying to make "institutional food" more attractive to students, staff, visitors, and patients. While some are employing more highly trained chefs and cooks to prepare more appealing meals, others are contracting out their food services. Many of the contracted companies emphasize fast-food and employ short-order and fast-food cooks instead of institutional and cafeteria cooks.

Earnings
Wages of chefs, cooks, and other kitchen workers depend greatly on the part of the country and the type of establishment in which they are employed. Wages generally are highest in elegant restaurants and hotels, with many executive chefs earning over $40,000 annually. According to a survey conducted by the National Restaurant Association, median hourly earnings of cooks in 1994 were $6.85, with most earning between $6.00 and $8.00. Assistant cooks had median hourly earnings of $6.25, with most earning between $5.50 and $7.00.

The same survey indicated that short-order cooks had median hourly earnings of $6.50 in 1994; most earned between $5.50 and $7.25. Median hourly earnings of bread and pastry bakers were $6.50; most earned within the range of $6.00 to $7.68. Salad preparation workers generally earned less, with median hourly earnings of $5.50; most earned between $5.25 and $6.50.

Some employers provide employees with uniforms and free meals, but Federal law permits employers to deduct from their employees' wages the cost or fair value of any meals or lodging provided, and some employers do so. Chefs, cooks, and other kitchen workers who work full time often receive paid vacation and sick leave and health insurance, but part-time workers generally do not.

In some large hotels and restaurants, kitchen workers belong to unions. The principal unions are the Hotel Employees and Restaurant Employees International Union and the Service Employees International Union.

Related Occupations
Workers who perform tasks similar to those of chefs, cooks, and other kitchen workers include butchers and meat cutters, cannery workers, and industrial bakers.

Sources of Additional Information

Information about job opportunities may be obtained from local employers and local offices of the State employment service.

Career information about chefs, cooks, and other kitchen workers, as well as a directory of 2- and 4-year colleges that offer courses or programs that prepare persons for food service careers, is available from:

☛The Educational Foundation of the National Restaurant Association, 250 South Wacker Dr., Suite 1400, Chicago, IL 60606.

For information on the American Culinary Federation's apprenticeship and certification programs for cooks, as well as a list of accredited culinary programs, write to:

☛American Culinary Federation, P.O. Box 3466, St. Augustine, FL 32085.

For general information on hospitality careers, write to:

☛Council on Hotel, Restaurant, and Institutional Education, 1200 17th St. NW., Washington, DC 20036-3097.

For general career information and a directory of accredited private career and technical schools offering programs in the culinary arts, write to:

☛Accrediting Commission of Career Schools and Colleges of Technology, 2101 Wilson Blvd., Suite 302, Arlington, VA 22201.

Food and Beverage Service Workers

(D.O.T. 310.137-010 and .357; 311.472, .477, .674-010, and -018, and .677; 312; 319.474, .677-014, and .687; 350.677-010, -026, -030; and 352.677-018)

Nature of the Work

Whether they work in small, informal diners or large, elegant restaurants, all food and beverage service workers deal with customers. The quality of service they deliver determines in part whether or not the patron will return.

Waiters and waitresses take customers' orders, serve food and beverages, prepare itemized checks, and sometimes accept payments. The manner in which they perform their tasks varies considerably, depending on the establishment where they work. In coffee shops, they are expected to provide fast and efficient, yet courteous, service. In fine restaurants, where gourmet meals are accompanied by attentive formal service, waiters and waitresses serve the meal at a more leisurely pace and offer more personal service to patrons. For example, they may recommend a certain kind of wine as a complement to a particular entree, explain how various items on the menu are prepared, or prepare some salads and other special dishes at table side.

Depending on the type of restaurant, waiters and waitresses may perform additional duties generally associated with other food and beverage service occupations. These tasks may include escorting guests to tables, serving customers seated at counters, setting up and clearing tables, or cashiering. However, larger or more formal restaurants frequently hire staff to perform these duties, allowing their waiters and waitresses to concentrate on customer service.

Bartenders fill the drink orders that waiters and waitresses take from customers seated in the restaurant or lounge, as well as orders from customers seated at the bar. They prepare standard mixed drinks and, occasionally, are asked to mix drinks to suit a customer's taste. Most bartenders know dozens of drink recipes and are able to mix drinks accurately, quickly, and without waste, even during the busiest periods. Besides mixing and serving drinks, bartenders collect payment, operate the cash register, clean up after customers have left, and on occasion serve food items to customers seated at the bar.

Bartenders who work at service bars have little contact with customers. They work at small bars in restaurants, hotels, and clubs where drinks are served only by waiters and waitresses. However, the majority who work in eating and drinking establishments directly serve and socialize with patrons.

Food and beverage service workers are on their feet a lot and often carry heavy trays of food, dishes, and glassware.

Some establishments, especially larger ones, use automatic equipment to mix drinks of varying complexity at the push of a button. However, bartenders still must be efficient and knowledgeable in case the equipment malfunctions or a customer requests a drink not handled by the equipment. Most customers frequent drinking establishments for the friendly atmosphere and would rather have their drinks prepared by a bartender than a lifeless machine.

Bartenders usually are responsible for ordering and maintaining an inventory of liquor, mixes, and other bar supplies. They form attractive displays out of the bottles and glassware, and wash the glassware and utensils after each use.

Hosts and hostesses try to evoke a good impression of the restaurant by warmly welcoming guests. They courteously direct patrons to where they may leave coats and other personal items, and indicate where they may wait until their table is ready. Hosts and hostesses assign guests to tables suitable for the size of their group, escort them to their seats, and provide menus.

Hosts and hostesses are restaurants' personal representatives to patrons. They try to insure that the service is prompt and courteous and that the meal meets expectations. Hosts and hostesses schedule dining reservations, arrange parties, and organize any special services that are required. In some restaurants, they also act as cashiers.

Dining room attendants and bartender helpers assist waiters, waitresses, and bartenders by keeping the serving area stocked with supplies, cleaning tables, and removing dirty dishes to the kitchen. They replenish the supply of clean linens, dishes, silverware, and glasses in the restaurant dining room, and keep the bar stocked with glasses, liquor, ice, and drink garnishes. Bartender helpers also keep the bar equipment clean and wash glasses. Dining room attendants set tables with clean tablecloths, napkins, silverware, glasses, and dishes and serve ice water, rolls, and butter to patrons. At the conclusion of the meal, they remove dirty dishes and soiled linens from the tables. Cafeteria attendants stock serving tables with food, trays, dishes, and silverware and may carry trays to dining tables for patrons.

Counter attendants take orders and serve food at counters. In cafeterias, they serve food displayed on counters and steam tables as requested by patrons, carve meat, dish out vegetables, ladle sauces and soups, and fill beverages. In lunchrooms and coffee shops, counter attendants take orders from customers seated at the counter, transmit the orders to the kitchen, and pick up and serve the food when it is ready. They also fill cups with coffee, soda, and other beverages and prepare fountain specialties such as milkshakes and ice cream sundaes. They prepare some short-order items, such as sandwiches and salads, and wrap or place orders in containers for carry out. Counter attendants also clean counters, write up itemized checks, and accept payment.

Fast-food workers take orders from customers standing at counters or drive-through windows at fast-food restaurants. They get the ordered beverage and food items, serve them to the customer, and accept payment. Many fast-food workers also cook and package french fries, make coffee, and fill beverage cups using a drink-dispensing machine.

Working Conditions

Food and beverage service workers are on their feet most of the time and often carry heavy trays of food, dishes, and glassware. During busy dining periods, they are under pressure to serve customers quickly and efficiently. The work is relatively safe, but care must be taken to avoid slips, falls, and burns.

Although some food and beverage service workers work 40 hours or more a week, the majority are employed part time—a larger proportion than in almost any other occupation. The majority of those working part-time schedules do so on a voluntary basis. The wide range in dining hours creates work opportunities attractive to homemakers, students, and other individuals seeking supplemental income. Many food and beverage service workers are expected to work evenings, weekends, and holidays. Some work split shifts—that is, they work for several hours during the middle of the day, take a few hours off in the afternoon, and then return to their jobs for the evening hours.

Employment

Food and beverage service workers held more than 4.5 million jobs in 1994. Waiters and waitresses held over 1.8 million of these jobs; counter attendants and fast-food workers, more than 1.6 million; dining room and cafeteria attendants and bartender helpers, 416,000; bartenders, 373,000; and hosts and hostesses, 248,000.

Restaurants, coffee shops, bars, and other retail eating and drinking places employed two-thirds of all food and beverage service workers. Of the remainder, nearly half worked in hotels and other lodging places, and others in bowling alleys, casinos, and country clubs and other membership organizations.

Jobs are located throughout the country but are typically plentiful in large cities and tourist areas. Vacation resorts offer seasonal employment, and some workers alternate between summer and winter resorts instead of remaining in one area the entire year.

Training, Other Qualifications, and Advancement

There are no specific educational requirements for food and beverage service jobs. Although many employers prefer to hire high school graduates for waiter and waitress, bartender, and host and hostess positions, completion of high school is generally not required for fast-food workers, counter attendants, and dining room attendants and bartender helpers. For many people, a job as a food and beverage service worker serves as a source of immediate income rather than a career. Many entrants to these jobs are in their late teens or early twenties and have a high school education or less. Usually, they have little or no work experience. Many are full-time students or homemakers. Food and beverage service jobs are a major source of part-time employment for high school students.

Most employers place an emphasis on personal qualities. Food and beverage service workers are in close contact with the public, so they should be well spoken and have a neat and clean appearance. They should enjoy dealing with all kinds of people, possess a pleasant disposition and a healthy sense of humor. State laws often require that food and beverage service workers obtain health certificates showing that they are free of communicable diseases.

Waiters and waitresses need a good memory to avoid confusing customers' orders and to recall the faces, names, and preferences of frequent patrons. They should be good at arithmetic so they can total bills without the assistance of a calculator or cash register. In restaurants specializing in foreign foods, knowledge of a foreign language

is helpful. Prior experience waiting on tables is preferred by restaurants and hotels which have rigid table service standards. Jobs at these establishments often have higher earnings, but may also have higher educational requirements than less formal establishments.

Generally, bartenders must be at least 21 years of age, and employers prefer to hire people who are 25 or older. They should be familiar with State and local laws concerning the sale of alcoholic beverages.

Most food and beverage service workers pick up their skills on the job by observing and working with more experienced workers. Some employers, particularly some fast-food restaurants, use self-instruction programs to teach new employees food preparation and service skills through audiovisual presentations and instructional booklets. Some public and private vocational schools, restaurant associations, and large restaurant chains also provide classroom training in a generalized food service curriculum.

Some bartenders acquire their skills by attending a bartending or vocational and technical school. These programs often include instruction on State and local laws and regulations, cocktail recipes, attire and conduct, and stocking a bar. Some of these schools help their graduates find jobs.

Due to the relatively small size of most food-serving establishments, opportunities for promotion are limited. After gaining some experience, some dining room and cafeteria attendants and bartender helpers are able to advance to waiter, waitress, or bartender jobs. For waiters, waitresses, and bartenders, advancement usually is limited to finding a job in a larger restaurant or bar where prospects for tip earnings are better. Some bartenders open their own businesses. Some hosts and hostesses and waiters and waitresses advance to supervisory jobs, such as maitre d'hotel, dining room supervisor, or restaurant manager. In larger restaurant chains, food and beverage service workers who excel at their work are often invited to enter the company's formal management training program. (For more information, see the *Handbook* statement on restaurant and food service managers.)

Job Outlook

Job openings for food and beverage service workers are expected to be abundant through the year 2005. Most openings will arise from the need to replace the high proportion of workers who leave this very large occupation each year. There is substantial movement into and out of the occupation because the education and training requirements are minimal, and the predominance of part-time jobs is attractive to people seeking a short-term source of income rather than a career. Many of these workers simply move to other occupations, while others stop working to assume household responsibilities or to attend school.

Employment of food and beverage service occupations is expected to grow about as fast as the average for all occupations through the year 2005. Since a significant proportion of food and beverage sales by eating and drinking places is associated with the overall level of economic activity, sales and employment will increase with the growth of the economy. Growth in demand also will stem from population growth, rising personal incomes, and increased leisure time. Since it is common for both husband and wife to be in the work force, families may increasingly find dining out a convenience.

Growth of the various types of food and beverage service jobs is expected to vary greatly. As the composition of the Nation's population becomes older, diners are expected to patronize full-service restaurants increasingly, spurring growth in demand for waiters and waitresses and hosts and hostesses. However, little change in the employment of dining room attendants is expected as waiters and waitresses increasingly assume their duties. The employment of bartenders is expected to decline as drinking of alcoholic beverages outside the home—particularly cocktails—continues to drop.

Workers under the age of 25 have traditionally filled a significant proportion of food and beverage service jobs, particularly in fast-food restaurants. The pool of these young workers in the labor force is expected to shrink through the 1990's, but begin to grow after the year 2000. To attract and retain workers, many employers will be forced to offer higher wages, better benefits, more training, and increased opportunities for advancement and full-time employment.

Because potential earnings are greatest in popular restaurants and fine dining establishments, keen competition is expected for the limited number of jobs in these restaurants.

Earnings

Food and beverage service workers derive their earnings from a combination of hourly wages and customer tips. Their wages and the amount of tips they receive varies greatly, depending on the type of job and establishment. For example, fast-food workers and hosts and hostesses generally do not receive tips, so their wage rates may be higher than those of waiters and waitresses, who may earn more from tips than from wages. In some restaurants, waiters and waitresses contribute a portion of their tips to a tip pool, which is distributed among many of the establishment's other food and beverage service workers and kitchen staff. Tip pools allow workers who normally do not receive tips, such as dining room attendants, to share in the rewards for a well served meal.

In 1994, median weekly earnings (including tips) of full-time waiters and waitresses were about $256. The middle 50 percent earned between $188 and $338; the top 10 percent earned at least $430 a week. For most waiters and waitresses, higher earnings are primarily the result of receiving more in tips rather than higher hourly wages. Tips generally average between 10 and 20 percent of guests' checks, so waiters and waitresses working in busy, expensive restaurants earn the most.

Full-time bartenders had median weekly earnings (including tips) of about $299 in 1994. The middle 50 percent earned from $226 and $395; the top 10 percent earned at least $514 a week. Like waiters and waitresses, bartenders employed in public bars may receive more than half of their earnings as tips. Service bartenders are often paid higher hourly wages to offset their lower tip earnings.

Median weekly earnings (including tips) of full-time dining room attendants and bartender helpers were about $228 in 1994. The middle 50 percent earned between $182 and $304; the top 10 percent earned over $446 a week. Most received over half of their earnings as wages; the rest was their share of the proceeds from tip pools.

Full-time counter attendants and fast-food workers had median weekly earnings (including any tips) of about $204 in 1994. The middle 50 percent earned between $160 and $266, while the highest 10 percent earned over $324 a week. Although some counter attendants receive part of their earnings as tips, fast-food workers generally do not.

In establishments covered by Federal law, workers beginning at the minimum wage earn $4.25 an hour. Federal law permits employers to credit an employee's tip earnings toward the minimum hourly wage, up to an amount equaling 45 percent of the minimum, and some employers exercise this right. Employers are also permitted to deduct from wages the cost, or fair value, of any meals or lodging provided. However, many employers provide free meals and furnish uniforms. Food and beverage service workers who work full time often receive paid vacation and sick leave and health insurance, while part-time workers generally do not.

In some large restaurants and hotels, food and beverage service workers belong to unions. The principal unions are the Hotel Employees and Restaurant Employees International Union and the Service Employees International Union.

Related Occupations

Other workers whose jobs involve serving customers and helping them feel at ease and enjoy themselves include flight attendants, butlers, and tour busdrivers.

Sources of Additional Information

Information about job opportunities may be obtained from local employers and local offices of the State employment service.

A guide to careers in restaurants, a list of 2- and 4-year colleges that have food service programs, and information on scholarships to those programs is available from:
☛The Educational Foundation of the National Restaurant Association, 250 South Wacker Dr., Suite 1400, Chicago, IL 60606.

For general information on hospitality careers, write to:
☛Council on Hotel, Restaurant, and Institutional Education, 1200 17th St. NW., Washington, DC 20036-3097.

For general career information and a directory of private career colleges and schools that offer training for bartender and other food and beverage service jobs, write to:
☛Accrediting Commission of Career Schools and Colleges of Technology, 2101 Wilson Blvd., Suite 302, Arlington, VA 22201.

Health Service Occupations

Dental Assistants

(D.O.T. 079.361-018)

Nature of the Work

Dental assistants perform a variety of patient care, office, and laboratory duties. They work at chairside as dentists examine and treat patients. They make patients as comfortable as possible in the dental chair, prepare them for treatment, and obtain dental records. Assistants hand instruments and materials to dentists and keep patients' mouths dry and clear by using suction or other devices. Assistants also sterilize and disinfect instruments and equipment; prepare tray setups for dental procedures; provide postoperative instruction; and

instruct patients in oral health care. Some dental assistants prepare materials for making impressions and restorations, expose radiographs, and process dental x-ray film as directed by a dentist. They may also remove sutures, apply anesthetics and cavity preventive agents to teeth and gums, remove excess cement used in the filling process, and place rubber dams on the teeth to isolate them for individual treatment.

Those with laboratory duties make casts of the teeth and mouth from impressions taken by dentists, clean and polish removable appliances, and make temporary crowns. Dental assistants with office duties schedule and confirm appointments, receive patients, keep treatment records, send bills, receive payments, and order dental supplies and materials.

Dental assistants should not be confused with dental hygienists, who are licensed to perform a wider variety of clinical tasks. (See the statement on dental hygienists elsewhere in the *Handbook*.)

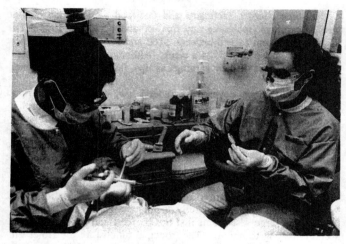

About 1 in 3 dental assistants works part time.

Working Conditions

Dental assistants work in a well-lighted, clean environment. Their work area is usually near the dental chair, so that they can arrange instruments, materials, and medication, and hand them to the dentist when needed. Handling radiographic equipment poses dangers, but they can be minimized with safety procedures. Likewise, dental assistants wear gloves and masks to protect themselves from infectious diseases like hepatitis.

Most dental assistants have a 32- to 40-hour workweek which may include work on Saturday or evenings.

Employment

Dental assistants held about 190,000 jobs in 1994. Almost 1 out of 3 worked part time, sometimes in more than one dentist's office.

Almost all dental assistants work in private dental offices. Some work in dental schools, private and government hospitals, State and local public health departments, or in clinics.

Training, Other Qualifications, and Advancement

Most assistants learn their skills on the job, though many are trained in dental assisting programs offered by community and junior colleges, trade schools, and technical institutes. Some assistants are trained in Armed Forces schools. Assistants must be a dentist's "third hand"; therefore, dentists look for people who are reliable, can work well with others, and have manual dexterity. High school students interested in careers as dental assistants should take courses in biology, chemistry, health, and office practices.

The American Dental Association's Commission on Dental Accreditation approved 235 training programs in 1995. Programs include classroom, laboratory, and preclinical instruction in dental assisting skills and related theory. In addition, students gain practical experience in dental schools, clinics, or dental offices. Most programs take 1 year or less to complete and lead to a certificate or diploma. Two-year programs offered in community and junior colleges lead to an associate degree. All programs require a high school diploma or its equivalent, and some require typing or a science course for admission. Some private vocational schools offer 4- to 6-month courses in dental assisting, but these are not accredited by the Commission on Dental Accreditation.

Certification is available through the Dental Assisting National Board. Certification is an acknowledgment of an assistant's qualifications and professional competence, but usually is not required for employment. In several States that have adopted standards for dental assistants who perform radiologic procedures, completion of the certification examination meets those standards. Candidates may qualify to take the certification examination by graduating from an

accredited training program or by having 2 years of full-time experience as a dental assistant. In addition, applicants must have taken a course in cardiopulmonary resuscitation.

Without further education, advancement opportunities are limited. Some dental assistants working the front office become office managers. Others, working chairside, go back to school to become dental hygienists.

Job Outlook

Job prospects for dental assistants should be good. Employment is expected to grow much faster than the average for all occupations through the year 2005. Also, the proportion of workers leaving and who must be replaced is above average. Many opportunities are for entry-level positions that offer on-the-job training.

Population growth and greater retention of natural teeth by middle-aged and older people will fuel demand for dental services. Also, dentists are likely to employ more assistants, for several reasons. Older dentists, who are less likely to employ assistants, will leave and be replaced by recent graduates, who are more likely to use one, or even two. In addition, as dentists' workloads increase, they are expected to hire more assistants to perform routine tasks, so they may use their own time more profitably.

Most job openings for dental assistants will arise from the need to replace assistants who leave the occupation. For many, this entry-level occupation provides basic training and experience and serves as a stepping-stone to more highly skilled and higher paying jobs. Other assistants leave the job to take on family responsibilities, return to school, or for other reasons.

Earnings

In 1993, median weekly earnings for dental assistants working full time were about $329. The middle 50 percent earned between $255 and $391 a week. According to the American Dental Association, dental assistants who worked 32 hours a week or more averaged $370 a week in 1993; the average hourly earnings for all dental assistants were $10.20.

Related Occupations

Workers in other occupations supporting health practitioners include medical assistants, physical therapy assistants, occupational therapy assistants, pharmacy assistants, and veterinary technicians.

Sources of Additional Information

Information about career opportunities, scholarships, accredited dental assistant programs, and requirements for certification is available from:

☛American Dental Assistants Association, 203 N. Lasalle, Suite 1320, Chicago, IL 60601-1225.

☛Commission on Dental Accreditation, American Dental Association, 211 E. Chicago Ave., Suite 1814, Chicago, IL 60611.

☛Dental Assisting National Board, Inc., 216 E. Ontario St., Chicago, IL 60611.

Medical Assistants

(D.O.T. 078.361-038 and .364-014, 079.362-010, .364-010, and -014, and .374-018, 355.667-010)

Nature of the Work

Medical assistants perform routine clinical and clerical tasks to keep the offices of physicians, podiatrists, chiropractors, and optometrists running smoothly. Medical assistants should not be confused with physician assistants who examine, diagnose and treat patients, under the direct supervision of a physician. (Physician assistants are discussed elsewhere in the *Handbook.*)

The duties of medical assistants vary from office to office, depending on office location, size, and specialty. In small practices, medical assistants are usually "generalists," handling both clerical and clinical duties and reporting directly to an office manager, physician, or other health practitioner. Those in large practices tend to specialize in a particular area under the supervision of department administrators.

Medical assistants perform many clerical duties. They answer telephones, greet patients, update and file patient medical records, fill out insurance forms, handle correspondence, schedule appointments, arrange for hospital admission and laboratory services, and handle billing and bookkeeping.

Clinical duties vary according to State law and include taking medical histories and recording vital signs, explaining treatment procedures to patients, preparing patients for examination, and assisting during the examination. Medical assistants collect and prepare laboratory specimens or perform basic laboratory tests on the premises, dispose of contaminated supplies, and sterilize medical instruments. They instruct patients about medication and special diets, prepare and administer medications as directed by a physician, authorize drug refills as directed, telephone prescriptions to a pharmacy, draw blood, prepare patients for x rays, take electrocardiograms, remove sutures, and change dressings.

Medical assistants may also arrange examining room instruments and equipment, purchase and maintain supplies and equipment, and keep waiting and examining rooms neat and clean.

Assistants who specialize have additional duties. *Podiatric medical assistants* make castings of feet, expose and develop x rays, and assist podiatrists in surgery. *Ophthalmic medical assistants* help ophthalmologists provide medical eye care. They administer diagnostic tests, measure and record vision, and test the functioning of eyes and eye muscles. They also show patients how to use eye dressings, protective shields, and safety glasses, and how to insert, remove, and care for contact lenses. Under the direction of the physician, they may administer medications, including eye drops. They also maintain optical and surgical instruments and assist the ophthalmologist in surgery.

Working Conditions

Medical assistants work in well-lighted, clean environments. They constantly interact with other people, and may have to handle several responsibilities at once.

Most full-time medical assistants work a regular 40-hour week. Some work part-time, evenings or weekends.

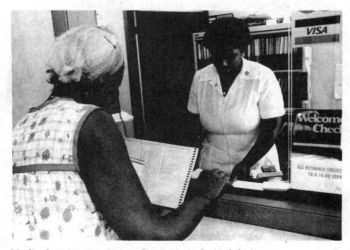

Medical assistants may perform many clerical duties.

Employment

Medical assistants held about 206,000 jobs in 1994. Seven in 10 jobs were in physicians' offices, and over 1 in 10 were in offices of other health practitioners such as chiropractors, optometrists, and podiatrists. The rest were in hospitals, nursing homes, and other health care facilities.

Training, Other Qualifications, and Advancement

Medical assisting is one of the few health occupations open to individuals with no formal training. Although formal training in medical assisting is available, such training–while generally preferred–is not always required. Some medical assistants are trained on the job. Applicants usually need a high school diploma or the equivalent. Recommended high school courses include mathematics, health, biology, typing, bookkeeping, computers, and office skills. Volunteer experience in the health care field is also helpful.

Formal programs in medical assisting are offered in vocational-technical high schools, postsecondary vocational schools, community and junior colleges, and in colleges and universities. College-level programs usually last either 1 year, resulting in a certificate or diploma, or 2 years, resulting in an associate degree. Vocational programs can take up to 1 year and lead to a diploma or certificate. Courses cover anatomy, physiology, and medical terminology as well as typing, transcription, recordkeeping, accounting, and insurance processing. Students learn laboratory techniques, clinical and diagnostic procedures, pharmaceutical principles and medication administration, and first aid. They study office practices, patient relations, and medical law and ethics. Some accredited programs include an internship that provides practical experience in physicians' offices, hospitals, or other health care facilities.

Two agencies recognized by the U.S. Department of Education accredit programs in medical assisting: the Commission on Accreditation of Allied Health Education Programs (CAAHEP) and the Accrediting Bureau of Health Education Schools (ABHES). In 1995, there were 221 medical assisting programs accredited by CAAHEP and 162 accredited by ABHES. The Joint Review Committee for Ophthalmic Medical Personnel has approved 16 programs in ophthalmic medical assisting.

Although there is no licensing for medical assistants, some States require them to take a test or a short course before they can take x rays, draw blood, or give injections. Employers prefer to hire experienced workers or certified applicants who have passed a national examination, indicating that the medical assistant meets certain standards of competence. The American Association of Medical Assistants awards the Certified Medical Assistant credential; the American Medical Technologists awards the Registered Medical Assistant credential; the American Society of Podiatric Medical Assistants awards the Podiatric Medical Assistant Certified credential; and the Joint Commission on Allied Health Personnel in Ophthalmology awards the Ophthalmic Medical Assistant credential at three levels: Certified Ophthalmic Assistant, Certified Ophthalmic Technician, and Certified Ophthalmic Medical Technologist.

Because medical assistants deal with the public, they must be neat and well-groomed and have a courteous, pleasant manner. Medical assistants must be able to put patients at ease and explain physicians' instructions. They must respect the confidential nature of medical information. Clinical duties require a reasonable level of manual dexterity and visual acuity.

Medical assistants may be able to advance to office manager. They may qualify for a wide variety of administrative support occupations, or may teach medical assisting. Some, with additional education, enter other health occupations such as nursing and medical technology.

Job Outlook

Employment of medical assistants is expected to grow much faster than the average for all occupations through the year 2005 as the health services industry expands due to technological advances in medicine, and a growing and aging population.

Employment growth will be driven by growth in the number of group practices, clinics, and other health care facilities that need a high proportion of support personnel, particularly the flexible medical assistant who can handle both clinical and clerical duties. Medical assistants primarily work in outpatient settings, where faster than average growth is expected.

In view of the preference of many physicians for trained personnel, job prospects should be excellent for medical assistants with formal training or experience, particularly those with certification.

Earnings

The earnings of medical assistants vary widely, depending on experience, skill level, and location. According to a 1995 survey by the Health Care Group, average hourly wages for medical assistants with less than 2 years of experience ranged from $7.51 to $10.20. Average hourly wages for medical assistants with more than 5 years of experience ranged from $9.60 to $13.12. Wages were higher in the Northeast and West and lower in the Midwest and South.

Related Occupations

Workers in other medical support occupations include medical secretaries, hospital admitting clerks, pharmacy helpers, medical record clerks, dental assistants, occupational therapy aides, and physical therapy aides.

Sources of Additional Information

Information about career opportunities, CAAHEP-accredited educational programs in medical assisting, and the Certified Medical Assistant exam is available from:

☛The American Association of Medical Assistants, 20 North Wacker Dr., Suite 1575, Chicago, IL 60606-2903.

Information about career opportunities and the Registered Medical Assistant certification exam is available from:

☛Registered Medical Assistants of American Medical Technologists, 710 Higgins Rd., Park Ridge, IL 60068-5765.

For a list of ABHES-accredited educational programs in medical assisting, write:

☛Accrediting Bureau of Health Education Schools, 2700 South Quincy St., Suite 210, Arlington, VA 22206.

Information about career opportunities, training programs, and the Certified Ophthalmic Assistant exam is available from:

☛Joint Commission on Allied Health Personnel in Ophthalmology, 2025 Woodlane Dr., St. Paul, MN 55125-2995.

Information about careers for podiatric assistants is available from:

☛American Society of Podiatric Medical Assistants, 2124 S. Austin Blvd., Cicero, IL 60650.

Nursing Aides and Psychiatric Aides

(D.O.T. 354.374-010, .377-010, and .677-010; 355.377-014 and -018, .674-014 and -018, and .677-014)

Nature of the Work

Nursing aides and psychiatric aides help care for physically or mentally ill, injured, disabled, or infirm individuals confined to hospitals, nursing or residential care facilities, and mental health settings. (Homemaker-home health aides, whose duties are similar but who work in clients' homes, are discussed elsewhere in the *Handbook*.)

Nursing aides, also known as nursing assistants or hospital attendants, work under the supervision of nursing and medical staff. They answer patients' call bells, deliver messages, serve meals, make beds, and help patients eat, dress, and bathe. Aides may also provide skin

care to patients, take temperatures, pulse, respiration, and blood pressure, and help patients get in and out of bed and walk. They may also escort patients to operating and examining rooms, keep patients' rooms neat, set up equipment, or store and move supplies. Aides observe patients' physical, mental, and emotional conditions and report any change to the nursing or medical staff.

Nursing aides employed in nursing homes are often the principal caregivers, having far more contact with residents than other members of the staff do. Since some residents may stay in a nursing home for months or even years, aides develop ongoing relationships with them and respond to them in a positive, caring way.

Psychiatric aides are also known as mental health assistants and psychiatric nursing assistants. They care for mentally impaired or emotionally disturbed individuals. They work under a team that may include psychiatrists, psychologists, psychiatric nurses, social workers, and therapists. In addition to helping patients dress, bathe, groom, and eat, psychiatric aides socialize with them and lead them in educational and recreational activities. Psychiatric aides may play games such as cards with the patients, watch television with them, or participate in group activities such as sports or field trips. They observe patients and report any signs which might be important for the professional staff to know. They accompany patients to and from wards for examination and treatment. Because they have the closest contact with patients, psychiatric aides have a great deal of influence on patients' outlook and treatment.

Working Conditions

Most full-time aides work about 40 hours a week, but because patients need care 24 hours a day, some aides work evenings, nights, weekends, and holidays. Many work part-time. Aides spend many hours standing and walking. Since they may have to move partially paralyzed patients in and out of bed or help them stand or walk, aides must guard against back injury.

Nursing aides often have unpleasant duties; they empty bed pans and change soiled bed linens. They also care for disoriented and irritable patients. Psychiatric aides must be prepared to care for patients whose disease may cause violent behavior. While their work can be emotionally demanding, many aides gain satisfaction from assisting those in need.

Employment

Nursing aides held about 1,265,000 jobs in 1994, and psychiatric aides held about 105,000 jobs. About one-half of all nursing aides worked in nursing homes, and about one-fourth worked in hospitals.

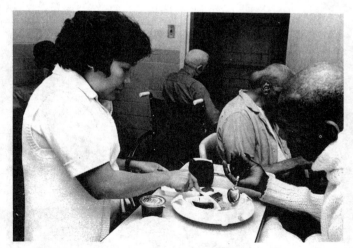

In many cases, neither a high school diploma nor previous work experience is necessary for a job as a nursing aide or a psychiatric aide.

Some worked in residential care facilities, such as halfway houses and homes for the aged or disabled, or in private households. Most psychiatric aides worked in State and county mental institutions, psychiatric units of general hospitals, private psychiatric facilities and community mental health centers.

Training, Other Qualifications, and Advancement

In many cases, neither a high school diploma nor previous work experience is necessary for a job as a nursing or psychiatric aide. A few employers, however, require some training or experience. Hospitals may require experience as a nursing aide or home health aide. Nursing homes often hire inexperienced workers who must complete a minimum of 75 hours of mandatory training and pass a competency evaluation program within 4 months of employment. Aides who complete the program are placed on the State registry of nursing aides. Some States require psychiatric aides to complete a formal training program.

These occupations can offer individuals an entry into the world of work. The flexibility of night and weekend hours also provides high school and college students a chance to work during the school year.

Nursing aide training is offered in high schools, vocational-technical centers, some nursing homes, and community colleges. Courses cover body mechanics, nutrition, anatomy and physiology, infection control, communication skills, and resident rights. Personal care skills such as how to help patients bathe, eat, and groom are also taught.

Some facilities, other than nursing homes, provide classroom instruction for newly hired aides, while others rely exclusively on informal on-the-job instruction from a licensed nurse or an experienced aide. Such training may last several days to a few months. From time to time, aides may also attend lectures, workshops, and in-service training.

Applicants should be healthy, tactful, patient, understanding, emotionally stable, dependable, and have a desire to help people. They should also be able to work as part of a team, and be willing to perform repetitive, routine tasks.

Opportunities for advancement within these occupations are limited. To enter other health occupations, aides generally need additional formal training. Some employers and unions provide opportunities by simplifying the educational paths to advancement. Experience as an aide can also help individuals decide whether to pursue a career in the health care field.

Job Outlook

Job prospects for nursing aides should be good through the year 2005. Employment of nursing aides is expected to grow faster than the average for all occupations in response to an emphasis on rehabilitation and the long-term care needs of a rapidly growing population of those 75 years old and older. Employment will increase as a result of the expansion of nursing homes and other long-term care facilities for people with chronic illnesses and disabling conditions, many of whom are elderly. Also increasing employment of nursing aides will be modern medical technology which, while saving more lives, increases the need for the extended care provided by aides. As a result, nursing and personal care facilities are expected to grow very rapidly and to provide most of the new jobs for nursing aides.

Employment of psychiatric aides is expected to grow about as fast as the average for all occupations. Employment will rise in response to the sharp increase in the number of older persons—many of whom will require mental health services. Employment of aides in private psychiatric facilities and community mental health centers is likely to grow because of increasing public acceptance of formal treatment for drug abuse and alcoholism, and a lessening of the stigma attached to those receiving mental health care. While employment in private psychiatric facilities may grow, employment in public mental hospitals is likely to be stagnant due to constraints on public spending.

Replacement needs will constitute the major source of openings for aides. Turnover is high, a reflection of modest entry requirements, low pay, and lack of advancement opportunities.

Earnings

Median weekly earnings of full-time salaried nursing aides and psychiatric aides were $275 in 1994. The middle 50 percent earned between $214 and $356. The lowest 10 percent earned less than $175; the top 10 percent, more than $482.

According to a University of Texas Medical Branch survey of hospitals and medical centers, the median annual salary of nursing aides, based on a 40-hour week and excluding shift or area differentials, was $14,612 in October 1994.

According to the Buck Survey conducted by the American Health Care Association, nursing aides in chain nursing homes had median annual earnings of about $12,800 in 1994. The middle 50 percent earned between $11,600 and $14,400.

Aides in hospitals generally receive at least 1 week's paid vacation after 1 year of service. Paid holidays and sick leave, hospital and medical benefits, extra pay for late-shift work, and pension plans also are available to many hospital and some nursing home employees.

Related Occupations

Nursing aides and psychiatric aides help people who need routine care or treatment. So do homemaker-home health aides, childcare attendants, companions, occupational therapy aides, and physical therapy aides.

Sources of Additional Information

For information on nursing careers in long-term care, write:
☛American Health Care Association, 1201 L St. NW., Washington, DC 20005.

Information about employment also may be obtained from local hospitals, nursing homes, psychiatric facilities, and State boards of nursing.

Occupational Therapy Assistants and Aides

(D.O.T. 076.364-010, 355.377-010)

Nature of the Work

Occupational therapy assistants and aides work under the direction of occupational therapists to provide rehabilitative services to patients suffering from mental, physical, emotional, or developmental impairments. The ultimate goal is to improve patients' quality of life by assisting them in overcoming limitations. For example, they help injured workers re-enter the labor force by improving their motor skills or help persons with learning disabilities increase their independence by teaching them to prepare meals or use public transportation.

Occupational therapy assistants help patients with the rehabilitative activities and exercises that are outlined in the treatment plan devised by the occupational therapist. The activities range from teaching the patient the proper method of moving from a bed into a wheelchair, to the best way to stretch and limber the muscles of the hand. Assistants monitor the individual to ensure the patient is performing the activities correctly and to provide encouragement. They also record their observations with regard to the patient's progress for use by the occupational therapist. If the treatment is not having the intended effect or the client is not improving as expected, the treatment program may be altered to obtain better results. They also document billing of the patient's health insurance provider.

Occupational therapy aides typically prepare materials and assemble equipment used during treatment and are responsible for a range of clerical tasks. Their duties may include scheduling appointments, answering the telephone, restocking or ordering depleted

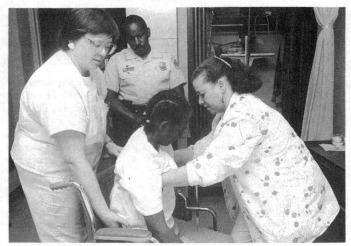

Occupational therapy assistants and aides may need to help lift or move patients.

supplies, and filling out insurance forms or other paperwork. Aides are not licensed, so by law they are not allowed to perform as wide a range of tasks as occupational therapy assistants.

Working Conditions

Occupational therapy assistants and aides usually work during the day, but may occasionally work evenings or weekends in order to accommodate the patient's schedule. They should be in good physical shape because they are on their feet for long periods of time and may be asked to help lift and move patients or equipment.

Assistants and aides must be responsible, patient, willing to take directions, and work as part of a team. Furthermore, they should be caring and want to help people who are not able to help themselves. The job can be rewarding and assistants and aides often feel a sense of accomplishment when patients show improvement or recover.

Employment

Occupational therapy assistants and aides held 16,000 jobs in 1994. Over one-third worked in hospitals and about 1 in 4 worked in nursing and personal care facilities. The rest primarily worked in offices of occupational therapists and other offices operated by health practitioners. A small, but increasing number of assistants and aides work in the home health services industry and provide care in patients' homes.

Training, Other Qualifications, and Advancement

Occupational therapy assistants need an associate's degree from an accredited community college or technical school. There were 77 accredited occupational therapy assistant programs in the United States in 1993. The first year of study typically involves an introduction to healthcare, and basic medical terminology, anatomy, and physiology. In the second year, courses are more rigorous and usually include occupational theory courses in areas like mental health, gerontology and pediatrics. Students also must complete supervised fieldwork in a clinic. Applicants to occupational therapy assistant programs can improve their chances of admission by taking high school courses in biology and health, and by performing volunteer work in nursing homes, occupational or physical therapist's offices, or elsewhere in the healthcare field.

After students receive their associate's degrees, they may have to take a State licensure exam to prove their competence. Thirty-seven States, Puerto Rico, and the District of Columbia required occupational therapy assistants to be licensed in 1994.

Occupational therapy aides usually receive most of their training on the job. Qualified applicants must have a high school diploma,

strong interpersonal skills, and a desire to help people in need. Applicants may increase their chances of getting a job by volunteering their services, thus displaying initiative and their aptitude to the employer.

Job Outlook

Opportunities for jobseekers should be favorable. Employment of occupational therapy assistants and aides is expected to grow much faster than the average for all occupations through 2005. Although the occupation is expected to be one of the fastest growing in the economy, the number of job openings will be low because the occupation is small.

Growth will result from an aging population, especially the "baby boom" cohort, that will need more occupational therapy services. Demand will also result from advances in medicine that allow more people with critical problems to survive, but then need rehabilitative therapy. Furthermore, employers seeking to reduce health care costs are expected to hire more occupational therapy assistants and aides for tasks currently being performed by more highly paid occupational therapists.

Earnings

According to a membership survey of the American Occupational Therapy Association, the median annual income for occupational therapy assistants was about $25,300 in 1993. Based on limited information, occupational therapy aides usually start between $6.00 and $7.00 an hour. Starting salaries for both occupations tend to be lower in hospitals and higher in privately owned practices and nursing homes.

Related Occupations

Occupational therapy assistants and aides work under the direction of occupational therapists. Other occupations in the healthcare field that work closely with and are supervised by professionals include dental assistants, medical assistants, optometric assistants, pharmacy assistants, and physical therapy assistants and aides.

Sources of Additional Information

Information on a career as an occupational therapy assistant or aide, and a list of accredited programs can be obtained from:
☛The American Occupational Therapy Association, 4720 Montgomery Lane., P.O. Box 31220, Bethesda, MD 20824-1220.

Physical Therapy Assistants and Aides

(D.O.T. 076.224-010, 355.354-010)

Nature of the Work

Physical therapy assistants and aides prepare patients both physically and psychologically for therapy under the watchful eye of a licensed physical therapist. The objective of physical therapy is two-fold: first prevent permanent disability from injury or illness, and second to have patients resume their regular activities as soon as they are physically capable. Physical therapy assistants and aides work towards these objectives by administering rehabilitation plans that are developed by a licensed physical therapist.

Physical therapy assistants instruct patients in a wide variety of treatments that may encompass manual exercises on a treadmill, stationary bike, or weight lifting equipment. For patients whose therapy requires non-weight bearing exercise, their treatment often includes exercises in a swimming pool. Other forms of treatment administered by the physical therapy assistant involve massages, electrical stimulation, paraffin baths, hot/cold packs and traction.

Assistants may also measure a patient's size, flexibility, and range of motion. They may also use ultrasound equipment to evaluate discomfort patients are experiencing with a knee or elbow. Physical therapists may use this data to fit the patient with an orthopedic brace, prostheses, or other support device. Assistants monitor the patient's progress during treatment and report all abnormalities and achievements to the physical therapist for periodic evaluation.

Physical therapy aides help make therapy sessions productive. They are usually responsible for keeping the treatment area clean and organized, and preparing for each patient's therapy. When patients needs assistance to or from the treatment area, aides may push them in a wheelchair, or provide them with a shoulder to lean on. Aides encourage patients during therapy sessions, and watch to see that exercises are performed correctly so as to attain the maximum benefit and to guard against further injury. Aides consult with the therapist or assistant if patients are experiencing difficulty with the treatment. Because they are not licensed, aides perform a smaller range of tasks than physical therapy assistants.

The duties of assistants and aides include some clerical tasks such as ordering depleted supplies, maintaining patient records, answering the phones, and filling out insurance forms and other paperwork. Records kept by the assistant or aide keep the therapist abreast of progress and any problems that may develop during treatment. The extent to which an aide, or even an assistant, performs clerical tasks depends on the size and location of the facility.

Working Conditions
The hours and days that physical therapy assistants and aides work vary depending on the facility and whether they are full-time or part-time employees. In 1994, approximately 4 out 5 assistants worked in a full-time, salaried capacity. Many private physical therapy offices have evening and weekend office hours to help coincide with patients' personal schedules.

Physical therapy assistants and aides need to have a moderate degree of strength due to the physical exertion required in assisting patients with their treatment. For example, constant kneeling, stooping and standing for long periods of time are all part of the job. In some cases assistants may need to help lift patients, therefore physical therapy programs strongly recommend against anyone prone to back problems becoming a physical therapy assistant.

Employment
Physical therapy assistants and aides held 78,000 jobs in 1994. They work alongside physical therapists in a variety of settings. Over half of all assistants and aides work in hospitals or private physical ther-

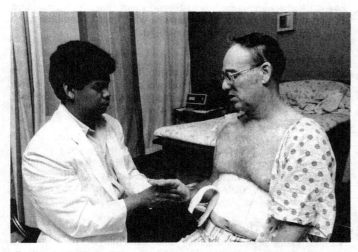

Earnings of physical therapy assistants and aides tend to be higher in private practice.

apy offices. Others work in clinics, nursing homes, schools and even inside patients' homes. In sports medicine, they may work part of the time on the sidelines of sporting events, or in swimming pools performing aqua therapy.

Training, Other Qualifications, and Advancement
Physical therapy assistants typically have earned an associate's degree from an accredited physical therapist assistant program. As of January 1996, 41 States and Puerto Rico required assistants to be certified or licensed. Other requirements include certification in CPR and First Aid, and a minimum number of hours of clinical experience.

According to the American Physical Therapy Association (APTA), there were 173 accredited physical therapist assistant programs in the United States, with another 54 in development as of June 1995. Accredited physical therapy assistant programs are designed to last 2 years, or four semesters, and culminate in an associate's degree. Admission into physical therapist assistant programs is competitive and it is not unusual for colleges to have long waiting lists of prospective candidates. The programs are divided into academic study and "hands on" clinical experience. Academic coursework initially includes algebra, anatomy and physiology, biology, chemistry, and psychology. Before students embark on their clinical field experience in a hospital or private clinic, many programs require that students complete a semester of anatomy and physiology and have certifications in CPR and First Aid. Both educators and prospective employers view clinical experience as an integral part of ensuring that students understand the responsibilities of a physical therapy assistant.

Employers typically require physical therapy aides to have a high school diploma, strong interpersonal skills, and a desire to assist people in need. Most employers provide aides clinical training on the job.

Job Outlook
Physical therapy assistants and aides is expected to be one of the fastest growing occupations through the year 2005. Opportunities should be especially favorable for assistants unless the number of new graduates increases significantly. Reports consistently indicate employers currently are having difficulty finding qualified candidates for job openings.

Demand for physical therapy assistants and aides will continue to rise as the median age of Americans increases. The elderly consume a disproportionate share of physical therapy services. As the "baby boom" generation ages, demand for services associated with geriatric medicine will grow significantly. Older patients often need more assistance in their treatment, making the roles of assistants and aides vital.

Shortages of physical therapists in many areas makes hiring licensed assistants an attractive alternative. After a patient is evaluated and a treatment plan is designed by the physical therapist, the patient can be turned over to an assistant. The licensed assistant can administer many aspects of the treatment prescribed by the therapist. By increasing the role of physical therapy assistants relative to physical therapists, more patients receive care and labor costs are substantially lower.

While the number of accredited programs has increased, enrollment in each has not thus limiting the growth in newly trained assistants. The size of many programs has been limited because of the difficulties in recruiting qualified instructors—educational institutions are often outbid for their services by other employers.

Earnings
According to the limited information available, starting salaries for physical therapy assistants average about $22,500 a year. Starting salaries of assistants working in hospitals tended to be lower than those in private practice. As an inducement, many hospitals offer assistants a structured path of advancement and a chance to work

with a varied patient population. In private practice, experienced physical therapy assistants earn, on average, about $24,000 a year.

Related Occupations

Physical therapy assistants and aides work under the supervision of physical therapists. Other occupations in the healthcare field that work under the supervision of professionals include dental, medical, occupational therapy, optometric, recreational therapy, and pharmacy assistants.

Sources of Additional Information

Information on a career as a physical therapy assistant or aide, and a list of schools offering accredited programs can be obtained from:

☛The American Physical Therapy Association, 1111 North Fairfax Street, Alexandria, VA 22314-1488.

Personal and Building Service Occupations

Barbers and Cosmetologists

(D.O.T. 330; 331; 332; 333; 339.361, .371)

Nature of the Work

Looking your best has never been easy. It requires the perfect hairstyle, exquisite nails, a neatly trimmed beard, or the proper make-up to accent your coloring. More and more, it also requires the services of barbers and cosmetologists. As people increasingly demand styles that are better suited to their individual characteristics and have available to them a vast array of cosmetic products, they rely on these workers to help them make sense of the different options. Although tastes and fashions change from year to year, the basic job of barbers and cosmetologists remains the same—to help people look their best.

Barbers cut, trim, shampoo, and style hair. Many people still go to a barber for just a haircut, but an increasing number seek more personalized hairstyling services. Barbers trained in these areas work in barber shops and styling salons that serve both men and women. Today, it is common for a barber to color or perm a customer's hair. In addition, barbers may fit hairpieces, provide hair and scalp treatments, shave male customers, or give facial massages. In most States, barbers are licensed to perform all the duties of cosmetologists except skin care and nail treatment.

Cosmetologists primarily shampoo, cut, and style hair, but they also provide a number of other services. These workers, who are often called hairstylists, may advise patrons on how to care for their hair, straighten or permanent wave a customer's hair, or lighten or darken hair color. In addition, most cosmetologists are trained to give manicures, pedicures, and scalp and facial treatments; provide makeup analysis for women; and clean and style wigs and hairpieces. Other workers include electrologists—who remove hair from skin by electrolysis—and estheticians—who cleanse and beautify the skin. Cosmetologists generally are licensed to provide all of the services that barbers do except shaving men.

In addition to their work with customers, barbers and cosmetologists are expected to keep their work area clean and their hairdressing implements sanitized. They may make appointments and keep records of hair color and permanent wave formulas used by their regular patrons. A growing number also actively sell hair products and other cosmetic supplies. Barbers and cosmetologists who operate their own salons have managerial duties that include hiring, supervising, and firing workers, as well as keeping records and ordering supplies.

Working Conditions

Barbers and cosmetologists generally work in clean, pleasant surroundings with good lighting and ventilation. Good health and stamina are important because these workers usually have to be on

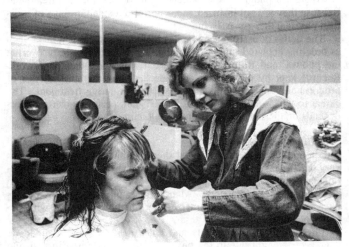

Barbers and cosmetologists must closely follow changes in hairstyles.

their feet for most of their shift. Prolonged exposure to some hair and nail chemicals may be hazardous and cause irritation, so special care must be taken when working with these chemicals.

Most full-time barbers and cosmetologists work 40 hours a week, but long hours are common in this occupation, especially among self-employed workers. This often includes evenings and weekends, when beauty and barber shops and salons are busiest. Although weekends and lunch periods are generally very busy, barbers and cosmetologists may have some time off during slack periods. One of every 3 barbers and cosmetologists works part time. The abundance of part-time jobs attracts many persons who want to combine a job with family, school, or other responsibilities.

Employment

Barbers and cosmetologists held about 709,000 jobs in 1994; 9 of every 10 were cosmetologists. Most worked in beauty salons, barber shops, or department stores, and a few were employed by hospitals, hotels, and prisons. Approximately 4 of every 5 barbers and half of all cosmetologists are self-employed.

Nearly every town has a barber shop or beauty salon, but employment in this occupation is concentrated in the most populous cities and States. Hairstylists usually work in cities and suburbs, where the greatest demand for their services exists. Stylists who set fashion trends with their hairstyles usually work in New York City, Los Angeles, and other centers of fashion and the performing arts.

Training, Other Qualifications, and Advancement

Although all States require barbers and cosmetologists to be licensed, the qualifications necessary to obtain a license vary. Generally, a person must have graduated from a State-licensed barber or cosmetology school, pass a physical examination, and be at least 16 years old. Some States require graduation from high school while others require as little as an eighth grade education. In a few States, completion of an apprenticeship can substitute for graduation from a school, but very few barbers or cosmetologists learn their skills in this way. Applicants for a license usually are required to pass a written test and demonstrate an ability to perform basic barbering or cosmetology services.

Some States have reciprocity agreements that allow licensed barbers and cosmetologists to practice in a different State without additional formal training. Other States do not recognize training or licenses obtained in another State; consequently, persons who wish to become a barber or a cosmetologist should review the laws of the State in which they want to work before entering a training program.

Public and private vocational schools offer daytime or evening classes in barbering and cosmetology. These programs usually last 6 to 12 months. An apprenticeship program can last from 1 to 2 years. Formal training programs include classroom study, demonstrations, and practical work. Students study the basic services—haircutting, shaving, facial massaging, and hair and scalp treatments—and, under supervision, practice on customers in school "clinics." Most schools also teach unisex hairstyling and chemical styling. Students attend lectures on barber services, the use and care of instruments, sanitation and hygiene, and recognition of certain skin ailments. Instruction also is given in selling and general business practices. There are also advanced courses for experienced barbers in hairstyling, coloring, and the sale and service of hairpieces. Most schools teach hairstyling of men's as well as women's hair.

After graduating from a training program, students can take the State licensing examination. The examination consists of a written test and, in some cases, a practical test of cosmetology skills. A few States include an oral examination in which the applicant is asked to explain the procedures he or she is following while taking the practical test. In many States, cosmetology training may be credited towards a barbering license, and vice versa. A few States have even combined the two licenses into one hair styling license. In most States, a separate examination is given for people who want only a manicurist, massage, or facial care license.

Persons who want to become barbers or cosmetologists must have finger dexterity and a sense of form and artistry. They should enjoy dealing with the public and be willing and able to follow patrons' instructions. Some cosmetology schools consider people skills to be so integral to the job that they require coursework in this area. Because hairstyles are constantly changing, barbers and cosmetologists must keep abreast of the latest fashions and beauty techniques. Business skills are important for those who plan to operate their own salons, and the ability to be an effective salesperson is becoming vital for nearly all barbers and cosmetologists.

Many schools help their graduates find jobs. During their first months on the job, new workers are given relatively simple tasks, such as giving shampoos, or are assigned the simpler hairstyling patterns. Once they have demonstrated their skills, they are gradually permitted to perform the more complicated tasks such as giving shaves, coloring hair, or applying a permanent.

Advancement usually is in the form of higher earnings as barbers and cosmetologists gain experience and build a steady clientele. Some barbers and cosmetologists manage large salons or open their own after several years of experience. Some teach in barber or cosmetology schools. Others become sales representatives for cosmetics firms, open businesses as beauty or fashion consultants, or work as examiners for State licensing boards.

Job Outlook

Overall employment of barbers and cosmetologists is expected to grow about as fast as the average for all occupations through the year 2005. Population growth, rising incomes, and a growing demand for the services that they provide will stimulate the demand for these workers. Within this occupation, however, different employment trends are expected. Cosmetologists will account for virtually all of the employment growth, reflecting the continuing shifts in consumer preferences to more personalized services in unisex establishments. Demand for manicurists and for cosmetologists who are trained in nail care will be particularly strong. Employment of barbers is expected to decline slightly, but in spite of this decline, a couple of thousand job openings will arise annually for new barber licensees as older barbers retire.

Many job openings will become available in the cosmetology field due to the large size of the occupation and the expected employment growth. This is especially true for entry-level workers who are licensed to provide a broad range of cosmetology services. The level of competition for employment and customers may be greater at the higher-paying, prestigious salons, though, as applicants vie with a large pool of licensed and experienced cosmetologists. The number of part-time and self-employed, booth-renting cosmetologists should continue to grow, creating many opportunities for ambitious people to enter the field.

Earnings

Barbers and cosmetologists receive income either from commissions or wages and tips. Their median annual income in 1994 was $14,800. A number of factors determine the total income for barbers and cosmetologists, including the size and location of the shop, the number of hours worked, customers' tipping habits, and the competition from other barber shops and salons. A cosmetologist's or barber's initiative and ability to attract and hold regular customers are also key factors, so these workers may play an important role in determining their earnings. In fact, 1 out of 10 barbers and cosmetologists earned over $26,800 in 1994. Earnings for entry-level workers are generally lower, ranging from the minimum wage to considerably more in prestigious or exceptionally busy salons.

A growing number of barbers and cosmetologists rent chairs or booths from salons on a daily or hourly basis. These workers are essentially self-employed, and their earnings are a function of their "book," or clientele list.

Related Occupations

Other workers whose main activity consists of improving a patron's personal appearance include beauty consultants, make-up and wig specialists, and salon and health club managers. Other related workers are employed in the cosmetology industry as instructors and beauty supply distributors.

Sources of Additional Information

A list of licensed training schools and licensing requirements for cosmetologists can be obtained from:

☛National Accrediting Commission of Cosmetology Arts and Sciences, 901 North Stuart St., Suite 900, Arlington, VA 22203-1816.

Information about barber and cosmetology schools also is available from:

☛American Association of Cosmetology Schools, 901 North Washington St., Suite 206, Alexandria, VA 22314.

☛Accrediting Commission of Career Schools and Colleges of Technology, 2101 Wilson Blvd., Suite 302, Arlington, VA 22201.

For details on State licensing requirements and approved barber or cosmetology schools, contact the State board of barber examiners or the State board of cosmetology in your State capital.

Preschool Teachers and Child-Care Workers

(D.O.T. 092.227-018; 355.674-010; 359.677-010, -018, -026)

Nature of the Work

Nurturing and teaching preschool children, those who are 5 years old or younger, is the job of preschool teachers and child-care workers.

Found in daycare centers, nursery schools, preschools, and family daycare homes, these workers play an important role in a child's development by caring for the child when the parents are at work or away for other reasons. Some parents enroll their children in nursery schools or child-care centers primarily to provide them with the opportunity to interact with other children. In addition to attending to children's basic needs, these workers organize activities that stimulate the children's physical, emotional, intellectual, and social growth. They help children explore their interests, develop their talents and independence, build self-esteem, and learn how to behave with others.

Preschool teachers and child-care workers must work in two different worlds—the child's and the parent's. At the same time that they create a safe, comfortable environment in which children can grow and learn, they must also keep records of each child's progress and discuss the children's progress and needs with the parents. They must try to involve the parents as much as possible in the child's learning process, encouraging parents to increase their child's learning and development at home. Some preschools and daycare centers actively recruit parent volunteers to work with the children and participate in administrative decisions and program planning.

Most preschool teachers and child-care workers perform a combination of basic care and teaching duties. Through many basic care activities, preschool teachers and child-care workers provide opportunities for children to learn. For example, a worker who shows a child how to tie a shoe teaches the child and also provides for that child's basic care needs. Through their experiences in preschool and child-care programs, children learn about trust and gain a sense of security.

Young children cannot be taught in the same manner as older students because they are less physically, emotionally, and mentally developed. Children at this age learn mainly through play. What results is a less structured approach to teaching preschool children, including small group lessons, one-on-one instruction, and learning through creative activities, such as art, dance, and music. Interaction with their peers is an important part of early childhood development. Preschool children are given an opportunity to engage in conversation and discussions, and learn to play and work cooperatively with their classmates. Preschool teachers and child-care workers play a vital role in preparing children to build the skills they will need in elementary school.

Preschool teachers and child-care workers greet children as they arrive, help them remove outer garments, and teach them how to dress and undress. When caring for infants, they feed and change them. In order to ensure a well-balanced program, preschool teachers and child-care workers prepare daily and long-term schedules of activities. Each day's activities must balance individual and group play with quiet and active time. Children must be given some freedom to participate in activities in which they are interested. Recognizing the importance of play, preschool teachers and child-care workers build their program around it. They capitalize on children's play to further language development (storytelling and acting games), improve social skills (working together to build a neighborhood in a sandbox), and introduce scientific and mathematical concepts (balancing and counting blocks when building a bridge or mixing colors when painting). (A statement on teacher aides—who assist classroom teachers—appears elsewhere in the *Handbook*.)

Helping to keep children healthy is an important part of the job. Preschool teachers and child-care workers serve nutritious meals and snacks and teach good eating habits and personal hygiene. They see to it that children have proper rest periods. They spot children who may not feel well or show signs of emotional or developmental problems and discuss these matters with their supervisor and the child's parents. In some cases, preschool teachers and child-care workers help parents identify programs that will provide basic health services.

Early identification of children with special needs, such as those with behavioral, emotional, physical, or learning disabilities, is

Preschool teachers and child-care workers help children learn daily skills and gain independence.

important to improve their future learning ability. Special education teachers often work with these preschool children to provide the individual attention they need. (Special education teachers are covered in a separate statement in the *Handbook*.)

Working Conditions

Preschool care facilities may be in private homes, schools, religious institutions, workplaces where employers provide care for employees' children, or private buildings. Individuals who provide care in their own homes are generally called family daycare providers. (Child-care workers who work in the child's home are covered in the statement on private household workers found elsewhere in the *Handbook*.)

Watching children grow, enjoy learning, and gain new skills can be very rewarding. Working with children, preschool teachers and child-care workers often improve their communication, learning, and other personal skills. Also, the work is never routine; each day is marked by new activities and challenges. However, child care can be physically and emotionally taxing, as workers constantly stand, walk, bend, stoop, and lift to attend to each child's interests and problems. Preschool teachers and child-care workers must be enthusiastic and constantly alert, anticipate and prevent problems, deal with disruptive children, and provide fair but firm discipline. They must be able to communicate effectively with the children and their parents, as well as other teachers and child-care workers.

To ensure that children receive proper supervision, State regulations require certain ratios of workers to children. The ratio varies with the age of the children. Child development experts generally recommend that a single caregiver be responsible for no more than 3 or 4 infants (less than 1 year old), 5 or 6 toddlers (1 to 2 years old), or 10 preschool-age children (between 2 and 5 years old).

The working hours of preschool teachers and child-care workers vary widely. Daycare centers are generally open year round with long hours so that parents can drop off and pick up their children before and after work. Daycare centers employ full-time and part-time staff with staggered shifts to cover the entire day. Some workers are unable to take regular breaks during the day due to limited staffing. Public and many private preschool programs operate during the typical 9- or 10-month school year, employing both full-time and part-time workers. Many preschool teachers may work extra unpaid hours each week on curriculum planning, parent meetings, and occasional fundraising activities. Family daycare providers have flexible hours and daily routines, but may work long or unusual hours to fit parents' work schedules. Some preschool employees suffer burnout due to long hours, stressful conditions, and low pay and benefits. Turnover in the occupation is high.

Employment

Preschool teachers and child-care workers held over 1 million jobs in 1994. Many worked part time. About 4 out of 10 preschool teachers and child-care workers are self-employed, most of whom are family daycare providers.

Over 60 percent of all salaried preschool teachers and child-care workers are found in child daycare centers and preschools, and about 15 percent work for a religious institution. The rest work in other service organizations and in government. Some employers run for-profit operations; many are affiliated with a local or national chain. Other employers, such as religious institutions, community agencies, school systems, and State and local governments, are nonprofit. A growing number of business firms operate daycare centers for the children of their employees.

Training, Other Qualifications, and Advancement

The training and qualifications required of preschool teachers and child-care workers vary widely. Each State has licensing requirements that regulate caregiver training, ranging from a high school diploma, to community college courses, to a college degree in child development or early childhood education. Some States require continuing education for workers in this field. For instance, Virginia requires that all workers in daycare centers receive 8 hours of courses related to child care each year. Formal education requirements in some private preschools and daycare centers are often lower than in public programs since they are not bound by State requirements. Often, child-care workers can obtain employment with a high school diploma and minimal experience.

Many States prefer preschool teachers and child-care workers to have a Child Development Associate (CDA) credential, which is offered by the Council for Early Childhood Professional Recognition. The CDA credential is recognized as a qualification for teachers and directors in 46 States and the District of Columbia. There are two ways to become a CDA—through direct assessment or by completing the Council's 1-year training program. Direct assessment is appropriate for people who already have some background and experience in early childhood education, while the training program is designed for people with little or no child development education or experience. To receive the credential, the applicant must demonstrate knowledge and skills acquired through formal training or experience, that meet certain nationally recognized standards for working with young children, to a team of child-care professionals from the Council for Early Childhood Professional Recognition.

Some employers may not require a CDA credential, but may require secondary or postsecondary courses in child development and early childhood education, and possibly work experience in a child-care setting. Other schools require their own specialized training. For example, Montessori preschool teachers must complete an additional year of training after receiving their bachelor's degree in early childhood education or a related field. Public schools typically require a bachelor's degree and State teacher certification. Teacher training programs include a variety of liberal arts courses, courses in child development, student teaching, and prescribed professional courses, including instruction in teaching gifted, disadvantaged, and other children with special needs.

Preschool teachers and child-care workers should be mature, patient, understanding, and articulate, and have energy and physical stamina. Skills in music, art, drama, and storytelling are also important. Those who work for themselves must have business sense and management abilities.

As preschool teachers and child-care workers gain experience, they may advance to supervisory or administrative positions in large child-care centers or preschools. Often, however, these positions require additional training, such as a bachelor's or master's degree. Other workers move on to work in resource and referral agencies, consulting with parents on available child services. Some workers become involved in policy or advocacy work related to child care and early childhood education. With a bachelor's degree, preschool teachers may become certified to teach in public schools at the kindergarten, elementary, and secondary school levels. Some workers set up their own child-care businesses.

Job Outlook

Employment of preschool teachers and child-care workers is projected to increase faster than the average for all occupations through the year 2005. Job openings should be plentiful as many preschool teachers and child-care workers leave the occupation each year for other—often better paying—jobs, family responsibilities, or other reasons. High turnover, combined with an increased demand for preschool teachers and child-care workers, is expected to create many openings. Qualified persons who are interested in this work should have little trouble finding and keeping a job.

Although the number of children under 5 years of age is expected to decline slightly through the year 2005, the proportion of youngsters in daycare and preschool will increase, reflecting a shift in the type of child-care arrangements parents choose. Many parents turn to formal child-care arrangements for a variety of reasons—they may need two incomes; they may find it too difficult to set up a satisfactory arrangement with a relative, babysitter, or live-in worker; or they may prefer the formal arrangements for personal reasons, such as a more structured learning and social environment.

Continuing high labor force participation among women of childbearing age will also contribute to employment growth among preschool teachers and child-care workers. Mothers of very young children have been joining the labor force in growing numbers, and this pattern is not expected to change. Moreover, women are returning to work sooner after childbirth. Many employers are increasing child-care benefits to their employees in the form of direct child-care assistance—such as vouchers and subsidies for community child-care centers—more flexible work schedules, and on-site daycare facilities.

Earnings

Pay depends on the employer and educational attainment of the worker. Although the pay is generally very low, more education means higher earnings in some cases.

In 1994, median weekly earnings of full-time, salaried child-care workers were $260. The middle 50 percent of child-care workers earned between $190 and $330. The top 10 percent of child-care workers earned at least $430; the bottom 10 percent earned less than $130.

Preschool teachers in public schools who have State teacher certification generally have salaries and benefits comparable to kindergarten and elementary school teachers. According to the National Education Association, public elementary school teachers earned an estimated average salary of $36,400 in 1995. (A statement on kindergarten, elementary, and secondary school teachers is found elsewhere in the *Handbook*.) Preschool teachers in privately funded child-care centers generally earn much lower salaries than other comparably educated workers.

Earnings of self-employed child-care workers vary depending on the hours worked, number and ages of the children, and the location.

Benefits for preschool teachers and child-care workers also vary. Many employers offer free or discounted child care to employees. Some offer a full benefits package, including health insurance and paid vacations, but others offer no benefits at all. Some employers offer seminars and workshops to help workers improve upon or learn new skills. A few are willing to cover the cost of courses taken at community colleges or technical schools.

Related Occupations

Child-care work requires patience; creativity; an ability to nurture, motivate, teach, and influence children; and leadership, organizational, and administrative abilities. Others who work with children and need these aptitudes include teacher aides, children's tutors, kindergarten and elementary school teachers, early childhood program directors, and child psychologists.

Sources of Additional Information

For information on careers in educating children and issues affecting preschool teachers and child-care workers, contact:

☛National Association for the Education of Young Children, 1509 16th St. NW., Washington, DC 20036.

☛Association for Childhood Education International, 11501 Georgia Ave., Suite 315, Wheaton, MD 20902-1924.

For information on the Federally sponsored Head Start program, contact:

☛Head Start Bureau, P.O. Box 1182, Washington, DC 20013.

For eligibility requirements and a description of the Child Development Associate credential, write to:

☛Council for Early Childhood Professional Recognition, 1341 G St. NW., Suite 400, Washington, DC 20005.

For information on salaries and efforts to improve compensation in child care, contact:

☛National Center for the Early Childhood Work Force, 733 15th St. NW., Suite 1037, Washington, DC 20005.

State Departments of Human Services or Social Services can supply State regulations and training requirements for child-care workers.

Flight Attendants

(D.O.T. 352.367-010)

Nature of the Work

It is the job of the flight attendants to see that all their passengers have a safe, comfortable, and enjoyable airplane flight.

At least 1 hour before each flight, attendants are briefed by the captain, the pilot in command, on such things as expected weather conditions and special passenger problems. The attendants check that the passenger cabin is in order, that supplies of food, beverages, blankets, and reading material are adequate, and that first aid kits and other emergency equipment are aboard and in working order. As passengers board the plane, attendants greet them, check their tickets, and assist them if necessary in storing coats and carry-on luggage.

Before the plane takes off, attendants instruct passengers in the use of emergency equipment and check to see that all passengers have their seat belts fastened and seat backs forward. In the air, they answer questions about the flight; distribute reading material, pillows, and blankets; and help small children, elderly or disabled persons, and any others needing assistance. They may administer first aid to passengers who become ill. Attendants also serve cocktails and other refreshments and, on many flights, heat and distribute precooked meals. After the plane has landed, flight attendants assist passengers as they leave the plane. They then prepare reports on medications given to passengers, lost and found articles, and cabin equipment conditions. Some flight attendants straighten up the plane's cabin.

Helping passengers in the event of an emergency is the most important responsibility of the flight attendant. This may range from reassuring passengers during occasional encounters with strong turbulence to directing passengers in evacuating a plane following an emergency landing.

Lead or first flight attendants aboard planes oversee the work of the other attendants while performing most of the same duties.

Working Conditions

Since airlines operate around the clock year round, attendants may work at night and on holidays and weekends. They usually fly 75 to 85 hours a month. In addition, they generally spend about 75 to 85 hours a month on the ground preparing planes for flights, writing reports following completed flights, and waiting for planes that arrive late. Because of variations in scheduling and limitations on flying

Flight attendants ensure that the ground crew delivers adequate supplies of food and beverage.

time, many attendants have 11 or more days off each month. Attendants may be away from their home base at least one-third of the time. During this period, the airlines provide hotel accommodations and an allowance for meal expenses.

The combination of free time and discount air fares provides flight attendants the opportunity to travel and see new places. However, the work can be strenuous and trying. Short flights require speedy service if meals are served. A rough flight can make serving drinks and meals difficult. Attendants stand during much of the flight and must remain pleasant and efficient regardless of how tired they are or how demanding passengers may be. Flight attendants are susceptible to injury because of the job demands in a moving aircraft.

Employment

Flight attendants held about 105,000 jobs in 1994. Commercial airlines employed the vast majority of all flight attendants, most of whom were stationed in major cities at the airlines' home bases. A small number of flight attendants worked for large companies that operate their own aircraft for business purposes.

Training, Other Qualifications, and Advancement

The airlines prefer to hire poised, tactful, and resourceful people who can deal comfortably with strangers. Applicants usually must be at least 19 to 21 years old. Flight attendants must have excellent health, good vision, and the ability to speak clearly.

Applicants must be high school graduates. Those having several years of college or experience in dealing with the public are preferred. More and more attendants being hired are college graduates. Flight attendants for international airlines generally must speak an appropriate foreign language fluently. Some of the major airlines prefer candidates who can speak two major foreign languages for their international flights.

Most large airlines require that newly hired flight attendants complete 4 to 6 weeks of intensive training in their own flight training centers. The airlines that do not operate training centers generally send new employees to the center of another airline. Transportation to the training centers and an allowance for board, room, and school supplies may be provided. Trainees learn emergency procedures such as evacuating an airplane, operating an oxygen system, and giving first aid. Attendants also are taught flight regulations and duties, and company operations and policies. Trainees receive instruction on personal grooming and weight control. Trainees for the international routes get additional instruction in passport and customs regulations and dealing with terrorism. Towards the end of their training, students go on practice flights. Attendants must receive 12 to 14 hours of training in emergency procedures and passenger relations annually.

After completing initial training, flight attendants are assigned to one of their airline's bases. New attendants are placed in "reserve status" and are called on either to staff extra flights or fill in for attendants who are sick or on vacation. Reserve attendants on duty must be available on short notice. Attendants usually remain on reserve for at least 1 year; at some cities, it may take 5 years or longer to advance from reserve status. Advancement takes longer today than in the past because experienced attendants are remaining in this career for more years than they used to. Attendants who no longer are on reserve bid for regular assignments. Because these assignments are based on seniority, usually only the most experienced attendants get their choice of base and flights.

Some attendants transfer within the company to flight service instructor, customer service director, recruiting representative, or various other administrative positions.

Job Outlook

Opportunities should be favorable for persons seeking flight attendant jobs as the number of applicants is expected to be roughly in balance with the number of job openings. Those with at least 2 years of college and experience in dealing with the public should have the best chance of being hired.

As more career minded people have entered this occupation, turnover—which traditionally has been very high—has declined somewhat. Still, most job openings through the year 2005 should flow from replacement needs. Many flight attendants are attracted to the occupation by the glamour of the airline industry and the opportunity to travel, but many eventually leave in search of jobs that offer higher earnings and require fewer nights be spent away from their families. Thousands of job openings will arise each year to replace flight attendants who transfer to another occupation or who leave the labor force.

Employment of flight attendants is expected to grow faster than the average for all occupations through the year 2005. Growth in population and income is expected to increase the number of airline passengers. Airlines enlarge their capacity by increasing the number and size of planes in operation. Since Federal Aviation Administration safety rules require one attendant for every 50 seats, more flight attendants will be needed.

Employment of flight attendants is sensitive to cyclical swings in the economy. During recessions, when the demand for air travel declines, many flight attendants are put on part-time status or laid off. Until demand increases, few new attendants are hired.

Earnings

Beginning flight attendants had median earnings of about $12,700 a year in 1994, according to data from the Association of Flight Attendants. Flight attendants with 6 years of flying experience had median annual earnings of about $18,700, while some senior flight attendants earned as much as $40,000 a year. Flight attendants receive extra compensation for overtime and for night and international flights. In addition, flight attendants and their immediate families are entitled to reduced fares on their own and most other airlines.

Many flight attendants belong to the Association of Flight Attendants. Others are members of the Transport Workers Union of America, The International Brotherhood of Teamsters, or other unions.

Flight attendants are required to buy uniforms and wear them while on duty. Uniform replacement items are usually paid for by the company. The airlines generally provide a small allowance to cover cleaning and upkeep of the uniforms.

Related Occupations

Other jobs that involve helping people as a safety professional and require the ability to be pleasant even under trying circumstances include emergency medical technician, firefighter, maritime crew and camp counselor.

Sources of Additional Information

Information about job opportunities in a particular airline and the qualifications required may be obtained by writing to the personnel manager of the company. For addresses of airline companies and information about job opportunities and salaries, contact:
☛FAPA, 4959 Massachusetts Blvd., Atlanta, GA 30337. (This organization may be called toll free at 1-800-Jet-Jobs, extension 190.)

Homemaker-Home Health Aides

(D.O.T. 309.354-010 and 354.377-014)

Nature of the Work

Homemaker-home health aides help elderly, disabled, and ill persons live in their own homes instead of in a health facility. Most work with elderly or disabled clients who need more extensive care than family or friends can provide. Some homemaker-home health aides work with families in which a parent is incapacitated and small children need care. Others help discharged hospital patients who have relatively short-term needs. These workers are sometimes called home care aides and personal care attendants.

Homemaker-home health aides provide housekeeping services, personal care, and emotional support for their clients. They clean clients' houses, do laundry, and change bed linens. Aides may also plan meals (including special diets), shop for food, and cook.

Home health aides provide personal care services, also known as "hands on" care because they physically touch the patient. These aides help clients move from bed, bathe, dress, and groom. They also check pulse, temperature, and respiration; help with simple prescribed exercises; and assist with medication routines. Occasionally, they change nonsterile dressings, use special equipment such as a hydraulic lift, give massages and alcohol rubs, or assist with braces and artificial limbs. Some accompany clients outside the home, serving as guide, companion, and aide.

Homemaker-home health aides also provide instruction and psychological support. For example, they assist in toilet training a severely mentally handicapped child or just listen to clients talk about their problems. Aides keep records of services performed and of the client's condition and progress.

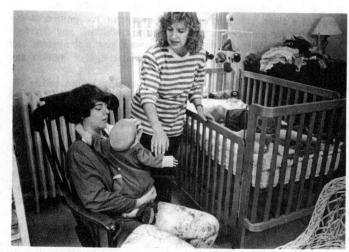

The number of jobs for homemaker-home health aides will more than double by 2005.

In home care agencies, homemaker-home health aides are supervised by a registered nurse, a physical therapist, or a social worker, who assigns them specific duties. Aides report changes in the client's condition to the supervisor or case manager. Homemaker-home health aides also participate in case reviews, consulting with the team caring for the client—registered nurses, therapists, and other health professionals.

Working Conditions

The homemaker-home health aide's daily routine may vary. Aides may go to the same home every day for months or even years. However, most aides work with a number of different clients, each job lasting a few hours, days, or weeks. Aides often go to four or five clients on the same day.

Surroundings differ from case to case. Some homes are neat and pleasant, while others are untidy or depressing. Some clients are angry, abusive, depressed, or otherwise difficult; others are pleasant and cooperative.

Homemaker-home health aides generally work on their own with periodic visits by their supervisor. They get detailed instructions explaining when to visit clients and what services to perform. Many aides work part time, and weekend hours are common.

Most aides generally travel by public transportation, but some need a car. In any event, they are responsible for getting to the client's home. Aides may spend a good portion of the working day traveling from one client to another.

Employment

Homemaker-home health aides held about 598,000 jobs in 1994. Most aides are employed by homemaker-home health agencies, home health agencies, visiting nurse associations, residential care facilities with home health departments, hospitals, public health and welfare departments, community volunteer agencies, and temporary help firms. Self-employed aides have no agency affiliation or supervision, and accept clients, set fees, and arrange work schedules on their own.

Training, Other Qualifications, and Advancement

In some States, this occupation is open to individuals with no formal training. On-the-job training is generally provided. Other States may require formal training, depending on Federal or State law.

The Federal Goverment has enacted guidelines for home health aides whose employers receive reimbursement from Medicare. Federal law requires home health aides to pass a competency test covering 12 areas: Communication skills; observation, reporting, and documentation of patient status and the care or services furnished; reading and recording vital signs; basic infection control procedures; basic elements of body function and changes; maintenance of a clean, safe, and healthy environment; recognition of and procedures for emergencies; the physical, emotional, and developmental characteristics of the patients served; personal hygiene and grooming; safe transfer techniques; normal range of motion and positioning; and basic nutrition.

A home health aide may also take training before taking the competency test. Federal law suggests at least 75 hours of classroom and practical training supervised by a registered nurse. Training and testing programs may be offered by the employing agency, but they must meet the standards of the Health Care Financing Administration. Training programs vary depending upon State regulations. Thirteen States have specific laws on personal care services.

The Foundation for Hospice and Home Care offers a National Homemaker-Home Health Aide certification. The certification is a voluntary demonstration that the individual has met industry standards.

Successful homemaker-home health aides like to help people and do not mind hard work. They should be responsible, compassionate, emotionally stable, and cheerful. Aides should also be tactful, honest, and discreet since they work in private homes.

Homemaker-home health aides must be in good health. A physical examination including State regulated tests like those for tuberculosis may be required.

Advancement is limited. In some agencies, workers start out performing homemaker duties, such as cleaning. With experience and training, they may take on personal care duties. The most experienced aides assist with medical equipment such as ventilators, which help patients breathe.

Job Outlook

A large number of job openings is expected for homemaker-home health aides, due to very rapid growth and very high turnover. Homemaker-home health aides is expected to be one of the fastest growing occupations through the year 2005—more than doubling in employment size.

The number of people in their seventies and beyond is projected to rise substantially. This age group is characterized by mounting health problems that require some assistance. Also, there will be an increasing reliance on home care for patients of all ages. This trend reflects several developments: Efforts to contain costs by moving patients out of hospitals and nursing facilities as quickly as possible; the realization that treatment can be more effective in familiar surroundings rather than clinical surroundings; and the development of portable medical equipment for in-home treatment.

In addition to jobs created by the increase in demand for these workers, replacement needs are expected to produce numerous openings. Turnover is high, a reflection of the relatively low skill requirements, low pay, and high emotional demands of the work. For these same reasons, many people are unwilling to do this kind of work. Therefore, persons who are interested in this work and suited for it should have excellent job opportunities, particularly those with experience or training as homemaker-home health aides or nursing aides.

Earnings

Earnings for homemaker-home health aides vary considerably. According to a National Association for Home Care survey of home care aides who work in Medicare-certified agencies, beginning aides' average starting hourly wage ranged from $4.90 to $6.86 in May 1994. More experienced aides' average starting hourly wage ranged from $5.69 to $8.11. Wages were somewhat higher in the Northeast and West and somewhat lower in the Midwest and South. Some aides are paid on a salary or per-visit basis.

Most employers give slight pay increases with experience and added responsibility. Aides usually are paid only for the time worked in the home. They normally are not paid for travel time between jobs. Most employers hire only "on-call" hourly workers and provide no benefits.

Related Occupations

Homemaker-home health aide is a service occupation that combines duties of health workers and social service workers. Workers in related occupations that involve personal contact to help or instruct others include attendants in children's institutions, childcare attendants in schools, child monitors, companions, nursing aides, nursery school attendants, occupational therapy aides, nursing aides, physical therapy aides, playroom attendants, and psychiatric aides.

Sources of Additional Information

General information about training and referrals to State and local agencies about opportunities for homemaker-home health aides, a list of relevant publications, and information on national certification are available from:

☛ Foundation for Hospice and Homecare/National Certification Program, 519 C St. NE., Washington, DC 20002.

Janitors and Cleaners and Cleaning Supervisors

(D.O.T. 321.137-010, -014; 323.137-010, .687; 350.137-026; 358.687-010; 381.137-010, .687 except -010; 382.664-010; 389.667-010, .683-010, .687-014; 739.687-198; 891.687-010 and -018; and 952.687-010)

Nature of the Work

Janitors and cleaners—also called building custodians, executive housekeepers, or maids—keep office buildings, hospitals, stores, apartment houses, hotels, and other types of buildings clean and in good condition. Some only do cleaning; others have a wide range of duties. They may fix leaky faucets, empty trash cans, do painting and carpentry, replenish bathroom supplies, mow lawns, and see that heating and air-conditioning equipment works properly. On a typical day, janitors may wet- or dry-mop floors, clean bathrooms, vacuum carpets, dust furniture, make minor repairs, and exterminate insects and rodents. In hospitals, where they are mostly known as maids or housekeepers, they may also wash bed frames, brush mattresses, make beds, and disinfect and sterilize equipment and supplies using germicides and sterilizing equipment. In hotels, aside from cleaning and maintaining the premises, they may deliver ironing boards, cribs, and rollaway beds to guests' rooms.

Janitors and cleaners use various equipment, tools, and cleaning materials. For one job, they may need a mop and bucket; for another, an electric polishing machine and a special cleaning solution. Improved building materials, chemical cleaners, and power equipment have made many tasks easier and less time consuming, but janitors must learn proper use of equipment and cleaners to avoid harming floors, fixtures, and themselves.

Cleaning supervisors coordinate, schedule, and supervise the activities of janitors and cleaners. They assign tasks and inspect building areas to see that work has been done properly; issue supplies and equipment; inventory stocks to ensure adequate supplies; screen and hire job applicants; and recommend promotions, transfers or dismissals. They also train new and experienced employees. Supervisors may prepare reports concerning room occupancy, hours worked, and department expenses. Some also perform cleaning duties.

Working Conditions

Because most office buildings are cleaned while they are empty, many cleaners work evening hours. Some, however, such as school and hospital custodians, work in the daytime. When there is a need full-time janitors and cleaners and supervisors worked about 40 hours

Janitors often bend, stoop, or stretch.

for 24-hour maintenance, janitors may be assigned to shifts. Most a week. Part-time cleaners usually work in the evenings and on weekends.

Janitors and cleaners usually work inside heated, well-lighted buildings. However, sometimes they work outdoors sweeping walkways, mowing lawns, or shoveling snow. Working with machines can be noisy, and some tasks, such as cleaning bathrooms and trash rooms, can be dirty and unpleasant. Janitors may suffer cuts, bruises, and burns from machines, handtools, and chemicals. They spend most of their time on their feet, sometimes lifting or pushing heavy furniture or equipment. Many tasks, such as dusting or sweeping, require constant bending, stooping, and stretching. As a result, janitors may also suffer back injuries and sprains.

Employment

Janitors and cleaners, including cleaning supervisors, held 3,168,000 jobs in 1994. More than one-third worked part time (less than 35 hours a week).

Janitors and cleaners held about 19 jobs out of 20. They worked in every type of establishment. One in 5 worked for a firm supplying building maintenance services on a contract basis. About 1 in 6 worked in a school, including colleges and universities. One in 8 worked in a hotel. Others were employed by hospitals, restaurants, operators of apartment buildings, office buildings, and other types of real estate, churches and other religious organizations, manufacturing firms, and government agencies.

Supervisors held about 1 job in 20. About 30 percent each were in hotels and hospitals. Others were employed by firms supplying building maintenance services on a contract basis, nursing care facilities, and educational facilities.

Although cleaning jobs can be found in all cities and towns, most are located in highly populated areas where there are many office buildings, schools, apartment houses, and hospitals.

Training, Other Qualifications, and Advancement

No special education is required for most cleaning jobs, but beginners should know simple arithmetic and be able to follow instructions. High school shop courses are helpful for jobs that involve repair work.

Most janitors and cleaners learn their skills on the job. Usually, beginners work with an experienced cleaner, doing routine cleaning. They are given more complicated work as they gain experience.

In some cities, programs run by unions, government agencies, or employers teach janitorial skills. Students learn how to clean buildings thoroughly and efficiently, how to select and safely use various cleansing agents, and how to operate and maintain machines, such as wet and dry vacuums, buffers, and polishers. Students learn to plan their work, to follow safety and health regulations, to interact positively with people in the buildings they clean, and to work without supervision. Instruction in minor electrical, plumbing, and other repairs may also be given. Those who come in contact with the public should have good communication skills. Employers usually look for dependable, hard-working individuals who are in good health, follow directions well, and get along with other people.

Janitors and cleaners usually find work by answering newspaper advertisements, applying directly to organizations where they would like to work, contacting local labor unions, or contacting State employment service offices.

Advancement opportunities for janitorial workers usually are limited in organizations where they are the only maintenance worker. Where there is a large maintenance staff, however, janitors can be promoted to supervisor and to area supervisor or manager. A high school diploma improves the chances for advancement. Some janitors set up their own maintenance business.

Supervisors usually move up through the ranks. In many establishments, they are required to take some in-service training to perfect housekeeping techniques and procedures, and to enhance supervisory skills.

Job Outlook

The occupation of janitors and cleaners is easy to enter because there are few requirements for formal education and training, turnover is high, and part-time and temporary jobs are plentiful. The need to replace workers who transfer to other occupations or leave the labor force will create most job openings.

Employment of building janitors and cleaners and cleaning supervisors is expected to grow about as fast as the average for all occupations through the year 2005 as the number of office buildings, apartment houses, schools, factories, hospitals, and other buildings increases. Businesses providing janitorial and cleaning services on a contract basis are expected to be one of the fastest growing employers of janitors and cleaners and cleaning supervisors as firms try to reduce costs by hiring independent contractors.

New technology is expected to have little effect on employment of janitors and cleaners. Robots now under development are limited to performing a single cleaning task and may not be usable in many places, particularly cluttered areas such as hotel and hospital rooms.

Earnings

Janitors and cleaners who usually worked full time averaged about $293 a week in 1994; the middle 50 percent earned between $219 and $401. Ten percent earned less than $178; 10 percent earned more than $527. Maids and housekeepers who usually worked full time averaged about $246 a week in 1994, with the middle 50 percent earning between $198 and $312. Ten percent earned less than $162 and 10 percent earned more than $407.

Cleaning supervisors who usually worked full time averaged about $361 a week in 1994; the middle 50 percent earned between $281 and $501. Ten percent earned less than $210 and 10 percent earned more than $686.

According to a survey of workplaces in 160 metropolitan areas, janitors had median earnings of $270 for a 40-hour week in 1993. The middle half earned between $206 and $374 a week.

Most building service workers receive paid holidays and vacations and health insurance.

Related Occupations

Private household workers have job duties similar to janitors and cleaners. Workers who specialize in one of the many job functions of janitors and cleaners include refuse collectors, floor waxers, street sweepers, window cleaners, gardeners, boiler tenders, pest controllers, and general maintenance repairers.

Sources of Additional Information

Information about janitorial jobs may be obtained from a local State employment service office.

For information about education and training or starting a janitorial company, contact:
☛Building Service Contractors Association International, 10201 Lee Hwy., Suite 225, Fairfax, VA 22030.

For information about careers in executive housekeeping, contact:
☛National Executive Housekeepers Association, Inc., 1001 Eastwind Dr., Suite 301, Westerville, OH 43081-3361.

Private Household Workers

(D.O.T. 301 except .687-018; 302; 305; 309 except .354-010 and .677-014)

Nature of the Work

Private household workers clean homes, care for children, plan and cook meals, do laundry, administer the household, and perform numerous other duties. They are employed by many types of households of various income levels. Although wealthy families may employ a large staff, it is much more common for one worker to be employed in a household where both parents work. Many workers are employed in households having one parent. A number of household workers work part time for two or more employers.

Most household workers are *general houseworkers* and usually the only worker employed in the home. They dust and polish furniture; sweep, mop, and wax floors; vacuum; and clean ovens, refrigerators, and bathrooms. They may also wash dishes, polish silver, and change and make beds. Some wash, fold, and iron clothes; a few wash windows. Other duties may include looking after a child or an elderly person, cooking, feeding pets, answering the telephone and doorbell, and calling and waiting for repair workers. General houseworkers may also take clothes and laundry to the cleaners, buy groceries, and do other errands.

Household workers whose primary responsibility is taking care of children are called *child-care workers*. Those employed on an hourly basis are usually called baby-sitters. Child-care workers bathe, dress, and feed children; supervise their play, wash their clothes, and clean their rooms. They may also put them to sleep and waken them, read to them, involve them in educational games, take them for doctors' visits, and discipline them. Those who are in charge of infants, sometimes called *infant nurses*, also prepare bottles and change diapers.

Nannies generally take care of children from birth to age 10 or 12, tending to the child's early education, nutrition, health, and other needs. They may also perform the duties of a general housekeeper, including general cleaning and laundry duties. *Governesses* look after children in addition to other household duties. They may help them with schoolwork, teach them a foreign language, and guide them in their general upbringing. (Child-care workers who work outside the child's home are covered in the statement on child-care workers elsewhere in the *Handbook*.)

Those who assist elderly, handicapped, or convalescent people are called *companions* or *personal attendants*. Depending on the employer's needs, a companion or attendant might help with bathing and dressing, preparing and serving meals, and keeping the house tidy. They also may read to their employers, write letters for them, play cards or games, and go with them on walks and outings. Companions may also accompany their employers to medical appointments and handle their social and business affairs.

Households with a large staff may include a housekeeper or a butler, a cook, a caretaker, and a launderer. *Housekeepers* and *butlers* hire, supervise, and coordinate the household staff to keep the household running smoothly. Butlers also receive and announce guests, answer telephones, deliver messages, serve food and drinks, chauffeur, or act as a personal attendant. *Cooks* plan and prepare meals, clean the kitchen, order groceries and supplies, and may also serve meals. *Caretakers* do heavy housework and general home maintenance. They wash windows, wax floors, and hang draperies. They maintain heating and other equipment and do light carpentry, painting, and odd jobs. They may also mow the lawn and do some gardening if the household does not have a gardener.

Working Conditions

Private household workers usually work in pleasant and comfortable homes or apartments. Most are dayworkers who live in their own homes and travel to work. Some live in the home of their employer, generally with their own room and bath. Live-ins usually work longer hours. However, if they work evenings or weekends, they may get other time off. Living in may isolate them from family and friends. On the other hand, they often become part of their employer's family and may derive satisfaction from caring for them. Being a general houseworker can also be isolating, since work is usually done alone.

Housekeeping is hard work. Both dayworkers and live-ins are on their feet most of the day and do much walking, lifting, bending, stooping, and reaching. In addition, some employers may be very demanding.

Job opportunities for private household workers are excellent.

Employment

Private household workers held about 808,000 jobs in 1994. Over 60 percent were general houseworkers, mostly dayworkers; 35 percent were child-care workers, including baby-sitters; less than 5 percent were housekeepers, butlers, cooks, and launderers. Most jobs are in big cities and their affluent suburbs. Some are on large estates or in resorts away from cities.

Training, Other Qualifications, and Advancement

Private household workers generally do not need any special training. Individuals who cannot find other work because of limited language or other skills often turn to this work. Most jobs require the ability to clean well, cook, or take care of children. These skills are generally learned by young people while helping with housework at home. Some training takes place on the job. Employers show the household workers what they want done and how. For child-care workers and companions, general education, background, and ability to get along with the person they will care for are most important.

Home economics courses in high schools and vocational and adult education schools offer training in cooking and child care. Courses in child development, first aid, and nursing in postsecondary schools are also useful.

Special schools for butlers, nannies, and governesses teach household administration, early childhood education, nutrition, child care, and bookkeeping.

Private household workers must be able to work well with others and be honest, discreet, dependable, courteous, and neat. They also need physical stamina.

There are very few opportunities for advancement within this occupation. Few large households exist with big staffs where general houseworkers can advance to cook, executive housekeeper, butler, or governess, and these jobs may require specialized training. Advancement usually consists of better pay and working conditions. Workers may move to similar jobs in hotels, hospitals, and restaurants, where the pay and fringe benefits are usually better. Others transfer into better paying unrelated jobs.

Job Outlook

Job opportunities for people wishing to become private household workers are expected to be excellent through 2005, as the demand for these services continues to far outpace the supply of workers willing to provide them.

For many years, demand for household help has outstripped the supply of workers willing to take domestic jobs. The imbalance is expected to persist—and possibly worsen—through the year 2005. Demand is expected to grow as more women join the labor force and need help running their households. Demand for companions and personal attendants is also expected to rise due to projected rapid growth in the elderly population.

The supply situation is not likely to improve. Unattractiveness of the work, low status, low pay, lack of fringe benefits, and limited advancement potential deter many prospective household workers. Due to the limited supply of household workers, many employers have turned to domestic cleaning firms, child-care centers, and temporary help firms to meet their needs for household help. This trend is expected to continue. (See the statements on janitors and cleaners, preschool teachers and child-care workers, and homemaker-home health aides elsewhere in the *Handbook*.)

Although employment of private household workers is expected to decline through 2005, many jobs will be available because of the need to replace the large number of workers who leave these occupations every year. Persons who are interested in and suited for this work should have no trouble finding and keeping jobs.

Earnings

Earnings of private household workers depend on the type of work, the number of hours, household and staff size, geographic location, training, and experience.

Most private household workers are employed part time, or less than 35 hours a week. Some work only 2 or 3 days a week, while others may work half a day 4 or 5 days a week. Earnings vary from about $10 an hour or more in a big city to less than the Federal minimum wage—$4.25 an hour—in some rural areas (some domestic workers are not covered by minimum wage laws). In addition, dayworkers often get carfare and a free meal. Live-in domestics usually earn more than dayworkers and also get free room and board. However, they often work longer hours. Baby-sitters usually have the lowest earnings.

In 1994, median earnings for full-time private household workers were about $180 a week. Some full-time live-in housekeepers, cooks, butlers, nannies, and governesses earn considerably more. Based on limited information, experienced workers employed by wealthy families in major metropolitan areas may earn $800 to $1,000 a week. Private household workers who live with their employers may be given room and board, medical benefits, a car, vacation days, and education benefits. However, most private household workers receive very limited or no benefits.

Related Occupations

Other workers with similar duties are building custodians, hotel and restaurant cleaners, child-care workers in daycare centers, home-health aides, cooks, kitchen workers, waiters and waitresses, and bartenders.

Sources of Additional Information

Information about job opportunities for private household workers is available from local private employment agencies and State employment service offices.

Agriculture, Forestry, Fishing, and Related Occupations

Animal Caretakers, Except Farm

(D.O.T. 410.674-010, -022; 412.674-010, -014; 418.381-010, .674-010, 677-010; and 449.674-010)

Nature of the Work

Most people like animals. But, as pet owners can attest, it is hard work taking care of them. Animal caretakers, sometimes called animal attendants or animal keepers, feed, water, groom, bathe, and exercise animals and clean and repair their cages. They also play with the animals, provide companionship, and observe behavioral changes that could indicate illness or injury.

Kennels, animal shelters, animal hospitals, pet stores, stables, veterinary facilities, laboratories, and zoological parks all house animals and employ caretakers. Job titles and duties vary by employment setting.

Kennel staff usually care for small companion animals like dogs and cats. Beginning attendants perform basic tasks, such as cleaning cages and dog runs. Experienced attendants may give basic treatment and first aid, bathe and groom animals, and clean their ears and teeth. "Dog groomers" specialize in maintaining the animals appearance. Some groomers work in kennels and others operate their own grooming business. Caretakers also sell pet food and supplies, teach obedience classes, help with breeding, or prepare animals for shipping.

In addition to providing the basic needs of the animals, caretakers in animal shelters screen applicants for animal adoption, vaccinate newly admitted animals, and euthanize (put to death) seriously ill, severely injured, or unwanted animals.

Pet store caretakers provide basic care, sell pet supplies, and give advice to customers.

Workers in stables saddle and unsaddle horses, give them rubdowns, and walk them through a cool-off after a ride. They also feed and groom the horses, muck out stalls, polish saddles, clean and organize the tack room, and store supplies and feed. Experienced staff may help train horses.

Animal caretakers in animal hospitals are like primary care nurses in human hospitals—they spend more time with the patients than anyone else. Busy veterinarians rely on caretakers to keep a constant eye on the condition of animals under their charge. Caretakers watch as animals recover from surgery, check whether dressings are still on correctly, observe the animals' overall attitude and notify a doctor if anything seems out of the ordinary. While among the animals, caretakers clean constantly to maintain sanitary conditions in the hospital.

In zoos, caretakers called keepers prepare the diets, clean the enclosures, monitor the behavior of exotic animals, and sometimes assist in research studies on their wards. Keepers also may answer questions from visitors about the natural habitat or eating habits of exhibited animals.

Keepers are generally assigned to work with a broad group of animals such as mammals, birds, or reptiles. In large zoological parks, keepers may work with a limited collection of animals such as primates, large cats, or dolphins.

Working Conditions

People who love animals get satisfaction from working with and helping animals. However, some of the work may be physically demanding and unpleasant. Caretakers have to clean animal cages and lift heavy animals, or supplies like bales of hay. Also, the work setting is often noisy. Some duties like euthanizing a hopelessly injured or aged animal may be emotionally stressful.

Animal caretakers can be exposed to bites, kicks, and disease from the animals they attend. Caretakers may work outdoors in all kinds of weather. Hours are irregular. Animals have to be fed every day, so caretakers rotate weekend shifts. In some animal hospitals and animal shelters an attendant is on duty 24 hours a day, which means night shifts. Most full-time caretakers work about 40 hours a week; some work 50 hours a week or more. Caretakers of show and sports animals travel to competitions.

Employment

Animal caretakers held about 125,000 jobs in 1994. Most were employed in veterinary facilities and boarding kennels. Other employers were animal shelters, stables, pet stores, grooming shops, zoological parks, and local, State, and Federal agencies. One out of every 6 caretakers is self-employed. More than a third work part time.

Training, Other Qualifications, and Advancement

Most animal caretakers working in kennels, pet stores, animal shelters, and stables are trained on the job. There are few formal training programs, but the American Boarding Kennel Association offers a home-study program for kennel technicians. Some States require certification of caretakers who euthanize animals. Training may be through a veterinarian or a State Humane Society. Otherwise, there are no formal training requirements in these settings; nonetheless, many employers look for people with some experience with animals. Caretakers start by cleaning cages and advance to giving medication

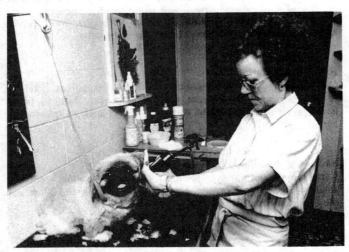

Employment of animal caretakers is expected to grow faster than average.

and grooming. Most dog groomers learn their trade through on-the-job training, but a few grooming schools do exist.

Dog groomers may receive professional registration or certification from the National Dog Groomers Association of America. The American Boarding Kennels Association accredits kennels and offers a Certified Kennel Operator program, both of which show professional competency.

There are no formal education requirements for animal caretakers in veterinary facilities. They are trained on the job.

Large zoological parks may require their caretakers to have a bachelor's degree in biology, animal science, or a related field. They also require experience with animals, preferably as a volunteer in a zoo or as a paid keeper in a smaller zoo.

Advancement varies with employment setting. Kennel caretakers may be promoted to kennel supervisor, assistant manager, and manager. Caretakers with enough capital may open up their own kennels. Pet store caretakers may become store managers. Caretakers in animal shelters may become a humane agent, animal control officer, assistant shelter manager, or shelter director. The Humane Society of the United States offers seminars for animal shelter and control personnel. Zoo keepers may advance to senior keeper, assistant head keeper, head keeper, and assistant curator but few openings occur, especially for the higher level positions.

Job Outlook

Employment opportunities for animal caretakers generally are expected to be good. Employment is expected to grow faster than the average for all occupations through the year 2005 as the population and economy expand and pet ownership grows. The number of dogs and cats has increased significantly over the last 10 years, and is expected to continue to increase in the future. More animals will require more caretakers to provide services.

Despite growth in demand for animal caretakers, the overwhelming majority of jobs will result from the need to replace workers leaving the field. Many animal caretaker jobs that require little or no training have work schedules which tend to be flexible; therefore, it is an ideal first job for people entering the labor force as well as for students and others looking for temporary or part-time work. Because turnover is quite high due to the hard physical labor and low pay, the overall availability of jobs should be very good. Much of the work of these animal caretakers is seasonal, particularly during vacation periods.

The outlook for caretakers in zoos, however, is not favorable. Jobseekers will face keen competition because of expected slow growth in zoo capacity, low turnover, and the fact that the occupation attracts many candidates.

Earnings

Animal caretakers who worked full time earned a median weekly salary of $275 in 1994. The middle 50 percent earned between $211 and $368. The bottom 10 percent earned less than $182; the top 10 percent earned more than $536 a week. Generally, veterinary technicians, laboratory animal technologists, and zookeepers earn more than other animal caretakers.

Related Occupation

Other occupations working with animals include agricultural and biological scientists, veterinarians, retail sales workers in pet stores, gamekeepers, game-farm helpers, poultry breeders, ranchers, and artificial-breeding technician.

Sources of Additional Information

For more information on animal caretaking and the animal shelter and control personnel training program, write to:

☛Animal Caretakers Information, The Humane Society of the United States, 2100 L St., NW, Washington, DC 20037.

To obtain a listing of grooming schools or the name of the nearest certified dog groomer in your area, send a stamped self-addressed envelope to:

☛National Dog Groomers Association of America, Box 101, Clark, PA 16113.

For information on training and certification of kennel staff and owners, contact:

☛American Boarding Kennel Association, 4575 Galley Rd., Suite 400-A, Colorado Springs, CO 80915.

Farm Operators and Managers

(D.O.T. 180.117, .161, and .167-018, -026 through -046, -058, and -066; 401.161; 402.161; 403.161; 404.161; 405.161; 407.161; 410.161; 411.161; 412.161; 413.161; 421.161; and 446.161)

Nature of the Work

American farm operators and managers direct the activities of one of the world's largest and most productive agricultural sectors. They produce enough food and fiber to meet the needs of our Nation and to export huge quantities to countries around the world.

Farm operators may be farmer-owners or tenant farmers, who rent the use of land. Their specific tasks are determined by the type of farm they operate. On crop farms—farms growing grain, cotton and other fibers, fruit, and vegetables—farm operators are responsible for planning, tilling, planting, fertilizing, cultivating, spraying, and harvesting. After the harvest, they make sure that the crops are properly stored or packaged, loaded, and promptly marketed. On livestock, dairy, and poultry farms, farm operators must plan, feed, and care for the animals and keep barns, pens, coops, and other farm buildings clean and in repair. They also oversee breeding, some slaughtering, and marketing activities. On horticultural specialty farms, farm operators oversee the production of ornamental plants, nursery products—such as flowers, bulbs, shrubbery, and sod—and fruits and vegetables grown in greenhouses.

Farm operators are required to make many managerial decisions. Their farm output is strongly influenced by the weather, disease, fluctuations in prices of domestic and foreign farm products, and Federal farm programs. Farm operators must determine the best time to seed, fertilize, cultivate, harvest, and market. They carefully plan the combination of crops they grow so if the price of one crop drops, they will have sufficient income from another to make up for the loss. Crop and livestock prices change frequently from one month to another. Farm operators who plan ahead may be able to store their crops or keep their livestock to take advantage of better prices later in the year. Farm operators may have to secure loans from credit agencies to finance the purchase of machinery, fertilizer, livestock, and feed. Increasingly, farm operators are using computers to keep their extensive financial and inventory records of their farming operations.

Farm operators perform tasks ranging from caring for livestock, to operating machinery, and erecting fences. The size of the farm often determines which of these tasks operators will handle themselves. Operators of large farms have employees who do much of the physical work that small-farm operators do themselves. Operators are responsible for training workers in the use of equipment and supervising them in the performance of their work. Although employment on most farms is limited to the farm operator and one or two family workers or hired employees, some large farms have 100 or more full-time and seasonal workers. Some of these workers are in nonfarm occupations, such as truckdriver, sales representative, bookkeeper, and computer specialist.

Farm managers have duties and responsibilities that vary widely.

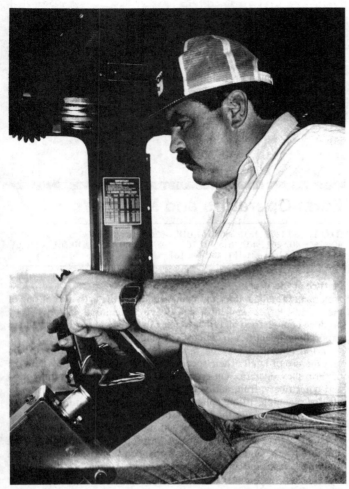

Small farm operators and managers perform much of the physical work themselves.

For example, the owner of a very large livestock farm may employ a farm manager to oversee a single activity such as feeding livestock. When managing a small crop farm for an absentee owner, on the other hand, a farm manager may assume responsibility for all functions, from planning the crop to participating in planting and harvesting activities. Farm management firms and corporations involved in agriculture employ highly trained professional farm managers who may manage farm operations or oversee tenant operators of several farms. In these cases, farm managers may establish output goals, determine financial constraints, and monitor production and marketing.

Working Conditions
The soil, topography of the land, and the climate of an area generally determine the type of farming that is done. For example, wheat, corn, and other grains are most efficiently grown on large farms on level land where large, complex machinery can be used. Thus, these crops are prevalent on the prairies and plains of Iowa, Illinois, Indiana, Nebraska, Ohio, Kansas, and southern Minnesota and Wisconsin. Crops that require longer growing seasons, such as cotton, tobacco, and peanuts, are grown chiefly in the South. Most of the country's fruits and vegetables come from California, Texas, and Florida. Many dairy herds are found in the areas with good pasture land, such as Wisconsin, New York, and Minnesota. In areas with large tracts of land—such as Texas, Nebraska, Iowa, and some

Western States—livestock and feed grain production flourish.

The work of farm operators and managers is often strenuous, their work hours are frequently long, and their days off are sometimes infrequent. Of those who worked full time, half worked 60 or more hours a week. Nevertheless, to those who enter farming, these disadvantages are outweighed by the opportunities for living in a more rural area, working outdoors, being self employed, and making a living working the land.

Many types of farming are seasonal. Although farm operators and managers on crop farms usually work from sunrise to sunset during the planting and harvesting seasons, they often work on the farm only 6 to 7 months a year. During the rest of the year they plan next season's crops, market their output, and repair machinery; some may earn additional income by working a second job off the farm.

On livestock producing farms, work goes on throughout the year. Animals must be fed and watered, and cows must be milked twice a day. Farm operators rarely get the chance to get away unless they hire an assistant or arrange for a temporary substitute.

Farm work can be hazardous. Farmers may be injured by planting and harvesting machinery or large livestock. In addition, they are subject to illnesses and diseases from improper handling and breathing of dangerous pesticides and chemicals.

On very large farms, farm operators spend substantial time meeting with farm managers or farm supervisors in charge of various activities. Professional farm managers overseeing several farms may divide their time between traveling to meet farm operators and planning the farm operations in their offices.

Employment
Farm operators and managers held about 1,327,000 jobs in 1994. About 90 percent were self employed farm operators. Most managed crop production activities while others managed livestock and dairy production. A relatively small number were involved in agricultural services such as contract harvesting and farm labor contracting.

Training, Other Qualifications, and Advancement
Growing up on a family farm and participating in agricultural programs for young people sponsored by the National Future Farmers of America Organization or the 4-H youth educational programs are important sources of training for those interested in pursuing agriculture as a career. However, modern farming requires increasingly complex scientific, business, and financial decisions. Therefore, even people who were raised on farms must acquire a strong educational background. High school training should include courses in mathematics and the sciences. Completion of a 2-year and preferably a 4-year program in a college of agriculture is becoming increasingly important.

Not all future farm managers grow up on farms. For these people, a bachelor's degree in agriculture is essential. In order to qualify for a farm manager position, they will need several years' work experience in the different aspects of farm operations.

Students should select the college most appropriate to their specific interests and location. In the United States, most State university systems have a college of agriculture. Common programs of study offered include agronomy, dairy science, agricultural economics and business, horticulture, crop and fruit science, pathobiology, and animal science. Also, colleges of agriculture usually offer special programs of study covering products important to the area in which they are located, such as animal science programs at colleges in the Western and Plains States. Whatever one's interest, the college curriculum should include courses in farm production, finance, and economics.

Professional status can be enhanced through voluntary certification as an Accredited Farm Manager (AFM) by the American Society of Farm Managers and Rural Appraisers. Certification requires several years' farm experience and the appropriate academic background—a bachelor's degree or preferably a master's degree in a field of agricultural science—and passing courses and examinations relating to business, financial, and legal aspects of farm management.

Farm operators and managers need to keep abreast of continuing advances in farming methods both in the United States and abroad. They should be willing to try new processes and adapt to constantly changing technologies to produce their crops or raise their livestock more efficiently. Keeping abreast of changing foreign agricultural policies and international exchange rates is important to operators of farms producing internationally traded crops and livestock. Operators also must have enough technical knowledge of crops, growing conditions, and plant and animal diseases to make decisions ensuring the successful operation of their farms. Knowledge of the relationship between farm operations—for example, the use of pesticides—and environmental conditions is essential. Mechanical aptitude and the ability to work with tools of all kinds also are valuable skills for the operator of a small farm, who often maintains and repairs machinery or farm structures.

Farm operators and managers must have the managerial skills necessary to organize and operate a business. A basic knowledge of accounting and bookkeeping can be helpful in keeping financial records, and a knowledge of credit sources is essential. They also must keep abreast of complex safety regulations, requirements of government agricultural support programs, and paperwork faced by other small businesses. Familiarity with computers is important, especially on large farms, where computers are often used for record keeping and business analysis. For example, some farmers use personal computers to get the latest information on prices of farm products and other agricultural news.

Job Outlook

Employment of farm operators and managers is expected to continue to decline through the year 2005. The expanding world population is increasing the demand for food and fiber. However, increasing productivity in the highly efficient U.S. agricultural sector is expected to easily meet domestic and export requirements with fewer but larger farms. Although requirements for machinery and equipment will remain stable or increase slightly, land and labor requirements in the agricultural sector will decrease, but at a slower rate than in the past. The overwhelming majority of job openings will result from the need to replace farmers who retire or leave the occupation for economic or other reasons.

The trend toward fewer and larger farms, primarily through mergers, is expected to continue to reduce the number of jobs for farm operators and managers. A farm can be acquired by inheritance; however, purchasing a farm is expensive and requires substantial capital. In addition, sufficient funds are required to withstand the adverse effects of climate and price fluctuations upon farm output and income and to cover operating costs—livestock, feed, seed, and fuel. Also, the complexity of modern farming and keen competition among farmers leave little room for the marginally successful farmer. Small and medium-size farms, many of which do not generate sufficient income to support the desired standard of living, are expected to decrease in number. However, the small but increasing number of horticultural farms may provide some employment opportunities.

Earnings

Farmers' incomes vary greatly from year to year, because prices of farm products fluctuate depending upon weather conditions and other factors that influence the amount and quality of farm output and the demand for those products. A farm that shows a large profit in one year may show a loss in the following year. Many farmers—primarily operators of small farms—have income from off-farm business activities often several times larger than their farm income.

Farm income also varies greatly depending upon the type and size of farm. According to the U.S. Department of Agriculture, average cash income net of expenses in 1993 was over $100,000 for operators of vegetable and fruit, cotton, and poultry and egg farms. On the other hand, cattle and tobacco farms generated less than $15,000 in cash income, on the average. Generally, large farms generate more income than small farms. Exceptions include some low volume specialty farms producing high-value horticultural and fruit products.

Farm operators and managers who were paid a wage or salary, and who worked full time had median earnings of $314 a week in 1994. The middle half earned between $237 and $445 a week. The highest paid managers earned over $594 a week in 1994, while the lowest paid made less than $173 a week.

Farmers and self-employed farm managers make their own provisions for benefits. As members of farm organizations, they may derive benefits such as group discounts on health and life insurance premiums. Salaried farm managers may receive housing and the usual benefits such as paid vacations and health insurance.

Related Occupations

Farmers and farm managers strive to improve the quality of agricultural products and the efficiency of farms. Workers with similar functions include agricultural engineers, animal breeders, animal scientists, county agricultural agents, dairy scientists, extension service specialists, feed and farm management advisors, horticulturists, plant breeders, and poultry scientists.

Sources of Additional Information

For general information about farming and agricultural occupations, contact:

☛American Farm Bureau Federation, 225 Touhy Ave., Park Ridge, IL 60068.

For information about certification as an accredited farm manager, contact:

☛American Society of Farm Managers and Rural Appraisers, 950 South Cherry St., Suite 106, Denver, CO 80222.

For general information about farm occupations, opportunities, and 4-H activities, contact your local county extension service office.

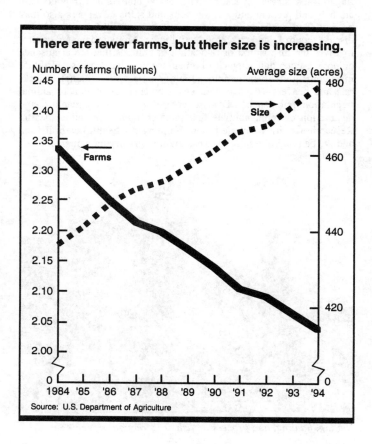

There are fewer farms, but their size is increasing.

Number of farms (millions) / Average size (acres)

Source: U.S. Department of Agriculture

Fishers, Hunters, and Trappers

(D.O.T. 197.133-010, -018; 441; 442; 443; 447; 449.664, .667; 461)

Nature of the Work

Fishers, hunters, and trappers gather aquatic and animal species for human consumption, animal feed, bait, and other uses, and manage animals for research and control purposes. The range of occupational functions reflects the wide variety of aquatic and animal life and their environments.

Gathering fish hundreds of miles from shore with commercial fishing vessels—large boats capable of hauling a catch of tens of thousands of pounds of fish—requires a crew that includes a captain, or skipper, a first mate and sometimes a second mate, boatswain, and deckhands.

The *captain* plans and oversees the fishing operation—the fish to be sought, the location of the best fishing grounds, the method of capture, the duration of the trip, and the sale of the catch. The captain ensures that the fishing vessel is in suitable condition; oversees the purchase of supplies, gear, and equipment such as fuel, netting, and cables; and hires qualified crew members and assigns their duties. The vessel's course is plotted with navigation aids such as compasses, sextants, and charts; it uses electronic equipment such as autopilots, a loran system, and satellites to navigate. The ships also use radar to avoid obstacles and depth sounders to indicate the water depth and the existence of marine life between the vessel and sea bottom. The captain directs the fishing operation through the officers, and records daily activities in the ship's log. Upon returning to port, the captain arranges for the sale of the catch directly to buyers or through a fish auction and ensures that each crew member receives the prearranged portion of the adjusted net proceeds from the sale of the catch.

The *first mate*—the captain's assistant, who must be familiar with navigation requirements and the operation of all electronic equipment—assumes control of the vessel when the captain is off duty. These duty shifts, called "watches," usually last 6 hours. The mate's regular duty, with the help of the boatswain and under the captain's oversight, is to direct the fishing operations and sailing responsibilities of the deckhands. These include the operation, maintenance, and repair of the vessel and the gathering, preservation, stowing, and unloading of the catch.

The *boatswain*, a highly experienced deckhand with supervisory responsibilities, directs the *deckhands* as they carry out the sailing and fishing operations. Prior to departure, the boatswain directs the deckhands to load equipment and supplies, either manually or with hoisting equipment, and untie lines from other boats and the dock. When necessary, boatswains repair fishing gear, equipment, nets, and accessories. They operate the fishing gear, letting out and pulling in nets and lines. They extract the catch, such as pollock, flounder, menhaden, and tuna, from the nets or lines' hooks. Deckhands use dip nets to prevent the escape of small fish and gaffs to facilitate the landing of large fish. The catch is then washed, salted, iced, and stowed away. Deckhands also must ensure that decks are clear and clean at all times and that the vessel's engines and equipment are kept in good working order. Upon return to port, they secure the vessel's lines to and from the docks and other vessels. Unless "lumpers," or laborers, are hired, the deckhands unload the catch.

Large fishing vessels that operate in deep water generally have more technologically advanced equipment, and some may have facilities on board where the fish are processed and prepared for sale. They are equipped for longer stays at sea and can perform the work of several smaller boats. (For information about merchant marine occupations, see the section on water transportation occupations elsewhere in the *Handbook*.)

Some full-time and many part-time fishers work on small boats in relatively shallow waters and often in sight of land. Navigation and communication needs are modest, and there is little need for much electronic equipment or provisions for long stays at sea. Crews are small—usually only one or two people collaborate on all aspects of the fishing operation. This may include placing gill nets across the mouths of rivers or inlets, entrapment nets in bays and lakes, or pots and traps for shellfish such as lobsters and crabs. Dredges and scrapes are sometimes used to gather shellfish such as oysters and scallops. A very small proportion of commercial fishing is conducted as diving operations. Depending upon the water's depth, divers—wearing regulation diving suits with an umbilical (air line) or a scuba outfit and equipment—use spears to catch fish and nets and other equipment to gather shellfish, coral, sea urchins, abalone, and sponges. In very shallow waters, fish are caught from small boats having an outboard motor, or from rowboats, or by wading. Fishers use a wide variety of hand-operated equipment—for example, nets, tongs, rakes, hoes, hooks, and shovels—to gather fish and shellfish, catch amphibians and reptiles such as frogs and turtles, and harvest marine vegetation such as Irish moss and kelp.

Although most fishers are involved with commercial fishing, some captains and deckhands are primarily employed in sport or recreational fishing. Typically a group of people charter a fishing vessel—for periods ranging from several hours to a number of days—for sport fishing, socializing, and relaxation, and employ a captain and possibly several deckhands.

Hunters track, stalk, and sometimes kill their quarry, either for a government agency or as a guide for other people. They may hunt alone or with others and may use dogs to locate the quarry. They use guns or poisons to kill predatory animals such as coyotes. Alligator hunters may shoot their quarry after snaring it with baited hooks. All legal hunting activities are approved and monitored by the appropriate Federal, State, or local government agencies. Exceptions are made for Native Americans on their own reservations and Alaska Natives.

Trappers catch animals or birds using baited, scented, or camouflaged traps, snares, cages, or nets. Many hunters and trappers skin animals and prepare and sell the pelts and skins. Trappers also may be involved with animal damage control, wildlife management, disease control, and research activities. Animal damage control involves the disposition or relocation of animals that are a nuisance or pose a potential danger to humans or populated areas. Wildlife management involves the relocation of animals—for example, muskrats and beavers—to deal with environmental disruption or animal population imbalance. Disease control involves the capture and destruction of rabid animals that threaten public or animal health. Research activities include blood sampling for health determination and the banding of wildfowl to ascertain migratory movements.

Netting, hauling, and processing fish are strenuous activities.

Working Conditions

Fishing, hunting, and trapping operations are conducted under various environmental conditions, depending on the region of the country and the kind of species being sought. Fishing vessels may be hampered or imperiled by storms, fog, or wind. Divers are affected by murky water and unexpected shifts in underwater currents. Hunters and trappers are hampered or disrupted by storms and rough terrain.

Fishers, hunters, and trappers work under hazardous conditions, and often help is not readily available. Malfunctioning navigation or communication equipment may lead to collisions or even shipwrecks. Malfunctioning fishing gear poses the danger of injury to the crew, who also must guard against entanglement in fishing nets and gear, slippery decks resulting from fish processing operations, ice formation in the winter, or being swept overboard—a fearsome situation. Treatment for serious injuries may have to await transfer to a hospital. Divers must guard against entanglement of air lines, malfunction of scuba equipment, decompression problems, or attacks by predatory fish. Hunters and trappers face numerous hazards such as assault by predators, falling branches and trees, slippery ground, danger of drowning by falling through ice on ponds, accidental self-inflicted gunshot and knife wounds, and snake and insect bites. Danger from incapacitating injuries is especially high, because these individuals often work alone in isolated areas. A disabled individual may die of injuries that could be routinely treated in an urban area.

This occupation entails strenuous outdoor work and long hours. Commercial fishing trips may require a stay of several weeks, or even months, hundreds of miles away from home port. The pace of work varies—intense while netting and hauling the catch aboard and relatively relaxed while traveling between home port and the fishing grounds. However, lookout watches—usually 6 hours long—are a regular responsibility and crew members must be prepared to stand watch at prearranged times of the day or night. Although fishing gear has improved and operations have become more mechanized, netting and processing fish are strenuous activities. Even though newer vessels have improved living quarters and amenities such as television and shower stalls, crews still experience the aggravations of confined conditions, continuous close personal contact, and the absence of family. Hunters and trappers generally must travel many miles by car or truck and then carry equipment and supplies on foot through swamps or forests, over rugged terrain. Long hours—dawn to dusk—often are the rule, and many spend lonely nights camped out in sparsely populated, forested, or mountainous areas.

Employment

Fishers, hunters, and trappers held an estimated 49,000 jobs in 1994. Over half were self-employed. About 1 in 6 of them worked part time, particularly in the summer, when demand for these workers peaks.

Captains, mates, and deckhands on fishing vessels accounted for the majority of these jobs. Trappers, and to a lesser extent hunters, accounted for the remaining jobs.

Outside of the fishing, hunting, and trapping industry, some people employed in this occupation are involved in sport fishing activities, while small numbers are employed by museums. Others work for government or buy and sell fur.

Training, Other Qualifications, and Advancement

Fishers generally acquire their occupational skills on the job, many as members of families involved in fishing activities. No formal academic requirements exist. Under a Coast Guard legislative proposal, operators of federally documented commercial fishing vessels will be required to complete a Coast Guard-approved training course. Young people can expedite their entrance into these occupations by enrolling in 2-year vocational-technical programs offered by secondary schools, primarily in coastal areas. In addition, the University of Rhode Island offers a bachelor's degree program in fishery technology that includes courses in seamanship, vessel operations, marine safety, navigation, vessel repair and maintenance, health emergencies, and fishing gear technology, and is accompanied by hands-on experience.

Experienced fishers may find short-term workshops offered through various postsecondary institutions especially useful. These programs provide a good working knowledge of electronic equipment used in navigation and communication and the latest improvements in fishing gear.

Captains and mates on larger fishing vessels of at least 200 gross tons must be licensed. Captains of sport fishing boats used for charter, regardless of size, also must be licensed. Crew members on certain fish processing vessels may need a merchant mariner's document. These documents and licenses are issued by the U.S. Coast Guard to individuals who meet the stipulated health, physical, and academic requirements.

Fishers must be in good health and possess physical strength. Coordination and mechanical aptitude are necessary to operate, maintain, and repair equipment and fishing gear. They need perseverance to work long hours on the sea, often under difficult conditions. On larger vessels, they must be able to work as members of a team. They must be patient, yet always alert, to overcome the boredom of long watches when not engaged in fishing operations. The ability to assume any deckhand's functions, on short notice, is important. Mates must have supervisory ability and be able to assume any deckhand's and the captain's duties, when necessary. The captain must be highly experienced, mature, decisive, and possess the necessary business skills. Captains with initiative and the required capital often become boat owners.

On fishing vessels, most fishers begin as deckhands. Deckhands whose experience and interests are in ship engineering—maintenance and repair of ship engines and equipment—can eventually become licensed chief engineers on large commercial vessels after meeting the U.S. Coast Guard's experience, physical, and academic requirements. Divers in fishing operations can enter commercial diving activity—for example, ship repair and pier and marina maintenance—usually after completion of a certified training program sponsored by an educational institution or industry association. Experienced, reliable deckhands who display supervisory qualities may become boatswains. Boatswains may, in turn, become second mates, first mates, and finally captains. Almost all captains become self-employed, and the overwhelming majority eventually own or have an interest in one or more fishing ships. Some may choose to run a sport or recreational fishing operation. When their seagoing days are over, experienced individuals may work in or, with the necessary capital, own stores selling fishing and marine equipment and supplies. Some captains may assume advisory or administrative positions in industry trade associations or government offices such as harbor development commissions, or teaching positions in industry-sponsored workshops or in educational institutions.

Hunters and trappers generally acquire their knowledge of wildlife and hunting and trapping equipment and supplies gradually, through experience. Some are members of rural families for whom hunting and trapping have been a way of life for generations. Formal training for hunters consists of a federally mandated and State sponsored hunter safety class, covering safety and ethics, which must be passed prior to being issued a hunting license in almost every State. Inexperienced individuals may join an established sports association to observe professional demonstrations and gain knowledge of hunting weapons and related equipment and tracking and survival techniques. After acquiring the mandatory State hunting license, they should hunt with an experienced hunter as an apprentice. Government hunters who hunt rabid or nuisance animals may be trained in the use of airplanes or helicopters.

Trappers may undergo various forms of training. For those interested in the sale of animals and their skins, pelts, or furs, experience is fundamental. Inexperienced trappers may serve an internship under the supervision of a professional trapper and take trapper education programs. Trapper education programs are offered by State wildlife departments or State trappers associations; in some States, these programs are mandatory. A trapper's license permits the trapping of animals forbidden to unlicensed trappers. Trappers interested in research associated with control and management of wildlife populations and disease may take courses, or even complete a degree program, in wildlife biology, wildlife management, or related fields.

Hunters and trappers must be in good health, possess physical strength and stamina, and have the desire, patience, and ability to work outdoors, sometimes for long periods, under difficult conditions. Maturity and judgment are important to deal with hazards. Good physical coordination and mechanical aptitude are necessary to safely and skillfully use hunting weapons and trapping equipment and to maintain camping and other gear.

Some hunters are employed by the Federal or State governments to work in such areas as predator control. Other hunters who have extensive experience may work as guides for hunting parties. Those with initiative, business skills, and the required capital may become self-employed outfitters, some of whom own sites in the wilds. Outfitters organize hunting parties, select hunting areas, and assume responsibility for the hunting expedition—providing equipment and supplies, instructing the party members in hunting techniques and safety measures, and overseeing leisure activities during the expedition. Most States require a license to work as a hunting guide.

Experienced trappers with the appropriate academic background may enter other occupations, such as wildlife technician, or wildlife refuge manager. Professional trappers with business skills and initiative may become self-employed fur traders.

Job Outlook

Employment of fishers, hunters, and trappers is expected to decline through the year 2005. Hunting, fishing, and trapping occupations depend on the natural ability of stock to replenish itself through growth and reproduction. Many operations are currently at or beyond maximum sustainable yield, and the number of workers who can earn an adequate income from fishing, hunting, and trapping is expected to decline. Most job openings will arise from the need to replace workers who retire or leave the occupation. Some fishers, hunters, and trappers leave the occupation because of the strenuous and hazardous nature of the job, and the lack of steady, year-round income.

Different factors will affect employment among these occupations. In many areas, particularly the North Atlantic, over fishing and pollution have adversely affected the stock of fish and, consequently, the demand for fishers. In some areas, States have greatly reduced permits to fishers to allow stocks of fish and shellfish to replenish themselves, idling many fishers. However, this also has helped spur the growth of a closely related field, aquaculture—the raising and harvesting of fish and other aquatic life in ponds or artificial bodies of water for commercial purposes. Aquaculture should be most prominent in the South, where the climate is best suited for the growth of most freshwater fish, except perhaps salmon and trout, which are farmed elsewhere.

Employment growth of fishers also may be somewhat restrained by the growing number of large fishing vessels; the use of sophisticated electronic equipment for navigation, communication, and fish location; and improvements in fishing gear, which have greatly increased the efficiency of fishing operations and have limited the expansion in crew size. Likewise, the use of highly automated "floating processors," where the catch is processed aboard the vessel, may limit employment opportunities. Sport fishing boats will continue to provide some job opportunities.

Employment of hunters and trappers is also expected to decline. The U.S. Forest Service and State fish and wildlife agencies may provide some jobs. Some qualified hunters should be able to obtain positions as hunting guides or outfitters, although the work generally is seasonal. Trapping activities increasingly are becoming ancillary duties of wildlife scientists and technicians and related workers. Opportunities should be best for trappers in pest control activities.

Earnings

Fishers, hunters, and trappers who worked full time in 1994 had median earnings of $508 a week. The middle 50 percent earned between $240 and $852 a week. The highest paid 10 percent earned over $1,891 a week, but the lowest paid 10 percent earned less than $198 a week.

Earnings of fishers, hunters, and trappers generally are highest in the summer and fall—when demand for their services peaks and environmental conditions are favorable—and lowest during the winter. Many full-time and most part-time workers supplement their income by working in other activities during the off-season. For example, fishers may work in seafood processing plants, establishments selling fishing and marine equipment, or in construction. Hunters may work as self-employed guides, for an outfitter, or in stores selling guns or hunting and related equipment. Trappers may work in stores selling trapping and related equipment.

Earnings of fishers vary widely depending upon the specific occupational function, the size of the ship, and the amount and value of the catch. The costs of the fishing operation—operating the ship, repair and maintenance of gear and equipment, and the crew's supplies—are deducted from the sale of the catch. The net proceeds are distributed among the crew members in accordance with a prearranged percentage. Generally, the ship's owner—usually its captain—receives half of the net proceeds, which covers any profit as well as the depreciation, maintenance, and replacement costs of the ship.

Related Occupations

Numerous occupations involve outdoor activities similar to those of fishers, hunters, and trappers. Among these are zoo keepers, loggers, animal control officers, forest rangers, fishing guides, fish hatchery and aquaculture workers, game wardens, harbor pilots, merchant marine officers and seamen, and wildlife management specialists.

Sources of Additional Information

For general information about fishing occupations, contact:
☛National Fisheries Institute, 1525 Wilson Blvd., Suite 500, Arlington, VA 22209.

Information about sport or recreational fishing occupations is available from:
☛Sport Fishing Institute, 1010 Massachusetts Ave. NW., Washington, DC 20001.

Names of postsecondary schools offering fishing and related marine educational programs are available from:
☛Marine Technology Society, 1828 L St. NW., Suite 906, Washington, DC 20036-5104.

Information on licensing of captains and mates and requirements for merchant mariner documentation is available from the U.S. Coast Guard Marine Inspection Office or Marine Safety Office in your State, or:
☛Licensing and Evaluation Branch (G-MPV-2), U.S. Coast Guard, 2100 Second St. SW., Washington, DC 20593.

For information about certified training programs for diving (umbilical) careers, contact:
☛College of Oceaneering, 272 S. Fries Ave., Wilmington, CA 90744-6399.

Information on licensing of hunting guides is available from the department of fish and game in your State.

Forestry and Logging Occupations

(D.O.T. 408.664, .667; 451.687; 452.364-010, .687-010, -018; 453; 454 except .134; 455 except .134; 459.387, .687; 669.485, .687-022; 921.364, .664-014, .667-014, .687-014 -022, -030; 922.687-082; and 929.663-010)

Nature of the Work

The Nation's forests are a rich natural resource, providing beauty and tranquillity, varied recreational areas, and wood for commercial use. Managing forests and woodlands requires many different kinds of workers. Forestry and conservation workers help develop, maintain, and protect these forests by growing and planting new tree seedlings, fighting insects and diseases that attack trees, and helping to control soil erosion. Timber cutting and logging workers harvest thousands of acres of forests each year for the timber that provides the raw material for countless consumer and industrial products.

Generally working under the direction of a professional forester, *forestry technicians* compile data on the characteristics of forest land tracts such as size, content, and condition. These workers travel through sections of forest to gather basic information such as species and population of trees, disease and insect damage, tree seedling mortality, and conditions that may cause fire danger. They also train and lead conservation workers in seasonal activities such as planting tree seedlings, putting out forest fires, and maintaining recreational facilities.

Forest workers are less skilled workers who perform a variety of different tasks to reforest and conserve timberlands and maintain forest facilities such as roads and campsites. Some forest workers, called tree planters, plant tree seedlings to reforest timberland areas, using digging and planting tools called dibble bars and hoedads. They also remove diseased or undesirable trees with a powersaw or handsaw and spray trees with insecticides or herbicides to kill insects and to protect against disease. Forest workers in private industry usually work for professional foresters, and paint boundary lines, assist with prescribed burning, and aid in tree marking and measuring by keeping a tally of the trees examined and counted. Those who work for Federal and State government also clear away brush and debris from camp trails, roadsides, and camping areas. Some clean kitchens and rest rooms at recreational facilities and campgrounds.

Other forest and conservation workers work in forest nurseries sorting out tree seedlings, discarding those that do not meet prescribed standards of root formation, stem development, and foliage condition.

Some forest workers work on tree farms, where they plant, cultivate, and harvest many different kinds of trees. Their duties vary depending on the type of tree farm. For example, those who work on specialty farms, such as Christmas tree farms or farms that grow ornamental trees for nurseries, are responsible for shearing the tops and limbs to control growth, increase limb density, and improve the shape, in addition to planting, spraying to control surrounding weed growth and insects, and harvesting.

Other forest workers gather products from the woodlands such as decorative greens, tree cones and barks, moss, or other wild plant life from the forest by hand or using handtools, and others tap trees for sap to make syrup or to produce chemicals.

The timber cutting and logging process is carried out by a variety of workers. Fallers cut down trees with chain saws or mechanical felling equipment. Buckers trim off the tops and branches and buck (cut) the resulting logs into specified lengths. These workers usually use gas-powered chain saws.

Choke setters fasten chokers (steel cables or chains) around logs to be skidded (dragged) by tractors or forwarded by the cable yarding system to the landing or deck area where the logs are separated by species and loaded onto trucks. Riggers set up and dismantle the cables and guy wires of the cable yarding system.

Most forestry and logging workers learn their skills on the job.

Logging tractor operators drive crawler or wheeled tractors called skidders, which drag logs from the felling site to the landing; grapple loaders, which load the logs into trucks; and tree harvesters, which cut and trim the trees, then cut the logs. Log handling equipment operators operate tracked or wheeled equipment to load logs and pulpwood off trucks or gondola railroad cars, usually in a sawmill or planing mill yard.

Log graders and scalers inspect logs for defects, measure logs to determine their volume, and estimate the marketable content or value of logs or pulpwood.

Other timber cutting and logging workers have a variety of responsibilities. Some workers hike through forests to assess logging conditions. Laborers clear areas of brush and other growth to prepare for logging activities and to promote growth of desirable species of trees.

The timber cutting and logging industry is characterized by a large number of small crews of four to eight workers. A typical crew might consist of one or two fallers or one feller machine operator, one bucker, two logging tractor operators to drag cut trees to the loading deck, and one equipment operator to load the logs onto trucks. Most of these crews work for self-employed logging contractors who possess substantial logging experience, the capital to purchase equipment, and the skills needed to run a small business successfully. Most contractors work alongside their crews as working supervisors and often operate one of the logging tractors, such as the grapple loader or the tree harvester. Many manage more than one crew and function as owner-supervisors.

Although timber cutting and logging equipment has greatly improved and operations are becoming increasingly mechanized, many logging jobs are still labor intensive. These jobs require various levels of skill, ranging from manually moving logs, branches, and equipment to skillfully using chain saws, peavies (hooked poles), and log jacks to cut and position logs for further processing or loading. Skillful operation of vehicles and equipment is necessary to avoid accidents and to minimize damage to the equipment and environment. The ability to maintain and repair equipment is increasingly necessary to reduce costs and increase productivity. A skillful, experienced logger is expected to handle a variety of logging operations.

Working Conditions

Forestry and logging occupations are physically demanding. Most forestry and logging workers often work outdoors in all kinds of weather, sometimes in isolated areas. A few lumber camps in Alaska house workers in bunkhouses or company towns. Workers in sparsely populated Western States commute long distances between their homes and logging sites. In the densely populated Eastern States, commuting distances are much shorter.

Most logging occupations involve lifting, climbing, and other strenuous activities. Loggers work under unusually hazardous conditions. Falling trees and branches are a constant menace, as are the dangers associated with log handling operations and use of sawing equipment, especially delimbing devices. Strong winds require special care and can even halt operations. Slippery or muddy ground and hidden roots or vines not only reduce efficiency but present a constant danger, especially in the presence of moving vehicles and machinery. Poisonous plants, brambles, insects, and heat and humidity are minor annoyances. Over long periods of time, if safety precautions are not taken, hearing may be impaired by the high noise level of sawing and skidding operations. Experience, exercise of caution, and use of proper safety measures and equipment—such as hardhats, eye and hearing protection, and safety clothing and boots— are extremely important to avoid injury.

The jobs of forest and conservation workers are generally much less hazardous although it may be necessary for some forestry aides or forest workers to walk long distances through densely wooded areas to carry out their work.

Employment

Forestry and logging workers held about 124,000 jobs in 1994, distributed among the following occupations:

Forest and conservation workers 42,000
Fallers and buckers 29,000
Logging tractor operators 20,000
Log handling equipment operators 16,000
All other timber cutting and related logging occupations 17,000

Most salaried logging workers are employed in the logging camps and logging contractors industry. Others work in sawmills and planing mills, or for services specializing in the care and maintenance of ornamental trees. Although logging operations are found in most States, Oregon and Washington account for about 1 out of every 5 logging workers.

Self-employed logging workers account for 1 of every 4 logging workers—a much higher proportion of self-employment than for most occupations.

Most forest and conservation workers work for government at some level. Of these workers, about 8,000 are employed by the U.S. Department of Agriculture's Forest Service, 8,500 work for State governments, and 5,800 work for local governments Most of the remainder work for companies that operate timber tracts, tree farms, or forest nurseries, or for establishments that supply forestry services. Although forestry workers and conservation workers are located in every State, employment is concentrated in the Western and Southeastern States where many national and private forests and parks are located.

Although seasonal demand for forestry and logging workers will vary slightly by region, employment generally is highest in the summer and lowest in the winter.

Training, Other Qualifications, and Advancement

Most forestry and logging workers develop their skills through on-the-job training. Instruction comes primarily from experienced workers. Logging workers must familiarize themselves with the character and potential dangers of the forest environment and the operation of logging machinery and equipment. However, larger logging companies and trade associations such as the Northeastern Loggers Association and the American Pulpwood Association may offer special programs, particularly for workers training to operate large, expensive machinery and equipment. Often, a representative of the manufacturer or company may spend several days in the field explaining and overseeing the operation of newly purchased

machinery. Safety training is a vital part of instruction for all logging workers.

In recent years, several States have established certification training programs for logging. To be certified, individuals must meet certain training requirements and pass an on-site field inspection that tests their skills.

Experience in other occupations can expedite entry into various logging occupations. For example, equipment operators such as truckdrivers and bulldozer and crane operators can assume skidding and yarding functions. Some loggers have worked in sawmills or on family farms with extensive wooded areas. Some logging contractors were formerly crew members of family-owned businesses operated over several generations.

Generally, little formal education is required for most forestry and logging occupations. The minimum requirement for a forestry technician or aide is a high school education. Many secondary schools, including vocational and technical schools, and a few community colleges offer courses, or even a 2-year degree in general forestry, wildlife, conservation, and forest harvesting which could be helpful in obtaining a job. A curriculum that includes field trips to observe or participate in forestry or logging activities provides a particularly good background. There are no educational requirements for forest worker jobs. Many of these workers may be high school or college students who are hired on a part-time or seasonal basis.

Forestry and logging workers must be in good health and be able to work outdoors every day and to work as part of a team. Many logging occupations require physical strength and stamina. Maturity and good judgment are important in making quick, intelligent decisions in dealing with hazards as they arise. Mechanical aptitude and coordination are necessary qualities for operators of machinery and equipment, who often are responsible for repair and maintenance as well. Initiative and managerial and business skills are necessary for success as a self-employed logging contractor.

Experience working at a nursery or as a laborer can be useful in obtaining a job as a forest worker. Logging workers generally advance from occupations involving primarily manual labor to those involving the operation of expensive, sometimes complicated machinery and equipment. Inexperienced entrants generally begin as laborers, carrying tools and equipment, clearing brush, and loading and unloading logs and brush. For some, familiarization with logging operations may lead to jobs such as log handling equipment operator. Further experience may lead to jobs involving the operation of more complicated machinery and yarding towers to transport, load, and unload logs. Those who have the motor skills required for the efficient use of power saws and other equipment may become fallers and buckers. Some logging workers who can readily assess the marketable volume of timber or identify defects in logs may become graders.

Job Outlook

Overall employment of forestry and logging workers is expected to decline through the year 2005. Most job openings will result from replacement needs. Many logging workers transfer to other jobs that are less physically demanding and dangerous. In addition, many forestry workers are younger workers who are not committed to the occupation on a long term basis. Some take jobs to earn money for school, others only take these jobs until they find a better paying job.

Employment of timber cutting and logging occupations is expected to decline. Despite steady demand for lumber and wood products, increased mechanization of logging operations and improvements in logging equipment will depress the demand for workers. In addition, forest conservation efforts may restrict the volume of public timber available for harvesting, further dampening demand for timber cutting and logging workers.

Employment of forest and conservation workers is expected to increase more slowly than the average for all occupations. Environmental concerns may spur the demand for workers who maintain and conserve our woodlands; however, budget cutting in the Federal Government will suppress faster growth.

Increasing mechanization will have differing effects on timber cutting and logging workers. Employment of fallers, buckers, choke setters, and other workers whose jobs are labor intensive should decline as safer, laborsaving machinery and equipment are increasingly used. Employment of machinery and equipment operators, such as logging tractor and log handling equipment operators, should be less adversely affected.

Weather can force curtailment of logging operations during the muddy spring season and cold winter months. Changes in the level of construction, particularly residential construction, also affect logging activities. In addition, logging operations must be relocated when timber harvesting in a particular area has been completed. During prolonged periods of inactivity, some workers may stay on the job to maintain or repair logging machinery and equipment; others are forced to find jobs in other occupations or be without work.

Earnings
Median weekly earnings for all full-time forestry and logging workers, including supervisors, who were not self-employed were $358 in 1994. The middle 50 percent earned between $229 and $513 weekly. The lowest 10 percent earned less than $158, while the highest 10 percent earned more than $789. Generally, earnings of more skilled workers, such as yarder operators, are substantially higher than those of less skilled workers, such as laborers and choke setters.

Earnings of logging workers vary widely by size of establishment and by geographic area. Earnings of workers in the largest establishments are much higher than those in the smallest establishments. Workers in Alaska and the Northwest earn substantially more than those in the South.

In 1995, forestry technicians and aides who worked for the Federal Government averaged about $23,090.

Forest and conservation workers who work for Federal, State, and local governments and large private firms, generally enjoy more generous benefits—for example, pension and retirement plans, health and life insurance, and paid vacations—than smaller firms. Small logging contractors generally offer timber cutting and logging workers few benefits. However, some employers offer full-time workers basic benefits such as medical coverage and provide safety apparel and equipment.

Related Occupations
Other occupations concerned with the care of trees and their environment include arborist, gardener, groundskeeper, landscaper, nursery worker, and soil conservation technician.

Sources of Additional Information
For information about forestry jobs with the Federal Government contact:

☛Chief, U.S. Forest Service, U.S Department of Agriculture, 14th St. and Independence Ave. SW., Washington, DC 20013.

For information about timber cutting and logging careers and secondary and postsecondary programs offering training for logging occupations, contact:

☛Northeastern Loggers Association, P.O. Box 69, Old Forge, NY 13420.
☛Timber Producers Association of Michigan and Wisconsin, P.O. Box 39, Tomahawk, WI 54487.
☛American Pulpwood Association, Inc., 600 Jefferson Plaza, Suite 350, Rockville, MD 20852.
☛American Forest and Paper Association, 1111 19th St., NW, Washington, DC 20036.

The school of forestry at your State land-grant college or university should also be able to provide useful information.

A list of State forestry associations and other forestry-related State associations is available at most public libraries.

Gardeners and Groundskeepers

(D.O.T. 182.167-014; 406.381-010, .683-010, .684-010, -014, -018, .687-010; 408.161-010, .662-010, .684-010, -014, -018, and .687-014)

Nature of the Work
Attractively designed, healthy, and well-maintained lawns, gardens, trees, and shrubbery create a positive first impression, establish a peaceful mood, and increase property values. A growing number of individuals and organizations rely on the services of gardeners and groundskeepers to care for their landscaping.

Some landscape gardeners work on large properties, such as office buildings and shopping malls. Following plans drawn up by a landscape architect, gardeners plant trees, hedges, flowering plants, and turf areas and apply mulch for protection. For residential customers, these workers install lawns, terrace hillsides, build retaining walls, and install patios, as well as plant flowers, trees and shrubs.

Gardeners working for homeowners, estates, and public gardens feed, water, and prune the flowering plants and trees, and mow and water the lawn. Some landscape gardeners, called lawn service workers, specialize in maintaining lawns and shrubs for a fee. A growing number of residential and commercial clients, such as managers of office buildings, shopping malls, multiunit residential buildings, and hotels and motels favor this full-service landscape maintenance. These workers perform a full range of duties, including mowing, edging, trimming, fertilizing, dethatching, and mulching. Those working for chemical lawn service firms are more specialized. They inspect lawns for problems and apply fertilizers, herbicides, pesticides, and other chemicals, as well as practice integrated pest management techniques.

Groundskeepers, often classified as either grounds managers or grounds maintenance personnel, maintain a variety of facilities including athletic fields, golf courses, cemeteries, university campuses, and parks. Grounds managers usually participate in many of the same tasks as maintenance personnel but typically have more extensive knowledge in horticulture, landscape design and construction, pest management, irrigation, and erosion control. In addition, managers usually have supervisory responsibilities.

Groundskeepers who care for athletic fields keep natural and artificial turf fields in top condition and mark out boundaries and paint turf with team logos and names before events. Groundskeepers must make sure the underlying soil on natural turf fields has the proper composition to allow proper drainage and support the appropriate grasses used on the field. They regularly mow, water, fertilize, and aerate the fields. In addition, groundskeepers apply chemicals and fungicides to control weeds, kill pests, and prevent diseases. Groundskeepers also vacuum and disinfect synthetic turf after use in order to prevent growth of harmful bacteria. They periodically remove the turf and replace the cushioning pad.

Workers who maintain golf courses are called greenskeepers. They do many of the same things other groundskeepers do. In addition, greenskeepers periodically relocate the holes on putting greens to eliminate uneven wear of the turf and add interest and challenge to the game. Greenskeepers also keep canopies, benches, ball washers, and tee markers repaired and freshly painted.

Cemetery workers prepare graves and maintain cemetery grounds. They dig graves to specified depth, generally using a back-hoe. They may place concrete slabs on the bottom and around the sides of the grave to line it for greater support. When readying a site for the burial ceremony, they position the casket-lowering device over the grave, cover the immediate area with an artificial grass carpet, erect a canopy, and arrange folding chairs to accommodate mourners. They regularly mow grass, apply fertilizers and other chemicals, prune shrubs and trees, plant flowers, and remove debris from graves.

Groundskeeping duties are increasingly contracted out to grounds management firms.

They also must periodically build the ground up around new gravesites to compensate for settling.

Groundskeepers in parks and recreation facilities care for lawns, trees, and shrubs, maintain athletic fields and playgrounds, clean buildings, and keep parking lots, picnic areas, and other public spaces free of litter. They may also remove snow and ice from roads and walkways, erect and dismantle snow fences, and maintain swimming pools. These workers inspect buildings and equipment, make needed repairs, and keep everything freshly painted.

Gardeners and groundskeepers use handtools such as shovels, rakes, pruning saws, saws, hedge and brush trimmers, and axes, as well as power lawnmowers, chain saws, snow blowers, and electric clippers. Some use equipment such as tractors and twin-axle vehicles. Park, school, cemetery, and golf course groundskeepers may use sod cutters to harvest sod that will be replanted elsewhere. Athletic turf groundskeepers use vacuums and other devices to remove water from athletic fields. In addition, some workers in large operations use spraying and dusting equipment.

In winter months, especially in the North, gardeners and groundskeepers may work removing snow from driveways, roadways, and parking lots.

Working Conditions

Many of the jobs for gardeners and groundskeepers are seasonal, mainly in the spring and summer, when cleanup, planting, and mowing and trimming take place. Gardeners and groundskeepers work outdoors in all kinds of weather. They frequently are under pressure to get the job completed, especially when they are preparing for scheduled events, such as athletic competitions or burials.

They work with pesticides, fertilizers, and other chemicals, and must exercise safety precautions to prevent exposure. They also work with dangerous equipment and tools such as power lawnmowers, chain saws, and power clippers.

Employment

Gardeners and groundskeepers held about 707,000 jobs in 1994. About 40 percent worked for lawn and garden service companies. More than 10 percent each worked for firms operating and building real estate and amusement and recreation facilities such as golf courses and race tracks. Others were employed by government, including parks departments, schools, hospitals, cemeteries, hotels, retail nurseries, and garden stores.

Almost 1 of every 4 gardeners and groundskeepers was self-employed, providing landscape maintenance directly to customers on a contract basis. One of every 3 worked part time, most likely students working their way through school. Others working part time were older workers who might have been cutting back their hours as they approached retirement.

Training, Other Qualifications, and Advancement

There usually are no minimum educational requirements for entry level jobs as gardeners and groundskeepers. Four in 10 workers do not have a high school diploma, although a high school diploma is necessary for some jobs. Experience can be obtained through home gardening or working in a nursery, a lawn care business, or a tree service. High school students may gain experience in the Future Farmers of America and other associations.

There are no national standards for gardeners and groundskeepers, but most States require certification for workers who apply pesticides. Certification requirements vary, but usually include passing a test on the safe use and disposal of insecticides, herbicides, and fungicides.

Employers prefer applicants with a good driving record and some experience driving a truck. Workers who deal directly with customers must get along well with people. Employers also look for responsible, self-motivated individuals, since many gardeners and groundskeepers work with little supervision.

Courses in agronomy, horticulture, and botany are helpful for advancement. There are many 2- and 4-year programs in landscape management, turfgrass management, interiorscape, and ornamental horticulture. Courses include equipment use and care, landscape design, plant biology, and irrigation. There are cooperative education programs in which students work alternate semesters or quarters for a lawn care or landscape contractor.

Generally, a gardener or groundskeeper can advance to supervisor after several years of progressively responsible experience, including the demonstrated ability to deal effectively with both coworkers and customers. Supervisors can advance to grounds manager or superintendent for a golf course or other athletic facility, a cemetery, a campus, a school system, or manager of a lawn maintenance firm. Many gardeners and groundskeepers become landscape contractors.

The Professional Grounds Management Society offers certification to those managers who have a combination of 8 years of experience and formal education beyond high school.

Job Outlook

Those wishing to become gardeners and groundskeepers should find excellent job opportunities in the future. Because of high turnover in this occupation, a large number of job openings are expected to result from the need to replace workers who transfer to other occupations or leave the labor force. This occupation attracts many people who are trying to make money but who are not committed to the occupation. Some take gardening or groundskeeping jobs to earn money for school, others only take these jobs until a better paying job is found. Because wages for beginners are low and the work is physically demanding, many employers have difficulty attracting enough workers to fill all openings.

Employment of gardeners and groundskeepers is expected to grow about as fast as the average for all occupations through the year 2005 in response to increasing demand for gardening and landscaping services. Expected growth in the construction of commercial and industrial buildings, shopping malls, homes, highways, and parks and recreational facilities should stimulate demand for these workers. Developers are increasingly using landscaping services, both interior and exterior, to attract prospective buyers and tenants. In addition, owners of many existing buildings and facilities are upgrading their landscaping. Also, a growing number of homeowners are using lawn maintenance and landscaping services to enhance the beauty and value of their property and to conserve their leisure time. Growth in the number of parks, athletic fields, golf courses, cemeteries, and similar facilities also can be expected to add to the demand for these workers.

Employment opportunities in landscaping are tied to local economic conditions. During economic downturns, many individuals turn to landscaping as a second source of income or a new career. At the same time, demand for landscaping services often slows as corporations, governments, and homeowners reduce spending on all nonessential expenditures, increasing the level of competition for available jobs.

Earnings
Median weekly earnings of gardeners and groundskeepers were about $287 in 1994; the middle 50 percent earned between $222 and $379. The lowest 10 percent earned less than $184, and the top 10 percent earned more than $508 a week.

Related Occupations
Gardeners and groundskeepers perform most of their work outdoors. Others whose jobs may be performed outdoors or are otherwise related are botanist, construction workers, landscape architects, nursery workers, farmers, horticultural workers, tree surgeon helpers, and forest conservation workers.

Sources of Additional Information
For career information, contact:

☞Associated Landscape Contractors of America, Inc., 12200 Sunrise Valley Dr., Suite 150, Reston, VA 22091.

☞Professional Lawn Care Association of America, 1000 Johnson Ferry Rd. NE., C-135, Marietta, GA 30068.

For career and certification information, contact:

☞Professional Grounds Management Society, 120 Cockeysville Rd., Suite 104, Hunt Valley, MD 21031.

Mechanics, Installers, and Repairers

Aircraft Mechanics, Including Engine Specialists

(D.O.T. 621.261-022, 621.281 except -030, .684-014; 806.384-038; 807.261, .381-014, and .684-018)

Nature of the Work

To keep aircraft in peak operating condition, aircraft mechanics and engine specialists perform scheduled maintenance, make repairs, and complete inspections required by the Federal Aviation Administration (FAA).

Many aircraft mechanics specialize in preventive maintenance. Following a schedule that is based on the number of hours the aircraft has flown, calendar days, cycles of operation, or a combination of these factors, mechanics inspect the engines, landing gear, instruments, pressurized sections, accessories—brakes, valves, pumps, and air-conditioning systems, for example—and other parts of the aircraft and do the necessary maintenance. They may examine an engine through specially designed openings while working from ladders or scaffolds, or use hoists or lifts to remove the entire engine from the craft. After taking the engine apart, mechanics may use precision instruments to measure parts for wear, and use x-ray and magnetic inspection equipment to check for invisible cracks. Worn or defective parts are repaired or replaced. They also may repair sheet-metal or composite surfaces, measure the tension of control cables, or check for corrosion, distortion, and cracks in the fuselage, wings, and tail. After completing all repairs, mechanics must test the equipment to ensure that it works properly.

Mechanics specializing in repair work rely on the pilot's description of a problem to find and fix faulty equipment. For example, during a preflight check, a pilot may discover that the aircraft's fuel gauge does not work. To solve the problem, mechanics may check the electrical connections, replace the gauge, or use electrical test equipment to make sure no wires are broken or shorted out. They work as fast as safety permits so that the aircraft can be put back into service quickly.

Aircraft mechanics inspect and service aircraft on a regularly scheduled basis.

Mechanics may work on one or many different types of aircraft, such as jets, propeller-driven airplanes, and helicopters; or, for efficiency, they may specialize in one section of a particular type of aircraft, such as the engine, hydraulic, or electrical system. As a result of technological advances, mechanics spend an increasing amount of time repairing electronic systems such as computerized controls. They also may be required to analyze and develop solutions to complex electronic problems. In small, independent repair shops, mechanics usually inspect and repair many different types of aircraft.

Working Conditions

Mechanics usually work in hangars or in other indoor areas, although they may work outdoors—sometimes in unpleasant weather—when the hangars are full or when repairs must be made quickly. This occurs most often to airline mechanics who work at airports because, to save time, minor repairs and preflight checks often are made at the terminal. Mechanics often work under time pressure to maintain flight schedules or, in general aviation, to keep from inconveniencing customers. At the same time, mechanics have a tremendous responsibility to maintain safety standards and this can cause the job to be stressful.

Frequently, mechanics must lift or pull objects weighing as much as 70 pounds. They often stand, lie, or kneel in awkward positions and occasionally must work in precarious positions on scaffolds or ladders. Noise and vibration are common when testing engines. Aircraft mechanics generally work 40 hours a week on 8-hour shifts around the clock. Overtime work is frequent.

Employment

Aircraft mechanics held about 119,000 jobs in 1994. Over three-fifths of all salaried mechanics worked for airlines, nearly one-fifth for aircraft assembly firms, and nearly one-sixth for the Federal Government. Most of the rest were general aviation mechanics, the majority of whom worked for independent repair shops or companies that operate their own planes to transport executives and cargo. Very few mechanics were self-employed.

Most airline mechanics work at major airports near large cities. Civilian mechanics employed by the Armed Forces work at military installations. A large proportion of mechanics who work for aircraft assembly firms are located in California or Washington. Others work for the FAA, many at its facility in Oklahoma City. Mechanics for independent repair shops work at airports in every part of the country.

Training, Other Qualifications, and Advancement

The majority of mechanics who work on civilian aircraft are certificated by the FAA as "airframe mechanic," "powerplant mechanic," or "repairer." *Airframe mechanics* are authorized to work on any part of the aircraft except the instruments, powerplants, and propellers. *Powerplant mechanics* are authorized to work on engines and to do limited work on propellers. Technicians called *repairers*—who are employed by FAA-certificated repair stations and air carriers—work on instruments and on propellers. *Combination airframe-and-powerplant mechanics*—called A & P mechanics—can work on any part of the plane, and those with an inspector's authorization can certify inspection work completed by other mechanics. Uncertificated mechanics are supervised by those with certificates.

The FAA requires at least 18 months of work experience for an airframe, powerplant, or repairer's certificate. For a combined A & P certificate, at least 30 months of experience working with both engines and airframes are required. To obtain an inspector's authorization, a mechanic must have held an A & P certificate for at least 3 years. Applicants for all certificates also must pass written and oral tests and demonstrate that they can do the work authorized by the certificate. Most airlines require that mechanics have a high school diploma and an A & P certificate.

Although a few people become mechanics through on-the-job training, most learn their job in one of about 192 trade schools certified by the FAA. Student enrollment in these schools varies greatly; some have as few as 50 students while at least one school has about 800 students. FAA standards established by law require that certificated mechanic schools offer students a minimum of 1,900 actual class hours. Courses in these trade schools generally last from 2 years to 30 months and provide training with the tools and equipment used on the job. For an FAA certificate, attendance at such schools may substitute for work experience. However, these schools do not guarantee jobs or FAA certificates. Aircraft trade schools are placing more emphasis on newer technologies such as turbine engines, aviation electronics, and composite materials—including graphite, fiberglass, and boron—all of which are increasingly being used in the construction of new aircraft. Less emphasis is being placed on older technologies such as woodworking and welding. Employers prefer mechanics who can perform a wide variety of tasks. Mechanics learn many different skills in their training that can be applied to other jobs.

Some aircraft mechanics in the Armed Forces acquire enough general experience to satisfy the work experience requirements for the FAA certificate. With additional study, they may pass the certifying exam. Generally, however, jobs in the military services are too specialized to provide the broad experience required by the FAA. Most mechanics have to complete the entire training program at a trade school, although a few receive some credit for the material they learned in the service. In any case, military experience is a great advantage when seeking employment; employers consider trade school graduates who have this experience to be the most desirable applicants.

Courses in mathematics, physics, chemistry, electronics, computer science, and mechanical drawing are helpful because many of their principles are involved in the operation of an aircraft and knowledge of the principles often is necessary to make repairs. Courses that develop writing skills are also important because mechanics are often required to submit reports.

As new and more complex aircraft are designed, more employers are requiring mechanics to take on-going training to update their skills. Recent technological advances in aircraft maintenance necessitate a strong background in electronics—both for acquiring and retaining jobs in this field. New FAA certification standards will make ongoing training mandatory. Every 24 months, mechanics will be required to take at least 16 hours of training to keep their certificate. Many mechanics take courses offered by manufacturers or employers, usually through outside contractors.

Aircraft mechanics must do careful and thorough work that requires a high degree of mechanical aptitude. Employers seek applicants who are self-motivated, hard-working, enthusiastic, and able to diagnose and solve complex mechanical problems. Agility is important for the reaching and climbing necessary for the job. Because they may work on the top of wings and fuselages on large jet planes, aircraft mechanics must not be afraid of heights.

As aircraft mechanics gain experience, they have the opportunity for advancement. Opportunities are best for those who have an aircraft inspector's authorization. A mechanic may advance to lead mechanic (or crew chief), inspector, lead inspector, and shop supervisor. In the airlines, where promotion is often determined by examination, supervisors may advance to executive positions. Those with broad experience in maintenance and overhaul have become inspectors with the FAA. With additional business and management training, some open their own aircraft maintenance facilities.

Job Outlook

Job prospects for aircraft mechanics are expected to vary among types of employers. Opportunities are likely to be the best at the smaller commuter and regional airlines, FAA repair stations, and in general aviation. Because wages in these companies tend to be relatively low, there are fewer applicants for these jobs than for jobs with the major airlines. Also, some jobs will become available as experienced mechanics leave for higher paying jobs with airlines or transfer to another occupation. Mechanics will face more competition for airline jobs because the high wages and travel benefits attract more qualified applicants than there are openings. Prospects will be best for applicants with significant experience. Mechanics who keep abreast of technological advances in electronics, composite materials, and other areas will be in greatest demand. The number of job openings for aircraft mechanics in the Federal Government should decline as the size of the Armed Forces is reduced.

Employment of aircraft mechanics is expected to increase about as fast as the average for all occupations through the year 2005 and provide some jobs. A growing population and rising incomes are expected to stimulate the demand for airline transportation, and the number of aircraft is expected to grow. However, employment growth will be restricted somewhat by increases in productivity resulting from greater use of automated inventory control and modular systems that speed repairs and parts replacement.

Most job openings for aircraft mechanics through the year 2005 will stem from replacement needs. Each year, as mechanics transfer to other occupations or retire, several thousand job openings will arise. Aircraft mechanics have a comparatively strong attachment to the occupation, reflecting their significant investment in training. However, because aircraft mechanics' skills are transferable to other occupations, some mechanics leave for work in a related field.

Declines in air travel during recessions force airlines to curtail the number of flights, which results in less aircraft maintenance and, consequently, layoffs for aircraft mechanics.

Earnings

In 1994, the median annual salary of aircraft mechanics was about $36,858. The middle 50 percent earned between $27,976 and $47,112. The top 10 percent of all aircraft mechanics earned over $53,872 a year and the bottom 10 percent earned less than $20,072. Mechanics who worked on jets generally earned more than those working on other aircraft. Airline mechanics and their immediate families receive reduced fare transportation on their own and most other airlines.

Earnings of airline mechanics generally are higher than mechanics working for other employers. Average hourly pay for beginning aircraft mechanics ranged from $8.70 at the smaller turbo-prop airlines to $13.56 at the major airlines in 1994, according to the Future Aviation Professionals of America. Earnings of experienced mechanics ranged from $14.48 to $21.12 an hour.

Almost one-half of all aircraft mechanics, including those employed by some major airlines, are covered by union agreements. The principal unions are the International Association of Machinists and Aerospace Workers and the Transport Workers Union of America. Some mechanics are represented by the International Brotherhood of Teamsters.

Related Occupations

Workers in some other occupations that involve similar mechanical and electrical work are electricians, elevator repairers, and telephone maintenance mechanics.

Sources of Additional Information

Information about jobs in a particular airline may be obtained by writing to the personnel manager of the company. For addresses of airline companies and information about job opportunities and salaries, contact:

☛FAPA, 4959 Massachusetts Blvd., Atlanta, GA 30337. (This organization may be called toll free at 1-800-JET-JOBS, extension 190.)

For general information about aircraft mechanics, write to:

☛Professional Aviation Maintenance Association, 500 Northwest Plaza, Suite 1016, St. Ann, MO 63074-2209.

For information on jobs in a particular area, contact employers at local airports or local offices of the State employment service.

Automotive Body Repairers

(D.O.T. 620.364, .684-034; 807.267; .281; .361-010; .381-010, -018, -022, and -030; .484; .684-010; and 865.684-010)

Nature of the Work

Thousands of motor vehicles are damaged in traffic accidents every day. Although some are sold for salvage or scrapped, most can be repaired to look and drive like new. Automotive body repairers straighten bent bodies, remove dents, and replace crumpled parts that are beyond repair. Usually, they can repair all types of vehicles, but most body repairers work on cars and small trucks. A few work on large trucks, buses, or tractor-trailers.

When a damaged vehicle is brought into the shop, body repairers generally receive instructions from their supervisors, who have determined which parts are to be restored or replaced and how much time the job should take.

Automotive body repairers use special machines to restore damaged metal frames and body sections to their original shape and location. They chain or clamp the frames and sections to alignment machines that usually use hydraulic pressure to align the damaged metal. "Unibody" designs, which are built without frames, must be returned to precise alignment, so repairers use bench systems to guide them and measure how much each section is out of alignment.

Body repairers remove badly damaged sections of body panels with a pneumatic metal-cutting gun or acetylene torch and weld in new sections to replace them. Repairers pull out less serious dents with a hydraulic jack or hand prying bar, or knock them out with handtools or pneumatic hammers. They smooth out small dents and creases in the metal by holding a small anvil against one side of the damaged area while hammering the opposite side. They remove very small pits and dimples with pick hammers and punches.

Body repairers also repair or replace the plastic body parts used increasingly on newer model vehicles. They remove the damaged panels and determine the type of plastic from which they are made. With most types, they can apply heat from a hot-air welding gun or by immersion in hot water, and press the softened panel back into its original shape by hand. They replace plastic parts which are badly damaged or more difficult to repair.

Body repairers use plastic or solder to fill small dents which cannot be worked out of the plastic or metal panel. On metal panels, they then file or grind the hardened filler to the original shape and sand it before painting. In many shops, automotive painters do the painting. (These workers are discussed in the *Handbook* statement on painting and coating machine operators.) In smaller shops, workers often do both body repairing and painting. A few body repairers specialize in repairing fiberglass car bodies.

In large shops, body repairers may specialize in one type of repair, such as frame straightening or door and fender repairing. Some body repairers also specialize in installing glass in automobiles and other vehicles. Glass installers remove broken, cracked, or pitted windshields and window glass. Curved windows sometimes must be cut from a sheet of safety glass. Glass installers apply a moisture-proofing compound along the edges of the glass, place it in the vehicle, and install rubber strips around the sides of the windshield or window to make it secure and weatherproof.

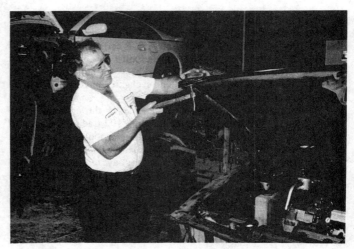

Automotive body repairers straighten bent bodies and remove dents.

Body repair work has variety and challenge—each damaged vehicle presents a different problem. Repairers must develop appropriate methods for each job, using their broad knowledge of automotive construction and repair techniques.

Body repairers usually work alone with only general directions from supervisors. In some shops, they may be assisted by helpers or apprentices.

Working Conditions

The majority of automotive body repairers work a standard 40 hour week, but those who are self employed may work 60 or more hours a week. They work indoors in body shops which are noisy because of the banging of hammers against metal and the whir of power tools. Most shops are well ventilated to partially disperse dust and paint fumes. Body repairers often work in awkward or cramped positions, and much of their work is strenuous and dirty. Hazards include cuts from sharp metal edges, burns from torches and heated metal, injuries from power tools, and fumes from paint.

Employment

Automotive body repairers held about 209,000 jobs in 1994. Most worked for shops that specialized in body repairs and painting, and for automobile and truck dealers. Others worked for organizations that maintain their own motor vehicles, such as trucking companies and automobile rental companies. A few worked for motor vehicle manufacturers. About 1 automotive body repairer out of 5 was self-employed.

Training, Other Qualifications, and Advancement

Most employers prefer to hire persons who have completed formal training programs in automotive body repair, but these programs are able to supply only a portion of employers' needs. Formal training is highly desirable because advances in technology in recent years have greatly changed the structure, the components, and even the materials used in automobiles. As a result, many new repair techniques have been created and many new skills are required. For example, the bodies of newer automobiles are increasingly made of a combination of materials—the traditional steel, plus aluminum and a growing variety of metal alloys and plastics—each requiring the use of somewhat different techniques to reshape and smooth out dents and small pits. Automotive body repair training programs are offered by high schools, vocational schools, private trade schools, and community colleges. Formal training in automotive body repair can enhance chances for employment and speed promotion to a journeyman position.

Employers also hire many persons without formal automotive body repair training. They learn the trade as helpers, picking up skills on the job from experienced body repairers. For helper jobs most employers prefer to hire high school graduates who know how to use handtools. Good reading and basic mathematics and computer skills are essential to becoming a fully skilled automotive body repairer. Restoring unibody automobiles to their original form requires such precision that body repairers often must follow instructions and diagrams in technical manuals and make very precise measurements of the position of one body section relative to another.

Helpers begin by assisting body repairers in tasks such as removing damaged parts and installing repaired parts. They learn to remove small dents and to make other minor repairs. They then progress to more difficult tasks such as straightening body parts and returning them to their correct alignment. Generally, to become skilled in all aspects of body repair requires 3 to 4 years of on-the-job training.

Certification by the National Institute for Automotive Service Excellence (ASE), which is voluntary, is recognized as a standard of achievement for automotive body repairers. To be certified, a body repairer must pass a written examination and must have at least 2 years of experience in the trade. Completion of a high school, vocational school, trade school, or community college program in automotive body repair may be substituted for 1 year of work experience. Automotive body repairers must retake the examination at least every 5 years to retain certification.

Automotive body repairers must buy their own handtools, but employers usually furnish power tools. Trainees generally accumulate tools as they gain experience, and many workers have thousands of dollars invested in tools.

Continuing education throughout a career in automotive body repair is becoming increasingly important. Automotive parts, body materials, and electronics continue to change and become more complex and technologically advanced. Gaining new skills, reading technical manuals, and attending seminars and classes is important for keeping up with these technological advances.

An experienced automotive body repairer with supervisory ability may advance to shop supervisor. Some workers open their own body repair shops. Others become automobile damage appraisers for insurance companies.

Job Outlook
Employment of automotive body repairers is expected to increase about as fast as the average for all occupations through the year 2005. Opportunities should be best for persons with formal training in automotive body repair and mechanics.

Requirements for body repairers will increase because, as the number of motor vehicles in operation grows with the Nation's population, the number damaged in accidents will increase as well. New automobile designs increasingly have body parts made of steel alloys, aluminum, and plastics—materials that are more difficult to work with than the traditional steel body parts. Also, new, lighter weight automotive designs are prone to greater collision damage than older, heavier designs and, consequently, are more time consuming to repair. Nevertheless, the need to replace experienced repairers who transfer to other occupations, retire, or stop working for other reasons will still account for the majority of job openings.

The automotive repair business is not very sensitive to changes in economic conditions, and experienced body repairers are rarely laid off. However, most employers hire fewer new workers during an economic slowdown. Although major body damage must be repaired if a vehicle is to be restored to safe operating condition, repair of minor dents and crumpled fenders can often be deferred.

Earnings
Body repairers earned median weekly earnings of $456 in 1994. The middle 50 percent earned between $321 and $624 a week. The lowest-paid 10 percent earned less than $249 a week, while the highest-paid 10 percent earned over $790 a week. Helpers and trainees usually earn from 30 to 60 percent of the earnings of skilled workers.

The majority of body repairers employed by automotive dealers and repair shops are paid on an incentive basis. Under this method, body repairers are paid a predetermined amount for various tasks, and earnings depend on the amount of work assigned to the repairer and how fast it is completed. Employers frequently guarantee workers a minimum weekly salary. Helpers and trainees usually receive an hourly rate until they are skilled enough to be paid on an incentive basis. Body repairers who work for trucking companies, buslines, and other organizations that maintain their own vehicles usually receive an hourly wage.

Many automotive body repairers are members of unions, including the International Association of Machinists and Aerospace Workers; the International Union, United Automobile, Aerospace and Agricultural Implement Workers of America; the Sheet Metal Workers' International Association; and the International Brotherhood of Teamsters. Most body repairers who are union members work for large automobile dealers, trucking companies, and buslines.

Related Occupations
Repairing damaged motor vehicles often involves working on their mechanical components as well as their bodies. Automotive body repairers often work closely with several related occupations including automotive and diesel mechanics, automotive repair service estimators, painters, and body customizers.

Sources of Additional Information
More details about work opportunities may be obtained from automotive body repair shops and motor vehicle dealers; locals of the unions previously mentioned; or local offices of the State employment service. The State employment service also is a source of information about training programs.

For general information about automotive body repairer careers, write to:
☛Automotive Service Association, Inc., 1901 Airport Freeway, Bedford, TX 76021-5732.
☛Automotive Service Industry Association, 25 Northwest Point, Elk Grove Village, IL 60007-1035.

For information on how to become a certified automotive body repairer, write to:
☛ASE, 13505 Dulles Technology Dr., Herndon, VA 22071-3415.

For a directory of certified automotive body repairer programs, contact:
☛National Automotive Technician Education Foundation, 13505 Dulles Technology Dr., Herndon, VA 22071.

For a directory of accredited private trade and technical schools that offer training programs in automotive body repair, write to:
☛Accrediting Commission of Career Schools and Colleges of Technology, 2101 Wilson Blvd., Suite 302, Arlington, VA 22201.

For a list of public automotive mechanic training programs, contact:
☛Vocational Industrial Clubs of America, P.O. Box 3000, 1401 James Monroe Highway, Leesburg, VA 22075.

Automotive Mechanics

(D.O.T. 620.261-010, -012, -030, and -034; .281-010, -026, -034, -038, -062, -066, and -070; .381-010 and -022; .682; .684-018 and -022; 706.381-046; 721.281-010; 806.361-026 and .684-038; 807.664 and .684-022; 825.381-014)

Nature of the Work
Automotive mechanics, often called *automotive service technicians*, repair and service automobiles and occasionally light trucks, such as vans and pickups, with gasoline engines. (Mechanics who work on diesel-powered trucks, buses, and equipment are discussed in the *Handbook* statement on diesel mechanics. Motorcycle mechanics—

who repair and service motorcycles, motorscooters, mopeds, and occasionally small all-terrain vehicles—are discussed in the *Handbook* statement on motorcycle, boat, and small-engine mechanics.)

Anyone whose car or light truck has broken down knows the importance of the mechanic's job. The ability to diagnose the source of the problem quickly and accurately, one of the mechanic's most valuable skills, requires good reasoning ability and a thorough knowledge of automobiles. In fact, many mechanics consider diagnosing "hard to find" troubles one of their most challenging and satisfying duties.

When mechanical or electrical troubles occur, mechanics first get a description of the symptoms from the owner or, if they work in a dealership or large shop, the repair service estimator who wrote the repair order. The mechanic may have to test drive the vehicle or use a variety of testing equipment, such as engine analyzers, spark plug testers, or compression gauges to locate the problem. Once the cause of the problem is found, mechanics make adjustments or repairs. If a part is damaged or worn beyond repair, or cannot be fixed at a reasonable cost, it is replaced, usually after consultation with the vehicle owner.

During routine service, mechanics inspect, lubricate, and adjust engines and other components, repairing or replacing parts before they cause breakdowns. They usually follow a checklist to be sure they examine all important parts, such as belts, hoses, steering systems, spark plugs, brake and fuel systems, wheel bearings, and other potentially troublesome items.

Mechanics use a variety of tools in their work. They use power tools such as pneumatic wrenches to remove bolts quickly; machine tools such as lathes and grinding machines to rebuild brakes and other parts; welding and flame-cutting equipment to remove and repair exhaust systems and other parts; jacks and hoists to lift cars and engines; and a growing variety of electronic service equipment, such as infrared engine analyzers and computerized diagnostic devices. They also use many common handtools such as screwdrivers, pliers, and wrenches to work on small parts and get at hard-to-reach places.

Automotive mechanics in larger shops have increasingly become specialized. For example, *automatic transmission mechanics* work on gear trains, couplings, hydraulic pumps, and other parts of automatic transmissions. Because these are complex mechanisms and include electronic parts, their repair requires considerable experience and training, including a knowledge of hydraulics. *Tune-up mechanics* adjust the ignition timing and valves, and adjust or replace spark plugs and other parts to ensure efficient engine performance. They

often use electronic test equipment to help them adjust and locate malfunctions in fuel, ignition, and emissions control systems.

Automotive air-conditioning mechanics install and repair air-conditioners and service components such as compressors and condensers. *Front-end mechanics* align and balance wheels and repair steering mechanisms and suspension systems. They frequently use special alignment equipment and wheel-balancing machines. *Brake repairers* adjust brakes, replace brake linings and pads, repair hydraulic cylinders, turn discs and drums, and make other repairs on brake systems. Some mechanics specialize in both brake and front-end work.

Automotive-radiator mechanics clean radiators with caustic solutions, locate and solder leaks, and install new radiator cores or complete replacement radiators. They also may repair heaters and air-conditioners, and solder leaks in gasoline tanks.

Working Conditions

Most automotive mechanics work a standard 40-hour week, but some self-employed mechanics work longer hours. Generally, mechanics work indoors. Most repair shops are well ventilated and lighted, but some are drafty and noisy. Mechanics frequently work with dirty and greasy parts, and in awkward positions. They often must lift heavy parts and tools. Minor cuts, burns, and bruises are common, but serious accidents are avoided when the shop is kept clean and orderly and safety practices are observed.

Employment

Automotive mechanics held about 736,000 jobs in 1994. The majority worked for retail and wholesale automotive dealers, independent automotive repair shops, and gasoline service stations. Others were employed at automotive service facilities at department, automotive, and home supply stores, or maintained the automobile fleets of taxicab and automobile leasing companies, Federal, State, and local governments, and other organizations. Motor vehicle manufacturers employed some mechanics to test, adjust, and repair cars at the end of assembly lines. Over 20 percent of automotive mechanics were self-employed.

Training, Other Qualifications, and Advancement

Automotive technology is rapidly increasing in sophistication, and most training authorities strongly recommend that persons seeking trainee automotive mechanic jobs complete a formal training program after graduating from high school. However, some automotive mechanics still learn the trade solely by assisting and working with experienced mechanics.

Automotive mechanic training programs are offered in high schools, community colleges, and public and private vocational and technical schools, but postsecondary programs generally provide more thorough career preparation than high school programs. High school programs, while an asset, vary greatly in quality. Some offer only an introduction to automotive technology and service for the future consumer or hobbyist, while others aim to equip graduates with enough skills to get a job as a mechanic's helper or trainee mechanic after graduation.

Postsecondary automotive mechanic training programs vary greatly in format, but generally provide intensive career preparation through a combination of classroom instruction and hands-on practice. Some trade and technical school programs provide concentrated training for 6 months to a year, depending on how many hours the student must attend each week. Community college programs normally spread the training out over 2 years, supplement the automotive training with instruction in English, basic mathematics, computers, and other subjects, and award an associate degree.

The various automobile manufacturers and their participating dealers sponsor 2-year associate degree programs at more than 100 community colleges across the Nation. The manufacturers provide service equipment and late model cars on which students practice

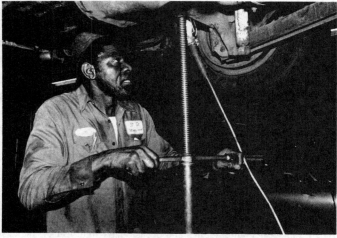

The majority of automotive mechanics work for retail and wholesale automotive dealers, independent automotive repair shops, and gasoline service stations.

new skills, and insure that the programs teach the latest automotive technology. Curriculums are updated frequently to reflect changing technology and equipment. Students in these programs typically spend alternate 6- to 12-week periods attending classes full time and working full time in the service departments of sponsoring dealers. Because students spend time gaining valuable work experience, these programs may take as long as 4 years to complete, instead of the normal 2 years required to earn an associate degree in automotive service technology. However, they offer students the opportunity to earn money while going to school and promise a job upon graduation. Also, some sponsoring dealers provide students with financial assistance for tuition or the purchase of tools.

The National Automotive Technicians Education Foundation (NATEF), an affiliate of the National Institute for Automotive Service Excellence (ASE), certifies automobile mechanic training programs offered by high schools and postsecondary trade schools, technical institutes, and community colleges. While NATEF certification is voluntary, and many institutions have not sought it, certification does signify that the program meets uniform standards for instructional facilities, equipment, staff credentials, and curriculum. In early 1995, over 850 high school and postsecondary automotive mechanic training programs had been certified by NATEF.

Knowledge of electronics is increasingly desirable for automotive mechanics because electronics is being used in a growing variety of automotive components. Engine controls and dashboard instruments were among the first components to use electronics, but now electronics are being used in brakes, transmissions, steering systems, and a variety of other components. In the past, problems involving electrical systems or electronics were usually handled by a specialist, but electronics are becoming so commonplace that most automotive mechanics must be familiar with at least the basic principles of electronics in order to recognize when an electronic malfunction may be responsible for a problem. In addition, automotive mechanics frequently must be able to test and replace electronic components.

For trainee mechanic jobs, employers look for people with good reading and basic mathematics and computer skills who can study technical manuals to keep abreast of new technology. People who have a desire to learn new service and repair procedures and specifications are excellent candidates for trainee mechanic jobs. Trainees also must possess mechanical aptitude and knowledge of how automobiles work. Most employers regard the successful completion of a vocational training program in automotive mechanics at a postsecondary institution as the best preparation for trainee positions. Experience working on motor vehicles in the Armed Forces or as a hobby is also valuable. Completion of high school is required by a growing number of employers. Courses in automotive repair, electronics, physics, chemistry, English, computers, and mathematics can provide a good basic educational background for a career as an automotive mechanic.

Beginners usually start as trainee mechanics, helpers, lubrication workers, or gasoline service station attendants and gradually acquire and practice their skills by working with experienced mechanics. Although a beginner can perform many routine service tasks and make simple repairs after a few months' experience, it usually takes 1 to 2 years of experience to acquire adequate proficiency to become a journey service mechanic and quickly perform the more difficult types of routine service and repairs. However, graduates of the better postsecondary mechanic training programs are often able to earn promotion to the journey level after only a few months on the job. An additional 1 to 2 years are usually required to become thoroughly experienced and familiar with all types of repairs. Difficult specialties, such as transmission repair, require another year or two of training and experience. In contrast, automotive radiator mechanics and brake specialists, who do not need an all-round knowledge of automotive repair, may learn their jobs in considerably less time.

In the past, many persons have become automotive mechanics through 3- or 4-year formal apprenticeship programs. However, as formal automotive training programs have increased in popularity, the number of employers willing to make such a long-term apprenticeship commitment has greatly declined.

Mechanics usually buy their handtools, and beginners are expected to accumulate tools as they gain experience. Many experienced mechanics have thousands of dollars invested in tools. Employers furnish power tools, engine analyzers, and other test equipment.

Employers increasingly send experienced automotive mechanics to manufacturer training centers to learn to repair new models or to receive special training in the repair of components such as electronic fuel injection or air-conditioners. Motor vehicle dealers may also send promising beginners to manufacturer sponsored mechanic training programs. Factory representatives come to many shops to conduct short training sessions.

Voluntary certification by ASE is widely recognized as a standard of achievement for automotive mechanics. Mechanics are certified in one or more of eight different service areas, such as electrical systems, engine repair, brake systems, suspension and steering, and heating and air conditioning. Master automotive mechanics are certified in all eight areas. For certification in each area, mechanics must have at least 2 years of experience and pass a written examination; completion of an automotive mechanic program in high school, vocational or trade school, or community or junior college may be substituted for 1 year of experience. Certified mechanics must retake the examination at least every 5 years.

Experienced mechanics who have leadership ability may advance to shop supervisor or service manager. Mechanics who work well with customers may become automotive repair service estimators. Some with sufficient funds open independent repair shops.

Job Outlook

Job opportunities in this occupation are expected to be good for persons who complete automotive training programs in high school, vocational and technical schools, or community colleges. Persons whose training includes basic electronics skills should have the best opportunities. Persons without formal mechanic training are likely to face competition for entry level jobs. Mechanic careers are attractive to many because extensive training is not required and they afford the opportunity for good pay and the satisfaction of skilled work with one's hands.

Employment of automotive mechanics is expected to increase about as fast as the average for all occupations through the year 2005. Growth in mechanic employment in automobile dealerships, independent automotive repair shops, specialty car care chains, and other establishments will be offset somewhat by declining employment in gasoline service stations, because fewer stations offer repair services.

Nevertheless, the number of mechanics is expected to increase because expansion of the driving age population will increase the number of motor vehicles on the road. The growing complexity of automotive technology, such as the use of electronic and emissions control equipment, increasingly necessitates that cars be serviced by skilled workers, contributing to growth in demand for highly trained mechanics. In addition, if the average age of automobiles in operation continues to be high, a significant proportion of consumers' vehicle operating expenditures will be spent on service and repairs, and less on purchasing vehicles. However, improvements in the reliability of automobiles, together with less frequent requirements for routine service, are expected to result in continued declines in the service and repair needs of cars.

More job openings are expected for automotive mechanics than for most other occupations because replacement needs, the main source of job openings, will be substantial, due in large part to the size of the occupation. Replacements will be needed as experienced workers transfer to other occupations or retire or stop working for other reasons.

Most persons who enter the occupation may expect steady work because changes in economic conditions have little effect on the automotive repair business. During a downturn, however, some employers may be more reluctant to hire inexperienced workers.

Earnings

Median weekly earnings of automotive mechanics who were wage and salary workers were $439 in 1994. The middle 50 percent earned between $308 and $624 a week. The lowest paid 10 percent earned less than $228 a week, and the top 10 percent earned more than $792 a week.

Many experienced mechanics employed by automotive dealers and independent repair shops receive a commission related to the labor cost charged to the customer. Under this method, weekly earnings depend on the amount of work completed by the mechanic. Employers frequently guarantee commissioned mechanics a minimum weekly salary.

Some mechanics are members of labor unions. The unions include the International Association of Machinists and Aerospace Workers; the International Union, United Automobile, Aerospace and Agricultural Implement Workers of America; the Sheet Metal Workers' International Association; and the International Brotherhood of Teamsters.

Related Occupations

Other workers who repair and service motor vehicles include diesel truck and bus mechanics, motorcycle mechanics, and automotive body repairers, painters, customizers, and repair service estimators.

Sources of Additional Information

For more details about work opportunities, contact local automotive dealers and repair shops, or the local office of the State employment service. The State employment service also may have information about training programs.

A list of certified automotive mechanic training programs may be obtained from:

☛National Automotive Technicians Education Foundation, 13505 Dulles Technology Dr., Herndon, VA 22071-3415.

Information on automobile manufacturer sponsored 2-year associate degree programs in automotive service technology may be obtained from:

☛ASSET Program, Training Department, Ford Parts and Service Division, Ford Motor Company, Room 109, 3000 Schaefer Rd., Dearborn, MI 48121.

☛Chrysler Dealer Apprenticeship Program, National C.A.P. Coordinator, CIMS 423-21-06, 26001 Lawrence Ave., Center Line, MI 48015, or by calling 1-800-626-1523.

☛General Motors Automotive Service Educational Program, National College Coordinator, General Motors Service Technology Group, 30501 Van Dyke Ave., Warren, MI 48090, or by calling 1-800-828-6860.

Information on how to become a certified automotive mechanic is available from:

☛ASE, 13505 Dulles Technology Dr., Herndon, VA 22071-3415.

For general information about the work of automotive mechanics, write to:

☛Automotive Service Association, Inc., 1901 Airport Freeway, Bedford, TX 76021-5732.

☛Automotive Service Industry Association, 25 Northwest Point, Elk Grove Village, IL 60007-1035.

For a directory of accredited private trade and technical schools that offer programs in automotive technician training, write to:

☛Accrediting Commission of Career Schools and Colleges of Technology, 2101 Wilson Blvd., Suite 302, Arlington, VA 22201.

For a list of public automotive mechanic training programs, contact:

☛Vocational Industrial Clubs of America, P.O. Box 3000, 1401 James Monroe Highway, Leesburg, VA 22075.

Diesel Mechanics

(D.O.T. 620.281-046, -050, and -058; 625.281-010, -014, -022, and .361)

Nature of the Work

Diesel engines are more durable and heavier than gasoline engines. In addition, they are more fuel efficient than gasoline engines, in part because the higher compression ratios found in diesel engines help convert a higher percentage of the fuel into power. Because of their greater durability and efficiency, diesel engines are used to power most of the Nation's heavy vehicles and equipment.

Diesel mechanics repair and maintain diesel engines that power transportation equipment, such as heavy trucks, buses, and locomotives; construction equipment such as bulldozers, cranes, and road graders; and farm equipment such as tractors and combines. A small number work on diesel-powered automobiles. Diesel mechanics also service a variety of other diesel-powered equipment, such as electric generators and compressors and pumps used in oil well drilling and irrigation systems.

Most diesel mechanics work on heavy trucks used in industries such as mining and construction to carry ore and building materials, and by private and commercial trucking lines for general freight hauling. Most light trucks are gasoline powered, and although some diesel mechanics may occasionally service gasoline engines, most work primarily on diesel engines. (For information on mechanics who work primarily on gasoline engines, see the *Handbook* statement on automotive mechanics.)

Mechanics who work for organizations that maintain their own vehicles may spend much time doing preventive maintenance to assure safe operation, prevent wear and damage to parts, and reduce costly breakdowns. During a maintenance check on a truck, for example, they usually follow a regular checklist that includes the inspection of brake systems, steering mechanisms, wheel bearings, and other important parts. They usually repair or adjust a part that is not working properly. Parts that cannot be fixed are replaced.

In many shops, mechanics do all kinds of repairs, working on a vehicle's electrical system one day and doing major engine repairs the next. In some large shops, mechanics specialize in one or two types of work. For example, one mechanic may specialize in major engine repair, another in transmission work, another in electrical systems, and yet another in suspension or brake systems.

Diesel mechanics use a variety of tools in their work, including power tools such as pneumatic wrenches to remove bolts quickly; machine tools such as lathes and grinding machines to rebuild brakes

Diesel mechanics usually work indoors, but occasionally make repairs on the road.

and other parts; welding and flame-cutting equipment to remove and repair exhaust systems and other parts; common handtools such as screwdrivers, pliers, and wrenches to work on small parts and get at hard-to-reach places; and jacks and hoists to lift and move large parts. Diesel mechanics also use a variety of testing equipment, including ohmmeters, ammeters, and voltmeters when working on electrical systems and electronic components; and tachometers, dynamometers, and engine analyzers to locate engine malfunctions.

For heavy work, such as removing engines and transmissions, two mechanics may work as a team, or a mechanic may be assisted by an apprentice or helper. Mechanics generally get their assignments from shop supervisors or service managers, who may check the mechanics' work or assist in diagnosing problems.

Working Conditions

Diesel mechanics usually work indoors, although they may occasionally make repairs on the road. They are subject to the usual shop hazards such as cuts and bruises. Mechanics handle greasy and dirty parts and may stand or lie in awkward or cramped positions to repair vehicles and equipment. Work areas usually are well lighted, heated, and ventilated, and many employers provide locker rooms and shower facilities.

Employment

Diesel mechanics held about 250,000 jobs in 1994. Nearly one-quarter serviced trucks and other diesel-powered equipment for customers of vehicle and equipment dealers, leasing companies, and independent automotive repair shops. Over one-fifth worked for local and long-distance trucking companies, and nearly one-seventh maintained the buses and trucks of buslines, public transit companies, school systems, and Federal, State, and local government. The remainder maintained the fleets of trucks and other equipment of manufacturing, construction, and other companies. A relatively small number were self-employed.

Diesel mechanics are employed in every section of the country, but most work in towns and cities where trucking companies, bus-lines, and other fleet owners have large repair shops.

Training, Other Qualifications, and Advancement

Although many persons are able to qualify for diesel mechanic jobs through years of on-the-job training in related, lesser skilled positions, training authorities recommend that persons seeking diesel mechanic jobs complete a formal diesel mechanic training program. Diesel technology is becoming more sophisticated and diesel engines increasingly use electronic components to control a growing variety of functions. Knowledge of basic electronics is becoming essential for diesel mechanics to diagnose whether a malfunction is caused by an electronic component or whether it can be traced to another source. Most employers prefer to hire graduates of formal training programs in diesel mechanics, and completion of such a program can speed advancement to the journey mechanic level. These 1- to 2-year programs, given by vocational and technical schools and community and junior colleges, lead to a certificate of completion or an associate degree. They provide a foundation in the basics of the latest diesel technology and electronics, and enable trainees to more quickly master the service and repair of the actual vehicles and equipment encountered on the job.

A formal 4-year apprenticeship is another good way to learn diesel mechanics. However, apprenticeships are becoming less common because employers are reluctant to make such a long-term investment in training, especially when graduates of postsecondary diesel mechanic programs are increasing in number. Competition for the limited number of apprenticeship slots is often extremely keen. Typical apprenticeship programs for diesel truck and bus mechanics consist of approximately 8,000 hours of practical experience working on transmissions, engines, and other components and at least 576 hours of formal instruction to learn blueprint reading, mathematics,

engine theory, and safety. Frequently, these programs include training in both diesel and gasoline engine repair.

Even though most employers prefer to hire graduates of formal post secondary training programs in diesel mechanics, the number of persons who complete such programs are too few to meet their needs. As a result, many diesel mechanics still learn their skills on the job. Unskilled beginners usually do tasks such as cleaning parts, fueling, lubricating, and driving vehicles in and out of the shop. As beginners gain experience and as vacancies become available, they usually are promoted to mechanics' helpers. In some shops, beginners—especially those having automobile service experience—start as mechanics' helpers.

Most helpers can perform routine service tasks and make minor repairs after a few months' experience. They advance to increasingly difficult jobs as they prove their ability. After they master the repair and service of diesel engines, they learn to work on related components such as brakes, transmissions, or electrical systems. Generally, at least 3 to 4 years of on-the-job experience is necessary to qualify as an all-round diesel truck or bus mechanic. Additional training on other components, such as hydraulic systems, may be necessary for mechanics who wish to specialize in other types of diesel equipment.

For unskilled entry level jobs, employers generally look for applicants who have mechanical aptitude and are at least 18 years of age and in good physical condition. Completion of high school is required by a growing number of employers. Courses in automotive repair, electronics, English, mathematics, and physics provide a good basic educational background for a career as a diesel mechanic. Good reading and basic mathematics skills are needed to study technical manuals to keep abreast of new technology and learn new service and repair procedures and specifications. A State commercial driver's license is needed for test driving trucks or buses on public roads. Practical experience in automobile repair in a gasoline service station, in the Armed Forces, or as a hobby also is valuable.

Employers sometimes send experienced mechanics to special training classes conducted by truck, bus, diesel engine, parts, and equipment manufacturers where they learn the latest technology or receive special training in subjects such as diagnosing engine malfunctions. Mechanics also must read service and repair manuals to keep abreast of engineering changes.

Voluntary certification by the National Institute for Automotive Service Excellence (ASE) is recognized as a standard of achievement for diesel mechanics. Mechanics may be certified as Master Heavy-Duty Truck Technician or may be certified in one or more of six different areas of heavy-duty truck repair: brakes, gasoline engines, diesel engines, drive trains, electrical systems, and suspension and steering. For certification in each area, mechanics must pass a written examination and have at least 2 years of experience. High school, vocational or trade school, or community or junior college training in gasoline or diesel engine repair may substitute for up to 1 year of experience. To retain certification, mechanics must retake the tests at least every 5 years.

Most mechanics must buy their own handtools. Experienced mechanics often have thousands of dollars invested in tools.

Experienced mechanics who have leadership ability may advance to shop supervisors or service managers. Mechanics who have sales ability sometimes become sales representatives. A few mechanics open their own repair shops.

Job Outlook

Employment of diesel mechanics is expected to increase about as fast as the average for all occupations through the year 2005. Because this is a large occupation, more job openings are expected for diesel mechanics than for most other occupations. Although employment growth will create many new jobs, most job openings will arise from the need to replace diesel mechanics who transfer to other fields of work or retire or stop working for other reasons.

Employment of diesel mechanics is expected to grow as freight transportation by truck increases. More trucks will be needed for both local and intercity hauling due to the increased production of goods. Additional diesel mechanics will be needed to repair and maintain growing numbers of buses and heavy construction graders, cranes, earthmovers, and other equipment. Due to the greater durability and economy of the diesel relative to the gasoline engine, buses and trucks of all sizes are expected to be increasingly powered by diesels, also creating new jobs for diesel mechanics.

Careers in diesel mechanics are attractive to many because wages are relatively high and skilled repair work is challenging and varied. Opportunities should be good for persons who complete formal training in diesel mechanics at community and junior colleges and vocational and technical schools, but others may face competition for entry level jobs.

Earnings

According to a survey of workplaces in over 160 metropolitan areas, diesel mechanics earned median earnings of $14.61 an hour in 1993. The middle 50 percent earned between $12.00 and $17.49 an hour. However, earnings may vary by industry and by geographic location.

Beginning apprentices usually earn from 50 to 75 percent of the rate of skilled workers and receive increases about every 6 months until they complete their apprenticeship and reach the rate of skilled mechanics.

The majority of mechanics work a standard 40 hour week, although many work as many as 70 hours per week, particularly if they are self employed. Those employed by truck and bus firms which provide service around the clock may work evenings, nights, and weekends. They usually receive a higher rate of pay for this work.

Many diesel mechanics are members of labor unions, including the International Association of Machinists and Aerospace Workers; the Amalgamated Transit Union; the International Union, United Automobile, Aerospace and Agricultural Implement Workers of America; the Transport Workers Union of America; the Sheet Metal Workers' International Association; and the International Brotherhood of Teamsters.

Related Occupations

Diesel mechanics repair trucks, buses, and other diesel-powered equipment and keep them in good working order. Related mechanic occupations include aircraft mechanics, automotive mechanics, boat engine mechanics, farm equipment mechanics, mobile heavy equipment mechanics, and motorcycle mechanics and small-engine specialists.

Sources of Additional Information

More details about work opportunities for diesel mechanics may be obtained from local employers such as trucking companies, truck dealers, or bus lines; locals of the unions previously mentioned; or the local office of the State employment service. Local State employment service offices also may have information about apprenticeships and other training programs.

For general information about careers as truck, bus, and diesel mechanics, write to:
☛Automotive Service Industry Association, 25 Northwest Point, Elk Grove Village, IL 60007-1035.
☛American Trucking Associations, Inc., Maintenance Council, 2200 Mill Rd., Alexandria, VA 22314-4677.

For a directory of accredited private trade and technical schools with training programs for diesel mechanics, contact:
☛Accrediting Commission of Career Schools and Colleges of Technology, 2101 Wilson Blvd., Suite 302, Arlington, VA 22201.
☛National Automotive Technicians Education Foundation, 13505 Dulles Technology Dr., Herndon, VA 22071-3415.

For a directory of public training programs for diesel mechanics, contact:
☛Vocational Industry Clubs of America, P. O. Box 3000, 1401 James Monroe Highway, Leesburg, VA 22075.

Information on how to become a certified heavy-duty diesel mechanic is available from:
☛ASE, 13505 Dulles Technology Dr., Herndon, VA 22071-3415.

Electronic Equipment Repairers

Nature of the Work

Electronic equipment repairers, also called service technicians or field service representatives, install, maintain, and repair electronic equipment used in offices, factories, homes, hospitals, aircraft, and other places. Equipment includes televisions, radar, industrial equipment controls, computers, telephone systems, and medical diagnosing equipment. Repairers have numerous job titles, which often refer to the kind of equipment they work with. (Electronics technicians, who use the principles and theories of science, engineering, and mathematics in their work, but may also do some repairs, are discussed in the statement on engineering technicians elsewhere in the *Handbook*. For information on workers who operate and maintain electronic equipment used to record and transmit radio and television programs, see the statement on broadcast technicians. Additional information about electronic equipment repairers is given in the separate statements in this section.)

Electronic repairers install, test, repair, and calibrate equipment to ensure that it functions properly. They keep detailed records on each piece of equipment to provide a history of tests, performance problems, and repairs.

When equipment breaks down, repairers first examine work orders, which indicate problems, or talk to equipment operators. Then they check for common causes of trouble such as loose connections or obviously defective components. If routine checks do not locate the trouble, repairers may refer to schematics and manufacturers' specifications that show connections and provide instruction on how to locate problems. They use voltmeters, ohmmeters, signal generators, ammeters, and oscilloscopes and run diagnostic programs to pinpoint malfunctions. It may take several hours to locate a problem but only a few minutes to fix it. However, more equipment now has self-diagnosing features, which greatly simplifies the work. To fix equipment, repairers may replace defective components, circuit boards, or wiring, or adjust and calibrate equipment, using test equipment, small handtools such as pliers, screwdrivers, and soldering irons.

Field repairers visit worksites in their assigned area on a regular basis to do preventive maintenance according to manufacturers' recommended schedules, and whenever emergencies arise. During these calls, repairers may also advise customers on how to use equipment more efficiently and how to spot problems in their early stages. They also listen to customers' complaints and answer questions, promoting customer satisfaction and good will. Some field repairers work full time at installations of clients with a lot of equipment.

Bench repairers work at repair facilities, in stores, factories, or service centers. They repair portable equipment—such as televisions and personal computers brought in by customers—or defective components and machines requiring extensive repairs that have been sent in by field repairers. They determine the source of a problem in the equipment, and may estimate whether it is wiser to buy a new part or machine or to fix the broken one.

Working Conditions

Some electronic equipment repairers work shifts, including weekends and holidays, to service equipment in computer centers, manufacturing plants, hospitals, and telephone companies which operate round the clock. Shifts are generally assigned on the basis of seniority. Repairers may also be on call at any time to handle equipment failure.

Repairers generally work in clean, well-lighted, air-conditioned surroundings—an electronic repair shop or service center, hospital, military installation, or a telephone company's central office. However, some, such as commercial and industrial electronic equipment repairers, may be exposed to heat, grease, and noise on factory floors. Some may have to work in cramped spaces. Telephone installers and repairers may work on rooftops, ladders, and telephone poles.

The work of most repairers involves lifting, reaching, stooping, crouching, and crawling. Adherence to safety precautions is essential to guard against work hazards such as minor burns and electrical shock.

Employment

Electronic equipment repairers held about 389,000 jobs in 1994. Many worked for telephone companies. Others worked for electronic and transportation equipment manufacturers, machinery and equipment wholesalers, hospitals, electronic repair shops, and firms that provide maintenance under contract (called third-party maintenance firms). The distribution of employment in each occupation is presented in the following tabulation:

Computer and office machine repairers	134,000
Communications equipment mechanics	118,000
Commercial and industrial electronic equipment repairers	66,000
Telephone installers and repairers	37,000
Electronic home entertainment equipment repairers	34,000

Training, Other Qualifications, and Advancement

Most employers prefer applicants with formal training in electronics. Electronic training is offered by public post secondary vocational-technical schools, private vocational schools and technical institutes, junior and community colleges, and some high schools and correspondence schools. Programs take 1 to 2 years. The military services also offer formal training and work experience.

Training includes general courses in mathematics, physics, electricity, electronics, schematic reading, and troubleshooting. Students also choose courses which prepare them for a specialty, such as computers, commercial and industrial equipment, or home entertainment equipment. A few repairers complete formal apprenticeship programs sponsored jointly by employers and locals of the International Brotherhood of Electrical Workers.

Applicants for entry-level jobs may have to pass tests that measure mechanical aptitude, knowledge of electricity or electronics, manual dexterity, and general intelligence. Newly hired repairers, even those with formal training, usually receive some training from their employer. They may study electronics and circuit theory and math. They also get hands-on experience with equipment, doing basic maintenance, and using diagnostic programs to locate malfunctions. Training may be in a classroom or it may be self-instruction, consisting of videotapes, programmed computer software, or workbooks that allow trainees to learn at their own pace.

Experienced technicians attend training sessions and read manuals to keep up with design changes and revised service procedures. Many technicians also take advanced training in a particular system or type of repair.

Good eyesight and color vision are needed to inspect and work on small, delicate parts and good hearing to detect malfunctions revealed by sound. Because field repairers usually handle jobs alone, they must be able to work without close supervision. For those who have frequent contact with customers, a pleasant personality, neat appearance, and good communications skills are important. Repairers must also be trustworthy because they may be exposed to money and other valuables in places like banks and securities offices, and some employers require that they be bonded. A security clearance may be required for technicians who repair equipment or service machines in areas where people are engaged in activities related to national security.

The International Society of Certified Electronics Technicians and the Electronics Technicians Association each administer a voluntary certification program. In both, an electronics repairer with 4 years of experience may become a Certified Electronics Technician. Certification, which is by examination, is offered in computer, radio-TV, industrial and commercial equipment, audio, avionics, wireless communications, video distribution, satellite, and radar systems repair. An Associate Level Test, covering basic electronics, is offered for students or repairers with less than 4 years of experience. Those who test and repair radio transmitting equipment, other than business and land mobile radios, need a General Operators License from the Federal Communications Commission.

Experienced repairers with advanced training may become specialists or troubleshooters who help other repairers diagnose difficult problems, or work with engineers in designing equipment and developing maintenance procedures.

Because of their familiarity with equipment, repairers are particularly well qualified to become manufacturers' sales workers. Workers with leadership ability also may become maintenance supervisors or service managers. Some experienced workers open their own repair services or shops, or become wholesalers or retailers of electronic equipment.

Job Outlook

Overall, employment of electronic equipment repairers is expected to decline through the year 2005. Although the amount of electronic equipment in use will grow very rapidly, improvements in product reliability and ease of service and lower equipment prices will cause a decline in the need for repairers. The following tabulation presents the expected job change in percent for the various electronic equipment repairer occupations:

Computer and office machine repairers	24
Commercial and industrial electronic equipment repairers	2
Electronic home entertainment equipment repairers	-10
Communications equipment mechanics	-35
Telephone installers and repairers	-70

Employment of computer equipment repairers will grow much faster the than average for all occupations through the year 2005 as the number of computers in service increases rapidly. Employment of industrial equipment repairers outside the Federal Government will increase faster than the average as the amount of equipment grows. Mainly because of cuts in the defense budget, employment of repairers in the Federal Government will decline. Employment of those who repair electronic home entertainment equipment will decline modestly as equipment becomes more reliable and easier to service. Employment of repairers who handle telephone industry equipment—telephone installers and repairers and communication equipment mechanics—is expected to decline sharply because of improvements in equipment reliability, ease of maintenance, and low equipment replacement cost.

Earnings

In 1994, median weekly earnings of full-time electronic equipment repairers were $592. The middle 50 percent earned between $434 and $765. The bottom 10 percent earned less than $317, while the top 10 percent earned more than $947. Earnings vary widely by occupation and the type of equipment repaired, as shown in the following tabulation:

Telephone installers and repairers	$679
Data processing equipment repairers	589
Electronic repairers, communications and industrial equipment	542
Office machine repairers	458

Central office installers, central office technicians, PBX installers, and telephone installers and repairers employed by AT&T and the

Bell Operating Companies and represented by the Communications Workers of America and the International Brotherhood of Electrical Workers earned between $469 and $1,063 a week in 1994.

According to a survey of workplaces in 160 metropolitan areas, beginning maintenance electronics technicians had median earnings of $10.75 an hour in 1993, with the middle half earning between $9.63 and $12.56 an hour. The most experienced repairers had median earnings of $18.40 an hour, with the middle half earning between $16.67 and $20.12 an hour.

Related Occupations

Workers in other occupations who repair and maintain the circuits and mechanical parts of electronic equipment include appliance and powertool repairers, automotive electricians, broadcast technicians, electronic organ technicians, and vending machine repairers. Electronics engineering technicians may also repair electronic equipment as part of their duties.

Sources of Additional Information

For career, certification, and FCC licensing information, contact:

☛The International Society of Certified Electronics Technicians, 2708 West Berry St., Fort Worth, TX 76109.

For certification, career, placement, and FCC licensing information, contact:

☛Electronics Technicians Association, 604 North Jackson, Greencastle, IN 46135.

For a list of FCC licensing administrators, write to:

☛Federal Communications Commission, Consumer Assistance Office, 1270 Fairfield Rd., Gettysburg, Pa 17325-7245 or call 1-800-322-1117.

For information on the telephone industry and career opportunities contact:

☛United States Telephone Association, 1401 H St. NW., suite 600, Washington, DC 20005-2136.

For information on electronic equipment repairers in the telephone industry, write to:

☛Communications Workers of America, 501 3rd St. NW., Washington, DC 20001.

Commercial and Industrial Electronic Equipment Repairers

(D.O.T. 726.361-022, .381-014, .684-090; 828.251-010, .261-014, -022, -026, and .281-022)

Nature of the Work

Commercial and industrial electronic equipment repairers, also called industrial electronics technicians, install and repair industrial controls, radar and missile control systems, medical diagnostic equipment, and communications equipment.

Those who work for the Defense Department install radar, missile control, and communication systems on aircraft, ships, and tanks, and in buildings and other structures. Some set up and service electronic equipment which controls machines and production processes in factories. They often coordinate their efforts with workers installing mechanical or electromechanical components. (See the statements on industrial machinery repairers and millwrights elsewhere in the *Handbook*).

Employment

Commercial and industrial electronic equipment repairers held about 66,000 jobs in 1994. About 1 out of 3 repairers was employed by the Federal Government, almost all in the Department of Defense at military installations around the country. Repairers also were employed by electronic and transportation equipment manufacturers, machinery and equipment wholesalers, telephone companies, hospi-

When making repairs, commercial and industrial electronic equipment repairers may refer to blueprints and manufacturers' specifications.

tals, electronic repair shops, and firms that provide maintenance under contract (called third-party maintenance firms).

Job Outlook

Overall employment of commercial and industrial electronic equipment repairers is expected to increase more slowly than the average for all occupations through the year 2005. Job prospects in private industry, however, should differ significantly from those within the Federal Government. Opportunities for employment outside of the Federal Government are expected to be good. Employment in nongovernment industries is expected to grow faster than the average for all occupations, as business and industrial firms install more electronic equipment to boost productivity and improve product quality. In addition, more electronic equipment will be used in energy conservation and pollution control. Because of cuts in the defense budget, however, employment in the Federal Government is expected to decline significantly.

(See introductory part of this section for information on working conditions, training requirements, earnings, and sources of additional information.)

Communications Equipment Mechanics

(D.O.T. 722.281; 726.381-014; 822.261-010, .281-010, -014, -022, -026, -030 and -034, .361-014, .381-010, -018, -022, and .684-010; 823.261-010, -018, -022, and -030, .281-014, and -022; 825.261-010; and 829.281-022)

Nature of the Work

Installing, repairing, and maintaining complex and sophisticated telephone communications equipment are the responsibilities of communications equipment mechanics. Most communications equipment mechanics—sometimes referred to as telecommunication technicians—work either in telephone company central offices or on customers' premises installing and repairing telephone switching and transmission systems.

Central office equipment installers, or equipment installation technicians, set up, rearrange, and remove the switching and dialing equipment used in central offices. They install equipment in new central offices, add equipment in expanding offices, or replace outdated equipment. *Central office repairers*, often referred to as central office technicians or switching equipment technicians, test, repair, and maintain all types of local and toll switching equipment that automatically connects lines when customers dial numbers.

When customers report trouble with their telephones, *trouble locators* working at special switchboards—sometimes called testboards—find the source of the problem. Trouble locators who work for cable television companies ensure that subscribers' television sets receive the proper signal. They may work with cable installers to track down the cause of the interference and make repairs.

Telephone companies have replaced trouble locators with *maintenance administrators*. Their jobs are largely automated; instead of using testboards and associated equipment to perform complex circuit tests, they enter instructions into a computer terminal and analyze the output. Maintenance administrators also update and maintain computerized files of trouble status reports.

PBX installers, also called systems technicians, install complex telephone equipment, often creating customized switching systems.

PBX repairers, with the assistance of maintenance administrators, locate the malfunction in customers' PBX or other telephone systems and make the necessary repairs. They also maintain associated equipment such as batteries, relays, and power supplies. Some PBX repairers maintain and repair equipment for mobile radiophones, microwave transmission equipment, switching equipment, and data processing equipment.

An increasing number of communications equipment repairers in the telephone industry are being trained to perform multiple tasks, ranging from splicing fiber optic cable, to programming switches, to installing telephones. As a result, the specific titles used above are becoming less common.

Radio repairers and mechanics install and repair stationary and mobile radio transmitting and receiving equipment. Some repair microwave and fiber optics installations. *Office electricians* handle submarine cable repeater and terminal circuits and related equipment. When trouble arises, they may rearrange cable connections to ensure that service is not interrupted. *Submarine cable equipment technicians* repair, adjust, and maintain the machines and equipment used in submarine cable offices or stations to control cable traffic.

Other communications equipment mechanics include *instrument repairers*, sometimes referred to as shop repairers or shop technicians, who repair, test, and modify a variety of communications equipment. *Data communications technicians* install and repair data communications lines and equipment for computer systems. They connect microcomputers or terminals to data communication lines.

Employment

Communications equipment mechanics held about 118,000 jobs in 1994. Most worked for telephone companies. Others worked for

PBX installers, also called systems technicians, install complex telephone equipment, often creating customized switchboard systems.

electrical repair shops, cable television firms, railroads, air transportation, and the Federal Government.

Job Outlook

Employment of communications equipment mechanics is expected to decline sharply through the year 2005. The telephone industry has almost completed a dramatic transformation from an electromechanical system to a completely electronic one. Digital systems, the most recent version of electronic switching, use computers and software to switch calls. Fewer workers are needed for maintenance and repair because the new systems are more reliable and compact and permit more efficient, centralized maintenance. In addition, the systems have self-diagnosing features which detect the source of problems and direct repairers to the defective part, which usually can simply be replaced. Once the transformation of the system has been completed, some time before 2005, the need for installers will drop sharply.

Decreased labor requirements due to improved technology have already caused some layoffs of communications equipment mechanics. Efficiencies resulting from consolidations and mergers of cable and telephone companies and pressure to reduce costs in the competitive environment following additional deregulation of the industry could cause further decreases in employment. Competition for available openings should intensify, making it much more difficult for other telephone workers to move into these positions without experience or formal training and virtually impossible for "outsiders" without the necessary skills to compete for jobs.

(See introductory part of this section for information on working conditions, training requirements, earnings, and sources of additional information.)

Computer and Office Machine Repairers

(D.O.T. 633.261-014, .281; 706.381-010 and -030)

Nature of the Work

Computer and office machine repairers install equipment, do preventive maintenance, and correct problems. Computer repairers work on computers (mainframes, minis, and micros), peripheral equipment, and word processing systems, while office machine repairers work on photocopiers, cash registers, mail processing equipment, and typewriters. Some repairers service both computer and office equipment. They make cable and wiring connections when installing equipment, and work closely with electricians, who install the wiring. (A description of the work of electricians can be found elsewhere in the *Handbook*)

Even with preventive maintenance, computers and other machines do break down. Repairers run diagnostic programs to locate malfunctions. Although some of the most modern and sophisticated computers have a self-diagnosing capacity that identifies problems, computer repairers must know enough about systems software to determine if the malfunction is in the hardware or in the software.

Employment

Computer and office machine repairers held about 134,000 jobs in 1994. Approximately 75,000 worked mainly on computer equipment, and the other 59,000 repaired mainly office machines. Three of every 5 were employed by wholesalers of computers and other office equipment, including the wholesaling divisions of equipment manufacturers, and by firms that provide maintenance services for a fee. Others worked for retail establishments and some with organizations that serviced their own equipment.

Repairers work throughout the country, even in relatively small

Computer and office machine repairers work throughout the country, even in relatively small communities.

Employment of electronic home entertainment equipment repairers will decline modestly as equipment becomes more reliable and easier to service.

communities. Most repairers, however, work in large cities, where computer and office equipment is concentrated.

Job Outlook

Employment of computer and office machine repairers is expected to grow faster than the average for all occupations through the year 2005. However, employment of repairers will grow less rapidly than the anticipated increase in the amount of equipment because of the improved reliability of computer and office machines and ease of repair. Applicants for computer repairer positions will have the most favorable job prospects.

Employment of those who repair computers is expected to grow much faster than the average for all occupations. Demand for computer repairers will increase as the amount of computer equipment increases—organizations throughout the economy should continue to automate in search of greater productivity and improved service. The development of new computer applications and lower computer prices, will also spur demand. More repairers will be needed to install, maintain, and repair these machines.

Employment of those who repair office machines is expected to grow more slowly than the average for all occupations. Slow growth in the amount of non-computer-based office equipment will dampen the demand for these repairers.

(See introductory part of this section for information on working conditions, training requirements, earnings, and sources of additional information.)

Electronic Home Entertainment Equipment Repairers

(D.O.T. 720.281, 729.281-010, 730.281-018, 823.361-010, and 828.261-010)

Nature of the Work

Electronic home entertainment equipment repairers, also called service technicians, repair radios, televisions, stereos, recorders, public address systems, slide and motion picture projectors, video cameras, video games, home security systems, microwave ovens, and electronic organs. Some repairers specialize in one kind of equipment; others repair many types.

They replace faulty parts or make adjustments, such as focusing and converging the picture or correcting the color balance of a television set. They may also make recordings and listen to playbacks to detect problems. Some install and repair automobile radios.

Employment

Electronic home entertainment equipment repairers held about 34,000 jobs in 1994. Nearly one-third were self-employed, a larger proportion than in most other repairer occupations. Most repairers work in electronic repair shops and service centers or in stores that sell and service electronic home entertainment products. Employment is distributed in much the same way as the population.

Job Outlook

Employment of electronic home entertainment equipment repairers is expected to decline through the year 2005. Improvements in reliability and ease of servicing should reduce service requirements even though the amount of equipment in use is expected to increase. Job opportunities should be good, nevertheless, due to the need to replace the many electronic home entertainment equipment repairers who transfer to higher paying occupations requiring a knowledge of electronics, such as computer and office machine repairer. (See introductory part of this section for information on working conditions, training requirements, earnings, and sources of additional information.)

Telephone Installers and Repairers

(D.O.T. 822.261-022 and .281-018)

Nature of the Work

Telephone installers and repairers install, service, and repair telephones and other communications equipment on customers' property. When customers move or request new types of service, installers relocate telephones or make changes to existing equipment. In buildings under construction, they install wiring and telephone jacks.

Telephone installers, sometimes called station installers or service technicians, assemble equipment and install wiring and switches on the customers' premises. They connect telephones to outside service wires and sometimes climb poles or ladders to make these connections. In apartment and office buildings, they connect wires and cables to terminals and test equipment to make sure it works properly.

Some experienced installers and repairers have multiple skills. They are considered especially valuable by many small companies. Installers and repairers may handle special cases such as complaints to public service commissions, illegal or unauthorized use of equipment, and electric or acoustic shocks.

Telephone installers and repairers may work on roofs, ladders, and telephone poles.

Employment

Telephone installers and repairers held about 37,000 jobs in 1994. More than 9 out of 10 worked full time for telecommunications companies.

Job Outlook

Employment of telephone installers and repairers is expected to decline sharply through the year 2005. Employment will continue to fall due to technological improvements. For example, prewired buildings that enable customers to buy telephones and plug them into prewired jacks have effectively eliminated the functions of the installer. The modular assembly of telephones, where components plug in and out, also will reduce the time and skills needed for repair. Also, fewer phones will be worth repairing as prices continue to decline. In addition, the use of portable terminals which hook into a central testing system makes repairers more efficient. Increased competition for customers due to consolidations and mergers of cable and telephone companies will further contribute to the decline of telephone installers and repairers.

With employment projected to decline, job openings will result exclusively from the need to replace persons who transfer to other occupations or leave the labor force. Traditionally, most openings for telephone installers and repairers have been filled by workers in other telephone company jobs. As technology continues to displace installers and repairers, it will remain difficult for telephone workers without additional training and virtually impossible for "outsiders" without the necessary skills to get these jobs.

(See introductory part of this section for information on working conditions, training requirements, earnings, and sources of additional information.)

Elevator Installers and Repairers

(D.O.T. 825.261-014, .281-030, -034, and .361-010)

Nature of the Work

Elevator installers and repairers—also called *elevator constructors* or *elevator mechanics*—assemble, install, and replace elevators, escala-

tors, dumbwaiters, moving walkways, and similar equipment in new and old buildings. Once the equipment is in service, they maintain and repair it. They are also responsible for modernizing older equipment.

In order to install, repair, and maintain modern elevators, which are almost all electronically controlled, elevator installers and repairers must have a thorough knowledge of electronics, electricity, and hydraulics. Many elevators today are installed with microprocessors, which are programmed to constantly analyze traffic conditions in order to dispatch elevators in the most efficient manner. With these computer controls, it is now possible to get the greatest amount of service with the least number of cars.

When installing a new elevator, elevator installers and repairers begin by studying blueprints in order to determine the equipment layout of the framework to install rails, machines, car enclosures, motors, pumps, cylinders, and plunger foundations. Once the layout analysis is completed, they begin equipment installation. Working on scaffolding or platforms, installers bolt or weld steel rails to the walls of the shaft to guide the elevator up and down.

Elevator installers put in electrical wires and controls by running tubing, called "conduit," along the shaft's walls from floor to floor. Once in place, mechanics pull plastic-covered electrical wires through the conduit. They then install electrical components and related devices required at each floor and at the main control panel in the machine room.

Installers bolt or weld together the steel frame of the elevator car at the bottom of the shaft, install the car's platform, walls, and doors, and attach guide shoes and rollers to minimize the lateral motion of the car as it travels through the shaft. They also install the outer doors and door frames at the elevator entrances on each floor.

For cabled elevators, these workers install geared or gearless machines with a traction drive sheave which moves heavy steel cables connected to the elevator car and counterweight. The counterweight moves in the opposite direction from the car and aids in its swift and smooth movement.

Elevator installers also install elevators in which a car sits on a hydraulic plunger that is driven by a pump. The plunger pushes the elevator car up from underneath, similar to a lift in an auto service station. They also install escalators. They put in place the steel framework, the electrically powered stairs, and the tracks, and install associated motors and electrical wiring. In addition to elevators and escalators, elevator installers also may install devices such as dumbwaiters and material lifts, which are similar to elevators in design, moving walkways, stair lifts, and wheelchair lifts.

The most highly skilled elevator installers and repairers, called "adjusters," specialize in fine-tuning all of the equipment after installation. Adjusters must make sure that the elevator is working according to specifications, such as stopping correctly at each floor within a specified time period. Once an elevator is operating properly, it must be maintained and serviced regularly to keep it in safe, working condition. Elevator maintenance mechanics generally do preventive maintenance—such as oiling and greasing moving parts, replacing worn parts, testing equipment with meters and gauges, and adjusting equipment for optimal performance. They also troubleshoot and may be called in to do emergency repairs.

A service crew usually handles major repairs—for example, replacing cables, elevator doors, or machine bearings. This may require cutting torches or rigging equipment—tools a maintenance mechanic would not normally carry. Service crews also do major modernization and alteration work, such as moving and replacing electrical motors, hydraulic pumps, and control panels.

Elevator installers and repairers usually specialize in installation, maintenance, or repair work. Maintenance and repair workers generally need more knowledge of electricity and electronics than installers because a large part of maintenance and repair work is troubleshooting. Similarly, construction adjusters need a thorough knowledge of electricity, electronics, and computers to ensure that newly installed elevators operate properly.

Most elevator installers and repairers begin as trainees or helpers, assisting experienced elevator mechanics on-the-job.

Working Conditions

Most elevator installers and repairers work a 40-hour week. However, maintenance and service mechanics often work overtime when repairing essential elevator equipment. They are sometimes on 24-hour call. Maintenance mechanics, unlike most elevator installers, are on their own most of the day and typically service the same elevators periodically.

Elevator installers lift and carry heavy equipment and parts and may work in cramped spaces or awkward positions. Hazards include falls, electrical shock, muscle strains, and other injuries related to handling heavy equipment. Because most of their work is performed indoors in buildings under construction or in existing buildings, elevator installers and repairers lose less work time due to inclement weather than other building trades workers.

Employment

Elevator installers and repairers held about 24,000 jobs in 1994. Most were employed by special trade contractors. Others were employed by field offices of elevator manufacturers; wholesale distributors; small, local elevator maintenance and repair contractors; or by government agencies or businesses that do their own elevator maintenance and repair.

Training, Other Qualifications, and Advancement

Most elevator installers and repairers apply for their jobs through a local of the International Union of Elevator Constructors. Applicants for trainee positions must be at least 18 years old, have a high school diploma or equivalent, and pass an aptitude test. Good physical condition and mechanical aptitude also are important.

Elevator installers and repairers learn their trade in a program administered by local joint educational committees representing the employers and the union. These programs, through which the trainee learns everything from installation to repair, combine on-the-job training with classroom instruction in electrical and electronic theory, mathematics, applications of physics, and safety. Elevator installers and repairers in nonunion shops may complete training programs sponsored by independent contractors.

Generally, trainees or helpers must complete a 6-month probationary period. After successful completion, they work toward becoming fully qualified mechanics within 4 to 5 years. In order to be classified a fully qualified mechanic, union trainees must pass a standard mechanics examination administered by the National Elevator Industry Educational Program. Most States and cities also require elevator constructors to pass a licensing examination.

Most trainees or helpers assist experienced elevator installers and repairers. Beginners carry materials and tools, bolt rails to walls, and assemble elevator cars. Eventually, they learn to do more difficult tasks, such as wiring, which requires a knowledge of local and national electrical codes.

High school courses in electricity, mathematics, and physics provide a useful background. As elevators become increasingly sophisticated, workers may find it necessary to acquire more advanced formal education—for example, in postsecondary technical school or junior college—with an emphasis on electronics. Workers with more formal education generally advance more quickly than their counterparts.

Many elevator installers and repairers also receive training from their employers or through manufacturers to become familiar with the company's particular equipment. Retraining is very important to keep abreast of technological developments in elevator repair. In fact, union elevator constructors typically receive continual training throughout their careers, either through correspondence courses, seminars, or formal classes. Although voluntary, this training greatly improves one's chances for promotion.

Some installers may receive further training in specialized areas and advance to mechanic-in-charge, adjuster, supervisor, or elevator inspector. Adjusters, for example, may actually be picked for the position because they possess particular skills or are seen to be more electronically inclined. Others workers may move into management, sales, or product design.

Job Outlook

Employment of elevator installers and repairers is expected to increase about as fast as the average for all occupations through the year 2005, but relatively few new job opportunities will be generated because the occupation is small. Replacement needs, another source of jobs, also will be relatively low, in part, because a substantial amount of time is invested in specialized training that yields high earnings and workers tend to remain in this field. The job outlook for new workers is largely dependent on activity in the construction industry and opportunities may vary from year to year as conditions within the industry change. Job prospects should be best for those with postsecondary training in electronics or more advanced formal education.

Demand for elevator installers and repairers will increase as the stock of equipment needing repairs and the construction of new buildings with elevators and escalators increases. Growth also should be driven by the need to continually update and modernize older equipment, including improvements in appearance and the installation of more sophisticated equipment and computerized controls. Since equipment must always be kept in working condition, economic downturns will have less of an effect on employment of elevator maintenance and repair mechanics. The need for people to service elevators and escalators should increase as equipment becomes more intricate and complex.

Earnings

Average weekly earnings for union elevator installers and repairers were about $820 in 1994, according to data from the International Union of Elevator Constructors. Rates vary with geographic location. Probationary helpers started at about 50 percent of the rate for experienced elevator mechanics, or about $410 a week. Non-probationary helpers earned about 70 percent of this rate, or an average of about $574 a week. Mechanics-in-charge averaged $923 a week.

In addition to free continuing education, elevator installers and repairers receive basic benefits enjoyed by most other workers.

The proportion of elevator installers and repairers who are union members is higher than nearly any other occupation. Over 90 percent of elevator installers and repairers are members of the International Union of Elevator Constructors.

Related Occupations

Elevator installers and repairers combine electrical and mechanical skills with construction skills such as welding, rigging, measuring, and blueprint reading. Other occupations that require many of these skills are boilermaker, electrician, industrial machinery repairer, millwright, sheet-metal worker, and structural ironworker.

Sources of Additional Information

For further details about opportunities as an elevator installer and repairer, contact elevator manufacturers, elevator repair and maintenance contractors, a local of the International Union of Elevator Constructors, or the nearest local public employment service office.

Farm Equipment Mechanics

(D.O.T. 624.281-010 and -014, .361-014, .381, and .684; and 629.281-018)

Nature of the Work

Today's farm is typically much larger than in the past, so few if any types of farming can be done economically without specialized machines. Farm equipment has grown in size, complexity, and variety. Many farms have several tractors equipped with from 40- to 400-horsepower diesel engines. Self-propelled combines, hay balers, swathers, crop dryers, planters, tillage equipment, grain augers, manure spreaders, and elevators are common, as well as spray and irrigation equipment.

As farm machinery has grown larger with more electronic and hydraulic controls, farmers have increasingly turned to farm equipment dealers for service and repair of the machines they sell. These dealers employ farm equipment mechanics, often called service technicians, to do this work and also to maintain and repair the smaller lawn and garden tractors many dealers sell to suburban homeowners.

Mechanics spend much of their time repairing and adjusting malfunctioning equipment that has been brought to the shop. But during planting and harvesting seasons, they may travel to farms to make emergency repairs on equipment so that important farming operations are not unduly delayed.

Mechanics also perform preventive maintenance. Periodically, they test, adjust, and clean parts and tune engines. In large shops, mechanics generally specialize in certain types of work, such as diesel engine overhaul, hydraulics, or clutch and transmission repair. Others specialize in repairing the air-conditioning units often included in the cabs of combines and large tractors, or in repairing certain types of equipment such as hay balers. Some mechanics also repair milking, irrigation, and other equipment on farms. In addition,

Farm equipment mechanics use many basic handtools such as wrenches, pliers, hammers, and screwdrivers.

some mechanics who work for dealers and equipment wholesalers assemble new implements and machinery and sometimes do body work, repairing dented or torn sheet metal on tractors or other machinery.

Mechanics use many basic handtools, including wrenches, pliers, hammers, and screwdrivers. They also use precision equipment, such as micrometers and torque wrenches; engine testing equipment, such as dynamometers to measure engine performance; and engine analysis units and compression testers, to find worn piston rings or leaking cylinder valves. They use welding equipment or power tools to repair broken parts.

Working Conditions

Generally, farm equipment mechanics work indoors. Modern farm equipment repair shops are well ventilated, lighted, and heated, but older shops may not offer these advantages. Farm equipment mechanics come in contact with grease, fuel and oil, hydraulic fluid, antifreeze, rust, and dirt, and there is danger of injury when they repair heavy parts supported on jacks or by hoists. Care must also be used to avoid burns from hot engine parts, cuts from sharp edges of machinery, and hazards associated with farm chemicals.

As with most agricultural occupations, the hours of work of farm equipment mechanics vary according to the season of the year. During the busy planting and harvesting seasons, mechanics often work 6 or 7 days a week, 10 to 12 hours daily. In winter months, however, mechanics may work fewer than 40 hours a week, and some may be laid off.

Employment

Farm equipment mechanics held about 41,000 jobs in 1994. Most worked in service departments of farm equipment dealers. Others worked in independent repair shops, and in shops on large farms. Most farm equipment mechanics worked in small repair shops. Nearly 1 out of 10 farm equipment mechanics was self-employed.

Because some type of farming is done in nearly every area of the United States, farm equipment mechanics are employed throughout the country. Employment is concentrated in small cities and towns, making this an attractive career choice for people who do not wish to live in a large city. However, many mechanics work in the rural fringes of metropolitan areas, so farm equipment mechanics who prefer the conveniences of city life need not live in rural areas.

Training, Other Qualifications, and Advancement

Farm equipment mechanics must have an aptitude for mechanical work. With the development of more complex farm implements, technical training has become more important. A growing number of employers prefer to hire trainee farm equipment mechanics who have completed a 1- or 2-year training program in agricultural or diesel mechanics at a vocational or technical school or community or junior college. In general, employers seek persons with training or previous experience in diesel and gasoline engines, the maintenance and repair of hydraulics, and welding, all of which may be learned in many high schools and vocational schools. Mechanics also need a basic knowledge of electronics and must be able to read circuit diagrams and blueprints in order to make complex repairs to electrical and other systems.

Most farm equipment mechanics enter the occupation as trainees and become proficient in their trade by assisting experienced mechanics. The length of training varies with the helper's aptitude and prior experience. At least 2 years of on-the-job training usually are necessary before a mechanic can efficiently do the more routine types of repair work, and additional training and experience are required for highly specialized repair and overhaul jobs.

Many farm equipment mechanics enter this occupation from a related occupation. For example, they may have experience working as diesel mechanics, mobile heavy equipment mechanics, or automotive mechanics. A farm background is an advantage since working on a farm usually provides experience in basic farm equipment repairs. Persons who enter from related occupations also may start as trainees or helpers, but they may not require as long a period of on-the-job training.

A few farm equipment mechanics learn the trade by completing an apprenticeship program, which lasts from 3 to 4 years and includes on-the-job as well as classroom training in all phases of farm equipment repair and maintenance. Applicants for these programs usually are chosen from shop helpers.

Keeping abreast of changing farm equipment technology requires a great deal of careful study of service manuals and analysis of complex diagrams. Many farm equipment mechanics and trainees receive refresher training in short-term programs conducted by farm equipment manufacturers. These programs usually last several days. A company service representative explains the design and function of equipment and teaches maintenance and repair on new models of farm equipment. In addition, some dealers may send employees to local vocational schools that hold special week-long classes in subjects such as air-conditioning repair or hydraulics.

Persons considering a career in this field should have the manual dexterity needed to handle tools and equipment. Occasionally, strength is required to lift, move, or hold heavy parts in place. Difficult repair jobs require problem-solving abilities to diagnose the source of the machine's malfunction. Experienced mechanics should be able to work independently with minimum supervision.

Farm equipment mechanics usually must buy their own handtools, although employers furnish power tools and test equipment. Trainee mechanics are expected to accumulate their own tools as they gain experience. Experienced mechanics have thousands of dollars invested in tools.

Farm equipment mechanics may advance to shop supervisor, service manager, or manager of a farm equipment dealership. Some mechanics open their own repair shops. A few farm equipment mechanics advance to service representatives for farm equipment manufacturers.

Job Outlook

Opportunities should be good for persons who have completed formal training in farm equipment repair or diesel mechanics; persons without such training are expected to encounter increasing difficulty entering mechanic jobs. Employment of farm equipment mechanics is expected to increase about as fast as the average for all occupations through the year 2005. The continued consolidation of farmland into fewer and larger farms and the use of new farming practices will cause farmers to invest in new, more efficient and specialized equipment, and the increasing complexity of equipment will force more farmers to rely on mechanics for service and repairs.

Most job openings will arise from the need to replace experienced mechanics who retire.

The increasing sophistication of newer farm equipment is making it more difficult for farmers to do their own repairs, forcing them to rely more on skilled mechanics in the future. For example, many newer tractors have much larger, electronically controlled engines and air-conditioned cabs and feature advanced transmissions with many speeds. New planting equipment uses electronics to spread seeds more uniformly, and electronic controls help harvesters reduce waste. Although farm machinery is expensive and generally designed and manufactured to withstand many years of rugged use, it nevertheless requires periodic service and repairs. Increasingly this work will require a farm equipment mechanic.

Sales of smaller lawn and garden equipment constitute a growing share of the business of most farm equipment dealers. Most of the large manufacturers of farm equipment now offer a line of these smaller tractors and sell them through their established dealerships. Although relatively few mechanics are required to service this equipment, more will be needed as household demand for lawn and garden equipment increases as the Nation's population grows.

The agricultural equipment industry experiences periodic declines—mostly in sales. Layoffs of mechanics, however, are uncommon because farmers often elect to repair old equipment rather than purchase new equipment.

Earnings

Farm equipment mechanics had median weekly earnings of about $382 in 1994. The middle 50 percent earned between $294 and $528 a week. The lowest paid 10 percent earned less than $248 a week, and the top 10 percent earned over $696 a week. Most farm equipment mechanics also have the opportunity to work overtime during the planting and harvesting seasons, for which they generally are paid time and one-half.

Very few farm equipment mechanics belong to labor unions, but those who do are members of the International Association of Machinists and Aerospace Workers; the International Union, United Automobile, Aerospace and Agricultural Implement Workers of America; and the International Brotherhood of Teamsters.

Related Occupations

Other workers who repair large mobile machinery include aircraft mechanics, automotive mechanics, diesel mechanics, and mobile heavy equipment mechanics.

Sources of Additional Information

Details about work opportunities may be obtained from local farm equipment dealers and local offices of the State employment service. For general information about the occupation, write to:

☛North American Equipment Dealers Association, 10877 Watson Rd., St. Louis, MO 63127.

☛Deere and Co., John Deere Rd., Moline, IL 61265.

General Maintenance Mechanics

(D.O.T. 899.261-014 and .381-010)

Nature of the Work

Most craft workers specialize in one kind of work such as plumbing or carpentry. General maintenance mechanics have skills in many different crafts. They repair and maintain machines, mechanical equipment, and buildings, and work on plumbing, electrical, and air-conditioning and heating systems. They build partitions, make plaster or drywall repairs, and fix or paint roofs, windows, doors, floors, woodwork, and other parts of building structures. They also

A general maintenance mechanic repairs a stove in an apartment.

maintain and repair specialized equipment and machinery found in cafeterias, laundries, hospitals, stores, offices, and factories. Typical duties include troubleshooting and fixing faulty electrical switches, repairing air-conditioning motors, and unclogging drains.

Those in small establishments, where they are often the only maintenance worker, do all repairs except for very large or difficult jobs. In larger establishments, their duties may be limited to the general maintenance of everything in a workshop or a particular area.

General maintenance mechanics inspect and diagnose problems and determine the best way to correct them, often checking blueprints, repair manuals, and parts catalogs. They obtain supplies and repair parts from distributors or storerooms. They use common hand and power tools such as screwdrivers, saws, drills, wrenches, and hammers as well as specialized equipment and electronic test devices. They replace or fix worn or broken parts, where necessary, or make adjustments.

These mechanics also do routine preventive maintenance and ensure that machines continue to run smoothly, building systems operate efficiently, and that the physical condition of buildings does not deteriorate. Following a check list, they may inspect drives, motors, and belts, check fluid levels, replace filters, and so forth. Maintenance mechanics keep records of maintenance and repair work.

Working Conditions

General maintenance mechanics often do a variety of tasks in a single day, generally at a number of different locations in a building, or in several buildings. They may have to stand for long periods, lift heavy objects, and work in uncomfortably hot or cold environments and in awkward and cramped positions or on ladders. They are subject to electrical shock, burns, falls, and cuts and bruises. Most general maintenance workers work a 40-hour week. Some work evening, night, or weekend shifts, or are on call for emergency repairs.

Those employed in small establishments, where they may be the only maintenance worker, often operate with only limited supervision. Those working in larger establishments often work under the direct supervision of an experienced craft worker.

Employment

General maintenance mechanics held about 1,273,000 jobs in 1994. They worked in almost every industry. More than one-third worked in service industries; most of these worked for elementary and secondary schools, colleges and universities, hotels, and hospitals and nursing homes. About 16 percent worked in manufacturing industries. Others worked for real estate firms that operate office and apartment buildings, wholesale and retail firms, or government agencies.

Training, Other Qualifications, and Advancement

Most general maintenance mechanics learn their skills informally on the job. They start as helpers, watching and learning from skilled maintenance workers. Helpers begin by doing simple jobs such as fixing leaky faucets and replacing light bulbs and progress to more difficult tasks such as overhauling machinery or building walls.

Others learn their skills by working as helpers to other repair or construction workers such as carpenters, electricians, or machinery repairers. Necessary skills can also be learned in high school shop classes and postsecondary trade or vocational schools. It generally takes from 1 to 4 years of on-the-job training or school, or a combination of both, to become fully qualified, depending on the skill level required.

Graduation from high school is preferred for entry into this occupation. High school courses in mechanical drawing, electricity, woodworking, blueprint reading, science, and mathematics are useful. Mechanical aptitude, ability to use shop math, and manual dexterity are important. Good health is necessary because the job involves much walking, standing, reaching, and heavy lifting. Difficult jobs require problem-solving ability, and many positions require the ability to work without direct supervision. A growing proportion of new buildings rely on computers to control building systems, so familiarity with computers is helpful.

Many general maintenance mechanics in large organizations advance to maintenance supervisor or to one of the crafts such as electrician, heating/air-conditioning mechanic, or plumber. In small organizations, promotion opportunities are limited.

Job Outlook

Job opportunities for people who want to be general maintenance mechanics should be plentiful through the year 2005. Employment is related to the number of buildings and amount of equipment needing maintenance and repair. Employment growth—expected to be about as fast as the average for all occupations through the year 2005—will occur as the number of office and apartment buildings, stores, schools, hospitals, hotels, and factories increases. Although the pace of construction of these facilities is expected to be slower than in the past, many opportunities arise because this is a large occupation with significant turnover, and many replacements are needed for those who leave the occupation.

General maintenance mechanics who work in manufacturing industries may be laid off during recessions.

Earnings

Earnings vary widely by industry, geographic area, and skill level. According to a survey of workplaces in 160 metropolitan areas, general maintenance mechanics had median earnings of about $9.40 an hour in 1993, with the middle half earning between $7.90 and $11.05 an hour. Median earnings were about $9.40 an hour in service businesses and about $10.20 an hour in manufacturing businesses. On average, workers in the Midwest and Northeast earned more than those in the West and South. Mechanics earn overtime pay for work in excess of 40 hours per week.

Some general maintenance mechanics are members of unions, including the American Federation of State, County and Municipal Employees and the United Automobile Workers.

Related Occupations

Some of the work of general maintenance mechanics is similar to that of carpenters, plumbers, industrial machinery mechanics, electricians, and air-conditioning, refrigeration, and heating mechanics.

Sources of Additional Information

Information about job opportunities may be obtained from local employers and local offices of the Job Service.

Heating, Air-Conditioning, and Refrigeration Technicians

(D.O.T. 637.261-014, -026, -030, and -034, and .381; 827.361-014; 862.281-018, .361-010; and 869.281-010)

Nature of the Work

What would those living in Chicago do without heating, those in Miami do without air-conditioning, or blood banks in all parts of the country do without refrigeration? Heating and air-conditioning systems control the temperature, humidity, and the total air quality in residential, commercial, industrial, and other buildings. Refrigeration systems make it possible to store and transport food, medicine, and other perishable items. Heating, air-conditioning, and refrigeration technicians install, maintain, and repair such systems.

Heating, air-conditioning, and refrigeration systems consist of many mechanical, electrical, and electronic components, including motors, compressors, pumps, fans, ducts, pipes, thermostats, and switches. In central heating systems, for example, a furnace heats air that is distributed throughout the building via a system of metal or fiberglass ducts. Technicians must be able to maintain, diagnose, and correct problems throughout the entire system. To do this, they may adjust system controls to recommended settings and test the performance of the entire system using special tools and test equipment.

Although they are trained to do both, technicians generally specialize in either installation or maintenance and repair. Some further specialize in one type of equipment—for example, oil burners, solar panels, or commercial refrigerators. Technicians may work for large or small contracting companies or directly for a manufacturer or wholesaler. Those working for smaller operations tend to do both installation and servicing, and work with heating, cooling, and refrigeration equipment.

Furnace installers, also called *heating equipment technicians*, follow blueprints or other specifications to install oil, gas, electric, solid-fuel, and multiple-fuel heating systems. After putting the equipment in place, they install fuel and water supply lines, air ducts and vents, pumps, and other components. They may connect electrical wiring and controls and check the unit for proper operation. To ensure the proper functioning of the system, furnace installers often use combustion test equipment such as carbon dioxide and oxygen testers.

After a furnace has been installed, technicians often perform routine maintenance and repair work in order to keep the system operating efficiently. During the fall and winter, for example, when the system is used most, they service and adjust burners and blowers. If the system is not operating properly, they check the thermostat, burner nozzles, controls, or other parts in order to diagnose and then correct the problem. During the summer, when the heating system is not being used, technicians do maintenance work, such as replacing filters and vacuum-cleaning vents, ducts, and other parts of the system that may accumulate dust and impurities during the operating season.

Air-conditioning and *refrigeration technicians* install and service central air-conditioning systems and a variety of refrigeration equipment. Technicians follow blueprints, design specifications, and manufacturers' instructions to install motors, compressors, condensing units, evaporators, piping, and other components. They connect this equipment to the duct work, refrigerant lines, and electrical power source. After making the connections, they charge the system with refrigerant, check it for proper operation, and program control systems.

When air-conditioning and refrigeration equipment breaks down, technicians diagnose the problem and make repairs. To do this, they may test parts such as compressors, relays, and thermostats. During the winter, air-conditioning technicians inspect the systems and do required maintenance, such as overhauling compressors.

Technicians use a wide variety of tools to install and repair heating and air-conditioning systems.

When servicing equipment, heating, air-conditioning, and refrigeration technicians must use care to conserve, recover, and recycle chlorofluorocarbon (CFC) and hydrochlorofluorocarbon (HCFC) refrigerants used in air-conditioning and refrigeration systems. The release of CFC's and HCFC's contributes to the depletion of the stratospheric ozone layer, which protects plant and animal life from ultraviolet radiation. Technicians conserve the refrigerant by making sure that there are no leaks in the system; they recover it by venting the refrigerant into proper cylinders; and they recycle it for reuse with special filter-dryers.

Heating, air-conditioning, and refrigeration technicians use a variety of tools, including hammers, wrenches, metal snips, electric drills, pipe cutters and benders, measurement gauges, and acetylene torches, to work with refrigerant lines and air ducts. They use voltmeters, thermometers, pressure gauges, manometers, and other testing devices to check air flow, refrigerant pressure, electrical circuits, burners, and other components.

Cooling and heating systems sometimes are installed or repaired by other craft workers. For example, on a large air-conditioning installation job, especially where workers are covered by union contracts, duct work might be done by sheet-metal workers; electrical work by electricians; and installation of piping, condensers, and other components by plumbers and pipefitters. Room air-conditioners and household refrigerators usually are serviced by home appliance repairers. (Additional information about each of these occupations appears elsewhere in the *Handbook*.)

Working Conditions

Heating, air-conditioning, and refrigeration technicians work in homes, supermarkets, hospitals, office buildings, factories—anywhere there is climate control equipment. They may be assigned to specific job sites at the beginning of each day, or if they are making service calls, they may be dispatched to jobs by radio or telephone.

Technicians may work outside in cold or hot weather or in buildings that are uncomfortable because the air-conditioning or heating equipment is broken. In addition, technicians often work in awkward or cramped positions and sometimes are required to work in high places. Hazards include electrical shock, burns, muscle strains, and other injuries from handling heavy equipment. Appropriate safety equipment is necessary when handling refrigerants since contact can cause skin damage, frostbite, or blindness. Inhalation of refrigerants when working in confined spaces is also a possible hazard, and may cause asphyxiation.

Technicians usually work a 40-hour week, but during peak seasons they often work overtime or irregular hours. Maintenance workers, including those who provide maintenance services under contract, often work evening or weekend shifts, and are on call. Most employers try to provide a full workweek the year round by doing both installation and maintenance work and many manufacturers and contractors now provide or even require service contracts. In most shops that service both heating and air-conditioning equipment, employment is very stable throughout the year.

Employment

Heating, air-conditioning, and refrigeration technicians held about 233,000 jobs in 1994. More than one-half of these worked for cooling and heating contractors. The remainder were employed in a wide variety of industries throughout the country, reflecting a widespread dependence on climate control systems. Some worked for fuel oil dealers, refrigeration and air-conditioning service and repair shops, and schools. Others were employed by the Federal Government, hospitals, office buildings, and other organizations that operate large air-conditioning, refrigeration, or heating systems. Approximately 1 of every 8 technicians was self-employed.

Training, Other Qualifications, and Advancement

Because of the increasing sophistication of heating, air-conditioning, and refrigeration systems, employers prefer to hire those with technical school or apprenticeship training. A sizable number of technicians, however, still learn the trade informally on the job.

Many secondary and postsecondary technical and trade schools, junior and community colleges, and the Armed Forces offer 6 month- to 2-year programs in heating, air-conditioning, and refrigeration. Students study theory, design, and equipment construction, as well as electronics. They also learn the basics of installation, maintenance, and repair.

Apprenticeship programs are frequently run by joint committees representing local chapters of the Air-Conditioning Contractors of America, the Mechanical Contractors Association of America, the National Association of Plumbing-Heating-Cooling Contractors, and locals of the Sheet Metal Workers' International Association or the United Association of Journeymen and Apprentices of the Plumbing and Pipefitting Industry of the United States and Canada. Other apprenticeship programs are sponsored by local chapters of the Associated Builders and Contractors and the National Association of Home Builders. Formal apprenticeship programs generally last 3 or 4 years and combine on-the-job training with classroom instruction. Classes include subjects such as the use and care of tools, safety practices, blueprint reading, and air-conditioning theory. Applicants for these programs must have a high school diploma or equivalent.

Those who acquire their skills on the job usually begin by assisting experienced technicians. They may begin performing simple tasks such as carrying materials, insulating refrigerant lines, or cleaning furnaces. In time, they move on to more difficult tasks, such as cutting and soldering pipes and sheet metal and checking electrical and electronic circuits.

Courses in shop math, mechanical drawing, applied physics and chemistry, electronics, blueprint reading, and computer applications provide a good background for those interested in entering this occupation. Some knowledge of plumbing or electrical work is also helpful. A basic understanding of microelectronics is becoming more important because of the increasing use of this technology in solid-state equipment controls. Because technicians frequently deal directly with the public, they should be courteous and tactful, especially when dealing with an aggravated customer. They also should be in good physical condition because they sometimes have to lift and move heavy equipment.

All technicians who purchase or work with refrigerants must be certified so that they know how to handle them properly. To become certified to purchase and handle refrigerants, a technician must pass a written examination specific to the type of work in which they specialize. The three possible areas of certification are: Type I—servicing small appliances, Type II—high pressure refrigerants, and Type III—low pressure refrigerants. Exams are administered by organizations approved by the Environmental Protection Agency, such as trade schools, unions, contractor associations, or building groups. Though no formal training is required for certification, training programs designed to prepare workers for the certification examination, as well as for general skills improvement training, are provided by heating and air-conditioning equipment manufacturers; the Refrigeration Service Engineers Society (RSES); the Air Conditioning Contractors of America (ACCA); the Mechanical Service Contractors of America; local chapters of the National Association of Plumbing-Heating-Cooling Contractors; and the United Association of Plumbers and Pipefitters. RSES, along with some other organizations, also offer basic self-study courses for individuals with limited experience. In addition to understanding how systems work, technicians must be knowledgeable about refrigerant products, and legislation and regulation that govern their use.

Advancement usually takes the form of higher wages. Some technicians, however, may advance to positions as supervisor or service manager. Others may move into areas such as sales and marketing. Those with sufficient money and managerial skill can open their own contracting business.

Job Outlook

Job prospects for highly skilled air-conditioning, heating, and refrigeration technicians are expected to be very good, particularly those with technical school or formal apprenticeship training to install, remodel, and service new and existing systems. In addition to job openings created by rapid employment growth, thousands of openings will result from the need to replace workers who transfer to other occupations or leave the labor force.

Employment of heating, air-conditioning, and refrigeration technicians is expected to increase faster than the average for all occupations through the year 2005. As the population and economy grow, so does the demand for new residential, commercial, and industrial climate control systems. Technicians who specialize in installation work may experience periods of unemployment when the level of new construction activity declines, but maintenance and repair work usually remains relatively stable. People and businesses depend on their climate control systems and must keep them in good working order, regardless of economic conditions.

Concern for the environment and energy conservation should continue to prompt the development of new energy-saving heating and air-conditioning systems. An emphasis on better energy management should lead to the replacement of older systems and the installation of newer, more efficient systems in existing homes and buildings. Also, demand for maintenance and service work should increase as businesses and home owners strive to keep systems operating at peak efficiency. Regulations prohibiting the discharge of CFC and HCFC refrigerants and banning CFC production by the year 2000 also should result in demand for technicians to replace many existing systems, or modify them to use new environmentally safe refrigerants. In addition, the continuing focus on improving indoor air quality should contribute to the growth of jobs for heating, air-conditioning, and refrigeration technicians.

Earnings

Median weekly earnings of air-conditioning, heating, and refrigeration technicians who worked full time were $494 in 1994. The middle 50 percent earned between $363 and $670. The lowest 10 percent earned less than $287 a week, and the top 10 percent earned more than $817 a week.

Apprentices usually begin at about 50 percent of the wage rate paid to experienced workers. As they gain experience and improve their skills, they receive periodic increases until they reach the wage rate of experienced workers.

Heating, air-conditioning, and refrigeration technicians enjoy a variety of employer-sponsored benefits. In addition to typical benefits like health insurance and pension plans, some employers pay for work-related training and provide uniforms, company vans, and tools.

Nearly 1 out of every 5 heating, air-conditioning, and refrigeration technicians is a member of a union. The unions to which the greatest numbers of technicians belong are the Sheet Metal Workers' International Association and the United Association of Journeymen and Apprentices of the Plumbing and Pipefitting Industry of the United States and Canada.

Related Occupations

Heating, air-conditioning, and refrigeration technicians work with sheet metal and piping, and repair machinery, such as electrical motors, compressors, and burners. Other workers who have similar skills are boilermakers, electrical appliance servicers, electricians, plumbers and pipefitters, sheet-metal workers, and duct installers.

Sources of Additional Information

For more information about employment and training opportunities in this trade, contact local vocational and technical schools; local heating, air-conditioning, and refrigeration contractors; a local of the unions previously mentioned; a local joint union-management apprenticeship committee; a local chapter of the Associated Builders and Contractors; or the nearest office of the State employment service or State apprenticeship agency.

For information on career opportunities and training, write to:

☛Associated Builders and Contractors, 1300 North 17th St., Rosslyn, VA 22209.

☛Refrigeration Service Engineers Society, 1666 Rand Rd., Des Plaines, IL 60016-3552.

☛Home Builders Institute, National Association of Home Builders, 1201 15th St. NW., Washington, DC 20005.

☛National Association of Plumbing-Heating-Cooling Contractors, 180 S. Washington St., P.O. Box 6808, Falls Church, VA 22046.

☛New England Fuel Institute, P.O. Box 9137, Watertown, MA 02272.

☛Mechanical Service Contractors of America, 1385 Piccard Dr., Rockville, MD 20850-4329.

☛Air Conditioning and Refrigeration Institute, 4301 North Fairfax Dr., Suite 425, Arlington, VA 22203.

☛Air Conditioning Contractors of America, 1712 New Hampshire Ave., NW., Washington, DC 20009.

Home Appliance and Power Tool Repairers

(D.O.T. 637.261-010 and -018; 723.381 and .584; 729.281-022; and 827.261, and .661)

Nature of the Work

Appliance and power tool repairers, often called service technicians, repair home appliances such as ovens, washers, dryers, refrigerators, window air-conditioners, and vacuum cleaners, as well as power tools such as saws and drills. Some repairers only service small appliances such as microwaves and vacuum cleaners; others specialize in major appliances such as refrigerators, dishwashers, washers, and dryers; and others only handle power tools or gas appliances.

To determine why an appliance or power tool fails to operate properly, repairers visually inspect it and run it to check for unusual noises, excessive vibration, fluid leaks, or loose parts. They may have to consult service manuals and troubleshooting guides to diagnose particularly difficult problems. They may disassemble the appliance or tool to examine its internal parts for signs of wear or corrosion. To check electrical systems for shorts and faulty connections, repairers follow wiring diagrams and use testing devices, such as ammeters, voltmeters, and wattmeters.

A power tool repairer uses needle-nosed pliers to repair a miter saw.

After identifying problems, they replace or repair defective belts, motors, heating elements, switches, gears, or other items. They tighten, align, clean, and lubricate parts as necessary. Repairers use common handtools, including screwdrivers, wrenches, files, and pliers, as well as soldering guns and special tools designed for particular appliances. When servicing appliances with electronic parts, they may replace circuit boards or other electronic components.

When servicing refrigerators, repairers must use care to conserve, recover, and recycle chlorofluorocarbon (CFC) and hydrochlorofluorocarbon (HCFC) refrigerants used in their cooling systems. The release of CFC's and HCFC's contributes to the depletion of the stratospheric ozone layer, which protects plant and animal life from ultraviolet radiation. Repairers conserve the refrigerant by making sure that there are no leaks in the system; they recover it by venting the refrigerant into proper cylinders; and they recycle it for reuse with special filter-dryers.

Repairers servicing gas appliances may check the heating unit and replace pipes, thermocouples, thermostats, valves, and indicator spindles. They also answer emergency calls for gas leaks. To install gas appliances, they may have to install pipes in customers' homes to connect the appliances to the gas line. They measure, lay out, cut, and thread pipe and connect it to a feeder line and to the appliance. They may have to saw holes in walls or floors and hang steel supports from beams or joists to hold gas pipes in place. Once the gas line is in place, they turn on the gas and check for leaks.

Repairers also answer customers' questions about the care and use of appliances. For example, they demonstrate how to load automatic washing machines, arrange dishes in dishwashers, or sharpen chain saws.

Repairers write up estimates of the cost of repairs for customers, keep records of parts used and hours worked, prepare bills, and collect payment.

Working Conditions

Home appliance and power tool repairers who handle portable appliances usually work in repair shops which generally are quiet, well lighted, and adequately ventilated. Those who repair major appliances usually make service calls to customers' homes. They carry their tools and a number of commonly used parts with them in a truck or van and may spend several hours a day driving. They may work in clean comfortable rooms such as kitchens, but sometimes the appliance is in an area of the home that is damp, dirty, or dusty. Repairers sometimes work in cramped and uncomfortable positions when replacing parts in hard-to-reach areas of appliances.

Repairer jobs generally are not hazardous, but they must exercise care and follow safety precautions to avoid electrical shocks and injuries when lifting and moving large appliances. When servicing gas appliances and microwave ovens, they must be aware of the dangers of gas and radiation leaks.

Many home appliance and power tool repairers work a standard 40-hour week. Some work early mornings, evenings, and Saturdays. During hot weather, repairers of air-conditioners and refrigerators are in high demand by consumers and many work overtime. Repairers of power tools such as saws and drills may also have to work overtime during spring and summer months when use of such tools increases and breakdowns are more frequent.

Home appliance and power tool repairers usually work with little or no direct supervision, a feature of the job that appeals to many people.

Employment

Home appliance and power tool repairers held about 70,000 jobs in 1994. More than 1 out of 10 was self-employed. Almost 2 out of 3 salaried repairers worked in retail establishments such as department stores, household appliance stores, and fuel dealers. Others worked for gas and electric utility companies, electrical repair shops, and wholesalers.

Appliance and power tool repairers are employed in almost every community, but jobs are concentrated in the more highly populated areas.

Training, Other Qualifications, and Advancement

Employers generally require a high school diploma for home appliance and power tool repairer jobs. Many repairers learn the trade primarily on the job. Mechanical aptitude is desirable, and those who work in customers' homes must be courteous and tactful.

Employers prefer to hire people with formal training in appliance repair and electronics, and many repairers complete 1-or 2-year formal training programs in appliance repair and related subjects in high schools, private vocational schools, and community colleges. Courses in basic electricity and electronics are becoming increasingly necessary as more manufacturers are installing circuit boards and other electronic control systems in home appliances.

Regardless of whether their basic skills are developed through formal training or on the job, trainees usually get additional training from their employer. In shops that fix portable appliances, they work on a single type of appliance, such as vacuum cleaners, until they master its repair. Then they move on to others, until they can repair all those handled by the shop. In companies that repair major appliances, beginners assist experienced repairers on service visits. They may also study on their own. They learn to read schematic drawings, analyze problems, determine whether to repair or replace parts, and follow proper safety procedures. Up to 3 years of on-the-job training may be needed to become skilled in all aspects of repair of the more complex appliances.

Some appliance and power tool manufacturers and department store chains have formal training programs which include home study and shop classes, where trainees work with demonstration appliances and other training equipment. Many repairers receive supplemental instruction through 2- or 3- week seminars conducted by appliance and power tool manufacturers. Experienced repairers also often attend training classes and study service manuals.

The Environmental Protection Agency (EPA) has mandated that all repairers who purchase or work with refrigerants must be certified in its proper handling. To become certified to purchase and handle refrigerants, repairers must pass a written examination. Exams are administered by organizations approved by the Environmental Protection Agency, such as trade schools, unions, and employer associations. Though no formal training is required for certification, many of these organizations offer training programs designed to prepare workers for the certification examination.

To protect consumers, some States and areas require repairers to

be licensed or registered. Applicants for licensure must meet standards of education, training, and experience; they also may have to pass an examination, which can include a written examination, a hands-on practical test, or a combination of both.

Repairers in large shops or service centers may be promoted to supervisor, assistant service manager, or service manager. A few advance to managerial positions such as regional service manager or parts manager for appliance or tool manufacturers. Preference is given to those who demonstrate technical competence and show an ability to get along with coworkers and customers. Experienced repairers who have sufficient funds and knowledge of small business management may open their own repair shop.

Job Outlook

Employment of home appliance and power tool repairers is expected to decline slightly through the year 2005. Although the number of home appliances and power tools in use is expected to increase as the number of households and businesses grows and new and improved appliances and tools are introduced, increasing use of electronic parts such as solid-state circuitry, microprocessors, and sensing devices in appliances reduce the frequency of repairs. Nevertheless, prospects should continue to be good for well-trained repairers, particularly those with a strong background in electronics. Most people with the electronics training needed to repair appliances go into other repairer occupations. Employment is relatively steady because the demand for appliance repair services continues even during economic downturns.

Earnings

Home appliance and power tool repairers who usually worked full time had median earnings of about $427 a week in 1994. The middle 50 percent earned between $308 and $674 a week. The lowest paid 10 percent earned $249 a week or less, while the highest paid 10 percent earned $838 a week or more. Earnings of home appliance and power tool repairers vary widely according to skill level, geographic location, and the type of equipment serviced. Trainees usually earn less and senior technicians more. Earnings tend to be highest in large firms and for those servicing gas appliances. Repairers are compensated when working overtime, weekends, or holidays. Many receive commission in addition to their hourly wage salary.

Many larger dealers and service stores offer benefits such as health insurance coverage, sick leave, and retirement and pension programs. Some home appliance and power tool repairers belong to the International Brotherhood of Electrical Workers.

Related Occupations

Other workers who service electrical and electronic equipment include heating, air-conditioning, and refrigeration mechanics; pinsetter mechanics; office machine and cash register servicers; electronic home entertainment equipment repairers; and vending machine servicers and repairers.

Sources of Additional Information

For information about jobs in the home appliance and power tool repair field, contact local appliance repair shops, appliance dealers, and utility companies, or the local office of the State employment service.

For general information about the work of home appliance repairers contact:

☛Appliance Service News, P.O. Box 789, Lombard, IL 60148.

☛National Association of Service Dealers, 10 East 22nd St., Suite 310, Lombard, IL 60148.

☛Service Dealers Newsletter, 1400 Easton Rd., Roslyn, PA 19001.

☛Professional Service Association, 71 Columbia St., Cohoes, NY 12047.

Industrial Machinery Repairers

(D.O.T. codes available on request. See p. 478.)

Industrial machinery mechanics often make repairs in places that are difficult to reach.

Nature of the Work

Industrial machinery repairers maintain and repair machinery found in a plant or factory. This must be done accurately and quickly because an idle machine will delay production. In addition, a machine that is not properly repaired and maintained may damage the final product and injure the operator. All these factors cost companies money.

Industrial machinery repairers—often called maintenance mechanics—spend much of their time doing preventive maintenance. This includes keeping machines and their parts well oiled, greased, and cleaned. Repairers regularly inspect machinery and check performance. For example, they adjust and calibrate automated manufacturing equipment such as industrial robots and rebuild components of other industrial machinery. By keeping complete and up-to-date records, mechanics try to anticipate trouble and service equipment before factory production is interrupted.

Maintenance mechanics must be able to spot minor problems and correct them before they become major ones. For example, after hearing a vibration from a machine, the mechanic must decide whether it is due to worn belts, weak motor bearings, or some other problem. Computerized maintenance-management, vibration analysis techniques, and self-diagnostic systems are making this task easier. Self-diagnostic features on new industrial machinery can determine the cause of a malfunction and, in some cases, can alert the mechanic to potential trouble spots before symptoms develop.

After diagnosing the problem, the mechanic disassembles the equipment and repairs or replaces the necessary parts. The final step is to test the machine to ensure that it is running smoothly. When repairing electronically controlled machinery, maintenance mechanics may work closely with electronic repairers or electricians who maintain the machine's electronic parts. However, industrial machinery repairers increasingly need electronic skills to repair sophisticated equipment on their own. (Additional information about commercial and industrial electronic equipment repairers as well as electricians appears elsewhere in the *Handbook*.)

A wide range of tools may be used when doing preventive maintenance or making repairs. For example, repairers may use a screwdriver and wrench to adjust an engine, or a hoist to lift a printing press off the ground. When replacements for broken or defective parts are not readily available, or when a machine must be quickly returned to production, repairers may sketch a part that can be fabricated by the plant's machine shop. Repairers use catalogs to order replacement parts and often follow blueprints and engineering specifications to maintain and fix equipment.

Some of the industrial machinery repairer's duties may be performed by millwrights. (See the statement on millwrights elsewhere in the *Handbook*.)

Working Conditions

Working conditions for repairers who work in manufacturing are similar to those of production workers. However, they often work underneath or above large machinery in cramped conditions or on the top of a ladder. These workers are subject to common shop injuries such as cuts and bruises and use protective equipment such as hard hats, protective glasses, and safety belts.

Because factories and other organizations cannot afford breakdowns in industrial machinery, industrial machinery repairers may be called to the plant at night or on weekends for emergency repairs. Overtime is common among industrial machinery repairers—half work more than 40 hours a week.

Employment

Industrial machinery repairers held about 464,000 jobs in 1994. About 7 of every 10 worked in manufacturing industries, primarily food processing, textile mill products, chemicals, fabricated metal products, and primary metals. Others worked for government agencies, public utilities, mining companies, and any other business that relies on machinery.

Because industrial machinery repairers work in a wide variety of plants, they are employed in every part of the country. Employment is concentrated, however, in heavily industrialized areas.

Training, Other Qualifications, and Advancement

Many workers learn their trade through a 4-year apprenticeship program that combines classroom instruction with on-the-job-training. These programs are usually sponsored by a local trade union. Other workers start as helpers and pick up the skills of the trade informally and by taking courses offered by machinery manufacturers and community colleges.

Repairers learn from experienced repairers how to operate, disassemble, repair, and assemble machinery. Classroom instruction focuses on subjects such as shop mathematics, blueprint reading, and welding. In addition, electronics and computer training are an increasingly important part of the apprenticeship program.

Most employers prefer to hire those who have completed high school. However, opportunities do exist for those without a high school diploma. High school courses in mechanical drawing, mathematics, blueprint reading, physics, and electronics are useful.

Mechanical aptitude and manual dexterity are important characteristics for workers in this trade. Good physical condition and agility are also necessary because repairers sometimes have to lift heavy objects or climb to reach equipment located high above the floor.

Opportunities for advancement are limited. Industrial machinery repairers advance either by working with more complicated equipment or by becoming a supervisor. Some of the most highly skilled repairers can be promoted to master mechanic or can become a machinist or a tool and die maker.

Job Outlook

Employment of industrial machinery repairers is expected to grow more slowly than the average for all occupations through the year 2005. As more firms introduce automated production equipment, industrial machinery mechanics will be needed to insure that these machines are well-maintained and consistently in operation. This growth will be moderated, however, by the self-diagnostic capabilities and growing reliability of many new machines that help to reduce the need for repairs. Most job openings will result from the need to replace repairers who transfer to other occupations or leave the labor force. Qualified applicants should find ample employment opportunities as older workers retire.

Unlike many other manufacturing occupations, industrial machinery repairers are not usually affected by seasonal changes in production. During slack periods, when some plant workers are laid off, repairers often are retained to do major overhaul jobs. Although these workers may face layoff or a reduced workweek when economic conditions are particularly severe, they generally are less affected than other workers because machines have to be maintained regardless of the level of production.

Earnings

Median weekly earnings of full-time industrial machinery repairers were about $530 in 1994; the middle 50 percent earned between $410 and $720 weekly. The lowest 10 percent earned less than $310, while the top 10 percent earned more than $950. Earnings vary by industry and geographic region. In addition to wages, most of these workers receive benefits such as health and life insurance, pension plans, annual leave, and sick days.

Labor unions to which some industrial machinery repairers belong include the United Steelworkers of America; the United Automobile, Aerospace and Agricultural Implement Workers of America; the International Association of Machinists and Aerospace Workers; and the International Union of Electronic, Electrical, Salaried, Machine, and Furniture Workers.

Related Occupations

Other occupations that involve repairing machinery include aircraft mechanics and engine specialists; elevator installers and repairers; machinists; millwrights; and automotive and motorcycle, diesel, farm equipment, general maintenance, mobile heavy equipment, and heating, air-conditioning, and refrigeration mechanics.

Sources of Additional Information

Information about employment and apprenticeship opportunities in this field may be obtained from local offices of the State employment service or from:

☛The Association for Manufacturing Technology, 7901 Westpark Dr., Mclean, VA 22102.

☛Associated General Contractors of America, 1957 E St. NW., Washington, DC 20006.

Line Installers and Cable Splicers

(D.O.T. 821.261-010, -014, -022, and -026, .281-010, .361-010, -018, -022, -026, -030, and -038, .684-022, .687-010; 822.381-014; 823.261-014; 829.361-010 and -014; and 959.367-010)

Nature of the Work

Vast networks of wires and cables transmit the electric power produced in generating plants to individual customers, connect telephone central offices to customers' telephones and switchboards, and extend cable television to residential and commercial customers. These networks are constructed and maintained by line installers and cable splicers and their helpers.

To install new electric power or telephone lines, line installers or line erectors install poles and terminals, erect towers, and place wires and cables. They usually use power equipment to dig holes and set poles. Line installers climb the poles or use truck-mounted buckets (aerial work platforms) and use handtools to attach the cables. When working with electric power lines, installers bolt or clamp insulators onto the pole before attaching the cable. They may also install transformers, circuit breakers, switches, or other equipment. To bury underground cable, they use trenchers, plows, and other power equipment.

Splicers connect individual wires or fibers within the cable when lines have to be moved.

Line installers also lay cable television lines underground or hang them on poles with telephone and utility wires. These lines transmit broadcast signals from microwave towers to customers' homes. Installers place wiring in the house, connect the customers' television sets to it, and check that the television signal is strong.

After telephone line installers place cables in position, cable splicers, also referred to as cable splicing technicians, complete the line connections. (Electric power line workers install and splice the cables simultaneously.) Splicers connect individual wires or fibers within the cable and rearrange wires when lines have to be changed. They first read and interpret service orders and circuit diagrams to determine splicing specifications. Splices are then made by joining wires and cables with small handtools, epoxy, or mechanical equipment. At each splice, they place insulation over the conductor, and seal the splice with some type of moisture proof covering. They may fill the cable sheathing on critical transmission routes with compressed air so that leaks in the sheathing can be monitored and repaired. Splicers work on poles, aerial ladders and platforms, in manholes, or in basements of large buildings.

Fiber optic cables are being used to replace worn or obsolete copper cables. These tiny hair-thin strands of glass are able to carry more signals per cable because they transmit pulses of light instead of electricity. Splices of fiber optic cables are completed in a van positioned near the splice point. These vans house workshops that contain all the necessary equipment, such as machines that heat the glass fibers so they can be joined.

Line installers and cable splicers also maintain and repair telephone, power, and cable television lines. They periodically make sure lines are clear of tree limbs or other obstructions that could cause problems and check insulation on cables and other equipment on line poles. When bad weather or earth quakes break wires or cables, knock poles down, or cause underground ducts to collapse, they make emergency repairs.

Working Conditions

Because telephone, electric, and television cables are strung from utility poles or are underground, line installers and cable splicers must climb and lift or work in stooped and cramped positions. They usually work outdoors in all kinds of weather and are subject to 24-hour call. Most usually work a 40-hour week, but, for example, when severe weather damages transmission and distribution lines, they may work long and irregular hours to restore service. At times, they may travel to distant locations—and occasionally stay for a lengthy period to help restore damaged facilities or build new ones.

Line installers and cable splicers face many situations in which safety procedures must be followed. They wear safety equipment when entering manholes and test for the presence of gas before going underground. They may be exposed to hazardous chemicals from the solvents and plugging compounds that they use when splicing cables. Electric power line workers have the most hazardous jobs. They typically work at higher elevations because the electric cable is always above telephone and cable television lines. Moreover, the voltages in electric power lines are lethal.

Employment

Line installers and cable splicers held about 302,000 jobs in 1994. More than half were telephone and cable television line installers and repairers. Nearly all worked for telephone, cable television companies, or electric power companies, or for construction companies specializing in power line, telephone, and cable television construction.

Training, Other Qualifications, and Advancement

Line installers are often hired as helpers or ground workers. Most employers prefer high school graduates. Many employers test applicants for basic verbal, arithmetic, and abstract reasoning skills. Some employers test for physical ability such as balance, coordination, and strength and mechanical aptitude. Because the work entails a lot of climbing, applicants should have stamina and must be unafraid of heights. Knowledge of basic electricity and training in installing telephone systems obtained in the Armed Forces or vocational education programs may be helpful. The ability to distinguish colors is necessary because wires and cables usually are coded by color. Motivation, self-discipline, and the ability to work as part of a team are needed to work efficiently and safely.

Line installers and cable splicers in electric companies and construction firms specializing in cable installation generally complete a formal apprenticeship program. These are administered jointly by the employer and the union representing the workers, either the International Brotherhood of Electrical Workers or the Communications Workers of America. These programs last several years and combine formal instruction with on-the-job training. Workers in telephone companies generally receive several years of informal on-the-job training, in some cases learning other skills like telephone installation and repair. They may also attend training provided by equipment manufacturers.

A growing number of employers are using computer-assisted instruction, video cassettes, movies, or "programmed" workbooks. Some training facilities are equipped with poles, cable-supporting clamps, and other fixtures, to simulate working conditions as closely as possible. Trainees learn to work on poles while keeping their hands free. In one exercise, for example, they play catch with a basketball while on the poles.

Formal training includes instruction in electrical codes, blueprint reading, and basic electrical theory. Afterwards trainees learn on the job and work with a crew of experienced line installers under a line supervisor. Line installers and cable splicers receive training throughout their careers to qualify for more difficult assignments and to keep up with technological changes.

Since deregulation of the telephone industry, many telephone companies have reduced the scope of their training programs in order to reduce their costs and to remain competitive. Increasingly, workers are responsible for their own training, which is provided by community colleges and postsecondary vocational schools.

For installers in the telephone industry, advancement may come about through promotion to splicer. Splicers can advance to engineering assistants or may move into other kinds of work, such as sales. Promotion to a supervisory position also is possible. In the electric industry, promotion is usually to a supervisory position.

Job Outlook

Job seekers are expected to face competition. Because prerequisite skills and training are minimal, and earnings are above average, applicants outnumber available job openings. Employment growth is not expected to provide many opportunities; most will result from the need to replace the larger than average number of older workers reaching retirement age. Job prospects will be best for electrical line workers employed by electric utilities and construction firms because the effects of new technology are expected to be less than for telephone line workers. In telephone companies, those who combine knowledge of line installation, fiber optic or copper cable splicing, and repair of many types of equipment should enjoy better prospects.

Overall employment of line installers and cable splicers is expected to show little or no growth through the year 2005. Technological advances will result in divergent trends within this occupation. Employment of electrical power line installers is expected to grow more slowly than the average for all occupations as the demand for electricity grows and the need to maintain existing lines continues. Employment of telephone and cable television line installers and repairers, however, is expected to decline despite growth in telephone and cable television usage. Layoffs of telephone line workers have already occurred, due to increased efficiency being built into telephone systems. New ways of transmitting information—satellites, microwave towers, and underground fiber optic cable, for example—are not as vulnerable to adverse weather conditions as aerial wires, and fewer workers are needed to maintain them. Fiber optic cables will continue to replace copper cables, and this will generate short-term demand for installers. Also, some will be needed to install the infrastructure for the new telecommunications system. Telephone, cable, and even utility companies are converting more of their networks to fiber optics which makes it possible to carry voice, data, and video signals over the same lines to a wide range of customers. Over the longer term, however, employment will fall as the conversion to fiber optics is completed and as maintenance requirements are reduced. Improved splicing techniques as well as new power tools and equipment also will continue to improve the efficiency of cable splicers. Finally, most areas of the country that can economically be served by cable television have already been wired, and fewer installers will be needed.

Earnings

Pay rates for line installers and cable splicers vary greatly across the country and depend on length of service; specific information may be obtained from local telephone, electric power, and cable television companies. It generally takes about 5 years to go from the bottom to the top of the pay scale. In 1994, line installers and repairers who worked full time earned a median weekly wage of $712. The middle 50 percent earned between $501 and $887. The bottom 10 percent earned less than $337; the top 10 percent earned more than $1,089 a week.

Line installers and cable splicers employed by AT&T and the Bell Operating Companies and represented by the Communications Workers of America and the International Brotherhood of Electrical Workers earned between $469 and $1,063 a week in 1994. Because of low job turnover in these occupations, many workers earn salaries near the top of the pay scale.

Most line installers and cable splicers belong to unions, principally the Communications Workers of America and the International Brotherhood of Electrical Workers. For these workers, union contracts set wage rates, wage increases, and the time needed to advance from one step to the next. These contracts require extra pay for overtime and for all work on Sundays and holidays. Most contracts provide for additional pay for night work. Time in service determines the length of paid vacations. Depending on the locality, there are 9 to 12 holidays a year.

Related Occupations

Workers in other skilled crafts and trades who work with tools and machines include communications equipment mechanics, biomedical equipment technicians, telephone installers and repairers, electricians, and sound technicians.

Sources of Additional Information

For more details about employment opportunities, contact the telephone or electric power company in your community or local offices of the unions that represent these workers. For general information on line installer and cable splicer jobs, write to:

☛Communications Workers of America, 501 3rd St. NW., Washington, DC 20001.

For additional information on the telephone industry and career opportunities contact:

☛United States Telephone Association,1401 H St. NW., Suite 600, Washington, DC 20005-2136.

For information on employment and training contact:

☛Utility Workers Union of America, 815 16th. St. NW, Washington, DC 20006.

☛International Brotherhood of Electrical Workers, 1125 15th. St. NW, Room 807, Washington, DC 20005.

Millwrights

(D.O.T. 638.261-010, -014, -018, -026, .281-018, -022)

Nature of the Work

Millwrights install, repair, replace, and dismantle the machinery and heavy equipment used in almost every industry. These responsibilities require a wide range of skills—from blueprint reading and pouring concrete to diagnosing and solving mechanical problems.

The millwright's responsibilities begin when machinery arrives at the job site. The new equipment must be unloaded, inspected, and then moved into position. To lift and move light machinery, millwrights may use rigging and hoisting devices such as pulleys and cables. In other cases, they require the assistance of hydraulic lift-truck or crane operators to position the machinery. Because millwrights often decide what device to use for moving machinery, they must know the load-bearing properties of ropes, cables, hoists, and cranes.

New machinery sometimes requires a new foundation. Millwrights either personally prepare the foundation or supervise its construction, so they must know how to read blueprints and work with building materials such as concrete, wood, and steel.

When assembling machinery, millwrights fit bearings, align gears and wheels, attach motors, and connect belts according to the manufacturer's blueprints and drawings. Precision leveling and alignment are important in the assembly process; millwrights must have good mathematical skills so that they can measure angles, material thickness, and small distances with tools such as squares, calipers, and micrometers. When a high level of precision is required, devices such as lasers may be used. They also use hand and power tools, cutting torches, welding machines, and soldering guns. Some millwrights use metalworking equipment such as lathes or grinders to modify parts to specifications.

The increasing level of automation found in most industries means that there are more sophisticated machines for millwrights to install and maintain. This machinery often requires special care and knowledge, so millwrights often work closely with computer or electronic experts, electricians, engineers, and manufacturer's representatives to install it. (Additional information about commercial

In addition to installing new equipment, millwrights may also perform maintenance and repairs.

and industrial electronic equipment repairers as well as electricians appears elsewhere in the *Handbook*.)

In addition to installing and dismantling machinery, many millwrights repair and maintain equipment. This includes preventive maintenance, such as lubrication, and fixing or replacing worn parts. (For further information on machinery maintenance, see the statement on industrial machinery repairers elsewhere in the *Handbook*.)

Working Conditions

Working conditions of millwrights vary by industry. Those employed in manufacturing often work in a typical shop setting and use protective equipment to avoid common hazards. For example, injuries from falling objects or machinery are avoided by protective devices such as safety belts, protective glasses, and hard hats. Those in construction may work outdoors in uncomfortable weather conditions.

Millwrights may work independently or as part of a team. They must work quickly and precisely because non-functioning machinery costs a company time and money. Most millwrights work overtime; nearly two-thirds report working more than 40 hours during a typical week.

Employment

Millwrights held about 77,000 jobs in 1994. Most worked in manufacturing, primarily in durable goods industries such as motor vehicles and equipment and basic steel products. Millwrights found in other sectors were employed primarily by construction firms and machining and equipment wholesalers. Many of these workers are contractors.

Although millwrights work in every State, employment is concentrated in heavily industrialized areas.

Training, Other Qualifications, and Advancement

Millwrights receive their training from a formal apprenticeship program, a community college, or informally on the job. Apprenticeship programs normally last 4 years and combine on-the-job training with classroom instruction. Apprenticeship programs include training in dismantling, moving, erecting, and repairing machinery. Apprentices may also work with concrete and receive instruction in related skills such as carpentry, welding, and sheet-metal work. Classroom instruction is given in mathematics, blueprint reading, hydraulics, electricity, and increasingly, computers or electronics.

Most employers prefer applicants with a high school diploma and some vocational training or experience. Courses in science, mathematics, mechanical drawing, and machine shop practice are useful.

Because millwrights assemble and disassemble complicated machinery, mechanical aptitude is very important.

Strength and agility also are important because the work can require a considerable amount of lifting and climbing. Millwrights need good interpersonal and communication abilities in order to work as part of a team and give detailed instructions to others.

Advancement for millwrights usually takes the form of higher wages. Some advance to supervisor.

Job Outlook

Employment of millwrights is projected to decline through the year 2005, due in part to an expected downturn in new industrial construction. When construction activity falls, jobs are scarce, and even experienced millwrights may face layoffs or shortened workweeks. In coming years, new industrial construction is expected to be insufficient to maintain existing employment levels. In addition, some of the duties of millwrights are being transferred to other workers, such as electronic technicians and industrial machinery mechanics, as new automation becomes more complicated and involves more electronic components. Finally, millwrights are becoming more productive through technologies like hydraulic torque wrenches, ultrasonic measuring tools, and laser shaft alignment that allow fewer of these workers to perform a greater amount of work.

Although employment is expected to decline, millwrights will still be needed to maintain and repair existing machinery, to dismantle old machinery, and to install and maintain new equipment. Workers with these skills will encounter a number of job openings that will arise annually as experienced millwrights transfer to other occupations or leave the labor force.

Earnings

Median weekly earnings of full-time millwrights were about $700 in 1994; the middle 50 percent earned between $520 and $880. The lowest 10 percent earned less than $380, while the top 10 percent earned more than $1,290. Earnings vary by industry and geographic location. Two-thirds of millwrights belong to labor unions, one of the highest rates of membership in the economy. Typical benefits for these workers include health and life insurance, pension plans, paid vacation, and sick leave.

Related Occupations

To set up machinery for use in a plant, millwrights must know how to use hoisting devices and how to assemble, disassemble, and in some cases repair machinery. Other workers with similar job duties are industrial machinery repairers, mobile heavy equipment mechanics, aircraft mechanics and engine specialists, diesel mechanics, farm equipment mechanics, ironworkers, and machine assemblers.

Sources of Additional Information

For further information on apprenticeship programs, write to the Apprenticeship Council of your State's labor department, local offices of your State employment service, or local firms that employ millwrights. In addition, you may contact:

☛The United Brotherhood of Carpenters and Joiners of America, 101 Constitution Ave. NW., Washington DC 20001.

☛Association for Manufacturing Technology, 7901 Westpark Dr., Mclean, VA 22102.

☛Associated General Contractors of America, 1957 E St. NW., Washington, DC 20006.

Mobile Heavy Equipment Mechanics

(D.O.T. 620.261-022, .281-042, .381-014)

Nature of the Work

Mobile heavy equipment is indispensable to construction, logging, surface mining, and other industrial activities. Mobile heavy equip-

Field service mechanics often work outdoors on construction sites because mobile heavy equipment is too difficult to bring into a repair shop.

ment mechanics service and repair the engines, transmissions, hydraulics, electrical systems, and other components of equipment such as motor graders, trenchers and backhoes, crawler-loaders, and stripping and loading shovels. (Mechanics who specialize in servicing only diesel engines are discussed in the section on diesel mechanics elsewhere in the *Handbook*.)

Mobile heavy equipment mechanics perform routine maintenance on the diesel engines that power most heavy equipment, and, if an operator reports a malfunction, they search for its cause. First, they inspect and operate the equipment to diagnose the nature of the repairs required. If necessary, they may partially dismantle the engine, examining parts for damage or excessive wear. Then they repair, replace, clean, and lubricate the parts as necessary, and reassemble and test the engine for operating efficiency. If repairs to the drive train are needed, mechanics remove and repair the transmission or differential.

Many types of mobile heavy equipment use hydraulics to raise and lower movable parts such as scoops, shovels, log forks, or scraper blades. Repairing malfunctioning hydraulic components is an important responsibility of mobile heavy equipment mechanics. When hydraulics loses power, mechanics examine them for hydraulic fluid leaks and replace ruptured hoses or worn gaskets on fluid reservoirs. Occasionally, more extensive repairs are required, such as replacing a defective hydraulic pump.

Mobile heavy equipment mechanics perform a variety of other types of repairs. They diagnose and correct electrical problems and replace defective electronic components. They also disassemble and repair crawler undercarriages and track assemblies. Occasionally, mechanics weld broken body and structural parts, using electric or gas welders.

Many mechanics work in small repair shops of construction contractors, logging and mining companies, and local government road maintenance departments. They typically perform routine maintenance and minor repairs necessary to keep the equipment in operation. Mechanics in larger repair shops—particularly those of mobile heavy equipment dealers and the Federal Government—perform more difficult repairs, such as rebuilding or replacing engines, repairing hydraulic fluid pumps, or correcting electrical problems. Mechanics in some large shops specialize in one or two types of work, such as hydraulics or electrical systems.

Mobile heavy equipment mechanics use a variety of tools in their work, including common handtools such as pliers, wrenches, and screwdrivers and power tools such as pneumatic wrenches. They use micrometers and gauges to measure wear on parts, and a variety of testing equipment. For example, they use tachometers and dynamometers to locate engine malfunctions; when working on electrical systems, they use ohmmeters, ammeters, and voltmeters.

Working Conditions

Most mobile heavy equipment repair shops are well ventilated, lighted, and heated. Many mechanics work indoors in shops, but others work as field service mechanics and spend much of their time away from the shop working outdoors. When mobile heavy equipment breaks down at a construction site, it may be too difficult or expensive to bring it into a repair shop, so a field service mechanic is sent to the job site to make repairs. Generally, the more experienced mobile heavy equipment mechanics specialize in field service; they usually drive specially equipped trucks and sometimes must travel many miles to reach disabled machinery. For many mechanics, the independence and challenge of field work outweigh the occasional long hours or bad weather, but other mechanics are more comfortable with the routine of shop work and the opportunity to work as part of a team.

Mechanics handle greasy and dirty parts and often work in awkward or cramped positions. They sometimes must lift heavy tools and parts, and must be careful to avoid burns, bruises, and cuts from hot engine parts and sharp edges of machinery. However, serious accidents may be prevented when the shop is kept clean and orderly and safety practices are observed.

Employment

Mobile heavy equipment mechanics held about 101,000 jobs in 1994. Over half worked for mobile heavy equipment dealers and construction contractors. About one-fifth were employed by Federal, State, and local governments; the Department of Defense is the primary Federal employer. Other mobile heavy equipment mechanics worked for surface mine operators, public utility companies, logging camps and contractors, and heavy equipment rental and leasing companies. Still others repaired equipment for machinery manufacturers, airlines, railroads, steel mills, and oil and gas field companies. About 1 out of 20 mobile heavy equipment mechanics was self-employed.

Mobile heavy equipment mechanics are employed in every section of the country, but most work near cities and towns, where most construction takes place.

Training, Other Qualifications, and Advancement

For trainee jobs, employers hire persons with mechanical aptitude who are high school graduates and at least 18 years of age. They seek persons knowledgeable about the fundamentals of diesel engines, transmissions, electrical systems, and hydraulics. Although some persons are able to acquire these skills on their own or by working as helpers to experienced mechanics, most employers prefer to hire graduates of formal training programs in diesel or heavy equipment mechanics.

Training programs in diesel and heavy equipment mechanics are given by vocational and technical schools and community and junior colleges. Training in the fundamentals of electronics is also essential because new mobile heavy equipment increasingly features electronic controls and sensing devices. Some 1- to 2-year programs lead to a certificate of completion; others lead to an associate degree if they are supplemented with additional academic courses. These programs provide a foundation in the basics of diesel and heavy equipment technology, including hydraulics, and enable trainee mechanics to advance more rapidly to the journey, or experienced worker, level.

Through a combination of formal and on-the-job training, trainee mechanics acquire the knowledge and skills to efficiently service and repair the particular types of equipment handled by the shop. Beginners are assigned relatively simple service and repair tasks. As they gain experience and become more familiar with the equipment, they are assigned increasingly difficult jobs, and are exposed to a greater variety of equipment.

Many employers send trainee mechanics to training sessions conducted by heavy equipment manufacturers. These sessions, which typically last up to 1 week, provide intensive instruction in the repair of a manufacturer's equipment. Some sessions focus on particular components found in all of the manufacturer's equipment, such as diesel engines, transmissions, axles, and electrical systems. Other sessions focus on particular types of equipment, such as crawler-loaders and crawler-dozers. As they progress, trainees may periodically attend additional training sessions. Experienced mechanics also occasionally attend training sessions to gain familiarity with new technology or with types of equipment they may never have repaired.

High school courses in automobile mechanics, physics, chemistry, and mathematics provide an essential foundation for a career as a mechanic. Good reading and basic mathematics skills and a basic understanding of scientific principles are needed to help a mechanic learn important job skills and to keep abreast of new technology through the study of technical manuals. Experience working on diesel engines and heavy equipment acquired in the Armed Forces also is valuable.

Mobile heavy equipment mechanics usually must buy their own handtools, although employers furnish power tools and test equipment. Trainee mechanics are expected to accumulate their own tools as they gain experience. Many experienced mechanics have thousands of dollars invested in tools.

Experienced mechanics may advance to field service jobs, where they have greater opportunity to tackle problems independently and earn overtime pay. Mechanics who have leadership ability may become shop supervisors or service managers. Some mechanics open their own repair shops.

Job Outlook

Opportunities should generally be good for persons who have completed formal training programs in diesel or heavy equipment mechanics. Persons without formal training are expected to encounter growing difficulty entering this occupation.

Employment of mobile heavy equipment mechanics is expected to grow more slowly than the average for all occupations through the year 2005. Increasing numbers of mechanics will be required in repair shops of equipment dealers and rental and leasing companies as the growing complexity of mobile heavy equipment necessitates more repairs being done by professionals. More mechanics also will be needed by all levels of government to service construction equipment that repairs and maintains the country's system of highways and bridges. But employment of mechanics will increase more slowly at the Federal level as defense-related spending is trimmed. Employment of mechanics by construction contractors will increase more slowly as more of the equipment in use is rented or leased.

As the economy expands, growth of construction activity should result in the use of more mobile heavy equipment, which would increase the necessity for periodic service and repair. Various kinds of equipment will be needed in increasing numbers to grade construction sites, excavate basements, lay water and sewer lines, and put in streets. In addition, construction of new highways and bridges and repair or rebuilding of existing ones will also require more mechanics for servicing the equipment.

Since construction and mining are sensitive to changes in the level of economic activity, mobile heavy equipment may be idled during downturns. In addition, winter is traditionally the slack season for construction activity, particularly in colder regions. Fewer mechanics may be needed during periods when equipment is used less intensively, but employers usually try to retain experienced workers. However, employers may be reluctant to hire inexperienced workers during slack periods.

Earnings

Median weekly earnings of mobile heavy equipment mechanics were about $554 in 1994. The middle 50 percent earned from around $409 to $684 a week; the lowest 10 percent earned less than $322 a week, and the top 10 percent earned over $864 a week in 1994.

Some mobile heavy equipment mechanics are members of unions. The unions include the International Association of Machinists and Aerospace Workers; the International Union of Operating Engineers; and the International Brotherhood of Teamsters.

Related Occupations

Workers in other occupations who repair and service diesel-powered vehicles and heavy equipment include rail car repairers and diesel, farm equipment, and mine machinery mechanics.

Sources of Additional Information

More details about work opportunities for mobile heavy equipment mechanics may be obtained from local mobile heavy equipment dealers, construction contractors, surface mining companies, and government agencies. Local offices of the State employment service may also have information on work opportunities and training programs.

Motorcycle, Boat, and Small-Engine Mechanics

(D.O.T. 620.281-054, .684-026; 623.261, .281-038, -042; 625.281-018, -026, -030, -034, .381; 721.281-022)

Nature of the Work

Although the engines that power motorcycles, boats, and lawn and garden equipment are usually smaller than those that power automobiles and trucks, they have many things in common, including breakdowns. Motorcycle, boat, and small-engine mechanics repair and service power equipment ranging from chain saws to yachts.

Small engines, like larger engines, require periodic servicing to minimize the possibility of breakdowns and keep them operating at peak efficiency. At routine intervals, mechanics adjust, clean, lubricate, and, when necessary, replace worn or defective parts such as spark plugs, ignition points, valves, and carburetors. Routine maintenance is normally a major part of the mechanic's work.

When breakdowns occur, mechanics diagnose the cause and repair or replace the faulty parts. The mark of a skilled mechanic is the ability to diagnose mechanical, fuel, and electrical problems and to make repairs in a minimum amount of time. A quick and accurate diagnosis requires problem-solving ability as well as a thorough knowledge of the equipment's operation. The mechanic first obtains a description of the symptoms of the problem from the owner, and then, if possible, operates the equipment to observe the symptoms. The mechanic may have to use special diagnostic testing equipment and disassemble some components for further examination. After pinpointing the cause of the problem, the needed adjustments, re-

pairs, or replacements are made. Some jobs require only the adjustment or replacement of a single item, such as a carburetor or fuel pump, and may be completed in less than an hour. In contrast, a complete engine overhaul may require a number of hours, because the mechanic must disassemble and reassemble the engine to replace worn valves, pistons, bearings, and other internal parts.

Motorcycle, boat, and small-engine mechanics use common handtools such as wrenches, pliers, and screwdrivers, as well as power tools such as drills and grinders. Engine analyzers, compression gauges, ammeters and voltmeters, and other testing devices help mechanics locate faulty parts and tune engines. Hoists may be used to lift heavy equipment such as motorcycles, snowmobiles, or boats. Mechanics often refer to service manuals for detailed directions and specifications while performing repairs.

Mechanics usually specialize in the service and repair of one type of equipment, although they may work on closely related products. *Motorcycle mechanics* repair and overhaul motorcycles, motor scooters, mopeds, and all-terrain vehicles. Besides engines, they may work on transmissions, brakes, and ignition systems, and make minor body repairs. Because many motorcycle mechanics work for dealers that service only the products they sell, mechanics may specialize in servicing only a few of the many makes and models of motorcycles.

Motorboat mechanics repair and adjust the engines and electrical and mechanical equipment of inboard and outboard marine engines. Most small boats have portable outboard engines that can be removed and brought into the repair shop. Larger craft, such as cabin cruisers and commercial fishing boats, are powered by diesel or gasoline inboard or inboard-outdrive engines, which are only removed for major overhauls. Motorboat mechanics may also work on propellers, steering mechanisms, marine plumbing, and other boat equipment.

Small-engine mechanics service and repair outdoor power equipment such as lawnmowers, garden tractors, edge trimmers, and chain saws. They also may occasionally work on portable generators, go-carts, and snowmobiles.

Working Conditions

Motorcycle, boat, and small-engine mechanics usually work in repair shops that are well lighted and ventilated, but which are sometimes noisy when engines are being tested. However, motorboat mechanics may work outdoors in all weather when repairing inboard engines aboard boats; they may have to work in cramped or awkward positions to reach a boat's engine.

In northern States, motorcycles, boats, lawnmowers, and other equipment are used less, or not at all, during the winter, and mechanics may work fewer than 40 hours a week; many mechanics are only hired temporarily during the busy spring and summer seasons. Some

Routine maintenance is a major part of motorcycle mechanics' work.

of the winter slack is taken up by scheduling time-consuming engine overhauls and working on snowmobiles and snowblowers. Many mechanics may work considerably more than 40 hours a week when the weather is warmer in the spring, summer, and fall.

Employment

Motorcycle, boat, and small-engine mechanics held almost 46,000 jobs in 1994. About 11,000 were motorcycle mechanics, while the remainder specialized in the repair of boats or outdoor power equipment such as lawnmowers, garden tractors, and chain saws. More than one-quarter of all motorcycle, boat, and small-engine mechanics worked for dealers of boats, motorcycles, and miscellaneous vehicles. Others were employed by independent repair shops, marinas and boat yards, equipment rental companies, and hardware and lawn and garden stores. Nearly one-third were self-employed.

Training, Other Qualifications, and Advancement

Due to the increasing complexity of motorcycles, most employers prefer to hire motorcycle mechanics who are graduates of formal training programs. However, because technology has not had as great an impact on boat and outdoor power equipment, most boat and small-engine mechanics learn their skills on the job. For trainee jobs, employers hire persons with mechanical aptitude who are knowledgeable about the fundamentals of small 2- and 4-cycle engines. Many trainees develop an interest in mechanics and acquire some basic skills through working on automobiles, motorcycles, boats, or outdoor power equipment as a hobby, or through mechanic vocational training in high school, vocational and technical schools, or community colleges. A growing number also prepare for their careers by completing training programs in motorcycle, marine, or small-engine mechanics, but only a relatively small number of such specialized programs exist.

Trainees begin by learning routine service tasks under the guidance of experienced mechanics, such as replacing ignition points and spark plugs, or taking apart, assembling, and testing new equipment. Equipment manufacturers' service manuals are an important training tool. As trainees gain experience and proficiency, they progress to more difficult tasks, such as diagnosing the cause of breakdowns or overhauling engines. Up to 3 years of training on the job may be necessary before an inexperienced beginner becomes skilled in all aspects of the repair of some motorcycle and boat engines.

Employers sometimes send mechanics and trainees to special training courses conducted by motorcycle, boat, and outdoor power equipment manufacturers or distributors. These courses, which can last as long as 2 weeks, are designed to upgrade the worker's skills and provide information on repairing new models.

Most employers prefer to hire high school graduates for trainee mechanic positions, but will accept applicants with less education if they possess adequate reading, writing, and arithmetic skills. Many equipment dealers employ students part time and during the summer to help assemble new equipment and perform minor repairs. Helpful high school courses include small-engine repair, automobile mechanics, science, and business arithmetic.

Knowledge of basic electronics is increasingly desirable for motorcycle, boat, and small-engine mechanics. Electronics are increasingly being used in engine controls, instrument displays, and a variety of other components of motorcycles, boats, and outdoor power equipment. Mechanics should be familiar with at least the basic principles of electronics in order to recognize when an electronic malfunction may be responsible for a problem, and be able to test and replace electronic components.

Motorcycle, boat, and small-engine mechanics are sometimes required to furnish their own handtools. Employers generally provide some tools and test equipment, but beginners are expected to gradually accumulate handtools as they gain experience. Some experienced mechanics have thousands of dollars invested in tools.

Some mechanics are able to use skills learned through repairing motorcycles, boats, and outdoor power equipment to advance to higher paying jobs as automobile, truck, or heavy equipment me-

chanics. In larger shops, mechanics with leadership ability can advance to supervisory positions such as shop supervisor or service manager. Mechanics who are able to raise enough capital may open their own repair shops or equipment dealerships.

Job Outlook

Employment of motorcycle, boat, and small-engine mechanics is expected to grow more slowly than the average for all occupations through the year 2005. The majority of job openings are expected to occur because many experienced motorcycle, boat, and small-engine mechanics leave each year to transfer to other occupations, retire, or stop working for other reasons. Job prospects should be especially favorable for persons who complete mechanic training programs.

Growth of personal disposable income over the 1994-2005 period should provide consumers with more discretionary dollars to buy boats, lawn and garden power equipment, and motorcycles—requiring more mechanics to keep the growing amount of equipment in operation. However, growth in the demand for mechanics will be slowed by design improvements that should continue to make equipment more reliable and lengthen intervals between routine service.

Employment of motorcycle mechanics should increase slowly as the popularity of motorcycles rebounds. Beginning in the late 1990's, the number of persons between the ages of 18 and 24 should begin to grow. Motorcycle usage should continue to be popular with persons in this age group, who historically have the greatest proportion of motorcycle enthusiasts. Motorcycles have also been increasing in popularity with persons between the ages of 25 and 40, a group with more disposable income to spend on recreational equipment such as motorcycles and boats.

Recreational boating is expected to continue to be popular, and construction of new single-family houses will result in an increase in the lawn and garden equipment in operation, increasing the need for mechanics. However, equipment growth will be slowed by trends toward smaller lawns and contracting out their maintenance to lawn service firms.

Earnings

Motorcycle, boat, and small-engine mechanics who usually worked full time had median earnings of about $407 a week in 1994. The middle 50 percent earned between $286 and $516 a week. The lowest paid 10 percent earned less than $202 a week, while the highest paid 10 percent earned over $644 a week.

Motorcycle, boat, and small-engine mechanics tend to receive few fringe benefits in small shops, but those employed in larger shops often receive paid vacations and sick leave and health insurance. Some employers also pay for work-related training and provide uniforms.

Related Occupations

The work of motorcycle, boat, and small-engine mechanics is closely related to that of mechanics and repairers who work on other types of mobile equipment powered by internal combustion engines. Related occupations include automotive mechanic, diesel mechanic, farm equipment mechanic, and mobile heavy equipment mechanic.

Sources of Additional Information

For more details about work opportunities, contact local motorcycle, boat, and lawn and garden equipment dealers, and boat yards and marinas. Local offices of the State employment service also may have information about employment and training opportunities.

General information about motorcycle mechanic careers may be obtained from:

☞Motorcycle Mechanics Institute, 2844 West Deer Valley Rd., Phoenix, AZ 85027.

General information about motorboat mechanic careers may be obtained from:

☞Marine Mechanics Institute, 2844 West Deer Valley Rd., Phoenix, AZ 85027.

Musical Instrument Repairers and Tuners

(D.O.T. 730.281-014, -026, -038, -050, -054, .361, .381-010, -026, -034, -038, -042, -058, .681-010, .684-022, -026, and -094)

Musical instrument repairers need good hearing, mechanical aptitude, and manual dexterity.

Nature of the Work

Musical instruments are a source of entertainment and recreation for millions of people. Maintaining these instruments so they perform properly is the job of musical instrument repairers and tuners. The occupation includes piano tuners and repairers (often called piano technicians); pipe-organ tuners and repairers; and brass, woodwind, percussion, or string instrument repairers.

Piano tuners adjust piano strings to the proper pitch. A string's pitch is the frequency at which it vibrates—and produces sound—when it is struck by one of the piano's wooden hammers. Tuners first adjust the pitch of the "A" string. Striking the key, the tuner compares the string's pitch with that of a tuning fork. Using a tuning hammer (also called a tuning lever or wrench), the tuner turns a steel pin to tighten or loosen the string until its pitch matches that of the tuning fork. The pitch of each of the other strings is set in relation to the "A" string. The standard 88-key piano has 230 strings and can be tuned in about an hour and a half.

A piano has thousands of wooden, steel, iron, ivory, and felt parts which can be plagued by an assortment of problems. It is the task of *piano repairers* to locate and correct these problems. In addition to repair work, piano repairers may also tune pianos.

To diagnose problems, repairers talk with customers before partially dismantling a piano to inspect its parts. Repairers may realign moving parts, replace old or worn ones, or completely rebuild pianos. Repairers use common handtools as well as special ones, such as regulating, repining, and restringing tools.

Some piano tuners service pianos that have built-in computers that control humidity, assist in recording, or allow the piano to operate as an automatic player-piano. Piano repair work will increasingly require some knowledge of electronics, as sales of sophisticated pianos increase, and people decide to upgrade their older pianos.

Pipe-organ repairers tune, repair, and install organs that make music by forcing air through flue pipes or reed pipes. (Repairers who service electronic organs are included in the statement on electronic home entertainment equipment repairers elsewhere in the *Handbook*.) The flue pipe sounds when a current of air strikes a metal lip in the side of the pipe. The reed pipe sounds when a current of air vibrates a brass reed inside the pipe.

To tune an organ, repairers first match the pitch of the "A" pipes with that of a tuning fork. The pitch of other pipes is set by comparing it to that of the "A" pipes. To tune a flue pipe, repairers move the metal slide that increases or decreases the pipe's "speaking length." To tune a reed pipe, the tuner alters the length of the brass reed. Most organs have hundreds of pipes, so often a day or more is needed to completely tune an organ.

Pipe-organ repairers locate problems, repair or replace worn parts, and clean pipes. Repairers also assemble organs on site in churches and auditoriums, following manufacturer's blueprints. They use hand and power tools to install and connect the air chest, blowers, air ducts, pipes, and other components. They may work in teams or be assisted by helpers. Depending on the size of the organ, a job may take several weeks or even months.

Violin repairers adjust and repair bowed instruments, such as violins, violas, and cellos, using a variety of handtools. They find defects by inspecting and playing instruments. They remove cracked or broken sections, repair or replace defective parts, and restring instruments. They also fill in scratches with putty, sand rough spots, and apply paint or varnish.

Guitar repairers inspect and play the instrument to determine defects. They replace levels using handtools, and fit wood or metal parts. They reassemble and string guitars.

Brass and woodwind instruments include trumpets, cornets, French horns, trombones, tubas, clarinets, flutes, saxophones, oboes, and bassoons. *Brass and wind instrument repairers* clean, adjust, and repair these instruments. They move mechanical parts or play scales to find defects. They may unscrew and remove rod pins, keys, and pistons, and remove soldered parts using gas torches. They repair dents in metal instruments using mallets or burnishing tools. They fill cracks in wood instruments by inserting pinning wire and covering them with filler. Repairers also inspect instrument keys and replace worn pads and corks.

Percussion instrument repairers work on drums, cymbals, and xylophones. In order to repair a drum, they remove drum tension rod screws and rods by hand or by using a drum key. They cut new drumheads from animal skin, stretch the skin over rimhoops and tuck it around and under the hoop using hand tucking tools. To prevent a crack in a cymbal, gong or similar instrument from advancing repairers may operate a drill press or hand power drill to drill holes at the inside edge of the crack. Another technique they may use involves cutting out sections around the cracks using shears or grinding wheels. They also replace the bars and wheels of xylophones.

Working Conditions

Although they may suffer small cuts and bruises, the work of musical instrument repairers and tuners is relatively safe. Most brass, woodwind, percussion, and string instrument repairers work in repair shops or music stores. Piano and organ repairers and tuners usually work on instruments in homes, schools, and churches and may spend several hours a day driving. Salaried repairers and tuners work out of a shop or store; the self-employed generally work out of their homes.

Employment

Musical instrument repairers and tuners held about 9,702 jobs in 1994. Most worked on pianos. About two-thirds were self-employed. Eight of 10 wage and salary repairers and tuners worked in music stores, and most of the rest worked in repair shops or for musical instrument manufacturers.

Training, Other Qualifications, and Advancement

For musical instrument repairer and tuner jobs, employers prefer people with post high school training in music repair technology. Some musical instrument repairers and tuners learn their trade on the job as apprentices or assistants, but employers willing to provide on-the-job training are difficult to find. A few music stores, large repair shops, and self-employed repairers and tuners hire inexperienced people as trainees to learn how to tune and repair instruments under the supervision of experienced workers. Trainees may sell instruments, clean up, and do other routine work. Usually 2 to 5 years of training and practice are needed to become fully qualified.

A small number of technical schools and colleges offer courses in piano technology or brass, woodwind, string, and electronic musical instrument repair. A few music repair schools offer 1- or 2-year courses. There are also home-study (correspondence school) courses in piano technology. Graduates of these courses generally refine their skills by working for a time with an experienced tuner or technician.

Music courses help develop the student's ear for tonal quality. The ability to play an instrument is helpful. Knowledge of woodworking is useful for repairing instruments made of wood.

Repairers and tuners need good hearing, mechanical aptitude, and manual dexterity. For those dealing directly with customers, a neat appearance and a pleasant, cooperative manner are important.

Musical instrument repairers keep up with developments in their fields by studying trade magazines and manufacturers' service manuals. The Piano Technicians Guild helps its members improve their skills through training conducted at local chapter meetings and at regional and national seminars. Guild members also can take a series of tests to earn the title Registered Piano Technician. The National Association of Professional Band Instrument Repair Technicians offers similar programs, scholarships, and a trade publication. Its members specialize in the repair of woodwind, brass, string and percussion instruments. Repairers and technicians who work for large dealers, repair shops, or manufacturers can advance to supervisory positions or go into business for themselves.

Job Outlook

Musical instrument repairer and tuner jobs are expected to increase about as fast as the average for all occupations through the year 2005. Replacement needs will provide the most job opportunities as many repairers and tuners near retirement age. Nonetheless, due to its small size the number of openings due to both growth and replacement needs is very low relative to other occupations. Because training is difficult to get—there are only a few schools that offer training programs and few experienced workers are willing to take on apprentices—opportunities for those who do get training should be excellent.

Several competing factors are expected to influence the demand for musical instrument repairers and tuners. Although the number of people employed as musicians will increase, the number of students of all ages playing musical instruments is expected to grow slowly. Yet, consumers should continue to buy more expensive instruments, so they should be willing to spend more on tuning and repairs to protect their value.

Earnings

According to the limited information available, repairers and tuners employed full-time by retail music stores averaged about $26,550 in 1994. Repairers and tuners who worked full-time plus supervised at least one other technician averaged $34,250.

Related Occupations

Musical instrument repairers need mechanical aptitude and manual dexterity. Electronic home entertainment equipment repairers, vending machine servicers and repairers, home appliance and power tool repairers, and computer and office machine repairers all require similar talents.

Sources of Additional Information

Details about job opportunities may be available from local music instrument dealers and repair shops.

For general information about piano technicians and a list of schools offering courses in piano technology, write to:
☛Piano Technicians Guild, 3930 Washington St., Kansas City, MO 64111-2963.

For general information on musical instrument repair, write to:
☛National Association of Professional Band Instrument Repair Technicians (NAPBIRT), P.O. Box 51, Normal, IL 61761.

Vending Machine Servicers and Repairers

(D.O.T. 319.464-014 and 639.281-014)

Nature of the Work

Coin-operated vending machines are a familiar sight. These machines dispense many types of refreshments, from cold soft drinks to hot meals. Vending machine servicers and repairers install, service, and stock these machines and keep them in good working order.

Vending machine servicers periodically visit coin-operated machines that dispense soft drinks, candy and snacks, and food items. They collect coins from the machines, restock merchandise, change labels to indicate new selections, and adjust temperature gauges so that items are kept at the right temperature. They are also responsible for keeping the machines clean. Because many vending machines dispense food, these workers must comply with State and local public health and sanitation standards.

Servicers make sure machines operate correctly. When checking complicated electrical and electronic machines, such as beverage dispensers, they make sure that the machines mix drinks properly and that refrigeration and heating units work correctly. On the relatively simple gravity-operated machines, servicers check handles, springs, plungers, and merchandise chutes. They also test coin and change-making mechanisms. When installing the machines, they make the necessary water and electrical connections and recheck the machines for proper operation. They also make sure installations comply with local plumbing and electrical codes.

Preventive maintenance—avoiding trouble before it starts—is a major job of these workers. For example, they periodically clean refrigeration condensers, lubricate mechanical parts, and adjust machines to perform properly.

If a machine breaks down, *vending machine repairers* inspect it for obvious problems, such as loose electrical wires, malfunctions of the coin mechanism, and leaks. If the problem cannot be readily located, they refer to technical manuals and wiring diagrams and use testing devices such as electrical circuit testers to find defective parts. Repairers sometimes fix faulty parts at the site, but they often install replacements and take broken parts to the company shop for repair. When servicing electronic machines, repairers may only have to replace a circuit board or other component. They also repair microwave ovens used to heat food dispensed from machines.

In repair and maintenance work, repairers use hammers, pliers, pipe cutters, soldering guns, wrenches, screwdrivers, and electronic testing devices. In the repair shop, they use power tools, such as grinding wheels, saws, and drills as well as voltmeters, ohmmeters, oscilloscopes, and other testing equipment.

Vending machine servicers and repairers employed by small companies may both fill and fix machines on a regular basis. These combination servicers-repairers stock machines, collect money, fill coin and currency changers, and repair machines when necessary.

Servicers and repairers also do some clerical work, such as filing reports, preparing repair cost estimates, ordering parts, and keeping daily records of merchandise distributed. However, many of the new computerized machines reduce the paperwork that a servicer performs.

Working Conditions

Some vending machine repairers work primarily in company repair shops, but many servicers and repairers spend much of their time on the road visiting machines wherever they have been placed. Vend-

Many vending machine repairs must be done on the site.

ing machines operate around the clock, so repairers often work at night and on weekends and holidays.

Vending machine repair shops generally are quiet, well lighted, and have adequate work space. However, when servicing machines on location, the work may be done where pedestrian traffic is heavy, such as in busy supermarkets, industrial complexes, offices, or schools. Repair work is relatively safe, although servicers and repairers must take care to avoid hazards such as electrical shocks and cuts from sharp tools and metal objects. They also must follow safe work procedures, especially when moving heavy vending machines or working with electricity and radiation from microwave ovens.

Employment

Vending machine servicers and repairers held about 19,000 jobs in 1994. Most repairers work for vending companies that sell food and other items through machines. Others work for soft drink bottling companies that have their own coin-operated machines. Some work for companies that own video games, pin-ball machines, juke boxes, and similar types of amusement equipment. Although vending machine servicers and repairers are employed throughout the country, most are located in areas with large populations and many coin and vending machines.

Training, Other Qualifications, and Advancement

Employers generally prefer to hire high school graduates and to train them to fill and fix machines informally on the job by observing, working with, and receiving instruction from experienced repairers. High school or vocational school courses in electricity, refrigeration, and machine repair are an advantage in qualifying for entry jobs. Employers usually require applicants to demonstrate mechanical ability, either through their work experience or by scoring well on mechanical aptitude tests. Because vending machine servicers and repairers sometimes handle thousands of dollars in merchandise and cash, employers hire persons who have a record of honesty and respect for the law. The ability to deal tactfully with people also is important. A commercial driver's license and a good driving record are essential for most vending machine repairer jobs.

Electronics are becoming more prevalent in vending machines, so employers increasingly prefer applicants to have some training in electronics. Technologically advanced machines with features such as multilevel pricing, inventory control, and scrolling messages extensively use electronics and microchip computers. Some vocational high schools and junior colleges offer 1- to 2-year training programs in basic electronics for vending machine servicers and repairers.

Beginners may start their training with simple jobs such as cleaning or painting machines. They then may learn to rebuild machines—removing defective parts, repairing, adjusting, and testing the machines. Next, they accompany an experienced repairer on service calls, and finally make visits on their own. This learning process may take from 6 months to 3 years, depending on the individual's abilities, previous education, types of machines, and the quality of instruction.

The National Automatic Merchandising Association has established an apprenticeship program for vending machine repairers. Apprentices receive 144 hours of home-study instruction in subjects such as basic electricity and electronics, blueprint reading, customer relations, and safety. Upon completion of the program, performance and written tests must be passed to become certified.

To learn about new machines, repairers and servicers sometimes attend training sessions sponsored by manufacturers, which may last from a few days to several weeks. Both trainees and experienced workers sometimes take evening courses in basic electricity, electronics, microwave ovens, refrigeration, and other related subjects. Skilled servicers and repairers may be promoted to supervisory jobs.

Job Outlook

Employment of vending machine servicers and repairers is expected to decline through the year 2005. More vending machines are likely to be installed in industrial plants, hospitals, stores, and other business establishments to meet the public demand for vending machine items. In addition, the range of products dispensed by machine can be expected to increase as vending machines continue to become more automated and more are built with microwave ovens, mini-refrigerators, and freezers. However, improvements in technology should require servicers and repairers to check on machines less frequently, reducing their employment. New machines will need to be repaired and restocked less often, and contain computers that record sales and inventory data, reducing time-consuming paperwork now done by servicers. Some new machines will even be able to signal the vending machine company when they need to be restocked or repaired, allowing servicers and repairers to be dispatched only when needed, instead of their having to check each machine on a regular schedule.

Although employment is expected to decline, job openings will nevertheless arise as experienced workers transfer to other occupations or leave the labor force. Persons with some background in electronics should have the best job prospects because electronic circuitry is an increasingly important component of vending machines. If firms cannot find trained or experienced workers for these jobs, they are likely to train qualified route drivers or hire inexperienced people who have acquired some mechanical, electrical, or electronic training by taking high school or vocational courses.

Earnings

According to a survey conducted by the National Automatic Merchandising Association, the average hourly wage rate for nonunion vending machine servicers was $8.30 in 1994, with rates ranging from just under $4.25 to nearly $16.00 an hour, depending on the size of the firm and the region of the country. Nonunion repairers averaged $10.21 an hour in 1994, but rates ranged from $5.00 to $22.00. Servicers and repairers who were members of unions generally earned slightly more.

Most vending machine repairers work 8 hours a day, 5 days a week, and receive premium pay for overtime. Some union contracts stipulate higher pay for night work and for emergency repair jobs on weekends and holidays.

Some vending machine repairers and servicers are members of the International Brotherhood of Teamsters.

Related Occupations

Other workers who repair equipment with electrical and electronic components include home appliance and power tool repairers, electronic equipment repairers, and general maintenance mechanics.

Sources of Additional Information

Further information on job opportunities in this field can be obtained from local vending machine firms and local offices of the State employment service. For general information and a list of schools offering courses in vending machine repair, write to:

☛National Automatic Merchandising Association, 20 N. Wacker Dr., Suite 3500, Chicago, IL 60606-3102.

Construction Trades Occupations

Bricklayers and Stonemasons

(D.O.T. 779.684-058; 861.361-010 and -014, .381-010 through -042, except -034, .684-010 and -014; and 899.364-010)

Nature of the Work

Bricklayers and stonemasons work in closely related trades that produce attractive, durable surfaces and structures. The work they perform varies in complexity, from laying a simple masonry walkway to installing the ornate exterior of a high-rise building. *Bricklayers* build walls, floors, partitions, fireplaces, chimneys, and other structures with brick, precast masonry panels, concrete block, and other masonry materials. Some specialize in installing firebrick linings in industrial furnaces. *Stonemasons* build stone walls as well as set stone exteriors and floors. They work with two types of stone—natural cut, such as marble, granite, and limestone, and artificial stone made from concrete, marble chips, or other masonry materials. Stonemasons usually work on structures such as houses of worship, hotels, and office buildings.

In putting up a wall, bricklayers build the corners of the structure first. Because of the necessary precision, these corner leads are very time consuming to erect and require the skills of the most experienced bricklayers on the job. After the corner leads are complete, less experienced bricklayers fill in the wall between the corners, using a line from corner to corner to guide each course or layer of brick. Because of the expense associated with building corner leads, an increasing number of bricklayers are using corner poles, also called masonry guides, that enable them to build the entire wall at the same time. They fasten the corner posts or poles in a plumb position to define the wall line and stretch a line between them. The line serves as a guide for each course of brick. Bricklayers then spread a bed of mortar (a cement, sand, and water mixture) with a trowel (a flat, bladed metal tool with a handle), place the brick on the mortar bed, and then press and tap it into place. As blueprints specify, they either cut brick with a hammer and chisel or saw them to fit around windows, doors, and other openings. Mortar joints are finished with jointing tools for a sealed, neat, and uniform appearance. Although bricklayers generally use steel supports or "lintels" at window and door openings, they sometimes build brick arches that support and enhance the beauty of the brickwork.

Bricklayers are assisted by hod carriers, or helpers, who bring brick and other materials, mix mortar, and set up and move the scaffolding.

Stonemasons often work from a set of drawings in which each stone has been numbered for identification. Helpers may locate and bring the prenumbered stones to the masons. A derrick operator using a hoist may be needed to lift large pieces into place.

When building a stone wall, masons set the first course of stones into a shallow bed of mortar. They align the stones with wedges, plumblines, and levels, and adjust them into position with a hard rubber mallet. Masons build the wall by alternating layers of mortar and courses of stone. As the work progresses, they remove the wedges and fill the joints between stones and use a pointed metal tool, called a "tuck pointer," to smooth the mortar to an attractive finish. To hold large stones in place, stonemasons attach brackets to the stone and weld or bolt them to anchors in the wall. Finally, masons wash the stone with a cleansing solution to remove stains and dry mortar.

When setting stone floors, which often consist of large and heavy pieces of stone, masons first trowel a layer of damp mortar over the surface to be covered. Using crowbars and hard rubber mallets for aligning and leveling, they then set the stone in the mortar bed. To finish, workers fill the joints and wash the stone slabs.

Masons use a special hammer and chisel to cut stone. They cut it along the grain to make various shapes and sizes. Valuable pieces often are cut with a saw that has a diamond blade. Some masons specialize in setting marble which, in many respects, is similar to setting large pieces of stone. Bricklayers and stonemasons also repair imperfections and cracks or replace broken or missing masonry units in walls and floors.

Most nonresidential buildings are now built with prefabricated panels made of concrete block, brick veneer, stone, granite, marble, tile, or glass. In the past, bricklayers did mostly interior work, such as block partition walls and elevator shafts. Now they must be more versatile and work with many materials. For example, bricklayers now install lighter-weight insulated panels used in new skyscraper construction.

Refractory masons are bricklayers who specialize in installing firebrick and refractory tile in high-temperature boilers, furnaces, cupolas, ladles, and soaking pits in industrial establishments. Most work in steel mills, where molten materials flow on refractory beds from furnaces to rolling machines.

Working Conditions

Bricklayers and stonemasons usually work outdoors. They stand, kneel, and bend for long periods and often have to lift heavy materials. Common hazards include injuries from tools and falls from scaffolds, but these can be avoided when proper safety practices are followed.

Employment

Bricklayers and stonemasons held about 147,000 jobs in 1994. The vast majority were bricklayers. Workers in these crafts are employed primarily by special trade, building, or general contractors. They work throughout the country but, like the general population, are concentrated in metropolitan areas.

Bricklayers spend much of their time standing, kneeling, or bending.

Nearly three of every 10 bricklayers and stonemasons are self-employed. Many of the self-employed specialize in contracting on small jobs such as patios, walks, and fireplaces.

Training, Other Qualifications, and Advancement
Most bricklayers and stonemasons pick up their skills informally by observing and learning from experienced workers. Many get training in vocational education schools. The best way to learn these skills, however, is through an apprenticeship program, which generally provides the most thorough training.

Individuals who learn the trade on the job usually start as helpers, laborers, or mason tenders. They carry materials, move scaffolds, and mix mortar. When the opportunity arises, they are taught to spread mortar, lay brick and block, or set stone. As they gain experience, they make the transition to full-fledged craft workers. The learning period generally lasts much longer than an apprenticeship program, however.

Apprenticeships for bricklayers and stonemasons usually are sponsored by local contractors or by local union-management committees. The apprenticeship program requires 3 years of on-the-job training in addition to a minimum 144 hours of classroom instruction each year in subjects such as blueprint reading, mathematics, layout work, and sketching.

Apprentices often start by working with laborers, carrying materials, mixing mortar, and building scaffolds. This period generally lasts about a month and familiarizes them with job routines and materials. Next, they learn to lay, align, and join brick and block. Apprentices also learn to work with stone and concrete. This enables them to be certified to work with more than one masonry material.

Applicants for apprenticeships must be at least 17 years old and in good physical condition. A high school education is preferable, and courses in mathematics, mechanical drawing, and shop are helpful. The International Masonry Institute, a division of the International Union of Bricklayers and Allied Craftsmen, operates training centers in several large cities that help job seekers develop the skills they will need to successfully complete the formal apprenticeship program.

Experienced workers can advance to supervisory positions or become estimators. They also can open contracting businesses of their own.

Job Outlook
Job opportunities for skilled bricklayers and stonemasons are expected to be good as the growth in demand outpaces the supply of workers trained in this craft. Employment of bricklayers and stonemasons is expected to grow about as fast as the average for all occupations through the year 2005, and additional openings will result from the need to replace bricklayers and stonemasons who retire, transfer to other occupations, or leave the trades for other reasons. However, the pool of young workers available to enter training programs will also be increasing slowly and many in that group are reluctant to seek training for jobs that may be strenuous and have uncomfortable working conditions.

Population and business growth will create a need for new factories, schools, hospitals, offices, and other structures, increasing the demand for bricklayers and stonemasons. Also stimulating demand will be the need to restore a growing stock of old masonry buildings, as well as the increasing use of brick for decorative work on building fronts and in lobbies and foyers. Brick exteriors should continue to be very popular as the trend continues toward more durable exterior materials requiring less maintenance. Employment of bricklayers who specialize in refractory repair will decline, along with employment in other occupations in the primary metal industries.

Employment of bricklayers and stonemasons, like that of many other construction workers, is sensitive to changes in the economy. When the level of construction activity falls, workers in these trades can experience periods of unemployment.

Earnings
Median weekly earnings for bricklayers and stonemasons were about $486 in 1994. The middle 50 percent earned between $338 and $648 weekly. The highest 10 percent earned more than $830 weekly; the lowest 10 percent, less than $261. Earnings for workers in these trades may be reduced on occasion because poor weather and downturns in construction activity limit the time they can work.

In each trade, apprentices or helpers usually start at about 50 percent of the wage rate paid to experienced workers. This increases as they gain experience.

Some bricklayers and stonemasons are members of the International Union of Bricklayers and Allied Craftsmen.

Related Occupations
Bricklayers and stonemasons combine a thorough knowledge of brick, concrete block, stone, and marble with manual skill to erect very attractive yet highly durable structures. Workers in other occupations with similar skills include concrete masons, plasterers, terrazzo workers, and tilesetters.

Sources of Additional Information
For details about apprenticeships or other work opportunities in these trades, contact local bricklaying, stonemasonry, or marble setting contractors; a local of the union listed above; a local joint union-management apprenticeship committee; or the nearest office of the State employment service or State apprenticeship agency.

For general information about the work of either bricklayers or stonemasons, contact:

☛International Union of Bricklayers and Allied Craftsmen, International Masonry Institute Apprenticeship and Training, 815 15th St. NW., Suite 1001, Washington, DC 20005.

Information about the work of bricklayers also may be obtained from:

☛Associated General Contractors of America, Inc., 1957 E St. NW., Washington, DC 20006.

☛Brick Institute of America, 11490 Commerce Park Dr., Reston, VA 22091-1525.

☛Home Builders Institute, National Association of Home Builders, 1201 15th St. NW., Washington, DC 20005.

☛National Concrete Masonry Association, 2302 Horse Pen Rd., Herndon, VA 22071.

Carpenters

(D.O.T. 806.281-058; 860.281-010 through .664-010 and .684-101 and -014; 863.684-010; 869.361-018, .381-010, -034, .684-018, -034, -042, and -058; and 962.281-010)

Nature of the Work
Carpenters are involved in many different kinds of construction activity. They cut, fit, and assemble wood and other materials in the construction of buildings, highways and bridges, docks, industrial plants, boats, and many other structures. Their duties vary by type of employer. A carpenter employed by a special trade contractor, for example, may specialize in one or two activities, such as setting forms for concrete construction or erecting scaffolding. However, a carpenter employed by a general building contractor may perform many tasks, such as framing walls and partitions, putting in doors and windows, hanging kitchen cabinets, and installing paneling and tile ceilings.

Local building codes often dictate where certain materials can be used, and carpenters have to know these requirements. Each carpentry task is somewhat different, but most tasks involve the same basic steps. Working from blueprints or instructions from supervisors, carpenters first do the layout—measuring, marking, and arranging mate-

Some carpenters specialize in setting forms for concrete construction.

rials. They then cut and shape wood, plastic, ceiling tile, fiberglass, or drywall using hand and power tools, such as chisels, planes, saws, drills, and sanders, and then join the materials with nails, screws, staples, or adhesives. In the final step, they check the accuracy of their work with levels, rules, plumb bobs, and framing squares and make any necessary adjustments. When working with prefabricated components, such as stairs or wall panels, the carpenter's task is somewhat simpler because it does not require as much layout work or the cutting and assembly of as many pieces. These components are designed for easy and fast installation and can generally be installed in a single operation.

Carpenters employed outside the construction industry do a variety of installation and maintenance work. They may replace panes of glass, ceiling tiles, and doors, as well as repair desks, cabinets, and other furniture. Depending on the employer, they may install partitions, doors, and windows; change locks; and repair broken furniture. In manufacturing firms, carpenters may assist in moving or installing machinery. (For more information on workers who install this machinery, see the statements on industrial machinery repairers and millwrights elsewhere in the *Handbook*.)

Working Conditions

As in other building trades, carpentry work is sometimes strenuous. Prolonged standing, climbing, bending, and kneeling often are necessary. Carpenters risk injury from slips or falls, from working with sharp or rough materials, and from the use of sharp tools and power equipment. Many carpenters work outdoors.

Some carpenters change employers each time they finish a construction job. Others alternate between working for a contractor and working as contractors themselves on small jobs.

Employment

Carpenters—the largest group of building trades workers—held about 992,000 jobs in 1994. Four of every 5 worked for contractors who build, remodel, or repair buildings and other structures. Most of the remainder worked for manufacturing firms, government agencies, wholesale and retail establishments, and schools. About 4 of every 10 were self-employed.

Carpenters are employed throughout the country in almost every community.

Training, Other Qualifications, and Advancement

Carpenters learn their trade through on-the-job training and through formal training programs. Some pick up skills informally by working under the supervision of experienced workers. Many acquire skills through vocational education. Others participate in employer training programs or apprenticeships.

Most employers recommend an apprenticeship as the best way to learn carpentry. Because the number of apprenticeship programs is limited, however, only a small proportion of carpenters learn their trade through these programs. Apprenticeship programs are administered by local joint union-management committees of the United Brotherhood of Carpenters and Joiners of America and the Associated General Contractors, Inc. or the National Association of Home Builders. Training programs are administered by local chapters of the Associated Builders and Contractors and by local chapters of the Associated General Contractors, Inc. These programs combine on-the-job training with related classroom instruction. Apprenticeship applicants generally must be at least 17 years old and meet local requirements. For example, some union locals test an applicant's aptitude for carpentry. The length of the program, usually about 3 to 4 years, varies with the apprentice's skill.

On the job, apprentices learn elementary structural design and become familiar with common carpentry jobs such as layout, form building, rough framing, and outside and inside finishing. They also learn to use the tools, machines, equipment, and materials of the trade. Apprentices receive classroom instruction in safety, first aid, blueprint reading and freehand sketching, basic mathematics, and different carpentry techniques. Both in the classroom and on the job, they learn the relationship between carpentry and the other building trades.

Informal on-the-job training usually is less thorough than an apprenticeship. The degree of training and supervision often depends on the size of the employing firm. A small contractor who specializes in home-building may only provide training in rough framing. In contrast, a large general contractor may provide training in several carpentry skills. Although specialization is becoming increasingly common, it is important to try to acquire skills in all aspects of carpentry to have the flexibility to be able to do whatever kind of work may be available. Carpenters with a well-rounded background can switch from residential building to commercial construction to remodeling jobs, depending on demand.

A high school education is desirable, including courses in carpentry, shop, mechanical drawing, and general mathematics. Manual dexterity, eye-hand coordination, physical fitness, and a good sense of balance are important. The ability to solve arithmetic problems quickly and accurately also is helpful. Employers and apprenticeship committees generally view favorably training and work experience obtained in the Armed Services and the job corps.

Carpenters may advance to carpentry supervisors or general construction supervisors. Carpenters usually have greater opportunities than most other construction workers to become general construction supervisors because they are exposed to the entire construction process. Some carpenters become independent contractors. To advance, carpenters should be able to estimate the nature and quantity of materials needed to properly complete a job. They also must be able to estimate with accuracy how long a job should take to complete and its cost

Job Outlook

Job opportunities for carpenters are expected to be plentiful through the year 2005, due primarily to extensive replacement needs. Well over 100,000 job openings will become available each year as carpenters transfer to other occupations or leave the labor force. The total number of job openings for carpenters each year usually is greater than for other craft occupations because the occupation is large and turnover is high. Since there are no strict training requirements for entry, many people with limited skills take jobs as carpenters but eventually leave the occupation because they find they dislike the work or cannot find steady employment.

Increased demand for carpenters will create additional job openings. Employment is expected to increase more slowly than the average for all occupations through the year 2005. Construction activity should increase slowly in response to demand for new housing and commercial and industrial plants and the need to renovate and modernize existing structures. Opportunities for frame carpenters will be particularly good. The demand for carpenters will be offset somewhat by expected productivity gains resulting from the increasing use of prefabricated components, such as prehung doors and windows and prefabricated wall panels and stairs, that can be installed much more quickly. Prefabricated walls, partitions, and stairs can be quickly lifted into place in one operation; beams, and in some cases entire roof assemblies, can be lifted into place using a crane. As prefabricated components become more standardized, their use will increase. In addition, stronger adhesives that reduce the time needed to join materials and lightweight cordless pneumatic and combustion tools such as nailers and drills, as well as sanders with electronic speed controls, will make carpenters more efficient as well as reduce fatigue.

Although employment of carpenters is expected to grow over the long run, people entering the occupation should expect to experience periods of unemployment. This results from the short-term nature of many construction projects and the cyclical nature of the construction industry. Building activity depends on many factors—interest rates, availability of mortgage funds, government spending, and business investment—that vary with the state of the economy. During economic downturns, the number of job openings for carpenters declines. The introduction of new and improved tools, equipment, techniques, and materials has vastly increased carpenters' versatility. Therefore, carpenters with all-round skills will have better opportunities than those who can only do relatively simple, routine tasks.

Job opportunities for carpenters also vary by geographic area. Construction activity parallels the movement of people and businesses and reflects differences in local economic conditions. Therefore, the number of job opportunities and apprenticeship opportunities in a given year may vary widely from area to area.

Earnings

Median weekly earnings of carpenters, excluding the self-employed, were $424 in 1994. The middle 50 percent earned between $315 and $591 per week. Weekly earnings for the top 10 percent of all carpenters were more than $785; the lowest 10 percent earned less than $252.

Earnings may be reduced on occasion because carpenters lose work time in bad weather and during recessions when jobs are unavailable.

Many carpenters are members of the United Brotherhood of Carpenters and Joiners of America.

Related Occupations

Carpenters are skilled construction workers. Workers in other skilled construction occupations include bricklayers, concrete masons, electricians, pipefitters, plasterers, plumbers, stonemasons, and terrazzo workers.

Sources of Additional Information

For information about carpentry apprenticeships or other work opportunities in this trade, contact local carpentry contractors, locals of the union mentioned above, local joint union-contractor apprenticeship committees, or the nearest office of the State employment service or State apprenticeship agency.

For general information about carpentry, contact:

☛Associated Builders and Contractors, 1300 North 17th Street, Rosslyn, VA 22209.

☛Associated General Contractors of America, Inc., 1957 E St. NW., Washington, DC 20006.

☛Home Builders Institute, National Association of Home Builders, 1201 15th St. NW., Washington, DC 20005.

☛United Brotherhood of Carpenters and Joiners of America, 101 Constitution Ave. NW., Washington, DC 20001.

Carpet Installers

(D.O.T. 864.381-010)

Nature of the Work

Many buildings—including homes, offices, stores, and restaurants—have carpet that was installed by a carpet installer. Before installing the carpet, these craft workers first inspect the surface to be covered to determine its condition and, if necessary, correct any imperfections that could show through the carpet. They must measure the area to be carpeted and plan the layout, keeping in mind expected traffic patterns and placement of seams for best appearance and maximum wear.

When installing wall-to-wall carpet without tacks, installers first fasten a tackless strip to the floor, next to the wall. They then install the padded cushion or underlay. Next, they roll out, measure, mark, and cut the carpet, allowing for 2 to 3 inches of extra carpet for the final fitting. Using a knee kicker, they position the carpet, stretching it to fit evenly on the floor and snugly against each wall and door threshold. They then rough cut the excess. Finally, using a power stretcher, they stretch the carpet, hooking it to the tackless strip to hold it in place. The installer then finishes the edges using a wall trimmer.

Because most carpet comes in 12-foot widths, wall-to-wall installations require installers to tape or sew sections together for large rooms. They join the seams by sewing them with a large needle and special thread or by using heat-taped seams—a special plastic tape made to join seams when activated with heat.

On special upholstery work, such as stairs, carpet may be held in place with staples. Also, in commercial installations, carpet is often glued directly to the floor or to padding which has been glued to the floor.

Carpet installers use handtools such as hammers, drills, staple guns, carpet knives, and rubber mallets. They also may use carpet-laying tools, such as carpet shears, knee kickers, wall trimmers, loop pile cutters, heat irons, and power stretchers.

Working Conditions

Carpet installers generally work regular daytime hours, but when recarpeting stores or offices, they may work evenings and weekends to avoid disturbing customers or employees. Installers usually work under better conditions than most other construction workers, although, the work is very labor intensive. Because carpets are installed in finished or nearly finished structures, work areas usually

When installing wall-to-wall carpet, carpet installers first lay a cushion or underlay.

are clean, well lighted, safe, and comfortable. Installers kneel, reach, bend, stretch, and frequently lift heavy rolls of carpet. They also may be required to move heavy furniture. Safety regulations may require that they wear knee pads or safety goggles when using certain tools.

Employment

Carpet installers held about 66,000 jobs in 1994. Many worked for flooring contractors or floor covering retailers. About two-thirds of all carpet installers are self-employed.

Although installers are employed throughout the Nation, they tend to be concentrated in urban areas where there are high levels of construction activity.

Training, Other Qualifications, and Advancement

The vast majority of carpet installers learn their trade informally on the job as helpers to experienced installers. Others learn through formal apprenticeship programs, which include on-the-job training as well as related classroom instruction.

Informal training is often sponsored by individual contractors and generally lasts from about 1 1/2 to 2 years. Helpers begin with simple assignments, such as installing stripping and padding, or helping stretch newly installed carpet. With experience, helpers take on more difficult assignments, such as measuring, cutting, and fitting.

Apprenticeship programs and some contractor-sponsored programs provide comprehensive training in all phases of carpet laying. Most apprenticeship programs are union sponsored and consist of weekly classes and on-the-job training that usually last 3 to 4 years.

Persons who wish to begin a career in carpet installation as a helper or apprentice should be 18 years old and have good manual dexterity. Since carpet installers frequently deal directly with customers, they should be courteous and tactful. High school graduation is preferred, though not necessary: courses in general mathematics and shop are helpful. Some employers may require a driver's license and a criminal background check.

Carpet installers may advance to positions as supervisors or installation managers for large installation firms. Some installers become salespersons or estimators. Many installers who begin working for a large contractor or installation firm also eventually go into business for themselves as independent subcontractors.

Job Outlook

Employment of carpet installers is expected to grow more slowly than the average for all occupations through the year 2005. Growth will be due primarily to the continued need to renovate and refurbish existing structures, which usually involves laying new carpet. Carpet as a floor covering continues to be popular and its usage is expected to grow in structures such as schools, offices, hospitals, and industrial plants.

Demand for carpet will also be stimulated by new, more durable fibers that are stain and crush resistant and which come in a wider variety of colors. More resilient carpet needs to be replaced less often, but these attractive new products may induce more people to replace their old carpeting, contributing further to the demand for carpet installers.

This occupation is less sensitive to changes in economic conditions than most other construction occupations. Because much of their work involves replacing carpet in existing buildings, renovation work usually allows employment of carpet installers to remain relatively stable even when new construction activity declines. In the many houses built with plywood, rather than hardwood floors, wall-to-wall carpeting is a necessity. Similarly, offices, hotels, and stores often cover concrete floors with wall-to-wall carpet, which must be periodically replaced.

Earnings

Median weekly earnings of all full-time carpet installers were about $412 in 1994. The middle 50 percent earned between $272 and $613 per week. The top 10 percent earned more than $751 and the lowest 10 percent earned less than $195.

Carpet installers get paid either on an hourly basis or by the number of yards installed. The rates vary widely depending on the geographic location and whether the installer is affiliated with a union. Nonunion carpet installers are usually paid by the number of yards installed. In 1994, they received between $1.50 and $3.00 a yard. According to limited information available, union carpet installers earned between $16 and $25 an hour in 1994, including benefits. Benefits average about $3.50 to $4.00 an hour, most of which is for health insurance. Apprentices and other trainees usually start out earning about half of what an experienced worker earns, though their wage rate increases as they advance through the training program. Some installers belong to the United Brotherhood of Carpenters and Joiners of America or the International Brotherhood of Painters and Allied Trades.

Related Occupations

Carpet installers measure, cut, and fit carpet materials. Workers in other occupations involving similar skills but using different materials include carpenters, cement masons, drywall installers, floor layers, lathers, painters and paperhangers, roofers, sheet-metal workers, terrazzo workers, and tilesetters.

Sources of Additional Information

For details about apprenticeships or work opportunities, contact local flooring contractors or retailers; locals of the unions previously mentioned; or the nearest office of the State apprenticeship agency or the State employment service.

For general information about the work of carpet installers, contact:

☛Floor Covering Installation Contractors Association, P.O. Box 948, Dalton, GA 30722-0948.

For information concerning training contact:

☛United Brotherhood of Carpenters and Joiners of America, 101 Constitution Ave. NW., Washington, DC 20001.

☛International Brotherhood of Painters and Allied Trades, 1750 New York Ave. NW., Washington, DC 20006.

☛New York City District Council of Carpenters Labor Technical College, 395 Hudson St., New York, NY 10014.

Concrete Masons and Terrazzo Workers

(D.O.T. 844.364-010, -014, . 461-010, .684-010; and 861.381-046, and -050)

Nature of the Work

Concrete—a mixture of Portland cement, sand, gravel, and water—is used for many types of construction projects. Whether small jobs, such as patios and floors, or huge dams or miles of roadway, *concrete masons* place and finish the concrete. They also may color concrete surfaces, expose aggregate (small stones) in walls and sidewalks, or fabricate concrete beams, columns, and panels.

Terrazzo workers create attractive walkways, floors, patios, and panels by exposing marble chips and other fine aggregates on the surface of finished concrete. Much of the preliminary work of terrazzo workers is similar to that of concrete masons.

In preparing a site for placing concrete, masons set the forms for holding the concrete to the desired pitch and depth and properly align them. They then direct the casting of the concrete and supervise laborers who use shovels or special tools to spread it. Masons then guide a straightedge back and forth across the top of the forms to "screed," or level, the freshly placed concrete. Immediately after leveling the concrete, masons carefully smooth the concrete surface with a "bull float," a long-handled tool about 8 by 48 inches that covers the coarser materials in the concrete and brings a rich mixture of fine cement paste to the surface.

After the concrete has been leveled and floated, finishers press an edger between the forms and the concrete and guide it along the edge and the surface. This produces slightly rounded edges and helps prevent chipping or cracking. They use a special tool called a "groover" to make joints or grooves at specific intervals that help control cracking. Next, finishers trowel the surface using either a powered or a hand trowel, a small, smooth, rectangular metal tool. Troweling removes most imperfections and brings the fine cement paste to the surface.

As the final step, masons retrowel the concrete surface back and forth with powered and hand trowels to create a smooth finish. For a coarse, nonskid finish, masons brush the surface with a broom or stiff-bristled brush. For a pebble finish, they embed small gravel chips into the surface. They then wash any excess cement from the exposed chips with a mild acid solution. For color, they use colored premixed concrete. On concrete surfaces that will remain exposed after forms are stripped, such as columns, ceilings, and wall panels, concrete masons cut away high spots and loose concrete with hammer and chisel, fill any large indentations with a Portland cement paste and smooth the surface with a rubbing carborundum stone. Finally, they coat the exposed area with a rich Portland cement mixture using either a special tool or a coarse cloth to rub the concrete to a uniform finish.

Attractive, marble-chip terrazzo requires three layers of materials. First, concrete masons or terrazzo workers build a solid, level concrete foundation that is 3 to 4 inches deep. After the forms are removed from the foundation, workers place a 1-inch deep mixture of sandy concrete. Before this layer sets, terrazzo workers partially embed metal divider strips into the concrete wherever there is to be a joint or change of color in the terrazzo. These strips separate the different designs and colors of the terrazzo panels and help prevent cracks. For the final layer, terrazzo workers blend and place a fine marble chip mixture that may be color-pigmented into each of the panels, then hand trowel each panel until it is level with the tops of the ferrule strips. While the mixture is still wet, workers toss additional marble chips of various colors into each panel and roll a lightweight roller over the entire surface.

When the terrazzo is thoroughly dry, helpers grind it with a terrazzo grinder (somewhat like a floor polisher, only much heavier). Slight depressions left by the grinding are filled with a matching grout material and hand troweled for a smooth, uniform surface.

Concrete masons set the forms for holding the concrete.

Terrazzo workers then clean, polish, and seal the dry surface for a lustrous finish.

Working Conditions

Concrete or terrazzo work is fast paced and strenuous. Since most finishing is done at floor level, workers must bend and kneel a lot. Many jobs are outdoors, but work is generally halted during rain or freezing weather. To avoid chemical burns from uncured concrete and sore knees from frequent kneeling, many workers wear kneepads. Workers usually wear water-repellent boots while working in wet concrete.

Employment

Concrete masons and terrazzo workers held about 126,000 jobs in 1994; terrazzo workers accounted for a very small proportion of the total. Most concrete masons worked for concrete contractors or for general contractors on projects such as highways, bridges, shopping malls, or large buildings such as factories, schools, or hospitals. A small number were employed by firms that manufacture concrete products. Most terrazzo workers worked for special trade contractors who install decorative floors and wall panels.

Fewer than 1 out of 10 concrete masons and terrazzo workers was self-employed, a smaller proportion than in other building trades. Most self-employed masons specialized in small jobs, such as driveways, sidewalks, and patios.

Training, Other Qualifications, and Advancement

Concrete masons and terrazzo workers learn their trades either through on-the-job training as helpers or through 3-year apprenticeship programs. Many masons first gain experience as construction laborers.

When hiring helpers and apprentices, employers prefer high school graduates who are at least 18 years old, in good physical condition, and licensed to drive. The ability to get along with others also is important because concrete masons frequently work in teams. High school courses in shop mathematics and blueprint reading or mechanical drawing provide a helpful background.

On-the-job training programs consist of informal instruction from experienced workers in which helpers learn to use the tools, equipment, machines, and materials of the trade. They begin with tasks such as edging and jointing and using a straightedge on freshly placed concrete. As they progress, assignments become more complex, and trainees usually can do finishing work within a short time.

Three-year apprenticeship programs, usually jointly sponsored by local unions and contractors, provide on-the-job training in addition to a recommended minimum of 144 hours of classroom instruction each year. A written test and a physical exam may be required. In the classroom, apprentices learn applied mathematics, blueprint reading, and safety. Apprentices generally receive special instruction in layout work and cost estimating.

Experienced concrete masons or terrazzo workers may advance to become supervisors or contract estimators. Some open their own concrete contracting businesses.

Job Outlook

Employment of concrete masons and terrazzo workers is expected to grow about as fast as the average for all occupations through the year 2005. In addition to job openings that will stem from the rising demand for the services of these workers, other jobs will become available as experienced workers transfer to other occupations or leave the labor force.

The demand for concrete masons and terrazzo workers will rise as the population and the economy grow. More masons will be needed to build highways, bridges, subways, factories, office buildings, hotels, shopping centers, schools, hospitals, and other structures. In addition, the increasing use of concrete as a building material—particularly in nonresidential construction—will add to the demand.

More concrete masons also will be needed to repair and renovate existing highways, bridges, and other structures.

Employment growth of concrete masons and terrazzo workers, however, will not keep pace with the growth of these construction projects. Nevertheless, their productivity will increase as a result of the use of improved concrete pumping systems, continuous concrete mixers, quicker setting cement, troweling machines, prefabricated masonry systems, and other improved materials, equipment, and tools.

Employment of concrete masons and terrazzo workers, like that of many other workers, is sensitive to the ups and downs in the economy. Workers in these trades may experience periods of unemployment when the level of nonresidential construction falls. On the other hand, shortages of these workers may occur in some areas during peak periods of building activity.

Earnings

Median weekly earnings of full-time concrete masons and terazzo workers were about $407 in 1994. The middle 50 percent earned between $310 and $528 per week. The top 10 percent earned more than $701 and the lowest 10 percent earned less than $231.

According to the limited information available, average hourly earnings—including benefits—for concrete masons who belonged to a union and worked full time ranged between $15.90 and $42.16 in 1994. Concrete masons in, New York, Boston, San Francisco, Chicago, Los Angeles, Philadelphia, and other large cities received the highest wages. Nonunion workers generally have lower wage rates than union workers. Apprentices usually start at 50 to 60 percent of the rate paid to experienced workers.

Concrete masons often work overtime, with premium pay, because once concrete has been placed, the job must be completed.

Annual earnings of concrete masons and terrazzo workers may be lower than the hourly rates suggest because bad weather and downturns in construction activity can limit the time they can work.

Many concrete masons and terrazzo workers belong to the Operative Plasterers' and Cement Masons' International Association of the United States and Canada, or to the International Union of Bricklayers and Allied Craftsmen. Some terrazzo workers belong to the United Brotherhood of Carpenters and Joiners of the United States.

Related Occupations

Concrete masons and terrazzo workers combine skill with knowledge of building materials to construct buildings, highways, and other structures. Other occupations involving similar skills and knowledge include bricklayers, form builders, marble setters, plasterers, stonemasons, and tilesetters.

Sources of Additional Information

For information about apprenticeships and work opportunities, contact local concrete or terrazzo contractors; locals of unions previously mentioned; a local joint union-management apprenticeship committee; or the nearest office of the State employment service or apprenticeship agency.

For general information about concrete masons and terrazzo workers, contact:

☛Associated General Contractors of America, Inc., 1957 E St. NW., Washington, DC 20006.

☛International Union of Bricklayers and Allied Craftsmen, International Masonry Institute Apprenticeship and Training, 815 15th St. NW., Suite 1001, Washington, DC 20005.

☛Operative Plasterers' and Cement Masons' International Association of the United States and Canada, 1125 17th St. NW., Washington, DC 20036.

☛National Terrazzo and Mosaic Association, 3166 Des Plaines Ave., Suite 132, Des Plaines, IL 60018.

☛Portland Cement Association, 5420 Old Orchard Rd., Skokie, IL 60077.

☛United Brotherhood of Carpenters and Joiners of America, 101 Constitution Ave. NW., Washington, DC 20001.

Drywall Workers and Lathers

(D.O.T. 842.361-010, -014, and -030, .664-010, .684-014; and 869.684-050)

Nature of the Work

Drywall consists of a thin layer of gypsum sandwiched between two layers of heavy paper. It is used today for walls and ceilings in most buildings because it is both faster and cheaper to install than plaster.

There are two kinds of drywall workers: installers and finishers. *Installers*, also called *applicators*, fasten drywall panels to the inside framework of residential houses and other buildings. *Finishers*, or *tapers*, prepare these panels for painting by taping and finishing joints and imperfections.

Because drywall panels are manufactured in standard sizes— usually 4 feet by 8 or 12 feet—installers must measure, cut, and fit some pieces around doors and windows. They also saw or cut holes in panels for electrical outlets, air-conditioning units, and plumbing. After making these alterations, installers may glue, nail, or screw the wallboard panels to the wood or metal framework. Because drywall is heavy and cumbersome, a helper generally assists the installer in positioning and securing the panel. A lift is often used when placing ceiling panels.

After the drywall is installed, finishers fill joints between panels with a joint compound. Using the wide, flat tip of a special trowel, they spread the joint compound into and along each side of the joint with brushlike strokes. They immediately use the trowel to press a paper tape—used to reinforce the drywall and to hide imperfections—into the wet compound and to smooth away excess material. Nail and screw depressions also are covered with this compound, as are imperfections caused by the installation of air-conditioning vents and other fixtures. On large commercial projects, finishers may use automatic taping tools that apply the joint compound and tape in one step. Finishers apply second and third coats, sanding the treated areas after each coat to make them as smooth as the rest of the wall surface. This results in a very smooth and almost perfect surface. Some finishers apply textured surfaces to walls and ceilings with trowels, brushes, or spray guns.

Lathers apply metal or gypsum lath to walls, ceilings, or ornamental frameworks to form the support base for plaster coatings. Gypsum lath is similar to a drywall panel, but smaller. Metal lath is used where the plaster application will be exposed to weather or water, or for curved or irregular surfaces for which drywall is not a practical material. Lathers usually nail, screw, staple, or wire-tie the lath directly to the structural framework.

Drywall workers install metal lathing around windows.

Working Conditions

As in other construction trades, drywall and lathing work sometimes is strenuous. Applicators, tapers, finishers, and lathers spend most of the day on their feet, either standing, bending, or kneeling. Some finishers use stilts to tape and finish ceiling and angle joints. Installers have to lift and maneuver heavy panels. Hazards include falls from ladders and scaffolds, and injuries from power tools. Because sanding joint compound to a smooth finish creates a great deal of dust, some finishers wear masks for protection.

Employment

Drywall workers and lathers held about 133,000 jobs in 1994. Most worked for contractors who specialize in drywall or lathing installation; others worked for contractors who do many kinds of construction. Nearly one-third were self employed independent contractors.

Most installers, finishers, and lathers are employed in urban areas. In other areas, where there may not be enough work to keep a drywall worker or lather employed full time, the work is usually done by carpenters and painters.

Training, Other Qualifications, and Advancement

Most drywall and lathing workers start as helpers and learn their skills on the job. Installer and lather helpers start by carrying materials, lifting and holding panels, and cleaning up debris. Within a few weeks, they learn to measure, cut, and install materials. Eventually, they become fully experienced workers. Finisher apprentices begin by taping joints and touching up nail holes, scrapes, and other imperfections. They soon learn to install corner guards and to conceal openings around pipes. At the end of their training, they learn to estimate the cost of installing and finishing drywall and gypsum lath.

Some installers and lathers learn their trade in an apprenticeship program. The United Brotherhood of Carpenters and Joiners of America, in cooperation with local contractors, administers an apprenticeship program in carpentry that includes instruction in drywall and lath installation. In addition, local affiliates of the Associated Builders and Contractors and the National Association of Home Builders conduct training programs for nonunion workers. The International Brotherhood of Painters and Allied Trades conducts a 2-year apprenticeship program for drywall finishers.

Employers prefer high school graduates who are in good physical condition, but they frequently hire applicants with less education. High school or vocational school courses in carpentry provide a helpful background for drywall work. Regardless of educational background, installers must be good at simple arithmetic.

Drywall workers and lathers with a few years' experience and leadership ability may become supervisors. Some workers start their own contracting businesses.

Job Outlook

Replacement needs will account for almost all job openings for drywall workers and lathers through the year 2005. Tens of thousands of jobs will open up each year because of the need to replace workers who transfer to jobs in other occupations or leave the labor force. Turnover in this occupation is very high, reflecting the lack of formal training requirements and the ups and downs of the business cycle, to which the construction industry is very sensitive. Because of their relatively weak attachment to the occupation, many workers with limited skills leave the occupation when they find they dislike the work or because they can't find steady employment.

Additional job openings will be created by the rising demand for drywall work. Employment is expected to grow more slowly than the average for all occupations, reflecting the slow growth of new construction and renovation. In addition to traditional interior work, the growing acceptance of insulated exterior wall systems will provide additional jobs for drywall workers.

Despite the growing use of exterior panels, most drywall installation, finishing, and lathing are usually done indoors. Therefore, these workers lose less work time because of bad weather than some other construction workers. Nevertheless, they may be unemployed between construction projects and during downturns in construction activity.

Earnings

Median weekly earnings for drywall workers and lathers were about $419 in 1994. The middle 50 percent earned between $311 and $596 weekly. The top 10 percent earned over $818 and the bottom 10 percent earned less than $257 a week. Trainees usually started at about half the rate paid to experienced workers and received wage increases as they became more highly skilled.

Some contractors pay these workers according to the number of panels they install or finish per day; others pay an hourly rate. A 40-hour week is standard, but sometimes the workweek may be longer. Those who are paid hourly rates receive premium pay for overtime.

Related Occupations

Drywall workers and lathers combine strength and dexterity with precision and accuracy to make materials fit according to a plan. Other occupations that require similar abilities include carpenters, floor covering installers, form builders, insulation workers, and plasterers.

Sources of Additional Information

For information about work opportunities in drywall application and finishing, contact local drywall installation contractors; a local of the unions previously mentioned; a local joint union-management apprenticeship committee; a State or local chapter of the Associated Builders and Contractors; or the nearest office of the State employment service or State apprenticeship agency.

For details about job qualifications and training programs in drywall application and finishing, write to:

☛Associated Builders and Contractors, Inc., 1300 North 17th St., Rosslyn, VA 22209.

☛International Brotherhood of Painters and Allied Trades, 1750 New York Ave. NW., Washington, DC 20006.

For information on training programs in drywall application and lathing, write to:

☛United Brotherhood of Carpenters and Joiners of America, 101 Constitution Ave. NW., Washington, DC 20001.

☛Home Builders Institute, National Association of Home Builders, 1201 15th St. NW., Washington, DC 20005.

Electricians

(D.O.T. 729.381-018; 806.381-062; 822.361-018, -022; 824.261, .281-010, -018, .381, .681; 825.381-030, -034; 829.261-018; and 952.364 and .381)

Nature of the Work

Electricity is essential for light, power, air-conditioning, and refrigeration. Electricians install, connect, test, and maintain electrical systems for a variety of purposes, including climate control, security, and communications. They also may install and maintain the electronic controls for machines in business and industry. Although most electricians specialize in either construction or maintenance, a growing number do both.

Electricians work with blueprints when they install electrical systems in factories, office buildings, homes, and other structures. Blueprints indicate the location of circuits, outlets, load centers, panel boards, and other equipment. Electricians must follow the National Electric Code and comply with State and local building codes when they install these systems. In factories and offices, they first place conduit (pipe or tubing) inside designated partitions, walls, or other concealed areas. They also fasten to the wall small metal or plastic boxes that will house electrical switches and outlets. They

Electricians join wires by twisting their ends together and covering them with plastic connectors.

then pull insulated wires or cables through the conduit to complete circuits between these boxes. In lighter construction, such as residential, plastic-covered wire usually is used rather than conduit.

Regardless of the type of wire being used, electricians connect it to circuit breakers, transformers, or other components. Wires are joined by twisting ends together with pliers and covering the ends with special plastic connectors. When stronger connections are required, electricians may use an electric "soldering gun" to melt metal onto the twisted wires, which they then cover with durable electrical tape. When the wiring is finished, they test the circuits for proper connections.

In addition to wiring a building's electrical system, electricians may install coaxial or fiber optic cable for computers and other telecommunications equipment. A growing number of electricians install telephone and computer wiring and equipment. They also may connect motors to electrical power and install electronic controls for industrial equipment.

Maintenance work varies greatly, depending on where the electrician is employed. Electricians who specialize in residential work may rewire a home and replace an old fuse box with a new circuit breaker to accommodate additional appliances. Those who work in large factories may repair motors, transformers, generators, and electronic controllers on machine tools and industrial robots. Those in office buildings and small plants may repair all kinds of electrical equipment.

Maintenance electricians spend much of their time in preventive maintenance. They periodically inspect equipment and locate and correct problems before breakdowns occur. Electricians also may advise management whether continued operation of equipment could be hazardous. When needed, they install new electrical equipment. When breakdowns occur, they must make the necessary repairs as quickly as possible in order to minimize inconvenience. Electricians may replace items such as circuit breakers, fuses, switches, electrical and electronic components, or wire. When working with complex electronic devices, they may work with engineers, engineering technicians, or industrial machinery repairers. (For information about each of these occupations, see the statements located elsewhere in the *Handbook*.)

Electricians use handtools such as screwdrivers, pliers, knives, and hacksaws. They also use power tools and testing equipment such as oscilloscopes, ammeters, and test lamps.

Working Conditions

Electricians' work is sometimes strenuous. They may stand for long periods and frequently work on ladders and scaffolds. They often work in awkward or cramped positions. Electricians risk injury from electrical shock, falls, and cuts; to avoid injuries, they must follow strict safety procedures. Some electricians may have to travel to job sites, which may be up to 100 miles away.

Most electricians work a standard 40-hour week, although overtime may be required. Those in maintenance work may have to work nights, on weekends, and be on call. Companies that operate 24 hours a day may employ 3 shifts of electricians. Generally, the first shift is primarily responsible for routine maintenance, while the other shifts perform preventive maintenance.

Employment

Electricians held about 528,000 jobs in 1994. More than half were employed in the construction industry. Others worked as maintenance electricians and were employed in virtually every industry. In addition, about 1 out of 10 electricians was self-employed.

Because of the widespread need for electrical services, jobs for electricians are found in all parts of the country.

Training, Other Qualifications, and Advancement

The best way to learn the electrical trade is by completing a 4- or 5-year apprenticeship program. Apprenticeship gives trainees a thorough knowledge of all aspects of the trade and generally improves their ability to find a job. Although more electricians are trained through apprenticeship than workers in other construction trades, some still learn their skills informally on the job.

Large apprenticeship programs are usually sponsored by joint training committees made up of local unions of the International Brotherhood of Electrical Workers and local chapters of the National Electrical Contractors Association. Training may also be provided by company management committees of individual electrical contracting companies and by local chapters of the Associated Builders and Contractors and the Independent Electrical Contractors. Because of the comprehensive training received, those who complete apprenticeship programs qualify to do both maintenance and construction work.

The typical large apprenticeship program provides at least 144 hours of classroom instruction each year and 8,000 hours of on-the-job training over the course of the apprenticeship. In the classroom, apprentices learn blueprint reading, electrical theory, electronics, mathematics, electrical code requirements, and safety and first aid practices. They also receive specialized training in welding and communications and fire alarm systems. On the job, under the supervision of experienced electricians, apprentices must demonstrate mastery of the electrician's work. At first, they drill holes, set anchors, and set up conduit. Later, they measure, fabricate, and install conduit, as well as install, connect, and test wiring, outlets, and switches. They also learn to set up and draw diagrams for entire electrical systems.

Those who do not enter a formal apprenticeship program can begin to learn the trade informally by working as helpers for experienced electricians. While learning to install conduit, connect wires, and test circuits, helpers also are taught safety practices. Many helpers supplement this training with trade school or correspondence courses.

Regardless of how one learns the trade, previous training is very helpful. High school courses in mathematics, electricity, electronics, mechanical drawing, science, and shop provide a good background. Special training offered in the Armed Forces and by postsecondary technical schools also is beneficial. All applicants should be in good health and have at least average physical strength. Agility and dexterity also are important. Good color vision is needed because workers frequently must identify electrical wires by color.

Most apprenticeship sponsors require applicants for apprentice positions to be at least 18 years old and have a high school diploma or its equivalent. For those interested in becoming maintenance electricians, a background in electronics is increasingly important because of the growing use of complex electronic controls on manufacturing equipment.

Most localities require electricians to be licensed. Although licensing requirements vary from area to area, electricians generally must pass an examination that tests their knowledge of electrical theory, the National Electrical Code, and local electric and building codes.

Electricians periodically take courses offered by their employer or union to keep abreast of changes in the National Electrical Code, materials, or methods of installation.

Experienced electricians can become supervisors and then superintendents. Those with sufficient capital and management skills may start their own contracting business, although this may require an electrical contractor's license.

Job Outlook

Job opportunities for skilled electricians are expected to be good as the growth in demand outpaces the supply of workers trained in this craft. There is expected to be a shortage of skilled workers during the next decade because of the anticipated smaller pool of young workers entering training programs.

Employment of electricians is expected to increase more slowly than the average for all occupations through the year 2005. As population and the economy grow, more electricians will be needed to install and maintain electrical devices and wiring in homes, factories, offices, and other structures. New technologies also are expected to continue to stimulate the demand for these workers. Increasingly, buildings will be prewired during construction to accommodate use of computers and telecommunications equipment. More and more factories will be using robots and automated manufacturing systems. Installation of this equipment, which is expected to increase, also should stimulate demand for electricians. Additional jobs will be created by rehabilitation and retrofitting of existing structures.

In addition to jobs created by increased demand for electrical work, many openings will occur each year as electricians transfer to other occupations, retire, or leave the labor force for other reasons. Because of their lengthy training and relatively high earnings, a smaller proportion of electricians than other craft workers leave their occupation each year. The number of retirements is expected to rise, however, as more electricians reach retirement age.

Employment of construction electricians like that of many other construction workers, is sensitive to changes in the economy. This results from the limited duration of construction projects and the cyclical nature of the construction industry. During economic downturns, job openings for electricians are reduced as the level of construction declines. Apprenticeship opportunities also are less plentiful during these periods.

Although employment of maintenance electricians is steadier than that of construction electricians, those working in the automotive and other manufacturing industries that are sensitive to cyclical swings in the economy may be laid off during recessions. Also, efforts to reduce operating costs and increase productivity through the increased use of contracting out for electrical services may limit opportunities for maintenance electricians in many industries. However, this should be partially offset by increased demand by electrical contracting firms.

Job opportunities for electricians also vary by geographic area. Employment opportunities follow the movement of people and businesses among States and local areas and reflect differences in local economic conditions. The number of job opportunities in a given year may fluctuate widely from area to area. Some parts of the country may experience an oversupply of electricians, for example, while others may have a shortage.

Earnings

Median weekly earnings for full-time electricians who were not self-employed were $574 in 1994. The middle 50 percent earned between $415 and $754 weekly. The lowest 10 percent earned less than $301, while the highest 10 percent earned more than $971 a week.

According to a survey of workplaces in 160 metropolitan areas, maintenance electricians had median hourly earnings of $17.45 in 1993. The middle half earned between $14.00 and $20.25 an hour. Annual earnings of electricians also tend to be higher than those of other building trades workers because electricians are less affected by the seasonal nature of construction.

Depending on experience, apprentices usually start at between 30 and 50 percent of the rate paid to experienced electricians. As they become more skilled, they receive periodic increases throughout the course of the apprenticeship program. Many employers also provide training opportunities for experienced electricians to improve their skills.

Many construction electricians are members of the International Brotherhood of Electrical Workers. Among unions organizing maintenance electricians are the International Brotherhood of Electrical Workers; the International Union of Electronic, Electrical, Salaried, Machine, and Furniture Workers; the International Association of Machinists and Aerospace Workers; the International Union, United Automobile, Aerospace and Agricultural Implement Workers of America; and the United Steelworkers of America.

Related Occupations

To install and maintain electrical systems, electricians combine manual skill and a knowledge of electrical materials and concepts. Workers in other occupations involving similar skills include air-conditioning mechanics, cable installers and repairers, electronics mechanics, and elevator constructors.

Sources of Additional Information

For details about apprenticeships or other work opportunities in this trade, contact offices of the State employment service, the State apprenticeship agency, local electrical contractors or firms that employ maintenance electricians, or local union-management electrician apprenticeship committees. This information may also be available from local chapters of the Independent Electrical Contractors, Inc.: the National Electrical Contractors Association; the Home Builders Institute; the Associated Builders and Contractors; and the International Brotherhood of Electrical Workers.

For general information about the work of electricians, contact:

☛Independent Electrical Contractors, Inc., 507 Wythe St., Alexandria, VA 22314.

☛National Electrical Contractors Association (NECA), 3 Metro Center, Suite 1100, Bethesda, MD 20814.

☛International Brotherhood of Electrical Workers (IBEW), 1125 15th St. NW., Washington, DC 20005.

☛Associated Builders and Contractors, 1300 North 17th St., Rosslyn, VA 22209.

☛Homebuilders Institute, National Association of Home Builders, 1201 15th St. NW., Washington, DC 20005.

Glaziers

(D.O.T. 865.361 and .381)

Nature of the Work

Glass serves many uses in modern buildings. Insulated and specially treated glass keeps in warmed or cooled air and provides good condensation and sound control qualities; tempered and laminated glass makes doors and windows more secure. In large commercial buildings, glass panels give skyscrapers a distinctive look while reducing the need for artificial lighting. The creative use of large windows, glass doors, skylights, and sun room additions make homes bright, airy, and inviting.

Glaziers generally work on four types of projects. Residential glazing involves work such as replacing glass in home windows, installing glass mirrors, shower doors and bathtub enclosures, and glass for table tops and display cases. On commercial interior projects, glaziers install items such as heavy, often etched, decorative room dividers and windows with speak holes and security glazing. Glazing projects may also involve replacement of storefront windows for establishments such as stores, supermarkets, auto dealerships, and banks. In construction of large commercial buildings, glaziers build metal framework extrusions and install glass panels or curtainwalls.

Glaziers select, cut, install, and remove all types of glass as well as plastics, granite, marble, and similar materials used as glass substitutes. They may mount steel and aluminum sashes or frames and attach locks and hinges to glass doors. For most jobs, the glass is precut and mounted in frames at a factory or a contractor's shop. It arrives at the job site ready for glaziers to position and secure it in place. They may use a crane or hoist with suction cups to lift large, heavy pieces of glass. They then gently guide the glass into position by hand.

Once glaziers have the glass in place, they secure it with mastic, putty, or other pastelike cement, or with bolts, rubber gaskets, glazing compound, metal clips, or metal or wood molding. When they secure glass using a rubber gasket—a thick, molded rubber half-tube with a split running its length—they first secure the gasket around the perimeter within the opening, then set the glass into the split side of the gasket, causing it to clamp to the edges and hold the glass firmly in place.

When they use metal clips and wood molding, glaziers first secure the molding to the opening, place the glass in the molding, and then force spring-like metal clips between the glass and the molding. The clips exert pressure and keep the glass firmly in place.

When a glazing compound is used, glaziers first spread it neatly against and around the edges of the molding on the inside of the opening. Next, they install the glass. Pressing it against the compound on the inside molding, workers screw or nail outside molding that loosely holds the glass in place. To hold it firmly, they pack the space between the molding and the glass with glazing compound and then trim any excess material with a glazing knife.

For some jobs, the glazier must cut the glass manually at the job site. To prepare the glass for cutting, glaziers rest it either on edge on a rack or "A-frame" or flat against a cutting table. They then measure and mark the glass for the cut.

Glaziers cut glass with a special tool that has a very hard metal wheel about 1/6 inch in diameter. Using a straightedge as a guide, the glazier presses the cutter's wheel firmly on the glass, guiding and rolling it carefully to make a score just below the surface. To help

Glaziers often work in pairs.

the cutting tool move smoothly across the glass, workers brush a thin layer of oil along the line of the intended cut or dip the cutting tool in oil. Immediately after cutting, the glazier presses on the shorter end of the glass to break it cleanly along the cut.

In addition to handtools such as glass cutters, suction cups, and glazing knives, glaziers use power tools such as saws, drills, cutters, and grinders. An increasing number of glaziers use computers in the shop or at the job site to improve their layout work and reduce the amount of glass that is wasted.

Working Conditions

Glaziers often work outdoors, sometimes in inclement weather. At times they work on scaffolds at great heights. They do a considerable amount of bending, kneeling, lifting, and standing. Glaziers may be injured by broken glass or cutting tools, falls from scaffolds, or from improperly lifting heavy glass panels.

Employment

Glaziers held about 34,000 jobs in 1994. Most worked for glazing contractors engaged in new construction, alteration, and repair. Others worked for retail glass shops that install or replace glass and for wholesale distributors of products containing glass. Glaziers work throughout the country, but jobs are concentrated in metropolitan areas.

Training, Other Qualifications, and Advancement

Many glaziers learn the trade informally on the job. They usually start as helpers, carrying glass and cleaning up debris in glass shops. They often practice cutting on discarded glass. After a while they are given an opportunity to cut glass for a job. Eventually, helpers assist experienced workers on simple installation jobs. By working with experienced glaziers, they eventually acquire the skills of a fully qualified glazier.

Employers recommend that glaziers learn the trade through a formal apprenticeship program that lasts 3 to 4 years. Apprenticeship programs, which are administered by the National Glass Association and local union-management committees or local contractors' associations, consist of on-the-job training, as well as 144 hours of classroom instruction or home study each year. On the job, apprentices learn to use the tools and equipment of the trade; handle, measure, cut, and install glass and metal framing; cut and fit moldings; and install and balance glass doors. In the classroom, they are taught basic mathematics, blueprint reading and sketching, general construction techniques, safety practices, and first aid. Learning the trade through an apprenticeship program usually takes less time and provides more complete training than acquiring skills informally on the job, but opportunities for apprenticeships are declining.

Local apprenticeship administrators determine how apprentices are recruited and selected. In general, applicants for apprenticeships and for helper positions must be in good physical condition and at least 17 years old. High school or vocational school graduates are preferred. In some areas, applicants must take mechanical aptitude tests. Courses in general mathematics, blueprint reading or mechanical drawing, general construction, and shop provide a good background.

Standards for acceptance into apprenticeship programs are rising to reflect changing requirements associated with new products and equipment. Glaziers need a basic understanding of electricity and electronics in order to be able to install electrochromatic glass and electronically controlled glass doors. In addition, the growing use of computers in glass layout requires more and more that glaziers be familiar with personal computers.

Because many glaziers do not learn the trade through a formal apprenticeship program, the National Glass Association (NGA) offers a series of written examinations which certify an individual's competency to perform glazier work at three progressively more difficult levels of proficiency. These levels include Level I, Glazier;

Level II, Commercial Interior/Residential Glazier or Storefront/Curtainwall Glazier; and Level III, Master Glazier.

Advancement generally consists of increases in pay for most glaziers; some advance to supervisory jobs or become contractors or estimators.

Job Outlook

Employment of glaziers is expected to increase more slowly than the average for all occupations through the year 2005 as a result of anticipated slow growth in residential and non-residential construction. Demand for glaziers will be spurred by the continuing need to modernize and repair existing structures and the popularity of glass in bathroom and kitchen design. Improved glass performance in insulation, privacy, safety, condensation control, and noise reduction are also expected to contribute to the demand for glaziers. In addition, job openings for glaziers will occur each year due to the need to replace experienced workers who retire or leave the occupation for other reasons.

People wishing to become construction glaziers should expect to experience periods of unemployment. These result from the limited duration of construction projects and the cyclical nature of the construction industry. During bad economic times, job openings for glaziers are reduced as the level of construction declines. Because construction activity varies from area to area, job openings—as well as apprenticeship opportunities—fluctuate with local economic conditions. Consequently, some parts of the country may experience an oversupply of these workers while others may have a shortage. Employment and apprenticeship opportunities should be greatest in metropolitan areas, where most glazing contractors and glass shops are located.

Earnings

The median weekly earnings of glaziers were about $420 a week in 1994. The middle 50 percent earned between $330 and $530 a week. The lowest paid 10 percent earned less than $240 a week, while 10 percent with the highest pay earned $660 or more a week.

According to the *Engineering News Record*, union glaziers received an average hourly wage of $26.05 in 1994, including benefits. Wages ranged from a low of $15.80 in Dallas to a high of $40.27 in New York City. Glaziers covered by union contracts generally earn more than their non-union counterparts. Apprentice wage rates usually start at 50 to 60 percent of the rate paid to experienced glaziers and increase every 6 months. Because glaziers can lose time due to weather conditions and fluctuations in construction activity, their overall earnings may be lower than their hourly wages suggest.

Many glaziers employed in construction are members of the International Brotherhood of Painters and Allied Trades.

Related Occupations

Glaziers use their knowledge of construction materials and techniques to install glass. Other construction workers whose jobs also involve skilled, custom work are bricklayers, carpenters, floor layers, paperhangers, terrazzo workers, and tilesetters.

Sources of Additional Information

For more information about glazier apprenticeships or work opportunities, contact local glazing or general contractors; a local of the International Brotherhood of Painters and Allied Trades; a local joint union-management apprenticeship agency; or the nearest office of the State employment service or State apprenticeship agency.

For general information about the work of glaziers, contact:
☛International Brotherhood of Painters and Allied Trades, 1750 New York Ave. NW., Washington, DC 20006.

For information concerning training for glaziers contact:
☛National Glass Association, Education and Training Department, 8200 Greensboro Dr., 3rd floor, McLean, VA 22102.
☛Glass Association of North America, White Lakes Professional Building, 3310 Southwest Harrison St., Topeka, KS 66611-2279.

Insulation Workers

(D.O.T. 863.364-010 and -014, .381-010 and -014, .664-010, and .685-010)

Nature of the Work

Properly insulated buildings reduce energy consumption by keeping heat in during the winter and out in the summer. Refrigerated storage rooms, vats, tanks, vessels, boilers, and steam and hot water pipes also are insulated to prevent the wasteful transfer of heat. Insulation workers install this insulating material.

Insulation workers cement, staple, wire, tape, or spray insulation. When covering a steam pipe, for example, insulation workers measure and cut sections of insulation to the proper length, stretch it open along a cut that runs the length of the material, and slip it over the pipe. They fasten the insulation with adhesive, staples, tape, or wire bands. Sometimes they wrap a cover of aluminum, plastic, or canvas over it and cement or band the cover in place. Sometimes insulation workers screw on sheet metal around insulated pipes to protect the insulation from weather conditions or physical abuse.

When covering a wall or other flat surface, workers may use a hose to spray foam insulation onto a wire mesh. The wire mesh provides a rough surface to which the foam can cling and adds strength to the finished surface. Workers may then install drywall or apply a final coat of plaster for a finished appearance.

In attics or exterior walls of uninsulated buildings, workers blow in loose-fill insulation. A helper feeds a machine with shredded fiberglass, cellulose, or rock wool insulation while another worker blows the insulation from the compressor hose into the space being filled.

In new construction or major renovations, insulation workers staple fiberglass or rockwool batts to exterior walls and ceilings before drywall, paneling, or plaster walls are put in place. In major renovations of old buildings or when putting new insulation around pipes and industrial machinery, insulation workers often must first remove the old insulation. In the past, asbestos—now known to cause cancer in humans—was used extensively in walls and ceilings and for covering pipes, boilers, and various industrial equipment. Because of this danger, U.S. Environmental Protection Agency regulations require that asbestos be removed before a building undergoes major renovations or is demolished. When removing asbestos, insulation workers must follow carefully prescribed asbestos removal techniques and work practices. First they seal and depressurize the area that contains the asbestos, then they remove it using hand tools and special filtered vacuum cleaners and air-filtration devices.

Insulation workers often use rolls of insulation to cover walls and pipes.

Insulation workers use common handtools—trowels, brushes, knives, scissors, saws, pliers, and stapling guns. They use power saws to cut insulating materials, welding machines to join sheet metal or secure clamps, and compressors for blowing or spraying insulation.

Working Conditions

Insulation workers generally work indoors. They spend most of the workday on their feet, either standing, bending, or kneeling. Sometimes they work from ladders or in tight spaces. However, the work is not strenuous; it requires more coordination than strength. Insulation work is often dusty and dirty. The minute particles from insulation materials, especially when blown, can irritate the eyes, skin, and respiratory system. Removing cancer-causing asbestos insulation is a hazardous task and is done by specially trained workers. To protect themselves from the dangers of asbestos and irritants, workers follow strict safety guidelines, wear protective suits, masks, and respirators, take decontamination showers, and keep work areas well ventilated.

Employment

Insulation workers held about 64,0000 jobs in 1994; most worked for insulation or other construction contractors. Others worked for the Federal Government, in wholesale and retail trade, in shipbuilding, and in other manufacturing industries that have extensive installations for power, heating, and cooling. Most worked in urban areas. In less populated areas, insulation work may be done by carpenters, heating and air-conditioning installers, or drywall installers.

Training, Other Qualifications, and Advancement

Most insulation workers learn their trade informally on the job, although some workers complete formal apprenticeship programs. For entry jobs, insulation contractors prefer high school graduates who are in good physical condition and are licensed to drive. High school courses in blueprint reading, shop math, sheet-metal layout, and general construction provide a helpful background. Applicants seeking apprenticeship positions must have a high school diploma or its equivalent, and be at least 18 years old.

Trainees are assigned to experienced insulation workers for instruction and supervision. They begin with simple tasks, such as carrying insulation or holding material while it is fastened in place. On-the-job training can take up to 2 years, depending on the work. Learning to install insulation in homes generally requires less training than insulation application in commercial and industrial settings. As they gain experience, trainees receive less supervision, more responsibility, and higher pay.

In contrast, trainees in formal apprenticeship programs receive in-depth instruction in all phases of insulation. Apprenticeship programs may be provided by a joint committee of local insulation contractors and the local union of the International Association of Heat and Frost Insulators and Asbestos Workers, to which many insulation workers belong. Programs normally consist of 4 years of on-the-job training coupled with classroom instruction, and trainees must pass practical and written tests to demonstrate a knowledge of the trade.

Insulation workers who work with asbestos usually have to be licensed. Although licensure requirements vary from area to area, most States require asbestos removal workers to complete a 3-day training program in compliance with the 1986 Asbestos Hazard Emergency Act (AHERA). The National Asbestos Council (NAC) provides this training in over 100 locations. This program emphasizes "hands-on" training. Typically, students build a decontamination unit, handle a respirator and filtered vacuum cleaners, and perform simulated asbestos removal. In addition, they receive classroom instruction on a wide variety of topics, such as government regulations, health effects and worker protection, sampling for asbestos, and work practices. NAC also offers a 2-day course on compliance with Occupational Safety and Health Administration (OSHA)

regulations governing industrial asbestos removal in plants and factories, and an annual AHERA recertification program.

Skilled insulation workers may advance to supervisor, shop superintendent, insulation contract estimator, or set up their own insulation or asbestos abatement business.

Job Outlook

Employment of insulation workers is expected to increase about as fast as the average for all occupations through the year 2005, reflecting the demand for insulation associated with new construction and renovation as well as the demand for asbestos removal in existing structures. Concerns about the efficient use of energy to heat and cool buildings will result in growth in demand for insulation workers in the construction of new residential, industrial, and commercial buildings. In addition, renovation and efforts to improve insulation in existing structures also will increase demand.

Asbestos removal also will provide many jobs for insulation workers, not only because insulation workers often remove asbestos, but because they replace it with another insulating material. The 1986 Asbestos Hazard Emergency Act requires that all public and private schools have an asbestos management plan. Federal regulations also require that asbestos be removed from buildings that are to be demolished or undergo major renovations. In addition, many banks require that buildings be free of asbestos before a real estate loan will be granted. All these regulatory requirements are expected to stimulate asbestos removal and employment growth. The need to maintain, remove, and replace asbestos insulation on old pipes, boilers, and a variety of equipment in chemical and refrigeration plants and petroleum refineries will also add to employment requirements.

Despite this growth in demand, replacement needs will account for most job openings. This occupation has the highest turnover of all the construction trades. Each year thousands of jobs will become available as insulation workers transfer to other occupations or leave the labor force. Since there are no strict training requirements for entry, many people with limited skills work as insulation workers for a short time and then move on to other types of work, creating many job openings.

Insulation workers in the construction industry may experience periods of unemployment because of the short duration of many construction projects and the cyclical nature of construction activity. Workers employed in industrial plants generally have more stable employment because maintenance and repair must be done on a continuing basis. Unlike other construction occupations, insulation workers usually do not lose work time when weather conditions are poor. Most insulation is applied after buildings are enclosed.

Earnings

Median weekly earnings for insulation workers who worked full time were $485 in 1994. The middle 50 percent earned between $337 and $653. The lowest 10 percent earned less than $276, and the top 10 percent earned more than $819.

According to the *Engineering News Record*, union insulation workers received an average hourly wage of $30.20 in 1994, including benefits. Wages ranged from a low of $20.38 an hour in New Orleans to a high of $46.67 in New York City. Insulation workers doing commercial and industrial work earn substantially more than those working in residential construction, which does not require as much skill.

Related Occupations

Insulation workers combine a knowledge of insulation materials with the skills of cutting, fitting, and installing materials. Workers in occupations involving similar skills include carpenters, carpet installers, drywall applicators, floor layers, roofers, and sheet-metal workers.

Sources of Additional Information

For information about training programs or other work opportunities in this trade, contact a local insulation contractor; a local of the International Association of Heat and Frost Insulators and Asbestos Workers; the nearest office of the State employment service or State apprenticeship agency, or:

☛National Insulation and Abatement Contractors Association, 99 Canal Center Plaza, Suite 222, Alexandria, VA 22314.

☛Insulation Contractors Association of America, 1321 Duke St., Suite 303, Alexandria, VA 22314.

Painters and Paperhangers

(D.O.T. 840.381, .681, and .684; 841.381)

Nature of the Work

Paint and wall coverings make surfaces clean, attractive and bright. In addition, paints and other sealers protect outside walls from wear caused by exposure to the weather. Although some people do both painting and paperhanging, each requires different skills.

Painters apply paint, stain, varnish, and other finishes to buildings and other structures. They choose the right paint or finish for the surface to be covered, taking into account customers' wishes, durability, ease of handling, and method of application. They first prepare the surfaces to be covered so the paint will adhere properly. This may require removing the old coat by stripping, sanding, wire brushing, burning, or water and abrasive blasting. Painters also wash walls and trim to remove dirt and grease, fill nail holes and cracks, sandpaper rough spots, and brush off dust. On new surfaces, they apply a primer or sealer to prepare them for the finish coat. Painters also mix paints and match colors, relying on knowledge of paint composition and color harmony.

There are several ways to apply paint and similar coverings. Painters must be able to choose the right paint applicator for each job, depending on the surface to be covered, the characteristics of the finish, and other factors. Some jobs only need a good bristle brush with a soft, tapered edge; others require a dip or fountain pressure roller; still others can best be done using a paint sprayer. Many jobs need several types of applicators. The right tools for each job not only expedite the painter's work but also produce the most attractive surface.

When working on tall buildings, painters erect scaffolding, including "swing stages," scaffolds suspended by ropes or cables attached to roof hooks. When painting steeples and other conical structures, they use a "bosun chair," a swinglike device.

Paperhangers cover walls and ceilings with decorative wall coverings made of paper, vinyl, or fabric. They first prepare the surface to be covered by applying "sizing," which seals the surface and makes the covering stick better. When redecorating, they may first remove the old covering by soaking, steaming, or applying solvents. When necessary, they patch holes and take care of other imperfections before hanging the new wall covering.

After the surface has been prepared, paperhangers must prepare the paste or other adhesive. Then they measure the area to be covered, check the covering for flaws, cut the covering into strips of the proper size, and closely examine the pattern to match it when the strips are hung.

The next step is to brush or roll the adhesive onto the back of the covering, then to place the strips on the wall or ceiling, making sure the pattern is matched, the strips are hung straight, and the edges butted together to make tight, closed seams. Finally, paperhangers smooth the strips to remove bubbles and wrinkles, trim the top and bottom with a razor knife, and wipe off any excess adhesive.

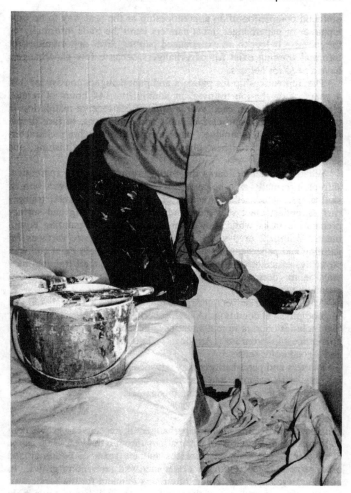

Remodeling, restoration, and maintenance projects often provide jobs for painters and paperhangers, even when new construction declines.

Working Conditions

Most painters and paperhangers work 40 hours a week or less; about 1 out of 6 works part time. Painters and paperhangers must stand for long periods. Their jobs also require a considerable amount of climbing and bending. These workers must have stamina because much of the work is done with their arms raised overhead. Painters often work outdoors, but seldom in wet, cold, or inclement weather.

Painters and paperhangers risk injury from slips or falls off ladders and scaffolds. They may sometimes work with materials that can be hazardous if masks are not worn or if ventilation is poor. Some painting jobs can leave a worker covered with paint.

Employment

Painters and paperhangers held about 439,000 jobs in 1994; most were painters. The majority of painters and paperhangers work for contractors engaged in new construction, repair, restoration, or remodeling work. In addition, organizations that own or manage large buildings, such as apartment complexes, employ maintenance painters, as do some schools, hospitals, and factories.

Self-employed independent painting contractors accounted for almost half of all painters and paperhangers, about twice the proportion of building trades workers in general.

Training, Other Qualifications, and Advancement

Painting and paperhanging are learned through apprenticeship or informal, on-the-job instruction. Although training authorities recommend completion of an apprenticeship as the best way to become a painter or paperhanger, most painters learn the trade informally on the job as a helper to an experienced painter. Few opportunities for informal training exist for paperhangers because few paperhangers have a need for helpers.

The apprenticeship for painters and paperhangers consists of 3 to 4 years of on-the-job training, in addition to 144 hours of related classroom instruction each year. Apprentices receive instruction in color harmony, use and care of tools and equipment, surface preparation, application techniques, paint mixing and matching, characteristics of different finishes, blueprint reading, wood finishing, and safety.

Whether a painter learns the trade through a formal apprenticeship or informally as a helper, on-the-job instruction covers similar skill areas. Under the direction of experienced workers, trainees carry supplies, erect scaffolds, and do simple painting and surface preparation tasks while they learn about paint and painting equipment. Within 2 or 3 years, trainees learn to prepare surfaces for painting and paperhanging, to mix paints, and to apply paint and wall coverings efficiently and neatly. Near the end of their training, they may learn decorating concepts, color coordination, and cost-estimating techniques.

Apprentices or helpers generally must be at least 16 years old and in good physical condition. A high school education or its equivalent that includes courses in mathematics is generally required to enter an apprenticeship program. Applicants should have manual dexterity and a good color sense.

Painters and paperhangers may advance to supervisory or estimating jobs with painting and decorating contractors. Many establish their own painting and decorating businesses.

Job Outlook

Employment of painters and paperhangers is expected to grow about as fast as the average for all occupations through the year 2005 as the level of new construction increases and the stock of buildings and other structures that require maintenance and renovation grows. In addition to job openings created by rising demand for the services of these workers, many tens of thousands of jobs will become available each year as painters and paperhangers transfer to other occupations or leave the labor force. There are no strict training requirements for entry, so many people with limited skills work as painters or paperhangers for a short time and then move on to other types of work, creating many job openings. Many fewer openings will occur for paperhangers because the number of these jobs is comparatively small.

Prospects for persons seeking jobs as painters or paperhangers should be quite favorable, due to the high turnover. Since there are no strict training requirements, a significant number of people work as painter for a short time and transfer to something else or work part-time. Despite the favorable overall conditions, job seekers considering these occupations should expect some periods of unemployment because many construction projects are of the short duration and construction activity is cyclical and seasonal in nature. Remodeling, restoration, and maintenance projects, however, often provide many jobs for painters and paperhangers even when new construction activity declines. The most versatile painters and paperhangers generally are most able to keep working steadily during downturns in the economy.

Earnings

Median weekly earnings for painters who were not self-employed were about $381 in 1994. Most earned between $288 and $516 weekly. The top 10 percent earned over $721 and the bottom 10 percent earned less than $721 a week. In general, paperhangers earn more than painters. Earnings for painters may be reduced on occasion because of bad weather and the short-term nature of many construction jobs.

Hourly wage rates for apprentices usually start at 40 to 50 percent of the rate for experienced workers and increase periodically.

Some painters and paperhangers are members of the International Brotherhood of Painters and Allied Trades. Some maintenance painters are members of other unions.

Related Occupations

Painters and paperhangers apply various coverings to decorate and protect wood, drywall, metal, and other surfaces. Other occupations in which workers apply paints and similar finishes include billboard posterers, metal sprayers, undercoaters, and transportation equipment painters.

Sources of Additional Information

For details about painting and paperhanging apprenticeships or work opportunities, contact local painting and decorating contractors; a local of the International Brotherhood of Painters and Allied Trades; a local joint union-management apprenticeship committee; or an office of the State apprenticeship agency or State employment service.

For general information about the work of painters and paperhangers, contact:

☛Associated Builders and Contractors, 1300 North 17th St., Rosslyn, VA 22209.

☛International Brotherhood of Painters and Allied Trades, 1750 New York Ave. NW., Washington, DC 20006.

☛Home Builders Institute, National Association of Home Builders, 1201 15th St. NW., Washington, DC 20005.

Plasterers

(D.O.T. 842.361-018, -022, and -026, and .381-014)

Nature of the Work

Plastering—one of the oldest crafts in the building trades—is enjoying a resurgence in popularity because of the introduction of newer, less costly materials and techniques. Plasterers apply plaster to interior walls and ceilings to form fire-resistant and relatively sound-proof surfaces. They also apply plaster veneer over drywall to create smooth or textured abrasion-resistant finishes. They apply durable plasters such as polymer-based acrylic finishes and stucco to exterior surfaces, and install prefabricated exterior insulation systems over existing walls for good insulation and interesting architectural effects. In addition, they cast ornamental designs in plaster. Drywall workers and lathers—a related occupation—use drywall instead of plaster when erecting interior walls and ceilings. (See the statement on drywall workers and lathers elsewhere in the *Handbook*.)

When plasterers work with interior surfaces such as cinder block and concrete, they first apply a brown coat of gypsum plaster that provides a base, followed by a second or finish coat—also called "white coat"—which is a lime-based plaster. When plastering metal lath (supportive wire mesh) foundations, they apply a preparatory or "scratch coat" with a trowel. They spread this rich plaster mixture into and over the metal lath. Before the plaster sets, they scratch its surface with a rake-like tool to produce ridges so the subsequent brown coat will bond to it tightly.

Laborers prepare a thick, smooth plaster for the brown coat. Plasterers spray or trowel this mixture onto the surface, then finish by smoothing it to an even, level surface.

For the finish coat, plasterers prepare a mixture of lime, plaster of Paris, and water. They quickly apply this onto the brown coat using a "hawk"—a light, metal plate with a handle—trowel, brush, and water. This mixture, which sets very quickly, produces a very smooth, durable finish.

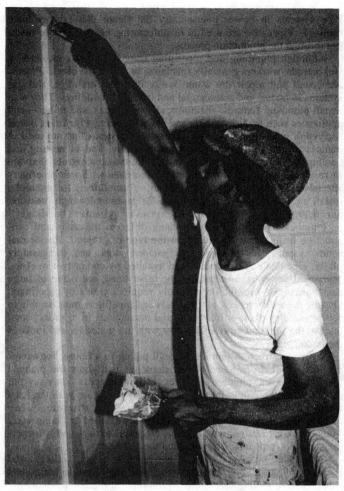

Plasterers trowel plaster onto a surface and smooth it until it is even and level.

Plasterers also work with a plaster material that can be finished in a single coat. This thin-coat or gypsum veneer plaster is made of lime and plaster of Paris and is mixed with water at the job site. It provides a smooth, durable, abrasion resistant finish on interior masonry surfaces, special gypsum base board, or drywall prepared with a bonding agent.

Plasterers create decorative interior surfaces as well. They do this by pressing a brush or trowel firmly against the wet plaster surface and using a circular hand motion to create decorative swirls.

For exterior work, plasterers usually apply a mixture of Portland cement, lime, and sand (stucco) over cement, concrete, masonry, and lath. Stucco is also applied directly to a wire lath with a scratch coat followed by a brown coat and then a finish coat. Plasterers may also embed marble or gravel chips into the finish coat to achieve a pebblelike, decorative finish.

Increasingly, plasterers apply insulation to the exteriors of new and old buildings. They cover the outer wall with rigid foam insulation board and reinforcing mesh and then trowel on a polymer-based or polymer-modified base coat. They apply an additional coat of this material with a decorative finish.

Plasterers sometimes do complex decorative and ornamental work that requires special skill and creativity. For example, they mold intricate wall and ceiling designs. Following an architect's blueprint, they pour or spray a special plaster into a mold and allow it to set. Workers then remove the molded plaster and put it in place according to the plan.

Working Conditions

Most plastering jobs are indoors; however, plasterers work outside when applying stucco or exterior wall insulation and decorative finish systems. Because plaster can freeze, heat is usually necessary to complete plastering jobs in cold weather. Sometimes plasterers work on scaffolds high above the ground.

Plastering is physically demanding, requiring considerable standing, bending, lifting, and reaching overhead. The work can be dusty and dirty; plaster materials also soil shoes and clothing and can irritate skin and eyes.

Employment

Plasterers held about 30,000 jobs in 1994. Most plasterers work on new construction, particularly where special architectural and lighting effects are part of the work. Some repair and renovate older buildings. Many plasterers are employed in Florida, California, and the Southwest, where exterior plasters with decorative finishes are very popular.

Most plasterers work for independent contractors. About 1 out of every 5 plasterers is self-employed.

Training, Other Qualifications, and Advancement

Although most employers recommend apprenticeship as the best way to learn plastering, many people learn the trade by working as helpers to experienced plasterers. Those who learn the trade informally as helpers usually start by carrying materials, setting up scaffolds, and mixing plaster. Later they learn to apply the scratch, brown, and finish coats.

Apprenticeship programs, sponsored by local joint committees of contractors and unions, generally consist of 2 or 3 years of on-the-job training, in addition to at least 144 hours annually of classroom instruction in drafting, blueprint reading, and mathematics for layout work.

In the classroom, apprentices start with a history of the trade and the industry. They also learn about the uses of plaster, estimating materials and costs, and casting ornamental plaster designs. On the job, they learn about lath bases, plaster mixes, methods of plastering, blueprint reading, and safety. They also learn how to use various tools, such as hand and powered trowels, floats, brushes, straightedges, power tools, plaster-mixing machines, and piston-type pumps. Some apprenticeship programs also allow individuals to obtain training in related occupations such as cement masonry and bricklaying.

Applicants for apprentice or helper jobs generally must be at least 17 years old, be in good physical condition, and have manual dexterity. Applicants who have a high school education are preferred. Courses in general mathematics, mechanical drawing, and shop provide a useful background.

Plasterers may advance to supervisors, superintendents, or estimators for plastering contractors, or may become self-employed contractors.

Job Outlook

Employment of plasterers is expected to increase about as fast as the average for all occupations through the year 2005. In addition to job openings due to rising demand for plastering work, additional jobs will open up as plasterers transfer to other occupations or leave the labor force.

In past years, employment of plasterers declined as more builders switched to drywall construction. This decline has halted, however, and employment of plasterers is expected to continue growing as a result of greater appreciation for the durability and attractiveness that troweled finishes provide. Thin-coat plastering—or veneering—in particular, is gaining greater acceptance as more builders recognize its ease of application, durability, quality of finish, and fire-retarding qualities. An increasing use of prefabricated wall systems and new polymer-based or polymer-modified acrylic exterior insulating finishes are also gaining popularity, not only because of their durability, attractiveness, and insulating properties, but also because of their lower cost. These wall systems and finishes are growing in popularity particularly in the South and Southwest regions of the country. In addition, plasterers will be needed to renovate plaster work in older structures and create special architectural effects such as curved surfaces, which are not practical with drywall materials.

Most plasterers work in construction, where prospects fluctuate from year to year due to changing economic conditions. Bad weather affects plastering less than other construction trades because most work is indoors. On exterior surfacing jobs, however, plasterers may lose time because materials cannot be applied under wet or freezing conditions. Best employment opportunities should continue to be in Florida, California, and the Southwest, where exterior plaster and decorative finishes are expected to remain popular.

Earnings
Median weekly earnings for plasterers working full time were about $385 a week in 1994. The middle 50 percent earned between $260 and $489 a week. The top 10 percent earned more than $626 and the lowest 10 percent less than $237 a week.

According to the limited information available, average hourly earnings—including benefits—for plasterers who belonged to a union and worked full time ranged between $15.80 and $37.63 in 1994. Plasterers in New York, Boston, Chicago, San Francisco, Los Angeles, and other large cities received the higher hourly earnings. Apprentice wage rates start at about half the rate paid to experienced plasterers. Annual earnings for plasterers and apprentices may be less than the hourly rate would indicate because poor weather and periodic declines in construction activity may limit their work time.

Many plasterers are members of unions. They are represented by the Operative Plasterers' and Cement Masons' International Association of the United States and Canada, or the International Union of Bricklayers and Allied Craftsmen.

Related Occupations
Other construction workers who use a trowel as their primary tool include drywall finishers, bricklayers, concrete masons, marble setters, stonemasons, terrazzo workers, and tilesetters.

Sources of Additional Information
For information about apprenticeships or other work opportunities, contact local plastering contractors; locals of the unions previously mentioned; a local joint union-management apprenticeship committee; or the nearest office of the State apprenticeship agency or the State employment service.

For general information about the work of plasterers, contact:
☛International Union of Bricklayers and Allied Craftsmen, 815 15th St. NW., Washington, DC 20005.
☛Operative Plasterers' and Cement Masons' International Association of the United States and Canada, 1125 17th St. NW., Washington, DC 20036.

Plumbers and Pipefitters

(D.O.T. 862.261; .281-010, -014, -022, and -026;.361-014, -018, and -022; .381 except -010 and -038; .681; .682-010; and .684-034)

Nature of the Work
Most people are familiar with plumbers who come to their home to unclog a drain or install an appliance. In addition to these activities, however, plumbers and pipefitters install, maintain, and repair many different types of pipe systems. For example, some systems move water to a municipal water treatment plant, and then to residential, commercial, and public buildings. Others dispose of waste. Some bring in gas for stoves and furnaces. Others supply air-conditioning.

Pipe systems in power plants carry the steam that powers huge turbines. Pipes also are used in manufacturing plants to move material through the production process.

Although plumbing and pipefitting sometimes are considered a single trade, workers generally specialize in one or the other. *Plumbers* install and repair the water, waste disposal, drainage, and gas systems in homes and commercial and industrial buildings. They also install plumbing fixtures—bathtubs, showers, sinks, and toilets—and appliances such as dishwashers and water heaters. *Pipefitters* install and repair both high and low-pressure pipe systems that are used in manufacturing, in the generation of electricity, and in heating and cooling buildings. They also install automatic controls that are increasingly being used to regulate these systems. Some pipefitters specialize in only one type of system. *Steamfitters*, for example, install pipe systems that move liquids or gases under high pressure. *Sprinklerfitters* install automatic fire sprinkler systems in buildings.

Plumbers and pipefitters use many different materials and construction techniques, depending on the type of project. Residential water systems, for example, use copper, steel, and increasingly plastic pipe that can be handled and installed by one or two workers. Municipal sewerage systems, on the other hand, are made of large cast iron pipes; installation normally requires crews of pipefitters. Despite these differences, all plumbers and pipefitters must be able to follow building plans or blueprints and instructions from supervisors, lay out the job, and work efficiently with the materials and tools of the trade.

When construction plumbers install piping in a house, for example, they work from blueprints or drawings that show the planned location of pipes, plumbing fixtures, and appliances. They lay out the job to fit the piping into the structure of the house with the least waste of material and within the confines of the structure. They measure and mark areas where pipes will be installed and connected. They check for obstructions, such as electrical wiring, and, if necessary, plan the pipe installation around the problem.

Sometimes plumbers have to cut holes in walls, ceilings, and floors of a house. For some systems, they may have to hang steel supports from ceiling joists to hold the pipe in place. To assemble the system, plumbers cut and bend lengths of pipe using saws, pipe cutters, and pipe-bending machines. They connect lengths of pipe with fittings; the method depends on the type of pipe used. For plastic pipe, plumbers connect the sections and fittings with adhesives. For copper pipe, they slide fittings over the end of the pipe and solder the fitting in place with a torch.

After the piping is in place in the house, plumbers install the fixtures and appliances and connect the system to the outside water or sewer lines. Using pressure gauges, they check the system to insure that the plumbing works properly.

Plumbers cut and bend pipe to meet the specifications of the job.

Working Conditions

Because plumbers and pipefitters frequently must lift heavy pipes, stand for long periods, and sometimes work in uncomfortable or cramped positions, they need physical strength as well as stamina. They may have to work outdoors in inclement weather. They also are subject to falls from ladders, cuts from sharp tools, and burns from hot pipes or from soldering equipment.

Plumbers and pipefitters engaged in construction generally work a standard 40-hour week; those involved in maintaining pipe systems, including those who provide maintenance services under contract, may have to work evening or weekend shifts, as well as be on call. These maintenance workers may spend quite a bit of time traveling to and from work sites.

Employment

Plumbers and pipefitters held about 375,000 jobs in 1994. About two-thirds worked for mechanical and plumbing contractors engaged in new construction, repair, modernization, or maintenance work. Others did maintenance work for a variety of industrial, commercial, and government employers. For example, pipefitters were employed as maintenance personnel in the petroleum and chemical industries, where manufacturing operations require the moving of liquids and gases through pipes. One of every 5 plumbers and pipefitters is self-employed.

Jobs for plumbers and pipefitters are distributed across the country in about the same proportion as the general population.

Training, Other Qualifications, and Advancement

Virtually all plumbers undergo some type of apprenticeship training. Many programs are administered by local union-management committees made up of members of the United Association of Journeymen and Apprentices of the Plumbing and Pipefitting Industry of the United States and Canada, and local employers who are members of either the Mechanical Contractors Association of America, Inc., the National Association of Plumbing-Heating-Cooling Contractors, or the National Fire Sprinkler Association, Inc.

Nonunion training and apprenticeship programs are administered by local chapters of the Associated Builders and Contractors, the National Association of Plumbing-Heating-Cooling Contractors, the American Fire Sprinkler Association, and the Home Builders Institute of the National Association of Home Builders.

Apprenticeships—both union and nonunion—consist of 4 to 5 years of on-the-job training, in addition to at least 144 hours annually of related classroom instruction. Classroom subjects include drafting and blueprint reading, mathematics, applied physics and chemistry, safety, and local plumbing codes and regulations. On the job, apprentices first learn basic skills such as identifying grades and types of pipe, the use of the tools of the trade, and the safe unloading of materials. As apprentices gain experience, they learn how to work with various types of pipe and install different piping systems and plumbing fixtures. Apprenticeship gives trainees a thorough knowledge of all aspects of the trade. Although most plumbers are trained through apprenticeship, some still learn their skills informally on the job.

Applicants for union or nonunion apprentice jobs must be 18 years old and in good physical condition. Apprenticeship committees may require applicants to have a high school diploma or its equivalent. Armed Forces training in plumbing and pipefitting is considered very good preparation. In fact, persons with this background may be given credit for previous experience when entering a civilian apprenticeship program. Secondary or post secondary courses in shop, plumbing, general mathematics, drafting, blueprint reading, and physics also are good preparation.

Although there are no uniform national licensing requirements, most communities require plumbers to be licensed. Licensing requirements vary from area to area, but most localities require workers to pass an examination that tests their knowledge of the trade and of local plumbing codes.

Some plumbers and pipefitters may become supervisors for mechanical and plumbing contractors. Others go into business for themselves.

Job Outlook

Job opportunities for skilled plumbers and pipefitters are expected to be good as the growth in demand outpaces the supply of workers trained in this craft. Employment of plumbers and pipefitters is expected to grow more slowly than the average for all occupations through the year 2005. However, the pool of young workers available to enter training programs will also be increasing slowly and many in that group are reluctant to seek training for jobs that may be strenuous and have uncomfortable working conditions.

Construction activity—residential, industrial, and commercial—is expected to grow slowly over the next decade. Demand for plumbers will stem from building renovation, including the increasing installation of sprinkler systems; repair and maintenance of existing residential systems, and maintenance activities for places that have extensive systems of pipes, such as power plants, water and wastewater treatment plants, pipelines, office buildings, and factories. However, the growing use of plastic pipe and fittings, which are much easier to use; more efficient sprinkler systems; and other technologies will mean that employment will not grow as fast as it has in past years. In addition, several thousand positions will become available each year from the need to replace experienced workers who leave the occupation.

Traditionally, many organizations with extensive pipe systems have employed their own plumbers or pipefitters to maintain their equipment and keep everything running smoothly. But, in order to reduce their labor costs, many of these firms no longer employ a full-time in-house plumber or pipefitter. Instead, when they need one they rely on workers provided, under service contracts, by plumbing and pipefitting contractors.

All construction projects provide only temporary employment, so when a project ends, plumbers and pipefitters working on it may experience short bouts of unemployment. Because construction activity varies from area to area, job openings, as well as apprenticeship opportunities, fluctuate with local economic conditions. However, employment of plumbers and pipefitters generally is less sensitive to changes in economic conditions than some of the other construction trades. Even when construction activity declines, maintenance, rehabilitation, and replacement of existing piping systems, as well as the growing installation of fire sprinkler systems, provide many jobs for plumbers and pipefitters.

Earnings

Median weekly earnings for plumbers and pipefitters who were not self-employed were $530 in 1994. The middle 50 percent earned between $373 and $742 weekly. The lowest 10 percent earned less than $284; the highest 10 percent earned more than $970 a week.

In 1993, the median hourly wage rate for maintenance pipefitters in 160 metropolitan areas were about $18.70. The middle 50 percent earned between about $16.90 and $20.90 an hour. In comparison, the average wage for all nonsupervisory and production workers in private industry, except farming, was $10.80. In general, wage rates tend to be higher in the Midwest and West than in the Northeast and South.

Apprentices usually begin at about 50 percent of the wage rate paid to experienced plumbers or pipefitters. This increases periodically as they improve their skills. After an initial waiting period, apprentices receive the same benefits as experienced plumbers and pipefitters.

Many plumbers and pipefitters are members of the United Association of Journeymen and Apprentices of the Plumbing and Pipefitting Industry of the United States and Canada.

Related Occupations

Other occupations in which workers install and repair mechanical systems in buildings are boilermakers, stationary engineers, electricians, elevator installers, industrial machinery repairers, millwrights, sheet-metal workers, and heating, air-conditioning, and refrigeration mechanics.

Sources of Additional Information

For information about apprenticeships or work opportunities in plumbing and pipefitting, contact local plumbing, heating, and air-conditioning contractors; a local or State chapter of the National Association of Plumbing, Heating, and Cooling Contractors; a local chapter of the Mechanical Contractors Association; a local of the United Association of Journeymen and Apprentices of the Plumbing and Pipefitting Industry of the United States and Canada; or the nearest office of the State employment service or State apprenticeship agency. This information is also available from:

☛The Home Builders Institute, National Association of Home Builders, 1201 15th St. NW., Washington, DC 20005.

For general information about the work of plumbers, pipefitters, and sprinklerfitters, contact:

☛National Association of Plumbing-Heating-Cooling Contractors, P.O. Box 6808, Falls Church, VA 22046.

☛Associated Builders and Contractors, 1300 North 17th St., Rosslyn, VA 22209.

☛National Fire Sprinkler Association, P.O. Box 1000, Patterson, NY 12563.

☛American Fire Sprinkler Association, Inc., 12959 Jupiter Rd., Suite 142, Dallas, TX 75238-3200.

☛Mechanical Contractors Association of America, 1385 Piccard Dr., Rockville, MD 20850.

Roofers

(D.O.T. 866.381-010, -014, and .684-010)

Nature of the Work

A leaky roof can damage ceilings, walls, and furnishings. To protect buildings and their contents from water damage, roofers repair and install roofs of tar or asphalt and gravel, rubber, thermoplastic, and metal; and shingles made of asphalt, slate, fiberglass, wood, tile, or other material. Repair and reroofing—replacing old roofs on existing buildings—provide many work opportunities for these workers. Roofers also may waterproof foundation walls and floors.

There are two types of roofs, flat and pitched (sloped). Most commercial, industrial, and apartment buildings have flat or slightly sloping roofs. Most houses have pitched roofs. Some roofers work on both types; others specialize.

Most flat roofs are covered with several layers of materials. Roofers first put a layer of insulation on the roof deck. Over the insulation, they then spread a coat of molten bitumen, a tar-like substance. Next, they install partially overlapping layers of roofing felt—a fabric saturated in bitumen—over the insulation surface and use a mop to spread hot bitumen over it and under the next layer. This seals the seams and makes the surface watertight. Roofers repeat these steps to build up the desired number of layers, called "plies." The top layer is either glazed to make a smooth finish, or has gravel embedded in the hot bitumen for a rough surface.

An increasing number of flat roofs are covered with a single-ply membrane of waterproof rubber or thermoplastic compounds. Roofers roll these sheets over the roof's insulation and seal the seams. Adhesive, mechanical fasteners, or stone ballasts hold the sheets in place. The building must be of sufficient strength to hold the ballast.

Most residential roofs are covered with shingles. To apply shingles, roofers first lay, cut, and tack 3-foot strips of roofing felt lengthwise over the entire roof. Then, starting from the bottom edge,

Repairing and replacing old roofs provides many work opportunities for roofers.

they nail overlapping rows of shingles to the roof. Workers measure and cut the felt and shingles to fit intersecting roofs, and to fit around vent pipes and chimneys. Wherever two roof surfaces intersect or shingles reach a vent pipe or chimney, roofers cement or nail "flashing," strips of metal or shingle, over the joints to make them watertight. Finally, roofers cover exposed nailheads with roofing cement or caulking to prevent water leakage.

Some roofers also waterproof and dampproof masonry and concrete walls and floors. To prepare surfaces for waterproofing, they hammer and chisel away rough spots or remove them with a rubbing brick before applying a coat of liquid waterproofing compound. They also may paint or spray surfaces with a waterproofing material or attach waterproofing membrane to surfaces. When dampproofing, they usually spray a bitumen-based coating on interior or exterior surfaces.

Working Conditions

Roofers' work is strenuous. It involves heavy lifting, as well as climbing, bending, and kneeling. Roofers risk injuries from slips or falls from scaffolds, ladders, or roofs, and burns from hot bitumen. In fact, of all construction industries, the roofing industry has the highest accident rate. Roofers work outdoors in all types of weather, particularly when making repairs. Roofs are extremely hot during the summer.

Employment

Roofers held about 126,000 jobs in 1994. Almost all wage and salary roofers worked for roofing contractors. Nearly one-third of all roofers were self-employed. Many self-employed roofers specialize in residential work.

Training, Other Qualifications, and Advancement

Most roofers acquire their skills informally by working as helpers for experienced roofers. They start by carrying equipment and material and erecting scaffolds and hoists. Within 2 or 3 months, they are taught to measure, cut, and fit roofing materials and then to lay asphalt or fiberglass shingles. Because some roofing materials are used infrequently, it can take several years to get experience working on all the various types of roofing applications.

Some roofers train through 3-year apprenticeship programs administered by local union-management committees representing roofing contractors and locals of the United Union of Roofers, Waterproofers, and Allied Workers. The apprenticeship program generally consists of a minimum of 1,400 hours of on-the-job training annually, plus 144 hours of classroom instruction a year in subjects such as tools and their use, arithmetic, and safety. On-the-job training for apprentices is similar to that for helpers, except that the apprenticeship program is more structured. Apprentices also learn to dampproof and waterproof walls.

Good physical condition and good balance are essential for roofers. A high school education or its equivalent is helpful, as are courses in mechanical drawing and basic mathematics. Most apprentices are at least 18 years old.

Roofers may advance to supervisor or estimator for a roofing contractor or become contractors themselves.

Job Outlook

Jobs for roofers should be plentiful through the year 2005, primarily because of the need to replace workers who transfer to other occupations or who leave the labor force. Turnover is high; roofing work is hot, strenuous, and dirty, and a significant number of workers treat roofing as a temporary job until something better comes along. Some roofers leave the occupation to go into other construction trades.

Employment of roofers is expected to increase about as fast as the average for all occupations through the year 2005. Roofs deteriorate faster than most other parts of buildings and periodically need to be repaired or replaced. About 75 percent of roofing work is repair and reroofing, a higher proportion than in most other construction work. As a result, demand for roofers is less susceptible to downturns in the economy than some of the other construction trades. In addition to repair and reroofing work on the growing stock of buildings, new construction of industrial, commercial, and residential buildings will add to the demand for roofers. However, many innovations and advances in materials, techniques, and tools have made roofers more productive and will restrict the growth of employment at least to some extent. Jobs should be easiest to find during spring and summer, when most roofing is done.

Earnings

Median weekly earnings for roofers working full time were about $371 a week in 1994. The middle 50 percent earned between $278 and $498 a week. The top 10 percent earned more than $630 weekly and the lowest 10 percent less than $219 a week.

According to the *Engineering News Record*, average hourly earnings—including benefits—for union roofers were $23.98 in 1994. Wages ranged from a low of $13.90 in Denver to a high of $38.58 in New York City. Apprentices generally start at about 40 percent of the rate paid to experienced roofers and receive periodic raises as they acquire the skills of the trade. Earnings for roofers are reduced on occasion because poor weather often limits the time they can work.

Some roofers are members of the United Union of Roofers, Waterproofers & Allied Workers.

Related Occupations

Roofers use shingles, bitumen and gravel, single-ply plastic or rubber sheets, or other materials to waterproof building surfaces. Workers in other occupations who cover surfaces with special materials for protection and decoration include carpenters, concrete masons, drywall installers, floor covering installers, plasterers, terrazzo workers, and tilesetters.

Sources of Additional Information

For information about roofing apprenticeships or work opportunities in this trade, contact local roofing contractors; a local of the Roofers union; a local joint union-management apprenticeship committee; or the nearest office of the State employment service or State apprenticeship agency.

For information about the work of roofers, contact:

☛National Roofing Contractors Association, 10255 W. Higgins Rd., Rosemont, IL 60018.

☛United Union of Roofers, Waterproofers and Allied Workers, 1125 17th St. NW., Washington, DC 20036.

Sheetmetal Workers

(D.O.T. 804.281-010 and -014)

Nature of the Work

Sheetmetal workers make, install, and maintain air-conditioning, heating, ventilation, and pollution control duct systems; roofs; siding; rain gutters and downspouts; skylights; restaurant equipment; outdoor signs; and many other building parts and products made from metal sheets. They may also work with fiberglass and plastic materials. Although some workers specialize in fabrication, installation, or maintenance, most do all three jobs. (Workers employed in the mass production of sheetmetal products in manufacturing are not included in this section.)

Sheetmetal workers usually fabricate their products at a shop away from the construction site. They first study plans and specifications to determine the kind and quantity of materials they will need. They then measure, cut, bend, shape, and fasten pieces of sheet metal to make duct work, counter tops, and other custom products. In an increasing number of shops, sheetmetal workers use computerized metalworking equipment. This enables them to experiment with different layouts and to select the one that results in the least waste of material. They cut or form the parts with computer-controlled saws, lasers, shears, and presses.

In shops without computerized equipment and for products that cannot be made on such equipment, sheetmetal workers use hand calculators to make the required calculations and use tapes, rulers, and other measuring devices for layout work. They then cut or stamp the parts on machine tools.

Before assembling the pieces, sheetmetal workers check each part for accuracy and, if necessary, finish it by using hand, rotary, or squaring shears and hacksaws. After the parts have been inspected, workers fasten the seams and joints together with welds, bolts, cement, rivets, solder, specially formed sheetmetal drive clips, or other connecting devices. They then take the parts to the construction site where they further assemble the pieces as they install them. These workers install ducts, pipes, and tubes by joining them end to end and hanging them with metal hangers secured to a ceiling or a wall. They also use shears, hammers, punches, and drills to make parts at the worksite or to alter parts made in the shop.

Some jobs are done completely at the job site. When installing a metal roof, for example, sheetmetal workers measure and cut the roofing panels that are needed to complete the job. They secure the first panel in place and interlock and fasten the grooved edge of the

Sheetmetal workers fabricate their products in a shop and take them to a construction site for assembly and installation.

next panel into the grooved edge of the first. Then they nail or weld the free edge of the panel to the structure. This two-step process is repeated for each additional panel. Finally, they fasten machine-made molding at joints, along corners, and around windows and doors for a neat, finished effect.

In addition to installation, some sheetmetal workers specialize in testing, balancing, adjusting, and servicing existing air-conditioning and ventilation systems to make sure they are functioning properly and to improve their energy efficiency. Some sheetmetal workers also remove asbestos and toxic materials.

Working Conditions

Sheetmetal workers usually work a 40-hour week. Those who fabricate sheetmetal products work in shops that are well lighted and well ventilated. They stand for long periods and lift heavy materials and finished pieces. Sheetmetal workers must follow safety practices because working around high-speed machines can be dangerous. They are subject to cuts from sharp metal, burns from soldering and welding, and falls from ladders and scaffolds. They generally wear safety glasses and must not wear jewelry or loose-fitting clothing that could easily get caught in a machine.

Those doing installation work do considerable bending, lifting, standing, climbing, and squatting, sometimes in close quarters or in awkward positions. Although installing duct systems and kitchen equipment is done indoors, the installation of siding, roofs, and gutters involves much outdoor work, requiring sheetmetal workers to work in all kinds of weather.

Employment

Sheetmetal workers held about 100,00 wage and salary jobs in the construction industry in 1994. Three-fourths worked for plumbing, heating, and air-conditioning contractors; most of the rest worked for roofing and sheetmetal contractors; and a few worked for other special trade contractors and for general contractors engaged in residential and commercial building. Unlike many other construction trades, very few sheetmetal workers are self-employed.

Jobs for sheetmetal workers are distributed throughout the country in about the same proportion as the total population.

Training, Other Qualifications, and Advancement

Sheetmetal contractors consider apprenticeship the best way to learn this trade. The apprenticeship program consists of 4 or 5 years of on-the-job training and a minimum of 144 hours per year of classroom instruction. Apprenticeship programs provide comprehensive instruction in both sheetmetal fabrication and installation. They are administered by local joint committees composed of the Sheet Metal Workers' International Association and local chapters of the Sheet Metal and Air-Conditioning Contractors National Association, or by local chapters of the Associated Builders and Contractors.

On the job, apprentices learn the basics of pattern layout and how to cut, bend, fabricate, and install sheet metal. They begin with basic ductwork and gradually advance to more difficult jobs, such as making more complex ducts, fittings, and decorative pieces. They also use materials such as fiberglass, plastics, and other non-metallic materials.

In the classroom, apprentices learn drafting, plan and specification reading, trigonometry and geometry applicable to layout work, the use of computerized equipment, welding, and the principles of heating, air-conditioning, and ventilating systems. Safety is stressed throughout the program. In addition, apprentices learn the relationship between sheetmetal work and other construction work.

A relatively small number of persons pick up the trade informally, usually by working as helpers to experienced sheetmetal workers. Most begin by carrying metal and cleaning up debris in a metal shop while they learn about materials and tools and their uses. Later, they learn to operate machines that bend or cut metal. In time, helpers go out on the job site to learn installation. Those who acquire their skills this way often take vocational school courses in mathematics or sheetmetal fabrication to supplement their work experience. To be promoted to the journey level, helpers usually must pass the same written examination as apprentices.

Applicants for jobs as apprentices or helpers should be in good physical condition and have mechanical and mathematical aptitude. Good eye-hand coordination, spatial and form perception, and manual dexterity are also important. Local apprenticeship committees require a high school education or its equivalent. Courses in Algebra, trigonometry, geometry, mechanical drawing, and shop provide a helpful background for learning the trade, as does work experience obtained in the Armed Services.

It is important that experienced sheetmetal workers keep abreast of new technological developments such as the growing use of computerized layout and laser cutting machines. Workers often take additional training provided by the union or by their employer in order to improve existing skills or to acquire new ones.

Sheetmetal workers may advance to supervisory jobs. Some take additional training in welding and do more specialized work. Others go into the contracting business for themselves. Because a sheetmetal contractor must have a shop with equipment to fabricate products, this type of contracting business is more expensive to start than other types of construction contracting.

Job Outlook

Opportunities should be good for individuals who acquire for apprenticeship training. Employment of sheetmetal workers in construction is expected to increase about as fast as the average for all occupations reflecting the growth of that sector. Demand for sheetmetal installation should increase as more industrial, commercial, and residential structures are built. Growing demand for more energy-efficient air-conditioning, heating, and ventilation systems in the growing stock of older buildings, as well as other types of renovation and maintenance work, also should boost employment. In addition, the greater use of decorative sheetmetal products and increased architectural restoration are expected to add to the demand for sheetmetal workers. Despite this growth in demand, most job openings will result from the need to replace workers who leave the occupation.

Job prospects are expected to be good for skilled sheetmetal workers over the long run, although workers may experience periods of unemployment when construction projects end and when economic conditions reduce the amount of construction activity. Because local economic conditions can vary so widely, there can be shortages of experienced workers in some areas and an oversupply in other parts of the country. The availability of training slots also fluctuates with economic conditions, so the number of openings may vary from year to year and by geographic area. Nevertheless, employment of sheetmetal workers is less sensitive to declines in new construction than employment of some other construction workers, such as carpenters. Maintenance of existing equipment—which is less affected by economic fluctuations than new construction—makes up a large part of the work done by sheetmetal workers. Installation of new air-conditioning and heating systems in existing buildings also continues during construction slumps as individuals and businesses seek more energy-efficient equipment to cut utility bills. In addition, a large proportion of sheetmetal installation and maintenance is done indoors so these workers usually lose less work time due to bad weather than other construction workers.

Earnings

Median weekly earnings for sheetmetal workers working full time were about $444 a week in 1994. The middle 50 percent earned between $317 and $692 a week. The top 10 percent earned more than $914 and the lowest 10 percent less than $283 a week.

According to the Engineering News Record, average hourly earnings—including benefits—for union sheetmetal workers were $29.40 in 1994. Wages ranged from a low of $19.92 in Birmingham, Alabama, to a high of $46.69 in New York City. Apprentices generally start at about 40 percent of the rate paid to experienced workers. As they acquire more skills of the trade throughout the course of the apprenticeship program, they receive periodic increases until their pay approaches that of experienced workers. In addition, union workers in some areas receive supplemental wages from the union when they are on layoff or shortened workweeks. Many sheetmetal workers are members of the Sheet Metal Workers' International Association.

Related Occupations

To fabricate and install sheetmetal products, sheetmetal workers combine metalworking skills and knowledge of construction materials and techniques. Other occupations in which workers lay out and fabricate metal products include layout workers, machinists, metal fabricators, metal patternmakers, shipfitters, and tool and die makers. Construction occupations requiring similar skills and knowledge include heating, air-conditioning, and refrigeration technicians and glaziers.

Sources of Additional Information

For more information about apprenticeships or other work opportunities, contact local sheetmetal contractors or heating, refrigeration, and air-conditioning contractors; a local of the Sheet Metal Workers; a local of the Sheetmetal and Air Conditioning Contractors Association; a local joint union-management apprenticeship committee; or the nearest office of the State employment service or apprenticeship agency.

For general information about sheetmetal workers, contact:

☛The Sheet Metal National Training Fund, 601 N. Fairfax St., Suite 240, Alexandria, VA 22314.

☛Associated Builders and Contractors, 1300 N. 17th St. NW., Rosslyn, VA 22209.

☛The Sheetmetal and Air Conditioning Contractors Association, 4201 Lafayette Center Dr., Chantilly, VA 22021.

☛The Sheet Metal Workers International Association, 1750 New York Ave. NW., Washington, DC 20006.

Structural and Reinforcing Ironworkers

(D.O.T. 801.361-014, -018, -022, .381-010, .684-026; and 809.381-022, and -026)

Nature of the Work

Materials made from iron, steel, aluminum, and bronze are used extensively in the construction of highways, bridges, office buildings, power transmission towers, and other large buildings. These structures have frames made of steel columns, beams, and girders. In addition, reinforced concrete—concrete containing steel bars or wire fabric—is an important material in buildings, bridges, and other structures. The steel gives the concrete additional strength. Metal stairways, catwalks, floor gratings, ladders, and window frames, as well as lampposts, railings, fences, and decorative ironwork are used to make these structures more functional and attractive. Structural and reinforcing ironworkers fabricate, assemble, and install these products. These workers also repair, renovate, and maintain older buildings and structures such as steel mills, utility plants, automobile factories, highways, and bridges.

Before construction can begin, ironworkers must erect the steel frames and assemble the cranes and derricks that move structural steel, reinforcing bars, buckets of concrete, lumber, and other materials and equipment around the construction site. This equipment arrives at the construction site in sections. There it is lifted into position by a mobile crane. Ironworkers then connect the sections and set up the cables that do the hoisting.

Once this job has been completed, *structural ironworkers* begin to connect steel columns, beams, and girders according to blueprints and instructions from supervisors and superintendents. Structural steel, reinforcing rods, and ornamental iron generally are delivered to the construction site ready for erection—cut to the proper size with holes drilled for bolts and numbered for assembly. This work is done by ironworkers in fabricating shops located away from the construction site. There they lay out the raw steel received from a steel mill and cut, bend, drill, bolt, and weld each piece according to the specifications for that particular job. Ironworkers at the construction site unload and stack the fabricated steel so it can be hoisted easily when needed.

To hoist the steel, ironworkers attach cables from the crane or derrick. One worker directs the hoist operator with hand signals. Another worker holds a rope (tag line) attached to the steel to prevent it from swinging. The steel is hoisted into place in the framework, where several workers using spud wrenches position it with connecting bars and jacks. Workers use driftpins or the handle of a spud wrench—a long wrench with a pointed handle—to align the holes in the steel with the holes in the framework. Then they bolt the piece in place temporarily, check vertical and horizontal alignment with plumb bobs, laser equipment, transits, or levels and then bolt or weld it permanently in place.

Reinforcing ironworkers set the bars in the forms that hold concrete, following blueprints that show the location, size, and number of reinforcing bars. They fasten the bars together by tying wire around them with pliers. When reinforcing floors, workers place blocks under the reinforcing bars to hold them off the deck. Although these materials usually arrive ready to use, ironworkers occasionally have to cut the bars with metal shears or acetylene torches, bend them by hand or machine, or weld them with arc-welding equipment. Some concrete is reinforced with welded wire fabric. Workers cut and fit the fabric and, while a concrete crew places the concrete, ironworkers use hooked rods to position it properly in the concrete.

Ornamental ironwork and related pieces are installed after the exterior of the building has been completed. As the pieces are hoisted into position, ironworkers bring them into position, make sure they fit correctly, and bolt, braze, or weld them for a secure fit. They also erect metal tanks used to store petroleum, water, or other fluids and assemble prefabricated metal buildings according to plans or specifications.

Working Conditions

Structural and reinforcing ironworkers usually work outside in all kinds of weather. However, those who work at great heights do not work when it is wet, icy, or extremely windy. Because the danger of

Reinforcing workers bolt or weld reinforcing tie rods in place.

injuries due to falls is so great, ironworkers use safety devices such as safety belts, scaffolding, and nets to reduce the risk.

Employment

Structural and reinforcing ironworkers held about 61,000 jobs in 1994. Almost all of these workers were employed in the construction industry. Nearly 6 of every 10 worked for structural steel erection contractors; most of the remainder worked for a variety of contractors specializing in the construction of homes, factories, commercial buildings, churches, schools, bridges and tunnels, and water, sewer, communications, and power lines. Very few were self-employed.

Ironworkers are employed in all parts of the country, but most work in metropolitan areas, where most commercial and industrial construction takes place.

Training, Other Qualifications, and Advancement

Most employers recommend apprenticeship as the best way to learn this trade. The apprenticeship consists of 3 years of on-the-job training and a minimum of 144 hours a year of classroom instruction. Apprenticeship programs are usually administered by joint union-management committees made up of representatives of local unions of the International Association of Bridge, Structural and Ornamental Ironworkers and local chapters of contractors' associations.

Ironworkers generally must be at least 18 years old. A high school diploma may be preferred by employers and may be required by some local apprenticeship committees. High School courses in general mathematics, mechanical drawing, and shop are helpful. Because materials used in ironworking are heavy and bulky, ironworkers must be in good physical condition. They also need good agility, balance, eyesight, and spatial perception in order to work at great heights on narrow beams and girders. Ironworkers should not be afraid of heights or suffer from dizziness.

In the classroom, apprentices study blueprint reading, mathematics for layout work, the basics of structural erecting, rigging, reinforcing, welding and burning, ornamental erection and assembling, and the care and safe use of tools and materials. On the job, apprentices work in all aspects of the trade, such as unloading and storing materials at the job site, rigging materials for movement by crane or derrick, connecting structural steel, and welding.

Some ironworkers learn the trade informally on the job without completing an apprenticeship. These workers generally do not receive classroom training, although some large contractors have extensive training programs. On-the-job trainees usually begin by assisting experienced ironworkers by doing simple jobs, like carrying various materials. With experience, they perform more difficult tasks like cutting and fitting different parts. Learning through work experience alone may not provide training as complete as an apprenticeship program, however, and usually takes longer.

Some experienced workers become supervisors. Others may go into the contracting business for themselves.

Job Outlook

Employment of structural and reinforcing ironworkers is expected to increase more slowly than the average for all occupations through the year 2005. The rehabilitation and maintenance of an increasing number of older buildings, factories, power plants, and highways and bridges is expected to increase, but employment growth will be slowed by the continued slow growth in industrial and commercial construction. In addition, more ironworkers will be needed to build incinerators and other structures to contain hazardous materials as part of ongoing toxic waste cleanup. Although employment growth will create many new jobs for structural and reinforcing ironworkers, most openings will result from the need to replace experienced ironworkers who transfer to other occupations or leave the labor force.

The number of job openings fluctuates from year to year as economic conditions and the level of construction activity change. During economic downturns, ironworkers can experience high rates of unemployment. Similarly, job opportunities for ironworkers may vary widely by geographic area. Job openings for ironworkers usually are more abundant during the spring and summer months, when the level of construction activity increases.

Earnings

Median weekly earnings of structural and reinforcing ironworkers employed full time were about $611 a week in 1994. The middle 50 percent earned between $494 and $813 a week. The top 10 percent earned more than $1,040 and the lowest 10 percent less than $414 a week.

According to the *Engineering News Record*, prevailing union wage rates—including benefits—for ironworkers averaged about $28.95 an hour in 1994. Their wages ranged from a low of about $18.50 in New Orleans, to a high of between $42.26 and $52.85 in New York City.

Apprentices generally start at about 40 percent of the rate paid to experienced workers. They receive periodic increases throughout the course of the apprenticeship program as they acquire the skills of the trade until their pay approaches that of experienced workers.

Earnings for ironworkers may be reduced on occasion because work can be limited by bad weather and the short-term nature of construction jobs.

Many workers in this trade are members of the International Association of Bridge, Structural and Ornamental Ironworkers.

Related Occupations

Structural and reinforcing ironworkers play an essential role in erecting buildings, bridges, highways, powerlines, and other structures. Others who also work on these construction jobs are operating engineers, concrete masons, and welders.

Sources of Additional Information

For more information on apprenticeships or other work opportunities, contact local general contractors; a local of the International Association of Bridge, Structural and Ornamental Ironworkers union; a local joint ironworkers' union-management apprenticeship committee; a local or State chapter of the Associated Builders and Contractors, or the nearest office of the State employment service or apprenticeship agency.

For general information about ironworkers, contact:

☛Associated General Contractors of America, Inc., 1300 North 17th St., Rosslyn, VA 22209-3883

☛International Association of Bridge, Structural and Ornamental Iron Workers, 1750 New York Ave. NW., Suite 400, Washington, DC 20006.

☛National Erectors Association, 1501 Lee Hwy., Suite 202, Arlington, VA 22209.

☛National Association of Reinforcing Steel Contractors, P.O. Box 280, Fairfax, VA 22030.

Tilesetters

(D.O.T. 861.381-054, -058, and .684-018)

Nature of the Work

In ancient Egypt and Rome, tile was used for mosaics—an art form using small, decorative ceramic squares. Over the years, tile has been a popular building material because it is durable, impervious to water, and easy to clean. It is used today, for instance, in shopping centers, hospitals, tunnels, lobbies of buildings, bathrooms, and kitchens.

Tilesetters, like the ancient artists, apply tile to floors, walls, and ceilings. To set tile, which generally ranges in size from 1 inch to 12 inches square, they use cement or "mastic," a very sticky paste. When using cement, tilesetters nail a support of metal mesh to the

After setting tile in cement, tilesetters fill the joints with grout.

wall or ceiling to be tiled. They use a trowel to apply a cement mortar—called a "scratch coat"—onto the metal screen and scratch the surface of the soft mortar with a small tool, similar to a rake. After the scratch coat has dried, tilesetters apply another coat of mortar to level the surface and then apply mortar to the back of the tile and place it onto the surface.

To set tile in mastic or a cement adhesive, called "thin set," tilesetters need a flat, solid surface such as drywall, concrete, plaster, or wood. They use a tooth-edged trowel to spread mastic on the surface or apply cement adhesive to the back of the tile and then properly position it.

Because tile varies in color, shape, and size, workers sometimes prearrange tiles on a dry floor according to a specified design. This allows workers to examine the pattern and make changes. In order to cover all exposed areas, including corners and around pipes, tubs, and wash basins, tilesetters cut tiles to fit with a machine saw or a special cutting tool. Once the tile is placed, they gently tap the surface with their trowel handle or a small block of wood to seat the tiles evenly.

When the cement or mastic has set, tilesetters fill the joints with "grout," a very fine cement. They then scrape the surface with a rubber-edged device called a "squeegee" to dress the joints and remove excess grout. Before the grout sets, they finish the joints with a damp sponge for a uniform appearance.

Working Conditions

Tilesetters generally work indoors. Because most of the structure has been completed, the work area is relatively clean and uncluttered.

Much of the workday is spent bending, kneeling, and reaching, activities that require endurance but not exceptional strength. To protect their knees, most workers wear kneepads.

Although workers are subject to cuts from tools or materials, falls from ladders, and strained muscles, the occupation is not as hazardous as some other construction occupations.

Employment

Tilesetters held about 27,000 jobs in 1994. Most wage and salary tilesetters were employed by tilesetting contractors who work mainly on nonresidential construction projects, such as schools, hospitals, and office buildings. Nearly one of every 2 tilesetters is self-employed, compared to 1 of every 4 construction workers. Most self-employed tilesetters work on residential projects.

Tilesetters are employed throughout the country but are found largely in urban areas.

Training, Other Qualifications, and Advancement

Most tilesetters acquire their skills on the job by working as helpers to experienced workers. They begin by learning about the tools of the trade, and then they learn to mix and apply cement and to apply mastic. As they progress, they learn to cut and install tile, apply grout, and do finishing work.

Employers recommend completion of a 3-year apprenticeship program, which consists of on-the-job training and related classroom instruction in subjects such as blueprint reading, layout, and basic mathematics.

When hiring apprentices or helpers, employers usually prefer high school graduates who have had courses in general mathematics, mechanical drawing, and shop. Good physical condition, manual dexterity, and a good sense of color harmony also are important assets.

Skilled tilesetters may start their own contracting businesses or may become supervisors or estimators for other contractors.

Job Outlook

Employment of tilesetters is expected to increase more slowly than the average for all occupations through the year 2005. Increased demand for tilesetters will stem from population and business growth, which should result in more construction of shopping malls, hospitals, schools, restaurants, and other structures where tile is used extensively. Tile is expected to continue to increase in popularity as a building material and be used more extensively, particularly in more expensive homes, whose construction is expected to increase. In more modestly priced homes, however, the use of tile substitutes, such as plastic or fiberglass tub and shower enclosures, is expected to increase, slowing the growth in demand for tilesetters.

Despite the increased demand for tilesetting, most job openings will result from the need to replace tilesetters who retire or leave the occupation for other reasons. Job opportunities will not be as plentiful as in other construction occupations because the occupation is small and turnover is relatively low.

Earnings

The median weekly earnings for tilesetters were about $450 a week in 1994. The middle 50 percent earned between $340 and $710 a week; 10 percent earned less than $280 a week; 10 percent earned more than $960 a week.

Apprentices usually start earning 50 percent of experienced workers' wages. Earnings vary greatly by geographic location. They tend to be highest in the North and lowest in the South.

Some tilesetters belong to the International Union of Bricklayers and Allied Craftsmen or the United Brotherhood of Carpenters and Joiners of America.

Related Occupations

Tilesetters use their knowledge of tools and masonry materials along with skill and dexterity to produce attractive, durable surfaces. Other workers with similar abilities include bricklayers, concrete masons, marblesetters, plasterers, stonemasons, and terrazzo workers.

Sources of Additional Information

For details about apprenticeship or other work opportunities in this trade, contact local tilesetting contractors; locals of the unions previously mentioned; or the nearest office of the State employment service or State apprenticeship agency.

For general information about the work of tilesetters, contact:

☛International Union of Bricklayers and Allied Craftsmen, International Masonry Institute, Apprenticeship and Training, 815 15th St. NW., Washington, DC 20005.

☛United Brotherhood of Carpenters and Joiners of America, Tile, Marble, and Terrazzo Finishers Division, 101 Constitution Ave. NW., Washington, DC 20001.

Production Occupations

Assemblers

Precision Assemblers

(List of D.O.T. codes available on request. See p. 478.)

Nature of the Work

Workers who put together the parts of manufactured products are called assemblers. In some instances, such as the building of a car, hundreds of assemblers work on a single product; in others, such as the assembly of a toy doll, a single assembler may be responsible for each product. Assembly work varies from simple, repetitive jobs that are relatively easy to learn to those requiring great precision and many months of experience and training. Precision assemblers are the highly experienced and trained workers who assemble complicated products.

The work of precision assemblers requires a high degree of accuracy. Workers must be able to interpret detailed specifications and instructions and apply independent judgment. Some experienced assemblers work with engineers and technicians, assembling prototypes or test products. Precision assemblers involved in product development must know how to read and interpret engineering specifications from text, drawings, and computer-aided drafting systems, and how to use a variety of tools and precision measuring instruments.

Precision assemblers may work on subassemblies or the final assembly of finished products or components of a vast array of products. For example, precision electrical and electronic equipment assemblers put together or modify prototypes or final assemblies of items such as missile control systems, radio or test equipment, computers, machine-tool numerical controls, radar, sonar, telemetering systems, and appliances. Precision electromechanical equipment assemblers prepare and test equipment or devices such as dynamometers, ejection seat mechanisms, magnetic drums, and tape drives. Precision machine builders construct, assemble, or rebuild engines and turbines, and office, agricultural, construction, oil field, rolling

mill, textile, woodworking, paper, printing, and food wrapping machinery. Precision aircraft assemblers put together and install parts of airplanes, space vehicles, or missiles, such as wings or landing gear. Precision structural metal fitters align and fit structural metal parts according to detailed specifications prior to welding or riveting.

The manufacturing process is changing. Flexible manufacturing systems, which include the manufacturing applications of robotics, computers, programmable motion control, and various sensing technologies, are changing the way goods are made and affecting the jobs of those who make them. Precision assemblers have had to learn to use these machines and adapt to changes in work processes. The advent of cellular manufacturing in American firms, for example, has meant that the assembly line is more likely to be composed of "cells" that place a premium on communication and teamwork. As the United States manufacturing sector continues to evolve in the face of growing international competition, the nature of precision assembly will change along with it.

Working Conditions

The conditions under which precision assemblers work depend on the manufacturing plant where they are employed. Electronics assemblers sit at tables in rooms that are clean, well lighted, and free from dust. Assemblers of aircraft and industrial machinery, however, usually come in contact with oil and grease, and their working areas may be quite noisy. They also may have to lift and fit heavy objects.

Most full-time assemblers work a standard 40-hour week, although overtime is fairly common. Work schedules of assemblers may vary at plants with more than one shift. In some plants, workers can accept or reject a certain job on a given shift, usually in order of seniority.

Employment

Virtually all of the 324,000 precision assembler jobs in 1994 were in plants that manufacture durable goods. One-third of all jobs involved assembly of electronic and electrical machinery, equipment, and supplies, including electrical switches, welding equipment, electric motors, lighting equipment, household appliances, and radios and television sets. Nearly one-quarter of all jobs involved assembly of industrial machinery—diesel engines, steam turbine generators, farm tractors, mining and construction machinery, and office machines. Other industries employing many precision assemblers were transportation equipment (aircraft, autos, trucks, and buses) and instruments manufacturing.

The following tabulation lists the wage and salary employment of precision assemblers in 1994 by industry.

Electronic and other electrical equipment manufacturing	109,000
Industrial machinery and equipment manufacturing	81,000
Transportation equipment manufacturing	57,000
Instruments and related products manufacturing	57,000
Fabricated metal products manufacturing	15,000
All other industries	5,000

Training, Other Qualifications, and Advancement

Precision assemblers often are promoted from the ranks of workers in less skilled jobs in the same firm. Sometimes, outside applicants may be hired if they possess suitable experience. The ability to do

Precision assembly requires concentration and manual dexterity.

accurate work at a rapid pace is a key job requirement. A high school diploma is helpful but usually is not required.

For some precision assembly jobs, applicants need specialized training. For example, employers may require that applicants for electrical or electronic assembler jobs be technical school graduates or have equivalent military training.

Good eyesight, with or without glasses, is required for assemblers who work with small parts. In plants that make electrical and electronic products, which may contain many different colored wires, applicants often are tested for color vision.

As precision assemblers become more experienced, they may progress to jobs that require more skill and be given more responsibility. Experienced assemblers who have learned many assembly operations and understand the construction of a product may become product repairers. These workers fix assembled articles that operators or inspectors have identified as defective. Assemblers also can advance to quality control jobs or be promoted to supervisor. In some firms, assemblers can become trainees for one of the skilled trades. Those with a background in math, science, and computers may advance to programmers or operators of more highly automated production equipment.

Job Outlook

Employment of precision assemblers is expected to decline through the year 2005, as increasing automation and internationalization of production will offset any increase in employment that would have resulted from industrial growth. As manufacturing firms strive for greater precision and productivity, jobs that can be performed more economically or more accurately by automated equipment will be upgraded or will disappear. Recent advancements have made robotics more applicable and affordable for manufacturing firms. The introduction of robots in these plants should continue to grow in coming years, raising the productivity of assembly workers and adversely affecting their employment.

The effects of automation will be felt more acutely in some industries than in others. Flexible manufacturing systems are expensive, and a large volume of repetitive work is required to justify their purchase. Also, where the assembly parts involved are irregular in size or location, new technology is only now beginning to make inroads. For example, much precision assembly in the aerospace industry is done in hard-to-reach locations unsuited for robots—inside airplane fuselages or gear boxes, for example—and replacement of these workers by automated processes will be slower and less comprehensive than replacement of other workers such as welders and painters. On the other hand, automation will continue to make more inroads in the precision assembly of electronic goods, where a third of these workers are employed.

An alternative to automation for many firms is sending their subassembly or component production functions to countries where labor costs are lower. This growing internationalization of production will be promoted by more liberal trade and investment. Although there will be some growth in exports of goods assembled in the United States as a result of this freer trade environment, growing imports and decisions by American corporations to relocate assembly in other nations will, on balance, lead to employment reductions for precision assemblers.

Despite the expected decline in employment, job openings will still arise as workers transfer to other occupations or leave the labor force. Moreover, the need for precision, independent judgment, and specialized knowledge will ensure the continued employment of many precision assemblers.

Earnings

Earnings information is somewhat limited for precision assemblers. Full-time workers who assemble electrical and electronic equipment had median weekly earnings of about $330 in 1994. Most earned between $260 and $430; the lowest 10 percent earned less than $210 a week while the highest 10 percent earned over $590. In addition to earnings, most precision assemblers receive typical benefits such as health and life insurance, a pension plan, paid vacation, and sick leave.

Many precision assemblers are members of labor unions. These unions include the International Association of Machinists and Aerospace Workers; the United Electrical, Radio and Machine Workers of America; the United Automobile, Aerospace and Agricultural Implement Workers of America; the International Brotherhood of Electrical Workers; and the United Steelworkers.

Related Occupations

Other occupations that involve operating machines and tools and assembling products include welders, ophthalmic laboratory technicians, and machine operators.

Sources of Additional Information

Information about employment opportunities for assemblers is available from local offices of the State employment service and from locals of the unions mentioned earlier.

Blue-Collar Worker Supervisors

(List of D.O.T. codes available on request. See p. 478.)

Nature of the Work

For the millions of workers who assemble manufactured goods, service electronics equipment, build office buildings, load trucks, or perform thousands of other activities, a blue-collar worker supervisor is the boss. These supervisors ensure that workers, equipment, and materials are used properly and efficiently to maximize productivity. They are often responsible for very expensive and complex equipment or systems. Supervisors make sure machinery is set up correctly and schedule or perform repairs and maintenance work. Supervisors create work schedules, keep production and employee records, monitor employees and ensure that work is done correctly and on time. They organize the workers' activities and make any necessary adjustments to ensure that work continues uninterrupted. Supervisors also train new workers and ensure the existence of a safe working environment.

Blue-collar worker supervisors may have other titles, such as first-line supervisor or foreman/forewoman. In the textile industry, they may be referred to as second hands; on ships they may be called boatswains. In the construction industry, they can be referred to as superintendents, crew chiefs, or foremen/forewomen, depending upon the type and size of their employer. Toolpushers or gang pushers are the common terms used to describe blue-collar supervisors in the oil drilling business.

Regardless of industry setting or job title, a supervisor's primary responsibility is to ensure that the work gets done. The way supervisors accomplish this task, however, is changing in some organizations. In companies that have restructured their operations for maximum efficiency, supervisors use computers to schedule work flow, monitor the quality of their workers' output, keep track of materials used, update their inventory control system, and perform other supervisory tasks. New management philosophies emphasize fewer levels of management and greater employee power and decision making. In the past, supervisors used their power and authority to direct the efforts of their subordinates; increasingly, supervisors are assuming the role of a facilitator for groups of workers, aiding in group decision making and conflict resolution.

Blue-collar worker supervisors have many interpersonal tasks related to their job as well. They inform workers about company plans and policies; recommend good performers for wage increases, awards, or promotions; and deal with poor performers by outlining expectations, counseling workers in proper methods, issuing warnings, or recommending disciplinary action. They also meet on a regular basis with their managers, reporting any problems and discussing possible solutions. Supervisors also meet among themselves to discuss goals, company operations, and performance. In companies with labor unions, supervisors must follow all provisions of labor-management contracts.

Working Conditions

Many blue-collar worker supervisors work in a shop environment. They may be on their feet much of the time overseeing the work of subordinates and may work near loud and dangerous machinery. Other supervisors, such as those in construction and oil exploration and production, may work outdoors and are subject to all kinds of weather conditions.

Supervisors may be on the job before other workers arrive and stay after they leave. Some supervisors work in plants that operate around the clock and may work any one of three shifts as well as on weekends and holidays. In some cases, supervisors work all three shifts on a rotating basis; in others, shift assignments are made on the basis of seniority.

Employment

Blue-collar worker supervisors held about 1.9 million jobs in 1994. Although salaried supervisors are found in almost all industries, 4 of every 10 worked in manufacturing—supervising the production of industrial machinery, motor vehicles, appliances, and thousands of other products. Other industries employing blue-collar worker supervisors included construction, wholesale and retail trade, public

Blue-collar worker supervisors are employed in nearly every industry.

utilities, repair shops, transportation, and government. Employment is distributed in much the same way as the population, and jobs are located in all cities and towns.

Training, Other Qualifications, and Advancement

When choosing supervisors, employers generally look for experience, job knowledge, organizational skills, and leadership qualities. Employers emphasize the ability to motivate employees, maintain high morale, and command respect. In addition, employers desire well rounded applicants who are able to deal with different situations and different types of people. Communication and interpersonal skills are extremely important attributes in this occupation.

Completion of high school is often the minimum educational requirement to become a blue-collar worker supervisor, but workers generally need training in human resources and management before they advance to these positions. Although many workers still rise through the ranks with high school diplomas, employers are increasingly hiring applicants with postsecondary technical degrees. In high-technology industries, such as aerospace and electronics, employers typically require a bachelor's degree or technical school training. Employers in the manufacturing sector generally prefer a background in engineering, mathematics, science, business administration, or industrial relations. Large companies usually offer better opportunities than smaller companies for promotion to blue-collar worker supervisor positions.

In most manufacturing companies, a degree in business or engineering combined with in-house training is needed to advance to department head or production manager. In the construction industry, supervisors increasingly need a degree in construction management or engineering, particularly if they expect to advance to project manager, operations manager, or general superintendent. Some use their skills and experience to start their own construction contracting firms. Supervisors in repair shops may open their own business.

Job Outlook

No change is expected in the employment of blue-collar worker supervisors through the year 2005. Because the occupation is so large, however, many openings will arise from the need to replace workers who transfer to other occupations or leave the labor force.

Job prospects vary by industry. In manufacturing, employment of supervisors is expected to decline slightly as the trend continues for supervisors to oversee more workers. This reflects the increasing use of computers to meet supervisory responsibilities such as scheduling, the effects of worker empowerment programs that relieve supervisors of some of the more time-consuming tasks, and corporate downsizing. In construction and most other nonmanufacturing industries, employment of blue-collar worker supervisors is expected to rise along with the employment of the workers they supervise.

Because of their skill and seniority, blue-collar worker supervisors often are protected from layoffs during a recession. However, some in the highly cyclical construction industry may be laid off when construction activity declines.

Earnings

Median weekly earnings for blue-collar worker supervisors were about $610 in 1994. The middle 50 percent earned between $450 and $810. The lowest 10 percent earned less than $360, while the highest 10 percent earned over $1,080. Most supervisors earn significantly more than their subordinates. While most blue-collar workers are paid by the hour, the majority of supervisors receive an annual salary. Some supervisors receive extra pay when they work overtime. Typical benefits for these workers include health and life insurance, pension plans, paid vacation, and sick leave.

Related Occupations

Other workers with supervisory duties include those who supervise professional, technical, sales, clerical, and service workers. Some of these are retail store or department managers, sales managers, clerical supervisors, bank officers, head tellers, hotel managers, postmasters, head cooks, head nurses, and surveyors.

Sources of Additional Information

For information on educational programs for blue-collar worker supervisors, contact:

☛American Management Association, 135 West 50th St., New York, NY 10020.

☛National Management Association, 2210 Arbor Blvd., Dayton, OH 45439.

☛American Institute of Constructors, 466 94th Ave. North, St. Petersburg, FL 33702.

☛Enterprises, 1429 Colonial Blvd., Suite 203, Fort Myers, FL 33907.

Food Processing Occupations

Butchers and Meat, Poultry, and Fish Cutters

(D.O.T. 316.681-010 and .684 except -014; 521.687-058, -106, and -126; 525.361, .381, .664, .684 except -026, -034, and -040, and .687-030, -066, and -074; and 529.686-022.)

Nature of the Work

Butchers and meat, poultry, and fish cutters carve animal carcasses into small pieces of meat suitable for sale to consumers. In meatpacking plants, *meatcutters* slaughter cattle, hogs, goats, and sheep and cut the carcasses into large wholesale cuts such as rounds, loins, ribs, and chucks to facilitate handling, distribution, and marketing. Meat trimmings are used to prepare sausages, luncheon meats, and other fabricated meat products. Meatcutters usually work on assembly lines, with each individual responsible for only a few of the many cuts needed to process a carcass. Depending on the type of cut, they may use knives, cleavers, meat saws, bandsaws, and other equipment.

In grocery stores, wholesale establishments that supply meat to restaurants, and institutional food service facilities, *butchers* separate the wholesale cuts of meat into retail cuts or individual size servings. They cut the meat into steaks and chops using knives and electric saws, shape and tie roasts, and grind beef for sale as chopped meat. Boneless cuts are prepared using knives, slicers, or power cutters, while bandsaws are required on bone-in pieces. Butchers in retail food stores also may weigh, wrap, and label the cuts and arrange them in refrigerated cases for display to customers. They also may prepare special cuts of meat ordered by customers.

Poultry cutters slaughter and cut up chickens, turkeys, and other types of poultry. The poultry processing industry is becoming increasingly automated, but many jobs such as trimming, packing, and deboning are still done manually.

Fish cleaners cut, scale, and dress fish in fish processing plants and wholesale and retail fish markets. They remove the head, scales, and other inedible portions and cut the fish into steaks or boneless fillets. In markets, they may wait on customers and clean fish to order.

Retail meat, poultry, and fish cutters also prepare ready-to-heat foods. This often entails filleting meat or fish or cutting it into bite-sized pieces, preparing and adding vegetables, or applying sauces or breading.

Working Conditions

Working conditions vary by the type and size of establishment. In meatpacking plants and larger retail food establishments, butchers and meatcutters work in large meatcutting rooms equipped with power machines and conveyors. In small retail markets, the butcher

or fish cleaner may work in a space behind the meat counter. To avoid viral and bacterial infections, work areas must be clean and sanitary.

Butchers and meat, poultry, and fish cutters often work in cold, damp rooms. Cutting rooms are refrigerated to prevent meat from spoiling; they are damp because meat cutting generates large amounts of blood and fat. The low temperature, combined with the need to stand for long periods of time, makes the work tiring. Butchers and meat, poultry, and fish cutters are more susceptible to

Meat cutters in grocery stores separate wholesale cuts of meat into retail cuts or individual sized servings.

injury than other workers. In 1992, meatpacking plants had the highest incidence of work-related injury and illness of any industry. Cuts and even amputations, occur when knives, cleavers, and power tools are used improperly. The cool damp floors of meat processing areas increase the likelihood of slips and falls. Repetitive slicing and lifting often leads to cumulative trauma injuries, such as carpal tunnel syndrome. To reduce the incidence of cumulative trauma disorders, many employers have reduced work loads, redesigned jobs and tools, and increased awareness of early warning signs. Nevertheless, workers in this occupation still face a serious threat of a disabling injury.

Employment
Butchers and meat, poultry, and fish cutters held about 351,043 jobs in 1994. Over four-fifths worked in meatpacking and poultry and fish processing plants and retail grocery stores, while others were employed by meat and fish markets, restaurants, hotels, and wholesale establishments. The majority of the 218,994 skilled butchers and meatcutters worked in retail grocery stores, while more than 9 out of 10 of the semiskilled meat, poultry, and fish cutters worked in meatpacking and poultry and fish processing plants. Skilled butchers and meatcutters are employed in almost every city and town in the Nation, while semiskilled meat, poultry, and fish cutter jobs are concentrated in communities with food processing plants.

Training, Other Qualifications, and Advancement
Most butchers and meat, poultry, and fish cutters acquire their skills informally on the job or through apprenticeship programs. A few learn their basic skills by attending trade and vocational schools. However, graduates of these schools may need additional on-the-job training and experience to work as butchers and meatcutters.

Generally, on-the-job trainees begin by doing less difficult jobs, such as removing bones. Under the guidance of experienced workers, they learn the proper use of tools and equipment and how to prepare various cuts of meat. After demonstrating skill with tools, they learn to divide quarters into wholesale cuts and wholesale cuts into retail and individual portions. Trainees may learn to roll and tie roasts, prepare sausage, and cure meat. Those employed in retail food establishments may learn marketing operations such as inventory control, meat buying, and record keeping.

Retail meatcutters and butchers who learn the trade through apprenticeship programs generally complete 2 years of supervised on-the-job training supplemented by classroom work. At the end of the training period, apprentices must pass a meatcutting test. In some areas, apprentices may become meatcutters or butchers without completing the entire training program if they can pass the test.

Skills important in meat, poultry, and fish cutting are manual dexterity, good depth perception, color discrimination, and good eye-hand coordination. Also, physical strength is often needed to lift and move heavy pieces of meat. Butchers and fish cleaners who wait on customers must have a pleasant personality, a neat appearance, and the ability to communicate clearly. In some States a health certificate may be required for employment.

Butchers and meat, poultry, and fish cutters may progress to supervisory jobs, such as meat or seafood department managers in supermarkets. A few become meat or seafood buyers for wholesalers and supermarket chains. Some become grocery store managers or open their own meat or fish markets. In processing plants, butchers and meat, poultry, and fish cutters may move up to supervisory positions.

Job Outlook
Overall employment of butchers and meat, poultry, and fish cutters is expected to grow more slowly than the average for all occupations through the year 2005 as more meat cutting and processing shifts from the retail store to the food processing plant. Nevertheless, job opportunities should be plentiful due to the need to replace experienced workers who transfer to other occupations or leave the labor force.

As the Nation's population grows, the demand for meat, poultry, and seafood should continue to increase. Successful marketing by the poultry industry is likely to increase demand for rotisserie chicken and ready-to-heat products. Similarly, the development of lower fat and ready-to-heat products promises to stimulate the consumption of red meat. The demand for fish and seafood should reach record levels in the coming years.

Employment growth of semiskilled meat, poultry, and fish cutters who work primarily in meatpacking, poultry, and fish processing plants is expected to increase faster than the average for all occupations through the year 2005. Although much of the production of poultry and fabricated poultry products is performed by machines, the growing popularity of labor-intensive ready-to-heat goods promises to spur demand for poultry workers. Semiskilled meat and fish cutters also will be in demand as the task of preparing ready-to-heat meat and fish goods slowly shifts from the retail store to the processing plant. Although the supply of edible ocean fish is limited, advances in fish farming, or "aquaculture," are expected to reduce the gap between supply and demand, and produce ample opportunities for fish cutters.

Employment of skilled butchers and meatcutters, who work primarily in retail stores, is expected to decline gradually. Although meat is increasingly cut and processed at meatpacking plants, this transformation is proceeding slowly. At present, most red meat arrives at the grocery store partially cut up. The retail butcher performs the final processing—cutting wholesale meat cuts into steaks, chops, and roasts and packaging them for sale.

Eventually, as ready-to-heat goods become more popular, both fresh meat and prepared foods will be completely processed and packaged at the plant. Consumers and the retail stores are slowly adjusting to this trend, and the demand for retail meat, poultry, and fish cutters should decline.

Earnings
Butchers and meatcutters had median weekly earnings of $329 in 1994. The middle 50 percent earned between $250 and $522 a week. The highest paid 10 percent earned over $702 a week. Meatcutters employed by retail grocery stores are generally among the highest paid workers.

Butchers and meat and fish cutters generally received paid vacations, sick leave, health insurance, and life insurance. Those who were union members and employed by grocery stores also had pension plans. However, poultry workers tended to rarely earn substantial benefits.

Many butchers and meat, poultry, and fish cutters are members of the United Food and Commercial Workers International Union. In 1992, nearly 30 percent of all butchers and meatcutters were union members or covered by a union contract.

Related Occupations
Butchers and meat, poultry, and fish cutters must be skilled at both hand and machine work and must have some knowledge of processes and techniques involved in handling and preparing food. Other occupations in food preparation which require similar skills and knowledge include bakers, chefs and cooks, and food preparation workers.

Sources of Additional Information
Information about work opportunities can be obtained from local employers or local offices of the State employment service. For information on training and other aspects of the trade, contact:

☛United Food and Commercial Workers International Union, 1775 K St. NW., Washington, DC 20006.

Inspectors, Testers, and Graders

(List of D.O.T. codes available on request. See p. 478.)

Nature of the Work
Inspectors, testers, and graders ensure that your food won't make you sick, your car will run when you buy it, and your pants won't split the first time you wear them. These workers monitor quality standards for virtually all manufactured products, including foods, textiles, clothing, glassware, motor vehicles, electronic components, computers, and structural steel.

Inspectors visually check products and may also listen to, feel, smell, or even taste them. They verify dimensions, color, weight, texture, strength, or other physical characteristics of objects, and look for imperfections such as cuts, scratches, bubbles, missing pieces, misweaves, or crooked seams. Many inspectors use micrometers, electronic equipment, calipers, alignment gauges, and other instruments to check and compare the dimensions of parts against the parts' specifications. Those testing electrical devices may use voltmeters, ammeters, and oscilloscopes to test the insulation, current flow, and resistance. Machinery testers generally check that parts fit and move correctly and are properly lubricated, check the pressure of gases and the level of liquids, test the flow of electricity, and do a test run to check for proper operation. Some jobs involve only a quick visual inspection; others require a much longer detailed one. Senior inspectors may also set up tests and test equipment.

Inspectors, testers, and graders are involved at every stage of the production process. Some inspectors examine materials received from a supplier before sending them to the production line. Others inspect components, subassemblies, and assemblies or perform a final check on the finished product.

Inspectors mark, tag, or note problems. They may reject defective items outright, send them for rework, or, in the case of minor problems, fix them themselves. If the product checks out, they may screw on a nameplate, tag it, stamp a serial number, or certify it in some other way. Inspectors, testers, and graders record the results of their inspections, compute the percentage of defects and other statistical parameters, prepare inspection and test reports, notify supervisors of problems, and help analyze and correct problems in the production process. They also calibrate precision instruments used in inspection work.

The recent emphasis on quality control in manufacturing has meant that inspection is becoming more fully integrated into the production process. Many machines are now self-monitoring to ensure that the product is produced within quality standards. Inspectors still test products to ensure that they meet specifications but, with the help of these machines, they direct the production line to adjust the machinery before the manufacturing line produces unusable parts. Also, many firms have automated inspection with the help of advanced vision systems, using machinery installed at one or several points in the production process. The inspectors in these firms generally are trained to operate this equipment.

Working Conditions
Working conditions vary from industry to industry. Some inspectors examine similar products for an entire shift; others examine a variety of items. Most remain at one work station, but some travel from place to place to do inspections. Some are on their feet all day; others sit. In some industries, inspectors are exposed to the noise and grime of machinery; in others, they work in a clean, quiet environment. Some may have to lift heavy objects.

Some inspectors work evenings, nights, or weekends. In these cases, shift assignments generally are made on the basis of seniority. Overtime may be required to meet production goals.

Employment
Inspectors, testers, and graders held about 654,000 jobs in 1994. More than 3 out of 4 worked in manufacturing industries, including industrial machinery and equipment, motor vehicles and equipment, primary and fabricated metals industries, electronic components and accessories, textiles, apparel, and aircraft and parts. Others worked in temporary help services, communications and utilities, wholesale trade, engineering and management services, and government agencies. Although they are employed throughout the country, most jobs are in large metropolitan areas where many large factories are located.

Training, Other Qualifications, and Advancement
A high school diploma is helpful and may be required for some jobs. Simple jobs are generally filled by beginners with a few days of training. More complex ones are filled by experienced assemblers, machine operators, or mechanics who already have a thorough knowledge of the products and production processes. Inspectors,

Inspection is becoming more integrated into the production process.

406

testers, and graders also need mechanical aptitude, good hand-eye coordination, and good vision.

In-house training for new inspectors may cover the use of special meters, gauges, computers, or other instruments; quality control techniques; blueprint reading; and reporting requirements. There are some postsecondary training programs in testing, but many employers prefer to train inspectors themselves.

Advancement for these workers frequently takes the form of higher pay. However, they also may advance to inspector of more complex products, supervisor, or quality control technician.

Job Outlook

Individuals wishing to become inspectors, testers, or graders may face competition. Although the occupation is large, giving rise to a large number of openings due to normal turnover, some jobs may be available only to those having experience with the production process. Also, like many other occupations concentrated in manufacturing, employment of these workers is projected to decline through the year 2005.

Even though the volume of manufactured goods will grow, employment of inspectors, testers, and graders will not grow for several reasons. Manufacturers are taking steps to improve production methods by using computers and statistical analysis to control the production process. In some cases, machines alert workers when items approach limits so that problems can be corrected before defects occur. This growing emphasis on quality will drive down the number of defective parts and help to reduce the demand for inspectors. In addition, assemblers, machine operators, and other production workers are becoming responsible for quality control in many firms, and they are correcting problems as they occur. As these responsibilities shift from inspectors to other workers, fewer inspectors, testers, and graders will be needed. Moreover, automated inspecting machinery is improving inspectors' speed and accuracy, resulting in higher productivity and adversely affecting employment of these workers.

In many industries, however, automation is not being aggressively pursued as an alternative to manual inspection. When key inspection elements are size oriented, such as length, width, or thickness, automation may play some role in the future. But when taste, smell, texture, appearance, or product performance are important, inspection will probably continue to be done by humans.

Earnings

Iinspectors, testers, and graders had median weekly earnings of about $430 in 1994. The middle 50 percent earned between $310 and $590 a week. The lowest 10 percent earned less than $240 a week; the highest 10 percent earned more than $780. In addition to these earnings, most inspectors, testers, and graders receive benefits including health and life insurance, pension plans, paid vacations, and sick leave.

Related Occupations

Other workers who inspect products or services are construction and building inspectors and inspectors and compliance officers, except construction, which includes consumer safety, environmental health, agricultural commodity, immigration, customs, postal, motor vehicle, safety, and other inspectors.

Sources of Additional Information

For general information about this occupation, contact:
☛The National Tooling and Machining Association, 9300 Livingston Rd., Fort Washington, MD 20744.
☛The American Society for Quality Control, 611 East Wisconsin Ave., Milwaukee, WI 53202-4606.

Metalworking and Plastics-Working Occupations

Boilermakers

(D.O.T. 805.261 .361, and .381)

Nature of the Work

Boilermakers and boilermaker mechanics make, install, and repair boilers, vats, and other large vessels that hold liquids and gases. Boilers supply steam to drive huge turbines in electric power plants and to provide heat or power in buildings, factories, and ships. Tanks and vats are used to process and store chemicals, oil, beer, and hundreds of other products.

Boilers and other high pressure vessels are usually made in sections by casting each piece out of molten iron or steel. Manufacturers are increasingly automating this process to increase quality. The boiler sections are then welded together, often using automated orbital welding machines, which make more consistent welds than possible by hand. Small boilers may be assembled in the manufacturing plant; larger boilers are usually assembled on site.

Following blueprints, boilermakers locate and mark reference points on the boiler foundation for installing boilers and other vessels, using straightedges, squares, transits, and tape measures. They attach rigging and signal crane operators to lift heavy frame and plate sections and other parts into place. They align sections, using plumb bobs, levels, wedges, and turnbuckles; use hammers, files, grinders, and cutting torches to remove irregular edges so they fit properly; and bolt or weld them together. Boilermakers align and attach water tubes, stacks, valves, gauges, and other parts and test complete vessels for leaks or other defects. Usually they assemble large vessels temporarily in a fabrication shop to insure a proper fit and again on their permanent site.

Because boilers last for a long time—35 years or longer—boilermakers regularly maintain them and update components such as burners and boiler tubes to make them as efficient as possible. Boilermaker mechanics maintain and repair boilers and similar vessels. They clean or direct others to clean boilers and inspect tubes, fittings, valves, controls, and auxiliary machinery. They repair or replace defective parts, using hand and power tools, gas torches, and welding equipment, and may operate metalworking machinery to repair or make parts. They also dismantle leaky boilers, patch weak spots with metal stock, replace defective sections, or strengthen joints.

Working Conditions

Boilermakers often use potentially dangerous equipment such as acetylene torches and power grinders, handle heavy parts, and work on ladders or on top of large vessels. Work may be done in cramped

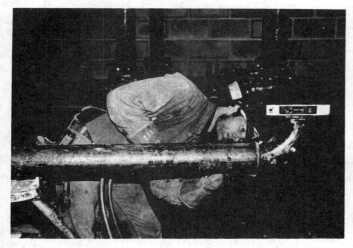

Boilermakers constantly check their work to ensure the safe operation of the installed boiler system.

quarters inside boilers, vats, or tanks that often are damp and poorly ventilated. To reduce the chance of injuries, they may wear hardhats, harnesses, respirators, protective clothing, and safety glasses and shoes. Boilermakers usually work a 40-hour week but may experience extended periods of overtime when equipment is shut down for maintenance. Overtime work may also be required to meet construction or production deadlines.

Employment

Boilermakers held about 20,000 jobs in 1994. About 44 percent worked in manufacturing, primarily in boiler manufacturing shops, iron and steel plants, petroleum refineries, chemical plants, and shipyards. One-third worked in the construction industry, assembling and erecting boilers and other vessels. Some also work for boiler repair firms, railroads, and in Navy shipyards and Federal power facilities.

Training, Other Qualifications, and Advancement

Most training authorities recommend a formal apprenticeship to learn this trade. Some people become boilermakers by working as helpers to experienced boilermakers, but generally lack the wide range of skills acquired through apprenticeship. Apprenticeship programs usually consist of 4 years of on-the-job training, supplemented by about 144 hours of classroom instruction each year in subjects such as set-up and assembly rigging, welding of all types, blueprint reading, and layout. Experienced boilermakers often attend apprenticeship classes to keep their knowledge current.

When an apprenticeship becomes available, the local union will publicize the opportunity by notifying local vocational schools and high school vocational programs. Qualified applicants take an aptitude test administered by the union specifically designed for boilermaking. The apprenticeship is awarded to the person scoring highest on this test.

When hiring helpers, employers prefer high school or vocational school graduates. Courses in shop, mathematics, blueprint reading, welding, and machine metalworking are useful. Mechanical aptitude and the manual dexterity needed to handle tools also are important.

Some boilermakers advance to supervisory positions; because of their broader training, apprentices generally have an advantage in promotion.

Job Outlook

Persons who wish to become boilermakers may face some competition, due to the limited number of apprenticeships available and the relatively good wages a journey boilermaker earns. In addition,

employment of boilermakers is expected to decline through the year 2005. However, a limited number of openings will arise from the need to replace experienced workers who leave the occupation.

Growth should be limited by several factors: The trend toward repairing and retrofitting rather than replacing existing boilers; the use of smaller boilers, which require less on-site assembly; automation of production technologies; and an increase in the use of imported boilers.

Most of the industries that purchase boilers are sensitive to economic conditions. Therefore, during economic downturns, construction boilermakers may be laid off. However, because boilers are maintained and repaired even during economic downturns, boilermaker mechanics generally have more stable employment.

Earnings

According to the limited data available, boilermakers who usually worked full time had median earnings of about $532 per week in 1994.

According to the International Brotherhood of Boilermakers, journey boilermakers earned $21.20 per hour in 1994. Apprentices started at 60 percent of journey wages, or about $12.70 hourly, with wages increasing gradually to the journey wage as progress is made in the apprenticeship. However, wages vary greatly around the country, with higher wages in Northeastern, Great Lakes, and Far Western cities than in other areas of the country.

Most boilermakers belong to labor unions. The principal union is the International Brotherhood of Boilermakers. Others are members of the International Association of Machinists, the United Automobile Workers, and the United Steelworkers of America.

Related Occupations

Workers in a number of other occupations assemble, install, or repair metal equipment or machines. These include assemblers, blacksmiths, instrument makers, ironworkers, machinists, millwrights, patternmakers, plumbers, sheet-metal workers, tool and die makers, and welders.

Sources of Additional Information

For further information regarding boilermaking apprenticeships or other training opportunities, contact local offices of the unions previously mentioned, local construction companies and boiler manufacturers, or the local office of the State employment service.

For general information regarding boilermaking and opportunities in the boiler manufacturing industry, contact:
☛American Boiler Manufacturing Association, 950 North Glebe Rd., Suite 160, Arlington, VA 22203-1824.

Jewelers

(D.O.T. 199.281; 700.281-010, -014, -022, and .381-030, -042, and -046)

Nature of the Work

Jewelers make, repair, and adjust rings, necklaces, bracelets, earrings, and other jewelry. Using drills, pliers, jeweler's soldering torches, saws, jeweler's lathes, and a variety of other handtools, they mold and shape metal and set gemstones. Jewelers also may use chemicals and polishing compounds, such as flux for soldering and tripoli and rouge for finishing.

Jewelers usually specialize in one or more areas of the jewelry field—buying, design, gem cutting, repair, sales, or appraisal. In small retail or repair shops, they may be involved in all aspects of the work. Regardless of the type of establishment or work setting, however, their work requires a high degree of skill and attention to detail. Those working in retail jewelry stores, in addition to their primary responsibility to sell jewelry, may spend some time repairing or adjusting it. In other cases, retailers send jewelry to specialized jewelry repair shops. Typical work includes enlarging or reducing rings, resetting stones, and replacing broken clasps and mountings. Some jewelers also design or make their own jewelry. Following their own designs or those created by designers or customers, they begin by shaping the metal or by carving wax to make a model for casting the metal. The individual parts are then soldered together, and the jeweler may mount a diamond or other gem or may engrave a design into the metal.

Jewelers who own or manage stores or shops hire and train employees; order, market, and sell merchandise; and perform other managerial duties. In manufacturing, jewelers usually specialize in a single operation. Some may make models or tools for the jewelry that is to be produced. Others do finishing work, such as setting stones, polishing, or engraving. A growing number of jewelers use lasers for cutting and improving the quality of stones.

Technology has not yet greatly affected the jewelry industry. However, some manufacturing firms use CAD/CAM (computer-aided design and manufacturing) to facilitate product design and automate some steps in mold and model making. Use of such systems should increase in the future as they become more affordable for smaller companies. In retail stores, computers are used mainly for inventory control; some jewelers use computers to design and create customized pieces according to their customers' wishes. With the aid of computers, customers visualize different combinations of styles, cuts, shanks, sizes, and stones to create their own pieces.

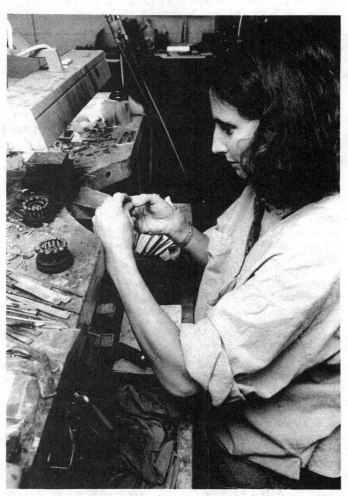

Jewelers need a keen eye for details.

Working Conditions

Jewelers usually do most of their work seated in comfortable surroundings, and the trade involves few physical hazards. While the work is not physically strenuous, there is a lot of work with detail and intricate designs which may be tiring to some. Caution must be taken because the chemicals, sawing and drilling tools, and torches a jeweler uses can cause serious injury. In addition, doing delicate work on precious stones or metals while trying to satisfy demands for speed and quality from customers and employers can cause stress, and bending over a workbench for long periods can be uncomfortable. In the future, the use of computers may ease some of these conditions since applications like CAD/CAM greatly increase the speed and accuracy of the design and manufacturing process.

Because many of the materials with which they work are very valuable, those working in retail stores must observe strict security procedures. These may include locked doors that are only opened by a buzzer, barred windows, burglar alarms, and the presence of armed guards.

In repair shops, jewelers generally work alone with little supervision. In retail stores, on the other hand, they may talk with customers about repairs, perform custom design work, and even do some sales work.

Employment

Jewelers held about 30,000 jobs in 1994. About 35 percent of all jewelers were self-employed; many operated their own store or repair shop, and some specialized in designing and creating custom jewelry.

Nearly 55 percent of all salaried jewelers worked in retail establishments, while another 30 percent were employed in manufacturing plants. Although jewelry stores and repair shops can be found in every city and many small towns, most job opportunities are in larger metropolitan areas. Many jewelers employed in manufacturing work in New York, California, or Rhode Island.

Training, Other Qualifications, and Advancement

Jewelers' skills usually are learned in technical schools, through correspondence courses, or informally on the job. Some aspiring jewelers begin working as clerks in department stores and transfer to jobs in jewelry shops or manufacturing firms after gaining experience. Colleges and art schools also offer programs which can lead to a bachelor's or master's degree of fine arts in jewelry design. Formal training in the basic skills of the trade enhances one's employment and advancement opportunities. Many employers prefer well-rounded jewelers with design, repair, and sales skills.

For those interested in working in a jewelry store or repair shop, technical schools or courses offered by local colleges are the best sources of training. In these programs, which vary in length from 6 months to 2 years, students learn the use and care of jewelers' tools and machines and basic jewelry making and repairing skills, such as design, casting, stone setting, and polishing. Technical school courses also cover topics like blueprint reading, math, and shop theory. Most employers feel that graduates need several more years of supervised on-the-job training to refine their repair skills and to learn more about the operation of the store or shop. In addition, some employers encourage workers to improve their skills by enrolling in short-term technical school courses such as sample making, wax carving, or gemology. Many employers pay all or part of the cost of this additional training.

The Gemological Institute of America offers programs lasting about 6 months, and self-paced correspondence courses lasting several years, leading to a gemologist diploma and a jeweler diploma. These advanced programs cover a wide range of topics including appraisal, evaluating diamonds and colored stones, identifying gems, and designing jewelry.

In jewelry manufacturing plants, workers traditionally have developed their skills through apprenticeships and informal on-the-job training. This training may last 3 to 4 years, depending on the difficulty of the specialty. Training usually focuses on casting, stonesetting, modelmaking, or engraving. In recent years, a growing number of technical schools and colleges have begun to offer training designed for jewelers working in manufacturing. Like employers in retail trade, those in manufacturing prefer graduates of these programs because they are familiar with the production process, allowing less in-house training.

To enter most technical school or college programs, a high school diploma or its equivalent is required. Courses in art, math, mechanical drawing, and chemistry are useful. Since computer-aided design is increasingly used in the jewelry field, it is recommended that students—especially those interested in design and manufacturing—obtain training in CAD.

The precise and delicate nature of jewelry work requires finger and hand dexterity, good hand-eye coordination, patience, and concentration. Artistic ability and fashion consciousness are major assets, because jewelry must be stylish and attractive. Those who work in jewelry stores have frequent contact with customers and should be neat, personable, and knowledgeable about the merchandise. In addition, employers require someone of good character because jewelers work with very valuable materials.

Advancement opportunities are limited and greatly dependent on an individual's skill and initiative. In manufacturing, some jewelers advance to supervisory jobs, such as master jeweler or head jeweler, but for most, advancement takes the form of higher pay for doing the same job. Jewelers who work in jewelry stores or repair shops may become salaried managers; some open their own businesses.

For those interested in starting their own business, a substantial financial investment is needed to acquire the necessary inventory. Also, because the jewelry business is highly competitive, jewelers who plan to open their own store should have experience in selling, as well as knowledge of marketing and business management. Courses in these areas often are available from technical schools and community colleges.

Job Outlook

Employment of jewelers is expected to increase more slowly than the average for all occupations through the year 2005. Traditionally, job opportunities for jewelers depended largely on jewelry sales and on demand for jewelry repair services. Now, however, non-traditional jewelry marketers such as discount stores, mail-order catalogue companies, and television shopping networks have limited the growth of sales made by traditional jewelers, limiting job opportunities because these types of establishments require few if any jewelers.

Because the demand for jewelry is largely affected by the amount of disposable income people have, the increasing number of affluent individuals, working women, double-income households, and fashion conscious men are expected to keep jewelry sales strong.

Jewelers have a relatively strong attachment to their occupations—reflecting the large proportion of self-employed workers. Nevertheless, job openings will largely result from the need to replace jewelers who transfer to other occupations, retire, or leave the labor force for other reasons.

Opportunities in jewelry stores and repair shops will be best for graduates from jeweler or gemologist training programs. Demand for repair workers will be strong because maintaining and repairing jewelry is an ongoing process, even during economic slowdowns. In fact, demand for jewelry repair may increase during recessions as people repair or restore existing pieces rather than purchase new ones.

Increasing automation within jewelry manufacturing will adversely affect employment of low-skilled occupations, like assembler and polisher. Automation will have a lesser impact on more creative, highly skilled positions, such as mold and model maker. Because of recent international trade agreements, exports are steadily increasing as manufacturers become more competitive in foreign markets.

Earnings

Median weekly earning of jewelers in all industries were $400 in 1994. Depending on the employer, jewelers may receive commis-

sions on what they sell or bonuses for outstanding work. According to the *Jewelers' Circular-Keystone* annual salary survey, the median salary of jewelers in retail stores was approximately $25,700 in 1993, while the median annual salary of jewelry repair workers was $26,200.

For those in manufacturing, earnings of experienced, unionized jewelry workers averaged between $12 and $17 an hour in 1994, according to the limited information available. According to the Manufacturing Jewelers and Silversmiths of America, the median average hourly wage of jewelers in companies with more than 10 employees was $11.64 in 1994. Beginners in jewelry factories generally start at considerably less than experienced workers; as they become more proficient, they receive periodic raises.

Most jewelers enjoy a variety of fringe benefits including reimbursement from their employers for work-related courses and discounts on jewelry purchases.

Related Occupations

Other skilled workers who do similar jobs include polishers, dental laboratory technicians, gemcutters, hand engravers, and watch makers and repairers.

Sources of Additional Information

Information on job opportunities and training programs for jewelers is available from:
☛Gemological Institute of America, 1660 Stewart St., Santa Monica, CA 90404.

General career information is available from:
☛Jewelers of America, 1185 Avenue of the Americas, New York, NY 10036.
☛Manufacturing Jewelers and Silversmiths of America, 1 State St., 6th Floor, Providence, RI 02908-5035.

To receive a list of technical schools accredited by the Accrediting Commission of Career Schools and Colleges of Technology that have programs in jewelry design, contact:
☛Accrediting Commission of Career Schools and Colleges of Technology, 2101 Wilson Blvd., Suite 302, Arlington, VA 22201.

Machinists and Tool Programmers

(D.O.T. 007.167-018; 600.260-022, .280-022, -026, -030, -034, -042, .281-010, .380-010; 609.262-010; and 714.281-018)

Nature of the Work

Machinists use machine tools such as lathes, drill presses, and milling machines to produce precision metal parts. Although they may produce large quantities of one part, machinists usually produce small batches or one-of-a-kind items. They use their knowledge of the working properties of metals—such as steel, cast iron, aluminum, and brass—and their skill with machine tools to plan and carry out the operations needed to make machined products that meet precise specifications.

Machinists first review blueprints or written specifications for a job. Next, they calculate where to cut or bore into the workpiece, how fast to feed the metal into the machine, and how much metal to remove. They then select tools and materials for the job, plan the sequence of cutting and finishing operations, and mark the metal stock to show where these cuts should be made.

After this layout work is completed, machinists perform the necessary machining operations. They position the metal stock on the machine tool—drill presses, lathes, milling machines, or others—set the controls, and make the cuts. Today, new machinery allows various functions to be performed with one setup, which reduces the need for additional, labor-intensive setups, saving time and money. During the machining process, they must constantly monitor the feed and speed of the machine. Machinists must also ensure that the workpiece is being properly lubricated and cooled because the machining of metal products generates a significant amount of heat.

Some machinists, often called production machinists, may produce large quantities of one part, especially parts requiring complex operations and great precision. For unusually sophisticated procedures, expensive machinery is used. Usually, however, large numbers of parts requiring more routine operations are produced by metalworking machine operators (see the statement on metalworking and plastics-working machine operators elsewhere in the *Handbook*). Other machinists do maintenance work—repairing or making new parts for existing machinery. For example, to repair a broken part, maintenance machinists may refer to blueprints and perform the same machining operations that were needed to create the original part.

Increasingly, the machine tools used to produce metal parts are numerically controlled (NC)—that is, they contain an electronic controller that directs the machine's operations. Most NC machines today are computer numerically controlled (CNC), which means that the controllers are computers. The controller "reads" a program—a coded list of the steps necessary to perform a specific machining job—and runs the machine tool's mechanisms through the steps.

The introduction of computer numerically controlled machines has greatly changed the nature of the work and productivity of machinists. These machines enable machinists to be more productive and to produce parts with a level of precision that is not possible with traditional machining techniques. Furthermore, because precise movements are recorded in the program, they allow this high level of precision to be consistently repeated.

The quality of the products these machines produce depends largely on the programs, which may be produced by machinists or by tool programmers—workers who specialize in programming machine tools.

Tool programmers begin as machinists do—by analyzing blueprints, computing the size and position of the cuts, determining the sequence of machine operations, selecting tools, and calculating the machine speed and feed rates. They then write the program in the language of the machine's controller and store it. Skilled machinists may also do programming. In fact, as computer software becomes more user friendly and CNC machines are used more widely, machinists are expected to perform this function more and more.

Machinists may work alone or with tool programmers to check new programs to ensure that machinery will function properly and the output will meet specifications. Because a problem with the program could damage the costly machinery and cutting tools, computer simulations may be used instead of a trial run to check the program. If errors are found, the program must be changed and retested until the problem is resolved. Some programs are modified for use on other jobs with similar specifications, thereby reducing the time and effort needed to start production of a part. A growing number of firms employ computer-aided design (CAD) systems to assist in writing programs.

Working Conditions

Most machine shops are well lighted and ventilated. Nevertheless, working around high-speed machine tools presents certain dangers, and workers must follow safety precautions. Machinists must wear protective equipment such as safety glasses to shield against bits of flying metal and earplugs to protect against machinery noise. They must also exercise caution when handling hazardous coolants and lubricants. The job requires stamina because machinists stand most of the day and may lift moderately heavy workpieces.

Some tool programmers work in offices that are near, but separate from, the shop floor. These work areas are usually clean, well lighted, and free of machine noise.

Most machinists and tool programmers work a 40-hour week. Evening and weekend shifts are becoming more common as companies invest in more expensive machinery. Overtime is common during peak production periods.

Employment

Machinists and tool programmers held about 376,000 jobs in 1994. Most machinists worked in small machining shops or in manufacturing firms that produce durable goods such as metalworking and industrial machinery, aircraft, or motor vehicles. Maintenance machinists work in most industries that use production machinery. Although machinists and tool programmers work in all parts of the country, jobs are most plentiful in areas where manufacturing is concentrated.

Training, Other Qualifications, and Advancement

A high school or vocational school education, including mathematics, blueprint reading, metalworking, and drafting, is desirable for becoming a machinist or tool programmer. A basic knowledge of computers and electronics is helpful because of the increased use of computer-controlled machine tools. Experience with machine tools also is helpful. In fact, many of the people who enter these occupations have previously worked as machine tool operators or setters.

Machinist training varies from formal apprenticeship and postsecondary programs to informal on-the-job training. Apprentice programs consist of shop training and related classroom instruction. In shop training, apprentices learn filing, handtapping, and dowel fitting, as well as the operation of various machine tools. Classroom instruction includes math, physics, blueprint reading, mechanical drawing, and shop practices. In addition, as machine shops have increased their use of computer-controlled equipment, training in the operation and programming of numerically controlled machine tools has become essential. A growing number of machinists and tool programmers receive most of their formal training from community colleges.

Qualifications for tool programmers vary widely depending upon the complexity of the job. Basic requirements parallel those of machinists. Employers often prefer skilled machinists, tool and die makers, or those with technical school training. For some specialized types of programming, such as with complex parts for the aerospace or shipbuilding industries, employers may prefer individuals with a degree in engineering.

For those entering tool programming directly, a basic knowledge of computers and electronics is necessary and experience with machine tools is extremely helpful. Classroom training includes an introduction to numerical control and the basics of programming and then advances to more complex topics such as computer-aided design. Trainees start writing simple programs under the direction of

Despite a slight projected decline, employment opportunities should be good for skilled machinists.

an experienced programmer. Although machinery manufacturers are trying to standardize programming languages, currently there are numerous languages in use. Because of this, tool programmers must be able to learn and adapt to new programming languages.

Established workers may also take courses to update their skills and to learn the latest technology and equipment. Some employers offer tuition reimbursement for job-related courses. In addition, when new machinery is introduced, workers receive training in its operation—usually from a representative of the equipment manufacturer.

Persons interested in becoming a machinist or tool programmer should be mechanically inclined. They also should be able to work independently and do highly accurate work that requires concentration as well as physical effort.

Workers may advance in several ways. Experienced machinists may become tool programmers; some move into supervisory or administrative positions in their firms; and a few may open their own shops.

Job Outlook
Employment of machinists and tool programmers is expected to decline slightly through the year 2005. Nevertheless, job opportunities will be good, as employers continue to report difficulties in attracting workers to machining and tool programming occupations. Therefore, candidates with the necessary mechanical and mathematical aptitudes should encounter ample demand for their skills. Many job openings also will arise each year from the need to replace experienced machinists and programmers who transfer to other occupations or retire.

The number of openings for machinists is expected to be far greater than the number of openings for tool programmers, primarily because the occupation is larger.

Automation is the major factor in the employment decline projected for machinists and tool programmers. The use of computer-controlled machine tools, for example, reduces the time required for machining operations and increases worker productivity. This allows fewer machinists to accomplish the same amount of work previously performed by more workers. Advanced machine tool technology is allowing some programming to be performed on the shop floor by machinists, tool and die makers, and machine operators. These simplified controls are one of the main factors behind the slight employment decline expected for tool programmers in the coming years.

Employment levels in these occupations is influenced by economic cycles; as the demand for machined goods falls, machinists and tool programmers involved in production may be laid off or be forced to work fewer hours. Employment of machinists involved in plant maintenance, however, is often more stable because proper maintenance and repair of costly equipment remain vital concerns even when production levels fall.

Earnings
Earnings of machinists compare favorably with those of other skilled workers. In 1994, median weekly earnings for machinists were about $520. Most earned between $400 and $690. The lowest paid ten percent of all machinists had median weekly earnings of less than $300; the 10 percent with the highest earnings made more than $880 a week. In addition to their hourly wage, most workers receive typical benefits such as health and life insurance, a pension plan, paid vacations, and sick leave.

Related Occupations
Occupations most closely related to that of machinist and tool programmer are the other machining occupations. These include tool and die maker, tool and die designer, tool planner, and instrument maker. Workers in other occupations that require precision and skill in working with metal include blacksmiths, gunsmiths, locksmiths, metal patternmakers, and welders.

Tool programmers apply their knowledge of machining operations, metals, blueprints, and machine programming to write programs that run machine tools. Computer programmers also write detailed instructions for a machine—in this case a computer.

Sources of Additional Information
For general information about this occupation, contact:
☛The Association for Manufacturing Technology, 7901 Westpark Dr., McLean, VA 22102.
☛The National Tooling and Machining Association, 9300 Livingston Rd., Fort Washington, MD 20744.
☛The Tooling and Manufacturing Association, ATTN: Education Department, 1177 South Dee Rd., Park Ridge, IL 60068.
☛Precision Metalforming Association, 27027 Chardon Rd., Richmond Heights, OH 44143.

Metalworking and Plastics-Working Machine Operators

(List of D.O.T. codes available on request. See p. 478.)

Nature of the Work
Consider the parts of a toaster—the metal or plastic housing or the lever that lowers the toast, for example. These parts, and many other metal and plastic products, are produced by metalworking and plastics-working machine operators. In fact, manual and numerical control machine tool operators in the metalworking and plastics industries play a major part in producing most of the consumer products on which we rely daily.

These workers can be separated into two groups—those who set up machines for operation and those who tend the machines during production. Set-up workers prepare the machines prior to production and may adjust the machinery during operation. Operators and tenders, on the other hand, primarily monitor the machinery during operation, sometimes loading or unloading the machine or making minor adjustments to the controls. Many workers do both—set up and operate the equipment. Because the set-up process requires an understanding of the entire production process, setters usually have more training and are more highly skilled than those who simply operate or tend the machinery.

Setters, operators, tenders, and set-up operators are usually identified by the type of machine with which they work. Some examples of specific titles are screw machine operator, plastics-molding machine set-up operator, punch press operator, and lathe tender. Although some workers specialize in one or two types of machinery, many are trained to set up or operate a variety of machines. Job duties usually vary based on the size of the firm as well as on the type of machine being operated.

Metalworking machine setters and operators set up and tend machines that cut and form all types of metal parts. Traditionally, set-up workers plan and set up the sequence of operations according to blueprints, layouts, or other instructions. They adjust speed, feed, and other controls, choose the proper coolants and lubricants, and select the instruments or tools for each operation. Using micrometers, gauges, and other precision measuring instruments, they may compare the completed work with the tolerance limits stated in the specifications.

Although there are many different types of metalworking machine tools that require specific knowledge and skills, most operators perform similar tasks. Whether tending grinding machines that remove excess material from the surface of machined products or presses that extrude metal through a die to form wire, operators usually perform simple, repetitive operations that can be learned quickly. Typically, these workers place metal stock in a machine on which the operating specifications have already been set. They may watch one or more machines and make minor adjustments according to their instructions. Regardless of the type of machine they operate, machine tenders usually depend on skilled set-up workers for major adjustments when the machines are not functioning properly.

Plastics working machine operators set up and tend machines that transform plastic compounds—chemical based products that can be produced in powder, pellet, or syrup form—into a wide variety of consumer goods such as toys, tubing, and auto parts. These products are produced by various methods, of which injection molding is the most common. The injection molding machine heats a plastic compound and forces it into a mold. After the part has cooled and hardened, the mold opens and the part is released. Many common kitchen products are produced using this method. To produce long parts such as pipes or window frames, on the other hand, an extruding machine is usually employed. These machines force a plastic compound through a die that contains an opening of the desired shape of the final product. Yet another type of plastics working technique is blow molding. Blow-molding machines force hot air into a mold which contains a plastic tube. As the air moves into the mold, the plastic tube is inflated to the shape of the mold and a plastic container is formed. The familiar 2-liter soft drink bottles are produced using this method.

Regardless of the process used, plastics-working machine operators check the materials feed, the temperature and pressure of the machine, and the rate at which the product hardens. Depending on the type of equipment in use, they may also load material into the machine, make minor adjustments to the machinery, or unload and inspect the finished products. Plastics-working machine operators also remove clogged material from molds or dies. Because molds and dies are quite costly, operators must exercise proper care to avoid damaging them.

Metalworking and plastics-working machine operators are increasingly being called upon to work with numerically controlled (NC) equipment. These machine tools have two major components—an electronic controller and a machine tool. Almost all NC machines today are computer numerically controlled (CNC), which means that the controllers are computers. The controller directs the mechanisms of the machine tool through the positioning and machining described in the program or instructions for the job. A program could contain, for example, commands that cause the controller to move a drill bit to certain spots on a workpiece and drill a hole at each spot.

Each type of CNC machine tool, such as a milling machine, a lathe, or a punch press, performs a specific task. A part may be worked on by several machines before it is finished. CNC machines are often used in computer-integrated manufacturing (CIM) systems. In these systems, automated material handling equipment moves workpieces through a series of work stations where machining processes are computer numerically controlled. In some cases, the workpiece is stationary and the tools change automatically. Although the machining is done automatically, numerically controlled machine tools must be set up and used properly in order to obtain the maximum benefit from their use. These tasks are the responsibility of numerical-control machine-tool operators or, in some instances, machinists. (See the statement on machinists and tool programmers elsewhere in the *Handbook*.)

Like the duties of manual metal and plastics machine operators, the duties of numerical-control machine-tool operators vary. In some shops, operators tend just one machine. More likely, however, they tend a number of machines or do some programming. As a result, the skill requirements of these workers vary from job to job. Although there are many variations in operators' duties, they generally involve many of the tasks described below.

Working from given instructions, operators load programs that are usually stored on disks into the controller. They also securely position the workpiece, attach the necessary tools, and check the coolants and lubricants. Many numerically controlled machines are equipped

with automatic tool changers, so operators may also load several tools in the proper sequence. In addition, heat generated by machining could damage the cutting tools and the part being machined, so operators must ensure that the proper coolants and lubricants are being used. This entire process may require a few minutes or several hours, depending on the size of the workpiece and the complexity of the job.

A new program must be "debugged," or adjusted, to obtain the desired results. If the tool moves to the wrong position or makes a cut that is too deep, for example, the program must be changed so that the job is done properly. NC operators rarely debug programs. More often, a machinist or tool programmer will perform this function, occasionally with the assistance of a computer automated design program that simulates the operation of machine tools. (See the statement on machinists and tool programmers elsewhere in the *Handbook*.) A new generation of machine tool technology called direct numerical control allows operators to make changes to the program and enter new specifications using minicomputers on the shop floor.

Because numerically controlled machine tools are very expensive, an important duty of operators is to monitor the machinery to prevent situations that could result in costly damage to the cutting tools or other parts. The extent to which the operator performs this function depends on the type of job as well as the type of equipment being used. Some numerically controlled machine tools automatically monitor and adjust machining operations. When the job has been properly set up and the program has been checked, the operator may

Computers are playing a vital role in the jobs of many machine operators.

only need to monitor the machine as it operates. These operators often set up and monitor more than one machine. Other jobs require frequent loading and unloading, tool changing, or programming. Operators may check the finished part using micrometers, gauges, or other precision inspection equipment to ensure that it meets specifications. Increasingly, however, this function is being performed by numerically controlled machine tools that are able to inspect products as they are being produced.

CNC machines are changing the nature of the work that machine setters and operators perform. For example, computer-controlled machines simplify setups by using formerly tested computer programs for new workpieces. If a workpiece is similar to one previously produced, small adjustments can be made to the old program instead of developing a new program from scratch. Also, operators of this equipment have less physical interaction with the machinery or materials. They primarily act as "troubleshooters," monitoring machines on which the loading, forming, and unloading processes are often controlled by computers.

Working Conditions

Most metalworking and plastics-working machine operators work in areas that are clean, well lit, and well ventilated. Regardless of setting, all of these workers operate powerful, high-speed machines that can be dangerous if strict safety rules are not observed. Most operators wear protective equipment such as safety glasses and earplugs to protect against flying particles of metal or plastic and noise from the machines. Other required equipment varies by work setting and by machine. For example, workers in the plastics industry who work near materials that emit dangerous fumes or dust must wear face masks or self-contained breathing apparatuses.

Most metal and plastics working machine operators work a 40-hour week, but overtime is common during periods of increased production. Because many metalworking and plastics working shops operate more than one shift daily, some operators work nights and weekends.

The work requires stamina because operators are on their feet much of the day and may do moderately heavy lifting. Approximately one-third of these workers are union members; the metalworking industries have a higher rate of unionization than the plastics industry.

Employment

Metalworking and plastics-working machine operators held about 1,445,000 jobs in 1994. Of these, 1,370,000 were manual machine operators, and 75,000 were NC machine operators. Eight out of every 10 of these workers are found in five manufacturing industries—fabricated metal products, industrial machinery and equipment, miscellaneous plastic products, transportation equipment, and primary metals. The following tabulation shows the distribution of employment of metalworking and plastics-working machine operators by detailed occupation.

Machine tool cutting and forming machine setters and operators	709,000
Molding machine setters and operators	205,000
Sheet metal workers and duct installers	116,000
Combination machine tool setters and operators	106,000
Numerical control machine operators	75,000
Metal fabricators, structural metal products	44,000
Plating machine setters and operators	42,000
Heat treating machine setters and operators	20,000
All other metal and plastics working machine operators	128,000

Training, Other Qualifications, and Advancement

Most metalworking and plastics-working machine operators learn their skills on the job. Trainees begin by observing and assisting experienced workers, often in formal training programs. Under supervision they may supply material, start and stop the machine, or remove finished products from the machine. As part of their training they advance to more difficult tasks like adjusting feed

speeds, changing cutting tools, or inspecting a finished product for defects. Eventually they become responsible for their own machine or machines.

The complexity of equipment largely determines the time required to become an operator. Most operators learn the basic machine operations and functions in a few weeks, but they may need several years to become a skilled operator or to advance to the more highly skilled job of set-up operator.

Although set-up operators perform many of the same tasks as skilled machine operators, they also need to have a thorough knowledge of the machinery and of the products being produced. Set-up operators often study blueprints, plan the sequence of work, make the first production run, and determine which adjustments need to be made. Strong analytical abilities are particularly important to perform this job. Some companies have formal training programs for set-up operators that combine classroom instruction with on-the-job training.

CNC machine tool operators undergo similar training. Working under a supervisor or an experienced operator, trainees learn to set up and run one or more kinds of numerically controlled machine tools. They usually learn the basics of their jobs within a few months. However, the length of the training period varies with the number and complexity of the machine tools the operator will run and with the individual's ability. If the employer expects operators to write programs, trainees may attend programming courses offered by machine tool manufacturers or technical schools. These courses usually last a couple of weeks.

Although no special education is required for most operating jobs, employers prefer to hire applicants with good basic skills. Many require employees to have a high school education and to read, write, and speak English. This is especially true for numerical control machine operators, who may need to be retrained often in order to learn to operate new equipment. Because machinery is becoming more complex and shop floor organization is changing, employers increasingly look for persons with good communication and interpersonal skills. Mechanical aptitude, manual dexterity, and experience working with machinery are also pluses. Those interested in becoming a metalworking or plastics-working machine operator can improve their employment opportunities by completing high school courses in shop, mathematics, and blueprint reading and by gaining a working knowledge of the properties of metals and plastics.

Advancement for operators usually takes the form of higher pay, although there are some limited opportunities for operators to advance to new positions as well. For example, they can become multiple machine operators, set-up operators, or trainees for the more highly skilled positions of machinist or tool and die maker. Manual machine operators can move on to CNC equipment when it is introduced into their establishments. Some set-up workers and CNC operators may advance to supervisory positions. CNC operators who have substantial training in numerical control programming may advance to the higher paying job of tool programmer. (See statements on machinists and tool programmers, and tool and die makers elsewhere in the *Handbook*.)

Job Outlook

Overall employment of metalworking and plastics-working machine operators is expected to decline through the year 2005. This decline is likely to affect metalworking machine operators more than those working with plastics machines. In addition, setters and more highly skilled operators are more likely to be retained by firms than are semi-skilled operators and tenders. In spite of the overall employment decline, however, a large number of jobs will become available each year as current operators and setters transfer to other occupations or leave the labor force.

A major factor driving the employment decline is the increasing productivity resulting from computer-controlled equipment. In order to remain competitive, many firms are adopting this technology to improve quality and lower production costs. Computer-controlled equipment allows operators to simultaneously tend a greater number of machines and often makes setup easier, thereby reducing the amount of time set-up workers spend on each machine. For these reasons, employment of CNC machine operators is expected to increase in the future despite the decline in machine operators as a whole. Lower-skilled positions like manual machine tool operators and tenders are more likely to be eliminated by increasing automation than those of setters and set-up operators, whose higher skills are more in demand and whose job functions are less easily automated.

The demand for metalworking and plastics-working machine operators largely mirrors the demand for the parts they produce. In recent years, plastic products have been substituted for metal goods in many consumer and manufacturing products. Although the rate of substitution may slow in the future, this process is likely to continue and should result in a relatively stronger demand for machine operators in plastics than in metalworking. Both industries, however, face stiff foreign competition that is limiting the demand for domestically-produced parts. One way that larger U.S. producers have responded to this competition is by moving production operations to other countries in order to reduce labor costs. These moves are likely to continue and will further reduce employment opportunities for metalworking and plastics-working machine tool operators in the United States.

Workers with a thorough background in machine operations, exposure to a variety of machines, and a good working knowledge of the properties of metals and plastics will be best able to adjust to this changing environment. In addition, new shopfloor arrangements will reward workers with good basic mathematics and reading skills, good communication skills, flexibility, and the ability and willingness to learn new tasks. Those interested in working with CNC machine tools will most likely need to have a high school education and should be familiar with several types of machines and operating systems.

Earnings
Median weekly earnings for most metalworking and plastics-working machine operators were about $420 in 1994. The middle 50 percent earned between $310 and $570. The top 10 percent earned over $760 and the bottom 10 percent earned less than $240. Metal and plastics molding, plating, heat-treating, and other processing machine operators earned somewhat less, about $390 a week. In addition to wages, most machine operators receive benefits such as health and life insurance, pension plans, paid vacation, and sick leave.

Earnings of production workers vary considerably by industry. The following tabulation shows 1994 average weekly wages for production workers in manufacturing industries where employment of metalworking and plastics-working machine operators is concentrated.

Transportation equipment	$730
Primary metals industries	640
Industrial machinery and equipment	570
Fabricated metal products	510
Rubber and miscellaneous plastics products	450

Related Occupations
Workers in occupations closely related to metalworking and plastics-working machine occupations include machinists, tool and die makers, extruding and forming machine operators producing synthetic fibers, woodworking machine operators, and metal patternmakers. Numerical-control machine-tool operators may program CNC machines or alter existing programs, which are functions closely related to those performed by NC machine tool programmers.

Sources of Additional Information
For general information about the metalworking trades, contact:
☛ The Association for Manufacturing Technology, 7901 Westpark Dr., McLean, VA 22102.

☛ The National Tooling and Machining Association, 9300 Livingston Rd., Fort Washington, MD 20744.
☛ The Tooling and Manufacturing Association, ATTN: Education Department, 1177 South Dee Rd., Park Ridge, IL 60068.
☛ The National Screw Machine Products Association, 6700 West Snowville Rd., Brecksville, OH 44141.
☛ The Precision Metalforming Association, 27027 Chardon Rd., Richmond Heights, OH 44143.

Information on educational programs in plastics technology and polymer sciences is available from:
☛ The Society of the Plastics Industry, Inc., 1275 K St. NW., Washington, DC 20005.

Tool and Die Makers

(D.O.T. 601.260-010, -014, .280 except -038 and -054, .281-010, -014, -026, .380, .381 except -018 and -038; 739.381-018, -022)

Nature of the Work
Tool and die makers are highly skilled workers who produce tools, dies, and special guiding and holding devices that are used in machines that produce a variety of products—from clothing and furniture to heavy equipment and parts for aircraft.

Toolmakers craft precision tools which are used to cut, shape, and form metal and other materials. They also produce jigs and fixtures (devices that hold metal while it is bored, stamped, or drilled) and gauges and other measuring devices. Diemakers construct metal forms (dies) that are used to shape metal in stamping and forging operations. They also make metal molds for diecasting and for molding plastics, ceramics, and composite materials. In addition, tool and die makers may repair worn or damaged tools, dies, gauges, jigs, and fixtures, and design tools and dies.

Tool and die makers must have a much broader knowledge of machining operations, mathematics, and blueprint reading than most other machining workers. They use many types of machine tools and precision measuring instruments and must be familiar with the machining properties, such as hardness and heat tolerance, of a wide variety of common metals and alloys.

Working from blueprints or instructions, tool and die makers plan the sequence of operations necessary to manufacture the tool or die. They measure and mark the pieces of metal that will be cut to form parts of the final product. They then cut, bore, or drill the part as required. They also check the accuracy of what they have done to ensure that the final product will meet specifications. Then they assemble the parts and perform finishing jobs such as filing, grinding, and smoothing surfaces.

Modern technology is helping to change tool and die makers' jobs. Firms commonly use computer aided design (CAD) to develop products. Specifications from the computer program can then be used to develop designs electronically for the required tools and dies. The designs can then be sent to computer numerically controlled (CNC) machines to produce the die. Programs can also be electronically stored and adapted for future use. This saves time and increases productivity of the workers.

In shops that use numerically controlled (NC) machine tools, tool and die makers' duties may be slightly different. For example, although they still manually check and assemble the tool or die, each of its components may be produced on an NC machine. In addition, they often assist in the planning and writing of NC programs.

Working Conditions
Tool and die makers usually work in toolrooms. These areas are quieter than the production floor because there are fewer machines in use at one time. Machines have guards and shields that minimize the

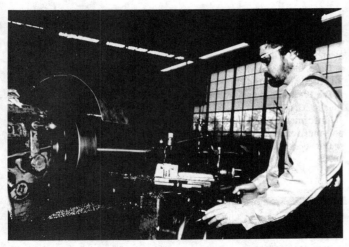

Tool and die makers are highly skilled workers with a broad knowledge of machining operations.

exposure of workers to moving parts. Tool and die makers, however, must follow safety rules and wear protective equipment, such as safety glasses to shield against bits of flying metal and earplugs to protect against noise. They also may be exposed to hazardous lubricants and cleaners. In addition, they spend much of the day on their feet and may do moderately heavy lifting.

Companies employing tool and die makers traditionally operate one shift per day. However, as the cost of new machinery and technology has increased, many employers now have more than one shift. Overtime and Saturday work are common, especially during peak production periods.

Employment
Tool and die makers held about 142,000 jobs in 1994. Most worked in industries that manufacture metalworking machinery and equipment, motor vehicles, aircraft, and plastics products. Although they are found throughout the country, jobs are most plentiful in the Midwest and Northeast, where many of the metalworking industries are located.

Training, Other Qualifications, and Advancement
Tool and die makers learn their trade through formal apprenticeship and postsecondary programs or informal on-the-job training. The best way to learn all aspects of tool and die making, according to most employers, is a formal apprenticeship program that combines classroom instruction and job experience. A growing number of tool and die makers, however, receive most of their formal training from community colleges.

Courses in math, blueprint reading, metalworking, and drafting, as well as machine shop experience, provide a helpful background.

During the 4 or 5 years of a tool and die apprenticeship, apprentices learn to operate milling machines, lathes, grinders, and other machine tools. They also learn to use handtools in fitting and assembling tools, gauges, and other mechanical and metal forming equipment, and they study metalworking processes such as heat treating and plating. Classroom training usually consists of mathematics, mechanical drawing, tool designing, tool programming, and blueprint reading.

Workers who become tool and die makers without completing formal apprenticeships generally acquire their skills through a combination of informal on-the-job training and classroom instruction at a vocational school or community college. They often begin as machine operators and gradually take on more difficult assignments. Many machinists become tool and die makers. In fact, tool and die makers are often considered highly specialized machinists. (See the statement on machinists and tool programmers elsewhere in the *Handbook*.)

Because tools and dies must meet strict specifications—precision to one ten-thousandth of an inch is not uncommon—the work of tool and die makers requires a high degree of patience and attention to detail. Good eyesight is essential. Persons entering this occupation should also be mechanically inclined, able to work independently, and capable of doing work that requires concentration and physical effort.

There are several ways for skilled workers to advance. Some move into supervisory and administrative positions in their firms; others become tool designers or tool programmers; and a few may open their own shops.

Job Outlook
Employment of tool and die makers is expected to decline through the year 2005. Nevertheless, jobseekers with the appropriate skills and background should find excellent opportunities, as employers across the Nation report difficulties in finding skilled workers to hire as tool and die makers. Many openings will be created each year by tool and die makers who retire. Three out of 10 tool and die makers are 50 years or older. As older workers begin to leave the occupation in larger numbers, employers in certain parts of the country may face more pronounced shortages.

The projected decline in employment reflects advancements in automation, including computer numerically controlled machine tools and computer aided design. CNC machine tools have made tool and die makers more productive, while CAD has allowed some functions of these workers to be carried out by a computer and tool programmer. In addition, because precision metal products are a primary component of manufacturing machinery, increased imports of finished goods and precision metal products may lessen the demand for tool and die makers. These workers, however, are highly skilled and play a key role in the operation of many firms. This fact, coupled with a growing demand for motor vehicles, aircraft, machinery, and other products that use machined metal parts, should help to moderate the decline in employment.

Earnings
Median weekly earnings for tool and die makers who worked full time were $660 in 1994. Most earned between $490 and $860 a week. Ten percent earned less than $380 a week, and the 10 percent with the highest weekly earnings made more than $1,130. In addition to their hourly wage, most workers receive health and life insurance, a pension plan, paid vacations, and sick leave.

Related Occupations
The occupations most closely related to the work of tool and die makers are the other machining occupations. These include machinist, mold maker, instrument maker, metalworking and plastics-working machine operator, and tool programmer.

Other occupations that require precision and skill in working with metal include blacksmith, gunsmith, locksmith, metal patternmaker, and welder.

Sources of Additional Information
For general information about tool and die makers, contact:
☛The Association for Manufacturing Technology, 7901 Westpark Dr., McLean, VA 22102.
☛The National Tooling and Machining Association, 9300 Livingston Rd., Ft. Washington, MD 20744.
☛The Tooling and Manufacturing Association, ATTN: Education Department, 1177 South Dee Rd., Park Ridge IL 60068.
☛Precision Metalforming Association, 27027 Chardon Rd., Richmond Heights, OH 44143.

Welders, Cutters, and Welding Machine Operators

(D.O.T. 613.667-010; 614.684-010; 709.684-086; 727.662, .684-022; 810; 811; 812; 814; 815; 816 except .482 and .682; 819.281-010, -014, -022, .361, .381, .384, .684, and .685)

Nature of the Work

Welding is the most common way of permanently joining metal parts. Heat is applied to the pieces to be joined, melting and fusing them to form a permanent bond. Because of its strength, welding is used to construct and repair parts of ships, automobiles, spacecraft, and thousands of other manufactured products. Welding is used to join beams when constructing buildings, bridges, and other structures, and pipes in nuclear power plants and refineries.

Welders use all types of welding equipment in a variety of positions, such as flat, vertical, horizontal, and overhead. They may perform manual welding, in which the work is entirely controlled by the welder, or semi-automatic welding, in which the welder uses machinery, such as a wire feeder, to perform welding tasks. They generally plan work from drawings or specifications or by analyzing damaged metal, using their knowledge of welding and metals. They select and set up welding equipment and may also examine welds to insure they meet standards or specifications. Some welders have more limited duties. They perform routine production work that has already been planned and laid out. These jobs do not require knowledge of all welding techniques.

In many production processes—where the work is repetitive and the items to be welded are relatively uniform—automated welding is used. In this process, a machine performs the welding tasks while monitored by a welding machine operator. Welding machine operators set up and operate welding machines as specified by layouts, work orders, or blueprints. Operators must constantly monitor the machine to ensure that it produces the desired weld.

The work of arc, plasma, and flame cutters is closely related to that of welders. However, instead of joining metals, cutters use the heat from burning gases or an electric arc to cut and trim metal objects to specific dimensions. Cutters also dismantle large objects, such as ships, railroad cars, automobiles or aircraft. Some operate and monitor cutting machines similar to those used by welding machine operators.

Working Conditions

Welders and cutters frequently are exposed to potential hazards. They use protective clothing, safety shoes, goggles, helmets with protective lenses, and other devices to prevent burns and eye injuries and to protect them from falling objects. Automated welding machine operators are not exposed to as many hazards. A face shield or goggles generally provide adequate protection. Because some metals may give off toxic gases and fumes as they melt, Federal regulations require ventilation to meet strict guidelines to minimize these hazards. Occasionally, some workers are in contact with rust, grease, and dirt on metal surfaces. Some welders are isolated for short intervals while they work in booths constructed to contain sparks and glare. Welders often work in a variety of awkward positions, having to make welds while bending, stooping, or working overhead. In some settings, however, working conditions are much better and few hazards or discomforts are encountered.

Employment

Welders, cutters, and welding machine operators held about 416,000 jobs in 1994. About 9 out of 10 welders and cutters were employed in manufacturing, services, construction, or wholesale trade. The majority of those in manufacturing were employed in transportation equipment, industrial machinery and equipment, or fabricated metal

Certification is the key to job mobility for welders.

products. All welding machine operators were employed in manufacturing industries, primarily fabricated metal products, machinery, and motor vehicles. Almost 2 of 5 welders are employed in six States: Texas, California, Ohio, Pennsylvania, Michigan, and Illinois—States heavily dominated by automobile and fabricated metal products manufacturing, and by the petroleum and chemical industry.

Training, Other Qualifications, and Advancement

Training for welders can range from a few weeks of school or on-the-job training for low skilled positions to several years of combined school and on-the-job training for highly skilled jobs. Formal training is available in high schools, vocational schools, and post-secondary institutions such as vocational-technical institutes, community colleges, and private welding schools. The Armed Forces operate welding schools as well. Some employers provide training to help welders improve their skills. Courses in blueprint reading, shop mathematics, mechanical drawing, physics, chemistry, and metallurgy are helpful.

Some welders become certified, a process whereby the employer sends a worker to an institution, such as an independent testing lab or technical school to weld a test specimen to specific codes and standards required by the employer. The testing procedures are usually based on the standards and codes set by one of several industry associations the employer may be affiliated with. If the welding inspector at the examining institution determines that the worker has performed according to the employer's guidelines, he or she then certifies that the welder being tested is able to work with a particular welding procedure.

Welders and cutters need manual dexterity, good eyesight, and good hand-eye coordination. They should be able to concentrate on detailed work for long periods and be able to bend, stoop, and work in awkward positions.

Welders can advance to more skilled jobs with additional training and experience. They may be promoted to welding technicians, supervisors, inspectors, or instructors. Some experienced welders open their own repair shops.

Job Outlook

Opportunities for those who wish to become welders, cutters, and welding machine operators should be good through the year 2005 as the number of qualified (certified) welders graduating from technical schools is expected to be in balance with the number of job openings resulting from the need to replace experienced workers who transfer to other occupations or leave the labor force. Employment of welders, cutters, and welding machine operators is expected to decline through the year 2005.

The growth of welders, cutters, and welding machine operators varies greatly by industry.

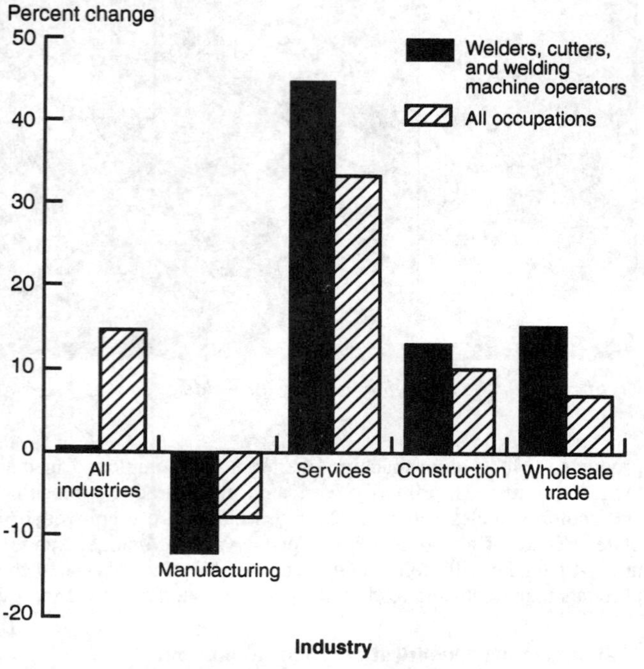

Percent change

In certain industries—construction, wholesale trade, and repair services, for example—employment of welders and cutters will increase (see accompanying chart). The level of construction is expected to expand, as is the number of metal products needing repair, increasing the need for welding and cutting. This work is generally less routine and more difficult to automate than other welding jobs. Greater use of welding automation in manufacturing using simple repetitive welds could cause manual welders to be replaced by or retrained to become welding machine operators. Automated welding systems are expected to cause a decline in the employment of welding machine operators. Despite the welding jobs eliminated by automated welding systems, manual welders, espe-

cially those with a wide variety of skills, will still be needed for the maintenance, repair, and other work in manufacturing that cannot be automated. Certified welders, especially those certified in more than one process, will have much better employment opportunities than non-certified welders.

Welders, cutters, and welding machine operators in construction and manufacturing are vulnerable to periodic layoffs due to economic downturns.

Earnings
Median earnings for welders and welding machine operators were about $460 a week in 1994. The middle 50 percent earned between $345 and $597. The top 10 percent earned more than $786, and the lowest 10 percent earned less than $281.

More than one-fourth of welders belong to unions. Among these are the International Association of Machinists and Aerospace Workers; the International Brotherhood of Boilermakers, Iron Ship Builders, Blacksmiths, Forgers and Helpers; the International Union, United Automobile, Aerospace and Agricultural Implement Workers of America; the United Association of Journeymen and Apprentices of the Plumbing and Pipe Fitting Industry of the United States and Canada; and the United Electrical, Radio, and Machine Workers of America.

Related Occupations
Welders and cutters are skilled metal workers. Other metal workers include blacksmiths, forge shop workers, all-round machinists, machine-tool operators, tool and die makers, millwrights, sheet-metal workers, boilermakers, and metal sculptors.

Welding machine operators run machines that weld metal parts. Others who run metalworking machines include lathe and turning, milling and planing, punching and stamping press, and rolling machine operators.

Sources of Additional Information
For information on training opportunities and jobs for welders, cutters, and welding machine operators, contact local employers, the local office of the State employment service, or schools providing welding training.

Information on careers in welding is available from:
☛American Welding Society, 550 NW. LeJeune Rd., Miami, FL 33126-5699.

For a list of accredited schools that offer training in welding, contact:
☛Career College Association, 750 1st Street NE, Suite 900, Washington, DC 20002.

Plant and Systems Operators

Electric Power Generating Plant Operators and Power Distributors and Dispatchers

(D.O.T. 820.662-010; 951.685-010; 952.167-014, .362, .367-014, and .382)

Nature of the Work
Although electricity is vital for most of our everyday activities, it only takes a downed powerline for us to realize how much we take it and the people who help generate it for granted. Power plant operators control the machinery that generates electricity. Power distributors and dispatchers control the flow of electricity through substa-

tions and over a network of transmission and distribution lines to users.

Electric power generating plant operators who work in plants fueled by coal, oil, or natural gas regulate and monitor boilers, turbines, generators, auxiliary equipment, such as coal crushers, and switching gear. They operate switches to distribute power demands among generators, combine the current from several generators, and regulate the flow of electricity into powerlines. When power requirements change, they start or stop generators and connect or disconnect them from circuits. Operators monitor instruments to see that electricity flows from the plant properly and that voltage is maintained. They also keep records of switching operations and loads on generators, lines, and transformers and prepare reports of unusual incidents or malfunctioning equipment during their shift.

Operators in newer plants with automated control systems work mainly in a central control room and usually are called control room operators and control room operator trainees or assistants. In older plants, the controls for the equipment are not centralized, and operators work throughout the plant, operating and monitoring valves, switches, and gauges. Job titles in older plants may be more varied than in newer plants. Auxiliary equipment operators work throughout the plant, while switchboard operators control the flow of electricity from a central point.

Operators of nuclear power plants are licensed by the Nuclear Regulatory Commission (NRC). NRC-licensed reactor operators are authorized to operate equipment that affects the power of the reactor in a nuclear power plant. In addition, an NRC-licensed senior reactor operator acts as the supervisor of the plant for each shift, and supervises operation of all controls in the control room.

Power distributors and dispatchers, also called load dispatchers or systems operators, control the flow of electricity through transmission lines to users. They operate current converters, voltage transformers, and circuit breakers. Dispatchers monitor equipment and record readings at a pilot board, which is a map of the transmission grid system showing the status of transmission circuits and connections with substations and large industrial users. Dispatchers anticipate power needs such as those caused by changes in the weather; they call control room operators to start or stop boilers and generators to bring production into balance with needs. They handle emergencies such as transformer or transmission line failures and route current around affected areas. They also operate and monitor equipment in substations, which step up or step down voltage, and operate switchboard levers to control the flow of electricity in and out of substations.

Working Conditions

Because electricity is provided around the clock, operators, distributors, and dispatchers usually work one of three daily 8-hour shifts on a rotating basis. Workers usually rotate to a different daily shift schedule periodically so that duty on less desirable shifts is shared by all operators. Work on rotating shifts can be stressful and fatiguing because of the constant change in living and sleeping patterns. Operators, distributors, and dispatchers who work in control rooms generally sit or stand at a control station. This work is not physically strenuous, but requires constant attention. Operators who work outside the control room may be exposed to danger from electric shock, falls, and burns.

Nuclear power plant operators are subject to random drug and alcohol tests.

Employment

Electric power generating plant operators and power distributors and dispatchers held about 43,000 jobs in 1994. Over 90 percent worked for electric utility companies and government agencies that produced electricity. Some worked for manufacturing establishments that produce electricity for their own use. Jobs are located throughout the country.

Training, Other Qualifications, and Advancement

Employers seek high school graduates for entry level operator, distributor, and dispatcher positions. Those with strong math and science skills are preferred. College level courses or prior experience in a mechanical or technical job may be helpful. Most entry level positions are in helper or laborer jobs in power plants or in other areas of the utility such as powerline construction. Workers may be assigned to train for any one of many utility positions in operations, maintenance, or other areas. Assignments depend on the results of aptitude tests, worker preferences, and availability of openings.

Workers selected for training as a power distributor or power plant operator at a conventionally fueled power plant undergo extensive on-the-job and classroom training provided by the employer. Several years of training and experience are required to become a fully qualified control room operator or power distributor. With further training and experience, workers may advance to shift supervisor. Because utilities generally promote from within, opportunities to advance by moving to another employer are limited.

Entrants to nuclear power plant operator trainee jobs must have strong math and science skills. Experience in other power plants or with Navy nuclear propulsion plants also is helpful. Extensive training and experience are necessary to pass the Nuclear Regulatory Commission's examinations for licensed reactor operator and senior reactor operator, including on-the-job and simulator training, classroom instruction, and individual study. Licensed reactor operators must pass an annual practical plant operation exam and a biennial written exam administered by their employer to maintain their license. With further training and experience, reactor operators may advance to senior reactor operators, who are qualified to be shift supervisors.

In addition to preliminary training as a power plant operator or power distributor or dispatcher, most workers are given periodic refresher training. Nuclear power plant operators are given frequent refresher training on a plant simulator.

Job Outlook

People who want to become power plant operators and power distributors and dispatchers are expected to encounter keen competition for jobs. With relatively modest qualifications for employment, good wages, and low turnover in this moderately sized occupation, job opportunities are expected to be few compared to the number of eligible candidates.

Power dispatchers work to balance the supply of power with the demands from different parts of the transmission circuit.

Opportunities for those interested in working as power plant operators, distributors, and dispatchers will be affected by the pace of new plant construction and equipment upgrading. The pace of expansion in power generating capacity through the year 2005 is expected to be moderate because capacity was somewhat overbuilt in the past. The increasing use of automatic controls and more efficient equipment should further offset the need for new plant construction and operators. Also, few new nuclear power plants are likely to be operational before the year 2005.

A recent development in the utility industry is the Energy Policy Act of 1992. This legislation has increased competition in power generating utilities by allowing independent power producers, who generally have lower prices, to sell their power directly to industrial customers. As a result, utilities are restructuring their operations to reduce costs and compete effectively, resulting in fewer jobs at all levels and reducing job security.

Overall, employment of electric power generating plant operators, distributors, and dispatchers is expected to decline through the year 2005.

Earnings

Earnings in the electric utility industry are relatively high. According to the limited information available, median weekly earnings for conventional power plant operators were about $857 in 1994. According to information from union contracts, wages for power plant operators ranged from $520 to $832 weekly. Nuclear power plant operators earned weekly wages of about $990 in 1994. Senior or chief operators in both nuclear and conventional power plants earned 10-15 percent more than operators.

Related Occupations

Other workers who monitor and operate plant and systems equipment include stationary engineers, water and sewage treatment plant operators, waterworks pumpstation operators, chemical operators, and refinery operators.

Sources of Additional Information

For information about employment opportunities, contact local electric utility companies, locals of unions mentioned below, or an office of the State employment service.

For general information about power plant and nuclear reactor operators and power distributors and dispatchers, contact:

☛International Brotherhood of Electrical Workers, 1125 15th St. NW., Washington, DC 20005.

☛Utility Workers Union of America, 815 16th St. NW., Washington, DC 20006.

For a copy of Careers in Electric Power and a catalog of other guidance information, send $5 to:

☛Edison Electric Institute, P.O. Box 2800, Kearneysville, WV 25430-2800.

Stationary Engineers

(D.O.T. 950.362-014, .382 except -014 and -022; and .485)

Nature of the Work

Heating, air-conditioning, and ventilation systems are what keep large buildings comfortable all year long. Industrial plants often have facilities to provide electrical power, steam, or other services as well. Stationary engineers operate and maintain these systems, which can include boilers, air-conditioning and refrigeration equipment, diesel engines, turbines, generators, pumps, condensers, and compressors. These workers are called stationary engineers because the equipment they operate is similar to equipment operated by locomotive or marine engineers except it is not on a moving vehicle.

Stationary engineers start up, regulate, and shut down equipment. They ensure that it operates safely and economically and within established limits by monitoring attached meters, gauges, other instruments, and computerized controls. They manually control equip-

ment, and if necessary, make adjustments. They use hand and power tools to perform repairs and maintenance ranging from a complete overhaul to replacing defective valves, gaskets, or bearings. They also record relevant events and facts concerning operation and maintenance in an equipment log. On steam boilers, for example, they observe, control, and record steam pressure, temperature, water level, power output, and fuel consumption. They watch and listen to machinery and routinely check safety devices, identifying and correcting any trouble that develops.

New building and plant systems are increasingly being run by stationary engineers using computers. These systems allow engineers to monitor, adjust, and diagnose systems from a central location or using a laptop computer linked into the buildings' communications network.

Stationary engineers also perform routine maintenance, such as lubricating moving parts, replacing filters, and removing soot and corrosion that can reduce operating efficiency. They test boiler water and add chemicals to prevent corrosion and harmful deposits. They also may check the air quality of the ventilation system and make adjustments to keep within mandated guidelines.

In a large building or industrial plant, a stationary engineer may be in charge of all mechanical systems in the building or an industrial power plant or engine room. Engineers may direct the work of assistant stationary engineers, turbine operators, boiler tenders, and air-conditioning and refrigeration operators and mechanics. In a small building or industrial plant, there may be only one stationary engineer.

Working Conditions

Stationary engineers generally have steady year-round employment. They usually work a 5-day, 40-hour week. Many work one of three daily 8-hour shifts, and weekend and holiday work often is required.

Engine rooms, power plants, and boiler rooms usually are clean and well lighted. Even under the most favorable conditions, however, some stationary engineers are exposed to high temperatures, dust, dirt, and high noise levels from the equipment. General maintenance duties may cause contact with oil and grease, as well as fumes or smoke. Workers spend much of their time on their feet; they also may have to crawl inside boilers and work in crouching or kneeling positions to inspect, clean, or repair equipment.

Because stationary engineers work around boilers as well as electrical and mechanical equipment, they must be alert to avoid burns, electric shock, and injury from moving parts. They also must be aware of exposure to hazardous materials such as asbestos and certain chemicals.

A stationary engineer begins the sequence of operations required to start up a boiler.

Employment

Stationary engineers held about 30,000 jobs in 1994. They worked in a wide variety of places, including factories, hospitals, hotels, office and apartment buildings, schools, and shopping malls.

Stationary engineers work throughout the country, generally in the more heavily populated areas where large industrial and commercial establishments usually are located.

Training, Other Qualifications, and Advancement

Most stationary engineers acquire their skills through a formal apprenticeship program or through informal on-the-job training which usually is supplemented by courses at trade or technical schools. In addition, a good background can be obtained in the Navy or the Merchant Marine because marine engineering plants are similar to many stationary power and heating plants. The increasing complexity of the equipment with which they work has made a high school diploma or its equivalent necessary; many stationary engineers have some college education.

Apprenticeship programs are sponsored by the International Union of Operating Engineers, the principal union to which stationary engineers belong. In selecting apprentices, most local labor-management apprenticeship committees prefer applicants who have received instruction in mathematics, computers, mechanical drawing, machine-shop practice, physics, and chemistry. Mechanical aptitude, manual dexterity, and good physical condition also are important.

An apprenticeship usually lasts 4 years. In addition to 8,000 hours of on-the-job training, apprentices receive 600 hours of classroom instruction in boiler design and operation, basic chemistry and water treatment, elementary physics, pneumatics, refrigeration and air conditioning, electricity and electronics, computer systems, and other technical subjects.

Those who acquire their skills on the job usually start as helpers to experienced stationary engineers or as boiler tenders. This practical experience may be supplemented by postsecondary vocational training in computerized controls and instrumentation. However, becoming a stationary engineer without going through a formal apprenticeship program usually requires many years of work experience.

Most large and some small employers encourage and pay for skill-improvement training for their employees. Training is almost always provided when new equipment is introduced, usually by a representative of the machinery manufacturer, or when regulations concerning some aspect of their duties change.

Most States and cities have licensing requirements for stationary engineers. Applicants usually must be at least 18 years of age, reside for a specified period in the State or locality, meet experience requirements, and pass a written examination. Because of regional differences in licensing requirements, a stationary engineer who moves from one State or city to another may have to pass an examination for a new license.

Generally, there are several classes of stationary engineer licenses, each specifying the type of equipment or the steam pressure or horsepower of the equipment the engineer can operate without supervision. A first-class license covers equipment of all types and capacities. A licensed first-class stationary engineer is qualified to run a large facility and to supervise others. An applicant for this license may be required to have a high school education, apprenticeship or on-the-job training, and several years of experience. Lower class licenses limit the types or capacities of equipment the engineer may operate without the supervision of a higher rated engineer.

Stationary engineers advance by being placed in charge of larger, more powerful, or more varied equipment. Generally, engineers advance to these jobs as they obtain higher class licenses. Some stationary engineers advance to boiler inspectors, chief plant engineers, building and plant superintendents, or building managers. A few obtain jobs as examining engineers or technical instructors.

Job Outlook

Persons wishing to become stationary engineers may face competition because of the small number of openings expected through the year 2005. Although growing commercial and industrial development will increase the amount of equipment to be operated and maintained, automated systems and computerized controls will make newly installed equipment more efficient and reduce the number of stationary engineers needed. Therefore, employment of stationary engineers is expected to decline through the year 2005. Most of the job openings will arise from the need to replace experienced workers who transfer to other occupations or leave the labor force. Because turnover in this occupation is low, partly due to its high wages, relatively few replacement openings are expected.

Due to the increasing complexity of power-generating systems, job opportunities will be best for those with apprenticeship training or vocational school courses in computerized controls and instrumentation.

Earnings

In 1994, the median weekly earnings for stationary engineers who worked full time were about $591. The middle 50 percent earned between $430 and $758 a week; 10 percent earned less than $304 a week; and 10 percent earned more than $977.

Related Occupations

Other workers who monitor and operate stationary machinery include nuclear reactor operators, power station operators, water and wastewater treatment plant operators, waterworks pump-station operators, chemical operators, and refinery operators.

Sources of Additional Information

Information about training or work opportunities is available from local offices of State employment services, locals of the International Union of Operating Engineers, and from State and local licensing agencies.

Specific questions about the occupation should be addressed to:

☛International Union of Operating Engineers, 1125 17th St. NW., Washington, DC 20036.

☛National Association of Power Engineers, Inc., 1 Springfield St., Chicopee, MA 01013.

☛Building Owners and Managers Institute International, 1521 Ritchie Hwy., Suite 3A, Arnold, MD 21403.

Water and Wastewater Treatment Plant Operators

(D.O.T. 954.382-010, -014; 955.362-010, .382, and .585)

Nature of the Work

Clean water is essential for many things: Health, recreation, fish and wildlife, and industry. Water treatment plant operators treat water so that it is safe to drink. Wastewater treatment plant operators remove harmful pollutants from domestic and industrial wastewater so that it is safe to return to the environment.

Water is pumped from wells, rivers, and streams to water treatment plants where it is treated and distributed to customers. Waste is collected from customers, carried by water through sewer pipes to wastewater treatment plants where it is treated and returned to streams, rivers, and oceans. Operators in both types of plants control processes and equipment to remove solid materials, chemical compounds, and micro-organisms from the water or to render them harmless. They also control pumps, valves, and other processing equipment to move the water or wastewater through the various treatment processes, and dispose of the waste materials removed from the water.

Operators read and interpret meters and gauges to make sure plant equipment and processes are working properly and adjust controls as needed. They operate chemical-feeding devices; take samples of the water or wastewater; perform chemical and biological laboratory analyses; and test and adjust the amount of chemicals such as chlorine in the water. Operators also make minor repairs to valves, pumps, and other equipment. They use gauges, wrenches, pliers, and other common handtools, as well as special tools.

Water and wastewater treatment plant operators increasingly rely on computers to help them monitor equipment, store sampling results, make process control decisions, and produce reports. When problems occur, operators may use their computers to determine the cause of and solution to the malfunction.

Occasionally operators must work under emergency conditions. A heavy rainstorm, for example, may cause large amounts of wastewater to flow into sewers, exceeding a plant's treatment capacity. Emergencies also can be caused by conditions inside a plant, such as chlorine gas leaks or oxygen deficiencies. To handle these conditions, operators are trained in emergency management response using special safety equipment and procedures to protect public health and the facility. During these periods, operators may work under extreme pressure to correct problems as quickly as possible. These periods may create dangerous working conditions and operators must be extremely cautious.

The specific duties of plant operators depend on the type and size of plant. In smaller plants, one operator may control all machinery, perform tests, keep records, handle complaints, and do repairs and maintenance. Some operators may handle both a water treatment and a wastewater treatment plant. In larger plants with many employees, operators may be more specialized and only monitor one process. The staff may also include chemists, engineers, laboratory technicians, mechanics, helpers, supervisors, and a superintendent.

Water pollution standards have become increasingly stringent since adoption of the Federal Water Pollution Control Act of 1972, which implemented a national system of regulation on the discharge of pollutants. Under the 1972 law and subsequent reauthorizations in 1977 and 1987, it is illegal to discharge any pollutant without a permit. Industrial facilities that send their wastes to municipal treatment plants must meet certain minimum standards and ensure that these wastes have been adequately pretreated so that they do not damage municipal treatment facilities. Municipal treatment plants also must meet stringent discharge standards set forth in the Clean Water Act of 1972 and the Safe Drinking Water Act of 1974. Operators must be familiar with the guidelines established by the Clean Water Act and how they affect their plant. In addition to Federal regulations, operators also must be aware of any guidelines imposed by the State or locality in which the plant operates.

A wastewater treatment plant operator checks the water temperature at the pump pushing sewage through the plant.

Working Conditions

Water and wastewater treatment plant operators work both indoors and outdoors and may be exposed to noise from machinery and some unpleasant odors, although chemicals may be used to minimize these. Operators have to stoop, reach, and climb and sometimes get their clothes dirty. They must pay close attention to safety procedures for they may be confronted with hazardous conditions, such as slippery walkways, dangerous gases, and malfunctioning equipment. Because plants operate 24 hours a day, 7 days a week, operators work one of three 8-hour shifts and on a rotational basis, weekends and holidays. Whenever emergencies arise, operators may be required to work overtime.

Employment

Water and wastewater treatment plant operators held about 95,000 jobs in 1994. The vast majority worked for local governments; some worked for private water supply and sanitary services companies, some of which provide operation and management services to local governments on a contract basis. About half worked as water treatment plant operators and half worked as wastewater treatment plant operators.

Water and wastewater treatment plant operators are employed throughout the country, with most jobs in larger towns and cities. Although nearly all work full time, those who work in small towns may only work part time at the water or wastewater treatment plant—the remainder of their time may be spent handling other municipal duties.

Training, Other Qualifications, and Advancement

Trainees usually start as attendants or operators-in-training and learn their skills on the job under the direction of an experienced operator. They learn by observing the processes and equipment in operation and by doing routine tasks such as recording meter readings; taking samples of wastewater and sludge; and doing simple maintenance and repair work on pumps, electric motors, and valves. They also clean and maintain plant equipment. Larger treatment plants generally combine this on-the-job training with formal classroom or self-paced study programs.

Operators need mechanical aptitude and should be competent in basic mathematics, as they need to apply data to formulas of treatment requirements, flow levels, and concentration levels. Because of the introduction of computer-controlled equipment and more sophisticated instrumentation, a high school diploma generally is required. In addition, employers prefer those who have had high school courses in chemistry, biology, and mathematics.

Some positions, particularly in larger cities and towns, are covered by civil service regulations, and applicants may be required to pass written examinations testing elementary mathematics skills, mechanical aptitude, and general intelligence.

Some 2-year programs leading to an associate degree in wastewater technology and 1-year programs leading to a certificate are available; these provide a good general knowledge of water treatment processes as well as basic preparation for becoming an operator. Because plants are becoming more complex, completion of such courses increases an applicant's chances for employment and promotion.

Most State water pollution control agencies offer training courses to improve operators' skills and knowledge. These courses cover principles of treatment processes and process control, laboratory procedures, maintenance, management skills, collection systems, safety, chlorination, sedimentation, biological treatment, sludge treatment and disposal, and flow measurements. Some operators take correspondence courses on subjects related to wastewater treatment, and some employers pay part of the tuition for related college courses in science or engineering.

As operators are promoted, they become responsible for more complex treatment processes. Some operators are promoted to plant supervisor or superintendent, while others advance by transferring to a larger facility. Some postsecondary training in water and wastewater treatment coupled with increasingly responsible experience as an operator may be sufficient to qualify for superintendent of a small plant, since at many small plants the superintendent also serves as an operator. However, educational requirements are rising as larger, more complex treatment plants are built to meet new water pollution control standards. With each promotion, the operator must have greater knowledge of Federal, State, and local regulations. Superintendents of large plants generally need an engineering or science degree. A few operators get jobs with State water pollution control agencies as technicians, who monitor and provide technical assistance to plants throughout the State. Vocational-technical school or community college training generally is preferred for technician jobs. Experienced operators may transfer to related jobs with industrial wastewater treatment plants, companies selling wastewater treatment equipment and chemicals, engineering consulting firms, or vocational-technical schools.

In 49 States, operators must pass an examination to certify that they are capable of overseeing wastewater treatment plant operations. A voluntary certification program is in effect in the remaining State. Water plant operators must also be certified in most States. Typically, there are different levels of certification depending on the operator's experience and training. Higher certification levels qualify the operator for a wider variety of treatment processes. Certification requirements vary by State, and by size of treatment plants.

There is no nationally mandated certification program for operators, and relocation may mean having to become certified in a new location. However, many States have begun accepting other States' certifications.

Job Outlook
Those who wish to become water and wastewater treatment plant operators should have good opportunities through the year 2005. Despite low turnover and job growth that is expected to be slower than average, the number of applicants in this field is normally low, making for good job prospects for qualified applicants.

The increasing population and growth of the economy are expected to increase demand for water and wastewater treatment services. As new plants are constructed to meet this demand, employment of water and wastewater treatment plant operators should increase. In addition, some job openings will occur as experienced operators transfer to other occupations or leave the labor force.

Although local government is the largest employer of water and wastewater treatment plant operators, increased reliance on private firms specializing in the operation and management of water and wastewater treatment facilities should shift some employment demand to these companies. Increased pre-treatment activity by manufacturing firms should also create new job opportunities.

Water and wastewater treatment plant operators generally have steady employment because the services they provide are essential even during economic downturns.

Earnings
Annual salaries of water and wastewater treatment plant operators averaged $27,100 in 1994; the lowest paid 10 percent of the occupation earned about $16,600, the middle 50 percent of the occupation earned between $22,300 and $35,200, and the top 10 percent earned about $42,100. Salaries depend, among other things, on the size and location of the plant, the complexity of the operator's job, and the operator's level of certification.

In addition to their annual salaries, water and wastewater treatment plant operators generally receive benefits that include health and life insurance, a retirement plan, and educational reimbursement for job-related courses.

Related Occupations
Other workers whose main activity consists of operating a system of machinery to process or produce materials include boiler operators, gas-compressor operators, power plant operators, power reactor operators, stationary engineers, turbine operators, chemical plant operators, and petroleum refinery operators.

Sources of Additional Information
For information on certification, contact:

☛Association of Boards of Certification, 208 Fifth St., Suite 1A, Ames, IA 50010-6259.

For educational information on careers as a water treatment plant operator, contact:

☛American Waterworks Association, 6666 West Quincy Ave., Denver, CO 80235.

☛Water Environment Federation, 601 Wythe St., Alexandria, VA 22314.

For information on jobs, contact State or local water pollution control agencies, State water and waste water operator associations, State environmental training centers, or local offices of the State employment service.

Printing Occupations

Bindery Workers

(D.O.T. 653.360, .382, .662, .682, .685; 692.685-146; 794.687-026; and 977.381 and .684-026)

Nature of the Work
The process of combining printed sheets into finished products such as books, magazines, catalogs, folders, or directories is known as "binding." Binding involves cutting, folding, gathering, gluing, stitching, trimming, sewing, wrapping, and other finishing operations. Bindery workers operate and maintain the machines performing these various tasks.

Job duties depend on the kind of material being bound. In firms that do *edition binding*, for example, workers bind books produced in large numbers or "runs." *Job binding* workers bind books produced in smaller quantities. In firms that specialize in *library binding*, workers repair books and provide other specialized binding services to libraries. *Pamphlet binding* workers produce leaflets and folders, and *manifold binding* workers bind business forms such as ledgers and books of sales receipts. *Blankbook binding* workers bind blank pages to produce notebooks, checkbooks, address books, diaries, calendars, and note pads.

Some binding consists of only one step. Preparing leaflets or newspaper inserts, for example, requires only folding. Binding of books, on the other hand, requires the following steps.

Bookbinders assemble books from large, flat, printed sheets of paper. Many skilled bookbinders also bind magazines. Machines are used extensively throughout the process. Skilled bookbinders operate machines that first fold printed sheets into units known as "signatures," which are groups of pages arranged sequentially. Bookbinders then sew, stitch, or glue the assembled signatures together, shape the book bodies with presses and trimming machines, and reinforce them with glued fabric strips. Covers are created separately, and glued, pasted, or stitched onto the book bodies. The books then undergo a variety of finishing operations, often including wrapping in paper jackets.

A small number of bookbinders work in hand binderies. These highly skilled workers design original or special bindings for limited editions or restore and rebind rare books. The work requires creativity, knowledge of binding materials, and a thorough background in the history of binding. Hand bookbinding gives individuals the opportunity to work at the greatest variety of jobs.

Bindery workers in small shops may perform many binding tasks, while those in large shops are usually assigned only one or a few operations, such as operating complicated paper cutters or folding machines. Others specialize in adjusting and preparing equipment, and may when necessary perform minor repairs.

Working Conditions
Binderies are often noisy and jobs can be fairly strenuous, requiring considerable lifting, standing, and carrying. They may also require stooping, kneeling, and crouching. Binding often resembles an assembly line, and workers should not mind performing repetitive tasks.

Employment
In 1994, bindery workers held about 78,000 jobs, including over 5,900 working as skilled bookbinders and nearly 72,000 working as lesser skilled bindery machine operators.

Although some bindery workers are employed by large libraries and book publishers, the majority of jobs are in commercial printing plants. Few publishers maintain their own manufacturing facilities, so most contract out the printing and assembly of books to commercial printing plants or bindery trade shops. Bindery trade shops, the second largest employer of bindery workers, specialize in binding for printers without binderies, or whose printing production exceeds their binding capabilities.

Bindery workers are employed in all parts of the country, but jobs are concentrated near large metropolitan areas such as New York, Chicago, Washington, DC, Los Angeles, Philadelphia, and Dallas.

Training, Other Qualifications, and Advancement
For bindery jobs, employers prefer high school graduates with basic mathematics and language skills. Accuracy, patience, neatness, and good eyesight are also important. Bindery work requires careful

Binding involves cutting, folding, gluing, trimming, and other finishing operations.

attention to detail, because mistakes at this stage in the printing process can cost a lot. Finger dexterity is essential to count, insert, paste, and fold, and mechanical aptitude is needed to operate the newer, more automated equipment. Artistic ability and imagination are necessary for hand bookbinding.

Most bindery workers learn the craft through on-the-job training. Inexperienced workers are usually assigned simple tasks such as moving paper from cutting machines to folding machines. They learn basic binding skills, including the characteristics of paper and how to cut large sheets of paper into different sizes with the least amount of waste. As workers gain experience, they advance to more difficult tasks and learn how to operate one or more pieces of equipment. Generally, it takes 1 to 3 months to learn how to operate the simpler machines well, but it can take up to 1 year to learn how to operate the more complex equipment, such as computerized binding machines.

Employers prefer to hire and train workers with some basic knowledge of binding operations. High school students interested in bindery careers can gain some exposure to the craft by taking shop courses or attending a vocational-technical high school. Occupational skill centers, usually operated by labor unions, also provide an introduction.

Formal apprenticeships are not as common as they used to be, but are still offered by some employers. They provide a more structured program that enables workers to acquire the high levels of specialization and skill needed for some bindery jobs. For example, a 4-year apprenticeship usually is necessary to teach workers how to restore rare books and to produce valuable collectors' items.

Training in graphic arts is also an asset. Postsecondary programs in the graphic arts are offered by vocational-technical institutes, skill updating or retraining programs, and community and junior colleges. Some updating and retraining programs require students to have bindery experience; other programs are available through unions for members. Four-year colleges also offer programs, but their emphasis on preparing people for careers as graphic artists or managers in the graphic arts field. To keep pace with ever-changing technology, occasional retraining will become increasingly important for bindery workers.

Advancement opportunities in bindery work are limited. In large binderies, experienced bookbinders may advance to supervisory positions.

Job Outlook
Employment of bindery workers is expected to grow more slowly than the average for all occupations through the year 2005 as demand for printed material grows but productivity in bindery operations increases. Most job openings for bindery workers will result from the need to replace experienced workers who change jobs or leave the labor force.

Growth of the printing industry will continue to spur demand for bindery workers by commercial printers. The volume of printed material should grow due to increased marketing of products through catalogs, newspaper inserts, and direct mail advertising. Book publishing is expected to continue to grow in response to rising school enrollments, and the expanding middle-aged and older population—age groups that do the most leisure reading.

Even though major technological changes are not anticipated, binding is becoming increasingly mechanized. New "in-line" equipment performs a number of operations in sequence, beginning with raw stock and ending with a complete finished product. Growth in requirements for bindery workers who assist skilled bookbinders will be slowed as binding machinery continues to become more efficient.

Opportunities for hand bookbinders are limited by the small number of establishments that do this highly specialized work. Experienced bindery workers will have the best opportunities.

Earnings

Bindery workers in 1994 had median weekly earnings of about $396. The middle 50 percent earned about $283 to $539 a week. The lowest paid 10 percent earned less than $205 a week, while the highest paid 10 percent earned $673 a week or more. Workers covered by union contracts generally had higher earnings.

Related Occupations

Other workers who set up and operate production machinery include papermaking machine operators, press operators, and various precision machine operators.

Sources of Additional Information

Information about apprenticeships and other training opportunities may be obtained from local printing industry associations, local bookbinding shops, local offices of the Graphic Communications International Union, or local offices of the State employment service.

For general information on bindery occupations, write to:

☛Graphic Communications International Union, 1900 L St. NW., Washington, DC 20036.

For information on careers and training programs in printing and the graphic arts, contact:

☛Education Council of the Graphic Arts Industry, 1899 Preston White Dr., Reston, VA 22091-4326.

☛PIA-PrintED Accreditation Program for the Graphic Arts, 100 Daingerfield Rd., Alexandria, VA 22314.

Prepress Workers

(A list of D.O.T. codes is available upon request. See page 478.)

Nature of the Work

The printing process has three stages—prepress, press, and binding or finishing. Prepress workers prepare material for printing presses. They perform a variety of tasks involved with transforming text and pictures into finished pages and making printing plates of the pages.

As personal computers recently have come into more widespread use, advances in computer software and printing technology have begun to greatly change prepress work. Much of the typesetting and page layout work formerly done by prepress workers is increasingly done by customers on their computers. Customers are able to use their computers to send material to printers that looks more and more like the desired finished product. This change, called "desktop publishing," poses new challenges for the printing industry. Instead of receiving simple typed text from customers, prepress workers increasingly get the material on a computer disk, and instead of relying on prepress workers to suggest a format, customers are increasingly likely to have already settled on one by experimenting on their personal computers. The printing industry is rapidly moving towards complete "digital imaging," by which customers' material received on computer disks is converted directly into printing plates. Other aspects of prepress work experiencing innovation include digital color page makeup systems, electronic page layout systems, and off-press color proofing systems.

As electronic imaging becomes more prevalent, the use of film in printing will decline. Film, however, is still often the most economical and efficient data storage and retrieval medium currently in use. Today, electronic imaging is limited to more advanced printing shops, but as costs decline and quality improves, the process will become the method of choice in the industry.

A growing number of printing companies do typesetting and page layout on the computer.

Typesetting and page layout have been greatly affected by technological changes. Today, composition work is done with computers and "cold type" technology. The old "hot type" method of text composition—which used molten lead to create individual letters, paragraphs, and full pages of text—is nearly extinct. Cold type, which is any of a variety of methods that create type without molten lead, has traditionally used "phototypesetting" to ready text and pictures for printing. Although this method has many variations, all use photography to create positive images on paper. The images are assembled into page format and rephotographed to create film negatives from which the actual printing plates are made. However, newer cold type methods are coming into increasing use; these automate the photography or make printing plates directly from material in a computer.

In one common form of phototypesetting, text is entered into a computer programmed to hyphenate, space, and create columns of text. Keyboarding of text may be done by typesetters or data entry clerks at the printing establishment or, increasingly, by the author before the job is sent out for composition. The computer stores the text on magnetic tape, floppy disk, or hard disk. The magnetically coded text is then transferred to a typesetting machine which uses photography, a cathode-ray tube, or a laser to create an image on typesetting paper or film. Once it has been developed, the paper or film is sent to a lithographer who makes the actual printing plate.

In another type of phototypesetting, a computer produces text on special paper in the desired format. In newspapers, for example, text is printed in long columns. Workers called *paste up artists* cut and arrange the columns of text and illustrations onto a special illustration board called a "mechanical." The special paper adheres easily to the board, yet is designed to allow easy removal and positioning. Once the text is arranged in final form, the board is sent to the camera department where a photographic negative used to create printing plates is produced. In small shops, *job printers* may be responsible for composition and page layout, reading proof for errors and clarity, correcting mistakes, and printing.

The most advanced method of typesetting, called "electronic pagination," is in growing commercial use. *Electronic pagination system operators* use a keyboard to enter and select the size and style of type, the column width, and appropriate spacing, and to store it in the computer. The computer then displays and arranges columns of type on a screen that resembles a television screen. An entire newspaper page—complete with artwork and graphics—can be made up on the screen exactly as it will appear in print. Operators transmit the pages for production into film and then into plates, or directly into plates, eliminating the role of paste up artists.

New technologies are also affecting the roles of other composition workers. Improvements in desktop publishing software will allow customers to do more typesetting directly. Laser printers read text from computer memory and then "beam" it directly onto film, paper, or plates, bypassing the slower photographic process traditionally used.

After the material has been arranged and typeset, in traditional processes that use photography it is passed on to workers who further prepare it for the presses. *Camera operators* are generally classified as line camera operators, halftone operators, or color separation photographers. Line camera operators start the process of making a lithographic plate by photographing and developing film negatives or positives of the material to be printed. They adjust light and expose film for a specified length of time, and then develop film in a series of chemical baths. They may load unexposed film in machines that automatically develop and fix the image.

Normal continuous-tone photographs cannot be reproduced by most printing processes, so halftone camera operators separate the photograph into pictures that are made up of tiny dots, which can be reproduced. Color separation photography is more complex. In this process, camera operators produce four-color separation negatives from a continuous-tone color print or transparency which is being reproduced.

More of this separation work will be done electronically in the future on scanners. *Scanner operators* use computerized equipment to create film negatives or positives of photographs or art. The computer controls the color separation or the scanning process, correcting for mistakes, or compensating for deficiencies in the original color print or transparency. Operators review all work to determine if corrections to the original are necessary and adjust the equipment accordingly. They then use a densitometer to measure the density of the colored areas, and adjust the scanner to obtain the best results. An original color photograph or transparency is scanned for each color to be printed. Each scan produces a dotted image, or halftone, of the original in one of four primary colors—yellow, magenta, cyan, and black. The images are used to produce printing plates that print each of these colors, one at a time. The printing is done with primary process color inks which are transparent, creating "secondary" color combinations of red, green, blue, and black. These secondary colors can be combined to produce all the colors and hues of the original photograph. The computer controls the color separation or the scanning process, correcting for mistakes or compensating for deficiencies in the original color print or transparency.

Scanners which can perform color correction during the color separation procedure are rapidly replacing *lithographic dot etchers*, who retouch film negatives or positives by sharpening or reshaping images. They do the work by hand, using chemicals, dyes, and special tools. Dot etchers must know the characteristics of all types of paper and must produce fine shades of color. Like camera operators, they are usually assigned to only one phase of the work, and may have job titles such as dot etcher, retoucher, or letterer.

New technology is also eliminating the need for *strippers*, who cut the film to required size and arrange and tape the negatives onto "flats"—or layout sheets used by platemakers to make press plates. When completed, flats resemble large film negatives of the text in its final form. In large printing establishments like newspapers, arrangement is done automatically.

Platemakers use a photographic process to make printing plates. The film assembly or flat is placed on top of a thin metal plate treated with a light-sensitive chemical. Exposure to ultraviolet light activates the chemical in those parts not protected by the film's dark areas. The plate is then developed in a special solution that removes the unexposed nonimage area, exposing bare metal. The chemical on areas of the plate exposed to the light hardens and becomes water repellent. The hardened parts of the plate form the text.

A growing number of printing plants use lasers to directly convert electronic data to plates without any use of film. Entering, storing, and retrieving information from computer-aided equipment requires technical skills. In addition to operating and maintaining the equipment, lithographic platemakers must make sure that plates meet quality standards.

During the printing process, the plate is first covered with a thin coat of water. The water adheres only to the bare metal nonimage areas, and is repelled by the hardened areas that were exposed to light. Next, the plate comes in contact with a rubber roller covered with an oil-based ink. Because oil and water do not mix, the ink is repelled by the water-coated area and sticks to the hardened areas. The ink covering the hardened text is transferred to paper.

Technological changes will continue in the prepress area as hand work is automated. Although computers will perform a wider variety of tasks, printing will still involve text composition, page layout, and plate making, so printing will still require prepress workers. Computer skills will be increasingly important to prepress workers. These workers will, however, need to demonstrate a desire and an ability to benefit from the frequent retraining that rapidly changing technology necessitates.

Working Conditions

Prepress workers usually work in clean, air-conditioned areas with little noise. Some workers, such as typesetters and compositors, may develop eyestrain from working in front of a video display terminal, as well as musculoskeletal problems, such as backaches. Lithographic artists and strippers may find working with fine detail tiring to the eyes. Platemakers, who work with toxic chemicals, face the hazard of skin irritations. Stress may be an important factor as workers are often subject to the pressures of shorter and shorter deadlines and tighter and tighter work schedules.

Prepress employees generally work an 8-hour day. Some workers—particularly those employed by newspapers—work night shifts, weekends, and holidays.

Employment

Prepress workers held about 169,000 jobs in 1994. Employment was distributed as follows:

Prepress precision workers

Strippers, printing	31,000
Paste-up workers	22,000
Electronic pagination systems workers	18,000
Camera operators	15,000
Job printers	14,000
Platemakers	13,000
Compositors and typesetters	11,000
Photoengravers	7,000
All other precision printing workers	13,000

Prepress machine operators

Typesetting and composing machine operators	20,000
Photoengraving and lithographic machine operators	5,000

Most prepress jobs were found in firms that handle commercial or business printing and in newspaper plants. Commercial printing firms print newspaper inserts, catalogs, pamphlets, and advertisements, while business form establishments print material such as sales receipts and paper used in computers. Additional jobs are found in printing trade service firms and "in-plant" operations. Establishments in printing trade services typically perform custom compositing, platemaking, and related prepress services.

The printing and publishing industry is one of the most geographically dispersed in the United States, and prepress jobs are found throughout the country. However, job prospects may be best in large printing centers such as New York, Chicago, Los Angeles, Philadelphia, Washington DC, and Dallas.

Training, Other Qualifications, and Advancement

The length of training required for prepress jobs varies by occupation. Some, such as typesetting, can be learned in only a few months, but they are the most likely to be automated. Others, such as stripping, require years of experience to master. Nevertheless, even workers in these occupations should expect to receive intensive retraining. Workers often start as helpers who are selected for on-the-job training programs once they demonstrate their reliability and interest in learning the job. They begin instruction with an experienced craft worker and advance based upon their demonstrated mastery of skills at each level of instruction. All workers should expect to be retrained from time to time to handle new, improved equipment.

Apprenticeship is another way to become a skilled prepress worker, although few apprenticeships have been offered in recent years. Apprenticeship programs emphasize a specific craft—such as camera operator, stripper, lithographic etcher, scanner operator, or platemaker—but apprentices are introduced to all phases of printing.

Generally, most employers prefer to hire high school graduates who possess good communication skills, both oral and written. Prepress workers need to be able to deal courteously with people because in small shops they may take customer orders. They may also need to add, subtract, multiply, divide, and compute ratios to estimate job costs. Persons interested in working for firms that use advanced printing technology need to know the basics of electronics and computers. Mathematical skills are also essential for operating many of the software packages used to run modern, computerized prepress equipment.

Prepress workers need manual dexterity, and they must be able to pay attention to detail and work independently. Good eyesight, including visual acuity, depth perception, field of view, color vision, and the ability to focus quickly, is an asset. Artistic ability is often a plus. Employers seek persons who are even-tempered and adaptable, important qualities for workers who often must meet deadlines and learn how to operate new equipment.

Formal graphic arts programs, offered by community and junior colleges and some 4-year colleges, also introduce persons to the industry. These programs provide job-related training, and enrolling in one demonstrates an interest in the graphic arts, which may impress an employer favorably. Bachelor's degree programs in graphic arts are generally intended for students who may eventually move into management positions, and 2-year associate degree programs are designed to train skilled workers.

Courses in various aspects of printing are also available at vocational-technical institutes, industry-sponsored update and retraining programs, and private trade and technical schools.

As workers gain experience, they advance to positions with greater responsibility. Some move into supervisory positions.

Job Outlook

Employment of prepress workers is expected to decline through the year 2005. Demand for printed material should grow rapidly spurred by rising levels of personal income, increasing school enrollments, and higher levels of educational attainment. However, increased use of computers in typesetting and page layout should eliminate many prepress jobs.

New technologies are also expected to spur demand for printed materials by expanding markets, allowing advertising dollars currently allotted to nonprint media, such as television, to be spent on direct mail. Work previously requiring a week or more can now be completed in a few days. Much faster turnaround time will permit printers to compete with nonprint media for time-sensitive business, providing advertisers with specialty advertisements used to target specific market segments, for example.

Technological advances will have a varying effect on employment among the prepress occupations. Employment of electronic pagination system operators is expected to much grow much faster than average, reflecting the increasing proportion of page layout and design that will be performed using computers. In contrast, prepress machine operators are expected to decline sharply as the work that these workers perform manually is increasingly automated. Occupa-

tions that are expected to experience moderate declines as hand work becomes automated include paste-up workers, job printers, precision compositors and typesetters, photoengravers, platemakers, and camera operators.

Job prospects also will vary by industry, most notably for compositors and typesetters. Changes in technology have shifted many employment opportunities away from the traditional printing plants into advertising agencies, public relations firms, and large corporations. Many companies are turning to in-house typesetting or "desktop publishing" due to the advent of inexpensive personal computers with graphic capabilities. Corporations are finding it more profitable to print their own newsletters and other reports than to send them out to trade shops. In addition, press shops themselves have responded to desktop publishers' needs by sending their own staff into the field to help customers prepare a disk that will live up to the customer's expectations.

Compositors and typesetters should find competition extremely keen in the newspaper industry, currently their largest employer. Computerized equipment that allows reporters and editors to specify type and style and to format pages at a desktop computer terminal has already eliminated many typesetting and composition jobs, and more are certain to disappear in the years ahead.

Many new jobs for prepress workers are expected to emerge in commercial printing establishments. New equipment should reduce the time needed to complete a printing job, and allow commercial printers to make inroads into new markets that require fast turn-around. Because small establishments predominate, commercial printing should provide the best opportunities for inexperienced workers looking to gain a good background in all facets of printing.

Opportunities for prepress workers should also be good in the printing trade services industry. Despite the fact that companies may have their own typesetting and printing capabilities, they usually turn to professionals in printing trade services if quality and time are of the essence.

Most employers prefer to hire experienced prepress workers. However, among persons without experience, opportunities should be best for those with a computer background who have completed postsecondary programs in printing technology. Many employers prefer graduates of these programs because the comprehensive training they receive helps them learn the printing process and adapt more rapidly to new processes and techniques.

Earnings

Wage rates for prepress workers vary according to occupation, level of experience and training, location and size of the firm, and whether they are union members. According to limited data available, the median earnings of full-time workers were $549 a week in 1994 for lithographers and photoengravers and $389 a week for typesetters and compositors.

Of the prepress workers who were unionized, scanner operators earned an hourly wage of $21.88 in 1995, and strippers earned $17.57 per hour, according to the Graphic Communications International Union, the principal union for prepress workers.

Related Occupations

Prepress workers use artistic skills in their work. These skills are also essential for sign painters, jewelers, decorators, engravers, and graphic artists. Other workers who operate machines equipped with keyboards like typesetters include clerk-typists, computer terminal system operators, keypunch operators, and telegraphic-typewriter operators.

Sources of Additional Information

Details about apprenticeship and other training programs may be obtained from local employers such as newspapers and printing shops or from local offices of the State employment service.

For information on careers and training in printing and the graphic arts, write to:

☛PIA-PrintED Accreditation Program for the Graphic Arts, 100 Daingerfield Rd., Alexandria, VA 22314.
☛Education Council of the Graphic Arts Industry, 1899 Preston White Dr., Reston, VA 22091-4326.
☛Graphic Communications International Union, 1900 L St. NW., Washington, DC 20212.

Printing Press Operators

(List of D.O.T. codes available on request. See p. 478.)

Nature of the Work

Printing press operators prepare, operate, and maintain the printing presses in a pressroom. Duties of press operators vary according to the type of press they operate—offset, gravure, flexography, screen printing, or letterpress. Offset is the dominant printing process and is expected to remain so into the next century. Gravure and flexography should increase in use, but letterpress should continue being phased out. In addition to the major printing processes, plateless or nonimpact processes are coming into general use. Plateless processes—including electronic, electrostatic, and ink-jet printing—are used for copying, duplicating, and document and specialty printing, generally by quick and in-house printing shops.

To prepare presses for printing, press operators install and adjust the printing plate, mix fountain solution, adjust pressure, ink the presses, load paper, and adjust the press to the paper size. Press operators check that paper and ink meet specifications, and adjust control margins and the flow of ink to the inking rollers accordingly. They then feed paper through the press cylinders and adjust feed and tension controls.

While printing presses are running, press operators monitor their operation and keep the paper feeders well stocked. They make adjustments to correct uneven ink distribution, speed, and temperatures in the drying chamber, if the press has one. If paper jams or tears—which can happen with some offset presses—and the press stops, operators quickly correct the problem to minimize downtime. Similarly, operators working with other high-speed presses constantly look for problems, making quick corrections to avoid expensive losses of paper and ink. Throughout the run, operators also occasionally pull sheets to check for any printing imperfections.

In many shops, press operators perform preventive maintenance. They oil and clean the presses and make minor repairs to keep them running smoothly.

Press operators' jobs differ from one shop to another because of differences in the kinds and sizes of presses. Small commercial shops tend to have relatively small presses which print only one or two colors at a time and are operated by one person. Operators who work with large presses have assistants and helpers. Large newspaper, magazine, and book printers use giant "in-line web" presses that require a crew of several press operators and press assistants. These presses are fed paper in big rolls, called "webs," up to 50 inches or more in width. Presses print the paper on both sides; trim, assemble, score, and fold the pages; and count the finished sections as they come off the press.

Most plants have or soon will have installed printing presses that have computers and sophisticated instruments to control press operations, making it possible to set up for jobs in much less time. Computers allow press operators to perform many of their tasks electronically. With this equipment, press operators monitor the printing process on a control panel that allows them to adjust the press electronically by pushing buttons.

Working Conditions

Operating a press can be physically and mentally demanding, and sometimes tedious. Press operators are on their feet most of the time.

To prepare presses for printing, press operators load and feed paper through the press cylinders.

Often, operators work under pressure to meet deadlines. Most printing presses are capable of high printing speeds, and adjustments must be made quickly to avoid waste. Pressrooms are noisy, and workers in certain areas wear ear protectors. Working with press machinery can be hazardous, but accidents can be avoided when safe work practices are observed. The danger of accidents is much less with newer computerized presses because operators make most adjustments from a control panel. Many press operators work evening, night, and overtime shifts.

Employment

Press operators held about 244,000 jobs in 1994. Employment was distributed as follows:

Printing press machine setters and operators	113,000
Offset lithographic press operators	79,000
Screen printing machine setters and setup operators	26,000
Letterpress operators	14,000
All other printing press setters and set-up operators	13,000

Most jobs were in newspaper plants or in firms that handle commercial or business printing. Commercial printing firms print newspaper inserts, catalogs, pamphlets, and the advertisements found in your mailbox, and business form establishments print items such as sales receipts and paper used in computers. Additional jobs were in the "in-plant" section of organizations and businesses that do their own printing—among them, banks, insurance companies, and government agencies.

The printing and publishing industry is one of the most geographically dispersed in the United States, and press operators can find jobs throughout the country. However, jobs are concentrated in large printing centers such as New York, Los Angeles, Chicago, Philadelphia, Washington, DC, and Dallas.

Training, Other Qualifications, and Advancement

Although completion of a formal apprenticeship or a post secondary program in printing equipment operation continue to be the best way to learn the trade, most printing press operators are trained informally on the job working as assistants or helpers to experienced operators. Beginning press operators load, unload, and clean presses. With time, they move up to operating one-color sheet-fed presses and eventually advance to multicolor presses. Operators are likely to gain experience on many kinds of printing presses during the course of their career.

Apprenticeship, once the dominant method of preparing for this occupation, is becoming less prevalent with the growing importance of formal post secondary programs in printing equipment operation offered by technical and trade schools and community and junior colleges. Apprenticeships for press operators in commercial shops take 4 years. In addition to on-the-job instruction, apprenticeships include related classroom or correspondence school courses. In contrast, although some post secondary school programs require 2 years of study and award an associate degree, most programs can be completed in 1 year or less. Post secondary courses in printing are increasingly important because they provide the theoretical knowledge needed to operate advanced equipment.

Persons who wish to become printing press operators need mechanical aptitude to make press adjustments and repairs and an ability to visualize color in order to work on color presses. Oral and writing skills also are required. Operators should be able to compute percentages, weights, and measures, and should possess adequate mathematical skills to calculate the amount of ink and paper needed to do a job. Because of technical developments in the printing industry, courses in chemistry, electronics, color theory, and physics are helpful.

Technological changes have had a tremendous effect on the skills needed by press operators. New presses require basic computer skills. Printing plants that change from sheet-fed offset presses to web-offset presses have to retrain the entire press crew because the skill requirements for the two types of presses are different. Web-offset presses, with their faster operating speeds, require faster decisions, monitoring of more variables, and greater physical effort. Even experienced operators periodically receive retraining and skill updating. In the future, workers are expected to need to retrain several times during their career.

Press operators may advance in pay and responsibility by taking a job working on a more complex printing press. For example, a one-color sheet-fed press operator may, through experience and demonstrated ability, become a four-color sheet-fed press operator. Others may advance to pressroom supervisor and become responsible for the work of the entire press crew.

Job Outlook

Persons seeking jobs as printing press operators will face keen competition from experienced operators and prepress workers who have been displaced by new technology, particularly those who have completed retraining programs. Opportunities to become printing press operators are likely to be best for persons who qualify for formal apprenticeship training or who complete postsecondary training programs.

Employment of press operators is expected to grow more slowly than the average for all occupations through the year 2005. Although demand for printed materials will grow, employment growth will be slowed by the increasing use of new, more efficient computerized printing presses. However, employment growth will vary among various press operator jobs. Employment of offset, gravure, and flexographic operators will increase, while employment of letterpress operators will decline sharply. Most job openings will result from the need to replace operators who retire or leave the occupation.

Most new jobs will result from expansion of the printing industry as demand for printed material increases in response to demographic trends, U.S. expansion into foreign markets, and growing use of direct mail by advertisers. Demand for books and magazines will increase as school enrollments rise, and as substantial growth in the middle-aged and older population spurs adult education and leisure reading. Additional growth should stem from increasing foreign demand for domestic trade publications, professional and scientific works, and mass-market books such as paperbacks.

Much of the growth in commercial printing will be spurred by increased expenditures for print advertising materials to be mailed directly to prospective customers. New market research techniques are leading advertisers to increase spending on messages targeted to specific audiences and should continue to require the printing of a wide variety of newspaper inserts, catalogs, direct mail enclosures, and other kinds of print advertising.

Other printing, such as newspapers, books, and periodicals, will also provide jobs. Experienced press operators will fill most of these jobs because many employers are under severe pressure to meet deadlines and have limited time to train new employees.

Earnings

The basic wage rate for a press operator depends on the type of press being run and the area of the country in which the work is located. Median weekly earnings of press operators who worked full time were about $432 in 1994. The middle 50 percent earned between $307 and $605 a week. The lowest 10 percent earned $239 or less a week, while the highest 10 percent earned over $787 a week.

Fewer than 1 out of 5 press operators belonged to a union.

Related Occupations

Other workers who set up and operate production machinery include papermaking machine operators, shoemaking machine operators, bindery machine operators, and various precision machine operators.

Sources of Additional Information

Details about apprenticeships and other training opportunities may be obtained from local employers such as newspapers and printing shops, local offices of the Graphic Communications International Union, local affiliates of Printing Industries of America, or local offices of the State employment service.

For general information about press operators, write to:

☛Graphic Communications International Union, 1900 L St. NW., Washington, DC 20036.

For information on careers and training in printing and the graphic arts, write to:

☛PIA-PrintED Accreditation Program for the Graphic Arts, 100 Daingerfield Rd., Alexandria, VA 22314.

☛Education Council of the Graphic Arts Industry, 1899 Preston White Dr., Reston, VA 22091-4326.

Textile, Apparel, and Furnishings Occupations

Apparel Workers

(A list of D.O.T. codes is available on request. See page 478.)

Nature of the Work

Apparel workers help to keep us warm, comfortable, and in style. They play this important role in our lives by transforming cloth, leather, and fur into clothing and other consumer products. Many apparel workers also repair and alter these products. (Some items that we think of as apparel, such as socks or pantyhose, are produced in knitting mills. Workers who are employed in these factories are classified as textile rather than as apparel workers. A separate statement on textile machinery operators is presented in this section of the *Handbook*.)

Apparel production begins with a designer's creation that has been made into a sample product. (A separate statement on designers is presented elsewhere in the *Handbook*.) Because many of these goods are to be mass produced, a pattern of the product must be developed. This is usually done with the aid of a computer. Sample makers often produce the sample garment for the designer.

Once the pattern has been created, the fabric must be spread and cut. Many layers of material may be spread on the cutting table, depending on the quantity being produced and the type of material. Workers known as markers must determine the best arrangement or layout of the pattern pieces to minimize waste. In most plants, this step depends on the judgment of the worker, but computers increasingly are used to determine the optimum arrangement of the pattern pieces.

Using an electric knife or other cutting tool, other workers cut out the various pieces of material following the outline of the pattern. On especially delicate or valuable items, this may be done by hand. Workers must pay close attention to detail because a mistake in the cutting process can ruin many yards of material. In more automated firms, electronic copies of layouts are sent to computer-controlled cutting machines. Workers then monitor the machine. Once the material has been cut, it is ready to be sewn together into a shirt, knapsack, dress, or other product.

Most sewing is done by sewing machine operators, who are classified by the type of machine and product on which they work. Because each product requires a variety of sewing operations that cannot be done on the same machine, companies producing apparel have many types of specialized sewing machines. Sewing machine operators' skills vary by the type of machine on which they work.

Sewing machine operators are also categorized by the specific product they produce. The most basic division, however, is between sewing machine operators who produce clothing and those who produce nongarment items such as towels, sheets, and curtains. Both garment and nongarment machine operators usually specialize in a single operation, such as bindings, collars, or hems.

Because of the value and delicate nature of some materials, sewing often is done by hand rather than on a machine. Hand sewers may specialize in a particular operation, such as sewing buttonholes or adding lace or other trimming. They also work with the designer to make a sample of a new product.

When sewing operations have been completed, workers remove loose threads, basting stitching, and lint from the finished product. Final inspection of the product is done at this time. Inspectors are found in all stages of the production process. They mark defects in uncut fabric so that layout workers can position the pattern to avoid them, or they mark defects in semifinished garments, which they may repair themselves or send back to be mended. (For a more detailed discussion, see the statement on inspectors, testers, and graders elsewhere in the *Handbook*.)

The shape and appearance of certain finished products depend, to a large extent, on the pressing that is done at different stages of production. Pressing is done by hand or by pressing machines. Some pressers specialize in a particular garment part; others do the final pressing before the product is shipped to the store.

Not all apparel goods are mass produced. Some people prefer clothing made especially for them. Custom tailors make garments from start to finish by taking measurements and helping the customer select the right fabric. These workers are highly skilled and must be knowledgeable in all phases of clothing production. Many work in retail outlets, where they make alterations and adjustments to ready-to-wear clothing.

Many apparel workers are employed by small firms that lack the capital resources to invest in new, more efficient equipment. Be-

Apparel production has been difficult to automate due to the flexibility and variety of fabrics.

cause of this, the nature of the work for many apparel workers has remained relatively unchanged. Nevertheless, in larger firms with modern facilities, some operations are computerized, and some of the product-moving operations are done by automated material handling systems. In addition, many firms are using modular manufacturing systems. In these systems, which often reduce production time while increasing product quality, operators work together in a module or group. Although each worker specializes in one operation, most are cross-trained in the various operations performed within the group. Not only do operators communicate more with other workers, they are given added responsibilities, including correcting problems, scheduling, and monitoring standards.

Working Conditions

Working conditions in apparel production vary by establishment and by the type of job. Older factories tend to be congested and poorly lit and ventilated, but more modern facilities are usually better planned, have more work space, and are well lighted and ventilated. Due to the nature of the work and the machinery being used, sewing and pressing areas are usually noisy, whereas patternmaking and spreading areas are quieter. Laundries and dry-cleaning establishments are often hot and noisy; retail stores, on the other hand, generally are relatively quiet and comfortable.

Most persons in apparel occupations work a standard 5-day, 35-to 40-hour week. Some apparel manufacturers add second shifts to justify the expense of new machinery. Also, those employed in retail stores and in laundry and dry-cleaning establishments may work evening and weekend hours.

Apparel production work can be physically demanding. Some workers sit for long periods, and others spend many hours on their feet, leaning over tables and operating machinery. In some instances, new machinery and production techniques have decreased the physical demands upon workers. For example, newer pressing machines are now operated by foot pedals or computer controls and don't require much strength to operate. Although there are no life-threatening dangers or health hazards associated with apparel occupations, operators must be attentive while running equipment such as sewing machines, pressers, and automated cutters. A few workers must use protective devices such as gloves.

In some areas of apparel production, the emphasis on individual performance is shifting to an emphasis on teamwork and cooperation. Incentive programs may also be based on a team's performance. The team or module often has managerial authority over itself, increasing the overall responsibility of each operator and allowing more interpersonal contact. It also means that groups and individual sewing machine operators are under pressure to improve their performance while maintaining quality.

Employment

Apparel workers held 924,000 jobs in 1994. The following tabulation shows that more than 7 out of 10 were sewing machine operators.

Garment sewing machine operators	531,000
Nongarment sewing machine operators	129,000
Custom tailors	84,000
Pressing machine operators	77,000
Hand cutters and trimmers	51,000
Hand sewers	19,000
Patternmakers and layout workers	17,000
Hand pressers	16,000

Production jobs are concentrated in California, New York, North Carolina, Pennsylvania, Tennessee, and Georgia. Most of these jobs are in the apparel and textile industries, except for pressers and custom tailors. Although pressing operations are an integral part of the apparel production process, more than one-half of all pressers are employed in the laundry and dry-cleaning industry. In addition, more than one-half of all custom tailors work in retail clothing establishments; many others are self-employed. For both of these occupations, jobs are found in every part of the country.

Training, Other Qualifications, and Advancement

Training requirements vary by industry. In the apparel industry, for example, few employers require production workers to have a high school diploma or previous work experience. Nevertheless, entrants with secondary or postsecondary vocational training or previous work experience in apparel production usually have a better chance of getting a job and advancing to a supervisory position.

Retailers prefer to hire custom tailors and sewers with previous experience in apparel manufacture, design, or alterations. Knowledge of fabrics, design, and construction is very important. Although laundries and dry cleaners prefer entrants with previous work experience, they routinely hire inexperienced workers.

Apparel workers need good hand-eye coordination and the ability to perform repetitive tasks for long periods. Knowledge of fabrics and their characteristics is sometimes required.

Regardless of setting, workers usually begin by performing simple tasks. As they gain experience, they are assigned more difficult operations. Further advancement is limited, however. Some production workers may become first-line supervisors, but the majority remain on the production line. Occasionally, a patternmaker may advance to designer, but usually only after additional training at a design school. Some experienced custom tailors open their own tailoring shop. Custom tailoring is a very competitive field, however, and training in small business operations can mean the difference between success and failure.

Machinery operators are usually trained on the job by more experienced employees or by machinery manufacturers' representatives. However, as machinery in the industry continues to become more complex, apparel workers will need training in the basics of computers and electronics. For example, some workers use computers to determine the best layout and then electronically send the layout to an automated cutting machine. In addition, the trend toward cross-training of operators will increase the time needed to learn different machines as well as increase an operator's skills.

Job Outlook

Employment of apparel workers is expected to decline through the year 2005. The job outlook of these workers depends largely on conditions in the apparel industry, where most apparel workers are employed. Increased imports, use of offshore assembly, and greater productivity through the introduction of labor-saving machinery will reduce the demand for these workers. Because of the large size of this occupation, however, many thousands of job openings will arise each year from the need to replace persons who transfer to other occupations, retire, or leave the occupation for other reasons.

Employment in the domestic apparel industry has declined in recent years as foreign producers have gained a greater share of the U.S. market. Imports now account for roughly half of domestic apparel consumption, and this share is expected to increase as the U.S. market is opened further by the North American Free Trade Agreement (NAFTA) and the Uruguay Round Agreement (URA) of the General Agreement on Tariffs and Trade (GATT). NAFTA allows apparel produced in Mexico and Canada to be imported, without tariffs, to the United States. Some apparel companies are expected to move their production facilities to Mexico to reduce costs. In addition, the URA will result in the elimination of quotas and a reduction in tariffs for many apparel products. As this agreement is phased in over the next 10 years, domestic production will continue to move abroad and imports into the U.S. market will increase, causing further employment decline for apparel workers in the United States.

To avoid losing more of the market, domestic manufacturers are developing the ability to take advantage of their closeness to the U.S. market by responding more quickly to changes in market demand. This is especially important in high-fashion items with unpredictable demand. U.S. producers are able to use computers and electronic data interchange to closely monitor the sales of the items that they produce and to respond rapidly to diminishing inventories. They are, therefore, able to keep retailers in stock of the most popular items and to reduce production of apparel that is not selling well.

Despite these advances in technology, it has been difficult to use automated equipment extensively in the apparel industry due to the soft properties of textile products. In addition, it is time consuming and expensive to adapt existing technology to the wide variety of items produced and the frequent style and seasonal changes. However, some of the larger firms and those that produce standardized items have automated pre-sewing functions, material handling, and some very simple sewing procedures. Technological developments, such as computer-aided marking and grading, computer-controlled cutters, semiautomatic sewing and pressing machines, and automated material handling systems, have increased output while reducing the need for workers in larger firms. As the apparel industry continues to restructure and consolidate, more of the smaller, less efficient producers will lose market share to larger firms.

Another strategy that domestic manufacturers have adopted to reduce costs is the use of offshore assembly. A provision in U.S. tariff regulations reduces tariffs on apparel imports from Caribbean nations that are assembled from pieces of fabric which were cut in the United States. This enables the most labor-intensive step in the production process—sewing—to be done at much lower wage rates. This trend is expected to continue, and will curtail job opportunities for sewing machine operators in the United States. Because many pre-sewing functions will continue to be done domestically, however, workers who perform these functions will not be as adversely affected. In fact, the only apparel worker occupation which is expected to grow—patternmakers and layout workers—will benefit from this program.

Earnings

Earnings of apparel workers vary by industry and by occupation. Average weekly earnings of production workers in the apparel industry were $275 in 1994, compared to about $510 for production workers in all manufacturing industries. Earnings vary significantly, depending on the product being manufactured. Average weekly earnings ranged from a low of $230 in firms producing women's blouses and shirts to a high of $440 in establishments making automotive and apparel trimmings.

Sewing machine operators—accounting for 7 of every 10 apparel workers—had median weekly earnings of $240 in 1994. Because many production workers in apparel manufacturing are paid according to the number of acceptable pieces they or their group produce, their total earnings depend on skill, speed, and accuracy.

Benefits also vary. Those offered by large employers usually include paid holidays and vacations, health and life insurance coverage, and increasingly, child care. Those employed in retail trade also may receive a discount of 10 to 30 percent on their purchases. In addition, some of the larger manufacturers operate company stores, where employees can purchase apparel products at significant discounts. Some small firms, however, offer only limited benefits. In addition to employer-sponsored benefits, the principal union—the Union of Needletrades, Industrial, and Textile Employees (UNITE)—provides benefits to its members.

Related Occupations
The work of apparel workers varies from that requiring very little skill and training to that which is highly complex, requiring several years of training. Those operating machinery and equipment, such as pressing or sewing machine operators, perform duties similar to metalworking and plastics-working machine operators, textile operatives, and shoe sewing machine operators. Other workers who perform handwork are precision woodworkers, precision assemblers, upholsterers, and shoe and leather workers.

Sources of Additional Information
Information regarding careers in apparel is available from numerous colleges and universities that have specialized textile and apparel programs. A list of these can be found in college guides. In addition, the local office of the State employment service or an apparel manufacturer can provide information on job opportunities in a specific area.

For general information on the apparel industry, write to:
☛American Apparel Manufacturers Association, 2500 Wilson Blvd., Suite 301, Arlington, VA 22201.

Shoe and Leather Workers and Repairers

(D.O.T. 365.361; 780.381-030; 781.381-018; 783.361-010, .381-018 through -026; 788.261-010, .381)

Nature of the Work
Creating stylish and durable leather products is the job of precision shoe and leather workers; keeping them in good condition is the work of repairers. Among the workers who do leather work and repair are custom orthopedic shoemakers, saddlemakers, and luggage makers. Although these workers produce different goods, their duties are actually quite similar.

Depending on the size of the factory or shop, a leather worker may perform one or more of the steps required to complete a product. In smaller factories or shops, workers generally perform several tasks, while those in larger facilities tend to specialize. However, most leather workers eventually learn the different skills involved in producing leather goods as they move from one task to another.

Leather workers must first check the leather for texture, color, and strength. They then place a pattern of the item being produced on the leather, trace the pattern onto the leather, cut along the outline, and sew the pieces together. Other steps may vary according to the type of good being produced.

Orthopedic shoemakers, for example, attach the insoles to shoe lasts (a wooden form shaped like a foot), affix the shoe uppers, and apply heels and outsoles. They shape the heels with a knife and then sand them on a buffing wheel for smoothness. Finally, they dye and polish the shoes. Custom shoe workers also may modify existing footwear for people with foot problems and special needs. This can involve preparing inserts, heel pads, and lifts from casts of customers' feet.

Saddlemakers often apply leather dyes and liquid top coats to produce a gloss finish on a saddle. They may also decorate the saddle surface by hand stitching or by stamping the leather with decorative patterns and designs. *Luggage makers* fasten leather to a frame and attach handles and other hardware. They also cut and secure linings inside the frames and sew or stamp designs onto the luggage exterior.

Shoe and leather repairers use their knowledge of leatherworking to give worn leather goods extended wearability. The most common type of shoe repair is replacing soles and heels. Repairers place the shoe on a last and remove the old sole and heel with a knife or pliers or both. They attach new soles and heels to shoes either by stitching them in place or by using cement or nails. Other leather goods, suitcases or handbags, for example, may need seams to be re-sewn or handles and linings to be replaced.

Leather workers and repairers use handtools and machines. The most commonly used handtools are knives, hammers, awls (used to poke holes in leather to make sewing possible), and skivers (for splitting leather). Power-operated equipment includes sewing machines, heel nailing machines, hole punching machines, and sole stitchers.

Self-employed shoe repairers and owners of custom-made shoe and leather shops have managerial responsibilities in addition to their regular duties. They must maintain good relations with their customers, make business decisions, and keep accurate records.

Workers in shoe repair shops may work irregular hours.

Working Conditions

Working conditions of leather workers vary according to the type of work performed, the size of the factory or business, and the practices of each individual shop.

Workers employed in custom leather goods manufacturing establishments generally work a regular 40-hour week. Those in repair shops work nights and weekends and often work irregular hours. For those who own their own repair shop, long hours are common. Although there are few health hazards if precautions are followed, work areas can be noisy and odors from leather dyes and stains are often present.

Employment

Shoe and leather workers and repairers held about 24,000 jobs in 1994. Self-employed individuals, who typically own and operate small shoe repair shops or specialty leather manufacturing firms, held about 7,000 of these jobs. Of the remaining workers, about half were employed in the manufacture of footwear products, and an additional one-fifth were employed in production of leather goods such as luggage, handbags, and apparel. Another fifth worked in shoe repair and shoeshine shops.

Training, Other Qualifications, and Advancement

Precision shoe and leather workers and repairers generally learn their craft on the job, either through in-house training programs or working as helpers to experienced workers. Helpers generally begin by performing simple tasks and then progress to more difficult projects like cutting or stitching leather. Trainees generally become fully skilled in 6 months to 2 years; the length of training varies according to the nature of the work and the aptitude and dedication of the individual.

A limited number of schools offer vocational training in shoe repair and leather work. These programs may last from 6 months to 1 year and impart basic skills including leather cutting, stitching, and dyeing. Students learn shoe construction, practice shoe repair, and study the fundamentals of running a small business. Graduates are encouraged to gain additional training by working with an experienced leather worker or repairer. National and regional associations also offer specialized training seminars and workshops in custom shoe making, shoe repair, and other leather work.

Manual dexterity and the mechanical aptitude to work with handtools and machines are important in the shoe repair and leather-working occupations. Shoe and leather workers who produce custom goods should have artistic ability as well. These workers must have self-discipline to work alone under little supervision. In addition, leather workers and repairers who own shops will need to have a knowledge of business practices and management as well as a pleasant manner when dealing with customers.

Many individuals who begin as workers or repairers advance to salaried supervisory and managerial positions. Some may open their own shop or business.

Job Outlook

Employment of shoe and leather workers is expected to decline through the year 2005. Inexpensive imports have made the cost of replacing shoes and leather goods cheaper or more convenient than repairing them, thus reducing the demand for shoe and leather repairers. These workers are also adversely affected by the rising cost of leather and higher rents in the high-traffic areas in which more shoe repairers are relocating. Some of the more expensive, fine leather products will continue to be repaired, however, and this demand will moderate the employment decline of shoe repairers. Consumers are also buying more comfort-soled leather shoes, which should also increase demand for the services provided by shoe repairers. In the future, though, most job openings in this occupation will arise from the need to replace experienced workers who transfer to other occupations or leave the work force.

Prospects for workers employed in the manufacture and modification of custom-made molded or orthopedic shoes are better than those for most other leather workers. This is a result of substantial expected growth in the elderly population and an increasing emphasis on preventive foot care. The employment effects of these trends may be limited, however, since the demand for orthopedic footwear is increasingly fulfilled by manufactured shoes that are modified to specification instead of totally custom made.

Earnings

Data on earnings of shoe and leather workers are very limited. Their earnings vary greatly depending upon the place of employment. Beginning workers often start near the minimum wage and can advance in just a few months. Owners of shoe repair and custom shoe manufacturing shops can earn substantially more.

Related Occupations

Other workers who make or repair items using handtools and machinery include dressmakers, designers and patternmakers, and furriers.

Sources of Additional Information

For information about the custom-made prescription shoe business, and about training opportunities in this field, contact:

☛Pedorthic Footwear Association, 9861 Broken Land Pkwy., Suite 255, Columbia, MD 21046-1151.

For information about opportunities in shoe repair, contact:

☛Shoe Service Institute of America, Educational Library, 5024-R Campbell Blvd., Baltimore, MD 21236-5974.

Textile Machinery Operators

(List of D.O.T. codes is available on request. See page 478.)

Nature of the Work

Textile machinery operators tend machines that manufacture a wide range of textile products. Hosiery, skirts, and socks are familiar examples of these products, but many people are surprised to learn that textile products are used in such things as roofs, tires, and roads. There are many phases in the textile production process, and operators' duties and responsibilities depend on the product and the type of machinery in use. Machinery operators control equipment that cleans, cards, combs, and draws the fiber; spins the fiber into yarn; and weaves, knits, or tufts the yarn into textile products. They are responsible for numerous machines that they start, stop, clean, and monitor for proper functioning.

The textile production process begins with the preparation of synthetic or natural fibers for spinning. Fibers are cleaned and aligned through carding and combing. To prepare the fiber for the spinning process, very short fibers and any foreign matter are removed and the fibers are drawn into a substance called sliver. During this process, different types of fibers may be combined to give products the desired textures, durability, or other characteristics. This is how "50 percent cotton, 50 percent polyester" blends, for example, are created. Operators constantly monitor their machines during this stage, checking the movement of the fiber, removing and replacing cans of sliver, repairing breaks in the sliver, and making minor repairs to the machinery.

The full cans of sliver are then taken to the spinning area. Spinning draws and twists the sliver to produce yarn which is then wound onto conical structures called bobbins or cones. This is an automated version of the old fashion spinning wheel.

Some workers oversee machinery that makes manufactured fibers. These fibers, used in many textile products, are created from materials that, unlike cotton, wool, and flax, are not fibrous in their natural form. To make this fiber, wood pulp or chemical compounds are dissolved or melted in a liquid which is then extruded, or forced, through holes in a metal plate, called a spinneret. The sizes and shapes of the holes in the spinneret determine the shape and the uses of the fiber. Workers adjust the flow of fiber base through the spinneret, repair breaks in the fiber, and make minor adjustments to the machinery. Because this fiber is created by a chemical process, the majority of these workers are employed by chemical companies, not textile mills.

When the yarn is ready, it is taken to be woven, knitted, tufted, or bonded with heat or chemicals. Each of these processes produces a different type of textile product and requires a different type of machine. For example, woven fabrics are made on looms that interlace the yarn. Knit products, such as socks or women's hosiery, are produced by intermeshing loops of yarn. Carpeting is made through the tufting process, in which the loops of yarn are pushed through a material backing. Although the processes are now highly automated, these concepts have been used for many centuries to produce textile products.

Even though operators work with many different kinds of machines, they share many responsibilities. Each operator oversees numerous machines—repairing breaks in the yarn, monitoring the supply of yarn, and making minor repairs to the machinery. As increasingly automated machinery is used in textile mills, more processes are controlled by computers, making it possible for each operator to monitor a larger area or number of machines. Because of the complexity of many machines, operators often specialize in a particular type of machine. In addition, operators prepare the machinery prior to a production run and help maintain the equipment. For example, they adjust the timing on a machine, thread the harnesses that create patterns in textile goods, and repair machinery.

Once the yarn has been woven, knitted, or tufted, the resulting fabric is ready to be dyed and finished either at the textile mill or at a plant specializing in textile finishing. Because of the variety of consumer preferences, manufacturers print and dye textiles in thousands of different designs and colors. Depending upon the end use of the yarn, it may be dyed before or after it is woven, knitted, or tufted. Some fabric is treated before it is dyed to remove other chemical additives that could affect the quality of the finished product.

In addition to dyeing and printing, products are often finished by treating them to prevent excessive shrinkage, to provide strength, to make them stain-resistant, or to give it a silky luster. In the production of hosiery and socks, for example, the stocking or sock is placed on a form and then exposed to steam and heat to give it shape.

The future of international trade is the greatest uncertainty facing textile workers.

Working Conditions

Most textile machine operators work in textile mills or chemical plants. Working conditions depend upon the age of the facility or equipment and its degree of modernization. Newer facilities usually offer better ventilation and climate control that reduce potential problems caused by airborne fibers and fumes. Workers in areas with high levels of these airborne materials often use protective glasses and masks that cover their nose and mouth.

Although some of the newer machinery has reduced the level of noise, workers in some areas still must wear ear protection. Because many machines operate at high speeds, workers must be careful not to wear clothing or jewelry that could get caught in moving parts. In addition, extruding and forming machine operators wear protective shoes and clothing when working with some types of chemical compounds.

Most textile machinery operators worked a standard 40-hour week. Because many textile and fiber mills operate 24 hours a day, night and weekend shifts are common. However, many employers use a rotating schedule of shifts so operators don't consistently work nights or weekends. Operators are on their feet moving between machines during most of their shift.

Although workers have traditionally worked under close supervision, new management philosophies are placing an increasing emphasis on teamwork, which will allow operators greater interpersonal contact and more initiative.

Employment

Textile machinery operators held about 281,000 jobs in 1994. Most of these workers were employed in weaving, finishing, yarn, and thread mills. Knitting mills and manufactured fiber producers also employed a substantial number of these workers. Most extruding and forming machine operators were employed in chemical plants.

North Carolina was the leading State in the employment of textile workers, accounting for about 30 percent of the total. Georgia and South Carolina combined accounted for another 30 percent. Most of the remaining workers were employed in other southern States and in the northeast.

Training, Other Qualifications, and Advancement

Education and training are becoming increasingly important for working with complex machinery and advanced manufacturing methods. A high school diploma in addition to extensive technical training is becoming a prerequisite for entry to many jobs. This training may be obtained, in part, at a formal training institution such as a technical school. Extensive on-the-job training by more experienced workers or representatives of machinery manufacturers is also common.

As the textile industry becomes more highly automated, operators will need to understand complex machinery and be able to diagnose problems. Because textile machinery is increasingly controlled electronically, many operators will need good computer skills.

Physical stamina and manual dexterity are important attributes for these jobs. In addition, self-direction and interpersonal skills are becoming more important for textile machinery operators. Organizational changes that promote teamwork and encourage fewer levels of management are leading operators to assume greater responsibility and to take more initiative.

Textile machinery operatives can advance in several ways. Some workers become instructors and train new employees. Others advance by taking positions requiring higher skills and greater responsibility. First-line supervisory positions usually are filled from the ranks of skilled operators.

Job Outlook

Employment of textile machinery operators is expected to decline over the 1994-2005 period. Changing trade regulations and greater productivity through the introduction of labor-saving machinery are the major factors influencing employment in this occupation. In spite of the projected decline, thousands of openings will be created annually as workers change occupations or leave the labor force.

The greatest uncertainty facing textile machinery operators is the future of trade. Recent trade agreements, like the North American Free Trade Agreement and the Uruguay Round of the General Agreement on Tariffs and Trade, will help to open export markets for textiles produced in the United States. At the same time, they will dismantle much of the protection that has been provided to the industry for decades. While the textile industry is highly efficient and will be able to compete in many product lines, the more labor-intensive U.S. apparel industry will be more adversely affected. Because the apparel industry is the largest consumer of American-made textiles, this will negatively affect the demand for textile machinery operators.

Textile firms will respond to this growing competition by investing in new equipment, reorganizing their work practices, and developing new uses for textiles. New machinery, such as faster shuttleless and air jet looms and computer-integrated manufacturing processes, increase productivity by producing goods at a faster rate. They also allow each operator to monitor a larger number of machines. Many factories are also reorganizing production floors to further increase productivity and to give workers more responsibility. In addition, textile firms are developing new uses for textiles that replace non-textiles, such as wallcoverings, medical products, and dome covers.

Because the textile industry is highly automated, persons with technical skills and some computer training will have the best opportunities. In particular, bleaching and dyeing machine operator employment is expected to grow in coming years. Also, extruding machine operators who produce synthetic fibers will encounter growing employment opportunities as the demand for synthetic fiber grows.

Earnings
Average weekly earnings for production workers in the textile and manufactured fiber industries were $380 in 1994, compared to about $510 for production workers throughout all manufacturing industries. Earnings vary significantly, depending upon the type of mill, job specialty, shift, and seniority. Average weekly earnings for production workers in the chemical industry, where most extruding machine operators are found, were around $660 in 1994.

Benefits usually include paid holidays and vacations, health and life insurance, a retirement plan, and sick leave. Some firms provide on-site daycare facilities. Employees may also receive discounts in company-owned outlet stores.

Related Occupations
Metalworking and plastics-working machine operators perform similar duties and have many of the same entry and training requirements as extruding and forming machine operators and tenders, textile machine operators and tenders, and textile bleaching and dyeing machine operators. Setters and setup operators in other industries—metal fabrication and plastics manufacturing, for example—perform duties comparable to those of textile machine setters and setup operators.

Sources of Additional Information
Information about job opportunities in textile and synthetic fiber production is available from local employers or local offices of the State employment service.

For general information on careers, technology, or trade regulations in the textile industry, write to:

☛American Textile Manufacturers Institute, Inc., 1801 K St. NW., Suite 900, Washington, DC 20006.

☛Institute of Textile Technology, P.O. Box 391, Charlottesville, VA 22901.

Upholsterers

(D.O.T. 780.381 except -030 and -034, .384, .684-034, -118, and -122)

Nature of the Work
Whether making a new piece of furniture, restoring a treasured antique, or simply giving an ordinary living room couch a facelift, upholsterers combine knowledge of fabrics and other materials with artistic flair and manual skill. Some repair and replace automobile upholstery and convertible and vinyl tops.

Upholsterers who make new furniture start with a bare wooden frame. Those who recondition old furniture first remove the old cover, padding, and springs, using hammers and tack pullers. They remove the material and padding that cover the arms, back, sides, and seat. They examine the springs and replace broken or bent ones. The springs sit on a cloth mat, called "webbing," that is attached to the frame. If the webbing is worn, upholsterers remove all the springs and webbing. They reglue loose sections of the frame and refinish exposed wood.

The first step in upholstering new furniture or reupholstering old pieces is to install webbing of nylon, jute, or cotton in the frame to hold the springs. Upholsterers tack webbing to one side of the frame, stretch it tight, and tack it to the opposite side. Additional webbing is woven across the first row of webbing and attached to the frame to form a new mat. After putting springs on the mat so they compress evenly, upholsterers sew or staple each spring to the webbing

About 1 out of 3 upholsterers is self-employed.

or frame and tie each spring to the ones next to it. Burlap then is stretched over the springs, cut, smoothed, and tacked to the frame. To form a smooth rounded surface over the springs and other parts of the frame, upholsterers cover the furniture with filling material. They then cover this with a layer of felt and heavy cloth, and tack the cloth to the frame. Upholsterers measure and cut fabric for arms, backs, and other sections with as little waste as possible. They temporarily stitch pieces together for fitting and after assuring tight and smooth fit of the cover—or noting where adjustments are necessary—they remove the cover, sew it together, and tack, staple, or glue it to the frame. To complete the job, upholsterers sew, tack, or glue on fringes, buttons, or other ornaments.

Upholsterers use common handtools, including tack hammers, staple guns, tack and staple removers, pliers, and shears, and special tools such as webbing stretchers and upholstery needles. They also use sewing machines.

Upholsterers who work in upholstery shops pick up and deliver furniture or help customers select new furniture coverings. Those who manage shops also order supplies and equipment and keep business records.

Working Conditions

Most upholsterers work inside a shop or factory. Working conditions in these facilities vary—many are spacious, adequately lighted, well ventilated, and well heated; others are small and dusty.

The work is not dangerous, but upholsterers must be careful to avoid cuts and bruises when they use sharp tools and when they lift and handle furniture or springs. Upholsterers stand most of the workday, and they do a lot of bending and heavy lifting. They also have to work in awkward positions for short periods of time.

Employment

Furniture upholsterers held about 63,000 jobs in 1994. About 1 out of 3 were self-employed. Of the remaining upholsterers, companies that manufacture household and office furniture employed 65 percent and shops that reupholster and repair furniture employed nearly another 17 percent. Over 10 percent worked in shops that specialize in reupholstering the seats of automobiles and other motor vehicles, and a few worked in furniture stores.

Training, Other Qualifications, and Advancement

Most upholsterers are trained on the job as a helper to an experienced worker. Usually about 3 years of on-the-job training are required to become a fully skilled upholsterer. On-the-job training in a furniture factory usually is much shorter because the range of skills required is more limited. Others learn upholstery through apprenticeship or formal training.

When hiring helpers, employers generally prefer people with some knowledge of the trade. Inexperienced persons may get basic training in upholstery in high school, vocational and technical schools, and some community colleges. Programs include sewing machine operation, measuring, cutting, springing, frame repair,

tufting, and channeling; as well as business and interior design courses. However, additional training and experience usually are required before graduates can perform as quickly and efficiently as experienced upholsterers.

Upholsterers should have manual dexterity, good coordination, and strength to lift heavy furniture. An eye for detail and flair for color and creative use of fabrics are helpful.

The major form of advancement for upholsterers is opening their own shop. It is relatively easy to open a shop because a small investment in handtools and a sewing machine are all that is needed. The upholstery business is extremely competitive, however, so operating a shop successfully is difficult. In large shops and factories, experienced or highly skilled upholsterers may become supervisors.

Job Outlook

Employment of upholsterers is expected to grow more slowly than the average for all occupations through the year 2005. Most of the growth will be in furniture manufacturing. Employment in reupholstery shops is expected to remain steady. Each upholstery job is unique, so upholstery work does not lend itself to automation; consequently, technology is not expected to affect employment of upholsterers. Most job openings will arise because of the need to replace experienced workers who transfer to other occupations or leave the labor force.

Opportunities for experienced upholsterers should be very good. The number of upholsterers with experience is limited because few young people want to enter the occupation and because few shops are willing to train people.

Earnings

Median weekly earnings of upholsterers were $359 in 1994; the middle 50 percent earned between $283 and $490 per week. The lowest 10 percent earned less than $198, and the top 10 percent earned more than $617.

Earnings of self-employed upholsterers depend not only on the size and location of the shop but also on the number of hours worked.

Related Occupations

Other workers who combine manual skills and knowledge of materials such as fabrics and wood are fur cutters, furniture finishers, pattern and model makers, and casket coverers.

Sources of Additional Information

For details about work opportunities for upholsterers in your area, contact local upholstery shops or the local office of the State employment service.

To receive a list of technical schools accredited by the Accrediting Commission of Career Schools and Colleges of Technology that have programs in upholstery, contact:
☛Accrediting Commission of Career Schools and Colleges of Technology, 2101 Wilson Blvd., Suite 302, Arlington, VA 22201.

Woodworking Occupations

(A list of D.O.T. codes is available on request. See page 478.)

Nature of the Work

Wood is one of the oldest, most basic building materials. Yet, even in our age of sophisticated composites and alloys, the demand for

wood products continues unabated. Helping to meet this demand are production and precision woodworkers. Production woodworkers can be found in primary industries, such as sawmills and plywood mills, as well as in secondary industries that manufacture furniture, kitchen cabinets, musical instruments, and other fabricated wood products. Precision woodworkers, on the other hand, usually work in small shops that make architectural woodwork, furniture, and many other specialty items.

Woodworkers are employed at some stage of the process through which logs of wood are transformed into finished products. Some of these workers produce the structural elements of buildings; others mill hardwood and softwood lumber; still others assemble finished wood products. They operate machines that cut, shape, assemble, and finish raw wood to make the doors, windows, cabinets, trusses, plywood, flooring, paneling, molding, and trim that are components of most homes. Others may fashion home accessories such as beds, sofas, tables, dressers, and chairs. In addition to these household goods, they also make sporting goods, including baseball bats, racquets, and oars, as well as musical instruments, toys, caskets, tool handles, and thousands of other wooden items.

Production workers usually set up, operate, and tend woodworking machines—such as power saws, planers, sanders, lathes, jointers, and routers—to cut and shape components from lumber, plywood, and other wood panel products. Working from blueprints, instructions from supervisors, or shop drawings that they produce, woodworkers determine the method of shaping and sequence of assembling parts. Before cutting, they must often measure and mark the materials to be cut. They verify dimensions to adhere to specifications and may trim parts to insure a tight fit, using handtools such as planes, chisels, wood files, or sandpaper.

Most production woodworkers operate a specific woodworking machine, but others are responsible for a variety of machines. Lower skilled operators may merely press a switch on a woodworking machine and monitor the automatic operation, while more highly skilled operators set up their equipment, cut and shape wooden parts, and verify dimensions using a template, caliper, or rule. In sawmills, machine operators cut logs into planks, timbers, or boards. In veneer mills, they cut veneer sheets from logs for making plywood. While in furniture plants, they make furniture components such as table legs, drawers, rails, and spindles.

Many companies have installed computer-controlled machinery, which raises worker productivity and reduces wasted resources. With computerized numerical controls, an operator can program a machine to perform a sequence of operations automatically, resulting in greater precision and reliability. The integration of computers with equipment has improved production speeds and capabilities, simplified setup and maintenance requirements, and increased the demand for workers with some computer skills.

Whether computer-controlled or manual equipment is used to machine the parts, the next step in the manufacturing process is the production of subassemblies using fasteners and adhesives. These pieces are then brought together to form a complete unit. The product is then finish sanded, stained, and if necessary, coated with a sealer such as lacquer or varnish. Woodworkers may perform this work in teams or be assisted by a helper.

Precision or custom woodworkers, such as cabinetmakers, model makers, wood machinists, and furniture and wood finishers, work on a customized basis, often building one-of-a-kind items. For this reason, they normally need substantial training and an ability to work from detailed instructions and specifications. They often are required to exercise independent judgment when undertaking an assignment. Precision woodworkers generally perform a complete cycle of cutting, shaping, surface preparation, and assembling prepared parts of complex wood components into a finished wood product.

Working Conditions

Working conditions vary from industry to industry, and job to job. In primary industries, such as logging and sawmilling, working conditions are physically demanding due to the handling of heavy, bulky material. Workers in this area may also encounter excessive noise and dust and other air quality pollutants. However, these factors can be controlled by using earplugs and respirators. Rigid adherence to safety precautions minimizes risk of injury from contact with rough woodstock, sharp tools, and power equipment. The risk of injury is

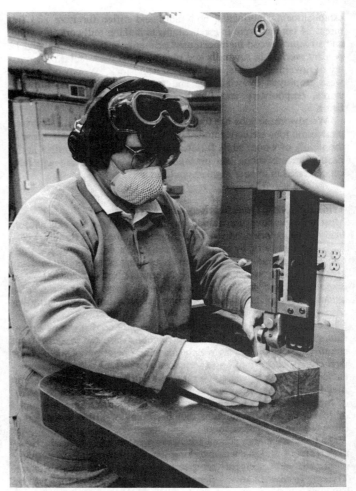

Woodworking requires skill and precision.

also lowered by the installation of computer-controlled equipment that reduces the physical labor and the hands-on contact with the machine.

In secondary industries, such as furniture and kitchen cabinet manufacturing, working conditions also depend on the industry and the particular job. Those employees who operate machinery must wear ear and eye protection, follow operating safety instructions, and use safety shields or guards when appropriate. Those who work in the finishing area must either be provided with an appropriate dust or vapor mask, a complete protective safety suit, or they must be in a finishing environment that removes all vapors and particle matter from the atmosphere. Prolonged standing, lifting, and fitting heavy objects are also common characteristics of the job.

Employment

Workers in woodworking occupations held about 367,000 jobs in 1994. Self-employed woodworkers, mostly cabinetmakers and furniture finishers, accounted for 50,000 of these jobs. Employment was distributed as follows:

Woodworkers, precision	241,000
Woodworking machine setters and operators	126,000
Head sawyers	62,000
Woodworking machine operators	64,000

Eighty percent of salaried woodworkers worked in manufacturing industries. Among these woodworkers, 31 percent were employed in establishments fabricating household and office furniture and fixtures; 24 percent were in establishments making millwork, plywood, and structural wood members, used primarily in construction; and 12 percent worked in sawmills and planing mills manufacturing a variety of raw, intermediate, and finished woodstock. Woodworkers also were employed by wholesale and retail lumber dealers, furniture stores, reupholstery and furniture repair shops, and construction firms.

Woodworking jobs are found throughout the country. However, production jobs are concentrated in the South and Northwest, close to the supply of wood, while furniture makers are more prevalent in the East. Custom shops can be found everywhere, but are generally concentrated in or near highly populated areas.

Training, Other Qualifications, and Advancement

Most woodworkers are trained on the job, picking up skills informally from experienced workers. Some acquire skills through vocational education or by working as carpenters on construction jobs. Others may attend colleges or universities that offer training in many areas including wood technology, furniture manufacturing, wood engineering, and production management. These programs prepare students for positions in production, supervision, engineering, or management.

Beginners usually observe and help experienced machine operators. They may supply material or remove fabricated products from the machine. Trainees do simple machine operating jobs and are at first closely supervised by experienced workers. As they gain experience, they perform more complex jobs with less supervision. Some may learn to read blueprints, set up machines, and plan the sequence of their work. Most woodworkers learn the basic machine operations or job tasks in a few months, but becoming a skilled woodworker often requires 2 years or more.

In the past, a high school education was seldom required. However, persons seeking woodworking jobs can enhance their employment and advancement prospects by completing high school. Training in mathematics, science, and computer applications will be beneficial in the future as woodworking technology becomes more sophisticated, and as more companies install computerized equipment. Employers often look for individuals with mechanical ability, manual dexterity, and the ability to pay attention to detail.

Advancement opportunities are often limited and depend upon availability, seniority, and a worker's skills and initiative. Experienced woodworkers may become inspectors or supervisors responsible for the work of a group of woodworkers. Production workers can advance into these positions by assuming additional responsibilities and by attending workshops, seminars, or college programs. Those who are highly skilled may set up their own woodworking shops.

Job Outlook

Little change is expected in the employment of woodworkers through the year 2005, as growth among precision woodworkers will be offset by the declining employment of woodworking machine operators. As the Nation's population, personal income, and business expenditures grow, the demand for wood products will increase. In addition, the continuing need for repair and renovation of residential and commercial properties is expected to stimulate demand. Opportunities for woodworkers who specialize in such items as moldings, cabinets, stairs, and windows should, therefore, be particularly good.

Several factors may limit the growth of woodworking occupations in coming years. Environmental measures designed to control various pollutants used in or generated by woodworking processes are likely to have a significant impact on employment, especially in secondary industries. Primary industries will be more affected by a shortage of timber as the harvesting of old growth forests on Federal lands becomes more restricted. Technological advances like computerized numerical control machinery and robots will prevent employment from rising as fast as the demand for wood products, particularly in the mills and manufacturing plants where many of the processes can be automated. In addition, some jobs will be lost in the United States as imports continue to grow and as U.S. firms move production to other countries. Finally, materials such as metal, plastic, and fiberglass will continue to be used as alternatives to wood in many products, primarily because they are cheaper, stronger, or easier to shape.

As a result of these trends, employment opportunities in the primary wood industries may be more limited than those in the secondary industries. Also, as firms automate production, the demand for highly skilled workers will increase. Employment in all of the woodworking occupations is highly sensitive to economic cycles, so the growth in these occupations will be primarily affected by the overall state of the economy. Although this growth will be modest, thousands of openings will arise each year because of the need to replace experienced workers who transfer to other occupations or leave the labor force.

Earnings

Median weekly earnings for salaried full-time precision woodworkers were about $390 in 1994. The middle 50 percent earned between $280 and $510. The lowest 10 percent earned less than $230, while the highest 10 percent earned over $650. Median weekly earnings for full-time woodworking machine operators were around $310 in 1994. The middle 50 percent earned between $250 and $420. The lowest 10 percent earned less than $200, while the highest 10 percent earned over $525. Earnings vary by industry, geographic region, skill, educational level, and complexity of the machinery operated. Woodworkers usually receive a basic benefit package including medical and dental benefits and a pension plan.

Some woodworkers, such as those in logging or sawmills, who are engaged in processing primary wood and building materials, are members of the International Association of Machinists. Others may belong to the United Furniture Workers of America or the United Brotherhood of Carpenters and Joiners of America.

Related Occupations

Many woodworkers follow blueprints and drawings and use machines to shape and form raw wood into a final product. Workers who perform similar functions working with other materials include precision metalworkers, metalworking and plastics-working machine operators, metal fabricators, molders and shapers, and leather workers.

Sources of Additional Information

For information about woodworking occupations, contact local furniture manufacturers, sawmills and planing mills, cabinetmaking or millwork firms, lumber dealers, a local of one of the unions mentioned above, or the nearest office of the State employment service.

For general information about furniture woodworking occupations, contact:

☛American Furniture Manufacturers Association, Manufacturing Services Division, P.O. Box HP-7, High Point, NC 27261.

Miscellaneous Production Occupations

Dental Laboratory Technicians

(D.O.T. 712.381-014, -018, -022, -026, -030, -042, -046, and -050, .664-010)

Nature of the Work

Dental laboratory technicians fill prescriptions from dentists for crowns, bridges, dentures, and other dental prosthetics. Dentists send a specification of the item to be fabricated along with an impression (mold) of the patient's mouth or teeth to the technicians. Then dental laboratory technicians, also called dental technicians, create a model of the patient's mouth by pouring plaster into the impression and allowing it to set. They place the model on an apparatus which mimics the bite and movement of the patient's jaw. The model serves as the basis of the prosthetic device. Technicians examine the model, noting the size and shape of the adjacent teeth or gaps within the gumline. Based upon these observations and the dentist's specifications, technicians build and shape a wax tooth or teeth using small hand instruments called wax spatulas and wax carvers. They use this wax model to cast the metal framework for the prosthetic device.

Once the wax tooth has been formed, dental technicians pour the cast and form the metal. Using small hand-held tools, they prepare the surface of the metal to allow the metal and porcelain to bond. They apply porcelain in layers to arrive at the precise shape and color of a tooth. Technicians place the tooth in a porcelain furnace to bake the porcelain onto the metal framework, then adjust the shape and color with subsequent grinding and addition of porcelain to achieve a sealed finish. The final product is an exact replica of the lost tooth or teeth.

In some laboratories, technicians perform all stages of the work, while in others, each does only a few. Dental laboratory technicians also may specialize in one of five areas: Orthodontic appliances, crown and bridge, complete dentures, partial dentures, or ceramics. Job titles may reflect specialization in these areas. For example, technicians who make porcelain and acrylic restorations are called *dental ceramists*.

Working Conditions

Dental laboratory technicians generally work in clean, well-lighted, and well-ventilated areas. Technicians usually have their own workbenches, which may be equipped with Bunsen burners, grinding and polishing equipment, and hand instruments, such as wax spatulas and wax carvers.

The work is extremely delicate and quite time consuming. Salaried technicians usually work 40 hours a week, but self-employed technicians frequently work longer hours.

Employment

Dental laboratory technicians held about 49,000 jobs in 1994. Most jobs were in commercial dental laboratories, which usually are small, privately owned businesses with fewer than five employees. However, some laboratories are larger; a few employ over 50 technicians.

Some dental laboratory technicians worked in dentists' offices. Others worked for hospitals that provide dental services, including Department of Veterans Affairs hospitals. Some technicians work in dental laboratories in their homes, in addition to their regular job. Approximately 1 technician in 7 is self-employed, a higher proportion than in most other occupations.

Training, Other Qualifications, and Advancement

Most dental laboratory technicians learn their craft on the job. They begin with simple tasks, such as pouring plaster into an impression, and progress to more complex procedures, such as making porcelain crowns and bridges. Becoming a fully trained technician requires an average of 3 to 4 years depending upon the individual's aptitude and ambition, but it may take a few more years to become an accomplished technician.

Training in dental laboratory technology is also available through community and junior colleges, vocational-technical institutes, and the Armed Forces. Formal training programs vary greatly both in length and the level of skill they impart.

In 1995, 37 programs in dental laboratory technology were approved (accredited) by the Commission on Dental Accreditation in conjunction with the American Dental Association (ADA). These programs provide classroom instruction in dental materials science, oral anatomy, fabrication procedures, ethics, and related subjects. In addition, each student is given supervised practical experience in the school or an associated dental laboratory. Accredited programs generally take 2 years to complete and lead to an associate degree.

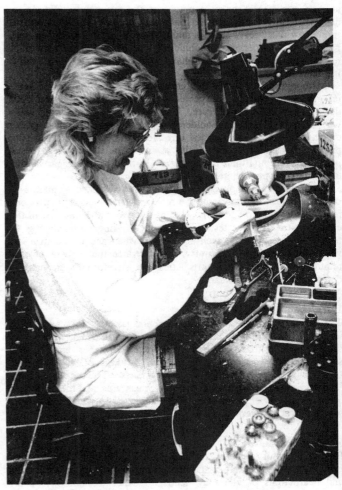

Dental laboratory technicians' earnings rise substantially with experience.

Graduates of 2-year training programs need additional hands-on experience to become fully qualified. Each dental laboratory owner operates in a different way, and classroom instruction does not necessarily expose students to techniques and procedures favored by individual laboratory owners. Students who have taken enough courses to learn the basics of the craft generally are considered good candidates for training, regardless of whether they have completed the formal program. Many employers will train someone without any classroom experience.

Certification, which is voluntary, is offered by the National Board for Certification in five specialty areas: Crown and bridge, ceramics, partial dentures, complete dentures, and orthodontic appliances.

In larger dental laboratories, technicians may become supervisors or managers. Experienced technicians may teach or take jobs with dental suppliers in such areas as product development, marketing, or sales. Still, for most technicians, opening one's own laboratory is the way toward advancement and higher earnings.

A high degree of manual dexterity, good vision, and the ability to recognize very fine color shadings and variations in shape are necessary. An aptitude for detailed and precise work also is important. Useful high school courses are art, metal and wood shop, drafting, and sciences. Courses in management and business may help those wishing to operate their own laboratories.

Job Outlook

Job opportunities for dental laboratory technicians should be favorable despite the absence of growth in the occupation. Employers have difficulty filling trainee positions, probably because of relatively low entry-level salaries and lack of familiarity with the occupation. Also, experienced technicians who have built up a favorable reputation with dentists should have good opportunities for establishing laboratories of their own.

Although job opportunities are favorable, employment of dental laboratory technicians is expected to decline through the year 2005, due to changes in dental care. The fluoridation of drinking water, which has reduced the incidence of dental cavities, and greater emphasis on preventive dental care since the early-1960s have improved the overall dental health of the population. As a result, people are keeping their teeth longer. Instead of full or partial dentures, most people will need a bridge or crown.

Office-based, computer-aided equipment, designed to measure a patient's mouth and fabricate the required prosthetic device, is currently under development and is beginning to come into use in this country after years of testing in Europe. While not replacing the technicians completely, such equipment, when and if it comes into widespread use in this country, could reduce the amount of time required to produce dental prosthetics and, therefore, the demand for dental laboratory technicians.

Earnings

The annual wage for all workers in dental laboratories was $22,269 in 1993. According to limited data, trainees in dental laboratories average only a little over minimum wage. However, earnings rise sharply with experience. In general, earnings of self-employed technicians exceed those of salaried workers. Technicians in large laboratories tend to specialize in a few procedures, and therefore tend to be paid a lower wage than those employed in small laboratories who perform a variety of tasks.

Related Occupations

Dental laboratory technicians fabricate artificial teeth, crowns and bridges, and orthodontic appliances following the specifications and instructions provided by dentists. Other workers who make medical devices include arch-support technicians, orthotics technicians (braces and surgical supports), prosthetics technicians (artificial limbs and appliances), opticians, and ophthalmic laboratory technicians.

Sources of Additional Information

For information about training and a list of approved schools, contact:

☛Commission on Dental Accreditation, American Dental Association, 211 E. Chicago Ave., Chicago, IL 60611.

General information on grants and scholarships is available from dental technology schools.

For information on career opportunities in commercial laboratories, contact:

☛National Association of Dental Laboratories, 3801 Mt. Vernon Ave., Alexandria, VA 22305.

For information on requirements for certification, contact:

☛National Board for Certification in Dental Technology, 3801 Mt. Vernon Ave., Alexandria, VA 22305.

Ophthalmic Laboratory Technicians

(D.O.T. 711.381-010; 713.381-010, .681-010; 716.280-010, -014, and -018, .381-014, .382-010, -014, -018, and -022, .462-010, .681-010,-014, and -018, .682-014, and -018)

Nature of the Work

Ophthalmic laboratory technicians—also known as manufacturing opticians, optical mechanics, or optical goods workers—make prescription eyeglass lenses. Prescription lenses are curved in such a way that light is correctly focused onto the retina of the patient's eye, improving vision. Some ophthalmic laboratory technicians manufacture lenses for other optical instruments, such as telescopes and binoculars. Ophthalmic laboratory technicians cut, grind, edge, and finish lenses according to specifications provided by dispensing opticians, optometrists, or ophthalmologists, and may insert lenses into frames to produce finished glasses.

Ophthalmic laboratory technicians should not be confused with workers in other vision care occupations. Ophthalmologists and optometrists are "eye doctors" who examine eyes, diagnose and treat vision problems, and prescribe corrective lenses. Ophthalmologists also perform eye surgery. Dispensing opticians, who may also do work described here, help patients select frames and lenses, and adjust finished eyeglasses. (See the statement on physicians, which includes ophthalmologists, and the statements on optometrists and dispensing opticians elsewhere in the *Handbook*.)

Ophthalmic laboratory technicians read prescription specifications, then select standard glass or plastic lens blanks and mark them to indicate where the curves specified on the prescription should be ground. They place the lens into the lens grinder, set the dials for the prescribed curvature, and start the machine. After a minute or so, the lens is ready to be "finished" by a machine which rotates the lens against a fine abrasive to grind it and smooth out rough edges. The lens is then placed in a polishing machine with an even finer abrasive, to polish it to a smooth, bright finish.

Next, the technician examines the lens through a lensometer, an instrument similar in shape to a microscope, and makes sure the degree and placement of the curve is correct. The technician then cuts the lenses and bevels the edges to fit the frame, dips each lens into dye if the prescription calls for tinted or coated lenses, polishes the edges, and assembles the lenses and frame parts into a finished pair of glasses.

In small laboratories, technicians generally handle every phase of the operation. In large ones, technicians may specialize in one or more steps, assembly-line style.

Working Conditions

Ophthalmic laboratory technicians work in relatively clean and well-lighted laboratories and have limited contact with the public. Surroundings are relatively quiet despite the humming of machines. At

Ophthalmic laboratory technicians work in clean, well-lighted laboratories and have limited contact with the public.

times, technicians may need to wear goggles to protect their eyes, and may spend a great deal of time standing.

Most ophthalmic laboratory technicians work a 5-day, 40-hour week, which may include weekends, evenings, or occasionally, some overtime. Some work part time.

Ophthalmic laboratory technicians need to take precautions against the hazards associated with cutting glass, handling chemicals, and working near machinery.

Employment

Ophthalmic laboratory technicians held about 19,000 jobs in 1994. More than half of these jobs were in optical laboratories. These laboratories manufacture eyewear for dispensing by retail stores that sell but do not fabricate prescription glasses, and by ophthalmologists and optometrists. Most of the rest were in retail stores that manufacture and sell prescription glasses—primarily chains of optical goods stores or independent retailers.

Training, Other Qualifications, and Advancement

Nearly all ophthalmic laboratory technicians learn their skills on the job. Employers filling trainee jobs prefer applicants who are high school graduates. Courses in science and mathematics are valuable; manual dexterity and the ability to do precision work is essential.

Technician trainees start on simple tasks such as marking or blocking lenses for grinding, then progress to lens grinding, lens cutting, edging, beveling, and eyeglass assembly. Depending on the

individual's aptitude, it may take 6 to 18 months to become proficient in all phases of the work.

Some ophthalmic laboratory technicians learn their trade in the Armed Forces. Others attend the few programs in optical technology offered by vocational-technical institutes or trade schools. These programs have classes in optical theory, surfacing and lens finishing, and the reading and applying of prescriptions. Programs vary in length from 6 months to 1 year, and award certificates or diplomas.

Ophthalmic laboratory technicians can become supervisors and managers. Some technicians become dispensing opticians, although further education or training may be required.

Job Outlook

Employment of ophthalmic laboratory technicians is expected to increase about as fast as the average for all occupations through the year 2005 due to rising demand for corrective lenses. Nonetheless, most job openings will come from the need to replace technicians who transfer to other occupations or leave the labor force. Relatively few opportunities will occur in any year because the occupation is small.

Demographic trends make it likely that many more Americans will wear glasses in the years ahead. Not only will the population grow, but the number of middle-aged and older adults will grow particularly rapidly. Middle age is a time when many people use corrective lenses for the first time, and older persons require appreciably more vision care than the rest of the population.

The public's heightened awareness of vision care should also increase demand for corrective lenses. The emergence of eyewear as a fashion item—eyewear now comes in an assortment of attractive shapes and colors—has been enticing many people to purchase two or three pair of glasses rather than just one. Most new jobs for ophthalmic laboratory technicians will be in retail optical chains that manufacture prescription glasses on the premises and provide fast service.

Earnings

Earnings vary greatly according to geographical region. According to the Opticians Association of America, the beginning average salary for laboratory technicians in retail optical stores was $14,185 in 1994. Those with 3 to 5 years of experience averaged $17,913; 6 to 10 years, $22,873; and 11 years or more, $23,980. Trainees may start at the minimum wage.

Related Occupations

Workers in other precision production occupations include biomedical equipment technicians, dental laboratory technicians, orthodontic technicians, orthotics technicians, prosthetics technicians, and instrument repairers.

Sources of Additional Information

For general information about a career as an ophthalmic laboratory technician and for a list of accredited programs in ophthalmic laboratory technology, contact:

☛Commission on Opticianry Accreditation, 10111 Martin Luther King, Jr. Hwy., Suite 100, Bowie, MD 20720-4299.

Painting and Coating Machine Operators

(List of D.O.T. codes available on request. See p. 478.)

Nature of the Work

Paints and coatings are an important part of most products. In manufacturing, everything from cars to candy is covered by either paint, plastic, varnish, chocolate, or some special coating solution. Often the paints and coatings are merely intended to enhance the products' appeal to consumers, as with the chocolate coating on candy. More often, however, the protection provided by the paint or coating is essential to the product, as with the coating of insulating material covering wires and other electrical and electronic components. Many paints and coatings have dual purposes, such as the paint finish on an automobile, which heightens the visual appearance of the vehicle while providing protection from corrosion.

Painting and coating machine operators control the machinery and equipment that applies these paints and coatings to a wide range of manufactured products. These workers use several basic methods to apply paints and coatings to manufactured articles. For example, dippers immerse racks or baskets of articles in vats of paint, liquid plastic, or other solutions using a power hoist. Tumbling barrel painters deposit articles of porous materials in a barrel of paint, varnish, or other coating, which is then rotated to insure thorough coverage.

Commonly, paints and coatings are applied by spraying the article with a solution. Spray-machine operators use spray guns to coat metal, wood, ceramic, fabric, paper, and food products with paint and other coating solutions. Following a formula, operators fill the equipment's tanks with a mixture of paints or chemicals, adding prescribed amounts or proportions. They screw nozzles onto the spray guns and adjust them to obtain the proper dispersion of the spray, and hold or position the guns to direct the spray onto the article. The pressure of the spray is regulated by adjusting valves. Operators check the flow and viscosity of the paint or solution and visually inspect the quality of the coating. They may also regulate the temperature and air circulation in drying ovens.

In response to concerns about air pollution and worker safety, manufacturers are increasingly using new types of paints and coatings on their products instead of high-solvent paints. Water-based paints and powder coatings are two of the most common. These compounds do not emit as many volatile organic compounds into the air and can be applied to a wide variety of products. Powder coatings are sprayed much like liquid paints and heated to melt and cure the coating.

The switch to new types of paints is often accompanied by a conversion to newer, more automated painting equipment that the operator sets and monitors. Operators position the automatic spray guns, set the nozzles, and synchronize the action of the guns with the speed of the conveyor carrying articles through the machine and drying ovens. The operator may also add solvents or water to the paint vessel that prepares the paint for application. During operation, the operator attends the painting machine, observes gauges on the control panel and randomly checks articles for evidence of any variation of the coating from specifications. The operator then "touches up" spots where necessary, using a spray gun.

Painting and coating machine operators use various types of spray machines to coat a wide range of products. Often their job title reflects the specialized nature of the machine or the coating being applied. For example, paper coating machine operators spray "size" on rolls of paper to give it its gloss or finish. Silvering applicators spray silver, tin, and copper solutions on glass in the manufacture of mirrors. Enrobing machine operators coat, or "enrobe," confectionery, bakery, and other food products with melted chocolate, cheese, oils, sugar, or other substances.

Although the majority of painting and coating machine operators are employed in manufacturing, the best known group of them work in automotive body repair and paint shops refinishing old and damaged cars, trucks, and buses. Automotive painters are among the most highly skilled manual spray operators because they often have to mix paint to match the original color, which can be very difficult, particularly if the color has faded.

To prepare a vehicle for painting, automotive painters or their helpers use power sanders and sandpaper to remove the original paint or rust, and then fill small dents and scratches with body filler. They also remove or mask parts they do not want painted, such as chrome trim, headlights, windows, and mirrors. Automotive painters use a spray gun to apply several coats of paint. They apply lacquer, enamel, or water-based primers to vehicles with metal bodies, and flexible primers to newer vehicles with plastic body parts. Controlling the spray gun by hand, they apply successive coats until the finish of the repaired sections of the vehicle matches that of the original undamaged portions. To speed drying between coats, they may place the freshly painted vehicle under heat lamps or in a special infrared oven. After each coat of primer dries, they sand the surface to remove any irregularities and to improve the adhesion of the next coat. Final sanding of the primers may be done by hand with a fine grade of sandpaper. A sealer is then applied and allowed to dry, followed by the final topcoat. When lacquer is used, painters or their helpers usually polish the finished surface after the final coat has dried; enamel dries to a high gloss and usually is not polished.

Working Conditions

Painting and coating machine operators work indoors and may be exposed to dangerous fumes from paint and coating solutions. Many operators wear masks or respirators that cover their nose and mouth, and painting is usually done in special ventilated booths that protect the operators from these hazards. The Clean Air Act of 1990 has led to a decrease in workers' exposure to hazardous chemicals by regulating emissions of volatile organic compounds from paints and other chemicals.

Operators have to stand for long periods of time and, when using a spray gun, they may have to bend, stoop, or crouch in uncomfortable positions to reach all parts of the article. Most operators work a normal 40-hour week, but self-employed automotive painters sometimes work more than 50 hours a week, depending on the number of vehicles customers bring in to be repainted.

Employment

Painting and coating machine operators held about 155,000 jobs in 1994. Eighty percent worked in manufacturing establishments—in the production of fabricated metal products, motor vehicles and related equipment, industrial machines, household and office furniture, and plastics, wood, and paper products, for example. Other workers included automotive painters employed by independent automotive repair shops and body repair and paint shops operated by retail automotive dealers. Five percent of painting and coating machine operators were self-employed; most of these were automotive painters.

Training, Other Qualifications, and Advancement

Most painting and coating machine operators acquire their skills on the job, usually by watching and helping experienced operators. For most operators, training lasts from a few days to several months. However, becoming skilled in all aspects of automotive painting usually requires 1 to 2 years of on-the-job training.

Most automotive painters start as helpers and gain their skills informally by working with experienced painters. Beginning helpers usually remove trim, clean and sand surfaces to be painted, mask surfaces that they do not want painted, and polish finished work. As helpers gain experience, they progress to more complicated tasks, such as mixing paint to achieve a good match and using spray guns to apply primer coats or final coats to small areas.

Painters should have keen eyesight and a good color sense. Completion of high school is generally not required but is advantageous. Additional instruction is offered at many community colleges and vocational or technical schools. Such programs enhance one's employment prospects and can speed promotion to the next level.

Painters wear protective equipment when using spray guns.

Some employers sponsor training programs to help their workers become more productive. This training is available from manufacturers of chemicals, paints, or equipment or from other private sources. It may include safety and quality tips and knowledge of products, equipment, and general business practices. Some automotive painters are sent to technical schools to learn the intricacies of mixing and applying different types of paint.

Voluntary certification by ASE (the National Institute for Automotive Service Excellence) is recognized as the standard of achievement for automotive painters. For certification, painters must pass a written examination and have at least 2 years of experience in the field. High school, trade or vocational school, or community or junior college training in automotive painting and refinishing may substitute for up to 1 year of experience. To retain certification, painters must retake the examination at least every 5 years.

Experienced painting and coating machine operators with leadership ability may advance to supervisory jobs. Those who acquire practical experience or college or other formal training may become sales or technical representatives to large customers or for chemical or paint companies. Some automotive painters open their own shops.

Job Outlook

Little change is expected in the employment of painting and coating machine operators through the year 2005, as technological improvements enable these operators to work more productively. Nevertheless, several thousand jobs will become available each year as employers replace experienced operators who transfer to other occupations or leave the labor force.

In manufacturing, employment of painting and coating machine operators is expected to decline, reflecting the increasing automation of paint and coating application. Improvements in the capabilities of industrial robots allow them to move and aim spray guns more like humans. As the cost of these machines continues to fall, they will be more widely used. The Clean Air Act of 1990, which sets limits on the emissions of ozone-forming volatile organic compounds, also is reducing the demand for operators in manufacturing. As firms switch to water-based and powder coatings to comply with the law, many are upgrading their equipment to increase the efficiency of the painting process. In fact, the powder coating process alone is much more efficient for work on assembly lines than liquid sprays because no drying time is required between coats and fewer operators are needed for touch-up painting. The expected employment decline resulting from these trends will be moderated, however, as painting and coating machine operators assume emissions monitoring and recording responsibilities.

Employment of these workers in the auto repair industry will grow slowly, as the improved quality of car finishes and the increasing use of nonrusting alloys slow the growth in demand for refinishing services. The employment outlook for skilled automotive painters, however, should remain bright.

The number of job openings for painting and coating machine operators may fluctuate from year to year due to cyclical changes in economic conditions. When demand for manufactured goods slackens, production may be suspended or reduced, and workers may be laid off or face a shortened workweek. Automotive painters, on the other hand, can expect relatively steady work because automobiles damaged in accidents require repair and refinishing regardless of the state of the economy.

Earnings

Painting and coating machine operators who usually worked full time had median weekly earnings of $370 in 1994. The middle 50 percent had usual weekly earnings between $280 and $560, while the highest 10 percent earned more than $750 weekly. Beginning automotive painter apprentices usually start at about half the hourly rate of fully qualified painters. As they progress, their wages gradually approach those of experienced automotive painters. Helpers start at lower wage rates than beginning apprentices.

Many automotive painters employed by automobile dealers and independent repair shops receive a commission based on the labor cost charged to the customer. Under this method, earnings depend largely on the amount of work a painter does and how fast it is completed. Employers frequently guarantee commissioned painters a minimum weekly salary. Helpers and apprentices usually receive an hourly rate until they become sufficiently skilled to work on a commission basis. Trucking companies, bus lines, and other organizations that repair their own vehicles usually pay by the hour.

Many painting and coating machine operators belong to unions, including the International Association of Machinists and Aerospace Workers; the International Brotherhood of Painters and Allied Trades; the International Union, United Automobile, Aerospace and Agricultural Implement Workers of America; the Sheet Metal Workers' International Association; and the International Brotherhood of Teamsters. Most union operators work for manufacturers and the larger automobile dealers.

Related Occupations

Other occupations in which workers apply paints and coatings include construction and maintenance painters, electrolytic metal platers, and hand painting, coating, and decorating occupations.

Sources of Additional Information

For more details about work opportunities, contact local manufacturers, automotive-body repair shops, automotive dealers, and vocational schools; locals of the unions previously mentioned; or the local office of the State employment service. The State employment service also may be a source of information about training programs.

For general information about a career as an automotive painter, write to:

☛Automotive Service Industry Association, 25 Northwest Point, Suite 425, Elk Grove Village, IL 60007-1035.

☛Automotive Service Association, Inc., P.O. Box 929, Bedford, TX 76021-0929.

Information on how to become a certified automotive painter is available from:

☛National Institute for Automotive Service Excellence (ASE), 13505 Dulles Technology Dr., Herndon, VA 22071-3415.

Photographic Process Workers

(D.O.T. 962.361; 970.281-010 and -018, .381-010 and -034; 972.384-014; 976.361, .380-010, .381-010, -018, and -022, .382-010, -018, -022, -030, and -038, .384-010 and -014, .385, .665, .681, .682-010, -014, -018, and -022, .684-014, and -030, .685-014, -018, -022, -026, -030, -034, and -038; 979.384)

Nature of the Work

Most photographers, both amateur and professional, rely on photo processing workers to develop their film, make prints or slides, and do related tasks such as enlarging or retouching photographs. Photographic processing machine operators and tenders operate various machines, such as motion picture film printing machines, photographic printing machines, film developing machines, and mounting presses. Precision photographic process workers perform more delicate tasks, such as retouching photographic negatives and prints to emphasize or correct specific features. They may restore damaged and faded photographs, and may color or shade drawings to create photographic likenesses using an airbrush. They also may color photographs, using oil colors to produce natural, lifelike appearances according to specifications.

The following jobs are examples of the work that machine operators perform. *Film process technicians* develop exposed photographic film or sensitized paper in a series of chemical and water baths to produce negative or positive images. They first mix the developing and fixing solutions, following a formula. They then immerse the exposed film in a developer solution to bring out the latent image, immerse the negative in stop-bath to halt the developer action, immerse it in hyposolution to fix the image, and finally immerse it in water to remove chemicals. The worker then dries the films. In some cases, these steps may be performed by hand.

Color printer operators control equipment which produces color prints from the negatives. They read customer instructions to determine processing requirements. They load the rolls into color printing equipment, examine the negatives to determine equipment control settings, set the controls, and produce a specified number of prints. They inspect the finished prints for defects, and remove any that are found, finally inserting the processed negatives and prints into an envelope for return to the customer.

Paper process technicians develop strips of exposed photographic paper; *takedown sorters* sort processed film; and *automatic mounters* operate equipment that cuts and mounts slide film into individual transparencies.

Precision photographic process workers, also known as digital imaging technicians, may take a conventional negative and, using a computer, vary the contrast of images, remove unwanted background, or even combine features from several different photographs. Precision photographic process workers in portrait studios, on the other hand, deal in very high volume, and tend to work directly on the photo negative, rather than on a computer. These workers include *airbrush artists,* who restore damaged and faded photographs; *photographic retouchers,* who alter photographic negatives and prints to accentuate the subject; *colorists,* who apply oil colors to portrait photographs to create natural, lifelike appearances; and *photographic spotters,* who spot out imperfections on photographic prints.

Working Conditions

In recent years, more commercial photographic processing has been done on computers than in darkrooms, and this trend is expected to continue. Work generally is performed in clean, appropriately lighted, well-ventilated, and air-conditioned offices, photofinishing laboratories, or 1-hour minilabs. At peak times, portrait studios hire individuals who work at home retouching negatives.

Photographic process machine operators must do repetitive work at a rapid pace without any loss of accuracy. Precision process

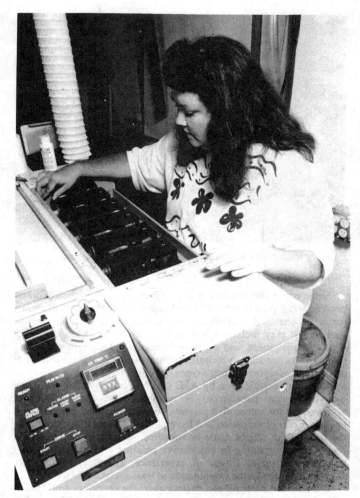

Photo processing has become a largely automated process that requires skilled operators.

workers do detailed tasks, such as airbrushing and spotting, which may contribute to eye fatigue.

Some photographic process workers are continuously exposed to the chemicals and fumes associated with developing and printing. These workers must wear rubber gloves and aprons and take precautions against chemical hazards.

Many photo laboratory employees work a 40-hour week, including weekends, and may work overtime during peak seasons.

Employment

Photographic process workers held about 57,000 jobs in 1994. Photofinishing laboratories and 1-hour minilabs employed about two-thirds. About 3 out of 10 worked for portrait studios and commercial laboratories that specialize in processing the work of professional photographers for advertising and other industries.

Employment fluctuates over the course of the year; peak periods include school graduation, summer vacation, and Christmas time.

Training, Other Qualifications, and Advancement

Most photographic process machine operators receive on-the-job training from manufacturers' representatives, company management, and more experienced workers. New employees gradually learn to use the machines and chemicals that develop and print film.

Employers prefer applicants who are high school graduates or those who have some experience or knowledge in the field. As preparation for precision work, proficiency in mathematics, art, chemistry, and computer science, as well as photography courses that include instruction in film processing are valuable. Such courses are available through high schools, vocational-technical institutes, private trade schools, and colleges and universities.

On-the-job training in photographic processing occupations can range from just a few hours for print machine operators to years for precision workers like airbrush artists, spotters, and negative retouchers. Some workers attend periodic training seminars to maintain a high level of skill. Manual dexterity, good hand-eye coordination, and good vision, including normal color perception, are important qualifications for precision photographic process workers. They must be comfortable with computers and able to adapt to technological advances.

Photographic process machine workers can advance from jobs as machine operators to supervisory positions in laboratories. Precision photographic process workers generally earn more as their skill level and the complexity of tasks they can perform increases.

Job Outlook

Employment of photographic process workers is expected to increase about as fast as the average for all occupations through the year 2005. Most openings will result from replacement needs, which tend to be higher for machine operators than for precision process workers.

Digital cameras, which use electronic memory rather than a film negative to record the image, are now available. However, these cameras are much more expensive than conventional cameras, and generally are not capable of producing an equally sharp image. Also, traditional photo development will coexist, rather than compete directly, with electronic photography for many years. As this technology improves and the prices decline, photographic process machine operators may be displaced.

Technological change is unlikely to affect demand for precision photographic process workers because the adjustments they make to pictures need to be done to digital images as well as to negatives. No matter what improvements occur in camera technology, there always will be some images which require precise manipulation.

Because photographic processing services are luxuries for most consumers, the number of job openings decreases during recessions.

Earnings

Earnings of photographic process workers vary greatly depending on skill level, experience, and geographic location. Median earnings for full-time photographic process workers in 1994 were about $327 a week. The middle 50 percent earned between $245 and $469 a week. The lowest 10 percent earned less than $201 a week while the highest 10 percent earned more than $611.

Related Occupations

Precision photographic process workers need a specialized knowledge of the photodeveloping process. Other workers who apply specialized technical knowledge include chemical laboratory technicians, crime laboratory analysts, food testers, medical laboratory assistants, metallurgical technicians, quality control technicians, engravers, and some of the printing occupations, such as photolithographer.

Photographic process machine operators perform work similar to that of other machine operators, such as computer and peripheral equipment operators and printing press operators.

Sources of Additional Information

For information about employment opportunities in photographic laboratories and schools that offer degrees in photographic technology, write to:

☛Photo Marketing Association International, 3000 Picture Place, Jackson, MI 49201.

Transportation and Material Moving Occupations

Busdrivers

(D.O.T. 913.363, .463-010, and .663-014 and -018)

Nature of the Work

Busdrivers provide transportation for millions of Americans every day. *Intercity busdrivers* transport people between regions of a State or of the country; *local transit busdrivers*, within a metropolitan area or county; and *school busdrivers*, to and from schools and related events. They follow time schedules and routes over highways and city and suburban streets to provide passengers with an alternative to the automobile and other forms of transportation.

Intercity busdrivers and local transit busdrivers report to their assigned terminal or garage, where they receive tickets and transfers and prepare trip report forms. School busdrivers do not always have to report to an assigned terminal or garage. Instead, school busdrivers often have the choice of taking their bus home, or parking it in another more convenient area. Before beginning their routes, drivers check their vehicle's tires, brakes, windshield wipers, lights, oil, fuel, water, and safety equipment, such as fire extinguishers, first aid kits, and emergency reflectors.

Drivers pick up and discharge passengers at bus stops or stations, or, in the case of students, at corners or in front of houses. Intercity and local transit busdrivers collect fares; answer questions about schedules, routes, and transfer points; and sometimes announce stops. School busdrivers do not collect fares. Instead, they prepare weekly reports with the number of students, trips or runs, work hours, and miles and the amount of fuel consumption. Time schedules and routes are set by their supervisors.

Busdrivers' days are run by the clock, as they must adhere to schedules. Drivers must operate safely, especially when traffic is heavier than normal. However, they cannot let light traffic put them ahead of schedule so that they miss passengers.

Busdrivers must be alert to prevent accidents, especially in heavy traffic or in bad weather, and to avoid sudden stops or swerves which jar passengers. School busdrivers must exercise particular caution when children are getting on or off the bus. They must know and reinforce the same set of rules used elsewhere in the school system.

Bus routes vary. Local transit busdrivers may make several trips each day over the same city and suburban streets, stopping as frequently as every few blocks. School busdrivers also drive the same routes each day, stopping frequently to pick up pupils in the morning and return them to their homes in the afternoon. School busdrivers may also transport students and teachers on field trips or to sporting events. Intercity busdrivers may make only a single one-way trip to a distant city or a round trip each day, stopping at towns just a few miles apart or only at large cities hundreds of miles apart. Drivers who operate chartered buses pick up groups, take them to their destination, and generally remain with them until they return. Trips frequently last more than 1 day, and if they are assigned to a tour, they may be away for a week or more.

Local transit busdrivers submit daily trip reports with a record of tickets and fares received, trips made, and significant delays in schedule, and report mechanical problems. All busdrivers must be able to fill out accident reports when necessary. Intercity drivers who drive across State or national boundaries must comply with U.S. Department of Transportation regulations. These include completing vehicle inspection reports and recording distances traveled and the periods of time they spend driving, performing other duties, and off duty.

Working Conditions

Driving a bus through heavy traffic while dealing with passengers is not physically strenuous, but it can be stressful and fatiguing. On the other hand, many drivers enjoy the opportunity to work without direct supervision, with full responsibility for the bus and passengers.

Intercity busdrivers may work nights, weekends, and holidays and often spend nights away from home, where they stay at hotels at company expense. Senior drivers with regular routes have regular weekly work schedules, but others do not have regular schedules and must be prepared to report for work on short notice. They report for work only when called for a charter assignment or to drive extra

Before beginning their routes, busdrivers check their vehicle's fuel, water, and oil levels.

buses on a regular route. Intercity bus travel and charter work tend to be seasonal. From May through August, drivers may work the maximum number of hours per week that regulations allow. During winter, junior drivers may work infrequently, except for busy holiday travel periods, and may be furloughed for periods of time.

School busdrivers work only when school is in session. Many work 20 hours a week or less, driving one or two routes in the morning and afternoon. Drivers taking field or athletic trips or who also have midday kindergarten routes may work more hours a week.

Regular local transit busdrivers usually have a 5-day workweek; Saturdays and Sundays are considered regular workdays. Some drivers work evenings and after midnight. To accommodate commuters, many work "split shifts," for example, 6 a.m. to 10 a.m. and 3 p.m. to 7 p.m., with time off in between.

Employment

Busdrivers held about 568,000 jobs in 1994. Over 40 percent worked part time. Nearly 3 out of 4 drivers worked for school systems or companies that provide school bus services under contract, as shown in the accompanying chart. Most of the remainder worked for private and local government transit systems; some also worked for intercity and charter buslines.

Training, Other Qualifications, and Advancement

Busdriver qualifications and standards are established by State and Federal regulations. Federal regulations require drivers who operate vehicles designed to transport 16 or more passengers to obtain a commercial driver's license from the State in which they live.

In order to be licensed, applicants for a commercial driver's license must take and pass a knowledge test and demonstrate that they have the skills necessary to operate a commercial motor vehicle safely. Applicants are also required to pass a behind-the-wheel road test in the type of vehicle that they will be operating. Trainees must be accompanied by another driver who has a commercial driver's license until they are issued their own commercial license.

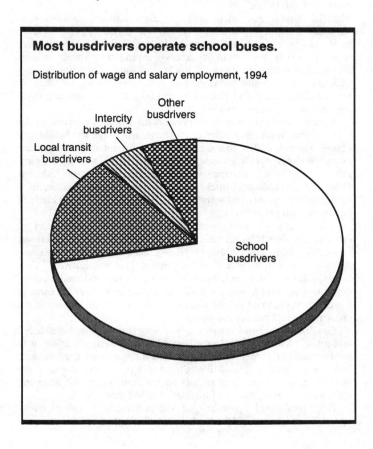

Most busdrivers operate school buses.

Distribution of wage and salary employment, 1994

Other busdrivers

Intercity busdrivers

Local transit busdrivers

School busdrivers

Interstate busdrivers must meet additional qualifications. For example, they must be at least 21 years old and pass a physical examination. State agencies and municipalities may also have additional requirements for drivers who operate within their jurisdictions.

Drivers should be in good health and have at least 20/40 vision with or without glasses, good hearing, and normal use of their arms and legs. Many employers prefer high school graduates and require a physical examination and a written test of ability to follow complex bus schedules. Many intercity and public transit bus companies prefer applicants who are at least 24 years of age; some require several years of bus or truck driving experience. Public transit and interstate busdrivers are also required to submit to drug and alcohol screening as a condition of employment. In some States, school busdrivers must pass a background investigation to uncover any criminal record or history of mental problems.

Because busdrivers deal with passengers, they must be courteous. They need an even temperament and emotional stability because driving in heavy, fast-moving, or stop-and-go traffic and dealing with passengers can be stressful.

Most intercity bus companies and local transit systems give driver trainees 2 to 8 weeks of classroom and "behind-the-wheel" instruction. In the classroom, trainees learn U.S. Department of Transportation and company work rules, safety regulations, State and municipal driving regulations, and safe driving practices. They also learn to read schedules, determine fares, keep records, and deal courteously with passengers.

School busdrivers are also required to obtain a commercial driver's license from the State in which they live. Many persons who enter school busdriving have never driven any vehicle larger than an automobile. They receive between 1 and 4 weeks of driving instruction plus classroom training on State and local laws, regulations, and policies of operating school buses; safe driving practices; driver-pupil relations; first aid; disabled student special needs; and emergency evacuation procedures.

During training, busdrivers practice driving on set courses. They practice turns and zigzag maneuvers, back up, and drive in narrow lanes. Then they drive in light traffic and, eventually, on congested highways and city streets. They also make trial runs, without passengers, to improve their driving skills and learn the routes. Local transit trainees memorize and drive each of the runs operating out of their assigned garage. New drivers begin with a "break-in" period. They make regularly scheduled trips with passengers, accompanied by an experienced driver who gives helpful tips, answers questions, and evaluates the new driver's performance.

New intercity and local transit drivers usually are placed on an "extra" list to drive charter runs, extra buses on regular runs, and special runs (for example, during morning and evening rush hours and to sports events). They also substitute for regular drivers who are ill or on vacation. New drivers remain on the extra list, and may work only part time, perhaps for several years, until they have enough seniority to get a regular run.

Senior drivers may bid for runs they prefer, such as those with more work hours, lighter traffic, weekends off, or, in the case of intercity busdrivers, higher earnings or fewer workdays per week.

Opportunities for promotion generally are limited. However, experienced drivers may become supervisors or dispatchers, who assign buses to drivers, check whether drivers are on schedule, reroute buses to avoid blocked streets or other problems, and dispatch extra vehicles and service crews to scenes of accidents and breakdowns. In transit agencies with rail systems, drivers may become train operators or station attendants. A few drivers become managers. Promotion in publicly owned bus systems is often by competitive civil service examination.

Job Outlook

Persons seeking jobs as busdrivers over the 1994-2005 period should encounter good opportunities. Opportunities should be best for individuals with good driving records who are willing to start on a part-time or irregular schedule, as well as for those seeking jobs as school busdrivers in metropolitan areas that are growing rapidly. Those seeking higher paying intercity and public transit busdriver positions may encounter competition.

Employment of busdrivers is expected to increase about as fast as average for all occupations through the year 2005, primarily to meet the transportation needs of a growing school-age population. Thousands of additional job openings are expected to occur each year because of the need to replace workers who take jobs in other occupations, retire or leave the occupation for other reasons.

School busdriving jobs should be easiest to get because most of these positions are part time and often have high turnover. The number of school busdrivers is expected to increase as a result of growth in elementary and secondary school enrollments. In addition, as more of the Nation's population is concentrated in suburban areas—where students generally ride school buses—and less in the central cities—where transportation is not provided for most pupils—more school busdrivers will be needed.

Employment of local transit and intercity drivers will grow as bus ridership increases. Local and intercity travel is expected to increase as the population and labor force grow and incomes rise, but most growth in intercity drivers will probably be in group charter travel, rather than scheduled intercity bus services, as more individual travelers opt to travel by airplane or automobile rather than by bus. There may continue to be competition for local transit and intercity busdriver jobs in some areas since many of these positions offer relatively high wages and attractive benefits. The most competitive positions will be those that offer regular hours and steady driving routes.

Full-time busdrivers are rarely laid off during recessions. However, hours of part-time local transit and intercity busdrivers may be reduced if bus ridership decreases, because fewer extra buses would be needed. Seasonal layoffs are common. Many intercity busdrivers with little seniority, for example, are furloughed during the winter when regular schedule and charter business falls off; school busdrivers seldom work during the summer or school holidays.

Earnings

Median weekly earnings of busdrivers who worked full time were $401 in 1994. The middle 50 percent earned between about $291 and $610 a week. The lowest 10 percent earned less than $227 a week, while the highest 10 percent earned more than $758 a week.

In 1994, according to the American Public Transit Association, local transit busdrivers in metropolitan areas with more than 2 million inhabitants were paid a median top hourly wage rate of $16.74 by companies with over 1,000 employees, and $14.39 by those with fewer than 1,000 employees. In smaller metropolitan areas, they had a median top hourly wage rate of $12.65 in areas with between 250,000 and 500,000 residents, and $10.96 in areas with populations below 50,000. Generally, drivers could reach the top rate in 3 or 4 years.

Earnings of intercity busdrivers depend primarily on the number of miles they drive. According to limited information, in 1994 beginning intercity drivers worked about 6 months out of the year and earned about $22,000 while many senior drivers who worked year round earned more than $48,000.

According to a survey by the Educational Research Service, the average rate for school busdrivers employed by public school systems was $10.35 an hour during the 1993-94 school year. Lowest hourly rates averaged $9.04 while highest hourly rate averaged $11.94.

The fringe benefits that busdrivers receive from their employers vary greatly. Most intercity and local transit busdrivers receive paid health and life insurance, sick leave, and free bus rides on any of the regular routes of their line or system. Drivers who work full time also get as much as 4 weeks of vacation annually. Most local transit busdrivers are also covered by dental insurance and pension plans. School busdrivers get sick leave, and many are covered by health and

life insurance and pension plans, but because they generally do not work when school is not in session, they do not get vacation leave. In a number of States, local transit and school busdrivers who are employed by local governments are covered by a State-wide public employee pension system.

Most intercity and many local transit busdrivers are members of the Amalgamated Transit Union. Local transit busdrivers in New York and several other large cities belong to the Transport Workers Union of America. Some drivers belong to the United Transportation Union and the International Brotherhood of Teamsters.

Related Occupations

Other workers who drive vehicles on highways and city streets are taxi drivers, truckdrivers, and chauffeurs.

Sources of Additional Information

For further information on employment opportunities, contact local transit systems, intercity buslines, school systems, or the local offices of the State employment service.

Information on school busdriving is available from:

☛National School Transportation Association, P.O. Box 2639, Springfield, VA 22152.

General information on local transit busdriving is available from:

☛American Public Transit Association, 1201 New York Ave. NW., Suite 400, Washington, DC 20005.

Material Moving Equipment Operators

(List of D.O.T. codes available on request. See p. 478.)

Nature of the Work

Material moving equipment operators use machinery to move construction materials, manufactured goods, earth, logs, petroleum products, grain, coal, and other heavy materials. Generally they move materials over short distances—around a construction site, factory, warehouse, or on or off trucks and ships. Operators control equipment by moving levers or foot pedals, operating switches, or turning dials. They may also set up and inspect equipment and make adjustments and minor repairs.

Material moving equipment operators usually are classified by the type of machines they operate. Those who operate bulldozers, cranes, loaders, and similar equipment are often called *construction equipment operators* even though they work in the mining, logging, utilities, and other industries as well as the construction industry. Others operate industrial trucks and tractors and similar equipment in manufacturing plants and warehouses. Some operate many kinds of equipment; others only one.

Crane and tower operators lift and move materials, machinery, or other heavy objects using mechanical or hydraulic booms and tower and cable equipment. Although some cranes are used on construction sites, most are used in manufacturing and other industries.

Excavation and loading machine operators run and tend machinery equipped with scoops, shovels, or buckets to excavate earth at construction sites and to load and move loose materials, mainly in the construction and mining industries.

Grader, dozer, and scraper operators remove, distribute, level, and grade earth with vehicles equipped with blades. In addition to the familiar bulldozers, they operate trench excavators, road graders, and similar equipment. Although many work in the construction industry, grader, dozer, and scraper operators also work for State and local governments, mainly in maintenance and repair work.

Hoist and winch operators lift and pull loads by using power-operated equipment. Most work in loading operations in construction, manufacturing, logging, transportation and public utilities, and mining.

Operating engineers are qualified to operate more than one type of the construction equipment discussed above. Although the term operating engineer often is applied to many construction equipment operators, many work for State and local governments.

Industrial truck and tractor operators drive and control industrial trucks or tractors. A typical industrial truck, often called a forklift or lift truck, has a hydraulic lifting mechanism and forks. Industrial truck operators use these to carry loads on a skid or pallet around a factory or warehouse. Industrial tractor operators pull trailers loaded with materials, goods, or equipment within factories and warehouses, or around outdoor storage areas.

Other material moving equipment operators tend air compressors or pumps at construction sites. Some operate oil or natural gas pumps and compressors at oil and gas wells and on oil and gas pipelines, and others operate ship loading and unloading equipment, conveyors, hoists, and other kinds of specialized material handling equipment such as mine or railroad tank car unloading equipment.

Material moving equipment operators may keep records of materials moved, and do some manual loading and unloading. They also may clean, fuel, and service their equipment.

Working Conditions

Many material moving equipment operators work outdoors, in hot and cold weather, and sometimes in rain or snow. Industrial truck and tractor operators work mainly indoors, in warehouses or manufacturing plants. Some machines, particularly bulldozers and scrapers, are noisy and shake or jolt the operator. To avoid injury while operating an industrial truck, operators must take care to avoid rollovers, collisions, and other accidents as well as protect materials and equipment from damage. While operating a bulldozer, care must be taken to keep it from overturning on a steep slope. However, these jobs have become much safer with the adoption of overhead guards on forklift trucks and roll bars on construction machinery. As with most machinery, most accidents can be avoided when proper operating procedures and safety practices are observed.

Employment

Material moving equipment operators held nearly 1,061,000 jobs in 1994. They were distributed among the detailed occupations of this group as follows:

Industrial truck and tractor operators	464,000
Operating engineers	146,000
Grader, dozer, and scraper operators	108,000
Excavation and loading machine operators	88,000
Crane and tower operators	45,000
Hoist and winch operators	9,000
All other material moving equipment operators	201,000

The largest proportion—one-third—of material moving equipment operators worked in manufacturing; most of these were industrial truck and tractor operators. More than one-fifth worked in the construction industry. Significant numbers also worked in State and local governments and in the trucking and warehousing, wholesale trade, and mining industries. A few material moving equipment operators were self-employed.

Material moving equipment operators work in every section of the country. Some work in remote locations on large construction projects, such as highways and dams, or in factory or mining operations.

Training, Other Qualifications, and Advancement

Operation of material moving equipment is usually learned on the job. Operators need a good sense of balance, the ability to judge distance, and good eye-hand-foot coordination. Employers of material moving equipment operators prefer to hire high school graduates, although, for some equipment, persons with less education may occasionally be accepted. Mechanical aptitude and high school training in automobile mechanics are helpful because workers may perform some maintenance on their machines. Experience operating mobile equipment, such as farm tractors or heavy equipment in the Armed Forces, is an asset.

Beginning material moving equipment operators handle light equipment under the guidance of an experienced operator. Later, they may operate heavier equipment such as bulldozers and cranes. Some construction equipment operators, however, are trained in formal 3-year apprenticeship programs administered by union-management committees of the International Union of Operating Engineers and the Associated General Contractors of America. Because apprentices learn to operate a wider variety of machines than other beginners, they usually have better job opportunities. Apprenticeship programs consist of at least 3 years or 6,000 hours of on-the-job training and 144 hours a year of related classroom instruction.

Private vocational schools offer instruction in the operation of certain types of construction equipment. Completion of such a program may help a person get a job as a trainee or apprentice. However, persons considering such training should check the reputation of the school among employers in the area.

Job Outlook

Employment of material moving equipment operators is expected to increase more slowly than the average for all occupations through the year 2005 as equipment improvements, including the growing automation of material handling in factories and warehouses, make operators more productive.

Opportunities for individuals who wish to become material moving equipment operators are related to the outlook of the industries in which they are employed. The majority of these workers are employed in construction and manufacturing industries; employment in construction is expected to grow more slowly than the average for all occupations, while jobs in manufacturing are expected to decline. Despite the projected slow growth, this is a large occupation with many opportunities arising from the need to replace experienced workers who transfer to other occupations or leave the labor force. However, both construction and manufacturing are very sensitive to changes in economic conditions, so the number of job openings for material moving equipment operators in these industries may fluctuate widely from year to year.

Many material moving equipment operators work outdoors, in hot and cold weather and sometimes in rain or snow.

Excavation and loading machine operators is the only occupation in this group that is expected to increase about as fast as the average for all occupations. Their growth is expected to stem from increased spending on improving the Nation's infrastructure of highways, bridges, and dams. The majority of excavation and loading machine operators work in mining and construction, the sector that constructs and maintains most of these facilities.

Employment of crane and tower operators and hoist and winch operators is expected to decline as more precise computerized controls and robotics allow many of these jobs to be automated. All of the remaining material moving equipment operating occupations are projected to grow more slowly than the average for all occupations, including industrial truck and tractor operators, the largest occupation in the group.

Growth of industrial truck and tractor operators—the largest occupation in this group—will be slower than average for all occupations due to productivity increases resulting from improved maneuverability and efficiency of industrial trucks and tractors. In addition, although the volume of goods to be moved will increase as the economy grows, fewer operator jobs will result as material handling systems in large factories and warehouses will continue to become more automated. Some systems use computerized dispatching or onboard data communication devices to enable industrial truck and tractor operators to move goods more efficiently. In other systems, some industrial trucks and tractors may be replaced by computer-controlled conveyor systems, overhead handling systems, and automated vehicles that don't require operators.

Earnings

Earnings for material moving equipment operators vary considerably. In 1994, median earnings of all material moving equipment operators were $459 a week; the middle 50 percent earned between $339 and $608. Ten percent earned less than $265 and 10 percent more than $839. Median weekly earnings of crane and tower operators were $535 in 1994; excavation and loading machine operators, $454; grader, dozer, and scraper operators, $497; industrial truck and tractor operators, $425; operating engineers, $527; hoist and winch operators, $514; and other material moving equipment operators, $463. Pay scales generally are higher in metropolitan areas. Annual earnings of some workers may be lower than weekly rates would indicate because the amount of time they work can be limited by bad weather.

Related Occupations

Other workers who operate mechanical equipment include truck and bus drivers, manufacturing equipment operators, and farmers.

Sources of Additional Information

For further information about apprenticeships or work opportunities for construction equipment operators, contact a local of the International Union of Operating Engineers; a local apprenticeship committee; or the nearest office of the State apprenticeship agency. In addition, the local office of the State employment service may provide information about apprenticeship and other training programs.

For general information about the work of construction equipment operators, contact:

☛Associated Builders and Contractors, National Center for Construction Education and Research, 1300 North 17th St., Rosslyn, VA 22209.

☛Associated General Contractors of America, Inc., 1957 E St. NW., Washington, DC 20006.

☛International Union of Operating Engineers, 1125 17th St. NW., Washington, DC 20036.

Information on industrial truck and tractor operators is available from:

☛Industrial Truck Association, 1750 K St. NW., Suite 460, Washington, DC 20006.

Rail Transportation Workers

(D.O.T. 184.167-278, 198; 850.663-018; 910.362, .363, .364, .367-010, -022, .382, .583, .664, .667-026, .683-010, -014, -022; 913.463-014; 919.663-014, .683-018, -026; 932.664-010)

Nature of the Work

Rail transportation workers operate our Nation's trains, subways, and streetcars to facilitate the movement of passengers and cargo. Railroad transportation workers deliver travelers and freight to destinations throughout the nation while subway and streetcar operators provide passenger service within a single metropolitan area.

Railroad transportation workers. *Locomotive engineers* and *rail yard engineers* are among the most highly skilled workers on the railroad. They operate locomotives in yards, stations, and over the track between distant stations and yards. Locomotive engineers operate trains carrying cargo and passengers between stations, while rail yard engineers move cars within yards to assemble or disassemble trains. In addition to those engineers who work for railroads, some engineers called *dinkey operators* work at industrial plants or mines operating smaller engines that pull cars loaded with coal, rock, or supplies around the site.

Engineers operate the throttle to start and accelerate the train and use air brakes or dynamic brakes to slow and stop it. They monitor gauges and meters that measure speed, fuel, temperature, battery charge, and air pressure in the brake lines. Both on the road and in the yard, they watch for signals that indicate track obstructions, other train movements, and speed limits. They must have a thorough knowledge of the signal systems, yards, and terminals along their routes and be constantly aware of the condition and makeup of their train. This is extremely important because trains react differently to acceleration, braking, and curves, depending on the number of cars, the ratio of empty to loaded cars, and the amount of slack in the train.

Most engineers run diesel locomotives; a few run electric locomotives. Before and after each run, engineers check locomotives for mechanical problems. Minor adjustments are made on the spot, but major problems are reported to the engine shop supervisor. In an effort to reduce costs, most railroads are phasing out *assistant engineers*, also known as firers, who monitor locomotive instruments and signals and observe the track for obstructions. Most of these duties are now performed by brake operators.

Road conductors and *yard conductors* are in charge of the train and yard crews. Conductors assigned to freight trains record each car's contents and destination and make sure that cars are added and removed at the proper points along the route. Conductors assigned to passenger trains collect tickets and fares and assist passengers. At stops, they signal engineers when to pull out of the station.

Before a train leaves the terminal, the road conductor and engineer discuss instructions received from the dispatcher concerning the train's route, timetable, and cargo. While underway, conductors receive additional information by radio. This may include information about track conditions ahead or instructions to pull off at the next available stop to let another train pass. During the run, conductors use two-way radios to contact engineers. They pass on instructions received from dispatchers and remind engineers of stops, reported track conditions, and the presence of other trains.

While underway, conductors receive information from *brake operators* regarding any equipment problems, and they may arrange for defective cars to be removed from the train for repairs at the nearest station or stop. They inform dispatchers of any problems using a radio or wayside telephone.

Yard conductors supervise the crews that assemble and disassemble trains. Some cars are sent to special tracks for unloading, while the rest are moved to other tracks to await assemblage into trains destined for different cities. Conductors tell engineers where to move cars. They tell brake operators which cars to couple and uncouple and which switches to throw to divert the locomotive or cars to the proper track. In yards that have automatic classification systems, conductors use electrical remote controls to operate the track switches that route cars to the correct track.

Brake operators play a pivotal role in making locomotives and cars into trains. Working under the direction of conductors, they do the physical work involved in adding and removing cars at railroad stations and assembling and disassembling trains in railroad yards.

Freight train crews include either one or two brake operators— one in the locomotive with the engineer and another in the rear car. An increasing number of freight trains use only one brake operator because new visual instrumentation and monitoring devices have eliminated the need for operators outside the locomotive. Before departure, brake operators inspect the train to make sure that all couplers and airhoses are fastened, that handbrakes on all the cars are released, and that the air brakes are functioning properly. While underway, they regularly look for smoke, sparks, and other signs of sticking brakes, overheated axle bearings, and other potentially faulty equipment. They may make minor repairs to airhoses and couplers. In case of unexpected stops, brake operators set up signals to protect both ends of the train.

When freight trains approach an industrial site, the brake operator in the locomotive gets off the train and runs ahead to switch the train to the proper track. They uncouple the cars and throw track switches to route them to certain tracks if they are to be unloaded, or to an outgoing train if their final destination is further down the line. They also set hand brakes to secure cars.

Many smaller railroads operate with only two crew members—an engineer and a conductor. Most passenger trains no longer employ brake operators but employ *assistant conductors* to help conductors collect tickets and assist passengers.

Subway and streetcar operators. *Subway operators* control trains that transport passengers throughout a city and its suburbs. The trains usually run on tracks in underground tunnels, but some systems have lines that run in part on tracks on the surface or elevated above streets. Observing the system's signals, operators start, slow, or stop the subway train. They make announcements to riders, open and close the doors, and ensure that passengers get on and off the subway safely. Operators should have a basic understanding of the operating system and be able to recognize common equipment problems. When breakdowns or emergencies occur, operators contact their dispatcher or supervisor and may have to evacuate cars. To meet predetermined schedules, operators must control the amount of time spent at each station.

Streetcar operators drive electric-powered streetcars or trolleys that transport passengers. Streetcars run on tracks that may be recessed in city streets, so operators must observe traffic signals and cope with car and truck traffic. Operators start, slow, and stop their cars so passengers may board or alight. They collect fares, and issue change and transfers. They also answer questions from passengers concerning fares, schedules, and routes.

Working Conditions

Because trains operate 24 hours a day, 7 days a week, many rail transportation employees often work nights, weekends, and holidays. On some days subway operators may work multiple shifts. Undesirable shifts are assigned to persons who have the least seniority.

Most freight trains are unscheduled, and few workers on these trains have scheduled assignments. Instead, their names are placed on a list, and when their turn comes they are assigned to the next train, usually on short notice and often at odd hours. Because road service personnel often work on trains that operate between stations that are hundreds of miles apart, they may spend several nights a week away from home.

Subway operators make announcements to riders and ensure that passengers get on and off safely.

Freight and yard conductors and brake operators spend most of their time outdoors in all kinds of weather. The work of brake operators on local runs—where trains frequently stop at stations to pick up and deliver cars—is physically demanding. Climbing up and down and getting off moving cars is strenuous and can be dangerous.

Employment

Rail transportation workers held about 86,000 jobs in 1994— including 26,000 conductors, 22,000 locomotive engineers, 19,000 brake operators, and 6,000 rail yard engineers and dinkey operators. Subway and streetcar operators accounted for over 12,000 jobs. Railroads employ about 82 percent of all rail transportation workers. The rest work for state and local governments as subway and streetcar operators, and for mining and manufacturing establishments that operate their own locomotives and rail cars to move ore, coal, and other bulk materials.

Training, Other Qualifications, and Advancement

Most railroad transportation workers begin as trainees for either engineer or brake operator jobs. Railroads prefer that applicants have a high school education. Applicants must have good hearing, eyesight, and color vision, as well as good hand-eye coordination, manual dexterity, and mechanical aptitude. Physical stamina is required for brake operator jobs. Most employers require that applicants for railroad transportation jobs pass a physical examination and tests that screen for drug and alcohol use.

Railroads prefer that applicants for locomotive engineer jobs be at least 21 years old. Engineer jobs are frequently filled by workers with experience in other railroad operating occupations, such as brake operators or conductors. Most beginning engineers undergo a 6-month training program, which includes classroom and hands-on instruction in locomotive operation. At the end of the training period, aspiring engineers must pass qualifying tests covering locomotive equipment, air brake systems, fuel economy, train handling techniques, and operating rules and regulations.

On most railroads, brake operators begin by making several trips with conductors and experienced operators to become familiar with the job. On some railroads, however, new brake operators undergo extensive training, including instruction in signaling, coupling and uncoupling cars, throwing switches, and boarding moving trains.

As railroads need new engineers and brake operators, newly trained workers who have the most seniority are placed on the "extra board." Extra board engineers and brake operators work only when the railroad needs substitutes for regular workers who are absent because of vacation, illness, or other personal reasons. Extra board engineers and brake operators frequently must wait years until they accumulate enough seniority to get a regular assignment. Seniority rules also may allow workers with greater seniority to select their type of assignment. For example, an engineer may move from an initial regular assignment in yard service to road service.

Engineers undergo periodic physical examinations and drug and alcohol testing to determine their fitness to operate locomotives. Unannounced safety and efficiency tests are also given to judge their overall conduct of operations. In some cases, engineers who fail to meet these physical and conduct standards are restricted to yard service; in other instances, they may be disciplined, trained to perform other work, or discharged.

Conductor jobs generally are filled from the ranks of experienced brake operators who have passed tests covering signals, timetables, operating rules, and related subjects. Some companies require these tests be passed within the first few years of employment. Until permanent positions become available, new conductors are put on the extra board, where they substitute for experienced conductors who are absent. On most railroads, conductors on extra board may work as brake operators if there are not enough conductor runs available that month. Seniority usually is the main factor in determining promotion from brake operator to conductor and from extra board to a permanent position. Advancement to conductor jobs is limited because there are many more brake operators than conductors.

Most railroads maintain separate seniority lists for road service and yard service conductors. Conductors usually remain in one type of service for their entire career. On some railroads, however, conductors start in the yards, then move to freight service, and finally to passenger service. Some conductors advance to managerial or administrative positions.

For subway and streetcar operator jobs, subway transit systems prefer applicants to have a high school education. Some systems require subway operators to work as busdrivers for a specified period of time. Applicants must be in good health, articulate, and able to make quick, responsible judgments.

New operators generally are placed in training programs that last from a few weeks to 6 months. At the end of the period of classroom and on-the-job training, operators usually must pass qualifying examinations covering the operating system, troubleshooting, and evacuation and emergency procedures. Some operators with sufficient seniority can advance to station managers.

Job Outlook

Competition for available opportunities is expected to be keen. Many persons qualify for rail transportation occupations because education beyond high school generally is not required and many more desire employment than can be hired because the pay is good and the work steady. While employment of railroad transportation workers is expected to decline for all occupations through the year

2005, employment of subway and streetcar operators is expected to grow faster than the average. The total number of new jobs, however, is not large. Also, relatively few opportunities resulting from replacement needs will occur because the attractive pay and job security results in relatively few rail transportation workers leaving their jobs.

Demand for railroad freight service will grow as the economy expands, but opportunities for railroad transportation workers will be limited because of ongoing reductions in the size of operating crews and improvements in the efficiency of railroad operations. Railroad freight service is expected to increase as the population and economy grow in size, and as intermodal freight transportation continues to become more efficient. Intermodal systems use trucks to pick-up and deliver the shippers' sealed trailers or containers, and trains to transport them long distance. Productivity and efficiency improvements cutting the time railroads need to deliver cargoes are also increasing shippers' use of railroads. In order to compete with other modes of transportation such as trucks, ships and barges, and aircraft, railroads are improving delivery times and on-time service while reducing shipping rates. As a result, businesses are expected to increasingly use railroads to carry their goods.

However, growth in the number of railroad transportation workers will be affected by innovations such as larger, faster, more fuel-efficient trains and computerized classification yards that make it possible to move passengers and freight more economically. Computers are used to keep track of freight cars, match empty cars with the closest loads, and dispatch trains. Computer-assisted devices alert engineers to train malfunctions, eliminating the need for brake operators in the rear car. Also, new work rules that allow trains to operate with two- or three-person crews instead of the traditional five-person crews are now becoming widespread. Many positions will not be filled as people leave the occupations, or the work will be restructured so that it can be done by other railroad employees. Employment opportunities for locomotive and yard engineers should be slightly better than other rail occupations because they should be less affected by technological changes and reductions in crew size. On the other hand, employment of brake operators should be the most adversely affected as visual instrumentation and monitoring devices eliminate the need for rear brake operators.

Subway and streetcar operator employment is expected to grow as cities build new rail systems and add new lines to existing systems. New construction is spurred by population growth in metropolitan areas that increases automobile traffic and makes streets and highways more congested. Improved rail systems offer an alternative to automobile transportation that can reduce road congestion and, by reducing automobile use, also contribute to government mandated improvements in air quality.

Earnings

Earnings of railroad transportation workers vary by occupation, size of the train, and type of service. According to the Brotherhood of Locomotive Engineers, in 1993, passenger engineers averaged about $63,900 a year, through-freight engineers about $62,900, local way freight engineers about $60,800, and yard engineers about $47,700 a year.

According to the Association of American Railroads, in 1994, annual earnings of conductors averaged $41,000 for through-freight and $39,200 for local and way freight. Brake operators averaged about $28,300 for through-freight and $31,000 for local and way freight. Yard brake operators averaged about $24,800 in 1994, while passenger brake operators averaged $21,600.

According to the American Public Transit Association, in 1994, operators for commuter rail had hourly earnings of about $19.20; operators for heavy rail about $17.30; and operators for light rail, about $15.90.

Most rail transportation employees in yards work 40 hours a week and receive extra pay for overtime. Most railroad workers in road service are paid according to miles traveled or hours worked, whichever leads to higher earnings. Full-time employees have steadier work, more regular hours, and higher earnings than those assigned to the extra board.

Most railroad transportation workers are members of unions. Many different railroad unions represent various crafts on the railroads, but most railroad engineers are members of the Brotherhood of Locomotive Engineers, while most other railroad transportation workers are members of the United Transportation Union. Many subway operators are members of the Amalgamated Transit Union, while others belong to the Transport Workers Union of North America.

Sources of Additional Information

Information on employment opportunities for railroad transportation workers may be obtained from the employment offices of the various railroads and rail transit systems, or State employment service offices.

For general information about career opportunities in passenger transportation, contact:

☛American Public Transit Association, 1201 New York Ave. NW., Suite 400, Washington, DC 20005.

General information on rail transportation occupations and career opportunities as a locomotive engineer is available from:

☛Brotherhood of Locomotive Engineers, 1370 Ontario Ave., Cleveland, OH 44113-1702.

Taxi Drivers and Chauffeurs

(D.O.T. 359.673-010 and -014; 913.463-018, .663-010; 919.663-010, and .683-014)

Nature of the Work

Taxi drivers and chauffeurs pick up and drive people to their destination in cars, limousines, or vans. Except for a small number of chauffeurs employed in private service, most charge passengers a fee.

Taxi drivers, also known as cab drivers, drive taxicabs, which are custom automobiles modified for transporting passengers. Taxi drivers take passengers to such places as airports, convention centers and hotels, or places of entertainment. Drivers collect fees from passengers based on the number of miles that are traveled or the amount of time spent reaching the destination. They record on a log, or trip sheet, the length of each trip, the point of pick-up, and the destination.

At the start of their driving shift, cab drivers usually report to a cab service or garage where they are assigned a cab. They are given a trip sheet, where they record their name, date of work, and cab identification number. They check the cab's fuel and oil levels, and make sure the lights, brakes, and windshield wipers are in good working order. Drivers adjust rear and side mirrors and their seat for comfort. Any equipment or parts not in good working order are reported to the dispatcher or company mechanic.

Taxi drivers pick up their passengers in one of three ways. Customers requesting transportation may call the cab company and give a place and an approximate time they wish to be picked up, and their destination. The cab company dispatcher then relays the information to a driver by two-way radio. In urban areas, drivers may cruise streets and pick up passengers who hail them, or "wave them down." Drivers also may get passengers by waiting at cab stands or in taxi lines at airports, train stations, hotels, and other places where people frequently seek taxis.

Drivers should be familiar with streets in the areas they service so they can use the most efficient route to destinations. They also should know the locations of frequently requested destinations, such as airports, bus and railroad terminals, convention centers, hotels, popular restaurants, sport facilities, museums, art galleries and other points of interest. Locations of the fire and police departments, as well as hospitals, should also be known in case of emergency.

Upon reaching the destination, drivers determine the fare and announce it to the rider. Fares often consist of many parts. One part is called a "drop charge," which is a flat fee just for using the cab. Another part of the fare is based on the length of the trip and the amount of time it took. In many taxicabs this is measured by a taximeter, a machine which drivers turn on as soon as passengers enter the cab and turn off when the destination is reached that displays the fare as it accrues. The fare may also include a surcharge for additional passengers or for handling luggage. In addition to paying the fare, most passengers will give the driver a tip. The amount of the gratuity depends on the passengers' satisfaction with the quality and efficiency of the ride and courtesy of the driver. When passengers request, a driver issues a receipt. Drivers enter onto the trip sheet all information regarding the trip, such as place and time of pick-up and drop-off and total fee. They also must fill out accident reports when necessary.

Chauffeurs drive passengers in private automobiles, limousines, or vans owned by limousine companies. Chauffeurs drive many types of passengers. Many transport travelers and other persons between hotels and airports or bus and train terminals in large vans. Others are hired to drive luxury automobiles, such as limousines, to popular entertainment and social events. Still others are employed full time by wealthy families and private companies to provide personal transportation.

At the start of the work day, chauffeurs make sure their automobile is ready for use. They inspect it for cleanliness and, when needed, vacuum the interior and wash windows, the exterior car body, and mirrors. They check fuel and oil levels and make sure the lights, tires, brakes, and windshield wipers are in good working order. Chauffeurs may perform routine maintenance and make minor repairs, such as changing tires or adding oil and other fluids when needed. If more serious repairs are needed, the chauffeur takes the vehicle to a professional mechanic.

Chauffeurs often strive to pamper their passengers with attentive service. They assist riders into the car, usually holding the door, holding umbrellas when raining, and loading packages and luggage into the trunk of the car. They may perform errands for their employers, such as delivering packages or picking up items. They also may meet persons arriving at airports. Many chauffeurs offer conveniences and luxuries in their limousines to insure a pleasurable ride, such as newspapers, music, drinks, televisions, and telephones.

Working Conditions

Taxi drivers and chauffeurs occasionally have to load and unload heavy luggage and packages. Driving for long periods of time can be

Taxi drivers may pick up their passengers by answering customers' requests for transportation.

tiring, especially in densely populated urban areas, and driving in bad weather, heavy traffic, or mountainous and hilly areas can be nerve racking. Sitting for long periods of time can be uncomfortable. Drivers must be alert to conditions on the road, especially in heavy and congested traffic or in bad weather, to prevent accidents and to avoid sudden stops, turns, and other driving maneuvers that would jar the passenger.

Work hours of taxi drivers and chauffeurs vary greatly. Some jobs offer full-time or part-time employment; in others hours are very flexible. Hours can change from day to day or be the same every day. Drivers sometimes must report to work on short notice. Chauffeurs who work for a single employer may be on call much of the time. For those who work for a limousine service, evening and weekend work is common.

The work schedule of chauffeurs is usually dictated by the needs of their client or employer. The work of taxi drivers is much less structured. Working free from supervision, they may break for a meal or a rest whenever their vehicle is unoccupied. However, taxi drivers risk robbery because they work alone and often carry a lot of cash.

Full-time taxi drivers usually work one shift a day, which may last from 8 to 12 hours. Part-time drivers may work half a shift each day, or work a full shift once or twice a week. Because most taxi companies offer services 24 hours a day, drivers must be on duty at all times of the day and night. Early morning and late night shifts are not uncommon. Drivers also work long hours during holidays, weekends, and other special events. Independent drivers, however, can often set their own hours and schedules.

Taxi drivers and chauffeurs meet many different types of people. Patience is required when waiting for passengers or when dealing with rude customers. Many municipalities and taxicab and chauffeur companies require dress codes. In many cities, taxicab drivers are required to wear clothes that are clean and neat. Many chauffeurs wear more formal attire, such as a coat and tie or a dress, or sometimes a uniform and cap or a tuxedo.

Employment

Taxi drivers and chauffeurs held about 129,000 jobs in 1994. About 5 out of 9 were wage and salary workers employed by a company or business. Of these, about 31 percent worked for local and suburban transportation companies and about 21 percent worked for taxicab companies. Others worked for automotive rental dealerships, private households, and funeral homes. About 4 out of 9 were self-employed.

Training, Other Qualifications, and Advancement

Local governments regulate taxicabs and set standards and tests required to be licensed as a taxi driver or chauffeur. Although requirements vary, most municipalities have minimum qualifications for age and driving experience. Many taxi and limousine companies have higher standards than the ones required by law: They ask to see a driving record and check credit and criminal records. In addition, many companies require a higher minimum age and prefer that drivers be high school graduates.

Persons interested in driving a limousine or taxicab must first have a regular automobile drivers license. They also must acquire a chauffeur or taxi driver's license, commonly called a "hacker's" license. Local authorities generally require applicants for a hacker's license to pass a written exam or complete a training program. To qualify either through an exam or a training program, applicants must know local geography, motor vehicle laws, safe driving practices, regulations governing taxicabs, and display some aptitude for being able to deal courteously with the public. In many municipalities, applicants sponsored by taxicab or limousine companies may be given a temporary permit that allows them to drive, even though they may not yet have finished the training program or taken the test. Many localities are adding a test on English usage, usually in the

form of listening comprehension. Applicants who do not pass the English exam must take an English course sponsored by the municipality. Many local authorities require that applicants pass a physical exam and many take applicants' fingerprints to check for a criminal record.

The majority of taxi drivers and chauffeurs are called "lease drivers." Lease drivers pay a monthly or weekly fee to the company that allows them to lease their vehicle and have access to the company dispatch system. The fee may also include a charge for vehicle maintenance and a deposit. Lease drivers may take their cars home with them when they are not on duty.

Some taxi and limousine companies give new drivers on-the-job training. They may show drivers how to operate the taximeter and two-way radio, and how to complete paperwork. Other topics covered may include driver safety and popular sightseeing and entertainment destinations. Many companies have contracts with social service agencies and transportation services to transport elderly and disabled citizens, so new drivers may get special training on how to properly handle wheelchair lifts and other mechanical devices.

Taxi drivers and chauffeurs should be able to get along with many different types of people. They must be patient when waiting for passengers or when dealing with rude customers, and driving in heavy and congested traffic requires tolerance and a mild temperament. Drivers should also be dependable because passengers rely on them to be picked up at prearranged times and taken to the correct destination. Because drivers work with little supervision, they must be responsible and self-motivated if they are to be successful.

Opportunities for advancement are limited for taxi drivers and chauffeurs. Experienced drivers may obtain preferred routes or shifts. Some advance to dispatcher or to manager jobs; others may start their own limousine company. On the other hand, many drivers like the independent, unsupervised work of driving their own automobile.

In many small and medium size communities, drivers are able to purchase their own taxi, limousine, or other type of automobile and go into business for themselves. These independent owner-drivers are usually required to get an additional permit that allows them to operate their vehicle as a company. In some big cities, however, the number of operating permits is limited and may only be obtained by purchasing one from an owner-driver who is leaving the business. Although many independent owner-drivers are successful, some fail to cover expenses and eventually lose their permit and their automobile. Independent owner-drivers should have good business sense and courses in accounting, business, and business arithmetic are helpful. Knowledge of mechanics can enable independent owner-operators to cut expenses and perform their own routine maintenance and minor repairs.

Job Outlook

Persons seeking jobs as taxi drivers and chauffeurs should encounter good opportunities. Thousands of job openings will occur each year as drivers transfer to other occupations or leave the labor force. However, driving jobs vary greatly in terms of earnings, work hours, and working conditions. Because driving does not require education beyond high school, competition is expected for jobs that offer regular hours and attractive earnings and working conditions. Opportunities should be best for persons with good driving records who are able to be flexible in their work schedules.

Employment of taxi drivers and chauffeurs is expected to grow faster than average for all occupations through the year 2005 as local and intercity travel increases with population growth. Opportunities should be best in metropolitan areas that are growing rapidly.

Job opportunities may fluctuate from season to season and from month to month. Extra drivers may be hired during holiday seasons and peak travel and tourist times. During economic slowdowns, drivers are seldom laid off but they may have to increase their working hours and their earnings may decline somewhat. Independent owner-operators are particularly vulnerable to economic slowdowns.

Earnings

Earnings of taxi drivers and chauffeurs vary greatly, depending on the number of hours worked, customers' tips, and other factors. Those who usually worked full time had median weekly earnings of $375 in 1994. The middle 50 percent earned between $262 and $510 a week. The lowest 10 percent earned less than $204, while the highest 10 percent earned more than $759 a week. Earnings were generally higher in more urban areas.

According to limited information available, the majority of independent taxi owner-drivers earned from about $20,000 to $30,000, including tips. However, professional drivers with a regular clientele often earn more. Many chauffeurs who worked full time earned from about $25,000 to $50,000 including tips.

Related Occupations

Other workers who drive vehicles on highways and city streets are ambulance drivers, busdrivers, and truckdrivers.

Sources of Additional Information

Information on licensing and registration of taxi drivers and chauffeurs is available from offices of local governments that regulate taxicabs. For information about work opportunities as a taxi driver or chauffeur, contact local taxi or limousine services or State employment service offices.

For general information about the work of taxi drivers, contact:
☛International Taxicab and Livery Association, 3849 Farragut Ave., Kensington, MD 20895.

For general information about the work of limousine drivers, contact:
☛National Limousine Association, 1300 L Street NW., Suite 1050, Washington, DC. 20005-4107.

Truckdrivers

(D.O.T. 292.353, .363, .463, .483, and .667; 900 through 905.683; 906; 909.663; 919.663-018, -022, -026; and 953.583)

Nature of the Work

Nearly all goods are transported by truck during some of their journey from producers to consumers. Goods may also be shipped between terminals or warehouses in different cities by train, ship, or plane. But truckdrivers usually make the initial pickup from factories, consolidate cargo at terminals for intercity shipment, and deliver goods from terminals to stores and homes.

Before leaving the terminal or warehouse, truckdrivers check their trucks for fuel and oil. They also inspect the trucks to make sure the brakes, windshield wipers, and lights are working and that a fire extinguisher, flares, and other safety equipment are aboard and in working order. Drivers adjust mirrors so that both sides of the truck are visible from the driver's seat, and make sure cargo has been loaded properly so it will not shift during the trip. Drivers report to the dispatcher any equipment that does not work or is missing, or cargo that is not loaded properly.

Once underway, drivers must be alert to prevent accidents. Because drivers of large tractor-trailers sit higher than cars, pickups, and vans, they can see farther down the road. They seek traffic lanes that allow them to move at a steady speed, and, when going downhill, they may increase speed slightly to gain momentum for a hill ahead.

Long-distance runs vary widely. On short "turnarounds," truckdrivers deliver a load to a nearby city, pick up another loaded trailer, and drive it back to their home base the same day. Other runs take an entire day, and drivers remain away from home overnight. On longer runs, drivers may haul loads from city to city for a week or more before returning home. Some companies use two drivers on very long runs. One drives while the other sleeps in a berth behind the cab. "Sleeper" runs may last for days, or even weeks, usually with the truck stopping only for fuel, food, loading, and unloading.

Some long-distance drivers who have regular runs transport freight to the same city on a regular basis. Because shippers request varying amounts of service to different cities every day, many drivers have unscheduled runs. Dispatchers tell these drivers when to report for work and where to haul the freight.

After long-distance truckdrivers reach their destination or complete their operating shift, they are required by the U.S. Department of Transportation to complete reports about the trip and the condition of the truck and to give a detailed report of any accident. In addition, drivers are subject to random alcohol and drug tests while on duty.

Long-distance truckdrivers spend most of their working time behind the wheel but may be required to unload their cargo. Drivers hauling specialty cargo often load or unload their trucks, since they may be the only one at the destination familiar with this procedure. Auto-transport drivers, for example, drive and position the cars on the trailers and head ramps and remove them at the final destination. When picking up or delivering furniture, drivers of long-distance moving vans hire local workers to help them load or unload.

When local truckdrivers receive assignments from the dispatcher to make deliveries, pickups, or both, they also get delivery forms. Before the drivers arrive for work, material handlers generally have loaded the trucks and arranged the items in order of delivery to minimize handling of the merchandise.

At the customer's place of business, local truckdrivers generally load or unload the merchandise. If there are heavy loads or many deliveries to make during the day, drivers may have helpers. Customers must sign receipts for goods and drivers may receive money for material delivered. At the end of the day, they turn in receipts, money, and records of deliveries made and report any mechanical problems their trucks may have.

The work of local truckdrivers varies, depending on the product they transport. Produce truckers usually pick up a loaded truck in the early morning and spend the rest of the day delivering produce to many different grocery stores. Lumber truckdrivers, on the other hand, make several trips from the lumber yard to one or more construction sites. Gasoline tank truckdrivers attach the hoses and operate the pumps on their trucks to transfer the gasoline to gas stations' storage tanks.

Some local truckdrivers have sales and customer relations responsibilities. These drivers—called "driver-sales workers" or "route drivers"—are primarily responsible for delivering their firm's products, but they also represent the company. Their reaction to customer complaints and requests for special services can make the difference between a large order and losing a customer. Route drivers also may use their selling ability to increase sales and to gain additional customers.

The duties of driver-sales workers vary according to the industry in which they are employed, the policies of their particular company, and how strongly their sales responsibilities are emphasized. Most have wholesale routes—that is, they deliver to businesses and stores rather than homes. A few distribute various foods, or pick up and deliver dry-cleaning to households, but these retail routes are now rare.

Wholesale bakery driver-sales workers, for example, deliver and arrange bread, cakes, rolls, and other baked goods on display racks in grocery stores. Paying close attention to the items that are selling well and those just sitting on the shelves, they estimate the amount and variety of baked goods that will be sold. They may recommend changes in a store's order or may encourage the manager to stock new bakery products. From time to time, they try to get the business of new stores along their route.

Driver-sales workers employed by laundries that rent linens, towels, work clothes, and other items visit businesses regularly to replace soiled laundry.

Some truckdrivers may be required to load and unload their trucks.

Vending machine driver-sales workers service machines in factories, schools, and other buildings. They check items remaining in the machines, replace stock, and remove money deposited in the cash boxes. They also examine each vending machine to see that merchandise and change are dispensed properly, make minor repairs, and clean machines.

After completing their route, driver-sales workers order items for the next day which they think customers are likely to buy, based primarily on what products have been selling well, the weather, time of year, and any customer feedback.

Working Conditions

Truckdriving has become less physically demanding because most trucks now have more comfortable seats, better ventilation, and improved cab designs. However, driving for many hours at a stretch, unloading cargo, and making many deliveries can be tiring, and driving in bad weather, heavy traffic, or mountains can be nerve racking. Local truckdrivers, unlike long-distance drivers, usually can return home in the evening. Some self-employed long distance truckdrivers who own as well as operate their trucks spend over 240 days a year away from home.

Local truckdrivers frequently work 48 hours or more a week. Many who handle food for chain grocery stores, produce markets, or bakeries drive at night or early in the morning. Although most drivers have a regular route, some have different routes each day. Many local truckdrivers—particularly driver-sales workers—load and unload their own trucks, which requires considerable lifting, carrying, and walking.

The U.S. Department of Transportation governs work hours and other matters of trucking companies engaged in interstate commerce. For example, a long-distance driver cannot be on duty for more than 60 hours in any 7-day period and cannot drive more than 10 hours following at least 8 consecutive hours off duty. Many drivers, particularly on long runs, work close to the maximum time permitted. Drivers on long runs may face boredom, loneliness, and fatigue. Although many drivers work during the day, travel at night and on holidays and weekends is frequently necessary in order to avoid traffic delays and deliver cargo on time.

Employment

Truckdrivers held 2,900,000 jobs in 1994. Jobs are concentrated in and around large cities. Some drivers are employed in almost all communities, however.

Trucking companies employed nearly one-third of all truckdrivers, and another one-third worked for companies engaged in wholesale or retail trade, such as auto parts stores, oil companies, lumber yards, or distributors of food and grocery products. The rest were scattered throughout the economy, including government agencies.

Fewer than 1 out of 10 truckdrivers are self-employed; of these, a significant number are owner-operators, who either operate independently, serving a variety of businesses, or lease their services and their trucks to a trucking company.

Training, Other Qualifications, and Advancement

Qualifications and standards for truckdrivers are established by State and Federal regulations. States must meet Federal standards, and some States have more stringent regulations. All truckdrivers must have a driver's license issued by the State in which they live, and most employers require a good driving record. All drivers of trucks designed to carry at least 26,000 pounds—which includes most tractor-trailers as well as bigger straight trucks—are required to obtain a special commercial driver's license (CDL) from the State in which they live; in many States a regular driver's license is sufficient for driving light trucks and vans. All truckdrivers who operate trucks that carry hazardous materials also must obtain a CDL.

To qualify for a commercial driver's license, applicants must pass a knowledge test and demonstrate that they can operate a commercial truck safely. A national data bank permanently records all driving violations incurred by persons who hold commercial licenses, so drivers whose commercial license is suspended or revoked in one State may not be issued a new one in another State. Trainees must be accompanied by a driver with a CDL until they get their own CDL. Information on how to apply for a commercial driver's license may be obtained from State motor vehicle administrations.

The U.S. Department of Transportation establishes minimum qualifications for truckdrivers who are engaged in interstate commerce. A driver must be at least 21 years old and pass a physical examination, which the employer usually pays for. Good hearing, 20/40 vision with or without glasses or corrective lenses, normal use of arms and legs (unless a waiver is obtained), and normal blood pressure are the main physical requirements. Persons with epilepsy or diabetes controlled by insulin are not permitted to be interstate truckdrivers, and drivers may not use any controlled substances unless prescribed by a licensed physician. In addition, drivers must take a written examination on the Motor Carrier Safety Regulations of the U.S. Department of Transportation.

Many trucking operations have higher standards than those described. Many firms require that drivers be at least 25 years old, be able to lift heavy objects, and have driven trucks for 3 to 5 years. Many prefer to hire high school graduates and require annual physical examinations. Federal regulations require employers to test their drivers for alcohol and drug use as a condition of employment, and require periodic random tests while on duty.

Since drivers often deal directly with the company's customers, they must get along well with people. For jobs as driver-sales workers, an ability to speak well and a neat appearance are particularly important, as are self-confidence, initiative, and tact. For all truckdriver jobs, employers also look for responsible, self-motivated individuals, since drivers work with little supervision.

Driver-training courses are a desirable method of preparing for truckdriving jobs and for obtaining a commercial driver's license. High school driver-training courses are an asset, and courses in automotive mechanics may help drivers make minor roadside repairs. Many private and public technical-vocational schools offer tractor-trailer driver training programs. Students learn to inspect the trucks and freight, to maneuver large vehicles on crowded streets and in highway traffic, and to comply with Federal, State, and local regulations. Some programs provide only a limited amount of actual driving experience, and completion of a program does not assure a job. Persons interested in attending one of these schools should check with local trucking companies to make sure the school's training is acceptable or should seek a school certified by the Professional Truck Driver Institute of America as providing training that meets

Federal Highway Administration guidelines for training tractor-trailer drivers.

Training given to new drivers by employers usually is informal and may consist only of a few hours of instruction from an experienced driver, sometimes on the new employee's own time. New drivers also may ride with and observe experienced drivers before being assigned their own runs. Additional training may be given if they are to drive a special type of truck or if they are handling hazardous materials. Some companies give 1 to 2 days of classroom instruction which covers general duties, the operation and loading of a truck, company policies, and the preparation of delivery forms and company records. Driver-sales workers also receive training on the various types of products they carry so they will be more effective sales workers and better able to handle customer requests.

Very few people enter truckdriving directly from school; most truckdrivers previously held jobs in other occupations. Driving experience in the Armed Forces can be an asset. In some instances, a person also may start as a truckdriver's helper, driving part of the day and helping to unload and load freight. When driving vacancies occur, senior helpers usually are promoted.

New drivers sometimes start on panel or other small "straight" trucks. As they gain experience and show good driving skills, they may advance to larger and heavier trucks, and finally to tractor-trailers.

Although most new truckdrivers are assigned immediately to regular driving jobs, some start as extra drivers, who substitute for regular drivers who are ill or on vacation. They receive a regular assignment when an opening occurs.

Advancement of truckdrivers is generally limited to driving runs that provide increased earnings or preferred schedules and working conditions. For the most part, a local truckdriver may advance to driving heavy or special types of trucks, or transfer to long-distance truckdriving. Working for companies that also employ long-distance drivers is the best way to advance to these positions. A few truckdrivers may advance to dispatcher, manager, or traffic work—for example, planning delivery schedules.

Some long-distance truckers purchase a truck and go into business for themselves. Although many of these owner-operators are successful, others fail to cover expenses and eventually lose their trucks. Owner-operators should have good business sense as well as truckdriving experience. Courses in accounting, business, and business arithmetic are helpful, and knowledge of truck mechanics can enable owner-operators to perform their own routine maintenance and minor repairs.

Job Outlook

Opportunities should be favorable for persons who are interested in truckdriving. This occupation has among the largest number of job openings each year. Although thousands of openings will be created by growth in demand for drivers, the majority will occur as experienced drivers transfer to other fields of work or retire or leave the labor force for other reasons. Truckdriver jobs vary greatly in terms of earnings, weekly work hours, number of nights that must be spent "on the road," and in the quality of equipment operated. Because truckdriving does not require education beyond high school, competition is expected for jobs with the most attractive earnings and working conditions.

Employment of truckdrivers is expected to increase about as fast as the average for all occupations through the year 2005 as the economy grows and the amount of freight carried by trucks increases. However, increased integration of truck and railroad long-distance freight transportation should continue to slow somewhat the growth of truckdriver jobs. Trailers are expected increasingly to be carried between distant regions on trains, thus requiring truckdrivers only to deliver and pick them up at rail depots. Perishable goods should continue to be shipped long distance by truck.

Average growth of local and long-distance truckdriver employment should outweigh the slow growth in driver-sales worker jobs.

The number of truckdrivers with sales responsibilities is expected to increase slowly because companies are increasingly splitting their responsibilities among other workers, shifting sales, ordering, and customer service tasks to sales and office staffs, and using regular truckdrivers to make deliveries to customers.

Job opportunities may vary from year to year because the amount of freight moved by trucks fluctuates with the economy. Many new truckdrivers are hired when the economy and the volume of freight are expanding, but fewer when these decline. During economic slowdowns, some truckdrivers are laid off and others have decreased earnings because of reduced hours or miles driven. Independent owner-operators are particularly vulnerable to slowdowns. Truckdrivers employed in industries such as wholesale food distribution, which is usually not affected much by recessions, are less likely to be laid off.

Earnings

As a rule, local truckdrivers are paid by the hour and receive extra pay for working overtime, usually after 40 hours. Long-distance drivers are generally paid primarily by the mile, and their rate per mile can vary greatly from employer to employer; their earnings increase with mileage driven, seniority, and the size and type of truck. Most driver-sales workers receive a commission based on their sales in addition to an hourly wage.

In 1993, truckdrivers had average straight-time hourly earnings of $12.73. Depending on the size of the truck, average hourly earnings were as follows:

Medium trucks $14.87
Tractor-trailers.. 13.29
Heavy straight trucks 11.80
Light trucks 8.06

Drivers employed by trucking companies had the highest earnings, averaging about $15.97 an hour in 1993. Truckdrivers in the Northeast and West had the highest earnings; those in the South had the lowest.

Most long-distance truckdrivers operate tractor-trailers, and their earnings vary widely, from as little as $20,000 to over $40,000 annually. Most self-employed truckdrivers are primarily engaged in long-distance hauling. After deducting their living expenses and the costs associated with operating their trucks, earnings of $20,000 to $25,000 a year are common.

Many truckdrivers are members of the International Brotherhood of Teamsters. Some truckdrivers employed by companies outside the trucking industry are members of unions that represent the plant workers of the companies for which they work.

Related Occupations

Other driving occupations include ambulance driver, busdriver, chauffeur, and taxi driver.

Sources of Additional Information

Information on truckdriver employment opportunities is available from local trucking companies and local offices of the State employment service.

Information on career opportunities in truckdriving may be obtained from:

☛American Trucking Associations, Inc., 2200 Mill Rd., Alexandria, VA 22314.

The Professional Truck Driver Institute of America, a nonprofit organization established by the trucking industry, manufacturers, and others, certifies truckdriver training programs that meet industry standards. A free list of certified tractor-trailer driver training programs may be obtained from:

☛Professional Truck Driver Institute of America, 8788 Elk Grove Blvd., Suite 20, Elk Grove, CA 95624.

Water Transportation Occupations

(D.O.T 197.130-010, .133 except -010 and -018, .137-010, .161-010, .163-010, -014, -018, .167 except -014; 911.131-010, .133-010, .137-010, -014, .263-010, .363-010, -014, .364-010, .584-010, .664-010, -014, .687-022 and -030, 951.685-018)

Nature of the Work

Workers in water transportation occupations operate and maintain deep sea merchant ships, tugboats, towboats, ferries, dredges, research vessels, and other waterborne craft on the oceans and the Great Lakes, in harbors, on rivers and canals, and on other waterways. (Workers who operate water craft used in commercial fishing are described in the section on fishers, hunters, and trappers elsewhere in the *Handbook*.)

Captains or *masters* are in overall command of the operation of a vessel and they supervise the work of the other officers and the crew. They set course and speed, maneuver the vessel to avoid hazards and other ships, and periodically determine position using navigation aids, celestial observations, and charts. They direct crew members who steer the vessel, operate engines, signal to other vessels, perform maintenance and handle lines, or operate towing or dredging gear. Captains insure that proper procedures and safety practices are followed, check that machinery and equipment are in good working order, and oversee the loading and unloading of cargo or passengers. They also maintain logs and other records of ships' movements and cargo carried.

Captains on large vessels are assisted by *deck officers* or *mates*. Merchant marine vessels—those carrying cargo overseas—have a chief or first mate, a second mate, and a third mate. Mates oversee the operation of the vessel, or "stand watch" for specified periods, usually 4 hours on and 8 off. On smaller vessels, there may be only one mate (called a pilot on some inland vessels) who alternates watches with the captain.

Engineers or *marine engineers* operate, maintain, and repair propulsion engines, boilers, generators, pumps, and other machinery. Merchant marine vessels usually have four engineering officers: A chief engineer and a first, second, and third assistant engineer. Assistant engineers stand periodic watches, overseeing the operation of engines and machinery.

Seamen, also called *deckhands*, particularly on inland waters, operate the vessel and its deck equipment under the direction of the ship's officers, and keep the nonengineering areas in good condition. They stand watch, looking out for other vessels, obstructions in the ship's path, and aids to navigation. They also steer the ship, measure water depth in shallow water, and maintain and operate deck equipment such as life boats, anchors, and cargo-handling gear. When docking or departing, they handle lines. They also perform maintenance chores such as repairing lines, chipping rust, and painting and cleaning decks and other areas. Seamen may also load and unload cargo. On vessels handling liquid cargo, they hook up hoses, operate pumps, and clean tanks. Deckhands on tugboats or tow vessels tie barges together into tow units, inspect them periodically, and disconnect them when the destination is reached. Larger vessels have a *boatswain* or head seaman.

Marine oilers work below decks under the direction of the ship's engineers. They lubricate gears, shafts, bearings, and other moving parts of engines and motors, read pressure and temperature gauges and record data, and may repair and adjust machinery.

A typical deep sea merchant ship has a captain, three deck officers or mates, a chief engineer and three assistant engineers, plus six or more seamen and oilers. Depending on their size, vessels operating in harbors, rivers, or along the coast may have a crew comprising only of a captain and one deckhand, or as many as a captain, a mate or pilot, an engineer, and seven or eight seamen. Large vessels also have a full-time cook and helper, while on small ones, a seaman does the cooking. Merchant ships also have an electrician, machinery

Many newer vessels are air-conditioned and soundproofed from noisy machinery.

mechanics, and a radio officer.

Pilots guide ships in and out of harbors, through straits, and on rivers and other confined waterways where a familiarity with local water depths, winds, tides, currents, and hazards such as reefs and shoals is of prime importance. Pilots on river and canal vessels usually are regular crew members, like mates. Harbor pilots are generally independent contractors, who accompany vessels while they enter or leave port. They may pilot many ships in a single day.

Working Conditions

Merchant mariners are away from home for extended periods, but earn long leaves. Most are hired for one voyage, with no job security after that. At sea, they usually stand watch for 4 hours and are off for 8 hours, 7 days a week. Those employed on Great Lakes ships work 60 days and have 30 days off, but do not work in the winter when the lakes are frozen over. Workers on rivers and canals and in harbors are more likely to have year-round work. Some work 8- or 12-hour shifts and go home every day. Others work steadily for a week or month and then have an extended period off. When working, they are usually on duty for 6 or 12 hours and are off for 6 or 12 hours.

People in water transportation occupations work in all weather conditions and although merchant mariners try to avoid severe storms while at sea, working in damp and cold conditions is unpleasant. It is uncommon for vessels to sink, but workers nevertheless face the possibility that they may have to abandon their craft on short notice if it collides with other vessels or runs aground. They also risk injury or death from falling overboard and hazards associated with working with machinery, heavy loads, and dangerous cargo.

Some newer vessels are air-conditioned, soundproofed from noisy machinery, and have comfortable living quarters. Nevertheless, some workers do not like the long periods away from home and the confinement aboard ship.

Employment

Water transportation workers held about 48,000 jobs in 1994. Many merchant marine officers and seamen worked only part of the year, so the total number who worked some time during the year was somewhat greater. The following tabulation shows employment in the occupations that make up this group:

Seamen and marine oilers	20,000
Captains and pilots	13,000
Engineers	7,600
Mates	7,300

A few of the captains and pilots were self-employed, operating their own vessel, or were pilots who were independent contractors.

About 45 percent of all water transportation workers were employed on board merchant marine ships or U.S. Navy Military Sealift ships operating on the oceans or Great Lakes. Another 42 percent were employed in transportation services, working on tugs, towboats, ferries, dredges, and other watercraft in harbors, on rivers and canals, and other waterways. Others worked in water transportation services such as piloting vessels in and out of harbors, operating lighters and chartered boats, and in marine construction, salvaging, and surveying. The remaining water transportation workers were employed on vessels that carry passengers, such as cruise ships, sightseeing and excursion boats, and ferries.

Training and Other Qualifications

Entry, training, and educational requirements for most water transportation occupations are established and regulated by the U.S. Coast Guard. All officers and operators of watercraft must be licensed by the U.S. Coast Guard, which offers nearly 60 different licenses, depending on the position and type of craft. Licensing differs somewhat between the merchant marine and others.

Deck and engineering officers in the merchant marine must be licensed. To qualify for a license, applicants must have graduated from the U.S. Merchant Marine Academy, or one of the six State academies, and pass a written examination. A physical examination and a drug test are also required. Persons with at least 3 years of appropriate sea experience also can be licensed if they pass the written exam, but it is difficult to pass without substantial formal schooling or independent study. Also, because seamen may work 6 months a year or less, it can take 5 to 8 years to accumulate the necessary experience. The academies offer 4-year bachelor's degree programs (one offers a 3-year associate program) in nautical science or marine engineering to prepare students to be third mates or third assistant engineers. With experience and passing of additional exams, third officers may qualify for higher rank. Because of keen competition, however, officers may have to take jobs below the grade for which they are qualified.

For employment in the merchant marine as an unlicensed seaman, a merchant mariner's document is needed. Applicants for merchant marine documents do not need to be U.S. citizens. A medical certificate of excellent health, and a certificate attesting to vision, color perception, and general physical condition may be required for higher-level deckhands. While no experience or formal schooling is required, training at a union-operated school is helpful. Beginners are classified as ordinary seaman and may be assigned to the deck or engineering department. With experience at sea, and perhaps union-sponsored training, an ordinary seaman can pass the able seaman exam.

Merchant marine officers and seamen, both experienced and beginners, are hired for voyages through union hiring halls or directly by shipping companies.

Harbor pilot training is usually an apprenticeship with a shipping company or a pilot employees' association. Entrants may be able seamen or licensed officers.

No training or experience is needed to become a seaman or deckhand on vessels operating in harbors or on rivers or other waterways. Newly hired workers generally learn skills on the job. With experience, they are eligible to take a Coast Guard exam to qualify as a mate, pilot, or captain. Substantial knowledge gained through experience, courses in seamanship schools, and independent study are needed to pass the exam.

Job Outlook

Keen competition is expected to continue for jobs in water transportation occupations. Overall, employment in these jobs is projected to change little through the year 2005, but opportunities will vary by sector.

Employment in deep sea shipping is expected to continue its long-term sharp decline as U.S.-staffed ships carry an even smaller proportion of international cargo. (In 1992, only 4 percent of our imports and exports were carried on U.S.-staffed ships.) Stringent Federal regulations require larger crews on U.S.-staffed ships, which allow vessels that fly foreign flags—and have smaller crew sizes—to operate at lower cost and charge lower shipping rates. A fleet of deep sea U.S.-staffed ships is considered to be vital to the Nation's defense, so they receive Federal support through operating subsidies and provisions in laws that limit certain Federal cargoes to ships that fly the U.S. flag.

Newer ships are designed to be operated safely by much smaller crews. Innovations include automated controls and computerized monitoring systems in navigation, engine control, watchkeeping, ship management, and cargo handling. As older vessels are replaced, crew sizes will shrink, and employed seamen will need greater skills.

Vessels on rivers and canals and on the Great Lakes mostly carry bulk products such as coal, iron ore, petroleum, sand and gravel, grain, and chemicals. Shipments of these products are expected to grow through the year 2005, but productivity increases should cause employment to decline. Employment in water transportation services is likely to show little or no change.

The decline in jobs has created competition for jobs, with many experienced merchant mariners going for long periods without work. As a result, unions generally accept few new members. Also, many merchant marine academy graduates have not found licensed shipboard jobs in the U.S. merchant marine, although most do find related jobs. All are commissioned as ensigns in the U.S. Naval Reserve, and many go on active duty in the Navy. Some find jobs on tugboats or other watercraft or on foreign-flag vessels, or take jobs as seamen on U.S. flag ships. Some take land-based jobs with shipping companies, marine insurance companies, manufacturers of boilers or related machinery, civilian jobs with the U.S. Navy, or other related jobs. Unless the number of people seeking merchant marine jobs declines sharply, the present keen competition is likely to continue.

Earnings

Water transportation workers who usually worked full time had median weekly earnings of $595 in 1994. The middle 50 percent earned between $403 and $856 a week. The lowest 10 percent earned less than $284, while the highest 10 percent earned more than $1,092 a week.

Captains and mates had median weekly earnings of $684 a week in 1994. The middle 50 percent earned between $522 and $908 a week. The lowest paid 10 percent earned less than $423, while the highest more than $1,112 a week.

Seamen had median weekly earnings of $533 a week in 1994. The middle 50 percent earned between $336 and $764 a week. The lowest 10 percent earned less than $264 a week, while the highest 10 percent earned more than $970 a week.

Related Occupations

Workers in occupations having duties and responsibilities similar to these occupations include fishing vessel captains, ferryboat operators, and hatchtenders.

Sources of Additional Information

Information on merchant marine careers, training, and licensing requirements is available from:

☛Maritime Administration, U.S. Department of Transportation, 400 7th St. SW., Washington, DC 20590.

☛Coast Guard, Licensing and Evaluation Branch, Merchant Vessel and Personnel Division, 2100 2nd St. SW., Washington, DC 20593.

Individuals interested in attending a merchant marine academy should contact:

☛Admissions Office, U.S. Merchant Marine Academy, Steamboat Rd., Kings Point, NY 11024.

☛Admissions Office, California Maritime Academy, P.O. Box 1392, Vallejo, CA 94590.

Handlers, Equipment Cleaners, Helpers, and Laborers

(A list of D.O.T. codes is available on request. See page 478.)

Nature of the Work

Employers in almost all industries hire entry level workers to do tasks that require little training, or to assist more skilled production, construction, operating, and maintenance workers. These workers perform a broad array of helper and laborer jobs, ranging from moving boxes and feeding machines to cleaning equipment and work areas. Many do tasks needed to make the work of more skilled employees flow smoothly. They often do routine, physical work under close supervision. They generally follow oral or written instructions from supervisors or more experienced workers, and have little opportunity to make decisions. In order to perform their jobs effectively, helpers and laborers must be familiar with the duties of workers they help, as well as with the materials, tools, and machinery they use.

Freight, stock, and material hand movers move materials to and from storage and production areas, loading docks, delivery vehicles, ships' holds, and containers. They move materials either manually or with forklifts, dollies, handtrucks, or carts. Their specific duties vary by industry and work setting. In factories, they may move raw materials, components, and finished goods between loading docks, storage areas, and work areas. They receive and sort materials and supplies and prepare them according to work orders for delivery to work or storage areas. In grocery stores, they stock shelves, bag groceries, carry packages to customers' cars, and return shopping carts to designated areas.

Helpers assist skilled construction trades workers, mechanics and repairers, and workers in production and extractive occupations. (Information on these occupations appears elsewhere in the *Handbook.*) They aid machine operators and tenders by moving materials, supplies, and tools to and from work areas. Some may tend machines during operation if an operator is not available. Helpers may sort finished products, keep records of machine processes, report malfunctions to operators, and clean machinery after use. Mechanics' helpers assist mechanics and service technicians who repair motor vehicles, industrial machinery, and electrical, electronic, and other equipment. They may fetch tools, materials, and supplies; hold materials or tools; take apart defective equipment; remove rivets; prepare replacement parts; or clean work areas. Construction trades' helpers carry tools, materials, and equipment to carpenters, electricians, plasterers, masons, painters, plumbers, roofers, and other construction trades workers. Helpers for bricklayers and plasterers, for example, mix cement or plaster and fetch bricks or other materials, set up and move scaffolding, and perform other lesser skilled tasks.

Construction craft laborers provide much of the routine physical labor at building, highway, and heavy construction projects, tunnel and shaft excavations, and demolition sites. They clean and prepare sites, dig trenches, set braces to support the sides of excavations, and clean up rubble and debris. In addition to performing a variety of excavation, tunneling, and pipe work, construction craft laborers work as individuals on highly specialized tasks. The installation of utility pipe, for example, requires the set up and operation of lasers guidance equipment for precise pipe elevation and placement. Tunnel and shaft projects may require workers to be trained and experienced in the use of drilling equipment and explosives. Construction craft laborers operate jackhammers, earth tampers, cement mixers, buggies, front-end loaders, "walk-behind" ditchdiggers, small mechanical hoists, laser beam equipment, and surveying and measuring equipment.

In addition to working on building and transportation projects, construction craft laborers work on other projects, such as hazardous waste cleanup and asbestos and lead abatement. In hazardous waste removal, they may operate, maintain, and read monitoring devices; perform material and atmospheric sampling; build, clean, or maintain facilities for hazardous material removal and decontamination; and package and transport hazardous or radioactive materials.

Hand packers and *packagers* manually package or wrap materials. They may inspect items for defects, label cartons and stamp information on products, keep records of items packed, and stack packages on loading docks.

Machine feeders and *offbearers* feed materials into or remove materials from automatic equipment or machines tended by other workers.

Service station attendants fill fuel tanks and wash windshields on automobiles, buses, trucks, and other vehicles. They may perform simple service and repair tasks under the direction of a mechanic, such as change oil, repair tires, and replace belts, lights, windshield wipers, and other accessories. They may also collect payment for services and supplies.

Refuse collectors gather trash, garbage, and recyclables from homes and businesses along a regularly scheduled route and deposit the refuse in their truck for transport to a dump, landfill, or recycling center. They lift and empty garbage cans by hand or operate a hydraulic lift truck that picks up and empties dumpsters.

Vehicle washers and *equipment cleaners* clean machinery, vehicles, storage tanks, pipelines, and similar equipment using water and other cleaning agents, vacuums, hoses, brushes, cloths, and other cleaning equipment.

Parking lot attendants assist customers in parking their cars in lots or storage areas and collect fees from customers.

Construction craft laborers perform much of the routine physical labor at construction and demolition sites.

Working Conditions

Most handlers, equipment cleaners, helpers, and laborers do repetitive, physically demanding work. They may lift and carry heavy objects, and stoop, kneel, crouch, or crawl in awkward positions. Some work at great heights, or outdoors in all weather conditions. Some jobs expose workers to harmful materials or chemicals, fumes, odors, loud noise, or dangerous machinery. These employees may need to wear safety clothing, such as gloves and hard hats, and devices to protect their eyes, mouth, or hearing. However, they can avoid injury if they constantly observe safety procedures.

In many industries, handlers, equipment cleaners, helpers, and laborers may have to work evening or "graveyard" shifts. Their shifts are generally 8 hours, but sometimes they may work 12 hour shifts. Service station and parking lot attendants may work at night since these establishments may be open at all hours; handlers in grocery stores may stock shelves at night when stores are closed. Garbage collectors often work early morning shifts, starting at 5:00 or 6:00 A.M.

Employment

Handlers, equipment cleaners, helpers, and laborers held about 4.8 million jobs in 1994. Their employment was distributed among the following detailed occupations:

Hand packers and packagers	942,000
Freight, stock, and material movers, hand	765,000
Helpers, construction trades	513,000
Machine feeders and offbearers	262,000
Vehicle washers and equipment cleaners	249,000
Service station attendants	167,000
Refuse collectors	111,000
Parking lot attendants	64,000
All other helpers, laborers, and material movers, hand	1,727,000

Handlers, equipment cleaners, helpers, and laborers are employed throughout the country in virtually all industries, with the greatest numbers concentrated in manufacturing, construction, and wholesale and retail trade. Nearly 1 out of 4 works part time. A growing number are employed on a temporary or contract basis. For example, companies that only need a laborer for a few days to move materials or clean up a site contract with temporary help agencies specializing in this type of worker.

Training, Other Qualifications, and Advancement

For most handler, equipment cleaner, helper, and laborer jobs, employers will hire people without work experience or specific training. Some require a high school diploma, others do not. Some jobs require union membership and may have long waiting lists. Most employers, however, require workers to be at least 18 years old and physically able to perform the work. For those jobs requiring physical exertion, employers may require that applicants pass a physical exam. Some employers require mandatory drug testing prior to employment.

For all of these jobs, employers look for people who are reliable and hard working. For those jobs that involve dealing with the public, such as grocery store helpers and garage and parking lot attendants, workers should be pleasant and tactful. Some jobs require reading and basic mathematics skills to read billing and other records and collect payment for services from customers. Handlers, equipment cleaners, helpers, and laborers are often younger than workers in other occupations—reflecting the limited training but significant physical requirements of these jobs.

Generally, handlers, equipment cleaners, helpers, and laborers learn skills informally from more experienced workers or supervisors. Workers who use dangerous equipment or handle toxic chemicals, for example, often receive special training in safety awareness and procedures.

Formal construction craft laborer apprenticeship programs provide more thorough preparation for these jobs. Local apprenticeship programs are operated under guidelines established by the Laborers-Associated General Contractors of America (AGC) Education and Training Fund. Programs include at least 4,000 hours of on-the job training, including 144 hours of classroom training. Most union contractors and laborer unions require some training before an apprentice is placed on the job. Apprentices are instructed in the correct use of numerous tools and equipment that must be mastered before they complete the program.

Experience in many of these jobs may allow workers to qualify for or become trainees for more skilled positions as construction trades workers, machine operators, assemblers, or other production workers; transportation, material moving equipment, or vehicle operators, or mechanics or repairers. Some may advance to become supervisors of handlers, equipment cleaners, helpers, and laborers. In fact, rather than directly hiring workers for mechanic, construction trade, production, or similar occupations, many employers prefer to promote qualified handlers, equipment cleaners, helpers, and laborers as openings arise.

Job Outlook

Employment of handlers, equipment cleaners, helpers, and laborers is expected to grow about as fast as the average for all occupations through the year 2005. Job openings should be numerous because the occupation is very large and turnover is relatively high—characteristic of occupations that require little formal training. Many openings will arise from the need to replace workers who retire, transfer to other occupations, or who leave the labor force for other reasons.

Employment changes for individual occupations, however, will vary. Among service station attendants and machine feeders and offbearers, for example, employment is expected to decline. A decline in employment has also been projected for freight, stock, and material movers. Employment of refuse collectors, on the other hand, should increase more slowly than the average. Vehicle washers and equipment cleaners, hand packers and packagers, and construction trades helpers can expect average employment growth. Employment of parking lot attendants is also expected to increase as fast as average.

Overall, demand for handlers, equipment cleaners, helpers, and laborers will depend on growth in the industries that employ these workers, as well as growth of the skilled workers whom they assist. Average growth among construction trade helpers and laborers, for example, is directly related to construction activity and the growing demand for construction trades workers. Growth of helper and laborer employment may be spurred by the Nation's emphasis on hazardous waste cleanup and other environmental projects, and on rebuilding infrastructure—roads, bridges, tunnels, and communications facilities, for example.

Employment growth will also be affected by automation. Some of these jobs are repetitive and, therefore, easily replaced by new machines and equipment that improve productivity and quality control. Some helper, handler, and hand packer and packaging jobs will be eliminated by automated material handling equipment, such as conveyor belts and computer-controlled lift mechanisms and machines that automatically load, unload, and package materials. As more skilled jobs, such as those of assemblers, become automated, demand for these types of employees who assist them will decline.

In addition to automation, many employers have adopted cost cutting measures such as consolidating or combining job responsibilities or contracting out labor. Job combinations may lead to displacement of handlers, equipment cleaners, helpers, and laborers because the tasks they perform may be assumed by more highly skilled workers, or they may be required to assist more than one type of worker. These types of occupations may increasingly be staffed by a growing group of contingent workers and as companies continue to downsize, more employers may turn to hiring temporary handlers, equipment cleaners, helpers, and laborers.

Earnings

Median weekly earnings for handlers, equipment cleaners, helpers, and laborers in 1994 were about $311. The middle 50 percent earned from $234 to $456 weekly. The top 10 percent earned over $632 weekly, and the bottom 10 percent earned less than $186 weekly. Construction craft laborers generally have higher weekly earnings than other workers in this group. However, they may be more likely to lose work time because of bad weather and the cyclical nature of construction work. Mechanics and repairers' helpers, garage and service station related occupations, and stock handlers and baggers have the lowest weekly earnings among workers in this group.

Over 20 percent of all handlers, equipment cleaners, helpers, and laborers are members of a union. Many helpers and laborers belong to the Laborers' International Union of North America.

Related Occupations

Other entry level workers who perform mostly physical work are roustabouts in the oil industry, certain timber cutting and logging occupations, and groundskeepers. The jobs of handlers, equipment cleaners, helpers, and laborers are often similar to those of the more experienced workers they assist, including machine operators, construction craft workers, assemblers, mechanics, and repairers.

Sources of Additional Information

For information about jobs as handlers, equipment cleaners, helpers, and laborers, contact local building or construction contractors, manufacturers, and wholesale and retail establishments, or the local office of the State employment service.

For general information about the work of construction craft laborers, contact:

☛Laborers' International Union of North America, 905 16th St. NW., Washington, DC 20006.

Job Opportunities in the Armed Forces

Nature of the Work

The mission of the Armed Forces is to: 1) Deter aggression and defeat attack against the Nation, 2) strengthen and build alliances, 3) prevent a hostile power from dominating a region critical to our interests, and 4) prevent conflicts by reducing sources of regional turmoil through various means, including humanitarian aid, counterterrorism, or limiting the spread of militarily significant technology.

The Army and Air Force prepare for defensive and offensive operations, on land and in the air, respectively. The Navy organizes and trains forces primarily for sea operations, while the Marine Corps, part of the Department of the Navy, prepares for land invasions in support of naval or amphibious operations. The Coast Guard, under the Department of Transportation (except in wartime, when it serves with the Navy), enforces Federal maritime laws, rescues distressed vessels and aircraft at sea, operates aids to navigation, and prevents smuggling.

Together, the Armed Forces constitute America's largest employer. Maintaining a strong defense encompasses such diverse activities as running a hospital, commanding a tank, programming computers, operating a nuclear reactor, and repairing and maintaining a helicopter. The military's occupational diversity provides educational opportunities and work experience in literally thousands of occupations. Military personnel hold managerial and administrative jobs; professional, technical, and clerical jobs; construction jobs; electrical and electronics jobs; mechanical and repair jobs; and many others. The military provides job training and work experience for people who can serve for a relatively brief period (3 to 6 years of active duty) or embark on a career that lasts 20 years or more.

There are more than 2,000 basic and advanced military occupational specialties for enlisted personnel and 1,600 for officers. Over 75 percent of these occupational specialties have civilian counterparts. A brief discussion of the major military occupational groups follows.

Infantry, gun crews, and seamanship specialists are the backbone of the Armed Forces. Officers plan and direct military operations, oversee security activities, and serve as combat troop leaders. Enlisted personnel serve as infantrymen, aircraft crew members, weapons specialists, armored vehicle operators, demolition experts, artillery crew, rocket specialists, special operations forces, and combat engineers. Although these functions are unique to the Armed Forces, some involve skills that can be applied to a number of civilian occupations such as police officers, firefighters, and heavy equipment operators. In addition, people in this category learn how to work as team members and can develop leadership, managerial, and supervisory skills.

Military personnel assigned to *electronic equipment repair occupations* are responsible for maintaining and repairing many different types of equipment. Officers manage the regular maintenance and repair of avionics, communications, radar, and air traffic control equipment. Enlisted personnel repair radio, navigation, missile guidance, and flight control equipment as well as telephone, teletype, and data processing equipment. Many of these skills are directly transferable to jobs in the civilian sector.

Communications and intelligence specialists in the military have civilian scientific and engineering counterparts. Officers serve as intelligence gatherers and interpreters, cryptologists, information analysts, translators, science and engineering researchers, and in related intelligence occupations. Enlisted personnel work as computer programmers, air traffic controllers, interpreters and translators, and radio, radar, and sonar operators.

Military *medical and dental occupations* all have civilian counterparts. Holding the rank of medical officer are physicians, dentists, optometrists, nurses, therapists, veterinarians, pharmacists, and others in health diagnosing and treating occupations. Enlisted personnel are trained to work as medical laboratory technologists and technicians, radiologic technologists, emergency medical technicians, dental assistants, optical assistants, pharmaceutical assistants, sanitation specialists, and veterinary assistants. Health professions training obtained in the military is usually recognized in the civilian sector; service-trained health professionals are eligible to apply for certification or registration, a hiring prerequisite in many civilian health settings.

Military experience in *other technical and allied specialty occupations* is often directly transferable to civilian life. Officers in this field work as meteorologists, mapping directors, television and motion picture directors, and band directors. Enlisted personnel are trained to work as photographers, motion picture camera operators, mapping and surveying specialists, illustrators, weather data collectors, explosives disposal specialists, divers, and musicians.

Functional support and administrative occupations in military service require the same skills as similar jobs in private businesses and government agencies. Officers in this category work as directors, executives, adjutants, administrative officers, personnel managers, training administrators, budget officers, finance officers, public affairs officers, accountants, hospital administrators, inspectors, computer systems managers, and lawyers. Enlisted personnel in this category work as accounting clerks, payroll clerks, personnel clerks, computer programmers, computer operators, chaplain assistants, counseling aides, typists, stenographers, storekeepers, and other clerks.

Those in *electrical and mechanical equipment repair occupations* maintain aircraft, motor vehicles, and ships. Officers manage the maintenance of aircraft, missiles, conventional and nuclear-powered ships, trucks, earth-moving equipment, and other vehicles. Enlisted personnel serve as mechanics, engine specialists, and boiler technicians. They also install and maintain wire communications systems such as telephones. Skills obtained in these jobs are readily transferable to those in the civilian sector.

Military forces train and work to be prepared in all climates, weather conditions, and settings.

Military personnel assigned to *craft occupations* are skilled craft workers. Officers serve as civil engineers and architects and manage the work of enlisted personnel who work as carpenters, construction equipment operators, metalworkers, machinists, plumbers, welders, electricians, and heating and air-conditioning specialists.

Military personnel in *service and supply occupations* handle food service, security, and personal services and supply. Officers work as logistics officers, supply managers, transportation and traffic managers, and procurement officers. Enlisted personnel include military police, correction specialists, detectives, firefighters, and food preparation and other service workers. They operate transportation equipment such as trucks, ships, boats, airplanes, and helicopters, and act as quartermasters, supply specialists, and cargo specialists. Many of these skills can be transferred to civilian occupations.

Working Conditions

Military life is much more regimented than civilian life, and one must be willing to accept the discipline. It is important to remember that by signing an enlistment contract, you sign a legal document that obligates you to serve for a specified period of time.

Dress and grooming requirements are stringent, and rigid formalities govern many aspects of everyday life. For instance, officers and enlisted personnel do not socialize together, and superior commissioned officers are saluted and addressed as "sir" or "ma'am." These and other rules encourage respect for superiors whose commands must be obeyed immediately and without question.

The needs of the military always come first. As a result, hours and working conditions can vary substantially. However, most military personnel usually work 8 hours a day, 5 days a week. Some assignments require night and weekend work, or require people to be on call at all hours. All may require substantial travel. Many require long periods at sea, sometimes in cramped quarters, or lengthy overseas assignments in countries offering few amenities. Some jobs are in isolated areas subject to extreme cold or heat. Others, such as carrier flight deck duty, are hazardous even in noncombat situations.

During times of conflict, many are in combat, and may find themselves in life or death situations. Countless hours of training produce teamwork that is highly critical to the success or failure of an operation, and possibly to the lives of individuals in the unit. Also, rapidly advancing military technology has made warfare more precise and lethal, further increasing the need for teamwork. Noncombatants may also face danger if their duties bring them close to the combat zone. They may also participate in dangerous training activities.

Military officers and enlisted personnel in all branches are paid according to the same pay scales and receive the same basic benefits.

Those aboard ship, on air crews, and others travel regularly, while others in the military are stationed at bases throughout the country or overseas. Military personnel usually are transferred to a new duty station every few years.

Military personnel enjoy more job security than their civilian counterparts. Satisfactory job performance generally assures one of steady employment and earnings.

Employment

In 1995, about 1.6 million persons were on active duty in the Armed Forces—about 523,000 in the Army; 405,000 in the Air Force; 442,000 in the Navy; 172,000 in the Marine Corps; and 34,000 in the Coast Guard. About one in eight of those on active duty were women.

Military personnel are stationed throughout the United States and in many countries around the world. California, Texas, North Carolina, and Virginia accounted for more than 1 in 3 military jobs. About 287,000 were stationed outside the United States in 1994. Over 142,000 of these were stationed in Europe (mainly in Germany); large numbers also were in the Western Pacific area.

Table 1 shows the occupational composition of enlisted personnel in 1995. Nearly 4 out of 10 held jobs that involved communications, electronic, mechanical, or related equipment, a reflection of the highly technical nature of the fighting forces today. Table 2 shows the occupational composition of officer personnel in 1995. Officers—who accounted for about 16 percent of all military personnel—are concentrated in combat activities, where they serve as ships' officers, aircraft pilots and crew members, and infantry or artillery officers. Officers also serve in engineering and maintenance, and medical and dental positions.

Qualifications, Training, and Advancement

General enlistment qualifications. As it has since 1973, the military expects to continue to meet its personnel requirements through volunteers. Enlisted members must enter a legal agreement called an enlistment contract, which usually involves a commitment to 8 years of service. Depending on the terms of the contract, 2 to 6 years are spent on active duty, the balance in the reserves. The enlistment contract obligates the service to provide the agreed-upon options— job, rating, pay, cash bonuses for enlistment in certain occupations, medical and other benefits, occupational training, and continuing education. In return, enlisted persons must serve satisfactorily for the specified period of time.

Requirements for each service vary, but certain qualifications for enlistment are common to all branches. Enlistees must be between the ages of 17 and 35, must be a U.S. citizen or immigrant alien holding permanent resident status, must not have a felony record, and must possess a birth certificate. Applicants who are 17 must have the consent of a parent or legal guardian before entering the service. Air Force enlisted personnel must enter active duty before their 28th birthday. Applicants must pass both a written examination—the Armed Services Vocational Aptitude Battery—and meet certain minimum physical standards such as height, weight, vision, and overall health. All branches prefer high school graduation or its equivalent and require it for certain enlistment options. In 1995, 95 percent of enlistees were high school graduates. Single parents are generally not eligible to enlist.

People thinking about enlisting in the military should learn as much as they can about military life before making a decision. This is especially important if you are thinking about making the military a career. Speaking to friends and relatives with military experience is a good idea. Determine what the military can offer you and what it will expect in return. Then talk to a recruiter, who can determine if you qualify for enlistment; explain the various enlistment options; and tell you which military occupational specialties currently have openings for trainees. Bear in mind that the recruiter's job is to recruit promising applicants into the military, so the information he or she gives you is likely to stress the positive aspects of military life.

Table 1. Military enlisted personnel by broad occupational category and branch of military service, 1995

Occupational Group	Total	Army	Navy	Marine Corps	Air Force
Total	1,300,937	439,471	381,241	153,841	326,384
Infantry, gun crews, and seamanship specialists	221,353	124,590	37,273	38,237	21,253
Electronic equipment repairers	127,110	25,177	56,765	9,119	36,049
Communications and intelligence specialists	119,392	45,543	39,158	12,150	22,541
Health care specialists	87,562	33,943	30,086	([1])	23,533
Other technical and allied specialists	32,685	12,799	4,121	3,609	12,156
Functional support and administration	212,637	75,035	39,947	25,361	72,294
Electrical/mechanical equipment repairers	258,114	60,608	97,884	23,008	76,614
Craftworkers	53,503	8,444	25,149	4,167	15,743
Service and supply handlers	116,900	49,313	20,133	21,183	26,271
Nonoccupational	68,974	1,369	30,703	16,992	19,910

[1]The Marine Corps employ no medical personnel. Their medical services are provided by the Navy.

SOURCE: U.S. Department of Defense

Table 2. Military officer personnel by broad occupational category and branch of service, 1995

Occupational Group	Total	Army	Navy	Marine Corps	Air Force
Total	240,986	83,930	60,325	17,825	78,905
General officers and executives	2,019	328	226	684[1]	781[3]
Tactical operations officers	93,263	33,623	23,007	8,697	27,936
Intelligence officers	12,580	5,987	2,251	716	3,626
Engineering and maintenance officers	31,814	9,755	7,543	1,752	12,763
Scientists and professionals	11,380	2,919	2,377	466	5,618
Medical officers	41,708	16,184	11,602	([2])	13,922
Administrators	16,264	5,070	3,150	1,588	6,456
Supply, procurement, and allied officers	20,441	8,038	3,597	2,078	6,728
Nonoccupational	9,433	137	6,517	1,735	1,044

[1]The Marine Corps includes colonels as general officers. There were 68 generals in the Marine Corps in 1995.
[2]The Marine Corps employ no medical personnel. Their medical services are provided by the Navy.
[3]There were 274 general officers and 507 executives, not elsewhere classified, in the Air Force in 1995.

SOURCE: U.S. Department of Defense

Ask the recruiter to assess your chances of being accepted for training in the occupation or occupations of your choice, or, better still, take the aptitude exam to see how well you score. The military uses the aptitude exam as a placement exam, and test scores largely determine an individual's chances of being accepted into a particular training program. Selection for a particular type of training depends on the needs of the service, general and technical aptitudes, and personal preference. Because all prospective recruits are required to take the exam, those who do so before committing themselves to enlist have the advantage of knowing in advance whether they stand a good chance of being accepted for training in a particular specialty. The recruiter can schedule you for the Armed Services Vocational Aptitude Battery without any obligation. Many high schools offer the exam as an easy way for students to explore the possibility of a military career.

Enlistment contract. If you decide to join the military, the next step is to pass the physical examination and then enter into the enlistment contract. This involves choosing, qualifying, and agreeing on a number of enlistment options such as length of active duty time, which may vary according to the enlistment option. (Most active duty programs have enlistment options ranging from 3 to 6 years, although there are some 2-year programs.) The contract will also list the date of enlistment and other options such as bonuses and types of training to be received. If the service is unable to fulfill its part of the contract (such as providing a certain kind of training) the contract may become null and void.

All services offer a "delayed entry program" by which an enlistee can delay entry into active duty for up to 1 year. High school students can enlist during their senior year and enter a service after graduation. Other enlistees choose this program because the job training they desire is not currently available but will be within the coming year, or because they need time to arrange personal affairs.

Women are eligible to enter almost all military specialties. Although many women serve in medical and administrative support positions, women also work as mechanics, missile maintenance technicians, heavy equipment operators, fighter pilots, and intelligence officers. Only some occupations involving a high probability of direct exposure to combat are excluded—for example, artilleryman and infantryman.

People planning to apply the skills gained through military training to a civilian career should look into several things before selecting their military occupation. First, they should determine how good the prospects are for civilian employment in jobs related to the military specialty which interests them. Second, they should know

Many occupations in the military have training applicable to civilian jobs.

The Coast Guard works to defend the Nation's shorelines from attack, smuggling, and illegal immigration.

the prerequisites for the related civilian job. Many occupations require a license, certification, or a minimum level of education. In such cases, it is important to determine whether military training is sufficient to enter the civilian equivalent or, if not, what additional training will be required.

Other *Handbook* statements discuss the job outlook for civilian occupations for which military training is helpful. Additional information often can be obtained from schools, unions, trade associations, and other organizations in the field of interest, or from a school counselor.

Training programs for enlisted personnel. Following enlistment, new members of the Armed Forces undergo recruit training. Better known as "basic" training, recruit training provides a 6- to 11-week introduction to military life with courses in health, first aid, and military skills and protocol. Days and nights are carefully structured and include rigorous physical exercises designed to improve strength and endurance.

Following basic training, most recruits take additional training at technical schools that prepare them for a particular military occupational specialty. The formal training period generally lasts from 10 to 20 weeks, although training for certain occupations—nuclear power plant operator is an example—may take as much as 1 year. Recruits not assigned to classroom instruction receive on-the-job training at their first duty assignment.

In addition to on-duty training, military personnel may choose from a variety of educational programs. Most military installations have tuition assistance programs for people wishing to take courses during off-duty hours. These may be correspondence courses or degree programs offered by local colleges or universities. Also available are courses designed to help service personnel earn high school equivalency diplomas. Each service branch provides opportunities for full-time study to a limited number of exceptional applicants. Military personnel accepted into these highly competitive programs receive full pay, allowances, tuition, and related fees. In return, they must agree to serve an additional amount of time in the service. Other very selective programs enable enlisted personnel to qualify as commissioned officers through additional military training.

Officer training. Officer training in the Armed Forces is provided through the Federal service academies (Military, Naval, Air Force, and Coast Guard); the Reserve Officers Training Corps (ROTC); Officer Candidate School (OCS); the National Guard (State Officer Candidate School programs); the Uniformed Services University of Health Sciences; and other programs. All are very selective and are good options for those wishing to make the military a career.

Federal service academies provide a 4-year college program leading to a bachelor of science degree. The midshipman or cadet is provided free room and board, tuition, medical care, and a monthly allowance. Graduates receive regular commissions and have a 5-year active duty obligation, or longer if entering flight training.

To become a candidate for appointment as a cadet or midshipman in one of the service academies, most applicants obtain a nomination from an authorized source (usually a Member of Congress). Candidates do not need to know a Member of Congress personally to request a nomination. Nominees must have an academic record of the requisite quality, college aptitude test scores above an established minimum, and recommendations from teachers or school officials; they also must pass a medical examination. Appointments are made from the list of eligible nominees.

Appointments to the Coast Guard Academy are made strictly on a competitive basis. A nomination is not required.

ROTC programs train students in about 950 Army, 60 Navy and Marine Corps, and 550 Air Force units at participating colleges and universities. Trainees take 2 to 5 hours of military instruction a week in addition to regular college courses. After graduation, they serve as officers on active duty for a stipulated period of time. In the last 2 years of an ROTC program, students receive a monthly allowance while attending school and additional pay for summer training. ROTC scholarships for 2, 3, and 4 years are available on a competitive basis. All scholarships pay for tuition and have allowances for subsistence, textbooks, supplies, and other fees.

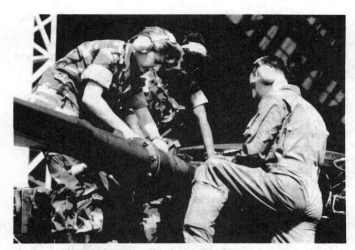

Most military occupations are open to women.

College graduates can earn a commission in the Armed Forces through OCS programs in the Army, Navy, Air Force, Marine Corps, Coast Guard, and National Guard.

Persons with training in certain health professions may qualify for direct appointment as officers. In the case of health professions students, financial assistance and internship opportunities are available from the military in return for specified periods of military service. Prospective medical students can apply to the Uniformed Services University of Health Sciences, which offers free tuition in a program leading to an M.D. degree. In return, graduates must serve for 7 years in either the military or the Public Health Service. Direct appointments also are available for those qualified to serve in other special duties, such as the judge advocate general (legal) or chaplain corps.

Flight training is available to commissioned officers in each branch of the Armed Forces. In addition, the Army has a direct enlistment option to become a warrant officer aviator.

Advancement opportunities. Each service has different criteria for promoting personnel. Generally, the first few promotions for both enlisted and officer personnel come easily. Subsequent promotions are much more competitive. Criteria for promotion may include time in service and grade, job performance, a supervisor's recommendation, and written examinations. Although the Armed Forces is a large organization that will continue to promote many of its people, the military drawdown continues to reduce the number of promotion slots. People who are continually passed over for promotion are eventually encouraged to leave the military.

Job Outlook

America's strategic position is stronger than it has been in decades. Due primarily to the reduction in the threat from Eastern Europe and Russia, the Armed Forces enacted a personnel reduction plan that is now nearly completed. From 1994 to 1999, planned reductions are as follows: Army, 18,000; Navy, 9,000; Air Force, 25,000; the Marine Corps has no further planned reductions. After 1997, the number of active duty personnel is expected to remain constant. The Armed Forces' goal is to maintain a sufficient force to fight and win two major regional conflicts occurring at the same time. However, political events could cause these plans to change. This personnel reduction has caused a decrease in recruiting levels and a toughening of advancement standards. In addition, many career personnel have been given the option of a severance payment to leave the service before their planned retirement.

In spite of this personnel reduction, job opportunities should be good in all branches of the Armed Forces through the year 2005. Persons entering the Armed Forces in the late-1990s will finish their first enlistment after 2000, and by then the planned personnel reduction should be complete. About 190,000 enlisted personnel and 15,000 officers must be recruited each year to replace those who complete their enlistment or retire. Educational requirements will continue to rise as military jobs become more technical and complex; high school graduates and applicants with some college background will be sought to fill the ranks of enlisted personnel.

Earnings, Allowances, and Benefits

Starting salaries. Annual salaries by rank and years of service of military personnel are shown in table 3. Most enlisted personnel started as recruits at Grade E-1 in 1995; however, those with special skills or above-average education started as high as Grade E-3. Most

---

Table 3. Military basic pay by grade for active duty personnel with fewer than 2 years service at grade, 1995

Rank and title				Basic monthly pay
Army	**Navy**	**Air Force**	**Marine Corps**	
Commissioned officers:				
O-6 Colonel	Captain	Colonel	Colonel	$3,449.70
O-5 Lieutenant Colonel	Commander	Lieutenant Colonel	Lieutenant Colonel	2,759.10
O-4 Major	Lieutenant Commander	Major	Major	2,325.60
O-3 Captain	Lieutenant	Captain	Captain	2,161.20
O-2 1st Lieutenant	Lieutenant (JG)	1st Lieutenant	1st Lieutenant	1,884.60
O-1 2nd Lieutenant	Ensign	2nd Lieutenant	2nd Lieutenant	1,636.20
Warrant officers:				
W-2 Chief Warrant Officer	Chief Warrant Officer	Chief Warrant Officer	Chief Warrant Officer	1,752.90
W-1 Warrant Officer	Warrant Officer	Warrant Officer	Warrant Officer	1,460.10
Enlisted personnel:				
E-6 Staff Sergeant	Petty Officer 1st Class	Technical Sergeant	Staff Sergeant	1,290.30
E-5 Sergeant	Petty Officer 2nd Class	Staff Sergeant	Sergeant	1,132.20
E-4 Corporal	Petty Officer 3rd Class	Airman 1st Class	Corporal	1,056.00
E-3 Private First Class	Seaman	Airman 2nd Class	Lance Corporal	995.10
E-2 Private	Seaman Apprentice	Airman 3rd Class	Private 1st Class	957.60
E-1 Recruit	Seaman Recruit	Basic Airman	Private	854.40
E-1[1]				790.20

[1]Fewer than 4 months active duty.

SOURCE: U.S. Department of Defense

warrant officers started at Grade W-1 or W-2, depending upon their occupational and academic qualifications and the branch of service. Most commissioned officers started at Grade O-1; highly trained officers—for example, physicians, engineers, and scientists—started as high as Grade O-3 or 0-4.

Allowances. In addition to basic pay, military personnel receive free room and board (or a housing and subsistence allowance), medical and dental care, a military clothing allowance, military supermarket and department store shopping privileges, 30 days of paid vacation a year, and travel opportunities. Other allowances are paid for foreign duty, hazardous duty, submarine and flight duty, and employment as a medical officer.

Athletic and other recreational facilities—such as libraries, gymnasiums, tennis courts, golf courses, bowling centers, and movies—are available on many military installations.

Military personnel are eligible for retirement benefits after 20 years of service.

Annual earnings. In 1995, the average compensation of all military personnel—including basic pay and housing and subsistence allowances—was $29,300. Enlisted personnel averaged $25,400; warrant officers averaged $42,400; and commissioned officers averaged $52,800.

Veterans' benefits. The Veterans Administration (VA) provides numerous benefits to those who have served at least 2 years in the Armed Forces. Veterans are eligible for free care in VA hospitals for all service-connected disabilities regardless of time served; those with other medical problems are eligible for free VA care if they are unable to pay the cost of hospitalization elsewhere. Admission to a VA medical center depends on the availability of beds, however.

Veterans are also eligible for certain loans, including home loans. Veterans, regardless of health, can convert a military life insurance policy to an individual policy with any participating company in the veteran's State of residence. In addition, job counseling, testing, and placement services are available.

Veterans who participate in the New Montgomery GI Bill Program receive educational benefits. Under this program, Armed Forces personnel may elect to deduct from their pay up to $100 a month to put toward their future education. Depending on the length of enlistment, the Government will contribute up to $9,600, until the combined contributions reach a maximum of $10,800. In addition, each service may provide its own additional contributions to put toward future education. This sum becomes the service member's educational fund. Upon separation from active duty, the fund can be used to finance an education at any VA-approved institution. VA-approved schools include many vocational, correspondence, business, technical, and flight training schools; community and junior colleges; and colleges and universities.

Information on educational and other veterans' benefits is available from VA offices located throughout the country.

Sources of Additional Information

Each of the military services publishes handbooks, fact sheets, and pamphlets that describe entrance requirements, training and advancement opportunities, and other aspects of military careers. These publications are widely available at all recruiting stations, most State employment service offices, and in high schools, colleges, and public libraries.

Data for Occupations Not Studied in Detail

Employment in the approximately 250 occupations covered in detail in the main body of the *Handbook* accounts for about 110 million or 87 percent of all jobs in the economy. Although occupations covering the full spectrum of work are included, those requiring lengthy education or training are generally given the most attention.

This chapter presents summary data on 79 additional occupations, for which employment projections are prepared, but for which detailed occupational information is not developed. These occupations account for about 5 percent of all jobs. For each occupation, a brief description of the nature of work, the number of jobs in 1994, a phrase describing the projected employment change from 1994 to 2005, and the most significant source of training are presented. For guidelines to interpreting the description of projected employment change, refer to an earlier chapter, Occupational Information Included in the *Handbook*.

The approximately 8 percent of all jobs not covered either in the detailed occupational descriptions in the main body of the *Handbook* or in the summary data presented in this chapter are mainly residual categories, such as "all other management support workers," for which little meaningful information could be developed.

Executive, Administrative, and Managerial Occupations

Communications, transportation, and utilities operations managers

Plan, organize, direct, control, or coordinate management activities related to: Communications by telephone, telegraph, radio, or television; transporting people or goods by air, highway, railway, water, or pipeline; transportation facilities, such as airports, harbors, or terminals; warehouse and storage facilities; and electricity, gas, water, steam, or sanitation services.

1994 employment: 154,000
Projected 1994-2005 employment change: A decline
Most significant source of training: Work experience plus bachelor's degree

Credit analysts

Analyze current data and financial statements of individuals or firms to determine the degree of risk involved in extending credit or lending money. Prepare reports with this credit information for use in making decisions.

1994 employment: 39,000
Projected 1994-2005 employment change: Faster than average
Most significant source of training: Bachelor's degree

Tax examiners, collectors, and revenue agents

Determine tax liability or collect taxes from individuals or business firms according to prescribed laws and regulations.

1994 employment: 63,000
Projected 1994-2005 employment change: Little change
Most significant source of training: Bachelor's degree

Professional Specialty Occupations

Athletes, coaches, umpires, and referees

Participate in competitive professional athletic events as a player, coach, manager, umpire, or judge.

1994 employment: 38,000
Projected 1994-2005 employment change: About as fast as average
Most significant source of training: More than 12 months of on-the-job training

Directors, religious activities and education

Direct and coordinate activities of a denominational group to meet religious needs of students. Plan, organize, and direct religious school programs designed to promote religious education. Provide counseling and guidance on marital, health, financial, and religious problems.

1994 employment: 81,000
Projected 1994-2005 employment change: About as fast as average
Most significant source of training: Bachelor's degree

Farm and home management advisors

Advise, instruct, and assist individuals and families engaged in agriculture and related processes or home economics activities. Apply research findings and procedures to solve problems and provide instruction and training in the development of products, sales, and the use of machinery and equipment.

1994 employment: 14,000
Projected 1994-2005 employment change: A decline
Most significant source of training: Bachelor's degree

Instructors and coaches, sports and physical training

Instruct or coach groups in the fundamentals of sports, and demonstrate techniques and methods of participation. Observe and inform participants of corrective measures to improve their skills. Includes those who are not required to hold teaching degrees.

1994 employment: 283,000
Projected 1994-2005 employment change: Faster than average
Most significant source of training: 1 to 12 months of on-the-job training

Residential counselors

Coordinate activities for residents of care and treatment institutions, boarding schools, college fraternities or sororities, children's homes, or similar establishments. Work includes developing or assisting in the development of program plans for individuals, maintaining household records, and assigning rooms. Counsel residents in identifying and resolving social or other problems. Order supplies and determine need for maintenance, repairs, and furnishings.

1994 employment: 266,000
Projected 1994-2005 employment change: About as fast as average
Most significant source of training: Bachelor's degree

Technicians and Related Support Occupations

Pharmacy technicians

Fill orders for unit doses and prepackaged pharmaceuticals and perform other related duties under the supervision and direction of a pharmacy supervisor or staff pharmacist. Duties include keeping records of drugs delivered to the pharmacy, storing incoming merchandise in proper locations, and informing supervisor or stock needs and shortages. May clean equipment used in the performance of duties and assist in the care and maintenance of equipment and supplies.

1994 employment: 81,000
Projected 1994-2005 employment change: Faster than average
Most significant source of training: Associate degree

Psychiatric technicians

Provide nursing care to mentally ill, emotionally disturbed, or mentally retarded patients, and participate in rehabilitation and treatment programs. Help with personal hygiene. Administer oral medications and hypodermic injections, following physician's prescriptions and hospital procedures. Monitor patients and their emotional well-being and report to medical staff.

1994 employment: 72,000
Projected 1994-2005 employment change: About as fast as average
Most significant source of training: Associate degree

Title examiners and searchers

Title examiners: Search public records and examine titles to determine legal status of property titles. Copy or summarize (abstract) recorded documents, such as mortgages, trust deeds, and contracts, affecting title to property. May prepare and issue policy that guarantees legality of title. *Abstractors*: Summarize pertinent legal or insurance details, or sections of statutes or case law from reference books for examination, proof, or ready reference. Search out titles to determine if title deed is correct. *Searchers*: Compile lists of mortgages, deeds, contracts, judgments, and other instruments pertaining to titles by searching public and private records for real estate or title insurance company.

1994 employment: 28,000
Projected 1994-2005 employment change: Little change
Most significant source of training: 1 to 12 months of on-the-job training

Veterinary technicians and technologists

Perform medical tests in a laboratory environment for use in the treatment and diagnosis of diseases in animals. Prepare vaccines and serums for prevention of diseases. Prepare tissue samples, take blood samples, and execute laboratory tests such as urinalysis and blood counts. Clean and sterilize instruments and materials and maintain equipment and machines.

1994 employment: 22,000
Projected 1994-2005 employment change: About as fast as average
Most significant source of training: Associate degree

Administrative Support Occupations, Including Clerical

Court clerks

Perform clerical duties in courts of law; prepare docket of cases to be called; secure information for judges; and contact witnesses, attorneys, and litigants to obtain information for court.

1994 employment: 51,000
Projected 1994-2005 employment change: About as fast as average
Most significant source of training: Up to 1 month of on-the-job training

Customer service representatives, utilities

Interview applicants for water, gas, electric, or telephone service. Talk with customers by phone or in person and receive orders for installation, turn-on, discontinuance, or change in service.

1994 employment: 151,000
Projected 1994-2005 employment change: About as fast as average
Most significant source of training: Up to 1 month of on-the-job training

Duplicating, mail, and other office machine operators

Duplicating machine operators: Operate one or a variety of duplicating machines to make copies of printed and other information. *Mail machine operators*: Operate machines to emboss names, addresses, and other matter onto metal plates for use in addressing machines; to print names, addresses and other similar information onto items, such as envelopes, accounting forms, and advertising literature; to address, fold, stuff, seal, and stamp mail; and to open envelopes. *Transit clerks*: Sort, record, proof, and prepare transit items for mailing to or from out-of-city banks to insure correct routing and prompt collection.

1994 employment: 222,000
Projected 1994-2005 employment change: A decline
Most significant source of training: Up to 1 month of on-the-job training

Municipal clerks

Draft agendas for town or city councils, record minutes of council meetings, answer official correspondence, keep fiscal records and accounts, and prepare reports on civic needs.

1994 employment: 22,000
Projected 1994-2005 employment change: A decline
Most significant source of training: Up to 1 month of on-the-job training

Proofreaders and copy markers

Read transcript or proof of type setup to detect and mark for correction any grammatical, typographical, or compositional errors.

1994 employment: 26,000
Projected 1994-2005 employment change: A decline
Most significant source of training: Up to 1 month of on-the-job training

Real estate clerks

Perform duties concerned with rental, sale, and management of real estate, such as typing copies of listings, computing interest owed or penalty payments, holding collateral in escrow, and checking due notices on taxes and renewal dates of insurance and mortgage loans.

1994 employment: 24,000
Projected 1994-2005 employment change: Slower than average
Most significant source of training: Up to 1 month of on-the-job training

Statistical clerks

Compile and compute data according to statistical formulas for use in statistical studies. May also perform actuarial computations, using algebra and trigonometry, and compile charts and graphs for use by actuaries.

1994 employment: 75,000
Projected 1994-2005 employment change: A decline
Most significant source of training: 1 to 12 months of on-the-job training

Service Occupations

Ambulance drivers and attendants, except emergency medical technicians

Drive ambulance or assist ambulance driver in transporting sick, injured, or convalescent persons. Assist in lifting patients and rendering first aid. May be required to have Red Cross first-aid training certificate.

1994 employment: 18,000
Projected 1994-2005 employment change: About as fast as average
Most significant source of training: Up to 1 month of on-the-job training

Amusement and recreation attendants

Perform one or more of the following duties at amusement or recreation facilities: Schedule use of recreation facilities, allocate equipment to participants in sporting events or recreational pursuits, collect fees, set pins, prepare billiard tables, provide caddying and other services for golfers, or operate carnival rides and amusement concessions.

1994 employment: 267,000
Projected 1994-2005 employment change: Much faster than average
Most significant source of training: Up to 1 month of on-the-job training

Baggage porters and bellhops

Carry baggage for travelers at transportation terminals or for guests at hotels or similar establishments. Perform additional duties, such as assisting handicapped persons, running errands, delivering ice, and directing people to their desired destinations.

1994 employment: 35,000
Projected 1994-2005 employment change: Faster than average
Most significant source of training: Up to 1 month of on-the-job training

Crossing guards

Guide or control vehicular or pedestrian traffic at such places as street and railroad crossings and construction sites.

1994 employment: 58,000
Projected 1994-2005 employment change: Little change
Most significant source of training: Up to 1 month of on-the-job training

Pest controllers and assistants

Spray or release chemical solutions or toxic gases and set mechanical traps to kill pests and vermin, such as mice, termites, and roaches, that infest buildings and surrounding areas.

1994 employment: 56,000
Projected 1994-2005 employment change: Much faster than average
Most significant source of training: 1 to 12 months of on-the-job training

Pharmacy assistants

Mix pharmaceutical preparations under direction of pharmacist. Duties include issuing medicine, labeling and storing supplies, and cleaning equipment and work areas.

1994 employment: 52,000
Projected 1994-2005 employment change: Faster than average
Most significant source of training: 1 to 12 months of on-the-job training

Ushers, lobby attendants, and ticket takers

Assist patrons at entertainment events, such as sporting events and motion picture performances. May assist in finding seats, searching for lost articles, and locating rest rooms and telephones. Collect admission tickets and passes from patrons.

1994 employment: 59,000
Projected 1994-2005 employment change: Faster than average
Most significant source of training: Up to 1 month of on-the-job training

Agricultural, Forestry, Fishing, and Related Occupations

Animal breeders and trainers

Breeders: Breed livestock or pets for purposes such as riding, working, or show; and for products such as milk, wool, meat, and hair. They select and breed animals according to knowledge of the animals' genealogy, characteristics, and offspring. *Trainers*: Train animals for riding, harness, security, or obedience. Accustom animals to human voice and contact; condition animals to respond to oral, hand, spur, and rein commands. Train animals according to standards for show or competition. May train animals to carry pack loads or work as part of pack team.

1994 employment: 16,000
Projected 1994-2005 employment change: A decline
Most significant source of training: Bachelor's degree

Farm workers

Plant, cultivate, harvest, and store crops; tend livestock and poultry; operate and maintain farm machinery; and maintain structures. May haul livestock and produce to market or terminal shipping point.

1994 employment: 906,000
Projected 1994-2005 employment change: A decline
Most significant source of training: Up to 1 month of on-the-job training

Lawn service managers

Plan, organize, direct, control, or coordinate activities of workers engaged in pruning trees and shrubs, cultivating lawns, and applying pesticides and other chemicals according to service contract specifications. Work may involve reviewing contracts to ascertain service, machine, and work force requirements; answering inquiries from potential customers regarding methods, material, and price ranges; and preparing service estimates according to labor, material, and machine costs.

1994 employment: 36,000
Projected 1994-2005 employment change: Faster than average
Most significant source of training: Work experience

Nursery and greenhouse managers

Plan, organize, direct, control, or coordinate activities of workers engaged in propagating, cultivating, and harvesting horticultural specialties, such as trees, shrubs, flowers, mushrooms, and other plants. Work may involve training new employees in gardening techniques, inspecting facilities for signs of disrepair, and delegating repair duties to staff.

1994 employment: 19,000
Projected 1994-2005 employment change: Much faster than average
Most significant source of training: Work experience

Nursery workers

Plant, cultivate, harvest, and transplant trees, shrubs, or plants in nursery facilities.

1994 employment: 83,000
Projected 1994-2005 employment change: Faster than average
Most significant source of training: Up to 1 month of on-the-job training

Supervisors, farming, forestry, and agricultural-related occupations

Directly supervise and coordinate the activities of agricultural, forestry, fishing, and related workers. May supervise helpers assigned to these workers.

1994 employment: 85,000
Projected 1994-2005 employment change: Slower than average
Most significant source of training: Work experience

Veterinary assistants

Examine animals for veterinarian; prepare animals for surgery; perform post-operational medical treatment as needed; and give medications to animals. Usually works directly under veterinarian. Receive extensive training on the job and may also have some post-secondary education, such as trade school or junior college.

1994 employment: 31,000
Projected 1994-2005 employment change: About as fast as average
Most significant source of training: Associate degree

Construction Trades and Extractive Occupations

Highway maintenance workers

Maintain highways, municipal and rural roads, airport runways, and rights-of-way in safe condition by patching broken or eroded pavement or erecting and repairing guard rails, highway markers, and snow fences. May also clear brush or plant trees along rights-of-way.

1994 employment: 167,000
Projected 1994-2005 employment change: Slower than average
Most significant source of training: Up to 1 month of on-the-job training

Mining, quarrying, and tunneling occupations

Rock splitters, quarry: Separate blocks of rough dimension stone from quarry mass using jackhammer, wedges, and feathers. *Roof bolters*: Operate self-propelled machine to install roof support bolts in underground mines. *Mining machine operators*: Operate mining machines, such as self-propelled or truck-mounted drilling machines, continuous mining machines, channeling machines, and cutting machines to extract coal, metal and nonmetal ores, rock, stone, or sand from underground or surface excavation. *Continuous mining machine operators*: Operate self-propelled mining machine that rips coal from the face and loads it onto conveyors or into shuttle cars in a continuous operation. *Mine cutting and channeling machine operators*: Cut or channel along the face or seams of coal, quarry stone, or other mining surfaces to facilitate blasting, separating, or removing minerals or materials from mines or from the earth's surface.

1994 employment: 18,000
Projected 1994-2005 employment change: A decline
Most significant source of training: More than 12 months of on-the-job training

Paving, surfacing, and tamping equipment operators

Operate equipment used for applying concrete, asphalt, or other materials to roadbeds, parking lots, or airport runways and taxiways; or equipment used for tamping gravel, dirt, or other materials.

1994 employment: 73,000
Projected 1994-2005 employment change: Faster than average
Most significant source of training: 1 to 12 months of on-the-job training

Pipelayers and pipelaying fitters

Pipelayers: Lay glazed or unglazed clay, concrete, plastic, or cast-iron pipe for storm or sanitation sewers, drains, water mains, and oil or gas lines. May grade trenches or culverts, position pipe, or seal joints. *Pipelaying fitters*: Align pipeline section preparatory to welding. Signal tractor driver in placing pipeline sections in proper alignment and insert steel spacers.

1994 employment: 57,000
Projected 1994-2005 employment change: About as fast as average
Most significant source of training: 1 to 12 months of on-the-job training

Roustabouts

Assemble or repair oil field equipment using hand and power tools. Perform other tasks as needed.

1994 employment: 28,000
Projected 1994-2005 employment change: A decline
Most significant source of training: Up to 1 month of on-the-job training

Mechanics, Installers, and Repairers

Bicycle repairers

Repair and service bicycles using hand tools.

1994 employment: 40,000
Projected 1994-2005 employment change: About as fast as average
Most significant source of training: 1 to 12 months of on-the-job training

Camera and photographic equipment repairers

Repair and adjust cameras and photographic equipment, including motion picture cameras and equipment, using specialized tools and testing devices.

1994 employment: 11,000
Projected 1994-2005 employment change: Slower than average
Most significant source of training: 1 to 12 months of on-the-job training

Electric meter installers and repairers

Install electric meters on pole or customer's premises, test meters, make necessary repairs, and turn current on/off by connecting or disconnecting service drop.

1994 employment: 12,000
Projected 1994-2005 employment change: A decline
Most significant source of training: More than 12 months of on-the-job training

Electromedical and biomedical equipment repairers

Test, adjust, and repair electromedical equipment using hand tools and meters.

1994 employment: 9,500
Projected 1994-2005 employment change: About as fast as average
Most significant source of training: More than 12 months of on-the-job training

Locksmiths and safe repairers

Repair and open locks, make keys, change locks and safe combinations, and install and repair safes.

1994 employment: 20,000
Projected 1994-2005 employment change: About as fast as average
Most significant source of training: 1 to 12 months of on-the-job training

Precision instrument repairers

Install, test, repair, maintain, and adjust indicating, recording, telemetering, and controlling instruments used to measure and control variables such as pressure, flow, temperature, motion, force, and chemical composition.

1994 employment: 40,000
Projected 1994-2005 employment change: Little change
Most significant source of training: More than 12 months of on-the-job training

Riggers

Set up or repair rigging for ships and shipyards, manufacturing plants, logging yards, construction projects, and for the entertainment industry—for example, motion picture production. Select cables, ropes, pulleys, winches, blocks, and sheaves according to weight and size of load to be moved. Coordinate and direct other workers and the movement of equipment to accomplish the task.

1994 employment: 11,000
Projected 1994-2005 employment change: A decline
Most significant source of training: More than 12 months of on-the-job training

Tire repairers and changers

Repair and replace tires, tubes, treads, and related products on automobiles, buses, trucks, and other vehicles. Mount tires on wheels, balance tires and wheels, and test and repair damaged tires and inner tubes.

1994 employment: 89,000
Projected 1994-2005 employment change: Slower than average
Most significant source of training: Up to 1 month of on-the-job training

Watchmakers

Repair, clean, and adjust mechanisms of instruments such as watches, time clocks, and timing switches using hand tools and measuring instruments.

1994 employment: 6,100
Projected 1994-2005 employment change: A decline
Most significant source of training: More than 12 months of on-the-job training

Production Occupations

Bakers, manufacturing

Mix and bake ingredients according to recipes to produce breads, pastries, and other baked goods. Goods are produced in large quantities for sale through establishments such as grocery stores. Generally, high-volume production equipment is used.

1994 employment: 36,000
Projected 1994-2005 employment change: About as fast as average
Most significant source of training: 1 to 12 months of on-the-job training

Boiler operators and tenders, low pressure

Operate or tend low-pressure stationary steam boilers and auxiliary steam equipment, such as pumps, compressors, and air-conditioning equipment, to supply steam heat for office buildings, apartment houses, or industrial establishments; to maintain steam at specified pressure aboard marine vessels; or to generate and supply compressed air for operation of pneumatic tools, hoists, and air lances.

1994 employment: 18,000
Projected 1994-2005 employment change: A decline
Most significant source of training: 1 to 12 months of on-the-job training

Cannery workers

Perform a variety of routine tasks in canning, freezing, preserving, or packing food products. May sort, grade, wash, peel, trim, or slice agricultural produce.

1994 employment: 73,000
Projected 1994-2005 employment change: About as fast as average
Most significant source of training: Up to 1 month of on-the-job training

Cementing and gluing machine operators and tenders

Operate or tend cementing and gluing machines to join together items, such as veneer sheets and plywood; paper and glass wool, cardboard, or paper; rubber and rubberized fabric parts; plastic; and simulated leather or other materials, to form completed product or to form product for further processing.

1994 employment: 36,000
Projected 1994-2005 employment change: A decline
Most significant source of training: 1 to 12 months of on-the-job training

Chemical equipment controllers, operators, and tenders

Controllers and operators: Control or operate equipment to control chemical changes or reactions in the processing of industrial or consumer products. Common types of equipment are reaction kettles, catalytic converters, continuous or batch treating equipment, saturator tanks, electrolytic cells, reactor vessels, recovery units, and fermentation chambers. *Tenders*: Tend equipment in which a chemical change or reaction takes place to process chemical substances into industrial or consumer products. Common types of equipment are devulcanizers, batch stills, fermenting tanks, steam-jacketed kettles, and reactor vessels.

1994 employment: 75,000
Projected 1994-2005 employment change: A decline
Most significant source of training: 1 to 12 months of on-the-job training

Chemical plant and system operators

Control and operate an entire chemical process or system of machines, such as reduction pots and heated air towers, using panel boards, control boards, or semiautomatic equipment.

1994 employment: 37,000
Projected 1994-2005 employment change: A decline
Most significant source of training: More than 12 months of on-the-job training

Coil winders, tapers, and finishers

Using coil winding machines, wind wire coils used in the manufacturing of electrical components, such as resistors and transformers, and electrical equipment, such as field cores, bobbins, and armature cores; and using coil making machines, form coils for electrical motors, generators, and control equipment.

1994 employment: 21,000
Projected 1994-2005 employment change: A decline
Most significant source of training: Up to 1 month of on-the-job training

Cooking and roasting machine operators and tenders

Cooking machine operators and tenders: Operate or tend cooking equipment, such as steam cooking vats, deep fry cookers, pressure cookers, kettles, and boilers, to prepare food products, such as meats, sugar, cheese, and grain. *Roasting, baking, and drying machine operators and tenders*: Operate or tend roasting, baking, or drying equipment, such as hearth ovens, kiln dryers, roasters, char kilns, steam ovens, and vacuum drying equipment, to reduce moisture content of food or tobacco products such as tobacco, cocoa and coffee beans, macaroni, and grain; to roast grain, nuts, or coffee beans; to bake bread or other bakery products; or to process food preparatory to canning.

1994 employment: 28,000
Projected 1994-2005 employment change: Slower than average
Most significant source of training: 1 to 12 months of on-the-job training

Crushing and mixing machine operators and tenders

Crushing, grinding, and polishing machine operators and tenders: Operate or tend machines to crush or grind materials such as coal, glass, plastic, dried fruit, grain, stone, chemicals, food, or rubber; or operate or tend machines to buff and polish materials such as stone, glass, slate, plastic or metal trim, bowling balls, or eyeglasses. *Mixing and blending machine operators and tenders*: Operate or tend machines to mix or blend materials such as spices, dough batter, tobacco, fruit juices, chemicals, livestock feed, food products, color pigments, or explosive ingredients.

1994 employment: 137,000
Projected 1994-2005 employment change: A decline
Most significant source of training: 1 to 12 months of on-the-job training

Cutting and slicing machine setters, operators, and tenders

Operators and tenders: Operate or tend machines to cut or slice materials such as tobacco, food, paper, roofing slate, glass, stone rubber, cork, and insulating material. *Setters and setup operators*: Set up and operate machines to cut or slice materials such as glass, stone, cork, rubber, crepe, wallboard, and fibrous insulating board, to specified dimensions for further processing.

1994 employment: 92,000
Projected 1994-2005 employment change: About as fast as average
Most significant source of training: 1 to 12 months of on-the-job training

Dairy processing equipment operators, including setters

Set up, operate, or tend continuous flow or vat-type equipment to process milk, cream, or other dairy products following specified methods and formulas.

1994 employment: 14,000
Projected 1994-2005 employment change: A decline
Most significant source of training: 1 to 12 months of on-the-job training

Electrical and electronic assemblers

Perform work at a level less than that required of the precision level. Includes occupations such as electronic wirers, armature connectors, electric motor winders, skein winders, carbon brush assemblers, battery parts assemblers, electric sign assemblers, and electronic assemblers.

1994 employment: 212,000
Projected 1994-2005 employment change: A decline
Most significant source of training: Up to 1 month of on-the-job training

Electronic semiconductor processors

Process materials used in the manufacture of electronic semiconductors; load semiconductor material into furnace; saw formed ingots into segments; load individual segment into crystal-growing chamber and monitor controls; locate crystal axis in ingot using x-ray equipment and saw ingots into wafers; clean, polish, and load wafers into series of special-purpose furnaces, chemical baths, and equipment used to form circuitry and change conductive properties. May scribe or separate wafer into dice.

1994 employment: 33,000
Projected 1994-2005 employment change: Little change
Most significant source of training: 1 to 12 months of on-the-job training

Extruding and forming machine setters, operators, and tenders

Operators and tenders: Operate or tend machines to shape and form manufactured products such as glass bulbs, molded food and candy, rubber goods, clay products, wax products, tobacco plugs, cosmetics, or paper products, by means of extruding, compressing, or compacting. *Setters and setup operators*: Set up and operate machines such as glass forming machines, plodder machines, and tuber machines, to manufacture products such as soap bars, formed rubber, glassware, soft candy, brick, and tile, by means of extruding, compressing, or compacting.

1994 employment: 102,000
Projected 1994-2005 employment change: Faster than average
Most significant source of training: 1 to 12 months of on-the-job training

Foundry mold assembly and shakeout workers

Prepare molds, such as cleaning and assembling foundry molds, for pouring. Assemble cores in fixture of automatic core-sorting machine, and bond cope and drags together to form completed shell mold.

1994 employment: 10,000
Projected 1994-2005 employment change: A decline
Most significant source of training: 1 to 12 months of on-the-job training

Furnace operators and tenders

Operate or tend furnaces, such as gas, oil, coal, electric-arc or electric induction, open-hearth, or oxygen furnaces, to melt and refine metal prior to casting or to produce specified types of steel.

1994 employment: 20,000
Projected 1994-2005 employment change: A decline
Most significant source of training: 1 to 12 months of on-the-job training

Furnace, kiln, or kettle operators and tenders

Operate or tend heating equipment other than basic metal or plastic processing equipment. *Furnace operators and tenders*: May anneal glass, roast sulfur, convert chemicals, or process petroleum. *Kiln operators and tenders*: May heat minerals, dry lumber, fire greenware, anneal glassware, or bake clay products. *Oven operators and tenders*: May bake fiberglass or painted products, fuse glass or enamel to metal products, carbonize coal, or cure rubber or other products. *Drier operators and tenders*: May remove moisture from paper, chemicals, ore, clay products, or slurry. *Kettle operators and tenders*: May melt antimony or asphalt materials, or boil soap.

1994 employment: 28,000
Projected 1994-2005 employment change: A decline
Most significant source of training: 1 to 12 months of on-the-job training

Gas and petroleum plant and systems occupations

Gaugers: Gauge and test oil in storage tanks and regulate flow of oil into pipelines at wells, tank farms, refineries, and marine and rail terminals following prescribed standards and regulations. *Petroleum refinery and control panel operators*: Analyze specifications or follow process schedules to operate and control panelboards and continuous petroleum refining and processing units. *Gas plant operators*: Distribute or process gas for utility companies and others. Distribute the gas for an entire plant or process, often using panel boards, control boards, or semiautomatic equipment. *Petroleum pump systems operators*: Operate and control manifold and pumping systems to circulate liquids through petroleum refinery.

1994 employment: 31,000
Projected 1994-2005 employment change: A decline
Most significant source of training: More than 12 months of on-the-job training

Grinders and polishers, hand

Perform work at a level less than that required of the precision level. Grind and polish a wide variety of metal, stone, clay, plastic, and glass objects or parts, using hand tools or hand-held power tools.

1994 employment: 74,000
Projected 1994-2005 employment change: A decline
Most significant source of training: Up to 1 month of on-the-job training

Laundry and drycleaning machine operators and tenders, except pressing

Operate and tend washing or drycleaning machines to clean or dryclean commercial, industrial, or household articles, such as suede, leather, and cloth garments, furs, blankets, draperies, fine linens, rugs, and carpets.

1994 employment: 175,000
Projected 1994-2005 employment change: About as fast as average
Most significant source of training: 1 to 12 months of on-the-job training

Machine assemblers

Perform work at a level less than that required of the precision level. Includes occupations such as air-conditioning coil assemblers, ball bearing ring assemblers, fuel injection assemblers, and subassemblers.

1994 employment: 51,000
Projected 1994-2005 employment change: Slower than average
Most significant source of training: Up to 1 month of on-the-job training

Motion picture projectionists

Set up and operate motion picture projection and sound-reproducing equipment to produce coordinated effects on screen.

1994 employment: 7,900
Projected 1994-2005 employment change: A decline
Most significant source of training: Up to 1 month of on-the-job training

Packaging and filling machine operators and tenders

Operate or tend machines, such as filling, casing-running, ham rolling, preservative filling, baling, wrapping, and stuffing machines, to prepare industrial or consumer products, such as gas cylinders, meat and other food products, tobacco, insulation, ammunition, stuffed toys and athletic equipment, and upholstered pads, as end products or for storage and shipment.

1994 employment: 329,000
Projected 1994-2005 employment change: Slower than average
Most significant source of training: 1 to 12 months of on-the-job training

Painting, coating, and decorating workers, hand

Paint, coat, and decorate, using handtools or hand-held power tools, a wide variety of manufactured items, such as furniture, glass and flatware, lamps, jewelry, books, or leather products.

1994 employment: 33,000
Projected 1994-2005 employment change: About as fast as average
Most significant source of training: 1 to 12 months of on-the-job training

Paper goods machine setters and setup operators

Set up and operate paper goods machines to convert, saw, corrugate, band, wrap, box, stitch, form, or seal paper or paperboard sheets into products such as toilet tissue, towels, napkins, bags, envelopes, tubing, cartons, wax rolls, and containers.

1994 employment: 51,000
Projected 1994-2005 employment change: A decline
Most significant source of training: 1 to 12 months of on-the-job training

Separating and still machine operators and tenders

Operate or tend machines, such as filter presses, shaker screens, centrifuges, condenser tubes, precipitator tanks, fermenting tanks, evaporating tanks, scrubbing towers, and batch stills, to extract, sort, or separate liquids, gases, or solid materials from other materials in order to recover a refined product or material.

1994 employment: 20,000
Projected 1994-2005 employment change: A decline
Most significant source of training: 1 to 12 months of on-the-job training

Shipfitters

Lay out and fabricate metal structural parts, such as plates, bulk heads, and frames, and brace them in position within hull or ship for riveting or welding. May prepare molds and templates for fabrication of nonstandard parts.

1994 employment: 12,000
Projected 1994-2005 employment change: A decline
Most significant source of training: More than 12 months of on-the-job training

Shoe sewing machine operators and tenders

Operate or tend single, double, or multiple-needle stitching machines to join or decorate shoe parts, reinforce shoe parts, or attach buckles.

1994 employment: 14,000
Projected 1994-2005 employment change: A decline
Most significant source of training: 1 to 12 months of on-the-job training

Solderers and brazers

Join together metal parts or components of metal products, and fill holes, indentations, and seams of fabricated metal products using hand soldering and brazing equipment as specified by job orders, work layouts, or blueprints.

1994 employment: 27,000
Projected 1994-2005 employment change: About as fast as average
Most significant source of training: Up to 1 month of on-the-job training

Soldering and brazing machine operators and setters

Operators and tenders: Operate or tend soldering and brazing machines to braze, solder, or spot-weld fabricated metal products or components as specified by job orders, work layouts, or blueprints. *Setters and setup operators*: Set up and operate soldering and brazing machines to bronze, solder, heat-treat, or spot-weld fabricated metal products or components as specified by job orders, work layouts, or blueprints.

1994 employment: 9,700
Projected 1994-2005 employment change: A decline
Most significant source of training: 1 to 12 months of on-the-job training

Tire building machine operators

Operate machines, such as collapsible drum devices, to build pneumatic tires from rubber components, such as beads, ply stock, tread, and sidewalls.

1994 employment: 14,000
Projected 1994-2005 employment change: A decline
Most significant source of training: 1 to 12 months of on-the-job training

Assumptions and Methods Used in Preparing Employment Projections

Occupational statements in the *Handbook* use one of five adjectives to describe projected change in employment. (See figure on page 20.) The adjectives are based on numerical projections developed using the Bureau's employment projections model system. The employment projections are the final output of the system, which also projects the size and composition of the labor force, the level of gross domestic product (GDP)—sales to all final consuming sectors in the economy—the total output of goods and services by industry, and employment by industry. A full description, including numerical projections of employment, appears in the November 1995 *Monthly Labor Review*, and in *Employment Outlook: 1994-2005*, BLS Bulletin 2472. The Fall 1995 *Occupational Outlook Quarterly* presents the projections in a series of charts.

The projections reflect the knowledge and judgment of staff in the Bureau's Office of Employment Projections, who prepared them, and of knowledgeable people from other offices in the Bureau, other government agencies, colleges and universities, industries, unions, professional societies, and trade associations, who furnished data and information, prepared reports, or reviewed the projections. The Bureau, of course, takes full responsibility for them.

Assumptions. Because the future course of the economy is uncertain, the Bureau prepares three scenarios of future economic growth—low, moderate, and high—with varying assumptions about growth of the labor force, output, productivity, inflation, and unemployment. The information in the *Handbook* is based on the moderate-growth scenario, which is characterized by slightly higher productivity growth than in the past, slowing labor force growth, a roughly constant unemployment rate, and a decreasing trade deficit. Other assumptions include real cuts in defense spending, a slight decline in consumer spending on automobiles, and an increase in consumer spending on durable goods such as computers and household electronics. Spending on food and beverages will grow more slowly than the average for all consumer expenditures, while spending on health care and other services, such as entertainment, recreation, and financial services, will grow faster. Investment in production equipment, including that for factory automation, communication, and computer items, will grow rapidly. Offsetting the expected slowdown in residential construction will be a relatively strong resumption of growth in nonresidential construction, leaving overall construction growing roughly as it did in the past.

While the Bureau considers these assumptions reasonable, the economy may well follow a different course, resulting in a different pattern of occupational growth. Growth also could be different from that projected here because most occupations are sensitive to a much wider variety of factors than those considered in the various models. Unforeseen changes in consumer, business, or government spending patterns and in the way goods and services are produced could greatly alter the growth of individual occupations.

Methods. This section summarizes the steps by which the Bureau arrives at projections of employment by occupation. BLS uses Bureau of the Census projections of the population by age, gender, and race, combined with projections of labor force participation rates, to arrive at estimates of the civilian labor force.

The projections of the labor force and assumptions about other demographic variables, fiscal policy, foreign economic activity, and energy prices and availability form the input to the macroeconomic model. This model provides a balanced and internally consistent representation of the U.S. economy. It projects GDP and the distribution of GDP by its major demand components—consumer expenditures, investment, government purchases, and net exports. These are broken down by detailed component, such as health or housing. The resulting estimates of demand for goods and services are used, in conjunction with detailed input-output tables, to project industry output of final products as well as of products required in the production process—total output by industry.

Industry output of goods and services is then converted to industry employment. Studies of trends in productivity and technology are used to estimate future output per worker hour, and regression analysis is used to estimate worker hours. These estimates, along with output projections, are used to develop the final industry employment projections.

An industry-occupation matrix is used to project employment for wage and salary workers. The matrix shows occupational staffing patterns—each occupation as a percent of the work force in every industry. It includes 260 detailed industries and 513 detailed occupations. Data for current staffing patterns in the matrix come primarily from the Bureau's Occupational Employment Statistics surveys, which collect data from employers on a 3-year cycle.

The occupational staffing patterns for each industry were projected based on anticipated changes in the way goods and services are produced, then applied to projected industry employment, and the resulting employment summed across industries to get total wage and salary employment by occupation. Using this method, employment is projected to grow faster than average in those occupations concentrated in fast-growing industries and more slowly in slow-growing industries. For example, health care workers are expected to grow rapidly, reflecting rapid growth of health care industries.

Employment in an occupation also may grow or decline as a result of many other factors. For example, rapid growth is expected among teacher aides and educational assistants as increasing attention to the quality of education leads schools to hire more support staff. Rapid growth is also expected among computer systems analysts as technology advances and organizations place more emphasis on network applications and maximizing the efficiency of their computer systems. On the other hand, automation, the expanding use of computers, and developments in computer software enhance productivity and will result in slower than average growth among many clerical workers, machine operators, and assemblers—thus lowering their proportion of the labor force. The projected-year matrix incorporates these expected changes.

Data on self-employed workers in each occupation come from the Current Population Survey. Self-employed workers were projected separately.

Replacement needs. In most occupations, replacement needs provide more job openings than growth. Replacement openings occur as people leave occupations. Some individuals transfer to other occupations as a step up the career ladder or to change careers. Some stop working temporarily, perhaps to return to school or care for a family. Other workers—retirees for example—leave the labor force permanently. A discussion of replacements, including separation rates for selected occupations, is presented in *Occupational Projections and Training Data*, 1996 Edition, BLS Bulletin 2471.

Dictionary of Occupational Titles Coverage

The *Dictionary of Occupational Titles (D.O.T.)* was designed to provide detailed standardized occupational information to facilitate public employment service activities involving classification and placement of jobseekers. Its coding structure also is used to help bridge or relate to other occupational classification systems used in the collection of employment data.

Columns 1 and 3 below list the numbers and titles, respectively, from the *D.O.T.*, Fourth Edition, Revised 1991. Column 4 gives the page of the *Handbook* on which the relevant occupational statement begins. Nearly all occupational statements in the *Handbook* list the *D.O.T.* codes that relate to or match the definitions used in the Bureau's Occupational Employment Statistics Survey—the major source of occupational staffing patterns used in the Occupational Outlook Program. However, the *D.O.T.* numbers associated with the following occupations are too numerous to list:

Apparel workers
Blue-collar worker supervisors
Clerical supervisors and managers
General managers and top executives
Handlers, equipment cleaners, helpers, and laborers
Industrial machinery repairers
Inspectors and compliance officers, except construction
Inspectors, testers, and graders
Manufacturers' and wholesale sales representatives
Material moving equipment operators
Material recording, scheduling, dispatching, and distributing
        occupations (except for dispatchers, stock clerks, and traffic,
        shipping, and receiving clerks)
Metalworking and plastics-working machine operators
Painting and coating machine operators
Precision assemblers
Prepress workers
Printing press operators
Retail sales workers
Science technicians
Textile machinery operators
Woodworking occupations

These, nevertheless, are available on request from the Chief, Division of Occupational Outlook, Bureau of Labor Statistics, U.S. Department of Labor, Washington, DC 20212.

Numbers in column 2 refer to the coding structure of the 1980 *Standard Occupational Classification Manual (S.O.C.)*. The *S.O.C.* is the basis for the occupational arrangement used in the National Industry-Occupation Employment Matrix—the *Handbook's* source of data on current and projected employment.

D.O.T. Number	SOC Code	D.O.T. Title	Page
007061030	1635	Tool-designer apprentice	82
007061034	1635	Utilization engineer	82
007061038	1635	Applications engineer, manufacturing	82
007061042	1635	Stress analyst	82
007161010	3720	Die designer	224
007161014	3720	Die-designer apprentice	224
007161018	3720	Engineering assistant, mechanical equipment	224
007161022	3713	Mechanical research engineer	82
007161026	3713	Mechanical-engineering technician	226
007161030	3713	Optomechanical technician	226
007161034	1635	Test engineer, mechanical equipment	82
007161038	1635	Solar-energy-systems designer	82
007167010	3713	Die-drawing checker	226
007167014	1635	Plant engineer	39
007167018	3974	Tool programmer, numerical control	410
007181010	3713	Heat-transfer technician	226
007261010	3720	Chief drafter	224
007261014	3720	Drafter, castings	224
007261018	3720	Drafter, patent	224
007261022	3720	Drafter, tool design	224
007267010	1635	Drawings checker, engineering	82
007267014	3713	Tool design checker	226
007281010	3720	Drafter, mechanical	224
008061010	1626	Absorption-and-adsorption engineer	80
008061014	1626	Chemical design engineer, processes	80
008061018	1626	Chemical engineer	80
008061022	1626	Chemical research engineer	80
008061026	1626	Chemical-test engineer	80
008167010	1626	Technical director, chemical plant	39
008261010	3719	Chemical-engineering technician	226
010061010	1624	Design engineer, mining-and-oil-field equipment	83
010061010	1624	Design engineer, mining-and-oil-field equipment	84
010061014	1624	Mining engineer	83
010061018	1625	Petroleum engineer	84
010061022	1624	Research engineer, mining-and-oil-well equipment	83
010061022	1624	Research engineer, mining-and-oil-well equipment	84
010061026	1624	Safety engineer, mines	83
010061030	1624	Test engineer, mining-and-oil-field equipment	83
010061030	1624	Test engineer, mining-and-oil-field equipment	84
010161010	1625	Chief engineer, research	39
010161014	1625	Chief petroleum engineer	39
010167010	1625	Chief engineer	84
010167014	1625	District supervisor, mud-analysis well logging	84
010167018	1260	Superintendent, oil-well services	39
010261010	3719	Field engineer, specialist	226
010261026	3719	Test-engine evaluator	226
010281010	3720	Drafter, directional survey	224
010281014	3720	Drafter, geological	224
010281018	3720	Drafter, geophysical	224
011061010	1623	Foundry metallurgist	82
011061014	1623	Metallographer	82
011061018	1623	Metallurgist, extractive	82
011061022	1623	Metallurgist, physical	82
011061026	1623	Welding engineer	82
011161010	1260	Supervisor, metallurgical-and-quality-control-testing	39
011261010	3719	Metallurgical technician	226
011261014	3719	Welding technician	226
011261018	3719	Nondestructive tester	226
011261022	3719	Laboratory assistant, metallurgical	226
011281014	3719	Spectroscopist	226
011361010	3719	Tester	226
012061018	1634	Standards engineer	81
012067010	1634	Metrologist	81
012167010	1634	Configuration management analyst	81
012167014	1634	Manager, quality control	81
012167018	1634	Factory lay-out engineer	81
012167030	1634	Industrial engineer	81
012167038	1634	Liaison engineer	81
012167042	1634	Manufacturing engineer	81
012167046	1634	Production engineer	81
012167050	1634	Production planner	81
012167054	1634	Quality control engineer	81
012167058	1634	Safety manager	39
012167062	7100	Supervisor, vendor quality	39
012167070	1634	Time-study engineer	81
012167074	1634	Tool planner	81
012167078	1634	Documentation engineer	81
012167082	1634	Material scheduler	81
012187014	1634	Shoe-lay-out planner	81
012261014	3712	Quality control technician	226
012267010	3712	Industrial engineering technician	226
013161010	3719	Agricultural-engineering technician	226
014281010	3720	Drafter, marine	224
015021010	1843	Health physicist	113
015061010	1627	Design engineer, nuclear equipment	84
015061014	1627	Nuclear engineer	84
015061018	1627	Research engineer, nuclear equipment	84
015061022	1627	Test engineer, nuclear equipment	84
015061026	1627	Nuclear-fuels reclamation engineer	84
015061030	1627	Nuclear-fuels research engineer	84
015067010	1627	Nuclear-criticality safety engineer	84
015137010	1627	Radiation-protection engineer	84
015167010	1627	Nuclear-plant technical advisor	84
015167014	1627	Nuclear-test-reactor program coordinator	84
017161010	3720	Drafter, chief, design	224
017261010	3713	Auto-design checker	226
017261014	3720	Design drafter, electromechanisms	224
017261018	3720	Detailer	224
017261022	3720	Detailer, furniture	224
017261026	3720	Drafter, commercial	224
017261030	3720	Drafter, detail	224
017261034	3720	Drafter, heating and ventilating	224
017261038	3720	Drafter, plumbing	224
017261042	3720	Drafter, automotive design	224
017281010	3720	Auto-design detailer	224
017281014	3720	Drafter apprentice	224
017281018	3720	Drafter, assistant	224
017281026	3720	Drafter, automotive design layout	224
017281030	3720	Drafter, oil and gas	224
017281034	3720	Technical illustrator	224
018131010	3734	Supervisor, cartography	89
018161010	1649	Surveyor, mine	89
018167010	3733	Chief of party	89
018167014	3739	Geodetic computator	89
018167018	1643	Land surveyor	89
018167022	1260	Manager, land surveying	39
018167026	1649	Photogrammetric engineer	89
018167030	3734	Supervisor, mapping	89
018167034	3733	Surveyor assistant, instruments	89
018167038	1649	Surveyor, geodetic	89
018167042	1649	Surveyor, geophysical prospecting	89
018167046	1649	Surveyor, marine	89
018261010	3734	Drafter, cartographic	89
018261014	3734	Editor, map	89
018261022	3734	Mosaicist	89
018261026	3739	Photogrammetrist	89
018262010	1644	Field-map editor	89
018281010	3734	Stereo-plotter operator	89
019061014	1623	Materials engineer	82
019161010	3720	Supervisor, estimator and drafter	224
019161014	3719	Test technician	226
019167014	1639	Project engineer	39
019167018	1628	Resource-recovery engineer	80
019261014	3720	Estimator and drafter	224
019261018	3890	Facilities planner	226
019261022	3890	Test technician	226
019261026	3710	Fire-protection engineering technician	226
019261034	3890	Laser technician	226
019267010	3719	Specification writer	226
019281010	3711	Calibration laboratory technician	226
020067014	1739	Mathematician	96
020067018	1721	Operations-research analyst	97
020067022	1733	Statistician, mathematical	99
020167010	1732	Actuary	91
020167026	1733	Statistician, applied	99
020167030	1739	Weight analyst	96
021067010	1842	Astronomer	113
022061010	1845	Chemist	107
022061014	1845	Chemist, food	107
022081010	3820	Toxicologist	103
022137010	1845	Laboratory supervisor	107
022161010	1845	Chemical laboratory chief	39
023061010	1843	Electro-optical engineer	113
023061014	1843	Physicist	113
023067010	1843	Physicist, theoretical	113
024061010	1847	Crystallographer	109
024061014	1649	Geodesist	89
024061018	1847	Geologist	109
024061022	1847	Geologist, petroleum	109
024061026	1847	Geophysical prospector	109
024061030	1847	Geophysicist	109

D.O.T. Number	SOC Code	D.O.T. Title	Page
197137010	8242	Dredge mate	458
197161010	8242	Dredge captain	458
197163010	8241	Ferryboat captain	458
197163014	8242	Master, passenger barge	458
197163018	8241	Master, riverboat	458
197167010	8241	Master, ship	458
198167010	8113	Conductor, passenger car	244
198167014	8113	Conductor, pullman	244
198167018	8113	Conductor, road freight	244
199167014	1920	Urban planner	126
199261010	3990	Parking analyst	226
199267014	1739	Cryptanalyst	96
199281010	3990	Gemologist	408
201162010	4622	Social secretary	287
201362010	4622	Legal secretary	287
201362014	4622	Medical secretary	287
201362018	4622	Membership secretary	287
201362022	4622	School secretary	287
201362026	4622	Script supervisor	287
201362030	4622	Secretary	287
202362010	4623	Shorthand reporter	289
202362014	4623	Stenographer	289
202362018	4623	Stenographer, print shop	289
202362022	4623	Stenotype operator	289
202382010	4623	Stenocaptioner	289
203362010	4624	Clerk-typist	294
203362014	4649	Credit reporting clerk	268
203362026	3290	Caption writer	184
203382014	4699	Cancellation clerk	254
203382018	4793	Magnetic-tape-composer operator	294
203382026	4793	Varitype operator	294
203382030	4624	Word processing machine operator	294
203582010	4793	Braille operator	294
203582014	4793	Braille typist	294
203582038	4793	Perforator typist	294
203582042	4793	Photocomposing-perforator-machine operator	294
203582046	4793	Photocomposition-keyboard operator	294
203582054	4793	Data entry clerk	294
203582058	4623	Transcribing-machine operator	289
203582062	4793	Typesetter-perforator operator	294
203582066	4624	Typist	294
203582078	4624	Notereader	294
205362010	4692	Civil-service clerk	287
205362014	4692	Employment clerk	287
205362018	4642	Hospital-admitting clerk	268
205362022	4692	Identification clerk	287
205362026	4642	Customer service representative	268
205362030	4642	Outpatient-admitting clerk	268
205367014	4642	Charge-account clerk	268
205367018	4782	Claims clerk II	254
205367022	4642	Credit clerk	263
205367026	4642	Creel clerk	268
205367034	4787	License clerk	254
205367038	4645	Registrar	268
205367042	4642	Registration clerk	268
205367046	4784	Rehabilitation clerk	254
205367054	4642	Survey worker	268
205367058	4642	Traffic checker	268
205367062	4692	Referral clerk, temporary help agency	287
205567010	4692	Benefits clerk II	287
206367014	4696	File clerk II	283
206367018	4696	Tape librarian	283
206387010	4696	Classification clerk	283
206387014	4696	Fingerprint clerk II	283
206387022	4696	Record clerk	283
206387034	4696	File clerk I	283
208382010	4793	Terminal-makeup operator	294
209362010	4783	Credit reference clerk	263
209362026	4692	Personnel clerk	287
209362030	4630	Congressional-district aide	264
209367042	4753	Reconsignment clerk	276
209382010	4624	Continuity clerk	294
209382014	4799	Special-certificate dictator	254
209387018	4664	Contact clerk	285
209387026	4694	Library clerk, talking books	284
209562010	4630	Clerk, general	264
209567014	4364	Order clerk, food and beverage	234
209587018	4744	Direct-mail clerk	270
209687010	4792	Checker II	282
209687014	4742	Mail handler	277
209687018	4699	Reviewer	254

D.O.T. Number	SOC Code	D.O.T. Title	Page
209687026	4744	Mail clerk	270
210362010	4712	Distribution-accounting clerk	282
210367010	4712	Account-information clerk	282
210367014	4712	Foreign-exchange-position clerk	282
210382010	4712	Audit clerk	282
210382014	4712	Bookkeeper	282
210382030	4712	Classification-control clerk	282
210382038	4712	Credit-card clerk	282
210382042	4712	Fixed-capital clerk	282
210382046	4712	General-ledger bookkeeper	282
210382050	4712	Mortgage-loan-computation clerk	282
210382054	4712	Night auditor	282
210382062	4712	Securities clerk	282
211362010	4364	Cashier I	234
211362014	4791	Foreign banknote teller-trader	258
211362018	4791	Teller	258
211367010	4364	Paymaster of purses	234
211382010	4791	Teller, vault	258
211462010	4364	Cashier II	234
211462014	4364	Cashier-checker	234
211462018	4364	Cashier-wrapper	234
211462022	4364	Cashier, gambling	234
211462026	4364	Check cashier	234
211462030	4364	Drivers'-cash clerk	234
211462034	4364	Teller	234
211462038	4364	Toll collector	234
211467010	4364	Cashier, courtesy booth	234
211467014	4364	Money counter	234
211467018	4364	Parimutuel-ticket cashier	234
211467022	4364	Parimutuel-ticket seller	234
211467026	4364	Sheet writer	234
211467030	4364	Ticket seller	234
211467034	4364	Change person	234
211482010	4364	Cashier, tube room	234
211482014	4718	Food checker	281
211482018	4364	Food-and-beverage checker	281
213362010	4612	Computer operator	261
213382010	4613	Computer peripheral equipment operator	261
213582010	4613	Digitizer operator	261
214267010	4716	Rate analyst, freight	281
214362010	4715	Demurrage clerk	281
214362014	4715	Documentation-billing clerk	281
214362022	4715	Insurance clerk	281
214362026	4715	Invoice-control clerk	281
214362030	4715	Rate clerk, passenger	269
214362038	4716	Traffic-rate clerk	281
214362042	4715	Billing clerk	281
214362046	4699	Statement clerk	282
214382010	4715	Billing typist	281
214382018	4715	C.o.d. clerk	281
214382022	4716	Interline clerk	281
214382026	4716	Revising clerk	281
214382030	4716	Settlement clerk	281
214387010	4715	Billing-control clerk	281
214387014	4716	Rate reviewer	281
214387018	4716	Services clerk	281
214462010	4718	Accounts-adjustable clerk	281
214467010	4716	Foreign clerk	281
214467014	4716	Pricer, message and delivery service	281
214482010	4718	Billing-machine operator	281
214482014	4715	Deposit-refund clerk	281
214482018	4716	Medical-voucher clerk	281
214482022	4716	Rater	281
214587010	4716	Telegraph-service rater	281
214587014	4753	Traffic clerk	276
215167010	4752	Car clerk, pullman	273
215362018	4713	Flight-crew-time clerk	286
215362022	4713	Timekeeper	286
215367018	4751	Taxicab coordinator	273
215382014	4713	Payroll clerk	286
215563010	4745	Caller	270
216362010	4712	Collection clerk	282
216362022	4718	Food-and-beverage controller	282
216362026	4712	Mortgage-accounting clerk	282
216362034	4712	Reserves clerk	282
216362038	4712	Electronic funds transfer coordinator	282
216362042	4712	Margin clerk I	282
216362046	4699	Transfer clerk	282
216382022	4712	Budget clerk	282
216382026	4712	Clearing-house clerk	282
216382034	4716	Cost clerk	281

D.O.T. Number	SOC Code	D.O.T. Title	Page
408684018	5614	Tree pruner	339
408687014	5622	Laborer, landscape	339
410161014	5514	Fur farmer	331
410161018	5514	Livestock rancher	331
410161022	5514	Hog-confinement-system manager	331
410674010	5624	Animal caretaker	330
410674012	5624	Stable attendant	330
411161014	5514	Poultry breeder	331
411161018	5514	Poultry farmer	331
412161010	5514	Game-bird farmer	331
412674010	5624	Animal keeper	330
412674014	5624	Animal-nursery worker	330
413161010	5514	Beekeeper	331
413161014	5514	Reptile farmer	331
418381010	5624	Horseshoer	330
418674010	5624	Dog groomer	330
418677010	5624	Dog bather	330
421161010	5512	Farmer, general	331
441132010	5830	Boatswain, otter trawler	334
441683010	5830	Skiff operator	334
441684010	5830	Fisher, net	334
441684014	5830	Fisher, pot	334
441684018	5830	Fisher, terrapin	334
441684022	5830	Fisher, weir	334
442684010	5830	Fisher, line	334
443664010	5830	Fisher, diving	334
443684010	5830	Fisher, spear	334
446161010	5514	Fish farmer	331
446161014	5514	Shellfish grower	331
447684010	5830	Sponge hooker	334
447687010	5830	Dulser	334
447687014	5830	Irish-moss bleacher	334
447687018	5830	Irish-moss gatherer	334
447687022	5830	Kelp cutter	334
447687026	5830	Sponge clipper	334
449664010	5830	Net repairer	334
449667010	5830	Deckhand, fishing vessel	334
449674010	5624	Aquarist	330
451687010	5720	Christmas-tree farm worker	337
451687014	5720	Christmas-tree grader	337
451687018	5720	Seedling puller	337
451687022	5720	Seedling sorter	337
452134010	5111	Smoke jumper supervisor	299
452167010	5122	Fire warden	299
452364010	5720	Forester aide	337
452364014	5123	Smoke jumper	299
452367010	5122	Fire lookout	299
452367014	5122	Fire ranger	299
452687010	5720	Forest worker	337
452687014	5123	Forest-fire fighter	299
452687018	5720	Tree planter	337
453687010	5720	Forest-products gatherer	337
453687014	5720	Laborer, tree tapping	337
454384010	5730	Faller I	337
454683010	5730	Tree-shear operator	337
454684010	5730	Bucker	337
454684014	5730	Faller II	337
454684018	5730	Logger, all-round	337
454684022	5730	River	337
454684026	5730	Tree cutter	337
454687010	5730	Chain saw operator	337
454687014	5730	Laborer, tanbark	337
454687018	5790	Log marker	337
455367010	7850	Log grader	337
455487010	5790	Log scaler	337
455664010	5790	Rafter	337
455684010	5790	Log sorter	337
455687010	5790	Log marker	337
459387010	5790	Cruiser	337
459687010	5730	Laborer, brush clearing	337
461134010	5840	Expedition supervisor	334
461661010	5840	Predatory-animal hunter	334
461664010	5840	Underwater hunter-trapper	334
461684010	5840	Sealer	334
461684014	5840	Trapper, animal	334
461684018	5840	Trapper, bird	334
522264010	2390	Training technician	138
525361010	6871	Slaughterer, religious ritual	404
525381010	6871	Butcher apprentice	404
525381014	6871	Butcher, all-round	404
525664010	6871	Meat dresser	404

D.O.T. Number	SOC Code	D.O.T. Title	Page
525684010	7753	Boner, meat	404
525684014	7753	Butcher, fish	404
525684018	7753	Carcass splitter	404
525684022	7753	Crab butcher	404
525684030	7753	Fish cleaner	404
525684038	7753	Offal separator	404
525684046	7753	Skinner	404
525684050	7753	Sticker, animal	404
525684054	7753	Trimmer, meat	404
525684058	7753	Turkey-roll maker	404
525687074	7753	Poultry eviscerator	404
553684010	7714	Heat welder, plastics	417
559361010	3690	Laboratory technician, pharmaceutical	200
579137030	7100	Dispatcher, concrete products	273
600260022	6813	Machinist, experimental	410
600280022	6813	Machinist	410
600280026	6813	Machinist apprentice	410
600280030	6813	Machinist apprentice, automotive	410
600280034	6813	Machinist, automotive	410
600280042	6813	Maintenance machinist	410
600281010	6130	Fluid-power mechanic	410
600380010	7329	Fixture maker	410
601260010	6811	Tool-and-die maker	415
601260014	6811	Tool-and-die-maker apprentice	415
601280010	6811	Die maker, stamping	415
601280014	6811	Die maker, trim	415
601280018	6811	Die maker, wire drawing	415
601280022	6811	Die sinker	415
601280030	6811	Mold maker, die-casting and plastic molding	415
601280034	6811	Tap-and-die-maker technician	415
601280042	6811	Tool maker	415
601280058	6811	Tool-maker apprentice	415
601281010	6811	Die maker, bench, stamping	415
601281014	6811	Die-try-out worker, stamping	415
601281026	6811	Tool maker, bench	415
601380010	6829	Carbide operator	415
601381010	6811	Die finisher	415
601381014	6811	Die maker	415
601381022	6811	Die-maker apprentice	415
601381026	6811	Piastic tool maker	415
601381030	6811	Plastic-fixture builder	415
601381034	6811	Saw maker	415
601381042	6811	Die maker, electronic	415
609262010	3974	Tool programmer, numerical control	410
613667010	7714	Liner assembler	417
614684010	7532	Billet assembler	417
620261010	6111	Automobile mechanic	345
620261012	6111	Automobile-mechanic apprentice	345
620261022	6117	Construction-equipment mechanic	368
620261030	6111	Automobile-service-station mechanic	345
620261034	6111	Automotive-cooling-system diagnostic technician	345
620281010	6111	Air-conditioning mechanic	345
620281026	6111	Brake repairer	345
620281034	6111	Carburetor mechanic	345
620281038	6111	Front-end mechanic	345
620281042	6117	Logging-equipment mechanic	368
620281046	6111	Maintenance mechanic	348
620281050	6112	Mechanic, industrial truck	348
620281054	6114	Motorcycle repairer	370
620281058	6112	Tractor mechanic	348
620281062	6111	Transmission mechanic	345
620281066	6111	Tune-up mechanic	345
620281070	6111	Vehicle-fuel-systems converter	345
620364010	6115	Squeak, rattle, and leak repairer	344
620381010	6111	Automobile-radiator mechanic	345
620381014	6117	Mechanic, endless track vehicle	368
620381022	6111	Repairer, heavy	345
620684018	6111	Brake adjuster	345
620684022	6111	Clutch rebuilder	345
620684026	6114	Motorcycle subassembly repairer	370
620684034	6115	Used-car renovator	344
621221010	2390	Field-service representative	138
621261010	6116	Experimental aircraft mechanic	342
621261018	8250	Flight engineer	215
621261022	6116	Experimental aircraft mechanic	342
621281014	6116	Airframe-and-power-plant mechanic	342
621281018	6116	Airframe-and-power-plant-mechanic apprentice	342
621684014	6179	Reclamation worker	342
623261010	6114	Experimental mechanic, outboard motors	370
623261014	6114	Outboard-motor tester	370
623281038	6114	Motorboat mechanic	370
623281042	6114	Outboard-motor mechanic	370

D.O.T. Number	SOC Code	D.O.T. Title	Page
801361014	6473	Structural-steel worker	397
801361018	6473	Structural-steel-worker apprentice	397
801361022	6473	Tank setter	397
801381010	6473	Assembler, metal building	397
801684026	6473	Reinforcing-metal worker	397
804281010	6824	Sheet-metal worker	395
804281014	6824	Sheet-metal-worker apprentice	395
805261010	6814	Boilermaker apprentice	407
805261014	6814	Boilermaker I	407
805361010	6814	Boilerhouse mechanic	407
805361014	6814	Boilermaker fitter	407
805381010	6814	Boilermaker II	407
806281058	6422	Carpenter, prototype	377
806361026	6111	New-car get-ready mechanic	345
806381062	6432	Installer, electrical, plumbing, mechanical	383
806384038	6116	Pressure sealer-and-tester	342
806684038	6111	Automobile-accessories installer	345
807261010	6116	Aircraft body repairer	342
807267010	6115	Shop estimator	344
807281010	6115	Truck-body builder	344
807361010	6115	Automobile-body customizer	344
807381010	6115	Automobile-body repairer	344
807381014	6116	Bonded structures repairer	342
807381018	6115	Frame repairer	344
807381022	6115	Service mechanic	344
807381030	6115	Auto-body repairer, fiberglass	344
807484010	6115	Frame straightener	344
807664010	6111	Muffler installer	345
807684010	6115	Automobile-bumper straightener	344
807684018	6116	Aircraft skin burnisher	342
807684022	6111	Floor service worker, spring	345
809381022	6479	Ornamental-iron worker	397
809381026	6479	Ornamental-iron-worker apprentice	397
810382010	7332	Welding-machine operator, arc	417
810384010	7714	Welder apprentice, arc	417
810384014	7714	Welder, arc	417
810664010	7714	Welder, gun	417
810684010	7714	Welder, tack	417
811482010	7332	Welding-machine operator, gas	417
811684010	7714	Welder apprentice, gas	417
811684014	7714	Welder, gas	417
812360010	7332	Welder setter, resistance machine	417
812682010	7332	Welding-machine operator, resistance	417
813684010	7714	Brazer, assembler	417
814382010	7532	Welding-machine operator, friction	417
814682010	7532	Welding-machine operator, ultrasonic	417
814684010	7532	Welder, explosion	417
815380010	7332	Welder setter, electron-beam machine	417
815382010	7332	Welding-machine operator, electron beam	417
815382014	7532	Welding-machine operator, electroslag	417
815682010	7532	Laser-beam-machine operator	417
815682014	7532	Welding-machine operator, thermit	417
816364010	7714	Arc cutter	417
816464010	7714	Thermal cutter, hand I	417
816684010	7714	Thermal cutter, hand II	417
819281010	7714	Lead burner	417
819281014	7714	Lead-burner apprentice	417
819281022	7714	Welder, experimental	417
819361010	7714	Welder-fitter	417
819361014	7714	Welder-fitter apprentice	417
819381010	7714	Welder-assembler	417
819384010	7714	Welder, combination	417
819384014	7714	Welder apprentice, combination	417
819684010	7714	Welder, production line	417
819685010	7532	Welding-machine tender	417
820662010	6932	Motor-room controller	418
821261010	6151	Cable television line technician	365
821261014	6433	Line maintainer	365
821261022	6159	Service restorer, emergency	365
821261026	6433	Trouble shooter II	365
821281010	6151	Cable television installer	365
821361010	6433	Cable installer-repairer	365
821361018	6433	Line erector	365
821361022	6433	Line installer, street railway	365
821361026	6433	Line repairer	365
821361030	6433	Line-erector apprentice	365
821361038	6433	Tower erector	365
821684022	6433	Trolley-wire installer	365
821687010	6433	Steel-post installer	365
822261010	6151	Electrician, office	352
822261022	6158	Station installer-and-repairer	354

D.O.T. Number	SOC Code	D.O.T. Title	Page
822281010	6151	Automatic-equipment technician	352
822281014	6151	Central-office repairer	352
822281018	6158	Maintenance mechanic, telephone	354
822281022	6151	Private-branch-exchange repairer	352
822281026	6151	Signal maintainer	352
822281030	6151	Technician, plant and maintenance	352
822281034	6151	Technician, submarine cable equipment	352
822361014	6151	Central-office installer	352
822361018	6432	Protective-signal installer	383
822361022	6432	Protective-signal repairer	383
822381010	6151	Equipment installer	352
822381014	6157	Line installer-repairer	365
822381018	6151	Private-branch-exchange installer	352
822381022	6151	Telegraph-plant maintainer	352
822684010	6151	Frame wirer	352
823261010	6151	Public-address servicer	352
823261014	6153	Radio interference investigator	365
823261018	6151	Radio mechanic	352
823261022	6151	Antenna installer, satellite communications	352
823261030	6151	Data communications technician	352
823281014	6151	Electrician, radio	352
823281022	6151	Rigger	352
823361010	6155	Television installer	354
824261010	6432	Electrician	383
824261014	6432	Electrician apprentice	383
824281010	6432	Airport electrician	383
824281018	6432	Neon-sign servicer	383
824381010	6432	Street-light servicer	383
824681010	6432	Electrician	383
825261010	6151	Electric-track-switch maintainer	352
825261014	6176	Elevator examiner-and-adjuster	355
825281030	6176	Elevator repairer	355
825281034	6176	Elevator-repairer apprentice	355
825361010	6176	Elevator constructor	355
825381014	6159	Automatic-window-seat-and-top-lift repairer	345
825381030	6432	Electrician	383
825381034	6432	Electrician apprentice	383
827261010	6156	Electrical-appliance servicer	362
827261014	6156	Electrical-appliance-servicer apprentice	362
827361014	6160	Refrigeration mechanic	360
827661010	6156	Household-appliance installer	362
828251010	6153	Electronic-sales-and-service technician	352
828261010	6155	Electronic-organ technician	354
828261014	6153	Field service engineer	352
828261018	3711	Senior technician, controls	226
828261022	6153	Electronics mechanic	352
828261026	6153	Electronics-mechanic apprentice	352
828281022	6153	Radioactivity-instrument maintenance technician	352
829261018	6153	Electrician, maintenance	383
829281022	6151	Sound technician	352
829361010	6157	Cable splicer	365
829361014	6157	Cable-splicer apprentice	365
840381010	6442	Painter	389
840381014	6442	Painter apprentice, shipyard	389
840381018	6442	Painter, shipyard	389
840681010	6442	Painter, stage settings	389
840684010	6442	Glass tinter	389
841381010	6443	Paperhanger	389
842361010	6424	Lather	382
842361014	6424	Lather apprentice	382
842361018	6444	Plasterer	390
842361022	6444	Plasterer apprentice	390
842361026	6444	Plasterer, molding	390
842361030	6424	Dry-wall applicator	382
842381014	6444	Stucco mason	390
842664010	6424	Taper	382
842684014	6424	Dry-wall applicator	382
844364010	6463	Cement mason	380
844364014	6463	Cement-mason apprentice	380
844461010	6463	Concrete-stone finisher	380
844684010	6463	Concrete rubber	380
845681010	6442	Railroad-car letterer	389
850387010	1472	Inspector of dredging	28
850467010	1472	Grade checker	28
850663018	8239	Lock tender II	244
860281010	6422	Carpenter, maintenance	377
860281014	6422	Carpenter, ship	377
860361010	6422	Boatbuilder, wood	377
860361014	6422	Boatbuilder apprentice, wood	377
860381010	6422	Acoustical carpenter	377
860381022	6422	Carpenter	377

D.O.T. Number	SOC Code	D.O.T. Title	Page
950382018	6931	Gas-engine operator	420
950382022	6932	Rotary-rig engine operator	420
950382026	6931	Stationary engineer	420
950382030	6931	Stationary-engineer apprentice	420
951685018	7668	Firer, marine	458
952167010	4751	Dispatcher, service or work	273
952167014	6932	Load dispatcher	418
952362010	6932	Auxiliary-equipment operator	418
952362014	6932	Feeder-switchboard operator	418
952362018	6932	Hydroelectric-station operator	418
952362022	6932	Power-reactor operator	418
952362026	6932	Substation operator	418
952362030	6932	Substation operator apprentice	418
952362034	6932	Switchboard operator	418
952362038	6932	Switchboard operator	418
952362042	6932	Turbine operator	418
952364010	6432	Trouble shooter I	206
952367014	6932	Switchboard operator assistant	418
952381010	6432	Switch inspector	383
952382010	6932	Diesel-plant operator	418
952382014	6932	Power operator	418
952382018	6932	Power-plant operator	418
952687010	5244	Hydroelectric-plant maintainer	327
953167010	4751	Gas dispatcher	273
953583010	8213	Drip pumper	455
954367010	4751	Water-service dispatcher	273
954382010	6910	Pump-station operator, waterworks	421
954382014	6910	Water-treatment-plant operator	421
955167010	4751	Dispatcher, radioactive-waste-disposal	273
955222010	6910	Instructor, wastewater-treatment plant	138
955362010	6910	Wastewater-treatment-plant operator	421
955382010	6910	Clarifying-plant operator	421
955382014	6910	Waste-treatment operator	421
955585010	6910	Wastewater-treatment-plant attendant	421
959167010	4751	Dispatcher, service	273
959167014	6433	Electric power line examiner	365
959367014	6151	Facility examiner	352
961364010	3240	Double	193
961667014	3280	Stand-in	193
962167010	3719	Manager, sound effects	220
962167014	3240	Program assistant	193
962281010	6422	Prop maker	377
962361010	6868	Optical-effects layout person	444
962382010	3990	Recordist	220

D.O.T. Number	SOC Code	D.O.T. Title	Page
969367010	4754	Custodian, athletic equipment	275
970131014	3250	Supervisor, artist, suspect	191
970281010	6863	Airbrush artist	444
970281018	6868	Photograph retoucher	444
970361018	3250	Artist, suspect	191
970381010	6868	Colorist, photography	444
970381034	6868	Spotter, photographic	444
972384010	7671	Platemaker, semiconductor packages	444
976361010	6868	Reproduction technician	444
976380010	7671	Computer-controlled-color-photograph-printer operator	444
976381010	6868	Film laboratory technician I	444
976381018	6868	Projection printer	444
976381022	6868	Template reproduction technician	444
976382010	7671	Camera operator, title	444
976382014	7671	Color-printer operator	444
976382018	7671	Film developer	444
976382022	6868	Photostat operator	444
976382030	7671	Photographic aligner, semiconductor wafers	444
976382038	7671	Photo mask pattern generator	444
976384010	7671	Photo technician	444
976384014	7671	Photo mask processor	444
976385010	7671	Microfilm processor	444
976665010	7671	Take-down sorter	444
976681010	6868	Developer	444
976682010	7671	Film printer	444
976682014	7671	Printer operator, black-and-white	444
976682018	7671	Rectification printer	444
976682022	7671	Microfilm-camera operator	444
976684014	7671	Film laboratory technician	444
976684030	7671	Contact printer, printed circuit boards	444
976685014	7671	Developer, automatic	444
976685018	7671	Film laboratory technician II	444
976685022	7671	Mounter, automatic	444
976685026	7671	Print developer, automatic	444
976685030	7671	Utility worker, film processing	444
976685034	7671	Developer, printed circuit board panels	444
976685038	7671	Photographic processor, semiconductor wafers	444
976687018	4753	Photofinishing laboratory worker	276
977381010	6844	Bookbinder	423
977381014	6844	Bookbinder apprentice	423
977684026	7759	Bench worker, binding	423
979361010	2520	Document restorer	140
979384010	6868	Screen maker, photographic process	444

Index

F

G

JIST's Revolutionary Career Information Software

America's Top 300 Jobs, 5th Edition, with Multimedia CD-ROM

This CD-ROM is the most powerful, lowest priced, and best program of its kind. Ideal for job seekers, students, and anyone wanting accurate and up-to-date information on careers. Includes *America's Top 300 Jobs, 5th Edition*, and our powerful CD-ROM for a compellingly low price. An awesome value!

The easy-to-use CD-ROM features:

☆ Every description from *America's Top 300 Jobs*

☆ Over 7,000 additional descriptions of more specific jobs

☆ Color photos, sound, and voice

☆ Effortless query by job title or within clusters

☆ Sorting of jobs by earnings, education, and employment queries

ISBN: 1-56370-280-0
$39.95
Order Code: JS2800

JIST Provides the Resources That Help America Work!

Call 1-800-JIST-USA

JIST FAX: 1-800-547-8329

JIST's America's Top Jobs Books

America's 50 Fastest Growing Jobs, 3rd Edition

Essential information for all job seekers, including descriptions of the fastest growing jobs in the U.S., labor market trends, and a section on career planning and job search skills.

ISBN: 1-56370-199-5
$14.95
Order Code: J1995

Career Guide to America's Top Industries, 2nd Edition

Detailed descriptions of the 40 industries that employ more than 75% of the American workforce, including working conditions; training and advancement; earnings and employment outlook.

ISBN: 1-56370-185-5
$14.95
Order Code: J18555

America's Federal Jobs

The ONLY source of this valuable information, includes details on all federal agencies, application procedures, pay scales, education requirements, and much more.

ISBN: 0-942784-81-2
$14.95
Order Code: AFJ

America's Top Jobs for College Graduates

This essential resource includes thorough descriptions for 60 jobs most often held by college grads, plus details on more than 500 jobs and a section on career planning and job search skills.

ISBN: 1-56370-281-9
$14.95
Order Code: ATCG

America's Top Medical and Human Services Jobs, 3rd Edition

Provides comprehensive information on more than 60 of the top jobs in this fast-growing field, for people with all levels of education and training.

ISBN: 1-56370-238-X
$14.95
Order Code: J238X

JIST Provides the Resources That Help America Work!

America's Top Office, Management, and Sales Jobs, 2nd Edition

More than 60 descriptions of jobs that offer great opportunities for those with and without college degrees, plus information on the top 500 jobs.

ISBN: 1-56370-117-0
$11.95
Order Code: ATO

America's Top Technical and Trade Jobs, 2nd Edition

Up-to-date information on more than 50 of the fastest growing jobs in the technical and trade areas, plus details on pay rates, training required, working conditions, and job search skills.

ISBN: 1-56370-116-2
$11.95
Order Code: ATT

America's Top Military Careers

An essential resource for anyone considering a career in the armed forces. Presents information on nearly 200 enlisted and officer occupations, plus their civilian counterparts.

ISBN: 1-56370-124-3
$19.95
Order Code: ATMC

Call 1-800-JIST-USA

JIST FAX: 1-800-547-8329

JIST's Essential Career References

Dictionary of Occupational Titles

U.S. Department of Labor

A standard reference describing 12,741 jobs. It is the primary source of information on most occupations and the best guide for specific job information.

Virtually all career reference products are cross-referenced to it.

Softcover (2 Volumes)	Hardcover (1 Volume)
ISBN 1-56370-000-X	ISBN 1-56370-006-9
$39.00	**$48.00**
Order Code DOT91	Order Code DOTH

Young Person's Occupational Outlook Handbook

Appropriate for children in grades 5 through 9, this exceptional new reference book covers the same 250 occupations as the adult edition, but in a simpler, graphically interesting way. Ideal to help young people explore the world of work.

ISBN 1-56370-201-0
$19.95
Order Code J2010

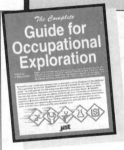

The Complete Guide for Occupational Exploration

Uses an intuitive occupational coding system developed by the U.S. Department of Labor to organize the 12,741 job titles in the **DOT** into 12 major "interest areas." A very good resource for career exploration.

Softcover	Hardcover
ISBN 1-56370-052-2	ISBN 1-56370-100-6
$39.95	**$49.95**
Order Code CGOE	Order Code CGOEH

The Enhanced Guide for Occupational Exploration, 2nd Edition

Organizes 2,800 of the most important jobs into 12 major interest areas with increasingly specific groupings of similar jobs. General information and specific job descriptions provided for each grouping.

Softcover	Hardcover
ISBN 1-56370-207-X	ISBN 1-56370-244-4
$34.95	**$44.95**
Order Code J207X	Order Code J2444

The Worker Traits Data Book

Provides coded information on more than 70 specific measures for all the jobs in the **DOT**. Based on the latest government sources, this essential career reource includes hard-to-find data never before available in one source.

ISBN 1-56370-110-3
$49.95
Order Code WTDB

Career Exploration Video

This unique video reviews all the essential career reference books described on this page, telling what they are and how to use them to best effect. This is a real time-saver for busy employment, training, and counseling professionals.

ISBN 1-56370-043-3
$99.00
Order Code CXV

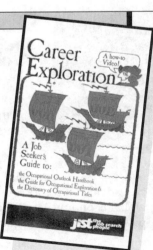

JIST Books to Change Your Life!

Career Satisfaction & Success, Revised Edition

A Guide to Job and Personal Freedom
By Bernard Haldane, Ph.D.

Bernard Haldane is a founder of the career counseling movement, and this completely revised edition of his career success classic reflects his years of experience helping people make the most of the their careers and lives. Readers will learn to identify skills, overcome job stress, increase productivity, and find more satisfaction and success!

ISBN: 1-56370-200-2
$14.95
Order Code: J2002

The PIE Method for Career Success

A Unique Way to Find Your Ideal Job
By Daniel Porot

A fresh, new approach to career planning and job seeking from one of Europe's leading experts. Featuring interesting graphics and an approach ideal for both left-brain and right-brain learners, Porot's unique PIE (Pleasure, Information, and Employment) method shows how to define and land the ideal job.

ISBN: 1-56370-182-0
$14.95
Order Code: J1820

Back to School

A College Guide for Adults
By LaVerne L. Ludden, Ed.D.

An essential resource for adults planning a return to school, this book shows how to select the right college, get credit for life experience, obtain financial aid, and match career goals to a college major. A special appendix lists 240 colleges with more than 1,000 programs designed specifically for adult students.

ISBN: 1-57112-070-X
$14.95
Order Code: P070X

Dare to Change Your Job and Your Life

By Carole Kanchier, Ph.D.

A powerful book based on interviews with more than 5,000 adults, this practical, thought-provoking guide is ideal for students, working adults, anyone wanting to improve their careers and lives. Filled with motivational profiles of successful individuals, solid advice on career advancement, and tips for increasing career satisfaction.

ISBN: 1-56370-224-X
$14.95
Order Code: J224X

Helping Your Child Choose a Career

By Luther B. Otto, Ph.D.

An invaluable resource for parents, teachers, and counselors, this book shows how to help your student make important life choices. Provides helpful, up-to-date information and advice on tomorrow's careers, technology, the global economy, labor force trends, and selecting and paying for the right education or training.

ISBN: 1-56370-184-7
$14.95
Order Code: J1847

Franchise Opportunities Handbook

A Complete Guide for People Who Want to Start Their Own Franchise
By LaVerne L. Ludden, Ed.D.

An essential resource for anyone considering opening a franchise, this directory provides information on 1,500 franchises in 39 business categories, including contact information, details on business type, number of outlets, years in operation, start-up money required, franchise fees, plus much more. Additional chapters provide information on starting your own business, plus solid advice on choosing the franchise that's right for you!

ISBN: 1-57112-073-4
$16.95
Order Code: P0734

Call 1-800-JIST-USA

JIST Provides the Resources That Help America Work!

JIST FAX:
1-800-547-8329

JIST Job Search Books Put You to Work!

The Very Quick Job Search, 2nd Edition

Get a Better Job in Half the Time!
By J. Michael Farr

A major revision of the most thorough career planning and job search book on the market, this is a must have for job seekers and career counselors! Completely updated with new information, techniques, and graphics, plus a "Quick Start" section to help you get your job search going *fast!*

ISBN: 1-56370-181-2
$14.95
Order Code: J1812

Getting the Job You Really Want, 3rd Edition

A Step-by-Step Guide
By J. Michael Farr

A complete revision of a best-seller with great advice on identifying skills, defining the ideal job, getting a job in less time, and surviving on the job, plus updated content, a fresh design, and lots of in-the-book activities. This book's results-oriented approach has made it the most widely used book of its kind in schools and programs throughout North America. Instructor's guide available.

ISBN: 1-56370-092-1
$9.95
Order Code: RWR

Instructor's Guide:
ISBN: 1-56370-196-0
$12.95
Order Code: RWRIG

The Resume Solution, 2nd Edition

How to Write (and Use) a Resume That Gets Results
By David Swanson

One of our best-selling books, this revised edition features greatly improved design, more examples, and updated content throughout. Swanson uses a step-by-step approach with lots of worksheets and examples, covers electronic resumes and job seeking, and offers solid advice on how to *use* a resume to get more interviews and job offers.

ISBN: 1-56370-180-4
$12.95
Order Code: J1804

The Quick Interview & Salary Negotiation Book

Dramatically Improve Your Interviewing Skills in Just a Few Hours!
By J. Michael Farr

This book provides you with everything you need to dramatically improve your interviewing skills and get the job you want! Includes specific answers for "problem" questions, salary negotiation strategies, average earnings for hundreds of jobs, plus thorough career planning and job search sections.

ISBN: 1-56370-162-6
$12.95
Order Code: J1626

Gallery of Best Resumes for Two-Year Degree Graduates

A Special Collection of Quality Resumes by Professional Resume Writers
By David F. Noble, Ph.D.

David Noble has put together a unique sampler of great resumes written by professionals especially for two-year degree grads. This book also includes helpful tips, sample cover letters, and advice on how to make your resume work for you. The 200 resumes represent an enormous variety of designs and styles to generate lots of ideas for your own outstanding resume!

ISBN: 1-56370-239-8
$14.95
Order Code: J2398

The Quick Resume & Cover Letter Book

Write and Use an Effective Resume in Only One Day
By J. Michael Farr

This book gets rave reviews for its great design, exceptional advice, ease-of-use, and excellent examples. Voted by Publishers' Marketing Association as one of the top three business books of the year, it offers a "Quick" section to create a functional resume in just a few hours, helpful worksheets and step-by-step directions, tips for handling problems, plus great advice on cover letters and thank-you notes.

ISBN: 1-56370-141-3
$12.95
Order Code: RCLQG

Call 1-800-JIST-USA

JIST Provides the Resources that Help America Work!

JIST FAX:
1-800-547-8329

JIST Workbooks Help You Discover Career and Life Skills

Hire Learning Series

Your Guide to Successful School-to-Work Transition
Patricia Duffy and T. Walter Wannie

This three-book series was field tested by thousands of students, incorporates the newest career education guidelines, and prepares students for successful transition from school to work.

Setting Your Career and Life Direction	Landing a Job	Succeeding in Your Work & Community
ISBN 1-56370-188-X	ISBN 1-56370-189-8	ISBN 1-56370-190-1
$6.95	**$6.95**	**$6.95**
Order Code J188X	Order Code J1898	Order Code J1901

Instructor's Guide	Hire Learning Set
ISBN 1-56370-191-X	ISBN 1-56370-192-8
$14.95	**$24.95**
Order Code J191X	Order Code J1928

I Am Already Successful

80 Activities on Developing Motivation and Self-Esteem
Dennis Hooker, Ph.D.

Provides activities that teach youth to accept and value themselves. Young people will learn how to work with others in a more productive and noncompetitive way. Good for at-risk and special needs programs.

Student Book	Instructor's Guide
ISBN 0-942784-4 1-3	ISBN 0-942784-42-1
$8.95	**$12.95**
Order Code AM	Order Code AMIG

jist

Pathfinder

Exploring Career and Educational Paths
Norene Lindsay

Pathfinder helps students develop future career plans through high school and into postsecondary training. It meets national career awareness guidelines and is excellent for school-to-work programs.

Student Book	Instructor's Guide
ISBN 1-56370-120-0	ISBN 1-56370-121-9
$59.95/package of 10	**$14.95**
Order Code PFP	Order Code PFTG

I Can Manage Life

Learning to Choose and Grow
Dennis Hooker, Ph.D.

Helps teens make the "right" choices for them. Over 90 activities help youth explore attitudes and behaviors—theirs and others. They will discover hidden strengths, talents, and opinions in the process.

Student Book	Instructor's Guide
ISBN 0-942784-77-4	ISBN 0-942784-78-2
$7.95	**$12.95**
Order Code ICAN	Order Code ICANIG

The JIST Job Search Course

A Young Person's Guide to Getting & Keeping a Good Job
J. Michael Farr and Marie Pavlicko

A comprehensive and results-oriented job search course designed for and field tested by high school students. Requires minimal preparation time to present the concepts, and features many teaching aids.

Student Book	Instructor's Guide	The Data Minder	Transparency Set
ISBN 0-942784-34-0	ISBN 0-942784-36-7	ISBN 0-942784-35-9	ISBN 1-56370-032-8
$8.95	**$12.95**	**$16.95/package of 10**	**$69.95**
Order Code YP	Order Code YPTM	Order Code J4359	Order Code YPTRAN

The World of Work and You

From the Exploring Careers Reference Set

A career exploration tool designed to help young adults make satisfying career choices by examining skills and interests used during school and extracurricular activities. Includes a self-guided career assessment.

ISBN 0-942784-28-6
$48.95/package of 25
Order Code WOW

Call 1-800-JIST-USA	*JIST Provides the Resources That Help America Work!*	JIST FAX: 1-800-547-8329

JIST Assessment Instruments Help You Discover . . . You

Career Interest Test Set

Includes:

- The Career Exploration Inventory

- The Leisure/Work Search Inventory

- The GOE Inventory

- The GOE Crosswalks Book (64 pages)

Use one or all of these self-scoring, self-interpreting tests to help clarify your career interests.

$12.95 • Order Code CC • TestsetA

Leisure/Work Search Inventory

Assessment Instrument
By John J. Liptak, Ed.D.

A new perspective for career assessment that relates interests in leisure activities to employment opportunities. By focusing on leisure activities, the *LSI* can be used with people who have limited work experience. A useful resource for people of all ages, from students just beginning their career exploration to seniors planning for retirement.

ISBN: 1-56370-125-1
$29.95/package of 25
Order Code: LSI

The *Guide for Occupational Exploration* Inventory

A Self-Directed Guide to Career, Learning, and Lifestyle Options
By J. Michael Farr

This self-scoring, self-interpreting device uses the 12 *GOE* interest areas and gives a graphic profile of career interests. Cross-references to all standard occupational reference sources. This device is designed to teach the user how to explore their options.

ISBN: 1-56370-245-2
$36.95/package of 25
Order Code: JA2452
Order Code: JA2479

The Career Exploration Inventory

A Guide for Exploring Work, Leisure, and Learning
By John J. Liptak, Ed.D.

After test takers reflect on 120 brief activity statements, a simple self-scoring grid totals the responses and the **CEI Interest Profile** provides a graphic picture of interest levels in 15 interest categories. Test takers then open the device to a clever 4-panel **Work, Learning & Leisure Activities Guide**, find the areas of strongest interest, and get information on related occupations.

ISBN: 1-56370-063-8
$29.95/package of 25
Order Code: CEI

Barriers to Employment Success Inventory (BESI)

A Self-Scoring Test to Identify Specific Barriers to Getting or Keeping a Job
By John J. Liptak, Ed.D.

In only 20 minutes, test takers can identify the key barriers keeping them from finding or succeeding on a job. By rating 50 simple statements, then scoring the items into five categories, they get a clear, graphic profile of their barriers to success. The BESI also suggests ways to overcome these barriers and succeed!

ISBN: 1-56370-243-6
$37.50/package of 25
Order Code: JA2436

Occupational Clues

A Career Interest Survey
By J. Michael Farr

Six checklists identify job possibilities from several perspectives, including occupational interests, work values, leisure activities, home activities, school, and work experience. The short, 24-page version of *Clues* does not require any specific occupational references, while the 32-page version includes information on using the *CGOE* to explore career alternatives.

32-page Long Form:
ISBN: 1-56370-088-3
$48.95/package of 25
Order Code: CLUES

24-page Short Form:
ISBN: 1-56370-108-1
$36.95/package
Order Code: SHORT

Call 1-800-JIST-USA   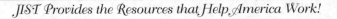 *JIST Provides the Resources that Help America Work!*   **JIST FAX: 1-800-547-8329**

JIST's Video Guide for Occupational Exploration

Real People, Real Jobs, Real Information

This excellent series of instructional videos introduces viewers to clusters of occupations through fascinating interviews with working people, who talk honestly and openly about how they chose their work, what they like and don't like about their jobs, what training and education they recommend, and tips for getting ahead. These high-quality videos emphasize the connections between education, work, and on-the-job success. An essential resource for libraries and career counseling centers, this 15-video series will appeal to both students and adults. Perfect for school-to-work programs!

Your Career—Series Introduction

J. Michael Farr, job search expert and author, explains the importance of career exploration.

ISBN: 1-56370-208-8
Order Code: JV2088

Artistic Careers

For those with a creative flair, this video introduces careers in writing, art, drama, music, and graphics. Features interviews with a writer, graphic artist, and radio announcer.

ISBN: 1-56370-209-6
Order Code: JV2096

Scientific Careers

This video will appeal to those with an interest in medicine, life sciences, and the natural sciences. Features interviews with a geologist, doctor, and veterinarian.

ISBN: 1-56370-210-X
Order Code: JV210X

Careers with Plants and Animals

Features careers in farming, animal training, forestry, and fishing. Interviews with an animal trainer and a greenskeeper.

ISBN: 1-56370-211-8
Order Code: JV2118

Protective Careers

People interested in action-oriented fields will like these interviews with a police officer, firefighter, and security consultant.

ISBN: 1-56370-212-6
Order Code: JV2126

Mechanical Careers, Part One

Engineering, building, repairing, crafts, and trades are covered. Interviews with a mechanical engineer, an architect, and a ship's captain.

ISBN: 1-56370-213-4
Order Code: JV2134

Mechanical Careers, Part Two

This video features interviews with a train engineer, a welder, and an auto body repairer.

ISBN: 1-56370-214-2
Order Code: JV2142

Industrial Careers

Those interested in mass-production techniques will enjoy these interviews with a machine set-up technician, an electronics tester, and a CNC machine operator.

ISBN: 1-56370-215-0
Order Code: JV2150

Business Detail Careers

Individuals interested in office work will want to check out these interviews with a finance manager, museum guide, and department supervisor.

ISBN: 1-56370-216-9
Order Code: JV2169

Selling Careers

Includes legal work, business negotiations, and advertising. Features interviews with people in advertising sales, printing sales, and automobile sales.

ISBN: 1-56370-217-7
Order Code: JV2177

Accommodating Careers

Featured interviews include a tour guide, hairstylist, taxi driver, casino dealer, and manicurist.

ISBN: 1-56370-218-5
Order Code: JV2185

Humanitarian Careers

People interested in helping others will enjoy these interviews with a pastor, a physical therapist, and an ambulance attendant.

ISBN: 1-56370-219-3
Order Code: JV2193

Leading & Influencing Careers, Part One

Those who want to lead others will be interested in the interviews with a computer programmer, a librarian, and a program director for a radio station.

ISBN: 1-56370-220-7
Order Code: JV2207

Leading & Influencing Careers, Part Two

Interviews include a museum curator, an editor, and a fund-raiser.

ISBN: 1-56370-221-5
Order Code: JV2215

Physical Performing Careers

Those who enjoy performing physical activities will be interested in these interviews with a pitching coach, an umpire, and a jockey.

ISBN: 1-56370-222-3
Order Code: JV2223

Individual videos: **$69.00 each**
15-Video Series
ISBN: 1-56370-223-1
Special Series Price—All 15 Videos
$729.00
Order Code: JV2231

jist

How to Be a Success at Work Video Series

All job seekers want to hear these words: "Congratulations! You've got the job." But for some, these words may cause as much anxiety as the stress of unemployment. Being a success at work requires a set of skills that, if practiced from day one, guarantee success. But without these skills, jobs that were hard to get can be quite easy to lose. That's why JIST created the *How to Be a Success at Work* video series.

The Three-Series Set Includes:

You've Got the Job . . . Now What?

Explains the importance of the employee/employer relationship and how it can benefit both worker and supervisor. You'll learn seven basic skills that employers look for in new employees.

ISBN 1-56370-165-0
$119.00
Order Code JV1650

Working 9 to 5

Puts you on the road to successful employment. You'll learn how to boost your self-confidence, how to interact with supervisors and coworkers, and how to make the workday more productive and enjoyable.

ISBN 1-56370-202-9
$119.00
Order CodeJV2029

Career Tips for Your Future

Shows you how to acquire and maintain work habits that make you a more valuable employee. You'll learn the importance of these skills and how they can influence your current and future positions.

ISBN 1-56370-203-7
$119.00
Order Code JV2037

Special series price—all three videos and one copy of the *Job Savvy* student book and instructor's guide!

ISBN 1-56370-204-5
$299.00
Order Code JV2045

Job Savvy
How to Be a Success at Work
LaVerne Ludden, Ed.D.

Helps entry-level youth and adults thrive, not just survive, in their jobs. It stresses the importance of basic job skills and explains what behaviors are most likely to get people hired, fired, or promoted.

ISBN 0-942784-79-0
$10.95
Order Code JS

Instructor's Guide
ISBN 0-942784-80-4
$12.95
Order Code JSTM

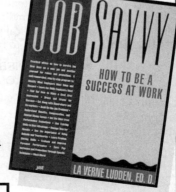

jist

The Video Guide to JIST's Self-Directed Job Search

This Telly Award-winning series is the most compelling and professional ever produced on this topic. Based on JIST's outcome-oriented, self-directed job search methods, these no-nonsense videos provide in-depth coverage of the practical techniques explained in *The Very Quick Job Search* by J. Michael Farr, techniques proven to cut job search time in half! Videos can be used individually to reinforce topics in job search training programs, or the entire series can be used to support the 20-session *The Very Quick Job Search Instructor's Curriculum.*

Self-Assessment I: Defining Your Skills

This video introduces the series and focuses on the importance of skills as a foundation for career planning.

ISBN: 1-56370-148-0
Order Code: JV1480

Self-Assessment II: Putting Your Skills to Work

This video show you how to identify your abilities, strengths, and assets, and to present weaknesses as positives.

ISBN: 1-56370-149-9
Order Code: JV1499

Evaluating a Job

The *Dictionary of Occupational Titles* lists more than 12,000 jobs. How is a job seeker to choose? This video gives tips to identify, select, and target the right job for you.

ISBN: 1-56370-150-2
Order Code: JV1502

Employment Applications and Tests

How can you use an application to be "screened *in*" for an interview? This video introduces employment applications and tests, and how to approach them.

ISBN: 1-56370-151-0
Order Code: JV1510

The Resume I: Their Styles and Use

Presents resume formats, such as chronological and functional, and tells when to use them, what to include, and how to make them more effective.

ISBN: 1-56370-152-9
Order Code: JV1529

The Resume II: JIST Cards, Cover Letters, and Thank-You Notes

The video shows how to get the best results from your resume by supplementing it with JIST Cards, cover letters, and thank-you notes.

ISBN: 1-56370-153-7
Order Code: JV1537

Traditional and Nontraditional Job Search Methods

An overview of traditional techniques, plus a look at nontraditional methods that can drastically reduce the time it takes to find jobs.

ISBN: 1-56370-154-5
Order Code: JV1545

The Interview I: Mastering the Job Interview

Discusses three types of interviews and the seven common interview phases, with tips for handling them.

ISBN: 1-56370-155-3
Order Code: JV1553

The Interview II: Answering Problem Questions

This video presents simple techniques for understanding what the interviewer is *really* asking and for answering problem questions.

ISBN: 1-56370-156-1
Order Code: JV1561

Organizing Your Job Search

Shows you how to make the best use of your time and energy, plus tips for meeting an employer's expectations and succeeding on the job.

ISBN: 1-56370-157-X
Order Code: JV157X

Individual videos: **$99.00 each**
10-Video Series
ISBN: 1-56370-147-2
Special Series Price—All 10 Videos
$795.00
Order Code: JV1472

An Unbelievable Introductory Offer:
America's Top Jobs™ *on CD-ROM! Only $12.95!*

America's Top Jobs™ *on CD-ROM!* is a revolutionary program—and it is superior to programs costing hundreds more! Yet we are offering it for **only $12.95** plus $4 shipping and handling to the first 5,000 who respond to this ad. This incredible value is available only if you mail or fax this response card to us and enclose your check or credit card billing information with your order. Or call our automated order line at 1-800-JIST-USA, mention item code JS2843, and have your credit card information ready.

Available July, 1996. No C.O.D. orders and no returns at this price, other than for a damaged program. Regular retail price is $24.95. For individual use only: contact us for price on multi-user or site license. Please direct questions or customer service calls to 1-317-264-3720.

If the response card is **not attached** call: **1-800-JIST-USA**
and ask for the **JS2843** Special Software Offer

(over)

Name: _____ Organization: _____

Street Address *(Please note that we can not deliver to P.O. boxes.)*:

_____

City: _____ State/Province: _____ Zip Code: _____

Daytime phone number *(for questions on your order)*: _____

☐ $16.95 check enclosed   ☐ Charge my credit card. Circle one: VISA   MC   Amex
(To assure privacy, consider sending charge card orders in an envelope.)

Name on card: _____

Card Number: _____   Expiration Date: _____

☐ Yes. Please send me additional information on JIST software and other products for schools, libraries, and other programs.

Thank You for Your Interest!   **FAX: 1-317-264-3709**

JS2843

Why is *America's Top Jobs*™ *on CD-ROM!* an incredible value?

✓ Descriptions for more than 7,000 specific jobs

✓ Capability to print or "cut and paste" any job description to your word processor

✓ Bonus career planning and job search advice from Mike Farr's *The Quick Job Search*

✓ Hundreds of color images

Based on the latest government information, *America's Top Jobs*™ *on CD-ROM!* is essential for: planning your career or education, identifying job targets, writing resumes, preparing for interviews, negotiating pay, and writing job descriptions. *America's Top Jobs*™ *on CD-ROM!* will run on PCs with Windows, CD-ROM drive, and graphics display capabilities.

Order now to get the special introductory price!

Post Office will not deliver without adequate postage.

JIST Works, Inc.
720 North Park Avenue
Indianapolis, IN 46202-3431